Lecture Notes in Artificial Intelligence 4733

Edited by J. G. Carbonell and J. Siekmann

Subseries of Lecture Notes in Computer Science

Roberto Basili   Maria Teresa Pazienza (Eds.)

AI*IA 2007:
Artificial Intelligence and
Human-Oriented Computing

10th Congress of the
Italian Association for Artificial Intelligence
Rome, Italy, September 10-13, 2007
Proceedings

 Springer

Series Editors

Jaime G. Carbonell, Carnegie Mellon University, Pittsburgh, PA, USA
Jörg Siekmann, University of Saarland, Saarbrücken, Germany

Volume Editors

Roberto Basili
Maria Teresa Pazienza
University of Rome "Tor Vergata"
Via del Politecnico 1, 00133 Rome, Italy
E-mail: {basili, pazienza}@info.uniroma2.it

Library of Congress Control Number: Applied for

CR Subject Classification (1998): I.2, F.1, F.4.1

LNCS Sublibrary: SL 7 – Artificial Intelligence

ISSN   0302-9743
ISBN-10   3-540-74781-8 Springer Berlin Heidelberg New York
ISBN-13   978-3-540-74781-9 Springer Berlin Heidelberg New York

Springer is a part of Springer Science+Business Media

springer.com

© Springer-Verlag Berlin Heidelberg 2007
Printed in Germany

Typesetting: Camera-ready by author, data conversion by Scientific Publishing Services, Chennai, India
Printed on acid-free paper   SPIN: 12119172   06/3180   5 4 3 2 1 0

Preface

*AI*IA 2007* was the tenth in a series of international conferences on advances in artificial intelligence held bi-annually in Italy by the Italian Association for Artificial Intelligence (*AI*IA*). With a history of 20 years, the first congress after the celebration of the 50th birthday of AI was a turning point and a good opportunity for reviewing the activities, research and achievements of these years.

AI research shows a growing impact on a variety of current problems according to the assessment of well-known methods and approaches as well as to novel paradigms (e.g, evolutionary computing). Most of today's IT challenges are strongly related to ideas, models and technological settings traditionally pursued by AI in the last 50 years. Human-centered practices are nowadays the main triggers of a variety of problems that the information society needs to tackle: from security-related issues to distributed information access, from life-critical applications to entertainment. It seems that most computer science interests are oriented towards the automation of relevant and traditionally human-centered tasks. In this perspective, AI takes a relevant, authoritative role, for its long-standing tradition in cognitive models and algorithms as well as for its large heritage of interests, experiences and best practices. Tools and systems that spread from non-traditional AI research are more and more rooted in paradigms well-known in AI. The case of the Semantic Web is an example, where the emphasis on representational aspects of data semantics, almost obvious for AI people, also became a target for many researchers and practitioners outside AI.

These new challenges are all characterized by the central role played by humans as users but also producers of information or services and owners of critical expertise on domains and processes. What AI brings into this game is the set of paradigms and knowledge able to determine solutions and computational models with a clear attitude: hiding the complexity of the underlying processes making the use, adoption and penetration of new technologies harmonic with existing human-centered practices. The attitude of making *"natural"* these transitions to new technological settings is what we call *human-oriented computing*, as a unifying paradigm for most of the traditional approaches in AI research. The cognitive assumptions characterizing the AI approaches make the difference here.

The AI*IA 2007 Congress summarized the results in the diversified AI fields and favored the interdisciplinary cross-fertilizations required. Advances in different broad areas were represented, ranging from knowledge representation to planning, from natural language processing to machine learning. Special tracks were designed to emphasize some specialized fields. The three Special Tracks were: *"AI and Robotics," "AI and Expressive Media"* and *"Intelligent Access to Multimedia Information"* dedicated to progresses in significant application fields that represent increasingly relevant topics.

The above contents are embodied in the proceedings of 52 papers together with 18 papers for the three Special Tracks. In total, 80 papers were submitted to the main conference of which 43 were selected as technical papers and 9 as posters. Papers are representative of a wide international research community with 15 countries involved and a percentage of 28% papers originating from research institutions located outside of Italy.

We would like to express our gratitude to the AI*IA Board that selected the Tor Vergata AI group for the organization of the 2007 congress. In particular, we thank Marco Schaerf and Salvatore Ruggieri for their continuous help and encouragement. A special thanks goes to Daniele Nardi and Vincenzo Lombardo, Chairs of the Special Tracks on *AI and Robotics* and *AI and Expressive Media*, respectively. They made these in-depth explorations of new fields possible, giving an excellent contribution to the technical quality of this volume. A crucial role was also played by the members of the Conference and Special Track Program Committees, and all the referees, for their major support in the hard review process. Our gratitude goes to all of them for the precious work in the selection of the high-quality papers appearing in these proceedings.

A particular thank-you goes to our supporting institutions: the University of Rome, Tor Vergata for hosting the event in the wonderful location of Villa Mondragone; the "Unione Industriale e delle Imprese di Roma e del Lazio" for its effort in the dissemination of the event at the industrial level; Rome Municipality for its general advice as the closest public institution. The congress industrial sponsors, IBM Italy, Google Inc., CELI, Exprivia S.p.A, also gave a vital support to the congress. In particular, we thank CELI for funding the Best Paper award, as well as IBM Italy, ENEA and Fondazione Bruno-Kessler[1] that supported the organization of three relevant workshops, hosted by the congress.

Last, but certainly not least, our thanks goes to the ART (AI Research @ Tor Vergata) group that acted as the local organization team: Diego De Cao, Francesca Fallucchi, Cristina Giannone, Alessandro Moschitti, Paolo Marocco, Daniele Pighin, Marco Pennacchiotti, Marzia Barbara Saraceno, Armando Stellato and Fabio Massimo Zanzotto. Without their invaluable effort in the organization and timely problem solving, AI*IA 2007 would not have been possible.

June 2007
Roberto Basili
Maria Teresa Pazienza

---

[1] previously ITC-Irst, Trento

Organization

AI*IA 2007 was organized by DISP (Department of Computer Science, Systems and Production), University of Rome, Tor Vergata in cooperation with the Italian Association for Artificial Intelligence (AI*IA).

Executive Committee

Conference Chairs	Roberto Basili
	Maria Teresa Pazienza

Special Track Chairs

Artificial Intelligence and Robotics	Daniele Nardi
Artificial Intelligence and Expressive Media	Vincenzo Lombardo
Intelligent Access to Multimedia Information	Roberto Basili

Workshop Chair	Alessandro Moschitti
Exhibition and Demonstration	Armando Stellato
Local Organization	Marzia Barbara Saraceno,
	Diego De Cao,
	Francesca Fallucchi,
	Cristina Giannone,
	Paolo Marocco,
	Daniele Pighin
Congress Web Pages	Marco Pennacchiotti

Program Committee

Khurshid Ahmad	Trinity College Dublin, Republic of Ireland
Luigia Carlucci Aiello	University of Rome, La Sapienza, Italy
Stefania Bandini	University of Milan Bicocca, Italy
Roberto Basili	University of Rome, Tor Vergata, Italy
Ernesto Burattini	CIB-CNR, Italy
Marc Cavazza	University of Teesside, UK
Roberto Cordeschi	University of Rome, La Sapienza, Italy
Walter Daelemans	CNTS, University of Antwerp, Belgium
Floriana Esposito	University of Bari, Italy
Salvatore Gaglio	University of Palermo, Italy

Attilio Giordana	University of Piemonte Orientale, Italy
Marco Gori	University of Siena, Italy
Gregory Grefenstette	CEA - LIC2M, France
Nicola Guarino	ISTC-CNR Trento, Italy
Eduard Hovy	Information Sciences Institute - USC, USA
Leonardo Lesmo	University of Turin, Italy
Robert Meersman	Free University of Brussels, Belgium
Enrico Motta	KMI, Open University, UK
Sergei Nirenburg	University of Maryland Baltimore County, USA
Andrea Omicini	University of Bologna, Italy
Patrizia Paggio	Centre for Language Technology, Denmark
Maria Teresa Pazienza	University of Rome, Tor Vergata, Italy
Lorenza Saitta	University of Turin, Italy
Kiril Simov	LMD, Bulgarian Academy of Sciences, Bulgaria
Giovanni Soda	Univesity of Florence, Italy
Konstantinos Spyropoulos	NCSR 'Demokritos', Greece
Steffen Staab	University of Koblenz-Landau, Germany
Oliviero Stock	Fondazione Bruno Kessler, Italy
Tokunaga Takenobu	Tokyo Institute of Technology, Japan
Roman Yangarber	University of Helsinki, Finland

Special Track on *"Artificial Intelligence and Robotics"* Committee

Andrea Bonarini	Politecnico Milano (Italy)
Antonio Chella	Università di Palermo (Italy)
Dorothy N. Monekosso	Kingston University (UK)
Daniele Nardi	Università di Roma, *"La Sapienza"* (Italy) (*Chair*)
Bernhard Nebel	Albert-Ludwigs-Universität Freiburg (Germany)
Stefano Nolfi	ICST-CNR, Rome (Italy)
Enrico Pagello	Università di Padova (Italy)
Fiora Pirri	Università di Roma, *"La Sapienza"* (Italy)
Alessandro Saffiotti	Orebro University, Sweden
Bruno Siciliano	Università "Federico II", Napoli (Italy)

Special Track on *"Artificial Intelligence and Expressive Media"* Committee

Marc Cavazza	University of Teesside, (UK)
David Cope	University of California, Santa Cruz, (USA)
Craig Lindley	Gotland University and Blekinge Tech. College, (Sweden)
Vincenzo Lombardo	Università di Torino, (Italy) (*Chair*)
Ramon Lopez de Mantaras	IIIA - AI Research Institute CSIC, (Spain)

Frank Nack	Université Claude Bernard, Lyon 1, (France)
Anton Nijholt	University of Twente, (The Netherlands)
Ana Paiva	Technical University of Lisbon, (Portugal)
Oliviero Stock	Fondazione Bruno Kessler, (Italy)

Special Track on *"Intelligent Access to Multimedia Information"* Committee

Werner Bailer	Joanneum Research (Austria)
Roberto Basili	University of Rome, "Tor Vergata" (Italy) (*chair*)
Fabio Crestani	University of Lugano (Switzerland)
Hamish Cunningham	University of Sheffield (UK)
Daniela D'Aloisi	Fondazione Ugo Bordoni (Italy)
Alberto Messina	RAI-CRIT (Italy)
Borislav Popov	Sirma Lab. Ontotext (Bulgaria)
Raimondo Schettini	University of Milan Bicocca (Italy)
Giovanni Semeraro	University of Bari (Italy)
Valentin Tablan	University of Sheffield (UK)
Daniel Teruggi	Institut National de l'Audiovisuel (France)
Fabio Vignoli	Philips Research Lab. Europe (The Netherlands)

Referees

Khurshid Ahmad	Gregory Grefenstette
Luigia Carlucci Aiello	Nicola Guarino
Werner Bailer	Eduard Hovy
Stefania Bandini	Leonardo Lesmo
Roberto Basili	Craig Lindley
Andrea Bonarini	Vincenzo Lombardo
Ernesto Burattini	Ramon Lopez de Mantaras
Marc Cavazza	Robert Meersman
Antonio Chella	Alberto Messina
David Cope	Dorothy N Monekosso
Roberto Cordeschi	Alessandro Moschitti
Fabio Crestani	Enrico Motta
Hamish Cunningham	Frank Nack
Daniela D'Aloisi	Daniele Nardi
Walter Daelemans	Bernhard Nebel
Floriana Esposito	Anton Nijholt
Salvatore Gaglio	Sergei Nirenburg
Aldo Gangemi	Stefano Nolfi
Attilio Giordana	Andrea Omicini
Alfio Massimiliano Gliozzo	Enrico Pagello
Marco Gori	Patrizia Paggio

Ana Paiva
Maria Teresa Pazienza
Marco Pennacchiotti
Fiora Pirri
Borislav Popov
Alessandro Saffiotti
Lorenza Saitta
Raimondo Schettini
Giovanni Semeraro
Kiril Simov
Giovanni Soda
Konstantinos Spyropoulos
Steffen Staab
Armando Stellato
Oliviero Stock
Valentin Tablan
Tokunaga Takenobu
Guido Tascini
Daniel Teruggi
Fabio Vignoli
Roman Yangarber
Fabio Massimo Zanzotto

Supporting Institutions

Comune di Roma (Italy)
Fondazione Bruno Kessler, previously ITC-Irst (Italy)
Monte dei Paschi di Siena (Italy)
Unione Industriale e delle Imprese di Roma e del Lazio (UIR), (Italy)

Sponsors

Italian Association for Artificial Intelligence, AI*IA (Italy)
CELI (Italy)
ENEA (Italy)
Exprivia (Italy)
Fondazione IBM Italia (Italy)
Google Inc. (USA)
Università di Roma, Tor Vergata (Italy)

Table of Contents

Invited Talks

Knowledge Representation and Reasoning

Multiagent Systems, Distributed AI

Knowledge Engineering, Ontologies and the Semantic Web

Machine Learning

Natural Language Processing

Information Retrieval and Extraction

Planning and Scheduling

AI and Applications

Special Track: *AI and Robotics*

Special Track: *AI and Expressive Media*

Special Track: *Intelligent Access to Multimedia Information*

Posters

Learning to Select Team Strategies in Finite-Timed Zero-Sum Games

Manuela Veloso

Carnegie Mellon University,
School of Computer Science
Pittsburgh PA, USA
`veloso@cmu.edu`

Abstract. Games, by definition, offer the challenge of the presence of an opponent, to which a playing strategy should respond. In finite-timed zero-sum games, the strategy should enable to win the game within a limited playing time. Motivated by robot soccer, in this talk, we will present several approaches towards learning to select team strategies in such finite-timed zero-sum games. We will introduce an adaptive playbook approach with implicit opponent modeling, in which multiple team strategies are represented as variable weighted plays. We will discuss different plays as a function of different game situations and opponents. In conclusion, we will present an MDP-based learning algorithm to reason in particular about current score and game time left. Through extensive simulated empirical studies, we will demonstrate the effectiveness of the learning approach. In addition, the talk will include illustrative examples from robot soccer. The major part of this work is in conjunction with my PhD student Colin McMillen.

R. Basili and M.T. Pazienza (Eds.): AI*IA 2007, LNAI 4733, p. 1, 2007.

Expressive Intelligence: Artificial Intelligence, Games and New Media

Michael Mateas

University of California, Santa Cruz
Computer Science Department
Santa Cruz, CA (USA)
michaelm@cs.ucsc.edu

Abstract. Artificial intelligence methods open up new possibilities in art and entertainment, enabling the creation of believable characters with rich personalities and emotions, interactive story systems that incorporate player interaction into the construction of dynamic plots, and interactive installations and sculptural works that are able to perceive and respond to the human environment. At the same time as AI opens up new fields of artistic expression, AI-based art itself becomes a fundamental research agenda, posing and answering novel research questions which would not be raised unless doing AI research in the context of art and entertainment. I call this agenda, in which AI research and art mutually inform each other, Expressive AI. These ideas will be illustrated by looking at several current and past projects, including the interactive drama Facade. As a new game genre, interactive drama involves socially and emotionally charged interaction with characters in the context of a dynamically evolving plot.

R. Basili and M.T. Pazienza (Eds.): AI*IA 2007, LNAI 4733, p. 2, 2007.

Artificial Ontologies and Real Thoughts: Populating the Semantic Web?

Khurshid Ahmad

Trinity College, Dublin Ireland

Abstract. Corpus linguistic methods are discussed in the context of the automatic extraction of a candidate terminology of a specialist domain of knowledge. Collocation analysis of the candidate terms leads to some insight into the ontological commitment of the domain community or collective. The candidate terminology and ontology can be easily verified and validated and subsequently may be used in the construction of information extraction systems and of knowledge-based systems. The use of the methods is illustrated by an investigation of the ontological commitment of four major collectives: nuclear physics, cell biology, linguistics and anthropology. An analysis of a diachronic corpus allows an insight into changes in basic concepts within a specialism; an analysis of a corpus comprising texts published during a short and fixed time period –a synchronic corpus- shows how different sub-specialisms within a collective commit themselves to an ontology.

1 Introduction

The discovery of *semantics* by artificial intelligence researchers in the mid 20th century will serve as an exemplar of what converts feel when discovering something for themselves. Latter-day AI researchers had the enthusiastic confidence of early converts. Broad and nebulous terms were coined to describe the scope of artificial intelligence: *frames* (Marvin Minsky), epistemological engineering (Donald Michie) *conceptual graphs* (John Sowa), *inheritance reasoning* (Terry Winograd) and *circumscription* (John McCarthy) gave way to *explicit conceptualizations, terminological logics,* and a whole host of web acronyms– such as *OIL, DAML.*

The term AI was coined in 1956 with a mission to develop an overarching view of knowledge, thought and cognition. This view was expected to inform the development of intelligent systems but led to systems that could only solve 'toy problems'. About 20 years later, the mission was revised and the focus of AI was on a narrow, application-driven view of knowledge, thought and cognition and this view led to the development of systems that can solve well-defined problems and have a limited learning capability. One of the major challenges facing the AI community is the development of systems for automatically extracting information and knowledge directly from documents. Documents originating from a specialist domain of knowledge are indexed according to keywords. The choice and usage of keywords is motivated by a desire for communicating information and knowledge as accurately

R. Basili and M.T. Pazienza (Eds.): AI*IA 2007, LNAI 4733, pp. 3–23, 2007.

and as precisely as possible. The choice and usage of keywords in a specialism is equally motivated by the ontological commitment of a specialist domain community or collective. The organisation of the keywords in hierarchies and networks enables an indexer to organise the documents. The organisation is also used to enable members of a collective to retrieve documents manually and latterly through search engines. The keywords and the organisational framework are surrogates of knowledge within a specialist domain – a trace of knowledge, which may be referred to as *domain ontology*. And indeed experts in a specialist domain have been enlisted to produce an ontology of their specialism (see [23], for example).

Language plays a key role in the communication of concepts. There are several ways of investigating language ([29]):

  (i) Introspection or observation that typically involve methods from philosophy and logic;

  (ii) Elicitation experiments that are rooted in methods and techniques of psychology or anthropology; and,

  (iii) Systematic study of archives of texts and artefacts involving methods of data archiving and curation used extensively in empirical linguistics for example.

One can argue that like other rationalists, a number of ontologists have relied on their introspection that formal logic will help to decipher the conceptual structure of a domain or the ontological commitment of the domain collective ([35,37,16]). The use of philosophical and deviant logics has also been suggested – this argument is put forward by the proponents of Bayesian systems and proponents of fuzzy logic ([10,26]). And elicitation experiments have been used by some ontologists to decipher the conceptual structure of a domain ([12]). There is discussion in the literature that these alternatives are complementary in nature ([17]).

The empirical route for deciphering the conceptual structure of a domain involves a systematic examination of domain texts using methods of text analysis ([4,3,15]). Hybrid methods using text analysis, for finding key 'patterns' in the discourse of medical collectives of differing interests, and formal logic have also been proposed ([31]). The use of established general language *a-priori* hand-crafted thesauri to check how 'clean' an existing, formalised taxonomy within an arbitrary collective has also been described ([33]).

The empirical data driven approach in this paper, however, relies solely on a text archive of a given collective for the identification and extraction of candidate single key words. The candidates are then used to populate a glossary of terms for the collective. This glossary is used to identify collocation patterns for the candidates, leading to a further population of the glossary, and establishing relationships between the keywords. The assumption is that a headword labels a key concept, describes an event, or denotes a person, place or thing. This keyword-based approach helps in the creation of a network that can be asserted directly into a representational system like PROTÉGÉ. If the text archive is updated with the addition of new texts, then the candidate keyword glossary can be re-populated, new terms will be taken into account and the influence of older, un-fashionable, and lesser-used terms will diminish in the frequency count. Our glossary is generated and not hand crafted. The results for creating a domain terminology and ontology using this empirical approach are encouraging.

In the next section on *writing ontology,* I will illustrate the use of the method for automatic term extraction and ontology construction by an analysis of the ontology collective itself: a synchronically organised corpus of texts in ontology is analysed to show the ontological commitment of a small, representative group of ontologists. Following *writing ontology*, I will introduce *a text-informed method for building thesauri* in specialist domains: I will try and demonstrate how the preferential use of certain words in the writings of specialists can be used for automatically extracting terminology and subsequently the ontology of their specialism.

The study of how a given language or a given science is used in the conceptualisation of a specialism is regarded by Barry Smith as *internal metaphysics:* 'the study of the ontological commitments of specific theories or systems of beliefs' ([36]). Smith notes that linguists, psychologists and anthropologists have sought to 'elicit the ontological commitments of [..] different cultures and groups' (ibid). In the section entitled *nuclei: nucleus, cell, language, ethnology* and *ideology,* I will seek to explore the ontological commitment of researchers in nuclear physics, cell biology, theoretical linguistics and cultural anthropology by exploring their use of vocabulary. This study was carried out by examining a randomly sampled collection of specialist texts. I will try and demonstrate that a diachronic analysis of texts in a specialism shows what is popularly regarded as 'paradigm shift'; I will look at the developments in nuclear physics over a 100 year period related to the nuclear atom and developments in linguistics, especially the variation in the terminology of Noam Chomsky over a 30 year period to identify possible paradigm shifts in the two subjects. An analysis of texts produced in the same time period within the sub-branches of a discipline suggests to me that the nuances of terms used across disciplines is changed so that sub-domains can be differentiated. To this end I have used my method to investigate two sub-branches in cell biology (mammalian and bacterial cell biology) and four in anthropology (cultural, social, medical, and psychological anthropology). The results appear encouraging.

My intention is to explore whether one can understand ontological commitment in a given domain without referring to a discourse external reality or to the mental state of the members of the domain collective (Teubert made this point very elegantly in the context of corpus linguistics, [38]).

2 Writing Ontology? Terminology and Ontological Commitments of Ontologists

Those involved in any collective exercise tend to develop a semiotic system of their own. This system has icons defining the collective usually through language and in most cases through imagery and sounds. Doing science, theoretical or experimental, involves joining a defined collective of scientists, either as an interested lay-person or as a potential member of the collective. In so doing, one has to learn the vocabulary of the given science to join a specific science collective. For example, a *cell,* a word borrowed from Old French into English, in biology is the 'ultimate element in organic structures; a minute portion of protoplasm usually in a membrane', but in the physics collective one has to define a cell as 'a vessel containing one pair of plates immersed in fluid' (OED Online - Oxford English Dictionary Online). OED Online tells us that the definition (of cell) in biology is related to the use of the word in general language where cell was used to refer to a compartment. In physics, or more accurately in physical chemistry, the term is related to its general language cousin 'cell' used to denote an enclosed space, cavity or sac. The first recorded use of the word as a biological cell was in 1672 and the use as chemical cell is found in documents dating back to 1828. In the 20th century the computing collective is defining a cell in three related ways: First as 'an address or location in memory', second as 'the basic unit of a spreadsheet or some other table of text', and third as 'the name given to a packet in a packet switching system' ([24]). It is no wonder Zellig Harris has remarked that special language is 'a splinter of ordinary language' ([20]).

It appears that once a word is drawn into a collective and used to express a concept, label an object, describe an event or scene, or articulate a feeling, that word is used repeatedly. If the word happens to relate to a name (of a person, place or thing), it is often used in its plural form and sometimes adapted to describe an act also. One of the best examples is the use of the neologism/acronym *laser beam* –a beam created through 'light-amplification by stimulated emission of radiation' ([25]). We now have different types of *lasers,* and the acronym is used as a modifier as in *laser printer* and *laser eye surgery* for example. And, in the context of *laser pointers* we are warned that it is possible to "accidentally laser someone's eye" ([39]). The collective, it appears, is economical: one word has many uses and all uses are well targeted so there is no confusion. A nuclear physicist is not looking for protoplasm in the nucleus and a biologist is not looking for neutrons, or protons or quarks, in animal or plant cells. This process of adapting words from general language, or occasionally creating a brand-new term (or neologism) is formalised through the agency of standardising organisations. The conformity shown by scientists and engineers to a given set of terms in established disciplines does not stop them from being as creative with the use of language as a painters' use of a paint or a musicians' plucking the string of a musical instrument.

Frequently used single-word terms are often used in compound formation. For instance, an examination of a corpus of texts on the topic of ontology[1] indicates that the most frequently used words in this domain, excluding the so-called closed class words or determiners, conjunctions, prepositions, and pronouns, include *ontology, ontologies and ontological*; these three terms appear once for every 100 words used in the ontology corpus (see Table 1).

---

[1] A corpus of 38 papers and research reports on the topic of ontology was compiled that contains texts written by 18 researchers including Brian Smith and Nicola Guarino, comprising over 336,311 words in all.

Table 1. Most frequent open class words in our ontology corpus (*N=336,311*)

RANK	TOKEN	FREQUENCY (*f*)	RELATIVE FREQUENCY (*f/N*)
16	ontology	1940	0.6%
30	particular	864	0.3%
39	web	714	0.2%
40	world	688	0.2%
41	knowledge	666	0.2%
42	ontologies	665	0.2%
48	ontological	647	0.2%
50	relation	645	0.2%
51	objects	639	0.2%
52	self	629	0.2%

The terms *ontology* (or *ontologies*) are frequently used either as *heads* of compounds, as in *application ontology, biomedical ontologies*, or, terms like *X+ontology (or ontologies)*. In addition, terms *ontology* (and *ontological*) are used as modifiers, for instance, in *ontology look-up service,* and *ontological commitment* (see Table 2 & 3 below.

Table 2. The uses of the term *ontology* as head in nominal compounds

TOKEN	+ONTOLOGY	+ONTOLOGIES	TOTAL
formal	81		81
application	34	9	43
gene	40		40
domain	13	8	21
method	19		19
fungalweb	18		18
core	18		18
generic		17	17
philosophical	15		15
foundational	10	5	15
biomedical		13	13
medical	6	5	11
top-level	10		10
applied	10		10
linguistic		9	9
representation	7		7
minimal	6		6
building		5	5
Total	287	71	358

Table 2 shows that in our small corpus, the term *ontology* appears to have 18 preferred neighbours out of a vocabulary of over 16,000 unique words. My ontology corpus is dominated by articles by Brian Smith and Nicola Guarino (22 out of 38 articles in the corpus are by them and their colleagues, see Table 6 for details). This domination is reflected by the very frequent use of highly theoretical terms like *formal ontology, philosophical ontology, foundational ontology* and *representational ontology* (See Table 2). The presence of terms like *gene ontology, fungalweb ontology* and *medical* and *bio-medical ontology,* indicates the increasing importance of ontology in genomics, agricultural sciences, and bio-medical sciences.

The adjective *ontological* shows similar preferences for key terms amongst all the tokens in the ontology corpus: In ontology literature, both the singular and plural forms of *ontological commitment* is used with about the same frequency, there no *ontological theories* but ontological theory is half as frequent as *ontological commitment.* (See Table 3).

Table 3. Compound terms that comprise *ontological* as modifier of nominals

ONTOLOGICAL +	SINGULAR	PLURAL	TOTAL
commitment	19	15	34
level	10	9	19
analysis	16		16
nature	15		15
engineering	12		12
theory	9		9
category		9	9
status	8		8
distinction		8	8
choice		7	7
sentence		7	7
criterion		6	6
TOTAL	89	72	161

Linguists have noted that a collocation pattern shows a 'habitual co-occurrence of individual lexical items [...][that] are linguistically predictable to a greater or lesser extent' ([11]). The frequently occurring compounds containing *ontology,* especially *formal ontology, gene ontology* and *ontology library,* appear to collocate with other terms to make longer compound terms that show further restrictions being placed on a notion expressed by a collocate (see Table 4).

Using a text-based approach, usually one can also identify and then find elaborations of a term which is not used frequently: The collocating patterns of terms *continuant* and its synonym *endurant,* suggest that there may be *contiuant entities* that may be dependent or independent, and that there are *physical* and *non-physical endurants* (see Table 5).

The empirical data driven approach described in the next section facilitates the generation of thesauri of specialist domain. Candidate keywords are identified and used to populate a glossary of terms for a specialist collective. Collocation patterns further expand this glossary and suggest relationships between terms. This keyword-based approach helps in the creation of a network that can be asserted directly into a representational system like PROTÉGÉ. If the text archive is renewed by the addition of new texts, then the candidate keyword glossary can be re-populated – new terms will be taken into account and the influence of older, non-fashionable, and lesser-used terms will lose prominence.

Table 4. Multiword candidate terms that involve the use of *ontology* and *ontological*. Superordinate terms are prefixed by the symbol (▼) and instances by ○[2].

ontology	*ontological*
▼ formal ontology	▼ ontological analysis
○ basic formal ontology	○ direct ontological analysis
▼ gene ontology	○ ontological analysis theory
○ gene ontology consortium	▼ ontological categories
○ gene ontology proceedings	○ basic ontological categories
○ gene ontology project	○ distinct ontological categories
○ gene ontology tool	○ relevant ontological categories
▼ ontology library	○ top-level ontological categories
○ generic ontology library	▼ ontological commitment
○ integrated ontology library	○ minimal ontological commitment
	○ well-founded ontological commitment

Table 5. Neologisms in the literature on ontology in our corpus (*N= 336,311*)

continuant	*endurant*
▼ continuant entities	▼ non-physical endurant
○ dependent continuant entities	○ non-physical endurant time
○ independent continuant entities	▼ physical endurant
○ continuant entity cells	○ eventive physical endurant

3   A Text-Informed Method for Building Thesauri

Quine's observations related to 'words' provide an inspiration for a text-informed method for building a thesaurus: "Words, or their inscriptions, unlike points, miles, classes, and the rest, are tangible objects of the size so popular in the marketplace, where men [or women] of unlike conceptual schemes communicate with each other" ([28]).

As early as the 1940's, Stanley Gerr ([14]) noted that the size of scientific vocabulary is in itself an indication of progress in that science and that language facilitates the verbalization of conceptualisations through the construction of compound terms for representing complex and/or derivative concepts. This verbalization is facilitated through a reduction in syntactic complexity. The syntactic reduction and the precision in use of terms appear to be an attempt by scientists to organise their thoughts using the apparatus of formal logic ([14]). The evidence of the verbalization of conceptualisation can be found in written texts and speech excerpts of members of a thought collective. There are four observations of leading pioneering corpus linguists that have guided me in the development of the automatic term and inter-term relationship extraction method from such written or spoken texts:

FIRST OBSERVATION: Frequency of a lexical token usually correlates with its acceptability within a linguistic community, [30].

---

[2] These hierarchies were produced automatically by marking up the collocational patterns in RDF and then processing the RDF file through the PROTÉGÉ system.

SECOND OBSERVATION: Semi-preconstructed phrases constitute single choices, even though they might appear to be analysable into segments', [32].

THIRD OBSERVATION: There are subsets of a natural language, for example, subject-matter sublanguages that are characterised by: 'a limited vocabulary [...] in which the occurrence of other words is rare', [20];

FOURTH OBSERVATION: What members of a collective, for instance, scientists, do is to 'take resources that already existed in English and bring them out of hiding for their own rhetorical purposes: to create a discourse that moves forward by logical and coherent steps, each building on what has gone before', [18].

Computationally, we can identify terms through a contrast by comparing the distribution of a token in a corpus of specialist texts with that of the distribution of the (same) token within a general language corpus. Consider the distribution of the 20 most frequent tokens in our small corpus of ontology articles together with the relative frequency of these terms in both our corpus (f_{SP}/N_{SP}) and in the 100-million word British National Corpus (BNC[3]) (f_{BNC}/N_{BNC}). The composition of our ontology corpus is shown below in Table 6.

The distribution of the word *the* is approximately the same in the two corpora once we take into account the size of the corpus. In our corpus *the* is used 17352 times in a corpus of 336,311 tokens, while *the* occurs over 6 million times in the BNC that comprises 100 million words. The ratio of the two relative frequencies is 0.83 – that is the word is distributed in a similar manner in both the corpora; the same is true for a number of other tokens like *is, or, in, of, a, and* and so on. However, note the token *ontology*, ranked the 15th most frequent token in our ontology corpus, occurs 1940 times out of 336,311 tokens, but *ontology* only occurs 52 times in the BNC – the ratio of two relative frequencies is 10895. This means that for every one occurrence of the token *ontology* in English of everyday usage, we will find 10895 occurrences of 'ontology' in 'ontology-speak' (see Table 7), thereby suggesting some kind of special use.

This ratio of relative frequencies is called a *weirdness* ratio ([6]) following the remarks of the British anthropologist, Bronsilaw Malinowksi that the South Sea shamans use the names of deities so frequently as to make their speech *weird*.

It appears that the token *ontology* is a high frequency token with high weirdness. In order to quantify the fuzzy notion of 'high', we compute the standardised z-score for the frequency and for weirdness score for each token. If both the standardised scores are above a given threshold, our system will signal that the token is a candidate term. The threshold set at zero, therefore only those tokens whose frequency and weirdness is greater than or equal to the average frequency and average weirdness are selected. Low frequency and high weirdness tokens are excluded, for example spelling mistakes, and high frequency and low weirdness tokens are excluded, as they are

---

[3] The BNC is a carefully sampled corpus comprising over 100 million words spread over 4,000+ texts published mainly between 1960-1990 and cover genre as diverse as magazine articles, newspaper excerpts, romance and crime fiction, and a few scientific papers.

usually closed class words. Table 7 shows that 5 most frequently occurring tokens in our corpus have a high z-score for frequency, but a negative z-score for weirdness. This is not the case for the token *ontology*, which has both high frequency and weirdness values with (large) positive *z*-scores for both.

Table 6. Composition of my Ontology corpus: texts were taken mainly from *Applied Ontology, Synthese, BMC Bioinformatics* journals

Author		Time Period	Collectives or Specialistation					TOTAL Authors
			Computing	Genomics (Human+Plants)	Infectious Disease	Philosophy & Logic	Physics & Chemistry	
Smith et al	Barry	1978-2006	2	3		7		*12*
Guarino et al	Nicola	1991-2004	10					*10*
Baker et al	Christopher	2006		1				*1*
Borson	Stig	2006			1			*1*
Côté	Richard G.	2006		1				*1*
Donnely	Maureen	2005				1		*1*
Goggans	P.	2000					1	*1*
Hacking	Ian	2001				1		*1*
Hale	Susan C	1991					1	*1*
Hartati	Sri	1995					1	*1*
Jaiswal et al	Pankaj	2006		1				*1*
McIntyre	Lee	2006					1	*1*
Musen et al	Mark	2007	1					*1*
Rector et al	Alan	2000	1					*1*
Romana et al	Dumitru	2005	1					*1*
St. Anna	Adonai S.	2000					1	*1*
Stanford	P. Kyle	2006			1			*1*
Steve	Geri	1995		1				*1*
TOTAL Domains			*15*	*7*	*2*	*9*	*5*	*38*

Table 7. Distribution of tokens in our ontology corpus (N_{sp}=331,669 words) and the BNC (N_{BNC} =100, 467,090). The numbers in parentheses for the token *ontology* and its morphological variants are the frequencies of the tokens in the BNC.

Rank	Token	f_{sp}	f_{sp}/N_{sp}	f_{BNC}/N_{BNC}	Weirdness	z-scores		Term?
			(a)	(b)	(a)/(b)	z_{fsp}	z_{weird}	
1	the	17352	5.16%	6.18%	0.83	40.67	-0.10	No
2	of	14321	4.26%	2.94%	1.45	33.54	-0.10	No
3	a	9532	2.83%	2.15%	1.32	22.28	-0.10	No
4	and	8253	2.45%	2.68%	0.92	19.27	-0.10	No
5	in	7279	2.16%	1.88%	1.15	16.98	-0.10	No
15	ontology (52)	1940	0.58%	0.00005%	10895	4.42	3.32	Yes
41	ontologies (1)	665	0.20%	0.000001%	197940	1.43	62.09	Yes
46	ontological (279)	647	0.19%	0.00028%	690	1.39	0.11	Yes

12 K. Ahmad

As already indicated, the writings and speech patterns of scientists extensively use collocation patterns through the use of compound terms and *frozen phrases*. Usually one thinks of a collocation pattern in terms of a contiguous unit such as *nuclear atom*. These collocation patterns constitute qualifications and statements of possession, causality and so on related to the two or more constituent terms. Consider, the collocation uses of two terms in nuclear and atomic physics –*atom* and *nucleus* including non-contiguous collocates (see Table 8).

Table 8. A concordance of the term *atom* from texts published between 1911 to 2002. (*) Niels Bohr 1911; (**) Phys Lett. A, 296, 2002; (***) Phys. Rev. 49, 324 (1936).

-5	-4	-3	-2	-1		1	2	3	4	5	Ref
				nuclear	*atom*[*]						N. Bohr 1911
			nuclear	hydrogen	*atom*						N. Bohr 1911
					atom						
	nuclear	interactions	in	kaonic	*atom*						
nuclear	transition	energy	for	muonic	*atom*						
				H	*atom*	**nuclear**	cusp[**]				Phys Lett. A, 296, 2002
				2-electron	*atom*	possessing	**nuclear**	spin[***]			Phys. Rev. 49, 324 (1936)
					atom	having	infinite	**nuclear**	mass		
					atom,	in	**its**	new	**nuclear**		

The collocation patterns show the effect of the ontological commitment in the domain of physics to the notion of a nuclear, sub-divisible atom. The relation this collocation expresses between the two notions, one, a self-contained identifiable unit (the *atom*) and the other, the existence of its centre, kernel or *nucleus*, is not only a container-contained phenomenon. The collocation reveals that the atom has *nuclear* properties. Extending this there are new forms of atom, *kaonic* and *muonic* atoms, comprising a *nucleus* around which *kaons* and *muons* revolve rather than the old *electron*.

The frequent use of collocation patterns has led to the claim that the language of science is becoming increasingly opaque ([21]). Despite the fact that many collocation patterns are deliberately introduced, it is still important to verify the fact of collocation through tests of statistical significance. And, here we face the difficulty in choosing an appropriate *measure of association* ([9], [13]). No matter, we will follow the two indicators of association developed by F. Smadja ([34]) because it takes into account longer-range collocations quite transparently. The terms to be collocated are those with positive z-scores for weirdness and frequency. The algorithm is set out below.

Let w_i denote a keyword that collocates with another word w_j in any of the k *neighbourhoods* indexed between $-k/2$ to $+k/2$, e.g. for k=10, we will have w_j occurring in 5 positions to left of w_i and 5 to the right;

Let f_{ij}^k be the frequency of the word w_j occurring in the k-th neighbourhood of w_i

Let U_i be the spread of the collocation between wi and wj defined in terms of a variance metric:

$$U_{ij} = \frac{\sum_{l=-k/2}^{k/2}(f_{ij}^l - \overline{f}_{ij})^2}{k}$$

where, $\overline{f}_{ij}$ is the average of f_{ij}^l over all k.

Let ζ_{ij} be the *strength* of the collocation between w_i and w_j, measured by the computing the normalised score z_{ij} for each of the frequencies

$$f_{ij} = \sum_{l=-k/2}^{k/2} f_{ij}^l \quad \text{and then computing the average frequency}$$

$$\overline{f}_i = \frac{\sum_{j=1}^{J} f_{ij}}{J}$$

of all the J collocates w_j of w_i standard deviation σ_{ij} around $\overline{f}_i$:

$$\zeta_{ij} = \frac{(f_{ij} - \overline{f}_i)}{\sigma_{ij}}$$

If the strength (ζ_{ij}) and spread (U_i) are both above a certain threshold then w_i and w_j are statistically acceptable collocates, otherwise such patterns are rejected.

Smadja suggests $\zeta_0 = 1$, and $U_0 = 10$ [34, pp155], which I have used.

4 NUCLEI: Nucleus, Cell, Language, Ethnology and Ideology – Ontological Commitments in Four Domains

In this section we demonstrate the extent to which the proposed method for text analysis facilitates the investigation of the ontological commitment for a given domain. The analysis automatically leads to a set of candidate terms and the compound terms are organised in a network that may be regarded as candidate *ontology* of the domain. The composition of the text corpora used in this study is shown below (Table 9).

4.1 Nuclear Physics

The atomist philosophy in physics was investigated towards the end of the 19th century as scientists tried to explain the origins of electricity. This attempted

Table 9. The composition of the 5 corpora of mainly British & American English special language used in my study

Corpus	Nuclear Physics	Mammalian Cell Biology	Bacterial Cell Biology	Linguistics	Anthropology
No. of texts	398	43	53	68	374 Volumes
No. of tokens	1,934,658	309,007	273,424	1,659,266	39,471,742
Time	1900-2007	1996-2006	1996-2006		1980-2002
Genre	Journals, Books, Letters, Popular Science	Journals	Journals and Books	Journals and Books	Journals, Book Reviews

explanation and a host of experimental discoveries – unique spectra for each chemical atom, black body radiation, and indeed radioactivity – led to the foundation of quantum mechanics at the turn of 20th century. Within the next 10 years or so Niels Bohr, Ernst Rutherford, Heidi Yukawa and Jean Perrin all proposed a model of the *nuclear atom*; Rutherford went on to experiment on the *artificial transmutation of elements* – where protons and helium atoms were fired upon heavier stable elements to create unstable and radio-active elements. The Second World War caused a mass migration of scientists and a team led by Enrico Fermi in Rome created an *atomic battery* – the first chain reaction involving neutrons producing fission in Uranium ([5]) which ultimately led to the construction and detonation of the first nuclear bomb.

Diachronic Measure of Weirdness and Atomic Theory

The creation of new compounds – and very seldom new single-word terms- indicates changes in a specialist domain that comprise innovations, revisions and rejections ([1]). This compound formations happens when members of the domain collective try to assert an idea. The developments in physics at the turn of 20th century illustrate this point. Some physicists were convinced that the atoms of all elements have a nucleus and they wanted to convince their peers that the atom indeed is divisible: the repeated use of the collocation pattern *atomic nuclei* helped in the denial and rejection of the atomist philosophy. This rejection led to an innovation –*nuclear physics*; another compound term but this time includes a derivation of the term nucleus, the adjective *nuclear* as a modifier in the compound term. The new sub-discipline *nuclear physics* has been defined as 'the physics of atomic nuclei and their interactions with particular reference to the generation of nuclear energy or nuclear physics for short' ([25]).

The development of both experimental and theoretical nuclear physics from a standing start in the 1930s –the term was not even used until the late 1940s- clearly shows a change in the ontological commitment of the physics collective with awesome and awful effects. The decline of atomist philosophy in physics can be seen when we look at the relative distribution of key terms used in physics at the beginning of 20th century (texts in our *Early Nuclear Physics corpus* are used for that purpose and comprise articles written by Niels Bohr, Ernst Rutherford and Enrico Fermi amongst others) through to the period soon after the Second World War (1945-1970) and thence on to modern times (c. 1980-2007).

Table 10 shows relative decline of the terms used in the early period when compared to the later two periods. If we use the BNC to identify terms, we will still get high weirdness for terms ranging from the composite *atom* and the constituents *nucleus and electrons,* and the constituents of the nucleus –neutron, protons and the super-ordinate *nucleon.* But if we use our early corpus as a base, then the weirdness declines dramatically indicating the increasing non-use of certain terms (especially *atom* and *electron*) and even the term *nuclei*! (Table 10 has the details).

Table 10. Change in the usage of key terms used in physics of atoms and nuclei in three periods when compared with a sample of English used generally (1960-1999)

	Relative	Frequency	of Usage		Weirdness	
	1900-1945 (N=201737)	1945-1970 (N=79773)	1980-2007 (N=1384317))	BNC	1900-1945 (45 texts)	1945-1970 (70 texts)
	a	b	c		(b)/(a)	('c)/(b)
Atom	0.48%	0.07%	*0.009%*	972	0.15	0.1
nucleus	**0.48%**	**0.31%**	***0.14%***	**964**	**0.65**	**0.4**
Electron	0.30%	0.22%	*0.03%*	605	0.74	0.1
neutron	**0.14%**	**0.19%**	**0.28%**	**1127**	**1.4**	**1.5**
Nuclei	0.24%	0.30%	0.25%	816	1.2	0.8
nucleon	*0.0003%*	**0.10%**	**0.16%**	**27262**	**344**	**1.7**
scattering	0.105%	0.26%	0.17%	208	3	1
Proton	**0.063%**	**0.17%**	**0.17%**	**307**	**3**	**1**

When we look at the collocates of the term *nuclear,* we see some dramatic changes in the collocation patterns – *nuclear atom* is less of a statistically significant collocate than was the case in the early period; nuclear physics and nuclear theory have become statistically significant collocates as measured by Smadja's U and ζ –scores (if U is greater than 10 then invariably ζ is greater than 1, but reverse is not the case; we omit the value of ζ unless it is less than the threshold 1 – see Table 11):

Table 11. Changes in the collocation 'strength' of compounds, comprising *nuclear* as a modifier, over a century in English special language of physics

nuclear	Collocate *U-score*						
Time Period	*atom*	*charge*	*theory*	*reactions*	*structure*	*matter*	*physics*
1890-1945	2	109	4	66	54	3	4
1980-2007	0.4	189	64	1333	9137	8303	18755
U-score ratio	0.2	1.7	16	20.2	169.2	2767.7	4688.8

Halo Nuclei

Having established their subject, the nuclear physicists have become more and more abstract. They talk about *unstable nuclei* and go on to create *Carbon-17* from the stable *Carbon-12* (6 neutrons and 6 protons) by artificially adding 5 extra neutrons making a *halo around* the *stable core C-12*. The unstable systems remain alive and the extra neutrons go around the stable core in an orbit that comprises three interlocking *rings, Borromean rings* to be 'precise'; but if one ring is removed the structure collapses. Currently these rings are also of interest in mathematical topology and the adjective *Borromeo* comes from the fact that three interlocking rings were an emblem of a minor Italian nobility – the Borromeo family. The stem 'halo' also refers to the observation that the planetary halo usually comprises dust particles: the 21st century artificially created nuclei have a *neutron (proton)* halo. The literal and metaphorical use of the term *halo* is quite firmly established and we find *halo nuclei* as the basis of other compounds; some of these are yet to 'establish' in that the U-score and ζ values are below our empirical threshold of 10 and 1 respectively (see Table 12).

Table 12. Collocations of the term nuclei and halo nuclei, where the compound is also found in other compounds. The symbol (▼) denotes a super-ordinate term and the instances are denoted by (○).

Nuclei	Collocate	U-score	z-score (ζ)	Acceptable ($U \geq 10$, $\zeta \geq 1$)?
▼ halo nuclei		6333	23	Yes
	▼ neutron halo nuclei	101	101	Yes
	▼ two- neutron halo nuclei	79	11	Yes
	○ borromean halo nuclei	46	9	Yes
	○ non-borromean halo nuclei	3	2	No
	▼ halo nuclei breakup	11	7	Yes
	▼ neutron halo nuclei breakup	0.4	3.5	No
	○ proton halo nuclei	2	1.9	No

4.2 Linguistics

Chomsky's contribution to linguistics is immense but he has been a controversial figure within the linguistic community (see [19] for a rather dramatic account). For this reason, we begin a diachronic study of changes in linguistics with the texts of Noam Chomsky and investigate whether Chomsky's terminology, and by implication his ontological commitment, is still intact in the current linguistic literature. The iconic terms introduced by Chomsky expressed his rationalist commitment through *universal grammar, innateness, language acquisition device* and other terms by inflecting the token *grammar* and using its derivations (*grammatical*) [2]. We examine the use of terminology in Chomsky's own work and its continuing effect in the linguistics domain in the publications of a randomly selected group of linguistics researchers.

Chomskyian Linguistics

I do not have Chomsky's books in digitised form and have to rely on the excellent facility provided by Amazon Inc., for 'searching inside' the books the organisation sells. Amazon provides a 'concordance' of each of the books they have in digitised form, comprising 100 most frequent words excluding closed class words. I have looked at eight of Chomsky's books published between 1957, his earliest, and 1995. These are very well cited books and are integral to many linguistics curricula. The ontological commitment to a universal (grammar) peaked in Chomsky's writings, as represented by the random sample of his eight books, in 1965 (f=0.25%) and has waned to the same level (f=0.02%) in 1995 as it was in 1957. *Language and Mind* comprises the key mission of Chomsky: establishing *linguistics* as a discipline, convincing his peers of the *innateness of language* and concomitantly of the existence of a *universal grammar* (see Table 13 below)

Table 13. Variation of the use of three key terms in Chomsly's texts between 1957-1995

	Syntactic Structures	Generative Grammar	Aspects of Syntax	Language and Mind	Rules and Representations	Government & Binding	Barriers	The Minimalist Prog.
Year of Pub	1957 (2000)	1964	1965	2006 (1968)	1980	1981 (1993)	1986	1995
Words	32,089	30,248	32,089	89,372	73,833	148,310	27,708	136,360
Linguistic	0.44%	0.53%	**0.53%**	0.27%	0.10%	0.02%	0.04%	0.04%
Universal	0.01%	0.02%	**0.25%**	0.24%	0.12%	0.00%	0.01%	0.02%
Innate	0.00%	0.01%	**0.07%**	0.12%	0.08%	0.00%	0.00%	0.00%

Chomsky is keen for us to think of language as a *system*; he seeks to create a theoretical foundation of the study of language and has taken a staunchly anti-empirical stance against corpus linguistics. As a rationalist, Chomsky works with *structures* and *rules (of grammar)*. Again, we see a peak in the use of these terms in *Aspects of the Theory of Syntax* (1965), after which the use of five key meta-theoretical terms reverts to his earlier usage of the terms (until *Government and Binding*) and then declines to almost zero in the publications in the 1980s and 1990s (see Figure 1).

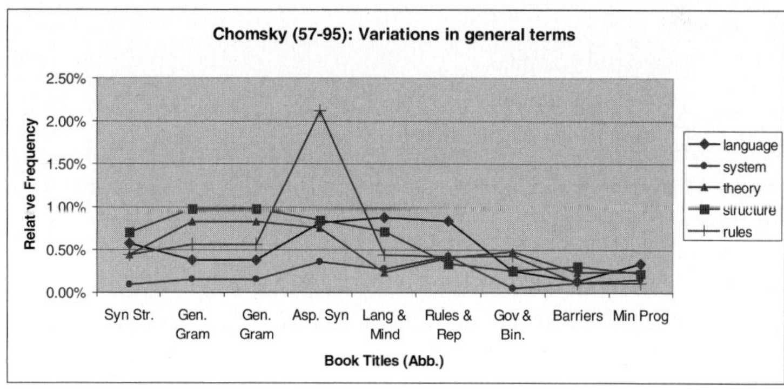

Fig. 1. Diachronic changes in 5 key terms in Chomsky over 28 years

The term grammar, terms used frequently to describe language either at different level of linguistic description, syntactic and semantic, and terms used to describe linguistic units, phrase and sentence, all show a decline in use in Chomsky's writings; except for *phrase* that has a massive peak in *Barriers* (1986) and comprises 2.54% of all the text in the book (See Figure 2).

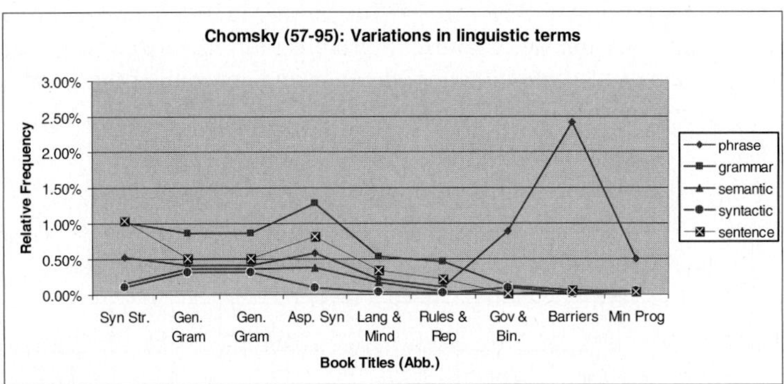

Fig. 2. Diachronic variation in 5 language-specific terms in Chomsky between 1957-1995

Modern Linguistics and Its Ontological Commitments

Noam Chomsky's influence can still be felt in our randomly sampled corpus that comprises papers from 1960-2006 comprising 1.65 million words. The key collocate used is *universal grammar* followed by *generative grammar*. But we also have frequent references to *phrase-structure grammar* and grammars that do not employ *phrase structure rules* like *head-driven* and *generalised phrase structure grammars*; *Lexical functional grammar* is also a strong collocate as are *tense* and *categorical grammar* (see Table 14).

Table 14. Collocation patterns of the the term *grammar* in our linguistics corpus

grammar (*f*=1979)	U-Score
○ universal grammar	803
○ generative grammar	514
▼ phrase structure grammar	334
○ head-driven phrase structure grammar	86
○ generalized phrase structure grammar	26
○ lexical-functional grammar	292
○ categorical grammar	80
○ tense grammar	154
○ transformational grammar	64
○ relational grammar	26
○ word grammar	24

Chomsky's contribution can still be felt through his original formulation of *phrase structure grammar* despite the fact that many of the recently developed *grammars* were formulated to improve upon his original idea.

4.3   Cell Biology: Commitments in Mammalian and Bacterial Cell Biology

The key ontological commitment in biology is the concept of *cell*. There are a variety of cell types and for the purposes of illustration we will consider *mammalian cells* and *bacterial cells*. Texts were selected from journals and public-information documents in two major areas that related to types of cells mentioned above: study of mammalian cells in immunology and that of bacterial cells in bacteriology for diagnosis and therapy. The differences in commitment appear both at cellular level and at the next level down when the constituents of the cell are discussed – for instance the *cytoskeleton* of a cell - the internal scaffolding of cells which determines 'cell shape, organizes structures within cells, and helps cells and growth cones of developing axons move.'(from *Wikipedia*). The different ways in which the knowledge of how a cell behaves – its movement or *migration* in the body of mammal or the *adhesion* of bacterial cells at a site – is denoted by the preferential use in the two related but divergent domains (Table 15).

Table 15 shows that whilst the super-ordinate terms appear with equal strength in the two sub-disciplines, the instances of these terms can be only found in one domain and not the other. So, for example, the compound term *cell migration* is strongly present in the bacterial cell biology corpus (U=14165), and is still strongly present in the bacterial cell biology (U=382). But, all the instances of *cell migration* are found in the bacterial cell corpus. The opposite is true of *cell adhesion*, showing different ontological commitments.

Table 15. Synchronic and contrastive analysis of two key ontological commitments (*cell* and *cytoskeleton*) in cell biology through the presence (or absence) of collocates of these terms. The symbol (▼) denotes a super-ordinate term and the instances are denoted by (○).

Concept	Collocates	U^B-score Bacterial Cell Biology (Bacteriology) (N=273,424)	U^M-score Mammalian Cell Biology (Immunology) (N=309,007)
▼ cell		*f(cell)*= 1,077	*f(cell)*=3,540
	▼ cell migration	382	14,165
	○germ cell migration	NF	490
	○endothelial cell migration	NF	13
	○border cell migration	NF	17
	▼ cell adhesion	746	333
	▼ tumor cell adhesion	51	NF
	▼ metastatic cell adhesion	19	NF
	○ metastatic tumor cell adhesion	13	NF
▼ cytoskeleton		65	248
	▼ microtubule cytoskeleton	20	31
	▼ actin cytoskeleton	1.4	1,842
	▼ cytoskeleton motility	NF	1,220

4.4 Anthropology

Anthropology is a well-established subject that has overlapping boundaries with sociology, psychology, economics, zoology, medicine, law and religious studies. It is defined as the "science of man, or of mankind, in the widest sense." (OED). In this section, I will present a synchronic analysis of the principal term in the subject *kinship*. Consider, first those collocates in which *kinship* appears as a modifier. The strength of the collocation *kinship system* is such that it appears as term in all the four domains –ethnology, cultural anthropology, medical anthropology and psychological anthropology. The two journals that cover all the domains, *Journal of the Royal Institute of Anthropology* (RIA) and the *American Anthropologist* (abbreviated as Am. Ant.) have all the five major collocates of *kinship: system, terminology, ties, theory* and *categories*. But except for articles in the journal on ethnology, *American Ethnologist* (Am. Ethn.), the other three branches of anthropology do not share the preference for these collocates. Here again, like the different branches of cell biology, a key concept (*kinship*) is shared across the domain, but not all of the compounds are so shared (Table 16 and 17). I have used the *Journal of Cultural Anthropolgy* (J. Cult. Ant.), *Journal of Medical Anthropology* (Med. Ant.) and *Ethos* – a journal of Psychological Anthropology.

The collocations where kinship is modified by other terms, have even wider distributions of these collocates. By looking at the two multi-disciplinary journals in anthropology (*Journal of the Royal Institute of Anthropology* and *American Anthropologist)*, we see that all collocations are present in these journals, except perhaps for *lesbian* and *gay kinship*. These terms are relatively more popular in cultural anthropology. There is no discernible collocate of *X+kinship* in either psychological or medical anthropology (Table 17).

Table 16. The right-collocates of *kinship* in 6 journals of anthropology covering 4 subjects

kinship+	Subjects in Anthropology					
	General	Ethnology	General	Culture	Psychology	Medicine
Journal	*RIA*	*Am. Ethn.*	*Am. Ant.*	*J. Cult. Ant.*	*Ethos*	*J. Med. Ant.*
$f_{Kinship}$	5071	3878	2657	671	276	246
system	2122	1159	478	17	19	3
terminology	1326	196	195	2	NF	NF
ties	239	659	128	7	4	6
theory	170	295	29	7	0.4	0.4
categories	78	11	3	0.3	0.1	1

If we agree that the frequent use of a term, say *kinship,* indicates an ontological commitment to the concept underlying the term, then we one can argue that the less frequent use of the term (*kinship*), and its collocates (*social kinship* to *gay kinship* in Table 17 above) in psychological anthropology and in medical anthropology suggests there is less of a commitment in these branches of anthropology then is the case in others.

Table 17. Strong collocates with *kinship* as head word, in 6 journals of anthropology covering 4 subjects

+*kinship*	Subjects in Anthropology					
	General	Ethnology	General	Culture	Psychology	Medicine
Journal	*RIA*	*Am. Ethn.*	*Am. Ant.*	*J. Cult. Ant.*	*Ethos*	*J. Med. Ant.*
$f_{Kinship}$	5,071	3,878	2,657	671	671	246
social	**222**	**392**	164	2	2	1
gender	**385**	**562**	133	60	4	6
ritual	37	117	56		1	
american	183	**212**	39	**377**	1	4
matrilineal	27	23	24	0.09	NF	0.09
fictive	85	47	17	0.16	0.36	6
bilateral	28	11	14	11		
lesbian	(1.45)	0.09	0.36	**117**	0.36	0.36
dravidian	**484**	42	2	NF	NF	NF
aboriginal	36	1	0.09	0.09	0.16	0.06
cognatic	46	3	1	1	0.09	0.36
gay	0.64	0.09	0.36	42	0.09	0.36

5 Afterword

I hope that the above tour de force of a range of disciplines and a rather straight-forward analysis of (randomly-selected) texts in the domain have given you some food for thought as to how we look at *what there is* synchronically and *what there was* which has now become *what there is* by a diachronic analysis of specialist domain texts

I have focused on compound terms throughout this paper. But two collocating words are not just in the head+modifier (or modifier+head) position. Causal relations (X causes Y), meronymic relations (X is_a part of Y) and many other lexical-semantic relations can be viewed as collocation patterns. Following Stanley Gerr and Zellig Harris, it is also possible to identify a *local grammar* that is exclusive to a domain of knowledge. Such a grammar, in principle, is a grammar of lexical semantic relations between terms of a domain.

Given the emergence of e-books and the fact that most journal publishers are publishing a parallel e-journal, the idea that we can literally feed books into a computer system is not such a fictional one. The availability of texts in almost all of science and technology opens up the possibility of thoroughly investigating the ontological commitments of the members of a domain community. This, I think, is the first step towards populating a semantic system that is designed for processing knowledge. Once we have the basic and comprehensive data related to a domain –its terminology and the inter-relationship of the terms- only then we can seriously discuss which formal method to use for representing knowledge. The semantic web needs to be populated systematically – hence the need for formal schema; the semantic web must have an exhaustive coverage- hence the need for large volumes of domain as typically written by members of a domain community.

Acknowledgement

The author wishes to thank Dr Ann Devitt (Trinity College, Dublin) and Prof Margaret Rogers (University of Surrey, England) for helping me to revise the paper so very thoroughly. I am grateful to Prof. Mike Fisher and Dr David Zettlyn, Department of Anthropology, University of Kent (UK) for allowing me to use their large collection of anthropology texts (c. 39 million words). Errors and omissions expected and they are all mine. My thanks to Roberto Basili and Maria Teresa Pazienza for inviting me to talk and for their infinite patience with this manuscript.

References

1. Ahmad, K.: Neologisms, Nonces and Word Formation. In: Heid, U., Evert, S., Lehmann, E., Rohrer, C. (eds.) Proceedings of the 9th EURALEX Int. Congress, Munich, 8-12 August 2000, vol. II, pp. 711–730. Universitat Stuttgart, Munich (2000)
2. Ahmad, K.: Writing Linguistics: When I use a word it means what I choose it to mean (Invited Talk). In: Klenner, M., Visser, H. (eds.) Computational Linguistics for the New Millennium: Divergence or Synergy? Proceedings of the International Symposium held at the Ruprecht-Karls-Universität, Heidelberg, 21-22 July 2000, pp. 15–38. Peter Lang Publishing Group, Bern (2002)
3. Ahmad, K., Gillam, L.: Automatic Ontology Extraction from Unstructured Texts. In: Meersman, R., Tari, Z. (eds.) On the Move to Meaningful Internet Systems 2005: CoopIS, DOA, and ODBASE. LNCS, vol. 3761, pp. 1330–1346. Springer, Heidelberg (2005)
4. Ahmad, K., Miles, L.: Specialist Knowledge and its Management. Journal of Hydroinformatics 24(4), 215–230 (2001)
5. Ahmad, K., Musacchio, M.T.: Enrico Fermi and the making of the language of nuclear physics. Fachsprache 25(3-4), 120–140 (2003)
6. Ahmad, K., Rogers, M.: Corpus Linguistics and Terminology Extraction. In: Wright, S.-E., Budin, G. (eds.) Handbook of Terminology Managemen, vol. 2, pp. 725–760. John Benjamins Publishing Company, Amsterdam & Philadelphia (2001)
7. Armstrong, S.: Using Large Corpora. The MIT Press, Cambridge & London (1993)
8. Aston, G., Burnard, L.: The BNC Handbook: Exploring the British National Corpus with Sara. Edinburgh Univ. Press, Edinburgh (1998)
9. Church, K.W., Mercer, R.L.: 'Introduction [...]'. In: Armstrong, S. (ed.), pp. 1–24 (1994)
10. Craven, M., DiPasquo, D., Freitag, D., McCallum, A., Mitchell, T., Nigam, K., Slattery, S.: Learning to construct knowledge bases from the World Wide Web. Artificial Intelligence 118, 69–113 (2000)
11. Crystal, D.: A Dictionary of Linguistics and Phonetics. Blackwell Publishers, Oxford (2002)
12. Dameron, O., Musen, M.A., Gibaud, B.: Using semantic dependencies for consistency management of an ontology of brain—cortex anatomy. Artificial Intelligence in Medicine 39, 217–225 (2007) (accessed June 20, 2007), available at: http://www.intl.elsevierhealth.com/journals/aiim
13. Dunning, T.: Accurate methods for the statistics of surprise and coincidence. In: Armstrong, S. (ed.), pp. 61–74 (1994)
14. Gerr, S.: Language and Science the Rational, Functional Language of Science and Technology. Philosophy of Science 9(2), 146–161 (1942)

15. Gillam, L., Tariq, M., Ahmad, K.: Terminology and the Construction of Ontology. Terminology 11(1), 55–81 (2005)
16. Guarino, N., Welty, C.: Evaluating ontological decisions with Ontoclean. Comms. of the ACM 45(2), 61–65 (2002)
17. Hacking, I.: Aristotelian Categories and Cognitive Domains. Synthese 126, 473–515 (2001)
18. Halliday, M.A.K., Martin, J.R.: Writing Science: Literacy and Discursive Power. The Falmer Press, London & Washington (1993)
19. Harris, R.A.: The Linguistic Wars. Oxford University Press, NewYork (1993)
20. Harris, Z.: A Theory of Language and Information: A Mathematical Approach. Clarendon Press, Oxford (1991)
21. Hayes, D.: The growing inaccessibility of science. Nature. 356, 739–740 (1992)
22. http://en.wikipedia.org/wiki/Cytoskeleton (accessed July 5, 2007)
23. Ilic, K., Kellogg, E.A., Jaiswal, P., Zapata, F., Stevens, P.F., Vincent Leszek, P., Avraham, S., Reiser, L., Pujar, A., Sachs, M.M., Whitman, N.T., McCouch Susan, R., Schaeffer, M.L., Ware, D.H., Stein, L.D., Rhee Seung, Y.: The Plant Structure Ontology, a Unified Vocabulary of Anatomy and Morphology of a Flowering Plant. Plant Physiology 143, 587–599 (2007)
24. Illingworth, V. (ed.): Oxford Dictionary of Computing. Oxford Univ. Press, Oxford (1996)
25. Issacs, A.: A Dictionary of Physics. Oxford University Press, Oxford (2003)
26. Lee, C.-S., Kao, Y.-F., Kuo, Y.-H., Wang, M.-H.: Automated ontology construction for unstructured text documents. Data & Knowledge Engineering 60(3), 547–566 (2007)
27. Oxford English Dictionary – The Online Version, available at http://www.oed.co.uk
28. van Orman Quine, W.: Word and Object. The MIT Press, Cambridge (1960)
29. Quirk, R.: Grammatical and Lexical Variance in English. Addison Wesley Longman, Harlow (1995)
30. Quirk, R., Greenbaum, S., Leech, G., Svartvik, J.: A Comprehensive Grammar of the English Language. Longman, London,New York (1985)
31. Serban, R., ten Teije, A., van Harmelen, F., Marcos, M., Polo-Conde, C.: Extraction and use of linguistic patterns for modelling medical guidelines. Artificial Intelligence in Medicine 39, 137–149 (2007)
32. Sinclair, J.M.: Collocation: a progress report. In: Steele, R., Threadgold, T. (eds.) Language Topics: essays in Honour of Michael Halliday, vol. 3, pp. 319–331. John Benjamins Pub. Co., Amsterdam (1987)
33. Sleeman, D., Reul, Q.: CleanONTO: Evaluating Taxonomic Relationships inOntologies. In: Proceedings WWW2006, Edinburgh, UK, May 22–26 (2006)
34. Smadja, F.: Retrieving collocations from text: Xtract. In: Armstrong, S. (ed.), pp. 143–177 (1994)
35. Smith, B.: An Essay in Formal Ontology. Grazer Philosophische Studien 6, 39–62 (1978)
36. Smith, B.: Ontology. In: Floridi, L. (ed.) Blackwell Guide to the Philosophy of Computingand Information, Basil Blackwell, Oxford (2003)
37. Smith, B.: Beyond Concepts: Ontology as Reality Representation. In: Varz, A., Vieu, L. (eds.) Proceedings of FOIS 2004. International Conference on Formal Ontology and Information Systems, Turin, 4-6 November, 2004 (2004)
38. Teubert, W.: Writing, hermeneutics and corpus linguistics. Logos and Language IV(2), 1–17 (2003)
39. Visual Being – A weblog for presentational technologies – (accessed July 8, 2007), www.visualbeing.com/2005/03
40. Wikipedia. (accessed July 5, 2007), http://en.wikipedia.org/wiki/Cytoskeleton

Model-Based Diagnosability Analysis for Web Services[*]

Stefano Bocconi[1], Claudia Picardi[1], Xavier Pucel[2], Daniele Theseider Dupré[3], and Louise Travé-Massuyès[2]

[1] Università di Torino, Dipartimento di Informatica, Torino, Italy
{Stefano.Bocconi,Claudia.Picardi}@di.unito.it
[2] LAAS-CNRS, Université de Toulouse, Toulouse, France
{xpucel,louise}@laas.fr
[3] Università del Piemonte Orientale, Dipartimento di Informatica, Alessandria, Italy
dtd@mfn.unipmn.it

Abstract. In this paper we deal with the problem of model-based diagnosability analysis for Web Services. The goal of diagnosability analysis is to determine whether the information one can observe during service execution is sufficient to precisely locate (by means of diagnostic reasoning) the source of the problem. The major difficulty in the context of Web Services is that models are distributed and no single entity has a global view of the complete model. In the paper we propose an approach that computes diagnosability for the decentralized diagnostic framework, described in [1], based on a Supervisor coordinating several Local Diagnosers. We also show that diagnosability analysis can be performed without requiring the Local Diagnosers different operations than those needed for diagnosis. The proposed approach is incremental: each fault is first analyzed independently of the occurrence of other faults, then the results are used to analyze combinations of behavioral modes, avoiding in most cases an exhaustive check of all combinations.

1 Introduction

Although many electronically controlled systems nowadays boast diagnostic capabilities, the actual performance of run-time diagnosis depends on several factors, and in particular on the design choices. This makes design-time diagnosability analysis a very important task in the design cycle of such systems.

In recent times automated diagnosis techniques have started being applied to the software domain; in particular model-based diagnosis approaches have been extended to deal with composed Web Services (WSs for short), as for example in [2,3,4]. However, for the diagnostic tools to be successful, diagnosability analysis becomes a design-time requirement also in these contexts.

Diagnosability tries to determine, given the current design and observability degree of the system, which faults can actually be diagnosed at run-time. This

---

[*] This work was partially supported by the EU, grant IST-516933, project WS-DIAMOND.

R. Basili and M.T. Pazienza (Eds.): AI*IA 2007, LNAI 4733, pp. 24–35, 2007.

type of analysis depends on the specific formalization of the notion of diagnosis that is being used for on-line software. In this paper we analyze the problem of diagnosability, with respect to the formalization of diagnosis introduced in [2] and the algorithm described in [1].

Before giving a short description of this framework, it is worth pointing out some peculiarities of the WS scenario, that pose some interesting problems with respect to existing literature on diagnosability analysis.

Web Services are often obtained by *composing* the functionalities of several simpler services. In this situation, it becomes important albeit difficult to find which of the simpler services did actually cause a malfunctioning. First of all, the parties that are involved in the composition, and then the model of the overall composition, cannot be assumed to be statically known[1]. For example, in an e-commerce scenario, it is easy to imagine that the shipment service is instantiated at run-time, depending on the customer requirements and type of delivery. Second, the internal models of the individual services are visible only to their owners, which can of course be different ones.

This scenario is addressed by the diagnosis approach in [2,1] as follows:

- Each WS is described, as in the component-oriented style of model-based diagnosis, by a **relation among finite-valued variables** that expresses both the process flow (workflow) and the dependencies between input and outputs of each workflow activity. Each activity is regarded as a possible source of errors.
- Diagnosis is defined as the task of finding which activity (or set of) may have caused the observed malfunctioning; formally the notion of **consistency-based diagnosis** [5] is adopted.
- Diagnosis is carried out through a **decentralized framework**. Diagnostic reasoning with respect to each WS model is performed by Local Diagnosers (one for each WS), while a Supervisor propagates solutions from one Local Diagnoser to the other, thanks to run-time information about the WSs interfaces and their connections.
- Diagnostic reasoning exploits a **least commitment** approach: solutions are represented as *partial* assignments to model variables, and variables that appear irrelevant to the diagnostic process are left unassigned. This has the twofold advantage of reducing the space needed to represent solutions and of avoiding the involvement of Local Diagnosers which have nothing to do with the observed problem. This approach has been generalized to any type of discrete constraint-based model in [1], while its specific tailoring to the WS case is discussed in [2].

In this paper we propose an algorithm for diagnosability analysis that builds upon those ideas, and that exploits, at the Supervisor level, operations analogous to those that Local Diagnosers implement for on-line diagnosis. We will show

---

[1] In the WS literature different ways exist to compose WSs; not all of them are based on a static model of the composition, therefore it is more general to assume that such model does not exist.

that, besides the above mentioned advantages, the usage of partial assignments allows to perform an incremental analysis that at each step takes into consideration more complex combinations of faults. Each step can reuse the results of previous ones, thereby gaining in efficiency. Moreover, the output at each step refines the analysis, so that a designer can interactively control the tradeoff between detail in the result and computational costs.

As a difference with respect to the diagnostic approach, we will assume that WSs are willing to disclose something more wrt their internal behavior: namely, the values of observable variables associated with each fault hypothesis. This, however, does not correspond to a centralized approach: the direct relation between fault hypotheses and observable is finally visible to the supervisor, but this relation must be computed in a decentralized way exploiting private models.

This paper is organized as follows: first, we present a brief description of the diagnosis approach in [1]. Then, we introduce some general notions related to diagnosability, and we use them to define our approach. We then present a complete example and discuss related work.

2   The Diagnosis Approach

As discussed in the previous section, the diagnosis framework we use as a reference has the following key features: it solves the problem of **consistency-based diagnosis** for **finite-valued relational models**, by adopting a **decentralized** approach and by exploiting a **least-commitment** strategy. Since the last point is central to the diagnosability algorithm we discuss in this paper, it is worth giving some more detail about it (see [1] for a more thorough description).

In the diagnosis algorithm, each Local Diagnoser has a threefold task: *(i)* explaining local observations and/or hypotheses on observations coming from other Local Diagnosers (and forwarded by the Supervisor); *(ii)* using local observations to discard hypotheses made by others; *(iii)* propagating the consequences of internal or external hypotheses so that others may discard them.

All these tasks are performed by finding those variable assignments that are consistent with the hypotheses to explain/propagate/discard. However, only variables that are relevant to the current task are considered, while the others are left unassigned. The operation that does this computation is called EXTEND, and it is also central to diagnosability analysis.

EXTEND works on *partial* assignments, that is functions that assign values to variables but whose domain is a *subset* of the variables of the local model.

EXTEND is either invoked by the Supervisor, or autonomously executed by the Local Diagnoser when it receives an alarm (the way diagnosis is activated). In both cases, the results are sent to the Supervisor.

The *input* to EXTEND is a partial assignment representing a projection over the local model variables of the current hypotheses in the system. The *output* is a (possibly empty) set of partial assignments that *extend* the input, propagating its values in the local model, and is meant to represent all the possible explanation/consequences locally consistent with it. In case the Local Diagnosers has also some local observations, these are incorporated in the input assignment before extending it.

Before returning the output set to the Supervisor, the Local Diagnoser restricts all the partial assignments in it to *public* variables, that is variables whose existence and value can be published to the Supervisor. These variables must include, but are not necessarily limited to, interface and behavior mode variables. Only the former are however shared by the Supervisor with the other Local Diagnosers, thus maintaining some privacy.

According to the framework in [1], the output set of extensions is built so that it meets two requirements.

1. The set of extensions is *sound and complete* with respect to the input. This means that the portion of model represented by the assignments in the set is equivalent to the portion of the model represented by the input assignment plus possibly the local observations.
2. Each extension in the set is *admissible* with respect to the local model. The notion of admissibility is meant to formalize the *least-commitment* strategy: intuitively, a partial assignment is admissible if it does not allow to infer anything about the unassigned variables that could not be inferred using the model alone.

3 Discriminability Analysis

Diagnosability analysis investigates the consequences of a fault on observable values in order to understand whether it is possible to uniquely isolate the fault starting from a given pattern of observables. More precisely, we need to distinguish the notion of *fault*, that is the individual state of one of the activities in a WS, and the notion of *fault mode*, that is the complete state of all the activities in the composite WS for which we want to do observability.

In the models we consider, each activity can either be *ok* (working as expected) or *ab* (faulty), so if there are n activities there are n faults that can occur in the system. A fault mode is instead a complete specification of *ok/ab* values for all the activities, therefore a system has 2^n possible fault modes[2].

Full diagnosability would mean that every possible fault mode in a system provides unique patterns of observable value; it is rather easy to see that this is close to impossible to achieve, and, in most cases, it is not even a requirement, given the improbability of some fault modes.

There are several ways for weakening this requirement so that it becomes practically interesting to study. For example, one could do the analysis only on fault modes that have a reasonable probability to occur, as for example those with single or double faults (i.e., 1 or 2 *ab* activities). Another possibility is to limit the study to *detectability*, i.e. the problem of finding whether the observables allow to distinguish a given fault mode from the "all ok" mode.

---

[2] We will consider in this context that the "all ok" state is one of the possible fault modes.

Since, depending on the particular situation, many of these properties can be of interest for the designer of a composite WSs, we prefer to focus on the notion of *discriminability*, which is given with respect to a *pair* of fault modes:

Definition 1 (Discriminability). *Two fault modes are* discriminable *if their patterns of observable values are disjoint. Since we consider relational models, this means that two fault modes f_1 and f_2 are discriminable if the portion $M(f_1)$ of the global model consistent with f_1, and the one $(M(f_2))$ consistent with f_2, are disjoint when projected on observable variables.*

Different types of "diagnosability analyses" can be obtained by choosing specific pairs for a discriminability test. The approach that we present here ultimately leads to a full discriminability analysis, but can be tuned to suit different needs.

As we discussed before, the diagnostic approach in [1] is centered around the notion of *partial* assignment, the idea being that by keeping track only of information that is relevant to the current analysis, one can store less information and avoid performing unnecessary reasoning.

Moreover, the kind of computation that is locally needed in order to perform a global consistency check through several local ones (namely, the EXTEND operation) naturally applies to partial assignments.

This leads us to the following definition:

Definition 2 (Partial fault mode). *A partial fault mode is an assignment of values (ok or ab) to* some *of the activity mode variables. A partial fault mode in which all mode variables are assigned is simply a* fault mode. *The* rank *of a partial fault mode is the number of mode variables it assigns, while its* domain *is the set of mode variables it assigns. Two partial fault modes are said to be* alternative *when they have the same domain, but assign a different value to at least one mode variable. A partial fault mode pfm_1 is a* refinement *for pfm_2 if every assigned variable in pfm_2 is assigned with the same value in pfm_1 and pfm_1 has a rank strictly greater than pfm_2. In this case we also say that pfm_2 is* a generalization *of pfm_1.*

The notion of discriminability in the case of relational models can be naturally extended to partial fault modes. It suffices to consider, in its definition, that f_1 and f_2 are partial fault modes.

Partial fault modes are actually more in number than "simple" fault modes: for n activities in a WS, there are 3^n partial fault modes. However, there are some advantages in doing discriminability analysis over partial fault modes, especially in the decentralized context. In fact, as we will shortly detail, we have that:

- the prediction of fault mode consequences (which is the part requiring the cooperation of several local diagnosers) is *only* performed for partial fault modes of rank 1. The actual discriminability analysis, that is, the comparison of the observable patterns of two partial fault modes, can then be performed by the Supervisor alone.
- The observable patterns are expressed in terms of partial assignments; that is, irrelevant variables are left unassigned. This provides some more information to the designer about the causes for non-discriminability.

- It is necessary to compare only *alternative* partial fault modes, that is, partial fault modes with the same rank and domain.
- The comparison of two alternative partial fault modes gives information also on their refinements, sometimes allowing to avoid performing the discriminability analysis for the refined pairs.

In particular, the algorithm exploits some properties that can be proved for *pfms* and their extensions. A first property allows the Supervisor to reuse the results of rank 1 analysis to compute extensions of *pfms* of higher ranks.

Property 1. *Let pfm_1 and pfm_2 be two consistent partial fault modes, and let us assume to have a complete set $\mathbf{Ext}(pfm_i)$ of admissible extensions for each of them. Then the set $\{\alpha_1 \wedge \alpha_2 \mid \alpha_1 \in \mathbf{Ext}(pfm_1), \alpha_2 \in \mathbf{Ext}(pfm_2), \alpha_1$ consistent with $\alpha_2\}$ is a complete set of admissible extensions for $pfm_1 \wedge pfm_2$.*

A second one shows how extensions can be used to assess discriminability:

Property 2. *Let pfm_1 and pfm_2 be two alternative partial fault modes, and let us assume to have a complete set $\mathbf{Ext}(pfm_i)$ of admissible extensions for each of them. Then pfm_1 and pfm_2 are discriminable if and only if for all $\alpha_1 \in \mathbf{Ext}(pfm_1), \alpha_2 \in \mathbf{Ext}(pfm_2)$, their restrictions α_1' and α_2' to observable variables are not consistent (i.e. there is at least one variable for which they assign two different values).*

For some pairs of *pfms* (in)discriminability can be inferred from lower rank results, without explicit analysis. This is straightforward for discriminability:

Property 3. *Let pfm_1' and pfm_2' be two discriminable partial fault modes. Then each pfm_1'', refinement of pfm_1', and pfm_2'', refinement of pfm_2', are discriminable.*

Indiscriminability can be inferred under appropriate conditions:

Property 4. *Let pfm_1 and pfm_2 be two alternative not discriminable partial fault modes. Let D denote their (coincident) domain and $\mathbf{Ext}(pfm_1)$, $\mathbf{Ext}(pfm_2)$ their complete sets of admissible extensions. Let m be a mode variable with $\mathbf{Dom}(m) \cap D = \emptyset$.*
If for every $\alpha_1 \in \mathbf{Ext}(pfm_1), \alpha_2 \in \mathbf{Ext}(pfm_2)$, consistent with each other when restricted to observable variables, it holds that $\mathbf{Dom}(\alpha_1) \cap \mathbf{Dom}(m) = \emptyset$ and $\mathbf{Dom}(\alpha_2) \cap \mathbf{Dom}(m) = \emptyset$, then the combinations $\{(pfm_1 \wedge m = v_1, pfm_2 \wedge m = v_2) \mid v_{1,2} \in \{ok, ab\}\}$ are non-discriminable as well.

This property tells us that whenever at rank k a pair of partial fault modes pfm_1, pfm_2 is non discriminable, and the extensions of pfm_1, pfm_2 do not mention a given additional mode variable m, then we can avoid to further refine this pair with m.

The algorithm can then be detailed as follows:

Step 1: The Supervisor computes a complete set of admissible extensions of all partial fault modes of rank 1. It does so by exploiting the EXTEND operation offered by Local Diagnosers and detailed in [1], with the only difference that Local Diagnoser treat all observable variables as public. In this way, for each partial fault mode *pfm* of rank 1, the Supervisor acquires a *complete set of admissible extensions* of *pfm* to observable, interface and mode variables.

Step 2: The Supervisor discards from the hypothesis table all the unobservable interface variables, thereby keeping only mode and observable variables. For each *pfm* the Supervisor has now a complete set of admissible extensions to observables and mode variables alone[3].

Step 3: The Supervisor performs discriminability analysis going rank by rank. A discriminability analysis of rank k consists in comparing two alternative partial mode assignments of rank k by exploiting their complete sets of admissible extensions. The procedure is as follows:

$\textsc{Output} = \emptyset; \textsc{Disc}_1 = \emptyset;$
$\textsc{ToDo}_1 = \{(m = ok, m = ab) \mid m \text{ mode variable}\};$
$\text{for } (k = 1; k \leq maxrank \wedge \textsc{ToDo}_k \neq \emptyset; k = k+1)$
$\quad \text{for each pair } (pfm_1, pfm_2) \in \textsc{ToDo}_k$
$\qquad \textsc{Ext}_1 = \textbf{Extend}(pfm_1); \textsc{Ext}_2 = \textbf{Extend}(pfm_2);$
$\qquad \textbf{AddDisc}(\textsc{Disc}_k, \textsc{Ext}_1, \textsc{Ext}_2, pfm_1, pfm_2);$
$\qquad \textbf{AddToDo}(\textsc{ToDo}_{k+1}, \textsc{Ext}_1, \textsc{Ext}_2, pfm_1, pfm_2);$
$\quad \textsc{Output} = \textsc{Output} \cup \textsc{Disc}_k;$
$\quad \textsc{Disc}_{k+1} = \textbf{Update}(\textsc{Disc}_k, k + 1);$
$\quad \textsc{ToDo}_{k+1} = \textsc{ToDo}_{k+1} \setminus \textsc{Disc}_{k+1};$
$\text{return } \textbf{Expand}(\textsc{Output}, k);$

The analysis proceeds rank by rank, that is it moves from more general partial fault modes, to more refined ones. It stops when either the maximum rank has been reached, or all the pairs of partial fault modes at higher ranks need not be analyzed because their discriminability status can already be assessed from the analysis of their generalizations at lower ranks. At the end of the algorithm $\textsc{Output}$ will contain the set of all pairs of discriminable alternative partial fault modes of all ranks (including those that the algorithm did not explicitly analyze).

At iteration k, $\textsc{ToDo}_k$ contains the set of pairs of alternative partial fault modes of rank k that should be analyzed for discriminability. The goal of iteration k is to find discriminable pairs of rank k, adding them to the output set, and to prepare the pairs that should be analyzed during iteration $k+1$. For these reasons it computes two sets: $\textsc{Disc}_k$ (discriminable pairs of rank k) and $\textsc{ToDo}_{k+1}$ (pairs to be analyzed in the next iteration).

For each element of a pair $(pfm_1, pfm_2) \in \textsc{ToDo}_k$ a complete set of admissible extensions is computed by **Extend** based on property 1.

AddDisc uses the results $\textsc{Ext}_1$, $\textsc{Ext}_2$ to assess, based on property 2, whether pfm_1 and pfm_2 are discriminable. If the pair is found discriminable, $\textsc{Disc}_k$ is updated adding (pfm_1, pfm_2).

---

[3] Due to space limits, it is not possible to discuss here the technical properties of admissible extensions; some more detail can be found in [1].

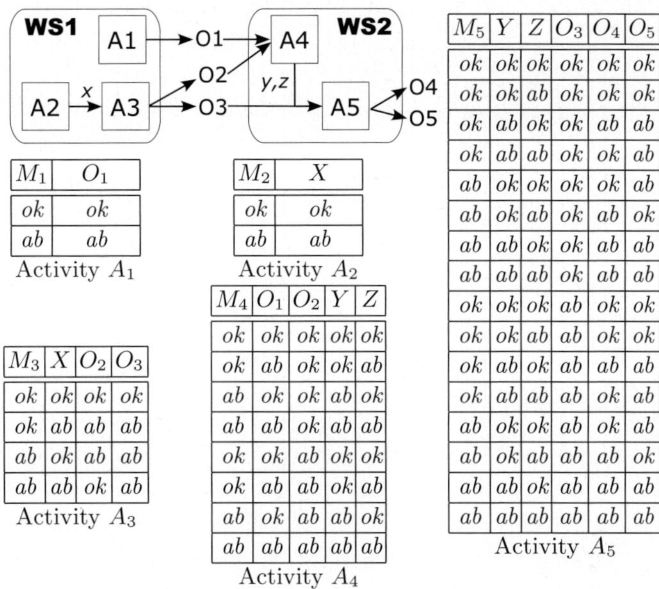

M_1	O_1
ok	ok
ab	ab

Activity A_1

M_2	X
ok	ok
ab	ab

Activity A_2

M_3	X	O_2	O_3
ok	ok	ok	ok
ok	ab	ab	ab
ab	ok	ab	ab
ab	ab	ok	ab

Activity A_3

M_4	O_1	O_2	Y	Z
ok	ok	ok	ok	ok
ok	ab	ok	ok	ab
ab	ok	ok	ab	ok
ab	ab	ok	ab	ab
ok	ok	ab	ok	ok
ok	ab	ab	ok	ab
ab	ok	ab	ab	ok
ab	ab	ab	ab	ab

Activity A_4

M_5	Y	Z	O_3	O_4	O_5
ok	ok	ok	ok	ok	ok
ok	ok	ab	ok	ok	ok
ok	ab	ok	ok	ab	ab
ok	ab	ab	ok	ok	ab
ab	ok	ok	ok	ok	ab
ab	ok	ab	ok	ab	ok
ab	ab	ok	ok	ab	ab
ab	ab	ab	ok	ab	ab
ok	ok	ok	ab	ok	ok
ok	ok	ab	ab	ok	ok
ok	ab	ok	ab	ab	ab
ok	ab	ab	ab	ok	ab
ab	ok	ok	ab	ok	ab
ab	ok	ab	ab	ab	ok
ab	ab	ok	ab	ab	ab
ab	ab	ab	ab	ab	ab

Activity A_5

Fig. 1. Illustrative example : two Web Services composed of five activities

Then, **AddToDo** updates the set ToDo_{k+1} by adding only those pairs of partial fault modes whose undiscriminability is not already certain, due to property 4, while property 3 allows **Update** to directly add in Disc_{k+1} the refinements of rank k discriminable pairs; this set can be subtracted from ToDo_{k+1}.

Since the analysis, thanks to search space pruning, could end before reaching the maximum rank, the final output set is obtained by expanding all the discriminable pairs found during the loop to higher ranks. In practice, the results could be left implicit, without such an expansion.

4   Example

In this example we apply the algorithm defined in the previous section to the Web Services whose model is described in figure 1. We assume that only interface variables are observed. A Web Service variable is considered observable if the observer is able to assess whether it is normal or not, thereby assigning a value *ok* or *ab* to the corresponding model variable. The behavior of an activity is described by a table; each tuple in the table corresponds to a valid combination of *ok* and *ab* values for its variables.

At step one the Supervisor computes a complete set of admissible extensions of all partial mode assignments of rank 1 (see figure 2). The information gathered at this stage suffices for the rest of the analysis, and the Supervisor does not need to invoke the Local Diagnosers anymore. As we said earlier, only observable and mode variables are kept, while interface variables are discarded (none in this case, since all interface variables are observable, see figure 1).

pfm	mode vars					observable vars				
	M_1	M_2	M_3	M_4	M_5	O_1	O_2	O_3	O_4	O_5
m_1	ok	$*$	$*$	ok	ok	ok	$*$	$*$	ok	ok
$= ok$	ok	$*$	$*$	ok	ab	ok	$*$	$*$	ok	ab
	ok	$*$	$*$	ab	$*$	ok	$*$	$*$	ab	ab
m_1	ab	$*$	$*$	ok	ok	ab	$*$	$*$	ok	ok
$= ab$	ab	$*$	$*$	ok	ab	ab	$*$	$*$	ab	ok
	ab	$*$	$*$	ab	ok	ab	$*$	$*$	ok	ab
	ab	$*$	$*$	ab	ab	ab	$*$	$*$	ab	ab
m_2	$*$	ok	ok	$*$	$*$	$*$	ok	ok	$*$	$*$
$= ok$	$*$	ok	ab	$*$	$*$	$*$	ab	ab	$*$	$*$
m_2	$*$	ab	ok	$*$	$*$	$*$	ab	ab	$*$	$*$
$= ab$	$*$	ab	ab	$*$	$*$	$*$	ok	ab	$*$	$*$
m_3	$*$	ok	ok	$*$	$*$	$*$	ok	ok	$*$	$*$
$= ok$	$*$	ab	ok	$*$	$*$	$*$	ab	ab	$*$	$*$

pfm	mode vars					observable vars				
	M_1	M_2	M_3	M_4	M_5	O_1	O_2	O_3	O_4	O_5
m_3	$*$	ok	ab	$*$	$*$	$*$	ab	ab	$*$	$*$
$= ab$	$*$	ab	ab	$*$	$*$	$*$	ok	ab	$*$	$*$
m_4	$*$	$*$	$*$	ok	ok	$*$	$*$	$*$	ok	ok
$= ok$	ok	$*$	$*$	ok	ab	ok	$*$	$*$	ok	ab
	ab	$*$	$*$	ok	ab	ab	$*$	$*$	ab	ok
m_4	$*$	$*$	$*$	ab	ab	$*$	$*$	$*$	ab	ab
$= ab$	ok	$*$	$*$	ab	$*$	ok	$*$	$*$	ab	ab
	ab	$*$	$*$	ab	ok	ab	$*$	$*$	ok	ok
m_5	$*$	$*$	$*$	ok	ok	$*$	$*$	$*$	ok	ok
$= ok$	ok	$*$	$*$	ab	ok	ok	$*$	$*$	ab	ab
	ab	$*$	$*$	ab	ok	ab	$*$	$*$	ok	ab
m_5	$*$	$*$	$*$	ab	ab	$*$	$*$	$*$	ab	ab
$= ab$	ok	$*$	$*$	ok	ab	ok	$*$	$*$	ok	ab
	ab	$*$	$*$	ok	ab	ab	$*$	$*$	ab	ok

Fig. 2. The admissible extensions of all partial mode assignments of rank 1

At this point the Supervisor starts diagnosability analysis from rank 1. We see that m_1 and m_4 are discriminable (i.e. $m_1 = ok$ is discriminable from $m_1 = ab$, and similarly for m_4) thanks to property 2. Thus, these assignments are inserted in the DISC_1 set; each refinement of $m_1 = ok$ is discriminable from each refinement of $m_1 = ab$, and analogously for $m_4 = ok$ and $m_4 = ab$. All these refinements will be inserted in the DISC_2 set so that the algorithm will not check them anymore. Continuing with rank 1 analysis, the algorithm determines that:

- m_2 is not discriminable (considering only restrictions to observable variables, the second tuple of $m_2 = ok$ is consistent with the first tuple of $m_2 = ab$)
- it needs to check m_2 in combination with m_3, since m_3 is present in the extensions of m_2 (property 4).

Therefore, the algorithm inserts in the TODO_2 set the combinations:

$$(m_2 = ok \wedge m_3 = ok, m_2 = ok \wedge m_3 = ab), (m_2 = ok \wedge m_3 = ok, m_2 = ab \wedge m_3 = ok)$$

$$(m_2 = ok \wedge m_3 = ok, m_2 = ab \wedge m_3 = ab), (m_2 = ok \wedge m_3 = ab, m_2 = ab \wedge m_3 = ok)$$

$$(m_2 = ok \wedge m_3 = ab, m_2 = ab \wedge m_3 = ab), (m_2 = ab \wedge m_3 = ok, m_2 = ab \wedge m_3 = ab)$$

Analyzing the last fault mode variable, m_5, the algorithm determines that it is also non discriminable (considering only restrictions to observable variables, the second tuple of $m_5 = ok$ is consistent with the first tuple of $m_5 = ab$), and that it needs to check at rank 2 combinations of m_5 with m_1 and m_4.

Since we saw that m_1 and m_4 are discriminable, not all combinations of m_5 with those mode variables need to be checked (more precisely, we do not need to check those that are in DISC_2, that is those where m_1 or m_4 have different values). The algorithm inserts therefore the following four combinations in TODO_2:

$$(m_5 = ok \wedge m_1 = ok, m_5 = ab \wedge m_1 = ok), (m_5 = ok \wedge m_1 = ab, m_5 = ab \wedge m_1 = ab)$$

$$(m_5 = ok \wedge m_4 = ok, m_5 = ab \wedge m_4 = ok), (m_5 = ok \wedge m_4 = ab, m_5 = ab \wedge m_4 = ab)$$

pfm	mode variables					observable variables				
	M_1	M_2	M_3	M_4	M_5	O_1	O_2	O_3	O_4	O_5
$(m_2 = ok \wedge m_3 = ok)$	*	ok	ok	*	*	*	ok	ok	*	*
$(m_2 = ok \wedge m_3 = ab)$	*	ok	ab	*	*	*	ab	ab	*	*
$(m_2 = ab \wedge m_3 = ok)$	*	ab	ok	*	*	*	ab	ab	*	*
$(m_2 = ab \wedge m_3 = ab)$	*	ab	ab	*	*	*	ok	ab	*	*
$(m_5 = ok \wedge m_1 = ok)$	ok	*	*	ab	ok	ok	*	*	ab	ab
	ok	*	*	ok	ok	ok	*	*	ok	ok
$(m_5 = ab \wedge m_1 = ok)$	ok	*	*	ok	ab	ok	*	*	ok	ab
	ok	*	*	ab	ab	ok	*	*	ab	ab
$(m_5 = ok \wedge m_1 = ab)$	ab	*	*	ok	ok	ab	*	*	ok	ok
	ab	*	*	ab	ok	ab	*	*	ok	ab
$(m_5 = ab \wedge m_1 = ab)$	ab	*	*	ok	ab	ab	*	*	ab	ok
	ab	*	*	ab	ab	ab	*	*	ab	ab
$(m_5 = ok \wedge m_4 = ok)$	*	*	*	ok	ok	*	*	*	ok	ok
$(m_5 = ok \wedge m_4 = ab)$	ok	*	*	ab	ok	ok	*	*	ab	ab
	ab	*	*	ab	ok	ab	*	*	ok	ab
$(m_5 = ab \wedge m_4 = ok)$	ok	*	*	ok	ab	ok	*	*	ok	ab
	ab	*	*	ok	ab	ab	*	*	ab	ok
$(m_5 = ab \wedge m_4 = ab)$	*	*	*	ab	ab	*	*	*	ab	ab

Fig. 3. The contents of the ToDo$_2$ set

At this stage, rank 2 analysis can start: combining the results of extend at rank 1, all extensions of the partial fault modes contained in ToDo$_2$ are calculated. Examining the six pairs of partial fault modes containing m_2 and m_3, the algorithm can determine that they are all discriminable except for $(m_2 = ok \wedge m_3 = ab, m_2 = ab \wedge m_3 = ok)$. The relative extensions do not mention any other mode variables, therefore the algorithm can conclude that each refinement of $(m_2 = ok \wedge m_3 = ab)$ is non-discriminable from each refinement of $(m_2 = ab \wedge m_3 = ok)$. Examining the 4 pairs of partial fault modes containing m_5 and m_1 or m_4, the algorithm can determine that $(m_5 = ok \wedge m_1 = ab, m_5 = ab \wedge m_1 = ab)$ and $(m_5 = ok \wedge m_4 = ok, m_5 = ab \wedge m_4 = ok)$ are discriminable. On the other hand, $(m_5 = ok \wedge m_1 = ok, m_5 = ab \wedge m_1 = ok)$ and $(m_5 = ok \wedge m_4 = ab, m_5 = ab \wedge m_4 = ab)$ are non-discriminable. The extensions of $(m_5 = ok \wedge m_1 = ok, m_5 = ab \wedge m_1 = ok)$ mention m_4, while the extensions of $(m_5 = ok \wedge m_4 = ab, m_5 = ab \wedge m_4 = ab)$ mention m_1.

The algorithm puts in the ToDo$_3$ set the following 2 combinations:

$$(m_5 = ok \wedge m_1 = ok \wedge m_4 = ok, m_5 = ab \wedge m_1 = ok \wedge m_4 = ok)$$

$$(m_5 = ok \wedge m_1 = ok \wedge m_4 = ab, m_5 = ab \wedge m_1 = ok \wedge m_4 = ab)$$

$$(m_5 = ok \wedge m_1 = ab \wedge m_4 = ab, m_5 = ab \wedge m_1 = ab \wedge m_4 = ab)$$

In fact, combinations with different values for m_1/m_4 are discarded due to property 2 (m_1 and m_4 are discriminable, thus these combinations are in DISC$_3$).

By checking the observable variables for each pair (see figure 4), the algorithm finds that the first and the third one are discriminable, while the second one is

pfm	mode variables					observable variables				
	M_1	M_2	M_3	M_4	M_5	O_1	O_2	O_3	O_4	O_5
$(m_5 = ok \wedge m_1 = ok \wedge m_4 = ok)$	ok	$*$	$*$	ok	ok	ok	$*$	$*$	ok	ok
$(m_5 = ab \wedge m_1 = ok \wedge m_4 = ok)$	ok	$*$	$*$	ok	ab	ok	$*$	$*$	ok	ab
$(m_5 = ok \wedge m_1 = ok \wedge m_4 = ab)$	ok	$*$	$*$	ab	ok	ok	$*$	$*$	ab	ab
$(m_5 = ab \wedge m_1 = ok \wedge m_4 = ab)$	ok	$*$	$*$	ab	ab	ok	$*$	$*$	ab	ab
$(m_5 = ok \wedge m_1 = ab \wedge m_4 = ab)$	ab	$*$	$*$	ab	ok	ab	$*$	$*$	ok	ab
$(m_5 = ab \wedge m_1 = ab \wedge m_4 = ab)$	ab	$*$	$*$	ab	ab	ab	$*$	$*$	ab	ab

Fig. 4. The contents of the ToDo_3 set

not. Since the extensions do not constrain other fault modes, the pair refinements are non-discriminable as well. Therefore the algorithm stops at rank 3.

As a final result, two partial fault modes are not discriminable if and only if they refine the pairs $(m_2 = ok \wedge m_3 = ab, m_2 = ab \wedge m_3 = ok)$ or $(m_1 = ok \wedge m_4 = ab \wedge m_5 = ok, m_1 = ok \wedge m_4 = ab \wedge m_5 = ab)$. All other pairs are discriminable. In this example a full discriminability analysis is obtained already at rank 3 (while the maximum rank is 5).

5   Conclusions and Related Work

The decentralized diagnosability approach proposed in this paper is based on the diagnosis algorithm developed in [2,1], and it is suited for the same application context for the same reason: it allows models of individual Web Services to be kept private. The main additional contribution of the diagnosability analysis in this paper is an incremental approach, where the implications of each individual fault on observable variables are analyzed, identifying those consequences that hold independently of the presence of other faults, and other observable consequences that only hold assuming the presence or absence of some other fault. Thanks to the newfound properties described in section 3, the results of this analysis can be used to compute or infer discriminability results for specific combinations of faults.

Distributed diagnosability analysis is also studied in [6,7], but the approach focuses on discrete event systems modeled by communicating automata. Diagnosability is analyzed in the context of event-based diagnosis, which means that the fault signatures are composed of sequences of events. In the discrete event systems framework, other well-known methods for diagnosability analysis, in particular [8], but also [9], [10], are devoted to centralized systems. In [11], diagnosability is analyzed upon a logic based formalism and within a state-based diagnosis framework that is closer to ours, however it focuses on centralized systems. The diagnosability analysis proposed in [12] also refers to a state-based diagnosis approach for centralized systems. [13,14,11] provide definitions of faults, fault modes, signatures and discriminability bridging different diagnosis approaches.

References

1. Console, L., Picardi, C., Theseider Dupré, D.: A framework for decentralized qualitative model-based diagnosis. In: IJCAI-07. Proc. 20th Int. Joint Conference on Artificial Intelligence (2007)
2. Ardissono, L., Console, L., Goy, A., Petrone, G., Picardi, C., Segnan, M., Theseider Dupré, D.: Enhancing Web Services with diagnostic capabilities. In: Proceedings of the 3rd IEEE European Conference on Web Services, IEEE Computer Society Press, Los Alamitos (2005)
3. Yan, Y., Cordier, M.O., Pencolé, Y., Grastien, A.: Monitoring web service networks in a model-based approach. In: Proceedings of the 3rd IEEE European Conference on Web Services, IEEE Computer Society Press, Los Alamitos (2005)
4. Mayer, W., Stumptner, M.: Debugging failures in web services coordination. In: DX'06. Proceedings of the 17th International Workshop on Principles of Diagnosis, pp. 171–179 (2006)
5. Reiter, R.: A theory of diagnosis from first principles. Artificial Intelligence 32(1), 57–96 (1987)
6. Pencole, Y.: Diagnosability analysis of distributed discrete event systems. In: 16th European Conference on Artificial Intelligence, 4th edn., pp. 43–47 (2004)
7. Schumann, A., Pencolé, Y.: Scalable diagnosability checking of event-driven systems. In: IJCAI'07, pp. 575–580 (2007)
8. Sampath, M., Sengputa, R., Lafortune, S., Sinnamohideen, K., Teneketsis, D.: Diagnosability of discrete-event systems. IEEE Trans. AC 40, 1555–1575 (1995)
9. Cimatti, A., Pecheur, C., Cavada, R.: Formal verification of diagnosability via symbolic model checking. In: Proceedings of IJCAI'03, pp. 363–369 (2003)
10. Jiang, S., Huang, Z., Chandra, V., Kumar, R.: A polynomial time algorithm for diagnosability of discrete event systems. IEEE Trans. AC 46(8), 1318–1321 (2001)
11. Struss, P., Dressler, O.: A toolbox integrating model-based diagnosability analysis and automated generation of diagnostics. In: DX'03. Proceedings of the 14th International Workshop on Principles of Diagnosis (2003)
12. Travé-Massuyès, L., Escobet, T., Olive, X.: Diagnosability analysis based on component supported analytical redundancy relations. IEEE Trans. SMC, Part A 36(6) (2006)
13. Cordier, M.O., Dague, P., Lévy, F., Montmain, J., Staroswiecki, M., Travé-Massuyès, L.: Conflicts versus analytical redundancy relations: A comparative analysis of the model-based diagnostic approach from the artificial intelligence and automatic control perspectives. IEEE Trans. SMC. Part B. 34(5), 2163–2177 (2004)
14. Cordier, M.O., Travé-Massuyès, L., Pucel, X.: Comparing diagnosability in continuous and discrete-event systems. In: DX'06. Proceedings of the 17th International Workshop on Principles of Diagnosis, pp. 55–60 (2006)

Finite Model Reasoning on UML Class Diagrams Via Constraint Programming*

Marco Cadoli[1], Diego Calvanese[2], Giuseppe De Giacomo[1], and Toni Mancini[1]

[1] Dip. di Informatica e Sistemistica Università di Roma "La Sapienza"
Via Ariosto 25, 00185 Roma, Italy
`cadoli,degiacomo,tmancini@dis.uniroma1.it`
[2] Faculty of Computer Science Free University of Bozen-Bolzano
P. Domenicani 3, 39100 Bolzano, Italy
`calvanese@inf.unibz.it`

Abstract. Finite model reasoning in UML class diagrams is an important task for assessing the quality of the analysis phase in the development of software applications in which it is assumed that the number of objects of the domain is finite. In this paper, we show how to encode finite model reasoning in UML class diagrams as a constraint satisfaction problem (CSP), exploiting techniques developed in description logics. In doing so we set up and solve an intermediate CSP problem to deal with the explosion of "class combinations" arising in the encoding. To solve the resulting CSP problems we rely on the use of off-the-shelf tools for constraint modeling and programming. As a result, we obtain, to the best of our knowledge, the first implemented system that performs finite model reasoning on UML class diagrams.

1 Introduction

The Unified Modelling Language (UML, [8], cf. `www.uml.org`) is probably the most used modelling language in the context of software development, and has been proven to be very effective for the analysis and design phases of the software life cycle.

UML offers a number of diagrams for representing various aspects of the requirements for a software application. Probably the most important diagram is the *class diagram*, which represents all main structural aspects of an application. A typical class diagram shows: *classes*, i.e., homogeneous collections of *objects*, i.e., instances; *associations*, i.e., relations among classes; *ISA hierarchies* among classes, i.e., relations establishing that each object of a class is also an object of another class; and *multiplicity constraints* on associations, i.e., restrictions on the number of links between objects related by an association.

---

* This research has been partially supported by FET project TONES (Thinking ONtologiES), funded within the EU 6th Framework Programme under contract FP6-7603, and by the PRIN 2006 project NGS (New Generation Search), funded by MIUR.

R. Basili and M.T. Pazienza (Eds.): AI*IA 2007, LNAI 4733, pp. 36–47, 2007.

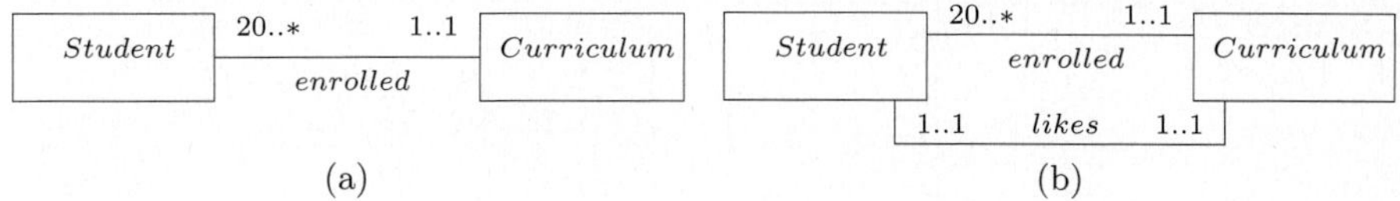

Fig. 1. UML class diagrams with (a) finitely satisfiable and (b) finitely unsatisfiable classes

Actually, a UML class diagram represents also other aspects, e.g., the attributes and the operations of a class, the attributes of an association, and the specialization of an association. Such aspects, for the sake of simplicity, will not be considered in this paper.

An example of a class diagram is shown in Figure 1(a), which refers to an application concerning management of administrative data of a university, and exhibits two classes (*Student* and *Curriculum*) and an association (*enrolled*) between them. The multiplicity constraints state that:

- Each student must be enrolled in at least one and at most one curriculum;
- Each curriculum must have at least twenty enrolled students, and there is no maximum on the number of enrolled students per curriculum.

It is interesting to note that a class diagram induces restrictions on the number of objects. As an example, referring to the situation of Figure 1(a), it is possible to have zero, twenty, or more students, but it is impossible to have any number of students between one and nineteen. The reason is that if we had, e.g., five students, then we would need at least one curriculum, which in turn requires at least twenty students.

In some cases the number of objects of a class is forced to be zero. As an example, if we add to the class diagram of Figure 1(a) a further association, *likes*, with the constraints that each student likes exactly one curriculum, and that each curriculum is liked by exactly one student (cf., Figure 1(b)), then it is impossible to have any finite non-zero number of students and curricula. In fact, the new association and its multiplicity constraints force the students to be exactly as many as the curricula, which is impossible. Observe that, with a logical formalization of the UML class diagram, one can actually perform such a form of reasoning making use of automated reasoning tools[1].

Referring to Figure 1(b), note that the multiplicity constraints do not rule out the possibility of having *infinitely many* students and curricula. When a class is forced to have either zero or infinitely many instances, it is said to be *finitely unsatisfiable*. For the sake of completeness, we mention that in some situations involving ISA hierarchies (not shown for brevity), classes may be forced to have zero objects, and are thus said to be unsatisfiable in the *unrestricted* sense. The above example shows that UML class diagrams do *not have the finite model property*, since unrestricted and finite satisfiability are different.

---

[1] Actually, current CASE tools do not perform any kind of automated reasoning on UML class diagrams yet.

Syntax	Semantics
$\neg B$	$\Delta^{\mathcal{I}} \setminus B^{\mathcal{I}}$
$D_1 \sqcap D_2$	$D_1^{\mathcal{I}} \cap D_2^{\mathcal{I}}$
$D_1 \sqcup D_2$	$D_1^{\mathcal{I}} \cup D_2^{\mathcal{I}}$
$\forall R.D$	$\{a : \forall b.\,(a,b) \in R^{\mathcal{I}} \to b \in D^{\mathcal{I}}\}$

Syntax	Semantics
$(\geq m\,R)$	$\{a : |\{b : (a,b) \in R^{\mathcal{I}}\}| \geq m\}$
$(\leq n\,R)$	$\{a : |\{b : (a,b) \in R^{\mathcal{I}}\}| \leq n\}$
P^-	$\{(a,b) : (b,a) \in P^{\mathcal{I}}\}$

Fig. 2. Syntax and semantics of $\mathcal{ALUNI}$

Unsatisfiability, either finite or unrestricted, of a class is a symptom of a bug in the analysis phase, since either such a class is superfluous, or a conflict has arisen while modeling different, antithetic, requirements. In particular, finite unsatisfiability is especially relevant in the context of applications, e.g., databases, in which the number of instances is intrinsically finite. Global reasoning on the whole class diagram is needed to show finite unsatisfiability. For large, industrial class diagrams, finite unsatisfiability could easily arise, because different parts of the same diagram may be synthesized by different analysts, and is likely to be nearly impossible to be discovered by hand.

In this paper, we address finite model reasoning on UML class diagrams, a task that, to the best of our knowledge, has not been attempted so far. This is done by exploiting an encoding of UML class diagrams in terms of Description Logics (DLs) [2], in order to take advantage of the finite model reasoning techniques developed for DLs [4,5].These techniques, which are optimal from the computational complexity point of view, are based on a reduction of reasoning on a DL knowledge base to satisfaction of linear constraints.

The contribution of this paper is on the practical realization of such finite modeling reasoning techniques by making use of off-the-shelf tools for constraint modelling and programming. In particular, by exploiting the finite model reasoning technique for DLs presented in [4,5], we propose an encoding of UML class diagram satisfiability as a Constraint Satisfaction Problem (CSP). We show that, in spite of the high computational complexity of the reasoning task in general, the aforementioned techniques are feasible in practice, if some optimizations are performed in order to reduce the exponential number of variables in the constraint problem. We do so by relying again on the constraint solver itself, by setting up and solving an auxiliary constraint problem that exploits the structure of real-world UML class diagrams.

We built a system that accepts as input an UML class diagram (written in the standard MOF syntax[2]), and reasons on it according to the ideas above making use of the ILOG's OPLSTUDIO constraint system. The system allowed us to test the technique on the industrial knowledge base CIM.

2   Description Logics

DLs [1] are logics for representing a domain of interest in terms of classes and relationships among classes and reasoning on it. They are extensively used to

---

[2] http://www.dmtf.org/

formalize conceptual models and object-oriented models in databases and software engineering [3,2], and lay the foundations for ontology languages used in the Semantic Web.

In DLs, the domain of interest is modeled through *concepts*, denoting classes of objects, and *roles*, denoting binary relations between objects. The semantics of DLs is given in terms of an *interpretation* $\mathcal{I} = (\Delta^{\mathcal{I}}, \cdot^{\mathcal{I}})$ consisting of an interpretation *domain* $\Delta^{\mathcal{I}}$ and an *interpretation function* $\cdot^{\mathcal{I}}$ that maps every concept D to a subset $D^{\mathcal{I}}$ of $\Delta^{\mathcal{I}}$ and every role R to a subset $R^{\mathcal{I}}$ of $\Delta^{\mathcal{I}} \times \Delta^{\mathcal{I}}$. In this paper we deal with the DL $\mathcal{ALUNI}$ [4,5], whose syntax and semantics are shown in Figure 2 (B and P denote respectively atomic concepts and roles, D and R respectively arbitrary concepts and roles, m a positive integer, and n a non-negative integer). The constructs $(\geq m\, R)$ and $(\leq n\, R)$ are called *number restrictions*. We refer to [1] for more details on DLs.

An $\mathcal{ALUNI}$ knowledge base (KB) is constituted by a finite set of *(primitive) inclusion assertions* of the form $B \sqsubseteq D$. An interpretation $\mathcal{I}$ is called a *model* of a KB if $B^{\mathcal{I}} \subseteq D^{\mathcal{I}}$ for each assertion $B \sqsubseteq D$ in the KB. The basic reasoning tasks in DLs are (finite) KB and concept satisfiability: a KB is *(finitely) satisfiable* if it admits a (finite) model; a concept C is *(finitely) satisfiable* in a KB, if the KB admits a (finite) model $\mathcal{I}$ such that $C^{\mathcal{I}} \neq \emptyset$.

Due to the expressiveness of the constructs present in $\mathcal{ALUNI}$ KBs, unrestricted and finite satisfiability are different problems, i.e., $\mathcal{ALUNI}$ does not have the *finite model property* (cf. [5]). Unrestricted model reasoning is a quite well investigated problem in DLs, and several DL reasoning systems that perform such kind of reasoning are available (e..g, Fact++[3] or Racer[4]).

Instead, finite model reasoning is less well studied, both from the theoretical and from the practical point of view. To the best of our knowledge, no implementation of finite model reasoners has been attempted till now. Some works provide theoretical results showing that finite model reasoning over a KB can be done in EXPTIME for variants of expressive DLs, including $\mathcal{ALUNI}$ [4,5,10]. Notice that this bound is tight, since (finite) model reasoning is already EXPTIME-hard even for much less expressive DLs (enjoying the finite model property) [1]. These results are based on an encoding of the finite model reasoning problem into the problem of finding particular integer solutions to a system of linear inequalities. Such solutions can be put in a direct correspondence with models of the KB in which the values provided by the solution correspond to the cardinalities of the extensions of concepts and roles. Also, the specific form of the system of inequalities guarantees that the existence of an arbitrary solution implies the existence of an integer solution. Moreover, from the encoding it is possible to deduce the existence of a bound on the size of an integer solution, as specified by the following theorem.

Theorem 1 ([5]). *Let $\mathcal{K}$ be an $\mathcal{ALUNI}$ KB of size K, C an atomic concept, $\Psi_{\mathcal{K},C}$ the system of linear inequalities derived from $\mathcal{K}$ and C, and N the maximum number appearing in number restrictions in $\mathcal{K}$. Then, C is satisfiable in $\mathcal{K}$ if and*

---

[3] http://owl.man.ac.uk/factplusplus/
[4] http://www.racer-systems.com/

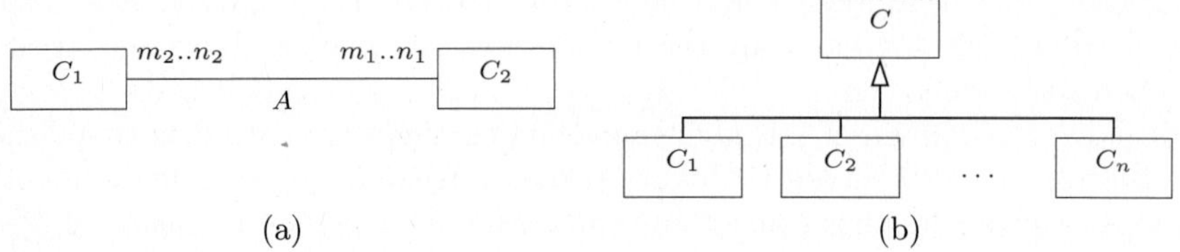

(a)   (b)

Fig. 3. (a) UML binary association with multiplicity constraints. (b) ISA hierarchy.

only if $\Psi K, \mathcal{B}$ admits a solution. Moreover, if a solution exists, then there is one whose values are bounded by $(K \cdot N)^{O(K)}$.

In the following, we will exploit the above result to derive a technique for reasoning on UML class diagrams that properly takes into account finiteness of the domain of interest. The technique is a based on an encoding of UML class diagrams in terms of DL KBs, which we present in the next section.

3 Formalizing UML Class Diagrams in DLs

UML class diagrams allow for modelling, in a declarative way, the static structure of an application domain, in terms of concepts and relations between them. Here, we briefly describe the core part of UML class diagrams, and specify the semantics of its constructs in terms of $\mathcal{ALUNI}$. An in-depth treatment on the correspondence between UML class diagrams and DLs can be found in [2].

A *class* in a UML class diagram denotes a set of objects with common features. Formally, a class C corresponds to a concept C. Classes may have attributes and operations, but for simplicity we do not consider them here, since they don't play any role in the finite class unsatisfiability problem.

A (binary) *association* in UML is a relation between the instances of two classes. An association A between two classes C_1 and C_2 is graphically rendered as in Figure 3(a). The *multiplicity* $m_1..n_1$ on the binary association specifies that each instance of the class C_1 can participate at least m_1 times and at most n_1 times to A, similarly for C_2. $*$ is used to specify no upper bound. [5]

An association A between the instances of classes C_1 and C_2, can be formalized as an atomic role A characterized by $C_1 \sqsubseteq \forall A.C_2$ and $C_2 \sqsubseteq \forall A^-.C_1$.

For an association as depicted in Figure 3(a), multiplicities are formalized by $C_1 \sqsubseteq (\geq m_1\, A) \sqcap (\leq n_1\, A)$ and $C_2 \sqsubseteq (\geq m_2\, A^-) \sqcap (\leq n_2\, A^-)$.

In UML, one can use a *generalization* between a parent class and a child class to specify that each instance of the child class is also an instance of the parent class. Hence, the instances of the child class inherit the properties of the parent class, but typically they satisfy additional properties that in general do

---

[5] In UML, an association can have arbitrary arity and relate several classes, but for simplicity we do not consider this case here (but see Conclusions). *Aggregations*, which are a particular kind of binary associations are modeled similarly to associations.

not hold for the parent class. Several generalizations can be grouped together to form a *class hierarchy* (also called *ISA hierarchy*), as shown in Figure 3(b). *Disjointness* and *completeness constraints* can also be enforced on a class hierarchy (graphically, by adding suitable labels). A class hierarchy is said to be disjoint if no instance can belong to more than one derived class, and complete if any instance of the base class belongs also to some of the derived classes.

A class C generalizing a class C_1 can be formalized as: $C_1 \sqsubseteq C$. A class hierarchy as shown in Figure 3(b) is captured by $C_i \sqsubseteq C$, for $i = 1, \ldots, n$.

Disjointness among $C_1, \ldots, C_n$ is expressed by $C_i \sqsubseteq \bigwedge_{j=i+1}^{n} \neg C_j$, for $i = 1, \ldots, n-1$. The *completeness constraint* expressing that each instance of C is an instance of at least one of $C_1, \ldots, C_n$ is expressed by $C \sqsubseteq \bigsqcup_{i=1}^{n} C_i$.

Here, we follow a typical assumption in UML class diagrams, namely that all classes not in the same hierarchy are a priori disjoint. Another typical assumption, called *unique most specific class assumption*, is that objects in a hierarchy must belong to a single most specific class. Hence, under such an assumption, two classes in a hierarchy may have common instances only if they have a common subclass. We discuss in the next section the effect of making the unique most specific class assumption when reasoning on an UML class diagram.

The basic form of reasoning on UML class diagrams is (finite) satisfiability of a class C, which amounts to checking whether the class diagram admits a (finite) instantiation in which C has a nonempty extension. Formally, this corresponds to checking whether the concept corresponding to C is (finitely) satisfiable in the KB formalizing the diagram. As mentioned, unrestricted and finite satisfiability in UML class diagrams (and also in $\mathcal{ALUNI}$) are different problems.

The formalization of UML class diagrams in terms of DLs [2], and the fact that instantiations of the UML class diagram must be finite, allows one to use on such diagrams the techniques for finite model reasoning in DLs discussed in Section 2. Specifically, the EXPTIME upper bounds apply also to finite model reasoning on UML class diagrams [2]. Instead, the exact lower bound of reasoning on UML class diagrams as presented above is still open. However, if one adds subsetting relations between associations or the ability of specializing the typing of an association for classes in a generalization, then both unrestricted and finite model reasoning are EXPTIME-hard (see [2]). This justifies the approach taken in the next section, where we address the problem of finite model reasoning on UML class diagrams also from a practical point of view.

4   Finite Model Reasoning on UML Class Diagr. Via CSP

We address now finite class satisfiability in UML class diagrams, and show how it is possible to encode the problem as a constraint satisfaction problem (CSP).

As mentioned, a technique for finite model reasoning in UML class diagrams can be derived from techniques developed in the context of DLs. Such techniques are based on translating a DL knowledge base into a set of linear inequalities [4,5]. The formalization of UML class diagrams in terms of DLs implies that the finite model reasoning techniques for the latter can be used also for the former.

In the rest of this paper, we will deal directly with the UML class diagram constructs, considered, from a formal point of view, as abbreviations for the corresponding DL concepts and roles.

Intuitively, consider a simple UML class diagram D with no generalizations and hierarchies. Figure 3(a) shows a fragment of such a diagram, in which we have two classes C_1 and C_2 and an association A between them. It is easy to see that such a class diagram D is always satisfiable (assuming $m_i \leq n_i$) if we admit infinite models. Hence, only finite model reasoning is of interest. We observe that, if D is finitely satisfiable, then it admits a finite model in which all classes are pairwise disjoint. Exploiting this property, we can encode finite satisfiability of class C_1 in D in a constraint satisfaction problem. The variables and the constraints of the CSP are modularly described considering in turn each association of the class diagram. Let A be an association between classes C_1 and C_2 such that the following multiplicity constraints are stated (cf. Figure 3(a)):

- There are at least m_1 and at most n_1 links of type A (instances of the association A) for each object of the class C_1;
- There are at least m_2 and at most n_2 links of type A for each object of C_2.

In the special case in which neither C_1 nor C_2 participates in an ISA hierarchy, the CSP is defined as follows:

- There are three non-negative variables `c1`, `c2`, and `a`, which stand for the number of objects of the classes and the number of links[6], respectively (upper bounds for these variables follow from Theorem 1; in practice, they can be set to a huge constant, e.g., `maxint`);
- There are the following constraints (we use, here and in what follows, a syntax similar to that of OPL[11]):

```
1.   m1 * c1 <= a;        3.   m2 * c2 <= a;        5.   a  <= c1 * c2;
2.   n1 * c1 >= a;        4.   n2 * c2 >= a;        6.   c1 >= 1;
```

Constraints 1–4 account for the multiplicity of the association; they can be omitted if either m_1 or m_2 is 0, or n_1 or n_2 is ∞ (symbol '*' in the class diagram). Constraint 5 sets an upper bound for the number of links of type A with respect to the number of objects. Constraint 6 encodes satisfiability of class C_1: we want at least one object in its extension. As an example, consider the Restaurant class diagram, shown in Figure 4: if A stands for *served_in*, C_1 stands for *menu*, and C_2 stands for *banquet*, then m_1 is 1, n_1 is ∞, m_2 is 1, and n_2 is 1.

Finally, to avoid the system returning an ineffectively large solution, an objective function that, e.g., minimizes the overall number of objects and links, may be added.

It is possible to show that, from a solution of such a constraint system we can construct a finite model of the class diagram in which the cardinality of

---

[6] The use of variables standing for the number of links stems from the technique proposed in [5], which ensures soundness and completeness of reasoning. It remains to be investigated whether a simpler encoding avoiding the use of such variables is possible.

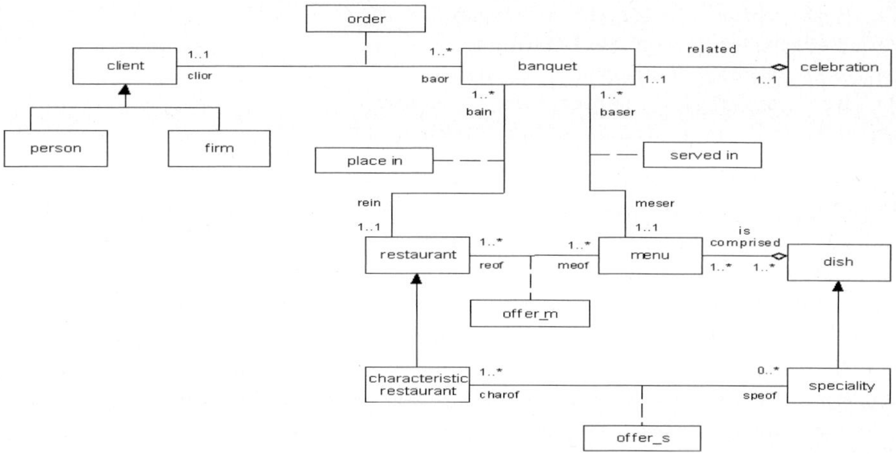

Fig. 4. The restaurant UML class diagram

the extension of each class and association is equal to the value assigned to the corresponding variable[7] [9].

When either C_1 or C_2 are involved in ISA hierarchies, the constraints are actually more complicated, because the meaning of the multiplicity constraints changes. As an example, the multiplicity 1..* of the *order* association in Figure 4 states that a *client orders* at least one *banquet*, but the client can be a *person*, a *firm*, both, or neither (assuming the generalization is neither disjoint nor complete). In general, for an ISA hierarchy involving n classes, 2^n non-negative variables corresponding to all possible combinations must be considered. For the same reason, in our example, we must consider four distinct specializations of the *order* association, i.e., one for each possible combination. Summing up, we have the following non-negative variables:

- **person**, **order_p**, for clients who are persons and not firms;
- **firm**, **order_f**, for clients who are firms and not persons;
- **person_firm**, **order_pf**, for clients who are both firms and persons;
- **client**, **order_c**, for clients who are neither firms nor persons;

plus the non-negative **banquet** variable.

The constraints which account for the *order* association are as follows:

```
/*  1 */   client <= order_c;
/*  2 */   firm <= order_f;
/*  3 */   person <= order_p;
/*  4 */   person_firm <= order_pf;
/*  5 */   banquet = order_c + order_f + order_p + order_pf;
```

---

[7] In fact, if one is interested just in the existence of a finite model, the nonlinear constraints $a \leq c_1 * c_2$ can be dropped. Indeed, any solution of the resulting constraint system can be transformed into one that satisfies also the nonlinear constraint by multiplying it with a sufficiently large constant, cf. [5].

```
/*  6 */   order_c <= client * banquet;
/*  7 */   order_f <= firm * banquet;
/*  8 */   order_p <= person * banquet;
/*  9 */   order_pf <= person_firm * banquet;
/* 10 */   client + firm + person + person_firm >= 1;
```

Constraints 1–4 account for the '1' in the 1..* multiplicity; Constraint 5 translates the 1..1 multiplicity; Constraints 6–9 set an upper bound for the number of links of type *order* with respect to the number of objects; Constraint 10 encodes satisfiability of the *client* class.

We refer the reader to [5] for formal details of the translation and the proof of its correctness. As for the implementation, the Restaurant example has been encoded in OPL as a CSP with 24 variables and 40 constraints. The solution has been found by the underlying constraint programming solver, i.e., ILOG's SOLVER, [7], in less than 0.01 seconds.

The exponential blow-up in the number of variables and constraints due to the presence of ISA hierarchies is a major obstacle when dealing with large class diagrams, such as those describing real-world applications. To this end, special care to reduce the size of the resulting CSP as much as possible is mandatory.

In particular, if a given ISA hierarchy (with C as parent class and $\{C_1, \ldots, C_n\}$ as children) is *complete*, the variable for C can be removed. Moreover, if the ISA is *disjoint*, we can omit all the variables that model instances that belong to *any* combination of two or more derived classes, hence reducing the overall number of variables to the number of classes in the hierarchy. As an example, if the ISA among *Client*, *Person*, and *Firm* in the Restaurant example is complete, variables `client` and `order_c` are superfluous. Similarly, if the ISA is disjoint, variables `person_firm` and `order_pf` can be omitted.

In order to derive the set of combinations of classes (called, in what follows, "types") that may have common instances, we show now that we can use CP technology again. Indeed, for a given UML class diagram, we can set up and solve an auxiliary constraint problem. The constraint problem is defined in such a way that the set of its solutions corresponds to the set of all those types that are consistent with the ISA hierarchies of the diagram, i.e., those types that can be populated without violating any of the constraints expressed by the ISA hierarchies. More precisely, assuming the classes of the diagram are represented by integers between 1 and `nclasses`, the constraint problem is defined as follows (we use again a pseudocode resembling the OPL syntax):

```
Given the set of ISA hierarchies of an UML class diagram
Find boolean legalType[1..nclasses] such that:

For each ISA (C1...Cn is-a C) {
  for each i = 1..n:  legalType[Ci] -> legalType[C];
  If ISA is disjoint:  at_most_one(i = 1..n)(legalType[Ci]);
  If ISA is complete:  legalType[C] -> exists i=[1..n] s.t. legalType[Ci];
}
legalType is a combination of at least one class;
Classes that belong to legalType must be connected by ISA hierarchies;
```

By computing all solutions of this auxiliary constraint problem, we obtain the set of all types that are consistent with the ISA hierarchies. Given a solution `legalType[]` (an array of booleans), the corresponding type is made of all classes `C` such that `legalType[C] = true`). Only variables for types found in this way need to be generated in order to solve the finite satisfiability problem. It is worth noting that in practical circumstances, the number of all possible types is not expected to be huge. In fact, well designed class diagrams, even if the unique most specific class assumption is not made (cf. end of Section 3), usually have a small amount of non-disjoint ISAs, since this helps to increase the overall quality of the diagram, by making the partitions of concepts that are important for the application explicit. Some experimental results that show the applicability of the approach when reasoning on real-world class diagrams are described in Section 5.

Once a UML class diagram is shown to be finitely satisfiable, a second problem is to return a model with non-empty classes and associations. To solve this problem, we can use again constraint technology, by writing a constraint program that encodes the semantics of the UML class diagram (cf. Section 3), and uses the output of the finite satisfiability problem to fix the size of the model. In fact, since in the finite satisfiability problem we have enforced the multiplicity constraints, we know that a finite model of the class diagram exists, and we also know an admissible number of instances for each class and association. We do not describe the relevant constraint program for space reasons, but just observe that, for the Restaurant example (encoded in OPL with about 40 lines of code, which resulted in a CSP with 498 variables and 461 constraints), the solution has been found by ILOG's SOLVER in less than 0.01 seconds, and no backtracking.

5   Implementation

In this section, we describe a system realized in order to automatically produce, given a UML class diagram as input, a constraint-based specification that decides finite class satisfiability. Two important choices were made in the design phase: the input language for class diagrams, and the output constraint language. As for the former, we decided to use a standard textual representation of UML class diagrams called "Managed Object Format" (MOF) (cf. footnote 2). Concerning the output language, instead, in order to use state-of-the-art solvers, we opted for the constraint programming language OPL. However, in order to have a strong decoupling between the two front-ends of the system, we realized it in two modules: the first one acts as a server, receiving a MOF file as input and returning a high-level, object-oriented complete internal representation of the described class diagram (actually, the system supports the concepts in the core UML, i.e., classes, associations, hierarchies among classes, and subset relationships between associations). A client module, then, traverses the internal model in order to produce the OPL specification encoding the finite satisfiability problem for the diagram (actually, subset relationships between associations are not taken into account). With this decoupling, we are able to change the language for the input (resp., output) by modifying only the MOF parser (resp., the OPL encoder) module of the system. Moreover, by decoupling the parsing module from the encoder into OPL, we are able to realize new tools to make additional forms of reasoning at low cost.

As for the handling of ISA hierarchies, it has already been mentioned that an exponential blow-up of the number of variables (one for each combination of classes involved in the hierarchy) cannot be avoided in the worst case. However, in case of disjoint or complete hierarchies, it is possible to strongly reduce the number of generated variables (cf. Section 4).

Hence, the system works in two stages. In the first one, after having built the internal representation of the input class diagram, it solves the OPL auxiliary constraint problem described in Section 4 in order to detect all possible combinations of classes (the so-called "types") belonging to the same hierarchy that may have objects in common. In the second stage, it uses this knowledge to build the OPL program that models the finite satisfiability problem for the class diagram.

In order to test whether using off-the-shelf tools for constraint programming is effective to decide finite satisfiability of real-world diagrams, we used our system to produce OPL specifications for several class diagrams of the "Common Information Model" (CIM)[8], a standard model used for describing overall management information in a network/enterprise environment. We don't describe the model in detail, but just observe that the class diagrams we used were composed of about 1000 classes and associations, and so can be considered good benchmarks to test whether current constraint programming solvers can be effectively used to perform the kind of reasoning shown so far.

Constraint specifications obtained from large class diagrams in the CIM collection were solved very efficiently by OPL. As an example, when the largest diagram, consisting of 980 classes and associations, was given as input to our system, we obtained an OPL specification consisting of a comparable number of variables and 862 constraints. Nonetheless, OPL solved it in less than 0.03 seconds of CPU time, by invoking ILOG SOLVER. This high efficiency is achieved also because of the "structural" aspects usually present in UML class diagrams that model real-world applications. In particular, multiplicity constraints on many associations had "0" or "1" as lower bounds, or "*" as upper bounds, and hence the corresponding OPL constraints were easily satisfiable. The consequence is that only a small portion of the constraints of the overall constraint model needed a deep search for finding a solution. Moreover, the exponential explosion of the number of variables for classes belonging to ISA hierarchies was not a problem, since the unique most specific class assumption is implicitly made in these diagrams (hence, non-disjointness among classes was always explicitly stated). This is encouraging evidence that current CP technology can be effectively used in order to make finite model reasoning on real-world class diagrams.

---

[8] http://www.dmtf.org/standards/cim

6   Conclusions

Finite model reasoning in UML class diagrams, e.g., checking whether a class is forced to have either zero or infinitely many objects, is important for assessing quality of the analysis phase in software development. Despite the importance of finite model reasoning, no implementation of this task has been attempted so far. In this paper we have shown how one can develop such a system by relying on off-the-shelf tools for constraint modeling and programming, using techniques for finite model reasoning in description logics, and putting special care in taming the class-combination explosion.

For simplicity, in this paper we have dealt with binary associations only, but in fact the technique can be straightforwardly extended to n-ary associations[9] as well, and in fact, our current implementation deals also with them.

This paper can also be seen as the first attempt to obtain a practical, computationally optimal finite model reasoner for expressive description logics. Indeed, the techniques developed here apply to $\mathcal{ALUNI}$ knowledge bases with primitive inclusion assertions [6]. More generally, the ideas of applying CSP tools and taking special care in limiting the "class combinations" explosion, could be applied to more expressive description logics as well [10].

References

1. Baader, F., Calvanese, D., McGuinness, D., Nardi, D., Patel-Schneider, P.F. (eds.): The Description Logic Handbook: Theory, Implementation and Applications. Cambridge University Press, Cambridge (2003)
2. Berardi, D., Calvanese, D., De Giacomo, G.: Reasoning on UML class diagrams. Artificial Intelligence 168(1–2), 70–118 (2005)
3. Borgida, A., Lenzerini, M., Rosati, R.: Description logics for data bases. In: Baader et al., ch. 16, pp. 462–484 [1]
4. Calvanese, D.: Finite model reasoning in description logics. In: Proc. of KR'96, pp. 292–303 (1996)
5. Calvanese, D.: Unrestricted and Finite Model Reasoning in Class-Based Representation Formalisms. PhD thesis, Dip. di Inf. e Sist., Univ. di Roma "La Sapienza" (1996)
6. Calvanese, D., Lenzerini, M., Nardi, D.: Unifying class-based representation formalisms. J. of Artificial Intelligence Research 11, 199–240 (1999)
7. ILOG OPL Studio system version 3.6.1 user's manual (2002)
8. Jacobson, I., Booch, G., Rumbaugh, J.: The Unified Modeling Language User Guide. Addison Wesley Publ. Co., Reading (1998)
9. Lenzerini, M., Nobili, P.: On the satisfiability of dependency constraints in entity-relationship schemata. Information Systems 15(4), 453–461 (1990)
10. Lutz, C., Sattler, U., Tendera, L.: The complexity of finite model reasoning in description logics. In: Baader, F. (ed.) Automated Deduction – CADE-19. LNCS (LNAI), vol. 2741, pp. 60–74. Springer, Heidelberg (2003)
11. Van Hentenryck, P.: The OPL Optimization Programming Language. The MIT Press, Cambridge (1999)

---

[9] We do not consider multiplicities for n-ary associations. For a discussion, see [2].

Model Checking and Preprocessing

Andrea Ferrara, Paolo Liberatore, and Marco Schaerf

Dipartimento di Informatica e Sistemistica, Università di Roma "La Sapienza",
Via Salaria 113, Roma, Italia
`lastname@dis.uniroma1.it`

Abstract. Temporal Logic Model Checking is a verification method having many industrial applications. This method describes a system as a formal structure called model; some properties, expressed in a temporal logic formula, can be then checked over this model. In order to improve performance, some tools allow to preprocessing the model so that a set of properties can be verified reusing the same preprocessed model. In this article, we prove that this preprocessing cannot possibly reduce complexity, if its result is bound to be of size polynomial in the size of the input. This result also holds if the formula is the part of the data that is preprocessed, which has similar practical implications.

Keywords: Model Checking, Complexity, Compilability.

1 Introduction

Temporal Logic Model Checking [10] is a verification method for discrete systems. It allows to verify whether a system has some properties. The system is described in a formal structure called model, which specifies the transitions of the system components. The properties to verify are encoded in a temporal modal logic. Model checking is used, for example, for the verification of protocols and hardware circuits [1]. Many tools, called *model checkers*, have been developed to this aim. The most famous ones are SPIN [15] and SMV [20] (with its many incarnations: NuSMV [9], RuleBase [2]), VIS [3], and FormalCheck [14]. There are many languages to express the model; the most widespread ones are Promela and SMV. Two temporal logics are mainly used to define the specification: CTL [10] and LTL [21]. In this paper we focus on the latter.

The two inputs of the model checking problem (the model and the formula) can in many cases be treated differently. If we want to verify several properties of the same system, it makes sense to spend more time on the model alone, if that simplifies the verification of the properties. Many tools allow to specify the model separately from checking the formula [8,25,16]; in this way, one can reuse the same model, compiled into a data structure, in order to check several formulae.

In the same way, we may wish to verify the same property on different systems: the property is this time the part we can spend more time on. Many tools allow populating a property database [8,25,16], i.e., a collection of temporal formulae which will be checked on the models. As an example, one may early establish

R. Basili and M.T. Pazienza (Eds.): AI*IA 2007, LNAI 4733, pp. 48–59, 2007.

the requirements of a system, even before the system is actually designed. These requirements can be therefore compiled into a database of temporal formulae, even if the system is not given yet. These formulae can be then preprocessing while the design/modeling of the system goes on. As soon as the system is given, in form of a model, we can use the result of this preprocessing step to check this model against the formulae.

In this paper, we study whether such preprocessing may improve performance. Using, as the technical tool, the compilability theory [7,18], we prove that model checking remains PSPACE-hard even if preprocessing is allowed, provided that its result is bounded to be polynomial in the size of its input. These theorems hold for all model checkers.

2   Preliminaries

2.1   Model Checking

In this section, we briefly recall the basic definitions about model checking that are needed in the rest of the paper. We follow the notation of [23,22]. LTL (Linear Temporal Logic) is a modal logic aimed at encoding how states evolve over time. It has three unary modal operators (X, G, and F) and a binary modal operator (U). A formula $X\phi$ is true in particular state if and only if the formula ϕ is true in the next state; $G\phi$ is true if and only ϕ is true from now on; $F\phi$ is true if ϕ is or will be true at some time in the future; $\phi U\psi$ is true if ψ will eventually become true and ϕ stays true until then. We indicate with $L(O_1, \ldots, O_n)$ the LTL fragment in which the only temporal operators allowed are $O_1, \ldots, O_n$; for instance, $L(F, X)$ is the fragment of LTL in which only F and X are allowed.

The semantics of LTL is based on Kripke models [13]. In the following, for an 'atomic proposition' we mean a Boolean variable. Given a set of atomic proposition, a Kripke structure for LTL is a tuple $\langle Q, R, \ell, I \rangle$, where Q is a set of states, R is a binary relation over states (the transition relation), ℓ is a function from states to atomic propositions (it labels every state with the atomic propositions that are true in that state), I is a set of initial states. A run of a Kripke structure is a Kripke model. A Kripke model for LTL is an infinite sequence of states, where the transition relation links each state with the one immediately following it in the sequence. The semantics of the modal operators is defined in the intuitive way: for example, $F\psi$ is true in a state of a Kripke model if ϕ is true in the state or in some following one.

The main problem of interest in practice is to verify whether all runs of a Kripke structure (all of its Kripke models) satisfy the formula; this is the Universal Model Checking problem. The Existential Model Checking problem is to verify whether there is a run of the Kripke structure that satisfies the formula. In formal verification, we encode the behavior of a system as a Kripke structure, and the property we want to check as an LTL formula. Checking the structure against the formula tells whether the system satisfies the property. Since the Kripke structure is usually called a "model" (which is in fact very different from a Kripke model, which is only a possible run), this problem is called Model Checking.

2.2   Composition of Transition Systems

In practice, all model checkers describe systems as a composition of their components, each expressed as a transition system [19,10]. By working on this formal settings, we obtain results which hold for all model checkers.

A transition system describse the possible transitions a system can go through by specifying the state variables, the possible initial states, and which transitions are possible, i.e., whether the transition from state s to state s' is possible for any pair of states s and s'. The formal definition is as follows [19,10].

Definition 1. *A finite-state transition system is a triple (V, I, ϱ), where $V = \{x_1, \ldots, x_n\}$ is a set of Boolean variables, I is a formula over V, and $\varrho(V, V')$ is a formula over $V \cup V'$, where $V' = \{x'_1, \ldots, x'_n\}$ is a set of new variables in one to one relation with elements of V.*

V is the set of state variables, I is a formula which is true on a truth assignment if and only if it represents a possible initial state, and ϱ is true on a pair of truth assignments if they represent a possible transition of the system. The set of variables V' is needed because ϱ refers the value of variables in the current and in the next state. For example, x_i is the value of x_i in the current state, while x'_i is the value of the same variable in the next state; therefore, the fact that x_i remains true is encoded by $\varrho = x_i \rightarrow x'_i$: if x_i is true now, then x'_i is true, i.e., x_i is true in the next state.

Formally, a *state* s is an assignment to the variables; a state s' is *successor* of a state s iff $\langle s, s' \rangle \models \varrho(V, V')$. A *computation* is an infinite sequence of states $s_0, s_1, s_2, \ldots$, satisfying the following requirements:

Initiality: s_0 is an initial state, i.e. $s_0 \models I$
Consecution: For each $j \geq 0$, the state s_{j+1} is a successor of the state s_j

For the sake of simplicity but without loss of any generality, in these definitions and in the following analisys we only consider Boolean variables and Boolean assertions. In fact, any assertion on enumerative variables is polynomially reducible to a Boolean assertion on Boolean variables.

In order to model a complex system, we assume that each of its parts can be modeled by a transition system. The interaction among these parts is modeled by variables shared among the corresponding transition systems. In the following, we consider k transition systems $M_1, \ldots, M_k$. Every M_i is described by $((V_i^L \cup V_i^S), I_i(V_i), \varrho_i(V_i, V'_i))$ for i $1 \leq i \leq k$ where V_i^L is the set variables local to M_i, V_i^S is the set of shared variables of M_i, and $V_i = V_i^L \cup V_i^S$. A group of transition systems can be composed in two basic ways: synchronous and interleaved.

In the synchronous parallel composition of k transition systems, the global transition is due to all processes M_i making a transition simultaneously. In other words, all processes make a transition at any time step.

Definition 2. *The synchronous parallel composition of processes $M_1, \ldots, M_k$, is the transition system $M = (V, I, \varrho)$ described by:*

$$V = \bigcup_{i=1}^{k} V_i \qquad I(V) = \bigwedge_{i=1}^{k} I_i(V_i) \qquad \varrho(V, V') = \bigwedge_{i=1}^{k} \varrho_i(V_i, V_i')$$

The synchronous parallel composition of $M_1, \ldots, M_k$ is denoted by $M_1 \| \ldots \| M_k$.

On the contrary, in the interleaved asynchronous composition, only one process at time is active (we omit the formal definition because of space limitations).

A model can be described as a composition of transition systems. The model checking problem for concurrent transition systems is the problem of verifying whether a model described by the composition of the transition systems satisfies a given formula.

2.3   Complexity and Compilability

We assume the reader knows the basic concepts of complexity theory [24,12]. What we mainly use in this paper are the concepts of polynomial reduction and the class PSPACE.

The Model Checking problem is PSPACE-complete [17], and is thus intractable. As said in the Introduction, it makes sense to preprocess one part of the problem (either the model or the formula), if this reduces the remaining running time. The analysis of how much can be gained by such preprocessing, however, cannot be done using the standard tools of the polynomial classes and reductions. The compilability classes [7] have to be used instead.

In order to denote problems in which one part can be preprocessed, we assume that their instances are composed of two parts, and that the part that can be preprocessed is the first one. As a result, the model checking problem written as $\langle M, \phi \rangle$ indicates that M can be preprocessed; written as $\langle \phi, M \rangle$ indicates that ϕ can be preprocessed.

The "complexity when preprocessing is allowed" is established by characterizing how hard a problem is *after* the preprocessing step. This is done by building over the usual complexity classes: if C is a "regular" complexity class such as NP, then a problem is in the (non-uniform) compilability class $\|{\rightsquigarrow}C$ if the problem is in C after a preprocessing step whose result takes polynomial space. In other words, $\|{\rightsquigarrow}C$ is "almost" C, but preprocessing is allowed and will not be counted in the cost of solving the problem. More details can be found in [7].

In order to identify how hard a problem is, we also need a concept of hardness. Since the regular polynomial reductions are not appropriate when preprocessing is allowed, ad-hoc reductions (called nu-comp reductions in [7]) have been defined.

In this paper, we do not show the hardness of problems directly, but rather use a sufficient condition called representative equivalence. For example, in order to prove that model checking is $\|{\rightsquigarrow}$PSPACE-hard, we first show a (regular) polynomial reduction from a PSPACE-hard problem to model checking and then show that this reduction satisfies the condition of representative equivalence.

Let us assume that we know that a given problem A is $\|{\rightsquigarrow}$C-hard and we have a polynomial reduction from the problem A to the problem B. Liberatore [18] shows a sufficient condition that ensures that a reduction also proves the $\|{\rightsquigarrow}$C-hardness of B. This condition involves the following definitions.

Definition 3 (Classification Function). *A classification function for a problem A is a polynomial function $Class$ from instances of A to nonnegative integers, such that $Class(y) \leq ||y||$.*

Definition 4 (Representative Function). *A representative function for a problem A is a polynomial function $Repr$ from nonnegative integers to instances of A, such that $Class(Repr(n)) = n$, and that $||Repr(n)||$ is bounded by some polynomial in n.*

Definition 5 (Extension Function). *An extension function for a problem A is a polynomial function from instances of A and nonnegative integers to instances of A such that, for any y and $n \geq Class(y)$, the instance $y' = Exte(y, n)$ satisfies the following conditions:*

1. *$y \in A$ if and only if $y' \in A$;*
2. *$Class(y') = n$.*

We now define the aforementioned condition over the polytime reduction from A to B. Since B is a problem of pairs, we can express a reduction from A to B as a pair of polynomial functions $\langle r, h \rangle$ such that $x \in A$ if and only if $\langle r(x), h(x) \rangle \in B$.

Definition 6 (Representative Equivalence). *Given a problem A (having the above three functions), a problem of pairs B, and a polynomial reduction $\langle r, h \rangle$ from A to B, the condition of representative equivalence holds if, for any instance y of A, it holds:*

$$\langle r(y), h(y) \rangle \in B \quad \text{iff} \quad \langle r(Repr(Class(y))), h(y) \rangle \in B$$

The condition of representative equivalence implies that the problem B is $||\!\rightsquigarrow$C-hard, if A is C-hard [18]. Given the limitation of space we cannot give the full definitions for compilability, which are reported elsewhere [7,6,5,18].

2.4   Planning

$PLANSAT_1^*$ is the following problem of planning: giving a STRIPS [11] instance $y = \langle P, O, I, G \rangle$ in which the operators have an arbitrary number of preconditions and only one postcondition, is there a plan for y? $PLANSAT_1^*$ is PSPACE-Complete [4]. Without loss of generality we consider $y = (P, O \cup o_0, I, G)$, where o_0 is a operator which is always usable (it has no preconditions) and does nothing (it has no postconditions). We use the following notation: $P = \{x_1, \ldots, x_n\}$, I is the set of conditions true in the initial state, $G = \langle \mathcal{M}, \mathcal{N} \rangle$. A state in STRIPS is a set of conditions. In the following we indicate with ϕ_i^h the hth positive precondition of the operator o_i, with ϕ_i all its the positive preconditions, with η_i^h its hth negative precondition, and with η_i all its negative preconditions; α_i is the positive postcondition of the operator o_i, β_i is the negative postcondition of the operator o_i. Since any operator has only one postcondition, for every operator i it holds that $||\alpha_i \cup \beta_i|| = 1$.

Since we shall use them in the following, we define a classification function, a representative function and a extension function for $PLANSAT_1^*$:

Classification Function: $Class(y) = \|P\|$. Clearly it satisfies the condition $Class(y) \leq \|y\|$.

Representative Function: $Repr(n) = \langle P_n, \emptyset, \emptyset, \emptyset \rangle$, where $P_n = \{x_1, \ldots, x_n\}$. Clearly it is polynomial and satisfies the following conditions: (i) Class(Repr(n))=n, (ii) $\|Repr(n)\| \leq p(n)$ where p(n) is a polynomial.

Extension Function: Let $y = \langle P, O, I, G \rangle$ and $y' = Exte(y, n) = \langle P_n, O, I, G \rangle$. Clearly for any y and n s.t. $n \geq Class(y)$ y' satisfies the following conditions: (i)$y \in A$ iff $y' \in A$, (ii) $Class(y') = n$.

Given the limitation of space we cannot give the full definitions for compilability, for which the reader should refer to [7] for an introduction, to [6,5] for an application to the succinctness of some formalisms, to [18] for further applications and technical advances.

3   Results

The Model Checking problem for concurrent transition systems is PSPACE-complete [17]. In this section, we prove that the Model Checking problem remains PSPACE-hard even if we can preprocess either the model or the formula, if this preprocessing step is constrained to have a polynomial size. In our proofs we consider Existential Model Checking problems, but the results also hold for the Universal case, since PSPACE is closed under complementation also for compilability.

Preprocessing of the formula is very relevant to those approaches to model checking that use automata theory, for instance in the on-the-fly model checking [10], implemented in [15], that represent and preprocess the formula in its related automata. More generally, in formal verification it is often the case that many properties (formulae) have to be verified over the same system (the model, in this case modeled by the transition systems), in all of these cases it is worth investigatine whether the complexity of model checking can be reduced by preprocessing the model.

On the other hand, there are many examples where the same property has to be verified on different models, in this case we investigate whether the formula can be processed.

We now consider the Model Checking problem for concurrent processes composed in a interleaved way when the model can be preprocessed.

Theorem 1. *The model checking problem for k interleaved concurrent process $MC_{asyn} = \langle (M_1 | \ldots | M_k), \varphi \rangle$ where $\varphi \in LTL$ is $\|\leadsto$PSPACE-complete, and remains $\|\leadsto$PSPACE-hard for $\varphi \in L(F, G, X)$.*

Proof. We show a reduction, that translates an instance $y \in PLANSAT_1^*$ into an instance $\langle r(y), h(y) \rangle \in M_{asyn}$, satisfying the condition of representative equivalence. Given $y = \langle P, O, I, G \rangle \in PLANSAT_1^*$

- $r(y)$ defines a concurrent transition systems $M_1, \ldots, M_n$, where each M_i is obtained from a variable $x_i \in P$ and it is described by:

$$V_i = \{x_i\}$$
$$I_i(V_i) = (x_i) \vee (\neg x_i)$$
$$\varrho_i(V_i, V_i') = (x_i = 0 \wedge x_i' = 0) \vee (x_i = 0 \wedge x_i' = 1) \vee$$
$$(x_i = 1 \wedge x_i' = 0) \vee (x_i = 1 \wedge x_i' = 1)$$

The process $M = M_1 \| \ldots \| M_n$ represents all possible computations, starting from all possible initial assignments, over the variables $x_1, \ldots, x_n$.

- $h(y) = h(I, G, O) = \neg(\phi_I \wedge \phi_G \wedge \phi_O)$

  where:

$$\varphi_I = \bigwedge_{i \in I} x_i \wedge \bigwedge_{i \notin I} \neg x_i$$

$$\varphi_G = F(\bigwedge_{i \in \mathcal{M}} x_i \wedge \bigwedge_{i \in \mathcal{N}} \neg x_i)$$

$$\varphi_O = G \bigvee_{i=0}^{m} [\bigwedge_{h=1}^{\|\phi_i\|} \phi_i^h \wedge \bigwedge_{h=1}^{\|\eta_i\|} \neg \eta_i^h \wedge X\gamma_i \wedge \bigwedge_{\substack{j \neq i \\ j=1}}^{n} (x_j \leftrightarrow Xx_j)]$$

where

$$\gamma_i = \begin{cases} \alpha_i & \text{if } \alpha_i \neq \emptyset \\ \neg\beta_i & \text{if } \beta_i \neq \emptyset \end{cases}$$

φ_I adds constraints about the initial states of y represented by I.

φ_G adds constraints about the goal states of y represented by G: it tells that a goal state will be reached.

φ_O describes the operators in O: globally (i.e. in every state) one of the operators must be used to go in the next state; φ_O also describes the nop operator o_0.

Now, we prove that $y \in PLANSAT_1^*$ iff $\langle r(y), h(y) \rangle \in M_{asyn}$. Given $y = \langle P, O, I, G \rangle$, a solution for y is a plan which generates the following sequence of states: $(s_1, \ldots, s_p)$ where s_1 is an initial state and s_p is a goal state. This sequence of states is obtained applying a sequence of operators $(o_{h_1}, \ldots, o_{h_p})$ chosen in $O = \{o_1, \ldots, o_m\}$ in the following way: for all i s.t. $1 \leq i \leq p$, preconditions for o_{h_i} are included in the state s_i, and the state s_{i+1} is obtained from the state s_i modifying the postcondition associated with o_{h_i}. We remark that a state in STRIPS is the set of conditions.

The model $M = r(y) = r(P)$ represents all possible traces starting from all possible initial configurations, over the variables $x_1, \ldots, x_n$. Thus, in this case the Existential Model Checking problem $\langle M, \varphi \rangle$ reduces to the satisfiability problem for φ: we check whether there exists a trace among all traces over the variables $x_1, \ldots, x_n$ that satisfies the LTL formula φ. Therefore, we have to prove that $y \in A$ iff $\varphi = h(y)$ is satisfiable:

$\Rightarrow$. Given a solution for $y \in A$, we identify a model for $\varphi = h(y)$; by construction such a model has:

- initial state s_1^M s.t. $\ell(s_1) = I \cup \{\neg x_i | x_i \notin I\}$
- a state s_p^M s.t. $\ell(s_p) \subseteq \mathcal{M} \cup \{\neg x_i | x_i \notin \mathcal{N}\}$
- given a state s_i^M, s_{i+1}^M is successor of s_i^M iff

- $\ell(s_i^M) \subseteq Precond(o_{h_i})$, where $Precond(o_{h_i}) = \{x_j | x_j \in \phi_{h_i}\} \cup \{\neg x_j | x_j \in \eta_{h_i}\}$
- $\ell(s_{i+1}^M) = \ell(s_i^M) \cup \alpha_i - \beta_i$

  where α_i is the positive postcondition of o_{h_i} and β_i is the negative post-condition of o_{h_i}.

- an infinite number of states: when the state s_p is reached this state is repeated for at least once or for ever (applying the nop operator o_0), or it is possible, it depends from y, to apply any operators whose preconditions are satisfied by $\ell(s_p^M)$.

$\Leftarrow$. Let $(s_1^M, \ldots, s_p^M, \ldots)$ a model for φ, and let s_p the goal state, that the first state satisfying φ_G. We obtain the sequence of states visited by a plan which is a solution for y, by cutting the states after the goal state s_p and assigning $s_i = \ell(s_i^M)$; thus this sequence of states $(s_1, \ldots, s_p)$, associated with the plan, has by construction:

- initial state s_1 s.t. $s_1 = I \cup \{\neg x_i | x_i \notin I\}$
- a state s_p s.t. $s_p \subseteq \mathcal{M} \cup \{\neg x_i | x_i \notin \mathcal{N}\}$
- given a state s_i, s_{i+1} is successor of s_i iff
    - $s_i \subseteq Precond(o_{h_i})$
    - $s_{i+1} = s_i \cup \alpha_i - \beta_i$

      where α_i is the positive postcondition of o_{h_i} and β_i is the negative post-condition of o_{h_i}. $\qquad\square$

This result shows that the complexity of model checking cannot be (significantly) decreased even if we have the model available and can preprocess it, no matter how much time we spend. This result does not rule out any improvement, but it proves that there is no preprocessing algorithm that guarantees a simplification (from a computational complexity point of view) of the model checking problem.

We now identify the complexity of the Model Checking problem when the preprocessing of the model (represented as the composition of transition systems) is allowed, in the synchronous case.

Theorem 2. *The model checking problem for k synchronous concurrent process $MC_{syn} = \langle (M_1 || \ldots || M_k), \varphi \rangle$ where $\varphi \in LTL$ is $\| \rightsquigarrow$PSPACE-hard, and remains $\| \rightsquigarrow$PSPACE-hard for $\varphi \in L(F, G, X)$.*

Proof. It is similar to the proof of the Theorem 1. We carry out a reduction from the $PLANSAT_1^*$ problem, that satisfies the conditions of representative equivalence; the main difference is about the LTL formula. $\qquad\square$

We now show the complexity results, in the synchronous case, when the formula can be preprocessed.

Theorem 3. *The model checking problem for k synchronous concurrent process $MC'_{syn} = \langle \varphi, (M_1 || \ldots || M_k) \rangle$ where $\varphi \in LTL$ is $\| \rightsquigarrow$PSPACE-complete, and remains $\| \rightsquigarrow$PSPACE-hard for $\varphi \in L(F, G, X)$.*

Proof. $PLANSAT_1^*$ is the following problem of planning: giving a STRIPS [11] instance $y = \langle P, O, I, G \rangle$ in which the operators have an arbitrary number of preconditions and only one postcondition, is there a plan for y? $PLANSAT_1^*$ is PSPACE-complete [4]. Without loss of generality we consider $y = (P, O \cup o_0, I, G)$, where o_0 is a operator which is always usable (it has no preconditions) and does nothing (it has no postconditions). We use the following notation: $P = \{x_1, \ldots, x_n\}$, I is the set of conditions true in the initial state, $G = \langle \mathcal{M}, \mathcal{N} \rangle$. A state in STRIPS is a set of conditions.

In the following we indicate with ϕ_i^h the hth positive precondition of the operator o_i, and with η_i^h the hth negative precondition of the operator o_i; α_i is the positive postcondition of the operator o_i, β_i is the negative postcondition of the operator o_i. Since any operator has only one postcondition, for every operator i it hold that $\|\alpha_i \cup \beta_i\| = 1$.

We show a polynomial reduction from the problem A to the problem B that satisfies the condition of representative equivalence. This proves that B is $\|\leadsto$C-hard, if A is C-hard; to apply this condition we must define a *Classification Function*, a *Representative Function* and a *Extension Function* for A. Thus we use such a proof schema: we define a *Classification Function*, a *Representative Function* and a *Extension Function* for $PLANSAT_1^*$, then we show a polynomial reduction from an instance $y \in PLANSAT_1^*$ to an instance $\langle r(y), h(y) \rangle \in MC'_{SYN}$ that satisfies the condition of representative equivalence.

Let $y = \langle P, O, I, G \rangle \in PLANSAT_1^*$. We define r and h as follows:

$$- \quad r(y) = r(P) = \neg \left\{ F(x_g) \wedge G \bigwedge_{i=0}^{n} \left[\neg(x_i \leftrightarrow X x_i) \rightarrow \bigwedge_{\substack{j=1 \\ j \neq i}}^{n} (x_j \leftrightarrow X x_j) \right] \right\}$$

- $h(y)$ defines the transition systems $M_1 \| \ldots \| M_k$. The generic M_i is obtained from the operators $o_{i_1}, \ldots, o_{i_{d_i}}$ whose postcondition involves the variable $x_i \in P$; d_i is the number of such operators. We add the variable x_g; thus we have at most as many processes as variables: if k is the number of variables used as postcondition of operators plus one, we have $k \leq n + 1$. Let M_k the process associated with the variable x_g; this variable is 0 at the beginning and it becomes 1 only when the goal of the $PLANSAT$ problem is reached. M_i, for i s.t. $1 \leq i < k$, is defined by:

$$V_i = \bigcup_{q=1}^{d_i} \phi_{i_q} \cup \eta_{i_q} \cup \alpha_{i_q} \cup \beta_{i_q}$$

$$I_i(V_i) = \bigwedge_{x_j \in I \cap V_i} x_j \wedge \bigwedge_{x_j \in \overline{I} \cup V_i} \neg x_j$$

$$\varrho_i(V_i, V_i') = \bigvee_{k=1}^{d_i} \bigwedge_{h=1}^{\|\phi_{i_k}\|} \phi_{i_k}^h \wedge \bigwedge_{h=1}^{\|\eta_{i_k}\|} \neg \eta_{i_k}^h \wedge \neg (\bigwedge_{i \in \mathcal{M}} x_i \wedge \bigwedge_{i \in \mathcal{N}} \neg x_i) \wedge (x_i' \equiv b_{i_k})$$

$$\text{where } b_{i_k} = \begin{cases} 1 \text{ if } \alpha_{i_k} \neq \emptyset \\ 0 \text{ if } \beta_{i_k} \neq \emptyset \end{cases}$$

The process M_k is defined by:

$$V_k = \{x_g\}$$

$$I_k(V) = (x_g = 0)$$

$$\varrho_k(V_k, V_k') = \bigwedge_{i \in \mathcal{M}} x_i \wedge \bigwedge_{i \in \mathcal{N}} \neg x_i \wedge x_g' = 1$$

Now we prove that this reduction is correct, i.e. $y \in PLANSAT_1^*$ iff $\langle r(y), h(y) \rangle \in MC'_{SYN}$.

$\Rightarrow$. Given a solution for $y \in PLANSAT_1^*$, we show a path of M which satisfies φ (r(y) defined above).

A solution for y is a plan which generates the following sequence of states: $(s_1, \ldots, s_p)$ where s_1 is a initial state and s_p is a goal state. This sequence of states is obtained by applying a sequence of operators $(o_{h_1}, \ldots, o_{h_p})$.

By construction M admits a path $(s_1^M, \ldots, s_p^M, s_{p+1}^M, \ldots)$ s.t.:

- $\ell(s_i^M) = s_i \cup \neg x_g$ for i $1 \leq i \leq p$
- $\ell(s_{p+1}^M) = s_p \cup x_g$

This path satisfies φ:

- φ does not constrain about the initial state, therefore every initial state of the model is legal;
- $x_g \subseteq \ell(s_{p+1}^M)$, therefore $F(x_g)$ is true;
- the path shown is s.t. only one variable change at a time, therefore the subformula under the Globally is true.

$\Leftarrow$. Given a path of M which satisfies φ, we show a solution for $y \in PLANSAT_1^*$. The path is a sequence $(s_1^M, \ldots, s_p^M, s_{p+1}^M, \ldots)$. We can obtain the sequence of states visited by a plan for y in this way:

- $s_i = \ell(s_i^M) - \{\neg x_g\}$ for i $1 \leq i \leq p$;
- we ignore the rest of the path of M. $\square$

The above theorem shows that even the availability beforehand of the formula to be tested does not guarantee an increase in the performances of model checking algorithms. A similar proof also holds for the interleaved case, which we state with only a proof sketch.

Theorem 4. *The model checking problem for k interleaved concurrent process* $MC'_{asyn} = \langle \varphi, (M_1 | \ldots | M_k) \rangle$ *where* $\varphi \in LTL$ *is* $\|\rightsquigarrow$*PSPACE-complete, and remains* $\|\rightsquigarrow$*PSPACE-hard for* $\varphi \in L(F)$.

Proof (sketch). We carry out a reduction from the $PLANSAT_1^*$ problem, that satisfies the conditions of representative equivalence. The proof is similar to the proof of the Theorem 3. $\square$

Summing up, we have shown that the model checking problem is inherently PSPACE-hard and that any algorithm that attempts to reduce the complexity by preprocessing either the model or the formula can only succeed in a limited number of cases.

4   Conclusions

We have proved that model checking remains PSPACE-hard even if a polynomial-size preprocessing step on either the model or the formula is allowed, if the formula is an LTL one and the model is represented as a synchronous or interleaved asynchronous composition of transition systems. In other words, preprocessing the model or the formula does not lead to a polynomial time algorithm for model checking.

Both cases, when the model is preprocessed or the formula is, are relevant to practical applications. The result about preprocessing of the formula applies to those approaches to model checking that use automata theory, for instance in the on-the-fly model checking [10,15], which represent and preprocess the formula in its related automata. More generally, in formal verification it is often the case that many properties (formulae) have to be verified over the same system (the model, in this case modeled by the transition systems), in all of these cases it is worth investigating whether the complexity of model checking can be reduced by preprocessing the model.

The result about preprocessing the model applies to the tools that allow to specify the model separately from checking the formula [8,25,16], as these tools allow the reuse of the same model on different properties.

References

1. Beer, I., Ben David, S., Geist, D., Gewirtzman, R., Yoeli, M.: Methodology and system for pratical formal verification of reactive hardware. In: Dill, D.L. (ed.) CAV 1994. LNCS, vol. 818, pp. 182–193. Springer, Heidelberg (1994)
2. Beer, I., Ben David, S., Landver, A.: On the fly model checking for rctl formulas. In: Vardi, M.Y. (ed.) CAV 1998. LNCS, vol. 1427, pp. 184–194. Springer, Heidelberg (1998)
3. Brayton, R.K., Hachtel, G.D., Vincetelli, A.S., Somenzi, F., Aziz, A., Cheng, S.T., Edwards, S., Khatri, S., Kukimoto, T., Pardo, A., Qadeer, S., Ranjan, R.K., Sarwary, S., Shiple, T.R., Swamy, G., Villa, T.: VIS: a system for verification and syntesis. In: Alur, R., Henzinger, T.A. (eds.) CAV 1996. LNCS, vol. 1102, pp. 428–432. Springer, Heidelberg (1996)
4. Bylander, T.: Complexity results for planning. In: Proceedings of the 12th International Joint Conference on Artificial Intelligence. LNCS, pp. 274–279. Morgan Kaufmann, San Mateo, CA (1991)
5. Cadoli, M., Donini, F.M., Liberatore, P., Schaerf, M.: Space efficency of propositional knowledge representation formalisms. Journal of Artificial Intelligence Research 13, 25–64 (1999)
6. Cadoli, M., Donini, F.M., Liberatore, P., Schaerf, M.: The size of a revised knowledge base. Artificial Intelligence 115, 1–31 (2000)
7. Cadoli, M., Donini, F.M., Liberatore, P., Schaerf, M.: Preprocessing of intractable problems. Information and Computation 176, 89–120 (2002)
8. Cavada, R., Cimatti, A., Jochim, C.A., Keighren, G., Olivetti, E., Pistore, M., Roveri, M., Tchaltsev, A.: NuSMV 2.4 User's Manual. IRST (2005), http://nusmv.irst.itc.it
9. Cimatti, A., Clarke, E.M., Giunchiglia, E., Giunchiglia, F., Pistore, M., Roveri, M., Sebastiani, R., Tacchella, A.: NuSMV 2: An opensource tool for symbolic model checking. In: Brinksma, E., Larsen, K.G. (eds.) CAV 2002. LNCS, vol. 2404, Springer, Heidelberg (2002)
10. Clarke, E.M., Grumberg, O., Peled, D.A.: Model Checking. MIT Press, Cambridge (2000)

11. Fikes, R., Nilson, N.: Strips: a new approach to the application of theorem proving to problem solving. Artificial Intelligence 2, 189–209 (1971)
12. Garey, M.R., Johnson, D.S.: Computers and Intractability: A Guide to the Theory of NP-Completeness. W.H. Freeman and Company, San Francisco, Ca (1979)
13. Goldblatt, R.: Logics of Time and Computation. CSLI Lecture Notes, vol. 7. Center for the Study of Language and Information, Stanford, CA (1987)
14. Hardin, R.H., Har'el, Z., Kurshan, R.P.: Cospan. In: Alur, R., Henzinger, T.A. (eds.) CAV 1996. LNCS, vol. 1102, pp. 423–427. Springer, Heidelberg (1996)
15. Holzmann, G.J.: The model checker spin. IEEE Transactions on Software Engineering 23(5), 279–295 (1997)
16. IBM Haifa, RuleBase User's Manual (2006), `http://www.haifa.ibm.com/projects/verification/Formal_Methods-Home/index.html`
17. Kupferman, O., Vardi, M.Y., Wolper, P.: An automata theoretic approach to branching-time model checking. Journal of ACM 47(2), 312–360 (2000)
18. Liberatore, P.: Monotonic reductions, representative equivalence, and compilation of intractable problems. Journal of ACM 48(6), 1091–1125 (2001)
19. Manna, Z., Pnueli, A.: Temporal Verification of Reactive Systems - Safety. Springer, Heidelberg (1995)
20. McMillan, K.L.: Symbolic Model Checking. Kluwer Academic Publishers, Boston, MA (1993)
21. Pnueli, A.: The temporal logic of programs. In: FOCS'77. Proceeding of the 18th IEEE Symposium on Foundations of Computer Science, pp. 46–57. IEEE Computer Society Press, Los Alamitos (1977)
22. Schnoebelen, Ph.: The complexity of temporal logic model checking. In: AiML'02. Proceedings of the 4th Internationa Workshop in Advances in Modal Logic, vol. 4, pp. 1–44. World Scientific Publishing, San Mateo, CA (2002)
23. Sistla, A.P., Clarke, E.M.: The complexity of propositional linear temporal logics. Journal of ACM 32(3), 733–749 (1985)
24. Stockmeyer, L.J.: The polynomial-time hierarchy. Theoretical Computer Science 3, 1–22 (1976)
25. Villa, T., Swarny, G., Shiple, T.: VIS User's Manual. VIS Group (2004), `http://vlsi.colorado.edu/~vis/`

Some Issues About
Cognitive Modelling and Functionalism

Francesco Gagliardi

Department of Physical Sciences — University of Naples *Federico II*
Via Cintia — I-80126 Napoli, Italy
francesco.gagliardi@libero.it

Abstract. The aim of this paper is to introduce some methodological issues about cognitive explanatory power of AI systems. We use the new concept of *mesoscopic functionalism* which is based on links between computational complexity theory and functionalism. This functionalism tries to introduce an unique intermediate, *mesoscopic,* descriptive level based on the key role of heuristics. The enforcement of constraints at this level can assure a cognitive explanatory power which is not guaranteed from mere selection of modelling technique. So we reconsider the discussions about empirical underdetermination of AI systems, proposed especially for classical systems, and about the research of the "right and unique" technique for cognitive modelling. This allows us to consider the several mainstreams of cognitive artificial intelligence as different attempts to resolve underdetermination and thus, in a way, we can unify them as a manifestation of scientific pluralism.

Keywords: Cognitive Modelling, Mesoscopic Functionalism, Heuristics, Empirical Underdetermination, Scientific Pluralism.

1 Introduction

Regarding computational modelling of human thought, philosopher Thagard states ([33] pg. 9,10): *"The central hypothesis of cognitive science is that thought can be understood in terms of computational procedures on mental representations. [...] Although there is considerable dispute within cognitive science concerning what kinds of procedures and representations are most important for understanding mental phenomena, the computational/representational approach is common to current work on how mind can be understood in terms of rules, concepts, analogies, images, and neural networks".*

In fact, the complete spectrum of computational techniques developed within artificial intelligence [30] field, is very wide including symbolic modelling, cognitive architectures, connectionism, a-life and evolutionary robotics. Due to all this diversification and to the absence of a *grand theory* [18][19] in social sciences for cognitive modelling, we consider useful to recall briefly the comprehensive conceptual framework of *Cognitive Naturalism* proposed by Thagard [33]. Then we try to draw some common aspects between different modelling techniques, with relation to the enforcement of cognitive plausibility to AI systems.

R. Basili and M.T. Pazienza (Eds.): AI*IA 2007, LNAI 4733, pp. 60–71, 2007.

2 Cognitive Naturalism and Heuristics

The *Cognitive Naturalism* is a computational conceptual framework for human mind understanding. It is well-rooted on concepts related to computational complexity, because it is based on the computational foundational formalization of the coherence as a combinatorial problem. This problem is proved to be computationally intractable and it is often efficiently faced with heuristics (see [34] for a comparison among connectionist and other techniques).

According to the cognitive naturalism much of the human thinking is naturally understood as heuristic-based solution to combinatorial problems, in domains as diverse as social impression formation, scientific-theory, choice, discourse comprehension, visual perception, and decision making (see [33] for a panorama and related bibliography).

Moreover in psychology the heuristics were proposed to explain how people make decisions, come to judgments and solve problems, typically when facing complex or incomplete information problems (e.g. [9]).

In fact in real-world problems there are too many uncertainties and conflicts for having any hope to obtain a best solution for an optimisation function which perhaps could be indeterminate. The alternative approach to maximizing is *satisficing*, an alternative to optimisation for cases in which one gives up the idea of obtaining the *best* solution.

Satisficing is a concept due to Herbert Simon ([31], chap. 14, 15; see also [32]) who identifies the decision making process whereby one chooses an option that is, while perhaps not the best, good enough. In this context of *bounded rationality*, humans search for good enough solutions by using heuristics.

Heuristics work well under many circumstances, but in certain cases leads to systematic cognitive poor performances. Tversky and Kahneman [35] are two key figures in the discovery of human heuristics which lead to cognitive bias or irrational behaviour (e.g. availability heuristic, clustering illusion, and others).

In particular, they originated the *prospect theory* [14] to explain irrational economic behaviour, these researches climaxed with the Nobel's prize at 2002.

Summarizing heuristic processes are able to explain both bounded rational and poor rational behaviours, according to experimental evidence of human behaviour.

Moreover, heuristics are relevant to understand also *unconscious* processes, such as perceptual categorization, in which many pieces of information are combined into a coherent whole.

For example, various perceptual processes such as stereoscopic vision and interpreting ambiguous figures are naturally interpreted in terms of combinatorial optimisation and constraint satisfaction [17] [7]. Hence, the natural neural net of visual cortex, with its complex topology, can be considered as a well-adapted connectionist heuristic for the very hard combinatorial problems of visual categorization.

In all these cases we can consider the heuristic internal realization of the cognitive functionality as responsible for the macroscopic external behaviour.

Put crudely and according to cognitive naturalism, the world is full of extremely large instances of intractable combinatorial problems, which are faced by heuristics based computational systems as, let us assume, human beings.

Therefore, the theory of computational complexity and the study of both natural and computational heuristics become theoretical interleaved core concepts to thought understanding.

3   Functional and Structural Models in Artificial Intelligence

The terms *'functional'* and *'structural'* refer to one of the fundamental debates in artificial intelligence, and cognitive science, about the legitimate description level of models. This conflict entangles the relationship between humans reasoning and AI procedures. Various researchers have different positions on what one means by: they are of the same type.

Functionalists propose a much looser definition of *same type*, based on identity of the functional macroscopic properties of the intelligent behaviour, that is, their input-output specifications. Functionalism was introduced in the philosophy of mind as a position critical of reductionist materialism in the mind-body problem, by Putnam in her seminal article *Minds and machines* [23]. Putnam argued that mental states could be studied not by referring them directly to brain states, but on the basis of their functional organization.

Other researchers looking for structural models, claim the not negligibility of how these functions are carried out. This perspective takes care of the human-likeness, or bio-psychological plausibility, of internal realization of a model as much as its intelligent behaviour.

But a literally structural model produces an «*asymptotic*» [28] regress to microscopic physical world until it reaches the paradox summarized in the well know Wiener sentence [28] «*The best material model of a cat is another, or preferably the same, cat*» and then, as matter of fact, the impossibility or the «*futility*» of building up a model of something.

In similar way Pylyshyn asserted about cognitive modelling ([24] p. 49) that if we do not formulate any restriction about model, we obtain the functionalism of Turing machine and, if we apply all possible restrictions, we reproduce a whole human being.

Then the key point is the research of a relevant descriptive level and the enforcement of constraints to this level to carry out a *human like* computation.

The explanatory level of functionalist models is the macroscopic one of stimulus-response relationship, at the opposite there is the microscopic level of physical re-production models according to a strong reductionist materialism. In the middle there are a lot of possible structural models.

4   The Mesoscopic Functionalism

In the paper [8] we introduce a novel way of characterizing the problem of multiple realizability in functionalism.

Thanks to computational complexity theory we relate the feasibility of the multiple realizability of internal implementation (viz. its *fungibility*) of a function with its computational tractability, and for intractable functions we propose the design of heuristic as a key aspect to model behaviour of real systems.

These considerations allow us to introduce the *mesoscopic functionalism* as a functionalism for which internal implementation is generally not negligible but that permits multiple realization only for the implementation of the heuristic. This kind of functionalism overcomes underdetermination of traditional functionalistic models and, at the same time, avoids a shift toward hyperdetermination. In fact it detects as a relevant descriptive level the one of functional specifications of heuristics.

The word *mesoscopic*, borrowed from the statistical physics, is meant as the intermediate level between the macroscopic one of the system behaviour and microscopic one of its implementation.

4.1 Intractability and Functionalism

All computable functions, in principle, are defined by an effective input-output relation, but intractable ones are *de facto* incomputable for almost all not trivial inputs.

Roughly speaking, a problem is called *intractable* [22] if the time required to solve problem instances grows at least exponentially, in the worst case, with the size of the instances.

This class contains many combinatorial problems that we all would like to be able to solve effectively, including the boolean satisfiability problem, the travelling salesman problem, max-cut graph problem and Thagard's foundational formalization of coherence-based cognitive problems [34].

The modeller of systems facing to intractable problems should strive to find smart way to bypass it. A computational inexpensive strategy must be pursued by means of heuristic computations.

In combinatorial optimisation [4], a heuristic is a technique designed to solve a problem that ignores whether the output can be proven to be correct, but which usually produces a good result. It is intended to gain computational performance or conceptual simplicity at the cost of accuracy or precision. The aim is to achieve a *good enough* output rather than exact output but this is rewarded with a great computational performance able to turn intractable problems into tractable ones.

The most known heuristic techniques are neural networks, Boltzman machines, genetic algorithms, hill climbing, tabu search, simulated annealing, swarm computing, ant colony optimisation, and others [27]. Many of these techniques are bio-inspired and they are widely used or created within bio-inspired AI researches.

The output of heuristic based systems becomes dependent from specific selected heuristic and also from its internal parameters. The concrete realized function is different from the exact intractable function because the choice of heuristic influences the carried output in addition to execution time (see figure 1).

So the heuristic between macroscopic functionality and microscopic implementation is the real responsible of the arising input-output behaviour of systems.

Due to this we can argue there is a coupling between functional (i.e. behavioural specification) and procedural   aspects (i.e. internal realization) of a system, this implies a *function-structure coupling* for intractable functions.

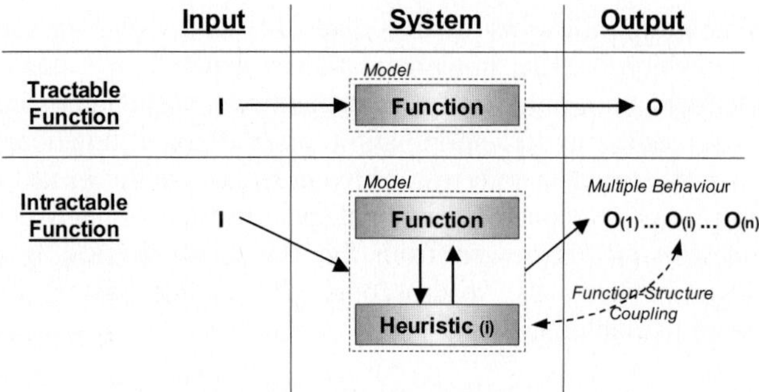

Fig. 1. Function-Structure Relationship

So intractable functions are not structure-independent entities: the internal realization is the *core* of the function because it is absolutely not a *fungible* interchangeable part of the computational system.

We observe that the multiple realizability for computationally intractable functions is *not realizable* at all because if we choose an exact fungible algorithm, the function becomes *de facto* incomputable and if we adopt a heuristic, the input-output behaviour is not more unambiguously defined. The multiple realizability produces a kind of "multiple behaviour" (more formally, we have a collection of heuristic functions, everyone with univocal output) (see figure 1).

For a heuristically computed intractable function, the *mesoscopic level* of the design of heuristic (that is a functional specification), is the essential aspect of the system, because it is just the heuristic that defines unambiguously the input-output relation.

Contrarily, for tractable functions input-output function specification is well posed and the used specific algorithm is entirely negligible because its choice do not influence input-output system behaviour.

So there is not a *function-structure coupling* for tractable functions. A system designed to perform these tasks can be rightly modelled at functional macroscopic level as black-box with well-known stimulus-response behaviour (see figure 1, on top). Thus the intermediate, *mesoscopic,* level of solution techniques between macroscopic functional specification and microscopic implementative details can be neglected. In other words, the internal realization is a *fungible* interchangeable part of the computational system hence we have the correctness of *multiple-realizability* and we can consider tractable functions as *structure-independent* entities without underdetermination.

4.2   The Mesoscopic Level of Functionalism

As we have shown above classical functionalism is well posed only for simple tractable functions because they can be considered structure independent entities.

However, this type of tractable functions are not much interesting for the cognitive modelling.

Thus for the intractable functions, which are of great cognitive interest, the descriptive level for explaining and predicting the macroscopic behaviour is the mesoscopic level of the computational heuristic. In fact, in accordance with the theoretical considerations of the computational complexity and the experimental cognitive evidences with the human beings, it is not possible to predict the system behaviour without considering the used specific heuristic.

So canonical functionalism neglecting the mesoscopic level of internal realization is unsuitable for human mind modelling.

But wholly agreeing with Harnad ([10] p. 299) one of the main risks, for overcoming underdetermination of simply functional models, is to push models up to synthetic bio-chemical or physical recreation. This kind of models tend to realism as much as possible, and so they can be *hyperdeterminated* because they consider physical or functional features which could be irrelevant to the understanding of bio-psychological phenomena, and this leads to a reduction of the explication power of models.

So we can set descriptive level of models at the mesoscopic one, taking into account subject-explicit heuristics as well as implicit unconscious heuristics.

In these mesoscopic models we are able to describe the heuristic in a functional way, because the internal realization of the heuristic at the lower microscopic-implementative level is absolutely irrelevant for the system behaviour.

Mesoscopic models can be considered functional and structural models at the same time. They are *functional* models of computational heuristics because they neglect theirs internal microscopic implementation and from a another viewpoint they are *structural* models of macroscopic functionality because they resolve underdetermination of macroscopic level (see figure 2).

We call this modelling approach *mesoscopic functionalism* because it shift down underdetermination at the mesoscopic level allowing multiple realizability only at microscopic level and because it resolves under-determination of macroscopic level (i.e. stimulus-response one) fixing a heuristic.

Furthermore, the *necessity* of a mesoscopic descriptive level due to intractability can be used [8] to support *design-stance* rather than *intentional-stance* proposed by Dennett [6] as explanatory strategies to human behaviour. This also justifies, in our view, AI practices as a kind of reverse engineering of bio-cognitive functionalities.

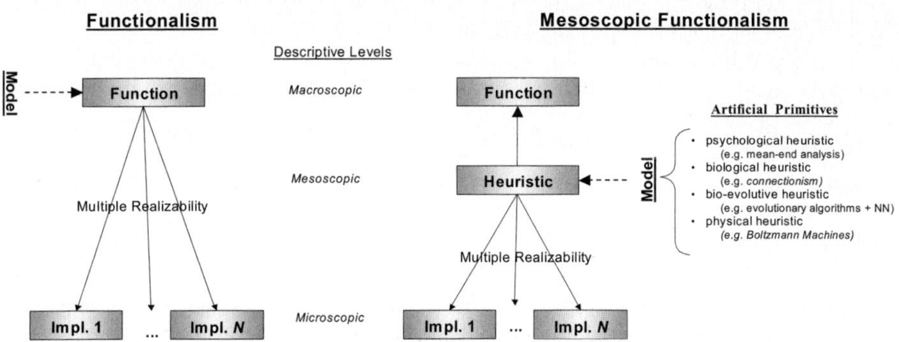

Fig. 2. Functionalism, Mesoscopic Functionalism and Artificial Primitives

5   Artificial Intelligence and Mesoscopic Functionalism

We can roughly divide artificial intelligence (AI) researches in two main schools of thought: *Classical* AI and *Nouvelle* AI.

Classical AI mostly involves the logical-symbolic techniques for the development of intelligent systems. This is also known as symbolic AI, neat AI or Good Old-Fashioned Artificial Intelligence (GOFAI) as it is called by Haugeland [11].

Two good examples of its successful fields are chess playing and theorem proving, the task environments preferred by early AI. Some early well known results obtained by this AI mainstream are production systems and notably *expert systems*. Nowadays, within this mainstream there are *cognitive architectures* such as ACT [1], SOAR [13] and theirs evolutions, which are systems based on symbolic-inferential techniques.

Nouvelle AI, also known as non-symbolic AI or 'scruffy' AI, is based on soft-computing and *bio-inspired* techniques as, for instance, neural networks, evolutionary computation and evolutionary robotics. Nouvelle AI applies biologically inspired design methods, including connectionism and evolutionism, to achieve an arising intelligent behaviour.

This bio-inspired computing, takes a *bottom-up*, decentralised approach, because these techniques often involve the method of specifying a set of simple rules (e.g. genetic operators or activation rule respectively for genetic algorithms or artificial neural nets), a set of simple organisms or node which adhere to those rules, and a method of iteratively applying those rules.

So nouvelle AI obtains an adaptive approach to intelligent behaviour and learning, as opposed to the what could be described as *top-down* 'creationist' method, used in classical AI.

5.1   Unifying Cognitive Artificial Intelligence

We think that both classical and nouvelle AI create models of cognitive functions at mesoscopic level.

In fact, classical AI does not build pure functional models because the intractability of combinatorial explosion in these systems is faced by heuristics.

As well within nouvelle AI the employed bio-plausible or only bio-inspired techniques can be seen as heuristic algorithms for approximated solution of hard intractable problems.

In classical AI (e.g. *Information Processing Psychology* (IPP) by Newell and Simon [21]), cognitive interested researchers designed artificial systems to re-create intermediate processes of human thinking beyond the pure stimulus-response intelligent behaviour.

For instance, in classical AI one of the early systems, *General Problem Solver* (GPS) [20], was designed from the beginning to recreate human problem-solving protocols. The main method of this system embodies the psychological plausible heuristic of *means-ends analysis* which is used, at the same time, to face combinatorial explosion of candidate solutions and to assure a human-likeness reasoning.

In cognitive architectures (e.g. ACT or SOAR), which are models of human reasoning based on production systems, the working memory of the system models human short-term memory, and the productions are part of long-term memory.

The order in which these programs generate subgoals and possible actions is similar to the bounded resources way (i.e. heuristic way) of humans approaching the same problems. So this family of models can be easily considered as mesoscopic models.

The nouvelle AI (e.g. *Parallel Distributed Processing* (PDP) [29]), following bio-plausibility modelling techniques, has tacitly detected a *mesoscopic* descriptive level (its models are often called *structural* models) which allow to reproduce the functionalities of biological structures (the heuristics) and to neglect the physical and chemical details.

Nouvelle AI reutilises the good heuristic solutions 'adopted' by nature to face intractable combinatorial problems as, for instance, the connectionism of biological neural nets or the evolutionary algorithms of natural selection.

Thus the mesoscopic functionalism, tacitly or consciously, has shared both from *top-down* approach of classical AI and *bottom-up* approach of nouvelle AI: classical AI facing the combinatorial explosion and nouvelle AI duplicating the nature.

According to this view, the prevalent attempt to lined up functional vs. structural model with classical AI vs. nouvelle AI is without real foundations (see also [5], chap. 7).

The differences among various approaches or modelling techniques within AI should be searched by means of some other subjects, including for example *symbol grounding* and the *embodiment* problems.

6 Cognitive Plausibility of Models

Thus mainstreams of AI build mesoscopic functionalist models, and for cognitive interested researchers, the core matter is not functional versus structural model problem, but it is the setting of the right bio-psychological constraints, for the mesoscopic level, to carry out a biological or psychological plausible computation.

Rethinking the concept of the *"fine-grain correspondence"* proposed by Pylyshyn ([25] p. 121), we propose that the explanatory abilities of mesoscopic models are guaranteed by the functional equivalence between the heuristic internally used and the heuristic realized by the natural systems (both psychological ones and biological ones).

Then, according to Cordeschi ([5], chap. 7), the difference between mesoscopic models of different AI mainstreams is due to the choice of distinctive *artificial primitives* [16]: psychological, neurological or bio-evolutive (see figure 2, right). By means of these different primitives the modeller builds the mesoscopic level of a intelligent artificial systems, and at this level the researcher enforces the constraints so that the models have some cognitive explanatory capability.

In fact, the choice of a given artificial primitive rather than another, does not suffice for assuring a cognitive explication power at built model. One can build a connectionist model that is irrelevant for cognitive science and a symbolic model that is interesting for cognitive explanation, or vice versa.

Hence, a computational cognitive model has to realize the particular considered cognitive function through the same heuristic used by the human being.

In this perspective cognitive oriented AI, both classical and nouvelle, attempt to recreates the "internal structure" of human mind functionalities: the classical AI mainly from a psychological perspective and the nouvelle AI mainly from a biological or bio-psychological one.

7 Underdetermination and Scientific Pluralism

Despite this methodological uniformity of building mesoscopic models, the classical AI models are often reproved from nouvelle AI researchers as *"in principle underdetermined"* ([36] p. 247) because they would allow multiple realizability of cognitive function, and then they would be ill-posed for cognitive explanations.

Conversely, many structural models within nouvelle AI are often considered *ipso facto* psychologically or biologically plausible, and not simply bio-inspired. (See [26] about some PDP connectionist models which are biologically implausible).

This intellectual attitude is not justified by evidences nor by theoretical reasons explained previously.

Moreover, the underdetermination of models is *"epidemic to science"* [12]. The existence of several alternative methodologies or theories that support experimental evidence, is common in all fields of science. Einstein had described this situation in physics as an *"embarrassment of riches"*(Cited in [12]).

In epistemology *underdetermination* (also *indeterminacy*) is used to refer to the dilemma of having several alternative theories, descriptive formalisms or models and consequently explanations, that are not falsified by experimental tests.

The underdetermination of the resulting empirically adequate multiplicity of scientific explanations and point of view is recognized by the pragmatist thesis as *scientific pluralism* [15].

In the social sciences underdetermination is a common outcome and scientific pluralism has been defended from both methodological and theoretical viewpoints [2] [3].

Hence the multiple internal realization of a computational model or theory which satisfies empirical data is a problem deeply rooted in whole scientific activity.

Cognitive researchers, exactly while attempting to resolve underdetermination of computational models, develop a wide spectrum of viewpoints and modelling techniques which we pose at a unifying mesoscopic level. (see figure 2, right).

In artificial intelligence, the concept of scientific pluralism leads to the observation that several artificial primitives are equally legitimate and scientists can choose among alternative mesoscopic models, including cognitive architectures, production systems or other logical-symbolic models, as well as connectionist models, a-life models or other bio-plausible.

Despite of this, most of debates within AI come from the attempt to legitimate a specific technique or methodology as the unique right one to recreate and explain human behaviour and intelligence. While following Merton [18] [19] and his concept of *middle range theory*, we should not try to explain the whole mind or to attempt to justify a modelling technique as a total theoretical system able to cover all, or almost all, aspects of mind (the *grand theory*); but we should concentrate to develop a computational partial models of some skills of human mind (*middle range theories*) using one of several techniques according to partial experimental data and available increasing knowledge.

8 Concluding Remarks

We have argued that several methodologies and techniques for cognitive modelling within artificial intelligence, lie in the same descriptive level and share the methodological approach of mesoscopic functionalism. The mesoscopic level of functional specification of heuristics is fixed by the necessity to deal with intractability for both natural and artificial systems.

Thus, the contraposition between functional and structural models is not so useful to cognitive modelling problem (and it should even be ill-posed from a hardly theoretical viewpoint), because cognitive relevance of a AI systems may be assured from constraint enforced to mesoscopic level. While different modelling techniques are all potentially well-posed, because according to scientific pluralism, complex mental phenomena require multiple, sometimes even incompatible, accounts achievable with the wide spectrum of models developed in the short and fruitful life of AI.

We think this pluralistic attitude is a key factor to progress artificial intelligence and cognitive science.

Acknowledgments. I wish to thank Prof. V. Cordeschi and Prof. G. Trautteur for the inspiring discussions about matters illustrated in the present paper.

References

1. Anderson, J.R.: The Architecture of Cognition. Harvard University Press, Cambridge, Massachusetts (1983)
2. Bohman, J.: New Philosophy of Social Science. In: Problems of Indeterminacy, MIT Press, Cambridge (1991)
3. Bohman, J.: Pluralism, Indeterminacy and the Social Sciences: Reply to Ingram and Meehan. Journal Human Studies 20(4), 441–458 (1997)
4. Cook, W.J., Cunningham, W.H., Pulleyblank, W.R, Schrijver, A.: Combinatorial Optimization. John Wiley & Sons, England (1997)
5. Cordeschi, R.: The Discovery of the Artificial: Behavior, Mind and Machines Before and Beyond Cybernetics. Kluwer Academic Publishers, Dordrecht (2002)
6. Dennett, D.: The Intentional Stance. MIT Press, Cambridge (1987)
7. Feldman, J.A.: A connectionist model of visual memory. In: Hinton, G.E., Anderson, J.A. (eds.) Parallel models of associative memory, pp. 49–81. Erlbaum, Hillsdale, NJ (1981)

8. Gagliardi, F.: Functionalism, Computational Complexity and Design Stance. In: Vosniadou, S., Kayser, D., Protopapas, A. (eds.) Proceedings of the European Cognitive Science Conference 2007 pp. 752–757. Lawrence Erlbaum Associates, Hove, East Sussex (2007)

9. Gigerenzer, G., Todd, P.M., & the ABC Research Group,: Simple Heuristics That Make Us Smart. Oxford University Press, Oxford (1999)

10. Harnad, S.: Levels of functional equivalence in reverse bioengineering. Artificial Life 1, 293–301 (1994)

11. Haugeland, J.: Artificial Intelligence: the Very Idea. MIT Press, Cambridge, MA (1985)

12. Hickey, T.J.: History of Twentieth-Century Philosophy of Science. T.J. Hickey Publisher (1995, 2005) (Link 2nd ed.), http://www.philsci.com

13. Laird, J.E., Newell, A., Rosenbloom, P.S.: SOAR: an architecture for general intelligence. Artificial Intelligence 33(1), 1–64 (1987)

14. Kahneman, D., e Tversky, A.: Prospect theory: An analysis of decision under risk. Econometrica 47, 263–291 (1979)

15. Kellert, S.H., Longino, H.E., Kenneth Waters, C. (eds.): Scientific Pluralism. University Of Minnesota Press (2006)

16. Langton, C.G.: Artificial Life. In: Langton, C.G. (ed.) Artificial Life, pp. 1–47. Addison-Wesley, Reading (1989)

17. Marr, D., Poggio, T.: Cooperative computation of stereo disparity. Science 194, 283–287 (1976)

18. Merton, R.K.: Social Theory and Social Structure. The Free Press, New York, NY (1949)

19. Merton, R.K.: Sociology of Science: Theoretical and Empirical Investigations. University of Chicago Press, Chicago, IL (1973)

20. Newell, A., Simon, H.A.: GPS, a program that simulates human thought. In: Billing, H. (ed.) Lernende Automaten, pp. 109–124. R. Oldenbourg, Munich, Germany (1961)

21. Newell, A., Simon, H.A.: Human problem solving. Prentice-Hall, Englewood Cliffs, NJ (1972)

22. Papadimitriou, C.H.: Computational Complexity. Addison-Wesley, Reading (1994)

23. Putnam, H.: Minds and machines. In: Hook, S. (ed.) Dimensions of Mind, pp. 138–164. Macmillan Publishers, London (1960)

24. Pylyshyn, Z.W.: Complexity and the study of artificial and human intelligence. In: Ringle, M. (ed.) Philosophical Perspectives in Artificial Intelligence, Harvester, Brighton (1979)

25. Pylyshyn, Z.W.: Computation and Cognition: Toward a Foundation for Cognitive Science. MIT Press, Cambridge, MA (1984)

26. Reeke, G.N., Sporns, O., e Edelman, G.M.: Synthetic neural modelling: comparisons of population and connectionist approaches. In: Pfeifer, R., Schreter, Z., Fogelman-Soulié, F., Steels, L. (eds.) Connectionism in Perspective, pp. 113–139. North Holland, Amsterdam (1989)

27. Reeves, C.R. (ed.): Modern Heuristic Techniques for Combinatorial Problems. John Wiley & Sons, Inc, New York, NY, USA (1993)

28. Rosenblueth, A., Wiener, N.: The role of Models in Sciences. Phil. Sci. 12, 316–321 (1945)

29. Rumelhart, D.E., McClelland, J.L., and the PDP Research Group: Parallel Distributed Processing: Explorations in the Microstructure of Cognition, vol. 1. MIT Press, Foundations, Cambridge, MA (1986)

30. Russell, S.J., Norvig, P.: Artificial Intelligence. A Modern Approach, 2nd edn. Prentice Hall, Englewood Cliffs (2002)

31. Simon, H.: Models of Man. John Wiley and Sons, New York (1957)
32. Slote, M.: Beyond Optimizing. Harvard University Press, Cambridge, Mass (1989)
33. Thagard, P.: Coherence in thought and action. MIT Press, Cambridge, MA (2000)
34. Thagard, P., Verbeurgt, K.: Coherence as constraint satisfaction. Cognitive Science 22, 1–24 (1998)
35. Tversky, A., Kahneman, D.: Judgment Under Uncertainty: Heuristics and Biases. Science 185, 1124–1131 (1974)
36. Verschure, P.F.M.J., Wray, J., Sporns, O., Tononi, T., Edelman, G.M.: Multilevel analysis of classical conditioning in a behaving real world artifact. Robotics and Autonomous Systems 16, 247–265 (1995)

Understanding the Environment Through Wireless Sensor Networks

Salvatore Gaglio, Luca Gatani, Giuseppe Lo Re, and Marco Ortolani

Dept. of Computer Engineering, University of Palermo
Viale delle Scienze, I-90128, Palermo, Italy
{gaglio, gatani, lore, ortolani}@unipa.it

Abstract. This paper presents a new cognitive architecture for extracting meaningful, high-level information from the environment, starting from the raw data collected by a Wireless Sensor Network. The proposed framework is capable of building rich internal representation of the sensed environment by means of intelligent data processing and correlation. Furthermore, our approach aims at integrating the connectionist, data-driven model with the symbolic one, that uses a high-level knowledge about the domain to drive the environment interpretation. To this aim, the framework exploits the notion of conceptual spaces, adopting a conceptual layer between the subsymbolic one, that processes sensory data, and the symbolic one, that describes the environment by means of a high level language; this intermediate layer plays the key role of anchoring the upper layer symbols. In order to highlight the characteristics of the proposed framework, we also describe a sample application, aiming at monitoring a forest through a Wireless Sensor Network, in order to timely detect the presence of fire.

1   Introduction

Wireless Sensor Networks (WSNs) are an emerging technology that allows pervasive environmental monitoring through measurement of characteristic quantities [1]. They can be thought of as "Google® for the physical world" [2] in that, while the primary purpose of a sensor node is data gathering, each of them also has limited processing capabilities that may be exploited in order to carry on preliminary operations on raw data. Despite the difficulty of collecting and managing huge amounts of measurements, meaningful information can be extracted by means of intelligent in-network processing and correlation of sensed data.

Although several interesting works present innovative applications where WSN pervasiveness has a dramatic impact in accomplishing monitoring and control tasks on well-defined scenarios, all these proposals are definitely application-specific [3], [4]. Our approach, on the other hand, aims at providing a comprehensive framework capable of general-purpose management of data streaming from the sensed environment to the highest level of knowledge representation. In particular, this paper proposes the adoption of a three-layer computational architecture, similar to the one presented in [5] and [6], where the authors exploit the idea of *conceptual spaces* [7] and describe a cognitive system for the interpretation of static and

R. Basili and M.T. Pazienza (Eds.): AI*IA 2007, LNAI 4733, pp. 72–83, 2007.
© Springer-Verlag Berlin Heidelberg 2007

dynamic scenes, starting from data obtained from video cameras. In order to generalize to more challenging scenarios, we devise an analogous architecture that employs WSNs as the sensing layer of an intelligent system. We describe the design of a flexible framework capable of collecting raw data through networked sensors, and of operating reductions and aggregations on them; processed data are then represented as vectors in ad-hoc geometric spaces (i.e., conceptual spaces), where the notion of *similarity* can be modeled in a natural way using opportune metrics. Meaningful concepts will finally be extracted and used for further higher-level inferences.

The remainder of the paper is organized as follows. Section 2 gives useful insights about the theory behind conceptual spaces, and about a few relevant data analysis and knowledge representation techniques. In Section 3 we introduce the cognitive architecture, we discuss the functionalities of each layer and detail our implementation choices. Section 4 illustrates how the architecture may be exploited in a sample scenario for wildfire monitoring. Finally, we draw our conclusions and outline some future developments in Section 5.

2   Technical Background

Cognitive science aims at understanding how information is represented and processed in different kinds of agents, biological as well as artificial. Finding the most appropriate way of modeling the information is a challenging issue and currently two approaches are dominating: the *symbolic* approach starts from the assumption that cognitive systems can be modeled as Turing machines, whereas the *connectionist* approach models such systems through artificial neuron networks.

According to Gärdenfors [7], neither approach can model complex aspects of cognitive phenomena in all situations; therefore, the author introduces a third form of representing information (*conceptual* representation), based on the exploitation of geometric structures. A conceptual space consists of a number of quality dimensions that can be generated by perceptual mechanisms, or can present a more abstract, non-sensory character. Examples of quality dimensions are colour, pitch, temperature, weight, and the three ordinary spatial dimensions. It is assumed that each of the quality dimensions is endowed with a certain topological or metric structure, so it is conceivable to define the similarity of two objects through the distance between their representing points in the space.

Conceptual spaces can serve as tools for categorization and concept formation, providing a natural way of representing similarities, which is typically very difficult to handle at the symbolic layer. In this model a categorization generates a partitioning of the conceptual space and Gärdenfors defines *natural concepts* as *convex regions*. However the fundamental issue concerns how to identify those regions in the space and, as those regions are supposed to group similar objects in the conceptual space together, a possible solution requires using a *clustering* technique. The arising of meaningful clusters is obviously closely related to the choice of an opportune metric for the space; moreover, once this crucial step is performed, the clusters that have been identified need to be analyzed in order to assess their validity with respect to their subsequent use in the knowledge representation system; to this aim it may be useful to identify representative objects for each cluster.

The interface of the proposed architecture with the real world is represented by the Wireless Sensor Network infrastructure, which accounts for the lowest layer of the whole complex cognitive system. Data manipulation may have significant impact on the efficiency of the overall architecture and, as will be detailed later, WSNs play an important role at this stage; a typical approach to lessening the burden of superfluous communication and processing in such context is to resort to data aggregation. A possible approach consists in reducing the overall amount of transmitted data by exploiting some spacial correlation; data may be merged as they traverse the network so that only the information that is actually needed is in fact transmitted. A somewhat similar approach relies on the observation that environmental phenomena are quite predictable, so they will likely present some temporal correlation that may be exploited if nodes try to establish collaborative relationships with each other. This leads to the formation of cluster of sensor nodes that delegate to a representative node the task of building a predictive model out of previous measurements [8].

In [9], several methods for feature extraction and dimensional reduction are surveyed. The author differentiates them into *projective methods*, and *manifold modeling methods*. The former class comprises those techniques that attempt to find low dimensional projections that extract useful information from the data and includes the projection pursuit method [10], and the well-known Principal Component Analysis (PCA) and its variants [11] among others, whereas the latter class contains those methods that model the manifold on which the data lies, such as multi-dimensional scaling (MDS) [12], graphical methods (Laplacian eigenmaps, spectral clustering) [13,14], and so on. Amongst projective techniques, great attention has been gathered by the so-called kernel methods, such as kernel PCA and, more importantly, by Support Vector Machines (SVMs) [15], which have been successfully applied to several research fields, such as text recognition, isolated handwritten digit recognition, and face detection.

Knowledge representation is a crucial aspect of AI and its main goal regards the expression of knowledge in computer-tractable form, such that it can be used to help intelligent agents in their activities. Knowledge engineering is the process of building a knowledge base in order to *understand* the considered domain and to represent the significant objects and relationships. The ability of a knowledge engineer resides in her capacity to represent very general concepts by means of a vocabulary, known as an *ontology*. Each of the approaches presented in literature offers a specific vision of some part of the world; moreover, ontologies can be formulated in a wide variety of languages and notations (e.g., logic, LISP, etc.); the essential information is not the form of the language, but the content, namely the set of ontological structures provided as a way of thinking about the world.

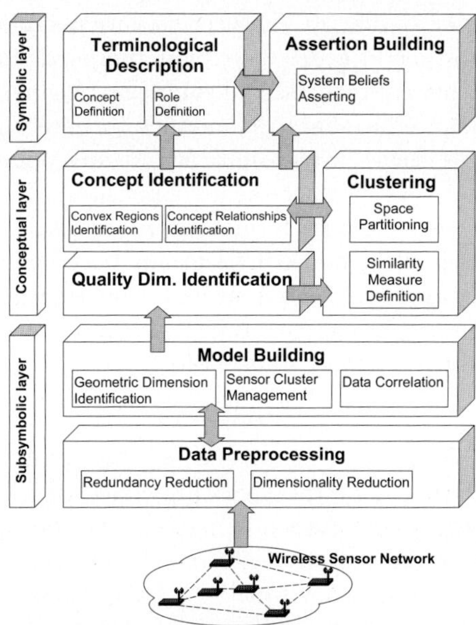

Fig. 1. The proposed architecture, showing the three levels of representation

3   The Proposed Architecture

This paper describes a multi-layer architecture for in-depth reasoning on large amount of data gathered by a Wireless Sensor Network. Our architecture is composed of three layers, as schematically represented in Figure 1: the *subsymbolic layer*, where information is still deeply embedded into raw data; the *conceptual layer*, where basic quantities are represented in geometric form as points in a vector space, and finally the *symbolic layer*, where information is eventually coded as high-level symbols on which logical inferences may be carried on.

3.1   Subsymbolic Layer

The subsymbolic layer exploits the computational capabilities of sensor nodes in order to implement data correlation techniques. Sensors capture raw, unprocessed data, so it is crucial to extract hidden correlations in order to capture the occurrence of unusual phenomena. Moreover, for the sake of our architectural scheme, the subsymbolic layer also needs to deal with adapting the dimensionality of the original data space to the requirements of the upper layer.

In [7], the notion of *dimension* is closely related to the measure of a distance, assuming that geometric proximity corresponds to the abstract notion of similarity. Identifying meaningful dimensions (named *quality dimensions*) in the subsymbolic space is both the primary goal and the challenging issue when relating raw data to concepts. They represent various "qualities" of real objects and affect the way in which an opportune distance metric may be interpreted as a natural way of expressing similarity. Our architecture assumes that sensor nodes collaborate with each other in order to exploit temporal correlation in sensed data and to build synthetical models. Following the original ideas of [8], neighboring sensor nodes help reduce data redundancy by entering into collaborative relationships and taking turns in transmitting. At any point in time, the node that is actively transmitting also acts as a representative for its collaborators, answering queries and participating in monitoring operation on their behalf. It shares a model with each of the nodes in its group, based on their past behavior, and exchanges information with them in order to make sure that its response on their behalf meets some accuracy constraints; in the ideal case very little data needs to be exchanged without any information loss.

3.2 Conceptual Layer

Environmental data gathered by the WSN are collected at a sink node, where they may be further processed and then mapped at the conceptual layer, in order to build a description of the sensed environment, in terms of a combination of geometric dimensions. The primary function of the geometric dimensions is to represent the significant "qualities" of perceived objects; they correspond to the different ways in which stimuli are judged to be similar or different and, therefore, they must be endowed with certain geometrical structures and topological metrics.

Following the definition of [5], we call *knoxel* a generic point in a conceptual space, representing main epistemological primitives. Formally, a knoxel is a vector whose components correspond to parameters associated with quality dimensions of the domain of interest. Unfortunately, the precise characterization of conceptual spaces poses severe difficulties, since finding dimensions and associated metrics is a complex and highly domain-specific task. It is clear that there is no identification technique that works well in every possible case, and that it is necessary to adopt methods carefully designed for the specific cognitive task. In particular, the structures of the dimensions should be as simple as possible, and tightly connected to the measurement methods that have been employed to determine the values of the dimensions in experimental situations.

Amongst the different available clustering techniques suitable for separating convex regions in the given space, we have chosen to use Support Vector Machines that, thanks to their general-purpose approach and their customizability with respect to the concepts of geometric space and metric, are promising for our specific purposes. They rely on the structural risk minimization principle in order to separate m classes through the best hyperplane. Although one of their drawbacks is their slowness during the training phase, this is not a serious limitation in our case, since we may as well rely on a single training phase to be performed at the beginning. However, if we wanted to add further knowledge at a later stage (as could happen, for instance, if we wanted to provide some feedback from the symbolic layer), we could resort to using a modified *incremental* version of SVMs [16] that allows for dynamic modifications of the model.

3.3   Symbolic Layer

At the symbolic layer our system must provide a concise description of the perceived environment in terms of a high-level logical language, capable of symbolic knowledge-based reasoning.

This layer aims to describing the relationships needed to infer complex events starting from "phenomena" extracted from the conceptual layer and, to this end, a description of the application domain ontology is needed. As in [5], the symbolic knowledge base description can be carried out by means of a hybrid representation formalism, in the sense of Nebel [17]. Such a hybrid formalism is constituted by two different components: a terminological module and an assertional module; the former contains the descriptions of the concepts relevant for the represented domain (e.g., types of objects and of relationships to be perceived), whereas the latter stores the assertions describing the particular perceived environment.

This distinction into two components is mirrored here by the use of two different formalisms. In particular, we adopt a KL-ONE-like notation [18] for representing the structured knowledge in the form of concept definitions, subsumption relationships, and roles. Furthermore, in order to enable the system to reason about instances of the defined terms, we represent them as one- and two-place predicate symbols, relying on a standard first-order logic.

4   Wildfire Detection: A Case Study

This Section describes a sample application of the proposed framework, aiming at monitoring a forest through a Wireless Sensor Network, in order to timely detect the presence of fire.

Fire is generated by a chemical reaction involving rapid oxidation or burning of a combustible material, and requires sufficient amounts of fuel and oxygen to be present in the proper conditions and proportions. One of the most important aspects in wildfire detection and prevention is fire behavior analysis; according to [19], this may be defined as "the manner in which fuel ignites, flame develops, and fire spreads and exhibits other related phenomena as determined by the interaction of fuel, weather, and topography." Fire behavior is heavily influenced by such factors as the fuel type, weather conditions (air temperature and humidity, wind speed and direction), and topography of the fire location; the products of burning include the gases carbon monoxide, carbon dioxide, and water vapour.

In the scenario considered here, the area to be monitored is covered with low-cost, resource-constrained wireless sensor nodes, deployed at known locations and at varying heights, and sufficiently close to each other so as to form a connected network. Similarly to other projects aiming at using Wireless Sensor Networks for fire prevention, such as FIRE [20] and Firebug [21], our system employs commonly available nodes equipped with sensors for monitoring environmental conditions such as wind speed and direction, air temperature, relative humidity, and barometric pressure, as well as more specific sensors such as detectors for carbon monoxide, carbon dioxide, water vapor, smoke, and flames.

For the purpose of the required monitoring actions, large amounts of data will need to be collected and processed, in order to extract meaningful information about the state of the environment; the information deduced by means of this higher-level analysis will then be used to promptly alert in case of likely dangerous conditions. Energy resources will be limited and non-renewable in the nodes, nevertheless they will still be able to perform selected computations on data. We adopt a model-based technique, in order to exploit correlation in the data through a distributed node grouping protocol [8]. This is motivated by the fact that in a typical sensor network monitoring task, the readings of sensor nodes show high temporal and spatial correlation; for instance, in the scenario considered here, environmental conditions will likely not be subject to significant changes over time, unless some disruptive event occurs. We are not interested in constant monitoring of weather conditions, but rather in capturing unusual phenomena that might be interpreted as fire alarms or, in other words, outliers with respect to the given prediction model. Nodes may thus organize themselves into clusters ruled by a collaboration relationship. A cluster head acts as a representative for the whole group, by building a model for predicting its collaborators' behavior; it will then transmit only those readings that differ from the predicted ones by more than a certain pre-specified error threshold; moreover, when no transmissions are received from the collaborating nodes, the monitoring entity uses the sensors' prediction models to infer their readings. Periodically, the cluster head will receive updated prediction models from its collaborators. Moreover, in order to provide resilience to natural variations in data, for instance as a consequence of different weather conditions depending on seasonal changes, we have modified the original collaboration protocol so that models are periodically updated to incorporate useful statistics, for instance about seasonal and daily trends of temperature, barometric pressure, and so on.

Sensor readings are used to characterize the conceptual spaces used in our system. When applying our architecture to the present scenario, we identify two conceptual spaces related to topology and environmental measurements respectively.

The dimensions of the former space correspond to the three spatial components of the known location of the sensor nodes, whereas for defining the latter space we interpret the different types of sensor readings as quality measures, thus individuating the following quality dimensions:

- variation of temperature with respect to the expected value;
- variation of toxic gases (e.g. carbon monoxide, carbon dioxide, nitrogen oxide) concentrations with respect to the expected values;
- water vapor concentration;
- barometric pressure;
- UV and IR spectra.

Similarity among knoxels is expressed in terms of two metric functions defined in the topological and environmental space, respectively. A perception cluster $pc = \{k_1, k_2, \ldots, k_l\}$ may thus be defined as a finite set of knoxels in one of the

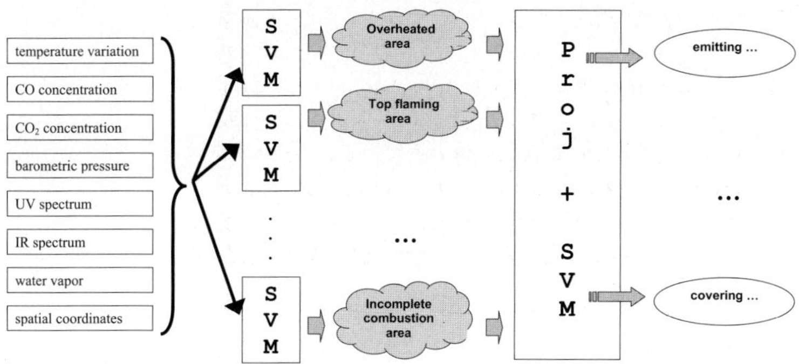

Fig. 2. The process of concepts and relationships extraction

conceptual spaces and such clusters may be identified through automated techniques, applying the similarity measure mentioned above. In particular, we have chosen to use Support Vector Machines (SVMs), thanks to their general-purpose approach and their customizability with respect to the concepts of geometric space and metric. By applying them to the above mentioned conceptual spaces, we are able to isolate specific regions, i.e basic concepts in our formulation.

Such concepts may individuate, for instance, a "smoke cloud", an "incomplete combustion area", an "overheated area", a "flaming area", and so on. Figure 2 shows a simplified case, where an initial clustering of the conceptual spaces by means of the SVMs has identified several convex regions, including for instance:

incomplete combustion area: a region identified by low water vapor concentration, low carbon monoxide and dioxide, and presence of nitrogen oxide;
top flaming area: a region identified by having ultraviolet and infrared spectra occupying specific ranges, and located at a certain height from the ground.

A projection technique, combined with the use of a SVM in the resulting projection space, is then used to extract relationships among those concepts. For instance, assuming that a smoldering fire was in fact present in the monitored area, we can compute the projection of the knoxels in the "overheated area", "smoke cloud", and "incomplete combustion area" regions onto the spatial dimensions, and cluster the resulting space. Provided that the original knoxels regarded phenomena occurring in the same topological area, the process would identify a region representing a set of relationships involving the above mentioned concepts. The same process would identify other analogous relationships that would then be mapped onto symbolic structures as will be detailed in the following.

A knowledge representation system is adopted at the upper layer, with the final goal to infer higher-level events and to correctly classify them. As already discussed in the previous Section, we adopt a logically oriented formalism that is constituted by two different components: a terminological component, building domain descriptions, and an assertional component, storing facts concerning

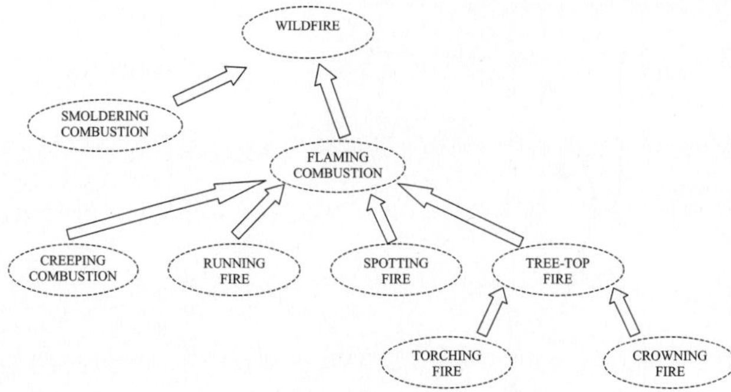

Fig. 3. Fragment of the terminological knowledge base describing the wildfire concepts taxonomy

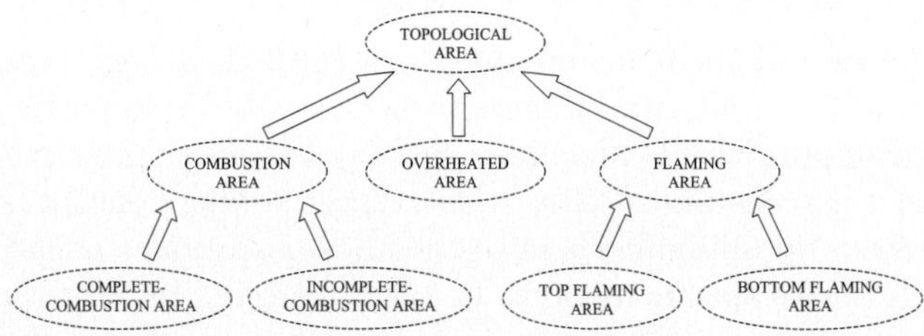

Fig. 4. Fragment of the terminological knowledge base describing the topological concepts taxonomy

a specific context. In particular, the descriptional task aims at forming an extensible repertoire of terms: a domain-specific vocabulary defining concepts on the basis of their taxonomical structure and their potential relationships (i.e., properties, parts, etc.). In our case study, we consider a simplified taxonomy of wildfires, and specify their necessary conditions in terms of the basic concepts that can be identified as regions on the conceptual spaces described above. The different kinds of wildfire can be informally defined as follows:

smoldering: a single-spot fire burning without flame, generating moderate heat, and emitting toxic gases (e.g., carbon monoxide) at a higher yield than flaming fires;

creeping: a flaming fire with low flame;

running: a flaming fire with high flame and with a well-defined front;

spotting: a flaming fire producing firebrands that fall beyond the main fire perimeter and result in spot fires;

torching: a flaming fire with high flame involving the foliage of a single tree (or a small clump of trees);

crowning: a flaming fire ascending into the crowns of trees and spreading from crown to crown.

Figure 3 depicts the subsumption relationships between these concepts, while Figure 4 presents another taxonomy fragment, dealing with some topological concepts (we adopt a network notation similar to that of Brachman and Schmolze

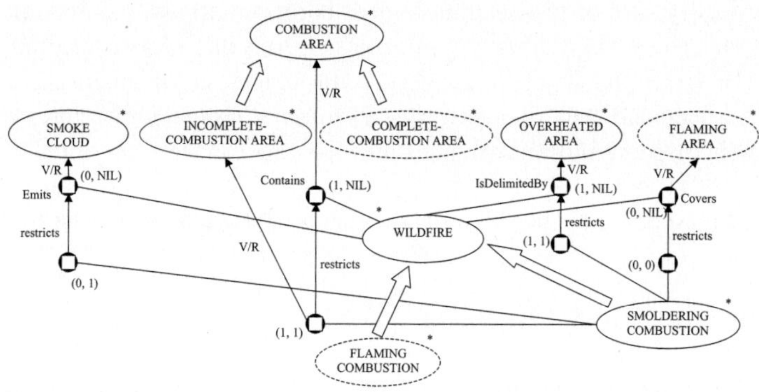

Fig. 5. Fragment of the terminological knowledge base describing the SMOLDERING COMBUSTION Concept

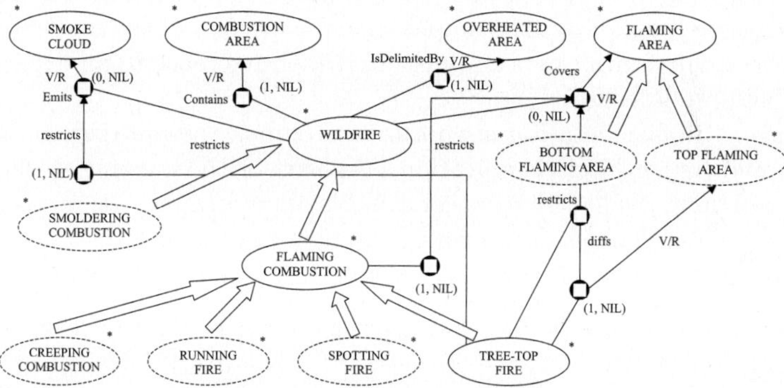

Fig. 6. Fragment of the terminological knowledge base describing the TREE-TOP FIRE Concept

[18]). The complete formalization captures the relationships that character-ize the wildfire taxonomy concepts in terms of the basic concepts singled out from measured data mapped into conceptual spaces. For example, Figure 5 represents a fragment of our terminological knowledge base, showing that a WILDFIRE is a THING that emits any number of SMOKE CLOUDs, contains at least one COMBUSTION AREA, is delimited by at least one OVERHEATED AREA, and covers any number of FLAMING AREAs. It also shows that SMOLDERING COMBUSTION rep-resents a a single-spot WILDFIRE, without any FLAMING AREA, and containing one INCOMPLETE COMBUSTION AREA. In a similar fashion, Figure 6 shows that a TREE-TOP FIRE is a WILDFIRE with flames (a FLAMING COMBUSTION), that emits at least one SMOKE CLOUD, and covers at least one flame area that satisfies the constraint of being a TOP FLAMING AREA.

The assertional component, on the other hand, maintains the linguistic in-formation concerning specific perceived contexts. In our sample case study, we represent the concepts of the terminological components as one-argument predicates, and the roles (e.g., *Emits*, *Contains*, and so on) as two-arguments relationships. For example, in order to assert the existence of an instance `SC#1` of the `SMOLDERING COMBUSTION` concept, the formula: *SmolderingCombustion*(`SC#1`) is added to the assertional knowledge base. To express that the filler of the role *Contains* for `SC#1` is an instance `ICA#1` (i.e., a specific knoxel) of the `INCOMPLETE COMBUSTION AREA` concept, the formula *Contains*(`SC#1`, `ICA#1`) is asserted.

5   Conclusion and Ongoing Work

In order to address the difficulty of gathering, managing, and understanding the huge amounts of data collected by WSNs, we proposed a novel architecture capable of understanding the sensed environment. Our proposal exploits the idea of representing knowledge through geometric structures which integrate the connectionist data-driven approach with the symbolic one. A cognitive architecture has been designed, detailing the computational aspects and the implementation choices. The architecture has been illustrated with reference to an experimental setup for wildfire detection.

The current implementation supports environment monitoring, basic event detection, and higher-level classifications. As part of the ongoing work, we are currently designing the logical reasoner capable of performing management tasks on the sensed environment. Furthermore, we plan to develop a distributed, grid-based implementation of the inference engine in order to improve the speedup of the overall system.

References

1. Akyildiz, I., Su, W., Sankarasubramaniam, Y., Cayirci, E.: A survey on sensor networks. IEEE Communication Magazine 40(8), 102–114 (2002)
2. Zhao, F., Guibas, L.: Wireless Sensor Networks: An Information Processing Approach. Morgan Kaufmann, San Francisco (2004)
3. He, T., Krishnamurthy, S., Luo, L., Yan, T., Gu, L., Stoleru, R., Zhou, G., Cao, Q., Vicaire, P., Stankovic, J.A., Abdelzaher, T.F., Hui, J., Krogh, B.: Vigilnet: An integrated sensor network system for energy-efficient surveillance. ACM Trans. Sen. Netw. 2(1), 1–38 (2006)
4. Tolle, G., Polastre, J., Szewczyk, R., Culler, D., Turner, N., Tu, K., Burgess, S., Dawson, T., Buonadonna, P., Gay, D., Hong, W.: A macroscope in the redwoods. In: SenSys '05. Proceedings of the 3rd international conference on Embedded networked sensor systems, pp. 51–63. ACM Press, New York, NY, USA (2005)
5. Chella, A., Frixione, M., Gaglio, S.: A cognitive architecture for artificial vision. Artificial Intelligence 89(1–2), 73–111 (1997)
6. Chella, A., Frixione, M., Gaglio, S.: Understanding dynamic scenes. Artificial Intelligence 123(1–2), 89–132 (2000)
7. Gärdenfors, P.: Conceptual Spaces. The Geometry of Thought. MIT Press, Cambridge MA (2000)

8. Goel, S., Imielinski, T., Passarella, A.: Using buddies to live longer in a boring world. In: Proc. IEEE PerCom Workshop, Pisa, Italy, pp. 342–346. IEEE Computer Society Press, Los Alamitos (2006)

9. Burges, C.J.: 1. In: Data mining and knowledge discovery handbook: A complete guide for practitioners and researchers, Kluwer Academic Publishers, Boston, MA (2005)

10. Friedman, J., Tukey, J.: A projection pursuit algorithm for exploratory data analysis. IEEE Transactions on Computers 23(9), 881–890 (1974)

11. Tipping, M., Bishop, C.: Probabilistic principal component analysis. Journal of the Royal Statistical Society 61(3), 611 (1999)

12. Borg, I., Groenen, P.: Modern Multidimensional Scaling: Theory and Applications. Springer, Heidelberg (1997)

13. Belkin, M., Niyogi, P.: Laplacian eigenmaps for dimensionality reduction and data representation. Neural Computation 15(6), 1373–1396 (2003)

14. Meila, M., Shi, J.: Learning segmentation by random walks. Advances in Neural Information Processing Systems 13 (2001)

15. Cristianini, N., Shawe-Taylor, J.: An Introduction to Support Vector Machines. Cambridge University Press, Cambridge (2000)

16. Cauwenberghs, C., Poggio, T.: Incremental and decremental support vector machine learning. In: NIPS. proc. of the 14th Conf. on Advances in Neural Infomation Processing Systems, pp. 409–415 (2000)

17. Nebel, B.: Reasoning and Revision in Hybrid Representation Systems. LNCS (LNAI), vol. 422. Springer, Heidelberg (1990)

18. Brachman, R., Schmoltze, J.: An overview of the KL-ONE knowledge representation system. Cognitive Science 9(2), 171–216 (1985)

19. Merrill, D.F., Alexander, M.E. (eds.): Glossary of Forest Fire Management Terms. Canadian Committee on Forest Fire Management. National Research Council Canada, Ottawa, Ontario, Canada (1987)

20. Wilson, J., Steingart, D., Romero, R., Reynolds, J., Mellers, E., Redfern, A., Lim, L., Watts, W., Patton, C., Baker, J., Wright, P.: Design of monocular head-mounted displays for increased indoor firefighting safety and efficiency. In: Proceedings of SPIE, vol. 5800, pp. 103–114. Helmet- and Head-Mounted Displays X: Technologies and Applications (May 2005)

21. Doolin, D.M., Sitar, N.: Wireless sensors for wildfire monitoring. In: Proceedings of the 2nd international conference on Mobile systems, applications, and services, San Diego, CA, USA (March 2005)

An Implementation of a Free-Variable Tableaux for KLM Preferential Logic P of Nonmonotonic Reasoning: The Theorem Prover FreeP 1.0

Laura Giordano[1], Valentina Gliozzi[2], Nicola Olivetti[3], and Gian Luca Pozzato[2]

[1] Dip. di Informatica - Univ. Piemonte O. "A. Avogadro"
`laura@mfn.unipmn.it`
[2] Dip. di Informatica - Università di Torino
`{gliozzi,pozzato}@di.unito.it`
[3] LSIS-UMR CNRS 6168 Univ. "P. Cézanne"
`nicola.olivetti@univ-cezanne.fr`

Abstract. We present FREEP 1.0, a theorem prover for the KLM preferential logic **P** of nonmonotonic reasoning. FREEP 1.0 is a SICStus Prolog implementation of a *free-variables*, labelled tableau calculus for **P**, obtained by introducing suitable modalities to interpret conditional assertions. The performances of FREEP 1.0 are promising. FREEP 1.0 can be downloaded at `http:// www.di.unito.it/` $\sim$`pozzato/FREEP 1.0`.

1   Introduction

The work of Kraus, Lehmann and Magidor (KLM) in the early 90s [1] is a milestone in the area of nonmonotonic reasoning. The postulates outlined by KLM have been widely accepted as the "conservative core" of nonmonotonic reasoning: they correspond to properties that any concrete reasoning mechanism should satisfy. Many different approaches to nonmonotonic reasoning are characterized by the properties of two of the KLM logics, namely preferential logic **P** and rational logic **R** [2].

According to the KLM framework, a defeasible knowledge base is represented by a (finite) set of nonmonotonic conditionals of the form $A \mathrel{|\!\sim} B$, whose reading is *normally (or typically) the A's are B's*. The operator "$\mathrel{|\!\sim}$" is nonmonotonic, in that $A \mathrel{|\!\sim} B$ does not imply $A \wedge C \mathrel{|\!\sim} B$. For instance, a knowledge base K may contain *sumo_wrestler* $\mathrel{|\!\sim}$ *fat*, *sumo_wrestler* $\mathrel{|\!\sim}$ *sumo_lover*, *sumo_lover* $\mathrel{|\!\sim}$ $\neg fat$, whose meaning is that sumo wrestlers are typically fat, sumo wrestlers typically love sumo, but people loving sumo typically are not fat. If $\mathrel{|\!\sim}$ were interpreted as classical implication, one would get *sumo_wrestler* $\mathrel{|\!\sim} \perp$, i.e. typically there are not sumo wrestlers, thereby obtaining a trivial knowledge base. One can derive new conditional assertions from the knowledge base by means of a set of inference rules, without incurring the trivializing conclusions of classical logic. In KLM framework, the set of inference rules defines some fundamental types of inference systems, namely, from the strongest to the weakest: Rational (**R**), Preferential (**P**), Loop-Cumulative (**CL**), and Cumulative (**C**) logic.

R. Basili and M.T. Pazienza (Eds.): AI*IA 2007, LNAI 4733, pp. 84–96, 2007.

In this paper we focus on **Preferential logic P**. Concerning the above example, in preferential logic **P** one can infer *sumo_lover* $\wedge$ *sumo_wrestler* $\mathrel{\vdash\mkern-7mu\sim}$ *fat*, giving preference to more specific information, and that *sumo_lover* $\mathrel{\vdash\mkern-7mu\sim}$ $\neg$*sumo_wrestler*. From a semantic point of view, the models of preferential logic **P** are possible-world structures equipped with a preference relation $<$ among worlds. The meaning of a conditional assertion $A \mathrel{\vdash\mkern-7mu\sim} B$ is that B holds in the *most preferred* worlds where A holds.

In [3] an analytic tableau calculus for propositional **P** is introduced. The basic idea there is to interpret the preference relation $<$ as an accessibility relation: a conditional $A \mathrel{\vdash\mkern-7mu\sim} B$ holds in a model if B is true in all worlds satisfying A that are minimal wrt $<$. The calculus provides a sort of run-time translation of **P** into Gödel-Löb modal logic of provability G. The relation with G is motivated by the fact that we assume, following KLM, the so-called *smoothness condition*, which is related to the well-known *limit assumption*. This condition ensures that minimal A-worlds exist whenever there are A-worlds, by preventing infinitely descending chains of worlds. This condition is therefore ensured by the finite-chain condition on the accessibility relation (as in modal logic G). The resulting calculus, called $\mathcal{T}\mathbf{P}^{\mathbf{T}}$, is a *non*-labelled, sound, complete and terminating proof method for the logic **P**. In [4] a SICStus Prolog implementation of $\mathcal{T}\mathbf{P}^{\mathbf{T}}$ is presented. The program, called KLMLean 2.0, is inspired to the "lean" methodology, and, as far as we know, it is the first theorem prover for the preferential logic **P**.

We extend our work on efficient theorem proving for KLM logics by introducing FREEP 1.0, a theorem prover for preferential logic **P** that implements a *free-variable* tableau calculus for this logic. Free-variable tableaux are a well-known and well-established technique for first order theorem proving [5], whose basic idea is to adopt free-variables as a meta-linguistic device for representing all labels/worlds that can be used in a proof search. To reduce the search space, the instantiation of these free-variables is postponed until more information is available (for instance to close a branch). Recently, Beckert and Goré have presented the theoretical foundations to extend the free-variable tableaux technique to all 15 basic propositional modal logics [6].

In our paper, we first introduce a *labelled* tableau calculus for the preferential logic **P**, based on the same translation into G adopted by $\mathcal{T}\mathbf{P}^{\mathbf{T}}$. This calculus, called $\mathcal{LABP}$, can be straightforwardly derived from the labelled calculus $\mathcal{T}\mathbf{R}^{\mathbf{T}}$ for the rational logic **R** introduced in [7]. We then show that $\mathcal{LABP}$ can be easily turned into a terminating calculus. Last, we present FREEP 1.0, an implementation of a free-variables version of $\mathcal{LABP}$ in SICStus Prolog. This last point is the main contribution of the paper.

2   KLM Preferential Logic P

In this section we briefly recall the axiomatization and semantics of the preferential logic **P**. For a complete description of KLM systems, see [1] and [8]. The language $\mathcal{L}$ we consider is defined from a set of propositional variables ATM, the boolean connectives and the conditional operator $\mathrel{\vdash\mkern-7mu\sim}$. We use $A, B, C, \ldots$ to denote propositional formulas, whereas $F, G, \ldots$ are used to denote all formulas (even conditionals). The formulas of $\mathcal{L}$ are defined as follows: if A is a propositional formula, $A \in \mathcal{L}$; if A and B are propositional formulas, $A \mathrel{|\!\sim} B \in \mathcal{L}$; if F is a boolean combination of formulas of $\mathcal{L}$, $F \in \mathcal{L}$. $\mathcal{L}$ corresponds to the fragment of the language of conditional logics without nested occurrences of the conditional operator $\mathrel{|\!\sim}$.

The axiomatization of $\mathbf{P}$ consists of all axioms and rules of propositional calculus together with the following axioms and rules ($\vdash_{PC}$ denotes provability in the propositional calculus, whereas $\vdash$ denotes provability in $\mathbf{P}$):

- REF. $A \mathrel{|\!\sim} A$ (reflexivity)
- LLE. If $\vdash_{PC} A \leftrightarrow B$, then $\vdash (A \mathrel{|\!\sim} C) \rightarrow (B \mathrel{|\!\sim} C)$ (left logical equivalence)
- RW. If $\vdash_{PC} A \rightarrow B$, then $\vdash (C \mathrel{|\!\sim} A) \rightarrow (C \mathrel{|\!\sim} B)$ (right weakening)
- AND. $((A \mathrel{|\!\sim} B) \wedge (A \mathrel{|\!\sim} C)) \rightarrow (A \mathrel{|\!\sim} B \wedge C)$
- CM. $((A \mathrel{|\!\sim} B) \wedge (A \mathrel{|\!\sim} C)) \rightarrow (A \wedge B \mathrel{|\!\sim} C)$ (cautious monotonicity)
- OR. $((A \mathrel{|\!\sim} C) \wedge (B \mathrel{|\!\sim} C)) \rightarrow (A \vee B \mathrel{|\!\sim} C)$

The semantics of $\mathbf{P}$ is defined by considering possible world structures with a preference relation (a strict partial order) $w < w'$ whose meaning is that w is preferred to w'. We have that $A \mathrel{|\!\sim} B$ holds in a model $\mathcal{M}$ if B holds in all *minimal A-worlds* (w.r.t. $<$). This definition makes sense provided minimal A-worlds exist (whenever there are A-worlds). This is ensured by the *smoothness condition* in the next definition.

Definition 1 (Semantics of P, Definition 16 in [1]). *A preferential model is a triple* $\mathcal{M} = \langle \mathcal{W}, <, V \rangle$ *where:* $\mathcal{W}$ *is a non-empty set of items called worlds;* $<$ *is an irreflexive and transitive relation on* $\mathcal{W}$; V *is a function* $V : \mathcal{W} \longmapsto pow(ATM)$, *which assigns to every world w the set of atoms holding in that world. We define the truth conditions for a formula F as follows: (i) if F is a boolean combination of formulas,* $\mathcal{M}, w \models F$ *is defined as for propositional logic; (ii) let A be a propositional formula; we define* $Min_<(A) = \{w \in \mathcal{W} \mid \mathcal{M}, w \models A$ *and* $\forall w', \, w' < w$ *implies* $\mathcal{M}, w' \not\models A\}$; (iii) $\mathcal{M}, w \models A \mathrel{|\!\sim} B$ *if for all* $w' \in \mathcal{W}$, *if* $w' \in Min_<(A)$ *then* $\mathcal{M}, w' \models B$.*

The relation $<$ satisfies the following smoothness condition: *if* $\mathcal{M}, w \models A$ *then* $w \in Min_<(A)$ *or* $\exists w' \in Min_<(A)$ *such that* $w' < w$.*

We say that a formula F is valid *in a model $\mathcal{M}$ ($\mathcal{M} \models F$), if $\mathcal{M}, w \models F$ for every $w \in \mathcal{W}$. A formula is* valid *if it is valid in every model $\mathcal{M}$.*

3   A Labelled Tableau Calculus for Preferential Logic P

In this section we present a labelled tableau calculus for preferential logic $\mathbf{P}$. This calculus, called $\mathcal{LAB}\mathbf{P}$ from $\mathcal{LAB}$elled $\mathbf{P}$, follows the same intuition as the calculus $\mathcal{T}\mathbf{P}^{\mathbf{T}}$ introduced in [3], i.e. to interpret the preference relation as an accessibility relation, thus implementing a sort of run-time translation into modal logic G. $\mathcal{LAB}\mathbf{P}$ is straightforwardly derived from the labelled calculus $\mathcal{T}\mathbf{R}^{\mathbf{T}}$ for rational logic $\mathbf{R}$ [7], by removing rule $(<)$, corresponding to modularity that differentiates $\mathbf{P}$ from $\mathbf{R}$.

$$(\mathbf{AX})\ \Gamma, x : P, x : \neg P \quad \text{with } P \in ATM \qquad\qquad (\neg)\frac{\Gamma, x : \neg\neg F}{\Gamma, x : F} \qquad\qquad (\mathbin{\vert\!\sim}^{-})\frac{\Gamma, u : \neg(A \mathbin{\vert\!\sim} B)}{\Gamma, x : A, x : \Box\neg A, x : \neg B}\ \begin{array}{l} x \text{ new} \\ \text{label} \end{array}$$

$$(\mathbin{\vert\!\sim}^{+})\frac{\Gamma, u : A \mathbin{\vert\!\sim} B}{\Gamma, u : A \mathbin{\vert\!\sim} B, x : \neg A \qquad \Gamma, u : A \mathbin{\vert\!\sim} B, x : \neg\Box\neg A \qquad \Gamma, u : A \mathbin{\vert\!\sim} B, x : B}\ x \text{ occurs in } \Gamma$$

$$(\Box^{-})\frac{\Gamma, x : \neg\Box\neg A}{\Gamma, y < x, y : A, y : \Box\neg A, \Gamma^{M}_{x \longrightarrow y}}\ \begin{array}{l} y \text{ new} \\ \text{label} \end{array} \qquad (\wedge^{+})\frac{\Gamma, x : F \wedge G}{\Gamma, x : F, x : G} \qquad (\wedge^{-})\frac{\Gamma, x : \neg(F \wedge G)}{\Gamma, x : \neg F \qquad \Gamma, x : \neg G}$$

Fig. 1. The calculus $\mathcal{LAB}\mathbf{P}$. To save space, rules for $\rightarrow$ and $\vee$ are omitted.

The calculus $\mathcal{LAB}\mathbf{P}$ makes use of labels to represent possible worlds. We consider a language $\mathcal{L}_P$ and a denumerable alphabet of labels $\mathcal{A}$, whose elements are denoted by x, y, z, ... $\mathcal{L}_P$ extends $\mathcal{L}$ by formulas of the form $\Box A$, where A is propositional, whose intuitive meaning is as follows: $\Box A$ holds in a world w if A holds in all the worlds w' such that $w' < w$, that is to say $\mathcal{M}, w \models \Box A$ if, for every $w' \in \mathcal{W}$, if $w' < w$ then $\mathcal{M}, w' \models A$. It can be observed that $\Box$ has (among others) the properties of the modal system G, whose characterizing axiom is $\Box(\Box A \rightarrow A) \rightarrow \Box A$. This axiom guarantees that the accessibility relation (defined as xRy if $y < x$) is transitive and does not have infinite ascending chains. From definition of $Min_<(A)$ in Definition 1, it follows that, for any formula A, $w \in Min_<(A)$ iff $\mathcal{M}, w \models A \wedge \Box\neg A$. As we will see, $\mathcal{LAB}\mathbf{P}$ only makes use of boxed formulas with a negated argument, i.e. formulas of the form $x : \Box\neg A$.

Our tableau calculus comprises two kinds of labelled formulas: (*i*) *world formulas* $x : F$, whose meaning is that F holds in the possible world represented by x; (*ii*) *relation formulas* of the form $x < y$, where $x, y \in \mathcal{A}$, used to represent the relation $<$.

We define $\Gamma^{M}_{x \rightarrow y} = \{y : \neg A, y : \Box\neg A \mid x : \Box\neg A \in \Gamma\}$. The calculus $\mathcal{LAB}\mathbf{P}$ is presented in Figure 1. We call *dynamic* the rules $(\mathbin{\vert\!\sim}^{-})$ and $(\Box^{-})$ that introduce new labels in their conclusion; all the other rules are called *static*. Notice that there is not a rule for positive boxed formulas, as the propagation of these formulas is performed by the set $\Gamma^{M}_{x \rightarrow y}$, when a new world is created by $(\Box^{-})$.

Definition 2 (Truth conditions of formulas of $\mathcal{LAB}\mathbf{P}$). *Given a model* $\mathcal{M} = \langle \mathcal{W}, <, V \rangle$ *and a label alphabet* $\mathcal{A}$, *we consider a mapping* $I : \mathcal{A} \mapsto \mathcal{W}$. *Given a formula* α *of the calculus* $\mathcal{LAB}\mathbf{P}$, *we define* $\mathcal{M} \models_I \alpha$ *as follows:* $\mathcal{M} \models_I x : F$ *iff* $\mathcal{M}, I(x) \models F$; $\mathcal{M} \models_I x < y$ *iff* $I(x) < I(y)$. *We say that a set* Γ *of formulas of* $\mathcal{LAB}\mathbf{P}$ *is satisfiable if there exist* $\mathcal{M}$ *and* I *s.t., for all formulas* $\alpha \in \Gamma$, *we have that* $\mathcal{M} \models_I \alpha$.

A tableau is a tree whose nodes are sets of labelled formulas Γ. Therefore, a branch is a sequence of sets of labelled formulas $\Gamma_1, \Gamma_2, \ldots, \Gamma_n, \ldots$ Each node Γ_i is obtained by its immediate predecessor Γ_{i-1} by applying a rule of $\mathcal{LAB}\mathbf{P}$, having Γ_{i-1} as the premise and Γ_i as one of its conclusions. A branch is closed if one of its nodes is an instance of $(\mathbf{AX})$, otherwise it is open. We say that a tableau is closed if all its branches are closed. In order to verify that a set of formulas Γ is unsatisfiable, we label all the formulas in Γ with a new label x, and verify that the resulting set of labelled formulas has a closed tableau.

The calculus $\mathcal{LABP}$ is sound and complete wrt the semantics. To save space, we omit the proofs, which are very similar to the ones for $\mathcal{T}\mathbf{R^T}$ in [7].

Theorem 1 (Soundness and Completeness of $\mathcal{LABP}$). *Given a set of formulas Γ, it is unsatisfiable if and only if there is a closed tableau in $\mathcal{LABP}$ starting with Γ.*

Let us now refine the calculus $\mathcal{LABP}$ in order to ensure termination. In general, non-termination in labelled tableau calculi can be caused by two different reasons: 1. dynamic rules can generate infinitely-many worlds, thus creating infinite branches; 2. some rules copy their principal formula in their conclusion(s), therefore they can be reapplied over the same formula without any control.

As far as $\mathcal{LABP}$ is concerned, we can show that the first source of non termination (point 1) cannot occur. Indeed, similarly to $\mathcal{T}\mathbf{R^T}$, we have that the only rules that can introduce new labels in the tableau are $(\vdash^-)$ and $(\Box^-)$. It can be proven that there can be only finitely many applications of these rules in a proof search. Intuitively, the rule $(\vdash^-)$ can be applied only once for each negated conditional occurring in the initial set Γ (hence it introduces only a finite number of labels). Furthermore, the generation of infinite branches due to the interplay between rules $(\vdash^+)$ and $(\Box^-)$ cannot occur. Indeed, each application of $(\Box^-)$ to a formula $x : \neg\Box\neg A$ (introduced by $(\vdash^+)$) adds the formula $y : \Box\neg A$ to the conclusion, so that $(\vdash^+)$ can no longer consistently introduce $y : \neg\Box\neg A$. This is due to the properties of $\Box$, that are similar to the properties of the corresponding modality of modal system G.

Concerning point 2, the calculus $\mathcal{LABP}$ does not ensure a terminating proof search due to the $(\vdash^+)$ rule, which can be applied without any control. It is easy to observe that it is useless to apply the rule on the same conditional formula more than once by using the same label x. Indeed, all formulas in the premise of $(\vdash^+)$ are kept in the conclusions, then we can assume, without loss of generality, that two applications of $(\vdash^+)$ on x are consecutive. We observe that the second application is useless, since each of the conclusions has already been obtained after the first application, and can be removed. We prevent redundant applications of $(\vdash^+)$ by keeping track of labels in which a conditional $u : A \vdash B$ has already been applied in the current branch. To this purpose, we add to each positive conditional a list L of *used* labels; we restrict the application of $(\vdash^+)$ only to labels not occurring in the corresponding list. The resulting terminating calculus $\mathcal{LABP}$ is obtained by replacing rule $(\vdash^+)$ in Figure 1 with the one presented in Figure 2. The proof of termination is similar to the one in [7] (Theorem 6).

4   Design of FreeP 1.0

Here we describe FREEP 1.0, an implementation of a free-variable extension of $\mathcal{LABP}$ calculus in SICStus Prolog. For expository reasons, we proceed in two

$$(\hspace{-1pt}\vdash^{+})\ \frac{\Gamma, u : A \hspace{1pt}\vdash\hspace{1pt} B^{L}}{\Gamma, x : \neg A, u : A \hspace{1pt}\vdash\hspace{1pt} B^{\,L,x} \qquad \Gamma, x : \neg\Box\neg A, u : A \hspace{1pt}\vdash\hspace{1pt} B^{\,L,x} \qquad \Gamma, x : B, u : A \hspace{1pt}\vdash\hspace{1pt} B^{\,L,x}}$$

with $x \notin L$

Fig. 2. The rule $(\vdash^{+})$ in the terminating tableau calculus $\mathcal{LABP}$

steps. First, in section 4.1 we present a simple implementation of $\mathcal{LABP}$ that does not use free-variables, yet. Second, in section 4.2 we refine it by introducing free-variables in order to increase its performances. Intuitively, this refinement consists in the fact that the $(\vdash^{+})$ rule introduces a *free-variable* in all its conclusions, rather than immediately choosing the label to use. The free-variables will then be instantiated to close a branch with an axiom, thus the choice of the label is postponed as much as possible.

4.1   A Simple Implementation of $\mathcal{LABP}$ (Without Free-Variables)

The Prolog program consists of a set of clauses, each representing a tableau rule or axiom; the proof search is provided for free by the mere depth-first search mechanism of Prolog, without any additional ad hoc mechanism. We represent each node of a proof tree (i.e. set of formulas) by a Prolog list. A world formula $x : A$ is represented by a *pair* [x,a], whereas a relation formula $x < y$ is represented by a triple [x,<,y]. The tableau calculus is implemented by the predicate **prove(Gamma,Cond,Labels,Tree)**, which succeeds if and only if the set of formulas Γ, represented by the list Gamma, is unsatisfiable. Cond is a list representing the set of *used conditionals*, and it is needed in order to control the application of the rule $(\vdash^{+})$, as described in the previous section. More in detail, the elements of Cond are pairs of the form [A=>B,Used], where Used is a Prolog list containing all the labels that have already been used to apply $(\vdash^{+})$ on $x : A \hspace{1pt}\vdash\hspace{1pt} B$ in the current branch. As we will discuss later in this section, this allows to apply this rule in a controlled way, ensuring termination of the proof search. Labels is the list of labels introduced in the current branch. When prove succeeds, Tree contains a representation of a closed tableau. For instance, to prove that $A \hspace{1pt}\vdash\hspace{1pt} B \wedge C, \neg(A \hspace{1pt}\vdash\hspace{1pt} C)$ is unsatisfiable in **P**, one queries FREEP 1.0 with the goal prove([[x,a => (b and c)], [x,neg (a => c)]],[ ], [x], Tree). The string "=>" is used to represent the conditional operator $\vdash$, "and" is used to denote $\wedge$, and so on. Each clause of prove implements one axiom or rule of the tableau calculus; for example, the clause implementing $(\vdash^{-})$ is as follows:

```
prove(Gamma,Cond,Labels,tree(...)):-
    select([X,neg (A => B)],Gamma,NewG),!,newLabel(Labels,Y),
    prove([[Y,neg B]|[[Y,box neg A]|[[Y,A]|NewG]]],Cond,[Y|Labels],...).
```

The clause for $(\vdash^{-})$ is applied when a formula $x : \neg(A \hspace{1pt}\vdash\hspace{1pt} B)$ belongs to Γ. The predicate select removes $x : \neg(A \hspace{1pt}\vdash\hspace{1pt} B)$ from Gamma, then the predicate prove is recursively invoked on the only conclusion of the rule. The predicate newLabel is used to generate a new label Y not occurring in the current branch.

To search a derivation of a set of formulas Γ, FREEP 1.0 proceeds as follows: first of all, if Γ is an instance of (**AX**), the goal will succeed immediately by using the clause for the axioms. If it is not, then the first applicable rule will be chosen, e.g. if `Gamma` contains a formula `[X,neg(neg F)]`, then the clause for $(\neg)$ rule will be used, invoking **prove** on its unique conclusion. FREEP 1.0 proceeds in a similar way for the other rules. The ordering of the clauses is such that the boolean rules are applied before the other ones. Let us now analyze the crucial rule $(\hspace{-2pt}\sim^{+})$, which is implemented by the two following clauses:

```
prove(Gamma,Cond,Labels,tree(...)):-
   member([_,A=>B],Gamma),\+member([A=>B,_],Cond),!,
   member(X,Labels),!,
   prove([[X,A->B]|Gamma],[[A=>B,[X]]|Cond],Labels,...),
   prove([[X,neg box neg A]|Gamma],[[A=>B,[X]]|Cond],...).
prove(Gamma,Cond,Labels,tree(...)):-
   member([_,A=>B],Gamma),select([A=>B,Used],Cond,NewCond),
   member(X,Labels),\+member(X,Used),!,
   prove([[X,A->B]|Gamma],[[A=>B,[X|Used]]|NewCond],Labels,...),
   prove([[X,neg box neg A]|Gamma],[[A=>B,[X|Used]]|NewCond],...).
```

The above clauses are applied when a conditional formula $u : A \hspace{-2pt}\sim\hspace{-2pt} B$ belongs to `Gamma`. If it is the first time the rule is applied on $A \hspace{-2pt}\sim\hspace{-2pt} B$ in the current branch, i.e. there is no `[A=>B,Used]` in the list `Cond`, then the first clause is applied. It chooses a label `X` to use (predicate `member(X,Labels)`), then the predicate **prove** is recursively invoked on the conclusions of the rule. Otherwise, i.e. if $(\hspace{-2pt}\sim^{+})$ has already been applied on $A \hspace{-2pt}\sim\hspace{-2pt} B$ in the current branch, the second clause is invoked: the theorem prover chooses a label `X` in the `Labels` list, then it checks if `X` belongs to the list `Used` of labels already used to apply $(\hspace{-2pt}\sim^{+})$ on $A \hspace{-2pt}\sim\hspace{-2pt} B$ in the current branch. If not, the predicate **prove** is recursively invoked on the conclusions of the rule. Notice that the above clauses implement an alternative version of the $(\hspace{-2pt}\sim^{+})$ rule, equivalent to the one presented in Figure 2. In order to build a binary tableau, the rule has two conclusions rather than three, namely the conclusions $\Gamma, u : A \hspace{-2pt}\sim\hspace{-2pt} B, x : \neg A$ and $\Gamma, u : A \hspace{-2pt}\sim\hspace{-2pt} B, x : B$ are replaced by the single conclusion $\Gamma, u : A \hspace{-2pt}\sim\hspace{-2pt} B, x : A \to B$.

Even if $(\hspace{-2pt}\sim^{+})$ is invertible, and it does not introduce any backtracking point in a proof search, choosing the right label in the application of $(\hspace{-2pt}\sim^{+})$ is highly critical for the performances of the theorem prover. Indeed, if the current set of formulas contains n different labels, say $x_1, x_2, \ldots, x_n$, it could be the case that a single application of $(\hspace{-2pt}\sim^{+})$ on $u : A \hspace{-2pt}\sim\hspace{-2pt} B$ by using x_n leads to an immediate closure of both its conclusions, thus ending the proof. However, if the deductive mechanism chooses the labels to use in the above order, then the right label x_n will be chosen only after $n - 1$ applications of $(\hspace{-2pt}\sim^{+})$ on each branch, thus creating a bigger tableau and, as a consequence, decreasing the performances of the theorem prover. In order to postpone this choice as much as possible, we have defined a **free-variables** version of the prover, whose basic idea is to use *Prolog variables* as *jolly* (or *wildcards*) in each application of the $(\hspace{-2pt}\sim^{+})$ rule. The refined version of the prover is described in the following section.

4.2   Free-Variables Implementation

A free-variable can be seen as a jolly representing *all the labels* that can be used in an application of $(\!\sim^+)$, that is to say the rule $(\!\sim^+)$ allows to step from the premise $\Gamma, u : A \!\sim B$ to the following conclusions: $\Gamma, u : A \!\sim B, X : A \to B$ and $\Gamma, u : A \!\sim B, X : \neg\Box\neg A$, where X is a free-variable. X will be then instantiated when further information is available on the tableau, that is to say when such an instantiation will lead to close the branch with an axiom.

In the following we will use another kind of free-variables, called *conditional free-variables*, in order to deal with boxed formulas. Intuitively, a boxed formula $x : \Box\neg A$ will be represented by $[V, x] : \neg A$, where V is a conditional free-variable, representing all the successors of x (V is called "conditional" since x might have no successors). The two kinds of free-variables should not be confused; we will denote "jolly" free-variables with $X, X_1, X_2, \ldots$, and "conditional" free-variables with $V, V_1, V_2, \ldots$. Similarly to Beckert and Goré's MODLEANTAP [6], FREEP 1.0 also adopts the following refinements:

- it makes use of integers starting from 1 to represent a single world; in this way, if `Max` is the maximal integer occurring in a branch, then we have that: a) `Max` is also the *number* of different labels occurring in that branch; b) the next new label to be generated is simply `Max`+1;
- the labels are *Prolog lists* representing *paths of worlds*; as a consequence, relation formulas, used in $\mathcal{LABP}$ to represent the preference relation, are replaced by *implicit relations* in the labels. Intuitively, when $(\Box^-)$ is applied to $[1] : \neg\Box\neg A$, a formula $[2, 1] : A$ is introduced rather than $[2] : A$ plus an explicit relation formula $[2, <, 1]$. In general, a label is a list $[n_k, n_{k-1}, \ldots, n_2, n_1]$, representing that $n_k < n_{k-1}, \ldots, n_2 < n_1$. From now on, we denote with $\sigma, \gamma, \ldots$, such "path labels";
- it replaces a boxed formula $\sigma : \Box\neg A$, where σ is a "path label", with a formula $[V, \sigma] : \neg A$, where V is a *conditional* free-variable, representing *all the paths descending from σ, if any*. The free-variable V is conditional in the sense that it could be the case that σ has no sons in the tableau;
- in order to distinguish "jolly" free-variables from "conditional" free-variables, we partition each node of a tableau in two different components $\langle \Gamma \mid \Sigma \rangle$. Σ contains formulas whose labels contain conditional free-variables, of the form $[V, \sigma] : \neg A$, corresponding to boxed formulas $\sigma : \Box\neg A$. Γ contains the other formulas. This distinction is needed in order to avoid unwanted unification between elements of Σ. For instance, we do not want that a branch closes because it contains two formulas such as $[V, \sigma] : A$ and $[V_1, \sigma] : \neg A$; indeed, such a branch would be satisfiable by a model in which σ has no successors.

We use a Prolog-like notation to denote a path label. In this respect, $[n_1, \ldots, n_k]$ denotes a label whose elements are $n_1, \ldots, n_k$, $[\ ]$ denotes the empty list, and $[n_1, \ldots, n_k, \sigma]$ denotes a list whose first k elements are $n_1, \ldots, n_k$ followed by the list σ. We also denote with $[\sigma_1, \sigma_2]$ the list obtained by appending σ_2 to σ_1. The basic ideas of the free-variables tableau implemented by FREEP 1.0 can be summarized as follows:

- when $(\hspace{-2pt}\vdash^{+})$ is applied, a jolly free-variable is introduced in the two conclusions; the free-variable represents all the labels occurring in the current
  branch, and will be instantiated later, when such an instantiation leads to
  close a branch with an axiom;
- when the $(\Box^{-})$ rule is applied to $\langle \Gamma, \sigma \; : \; \neg\Box\neg A \mid \Sigma \rangle$, then the formula
  $[n, \sigma] : A$ is added to Γ, where n is Max+1 and Max is the maximal integer
  occurring in the branch, whereas $[V, n, \sigma] : \neg A$ is added to Σ. The conditional
  free-variable V will then be instantiated to close a branch with an axiom.
  As an example, if another formula $[m, n, \sigma] : A$ (or $[m_2, m_1, n, \sigma] : A$) will
  be introduced in the branch, then the branch will close since V can be
  instantiated with $[m]$ (resp. $[m_2, m_1]$);
- given a tableau node $\langle \Gamma \mid \Sigma, [V, \sigma] : \neg A \rangle$, the branch is closed when there is
  a formula of the form $[\gamma, \sigma] : A$ belonging to Γ, where γ is a list of numbers.
  This machinery is used to perform the propagation of boxed formulas, rather
  than explicitly computing, step by step (when a new world is generated), the
  set $\Gamma^{M}_{x \to y}$. In fact, at the world $[\gamma, \sigma]$ reachable from σ, the formula $\neg A$ holds
  as the labelled formula $[V, \sigma] : \neg A$ says that $\neg A$ must hold in all the worlds
  reachable from σ (and V stands for any path from σ).

Observe that the improved implementation of the tableau for $\mathbf{R}$ given in [4]
already makes use of jolly free-variables. However, it does not introduce neither
path labels nor conditional free-variables, thus requiring to explicitly compute
$\Gamma^{M}_{x \to y}$ step by step.

Coming back to FREEP 1.0, by looking carefully at how free-variables are introduced, it can be shown that labels containing jolly free-variables have the form
$[n_1, n_2, \ldots, n_k, X]$, where $n_1, \ldots, n_k$ are integers and X is a jolly free-variable.
On the contrary, labels containing conditional free-variables have the form $[V, \sigma]$,
where V is a conditional free-variable and σ is a path label that might contain a
jolly free-variable. In Figure 3 two derivations of $\{A \mathrel{\vdash\!\!\!\sim} B \wedge C, \neg(A \mathrel{\vdash\!\!\!\sim} B), \neg(D_1 \mathrel{\vdash\!\!\!\sim}$
$E_1), \neg(D_2 \mathrel{\vdash\!\!\!\sim} E_2)\}$ are presented. The upper tableau is obtained by applying
the simple implementation of $\mathcal{LABP}$ introduced in section 4.1, has height 9 and
contains 59 nodes. The lower one, obtained by applying FREEP 1.0, is a tableau
of height 6 and contains only 9 nodes.

Here again, the free-variables tableau calculus is implemented by the predicate **prove(Gamma,Sigma,Max,Cond,Tree)**, where Gamma and Sigma are Pro-
log lists representing a node $\langle \Gamma \mid \Sigma \rangle$ as described above and Max is the maximal
integer in the current branch. Cond is used to apply $(\hspace{-2pt}\vdash^{+})$ in a controlled way;
it is a list whose elements are triples of the form [A=>B,N,Used], representing
that $(\hspace{-2pt}\vdash^{+})$ has been applied N times on $A \mathrel{\vdash\!\!\!\sim} B$ in the current branch, by introducing the free-variables of the list Used. In general, Used is a list of paths
partially instantiated. This machinery is used to control the application of $(\hspace{-2pt}\vdash^{+})$
as described in the previous section, in order to ensure termination by prevent-
ing that the rule is applied more than once by using the same label. Indeed,
as we will see later, the rule is only applied to a conditional $A \mathrel{\vdash\!\!\!\sim} B$ if it has
already been applied less than Max times in the current branch, i.e. N<Max. Furthermore, it must be ensured that all labels in Used are different. When the

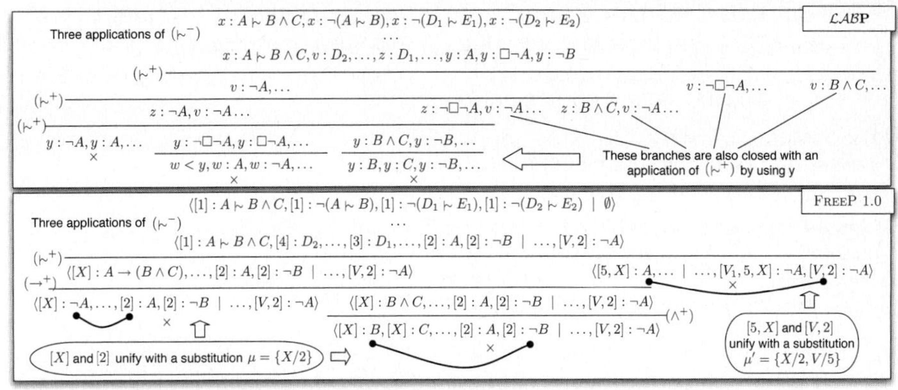

Fig. 3. A derivation in $\mathcal{LAB}\mathbf{P}$ and in FREEP 1.0

predicate `prove` succeeds, the argument `Tree` is instantiated by a Prolog functor representing the closed tableau found by the theorem prover. For instance, to prove that $A \mathrel{\mid\!\sim} B \wedge C, \neg(A \mathrel{\mid\!\sim} B)$ is unsatisfiable in **P**, one queries FREEP 1.0 with the following goal: `prove([[[1],a=>b and c],[[1],neg(a=>b)]],[ ],1,[ ], Tree)`.

Before introducing some examples of the clauses of FREEP 1.0, we introduce the following two definitions of the *unification* of path labels. A branch of a tableau is closed if it contains two formulas $\sigma : F$ and $\gamma : \neg F$ such that the two labels (paths) σ and γ unify, i.e. there exists a substitution of the free-variables occurring in them such that the two labels represent the same world. We distinguish the case where the two formulas involved in a branch closure are both in Γ, i.e. their labels only contain jolly free-variables, from the case where one of them belongs to Σ, i.e. its label also contains a conditional free-variable. The first case is addressed in Definition 3, whereas the second case is addressed in Definition 4.

Definition 3 (Unification of labels in Γ). *Given two formulas $\sigma : F \in \Gamma$ and $\gamma : G \in \Gamma$, the labels σ and γ unify with substitution μ if the following conditions hold:*

(A)
- *if $\sigma = \gamma = [\,]$, then $\mu = \epsilon$;*
- *if $\sigma = [n_1, \sigma']$ and $\gamma = [n_1, \gamma']$, where n_1 is an integer (Prolog constant), and σ' and γ' unify with a substitution μ', then $\mu = \mu'$;*
- *if $\sigma = [n_1, \sigma']$ and $\gamma = X$, where X is a jolly free-variable, and X does not occur in σ', then $\mu = X/[n_1, \sigma']$;*
- *if $\sigma = X_1$ and $\gamma = X_2$, where X_1 and X_2 are jolly free-variables, then $\mu = X_1/X_2$.*

(B) the substitution μ is such that, given two jolly free-variables X_1 and X_2 introduced on a branch by applying $(\mathrel{\mid\!\sim}^+)$ on the same conditional $A \mathrel{\mid\!\sim} B$, X_1 and X_2 are not instantiated with the same path by μ.

Definition 4 (Unification of labels in Γ and Σ). *Given two formulas $\sigma : F \in \Sigma$ and $\gamma : G \in \Gamma$, where $\sigma = [V, n_1, \ldots, n_k]$, the labels σ and γ unify with substitution $\mu = \mu' \circ \{V/\gamma_1\}$ if the following conditions hold:*

- *one can split γ in two parts, i.e. $\gamma = [\gamma_1, \gamma_2]$, such that $\gamma_1 \neq \epsilon$ and $\gamma_2 \neq \epsilon^1$;*
- *γ_2 and $[n_1, \ldots, n_k]$ unify w.r.t. Definition 3 with a substitution μ'.*

Here below are the clauses implementing axioms:

```
prove(Gamma,_,_,Cond,...):-
   member([X,A],Gamma),member([Y,neg A],Gamma),
   matchList(X,Y),constr(Cond),!.
prove(Gamma,Sigma,_,Cond,...):-
   member([[V|X],A],Sigma),member([Y,neg A],Gamma),
   copyFormula([[V|X],A],Fml),split(Y,PrefY,SuffY),V=PrefY,
   matchList(SuffY,X),constr(Cond),!.
```

The first clause is applied when two formulas [X,A] and [Y,neg A] belong to Gamma. The predicate matchList(X,Y) implements the point (A) of Definition 3, i.e. it checks if there exists a substitution of the jolly free-variables belonging to X and Y such that these two labels unify. The predicate constr(Cond) implements point (B) in Definition 3. This ensures the condition of termination of the proof search; indeed, as an effect of the matching between labels, the instantiation of some free-variables could lead to duplicate an item in Used, resulting in a redundant application of $(\vdash^+)$ on $A \vdash B$ in the same world/label. The predicate constr avoids this situation.

The second clause checks if a branch can be closed by applying a free-variable substitution involving a formula in Sigma, i.e. a formula whose label has the form [V|X], where V is a conditional free-variable. Given a formula [Y,neg A] in Gamma and a formula [[V|X],A] in Sigma, if the two path labels unify, then the branch can be closed. The clause implements Definition 4 by means of the auxiliary predicates split,V=PrefY, and matchList. In order to allow further instantiations of the conditional free-variable V in other branches, the predicate copyFormula makes a new copy the labelled formula [[V|X],A], generating a formula Fml of the form [[V'|X'],A], where V' is a conditional free-variable whose instantiation is *independent* from the instantiation of V.

To search a derivation for a set of formulas, FREEP 1.0 proceeds as follows: first, it checks if there exists an instantiation of the free-variables such that the branch can be closed, by applying the clauses implementing axioms. Otherwise, the first applicable rule will be chosen. The ordering of the clauses is such that boolean rules are applied in advance. As another example of clause, here below is one of the clauses implementing $(\vdash^+)$. It is worth noticing that the following clause implements a further refinement of the calculus $\mathcal{LABP}$, namely the $(\Box^-)$ rule is "directly" applied to the conclusion of $(\vdash^+)$, which is the only rule that introduces a negated boxed formula $X : \neg\Box\neg A$ in the branch. In this way, an application of $(\vdash^+)$ to $\langle \Gamma, \sigma : A \vdash B \mid \Sigma \rangle$ leads to the following conclusions: $\langle \Gamma, \sigma : A \vdash B, X : A \to B \mid \Sigma \rangle$ and $\langle \Gamma, \sigma : A \vdash B, [n, X] : A \mid [X', n, X] : \neg A, \Sigma \rangle$. The rule $(\Box^-)$ can then be removed from the calculus.

```
prove(Gamma,Sigma,Max,Cond,...):-
   member([Label,A=>B],Gamma),
```

---

^{1} Given the form of labels in Γ, these conditions ensure that γ_1 does not contain free-variables.

```
select([A=>B,NumOfWildCards,PrevWildCards],Cond,NewCond),
NumOfWildCards<Max,!,NewWildCards#=NumOfWildCards+1,
prove([[[X],A->B]|Gamma],Sigma,Max,[[A=>B,NewWildCards,
        [[X]|PrevWildCards]]|NewCond],...),!,N#=Max+1,
prove([[[N|[X]],A]|Gamma],[[[_|[N|[X]]],neg A]|DefSigma],N,
        [[A=>B,NewWildCards,[[X]|PrevWildCards]]|NewCond],...).
```

If a formula [Label,A=>B] belongs to Gamma, then the above clause is invoked. If
$(\mathbin{\vdash}^+)$ has already been applied to $A \mathbin{\vdash} B$ in the current branch, then an element
[A=>B,NumOfWildCards,PrevWildCards] belongs to Cond: the predicate prove
is recursively invoked on the two conclusions of the rule only if the predicate
NumOfWildCards<Max succeeds, by preventing that the rule is applied a redundant number of times. As mentioned above, this machinery, together with the
predicate constr described above, ensure a terminating proof search.

4.3   Performances of FreeP 1.0

The performances of FREEP 1.0 are promising. We have tested FREEP 1.0 over
300 sets of formulas randomly generated, each one containing 100 conditional
formulas, and we have compared its performances with KLMLean 2.0, a theorem
prover implementing the non-labelled calculus $\mathcal{T}\mathbf{P}^\mathbf{T}$. The statistics obtained are
shown in Table 1 and present the number of successes within a fixed time limit:

Table 1. Some statistics comparing FREEP 1.0's performances with KLMLean 2.0's

Implementation	1 ms	10 ms	100 ms	1 s	2.5 s	5 s
KLMLean 2.0	113	113	177	240	255	267
FREEP 1.0	157	158	207	255	269	276

In future research we intend to improve the performances of FREEP 1.0 by
experimenting standard refinements and heuristics. For instance, we intend to
investigate how to increase the efficiency of the machinery adopted in order to
ensure a terminating proof search by means of the constraint logic programming.
Moreover, we aim to extend the free-variables technique to the case of the other
KLM logics.

References

1. Kraus, S., Lehmann, D., Magidor, M.: Nonmonotonic reasoning, preferential models
   and cumulative logics. Artificial Intelligence 44(1-2), 167–207 (1990)
2. Friedman, N., Halpern, J.Y.: Plausibility measures and default reasoning. Journal
   of the ACM 48(4), 648–685 (2001)
3. Giordano, L., Gliozzi, V., Olivetti, N., Pozzato, G.L.: Analytic Tableaux for KLM
   Preferential and Cumulative Logics. In: Sutcliffe, G., Voronkov, A. (eds.) LPAR
   2005. LNCS (LNAI), vol. 3835, pp. 666–681. Springer, Heidelberg (2005)

4. Giordano, L., Gliozzi, V., Pozzato, G.L.: Klmlean 2.0: A theorem prover for KLM Logics of Nonmonotonic Reasoning. In: Olivetti, N. (ed.) TABLEAUX 2007. LNCS (LNAI), vol. 4548, pp. 238–244. Springer, Heidelberg (2007)
5. Fitting, M.: First-Order Logic and Automated Theorem Proving, 2nd edn. (1996)
6. Beckert, B., Goré, R.: Free-variable tableaux for propositional modal logics. Studia Logica 69(1), 59–96 (2001)
7. Giordano, L., Gliozzi, V., Olivetti, N., Pozzato, G.L.: Analytic Tableaux Calculi for KLM Rational Logic R. In: Fisher, M., van der Hoek, W., Konev, B., Lisitsa, A. (eds.) JELIA 2006. LNCS (LNAI), vol. 4160, pp. 190–202. Springer, Heidelberg (2006)
8. Lehmann, D., Magidor, M.: What does a conditional knowledge base entail? Artificial Intelligence 55(1), 1–60 (1992)

Ranking and Reputation Systems in the QBF Competition

Massimo Narizzano, Luca Pulina, and Armando Tacchella*

DIST, Università di Genova, Viale Causa, 13 – 16145 Genova, Italy
{Massimo.Narizzano,Luca.Pulina,Armando.Tacchella}@unige.it

Abstract. Systems competitions play a fundamental role in the advancement of the state of the art in several automated reasoning fields. The goal of such events is to answer the question: "Which system should I buy?". In this paper, we consider voting systems as an alternative to other procedures which are well established in automated reasoning contests. Our research is aimed to compare methods that are customary in the context of social choice, with methods that are targeted to artificial settings, including a new hybrid method that we introduce.

1 Introduction

Systems competitions play a fundamental role in the advancement of the state of the art in several automated reasoning fields. A non-exhaustive list of such events includes the CADE ATP System Competition (CASC) [1] for theorem provers in first order logic, the SAT Competition [2] for propositional satisfiability solvers, the International Planning Competition (see, e.g., [3]) for symbolic planners, the CP Competition (see, e.g., [4]) for constraint programming systems, the Satisfiability Modulo Theories (SMT) Competition (see, e.g., [5]) for SMT solvers, and the evaluation of quantified Boolean formulas solvers (QBFEVAL, see [6,7,8] for previous reports). The main purpose of the above events is to designate a winner, i.e., to answer the question: "Which system should I buy?". Even if such perspective can be limiting, and the results of automated reasoning systems competitions may provide less insight than controlled experiments in the spirit of [9], there is a general agreement that competitions raise interest in the community and they help to set research challenges for developers and assess the current technological frontier for users. The usual way to designate a winner in competitions is to compute a ranking obtained by considering a pool of problem instances and then aggregating the performances of the systems on each member of the pool. While the definition of performances can encompass many aspects of a system, usually it is the capability of giving a sound solution to a high number of problems in a relatively short time that matters most. Therefore, one of the issues that occurred to us as organizers of QBFEVAL, relates to the procedures used to compute the

---

* The authors wish to thank the Italian Ministry of University and Research for its financial support.

R. Basili and M.T. Pazienza (Eds.): AI*IA 2007, LNAI 4733, pp. 97–108, 2007.

final ranking of the solvers, i.e., we had to answer the question "Which aggregation procedure is best?". Indeed, even if the final rankings cannot be interpreted as absolute measures of merit, they should at least represent the relative strength of a system with respect to the other competitors based on the difficulty of the problem instances used in the contest.

Our analysis of aggregation procedures considers three voting systems, namely Borda's method [10], range voting [11] and Schulze's method [12], as an alternative to methods which are well estabished in automated reasoning contests, namely CASC [1], the SAT competitions [2], and QBFEVAL [13] (before 2006). We adapted voting systems to the artificial setting of systems competition by considering the systems as candidates and the problem instances as voters. Each instance casts its vote on the systems in such a way that systems with the best performances on the instance will be preferred over other candidates. The individual preferences are aggregated to obtain a collective choice that determines the winner of the contest. Our motivation to investigate methods which are customary in the context of social choice by applying them to the artificial setting of systems competitions is twofold. First, although voting systems do not enjoy a great popularity in automated reasoning systems contests (one exception is Robocup [14] using Borda's method), there is a substantial amount of literature in social choice (see, e.g., [15]) that deals with the problem of identifying and formalizing appropriate methods of aggregation in specific domains. Second, voting can be seen as a way to "infer the candidates' absolute goodness based on the voters' noisy signals, i.e., their votes." [16]. Therefore, the use of voting systems as aggregation procedures could pave the way to extracting hints about the absolute value of a system from the results of a contest. In the paper, we also propose a new procedure called YASM ("Yet Another Scoring Method")[1] that we selected as an aggregation procedure for QBFEVAL'06. YASM is an hybrid between a voting system and traditional aggregation procedures used in automated reasoning contests. Our results show that YASM provides a good compromise when considering some measures that should quantify desirable properties of the aggregation procedures.

The paper is structured as follows. In Section 2 we introduce the case study of QBFEVAL'05 [8], and we introduce the state of the art aggregation procedures. In Section 3 we introduce our new aggregation procedure, and then we compare it with other methods in Section 4 using several effectiveness measures. We conclude the paper in Section 5 with a discussion about the presented results.

2   Preliminaries

2.1   QBFEVAL'05

QBFEVAL'05 [8] is the third in a series of non-competitive events that preceded QBFEVAL'06. QBFEVAL'05 accounted for 13 competitors, 553 quantified

---

[1] The terminology "scoring method" is somewhat inappropriate in the context of social choice, as it recalls a positional scoring procedure such as Borda's method and range voting; we decided to keep the original terminology for consistency across the previous works [17,18,21].

Boolean formulas (QBFs) and three QBF generators submitted. The test set was assembled using a selection of 3191 QBFs obtained considering the submissions and the instances archived in QBFLIB [19]. The results of QBFEVAL'05 can be listed in a table RUNS comprised of four attributes (column names): SOLVER, INSTANCE, RESULT, and CPUTIME. The attributes SOLVER and INSTANCE report which solver is run on which instance. RESULT is a four-valued attribute: SAT, i.e., the instance was found satisfiable by the solver, UNSAT, i.e., the instance was found unsatisfiable by the solver, TIME, i.e., the solver exceeded a given time limit without solving the instance (900 seconds in QBFEVAL'05), and FAIL, i.e., the solver aborted for some reason (e.g., a run-time error, an inherent limitation of the solver, or any other reason beyond our control). Finally, CPUTIME reports the CPU time spent by the solver on the given instance, in seconds. In the analysis herewith presented we used a subset of QBFEVAL'05 RUNS table, including only the solvers that admitted to the second stage of the evaluation, namely QUANTOR, QMRES, SEMPROP, YQUAFFLE, SSOLVE, WALKQSAT, OPENQBF and QBFBDD, and the QBFs coming from classes of instances having fixed structure (see [8] for more details). Under these assumptions, RUNS table reduces to 4408 entries, one order of magnitude less than the original one. This choice allows us to disregard correctness issues, to reduce considerably the overhead of the computations required for our analysis, and, at the same time, maintain a significant number of runs. The aggregation procedures that we evaluate, the measures that we compute and the results that we obtain, are based on the assumption that a table identical to RUNS as described above is the only input required by a procedure. As a consequence, the aggregation procedures (and thus our analysis) do not take into account (i) memory consumption, (ii) correctness of the solution, and (iii) "quality" of the solution.

2.2   State of the Art Aggregation Procedures

In the following we describe in some details the state of the art aggregation procedures used in our analysis. For each method we describe only those features that are relevant for our purposes. Further details can be found in the references provided.

CASC [1]. Using CASC methodology, the solvers are ranked according to the number of problems solved, i.e., the number of times RESULT is either SAT or UNSAT. Under this procedure, solver A is better than solver B, if and only if A is able to solve at least one problem more than B within the time limit. In case of a tie, the solver faring the lowest average on CPUTIME fields over the problems solved is the one which ranks first.

QBF evaluation [13]. QBFEVAL methodology is the same as CASC, except for the tie-breaking rule, which is based on the sum of CPUTIME fields over the problems solved.

SAT competition [2]. The last SAT competition uses a *purse-based method*, i.e., the measure of effectiveness of a solver on a given instance is obtained by adding up three purses:

- the solution purse, which is divided equally among all solvers that solve the problem;
- the speed purse, which is divided unequally among all the competitors that solve the problem, first by computing the speed factor $F_{s,i}$ of a solver s on a problem instance i:

$$F_{s,i} = \frac{k}{1 + T_{s,i}} \qquad (1)$$

where k is an arbitrary scaling factor (we set $k = 10^4$ according to [20]), and $T_{s,i}$ is the time spent by s to solve i; then by computing the speed award $A_{s,i}$, i.e., the portion of speed purse awarded to the solver s on the instance i:

$$A_{s,i} = \frac{P_i \cdot F_{s,i}}{\sum_r F_{r,i}} \qquad (2)$$

where r ranges over the solvers, and P_i is the total amount of the speed purse for the instance i.

- the series purse, which is divided equally among all solvers that solve at least one problem in a given series (a series is a family of instances that are somehow related, e.g., different QBF encodings for some problem in a given domain).

The overall ranking of the solvers under this method is obtained by considering the sum of the purses obtained on each instance, and the winner of the contest is the solver with the highest sum.

Borda's method [10]. Suppose that n solvers (candidates) and m instances (voters) are involved in the contest. Consider the sorted list of solvers obtained for each instance by considering the value of the CPUTIME field in ascending order. Let $p_{s,i}$ be the position of a solver s ($1 \leq s \leq n$) in the list associated with instance i ($1 \leq i \leq m$). According to Borda's method, each voter's ballot consists of a vector of individual scores given to candidates, where the score $S_{s,i}$ of solver s on instance i is simply $S_{s,i} = n - p_{s,i}$. In cases of time limit attainment or failure, we default $S_{s,i}$ to 0. The score of a candidate, given the individual preferences, is just $S_s = \sum_i S_{s,i}$, and the winner is the solver with the highest score.

Range voting [11]. Again, suppose that n solvers and m instance are involved in the contest and $p_{s,i}$ is obtained as described above for Borda's method. We let the score $S_{s,i}$ of solver s on instance i be the quantity $ar^{n-p_{s,i}}$, i.e., we use a positional scoring rule following a geometric progression with a common ratio $r = 2$ and a scale factor $a = 1$. We consider failures and time limit attainments in the same way (we call this the failure-as-time-limit model in [21]), and thus we assume that all the voters express an opinion about all the solvers. The overall score of a candidate is again $S_s = \sum_i S_{s,i}$ and the candidate with the highest score wins the election.

Schulze's method. We denote as such an extension of the method described in Appendix 3 of [12]. Since Schulze's method is meant to compute a single overall winner, we extended the method according to Schulze's suggestions [22] in order to make it capable of generating an overall ranking.

3   YASM: Yet Another Scoring Method (Revisited)

While the aggregation procedures used in CASC and QBF evaluations are straight-forward, they do not take into account some aspects that are indeed considered by the purse-based method used in the last SAT competition. On the other hand, the purse-based method used in SAT requires some oracle to assign purses to the problem instances, so the results can be influenced heavily by the oracle. In [17] a first version of YASM was introduced as an attempt to combine the two approaches: a rich method like the purse-based one, but using the data obtained from the runs only. As reported in [17], YASM featured a somewhat complex calculation, yielding unsatisfactory results, particularly in the comparison with the final ranking produced by voting systems. Here we revise the original version of YASM to make its computation simpler, and to improve its performance using ideas borrowed from voting systems. From here on, we call YASMv2 the revised version, and YASM the original one presented in [17]. YASMv2 requires a preliminary classification whereby a hardness degree H_i is assigned to each problem instance i using the same equation as in CASC [1] (and YASM):

$$H_i = 1 - \frac{S_i}{S_t} \qquad (3)$$

where S_i is the number of solvers that solved i, and S_t is the total number of participants to the contest. Considering equation (3), we notice that $0 \le H_i \le 1$, where $H_i = 0$ means that i is relatively easy, while $H_i = 1$ means that i is relatively hard. We can then compute the measure of effectiveness $S_{s,i}$ of a solver s on a given instance i (this definition changes with respect to YASM):

$$S_{s,i} = k_{s,i} \cdot (1 + H_i) \cdot \frac{L - T_{s,i}}{L - M_i} \qquad (4)$$

where L is the time limit, $T_{s,i}$ is the CPU time used up by s to solve i ($T_{s,i} \le L$), and $M_i = min_s\{T_{s,i}\}$, i.e., M_i is the time spent on the instance i by the *SOTA solver* defined in [8] to be the ideal solver that always fares the best time among all the participants. The hybridization with voting systems comes into play with the coefficient $k_{s,i}$ which is computed as follows. Suppose that n solvers are participating to the contest. Each instance ranks the solvers in ascending order considering the value of the CPUTIME field. Let $p_{s,i}$ be the position of a solver s in the ranking associated with instance i ($1 \le p_{s,i} \le n$), then $k_{s,i} = n - p_{s,i}$. In case of time limit attainment and failure, we default $k_{s,i}$ to 0, and thus also $S_{s,i}$ is 0. The overall ranking of the solvers is computed by considering the values $S_s = \sum_i S_{s,i}$ for all $1 \le s \le n$, and the solver with the highest sum wins.

We can see from equation (4) that in YASMv2 the effectiveness of a solver on a given instance is influenced by three factors, namely (i) a Borda-like positional weight ($k_{s,i}$), (ii) the relative hardness of the instance ($1 + H_i$), and (iii) the relative speed of the solver with respect to the fastest solver on the instance ($\frac{L - T_{s,i}}{L - M_i}$). Intuitively, coefficient (ii) rewards the solvers that are able to solve hard instances, while (iii) rewards the solvers that are faster than other competitors.

Table 1. Homogeneity of aggregation procedures

	CASC	QBF	SAT	YASM	YASMv2	Borda	r.v.	Schulze
CASC	–	1	0.71	0.86	0.79	0.86	0.71	0.86
QBF		–	0.71	0.86	0.79	0.86	0.71	0.86
SAT			–	0.86	0.86	0.71	0.71	0.71
YASM				–	0.86	0.71	0.71	0.71
YASMv2					–	0.86	0.86	0.86
Borda						–	0.86	1
r. v.							–	0.86
Schulze								–

The coefficient $k_{s,i}$ has been added to stabilize the final ranking and make it less sensitive to an initial bias in the test set. As we show in the next Section, this combination allows YASMv2 to reach the best compromise among different effectiveness measures.

4   Experimental Evaluation

4.1   Homogeneity

The rationale behind this measure (introduced in [17]) is to verify that, on a given test set, the aggregation procedures considered (i) do not produce exactly the same solver rankings, but, at the same time, (ii) do not yield antithetic solver rankings. Thus, homogeneity is not an effectiveness measure per se, but it is a preliminary assessment that we are performing an apple-to-apple comparison and that the apples are not exactly the same.

Homogeneity is computed as in [17] considering the Kendall rank correlation coefficient τ which is a nonparametric coefficient best suited to compare rankings. τ is computed between any two rankings and it is such that $-1 \leq \tau \leq 1$, where $\tau = -1$ means perfect disagreement, $\tau = 0$ means independence, and $\tau = 1$ means perfect agreement. Table 1 shows the values of τ computed for the aggregation procedures considered, arranged in a symmetric matrix where we omit the elements below the diagonal (r.v. is a shorthand for range voting). Values of τ close to, but not exactly equal to 1 are desirable. Table 1 shows that this is indeed the case for the aggregation procedures considered using QBFEVAL'05 data. Only two couples of methods (QBF-CASC and Schulze-Borda) show perfect agreement, while all the other couples agree to some extent, but still produce different rankings.

4.2   Fidelity

We introduce this measure to check whether the aggregation procedures under test introduce any distortion with respect to the true merits of the solvers. Our motivation is that we would like to extract some scientific insight from the final ranking of QBFEVAL'06 and not just winners and losers. Of course, we have no way to know the true merits of the QBF solvers: this would be like knowing the true statistic of some population. Therefore, we measure fidelity by

Table 2. Fidelity of aggregation procedures. As far as **SAT** is concerned, the series purse is not assigned.

Method	Mean	Std	Median	Min	Max	IQ Range	F
QBF	182.25	7.53	183	170	192	13	88.54
CASC	182.25	7.53	183	170	192	13	88.54
SAT	87250	12520.2	83262.33	78532.74	119780.48	4263.94	65.56
YASM	46.64	2.22	46.33	43.56	51.02	2.82	85.38
YASMv2	1257.29	45.39	1268.73	1198.43	1312.72	95.11	91.29
Borda	984.5	127.39	982.5	752	1176	194.5	63.95
r. v.	12010.25	5183.86	12104	5186	21504	8096	24.12
SCHULZE	–	–	–	–	–	–	–

feeding each aggregation procedure with "white noise", i.e., several samples of table RUNS having the same structure outlined in Subsection 2.1 and filled with random results. In particular, we assign to RESULT one of SAT/UNSAT, TIME and FAIL values with equal probability, and a value of CPUTIME chosen uniformly at random in the interval [0;1]. Given this artificial setting, we know in advance that the true merit of the competitors is approximately the same. A high-fidelity aggregation procedure is thus one that computes approximately the same scores for each solver, and thus produces a final ranking where scores have a small variance-to-mean ratio.

The results of the fidelity test are presented in Table 2 where each line contains the statistics of a aggregation procedure. The columns show, from left to right, the mean, the standard deviation, the median, the minimum, the maximum and the interquartile range of the scores produced by each aggregation procedure when fed by white noise. The last column is our fidelity coefficient F, i.e., the percent ratio between the lowest score (solver ranked last) and the highest one (solver ranked first): the higher the value of F, the more the fidelity of the aggregation procedure. As we can see from Table 2, the fidelity of YASMv2 is better than that of all the other methods under test, including QBF and CASC which are second best, and have higher fidelity than YASM. Notice that range voting, and to a lesser extent also SAT and Borda's methods, introduce a substantial distortion. In the case of range voting, this can be explained by the exponential spread that separates the scores, and thus amplifies even small differences. Measuring fidelity does not make sense in the case of Schulze's method. Indeed, given the characteristics of the "white noise" data set, Schulze's method yields a tie among all the solvers. Thus, checking for fidelity would essentially mean checking the tie-breaking heuristic, and not the main method.

4.3   RDT-Stability and DTL-Stability

Stability on a randomized decreasing test set (RDT-stability), and stability on a decreasing time limit (DTL-stability) have been introduced in [17] to measure how much an aggregation procedure is sensitive to perturbations that diminish the size of the original test set, and how much an aggregation procedure is sensitive to perturbations that diminish the maximum amount of CPU time granted to the solvers, respectively. The results of RDT- and DTL-stability tests

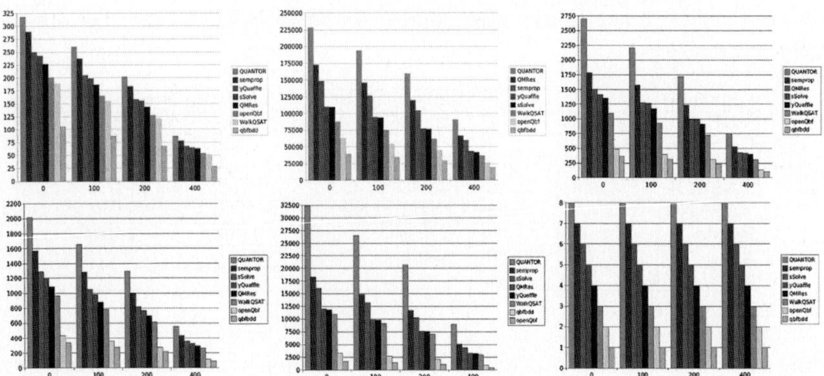

Fig. 1. RDT-stability plots

are presented in the plots of Figures 1 and 2. We obtained such plots considering the CPU time noise model in [18], and considering YASMv2 instead of YASM and the Schulze's method instead of the sum of victories method.

On Figure 1, the first row shows, from left to right, the plots regarding QBF/CASC, SAT and YASMv2 procedures, while the second row shows, again from left to right, the plots regarding Borda's method, range voting and Schulze's method. Each histogram reports, on the x-axis the number of problems m discarded uniformly at random from the original test set (0, 100, 200 and 400 out of 551) and on the y-axis the score. Schulze's scores are the straightforward translation of the ordinal ranking derived by applying the method which is not based on cardinal ranking. For each value of the x-axis, eight bars are displayed, corresponding to the scores of the solvers. The legend is sorted according to the ranking computed by the specific procedure, and the bars are also displayed accordingly. This makes easier to identify perturbations of the original ranking, i.e., the leftmost group of bars in each plot corresponding to $m = 0$. On Figure 2, the histograms are arranged in the same way as Figure 1, except that the x-axis now reports the amount of CPU time seconds used as a time limit when evaluating the scores of the solvers. The leftmost value is $L = 900$, i.e., the original time limit that produces the ranking according to which the legend and the bars are sorted, and then we consider the values $L' = \{700, 500, 300, 100, 50, 10, 1\}$. The conclusion that we reach are the same of [17], and precisely:

- All the aggregation procedures considered are RDT-stable up to 400, i.e., a random sample of 151 instances is sufficient for all the procedures to reach the same conclusions that each one reaches on the heftier set of 551 instances used in QBFEVAL'05.
- Decreasing the time limit substantially, even up to one order of magnitude, is not influencing the stability of the aggregation procedures considered, except for some minor perturbations for QBF/CASC, SAT and Schulze's methods. Moreover, independently from the procedure used and the amount of CPU time granted, the best solver is always the same.

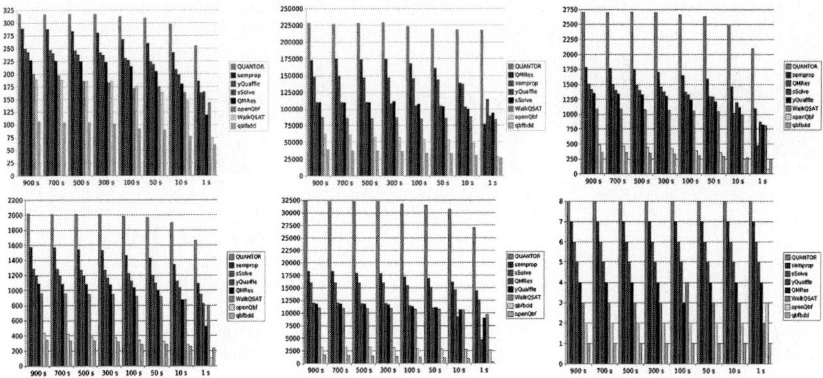

Fig. 2. DTL-stability plots

Indeed, while the above measures can help us extract general guidelines about running a competition, in our setting they do not provide useful insights to discriminate the relative merits of the procedures.

4.4 SBT-Stability

Stability on a solver biased test set (SBT-stability) is introduced in [17] to measure how much an aggregation procedure is sensitive to a test set that is biased in favor of a given solver. Let Γ be the original test set, and Γ_s be the subset of Γ such that the solver s is able to solve exactly the instances in Γ_s. Let $R_{q,s}$ be the ranking obtained by applying the aggregation procedure q on Γ_s. If $R_{q,s}$ is the same as the original ranking R_q, then the aggregation procedure q is SBT-stable with respect to the solver s. Notice that, contrarily to what stated in [17], SBT-stability alone is not a sufficient indicator of the capacity of an aggregation procedure to detect the absolute merit of the participants. Indeed, it turns out that a very low-fidelity method such as range voting is remarkably SBT-stable. This because we can raise the SBT-stability of a ranking by decreasing its fidelity: in the limit, a aggregation procedure that assigns fixed scores to each solver, has the best SBT-stability and the worst fidelity. Therefore, an aggregation procedure showing a high SBT-stability is relatively immune to bias in the test set, but it must also feature a high fidelity if we are to conclude that the method provides a good hint at detecting the absolute merit of the solvers.

Figure 3 shows the plots with the results of the SBT-stability measure for each aggregation procedure considering the noise model and YASMv2 (the layout is the same as Figures 1 and 2). The x-axis reports the name of the solver s used to compute the solver-biased test set Γ_s and the y-axis reports the score value. For each of the Γ_s's, we report eight bars showing the scores obtained by the solvers using only the instances in Γ_s. The order of the bars (and of the legend) corresponds to the ranking obtained with the given aggregation procedure on the original test set Γ. As we can see from Figure 3 (top-left), CASC/QBF aggregation procedures are not SBT-stable: for each of the Γ_s, the original ranking is perturbed

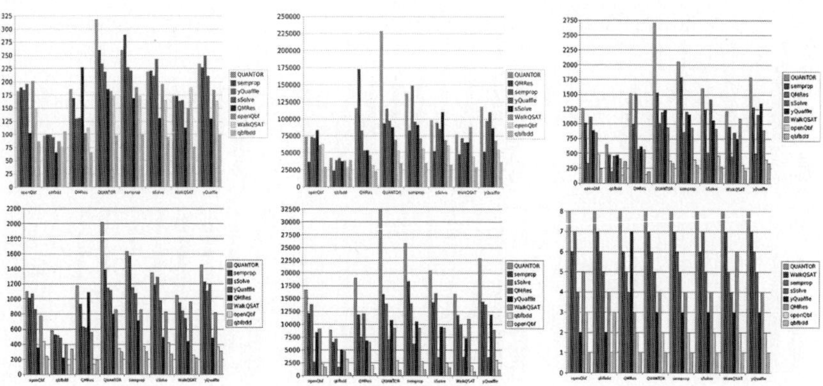

Fig. 3. SBT-stability plots

and the winner becomes s. Notice that on $\Gamma_{\mathrm{QUANTOR}}$, CASC/QBF yield the same ranking that they output on the complete test set Γ. The SAT competition procedure (Figure 3, top-center) is not SBT-stable, not even on the test set biased on its alleged winner QUANTOR. YASMv2 is better than both CASC/QBF and SAT, since its alleged winner QUANTOR is the winner on biased test sets as well. Borda's method (Figure 3, bottom-left) is not SBT-stable with respect to any solver, but the alleged winner (QUANTOR) is always the winner on the biased test sets. Moreover, the rankings obtained on the test sets biased on QUANTOR and SEMPROP are not far from the ranking obtained on the original test set. Also range voting (Figure 3, bottom-center), is not SBT-stable with respect to any solver, but the solvers ranking first and last do not change over the biased test sets and it is true for the Schulze's method (Figure 3, bottom-right) too.

Looking at the results presented above, we can see that YASMv2 performance in terms of SBT stability lies in between classical automated reasoning contests methods and methods based on voting systems. This fact is highlighted in Table 3, where for each procedure we compute the Kendall coefficient between the ranking obtained on the original test set Γ and each of the rankings obtained on the Γ_s test sets, including the mean coefficient observed. Overall, YASMv2 turns out to be, on average, better than CASC/QBF, SAT, and YASM, while it is worse, on average, than the methods based on voting systems. However, if we consider also the results of Table 2 about fidelity, we can see that YASMv2 offers the best compromise between SBT-stability and fidelity. Indeed, while CASC/QBF methods have a relatively high fidelity, they perform poorly in terms of SBT-stability, and SAT method is worse than YASMv2 both in terms of fidelity and in terms of SBT-stability. Methods based on voting systems are all more SBT-stable that YASMv2, but they have poor fidelity coefficients. We consider this good performance of YASMv2 a result of our choice to hybridize classical methods used in automated reasoning contests and methods based on voting systems. This helped us to obtain an aggregation procedure which is less sensitive to bias, and, at the same time, a good indicator of the absolute merit of the competitors.

Table 3. Kendall coefficient between the ranking obtained on the original test set and each of the rankings obtained on the solver-biased test sets

	CASC/QBF	SAT	YASM	YASMv2	Borda	r. v.	Schulze
OPENQBF	0.43	0.57	0.36	0.64	0.79	0.79	0.79
QBFBDD	0.43	0.43	0.36	0.64	0.79	0.86	0.79
QMRES	0.64	0.86	0.76	0.79	0.71	0.86	0.79
QUANTOR	1	0.86	0.86	0.86	0.93	0.86	0.93
SEMPROP	0.93	0.71	0.71	0.79	0.93	0.86	0.93
SSOLVE	0.71	0.57	0.57	0.79	0.86	0.79	0.86
WALKQSAT	0.57	0.57	0.43	0.71	0.64	0.79	0.79
YQUAFFLE	0.71	0.64	0.57	0.71	0.86	0.86	0.93
Mean	0.68	0.65	0.58	0.74	0.81	0.83	0.85

5 Conclusions

Summing up, the analysis presented in this paper allowed us to make some progress in the research agenda associated to QBFEVAL. YASMv2 features a simpler calculation, yet it is more powerful than YASM in terms of SBT-stability and fidelity. We confirmed some of the conclusions reached in [17], namely that independently of the specific procedure used, a larger test set is not necessarily a better test set, and that a higher time limit does not necessarily result in a more informative contest. On the other hand, while aggregation procedures based on voting systems emerged from [17] as "moral" winners over other procedures, the analysis presented in this paper shows that better results could be achieved using hybrid techniques such as YASMv2.

References

1. Sutcliffe, G., Suttner, C.: The CADE ATP System Competition (April 22, 2007), http://www.cs.miami.edu/~tptp/CASC
2. Le Berre, D., Simon, L.: The SAT Competition (April 22, 2007), http://www.satcompetition.org
3. Long, D., Fox, M.: The 3rd International Planning Competition: Results and Analysis. Artificial Intelligence Research 20, 1–59 (2003)
4. van Dongen, M.R.C.: Introduction to the Solver Competition. In: CPAI 2005 proceedings (2005)
5. Barrett, C.W., de Moura, L., Stump, A.: SMT-COMP: Satisfiability Modulo Theories Competition. In: Etessami, K., Rajamani, S.K. (eds.) CAV 2005. LNCS, vol. 3576, pp. 20–23. Springer, Heidelberg (2005)
6. Le Berre, D., Simon, L., Tacchella, A.: Challenges in the QBF arena: the SAT'03 evaluation of QBF solvers. In: Giunchiglia, E., Tacchella, A. (eds.) SAT 2003. LNCS, vol. 2919, Springer, Heidelberg (2004)
7. Le Berre, D., Narizzano, M., Simon, L., Tacchella, A.: The second QBF solvers evaluation. In: Hoos, H.H., Mitchell, D.G. (eds.) SAT 2004. LNCS, vol. 3542, Springer, Heidelberg (2005)
8. Narizzano, M., Pulina, L., Tacchella, A.: The third QBF solvers comparative evaluation. Journal on Satisfiability, Boolean Modeling and Computation 2, 145–164 (2006), Available on-line at http://jsat.ewi.tudelft.nl/

9. Hooker, J.N.: Testing Heuristics: We Have It All Wrong. Journal of Heuristics 1, 33–42 (1996)

10. Saari, D.G.: Chaotic Elections! A Mathematician Looks at Voting. American Mathematical Society (2001)

11. Smith, W.D.: Range voting (April 22, 2007), Available on-line at `http://www.math.temple.edu/~wds/homepage/rangevote.pdf`

12. Schulze, M.: A New Monotonic and Clone-Independent Single-Winner Election Method. Voting Matters, 9–19 (2003)

13. Narizzano, M., Pulina, L., Taccchella, A.: QBF solvers competitive evaluation (QBFEVAL), `http://www.qbflib.org/qbfeval`

14. RoboCup, `http://www.robocup.org`

15. Arrow, K.J., Sen, A.K., Suzumura, K. (eds.): Handbook of Social Choice and Welfare, vol. 1. Elsevier, Amsterdam (2002)

16. Conitzer, V., Sandholm, T.: Common Voting Rules as Maximum Likelihood Estimators. In: EC-05. 6th ACM Conference on Electronic Commerce. LNCS, pp. 78–87. Springer, Heidelberg (2005)

17. Pulina, L.: Empirical Evaluation of Scoring Methods. In: Proc. STAIRS 2006. Frontiers in Artificial Intelligence and Applications, vol. 142, pp. 108–119 (2006)

18. Narizzano, M., Pulina, L., Tacchella, A.: Competitive Evaluation of QBF Solvers: noisy data and scoring methods. Technical report, STAR-Lab - University of Genoa (May 2006)

19. Giunchiglia, E., Narizzano, M., Pulina, L., Tacchella, A.: Quantified Boolean Formulas satisfiability library (QBFLIB), `www.qbflib.org`

20. Van Gelder, A., Le Berre, D., Biere, A., Kullmann, O., Simon, L.: Purse-Based Scoring for Comparison of Exponential-Time Programs (2006) (unpublished draft)

21. Narizzano, M., Pulina, L., Tacchella, A.: Competitive Evaluation of Automated Reasoning Tools: Statistical Testing and Empirical Scoring. In: EMAA 2006. First Workshop on Empirical Methods for the Analysis of Algorithms (2006)

22. Schulze, M.: Extending schulze's method to obtain an overall ranking. Personal communications

A Top Down Interpreter for LPAD and CP-Logic

Fabrizio Riguzzi

Dip. di Ingegneria – Università di Ferrara – Via Saragat, 1 – 44100 Ferrara, Italy
`fabrizio.riguzzi@unife.it`

Abstract. Logic Programs with Annotated Disjunctions and CP-logic
are two different but related languages for expressing probabilistic information in logic programming. The paper presents a top down interpreter for computing the probability of a query from a program in one
of these two languages. The algorithm is based on the one available for
ProbLog. The performances of the algorithm are compared with those
of a Bayesian reasoner and with those of the ProbLog interpreter. On
programs that have a small grounding, the Bayesian reasoner is more
scalable, but programs with a large grounding require the top down interpreter. The comparison with ProbLog shows that the added expressiveness effectively requires more computation resources.

1 Introduction

Logic Programs with Annotated Disjunctions (LPADs) [9] and CP-logic [8] are
two recent formalisms combining logic and probability. They are interesting for
the simplicity and clarity of their semantics that makes the reading of their
programs very intuitive.

Even if the semantics of these two formalisms were defined in a different way,
there exists a syntactic transformation that makes CP-logic programs equivalent
to a large subset of LPADs, in particular to the most interesting subset of LPADs.

The LPADs and CP-logic semantics assigns a probability value to logic queries.
In this paper, we consider the problem of computing this probability given a program and a query. In particular, we propose a top down interpreter that computes
derivations for a query and then computes the probability of the query by using
Boolean decision diagrams. The algorithm is based on the top down interpreter
for ProbLog presented in [4]. This interpreter is highly optimized and answers
queries from programs containing thousands of clauses. Due to the difference between ProbLog and LPADs, it was not possible to use all the optimizations.

Besides the interpreter, we consider an approach that exploits the possibility
of translating an LPAD into a Bayesian network shown in [9]. The approach
allows the use of Bayesian network reasoners on the problem.

In order to compare the algorithm with the Bayesian approach and with the
ProbLog interpreter, we performed a number of experiments on a simple game
of dice and on graphs of biological concepts. For the first problem the grounding
of the program is small and the Bayesian reasoner is more scalable. For the
second problem, the grounding is so large that the Bayesian approach could not

R. Basili and M.T. Pazienza (Eds.): AI*IA 2007, LNAI 4733, pp. 109–120, 2007.

be applied. As expected, the size of problems that were successfully solved is smaller than the one of ProbLog.

The paper is organized as follows. In Section 2 we present the syntax and semantics of ProbLog, LPADs and CP-logic, together with the approach for translating them into Bayesian networks. Section 3 describes the top down interpreter for ProbLog presented in [4]. Section 4 presents the top down interpreter for LPADs and CP-logic. In Section 5 we discuss the experiments performed and in Section 6 we conclude and present directions for future work.

2   Preliminaries

A ProbLog program [4] T is a set of clauses of the form

$$\alpha : h \leftarrow b_1, \ldots, b_n \tag{1}$$

where α is a real number between 0 and 1 and h and $b_1, \ldots, b_n$ are atoms.

The semantics of such programs is defined in terms of instances: an instance is a definite logic program obtained by selecting a subset of the clauses and removing the α. Its probability is given by the product of the α factor for all the clauses that are included in the instance and of $1 - \alpha$ for all the clauses not included. The probability $P_{PB}^T(Q)$ of a query Q according to program T is given by the sum of the probabilities of the instances that have the query as a consequence according to the least Herbrand model semantics.

A Logic Program with Annotated Disjunctions T [9] consists of a set of formulas of the form

$$h_1 : \alpha_1 \vee \ldots \vee h_n : \alpha_n \leftarrow b_1, \ldots b_m \tag{2}$$

In such a clause the h_i are logical atoms, the b_i are logical literals and the α_i are real numbers in the interval $[0, 1]$ such that $\sum_{i=1}^{n} \alpha_i = 1$.

The semantics of LPADs is given as well in terms of instances: an instance is a ground normal program obtained by selecting for each clause of the grounding of T one of the heads and by removing the α_i. The probability of the instance is given by the product of the α factors associated with the heads selected. The probability $P_{LP}^T(Q)$ of a formula Q according to program T is given by the sum of the probabilities of the instances that have the formula as a consequence according to the well founded [7] semantics.

A CP-logic program T [8] consists of a set of formulas of the form (2) where it is imposed that $\sum_{i=1}^{n} \alpha_i \leq 1$. The semantics of CP-logic was given in terms of probabilistic processes. However, it was shown in [8] that this semantics, when it is defined, is equivalent to the instance based semantics of the LPAD T' obtained from the CP-logic program T by replacing each clause of the form (2) with the clause

$$h_1 : \alpha_1 \vee \ldots \vee h_n : \alpha_n \vee none : 1 - \sum_{i=1}^{n} \alpha_i \leftarrow b_1, \ldots b_m \tag{3}$$

where $none$ is a special atom that does not appear in the body of any clause.

It was shown in [9] that an LPAD can be translated into a Bayesian Logic Program (BLP) preserving the semantics. Since BLP encode Bayesian networks, this provides a way of translating an LPAD into a Bayesian network. This means that we can answer a query by using a Bayesian inference algorithm.

In order to convert an LPAD into a Bayesian network, its grounding must be generated. If the program contains function symbols, the number of different terms is infinite so the user has to provide a finite set of terms for instantiating the clauses, thus restricting the translation to the portion of the ground program of interest to the user. Moreover, the user has also to ensure that the grounded program is acyclic.

Even if the program does not contain function symbols, grounding each clause with every possible constants may generate a very large and cyclic network. Therefore, also in this case the intervention of the user is required.

3   The Top Down Interpreter for ProbLog

In [4] a proof procedure was given for computing the probability of a query Q from a ProbLog program T. The procedure involves the computation of all the possible SLD derivations for Q.

Consider a single derivation d for Q that uses the set of clauses $C_d = \{\alpha_1 : c_1, \ldots, \alpha_k : c_k\}$. Let us assign a Boolean random variable X_i to every clause c_i of T. X_i assumes value 1 if the clause c_i is selected and value 0 if the clause is not selected. The probability

$$P(X_1 = 1 \wedge \ldots \wedge X_k = 1)$$

is the sum of the probabilities of the instances containing these clauses, thus it is the probability of Q if it has only derivation d. Since each clause is independent from the other clauses, the probability above is given by $\prod_{i=1}^{k} \alpha_i$.

If Q has multiple derivations $pr(Q) = \{d_1, \ldots, d_l\}$, then its probability is given by

$$P\left(\bigvee_{d \in pr(Q)} \bigwedge_{\alpha_i : c_i \in C_d} X_i = 1 \right)$$

Thus the problem of computing the probability of a query is reduced to the problem of computing the probability of a DNF formula. This problem is known to be NP-hard. In order to solve it, the authors of [4] use Binary Decision Diagrams (BDD) [2]. BDD represent a Boolean formula as a binary decision graph: one can compute the value of the function given an assignment of the variables by navigating the graph from the root to a leaf. The nodes of the graph are divided into levels and each level is associated with a Boolean variable. The next node is chosen on the basis of the value of the variable associated to that level: if the variable is 1 the high child is chosen, if the value is 0 the low child is chosen. The leaves are associated either with the value 1 or with the value 0: when we reach a leaf we return the value stored there. For example, a BDD for the Boolean function

$$X_{1,1} = 0 \vee X_{2,1} = 0 \wedge X_{2,2} = 1 \wedge X_{3,1} = 0 \vee X_{2,1} = 1 \wedge X_{2,2} = 0 \wedge X_{3,1} = 0 \quad (4)$$

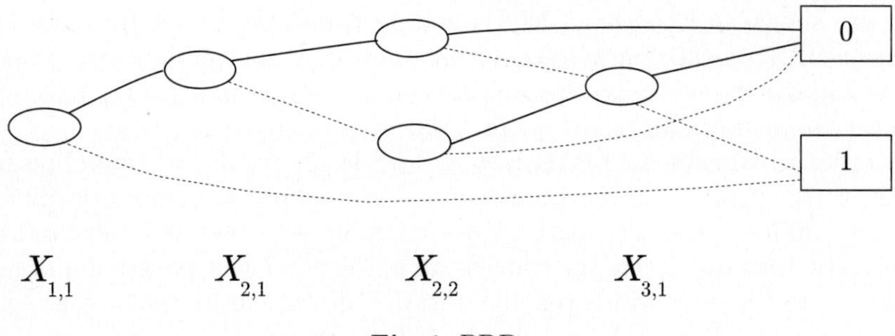

$X_{1,1}$ $X_{2,1}$ $X_{2,2}$ $X_{3,1}$

Fig. 1. BDD

is represented in Figure 1, where all the $X_{i,j}$ are Boolean variables, high children are reached by solid edges, low children by dashed edges and the leaves are represented by rectangular nodes.

A BDD is built by first building a full binary decision tree having 2^n nodes for level n and then simplifying it by merging isomorphic subgraphs until no further reduction is possible. Since the number of reductions depends on the order chosen for the variables, practical BDD tools use sophisticated heuristics for choosing a good order.

Given a BDD of a Boolean formula F, we can easily compute its probability because F can be represented as $F = (X = 1) \wedge F_1 \vee (X = 0) \wedge F_0$ where X is the variable associated to the root of the BDD, F_1 is the formula associated to the high child and F_0 is the formula associated to the low child. Since the two disjuncts are now mutually disjoint, the probability of F can be computed as $P(F) = P(X = 1) \cdot P(F_1) + P(X = 0) \cdot P(F_0)$. The probabilities $P(F_1)$ and $P(F_0)$ can then be computed recursively.

4 A Top Down Interpreter for LPAD and CP-Logic

The notion of derivation presented above must be extended in three ways in order to compute the probability of an LPAD query. First, we must take into account the fact that clauses have more than one atom in the head, therefore each clause is not represented by a Boolean variable but by a multivalued variable with as many values as there are atoms in the head. Second, a variable is not associated with a clause but with a grounding of a clause, thus we have different variables for different groundings. Third, the body of LPAD clauses can contain negative literals: roughly speaking, a negative goal is treated by computing all the possible derivations for the goal, by selecting, for each derivation, a grounded clause and by including in the current derivation the clause with a head different from the one used for deriving the negative goal.

The interpreter we present is based on SLDNF and therefore is valid only for programs for which the Clark's completion semantics [3] and the well founded semantics coincide, as for acyclic programs [1].

In the following, we give an algorithmic definition of derivation. We adopt a mixed pseudo code: we use procedural features, such as assignments and functions, and declarative features, such as non-determinism, unification and coroutining (the predicate *dif* in particular).

A *derivation* from (G_1, C_1) to (G_n, C_n) in T of depth n is a sequence

$$(G_1, C_1), \ldots, (G_n, C_n)$$

such that each G_i is a goal of the form $\leftarrow l_1, \ldots, l_k$, C_i is a set of couples that stores the instantiated clauses and the heads used and (G_{i+1}, C_{i+1}) is obtained according to one of the following rules

- if l_1 is built over a built-in predicate, then l_i is executed, $G_{i+i} = \leftarrow l_2, \ldots, l_k$ and $C_{i+1} = C_i$
- if l_1 is a positive literal, then let $c = h_1 : \alpha_1 \vee \ldots \vee h_n : \alpha_n \leftarrow B$ be a fresh copy of a clause of T that resolves with G_i on l_1, let h_j be a head atom of c that resolves with l_1 and let θ be the mgu substitution of l_1 and h_j. For every couple $(c\delta, m) \in C_i$ such that $m \neq j$ and $c\delta$ unifies with $c\theta$, we impose the constraint $dif(c\delta, c\theta)$ so that further instantiations of $c\delta$ or $c\theta$ do not make the two clauses equal. Then $G_{i+1} = r$ where r is the resolvent of $h_j \leftarrow B$ with G_i on the literal l_1 and $C_{i+1} = C_i \cup \{(c\theta, j)\}$.
- if l_1 is a negative literal $\neg a_1$, then let $\mathcal{C}$ be the set of all the sets C such that there exists a derivation from $(\leftarrow a_1, \emptyset)$ to $(\leftarrow, C)$. Then $G_{i+1} = \leftarrow l_2, \ldots, l_k$ and $C_{i+1} = $Select$(\mathcal{C}, C_i)$, where Select is the function shown in Figure 2.

A derivation is *successful* if $G_n = \leftarrow$.

From the set $\mathcal{C}$ of the all the C such that there exists a derivation from $(\leftarrow Q, \emptyset)$ to $(\leftarrow, C)$ we can build the formula

$$F = \bigvee_{C \in \mathcal{C}} \bigwedge_{(c\theta, j) \in C} (X_{c\theta} = j)$$

where $X_{c\theta}$ is the multivalued variable associated to the clause $c\theta$. In order to deal with multivalued variables using BDD, an approach [6] consists in using a binary encoding: if multivalued variable X_i can assume p different values, we use $q = \lceil \log_2 p \rceil$ binary variables $X_{i,1}, \ldots, X_{i,q}$ where $X_{i,1}$ is the most significant bit. The equation $X_i = j$ can be represented with binary variables in the following way

$$X_{i,1} = j_1 \wedge \ldots \wedge X_{i,q} = j_q$$

where $j_1 \ldots j_q$ is the binary representation of j. Once we have transformed all multivalued equations into Boolean equations we can build the BDD.

In order to compute the probability of a multivalued formula represented by a BDD, we exploit the possibility offered by many BDD packages of specifying that the variables belonging to a certain set must be kept together and in the order given when building the diagram. Therefore, for every multivalued variable, we enclose in one such set all the binary variables associated to it.

114   F. Riguzzi

function Select(
   inputs : $\mathcal{C}$: C sets for successful derivations of
       the negative goal,
     C_i : current set of used clauses
   returns : C_{i+1} : new set of used clauses)
$C_{i+1} := C_i$
for each $C \in \mathcal{C}$
   select a $(c\theta, j) \in C$// If the program is range restricted,
     // $c\theta$ is ground, see the discussion below
   for all δ such that $(c\delta, j) \in C_{i+1}$ and $c\delta$ unifies with $c\theta$
     impose the constraint $dif(c\delta, c\theta)$
   perform one of the following operations
     1. select $(c\delta, m) \in C_{i+1}$ such that $m \neq j$ and $c\delta$ unifies with $c\theta$,
       then $C_{i+1} := C_{i+1} \setminus \{(c\delta, m)\} \cup \{(c\theta, m)\}$
     2. select $(c\delta, m) \in C_{i+1}$ such that $m \neq j$ and $c\delta$ unifies with $c\theta$,
       then impose the constraint $dif(c\delta, c\theta)$ and $C_{i+1} := C_{i+1} \cup \{(c\theta, m)\}$
     3. select $m \neq j$ such that $\nexists c\delta \ (c\delta, m) \in C_{i+1}$ with $c\delta$ that unifies with $c\theta$,
       then $C_{i+1} := C_{i+1} \cup \{(c\theta, m)\}$.
return C_{i+1}

Fig. 2. Function Select

Consider for example the program
$$c_1 = a : 0.1. \quad c_2 = b : 0.3 \vee c : 0.6. \quad c_3 = a : 0.2 \leftarrow \neg b.$$
This program has three successful derivations from $(\leftarrow a, \emptyset)$ to $(\leftarrow, C)$. Their C sets are
$$C^1 = \{(c_1\emptyset, 0)\}$$
$$C^2 = \{(c_2\emptyset, 1), (c_3\emptyset, 0)\}$$
$$C^2 = \{(c_2\emptyset, 2), (c_3\emptyset, 0)\}$$
These C sets produce the following formula with multivalued variables
$$X_1 = 0 \vee X_2 = 1 \wedge X_3 = 0 \vee X_2 = 2 \wedge X_3 = 0$$
where X_i corresponds to $c_i\emptyset$. The formula is then converted into formula (4) that produces the BDD of Figure 1.

The algorithm shown in Figure 3 computes the probability of a multivalued formula encoded by a BDD. It consists of two mutually recursive functions, Prob and ProbBool. The idea is that we call Prob in order to take into account a new multivalued variable and we call ProbBool to consider the individual binary variables. In particular, $\text{Prob}(n)$ returns the probability of node n while the calls of ProbBool build a binary tree with a level for each bit of the multivalued variable, so that the last calls of ProbBool (the leaves) identify a single value and are called with a node whose binary variable belongs to the next multivalued variable. Then ProbBool calls Prob on the node to compute the probability of the subgraph and returns the product of the result and the probability associated to the value. The intermediate ProbBool calls sum up these partial results and return them to the parent Prob call. Note that ProbBool builds a full binary tree for a variable even if there is not a node for every binary variable (for example, because the result is not influenced by the value of one bit). As in [4], Prob is

function Prob(
    inputs : n : BDD node,
    returns : P : probability of the formula)
if n is the 1-terminal then return 1
if n is the 0-terminal then return 0
let $mVar$ be the multivalued variable
    corresponding to the Boolean variable associated to n
$P :=$ProbBool$(n, 0, 1, mVar)$
return P

function ProbBool(
    inputs : n : BDD node,
        $value$: index of the value of the multivalued variable
        $posBVar$: position of the Boolean variable, 1 most significant
        $mVar$: multivalued variable
    returns : P : probability of the formula)
if $posBVar = mVar.nBit + 1$ then // the last bit has been reached
    let p_{value} be the probability associated with value of index
        $value$ of variable $mVar$
    return $p_{value} \times$ Prob(n)
else
    let b_n be the Boolean variable associated to n
    let b_p be the Boolean variable in position $posBVar$ of $mVar$
    if $b_n = b_p$
        // variable b_p is present in the BDD
        let h and l be the high and low children of n
        shift left 1 position the bits of $value$
        $P :=$ProbBool$(h, value + 1, posBVar + 1, mVar)+$
            ProbBool$(l, value, posBVar + 1, mVar)$
        return P
    else
        // variable b_p is absent from the BDD
        shift left 1 position the bits of $value$
        $P :=$ProbBool$(n, value + 1, posBVar + 1, mVar)+$
            ProbBool$(n, value, posBVar + 1, mVar)$
        return P

Fig. 3. Function Prob

optimized by storing, for each computed node, the value of its probability, so that if the node is visited again the probability can be retrieved.

Note that for the algorithm to behave correctly the program must be range restricted, i.e., all the variables in the head of clauses must appear in the body. Consider for example the following program T

$c_1 = a(1) : 0.3 \leftarrow p(X).$
$c_1 = a(2) : 0.4 \leftarrow p(X).$
$c_3 = p(X) : 0.5.$

where the third clause (c_3) is not range restricted.

The only derivation from $(\leftarrow a(1), \emptyset)$ to $(\leftarrow, C)$ has the following C set
$$C = \{((c_1\emptyset, 0), (c_3\emptyset, 0)\}$$
and thus gives a probability of 0.15. The grounding T' of T is

$c_1 = a(1) : 0.3 \leftarrow p(1).$ $c_2 = a(1) : 0.3 \leftarrow p(2).$
$c_3 = a(2) : 0.4 \leftarrow p(1).$ $c_4 = a(2) : 0.4 \leftarrow p(2).$
$c_5 = p(1) : 0.5.$ $c_6 = p(2) : 0.5.$

thus there are two successful derivations of $a(1)$ whose C sets are
$$C^1 = \{(c_1\emptyset, 0), (c_5\emptyset, 0)\}   C^2 = \{(c_2\emptyset, 0), (c_6\emptyset, 0)\}$$
for a probability of 0.2775.

If the program is range restricted, every derivation from $(\leftarrow G, \emptyset)$ to $(\leftarrow, C)$ will contain in C couples $(j, c\theta)$ such that $c\theta$ is ground and thus the above problem does not appear.

However, the query can contain variables: from the program T', the algorithm for the query $a(X)$ would return probability 0.2775 for $X = 1$ and probability 0.36 for $X = 2$.

In [4] an algorithm was given for computing the probability of the query in an approximate way, returning an upper and a lower bound of the probability. This involves the use of iterative deepening: the SLD-tree is built only up to a given depth d and at each iteration we increment the value of d. At the end of each iteration we have a set of C sets of successful derivations *Successful* and a set of C sets for still open derivations *Open*. The true probability $P_{PB}^T(Q)$ of a query is such that

$$P(F_1) \le P_{PB}^T(Q) \le P(F_1 \vee F_2)$$

where F_1 (F_2) is the formula corresponding to *Successful* (*Open*) Thus we have an upper and a lower bound on $P_{PB}^T(Q)$.

The cycle terminates when $P(F_1 \vee F_2) - P(F_1) \le \epsilon$, where ϵ is a used defined precision.

However, this approach cannot be used for LPADs. In fact, consider the following program

$c_1 = a : 0.1 \leftarrow p(X).$ $c_2 = p(1) : 0.9.$ $c_3 = p(2) : 0.9.$

If we have the query a and a depth bound $d = 1$, then at the end of the first iteration *Successful* is empty and *Open* contains the only set $\{(c_1\emptyset, 0)\}$. Thus $P(F_1) = 0$ and $P(F_1 \vee F_2) = 0.1$. However $P_{LP}^T(Q)$ is 0.1719 so $P(F_1 \vee F_2)$ is not an upper bound on $P(Q)$. In fact, there are two successful derivations of a, one has the C set $\{(c_1\{X/1\}, 0), (c_2\emptyset, 0)\}$ and the other has the C set $\{(c_1\{X/2\}, 0), (c_3\emptyset, 0)\}$. Thus the formula F is

$$X_{c_1\{X/1\}} = 0 \wedge X_{c_2} = 0 \vee X_{c_1\{X/2\}} = 0 \wedge X_{c_3} = 0$$

Since the two disjunct are not mutually exclusive, we can use the law for the probability of an or and obtain

$$0.1 \cdot 0.9 + 0.1 \cdot 0.9 - 0.1 \cdot 0.9 \cdot 0.1 \cdot 0.9 = 0.18 - 0.0081 = 0.1719$$

This problem depends on the fact that, while in ProbLog we consider non ground clauses, in LPAD we consider instantiated ones and a clause in a partial derivation may not be fully instantiated. When the derivation is continued, it may generated more than one derivation with different instantiation of the clause.

5   Experiments

We report here on two experiments performed in order to evaluate the performances of the top down interpreter: the first involves a game of dice and the second graphs of biological concepts. All the experiments were performed on a Linux machine with a 3.40 GHz Pentium D processor and 1 GB of RAM.

In the first experiment we consider two versions of a dice game proposed in [9]: the player throws a die a number of times and stops only when a certain number comes out. We want to predict the probability of a given outcome at a given time point.

The two versions differ only for the number of faces of the (idealized) die: the first version considers a two face die and the second version a three face die. The LPAD describing the first version is shown below:

$on(0, 1) : 1/2 \vee on(0, 2) : 1/2.$

$on(T, 1) : 1/2 \vee on(T, 2) : 1/2 \leftarrow T1\ is\ T - 1, T1 >= 0, on(T1, 1).$

Atom $on(T, N)$ means that at time T we rolled a die and face N came out. The first rule states that at time 0 (the beginning of the game) we rolled a die and we got a 1 or a 2 with equal probability. The second rule states that at time T we roll a die if a die was rolled at the previous time point and we got a 1. If we roll a die, we get a 1 or a 2 with equal probability. Thus, we stop when we get a 2.

The LPAD describing the second version is similar to the one above and states that we stop throwing dice only when we get a 3.

For the top down interpreter we used an implementation of it in Yap Prolog[1] that uses CUDD[2] as the BDD manipulation package.

For the Bayesian reasoner, we used the implementation of the junction tree inference algorithm [5] available in BNJ[3] version 2 release 7 2004.

The query $on(T, 1)$ was tried against both programs with T ranging from 0 to 15. The execution times of the top down interpreter (cplint) and of the Bayesian reasoner (bnj) are shown in Figures 4(a) and 4(b) for the two sided die and for the three sided die respectively.

When generating the ground program to be translated into a Bayesian network, only the constants relevant to the query were considered. So, for example, if the query was $on(3, 1)$, only constants 0, 1, 2 and 3 were considered for T and $T1$. For N, the constants 1 and 2 were considered for the first program and 1, 2 and 3 for the second program.

For the point not shown for cplint in Figure 4(b), the system started thrashing and the computation was interrupted after four hours.

We consider now two programs with the same meaning as those above but that use negation. The one for the three sided die is

$on(0, 1) : 1/3 \vee on(0, 2) : 1/3 \vee on(0, 3) : 1/3.$

$on(T, 1) : 1/3 \vee on(T, 2) : 1/3 \vee on(T, 3) : 1/3 \leftarrow$
$\qquad T1\ is\ T - 1, T1 >= 0, on(T1, N), \neg on(T1, 3).$

---

[1] http://www.ncc.up.pt/~vsc/Yap/
[2] http://vlsi.colorado.edu/~fabio/
[3] http://sourceforge.net/projects/bndev

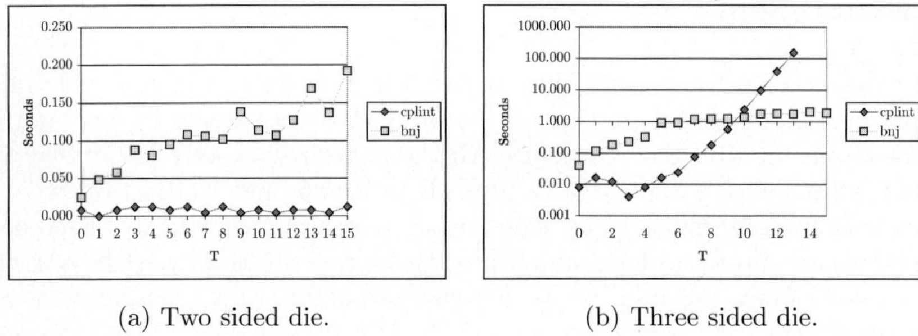

(a) Two sided die.   (b) Three sided die.

Fig. 4. Execution times for the die programs

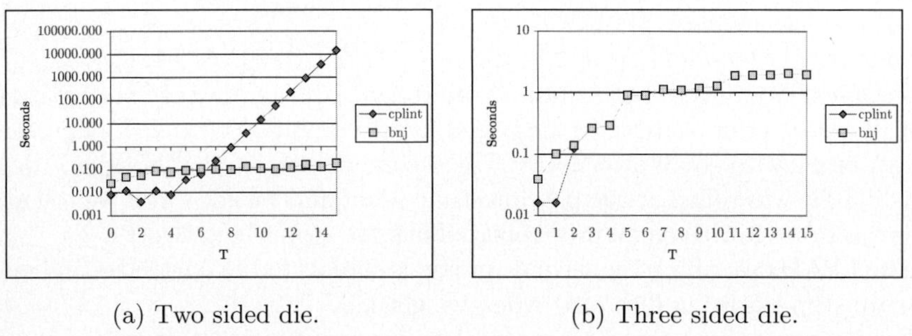

(a) Two sided die.   (b) Three sided die.

Fig. 5. Execution times for the die programs with negation

The computation times are shown in Figures 5(a) and 5(b) respectively under the same experimental settings discussed before.

The points not shown for cplint in Figure 5(b) are those for which Yap stopped returning an "out of database space" error.

The second experiment involves computing the probability of a path between two nodes in a graph. This experiment was chosen in order to compare the results with those [4] where the authors use the ProbLog interpreter for evaluating the probability of paths between nodes in a network of biological concepts. The dataset was kindly provided by the authors of [4] and is the same as the one used in the paper. The dataset consists of a number of subgraphs $G_1, G_2, \ldots G_n$ extracted from a complete graph built around four Alzheimer genes. The complete graph contains 11530 edges and 5220 nodes. The subgraphs are obtained by subsampling, they have the sizes 200, 400, ..., 5000 edges and are such that $G_1 \subset G_2 \subset \ldots \subset G_n$. Subsampling was repeated 10 times.

The query $can\_reach(620, 983)$ was issued on every subgraph, where 620 and 683 are the identifiers of a couple of genes and can_reach is defined recursively with definite clauses in the usual way.

The computation time for the probability of the query is shown in Figure 6(a) in seconds as a function of the number of edges. The time shown is the average computation time on the subgraphs on which the interpreter was successful.

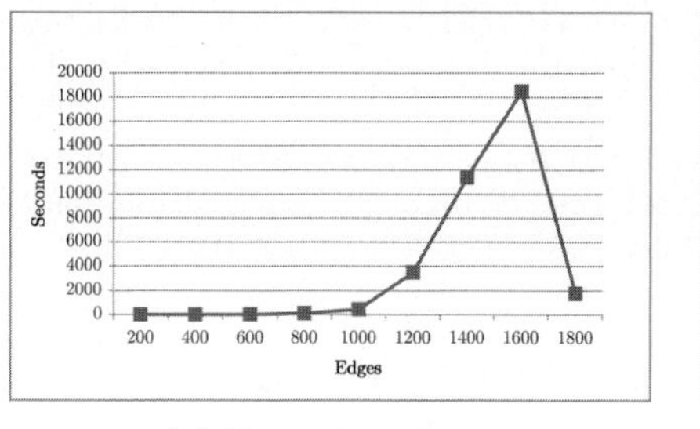
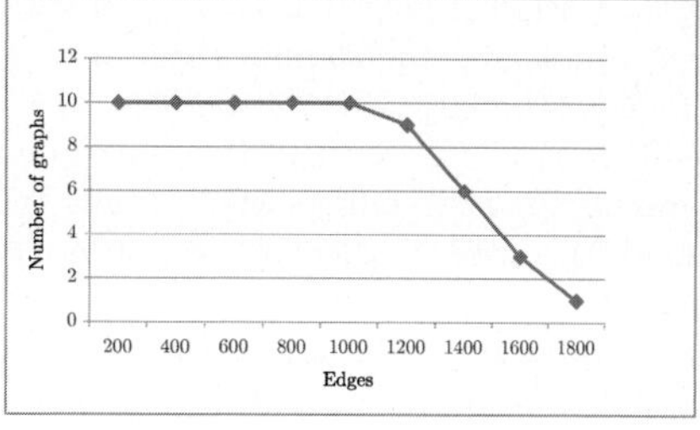

(a) Execution times.   (b) Number of successes.

Fig. 6. Biological graph experiments

Figure 6(b) shows the number of graphs for which the computation succeeded: for the other graphs, the computer did not return an answer after 10 hours.

A comparison with bnj was not possible because the conversion program exhausted the available memory: the grounding of the definition for *can_reach* was too large.

These experiments show that, for small problems, Bayesian inference is more scalable. However, when problems with many constants are considered, using Bayesian inference is not possible. Comparing cplint with the ProbLog interpreter of [4], we see that the added expressiveness of LPAD and CP-Logic has an impact on performances, since the ProbLog interpreter was able to answer the query for up to 4600 edges.

6   Conclusions

We have presented a top down interpreter for computing the probability of LPADs and CP-logic queries that is inspired to the one presented in [4].

We have experimentally compared the algorithm with a Bayesian inference algorithm and with the ProbLog interpreter.

In the future, we plan to extend the interpreter by considering also aggregates and the possibility of having the probabilities in the head depend on literals in the body.

References

1. Apt, K.R., Bol, R.N.: Logic programming and negation: A survey. J. Log. Program 19/20, 9–71 (1994)
2. Bryant, R.E.: Graph-based algorithms for boolean function manipulation. IEEE Trans. on Computers 35(8), 677–691 (1986)
3. Clark, K.L.: Negation as failure. In: Logic and Databases, Plenum Press, New York (1978)
4. De Raedt, L., Kimmig, A., Toivonen, H.: Problog: A probabilistic prolog and its application in link discovery. In: Proceedings of the 20th International Joint Conference on Artificial Intelligence, pp. 2462–2467 (2007)

5. Lauritzen, S., Spiegelhalter, D.J.: Local computations with probabilities on graphical structures and their application to expert systems. Journal of the Royal Statistical Society, B 50(2), 157–224 (1988)
6. Miller, D.M., Drechsler, R.: On the construction of multiple-valued decision diagrams. In: Proceedings 32nd IEEE International Symposium on Multiple-Valued Logic, pp. 245–253. IEEE Computer Society Press, Los Alamitos (2002)
7. Van Gelder, A., Ross, K.A., Schlipf, J.S.: The well-founded semantics for general logic programs. Journal of the ACM 38(3), 620–650 (1991)
8. Vennekens, J., Denecker, M., Bruynooghe, M.: Representing causal information about a probabilistic process. In: Fisher, M., van der Hoek, W., Konev, B., Lisitsa, A. (eds.) JELIA 2006. LNCS (LNAI), vol. 4160, Springer, Heidelberg (2006)
9. Vennekens, J., Verbaeten, S., Bruynooghe, M.: Logic programs with annotated disjunctions. In: Demoen, B., Lifschitz, V. (eds.) ICLP 2004. LNCS, vol. 3132, Springer, Heidelberg (2004)

A Multi-layered
General Agent Model

Stefania Costantini[1], Arianna Tocchio[1], Francesca Toni[2],
and Panagiota Tsintza[1]

[1] Università degli Studi di L'Aquila
Dipartimento di Informatica
Via Vetoio, Loc. Coppito, I-67010 L'Aquila - Italy
{stefcost, tocchio, tsintza}@di.univaq.it
[2] Department of Computing
Imperial College London
South-Kensington Campus, SW7 2AZ London, UK
ft@doc.ic.ac.uk

Abstract. We propose a layered representation of general agent models with a base layer, composed of basic agent features including control, and a higher layer, consisting of a meta-control with the task of tuning, supervising and modifying the base layer. This provides higher flexibility in how an agent is built and may evolve.

1 Introduction

Nowadays, there is a clear tendency toward employing software agents instead of traditional programs, so as to reach in perspective a higher flexibility of use and interaction. Agents should be *intelligent* so as to face changing situations by modifying their behavior, or their goals, or the way to achieve their goals. This requires agents to be able to perform, interleave and combine various forms of commonsense reasoning, possibly based upon different kinds of representation. Several generic agent-oriented languages and architecture exist and in particular several computational logic-based agent architectures and models. A common feature is the aim at building agents that are able to adapt or change their behavior when they encounter a new or different situation.

Since long it has been observed that, in order to reach real flexibility and improve their behavior, intelligent entities would need an *understanding* of how they do things. Beyond understanding, *awareness* should be a process whereby appropriate sentences about the world and its own mental situation come into the entity's consciousness, usually without intentional actions.

More recently, Singh, Minski and Eslick [6] consider awareness as the result of introspective (reflective, self-reflective and in the end self-conscious) layers of thought that are on top of deliberative thinking and of all the other forms of reasoning and reacting that constitute intelligent behavior. In this approach, an agent is seen as a collection of several agents, each one either encoding distinct kinds of ability or distinct ways of thinking, or representing different ways of

R. Basili and M.T. Pazienza (Eds.): AI*IA 2007, LNAI 4733, pp. 121–132, 2007.

doing the same thing. An architecture resulting form these considerations is being implemented at the MIT Media Lab [6].

In this paper, we propose a general agent model that goes in the direction of flexibility and adaptability. This is obtained by providing higher flexibility in how an agent is built and may evolve, and by equipping an agent with forms of understanding and awareness that we "situate" at different control layers. Beyond the basic control layer we in fact introduce a meta-control, where non-trivial supervising and tuning tasks (including agent reconfiguration) can be performed, based on suitable control and meta-control information. After a general discussion about the potentials of this new model, we shortly demonstrate by means of specific case-studies how the meta-control might be exploited, abstracting away from the details of the specific instance of the general model.

2   A General Agent Model

Below we define a general agent model by listing a set of aspects that we believe to be fundamental of the agent-oriented paradigm. We restrict ourselves to a high-level description of these aspects, leaving their specific description to the actual definition of specific instances of the general model. An *agent model* $\mathcal{M}$ which is an instance of this general model will encompass all or some of the aspects that we list, and will provide a specification of how they should be formalized. In fact, when realising an agent according to the agent model $\mathcal{M}$, every aspect present in $\mathcal{M}$ will correspond to a software component that will be described according to the languages/formalisms the components of $\mathcal{M}$ rely upon.

$\mathcal{M}$ is associated with an *underlying control mechanism* $\mathcal{U}^{\mathcal{M}}$ (or simply $\mathcal{U}$ when $\mathcal{M}$ is clear from the context). This control mechanism implements the run-time behavior of the agents. In some agent models this behavior may be implemented according to a given semantics, in other models there may be some other kind of specification. In practice, $\mathcal{U}$ can be an interpreter, or an inference engine, or a virtual machine, or any other kind of implementation.

Definition 1. *An agent model $\mathcal{M}$ results from the choice of (some of) the aspects listed below.*

- *A set of* beliefs, *possibly divided into various modules/theories, encompassing (some of) the following activities: reasoning, planning, proactivity, reaction, constraint solving, goal identification, preferences, history, communication management.*
- *A set of* desires *(goals that have been adopted or goals that are under considerations) and* intentions *(plans in execution and plans under analysis).*
- *A set of* constraints, *including temporal constraints that either induce or verify a partial order among actions in intentions and goals.*
- *A set of mechanisms for interacting with the environment including: a sensing mechanism/device, an actuating mechanism/device, a mechanism/device supporting communication to and from other agents.*

- *A set of mechanisms for* managing beliefs *including: a learning mechanism, a belief revision mechanism.*
- *A* control component *for combining, exploiting and supervising the above* components, *based on* control information *aimed at improving the control* mechanism effectiveness.

Agents defined according to a model $\mathcal{M}$ will be referred to as $\mathcal{M}$-agents.

2.1 About Beliefs

The set of beliefs expresses what the agent knows, can do and is able to remember. Thus, beliefs are not only facts but can also be: sets of facts annotated in various ways (e.g. histories, preferences); modules including sets of rules and/or procedural knowledge, capable in principle to exploit factual knowledge, possibly with the help of annotations expressing preferences or biases about which module to use when. Beliefs can be expressed by means of logical theories and/or by means of other formalisms/languages. The agent life starts with an initial set of beliefs that evolves over time according to the agent's interactions with the environment. These interactions are supported by the mechanisms of sensing, actuating and communication, that will vary depending on the kind of world where the agent operates.

The desires and intentions encode what the agent is doing or is intending to do during its operation. They are the outcome of putting beliefs at work in a given setting. The execution of intentions determines an evolution of the beliefs. This in accordance to the given mechanisms for managing beliefs (learning and belief revision), that affect what new knowledge an agent will acquire (which includes what the agent is able/wishing to remember, and in which form) and how it will process (by belief revision) its own knowledge, possibly by incorporating new learned knowledge or by eliminating (forgetting) what is considered to be no longer useful.

In fact (as discussed in depth in [3] and in the references therein), it is useful for an agent to have a "memory", that makes the agent potentially able to learn from experiences and ground what is believed through these experiences. Most methods to design agent memorization mechanisms distinguish among a "working memory", i.e., a workspace for reflective and reactive processes where explicit design-based reasoning occurs, and the "stored" knowledge and experiences. Stored items can be manipulated, interpreted and recombined to develop new knowledge, assist learning, form goals, and support interaction with the external environment.

The simplest way of defining the "static" agent memory [3]) is to see it as composed of the original beliefs augmented with *past events* that record the external stimuli perceived, the internal conclusions reached and the actions performed. Past events can play a role in reaching internal conclusions. These conclusions, that can be proactively pursued, can take the role of "dynamic" memory that supports decision-making and actions.

With time, a past event can be overridden on the one hand by more recent ones of the same kind (where the last one is the "current" one) and on the other hand by more recent ones of different kind, which are however somehow related to it. The old version will be kept in case the agent has to maintain a record of the state of the world and of its changes or otherwise they will be removed, according to given conditions.

Concerning rules or sets of rules (or other forms of "procedural" knowledge), if either they have not fulfilled the agent's expectations or a better version has been learned, then they can be de-activated and, later, even removed, again according to specific conditions or properties that define their usefulness. This topic will be further pursued in Section 4 and has been discussed in [2].

2.2   About Control

The control component is responsible for deploying the other components of the agent model, with the help of the control information, in order to render the agent operative. The control mechanism usually guarantees liveliness (the agent tries to stay alive at least until its objectives have been reached) and decides which features have to be employed at each stage (according to preferences). The control information may be partly provided in advance, e.g., by indicating: which order, which priorities and which preconditions are to be assigned to the application of different control functionalities; and which is the time limit or minimum frequency in performing some activities, for instance reaction. Other control information can be generated by the control itself, e.g. concerning: whether an intention has either been achieved or is failed or is timed-out or is still under work; whether constraint verification on some aspects of the agent work has been successful or not. The control information could be seen as part of the beliefs, and the beliefs themselves concur to form it, but we believe it is useful to separate it.

2.3   Concrete Agent and Agent Evolution

A concrete agent *program* will result from the choice of a component for each of the features of the model. An agent will then result from activating the control in the context of an environment where the sensing, actuating and communication capabilities can be put at work.

The working agent (following the concrete agent program according to the underlying control) can be given a meaning (e.g. a semantics, or at least a description) in terms of either a declarative or an operational semantics, or by means of some other characterization. The agent will in general pass through a sequence of stages, in that it will be affected by the interaction with the environment, that will lead it to respond, to set and pursue goals, to either record or prune items of information, etc. This process, that we can call the agent *life*, can be understood in at least two ways: the same agent proceeding into a sequence of states, each state encoding the present version of beliefs, desires, intentions and each state transition encoding what kind of control step has been done, including steps of learning and belief revision; successive transformations of the initial agent into new agents, that are its descendants in that the program has changed by modifying the beliefs, desires, intentions, and by learning and belief revision steps; each transformation is determined by the step that has been done. Formally, an agent starts from a program that defines it, according to the given agent model.

Definition 2. *Let $\mathcal{M}$ be an agent model. An agent program $\mathcal{P}_\mathcal{M}$ is a tuple $\langle \mathcal{B}, \mathcal{DI}, \mathcal{SC}, \mathcal{BM}, \mathcal{CS}, \mathcal{C}, \mathcal{CI} \rangle$ of software components where $\mathcal{B}$ is the set of beliefs, $\mathcal{DI}$ the set of desires and intentions, CS the set of constraints, $\mathcal{SC}$ the sensing, actuating and communication component, $\mathcal{BM}$ the belief management, $\mathcal{C}$ the control component and $\mathcal{CI}$ the control information. Each component of the tuple is defined (or omitted) according to $\mathcal{M}$.*

We can take the agent program $\mathcal{P}_\mathcal{M}$ as the *initial state* of the agent where nothing has happened yet. below, we represent an agent program simply as $\mathcal{P}$ when $\mathcal{M}$ is clear from the context.

Definition 3. *The* initial agent A_0 *is an agent program* $\mathcal{P} = \langle \mathcal{B}_0, \mathcal{DI}_0, \mathcal{SC}_0, \mathcal{BM}_0, \mathcal{CS}_0, \mathcal{C}_0, \mathcal{CI}_0 \rangle$.

The operational behavior of the agent will result from the control component and the control information, which rely on the underlying control mechanism that implements the operational counterpart of the agent model.

Definition 4. *Given an agent model $\mathcal{M}$, the* underlying control mechanism $\mathcal{U}^\mathcal{M}$ *(or $\mathcal{U}$ in short), able to put in operation the various components of $\mathcal{M}$, is a transformation function operating in terms of a set of distinguishable steps, starting from A_0 and transforming it step by step into A_1, A_2, ..., given $\mathcal{C}$ and $\mathcal{CI}$ as defined in $A_0, A_1, A_2, \ldots$ respectively.*

Definition 5. *Let M be an agent model, $\mathcal{U}$ the control mechanism associated to it, and $\mathcal{P}$ an agent program. Then, $\forall i \geq 0$, $A_i \rightarrow^{\mathcal{U}(\mathcal{C}_i, \mathcal{CI}_i)} A_{i+1}$.*

Notice that the A_js do not deterministically follow from A_0, as there is the unforeseen interaction with the external environment, and the agent internal choices that are not in general deterministic.

Each transition step can in principle modify all the agent components. The most likely to be modified are the beliefs, desires and intentions but also the constraints (by adding/dropping constraints) and the control information. However, the control component replacing itself appears to be awkward, circular and not so easily feasible. Also, the agent evolution as defined above is determined on the one hand by interactions with the environment and on the other hand by the agent inner non-determinism. One might wonder how the evolution might be constrained to follow desirable directions or, symmetrically, to avoid unwanted behavior. We will discuss in the rest of the paper possible enhancements of the general agent model aimed at providing flexible and more powerful control.

2.4 Instances

Several agent models are in fact instances if the proposed abstract model. To demonstrate this claim, we consider the following well-known and fully implemented models.

The KGP agent model [5] is an instance of this abstract model. In fact, KGP agents are equipped with the following components.

(1) A set of bcliefs, equipped with a set of *reasoning capabilities*, for reasoning with the information available in the agent state. These capabilities include Planning, Temporal Reasoning, Reactivity, Goal Decision, and Temporal Constraint Satisfiability. The beliefs include a component (KB_0), recording any information sensed from the environment, as well as a history of executed actions.

(2) A set of *goals* and *plans*; goals and plan components have associated times and temporal constraints, inducing a partial order. The agent is committed to all its goals and plans, at any given time.

(3) A sensing capability, allowing agents to observe their environment and actions (including utterances) by other agents.

(3) An actuating capability, allowing agents to affect their environment (including by performing utterances).

(4) Control information, including: a set of *transition rules*, changing the agent's state; the transition rules are defined in terms of the capabilities, and their effect is dependent on the concrete time of their application; a set of *selection functions* to select inputs to transitions.

(5) A control component, for deciding which enabled transition should be next, based on the selection functions, the current time, and the previous transition. This component is defined in declarative terms [4].

The DALI agent model is also an instance of this abstract model in that includes: (i) A set of beliefs, including reactive rules, support for proactivity and reasoning, planning, constraint satisfiability. Beliefs also include the *past events* that record (with a time-stamp) what has happened in the past: events perceived and reacted to, proactive initiatives, goals reached, etc. The past events can be organized into histories on which properties can be verified by means of constraints.

(ii) A sensing capability, allowing agents to observe their environment and actions by other agents.

(iii) A set of constraints for verifying that the agent's course of actions respects some properties and does not present anomalies.

(iv) A learning component for recording past events and building histories; a belief revision component for removing old information based on conditions. More advanced components are also provided, for acquiring, testing and finally either incorporating or dropping knowledge acquired from other agents.

(v) Control information defining: the frequency and the time intervals for attempting specific goals, that trigger proactive behavior; which past events should be recorded, and for how long they should be kept. These directives may involve significant (temporal) conditions.

(vi) The control component is missing, as the control information is directly exploited by the underlying control mechanism.

3   Enhancing the Agent Model

We may notice that while beliefs, desires, intentions and interaction components deal with the relationship between the agent and its environment, control deals with the need that an agent has of self-activating and self-tuning its own behavior, according to conditions that may vary over time. That is why in our general model we have made aspects of control explicit. For the specific agent models we have considered: KGP introduces a control theory that describes the control behavior in terms of which transitions to activate when; DALI provides explicit directives based on constraints so as to influence the standard behavior of an underlying operational mechanism with respect to which activities are allowed and at which frequency they should be attempted.

Then control, or at least the aspects of control which are made explicit, can be seen as the meta-level part of the agent. However, the control component can affect in general many aspects of the agent, besides its own behavior. It can supervise and monitor the agent evolution and possibly verify some properties. However, in the setting introduced up to now it can do so in only a pre-defined, hard-wired manner.

Going a step further, it can be useful to introduce a higher layer of *meta-control*, where supervising, tuning and monitoring capabilities are made explicit. In fact, as beliefs, desires and intentions change over time, more general forms of change might occur. Every agent component might in principle be either changed or replaced when needed, i.e., when either the agent evolution or environmental changes call for these modifications. Below we list some potential higher-level modifications that can be made by the meta-control.

(a) The control component itself can be chosen among different possible alternatives: the control component presently at work can be replaced by another one based on specific needs at certain stages of the agent life. For instance, an agent may find itself in a critical situation where it needs to be quick and eager on reacting, while later it may need to reason on what happened so as to set or revise its goals, even at the expense of being slower in reaction.

(b) The components defining mechanisms for managing beliefs can be tuned or replaced by others. For instance, with respect to learning, an agent at the beginning of its life can be either poor of devoid of knowledge, and thus can be wishful to acquire and incorporate new knowledge coming from its environment. Later, when the agent becomes more knowledgeable and competent, it can choose to be more cautious in incorporating external knowledge.

(c) Intentions can be filtered according to *a posteriori* preferences based on how the plans are going on.

(d) High-level aspects of the agent behavior can be monitored, e.g. how many goals are pursued, or how often a certain goal succeeds, or whether some general properties are verified.

(e) In the beliefs, non-trivial modifications can also be made, for instance for replacing/adding/dropping knowledge modules that were already available to the agent, but had not been chosen in its first instantiations, or for adding/dropping new knowledge modules that have been acquired by means of learning.

4   Meta-control

In this Section, we explicitly augment the basic abstract agent model by formally introducing the meta-control. We then discuss how the meta-control might be exploited, and propose specific case-studies.

The meta-control acts by means of single steps, similarly to the control. We may assume that also the meta-control, that we call $\mathcal{MC}$, relies upon some suitable form of control information that we indicate by $\mathcal{MCI}$. We assume to perform some steps of meta-control after a number of steps of control. We do not specify here how many these steps are: they may be specified either in advance (built-in in $\mathcal{U}^{\mathcal{M}}$) or in the control information. Accordingly, in the definition below we assume that agent A_i evolves through n_i steps of control from stage A_i to stage A_{i+n_i}. Then, we assume that a number m_i of meta-control steps take place, until stage $A_j = A_{i+n_i+m_i}$.

Definition 6. *Let $\mathcal{M}$ be an agent model and $\mathcal{U}^{\mathcal{M}}$ be a control mechanism associated to it. Let $\mathcal{MC}$ and $\mathcal{MCI}$ be the meta-control and the meta-control information, respectively, associated with $\mathcal{M}$. Then, given an agent program $\mathcal{P}_{\mathcal{M}}$,*

- *the* extended agent program *is $\mathcal{P}'_{\mathcal{M}} = (\mathcal{P}_{\mathcal{M}}, \mathcal{MC}, \mathcal{MCI})$;*
- *the* meta-control *$\mathcal{H}^{\mathcal{M}}$ ($\mathcal{H}$ in short) associated with $\mathcal{M}$ is such that $\mathcal{H}(\mathcal{MC}, \mathcal{MCI})$ denotes a transformation/transition function responsible for the agent extended program;*
- *the operational behavior of the agent equipped with $\mathcal{P}'_{\mathcal{M}}$, is obtained as follows: $\forall i > 0\ A_i \to^{\mathcal{U}(\mathcal{C}_i, \mathcal{CI}_i)} \ldots A_{i+n_i} \to^{\mathcal{H}(\mathcal{MC}_i, \mathcal{MCI}_i)} A_j$ where $A_j = A_{i+n_i+m_i}$ and $\forall k \geq 0\ A_k = \langle \mathcal{B}_k, \mathcal{DI}_k, \mathcal{SC}_k, \mathcal{BM}_k, \mathcal{CS}_k, \mathcal{C}_k, \mathcal{CI}_k \rangle$.*

Based on suitable meta-control information, the meta-control can be exploited either in a domain-dependent or in a domain-independent fashion for supervising, checking, tuning many aspects. To illustrate this point we will consider at some length the following two possible applications of the meta-control.

- Detect anomalies in the agent behavior, concerning the management of events and goals, and check temporal properties about the overall agent life.
- In case of execution of parallel plans for goals that are not compatible (i.e., the agent may profit from keeping several ways open, before being forced to choose eventually) evaluate the state of plans and consider whether one should be chosen and the others dropped.

4.1   Detecting Anomalies, Checking and Enforcing Properties

Another example of the useful role that the meta-control can assume concerns supervising how the agent itself proceeds and reflecting on the techniques that are being used. The latter may lead to a reconfiguration of the agent by replacing some of its components.

Supervising activities may rely upon a *meta-history* generated during the agent operation, that integrates in time the existing meta-control information $\mathcal{MCI}$. For instance, the meta-history may contain a list of: which goals have been set, at which time; which goals result to be successful/failed/timed-out, at which time. Which incoming external events were known to the agent (and thus has been reacted to) and which ones instead were unknown.

Various properties that should be respected by the agent behavior can be expressed on the meta-history, also in terms of (adapted versions of) temporal statements. We propose below some examples.

(1) There cannot be too many unknown events:
$$prop1 :\text{-} ALWAYS \, \sharp known\_evs \, > \, \sharp unknown\_evs$$
(2) A certain goal g should never fail or be timed-out:
$$prop2 :\text{-} NEVER \, failed(g) \, OR \, timed\_out(g)$$
(3) A certain goal g should eventually succeed (by time t):
$$prop3 :\text{-} EVENTUALLY \, successful(g) : t$$
(4) A certain goal g should not fail too often (i.e., more than n times) in a time interval $t_1 - t_2$:
$$prop4 :\text{-} NEVER \, \sharp failed(g) \, > \, n \, : \, t_1 - t_2$$

If a property is not respected, the meta-control may take suitable countermeasures. One could be to inform either a supervisor agent or the user. Otherwise, better, it might operate on the agent so as to try to enforce the properties for the future. In the above cases, the following measures might be respectively taken: (1), the learning module should be explicitly activated so as to learn reactive rules for the unknown events; (2) the planning module should be replaced; (3)-(4) preferences among goals should be modified, so as to give goal g higher priority.

The meta-control can also detect various anomalies in the agent behavior by extracting information from the agent "memory" discussed in Section 2 (for an extensive and formal discussion refer to [3]). In particular, let P be the set of the last versions of past events and let PNV be the set of the previous versions that have been kept.

Actions performed (or goals pursued) in an incorrect order. Suppose for instance that an agent bought a goldfish and an aquarium. To keep the fish safe, it is necessary to first fills the aquarium and then put the animal inside. So, the expected action sequence will be (where actions are indicated by the postfix A for the sake of readability): $fill\_the\_aquarium_A$, $put\_inside\_fish_A$.

In order to control the action execution correctness, one has to verify that agent does not perform the second action before the first one. To this aim, we can adopt the following *existential constraint*. It is based on the assumption that every action, after being performed, is recorded in P as a past event (with postfix P instead of A), associated to a time-stamp indicating when it has been accomplished.

$$fill\_the\_aquarium_P : T_1 \; \exists \triangleleft \, put\_inside\_fish_P : T_2, \{T_2 < T_1\}.$$

It states that, if the agent has accomplished the action $put\_inside\_fish_A$ at the time T_2 and the action $fill\_the\_aquarium_A$ at time T_1 where $T_2 < T_1$, then the action sequence is not correct and we are in the presence of *Incorrect time execution* anomaly. The connective $\exists\triangleleft$ indicates a constraint which is violated whenever the left-hand side is implied by the current history and at least an occurrence of the right-hand side is implied as well.

An action (goal) is executed (pursued) a number of times greater than an expected threshold. This anomaly is strictly related to PNV events. Consider for instance an agent that has bought something, i.e., a car. It has to pay a number of instalments during the current year. If it pays a further instalment, the expected behavior is violated, and the violation can be detected by the following *existential constraint*. It controls whether the cardinality of the set of past events *pay_instalment* in PNV is greater than the threshold, in which case trying to pay a further instalment constitutes a wrong behavior.

$$pay\_instalment(Value, Date))_P : T \; \exists \triangleleft$$
$$\{N = \Delta_n^{PNV}(pay\_instalment(Value, Date)), \; N > 20, \; T > 0\}.$$

These *Behavioral constraints* are to be checked from time to time by the meta-control in order to point out the anomalies and take appropriate counter-measures.

4.2   Parallel Plans

Normally, a plan (intention) can be either under consideration, or successful, or failed or timed-out. Let us us introduce the notion of *feasible* plan, namely a plan where all preliminary non-committal actions have been successfully performed (i.e., if the goal is to go to the theatre, a corresponding plan is feasible if by calling the booking office we ensure that tickets are still available) but all proper unrecoverable actions (i.e., buying the tickets) have not been performed yet. A goal is feasible if it admits a feasible plan.

If we have a meta-control, instead of choosing the most preferred among a set of goals and try to achieve it, a more general strategy can be adopted. The agent might in fact try to achieve all goals in parallel, where however the achievement process should be divided into two stages: (i) feasibility verification and (ii) actual achievement of a feasible goal. The meta-control can (in the perspective of resource-bounded reasoning) wait until some predefined time amount has elapsed. Then, it can verify which of the attempted goals result to be feasible at that time (the others will be considered to be timed-out). Finally, the meta-control can choose the most preferred goal among feasible ones. This is the goal which will actually proceed to be completed.

Assuming that the agent is able to exploit real parallelism in executing plans (e.g., by means of delegation to "children" agents) we have the following:

Property 1. In presence of meta-control the number of achieved goals increases or stays the same over time. It stays the same if the most preferred goal is always feasible, strictly increases otherwise.

Notice that previously defined controls can take a role in enforcing the above-defined property. In fact, ensuring that goal achievement proceeds without apparent anomalies brings advantages to subsequent goals that depend (explicitly or implicitly) on previous ones. E.g., referring to the above examples, the goal of, for instance, saving a certain amount of money by the end of the year becomes more feasible if one avoids useless expenses (like e.g., paying extra instalments or making other expenses that can be catched by similar constraints).

5   Learning

In [1] we have introduced the possibility for an agent to learn reactive rules and plans. Once acquired, the new knowledge is stored in two forms: as plain knowledge added to the set of beliefs, so that the agent is able to use it and as meta-information, that permits the agent to "trace" the new knowledge, in the sense of recording what has been acquired, when and with what expectations. The meta-control, if present, can exploit this meta-information to reason about these aspects. If the agent should conclude that the new rules must be removed because the expectations have not been met, the meta-information will be used to locate the rules in the set of beliefs and remove them.

In [2] we envisage a setting where agents interact with users with the objective of training them in some particular task, and/or with the aim of monitoring them for ensuring some degree of consistence and coherence in user behavior. We assume that agents are able to elicit (e.g. by inductive learning) the behavioral patterns that the user is adopting, and are also able to learn rules and plans from other agents by imitation (or by being told). An internal meta-control component can perform an appropriate evaluation of the learned knowledge.

The meta-control may also manage social aspects. In fact, in many applications the role of the society is crucial. As a future development, we mean to specify a meta-meta-control which is present in every agent which participates in a society. This higher level should be responsible for social information exchange, by exploiting and developing techniques based on social evaluation and consensus, involving credibility measures and overall preferences. According to this vision, the society will have the role of proposing behavioral rules (that are socially accepted) to its agents, which have the freedom to accept them in accordance to their experience and to the type of user they are monitoring.

6   Conclusions

We have presented a very general, abstract agent model, and we have shown, informally, how this general model instantiates to some existing agent models. We have extended the model with "meta-control" features. We have argued that this meta-control feature can be very useful for guaranteeing properties of the agent behavior. In the future, we will study whether for particular instances of the abstract agent model, it would be possible to prove concretely these properties.

Acknowledgements

This research was partially funded by a Senior Visiting Fellowship in Communications supported by The Royal Academy of Engineering and the Vodafone Group Foundation, UK.

References

1. Costantini, S., Dell'Acqua, P., Pereira, L.M., Tocchio, A.: Conditional learning of rules and plans in logical agents (submitted)
2. Costantini, S., Dell'Acqua, P., Pereira, L.M., Toni, F.: Towards a model of evolving agents for ambient intelligence. In: ASAmI'07. Proc. of Symposium on Artificial Societies for Ambient Intelligence (2007)
3. Costantini, S., Tocchio, A.: Memory-driven dynamic behavior checking in logical agents. In: Electronic Proceedings of CILC'06, Italian Conference on Computational Logic (2006), `http://cilc2006.di.uniba.it/programma.html`
4. Kakas, A.C., Mancarella, P., Sadri, F., Stathis, K., Toni, F.: Declarative agent control. In: Leite, J.A., Torroni, P. (eds.) Computational Logic in Multi-Agent Systems. LNCS (LNAI), vol. 3487, Springer, Heidelberg (2005)
5. Kakas, A.C., Mancarella, P., Sadri, F., Stathis, K., Toni, F.: The KGP model of agency. In: Proc. ECAI-2004 (2004)
6. Singh, P., Minski, M., Eslick, I.: Computing commonsense. BT Technology Journ. 22(4), 201–210 (2004)

Goal Generation with Ordered Beliefs

Célia da Costa Pereira and Andrea G.B. Tettamanzi

Università degli Studi di Milano
Dipartimento di Tecnologie dell'Informazione
Via Bramante 65, I-26013 Crema (CR), Italy
`pereira@dti.unimi.it`, `andrea.tettamanzi@unimi.it`

Abstract. A rational agent adopts (or changes) its desires/goals when new information becomes available or its "desires" (e.g., tasks it is supposed to carry out) change. In conventional approaches on goal generation a desire is adopted if and only if *all* conditions leading to its generation are satisfied. The fact that certain beliefs might be differently relevant in the process of desire/goal generation is not considered. As a matter of fact, a belief could be crucial for adopting a given goal but less crucial for adopting another goal. Besides, a belief could be more influent than another in the generation of a particular goal.

We propose an approach which takes into account the relevance of beliefs (more or less *useful* and more or less *prejudicial*) in the desire/goal generation process. More precisely, we propose a logical framework to represent changes in the mental state of an agent depending on the acquisition of new information and/or on the arising of new desires, by taking into account the fact that some beliefs may help the generation of a goal while others may prevent it.

We compare this logical framework with one where relevance of beliefs is not accounted for, and we show that the novel framework favors the adoption of a broader set of goals, exhibiting a behavior which imitates more faithfully how goals are generated/adopted in real life.

1   Introduction

Although there has been much discussion on belief change, goal change has not received much attention. Most of the works on goal *change* found in the literature do not build on results on belief change. That is the case of [3], in which the authors propose a formal representation for goals as rational desires and introduce and formalize dynamic goal hierarchies, but do not formalize explicitly beliefs and plans; or of [10], in which the authors propose an explicit representation of goals suited to conflict resolution based on a preference ordering of sets of goals. Another approach is [9], which models a multi-agent system in which an agent adopts a goal if requested to do so and the new goal is not conflicting with existing goals. This approach is based on goal persistence, i.e., an agent maintains its goals unless explicitly requested to drop them by the originating agent. The main lack of the above approaches is that they suppose that an agent does not use its own beliefs for updating goals in a general way. The work presented in [5], which is an extension and an adaptation of framework [11], consists

R. Basili and M.T. Pazienza (Eds.): AI*IA 2007, LNAI 4733, pp. 133–144, 2007.

in constructing dynamically the goal set to be pursued by a rational agent, by considering changes in its mental state. However, the fact that a belief might be more or less relevant for a given goal generation process is not considered.

In this work, we consider the direct relevance relation among beliefs with respect to a given goal, and how this relation influences the goal generation process. We divide the beliefs influencing the generation of a goal into two parts — the positive and the negative, which correspond, respectively, to beliefs which favor the generation of a goal and beliefs which may prevent it. In previous works on goal generation, positive (or negative) beliefs were implicitly represented by beliefs which must be true (or false) for generating a goal. If one of the beliefs does not abide by these requirements, the relevant goal is not generated. This is a strong restriction to the goal generation process. Indeed, in real life, depending on the importance an agent gives to each belief related to a goal, it may decide to generate the goal even if not all those conditions are verified. When making decisions or when choosing goals to realize, we often accept trade-offs. It is almost always impossible to have everything we really want. When considering beliefs, generating or not generating a goal depends essentially on the importance each belief has for the agent with respect to the the goal to be generated.

Let us consider the following example which we will use throughout the paper. Suppose you know one of your colleagues whom you trust is selling her house while you are looking for a house. Of course, you have some preferences concerning the house you would like to buy. Let us suppose that those preferences are expressed by the following rule: "if the house has a garden, is in the center of the town, and if it is not close to an airport, I would like to buy it". If your colleague tells you that the house has a garden and is in the center of the town but close to an airport, what will you do? If the fact that the house is not close to an airport is the most important requirement for you, you will never buy your colleague's house. Instead, if you deem more important to have a house with a garden, it would not be unthinkable that you buy a house with a garden even if it is close to an airport.

In this paper, we attempt to take into account this kind of relevance relation among beliefs in the goal generation process.

2   Preliminaries

In this section, we present the formalism which will be used throughout the paper. Such formalism is inspired by the formalisms used in [11,5]. However, unlike [11], but like [5], the objective of our formalism is to analyze, not to develop, agent systems. Precisely, our agent must single out a *largest* set of goals to be given as an input to a traditional planner component. That is because the intentions of the agent are not considered. We merely consider beliefs (the agent has about the world states), desires (or motivations) and relations (desire-adoption rules) wich define how the desire base will change with the acquisition of new beliefs and/or new desires. Unlike conventional approches [11,7,6,4,5] in which *all* beliefs influencing the generation of a desire *must* be considered, here, we merely consider those which *really* influence the generation of the desire according to a relevance relation among the beliefs.

2.1   Beliefs, Desires and Goals

The basic components of our language are *beliefs* and *desires*. Beliefs are represented by means of a *belief base*. A belief base consists of a consistent set of propositional formulas which describe the information an agent has about the world, as well as internal information. Desires are represented by means of a desire base. A desire base consists of a set of propositional formulas which represent the situations an agent would like to achieve. However, unlike the belief base, a desire base may be inconsistent, i.e., $\{\phi, \neg\phi\}$ may be a desire base. Goals, on the other hand, are represented by consistent desire bases.

Definition 1 (Belief Base and Desire Base). *Let $\mathcal{L}$ be a propositional language with $\top$ a tautology, and the logical connectives $\wedge$ and $\neg$ with the usual meaning. The agent belief base, denoted by σ, is a subset of $\mathcal{L}$, i.e., $\sigma \subseteq \mathcal{L}$. Similarly, the agent's desire base is denoted by γ, where $\gamma \subseteq \mathcal{L}$.*

We use the modal operator $\mathbf{B}$ to talk about the belief base and $\mathbf{D}$ to talk about the desire bases of an agent. Since the belief and desire bases of an agent are completely separated, there is no need to nest the operators $\mathbf{B}$ and $\mathbf{D}$.

Definition 2 (Belief and Desire Formulas). *Let ϕ be a formula of $\mathcal{L}$. An element, β, of the set of belief formulas $\mathcal{L}_B$ and an element κ of the set of desire formulas $\mathcal{L}_D$ are defined as follows:*

$$\beta ::= \top \mid \mathbf{B}\phi \mid \neg\mathbf{B}\phi \mid \beta_1 \wedge \beta_2,$$
$$\kappa ::= \top \mid \mathbf{D}\phi \mid \neg\mathbf{D}\phi \mid \kappa_1 \wedge \kappa_2.$$

2.2   Relevance Relation Among Beliefs w.r.t. a Desire

We extend the notion of useful and prejudicial beliefs, implicit in conventional approaches, by defining them as beliefs which *may* favor or prevent the generation of a desire. This is a more realistic setting, because it allows us to make trade-offs among beliefs in general, and between useful and prejudicial beliefs in particular, as it happens in real life. Indeed, even if a secondary useful belief is false or a secondary prejudicial belief is true we often generate a desire anyway. It all depends on the relevance/importance useful and prejudicial beliefs have in the process of goal generation. We will assume that these two kinds of beliefs are mutually exclusive for a given desire and, depending on the desire, a belief may be more or less relevant than another. Useful beliefs will be said in the rest of the paper *positive beliefs* (P_β), while prejudicial beliefs will be said *negative beliefs* (N_β).

Definition 3 (Positive and Negative Beliefs). *Given a belief $\beta \in \mathcal{L}_B$, let*

- P_β *denote the set of atoms $\mathbf{B}\phi$ such that the literal $\mathbf{B}\phi$ occurs in β, and*

— N_β *denote the set of atoms* $\mathbf{B}\phi$ *such that the literal* $\neg\mathbf{B}\phi$ *occurs in* β.

Note that a belief may be negative for a desire but positive for another.

Let us reconsider the example introduced in Section 1. Suppose you know one of your colleagues whom you trust is selling her house while you are looking for a house. Of course, you have some preferences concerning the house you would like to buy. Let us suppose that those preferences are expressed by the following rule for generating your desire "to buy a house", *bh*: "if the house has a garden, is in the center of the town, and if it is not close to an airport, I would like to buy it". If your colleague tells you the house has a garden and it is in the center of the town but close to an airport, your beliefs will be that the house has a garden ($\mathbf{B}hg$), it is in the center of the town ($\mathbf{B}hc$) but close to an airport ($\mathbf{B}ha$). $\mathbf{B}hg$ and $\mathbf{B}hc$ are positive beliefs, i.e., $P_\beta = \{\mathbf{B}hg, \mathbf{B}hc\}$, and $\mathbf{B}ha$ is a negative belief, i.e., $N_\beta = \{\mathbf{B}ha\}$. What will you do? Following a conventional approach, you would not desire to buy your collegue's house because it is close to an airport! However, in real life this kind of rule is less restrictive in the sense that you could decide to buy the house despite the fact it is close to an airport. Indeed, if your dream is to own a house with a garden and if possible in the center of the town, the rule would be expressed as "if the house has a garden, maybe it is also situated in the center of the town, and, if possible, it is not close to an airport, I would like to buy it". This rule corresponds to the previous rule, plus a relevance order among the beliefs. In this more realistic case, the answer to the above question depends on how relevant the beliefs you dispose of are for adopting your desire to buy that house. We define the relevance relation among beliefs as follows:

Definition 4 (Relevance Relation Among Beliefs). *Let* $\phi \in \mathcal{L}$ *be a desire,* $\beta, \beta' \in \mathcal{L}_B$ *be two belief formulas.* β *is at least as relevant as* β' *for generating desire* ϕ, *noted* $\beta \succeq_\phi \beta'$, *iff the information brought by* β *is at least as influential for generating* ϕ *as the information brought by* β'.

Remark 1. For all belief $\beta(\neq \top) \in \mathcal{L}_B$ we have $\beta \succ_\phi \top$. This means that having information is strictly more relevant than not.

In the example, if knowing that the house has a garden were more relevant for you than knowing that the house is in the center of the town, this could be represented by stating $\mathbf{B}hg \succeq_{bh} \mathbf{B}hc$. Besides, if you could not stand loud noise, this would be represented as $\mathbf{B}ha \succeq_{bh} \mathbf{B}hg$.

In the rest of the paper we will assume that an agent disposes of a total order $\succeq_\phi$ on beliefs for every desire ϕ. We can extend this relation from beliefs to sets of beliefs.

Definition 5 (Most Relevant Formulas). *Given a set* B *of belief formulas, the subset of the most relevant formulas of* B, *noted* $\mathrm{MRF}(B)$, *is defined as follows:*

$$\mathrm{MRF}(B) = \{\beta \in B : \neg\exists\beta' \in B, \beta' \succ \beta\}.$$

In the case of the example, $\mathrm{MRF}(\{\mathbf{B}hg, \mathbf{B}hc, \mathbf{B}ha\}) = \{\mathbf{B}ha\}$, if you cannot stand loud noise, or $\mathrm{MRF}(\{\mathbf{B}hg, \mathbf{B}hc, \mathbf{B}ha\}) = \{\mathbf{B}hg\}$, if your dream is to own a house with a garden.

Definition 6 (Comparing Sets of Beliefs w.r.t. a Desire). *Let B_1 and B_2 be two sets of beliefs. Let $\succeq_\phi$ be the relevance relation over the beliefs w.r.t. desire ϕ. $B_1 \succeq_\phi B_2$ iff $\exists \beta \in B_1 : \forall \beta' \in B_2, \beta \succeq_\phi \beta'$.*

Following [11] and [5], the antecedent of a desire-adoption rule consists of a belief condition and a desire condition; the consequent is a propositional formula. Intuitively, this means that if the belief and the desire conditions in the antecedent hold, the formula in the consequent is adopted as a desire. Unlike in the above-mentioned approaches, in which a belief holds if and only if all of its antecedent conditions are satisfied, here we consider that a belief β holds if and only if the most relevant positive beliefs in P_β hold and the most relevant negative belief in N_β that holds is not more relevant than the most relevant positive beliefs.

Coming back to the example, if your dream is to own a house with a garden, despite the information provided by your collegue that the house is close to an airport, your belief $\beta = \mathbf{B}hg \wedge \mathbf{B}hc \wedge \neg\mathbf{B}ha$ holds.

Definition 7 (Desire-Adoption Rules). *The language of desire-adoption rules $\mathcal{L}_R$ is defined as follows: $\mathcal{L}_R = \{\beta, \kappa \Rightarrow_D^+ \phi \mid \beta \in \mathcal{L}_B, \kappa \in \mathcal{L}_D, \phi \in \mathcal{L}\}$.*
The set of desire-adoption rules $\mathcal{R}_D$ of an agent is a finite subset of $\mathcal{L}_R$.

The desire adoption rule for the house example may be represented as $\mathbf{B}hg \wedge \mathbf{B}hc \wedge \neg\mathbf{B}ha, \top \Rightarrow_D^+ bh$ with $P_\beta = \{\mathbf{B}hg, \mathbf{B}hc\}$ and $N_\beta = \{\mathbf{B}ha\}$.

Remark 2. $P_\beta = \emptyset$ counts as $\top$ and $N_\beta = \emptyset$ counts as $\bot$.

If the only information relevant for you is that you would not like that the house were close to an airport, the rule may be written as $\neg\mathbf{B}ha, \top \Rightarrow_D^+ bh$, with $P_\beta = \emptyset$ and $N_\beta = \{\mathbf{B}ha\}$. Instead, if the only information relevant for you is that you would like a house with a garden, the desire-adoption rule may be written as $\mathbf{B}hg, \top \Rightarrow_D^+ bh$ with $P_\beta = \{\mathbf{B}hg\}$ and $N_\beta = \emptyset$.

Given a desire adoption rule R, we shall denote $\mathrm{lhs}(R)$ the antecedent of R, and $\mathrm{rhs}(R)$ the consequent of R. Furthermore, if S is a set of rules, we define $\mathrm{rhs}(S) = \{\mathrm{rhs}(R) : R \in S\}$.

3   Mental State Representation

We assume that an agent is equipped with three bases:

- Belief base $\sigma \subseteq \mathcal{L}$;
- Desire base $\gamma \subseteq \mathcal{L}$;
- Desire-adoption rule base $\mathcal{R}_D$.

The state of an agent is completely described by a triple $\mathcal{S} = \langle \sigma, \gamma, \mathcal{R}_D \rangle$.

The belief base, σ, represents the agent's beliefs about the world, $\mathcal{R}_D$ contains the rules which generate desires from beliefs and other (more basic) desires, and the desire base, γ, contains all desires which may be deduced from the agent's beliefs and the agents's desire-adoption rule base. In addition, we assume that an agent can be described using a relation of relevance among beliefs for every desire $\phi \in \mathcal{L}$ and a belief revision operator $*$, as discussed below.

The semantics we adopt for the belief and desire formulas are inspired by the semantics of belief and "goal" formulas proposed in [11,5].

Semantics of Belief Formulas. Let $\phi \in \mathcal{L}$ and $\mathcal{S} = \langle \sigma, \gamma, \mathcal{R}_D \rangle$ be the mental state of an agent. Let $\beta_1, \beta_2 \in \mathcal{L}_B$ and B be a set of belief formulas. The semantics of belief formulas and sets of beliefs formulas is given as

$$\mathcal{S} \models_{\mathcal{L}_B} \top,$$
$$\mathcal{S} \models_{\mathcal{L}_B} \mathbf{B}\phi \Leftrightarrow \sigma \models \phi,$$
$$\mathcal{S} \models_{\mathcal{L}_B} \neg\mathbf{B}\phi \Leftrightarrow \mathcal{S} \not\models_{\mathcal{L}_B} \mathbf{B}\phi,$$
$$\mathcal{S} \models_{\mathcal{L}_B} \beta_1 \wedge \beta_2 \Leftrightarrow \mathcal{S} \models_{\mathcal{L}_B} \beta_1 \text{ and } \mathcal{S} \models_{\mathcal{L}_B} \beta_2,$$
$$\mathcal{S} \models_{\mathcal{L}_B} B \Leftrightarrow \forall \beta \in B, \mathcal{S} \models_{\mathcal{L}_B} \beta.$$

Semantics of Desire Formulas. Let $\phi \in \mathcal{L}$ and $\mathcal{S} = \langle \sigma, \gamma, \mathcal{R}_D \rangle$ be the mental state of an agent. Let $\kappa_1, \kappa_2 \in \mathcal{L}_D$. The semantics of desire formulas is given as

$$\mathcal{S} \models_{\mathcal{L}_D} \top,$$
$$\mathcal{S} \models_{\mathcal{L}_D} \mathbf{D}\phi \Leftrightarrow \exists \gamma' \subseteq \gamma : (\gamma' \not\models \bot \text{ and } \gamma' \models \phi),$$
$$\mathcal{S} \models_{\mathcal{L}_D} \neg\mathbf{D}\phi \Leftrightarrow \mathcal{S} \not\models_{\mathcal{L}_D} \mathbf{D}\phi,$$
$$\mathcal{S} \models_{\mathcal{L}_D} \kappa_1 \wedge \kappa_2 \Leftrightarrow \mathcal{S} \models_{\mathcal{L}_D} \kappa_1 \text{ and } \mathcal{S} \models_{\mathcal{L}_D} \kappa_2.$$

In [6,4] a rule R is said to be active in state $\mathcal{S}$, noted by $\mathcal{S} \models_a \mathrm{lhs}(R)$, if and only if both, belief and desire conditions hold, i.e.,

$$\mathcal{S} \models_a \mathrm{lhs}(R) \Leftrightarrow (\mathcal{S} \models_{\mathcal{L}_B} \beta) \wedge (\mathcal{S} \models_{\mathcal{L}_D} \kappa).$$

With this definition, all belief literals in β of the form $\mathbf{B}\phi$ or $\neg\mathbf{B}\phi$ are regarded as having the same importance in the desire adoption process. The fact that an agent might adopt a desire/goal even if one of the beliefs in β were not satisfyed could not be taken into account.

In the example, your rule for adopting the desire to buy the house (bh) is "if the house has a garden, it is also situated in the center of the town and it is not situated near of the airport, I would buy it". Your colleague, whom you trust, tells you the house has a garden and it is situated in the center of the town but near to the airport, your beliefs will be that the house has a garden $(\mathbf{B}hg)$, it is in the center of the town $(\mathbf{B}hc)$ but near of the airport $(\mathbf{B}ha)$. Your desire-adoption rule is represented as $\mathbf{B}hg \wedge \mathbf{B}hc \wedge \neg\mathbf{B}ha, \top \Rightarrow_D^+ bh$ with $P_\beta = \{\mathbf{B}hg, \mathbf{B}hc\}$ and $N_\beta = \{\mathbf{B}ha\}$. If the relevance order among your beliefs is $\mathbf{B}hg \succeq_{bh} \mathbf{B}hc \succeq_{bh} \mathbf{B}ha$, by using the $\models_a$ approach you could not obtain a sensible decision, i.e., a decision which would consist of adopting the desire to buy your collegue's house anyway. It is because your desire-adoption rule would not be activated in a $\models_a$ based approach. To overcome such problem, we propose the following definition instead:

Definition 8 (Active Desire Adoption Rule). *Let $R \in \mathcal{R}_D$ be a desire adoption rule. R is active iff $\mathcal{S} \models_{\mathcal{L}_R} \mathrm{lhs}(R)$, i.e.,*

$$\begin{aligned}
\mathcal{S} \models_{\mathcal{L}_R} \mathrm{lhs}(R) \Leftrightarrow\; & (\mathcal{S} \models_{\mathcal{L}_B} \mathrm{MRF}(P_\beta)) \wedge \\
& (\neg \exists \beta' \in N_\beta | (\mathcal{S} \models_{\mathcal{L}_B} \beta') \wedge (\{\beta'\} \succ_{\mathrm{rhs}(R)} \mathrm{MRF}(P_\beta))) \wedge \quad (1) \\
& (\mathcal{S} \models_{\mathcal{L}_D} \kappa).
\end{aligned}$$

Rule R is active iff (i) the most relevant positive beliefs hold in state $\mathcal{S}$ and the most relevant negative beliefs in N_β that hold in $\mathcal{S}$ are not more relevant than the most relevant positive beliefs, and, (ii) the desire condition κ in the antecedent holds.

In the example, consider the rule $R : \mathbf{B}hg \wedge \mathbf{B}hc \wedge \neg \mathbf{B}ha, \top \Rightarrow_D^+ bh$. If $\mathbf{B}hg \succeq_{bh} \mathbf{B}ha$, i.e., loud noise does not disturb you very much while it is very importatnt for you to own a house with a garden, R is active. Instead, if $\mathbf{B}ha \succeq_{bh} \mathbf{B}hg$, R is not active.

Note that the rule $\top, \top \Rightarrow_D^+ \phi$ with $\beta = \top$ ($P_\beta = \emptyset$, $N_\beta = \emptyset$), is always active. Intuitively, this means that no matter what beliefs or other desires you have, you adopt desire ϕ.

Observation 1. $(\mathrm{MRF}(P_\beta) \succ_\phi \mathrm{MRF}(N_\beta)) \wedge (\mathcal{S} \models_{\mathcal{L}_B} \mathrm{MRF}(P_\beta)) \Rightarrow \mathcal{S} \models_{\mathcal{L}_R} \mathrm{lhs}(R)$.

Observation 2. $(\mathrm{MRF}(N_\beta) \succeq_\phi \mathrm{MRF}(P_\beta)) \wedge (\mathcal{S} \models_{\mathcal{L}_B} \mathrm{MRF}(N_\beta)) \Rightarrow \mathcal{S} \not\models_{\mathcal{L}_R} \mathrm{lhs}(R)$.

We can prove that $\models_{\mathcal{L}_R}$ is an extension of $\models_a$. Indeed,

Proposition 1. *If a rule R is active with $\models_a$, R is also active with $\models_{\mathcal{L}_R}$, i.e.,*

$$\mathcal{S} \models_a \mathrm{lhs}(R) \Rightarrow \mathcal{S} \models_{\mathcal{L}_R} \mathrm{lhs}(R).$$

The inverse is not true.

Proof.

$$\begin{aligned}
\mathcal{S} \models_a \mathrm{lhs}(R) \Rightarrow\; & (\mathcal{S} \models_{\mathcal{L}_B} \beta) \wedge (\mathcal{S} \models_{\mathcal{L}_D} \kappa); \\
\mathcal{S} \models_{\mathcal{L}_B} \beta \Rightarrow\; & (\forall \phi \in P_\beta, \mathcal{S} \models_{\mathcal{L}_B} \phi) \wedge (\forall \phi' \in N_\beta, \mathcal{S} \not\models_{\mathcal{L}_B} \phi'), \\
\Rightarrow\; & (\mathcal{S} \models_{\mathcal{L}_B} \mathrm{MRF}(P_\beta)) \wedge (\neg \exists \phi' \in N_\beta, \mathcal{S} \models_{\mathcal{L}_B} \phi'), \\
\Rightarrow\; & (\mathcal{S} \models_{\mathcal{L}_B} \mathrm{MRF}(P_\beta)) \wedge (\neg \exists \phi' \in N_\beta, (\mathcal{S} \models_{\mathcal{L}_B} \phi') \\
& \wedge (\{\phi'\} \succ_{\mathrm{rhs}(R)} \mathrm{MRF}(P_\beta)));
\end{aligned}$$

Therefore, $\mathcal{S} \models_a \mathrm{lhs}(R) \Rightarrow \mathcal{S} \models_{\mathcal{L}_R} \mathrm{lhs}(R)$. $\qquad\qquad\square$

Semantics of Desire-Adoption Rules. Let $\phi \in \mathcal{L}$ and let $\mathcal{S}$ be the mental state of an agent.

$$\phi \in \gamma \Leftrightarrow \exists R \in \mathcal{R}_D : \mathrm{rhs}(R) = \phi \wedge \mathcal{S} \models_{\mathcal{L}_R} \mathrm{lhs}(R).$$

Such a desire is said to be a *justified* desire.

Observation 3. *If γ' is the set of desires justified with $\models_a$ and γ the set of desires justified with $\models_{\mathcal{L}_R}$, we have $\gamma' \subseteq \gamma$.*

Goals, unlike desires, are represented by consistent desire sets.

Definition 9 (Candidate Goals). *A candidate goal set γ^* is a subset of the desire base which is consistent, i.e., it is a consistent set of justified desires.*

In the example, if in addition you believe that you will soon move abroad ($\mathbf{B}ma$), you will likely adopt the desire to abstain from buying a house ($\neg bh$). This fact may be represented with the rule $\mathbf{B}ma, \top \Rightarrow_D^+ \neg bh$. The initial desire-adoption rule was $\mathbf{B}hg \wedge \mathbf{B}hc \wedge \neg\mathbf{B}ha, \top \Rightarrow_D^+ bh$ and your belief base is now $\sigma = \{hg, hc, ha, ma\}$. In this case, your desire base is $\gamma = \{bh, \neg bh\}$ which is inconsistent. You cannot pursue these two desires at the same time. The two possible candidate goal sets are $\{bh\}$ and $\{\neg bh\}$.

Observation 4. *From Observation 3 and Definition 9 we may conclude that every candidate goal set for $\models_a$ is also a candidate goal set for $\models_{\mathcal{L}_R}$.*

More generally, if a set of goals is candidate to be pursued by an agent according to $\models_a$, it is also guaranted that all the elements of this set belong to a candidate goal set according to $\models_{\mathcal{L}_R}$.

Proposition 2. *Let γ' be the set of desires justified with $\models_a$ and γ be the set of desires justified with $\models_{\mathcal{L}_R}$. For all candidate goal sets $\gamma'^* \subseteq \gamma'$ there exists a candidate goal set $\gamma^* \subseteq \gamma$ such that $\gamma'^* \subseteq \gamma^*$.*

Proof. By Observation 4, γ'^* is also a candidate goal set in γ; therefore, there exists at least a candidate goal set $\gamma^* = \gamma'^* \subseteq \gamma$. In addition, there might be some desire in $\gamma \setminus \gamma'$ which is consistent with γ'^*; such desire could be added to γ'^* to obtain a candidate goal set $\gamma^* \supset \gamma'^*$. $\square$

4   Changes in the Mental State of an Agent

The acquisition of a new belief in state $\mathcal{S}$ may cause a change in the belief base σ and this may also cause a change in the desire set γ with the retraction of existing desires and/or the assertion of new desires. A desire ϕ is retracted from the desire set γ if and only if ϕ becomes not justified, i.e., all active desire-adoption rules such that $\mathrm{rhs}(R) = \phi$ become inactive. A desire ϕ is asserted into a desire set γ if and only if the new information activates a desire adoption rule R with $\mathrm{rhs}(R) = \phi$.

4.1   Changes Caused by a New Belief

The next definition introduces a notation to refer to the set of rules that become active, resp. inactive, after the acquisition of new information β in a given state $\mathcal{S} = \langle \sigma, \gamma, \mathcal{R}_D \rangle$. Let $*$ be the well known AGM operator for belief revision [1] and $\mathcal{S}' = \langle \sigma * \beta, \gamma, \mathcal{R}_D \rangle$ be the new resulting state.

Definition 10 (Rule activated/deactivated by a Belief). *We define the subsets* $\mathrm{Act}_\beta^{\mathcal{S}}$ *of* $\mathcal{R}_D$ *composed by the rules which become activated because of* β *as follows:*

$$\mathrm{Act}_\beta^{\mathcal{S}} = \{R : (\mathcal{S} \not\models_{\mathcal{L}_R} \mathrm{lhs}(R)) \wedge (\mathcal{S}' \models_{\mathcal{L}_R} \mathrm{lhs}(R))\}. \tag{2}$$

$\mathrm{Act}_\beta^{\mathcal{S}}$ *contains rules which are directly or indirectly activated by* β. *In the same way, we define the subset of* $\mathcal{R}_D$, $\mathrm{Deact}_\beta^{\mathcal{S}}$, *containing the rules which become directly or indirectly deactivated because of* β.

Three considerations must be taken into account:

1. By definition of the revision operator $*$, $\mathcal{S}' \models_{\mathcal{L}_B} \beta$, thus all desire-adoption rules $R \in \mathrm{Act}_\beta^{\mathcal{S}}$ become active and all new desires $\phi = \mathrm{rhs}(R)$ are asserted into the desire base γ;
2. If, before the arrival of β, $\mathcal{S} \models_{\mathcal{L}_B} \neg\beta$, then all active desire-adoption rules R, such that $\neg\beta \in \mathrm{MRF}(P_\beta)$ become inactive and, if there is not an active desire-adoption rule R', such that $\mathrm{rhs}(R') = \mathrm{rhs}(R)$, then the desire $\phi = \mathrm{rhs}(R)$ is retracted from the desire set γ;
3. Every active rule R such that $\beta \in N_\beta$ and $\{\beta\} \succ_{\mathrm{rhs}(R)} \mathrm{MRF}(P_\beta)$ becomes inactive and, if there is not an active desire-adoption rule R', such that $\mathrm{rhs}(R') = \mathrm{rhs}(R)$, then the desire $\phi = \mathrm{rhs}(R)$ is retracted from the desire set γ.

Let us suppose that your initial belief base is $\sigma = \{hg, hc, ha\}$, with $\mathbf{B}hg \succeq_{bh} \mathbf{B}hc \succeq_{bh} \mathbf{B}ha$, and that another condition to desire to buy a house is that you do not desire to save money (sm). Your initial desire-adoption rule may then be written as $R_1 : \mathbf{B}hg \wedge \mathbf{B}hc \wedge \neg\mathbf{B}ha, \neg\mathbf{D}sm \Rightarrow_D^+ bh$. Because your initial desire base is $\gamma = \emptyset$ (and then is such that $\mathcal{S} \not\models_{\mathcal{L}_D} sm$), it now becomes $\gamma = \{bh\}$. If same new information lets you think that you will lose your job (lj), you will likely adopt the desire to save money (sm). This fact may be represented with rule $R_2 : \mathbf{B}lj, \top \Rightarrow_D^+ sm$. Your believe base becomes $\sigma = \{hg, hc, ha, lj\}$ and your desire base becomes $\gamma = \{sm\}$. Indeed, the acquisition of belief lj implies the activation of rule R_2 which in turn implies the deactivation of rule R_1. Thus, if you belief that you will lose your job you do not adopt the desire to buy a house because you have to save money.

We can summarize the above considerations into one desire-updating formula which tells how the desire set γ of a rational agent in state $\mathcal{S}$ should change in response to the acquisition of a new belief β. Let $A_\beta^{\mathcal{S}}$ be the set of desires acquired because of the new belief β:

$$A_\beta^{\mathcal{S}} = \mathrm{rhs}(\mathrm{Act}_\beta^{\mathcal{S}}). \tag{3}$$

Let $L_\beta^{\mathcal{S}}$ be the set of desires lost because of the acquisition of the new belief β:

$$L_\beta^{\mathcal{S}} = \{\phi : \phi \in \mathrm{rhs}(\mathrm{Deact}_\beta^{\mathcal{S}}) \wedge \\ \neg\exists R\,(\mathcal{S} \models_{\mathcal{L}_R} \mathrm{lhs}(R) \wedge \mathrm{rhs}(R) = \phi)\}. \tag{4}$$

Let $\oplus$ be our operator for desire updating, and γ the base of agent's desires. According to the above considerations, we have:

$$\gamma \oplus \beta = (\gamma \cup A_\beta^{\mathcal{S}}) \setminus L_\beta^{\mathcal{S}}. \tag{5}$$

It is easy to verify that $A_\beta^{\mathcal{S}} \cap L_\beta^{\mathcal{S}} = \emptyset$, for all state $\mathcal{S}$.

In the approach [5] based on $\models_a$, in which relevances among beliefs are not considered, two considerations were made concerning the activation and the deactivation of a rule:

1. A rule R becomes active in state $\mathcal{S}$ if and only if all the components in its left hand side, $\mathrm{lhs}(R)$, are satisfied in $\mathcal{S}$;
2. If, before the arrival of β, $\neg\beta$ is satisfyied in state $\mathcal{S}$, then all active desire-adoption rules R, such that $\neg\beta \in \mathrm{lhs}(R)$, become inactive and, if there is not an active desire-adoption rule R', such that $\mathrm{rhs}(R') = \mathrm{rhs}(R)$, then the desire $\phi = \mathrm{rhs}(R)$ is retracted from the desire set γ.

We can note that these considerations are more restrictive than the considerations made in the approach presented here. Indeed,

Observation 5. *If $A'^{\mathcal{S}}_\beta$ and $A_\beta^{\mathcal{S}}$ are sets of rules activacted by new belief β according to $\models_a$ and $\models_{\mathcal{L}_R}$ respectively, we have $A'^{\mathcal{S}}_\beta \subseteq A_\beta^{\mathcal{S}}$.*

Observation 6. *If $L'^{\mathcal{S}}_\beta$ and $L_\beta^{\mathcal{S}}$ are sets of rules deactivacted by new belief β according to $\models_a$ and $\models_{\mathcal{L}_R}$ respectively, we have $L_\beta^{\mathcal{S}} \subseteq L'^{\mathcal{S}}_\beta$.*

Proposition 3. *The set corresponding to desires acquired because of β according to $\models_a$ are also acquired according to $\models_{\mathcal{L}_R}$, i.e., $\gamma' \oplus \beta \subseteq \gamma \oplus \beta$.*

Proof. From Observations 3,5,6 we have:

$$\phi \in \gamma' \oplus \beta \Rightarrow \phi \in \gamma' \cup A'^{\mathcal{S}}_\beta \text{ and } \phi \notin L'^{\mathcal{S}}_\beta$$
$$\Rightarrow \phi \in \gamma \cup A_\beta^{\mathcal{S}} \text{ and } \phi \notin L_\beta^{\mathcal{S}}$$
$$\Rightarrow \phi \in \gamma \oplus \beta. \qquad \square$$

4.2   Changes Caused by a New Desire

In [5] we have considered that a new desire ϕ might only be represented by a desire adoption rule R with an empty left hand side and such that $\mathrm{rhs}(R) = \phi$. Such a desire may be considered as an unconditional desire. Here, we relax this hypothesis by allowing a new desire to be represented with a desire-adoption rule with a non-empty left-hand side, i.e., as a conditional desire.

Let $\phi \in \mathcal{L}$ be a new desire arising in state $\mathcal{S} = \langle \sigma, \gamma, \mathcal{R}_D \rangle$. Let $\mathcal{S}' = \langle \sigma, \gamma \oplus \phi, \mathcal{R}_D \rangle$ be the resulting mental state.

Definition 11 (Rule Activated by a New Desire). *We define the subsets* $\mathrm{Act}_\phi^{\mathcal{S}}$ *of* $\mathcal{R}_D$ *composed by the rules which become activated because of* ϕ *as follows:*

$$\mathrm{Act}_\phi^{\mathcal{S}} = \{R : (\mathcal{S} \not\models_{\mathcal{L}_R} \mathrm{lhs}(R)) \wedge (\mathcal{S}' \models_{\mathcal{L}_R} \mathrm{lhs}(R))\}. \tag{6}$$

$\mathrm{Act}_\phi^{\mathcal{S}}$ contains rules which are directly or indirectly activated because of ϕ. Because the desire base may be inconsistent, the new acquired desire ϕ and the desires in the consequent of the rules activated because of ϕ are automatically asserted into γ.

In the same way, we may define the subset of $\mathcal{R}_D$, $\mathrm{Deact}_\phi^{\mathcal{S}}$ containing the rules which become directly or indirectly deactivated because of ϕ.

Let $\mathcal{S}$ be the state of the agent, and $A_\phi^{\mathcal{S}} = \{\mathrm{rhs}(R) : R \in \mathrm{Act}_\phi^{\mathcal{S}}\}$ be the set of desires acquired with the arising of ϕ in state $\mathcal{S}$. Let $\otimes$ be the operator for updating the desire-adoption rule base.

How does $\mathcal{S}$ change with the arising of the new desire ϕ?

1. The desire-adoption rule $R : \beta, \kappa \Rightarrow_D^+ \phi$ is added to $\mathcal{R}_D$,
2. If $\mathcal{S} \models_{\mathcal{L}_R} \mathrm{lhs}(R)$ then:
   - ϕ is added to γ,
   - All desire-adoption rules R' in $\mathrm{Act}_\phi^{\mathcal{S}}$ become activated, and all desires appearing in the right hand side of these rules are also added to γ.

Therefore,

$$\mathcal{R}_D \otimes \phi = \mathcal{R}_D \cup \{\beta, \kappa \Rightarrow_D^+ \phi\} \tag{7}$$

and, if $\mathcal{S} \models_{\mathcal{L}_R} \mathrm{lhs}(R)$,

$$\gamma \oplus \phi = \gamma \cup \{\phi\} \cup A_\phi^{\mathcal{S}}; \tag{8}$$

otherwise,

$$\gamma \oplus \phi = \gamma. \tag{9}$$

which means that a conditional desire is adopted if and only if the desire-adoption rule representing it is active.

5 Conclusion

A new approach to goal generation has been proposed. This approach takes into consideration desire changes, belief changes and the relevance order among the beliefs which influence the goal generation process for a goal. This order represents the fact that a belief which influences the generation of a desire/goal may be more or less relevant than another belief and then its occurrence may be more or less decisive for generating the goal.

An important result of this approach is that it is possible to generate goals using less information than in conventional approaches. In particular, concerning beliefs it is enough to dispose of information about the more relevant positive (useful) and negative (prejudicial) beliefs which really influence the goal generation process. Another important result is that the set of desires/goals obtained using this approach is a superset of the set of goals obtained by using the approaches which do not take into consideration the relevance order among beliefs. More precisely, this approach allows us to decrease the risk of not generating some "valid" desires/goals.

References

1. Alchourrón, C.E., Gärdenfors, P., Makinson, D.: On the logic of theory change: Partial meet contraction and revision functions. J. Symb. Log. 50(2), 510–530 (1985)
2. Amgoud, L., Kaci, S.: On the generation of bipolar goals in argumentation-based negotiation. In: Rahwan, I., Moraïtis, P., Reed, C. (eds.) ArgMAS 2004. LNCS (LNAI), vol. 3366, pp. 192–207. Springer, Heidelberg (2005)
3. Bell, J., Huang, Z.: Dynamic goal hierarchies. In: PRICAI '96. Proceedings from the Workshop on Intelligent Agent Systems, Theoretical and Practical Issues, pp. 88–103. Springer, London, UK (1997)
4. da Costa Pereira, C., Tettamanzi, A.: Towards a framework for goal revision. In: Pierre-Yves Schobbens, W.V., Schwanen, G. (eds.) BNAIC-06. Proceedings of the 18th Belgium-Netherlands Conference on Artificial Intelligence, October 5-6, University of Namur, Namur, Belgium (2006)
5. da Costa Pereira, C., Tettamanzi, A.: A belief-desire framework for goal revision. In: Jain, L.C., Howlett, R.J. (eds.) Proceedings of KES 2007, Vietri sul mare, September 12–14, Springer, Heidelberg (2007) (to appear)
6. da Costa Pereira, C., Tettamanzi, A., Amgoud, L.: Goal revision for a rational agent. In: Brewka, G., Coradeschi, S., Perini, A., Traverso, P. (eds.) ECAI 2006. Proceedings of the 17th European Conference on Artificial Intelligence, August 29–September 1, pp. 747–748. IOS Press, Riva del Garda, Italy (2006)
7. Hulstijn, J., Broersen, J., Dastani, M., van der Torre, L.: Goal generation in the boid architecture. Cognitive Science Quarterly Journal 2(3–4), 428–447 (2002)
8. Rahwan, I., Amgoud, L.: An argumentation based approach for practical reasoning. In: AAMAS '06. Proceedings of the fifth international joint conference on Autonomous agents and multiagent systems, pp. 347–354. ACM Press, New York, USA (2006)
9. Shapiro, S., Lespérance, Y., Hector, J., Levesque, H.J.: Goal change. In: Kaelbling, L.P., Saffiotti, A. (eds.) IJCAI-05. Proceedings of the Nineteenth International Joint Conference on Artificial Intelligence, July 30–August 5, pp. 582–588. Professional Book Center, Edinburgh, Scotland, UK (2005)
10. Thangarajah, J., Padgham, L., Harland, J.: Representation and reasoning for goals in bdi agents. In: CRPITS '02. Proceedings of the twenty-fifth Australasian conference on Computer science, pp. 259–265. Australian Computer Society, Inc, Darlinghurst, Australia, Australia (2002)
11. van Riemsdijk, M.B.: *Cognitive Agent Programming: A Semantic Approach*. PhD thesis, Ludwig-Maximilians-Universität München (2006)

Verifying Agent Conformance with Protocols Specified in a Temporal Action Logic[*]

Laura Giordano[1] and Alberto Martelli[2]

[1]Dipartimento di Informatica, Università del Piemonte Orientale, Alessandria
[2]Dipartimento di Informatica, Università di Torino, Torino

Abstract. The paper addresses the problem of agents compatibility and their conformance to protocols. We assume that the specification of protocols is given in an action theory by means of temporal constraints and, in particular, communicative actions are defined in terms of their effects and preconditions on the social state of the protocol. We show that the problem of verifying the conformance of an agent with a protocol can be solved by making use of an automata based approach, and that the conformance of a set of agents with a protocol guarantees that their interaction cannot produce deadlock situations and it only gives rise to runs of the protocol.

1   Introduction

One of the central problems in the area of multi-agent systems, as well as in the area of web services, concerns the interoperability of software agents in an open environment. Agents are usually loosely coupled, as they are written by different organizations, and their interoperability with other agents cannot be guaranteed a-priori. This has raised the problem of introducing conditions which enforce that a set of agents can interact properly, thus leading to the introduction of different notions of *compatibility* among agents [5] as well as to the definition of notions of *conformance* of an agent with a protocol [13,3,6]. The fact that an agent conforms with a protocol must guarantee that all the interactions of the agent with other conformant agents are correct: they produce executions of the protocol and do not lead to deadlock situations.

In our proposal, the interaction protocol which rules the communications among agents is specified in an action theory based on a temporal logic, namely dynamic linear time temporal logic (DLTL) [11]. In this framework, as described in the next section, protocols are given a *declarative specification* consisting of: (i) specification of communicative actions by means of their effects and preconditions on the social state which, in particular, includes commitments; (ii) a set of temporal constraints, which specify the wanted interactions (under this respect, our approach to protocol specification is similar to the one proposed in

---

[*] This research has been partially supported by the project PRIN 2005 "Specification and verification of agent interaction protocols".

DecSerFlow [1]). Protocols with nonterminating computations, modeling reactive services [7], can also be captured in this framework. Communication among agents is assumed to be synchronous and, in this concern, we diverge from [7] and [13], where asynchronous message passing is considered.

In [9,10], we have shown that several verification problems can be modelled as satisfiability and validity problems in the logic, by making use of an automata based approach and, in particular, by working on the Büchi automaton which can be extracted from the logical specification of the protocol. In this paper we focus on the problem of agent interoperability and we define a notion of conformance of an agent with a protocol which guarantees interoperability. In the verification of conformance, we make use of the protocol automaton.

In Section 3, we introduce a notion of conformance of an agent with a protocol by comparing the runs of the agent and the runs of protocol. Then, in Section 4, we define an algorithm which verifies the conformance of an agent with a protocol, assuming that both the agent and the protocol are represented as Büchi automata. The protocol automaton obtained from the temporal specification is a general (non deterministic) Büchi automaton, while agents are assumed to be modelled by deterministic Büchi automata. The non deterministic behaviors of agents can however be modelled through the "non deterministic choice" among different actions.

In the general case, the verification algorithm works in exponential time in the size of the automata. However, when the protocol automaton is deterministic, conformance can be checked in polynomial time.

For lack of space, in the paper we only address in detail the case of protocols with two participants. We shortly discuss the general problem in the conclusions.

2   Protocol Specification

The specification of interaction protocols [9,10] is based on Dynamic Linear Time Temporal Logic (DLTL) [11], a linear time temporal logic which extends LTL by allowing the until operator to be indexed by programs in Propositional Dynamic Logic (PDL) as follows: $\alpha \mathcal{U}^\pi \beta$, where π is a program (a regular expression), built from a set Σ of atomic actions.

As for LTL, DLTL models are infinite linear sequences of worlds (propositional interpretations), each one reachable from the initial one by a finite sequence τ of actions in Σ. A valuation function V, defines the interpretation of propositions at each world τ.

A formula $\alpha \mathcal{U}^\pi \beta$ is true at a world τ if "α until β" is true on a finite stretch of behavior which is in the linear time behavior of the program π. The derived modalities $\langle \pi \rangle$ and $[\pi]$ can be defined as follows: $\langle \pi \rangle \alpha \equiv \top \mathcal{U}^\pi \alpha$ and $[\pi]\alpha \equiv \neg \langle \pi \rangle \neg \alpha$. When π is Σ^*, we replace $\langle \pi \rangle$ with $\Diamond$ and $[\pi]$ with $\Box$. As shown in [11], DLTL(Σ) is strictly more expressive than LTL(Σ). The satisfiability and validity problems for DLTL are PSPACE complete problems [11].

We illustrate how a protocol can be specified in this framework trough the specification of a *Purchase protocol*. We have two roles: the merchant (mr) and

the customer (ct). The customer sends a request to the merchant, the merchant
replies with an offer or by saying that the requested good is not available, and, if
the customer receives the offer, it may accept or refuse it. If the customer accepts
the offer, then the merchant delivers the goods. After receiving the goods, the
customer sends the payment.

The two agents share all the communicative actions, which are: *sendOffer*,
sendNotAvail, sendGoods whose sender is the merchant; *sendRequest, sendAc-
cept, sendRefuse, sendPayment*, whose sender is the customer. Communication
is synchronous: the agents communicate by synchronizing on the execution of
communicative actions.

The Purchase protocol Pu is specified by a *domain description* D_{Pu}, which
is a pair $(\Pi, \mathcal{C})$, where Π is a set of formulas describing the action theory, and
$\mathcal{C}$ is a set of *constraints*.

We adopt a social approach where an interaction protocol is specified by describing the effects of communicative actions on the social state. The social state
contains the domain specific fluents describing observable facts concerning the
execution of the protocol. Examples of fluents are: *requested* (the customer has
requested a quote), *accepted* (the customer has accepted the quote), *goods* (the
merchant has sent the goods). Also special fluents are introduced to model *commitments* among the agents [15]: $C(i, j, \alpha)$, means that agent i is committed to
agent j to bring about α. Furthermore, a *conditional commitments* $CC(i, j, \beta, \alpha)$
means that agent i is committed to agent j to bring about α, if the condition β
is brought about.

The action theory Π consists of *action laws, causal laws, precondition laws*,
and an *initial state*.

Action laws. $\mathcal{AL}$ in Π have the form: $\Box(\alpha \rightarrow [a]l)$, with $a \in \Sigma$, l a fluent literal[1]
and α a conjunction of literals, meaning that executing action a in a state where
precondition α holds causes the effect l to hold.

Although the framework has been extended in [12] to model incomplete information by including epistemic operators, for simplicity here we do not consider
the epistemic extension of the formalism. Also, actions are assumed to be *deterministic*, i.e. executing an action in a state gives a unique successor state.

Some of the effects of communicative actions in protocol Pu are the following:

$$\Box([sendOffer]CC(mr, ct, accepted, goods))$$
when the merchant sends the quote for the good, then he commits to send the
goods if the customer accepts the request,
$$\Box(requested \rightarrow [sendOffer]\neg requested)$$
when the merchant sends the quote for the good, if there is a request, the request
is cancelled.

Causal laws. $\mathcal{CL}$ in Π have the form: $\Box((\alpha \wedge \bigcirc \beta) \rightarrow \bigcirc l)$ (where l a fluent literal
and α, β conjunctions of literals), meaning that if α holds in a state and β holds
in the next state, then l also holds in the next state. Such laws are intended to
expresses "causal" dependencies among fluents. For instance, the *causal law*:

---

[1] A *fluent literal l* stands for a fluent name f or its negation $\neg f$.

$$\Box(\bigcirc\alpha \to \bigcirc\neg C(i,j,\alpha))$$

says that a commitment to bring about α is cancelled when α holds. Other causal laws are needed for dealing with conditional commitments.

Precondition laws. $\mathcal{PL}$ have the form: $\Box(\alpha \to [a]\bot)$, meaning that the execution of an action a is not possible if α holds (i.e. there is no resulting state following the execution of a if α holds). The *precondition laws* for the actions of the customer are the following ones:

$$\Box(\neg offer \to [sendAccept]\bot)$$
$$\Box(\neg offer \to [sendRefuse]\bot)$$
$$\Box(\neg goods \to [sendPayment]\bot).$$

meaning that: the customer may send an accept or refuse only if an offer has been done. The customer may send a payment for the goods only if he has received the goods (all other actions are always executable for the customer).

The *initial state* $\mathcal{IS}$ of the protocol defines the initial value of all the fluents. Here, differently from [12], we assume that the initial state is complete.

Action laws and causal laws describe the changes to the state. All other fluents which are not changed by the actions are assumed to persist unaltered to the next state. To cope with the *frame problem* [14] we use a completion construction $Comp$, which is applied to the action laws and to the causal laws [10]. Thus Π is defined as:

$$\Pi = Comp(\mathcal{AL} \wedge \mathcal{CL}) \wedge \mathcal{PL} \wedge \mathcal{IS}$$

The second component $\mathcal{C}$ of the domain description D_{Pu} defines constraints as arbitrary temporal formulas of DLTL. For instance, to model the fact that, for each request, the customer answers only once sending an Offer or NotAvail, we introduce the following constraint:

$$\neg\Diamond < sendOffer + sendNotAvail > \Diamond < sendOffer + sendNotAvail > \top$$

where $+$ is the nondeterministic choice among actions. It is not possible that the merchant sends an offer or informs that good is not available, and then, later on, he sends again one of these two messages.

We are interested in those execution of the purchase protocol in which all commitments have been fulfilled. Hence, we add, for each commitment $C(i,j,\alpha)$ the constraint:

$$\Box(C(i,j,\alpha) \to \Diamond\alpha).$$

Given the domain description $D_{Pu} = (\Pi,\mathcal{C})$ of Purchase protocol, the *runs* of the protocol are the linear models of $\Pi \wedge \mathcal{C}$.

Note that protocol "runs" are always infinite, as logic DLTL is characterized by infinite models. When we want to model terminating protocols, as the one above, we assume the domain description of the protocol to be suitably extended with an action *noop* which does nothing and which can be executed forever after termination of the protocol.

Once the specification of a protocol has been given, several kinds of verification can be performed on it, including the verification of properties of the protocol per-se, as well as the verification that a set of agents are compliant with a given interaction protocol at runtime. We refer to [9,10] for a description of these verification problems which can be modelled as satifiability or validity problems in the temporal logic.

3   Conformance

Given a protocol P with two roles i and j, and an agent S_i (playing the role of i), we want to define a notion of conformance of S_i with the protocol P which guarantees that the interactions of S_i with any other conformant agent S_j gives rise to legal runs of the protocol and it does not produce deadlock situations.

Consider for instance a customer agent S_{ct} whose behavior differs from that of the role "customer" of protocol Pu as follows: whenever it receives an offer from the merchant, it always accepts it; after accepting the offer it expects to receive from the merchant either the goods or a warning that the delivery has been cancelled.

Although the behavior of the customer agent and that of the corresponding role of the protocol are different, we can consider however the agent to be compliant with the protocol, according to the following observations. The customer, is not forced to send all the messages that could be sent according to the protocol. For instance, it can always accepts an offer, and never send the message *sendRefuse*. On the other hand, an agent can receive more messages than those it should actually receive according to the protocol (an agent can serve more requests than expected from the protocol). The customer S_{ct} can also receive the message that the delivery has been cancelled, even if no merchant conformant with the protocol will ever send it (for further comments on this notion of conformance see [5,3]). Informally, a protocol S_i conforms with a protocol P if the following conditions hold:

(i) The messages sent from S_i are *correct*: that is, if S_i sends a message m at some stage, then, the role i of the protocol can send message m at that stage.

(ii) S_i must receive all the messages which it could receive according to the protocol. This is a *completeness* requirement for S_i.

(iii) If, in a state of the protocol, role i is expected to send a message, in the corresponding state of agent S_i, it must send at least a message. This condition is required to avoid deadlock situations when the two agents S_i and S_j interact: they cannot be both waiting to receive a message.

The third condition is needed because our notion of conformance includes also interoperability of interacting agents.

Notice again that we are considering in two different ways the nondeterministic choices concerning emissions (the customer can accept or refuse an offer) and those concerning receptions (the customer receives the messages *sendOffer* or *sendNotAvail*). As usual in agent applications, we assume that, in the first case, the choice is internal to the agent (internal non determinism), while, in the second case, the choice is of the partner agents, here, the merchant (external non determinism). We refer to [13] for a distinction between internal and external non-determinism.

In the following, we define a notion of conformance of an agent with respect to a protocol by comparing the runs of the agents and the runs of the protocol. In particular, in this definition, we will not consider the value of fluents at the different worlds in the runs, but only the sequences of actions that can be executed according to the protocol and to the agent.

Let us consider a protocol P involving two roles, i and j.

Definition 1. *An agent S_i is conformant with a protocol P if, whenever there are two runs, σ_S of S_i and σ_P of P, with a common prefix π, the following conditions are satisfied:*

(1) if the action $send_{i,j}$ is executed after the prefix π in σ_S, then there exist a run σ common to P and S_i with prefix $\pi send_{i,j}$;

(2) if the action $send_{j,i}$ is executed after the prefix π in σ_P, then there is a run σ common to P and S_i with prefix $\pi send_{j,i}$;

(3) if the action $send_{i,j}$ is executed after the prefix π in σ_P, then there is a run σ common to P and S_i with prefix $\pi send'_{i,j}$, with $send'_{i,j}$ possibly different from $send_{i,j}$.

Item (1) says that the messages sent by agent S_i are correct. It corresponds to condition (i). Item (2) says that S_i receives all the messages he can get according to its role, and corresponds to condition (ii). Finally, item (3) corresponds to condition (iii).

We can prove that if two agents S_i and S_j are conformant with respect to a protocol P, then the interaction of S_i and S_j cannot produce deadlock situations and it only gives rise to runs of the protocol P.

Theorem 1. *Let P be a protocol with a nonempty set of runs. Let S_i and S_j be two agents that are conformant with P. If there are two runs σ_i of S_i and σ_j of S_j that have a common prefix π, then there are two runs σ'_i of S_i and σ'_j of S_j, that have a common prefix πa, for some action a. Moreover, πa is a prefix of a run of P.*

Proof. Let π be the prefix common to σ_i and σ_j. First, we show that there is a run of P with prefix π. We prove it by induction on the length l of the prefix π. For $l = 1$, let $\pi = a$. Let us assume that action a is $send_{i,j}$. As there is a run of P with a common prefix ϵ with σ_i, by the conformance of S_i with P, case (1), there is a run σ common to P and S_i with prefix $send_{i,j}$. In case action a is $send_{j,i}$, we proceed similarly, using conformance of S_j with P. For the inductive case $l + 1$, let $\pi = \pi' a$. By inductive hypothesis we know that there is as run of P starting with π'. From the hypothesis, the runs σ_i of S_i and σ_j of S_j have a common prefix π, and hence π'. Let us assume that $a = send_{i,j}$. Then, by the conformance of S_i with P, case (1), there is a run σ common to P and S_i with prefix $\pi' send_{i,j}$ of length $l + 1$. Hence, there is a run of P with prefix π. For $a = send_{j,i}$, we proceed similarly.

We can now prove the thesis. Let us now consider, for a given π, the different actions that can be executed in σ_i and σ_j after π.

Case 1. Assume that in σ_i action $send_{i,j}$ is executed after π. As there is a run of P starting with π, by the conformance of S_i with P, case (1), there is a run σ'_i common to P and S_i with prefix $\pi send_{i,j}$. By the conformance of S_j to P, case (2), there is a run σ'_j common to P and S_j with prefix $\pi send_{i,j}$. And the thesis follows.

Case 2. If in σ_j action $send_{j,i}$ is executed after π, the proof is as in case 1.

Case 3. Assume that in σ_i action $send_{j,i}$ is executed after π and in σ_i action $send_{i,j}$ is executed after π (both S_i and S_j execute a receive after π). As there is a run σ_P of P with prefix π, let $send_{i,j}$ be the action executed on σ_P after π (in case the action is $send_{j,i}$, we proceeds similarly). Then, by the conformance of S_i, case (3), there is a run σ'_i common to P and S_i with prefix $\pi send'_{i,j}$. By the conformance of S_j, case (2), there is a run σ'_j common to P and S_j with prefix $\pi send'_{i,j}$. And the thesis follows.

Corollary 1. *Let S and J be two agents that are conformant with P. The interaction of S and P does not produce deadlock situations and it only produces executions of the protocol P.*

The proof is omitted for lack of space.

4   Verifying the Conformance of an Agent with a Protocol

4.1   Reasoning About Protocols Using Automata

Verification and satisfiability problems can be solved by extending the standard approach for verification of Linear Time Temporal Logic, based on the use of Büchi automata. We recall that a *Büchi automaton* has the same structure as a traditional finite state automaton, with the difference that it accepts infinite words. More precisely a Büchi automaton over an alphabet Σ is a tuple $\mathcal{B} = (Q, \rightarrow, Q_{in}, F)$ where:

- Q is a finite nonempty set of states;
- $\rightarrow\, \subseteq Q \times \Sigma \times Q$ is a transition relation;
- $Q_{in} \subseteq Q$ is the set of initial states;
- $F \subseteq Q$ is a set of accepting states.

Let $\sigma \in \Sigma^\omega$. Then a run of $\mathcal{B}$ over σ is a map $\rho : prf(\sigma) \rightarrow Q$ such that:

- $\rho(\varepsilon) \in Q_{in}$
- $\rho(\tau) \xrightarrow{a} \rho(\tau a)$ for each $\tau a \in prf(\sigma)$

The run ρ is *accepting* iff $inf(\rho) \cap F \neq \emptyset$, where $inf(\rho) \subseteq Q$ is given by $q \in inf(\rho)$ iff $\rho(\tau) = q$ for infinitely many $\tau \in prf(\sigma)$.

As described in [11], the satisfiability problem for DLTL can be solved in deterministic exponential time, as for LTL, by constructing for each formula $\alpha \in DLTL(\Sigma)$ a Büchi automaton $\mathcal{B}_\alpha$ such that the language of ω-words accepted by $\mathcal{B}_\alpha$ is non-empty if and only if α is satisfiable.

The construction given in [11] is highly inefficient since it requires to build an automaton with an exponential number of states, most of which will not be reachable from the initial state. A more efficient approach for constructing on-the-fly a Büchi automaton from a DLTL formula has been proposed in [8], by generalizing the tableau-based algorithm for LTL. Given a formula φ, the algorithm builds a *labelled* Büchi automaton, i.e. a Büchi automaton extended with a *labeling function* $\mathcal{L} : S \rightarrow 2^F$, which associates a set of fluents with each state. Given an accepting run of the automaton, a model of the given formula φ can be obtained by completing the label of each state of the run in a consistent way.

For a given a domain description $\Pi \wedge \mathcal{C}$ specifying a protocol, the above algorithm can be used to construct the corresponding labelled Büchi automaton, such that all runs accepted by the automaton represent runs of the protocol.

Here, we adopt a technique similar to the one adopted for *model checking*, i.e. by building separately the two Büchi automata corresponding to Π and $\mathcal{C}$ and by making their synchronous product. The Büchi automaton for $\mathcal{C}$ can be constructed with the general algorithm mentioned above. In the following we will call this non-deterministic automaton $\mathcal{M}_\mathcal{C}$.

Instead, the Büchi automaton corresponding to Π can be easily obtained by means of a more efficient technique, exploiting the fact that in our action theory we assume to have *complete states* and *deterministic actions*. We can obtain from the domain description a function $next\_state_a(S)$, for each action a, for transforming a state to the next one, and then build the automaton by repeatedly applying these functions to all states where the preconditions of the action hold, starting from the initial state. In the following we will call this deterministic automaton $\mathcal{M}_{det}^P$.

The runs of the deterministic automaton $\mathcal{M}_{det}^P$ are all possible executions of the protocol according to the action theory, while the runs of $\mathcal{M}_\mathcal{C}$ describe all possible executions satisfying the constraints in $\mathcal{C}$.

The Büchi automaton $\mathcal{M}_P$ describing all runs of the protocol can thus be obtained as follows:

1. Build a labelled Büchi automaton $\mathcal{M}_{det}^P$ obtained from the action and causal laws, precondition laws and the initial state, as described above. This automaton is deterministic, all states can be considered as accepting states, and the labels are complete.
2. Build a labelled Büchi automaton $\mathcal{M}_\mathcal{C}$ obtained from the set of DLTL formulas expressing constraints [8]. This automaton will, in general, be nondeterministic. It is well-known that not every Büchi automaton has an equivalent deterministic Büchi automaton.
3. Build the product of the two automata $\mathcal{M}_P = \mathcal{M}_{det}^P \otimes \mathcal{M}_\mathcal{C}$. $\mathcal{M}_P$ will be a labelled nondeterministic Büchi automaton. Since all states of $\mathcal{M}_{det}^P$ are accepting, $\mathcal{M}_P$ is a standard Büchi automaton (not a generalized one).

4.2   An Automata-Based Verification Algorithm

In this section we define an algorithm to verify the conformance of an agent S with a protocol P. The specification of the protocol is given by the non deterministic automaton $\mathcal{M}_P$, defined in the previous section. In the following, we disregard state labels of $\mathcal{M}_P$, and consider it as a standard non-deterministic Büchi automaton. The behavior of the agent S is given by a *deterministic* Büchi automaton $\mathcal{M}_S$, whose accepted runs provide all the possible executions of the agent. Observe that, although $\mathcal{M}_S$ is deterministic, the non deterministic behaviors of the agent can be modelled through the "nondeterministic choice" among different actions.

We assume that the automata $\mathcal{M}_P$ and $\mathcal{M}_S$ have been pruned by eliminating all the states which do not occur on any accepted run. This can be achieved by starting from the accepting states, and by propagating backwards the information on the states for which a path to an accepting state exists.

In order to verify the conformance of agent an S with a protocol P, we define the synchronous product between $\mathcal{M}_P$ and $\mathcal{M}_S$, $\mathcal{M} = \mathcal{M}_P \otimes \mathcal{M}_S$, whose runs are all the runs of S which are also runs of P. $\mathcal{M}$ is a non-deterministic generalized Büchi automaton.

The states of $\mathcal{M}$ are triples $< q_D, q_C, q_S >$, where $q_D \in \mathcal{M}^P_{det}$, $q_C \in \mathcal{M}_C$ and $q_S \in \mathcal{M}_S$. We assume that all the states of $\mathcal{M}$ which are on an accepting run are marked as *alive*.

In order to verify the conformance we must be able to consider all states of $\mathcal{M}$ which are reachable with the same prefix. Unfortunately we know that it is not possible to transform $\mathcal{M}$ into an equivalent deterministic Büchi automaton. Therefore, we proceed as follows.

Let $\mathcal{M}' = (Q, \Delta, Q^0)$ be a non-deterministic finite state automaton obtained by deleting the accepting states from $\mathcal{M}$. We can now apply to $\mathcal{M}'$ the classical powerset construction for obtaining a deterministic automaton $\mathcal{M}_{PS} = (Q_{PS}, \Delta_{PS}, q^0_{PS})$, where

- $Q_{PS} = 2^Q$
- $(q_{PS}, a, q'_{PS}) \in \Delta_{PS}$ iff $q'_{PS} = \{q' \in Q : \exists q \in q_{PS} \text{ and } (q, a, q') \in \Delta\}$
- $q^0_{PS} = Q^0$
- $F_{PS} = Q_{PS}$.

Let $Q^R_{PS} \subset Q_{PS}$ be the subset of states of $\mathcal{M}_{PS}$ reachable from the initial state q^0_{PS}. Let $q^R_{PS} = \{q_1, \ldots, q_n\}$ be a state of Q^R_{PS}, and let σ be a prefix with which this state can be reached from the initial state. By construction of $\mathcal{M}_{PS}$, the states in q^R_{PS} are all the states which are reachable in $\mathcal{M}$ from an initial state through the prefix σ. As pointed out before, every state $q_i \in q^R_{PS}$ has the form $< q^i_D, q^i_C, q^i_S >$. Since the first and third component of q_i are states of a deterministic automaton, all q^i_D of all states in q_i will be equal, and the same for q^i_S.

For verifying the conformance of an agent S with a protocol P (P involving two roles i and j and S playing role i), we will refer to the automaton $\mathcal{M}$, but we will also make use of the states of the automaton $\mathcal{M}_{PS}$ to reason on the set of states of $\mathcal{M}$ reachable with the same prefix. We give the following algorithm.

Algorithm (for verifying the conformance of S with P)

For each state $q_{PS}^R = \{< q_D, q_C^1, q_S >, \ldots, < q_D, q_C^n, q_S >\}$ of Q_{PS}^R, verify the following conditions:

- If in $\mathcal{M}_S$ there is an outgoing action $send_{i,j}$ from q_S, then there must be a state (q_D, q_C^k, q_S) of $\mathcal{M}$ with an outgoing edge labelled with action $send_{i,j}$, leading to an alive state.
- For all the states (q_D, q_C^k) of $\mathcal{M}_P$, if there is an outgoing action $send_{j,i}$ from (q_D, q_C^k), then there must be a state $< q_D, q_C^l, q_S >$ of q_{PS}^R, so that in $\mathcal{M}$ there is an outgoing edge from $< q_D, q_C^l, q_S >$ labelled with action $send_{j,i}$, leading to an alive state.
- For all the states (q_D, q_C^k) of $\mathcal{M}_P$, if there is an outgoing action $send_{i,j}$ from (q_D, q_C^k), then there must be a state $< q_D, q_C^l, q_S >$ of q_{PS}^R, so that in $\mathcal{M}$ there is an outgoing edge from $< q_D, q_C^l, q_S >$ labelled with action $send'_{i,j}$, leading to an alive state.

We want to evaluate the complexity of the algorithm with respect to the size n of the protocol automaton. We assume that the size of the agent automaton $\mathcal{M}_S$ is $O(n)$. Although the size of the product automaton is polynomial in n (namely, $O(n^2)$), the size of the automaton $\mathcal{M}_{PS}$ is exponential in the size of $\mathcal{M}$. Hence, the algorithm requires exponential time in n. It has to be observed, however, that, when the protocol automaton is deterministic, the automaton $\mathcal{M}_{PS}$ is useless (each state, q_{PS}^R of Q_{PS}^R contains a single triple) and the complexity of the algorithm becomes polynomial in n.

5   Conclusions and Related Work

In this paper we have addressed the problem of conformance between an agent and a protocol, assuming that the specification of the protocol is given in a temporal action logic. We have addressed the case when the protocol involves two agents and we have defined an algorithm which verifies the conformance of an agent with a protocol, by making use of automata-based techniques. The notion of conformance we have defined guarantees the interoperability among the agents.

In [3] a similar approach is used for conformance verification, by taking into account the asymmetry between messages that are sent and messages that are received. Agents and protocols are represented as deterministic finite automata, and protocols are limited to protocols with only two roles. The results of that paper have been extended in [4], where conformance of web services is considered. First of all, protocols can contain an arbitrary number of roles. Furthermore, by referring to nondeterministic automata, the proposed approach also accounts for the case of agents and roles producing the same interactions but having different branching structures. This case cannot be handled in the framework in [3] as well as in our framework, due to the fact that they are exclusively based on a trace semantics.

A similar approach is also used in [2], where an abductive framework is used to verify the conformance of agents to a choreography with any number of roles.

The notions of conformance, coverage and interoperability are defined in a different way in [6]. A distinctive feature of that formalization is that the three notions are orthogonal to each other. Conformance and coverage are based on the semantics of runs (a run being a sequence of states), whereas interoperability among agents is based upon the idea of blocking.

In [5], several notions of *compatibility* among agents have been analyzed, in which agents are modelled by Labelled Transition Systems, communication is synchronous, and models are deterministic (no two actions labelled by the same name can be applied in a given state). While compatibility is concerned with the interoperablility of agents, in [5] a notion of *substitutability* is introduced, which is related to the notion of conformance. The problem of substitutability is that of determining if an agent A' can substitute an agent A, while preserving the compatibility with all the agents B with whom A is compatible. [5] introduces two distinct notions of substitutability: the first one requires that A' at each state can have less emissions and more receptions than A, and this, in essence, corresponds to requirements (1) and (2) in our definition of conformance. This notion of substitutability does not preserves deadlock-freeness. The second notion of substitutability is more restrictive and requires that A' and A have the same emissions and receptions in the corresponding states. As a difference with our proposal, in [5] agent executions are always terminating.

In [13] a notion of conformance is defined to check if an implementation model I extracted from a message-passing program conforms with a signature S. Both I and S are CCS processes, communication is asynchronous, and the paper, in particular, focuses on stuck-freeness of communication.

The approach presented in the paper can be generalized to an arbitrary number n of agents, although the generalization is not straightforward. More precisely, in the general case, we would like to show that, given a protocol P with k roles and a set of agents $S_1, \ldots, S_k$, if the behavior of each agent S_i is conformant with the protocol P, then the interaction of the agents does not lead to deadlock situations and it gives rise only to executions of the protocol P.

The main difficulty in generalizing the proposed approach to an arbitrary number of agents comes from the fact that, given a protocol P involving k agents, it is not guaranteed that the constraints in P (which declaratively define which are the wanted executions) can be enforced directly on the agents $S_1, \ldots, S_k$. Consider, for instance, a protocol involving four agents A, B, C, D containing the constraint:

$$[m_1(A, B)] < m_2(C, D) > T$$

meaning that message m_2, sent from C to D has to be executed after m_1, sent from A to B. Assume that A and B do not exchange messages with C and D. It is clear that this constraint cannot be enforced by agents A or B alone, as they do not see message m_2, nor by agents C or D alone, as they do not see message m_1, while both the messages are involved in the constraint. Intuitively, only constraints which are defined on the language (fluents and actions) of single agents should be allowed, as they can be enforced by single agents. A full discussion of the general problem and its solutions will be subject of further work.

References

1. van der Aalst, W.M.P., Pesic, M.: DecSerFlow: Towards a Truly Declarative Service Flow Language. In: Bravetti, M., Núñez, M., Zavattaro, G. (eds.) WS-FM 2006. LNCS, vol. 4184, pp. 1–23. Springer, Heidelberg (2006)
2. Alberti, M., Chesani, F., Gavanelli, M., Lamma, E., Mello, P., Montali, M.: An abductive framework for a-priori verification of web agents. In: PPDP06. Principles and Practice of Declarative Programming, ACM Press, New York (2006)
3. Baldoni, M., Baroglio, C., Martelli, A., Patti: Verification of protocol conformance and agent interoperability. In: Toni, F., Torroni, P. (eds.) Computational Logic in Multi-Agent Systems. LNCS (LNAI), vol. 3900, pp. 265–283. Springer, Heidelberg (2006)
4. Baldoni, M., Baroglio, C., Martelli, A., Patti: A Priori Conformance Verification for Guaranteeing Interoperability in Open Environments. In: Dan, A., Lamersdorf, W. (eds.) ICSOC 2006. LNCS, vol. 4294, pp. 339–351. Springer, Heidelberg (2006)
5. Bordeaux, L., Salaün, G., Berardi, D., Mecella, M.: When are two web-agents compatible. In: VLDB-TES 2004,
6. Chopra, A.K., Singh, M.P.: Producing Compliant Interactions: Conformance, Coverage, and Interoperability. In: Baldoni, M., Endriss, U. (eds.) DALT 2006. LNCS (LNAI), vol. 4327, pp. 1–15. Springer, Heidelberg (2006)
7. Fu, X., Bultan, T., Su, J.: Conversation protocols: a formalism for specification and verification of reactive electronic services. Theor. Comput. Sci. 328(1-2), 19–37 (2004)
8. Giordano, L., Martelli, A.: Tableau-based Automata Construction for Dynamic Linear Time Temporal Logic. Annals of Mathematics and Artificial Intelligence 46(3), 289–315 (2006)
9. Giordano, L., Martelli, A., Schwind, C.: Verifying Communicating Agents by Model Checking in a Temporal Action Logic. In: Alferes, J.J., Leite, J.A. (eds.) JELIA 2004. LNCS (LNAI), vol. 3229, pp. 57–69. Springer, Heidelberg (2004)
10. Giordano, L., Martelli, A., Schwind, C.: Specifying and Verifying Interaction Protocols in a Temporal Action Logic. Journal of Applied Logic (Special issue on Logic Based Agent Verification) (2006) (Accepted for publication)
11. Henriksen, J.G., Thiagarajan, P.S.: Dynamic Linear Time Temporal Logic. Annals of Pure and Applied logic 96(1-3), 187–207 (1999)
12. Martelli, A., Giordano, L.: Reasoning About Web Services in a Temporal Action Logic. In: Stock, O., Schaerf, M. (eds.) Reasoning, Action and Interaction in AI Theories and Systems. LNCS (LNAI), vol. 4155, pp. 229–246. Springer, Heidelberg (2006)
13. Rajamani, S.K., Rehof, J.: Conformance checking for models of asynchronous message passing software. In: Brinksma, E., Larsen, K.G. (eds.) CAV 2002. LNCS, vol. 2404, pp. 166–179. Springer, Heidelberg (2002)
14. Reiter, R.: Knowledge in Action. The MIT Press, Cambridge (2001)
15. Yolum, P., Singh, M.P.: Flexible Protocol Specification and Execution: Applying Event Calculus Planning using Commitments. In: Falcone, R., Barber, S., Korba, L., Singh, M.P. (eds.) AAMAS 2002. LNCS (LNAI), vol. 2631, pp. 527–534. Springer, Heidelberg (2003)

Harvesting Relational and Structured Knowledge for Ontology Building in the *WPro* Architecture

Daniele Bagni[1], Marco Cappella[1], Maria Teresa Pazienza[1], Marco Pennacchiotti[2], and Armando Stellato[1]

[1] DISP, University of Rome "Tor Vergata", Italy
{pazienza,stellato}@info.uniroma2.it
[2] Computational Linguistics, Saarland University, Germany
pennacchiotti@coli.uni-sb.de

Abstract. We present two algorithms for supporting semi-automatic ontology building, integrated in *WPro,* a new architecture for ontology learning from Web documents. The first algorithm automatically extracts ontological entities from tables, by using specific heuristics and WordNet-based analysis. The second algorithm harvests semantic relations from unstructured texts using Natural Language Processing techniques. The integration in *WPro* allows a friendly interaction with the user for validating and modifying the extracted knowledge, and for uploading it into an existing ontology. Both algorithms show promising performance in the extraction process, and offer a practical means to speed-up the overall ontology building process.

1 Introduction

Ontology learning from text [3] is today receiving growing attention, as a means to (semi-)automatically build ontologies from document collections. From the one side, the development of accurate and scalable Natural Language Processing (NLP) techniques for automatically harvesting different types of information, such as relations [12] and facts [5], has urged the creation of algorithms and applications for structuring and organizing this knowledge into formal ontological repositories. From the other side, the Semantic Web and the Knowledge Representation communities have reached a stage in which the formalisms (such as OWL) and the reasoning engines are ready to host and process the large amount of knowledge harvested by the NLP algorithms. As a further point, the impressive amount of unstructured (textual) and structured (tables and templates) information that we have at our disposal via the Web and other *e*-collections, indicate that the time is mature for integrating NLP techniques into Semantic Web oriented applications aimed at ontologically structuring the Web and other textual content. As a matter of fact, in recent years many tools have been created for semi-automatically supporting human experts in the task of ontology building from documents (e.g. KIM [10], Text-to-Onto [11], etc.).

In this paper we present two algorithms for supporting the ontology building process from Web pages in a semi-automatic fashion. Specifically, we present an algorithm for automatically inducing from structured data (i.e. HTML tables) in an existing ontology, new ontological entities (classes, instances, properties); and an

R. Basili and M.T. Pazienza (Eds.): AI*IA 2007, LNAI 4733, pp. 157–169, 2007.

algorithm for automatically extracting semantic relations between ontological instances from unstructured texts. Both algorithms are implemented as two independent modules into *WPro*, a new prototypical architecture for ontology building and engineering. By relying on their integration into the *WPro* graphical interface, the two algorithms offer a direct interaction with the user, for activating, managing and validating the extracted knowledge, and integrating it into an existing ontology.

The goal of *WPro* is to offer a means to support a user or an ontology engineer during the process of ontology building from the Web. It provides a friendly graphical interface divided in two main areas. A first area is the actual Firefox browser, which embodies the second area. This latter includes the ontology which the user is building, together with various tools for ontology engineering, i.e. to manually create and delete entities and to add new entities from the text of Web pages by simple drag-and-drop operations. The ontology is maintained and modified by relying on a background Protègè-based engine [7], which guarantees efficiency and robustness in the ontology engineering operations, and the possibility of producing a final ontology in different formalisms, such as OWL. The *WPro* architecture is implemented using various languages. It is based on XUL for the general integration in Mozilla Firefox, and interfaces to Protégé through the specific Protégé API. *WPro* also provides a set of APIs, which can be used to easily extend the architecture with further tools and modules to better automate and support the ontology building process. The two modules presented in the paper are directly integrated into *WPro* by using these APIs. In the rest of the paper we present our two novel algorithms: in Section 0 we introduce TOE, the *WPro* module implementing the algorithm for inducing ontological entities from HTML tables; in Section 0, we describe the *WPro* module for relation extraction. Both modules show promising and close to state of the art performance. Finally, in Section 0 we draw some final conclusions.

2 The TOE Module

Structured information, such as tables, lists and templates, offer a rich source of knowledge to enrich ontologies. Structured sources have the major advantage that the data they contain are structurally coherently organized, making their ontological interpretation easier with respect to unstructured documents. Also, structured information typically contain *dense* meaningful content which tends to be ontology-oriented, unlike unstructured text, where relevant information are scattered throughout sentences. Despite this, not much attention has been paid so far on the extraction of ontological information from tables. [14] propose *TARTAR*, a system for the automatic generation of semantic ontological frames in Frame Logic, from HTML, Excel, PDF tables and others. The methodology leverages the structural, functional and semantic aspect of tables. Our approach differs from TARTAR, both in the input considered (we focus on HTML), the final goal (we enrich an OWL based ontology, TARTAR builds independent frames) and in the adopted methodology (we rely on heuristics based on the content, structure and presentation, while TARTAR mostly focuses on functional aspects). [16] present *TANGO*, a system which automatically creates *mini-ontologies* from tables, that can be successfully integrated into larger *inter-ontologies*, using ontology mapping techniques. The approach is intended as a process of reverse engineering from an actual table to a conceptual model. The output is a set of concepts and relationships among them. Unlike *TANGO* we have a more practical focus, as described hereafter.

The TOE module extracts ontological entities (classes, instances and properties) from this type of structured information. Specifically, TOE implements an algorithm for analyzing HTML tables embodied in Web pages, and for proposing a possible ontological interpretation to the user of the *WPro* application. Also, the user can accept, reject or modify TOE's interpretation through an easy to use graphical interface, and then start an automatic process to upload the new information into the existing *WPro* ontology. The TOE module is fully integrated in the *WPro* architecture, and can be activated over a Web page by a simple listener.

2.1 Tables' Structure and Ontological Types

Many models have been proposed in the literature to describe tables (e.g. [9]). We here adopt a simple approach, specifically oriented to our task. In our framework, a table is intended as a matrix of cells (see Fig. 1), whose structure can be divided in four main areas, which in most cases contain different type of information: (1) *First*

$\langle 1,1 \rangle$	$\langle 1,2 \rangle$	$\langle 1,3 \rangle$	...	$\langle 1,n \rangle$
$\langle 2,1 \rangle$	$\langle 2,2 \rangle$	$\langle 2,3 \rangle$	...	$\langle 2,n \rangle$
...	...	...	...	...
$\langle m,1 \rangle$	$\langle m,2 \rangle$	$\langle m,3 \rangle$	...	$\langle m,n \rangle$

Fig. 1. Structure of a $n \times m$ table

row (cells *<1,2>* ... *<1,n>*) , which usually contains a *column header*, i.e. a short description of the information enclosed in each column. (2) *First column* (cells *<2,1>* ... *<2,m>*), typically containing a *row header*, describing the content of a single row. (3) *First cell* (cell *<1,1>*), sometimes used to give a short indication on the type of data contained in the table (*table header*); in other cases, it is part of the first row or the first column. (4) *Internal cells* (other cells), containing the actual *data* of the table, whose meaning is described by the related cells in the first row/column.

The above represents a typical structure, which is verified in most but not all cases. Our empirical investigation on a set of hundreds of tables revealed that most tables follow this structure, apart from two simple variants, in which the row or column headers are absent. TOE's heuristics have been then implemented to treat both the basic structure and these two variants.

The above structure indicates that from an information-content perspective, a table is at least *three-dimensional*, i.e. it can contain three types of information: *row header*, *column header* and *data*. *Table header* is not included, as it is a simple singleton value, which does not express an actual content. A table can also be *two-dimensional* (when either the row or column header is not present). Mono-dimensional tables are seldom, as the value of internal rows and columns must be somehow described by a header (these seldom cases assume that the description of the internal cells is given in the table caption). This observation implies that the ontological content of a table cannot be too complex. We can assume two basic facts: *(a)* in most cases tables contain simple *flat* non-hierarchical knowledge, i.e. they embody only knowledge describing entities and no hierarchical information; *(b)* a table cannot contain knowledge about more than one class. In facts, this would imply the table to be four-dimensional, as it should represent class names, property names, instance names, property values. From these assumptions it follows that to leverage tables in the ontology building process we can classify them in three categories, based on the allowed types of ontological content:

Class Tables: These contain the definition of a class (the name of its properties) and a set of its instances. The information that must be enclosed in the table are: property names, instance names and property values. Potentially, the name of the class can be also represented. The table must then be three-dimensional, i.e. *it must have row header and column header*. Structurally, property names and instance names can be either reported in the row or column headers. Property values are reported in the internal cells, while the class name, if present, is typically in the table header. An example of class table is reported in Fig. 2: the class is *"Business District"*, with the property names indicated in the column header (e.g. *"Office Space"*), the instance names in the row header (e.g. *"The City"*), and the property values in the inner cells.

Instance Tables: These contain information about a single instance. The information enclosed in the table are property name and property value. *These tables are typically two dimensional and have either exactly two columns or rows.* The column (row) header indicates the name of the properties, while the second column contains the property values. A typical example is in Fig. 3: the table contains information for the instance *"London"* of a class *capital cities*, with property names in the first column, and values in the second.

Empty tables: These are tables which do not contain any ontological interesting content. Typical cases of empty tables are those containing graphical elements.

2.1.1 Table Extraction and Selection

TOE takes as input the Web page currently displayed in the browser window. Once the user activates the module, it automatically extracts from the HTML source all the well-formed tables (a well-formed table is one which is compliant with the HTML 1.0 specifications), using a simple HTML parser.

Business District	Office Space (m²)	Business Concentration
The City	7,740,000	finance, broking, insurance, legal
Westminster	5,780,000	head offices, real estate, private banking, hedge funds, government
Camden & Islington	2,294,000	creative industries, finance, design, art, fashion, architecture
Canary Wharf	2,120,000	banking, media, legal
Lambeth & Southwark	1,780,000	accountancy, consultancy, local government

Fig. 2 . A typical example of a *class table* representing an the class *"Business District"*

Sovereign state:	United Kingdom
Constituent country:	England
Region:	London
Regional authority:	Greater London Authority
Regional assembly:	London Assembly
HQ:	City Hall
Mayor:	Ken Livingstone

City of Rome
Population by year

350 BC	30,000
250 BC	100,000
100 BC	500,000
25 BC	1,000,000
120	1,650,000

Fig. 3 (left). A typical example of a *instance table* representing the instance *"London"*
Fig. 4 (right). An example of table with missing column header

A special case regards nested tables, i.e. tables which recursively contain other tables. In that case, TOE applies the heuristic that the outermost table is that which is informative, while the content of the inner tables is discarded. The motivation of this choice is that our empirical study on a set of table revealed that inner tables tend to contain in most cases graphical objects, or are used for a mere presentation purpose.

Once all tables are extracted, the user selects in the graphical interface, the set of tables to analyse. TOE then starts the analysis of one table at time, as follows.

2.1.2 Identifying Table Type: Header Analysis

Given an input table, the goal of the first step of the TOE algorithm is to recognize if the table is an *instance table* or a *class table*. A first simple heuristic is applied, according to the assumption in Section 0: if a table has more than two column, it cannot be an *instance table*. In this case, TOE predicts that it is a *class table[1]* and goes directly to the ontological analysis step (Section 2.1.3). If a table has two columns, its type must be decided by verifying if it has a *column header*, as in the following.

From the assumptions is Section 0, a table without a header is two-dimensional, and is then an *instance table*. A table with both headers is three-dimensional, and then is a *class table*. Specifically, we here make the further assumption that a row header must be always present in a table. Otherwise, the meaning of the rows would be unknown. On the contrary, the column header can be missing in the case the description of the column is directly indicated in the table caption, as in Fig. 4. Again, this assumption comes from our empirical investigation. The header analysis step is then reduced to the problem of understanding if the table has or not a column header, by using the two following types of heuristics.

Style-based heuristics. The assumption of these heuristics is that a column header has a different style with respect to the rest of the table, e.g. a different background colour or a different font style (bold, italic, etc.). Both background colour and font-style are checked by relying on the information enclosed in related HTML tags (e.g <b> indicates a bold-style, and <TR bgcolor="red"> indicates a row with a red background). Fig. 2 shows an example captured by these heuristics. A third heuristic looks at the content of the cell *<1,1>*. If it is empty, the first row is assumed to be a column header, otherwise the row would not be meaningful.

---

[1] The decision if a table is an *empty table* is left to the user in the later validation phase. TOE only discards as empty, those table which contains only figures and symbols.

Value-based heuristics. If the style-based heuristics fail, a second (less certain) check is made on the values of the cells in the different rows. One of the basic assumption is that when the column header is present, its row is likely to contain cells of the same type, and that this data type is most likely `string` (as it is the most descriptive, as required in a header). Different heuristics are implemented to treat different cases. For example, if rows $2...m$ contain all numeric values (excluding the first column, which represents the row header) and also row 1 contains the same type of numeric values, then the column header is likely to be absent. As another example, if rows $2...m$ contain numeric values and row 1 is formed by `string`, then this latter is likely to be a header. Once the presence of the column header has been verified, the first step decides the table type according to the following heuristic: if the column header is present then the table is a *class table*, otherwise it is an *instance table*. This information is then given to the second step, together with the table itself.

2.1.3 Ontological Analysis

on a second step TOE identifies what ontological entity each cell contains. The analysis varies according to the table type.

Class table analysis. Class tables describe instances of a given class, i.e. they must contain the property names of the class, the instances names and the related property values. Instance and property names can be alternatively coded in the row or in the column headers, while the property values are in the internal cells.

The only problem is then to understand which header contains which name. For this purpose, the assumption is that an ontological property (either datatype- or object-property) has always the same range. Consequently, if the column header contains the property names, the first element of a column (property name) must be followed by cells of the same data type (property values). The same observation stands for the row header. An example is reported in Fig. 5.In the case that all internal cells are of the same data type, the system simply guesses as default that the column header represents the property names.

In class tables, cell $<1,1>$ represents the table header. This cell can either be empty, contain the class name to which the table refers, or contain additional information not interesting for the ontology. The treatment of the table header is left to the user during the validation step.

1971-2000	Jan	Feb	Mar	Apr	May	June	July	Ago	Sep	Oct	Nov	Dec	*Total*
Maximum temperature (°C)	9,7	12,0	15,7	17,5	21,4	26,9	31,2	30,7	26,0	19,0	13,4	10,1	*19,4*
Minimum temperature (°C)	2,6	3,7	5,6	7,2	10,7	15,1	18,4	18,2	15,0	10,2	6,0	3,8	*9,7*
Rainfall (mm)	37	35	26	47	52	25	15	10	28	49	56	56	*436*

Fig. 5. An example of system complete ontological interpretation for a *class table "Monthly Weather"*. In the column header (*Jan...Dec*) are reported instance names; in the row header (first column) are property names; other cells are property values.

Instance table analysis. Instance tables describe a single instance, and are assumed to be formed by two column: the left columns (row header) containing property names, and the right column containing the properties' values (internal cells).Then, in this case TOE does not have to perform any specific operation.

A the end of the ontological analysis step, TOE returns an ontological interpretation of the table, by indicating the ontological type of each cell (property name or property value). This interpretation is then reported to the user for validation.

2.1.4 Validation and Ontology Uploading

In this phase, TOE shows to the user the results of the ontological analysis (see Fig.6). The user can then decide either to reject the table as not interesting (*empty table*) to accept completely TOE's interpretation, or to modify it. In the latter case, the user is provided with different tools to change the ontological type of cells. Once the correct ontological interpretation of the table is decided, the information is automatically uploaded in the ontology. Yet, the user has to manually specify some information:

- *Class/Instance name*, for *class/instance tables*. In the case of class tables, TOE gives as suggested name the value in the table header (cell *<1,1>*), or a name induced by a lexical-semantic analysis of the table (see Section 2.1.2).
- *Ontological Attachment*: the user must specify where in the existing *WPro* ontology the information must be added. For *class table* it must be indicated the parent class of the new class, for *instance table* which is its class in the ontology.
- *Properties range*: the user has to indicate the range of each property.

Before information are finally uploaded in the ontology, TOE performs correctness checks on all entities, and consistency checks on the (possible) new properties and on the (possibly) discrepancies in the ranges of existing ones. In case of incorrect data, the user is requested to perform the needed correction.

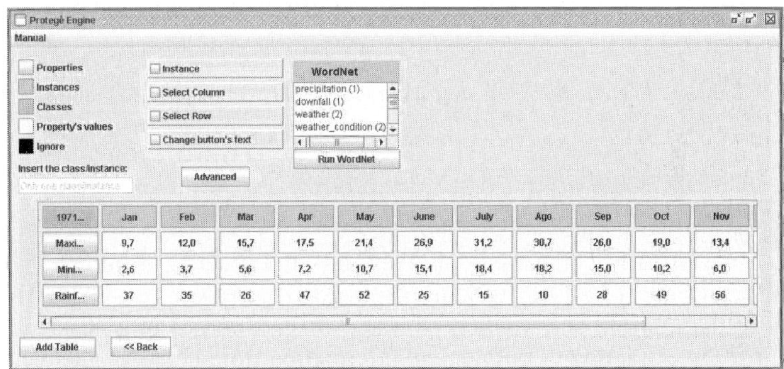

1971...	Jan	Feb	Mar	Apr	May	June	July	Ago	Sep	Oct	Nov
Maxi...	9,7	12,0	15,7	17,5	21,4	26,9	31,2	30,7	26,0	19,0	13,4
Mini...	2,6	3,7	5,6	7,2	10,7	15,1	18,4	18,2	15,0	10,2	6,0
Rainf...	37	35	26	47	52	25	15	10	28	49	56

Fig. 6. Validation interface of the TOE module. Different cells' colors indicate different ontological entities (*blue*, row header*:* property names ; *green*, column header*:* instance names; *white*, internal cells: property values; *gray*, cell <1,1>*:* table header).

2.1.5 Naming Classes: WordNet Semantic Analysis

If requested, TOE can optionally propose a name for the new class of a *class table*. The name is induced by a lexical-semantic analysis of the table, carried out using WordNet [6] as support. The intuition is that a class name is likely to be a common ancestor of the instances' names in the WordNet hierarchy. Then, for each cell k containing an instance name, TOE extracts its content W^k, which can be formed by one or more word $w^k_i \in W^k$. It then finds the *least common subsumer* [17] of at least one word w^k_i in each of the k cells, up to a given degree of generalization chosen by the user through the graphical interface. In order to cope with acronyms and abbreviations (which are in most cases not present in WordNet), TOE uses as support a gazetteer of acronyms and abbreviations, which is used to expand them into their original form (e.g. *"fifa"*→*"international football federation"*).

2.2 Experimental Investigation

The goal of the experiment is to verify the TOE's accuracy in proposing the correct ontological interpretation of a table. We chose as corpus a set of 100 Web pages of European and Asian capitals taken from *Wikipedia*. These pages contain in all 207 tables. We evaluated TOE on three tasks: **(1)** *table type identification*: the accuracy a_{ident} (fraction of correct predictions) in predicting the table type (i.e. *class* or *instance table*). **(2)** *ontological interpretation*: the accuracy a_{ont} in predicting a completely correct interpretation of the table (in all cells). **(3)** *WordNet analysis*: the accuracy a_{WN} of WordNet in predicting a correct name for class tables. The performance evaluation has been carried out by an expert ontology engineer[2]. Results, reported in Table 1, show that TOE guarantees a high accuracy in both tasks (1) and (2). In particular, TOE is highly accurate in predicting the correct table type, revealing that the simple heuristics implemented are effective. Yet, the accuracy in the WordNet prediction is low. This indicates that in general the use of linguistic analysis in tables is not particularly effective, as the linguistic content is very limited. Also, in many cases we verified problems of coverage: authors of tables often tend to use atypical word abbreviation and truncations in order to limit the cell content. This causes WordNet and the gazetteer do fail in interpreting many expressions. In the future we plan to expand our evaluation to more heterogeneous and large sets of Web pages.

Table 1. Accuracy of TOE over a corpus of 100 Web pages (207 tables)

task	(1)	(2)	(3)
accuracy	0.91	0.77	0.25

Even if not directly comparable, as they aim at extracting different knowledge, both TOE and the TARTAR systems show good performance (TARTAR has an accuracy of 0.85 on the construction of frames over a corpus of 158 tables), which indicate that the extraction of ontological information from table is valuable, feasible and effective.

3   The Relation Extraction Module

Relation extraction is generically intended as the task of extracting generic and specific binary semantic relations between entities from textual corpora, such as *is-a(bachelor, man)* and *capital-of(Roma, Italy)*. It plays a key role in ontology learning from text, and in general in NLP applications which leverage ontological information,

---

[2] Table recognized as *empty tables* are not considered in the evaluation.

such as Question Answering (QA) and Textual Entailment. Consider for example a web portal application supporting on-line questions regarding geographical knowledge. It could answer questions such as: *"Where is Cape Agulhas located?"* or *"What is the longest river of Mozambico?"* by relying on a domain ontology built using a relation extraction engine applied to the relations *located-in(x,y)* and *longest-river-of(x,y)*. It is here important to note that many applications which leverage domain ontologies require information which are in most cases relational, or that can be reduced to a relational format. Relation extraction is then often a key issue.

Most approaches to relation extraction are either pattern- or clustering-based. *Pattern-based approaches* are the most used: [8] pioneered, using patterns to extract hyponym (*is-a*) relations. Manually building three lexico-syntactic patterns, [8] sketched a bootstrapping algorithm to learn more patterns from instances, which has served as the model for most subsequent pattern-based algorithms, such as [1] for the *part-of* relation. [15] focused on scaling relation extraction to the Web, proposing a simple and effective algorithm to discover surface patterns from a small set of seeds. [12] propose an approach inspired by [8] to infer patterns, making use of generic patterns and applying refining techniques to deal with wide variety of relations and principled reliability measures for patterns and instances. Our   approach uses a technique similar to [12]: yet, it uses a dependency parser to extract patterns, allowing the exploitation of long distance dependencies. *Clustering approaches* have so far been applied only to *is-a* extraction (e.g. [4],[13]) : they use clustering to group words, label the clusters using their members' lexical or syntactic dependencies, and extract an *is-a* relation between cluster members and labels. These approaches fail to produce coherent clusters from less than 100 million words, being then unreliable for small corpora.

In the framework of the *WPro* environment, which aims at supporting the creation of domain ontologies from the Web, the relation extraction module plays a primary role. Suppose for example that the *WPro* ontology contains the entities *Madrid* and *Spain*, related by the property *capital-of*. It can then be assumed that the semantic relation *capital-of* between *cities* and *nations* is interesting for the ontology. The module should then allow the *WPro* user to extract automatically other instances of *capital-of* from the web collection. Our relation extraction module aims at providing such a service. Given a pair of entities related by an ontological property, the module provides the user a dedicated interface to start a *relation extraction engine* for the relation. The engine implements an algorithm based on the framework adopted in [8]. It uses the pair of entities as seeds (e.g. *(Madrid,Spain)*) and starts the extraction of other pairs implementing the following steps. First, it collects from the corpus of Web pages all sentences containing the seed (e.g *"Madrid is a beautiful city and is the capital of Spain"*). Secondly, the syntactic patterns connecting the entities in the seed are extracted from the sentences (e.g *Madrid-is-the-capital-of-Spain*). Then, patterns are used to extract new instances from the corpus (e.g. *(Roma,Italy)* is extracted from the snippet *"Roma has been the capital of Italy since 1870"*). Finally, the engine returns to the user a list of extracted instances, ranked according to a reliability measure; the user can then validate the instances using an interface and upload them in the ontology. The module guarantees: (1) *minimal supervision*, by using as input one of few instance(s) already in the ontology, and by presenting as output a list of ranked instances which can be easily validated and uploaded; (2) *high accuracy*, by adopting a dedicated reliability measure to weight the extracted instances; (3) *easing data sparseness*: as *WPro* must efficiently work in small domain corpora, our algorithm implements specific techniques, such as syntactic expansion and the use of dependency parsing to exploit long distance dependencies; (4) *generality*, as it is applicable to a wide variety of relations; (5)*WPro integration*, being explicitly integrated in the *WPro* architecture, leveraging the APIs and dedicated user interfaces.

3.1 Module Components and Algorithm

Hereafter we present the different components of the module.

Input Interface. This provides to the user the functionalities needed for starting the relation extraction process, by allowing to select a seed pair $s=(x_s,y_s)$ for a given relation. The pair consists in two entities of the *WPro* ontology, related by an object property. Fig.7 shows an example, in which the user selects as seed words the pair $s=(Madrid,Spain)$. The extraction process is then executed as follows[3].

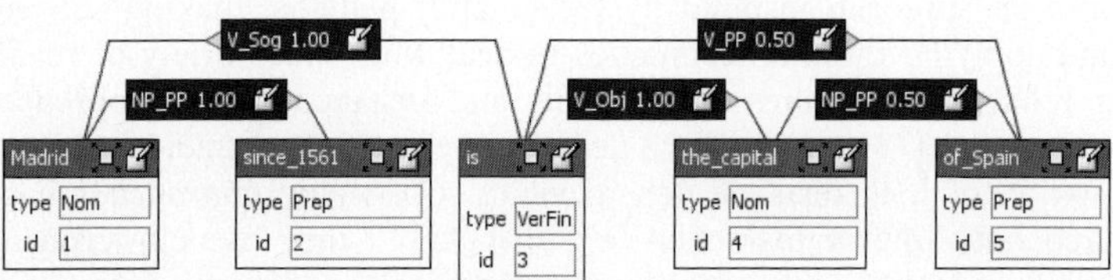

Fig. 7. A dependency graph output by *Chaos*. *Lower boxes* are constituents. *Upper boxes* are dependencies, with the related *plausibility,* i.e. a representation of ambiguous relations.

Pattern Induction and Expansion. Given an input seed instance *s*, the algorithm looks in the corpus for all sentences containing the two terms. These sentences are parsed by the *Chaos* constituent-dependency parser [1]. Then, all dependency paths connecting the seed words are extracted as patterns *P*. The use of Chaos guarantees two main advantages with respect to simple surface approaches such as [15]. First, the use of dependency information allows to extract more interesting patterns. Second, Chaos explicitly represents ambiguous relations between constituents, allowing to infer patterns also when the syntactic interpretation is not complete. Fig. 7 shows a parsed sentence connecting the seeds *Madrid* and *Spain*. The algorithm extracts as patterns the paths: *"X is the capital of Y"* and *"X is of Y"*, which connect the two words[4]. Notice that a simple surface approach would have extracted the only irrelevant pattern *"X since 1561 is the capital of Y"*. The dependency analysis thus allows our algorithm to extract more useful patterns, helping to deal with data sparseness, i.e. cases in which only few sentences are retrieved for a given seed, and then patterns must be carefully created. Yet, the algorithm is prone to capture too generic patterns such as *"X of Y"*: a reliability measure is applied to cope with this problem. Also, to further deal with data sparseness, the algorithm expands the

---

[3] In the present implementation the system carries out the following phases only once. We also experimented bootstrapping iterative calls over these phase, as suggested in [**Error! Reference source not found.**]. In Section 0 we report early results.

[4] For clarity, we here do not report the grammatical dependencies of the pattern, but only its surface form.

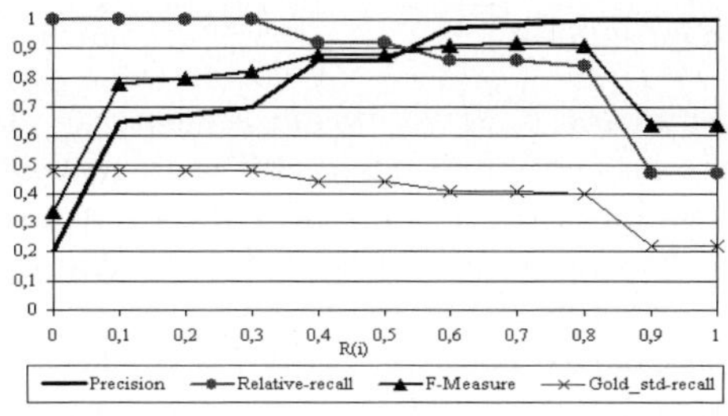

Fig. 8. Precision, Relative-Recall, F-measure and GoldStd-Recall at different levels of τ for the relation *capital-of*

patterns *P* in a bigger set *P'*, by including different morphological variations of the main verb (e.g. "*X being the capital of Y*", "*X was the capital of Y*", etc.).

Instance Induction and Reliability Ranking. Given the set *P'*, the algorithm retrieves all the sentences containing the words of any $p \in P'$. Each sentence is then parsed by *Chaos*. The constituents connected by a dependency path corresponding to a pattern in *P'* are then extracted as new instances *I*. For example from the sentence *"New Delhi being the capital of India, is an important financial market"*, it is extracted the new instance *(New Delhi, India)*.

Each instance $i=(x,y) \in I$ is then assigned a *reliability score*, according to a measure $R(i)$, which accounts for the intuition that an instance is reliable, i.e. it is likely to be correct, if: *(1)* it is activated by many patterns; *(2)* the Part-of-Speech (PoS) of the instance and of the seed *s* are the same; *(3)* the semantic class of *x* and *y* are respectively similar to those of x_s and y_s. The measure is then:

$$R(i) = \alpha \frac{|P_i|}{|i|} + \beta POS_i + \gamma \left(\frac{1}{k} + \frac{1}{j} \right)$$

where P_i are the patterns activating *i*; POS_i is a binary value which is 1 if the PoS of *i* and *s* are the same, 0 otherwise; *k* and *j* are the depths of the *least common subsumer* [17] respectively between *x* and x_s and between *y* and y_s in the WordNet [6] hyperonymy hierarchy. α, β, and γ parameters sum to 1, and weight the contribution of respectively point *(1),(2)* and *(3)*. The value of the parameters can be manually set, or induced using exploratory experiments.

Validation Interface and Ontology Uploading. The ranked list of extracted instances *I* according to $R(i)$, is returned to the user, via a validation interface. The user can select the instances to be uploaded in the ontology by a simple click. To support the user and speed-up the validation, instances with different degrees of reliability are displayed in the interface with different colors. Once the validation is finished, selected instances are uploaded in the *WPro* ontology: *x* and *y* are inserted in the same ontology class of x_s and y_s and the related object property is activated. For example, if x_s=*Madrid* is an instance of the ontology class *city* and y_s=*Spain* is instance of *nation*, then the new ontological entities *New Delhi* and *India* are added as instances of the class *city* and *nation*, and related by the object property *capital-of*.

3.2 Experimental Investigation

The goal of the experiments is to verify the accuracy of the relation extraction algorithm in harvesting instances in a typical *WPro* framework, i.e. a small domain specific corpus of Wikipedia documents, and the extraction of domain related relations. We chose as domain of interest the domain of *European and Asian cities*, and *capital-of* and *located-in* as target relations. The corpus is composed of 80 Wikipedia pages about capitals, consisting in 207,555 tokens. The seed instance for the algorithm is *s=(Madrid,Spain)*, and the parameters α, β, and γ are set to 0.05, 0.25 and 0.75, by using a small annotated development corpus of 10 pages. As gold standard we use a list of instances I_{gs} manually extracted from the corpus. As the goal of the experiment is also to evaluate the effectiveness of the reliability measure $R(i)$, we measure performance in term of *precision P*, *relative-recall R*, *F-measure*, and *goldStd-recall G* at different levels of a threshold τ. The set of instances $I_\tau \in I$ which have a score $R(i)$ above the threshold are taken as accepted by the system. At each level of τ, P_τ and R_τ, F_τ and G_τ are then defined as follows:

$$P_\tau = \frac{\left| I_\tau \cap I_{gs} \right|}{\left| I_\tau \right|} \qquad R_\tau = \frac{\left| I_\tau \cap I_{gs} \right|}{\left| I \right|} \qquad F_\tau = 2\frac{P_\tau * R_\tau}{P_\tau + R_\tau} \qquad G_\tau = \frac{\left| I_\tau \cap I_{gs} \right|}{\left| I_{gs} \right|}$$

GoldStd-recall is intended to capture the recall over the gold standard, while relative-recall captures recall at a given threshold over all extracted instances. Results for the *capital-of* relation are reported in Figs. 8-9. They reveal that in general our algorithm is able to extract instances with high precision and recall. For example, at τ=0.5, precision is high (almost 0.90) while goldStd recall is still acceptable, about 0.45. Precision is in general comparable to that obtained by state of the art algorithms: for example [12] obtain 0.91 on a chemistry corpus of the same size as our for the *reaction* relation. Yet, our recall is lower, as we do not exploit generic patterns. Figures indicates that according to the intuition, as the threshold grows, precision improves, while recall decreases. This indicate that our reliability measure is coherent and can be effectively used to select correct/incorrect instances ad different levels of reliability. Fig.9 reports some of the best scoring instances extracted by the algorithm for both *capital-of* and *located-in* relations (in all, the algorithm extracted around 50 instances for both relations). From a qualitative perspective, most of the erroneous extracted instances correspond to parsing errors or to the induction of wrong patterns (e.g. the incorrect instance *(Antananarivo, University)* for the *capital-of* relation is fired by the wrong pattern *"X is home of Y"*). As a further exploratory study we experimented our algorithm using two iterations over the loop *pattern induction – instance extraction*, hoping to improve recall. Results show that we extract more correct instances, without losing much precision. It is interesting to notice that the best choice of α, β, and γ values indicates that the semantic information conveyed by the WordNet measure is the most important to select correct instances (as γ=0.75).

4 Conclusions

We presented two modules for supporting the semi-automatic enrichment and building of ontologies from Web pages, in the framework of *WPro*. Both modules guarantee a significant speed-up in the construction process, by automatically extracting information that otherwise would require time consuming manual analysis. The modules guarantee high level of precision and recall. In the future, we plan to integrate other linguistically-based modules in the *WPro* architecture, such as terminology and event extractors; and to improve the performance of TOE and the relation extractor, by using new heuristics for pattern induction. We will expand and improve the functionalities of *WPro*, to guarantee more usability and robustness in the architecture, which at the moment is intended as a prototypical framework.

References

1. Basili, R., Zanzotto, F.M.: Parsing engineering and empirical robustness. Natural Language Engineering 8/2-3, 1245–1262 (2002)
2. Berland, M., Charniak, E.: Finding parts in very large corpora. In: Proceedings of ACL-1999, College Park, MD, pp. 57–64 (1999)
3. Buitelaar, P., Cimiano, P., Magnini, B.: Ontology learning from texts: methods, evaluation and applications. IOS Press, Amsterdam (2005)
4. Caraballo, S.: Automatic acquisition of a hypernym labeled noun hierarchy from text. In: Proceedings of ACL-99, Baltimore, MD, pp. 120–126 (1999)
5. Etzioni, O., Cagarella, M.J., Downey, D., Popescu, A.M., Shaked, T., Soderland, S., Weld, D.S., Yates, A.: Unsupervised named entity extraction from the web: An experimental study. Artificial Intelligence 165(1), 91–143 (2002)
6. Christiane, F. (ed.): WordNet: Electronic Lexical Database. MIT Press, Cambridge (1998)
7. Grosso, W.E., Eriksson, H., Fergerson, R.W., Gennari, J.H., Tu, S.W., Musen, M.A.: Knowledge Modeling at the Millennium (1999)
8. Hearst, M.: Automatic acquisition of hyponyms from large text corpora. In: Proceedings of COLING-92, Nantes, France, pp. 539–545 (1992)
9. Hurst, M.: Layout and language: Beyond simple text for information interaction-modelling the table. In: Proceedings of the 2nd ICMI, Hong Kong (1999)
10. Jüling, W., Maurer, A.: Karlsruher Integriertes InformationsManagement. In: PIK 28 (2005)
11. Maedche, Volz: The Text-To-Onto Ontology Extraction and Maintenance Environment. In: Proceedings of the ICDM Workshop on integrating data mining and knowledge management, San Jose, California, USA (2001)
12. Pantel, P., Pennacchiotti, M.: Espresso: A Bootstrapping Algorithm for Automatically Harvesting Semantic Relations. In: Proceedings of COLING/ACL-06, Sydney, Australia (2006)
13. Pantel, P., Ravichandran, D.: Automatically labeling semantic classes. In: Proceedings of HLT/NAACL-04, Boston, MA, pp. 321–328 (2004)
14. Pivk, A., Cimiano, P., Sure, Y., Gams, M., Rajkovič, V., Studer, R.: Transforming arbitrary tables into logical form with TARTAR. Data & Knowledge Engineering 60, 3 (2007)
15. Ravichandran, D., Hovy, E.H.: Learning surface text patterns for a question answering system. In: Proceedings of ACL-2002, Philadelphia, PA, pp. 41–47 (2002)
16. Tiberino, A.J., Embley, D.W., Lonsdale, D.W., Ding, Y., Nagy, G.: Towards Ontology Generation from Tables. World Wide Web: Internet and Web Information Systems 8, 261–285 (2005)
17. Wu, Z., Palmer, M.: Verb semantics and lexical selection (1994)

English Querying over Ontologies: E-QuOnto[*]

Raffaella Bernardi[1], Francesca Bonin[1,2], Diego Calvanese[1],
Domenico Carbotta[1], and Camilo Thorne[1]

[1] Faculty of Computer Science
Free University of Bozen-Bolzano, Italy
`lastname@inf.unibz.it`
[2] Dipartimento di Linguistica - Università di Pisa

Abstract. Relational database (DB) management systems provide the standard means for structuring and querying large amounts of data. However, to access such data the exact structure of the DB must be know, and such a structure might be far from the conceptualization of a human being of the stored information. Ontologies help to bridge this gap, by providing a high level conceptual view of the information stored in a DB in a cognitively more natural way. Even in this setting, casual end users might not be familiar with the formal languages required to query ontologies. In this paper we address this issue and study the problem of ontology-based data access by means of natural language questions instead of queries expressed in some formal language. Specifically, we analyze how complex real life questions are and how far from the query languages accepted by ontology-based data access systems, how we can obtain the formal query representing a given natural language question, and how can we handle those questions which are too complex wrt the accepted query language.

1 Introduction

Relational database management systems (RDBMs) provide the standard means for structuring, modeling, declaring, updating and querying large amounts of structured data. The interfaces of these systems are based on formal query languages, such as SQL, that combine both declarative and imperative features (cf. [1]). Crucially, the expressive power of these formal languages is well-known, and query answering in relational databases (DBs) can be carried out efficiently in the size of the data. More precisely, the *data complexity* (i.e., the complexity measured in the size of the DB) of answering SQL (or First-Order) queries is in LOGSPACE [1], and it is precisely this property that allows RDBMSs to handle in practice very large amounts of data. However, access to these data requires knowledge of the exact structure of the DB, which might be far from the conceptualization that human beings have of the represented information. Ontologies

---

[*] This research has been partially supported by FET project TONES (Thinking ONtologiES), funded within the EU 6th Framework Programme under contract FP6-7603.

R. Basili and M.T. Pazienza (Eds.): AI*IA 2007, LNAI 4733, pp. 170–181, 2007.

help to overcome these limitations by providing a high level conceptual view of the stored information in a cognitively more natural way[12]. Recently, the problem of ontology based access to DBs has been studied. This problem poses particular challenges since on the one hand, it requires to deal with the large amount of information stored in DBs, and on the other hand, it requires to cope with incomplete knowledge[1]. In fact, the ontology encodes constraints on the domain of interest w.r.t. which data in the DB might be incomplete. For instance, the ontology might require that all instances of some class have to participate to a relation, but for some instance the DB does not contain the corresponding facts. For a concrete example, let's assume, that the ontology requires that each student attends at least one course, but the DB happens not to have any information about the course attended by the student John.

Against this background, a family of ontology languages has been proposed recently that is based on Description Logics [3], namely the *DL-Lite* family [9,8]. The kind of constraints that can be expressed in variants of *DL-Lite* tightly correspond to constraints typically encountered in conceptual data models used in DBs and software engineering. A distinguishing feature of the logics of the *DL-Lite* family is that they allow for efficiently answering queries posed to an ontology with an underlying DB, taking into account that the latter may be incomplete with respect to the constraints expressed by the ontology. The kind of queries supported in *DL-Lite* are *unions of conjunctive queries* (UCQs): *conjunctive queries* (CQs) correspond to the fragment of First-Order Logic (FOL) whose formulas are conjunctions of atoms over constants, existentially quantified variables that may be shared across the atoms, and free variables (also called *distinguished variables*)[2]. An UCQ corresponds to a disjunction of CQs, all with the same number of distinguished variables.

This paper builds on these results and considers a further problem, namely the fact that using formal query languages requires some previous training and can prove counter-intuitive to a casual end user. For such a user the intuitive appeal and understanding of the machine interface can be crucial. It would thus be suitable in such cases to shift to natural language (NL) and to use natural language questions instead of queries expressed in some formal language. In order to reach this goal, in this paper we try to answer the following questions: (*i*) how complex are natural language questions a user would ask to access data in a DB; (*ii*) how far are these real life questions from conjunctive queries; (*iii*) given a natural language question how can we obtain the formal query (in a suitable query language) representing it; (*iv*) how can we handle those questions which cannot be represented by conjunctive queries. Question (*i*) is addressed in Section 3 whereas (*ii*)–(*iv*) are the focus of Section 4. Before presenting our results, we introduce in Section 2 some preliminary technical notions. The paper presents work in progress, the ideas we are planning to further explore are summarised in Section 5.

---

[1] A further important issue that may arise in the presence of an ontology is inconsistency w.r.t. the ontology. However, we do not deal with inconsistency here.

[2] In terms of SQL, CQs correspond to the SELECT-PROJECT-JOIN fragment.

2   Preliminaries

We provide now the technical preliminaries underlying languages used in the context of ontology-based data access, both for the specification of the ontology, and for specification of queries over the ontology to access underlying data sources. When asking ourselves which are the formalisms most suited to represent the information about a domain of interest in an ontology, we can draw on the large body of research carried out in the last twenty years in structured knowledge representation, and specifically in the area of Description Logics. Description Logics (DLs) [3] are logics that allow one to structure the domain of interest by means of *concepts*, denoting sets of objects, and *roles*, denoting binary relations between (instances of) concepts. Complex concepts and role expressions are constructed starting from a set of atomic concepts and roles by applying suitable constructs. The domain of interest is then represented by means of a DL knowledge base (KB), consisting of a TBox, storing intensional information, and an ABox, storing assertional information about individual objects of the domain of interest.

We start by defining the ontology language we make use of, which is based on the recently introduced *DL-Lite* family of DLs [9,8]. Such a family of DLs is specifically tailored for an optimal tradeoff between expressive power and computational complexity of inference in the context of ontology-based data access. In the logics of the *DL-Lite* family, the TBox is constituted by a set of *assertions* of the form

$$Cl \sqsubseteq Cr \quad \text{(concept inclusion assertion)} \quad (\mathsf{funct}\ R) \quad \text{(functionality assertion)}$$
$$R_1 \sqsubseteq R_2 \quad \text{(role inclusion assertion)}$$

In the above assertions, Cl and Cr denote concepts that may occur respectively on the left and right-hand side of inclusion assertions, and R, R_1, R_2 denote roles, constructed according to the following syntax:

$$Cl \longrightarrow A \mid \exists R \mid Cl_1 \sqcap Cl_2 \qquad\qquad R \longrightarrow P \mid P^-$$
$$Cr \longrightarrow A \mid \exists R \mid Cr_1 \sqcap Cr_2 \mid \exists R.A \mid \neg A \mid \neg\exists R$$

where A denotes an atomic concept, and P denotes an atomic role.

The $\exists R$ construct is called *unqualified existential quantification*, and intuitively denotes all objects that are connected through role R to some (not further specified) object. The $\exists R.A$ construct, called *qualified existential quantification*, allows one to further qualify the object connected through role R as being an instance of concept A. Also, $\sqcap$ denotes conjunction, and $\neg$ negation (or complement). Finally, P^- denotes the binary relation that is the inverse of the one denoted by P.

We formally specify the semantics of *DL-Lite*, by providing its translation to FOL. Specifically, we map each concept C (we use C to denote an arbitrary concept, constructed applying the rules above) to a FOL formula $\varphi(C, x)$ with one free variable x (i.e., a unary predicate), and each role R to a binary predicate $\varphi(R, x, y)$ as follows:

$$\varphi(A, x) = A(x) \qquad\qquad \varphi(\exists R, x) = \exists y(\varphi(R, x, y))$$
$$\varphi(\neg C, x) = \neg\varphi(C, x) \qquad\qquad \varphi(\exists R.C, x) = \exists y(\varphi(R, x, y) \wedge \varphi(C, y))$$
$$\varphi(C_1 \sqcap C_2, x) = \varphi(C_1, x) \wedge \varphi(C_2, x)$$
$$\varphi(P, x, y) = P(x, y) \qquad\qquad \varphi(P^-, x, y) = P(y, x)$$

An inclusion assertion $Cl \sqsubseteq Cr$ of the TBox corresponds then to the universally quantified FOL sentence $\forall x(\varphi(Cl, x) \rightarrow \varphi(Cr, x))$. Similarly, $R_1 \sqsubseteq R_2$ corresponds to $\forall x\forall y(\varphi(R_1, x, y) \rightarrow \varphi(R_2, x, y))$. Instead, a functionality assertion (funct R), imposes that the binary predicate R is functional, i.e., $\forall x\forall y\forall z(\varphi(R, x, y) \wedge \varphi(R, x, z) \rightarrow y = z)$.

In *DL-Lite*, an ABox is constituted by a set of assertions on *individuals*, of the form $A(c)$ or $P(a, b)$, where A and P denote respectively an atomic concept and an atomic role, and a, and b denote constants. As in FOL, each constant is interpreted as an element of the interpretation domain, and we assume that distinct constants are interpreted as distinct individuals, i.e., we adopt the *unique name assumption* (UNA). The above ABox assertions correspond to the analogous FOL facts, or, by resorting to the above mapping, to $\varphi(A, x)(c)$ and $\varphi(R, x, y)(a, b)$, respectively.

A *model* of a *DL-Lite* KB is a FOL model of the conjunction of FOL formulas representing its semantics.

It is worth noticing that, by means of the constructs present in *DL-Lite*, one can capture almost all features of conceptual data models used in DBs and software engineering, such as the Entity-Relationship model [4] or UML class diagrams[3] Hence, the DLs of the *DL-Lite* family are well suited also to represent data stored in commercial DBMSs.

Indeed, in the setting where such data are accessed through an ontology, the DL ABox is actually represented by the DB. Alternatively, the ABox may be reconstructed from the data present in the DB through suitable mappings, that allow one also to overcome the impedance mismatch between the data values stored in the DB and the objects at the conceptual level [7].

Reasoning has been studied for several variants of logics of the *DL-Lite* family. Specifically, the logic obtained by dropping functionality assertions is called $DL\text{-}Lite_R$, and has already been adopted in the context of natural language specification of ontologies [6,5]. Instead, the logic obtained by dropping role inclusion assertions and also the construct for qualified existential quantification is called $DL\text{-}Lite_F$, and is quite close to formalisms used in conceptual modeling, such as the Entity-Relationship model. A combination of all constructs and types of assertions considered above, with some restriction on the possible interaction of functionality and role inclusions, has also been studied [7].

It has been shown in [9,8] that for the above mentioned variants of *DL-Lite* all relevant reasoning services (e.g., KB satifiability, subsumption, ecc.), are polynomial in the size of the knowledge base, and LOGSPACE in the size of the ABox only, i.e., in *data complexity* (cf. [1]).

---

[3] Complete (also called covering) hierarchies are an exception, since they require some form of disjunction, which is *not* present in *DL-Lite* (see [8] for motivations).

Given an *DL-Lite* KB $\mathcal{K}$, queries over $\mathcal{K}$ are *unions of conjunctive queries* (UCQs), which are expressions of the form $\{\boldsymbol{x} \mid \exists\boldsymbol{y}_1\, conj_1(\boldsymbol{x}, \boldsymbol{y}_1) \vee \cdots \vee \exists\boldsymbol{y}_n\, conj_n(\boldsymbol{x}, \boldsymbol{y}_n)\}$, where $\boldsymbol{x}$ is a (possibly empty) finite sequence of *distinguished variables*, each $\boldsymbol{y}_i$ is a finite sequences of (existentially quantified) variables and constants, and each $conj_i$ is a conjunction of atoms whose predicates are the concept and role symbols of the KB. If there is only one disjunct (i.e., $n = 1$), the query is called a *conjunctive query* (CQ). The FOL formula following $\mid$ is called the *body* of the query. Each distinguished variable must appear also in the body of the query. A *boolean query* is one where sequence of distinguished variables is empty.

As an example, consider the natural language questions *"Which are the red books"?*, corresponding to the CQ $\{x \mid \mathsf{book}(x) \wedge \mathsf{red}(x)\}$, and *"Which are the books read by John?"*, corresponding to the CQ $\{x \mid \mathsf{book}(x) \wedge \mathsf{read}(\mathsf{john}, x)\}$. Also, CQs may allow one to represent complex dependencies coming from relative pronouns, e.g., *"which are the students who attend a course which is taught by their father?"* can be represented by $\{x \mid \exists y_1 \exists y_2 (\mathsf{student}(x) \wedge \mathsf{attend}(x, y_1) \wedge \mathsf{teach}(y_2, y_1) \wedge \mathsf{father}(y_2, x))\}$.

Note that UCQs may contain no negation, no universal quantification, and that disjunction may appear only at the outermost level. Hence, CQs and UCQs constitute a *proper* fragment of FOL (in particular, we lack a complete set of boolean operators). In terms of SQL, it is well known that CQs correspond to the SELECT-PROJECT-JOIN fragment of SQL.

As an example, the questions *"What is causing all the joint pain?"* and *"What is the chance that aspirating a joint effusion that is not red will help the patient?"* cannot be translated into CQs or UCQs.

Given an interpretation $\mathcal{I}$ of $\mathcal{K}$, the *semantics* of a UCQ $q(\boldsymbol{x})$, denoted $q^{\mathcal{I}}$, is given by the set of tuples $\boldsymbol{c}$ of *constants*, such that, if each constant in $\boldsymbol{c}$ is assigned to the corresponding variable in $\boldsymbol{x}$, the formula that constitutes the body of q evaluates to true in $\mathcal{I}$. Notice that for a boolean query q, $q^{\mathcal{I}}$ is either empty or constituted by the empty tuple only.

It is well-known (cf. [1]) that given a finite interpretation $\mathcal{I}$ (that in our setting plays the role of a traditional database), $q^{\mathcal{I}}$ can be computed in LOGSPACE in the size of $\mathcal{I}$, i.e., in *data complexity*. However, the setting we are considering here is complicated by the fact the we are usually not given a single interpretation $\mathcal{I}$, but rather a DL KB $\mathcal{K}$, and are interested in reasoning with respect to all models of $\mathcal{K}$. In other words, we are interested in the answers to queries in the presence of *incomplete information* in the ABox/database with respect to the constraints specified by the TBox. Formally, given $\mathcal{K}$ and a UCQ $q(\boldsymbol{x})$, we are interested in computing the so-called *certain answers* to q over $\mathcal{K}$, which are defined as the set of tuples $\boldsymbol{c}$ of constants that are in $q^{\mathcal{I}}$ for *every* model $\mathcal{I}$ of $\mathcal{K}$. The problem of computing certain answers has been studied for various variants of *DL-Lite*, and it has been shown that is polynomial in the size of $\mathcal{K}$ and LOGSPACE in data complexity, i.e., in the size of the data constituted by the ABox (or the database representing it) [9,8]. However, this property crucially depends on the constructs in the DL and on the adopted query language, and does not carry over if we e.g., allow for negation or universal quantification in queries.

Recently, the system QuOnto [2] has been developed, which implements (sound and complete) algorithms for computing certain answers to UCQs over *DL-Lite* ontologies, by relying on the underlying DBMS for the actual execution of the queries and retrieval of the data.

3   Analysis of Questions Asked by Users

We are interested in understanding which natural language questions can be expressed by CQs (and UCQs) and which ones cannot. "How" and "why" questions are clearly outscoping CQs, which return only sets of tuples of objects. On the other hand, both boolean (i.e., yes/no) questions and the wh-questions built out of "which", "what", "when", "where", and "who" could be expressed as CQs if their semantic representation does not contain any of the operations not admitted in CQs, specifically disjunction, negation, and universal quantification. The question we try to address in this section is how frequent this happens and how complex are the structures of these questions. To this end, we have analysed several corpora of questions on different domains and asked in different settings:

Clinical Questions: contains users' questions on the clinical domain, mostly asked by doctors to colleagues; 435 questions, vocabulary: 3495, total tokens: 40489 (questions with introduction).

Answer.com: contains questions on different topics (e.g., art, sport, computers) asked by internet users; 444 questions[4], vocabulary: 1639, total tokens: 5791 (without introduction)[5].

TREC: we have used the TREC 2004 corpus that contains 408 questions.

Table 1. Searched Terms

Operator	Linguistic terms
Universal quantification	all, both, each, every, everybody, everyone, any (in positive context), none, nothing
Disjunction	or
Negation	not (and its abbreviations), without
Existential quantification	any, anything, anyone, anybody, some, something, someone, somebody, there is a, there are a, there was a

To understand how often FOL constructs outside the CQ fragment occur in real life questions, we have checked the occurrences of universal quantification, negation and disjunction in the corpora listed above, by searching for the frequency of the terms shown in Table 1. We are aware that these terms might not cover all the possible ways of expressing the operations under investigation,

---

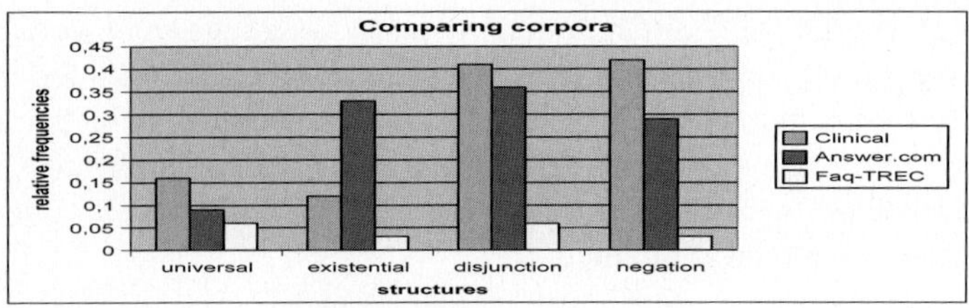

Fig. 1. Summary of the analysis

however, we believe the results do help revealing features of natural language questions with respect to the problem we are trying to tackle. To have a more general picture of the occurrences of logical operators in questions, we considered also the frequency of existential quantifiers. This was also needed in order to check whether the latter were negated, hence resolving into universal quantification. Similar studies have been conducted on other corpora containing declarative sentences and the results were different than those reported here, which highlights the peculiarity of questions.

In Figure 1, we report the results of such analyses. The chart shows the frequency of each class of terms in the three corpora. Frequency values refer to the normalized relative frequency (number of tokens/total word count multiplied by 100). As the figure shows, the use of the "forbidden" constructs is particularly frequent in natural questions even in a free text access to data. The details about the number of questions in which these operators occur are given in Table 2.

More specifically, the comparison among the corpora shows that: (i) universal quantifiers are rare in all the analysed questions; they are slightly more frequent in the Clinical Questions corpus where, anyway, they mostly occur in the declarative sentences preceding the question; (ii) existentials do occur in questions but never negated; (iii) negation and disjunction are more frequent particularly in real free text access, but still rare in questions like those in TREC.

Table 2. Number of questions

	Clinical Questions Tot: 435	Answer.com Tot: 444	TREC Tot: 408
universal	12	6	2
existential	111	22	1
disjunction	132	15	2
negation	52	13	1

Though rare, still there is the need of handling those questions that outscope the expressivity of CQs. Therefore, we now turn to analyse them in detail.

Universal quantification. Universal quantifiers have been found to occur in any syntactic position: as subject (1a) or object (1b) as well as in prepositional phrases (1c), as exemplified by the following questions taken from the Clinical Questions corpus:

(1a) *Should* all *pregnant women take a test for human immunodeficiency virus?*
(1b) *What is causing* all *the joint pain?*
(1c) *Can we use Energix for* all *five doses of DPT?*

Negation. In the analysed corpora, "negation" is used only to negate the verb of an embedded clause (2a) (never the main verb of the question or the auxiliary), or to negate adjectives (2b) or in the form of *without* (2c), as exemplified again by the Clinical Questions corpus:

(2a) *Should you give a full series of tetanus shots to an adult who* does not *know their immunization history?*
(2b) *What is the chance that aspirating a joint effusion that is* not *red or tender will yield anything diagnostically?*
(2c) *Is it possible for someone to get recurrent pelvic disease* without *a new exposure?*

Disjunction. Finally, disjunction occurs only coordinating nouns and really rarely between propositions. See the examples below taken from Answer.com.

(3a) *What is the word for the fear if viewing sports* or *playing sports?*
(3b) *Is Liberia considered a rural* or *a urban country?*

In such rare cases, we would need to resort to a UCQ, rather than a CQ, obtained by splitting up the query at each occurrence of a disjunction.

The analysed corpora contain questions whose structure is rather simple and not too far away from CQs' constructs. This could be claimed even strongly if we focus on questions asked by users to DBs. For English, we have looked into Geoquery[6] (304 questions on the geographical domain) where there is only one question of the "forbidden" class, namely one containing negation –though the corpus contains several (75) questions falling outside CQs, viz. aggregation questions (how high, how many, etc.). Similar studies have been carried out for Italian obtaining similar results.

In the remainder of the paper, we show how to build the CQ representation of a given question, and propose a method, based on *semantic weakening*, that allows us to extend the kinds of natural language questions that query answering tools over ontologies can handle.

4   Answering Natural Language Questions over Ontologies

Our third question, namely "how can we obtain a formal query (in a suitable query language) representing a given natural language question?", can be re-phrased in how well current Computational Semantics tools will perform when their output is used as input for query answering tools, as e.g., QuOnto, which accepts UCQs. Hence, we start from off-the-shelf wide-coverage parsing tools producing

---

[6] http://www.cs.utexas.edu/users/ml/geo.html

FOL meaning representation of the parsed questions. In this paper we are considering a CCG parser (paired with Boxer) [11] which outputs questions of the form[7]:

$$\{x \mid \exists \boldsymbol{y}(\varphi(\boldsymbol{y}) \wedge D(x) \wedge \exists \boldsymbol{z}(\psi(x, \boldsymbol{y}, \boldsymbol{z})))\} \tag{1}$$

where x represents the answer to the question, D is the domain of the question, ψ represents the body of the question, and φ represents the knowledge that is presupposed by the user posing the question. We consider wh-questions and boolean questions. In the first case, if the wh-phrase is *where, who/whom, how, when, what,* or *why,* then D refers to *location, person, manner, unit_of_time, thing* and *reason,* respectively. If the wh-phrase is *which,* then the domain is the head noun of the noun phrase. For example, in the question *"Which services are offered by the library?"* the domain is *services.* If the question is boolean, then the domain of the question is empty. In both cases the body of the question contains a conjunction of conditions.

For instance, the question *"Who may use the Interlibrary Loan service?"* is represented as follows:

$$\{x \mid \exists y_1 \exists y_2 (\mathsf{loan}(y_1) \wedge \mathsf{interlibrary}(y_2) \wedge \mathsf{service}(y_2) \wedge \mathsf{nn}(y_1, y_2) \wedge \mathsf{person}(x) \wedge \\ \exists z(\mathsf{use}(z) \wedge \mathsf{event}(z) \wedge \mathsf{agent}(z, x) \wedge \mathsf{patient}(z, y_2)))\}$$

As the example shows, besides the predicates introduced by the words in the question, the meaning representation produced by Boxer contains information about thematic roles too, namely **agent, patient, theme,** whose first argument appears also as argument of the unary predicate **event,** which in itself is introduced by a verb. Also, the formula in the example contains the predicate **nn,** which relates nouns that in the question occur as multi words (e.g., interlibrary loan).

In short, Boxer produces formulas of the fragment of FOL with equality and without function symbols, where predicate symbols are either unary or binary. This output must be translated into queries suitable for query answering tools. Here we focus on the structure of the logical form rather than on the predicates to be used for properly matching the ontology vocabulary.

4.1   Translation

The translation to an UCQ starts from the FOL representation of the question, as calculated by Boxer, and hence in form (1). We deal first with the easy case where both φ and ψ in that formula contain conjunctions and disjunctions only. Let $\mathsf{dnf}(\varphi) = \alpha_1 \vee \cdots \vee \alpha_n$ and $\mathsf{dnf}(\psi) = \beta_1 \vee \cdots \vee \beta_m$ be the disjunctive normal form (DNF) expansions of φ and ψ, respectively. Query (1) is then expanded into an UCQ as follows:

---

[7] Boxer actually outputs such open FOL formulas as closed formulas in which the free variable is universally quantified and the second conjunction is represented by an implication.

$$\begin{aligned}
q(x) &= \{x \mid \exists\boldsymbol{y}\exists\boldsymbol{z}(\varphi(\boldsymbol{y}) \wedge D(x) \wedge \psi(x,\boldsymbol{y},\boldsymbol{z}))\} \\
&= \{x \mid \exists\boldsymbol{y}\exists\boldsymbol{z}((\alpha_1(\boldsymbol{y}) \vee \cdots \vee \alpha_n(\boldsymbol{y})) \wedge D(x) \wedge (\beta_1(x,\boldsymbol{y},\boldsymbol{z}) \vee \cdots \vee \beta_m(x,\boldsymbol{y},\boldsymbol{z})))\} \\
&= \{x \mid \exists\boldsymbol{y}\exists\boldsymbol{z}((\alpha_1(\boldsymbol{y}) \wedge D(x) \wedge \beta_1(x,\boldsymbol{y},\boldsymbol{z})) \vee \cdots \vee (\alpha_1(\boldsymbol{y}) \wedge D(x) \wedge \beta_m(x,\boldsymbol{y},\boldsymbol{z})) \vee \\
&\qquad\qquad \cdots \\
&\qquad (\alpha_n(\boldsymbol{y}) \wedge D(x) \wedge \beta_1(x,\boldsymbol{y},\boldsymbol{z})) \vee \cdots \vee (\alpha_n(\boldsymbol{y}) \wedge D(x) \wedge \beta_m(x,\boldsymbol{y},\boldsymbol{z})))\} \\
&= \{x \mid \exists\boldsymbol{y}\exists\boldsymbol{z}(\alpha_1(\boldsymbol{y}) \wedge D(x) \wedge \beta_1(x,\boldsymbol{y},\boldsymbol{z})) \vee \cdots \vee \exists\boldsymbol{y}\exists\boldsymbol{z}(\alpha_n(\boldsymbol{y}) \wedge D(x) \wedge \beta_m(x,\boldsymbol{y},\boldsymbol{z}))\}
\end{aligned}$$

4.2 Semantic Weakening

Though rarely, universal quantifiers do occur in questions asked by users. Here we discuss a way to deal with this kind of questions. Techniques (and systems for) query answering in the setting of incomplete information provide the *certain answers* to a query – i.e., given a query in the form $q(\boldsymbol{x}) = \{\boldsymbol{x} \mid \exists\boldsymbol{y}(\varphi(\boldsymbol{x},\boldsymbol{y}))$, it returns the tuples of constants $\boldsymbol{c}$ that are guaranteed to satisfy the formula $\exists\boldsymbol{y}(\varphi(\boldsymbol{c},\boldsymbol{y}))$ in all models of the ontology. Certain answers can also be characterized by resorting to the minimal knowledge operator $\mathbf{K}$ [14,15], where $\mathbf{K}\varphi$ denotes that "φ is known to hold by the ontology". In this way, the answers to the query q above can be defined as the tuples $\boldsymbol{c}$ of constants that satisfy the epistemic formula $\mathbf{K}\exists\boldsymbol{y}(\varphi(\boldsymbol{c},\boldsymbol{y})))$.

A question containing universal quantification results in a query of the form:

$$\varphi(\boldsymbol{x}) \wedge \forall\boldsymbol{y}(D(\boldsymbol{y}) \rightarrow \exists\boldsymbol{z}(\psi(\boldsymbol{x},\boldsymbol{y},\boldsymbol{z})))$$

Its intended semantics are captured by the equivalent epistemic query:

$$\mathbf{K}(\varphi(\boldsymbol{x}) \wedge \forall\boldsymbol{y}(D(\boldsymbol{y})\rightarrow\exists\boldsymbol{z}(\psi(\boldsymbol{c},\boldsymbol{y},\boldsymbol{z})))) \equiv \mathbf{K}\varphi(\boldsymbol{x}) \wedge \mathbf{K}\,\forall\boldsymbol{y}(D(\boldsymbol{y})\rightarrow\exists\boldsymbol{z}(\psi(\boldsymbol{c},\boldsymbol{y},\boldsymbol{z})))$$

The occurrence of a universal quantification in the scope of the $\mathbf{K}$ operator leads to a query that cannot be handled directly by systems like QuOnto. In order to make the query answerable, we can apply to it some kind of *semantic weakening*. The intuition behind the proposed weakening follows from the fact that all the system can do is try to find a counterexample to the given implication: if it fails, then the implication can be assumed to hold. Hence, the key step consists in substituting the knowledge operator $\mathbf{K}$ enclosing the universal quantification with the belief operator $\mathbf{B}$, i.e., $\mathbf{K}\varphi(\boldsymbol{x})\wedge\mathbf{B}\,\forall\boldsymbol{y}(D(\boldsymbol{y}) \rightarrow \exists\boldsymbol{z}(\psi(\boldsymbol{x},\boldsymbol{y},\boldsymbol{z})))$.

The derived formula expresses the fact that all the system can do is test whether the universally quantified subformula is consistent with the knowledge base – i.e., the knowledge base does not entail the existence of a counterexample. Making use of the standard equivalence $\mathbf{B}\varphi \equiv \neg\mathbf{K}\neg\varphi$, the whole query can be rewritten as follows (in NNF), i.e., $\mathbf{K}\varphi(\boldsymbol{x}) \wedge \neg\mathbf{K}\,\exists\boldsymbol{y}(D(\boldsymbol{y}) \wedge \forall\boldsymbol{z}(\neg\psi(\boldsymbol{x},\boldsymbol{y},\boldsymbol{z})))$.

This newly introduced universal quantification poses the same problem with respect to query answering. We apply the same kind of weakening, replacing again the knowledge operator with the belief operator, i.e., $\mathbf{K}\varphi(\boldsymbol{x}) \wedge \neg\mathbf{K}\,\exists\boldsymbol{y}(D(\boldsymbol{y})\wedge\mathbf{B}\,\forall\boldsymbol{z}(\neg\psi(\boldsymbol{x},\boldsymbol{y},\boldsymbol{z})))$, which is equivalent to the final query $\mathbf{K}\varphi(\boldsymbol{x})\wedge \neg\mathbf{K}\,\exists\boldsymbol{y}(D(\boldsymbol{y}) \wedge \neg\mathbf{K}\,\exists\boldsymbol{z}(\psi(\boldsymbol{x},\boldsymbol{y},\boldsymbol{z})))$.

Queries in this form correspond to the `SELECT/FROM/WHERE/NOT_IN` fragment of SQL, which can be efficiently answered by systems for query answering over ontologies such as QuOnto, by combining the computation of certain answers with the computation of a set difference (cf. [10])

Going back to natural language, this process would correspond to answer a question like *"What is causing all the joint pain?"* with *"I am not aware of any joint pain that is not caused by the following diseases"*, when the system does retrieve some disease.

5   Conclusions and Future Work

The analysed corpora have shown that (*i*) the natural language questions a user would ask in order to access data in a DB are rather simple (compared to other forms of free text); (*ii*) often these real life questions are actually representable by CQs; (*iii*) given a natural language question, its corresponding query can be obtained by translating FOL representation outputs of state-of-the-art (wide coverage) parsers; (*iv*) questions that cannot be represented by CQs (or UCQs) could be handled via some form of semantic weakening, as illustrated by the case of universal quantifier. A similar method could be used to answer questions containing negation. Also, strategies for handling aggregations could be considered in the described framework. The observed data have also shown that quite often users would use plurals rather that an explicit universal quantifier. Hence, it would be interesting to check how the proposed method could be extended to properly capture their meaning. The work described in [17] could be taken as the starting point.

The output of the parser suggests an improvement to the application of the query answering tool to better meet the user expectations, viz. treat differently the presupposed knowledge in the question representation from the one in the body of the question. In the example considered in Section 4, "Who may use the Interlibrary Loan service?" the existence of an "interlibrary loan service" is presupposed. The system could verify the presupposition before answering the actual questions and give feedback to the user in case the presupposition is actually falsified. Evaluations of the proposed approach should be carried out.

Our work shows that the syntactic constructs present in user questions might in general not constitute a problem, and presents techniques to handle the more problematic cases. However, an important aspect that is largely left open in the present paper, while being addressed in other systems, e.g., Aqualog [16], is the problem of bridging the gap between the terminology of the user and the ontology terms and structure. To address this problem, on the one hand, lexical resources can be used to overcome differences in the terminology, by substituting user terms with appropriate synonyms present in the ontology. Notice also that QuOnto itself may expand a CQ into an UCQ by substituting a term with a collection of terms related to the first one through a (generalization) hierarchy. On the other hand, we are working on enriching our framework with mappings (in the style of local-as-view mappings used in data integration [13]) from the ontology structures to suitable meaning representations, corresponding to the various ways in which users may query the ontology structures. We aim at constructing the mappings semi-automatically, by exploiting verbalizations of the ontology structures.

References

1. Abiteboul, S., Hull, R., Vianu, V.: Foundations of Databases. Addison Wesley Publ. Co., London (1995)
2. Acciarri, A., Calvanese, D., De Giacomo, G., Lembo, D., Lenzerini, M., Palmieri, M., Rosati, R.: QuOnto: QUerying ONTOlogies. In: Proc. of AAAI 2005 (2005)
3. Baader, F., Calvanese, D., McGuinness, D., Nardi, D., Patel-Schneider, P.F. (eds.): The Description Logic Handbook: Theory, Implementation and Applications. Cambridge University Press, Cambridge (2003)
4. Batini, C., Ceri, S., Navathe, S.B.: Conceptual Database Design, an Entity-Relationship Approach. Benjamin and Cummings Publ. Co. (1992)
5. Bernardi, R., Calvanese, D., Thorne, C.: Expressing DL-Lite ontologies with controlled english. In: Proc. of DL 2007 (2007)
6. Bernardi, R., Calvanese, D., Thorne, C.: Lite natural language. In: IWCS-7. Proc. of the 7th Int. Workshop on Computational Semantics (2007)
7. Calvanese, D., De Giacomo, G., Lembo, D., Lenzerini, M., Poggi, A., Rosati, R.: Linking data to ontologies: The description logic DL-Lite$_A$. In: Proc. of OWLED 2006 (2006)
8. Calvanese, D., De Giacomo, G., Lembo, D., Lenzerini, M., Rosati, R.: Data complexity of query answering in description logics. In: Proc. of KR 2006 (2006)
9. Calvanese, D., De Giacomo, G., Lembo, D., Lenzerini, M., Rosati, R.: DL-Lite: Tractable description logics for ontologies. In: Proc. of AAAI 2005 (2005)
10. Calvanese, D., De Giacomo, G., Lembo, D., Lenzerini, M., Rosati, R.: EQL-Lite: Effective first-order query processing in description logics. In: Proc. of IJCAI 2007 (2007)
11. Curran, J.R., Clark, S., Bos, J.: Linguistically motivated large-scale NLP with C&C and Boxer. In: ACL 2007. Proc. of the Demonstrations Session of the 45th Annual Meeting of the Association for Computational Linguistics (2007)
12. Guarino, N.: Formal ontology in information systems. In: FOIS'98. Proc. of the Int. Conf. on Formal Ontology in Information Systems, IOS Press, Amsterdam (1998)
13. Lenzerini, M.: Data integration: A theoretical perspective. In: Proc. of PODS 2002 (2002)
14. Levesque, H.J.: Foundations of a functional approach to knowledge representation. Artificial Intelligence 23 (1984)
15. Levesque, H.J., Lakemeyer, G.: The Logic of Knowledge Bases. The MIT Press, Cambridge (2001)
16. Lopez, V., Pasin, M., Motta, E.: AquaLog: An ontology-portable question answering system for the Semantic Web. In: Gómez-Pérez, A., Euzenat, J. (eds.) ESWC 2005. LNCS, vol. 3532, Springer, Heidelberg (2005)
17. Schwertel, U.: Plural Semantics for Natural Language Understanding – A Computational Proof-Theoretic Approach. PhD thesis, University of Zurich (2004)

Use of Ontologies in Practical NL Query Interpretation

Leonardo Lesmo and Livio Robaldo

Dipartimento di Informatica – Università di Torino,
C.so Svizzera 185, 10149, Torino, Italy
{lesmo, robaldo}@di.unito.it

Abstract. This paper describes how a domain ontology has been used in practical system of query interpretation. It presents a general methodology for building a semantic and language-independent representation of the meaning of the query on the basis of the contents of the ontology. The basic idea is to look for paths on the ontology connecting concepts related to words appearing in the NL query. The final result is what has been called *Ontological Query*, i.e. a semantic description of the user's target. Since the domain is restricted, the problem of semantic ambiguity is not as relevant as in unrestricted applications, but some hints about how to obtain unambiguous representation will be given.

Keywords: NLP, Semantics, Ontologies.

1 Introduction

In the attempt to access information via NL, coverage and depth of analysis are competing. In case of complete coverage (any domain and any kind of structuring of the data, from Web pages to structured DB), the current technology puts at disposal mainly keyword search, possibly enhanced via some morphological adjustment [6]. EuroWordNet has been used for overcoming the language barrier [13]. Also, taxonomic-ontological information has been used to exploit knowledge about subordinate terms [9]. Partial syntactic analysis has been proposed, as chunk parsing [1], in order to extract NP from pieces of text, so that complex descriptions may be used [2]. An overview of methods, tool and approaches for using ontologies in natural language understanding is [12].

On the other hand, in limited domains, deep NL understanding could be a reasonable approach. It is "knowledge intensive", in the sense that the a wide-coverage, robust grammar is needed for the language under investigation, as well as an ontology describing the domain. In this paper, we aim at showing that the approach is feasible, by describing a platform based on general linguistic and semantic tools. The Natural Language Processor that we describe is embedded within a dialogue system that keeps track of the interaction and of the user needs and decides when the information provided by the user is sufficient to access the data on the backend database. Moreover, the system includes a speech interface in order to enable the user to interact via voice through a telephone call. However, the present paper is focused on the linguistic processing, so that only a few details will be given about the whole system architecture.

R. Basili and M.T. Pazienza (Eds.): AI*IA 2007, LNAI 4733, pp. 182–193, 2007.

One of the main features of the platform is the approach to multilinguality. Since the partners in the project involved the municipalities of Barcelona (Spain), Torino (Italy), and the London borough of Camden, four languages were selected for the prototype, i.e. Catalan, English, Italian, and Spanish. However, the original idea of the project was that new languages had to be added with limited effort, so the architecture had to constrain as much as possible the impact of language-dependent knowledge. The solution found requires, for any new language, the representation of lexical knowledge (which is, of course, language dependent) and the adaptation of the syntactic knowledge base (which, again, is largely language-dependent).

After these pieces of language-dependent knowledge are used by the processor, the result is a syntactic tree, annotated with references to semantic concepts. The basic assumption is that, starting from this representation of the user's input, the remaining part of the process can be carried out in a completely language-independent way. This remaining part concerns the actual representation of the meaning of the sentence, i.e. the actual process of semantic interpretation (apart from lexical access). The semantic interpretation is carried out on the basis of semantic knowledge stored in an ontology. It contains data about the types of events that the user may refer to (concerts, movies, theatre plays, etc.), to the dates and the places where they are given, and to the participants (e.g. the concert director) in the event. The ontology, is, of course, language independent, so that a new language can be added without affecting in any way the ontological knowledge base. In this way, we preserve the locality of linguistic knowledge and use effectively, in the interpretation process, in-depth ontological knowledge of the domain of application.

Two modules that are worth mentioning, though they are not in the focus of this paper, concern the speech analysis and the translation of the abstract semantic representation (which we call Ontological Query) in terms understandable by the Dialogue Manager (DM) and useful for accessing the Backend database that stores the actual data about the cultural events. The first module gets the sound stream and, according to a compiled probabilistic language model returns the most probable string corresponding to the input. Then, this string is treated as if it were a textual input (so that the same syntactic-semantic interpreter is used in both cases). The DM models the dialogue in terms of "attributes", i.e. feature-value pairs: the dialogue manager collects these pairs and, according to the pairs obtained so far, decides if another question must be asked to the user (so that the dialogue continues), or the collected information is sufficient for an efficient access to the backend DB. Some more details about this last module will be given in section 5.

This paper aims at describing the way the ontological query is built, starting from the input string. In fig.1, we report the architecture of the whole system. (some details about the parser are reported in [7]).

2 Multilinguality

The parser that analyses the input is a robust chunk-based parser that produces a dependency tree, i.e. a tree such that, approximately, each word of the input sentence corresponds to a node of the tree, and viceversa. Dependency parsing has received great attention in the linguistic literature (e.g. [11], [5]); among its features, the one which is most relevant here is the strict correspondence between a dependency tree and a predicate-argument structure.

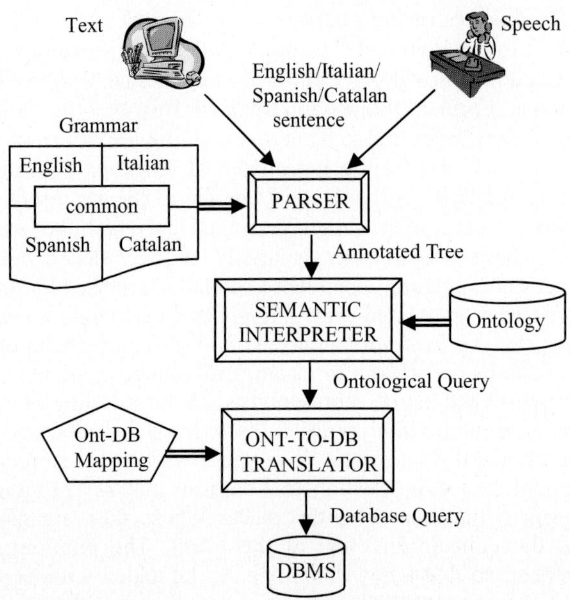

Fig. 1. The architecture of the system

In order to describe in a clearer way the operations of the system, in this paper we follow the processing steps for the sentence:

- *"Can you tell me which cabaret events I can see tomorrow?"*
- *"Puoi dirmi che spettacoli di cabaret posso vedere domani?"*

The syntactic analysis is carried out in two main steps. First, chunks corresponding to non-verbal subtrees are built, then they are assembled in a whole connected structure using information about verbal subcategorization. The first step produces the following result on the example sentence:

- $Could_{V\text{-}modal\text{-}past}$ $[you_{Pron\text{-}2nd}]_{Pron}$ $tell_{V\text{-}inf}$ $[me_{Pron\text{-}1st\text{-}dative}]_{Pron}$ $[which_{Adj\text{-}interr}$ $cabaret_{Noun}$ $events_{Noun}]_{N\text{-}group}^{1}$ $[I_{Pron\text{-}1st\text{-}nom}]_{Pron}$ $can_{V\text{-}modal\text{-}pres}$ $see_{V\text{-}inf}$ $[tomorrow_{Adv}]_{A\text{-}group}$?

- $Puoi_{V\text{-}modal\text{-}2nd\text{-}sing\text{-}pres}$ $dir_{V\text{-}inf}$ $[mi_{Pron\text{-}1st\text{-}dative}]_{Pron}$ $[che_{Adj\text{-}interr}$ $spettacoli_{Noun}$ $[di_{Prep}$ $cabaret_{Noun}]_{P\text{-}group}]_{N\text{-}group}$ $posso_{V\text{-}modal.1st\text{-}sing\text{-}pres}$ $[vedere_{V\text{-}inf}$ $[domani_{Adv}]_{A\text{-}group}$?

Actually, the chunks are internally structured as subtrees. For space reasons, this structure will be presented only in the final result of the analysis (see fig.2). Before the second step, some heuristic rules take care of determining clause boundaries, as shown below:

---

[1] The label *N-group* roughly corresponds to NP. It has been adopted to recall that we are working with dependency structures, and not with standard constituents.

- $\{Could_{V\text{-}modal\text{-}past}\ [you_{Pron\text{-}2nd}]_{Pron}$

  $\{tell_{V\text{-}inf}\ [me_{Pron\text{-}1st\text{-}dative}]_{Pron}$

  $\{[which_{Adj\text{-}interr}\ cabaret_{Noun}\ events_{Noun}]_{N\text{-}group}\ [I_{Pron\text{-}1st\text{-}nom}]_{Pron}\ can_{V\text{-}modal\text{-}pres}$

  $\{see_{V\text{-}inf}\ [tomorrow_{Adv}]_{A\text{-}group}?\}\}\}$

- $\{Puoi_{V\text{-}modal\text{-}2nd\text{-}sing\text{-}pres}$

  $\{\ dir_{V\text{-}inf}\ [mi_{Pron\text{-}1st\text{-}dative}]_{Pron}$

  $\{[che_{Adj\text{-}interr}\ spettacoli_{Noun}[di_{Prep}cabaret_{Noun}]_{P\text{-}group}]_{N\text{-}group}posso_{V\text{-}modal.1\text{-}sing\text{-}pres}$

  $\{\ [vedere_{V\text{-}inf}\ [domani_{Adv}]_{A\text{-}group}?\}\}\}\}$

Finally, subcategorization information is applied. Since "to can" is a *modal-verb*, it expects two arguments: a nominal group and a verbal group headed by an infinite verb. In the English version, the two arguments are found, while in Italian the first one is missing (pro-drop), so a trace is inserted. This trace (Italian) and "you" (English) are linked to the verb via a *verb-subj* arc, while the governed subordinate is linked via *verb+modal-indcompl* (fig.2). The "to tell" (dire) verb licenses three arguments: *verb-subj*, *verb-obj*, and *verb-indobj* (where *verb-obj* can be either a *N-group* or a *V-group*, and *verb-indobj* must either be in the dative case, or be introduced by a suitable preposition). Moreover, a movement is induced by the governing modal, so that *verb-subj* is filled by a trace co-referring to the *verb-subj* of the modal. The match of the expected arguments with the input produces the linking of "me" ("mi") as *verb-indobj*, and the inner clause governed by "to can" (potere) as *vern-obj* (see fig.2). Finally, the inner clause is analysed in similar way[2].

The dependency tree of the English example is shown in fig.2. In the tree, there appear the three traces mentioned above. The labels on the arcs are organized in order to mark the syntactic/semantic role of the dependent with respect to the governor [3]. The labels seem to be reasonably readable. We note that we keep apart arguments via the *arg* or *indcompl* component of the label (*verb-subj, verb-obj,* and *verb-indobj* are implicitly *arg*) from adjuncts (called "modifiers", see the *advb-rmod-time* label in the figure). Note that the Noun Groups are headed by the determiner, an approach which is widely accepted in dependency grammar (see, for instance [5]).

Could you tell me which cabaret concerts I can see tomorrow?

The parser was not developed expressly for the project, but it is a wide-coverage parser used for parsing general texts. It has been used for supporting the construction of the TUT Italian Treebank [4], and a small set of annotated sentences exist for English. During the project activity, it was extended to cover Spanish and Catalan. It includes about 300 chunking rules, 70% of which are common to different languages, while 30% are language specific.

---

[2] The match between the expected arguments and the input structure is much more complex than this, since it has to take into account transformations (e.g. passivization) and adjuncts.

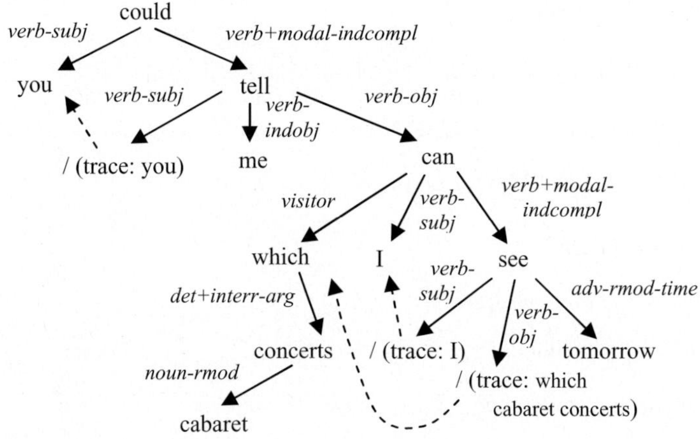

Fig. 2. The dependency tree of

3   Semantic Knowledge

The description of the domain is contained in an ontological KB. Since the whole NLP component of the system was developed in LISP, the ontology has been implemented in LISP[3]. However, in order to have a friendly interface for maintaining it, a translator from OWL ([10]) to LISP has been implemented, by the ISOCO partners of the Project. We adopt here a graphical representation similar to KL-one (see fig.3) in order to increase readability. In the figure, we include some concepts needed to cover the analysis of our example. Note, in particular, the role of *descriptions*. They have been introduced in order to keep apart the concept itself from the way it can be "communicated" outside (e.g. to the user)[4]. See the *&description* relation, whose range is a subconcept of *££datatype*.

In order to get access to the ontology, the syntactic tree (see fig.2) is annotated with word meanings. The mapping is simply expressed as a mapping between words and concepts (nodes) in the ontology. It is just a set of pairs *<word concept>*, as shown in fig.4, where the ££ prefix marks concepts in the ontology[5]. With respect to semantic ambiguity, it is represented by including in the table a list of concepts in a

---

[3] The ontology used in the current prototype includes about 210 concepts and 95 relations. Relations (e.g. *event-day*, in fig.3) are implemented, in the LISP version, as concepts having explicit *range* and *domain* links to other concepts. With respect to instances, their number is not fixed, since it depends on the current content of the Backend DB (currently, there are about 2000 instances, but see footnote 1 above).

[4] In the figure, we have omitted for space reasons the *££, &* and *£* prefixes the we use as mnemonics to keep apart concepts, relations, and instances.

[5] The correspondence between the English dictionary and the concept names is only aimed at enhancing readability; nothing changes in the behaviour of the system, in case a name such as *££location* is consistently changed into *&%$X7723*.

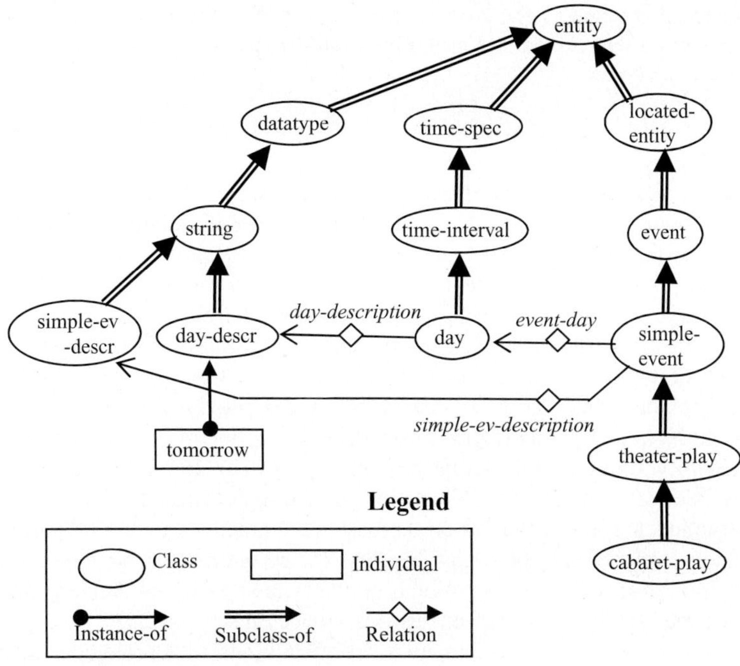

Fig. 3. A portion of the Ontology

Italian	English	Concept
potere	can	££can
dire	tell	££tell
cabaret	cabaret	££cabaret
domani	tomorrow	£tomorrow
…	…	…

Fig. 4. The word (stem) to concept mapping. Shown only for Italian and English. Similar tables exist for Spanish and Catalan.

single row. So, the lemma "theatre" corresponds to the pair <*££theatre ££theatre-loc*>, where the first one is the artistic genre, while the second is the physical place.

Not much has been done to date to handle non-content words (as articles and, at least in part, prepositions), which deserve further study. However, as a first solution, for prepositions we adopted a two-level solution: preposition in a language are mapped to a language-independent preplate table that, given two concepts connected via the preposition, returns a list of possible connecting relations. For instance, Italian "di", English "of", and Spanish "de" are mapped to --*of-relation*. In the preplate table, it is specified that when *--of-relation* is used to connect, e.g. *££office* and *££complex-event*, it has to be interpreted as a reference to *&has-office*[6].

4 Semantic Interpretation

The semantic interpreter takes apart two different types of user input: information givings and queries. This is due to the fact that, during the dialogue flow, two main situations may arise: the user asks an explicit question (usually at the beginning of the dialogue) as "Which concerts of classical music may I see?", or s/he answers a previous system question, as "Tonight or tomorrow", in reply to "When do you want to see it?". In the first case, a full query must be built, since the system could, in principle, access the DB (in case sufficient information was provided); in the second case, the provided data must be integrated in the previously collected pieces of information. Note that the dialogue is user-driven: in principle, the user can start with any sentence, without explicit requests from the system. For instance, simple noun groups as "Concerts of January 25" are interpreted as full queries. However, the two classes of inputs are not kept apart on the basis of syntactic structure: "I would like to know which concerts take place on January 25" is interpreted in the same way as "Concerts of January 25" or as "Which concerts take place on January 25?" or as "Could you please tell me which concerts take place on January 25?".

According to this categorization, two different kinds of Ontological queries are built. In case of answers, we get the following structure: *(ABOUT … WHERE …)*, while in case of queries we get *(SELECT … FROM … WHERE …)*. Since the first structure is simpler, we focus the description on the second one. It is clear that the second form mirrors classical DB query languages. In fact, in a version of the system not based on dialogue, the single user input was always interpreted as full DB query (see [8]). However, the structure is general enough to cope with any kind of request, since it keeps apart the focused concept (FROM clause), what is asked about it (SELECT clause) and what are the criteria for choosing the specific individuals of interest (WHERE clause). Our example produces the query:

SELECT
    (domain-of *&simple-ev-description* range *££simple-ev-descr* subclass-of *$string*)
FROM *££simple-event*
WHERE
    (*££simple-event* subclass-of *££event* (cardinality pl) has-subclass *££simple-event*
        (and ((has-subclass *££theater-play* has-subclass *$$cabaret-play*)
          (domain-of *&event-day* range *££day* domain-of *&day-description*
            range *££day-descr* (eq *£tomorrow*)))))

In this Ontological Query, the focused concept is *££simple-event*. A *££simple-event* is externally given as a *££simple-ev-descr*, which is a subclass of *$string* (the $ prefix identifies basic datatypes), which is connected to *££simple-event* via the

---

[6] The fact that the preplate table is language-independent has not to be taken as a theoretical claim. It is clear that "of" in English has a different meaning than "de" in Spanish. But this has been proven as a viable solution in the application domain.

££simple-ev-description relation[7]. The *WHERE* clause gives the ontological specification of the relevant events. It expresses the path that links the *££simple-event* concept to the subtype *££cabaret* and to the time *£tomorrow*.

The construction of the query is based on a separation between the topic and the focus of the sentence. In our example, "Which events" is the topic, while the focus is built by combining "cabaret" and "tomorrow". Usually, the topic is marked by a question element, i.e. an adverb ("where"), or a question adjective ("which" in our example), while the focus is given by other dependents. However, in order to build up the ontological query, it is more useful to think in terms of "goal" and "restrictions". The goal consists in the semantic "head" of the focus, while the restrictions are determined on the basis of possible modifiers of the head plus other components of the sentence[8]. The interpretation process is carried out in two main steps: first the syntactic tree is annotated with semantic information, then the annotated tree is used to produce the ontological query.

The input sentence often includes elements which are not useful for determining topic and focus, as, for instance, "Puoi dirmi" (can you tell me), "Vorrei sapere" (I would like to know), "per favore" (please). Some of these elements are governors of the actual query sentence (i.e. they occur higher in the parse tree). Others (as 'please') depend on the main verb of the sentence. The first step of the translator is to travel down the tree in order to skip the upper elements. When the actual top verb (the useful one) is found, then the query elements are sought below it. The topic and the focus are interpreted separately, but some join element is used. In this example, the join element is the word "events" (spettacoli), which, in the tree, has been associated with the concept *££event* during the annotation phase. Intuitively, the sentence is interpreted as follows:

a)   what is desired is the "which" (list) of some "events"
b)   the involved "events" are of type "cabaret" and must occur "tomorrow"

Now, the problem is to find two subpaths, the first describing how is built an event list (i.e. how can it be given in a readable way) and the second that links "events" to "cabaret" (notice that, until now, we do not know that cabaret is a subtype of event, cfr. "evening events"), and to "tomorrow". We adopted two different solutions.

As concerns the path from a concept to a "goal" (i.e. useful information) we adopted a knowledge-intensive solution, in the sense that an additional knowledge repository has been built that contains information about the reasonable answer. Note that this is a kind of inverse index, where ontology concepts are the keys and paths from concepts to basic data types are indexed. So that the number of entries cannot exceed the number of concepts in the ontology. In the case of the example, it specifies the path from *££simple-event:*

££simple-event domain-of *&simple-ev-description* range *££simple-ev-descr* subclass-of *$string*

---

[7] About 35 concepts in the ontology are related to descriptions.

[8] Some yes/no questions are handled as implicit requests of information. So, in *Ci sono concerti al Regio domani?[Are there concerts at the Regio tomorrow?],* in case the answer is affirmative, the list of relevant concerts are returned.

This is intended to mean that simple events have an associated description (their name), which is a string.

For what concerns the "restriction" of the query, i.e. the part regarding the fact that the event is related to cabaret and has to occur tomorrow), we adopted a substantially different approach, i.e. we assumed that it is possible to automatically find a path from the concept *££event* and the concept *££cabaret* (and from *££event* to *£tomorrow*). This is carried out by looking for the shortest path connecting the two concepts in the ontology (without counting *subclass-of* links, in order to account for inheritance). In our example, this is done twice. First, the shortest path between *££event* and *££cabaret-play* is looked for[9]. This returns the following path:

> *££event* has-subclass *££simple-event* has-subclass *££theater-play* has-subclass *££cabaret-play*

Then, the path from *££event* to *£tomorrow* is retrieved in an analogous way. The result is the following:

> *££event* has-subclass *££simple-event* domain-of *&event-day* range *££day* domain-of *&day-description* range *££day-descr* (eq *£tomorrow*)

Then since we have two subconditions, the "and" logical connective is including in the resulting ontological query, and the result is simplified by merging the common prefix.

With respect to semantic ambiguity, we note that the strategy described above has been successful in disambiguation, by launching the search for the shortest path on the ambiguous concepts (e.g. from *££event* to <*££theatre-play ££theatre-loc*> wrt. from *££location* to <*££theatre-play ££theatre-loc*>). We repeat, however, that this is useful on limited domains, while semantic disambiguation requires more complex techniques in unrestricted domains.

5   Translation into Attributes

In this short section, we provide some details about the last step of the process, i.e. the translation of the Ontological Query into objects usable by the Dialogue Manager. Although this is not the focus of the paper, it is useful to understand in what sense the Ontological Query is independent not only of the particular language, but also of the processes that lead to the actual access to the requested data.

The Dialogue Manager (DM) is based on <feature, value> pairs. These objects are collected by the DM, in order to enable the access to the data base of events. Upon receiving a set of pairs from the NL processor, it checks of the number of items that will be retrieved by using the pairs as selection criteria is below a certain threshold. In such a case, the database is accessed and the results are returned to the user, who is then asked if s/he wants further details. If the retrieved items are too many to be successfully presented to the user (e.g a list of 100 titles), then the DM asks for further conditions (e.g. constraints on the date, the place, the type of event).

---

[9] Note that in the Italian version, during the interpretation of "spettacoli di cabaret" the preplate table mentioned above is used.

The mapping from the ontological query to the DM objects is represented as simple patterns associated with the concepts that may appear in the query. Two examples of such mappings are reported below.

(££cabaret-event (|channelName| "theatre") (|subChannelName| "cabaret"))
(£tomorrow (|date| (fun (get-tomorrow-date)))))

The first example is the simplest one, where to the concept *££cabaret-event* the attributes *|channelName|*, and *|subChannelName|*, with values "theatre" and "cabaret" are associated. In the second example *£tomorrow* is associated with a procedure (*get-tomorrow-date*) that gets the absolute expression for the tomorrow date and associates it to the *|date|* attribute. The final result of the translation is reported below.

((|queryFocus| (|date| |subchannelName| |channelName|))
  (|channelName| "theatre")
  (|subchannelName| "cabaret")
  (|date| |20070424|)   )

6   Conclusions

This paper describes a multilingual system enabling a user to ask for information either via voice or via written queries in a limited domain. The main features of the system are the modular approach, allowing for extensions to new language without concern to the conceptual description of the domain (apart the mapping from word to concepts), and the exploitation of an ontological knowledge base as a way to express the queries in a language-independent and DB-independent way. The last feature, which has not been in the focus of the paper, is particularly important in the present phase of the project, where a new version of the Dialogue Manager is being implemented. In fact, the current architecture allows us to carry out the required changes without affecting in any way the syntactic-semantic module. Also, the ontology proper is not affected in any way, since the features of the application domain remain the same, and the only modifications concern the mapping between concepts and objects used by the dialogue manager (the <attribute, value> pairs).

The actual implementation of the system shows that the current technology (including, beyond the modules that have been described in the paper, the speech interface) is able to provide the basis for deep syntactic and semantic analysis, overcoming, in limited domains, the problems associated with simple keyword search or with shallow linguistic processing.

We must stress again that the grammars used for the syntactic analysis were not designed for the project, but they are wide-coverage grammars able to cope with any type of text. Only some limited refinements were needed to cope with the peculiarities of the application domain. This is further evidence for the claim that current linguistic resources can really be applied to different kinds of applications. This has in fact been verified in the last phase of the project, where the system has been applied to a completely different application domain (a service that allows user to ask for support in the collection of large objects being thrown away by the user).

However, one of the main drawbacks of the current implementation is its failure to have the ontology linked to a well-founded top-level ontology. A work which is planned for the next future is its integration with the DOLCE top-level [http://www.loa-cnr.it/DOLCE.html].

Finally, we remind that the system does not include four separate grammars, but a single one, including specific rules for different languages. This is, of course, favoured by the fact that all involved languages are western languages and, in particular, Catalan, Italian, and Spanish have strong similarities. We are currently planning, with the support of a new international project, to check the approach also on Hindi, i.e. a language having very different features.

Acknowledgements

This work described has been carried out within the HOPS project funded by the EC (IST-2002-507967). HOPS means "Enabling an Intelligent Natural Language Based Hub for the Deployment of Advanced Semantically Enriched Multi-channel Mass-scale Online Public Services" and is devoted to the access via speech and text to public services. Although the work described here has been carried out at the University of Torino (but Speech Interface is due to Loquendo, the Dialogue Manager to the Polytechnic University of Cataluna, and the OWL to Lisp converter to ISOCO) it could not have been possible without the continuous interaction with the partners in the project. All of them made significant contributions, but we want to mention here especially Marta Gatius and Meritxell Gonzales (TALP, University of Barcelona). Also, Morena Danieli and Sheyla Militello (Loquendo S.p.A., Torino), helped us to clarify some points of the approach described herein.

References

1. Abney, S.P.: Parsing by Chunks. In: Berwick, R.C., Abney, S.P., Tenny, C. (eds.) Principle-Based Parsing: Computation and Psycholinguistics, Kluwer, Dordrecht (1991)
2. Alfonseca, E., Guirao, J.M., Moreno-Sandoval, A.: A study of chunk-based and keyword-based approaches for generating headlines. In: Vicedo, J.L., Martínez-Barco, P., Muñoz, R., Saiz Noeda, M. (eds.) EsTAL 2004. LNCS (LNAI), vol. 3230, pp. 395–406. Springer, Heidelberg (2004)
3. Bosco, C., Lombardo, V.: A relation-based schema for treebank annotation. In: Cappelli, A., Turini, F. (eds.) AI*IA 2003: Advances in Artificial Intelligence. LNCS, vol. 2829, pp. 462–473. Springer, Heidelberg (2003)
4. Bosco, C., Lombardo, V.: Comparing linguistic information in treebank annotations. In: LREC06. 5th Edition of the International Conference on Language Resources and Evaluation, Genova, Italy (2006)
5. Hudson, R.: English word grammar. Basil Blackwell, Oxford, Cambridge, MA (1990)
6. Järvelin, K., Pirkola, A.: Morphological Processing in Mono- and Cross-Lingual Information Retrieval. In: Arppe, A., et al. (eds.) Inquiries into Words, Constraints and Contexts, pp. 214–226 (2005)

7. Lesmo, L., Lombardo, V., Bosco, C.: Treebank Development: the TUT Approach. In: Sangal, Bendre (eds.) Recent Advances in Natural Language Processing, pp. 61–70. Vikas Publ. House, New Delhi (2002)
8. Lesmo, L., Robaldo, L.: From Natural Language to Databases via Ontologies. In: LREC06. 5th Edition of the International Conference on Language Resources and Evaluation, Genova, Italy (2006)
9. Maynard, D., Yankova, M., Kourakis, A., Kokossis, A.: Ontology-based information extraction for market monitoring and technology watch. In: Proceedings of the Workshop on User Aspects of the Semantic Web, Heraklion, Greece (2005)
10. McGuinness, D.L., Smith, K., Welty, C.: Owl Web Ontology Language Guide, http://www.w3.org/TR/owl-guide/
11. Mel'cuk, I.: Dependency syntax: theory and practice, SUNY University Press (1988)
12. Nirenburg, S., Raskin, V.: Ontological Semantics. MIT Press, Cambridge (2004)
13. Stevenson, M., Clough, P.: EuroWordNet as a Resource for Cross-language Information Retrieval. In: LREC04. 4th Edition of the International Conference on Language Resources and Evaluation, Lisbon, pp. 777–780 (2004)

Evolving Complex Neural Networks

Mauro Annunziato[1], Ilaria Bertini[1], Matteo De Felice[2], and Stefano Pizzuti[1]

[1] Energy, New technology and Environment Agency (ENEA)
Via Anguillarese 301, 00123 Rome, Italy
{mauro.annunziato, ilaria.bertini,
stefano.pizzuti}@casaccia.enea.it
[2] Dipartimento di Informatica ed Automazione, Università degli Studi di Roma "Roma Tre",
Via della Vasca Navale 79, 00146 Rome, Italy
matteo.defelice@casaccia.enea.it

Abstract. Complex networks like the scale-free model proposed by Barabasi-Albert are observed in many biological systems and the application of this topology to artificial neural network leads to interesting considerations. In this paper, we present a preliminary study on how to evolve neural networks with complex topologies. This approach is utilized in the problem of modeling a chemical process with the presence of unknown inputs (disturbance). The evolutionary algorithm we use considers an initial population of individuals with differents scale-free networks in the genotype and at the end of the algorithm we observe and analyze the topology of networks with the best performances. Experimentation on modeling a complex chemical process shows that performances of networks with complex topology are similar to the feed-forward ones but the analysis of the topology of the most performing networks leads to the conclusion that the distribution of input node information affects the network performance (modeling capability).

Keywords: artificial life, complex networks, neural networks.

1 Introduction

Artificial Neural Networks (ANN) and Evolutionary Algorithms (EA) are both abstractions of natural processes. They are formulated into a computational model so that the learning power of neural networks and adaptive capabilities of evolutionary processes can be harnessed in an artificial life environment. "Adaptive learning", as it is called, produces results that demonstrate how complex and purposeful behavior can be induced in a system by randomly varying the topology and the rules governing the system. Evolutionary algorithms can help determine optimized neural network architectures giving rise to a new branch of ANN known as Evolutionary Neural Networks [1] (ENN). It has been found [2] that, in most cases, the combinations of evolutionary algorithms and neural nets perform equally well (in terms of accuracy) and were as accurate as hand-designed neural networks trained with backpropagation [3]. However, some combinations of EAs and ANNs performed much better for some data than the hand-designed networks or other EA/ANN combinations. This suggests

R. Basili and M.T. Pazienza (Eds.): AI*IA 2007, LNAI 4733, pp. 194–205, 2007.

that in applications where accuracy is a premium, it might pay off to experiment with EA and ANN combinations. A new and very interesting research area which recently emerged is that of *Complex Networks* (CN). CN (mainly *scale-free* networks) are receiving great attention in the physics community, because they seem to be the basic structure of many natural and artificial networks like proteins, metabolism, species network, biological networks [4, 5, 6], the Internet, the WWW, the e-mail network, metabolic networks, trust network and many more [7].

In this context, using complex ANN topologies driven by evolutionary mechanisms is a new idea and we used them in order to model complex processes.

2 The Methodology

In this context, the goal of the proposed work is the study of evolutionary neural networks with a directed-graph based topology, obtained using an iterative algorithm similar to that proposed by Barabasi-Albert in 1999 [8].

2.1 Complex Networks

A unique definition of "complex network" doesn't exist, this term refers to networks with non-trivial topology and high number of nodes and connections. However, complex networks can be classified, according to some topology descriptors, into two main classes : *Small World* and *Scale Free.*

The most important topology descriptors are: the node degree distribution, the shortest path length and the clustering coefficient.

Properties of these networks are often compared with random graphs [9] that are to be considered "simple" networks. Random networks have a Poisson node degree distribution, a small shortest path length and a small clustering coefficient.

Small World networks [4, 10] have a Poisson node degree distribution, a small shortest path length and a high clustering coefficient. They are in the middle between regular and random networks (see Figure 1) and it has been shown [4] that this topology is the optimal one for communication tasks.

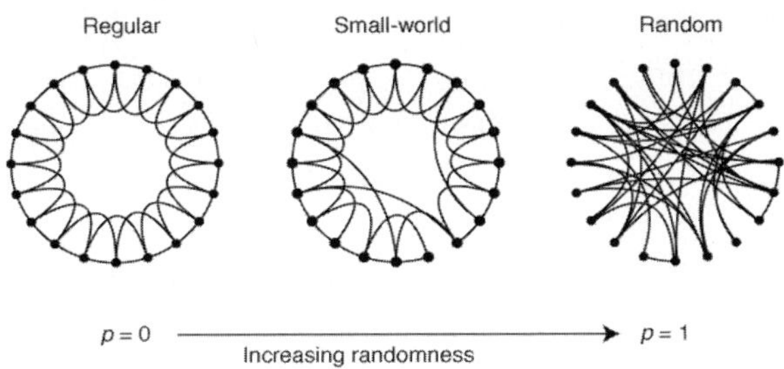

Fig. 1. Networks topologies

The scale-free model [11] have a node degree distribution which follows the power law distribution. It means that we have few nodes with high connectivity (*hubs*) and many nodes with few links (see Figure 2). These networks show the so-called "small-world" property [4], every two nodes of the network are placed at a distance of a relative small number of edges. These types of networks are receiving great attention in the physics community, because many networks have been reported recently to follow a scale free degree distribution. Just as examples we can cite the Internet, the WWW, the e-mail network, metabolic networks, trust network and many more [7]. Their inspiring philosophy could be synthesized in the sentence "the rich gets richer", because each node has a probability to get a new link that is proportional to the number of its current links.

Fig. 2. Scale free network

In this study, we focussed on scale-free networks.

2.2 The Algorithm

We used ANNs based on a complex network created with the algorithm whose pseudo-code is shown in Table 1. The algorithm starts creating an initial set of nodes connected each other and then each added node is connected with a selected destination node with a *preferential-attachment* function: this function defines the probability that a node in network receive a link from a newly inserted node [8, 12]. The analytic form of this function is:

$$\Pi(k_i) = \frac{k_i^{\alpha}}{\sum_j k_j^{\alpha}} \tag{1}$$

In this function k_i is the degree of node i. This function is monotonically increasing, the α parameter influences the numbers of dominant hubs with high connectivity. In figures 3 e 4 we show the node degree distributions of networks with 4000 nodes built with the presented algorithm with different α values, fitting with a power function like $k^{-\gamma}$ is shown in following plots (figures 3, 4).

The output node of the network is randomly chosen after the insertion of the nodes of the hidden layer. At the selection of the output node, input nodes are inserted.

Table 1. Algorithm pseudo-code

```
BEGIN
    /* Initial set of nodes */
    FOR i = 1 to m_0
            ADD node_i
            CONNECT node_i to ALL
    END FOR
    /* Add nodes and connect them with PA function */
    FOR i = 1 to TOTAL_NODES
            ADD node_i
            FOR j = 1 to m
                    x = GET_NODE_WITH_PREFERENTIAL_ATTACHMENT
                    CONNECT node_i to node_x
                    CONNECT node_x to node_i
            END FOR
    END FOR
    /* Select output node */
    x = RANDOM(TOTAL_NODES)
    OUTPUT_NODE = node_x
    /* Add and connect input nodes */
    CASE INPUT_CONNECTION_TYPE OF:
            /* CONNECTION TYPE A */
            A: ADD ALL_INPUT_NODES
            FOR i = 1 to m
                    x = RANDOM(TOTAL_NODES)
                    CONNECT ALL_INPUT_NODES to node_x
            END FOR
            /* CONNECTION TYPE B */
            B: FOR i = 1 to TOTAL_INPUT_NODES
                    ADD input_node_i
                    FOR j = 1 to m
                            x = GET_NODE_WITH_PREFERENTIAL_ATTACHMENT
                            CONNECT input_node_i to node_x
                    END FOR
            END FOR
    END CASE
END
```

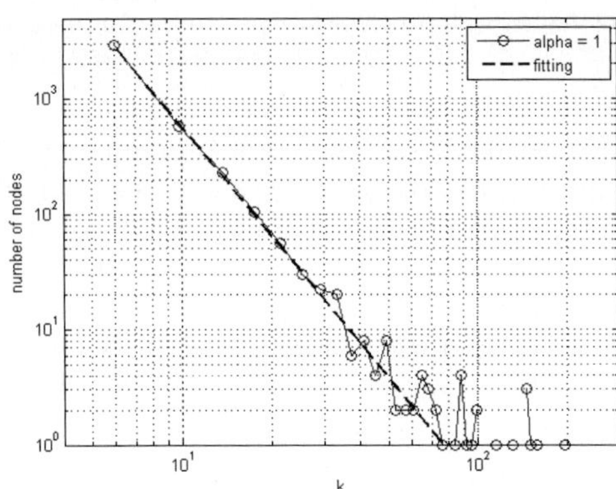

Fig. 3. Degree distribution of a 4000 nodes network created with $\alpha = 1$ fitted with a power-law function with gamma = 3.1 (dashed line)

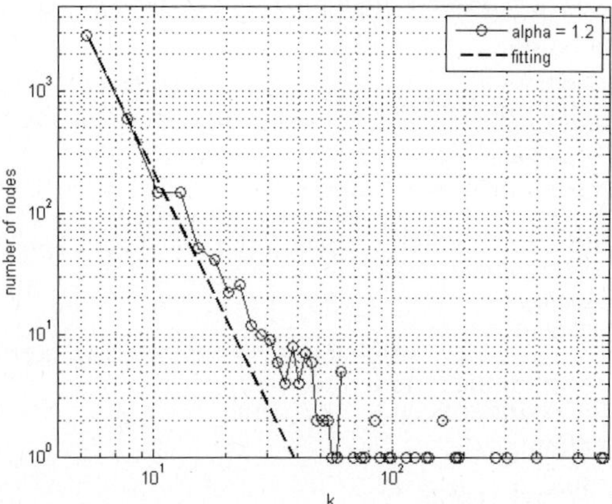

Fig. 4. Degree distribution of a 4000 nodes network created with $\alpha = 1.2$ fitted with a power-law function with gamma = 4 (dashed line)

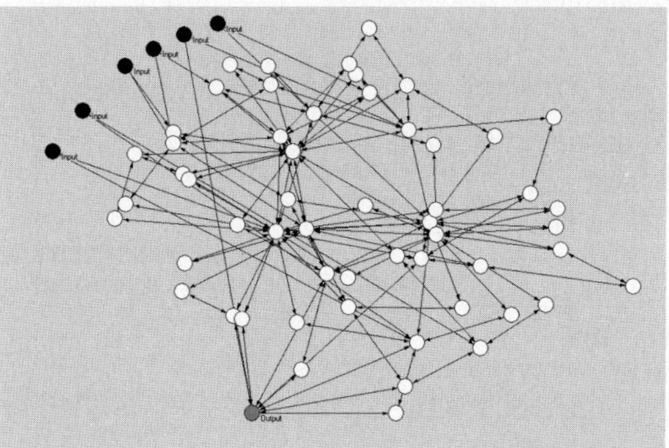

Fig. 5. An example of complex neural network. Input nodes are black and the output node is grey.

In this algorithm we considered two types of connections between the network and the input nodes (in the pseudo-code these methods are indicated by the variable INPUT_CONNECTION_TYPE). In case A we have all the input nodes connected to the same m nodes of the hidden layer. Otherwise in case B we have each input node linked to m random nodes of the hidden layer.

A network created with this algorithm is presented in Figure 5.

We used the values of the parameters presented in the Table 2 for the execution of the algorithm.

2.3 The Evolutionary Environment

The implemented evolutionary environment is an *Artificial Life* (ALIFE) environment [13]. This approach has been tested on the optimization of static well known benchmarks, as the Travelling Salesman Problem, the Chua's circuit and the Kuramoto dynamical system [14], as well as real cases [15, 16, 17, 18]. The ALIFE context is a two-dimensional lattice (life space) representing a flat physical space where the artificial individuals (or autonomous agents) can move around. At each iteration (or life cycle), individuals move in the life space and, in case of meeting with other individuals, interaction occurs. Each individual has a particular set of rules that determines its interactions with other agents basically based on a competition for energy in relation to the performance value. Individuals can self-reproduce via haploid mutation which occurs only if the individual has an energy greater than a specific birth energy. In fact, during reproduction, an amount of energy equal to the birth energy is transferred from the parent to the child. In the haploid reproduction a probabilistic test for self reproduction is performed at every life cycle and a probabilistic-random mutation occurs on the genes according to the mutation rate and the mutation amplitude, which are evolutionary themselves [19]. When two individuals meet, fight occurs. The winner is the individual characterized by a greater value of performance and the loser transfers an amount of energy (fighting energy) to the winner. At every life cycle each individual age is increased and when the age reaches a value close to the average lifetime, the probability of natural death increases. This ageing mechanism is very important to warrant the possibility to lose memory of very old solutions and follow the process evolution. Another mechanism of death occurs when the individual reaches the null energy due to reproduction or fighting with other individuals. For interested readers, a detailed description of the methodology is reported in [15, 16]. The characteristic Artificial Life environment we used is called "Artificial Societies", introduced in [20], but we made some modifications to the original one. In our implementation each individual of the initial population is initialized with a different network topology in his genotype. Initial networks are created with a value of the parameter m that varies from 2 to 6. Network weights and activation functions, but not the topology, are subject to random mutations and no crossover mechanism among different network topologies has been implemented because in the artificial life algorithm we used there is not present a bi-sexual reproduction mechanism.

Table 2. Parameters of the algorithm

m_0	4
m	2-6
α	1.2
Life space dimension	25 x 25
Initial population	215

3   The Benchmark Model

The model we used is a process consisting of two linearized *Continuous flow Stirred Tank Reactor* (CSTR) models in parallel (figure 4). The CSTR model describes an exothermic diabatic reaction of the first order and it is commonly studied for his characteristics [21, 22]. The equations, written in dimensionless form [23], are the following:

$$\dot{x}_1 = q(x_{1s} - x_1) - \Phi x_1 \kappa(x_2)$$
$$\dot{x}_2 = q(x_{2s} - x_2) - \delta(x_2 - x_3) + \beta \Phi \kappa(x_2) \tag{2}$$
$$\dot{x}_3 = \delta_1 [q_c(x_{3s} - x_3) + \delta \delta_2(x_2 - x_3)]$$

where x_1, x_2 and x_3 are respectively dimensionless concentration, reaction temperature and cooling-jacket temperature. The first manipulated input is q_c which represents the cooling-jacket flow rate and the second input q is the reactor flow rate. The output of the system is the dimensionless concentration x_1. The other parameters are explained in Table 3 with the values we set. The model we used is represented in the schema in figure 6. As stated before, the process consists of two CSTR linearized models with different Damkholer numbers, therefore we have two different inertias (the length of the transient regime), one fast and one slow. In order to simulate a non-stationary environment (like most of real situations are), we consider the input q (reactor flow rate) of the CSTR model as "disturbance", because it is not given to the neural models. The whole output of the system, $s(t)$, is the sum of the two CSTR's output normalized between 0 and 1 and sampled every 0,3 s.

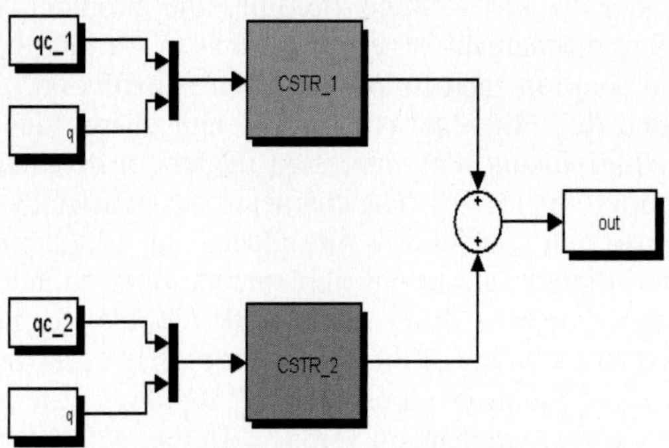

Fig. 6. Model layout

The system matrices of the model with "disturbance" are the following:

$$A = \begin{bmatrix} -q_s - \Phi K & -\Phi x_{1s} K' & 0 \\ \beta \Phi K & -q_s - \delta - \beta \Phi x_{1s} K' & \delta \\ 0 & \delta \delta_1 \delta_2 & -\delta_1 q_{cs} - \delta \delta_1 \delta_2 \end{bmatrix} \tag{3}$$

$$B = \begin{bmatrix} 0 & (x_{1f} - x_{1s}) \\ 0 & (x_{2f} - x_{2s}) \\ \delta_1(x_{3f} - x_{3s}) & 0 \end{bmatrix} \tag{4}$$

With $K = e^{\dfrac{x_{2s}}{1+\dfrac{x_{2s}}{\gamma}}}$ and $K' = e^{\dfrac{x_{2s}}{1+\dfrac{x_{2s}}{\gamma}}} \dfrac{1}{\left(1+\dfrac{x_{2s}}{\gamma}\right)^2}$.

The reactor flow rate q (disturbance) is modeled as a train pulse of 0.1 Hz of frequency, 0.15 of amplitude and a pulse width of 40%.

Both CSTR have in input a random step ranging between 0 and 0.5 every 6.5 seconds. The step is filtered by a $\dfrac{1}{s+1}$ transfer function.

Table 3. Model parameters

Name	Value	Explanation
x_{1s}	0.2028	Steady state of concentration
x_{2s}	5	Steady state of reaction temperature
x_{3s}	0.4079	Steady state of cooling-jacket temperature
x_{1f}	1	Dimensionless reactor feed concentration
x_{2f}	0	Dimensionless reactor feed temperature
x_{3f}	-1	Dimensionless cooling-jacket feed temperature
Φ	0.25-0.53	Damkholer number
q_{cs}	0.9785	Steady state of cooling-jacket flow rate
q_s	1	Steady state of reactor flow rate
β	8	Dimensionless heat of reaction
δ	0.3	Dimensionless heat transfer coefficient
δ_1	10	Reactor to cooling jacket volume ratio
δ_2	1	Reactor to cooling jacket density heat capacity ratio
γ	20	Dimensionless activation energy

The term $k(\cdot)$ represents the dimensionless Arrhenius reaction rate which corresponds to:

$$\kappa(x) = e^{\frac{x}{1+\frac{x}{\gamma}}} \tag{5}$$

4   Experimental Results

The output of the network is the prediction of the signal s(t+h), with h the prediction horizon, and the inputs are the six past samples of the signal, s(t-1)…s(t-6). All the experimentations are carried out with the prediction horizon (h) as 5.

We made a set of 10 tests and calculated the mean RMSE :

$$E_{rmse} = \sqrt{\frac{\frac{1}{2}\sum_{i=1}^{M}(y(i)-\bar{y}(i))^2}{M}} \tag{6}$$

In Table 4 it is presented a comparison of the performance of different ANN typologies: feed-forward network, fully-connected network and scale free networks trained with ALIFE algorithm and feed-forward network trained with classic back-propagation algorithm. An example of target signal and neural network output is show in figure 7.

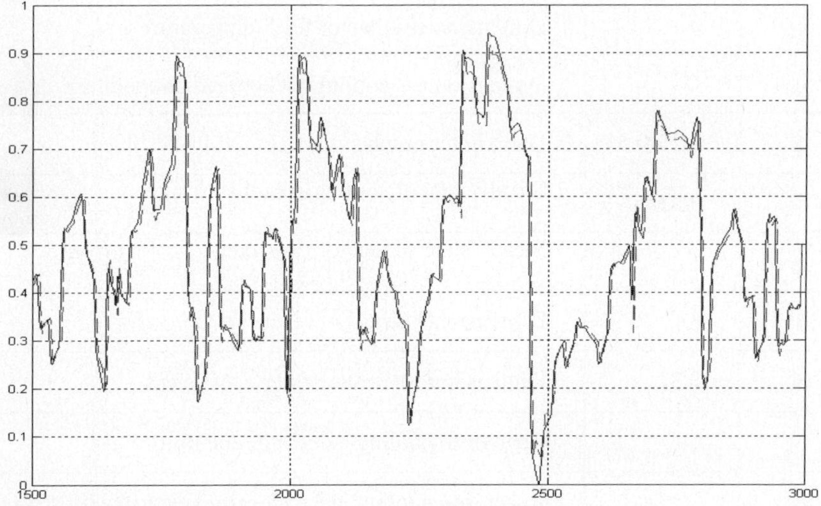

Fig. 7. Comparison between the model output and the output of the ANN (dotted line)

Table 4. Performance comparison

ANN typology	RMSE
Feed-forward network with ALIFE	0.039
Feed-forward network with back-propagation	0.072
Fully-connected with ALIFE	0.039
ANN with scale-free topology with ALIFE	0.041

At the end of the tests a topology analysis on the "best" networks was performed. In fact, natural selection mechanism, intrinsic in evolutive algorithms, generates a drastic reduction of the number of different topologies which are inside the solutions of the overall population. An example of this mechanism is shown in figure 8: on the horizontal axis time it is reported, while on the vertical axis there are the different network topologies. In this plot it is clearly shown the process leading to the elimination of most network topologies.

An analysis of the average connectivity, the m parameter of tables 1 and 2, of the "best" networks shows that, at the end of 10 simulations, the value was 3.9, an outcome very close to the arithmetic mean (the m parameter ranges from 2 to 6). In this way, it seems that connectivity doesn't affect the performance of the neural network.

A network analysis considering parameters like clustering coefficient or shortest path length has not been performed because of the small dimension of the networks considered, in fact with small networks some parameters commonly used in complex networks analysis are to be considered not meaningful.

Moreover, we analyzed the type of input nodes connection and we observed that the 80% of the "best" networks had used an input nodes connection of type B (see variable INPUT_CONNECTION_TYPE in the pseudo-code presented in Table 1), so after these tests we can see that input distributed information leads to a better performance than an information focussed on little sets of nodes.

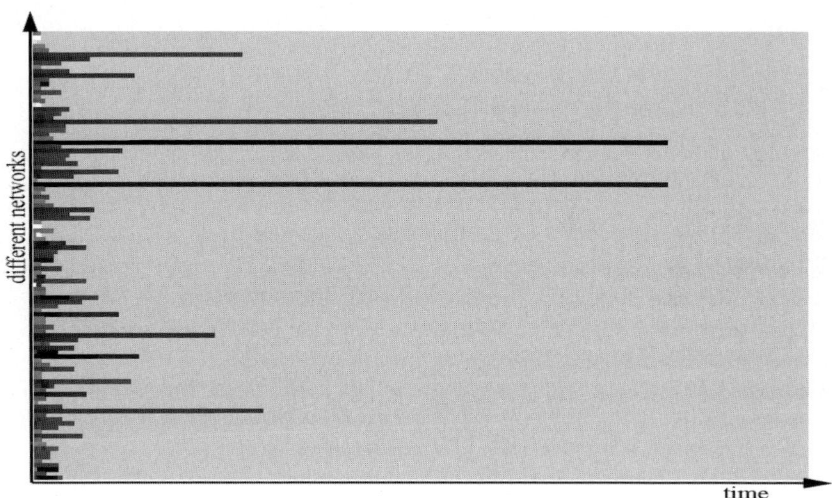

Fig. 8. Example of natural selection mechanism

5 Conclusion

Complex networks like the scale-free model proposed by Barabasi-Albert are observed in many biological systems and the application of this topologies to artificial neural network leads to interesting considerations.

In this paper, we presented a preliminary study on how to evolve neural networks with complex topologies and in particular we focused on the scale-free model. As benchmark we faced the problem of modeling a chemical process with the presence of unknown inputs (disturbance). The evolutionary environment has an initial population of individuals with differents scale-free networks in the genotype and at the end of the algorithm we observed and analyzed the topologies of networks with the best performances.

The experimentation we did is to be considered only the beginning of the exploration of the union between neural networks and complex topologies. It is necessary to perform more extended tests and to compare the structures object of this paper with another optimization and modeling methods like kernel machines (SVRs).

Testing showed that performances of complex networks on the proposed modeling problem are similar to those achieved with classic feed-forward networks. The possibility to perform topological analysis at the end of the evolutionary process, typical of the algorithms like that one we used, could be considered as the basis for a profitably union between the two paradigms of cognitive systems par excellence: artificial neural networks and complex networks. In fact, the analysis at the end of a set of tests, showed on one hand that connectivity has little influence on the network performance, while on the other hand the input connectivity seems to be more effective. These results suggest a direction to the purpose of creating networks that are able to accomplish complex modeling tasks.

References

1. Yao, X.: Evolving Artificial Neural Networks. Proceedings of the IEEE 87(9), 1423–1447 (1999)
2. Alander, J.T.: An indexed bibliography of genetic algorithms and neural networks, Technical Report 94-1-NN, University of Vaasa, Department of Information Technology and Production Economics (1998)
3. Cant-Paz, E., Kamath, C.: An empirical comparison of combinations of evolutionary algorithms and neural networks for classification problems. IEEE Transactions on Systems, Man, and Cybernetics-Part B: Cybernetics, 915–927 (2005)
4. Watts, D.J., Strogatz, S.: Collective dynamics of 'small-world' networks. Nature 393(6684), 440–442 (1998)
5. Burns, G.A.P.C., Oung, M.P.Y: Analysis of the connectional organization of neural systems associated with the hippocampus in rats. Philosophical Transactions of the Royal Society B: Biological Sciences 355(1393), 55–70 (2000)
6. Eguiluz, V.M., Chialvo, D.R., Cecchi, G.A., Baliki, M., Apkarian, A.V.: Scale-Free Brain Functional Networks. Phys. Rev. Lett. 94, 18–102 (2005)
7. Dorogotvsev, S.N., Mendes, J.F.F.: Evolution of Networks. Advances in Physics 51(4), 1079–1187 (2002)
8. Barabasi, A.-L., Albert, R.: Emergence of scaling in random networks. Science 286, 509–512 (1999)
9. Erdos, P., Renyi, A.: On random graphs, Publ. Math. Debrecen (1959)
10. Watts, D.J.: Small Worlds: The Dynamics of Networks Between Order and Randomness. Princeton University Press (1999)
11. Coven, R., Havlin, S., ben-Avraham, D.: Structural Properties of Scale-Free Networks. In: Bornholdt, S., Schuster, H.G. (eds.) Handbook of graphs and networks, ch. 4, Wiley-VCH, Chichester (2002)

12. Jeong, H., Neda, Z., Barabasi, A.-L.: Measuring preferential attachment for evolving networks. Euro. Phys. Lett. 61, 567 (2003)
13. Langton, C.: Artificial Life. Addison-Wesley, Redwood City/CA, USA (1989)
14. Annunziato, M., Bertini, I., Lucchetti, M., Pannicelli, A., Pizzuti, S.: Adaptivity of Artificial Life Environment for On-Line Optimization of Evolving Dynamical Systems. In: Proc. EUNITE01, Tenerife, Spain (2001)
15. Annunziato, M., Bertini, I., Pannicelli, A., Pizzuti, S., Tsimring, L.: Complexity and Control of Combustion Processes in Industry. In: Proc. of CCSI 2000 Complexity and Complex System in Industry, Warwick, UK (2000)
16. Annunziato, M., Lucchetti, M., Orsini, G., Pizzuti, S.: Artificial life and on-line flows optimisation in energy networks. In: IEEE Swarm Intelligence Sympusium, Pasadena (CA), IEEE Computer Society Press, Los Alamitos (2005)
17. Annunziato, M., Bertini, I., Pannicelli, A., Pizzuti, S.: A Nature-inspired-Modeling-Optimization-Control system applied to a waste incinerator plant. In: 2nd European Symposium NiSIS'06, Puerto de la Cruz, Tenerife (Spain) (2006)
18. Annunziato, M., Bertini, I., Pannicelli, A., Pizzuti, S.: Evolutionary Control and On-Line Optimization of an MSWC Energy Process. Journal of Systemics, Cybernetics and Informatics 4(4) (2006)
19. Annunziato, M., Bertini, I., Iannone, R., Pizzuti, S.: Evolving feed-forward neural networks through evolutionary mutation parameters. In: Corchado, E., Yin, H., Botti, V., Fyfe, C. (eds.) IDEAL 2006. LNCS, vol. 4224, pp. 554–561. Springer, Heidelberg (2006)
20. Annunziato, M., Bruni, C., Lucchetti, M., Pizzuti, S.: Artificial life approach for continuous optimisation of non stationary dynamical systems. Integrated Computer-Aided Engineering 10(2), 111–125 (2003)
21. Russo, L.P., Bequette, B.W.: Impact of process design on the multiplicity behaviour of a jacketed exothermic CSTR. AIChE Journal 41, 135–147 (1995)
22. Saraf, V.S., Bequette, B.W.: Auto-tuning of cascade controlled open-loop unstable reactors. In: American Control Conference, Proceedings of the 2001, vol. 3, pp. 2021–2026 (2026)
23. Russo, L.P., Bequette, B.W.: State-Space versus Input/Output Representations for Cascade Control of Unstable Systems. Ind. Eng. Chem. Res. 36(6), 2271–2278 (1997)

Discovering Relational Emerging Patterns

Annalisa Appice, Michelangelo Ceci, Carlo Malgieri, and Donato Malerba

Dipartimento di Informatica, Università degli Studi di Bari
via Orabona, 4 - 70126 Bari - Italy
{appice,ceci,malerba}@di.uniba.it

Abstract. The discovery of emerging patterns (EPs) is a descriptive data mining task defined for pre-classified data. It aims at detecting patterns which contrast two classes and has been extensively investigated for attribute-value representations. In this work we propose a method, named Mr-EP, which discovers EPs from data scattered in multiple tables of a relational database. Generated EPs can capture the differences between objects of two classes which involve properties possibly spanned in separate data tables. We implemented Mr-EP in a pre-existing multi-relational data mining system which is tightly integrated with a relational DBMS, and then we tested it on two sets of geo-referenced data.

1   Introduction

The discovery of emerging patterns (EPs) is a descriptive data mining task aiming at the detection of significant differences between objects belonging to separate classes. EPs are introduced in [4] as a particular kind of patterns (or multi-variate features) whose support significantly changes from one data class to another: the larger the difference of pattern support, the more interesting the patterns. Due to the sharp change in support, EPs can be used to characterize object classes. For example, EPs have been used to predict the likelihood of diseases such as acute lymphoblastic leukemia [13] and to explore high-dimensional data such as gene expression data [12].

Several algorithms [18,4,10] have been proposed to discover EPs from data belonging to separate classes (data populations) and stored in a single relational table. Independent units of each data population D_i are described by a fixed vector S of explanatory attributes $X_1, X_2, \ldots, X_m$ and are tagged with a class label $Y = C_i$. The EPs which distinguish a target data population D_i from the background data D_j are in the form $P(GR^{D_j \to D_i}(P))$, where P is a set of items $(P \subseteq S)$ and $GR^{D_j \to D_i}(P)$ is the support ratio (or *growth rate*) of P over D_j to D_i. Formally $GR^{D_j \to D_i}(P) = \frac{s_{D_i}(P)}{s_{D_j}(P)}$, where $s_{D_i}(P)$ $(s_{D_j}(P))$ is the support of P on D_i (D_j). Since an item refers to an attribute-value pair, the *itemset* P can be interpreted as a conjunction of attribute values. Formally, given a growth rate threshold $minGR \geq 1$, an EP from D_j to D_i is an itemset P whose growth rate from D_j to D_i is greater than $minGR$.

Although research on EPs has reached relative maturity over the last years, there is still a number of interesting issues which remain open. One issue concerns

R. Basili and M.T. Pazienza (Eds.): AI*IA 2007, LNAI 4733, pp. 206–217, 2007.

the need to face the challenges of real-world data mining tasks involving complex and heterogeneous data with different properties which are modeled by as many relations as the number of object types. Mining data scattered over the multiple tables of a relational database (*relational data*) poses the problem of taking into account attributes of related (i.e. *task-relevant*) objects when investigating properties of some *reference* objects which are the main subject of analysis. Classical EPs discovery methods do not distinguish task-relevant from reference objects, nor do they allow the representation of any kind of interaction. Therefore, we propose to resort to a Multi-Relational Data Mining (MRDM) approach [6] in order to deal with both relational data and relational patterns.

In this paper, we propose a novel method, called Mr-EP (*M*ulti-*R*elational *E*merging *P*atterns), which discovers EPs from relational data and is capable to capture the change in properties of separate classes of data spanned in multiple data tables. The class variable is associated with the reference objects, while explanatory attributes refer to either the reference objects or the task-relevant objects which are someway related to the reference objects. The structural information required to mine such *relational* EPs can be automatically obtained from the database schema by navigating foreign key constraints. For each class, relational EPs are expressed as SQL queries stored in XML format.

The paper is organized as follows. In the next section the background of this research and related works are discussed, while in Section 3 the problem of EPs discovery is formalized in the multi-relational framework. Relational emerging patterns discovery is described in Section 4. Lastly, experimental results are reported in Section 5 and then some conclusions are drawn.

2   Related Works

The combination of relational representation with pattern discovery has been deeply investigated for several data mining tasks. Data mining research has provided several solutions for the task of frequent pattern and association rule discovery both in a propositional and a relational setting, but, at the best of our knowledge, this work represents the first attempt at extracting relational EPs.

In [1], a frequent pattern is defined as an itemset whose support is greater than a predefined minimum threshold value (minimum support), while an association rule is an implication in the form $A \Rightarrow C(s, c)$, where A and C are itemsets and $A \cap C = \oslash$. The support s provides an estimate of the probability $p(A \cup C)$, while the confidence c provides an estimate of the probability $p(C|A)$. An association rule $A \rightarrow C$ ($s\%$, $c\%$) is *strong* if the pattern $A \cup C$ ($s\%$) is frequent and the confidence of the rule is greater than a predefined minimum threshold value (minimum confidence).

The two best known association rule discovery methods defined in the relational framework are WARMR [3] and SPADA [14]. They are both based on an Inductive Logic Programming (ILP) approach, where both data and background (or domain) knowledge is represented in a first-order logic formalism, such as Horn clausal logic. Relational frequent patterns are discovered according to the levelwise method described in [16], which consists in a level-by-level exploration of the lattice of patterns ordered by θ-subsumption [17]. Strong association rules are then generated from frequent patterns.

Unlike frequent patterns and/or association rules which capture regularities in data describing unclassified objects, EPs capture changes in data describing objects of different classes. This adds one main source of complexity to the learning task, since the monotonicity property does not hold for EPs. Suppose a pattern P is not an EP from D_j to D_i, that is, the growth rate of P from D_j to D_i is not greater than the user-defined threshold. For any super-pattern Q of P ($P \subseteq Q$), its support is less than or equal to that of P for both classes C_i and C_j, while its growth rate (the support ratio) is free to be any real value between 0 and ∞. Therefore, a superset of a non-EP may or may not be an EP.

In the seminal work by Dong and Li [4], EPs are discovered by assuming that each data set is stored in a single data table. A border-based approach is adopted to discover the EPs discriminating between separate classes. Borders are used to represent both candidates and subsets of EPs; the border differential operation is then used to discover the EPs. Zhang et al. [18] have described an efficient method, called ConsEPMiner, which adopts a level-wise generate-and-test approach to discover EPs which satisfy several constraints (e.g., growth-rate improvement). Finally, Fan and Ramamohanarao [7] have proposed a method which improves the efficiency of EPs discovery by adopting a CP-tree data structure to register the counts of both the positive and negative class.

A further direction of research concerns the usage of EPs in learning accurate data classifiers [5,8,11,9]. EP-based classification is related to the associative classification framework [15] where classifiers are built by carefully selecting high quality association rules. The advantage of EPs over association rules is that EPs provide features which better discriminate objects of distinct classes.

3   Problem Definition

In this work we assume that both reference objects and task-relevant objects are tuples stored in tables of a relational database D according to a schema S. The set R of reference objects is the collection of tuples stored in a table T of D called *target* table. Similarly, each set R_i of task-relevant objects corresponds to a distinct table of D. The inherent "structure" of data, that is, the relations between reference and task-relevant objects, is expressed in the schema S by foreign key constraints (FK). Foreign keys make it possible to navigate the data schema and retrieve all the task-relevant objects in D which are related to a reference object and, thus, are capable of discriminating between the values of the target attribute Y.

Before providing a formal definition of the problem to be solved, some other definitions need to be introduced.

Definition 1 (Key predicate). *Let S be a database schema and T be a table of S representing the target table for the task at hand. The "key predicate"* *associated with T in S is a first order unary predicate $p(t)$ such that p denotes the table T and the term t is a variable that represents the primary key of T.*

Definition 2 (Structural predicate). *Let S be a database schema and $\{T_i, T_j\}$ be a pair of tables in S such that there exists a foreign key FK in S between T_i and T_j. A "structural predicate" associated with the pair of tables $\{T_i, T_j\}$ in S is a first order binary predicate $p(t, s)$ such that p denotes FK and the term t (s) is a variable that represents the primary key of T_i (T_j).*

Definition 3 (Property predicate). *Let S be a database schema, T_i a table of S and ATT be an attribute of T_i which is neither primary key nor foreign key for T_i in S. A "property predicate" associated with the attribute ATT of the table T_i is a binary predicate $p(t, s)$ such that p denotes the attribute ATT, the term t is a variable representing the primary key of T_i and s is a constant which represents a value belonging to the range of ATT in T_i.*

A relational pattern over S is a conjunction of predicates consisting of the key predicate and one or more (structural or property) predicates over S. More formally, a relational pattern is defined as follows:

Definition 4 (Relational pattern). *Let S be a database schema. A "relational pattern" P over S is a conjunction of predicates:*

$$p_0(t0_1), p_1(t1_1, t1_2), p_2(t2_1, t2_2), \ldots, p_m(tm_1, tm_2)$$

where $p_0(t0_1)$ is the key predicate associated with the target table of the task at hand and $\forall i = 1, \ldots, m$ $p_i(ti_1, ti_2)$ is either a structural predicate or a property predicate over S.

Henceforth, we will also use the set notation for relational patterns, that is, a relational pattern is considered a set of atoms.

Definition 5 (Key linked predicate).
Let $P = p_0(t0_1), p_1(t1_1, t1_2), p_2(t2_1, t2_2), \ldots, p_m(tm_1, tm_2)$ be a relational pattern over the database schema S. For each $i = 1, \ldots, m$, the (structural or property) predicate $p_i(ti_1, ti_2)$ is "key linked" in P if

- *$p_i(ti_1, ti_2)$ is a predicate with $t0_1 = ti_1$ or $t0_1 = ti_2$, or*
- *there exists a structural predicate $p_j(tj_1, tj_2)$ in P such that $p_j(tj_1, tj_2)$ is key linked in P and $ti_1 = tj_1 \lor ti_2 = tj_1 \lor ti_1 = tj_2 \lor ti_2 = tj_2$.*

Definition 6 (Completely linked relational pattern). *Let S be a database schema. A "completely linked" relational pattern is a relational pattern $P = p_0(t0_1), p_1(t1_1, t1_2), \ldots, p_m(tm_1, tm_2)$ such that $\forall i = 1 \ldots m$, $p_i(ti_1, ti_2)$ is a predicate which is key linked in P.*

Definition 7 (Relational emerging patterns). *Let D be an instance of a database schema S that contains a set of reference objects labeled with $Y \in \{C_1, \ldots, C_L\}$ and stored in the target table T of S. Given a minimum growth* *rate value (minGR) and a minimum support value (minsup), P is a "relational emerging pattern" in D if P is a completely linked relational pattern over S and some class label C_i exists such that $GR^{\overline{D_i} \to D_i}(P) > minGR$ and $s_{D_i}(P) > minsup$, where:*

- *D_i is an instance of database schema S such that $D_i.T = \{t \in D.T | D.T.Y = C_i\}$ and $\forall T' \in S, T' \neq T: D_i.T' = \{t \in D.T' |$ all foreign key constraints FK are satisfied in $D_i\}$.*
- *$\overline{D_i}$ is an instance of database schema S such that $\overline{D_i}.T = \{t \in D.T | D.T.Y \neq C_i\}$ and $\forall T' \in S, T' \neq T: \overline{D_i}.T' = \{t \in D.T' |$ all foreign key constraints FK are satisfied in $\overline{D_i}\}$.*

The support $s_{D_i}(P)$ of P on database D_i is computed as follows:

$$s_{D_i}(P) = \frac{|O_P|}{|O|}, \tag{1}$$

where O denotes the set of reference objects stored as tuples of $D_i.T$, while O_P denotes the subset of reference objects in O which are covered by the pattern P. The growth rate of P for distinguishing D_i from $\overline{D_i}$ is the following:

$$GR^{\overline{D_i} \to D_i}(P) = \frac{s_{D_i}(P)}{s_{\overline{D_i}}(P)} \tag{2}$$

As in [4], we assume that $GR(P) = \frac{0}{0} = 0$ and $GR(P) = \frac{\geq 0}{0} = \infty$.

The problem of discovering relational EPs can now be formalized as follows. *Given:*

- a relational database D with a data schema S,
- a set R of reference objects tagged with a class label $Y \in \{C_1, C_2, \ldots, C_L\}$,
- some sets R_i, $1 \leq i \leq h$ of task-relevant objects,
- a pair of thresholds, that is, the minimum growth rate $(minGR \geq 1)$ and the minimum support $(minsup > 0)$.

Find:
the set of *relational emerging patterns* which discriminate between reference objects belonging to distinct classes in D.

In this work, we resort to the relational algebra formalism to express a relational emerging pattern P by means of an SQL query. The SELECT statement selects primary key values for distinct reference objects of the task at hand. The FROM statement describes the joins between all the tables of S which are involved in P (i.e., the target table associated with the key predicate and the tables which are included in separate structural predicates of the pattern P). A structural predicate is translated into a join condition. The property of linkedness in relational patterns guarantees the soundness of joins. The WHERE statement describes the conditions expressed in the property predicates. Reference objects contributing to the support of the EP on each D_i are obtained as result set by running this SQL query on the database instance D_i.

Example 1. Let us consider a set of molecules (reference objects) described in terms of the "logP" property and the "mutagenicity" class. Each molecule is composed by one or more atoms (task-relevant objects) and each atom is described by the "charge". An example of relational pattern P is the following:

> molecule(MolID), logPInMolecule(MolId,[5..10[),atom(MolId,AtomId1),
> chargeInAtom(AtomId1,[3.2,5.8[),atom(MolID,AtomId2),
> chargeInAtom(AtomId2,[5.0,7.1[)

P can be expressed by means of the SQL query:
SELECT distinct M.MolID
FROM (Molecule M INNER JOIN Atom A1 on M.MolId=A1.MolId)
    INNER JOIN Atom A2 on M.MolId=A2.MolId
WHERE M.logP>=5 AND M.logP<10 AND
    A1.Charge >=3.2 AND A1.Charge<5.8 AND
    A2.Charge >=5.0 AND A2.Charge<7.1

4   Relational EPs Discovery

We address EP discovery by adapting the algorithms proposed for frequent pattern discovery to the special case of EPs. The blueprint for the frequent patterns discovery algorithms is the levelwise method [16] that explores level-by-level the lattice of patterns ordered according to a generality relation ($\geqslant$) between patterns. Formally, given two patterns $P1$ and $P2$, $P1 \geqslant P2$ denotes that $P1$ ($P2$) is more general (specific) than $P2$ ($P1$). The search proceeds from the the most general pattern and iteratively alternates the candidate generation and candidate evaluation phases.

In this paper, we propose an enhanced version of the aforementioned levelwise method which works on EPs rather than frequent patterns. The space of candidate EPs is structured according to the θ-subsumption generality order [17].

Definition 8 (θ-subsumption). *Let $P1$ and $P2$ be two relational patterns on a data schema S such that both $P1$ and $P2$ are key completely linked patterns with respect to a target table T in S. $P1$ θ-subsumes $P2$ if and only if a substitution θ exists such that $P2\, \theta \subseteq P1$.*

Having introduced θ-subsumption, we now go to define generality order between completely linked relational patterns.

Definition 9 (Generality order under θ-subsumption). *Let $P1$ and $P2$ be two completely linked relational patterns. $P1$ is more general than $P2$ under θ-subsumption, denoted as $P1 \geqslant_\theta P2$, if and only if $P2$ θ-subsumes $P1$.*

θ-subsumption defines a quasi-ordering, since it satisfies the reflexivity and transitivity property but not the anti-symmetric property. The quasi-ordered set spanned by $\geqslant_\theta$ can then be searched according to a downward refinement operator which computes the set of refinements for a completely linked relational pattern.

Definition 10 (Downward refinement operator under θ-subsumption). *Let $\langle G, \geqslant_\theta \rangle$ be the space of completely linked relational patterns ordered according to $\geqslant_\theta$. A downward refinement operator under θ-subsumption is a function ρ such that $\rho(P) \subseteq \{Q \in G | P \geqslant_\theta Q\}$.*

We now define the downward refinement operator ρ' to explore the space of candidate EPs for distinguishing D_i from $\overline{D_i}$.

Definition 11 (Downward refinement operator for EPs). *Let P be a relational EP for distinguishing D_i from $\overline{D_i}$. Then $\rho'(P) = \{P \cup \{p(t1, t2)\} | p(t1, t2)$ is a structural or property predicate key linked in $P \cup \{p(t1, t2)\}$ and $P \cup \{p(t1, t2)\}$ is an EP for distinguishing D_i from $\overline{D_i}\}$.*

The downward refinement operator for EPs is a refinement operator under θ-subsumption. In fact, it can be easily proved that $P \geqslant_\theta Q$ for all $Q \in \rho'(P)$. This makes Mr-EP able to perform a levelwise exploration of the lattice of EPs ordered by θ-subsumption. More precisely, for each class C_i, the EPs for distinguishing D_i from $\overline{D_i}$ are discovered by searching the pattern space one level at a time, starting from the most general EP (the EP that contains only the key predicate) and iterating between candidate generation and evaluation phases. In Mr-EP, the number of levels in the lattice to be explored is limited by the user-defined parameter $MAX_M \geq 1$. In other terms, MAX_M limits the maximum number of structural predicates (joins) within a candidate EP. Since joins affects the computational complexity of the method, a low value of MAX_M guarantees the applicability of the algorithm to reasonably large data The monotonicity property of the generality order $\geqslant_\theta$ with respect to the support value (i.e., a superset of an infrequent pattern cannot be frequent) is exploited to avoid the generation of infrequent relational patterns. In fact, an infrequent pattern on D_i cannot be an EP for distinguishing D_i from $\overline{D_i}$.

Proposition 1 (Property of θ-subsumption monotonicity). *Let $\langle G, \geqslant_\theta \rangle$ be the space of relational completely linked patterns ordered according to $\geqslant_\theta$. P1 and P2 are two patterns of $\langle G, \geqslant_\theta \rangle$ with $P1 \geqslant_\theta P2$ then $O_{P1} \supseteq O_{P2}$.*

Therefore, when $P1 \geqslant_\theta P2$, we have $s_{D_i}(P1) \geq s_{D_i}(P2)$ and $s_{\overline{D_i}}(P1) \geq s_{\overline{D_i}}(P2)$ $\forall i = 1, \ldots, L$. This is the counterpart of one of the properties exploited in the family of the Apriori-like algorithms [1] to prune the space of candidate patterns. To efficiently discover relational EPs, Mr-EP prunes the search space by exploiting the θ-subsumption monotonicity of support (*prune1* criterion). Let P' be a refinement of a pattern P. If P is an infrequent pattern on D_i ($s_{D_i}(P) < minsup$), then P' has a support on D_i that is lower than the user-defined threshold (*minsup*). According to the definition of EP, P' cannot be an EP for distinguishing D_i from $\overline{D_i}$, hence Mr-EP does not refine patterns which are infrequent on D_i.

Unluckily, the monotonicity property does not hold for the growth rate: a refinement of an EP whose growth rate is lower than the threshold $minGR$ may or may not be an EP. Anyway, as in the propositional case [18], some mathematical considerations on the growth rate formulation can be usefully exploited to define two further pruning criteria.

First (*prune2* criterion), Mr-EP avoids generating the refinements of a pattern P in the case that $GR^{\overline{D_i} \to D_i}(P) = \infty$ (i.e., $s_{D_i}(P) > 0$ and $s_{\overline{D_i}}(P) = 0$). Indeed, due to the θ-subsumption monotonicity of support $\forall P' \in \rho'(P)$: $s_{\overline{D_i}}(P) \geq s_{\overline{D_i}}(P')$ then $s_{\overline{D_i}}(P') = 0$. Thereby, $GR^{\overline{D_i} \to D_i}(P') = 0$ in the case that $s_{D_i}(P') = 0$, while $GR^{\overline{D_i} \to D_i}(P') = \infty$ in the case that $s_{D_i}(P') > 0$. In the former case, P' is not worth to be considered (*prune1*). In the latter case, $P \succeq_\theta P'$ and $s_{D_i}(P) \geq s_{D_i}(P')$. Therefore, P' is useless since P has the same discriminating ability than P' ($GR^{\overline{D_i} \to D_i}(P) = GR^{\overline{D_i} \to D_i}(P') = \infty$). We prefer P to P' based on the Occams razor principle, according to which all things being equal, the simplest solution tends to be the best one.

Second (*prune3* criterion), Mr-EP avoids generating the refinements of a pattern P which add a property predicate in the case that the refined patterns have the same support of P on $\overline{D_i}$. We denote by:
$$SameSupport(P)_{\overline{D_i}} = \{P' \in \rho'(P) | s_{\overline{D_i}}(P) = s_{\overline{D_i}}(P'),\ P' = P \wedge p(t1, t2),$$
$$p(t1, t2) \text{ is a property predicate}\}.$$

For the monotonicity property, $\forall P' \in SameSupport_{\overline{D_i}}(P)$: $s_{D_i}(P) \geq s_{D_i}(P')$. This means that $GR^{\overline{D_i} \to D_i}(P) \geq GR^{\overline{D_i} \to D_i}(P')$. P' is more specific than P but, at the same time, P' has a lower discriminating power than P. This pruning criterion prunes EPs that could be generated as refinements of patterns in $SameSupport_{\overline{D_i}}(P)$. However, it is possible that some of them may be of interest for our discovery process. Their identification is guaranteed by the following:

Proposition 2. *Let $P' \in SameSupport_{\overline{D_i}}(P)$ such that $P' = P \cup \{p(t1, t2)\}$ with $p(t1, t2)$ being a property predicate. Let $P'' \in \rho'(P')$ such that $P'' = P' \cup \{q(t3, t4)\}$ with $q(t3, t4)$ being a property predicate. If P'' is an EP discriminating D_i from $\overline{D_i}$ and $s_{\overline{D_i}}(P'') \neq s_{\overline{D_i}}(P)$ then $P''' = P \cup \{q(t3, t4)\} \notin SameSupport_{\overline{D_i}}(P)$.*

Proof: *Let $O_P^{\overline{D_i}}$ denote the set of reference objects in $\overline{D_i}$ covered by a pattern P. By construction, $P'' \in \rho'(P') \cap \rho'(P''')$ and $O_{P''}^{\overline{D_i}} = O_{P'}^{\overline{D_i}} \cap O_{P'''}^{\overline{D_i}}$. Since $P' \in SameSupport_{\overline{D_i}}(P)$, we have $s_{\overline{D_i}}(P) = s_{\overline{D_i}}(P')$, that is, $O_P^{\overline{D_i}} = O_{P'}^{\overline{D_i}}$. Moreover, for the θ-subsumption monotonicity property, we have $O_{P'''}^{\overline{D_i}} \subseteq O_P^{\overline{D_i}}$. Therefore, we have: $O_{P''}^{\overline{D_i}} = O_{P'}^{\overline{D_i}} \cap O_{P'''}^{\overline{D_i}} = O_P^{\overline{D_i}} \cap O_{P'''}^{\overline{D_i}} = O_{P'''}^{\overline{D_i}}$. Since $s_{\overline{D_i}}(P'') \neq s_{\overline{D_i}}(P)$ by hypothesis, then it is also true that $s_{\overline{D_i}}(P''') \neq s_{\overline{D_i}}(P)$. Therefore, $P''' \notin SameSupport_{\overline{D_i}}(P)$.*

According to proposition 2, we can prune P' (but not P''') without preventing the generation of EPs more specific than P'. It is noteworty to observe that this pruning criterion operates only when $p(t1, t2)$ is a property predicate. Differently, pruning of structural predicates would avoid the introduction of a new variable thus avoiding the discovery of further EPs obtained by adding property or structural predicates involving such variable.

Finally, additional candidates not worth being evaluated are those equivalent under θ-subsumption to some other candidate (*prune4*).

5   Experimental Results

Mr-EP has been implemented as a module of the MRDM system MURENA (MUlti RElational aNAlyzer) which interfaces the Oracle 10g DBMS. We tested the method on two real world geo-referenced data sets: the North-West England Census Data and the Munich Census Data. Both data sets include numeric attributes, which are handled through an equal-width discretization to partition the range of values into a fixed number of bins. EPs have been discovered with $minGR = 1.1$, $minsup = 0.1$. MAX_M is set to 3 for North-West England Census Dataset and to 5 for Munich Census Dataset. In this work, we present only a qualitative interpretation of EPs. Each EP is analyzed in terms of a human interpretable pattern that is descriptive of characteristics discriminating between separate classes of relational data.

The North-West England Census Data. Data were obtained from both census and digital maps provided by the European project SPIN! (http://www.ais. fraunhofer.de/KD/SPIN/project.html). They concern Greater Manchester, one of the five counties of North West England (NWE). Greater Manchester is divided into into 214 census sections (wards). Census data are available at ward level and provide socio-economic statistics (e.g. mortality rate) as well as some measures of the deprivation of each ward according to information provided by Census combined into single index scores. We employed the Jarman score that estimates the need for primary care, the indices developed by Townsend and Carstairs to perform health-related analyses, and the DoE index which is used in targeting urban regeneration funds. The higher the index value the more deprived the ward. In this application, the mortality percentage rate (target attribute) takes values in the finite set $\{low = [0.001, 0.01], high =]0.01, 0.18]\}$. The analysis we performed was based on deprivation factors and geographical factors represented in topographic maps of the area. Vectorized boundaries of the 1998 census wards as well as of other Ordnance Survey digital maps of NWE are available for several layers such as urban area (115 lines), green area (9 lines), road net (1687 lines), rail net (805 lines) and water net (716 lines). Objects of each layer are stored as tuples of relational tables including information on the object type (TYPE). For instance, an urban area may be either a "large urban area" or a "small urban area". Topological relationships between wards and objects in these layers are materialized as relational tables expressing non-disjoint relations. The number of materialized "non disjoint" relationships is 5313.

Mr-EP discovered 60 EPs to discriminate high mortality rate wards from the class of wards with low mortality rate and 55 EPs to discriminate low mortality rate wards from high mortality rate wards. An example of EP extracted for the class *mortality_rate=high* is:

$wards(A) \wedge wards\_rails(A, B) \wedge wards\_doeindex(A, [6.598..9.232])$

where *wards(A)* is the key predicate, *wards_rails(A, B)* is the structural predicate representing an interaction between the ward A and a ward B (this means that A is crossed by at least one railway) and *wards_doeindex(A, [6.598..9.232])* (i.e. A is a deprived zone to be considered as target zone for regeneration fundings) is a property predicate. This pattern presents a support of 0.22 and growth rate 3.77. This means that wards crossed by railways and with a relatively high doeindex value present a high percentage of mortality. This could be due to urban decay condition of the area. The pattern corresponds to the SQL query:

SELECT distinct W.ID
FROM (WARDS W INNER JOIN WARDS_RAILS WR on W.ID=WR.WardID)
WHERE W.DOEINDEX <= 9.232 AND W.DOEINDEX >= 6.598

A different conclusion can be drawn from the following relational EP extracted for the class *mortality_rate=low*:

$$wards(A) \wedge wards\_townsendidx(A, [-3.86431.. - 2.01452])$$
$$\wedge\ wards\_greenareas(A, B)$$

This pattern has a support of 0.113 and a growth rate of 2.864. It captures the event that a ward with a relative low Townsend deprivation level (i.e., the ward A cannot be considered as deprived with respect to health-related analyses) and overlaps at least one green area (i.e., a park) discriminates wards with low mortality rate from the others.

The Munich Census Data. These data concern the level of monthly rent per square meter for flats in Munich expressed in German Marks. They have been collected on 1998 to develop the 1999 Munich rental guide and describe 2180 flats located in the 446 subquarters of Munich obtained by dividing the Munich metropolitan area up into three areal zones and decomposing each of these zones into 64 districts. The vectorized boundaries of subquarters, districts and zones as well as the map of public transport stops (56 subway (U-Bahn) stops, 15 rapid train (S-Bahn) stops and 1 railway station) within Munich are available for this study (http://www.di.uniba.it/~ceci/mic Files/munich_db.tar.gz). The objects included in these layers are stored in different relational tables (SUBQUARTERS, TRANSPORT_STOPS and APARTMENTS). Information on the "area" of subquarters is stored in the corresponding table. Transport stops are described by means of their type (U-Bahn, S-Bahn or Railway station), while flats are described by means of their "monthly rent per square meter", "floor space in square meters" and "year of construction". The monthly rent per square meter (target attribute) has been discretized into the two intervals $low = [2.0, 14.0]$ or $high =]14.0, 35.0]$. The "close to" relation between subquarters areas and the "inside" relation between public train stops and metropolitan subquarters are materialized into relational tables (*ward_close_to_ward* and *apartment_inside_district*). Similarly, the "cross" relation between districts and public train stops is materialized into the relational table *district_crossedby_tranStop*.

Mr-EP discovered 31 (31) EPs to discriminate apartment with high (low) rent rate per square meters from the class of apartments with low (high) rent rate per square meters. An example of EP extracted for the class *rate_per_squaremeters =high* is:

$$apartment(A) \wedge apartment\_inside\_district(A, B) \wedge$$
$$district\_close\_to\_district(B, C) \wedge district\_ext\_19\_69(B, [0.875..1.0])$$

This pattern has a support of 0.125 and a growth rate of 1.723. It represents the event that an apartment A is inside a district B which contains a high percentage (between 87.5% and 100%) of apartments with a relatively low extension (between 19 m^2 and 69 m^2). This pattern distriminates apartments with high rate per square meters form the others. It can be motivated by considering that the rent rate is not directly proportional to the apartment extension but it includes fixed expenses that do not vary with the apartment size.

For the class $rate\_per\_squaremeters=low$ the following EP was discovered:

$$apartment(A) \wedge apartment\_inside\_district(A, B) \wedge$$
$$district\_crossedby\_tranStop(B, C) \wedge apartment\_year(A, [1893..1899])$$

This pattern has a support of 0.265 and a growth rate of 2.343. It represents the event that an apartment A built between 1893 and 1899 is inside a district B that contains a railway public stop. This pattern discriminates apartments with low rate per square meters from the others. It can be motivated by considering that old buildings do not offer the same facilities of a recently built apartment.

6 Conclusions

In this paper, we presented a novel MRDM method, called Mr-EP, which discovers a characterization of classes in terms of relational EPs thus providing a human-interpretable description of the differences between separate classes. The method was implemented in a MRDM system which is tightly integrated with a relational DBMS. The tight-coupling with the database makes the knowledge on data structure available free of charge to guide the search in the relational pattern space. Experimental results have been obtained by running Mr-EP to capture data changes among several populations of geo-referenced data. As future work, we plan to exploit relational EPs for associative classification tasks and to compare results with those already reported in a previous study [2].

Acknowledgment

This work is partial fulfillment of the research objective of ATENEO-2007 project "Metodi di scoperta della conoscenza nelle basi di dati: evoluzioni rispetto allo schema unimodale". The authors thank Nicola Barile for his help in reading a first draft of this paper.

References

1. Agrawal, R., Imielinski, T., Swami, A.N.: Mining association rules between sets of items in large databases. In: Buneman, P., Jajodia, S. (eds.) International Conference on Management of Data, pp. 207–216 (1993)
2. Ceci, M., Appice, A.: Spatial associative classification: propositional vs structural approach. Journal of Intelligent Information Systems 27(3), 191–213 (2006)
3. Dehaspe, L., Toivonen, H.: Discovery of frequent datalog patterns. Journal of Data Mining and Knowledge Discovery 3(1), 7–36 (1999)

4. Dong, G., Li, J.: Efficient mining of emerging patterns: Discovering trends and differences. In: International Conference on Knowledge Discovery and Data Mining, pp. 43–52. ACM Press, New York (1999)
5. Dong, G., Zhang, X., Wong, L., Li, J.: CAEP: Classification by aggregating emerging patterns. In: Arikawa, S., Furukawa, K. (eds.) DS 1999. LNCS (LNAI), vol. 1721, pp. 30–42. Springer, Heidelberg (1999)
6. Džeroski, S., Lavrač, N.: Relational Data Mining. Springer, Heidelberg (2001)
7. Fan, H., Ramamohanarao, K.: An efficient singlescan algorithm for mining essential jumping emerging patterns for classification. In: Chen, M.-S., Yu, P.S., Liu, B. (eds.) PAKDD 2002. LNCS (LNAI), vol. 2336, pp. 456–462. Springer, Heidelberg (2002)
8. Fan, H., Ramamohanarao, K.: A bayesian approach to use emerging patterns for classification. In: Australasian Database Conference, vol. 143, pp. 39–48. Australian Computer Society, Inc. (2003)
9. Fan, H., Ramamohanarao, K.: A weighting scheme based on emerging patterns for weighted support vector machines. In: Hu, X., Liu, Q., Skowron, A., Lin, T.Y., Yager, R.R., Zhang, B. (eds.) IEEE International Conference on Granular Computing, pp. 435–440. IEEE Computer Society Press, Los Alamitos (2005)
10. Li, J.: Mining Emerging Patterns to Construct Accurate and Efficient Classifiers. PhD thesis, University of Melbourne (2001)
11. Li, J., Dong, G., Ramamohanarao, K., Wong, L.: DeEPs: A new instance-based lazy discovery and classification system. Machine Learning 54(2), 99–124 (2004)
12. Li, J., Liu, H., Downing, J.: Simple rules underlying gene expression profiles of more than six subtypes of acute lymphoblastic leukemia. Bioinformatics 19(1), 71–78 (2003)
13. Li, J., Liu, H., Ng, S.-K., Wong, L.: Discovery of significant rules for classifying cancer diagnosis data. In: European Conference on Computational Biology, Supplement of Bioinformatics, pp. 93–102 (2003)
14. Lisi, F.A., Malerba, D.: Inducing multi-level association rules from multiple relations. Machine Learning 55, 175–210 (2004)
15. Liu, B., Hsu, W., Ma, Y.: Integrative classification and association rule mining. In: Proceedings of AAAI Conference of Knowledge Discovery in Databases (1998)
16. Mannila, H., Toivonen, H.: Levelwise search and borders of theories in knowledge discovery. Data Mining and Knowledge Discovery 1(3), 241–258 (1997)
17. Plotkin, G.D.: A note on inductive generalization 5, 153–163 (1970)
18. Zhang, X., Dong, G., Ramamohanarao, K.: Exploring constraints to efficiently mine emerging patterns from large high-dimensional datasets. In: Terano, T., Chen, A.L.P. (eds.) PAKDD 2000. LNCS, vol. 1805, pp. 310–314. Springer, Heidelberg (2000)

Advanced Tree-Based Kernels for Protein Classification

Elisa Cilia[1] and Alessandro Moschitti[2]

[1] Department of Information and Communication Technology
University of Trento,
Via Sommarive 14, 38100, Povo (Trento), Italy
cilia@dit.unitn.it
[2] Department of Computer Science, System and Production
University of Rome, Tor Vergata,
Via Della Ricerca Scientifica s.n.c., 00133, Roma, Italy
moschitti@info.uniroma2.it

Abstract. One of the aims of modern Bioinformatics is to discover the
molecular mechanisms that rule the protein operation. This would allow us to understand the complex processes involved in living systems
and possibly correct dysfunctions. The first step in this direction is the
identification of the functional sites of proteins.

In this paper, we propose new kernels for the automatic protein active
site classification. In particular, we devise innovative attribute-value and
tree substructure representations to model biological and spatial information of proteins in Support Vector Machines. We experimented with such
models and the Protein Data Bank adequately pre-processed to make explicit the active site information. Our results show that structural kernels
used in combination with polynomial kernels can be effectively applied
to discriminate an active site from other regions of a protein. Such finding is very important since it firstly shows a successful identification of
catalytic sites for a very large family of proteins belonging to a broad
class of enzymes.

1   Introduction

Recent research in Bioinformatics has been devoted to the production and understanding of genomic data. The availability of the human genome sequence has
shown how small our knowledge about the relation between molecular structures
and their functions is. There are about 10,000 genes encoding approximately the
same number of well characterized proteins, but apparently, the number of protein functions seems to be higher. Current methods rarely allow us to recognize
all the functions that a protein can carry out.

From a biological point rof view, it is clear the importance of understanding the
molecular mechanisms which rule the correct operation of a protein or, in case
of pathologies, which lead to an altered or null protein function. Through the
knowledge of these mechanisms it is possible to eventually correct dysfunctions.

R. Basili and M.T. Pazienza (Eds.): AI*IA 2007, LNAI 4733, pp. 218–229, 2007.
© Springer-Verlag Berlin Heidelberg 2007

Such research is quite complex to carry out as a protein function is the result of a combination of several factors. One important step in this direction is the study of the relation between molecular structures and their functions, which in turn depends on the discovering of the protein active sites. As there is a large number of synthesized proteins which have no associated function yet, automatic approaches for active site detection are critical.

Currently, the general strategy used to identify a protein active site involves the expertise of researchers and biologists accumulated in years of study on the target protein. This manual approach is conducted essentially using homology based strategies, i.e. inferring the function of a new protein based on a close similarity to already annotated proteins [1]. Sometimes proteins with the same overall tertiary structure can have different active sites, i.e. different functions and proteins with different overall tertiary structure can show the same function and similar active sites. In these cases homology based approaches are inadequate. In general, there is no automated approach to protein active site detection, although it is evident its usefulness to restrict the number of candidate sites and also to automatically learn rules characterizing an active site [2].

In this paper we define the problem of determining protein active sites in terms of a classification problem. We modeled protein active site based on both attribute/value and structural representations [3]. The former representation is a set of standard linear features whereas the latter is constituted by tree structures extracted from graphs associated with proteins or their candidate sites. The graph nodes (or vertexes) represent amino acids (or better residues) and edges represent distances in the three-dimensional space between these residues.

We applied these representations to SVMs using polynomial kernels, tree kernels and some combinations of them. To experimentally evaluate our approach, we created a data set, using the protein structures retrieved from the *Protein Data Bank* (PDB) [4] maintained by the *Research Collaboratory for Structural Bioinformatics* (RCBS) at http://www.rcbs.org. The combined kernels show the highest F_1 measure, i.e. 68%, in the detection of active sites. This is an important and promising result considering that the baseline based on a random selection of active sites has an upperbound of only 2%.

In the remainder of this article Section 2 describes the faced problem. Section 3 describes the proposed linear and structural features. Section 4 describes the experimental evaluation and reports the results of the classification experiments. Finally, in Section 5, we summarize the results of the previous sections and propose other interesting future research lines.

2   Definition of the Protein Active Site Classification Task

In this section we formally define the task of protein active site classification: first, we give the protein active site definition then we provide a formal description of our computational model.

2.1   Protein Active Site Definition

An active site in a protein is a topological region which defines the protein function, in other words it is a functional domain in the protein three-dimensional structure (see also [2]). In a cell there are many types of proteins which carry out different functions. The enzymes are those proteins able to accelerate chemical processes inside a cell. This type of proteins are distinguished from structural and supplying proteins for their catalytical action on the large part of molecules constituting the living world. We limit our research to a particular class of enzymes, the hydrolases.

Hydrolases are maybe the most studied and known type of enzymes. They catalyze hydrolysis reactions, generically consisting in the cleavage of a biochemical compound thanks to the addition of a water molecule (H_2O). The characteristic of some hydrolases to catalyze reactions in the presence of a water molecule motivates our model: as a hydrolase active site, we choose a sphere in a three-dimensional space centered in the coordinates of the oxygen atom of a water molecule. This sphere includes a portion of the protein within its volume, which is a number of amino acids which could reciprocally interact with other amino acids in the surrounding space, or with water molecules. In this first analysis, we consider a sphere with a radius of 8 Å, which is the maximum distance needed for the water-residue interaction.

Figure 1(a), shows the active site of 1A2O protein structure and its representation according to our model. The protein residues are colored in light gray whereas the particular catalytic residues are in dark gray. The center of the sphere is the black colored oxygen atom of a water molecule.

2.2   The Computational Model

We defined the functional site identification as a classification problem, where the objects we want to classify are protein active sites. We represent the portion of the protein contained in a spherical three-dimensional region with a completely

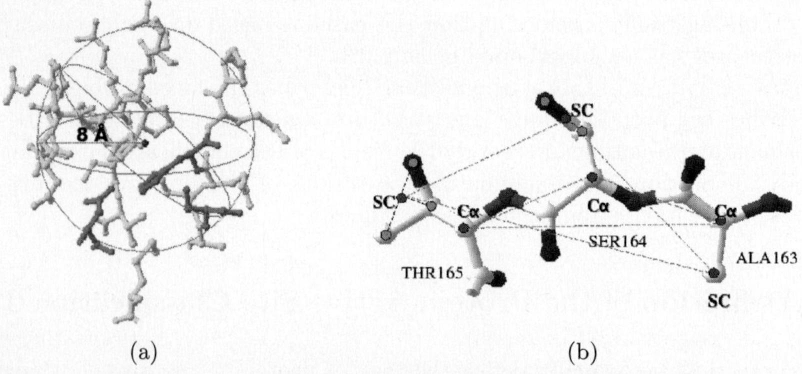

(a)   (b)

Fig. 1. (a) A sphere (positive example). (b) Distances.

connected graph. Each vertex of this graph is a residue and each edge represents the distance in the three-dimensional space between a pair of vertexes.

Every amino acid is represented by two points in the three-dimensional space: the first represents an amino acid main-chain (the α-carbon atom of the amino acid, $C\alpha$) and the second represents an amino acid side-chain (the centroid between the coordinates of the atoms belonging to the amino acid side-chain, SC) (see figure 1(b)). The same kind of approximation has been described in [5] because it seems to provide a good balance between fuzziness and specificity in these kind of applications.

In figure 1(b) the three-dimensional SC-SC distances and $C\alpha$-$C\alpha$ distances are indicated between the represented chain of three residues.

An object (modeled by a graph centered on a water molecule) can be classified as being an active site or not with a binary classifier. Thus, we consider as a positive example, a graph whose set of vertices includes all the catalytic amino acids and as a negative example a graph which contains no catalytic amino acid. Moreover, to reduce the task complexity, we extract, from the initial completely connected graph, some spanning substructures which preserve the edges within the maximum interaction distance of 5 Å between the side-chains of the residues.

The next section shows how the above representation model can be used along with Support Vector Machines to design an automatic active site classifier.

3   Automatic Classification of Active Sites

Previous section has shown that the active site representation is based on graphs. To design the computational model of these latter, we have two possibilities: (1) we extract scalar features able to capture the most important properties of the graph and (2) we can use graph based kernels [6] in kernel-based machines such as Support Vector Machines [7]. Point (2) often leads to high computational complexity. We approached such problem by extracting a tree forest from the target graph and applying efficient tree kernels [8].

3.1   Tree Kernels

Tree-kernel functions are viable alternative to attribute/value representations of tree structures. Such functions implicitly define a feature space based on all possible tree substructures. Given two trees T_1 and T_2, the kernel function evaluates the number of common fragments.

More formally, let $\mathcal{F} = \{f_1, f_2, \ldots, f_{|\mathcal{F}|}\}$ be a tree fragment space, the indicator function $I_i(n)$ is equal to 1 if the target f_i is rooted at node n and equal to 0 otherwise. A tree-kernel function over t_1 and t_2 is $K_t(t_1, t_2) = \sum_{n_1 \in N_{t_1}} \sum_{n_2 \in N_{t_2}} \Delta(n_1, n_2)$, where N_{t_1} and N_{t_2} are the sets of the t_1's and t_2's nodes, respectively. In turn $\Delta(n_1, n_2) = \sum_{i=1}^{|\mathcal{F}|} \lambda^{l(f_i)} I_i(n_1) I_i(n_2)$, where $0 \leq \lambda \leq 1$ and $l(f_i)$ is the height of the subtree f_i. Thus $\lambda^{l(f_i)}$ assigns a lower weight to larger fragments. When $\lambda = 1$, Δ is equal to the number of common fragments rooted at nodes n_1 and n_2.

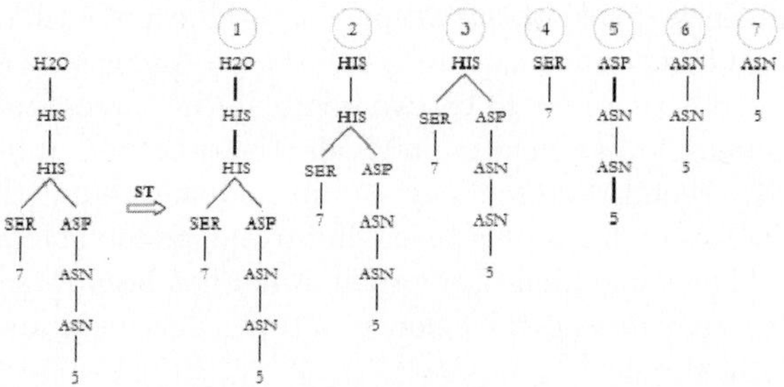

Fig. 2. A tree with its *SubTrees*

The Δ function depends on the type fragments that we consider as a *basic* features. For example, in [9], the SubSet Trees (SSTs) are proposed. These are any portion p of the initial tree T subject to the constraint that for each node $n \in p$ either n has no children or it has all children described in T. The evaluation of Δ computing such fragment space can be carried out in $O(|N_{t_1}| \times |N_{t_2}|)$.

In figure 2 all the subtrees of a given tree are represented while in figure 3 there are some of the fragments in the SST structure space for the same given tree.

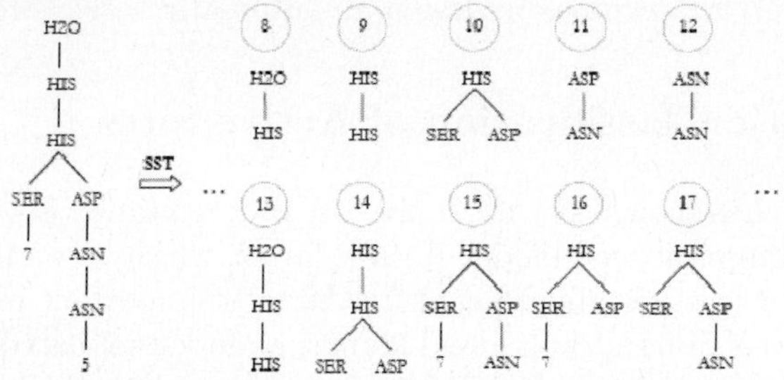

Fig. 3. A tree with some of its *SubSet Trees*

A more general form of fragments has been given in [8]. In this case any portion p of T, namely Partial Trees (PT), is considered and an efficient evaluation is provided. Note that the SST space is less rich, i.e. it is a subspace of the PT set. Nevertheless, the SST-based kernel can provide higher accuracy since its parameterization is simpler and it usually contains less irrelevant fragments than the PT kernel. In figure 4 some of the partial trees of a given tree are represented. Note that ST $\subset$ SST $\subset$ PT, if we consider ST, SST and PT respectively as the sets of all subtress, all subset trees and all the partial trees of a given tree.

To compute the PT space, we need to define a different Δ function as follows:

- if the node labels of n_1 and n_2 are different then $\Delta(n_1, n_2) = 0$;
- else

$$\Delta(n_1, n_2) = 1 + \sum_{J_1, J_2, l(J_1) = l(J_2)} \prod_{i=1}^{l(J_1)} \Delta(c_{n_1}[J_{1i}], c_{n_2}[J_{2i}]) \tag{1}$$

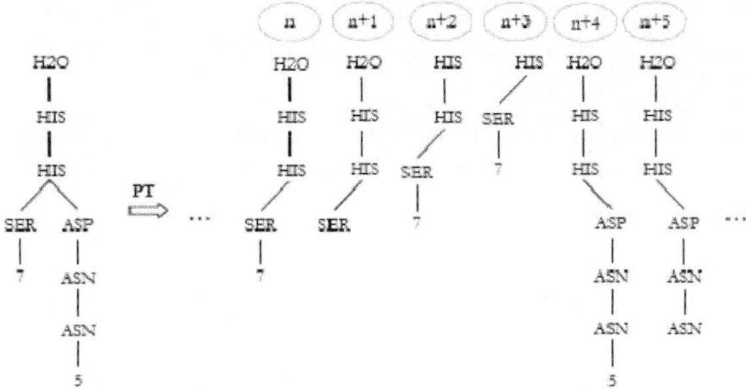

Fig. 4. A tree with some of its *Partial Trees*

where $\boldsymbol{J}_1 = \langle J_{11}, J_{12}, J_{13}, ..\rangle$ and $\boldsymbol{J}_2 = \langle J_{21}, J_{22}, J_{23}, ..\rangle$ are index sequences associated with the ordered child sequences c_{n_1} of n_1 and c_{n_2} of n_2, respectively, $\boldsymbol{J}_{1i}$ and $\boldsymbol{J}_{2i}$ point to the i-th child in the corresponding sequence, and $l(\cdot)$ returns the sequence length.

Furthermore, we add two decay factors: μ for the height of the tree and λ for the length of the child sequences. It follows that

$$\Delta(n_1, n_2) = \mu\Big(\lambda^2 + \sum_{\boldsymbol{J}_1, \boldsymbol{J}_2, l(\boldsymbol{J}_1)=l(\boldsymbol{J}_2)} \lambda^{d(\boldsymbol{J}_1)+d(\boldsymbol{J}_2)} \prod_{i=1}^{l(\boldsymbol{J}_1)} \Delta(c_{n_1}[\boldsymbol{J}_{1i}], c_{n_2}[\boldsymbol{J}_{2i}])\Big) ,$$

(2)

where $d(\boldsymbol{J}_1) = \boldsymbol{J}_{1l(\boldsymbol{J}_1)} - \boldsymbol{J}_{11}$ and $d(\boldsymbol{J}_2) = \boldsymbol{J}_{2l(\boldsymbol{J}_2)} - \boldsymbol{J}_{21}$. In this way, we penalize both larger trees and subtrees built on child subsequences that contain gaps. Moreover, to have a similarity score between 0 and 1, we also apply a normalization in the kernel space, $K'(T_1, T_2) = \dfrac{K(T_1,T_2)}{\sqrt{K(T_1,T_1) \times K(T_2,T_2)}}$.

Equation 2 is a more general one, the kernel can be applied to PTs. Also note that if we only consider the contribution of the longest child sequence from node pairs that have the same children, we implement the SST kernel. For the ST computation we also need to remove the λ^2 term from Eq. 2.

3.2   Scalar Features

Scalar features refer to typical chemical values of the molecules described in the target graph. We defined 5 different types of such features (see Table 1):

The first class (C1) encodes chemical and physical properties of the graph. This class represents properties such as hydrophobicity, polarity, polarizability and Van der Waals volume of the amino acids composing the sphere. The encoding is the same used in [10] where the features were used to classify the function of proteins.

The second class (C2) encodes the amino acid composition of a spherical region. There is a feature associated with every labeled vertex (amino acid) in the graph, weighted with the inverse of the distance from the oxygen atom of the water molecule which is the center of the sphere. This group of features emphasizes the importance of the interaction distance of a residue with respect to a water molecule.

The third class (C3) represents charge or neutrality of a spherical region. This is measured by counting the number of positively or negatively charged amino acids.

Another group of linear features (C5) encodes the quantity of water in a sphere. This is measured by counting the number of water molecules within the sphere radius. This group of features is motivated by the fact that biologists observed that an active site is usually located in a hydrophobic core of the protein while on the surface the quantity of water is higher and the residues exposed to the solvent are not hydrophobic.

Finally, the last class of linear features (C6) is the one which measures the atomic density of the sphere calculated as the total number of atoms in the sphere.

Table 1. Representation: feature classes

Linear Features	Description
1st Class	Physical and chemical properties (amino acid attributes)
2nd Class	Amino acidic Composition
3rd Class	Charge/Neutrality
5th Class	Water molecule quantity
6th Class	Atomic density
Structural Features	**Description**
4th Class	Tree substructures from tertiary structure

It should be noted that (a) the last two classes of linear features are made discrete using a different number of value intervals. A feature is associated with an example if the measured value of a certain property falls in the correspondent range. (b) These features are often used to describe protein structures in similar tasks of Bioinformatics [10] and to develop software for protein structure prediction like Modeler 7v7.

3.3   Structural Features

We designed a class of structural features to encode the three-dimensional structure (tertiary structure) or better, the spatial configuration characterizing a spherical region, i.e. the set of amino acids composing it with their 3D distances. As previously mentioned this representation results in a completely connected graph since every vertex is connected to any other vertex in the sphere graph through an edge labeled with the 3D distance of the pair.

Starting from this completely connected graph, we extract some tree substructures using heuristics: we fix the maximum interaction distance to 5 Å between the side-chains of the residues and we use the minimum spanning tree algorithm to extract tree structures from the graph.

Such heuristics are motivated by the observation that to perform the catalytic function it is necessary that the side-chains of the catalytic residues can interact with each other and with the substrate. The maximum interaction distance between atoms in different residue side-chains is usually of about 3-4 Å. We chose a cut-off distance of 5 Å to take into consideration our approximation in the representation of residues (figure 1(b)).

The applied cut-off possibly leads to the separation in disconnected components of the initial graph. From each of these components, using the Prim algorithm [11], we extract the spanning tree which minimizes the interaction distances d_{xy} between the side-chains of the residues x and y. Note that as some graphs contain more than one connected component, the Prim algorithm is applied to each of them, therefore the final output is a tree forest.

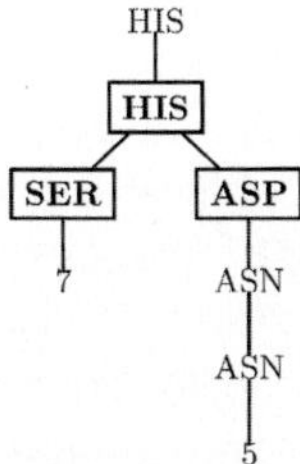

Fig. 5. Graphical representation of a tree of a sphere

We add the water molecule (center of the sphere) as root node to the obtained spanning tree. In figure 5, we show a tree which can represent the spherical region in figure 1(a). In bold within the boxes, we highlight the nodes which represent catalytic amino acids.

The tree substructures generated for each example constitute the features analyzed by our tree kernel function. If two examples are described by two tree forests, we can use as a kernel function the summation of the tree kernels applied to all possible pairs coming from such forests.

4   Experiments

In the next subsections, we describe our classification experiments carried out on the data set that we generated from the Protein Data Bank.

4.1   Experimental Set-Up

The evaluations were carried out using the SVM-light-TK software [12] (available at http://ai-nlp.info.uniroma2.it/moschitti/) which encodes tree kernels in SVM-light [13]. We applied polynomial kernels to the linear features and tree kernels to the structural features.

More precisely, we used the SST and the PT kernels described in [8] on a simple tree, i.e. the main tertiary structure[1], or on a tree forest (see Section 3.3). The former kernels are indicated with SST_T and PT_T whereas the latter

---

[1] The most relevant tree structure in the forest, that is, the tree which contains at least a catalytic amino acid and the two nearest residue side-chains of the sphere.

Table 2. (a) Linear feature performance. (b) Combined kernel performance.

(a)

Linear	Precision	Recall	F_1
C1	5.5%	66.7%	**10.2%**
C2	55.9%	63.3%	**59.4%**
C3	20%	3.3%	**5.7%**
C5	2.2%	30%	**4.1%**
C6	5.5%	13.3%	**7.8%**

(b)

	Precision	Recall	$F_1 \pm Std.Dev.$
L	62.3%	55.4%	**56.2%** ±6.8
SST_F	66.2%	31.8%	**39.9%** ±13.7
L+SST_F	82.9%	58.6%	**68.3%** ±14.5

are called SST_F and PT_F. The kernel for tree forest is simply the summation of all possible pairs of trees contained in two examples.

We experimented with our models and the protein structures downloaded from the Protein Data Bank (PDB). We adequately pre-processed PDB files to obtain all the information of interest for this task. In particular, we created a data set of 14,688 examples from 48 hydrolases from the PDB structures. The data set is composed of 171 positive examples and 14,571 negative examples, which means a $\frac{1}{125}$ ratio between positive and negative examples.

The results were evaluated by applying a 5-fold cross validation[2] on this data set measuring the performance with the F_1 measure[3]. A noticeable attention was devoted to parameterization (cost factor, decay factor, etc.)

4.2 Experiment Results

Table 2(a) reports the results on the 5 types of linear features using the polynomial kernel (degree 3). These results are only indicative as we did not run a cross validation procedure. We note that most linear features cannot discriminate between active and non-active site. Only, the second class, which encodes the structural information, shows a meaningful F_1. The general low results of linear features is caused by the remarkable complexity of the task as suggested by the F_1 upperbound of the random selection, i.e. $\simeq 1.6\%$.

Table 3. Tree kernel impact

L+TK	Precision	Recall	$F_1 \pm Std.Dev.$
SST_F	82.9%	58.6%	**68.3%** ±14.5
SST_T	79.7%	51.7%	**62.3%** ±10.4
PT_T	80.4%	41.2%	**54.4%** ±9.1

In order to boost the classification performance, we experimented with the structural kernels. Table 2(b) summarizes the cross validation results: Row 2 reports the outcome with polynomial kernels on all the linear features (L), Row 3

---

[2] We separated the data set into five parts, each one composed of examples belonging to a set of nine or ten protein structures randomly assigned to this set.

[3] F_1 assigns equal importance to Precision P and Recall R i.e. $F_1 = \frac{2P \cdot R}{P+R}$

shows the outcomes of the SST kernels on the tree forest (SST_F) and Row 4 illustrates the performance of the polynomial kernel summed to the SST kernel on the tree forest (L+SST_F). The $\pm$ sign precedes the standard deviation evaluated on the 5 folds.

It is worth to note that the F_1 obtained with the linear features (56.24%) improves by 12 absolute points if we use the combined model (L+SST_F), i.e. 68%.

We also experimented with the PT kernel. The results of the cross validation experiments are summarized in Table 3: Row 2 reports the results with polynomial kernel plus SST_F (applied to linear features and a forest structure), Row 3 reports the cross validation results of polynomial kernel plus SST_T (applied to linear features and a tree structure) and finally Row 4 illustrates the performance of the additive combination of polynomial with the PT kernel (PT_T) (on linear features and a tree structure).

The results show that the highest F_1 measure can be achieved with the SST_F but quite similar performance can be obtained representing examples with only a tree structure in the forest, i.e. SST_T.

In contrast to our expectations the PT kernel, which may be considered the most appropriate for this task, shows the lowest F_1. A plausible explanation of such low F_1 is the higher complex parameterization needed by the PT kernel.

Overall, the very good F_1 of our best model suggests that our classification system can be a useful tool to help biology researchers in the study of protein functions.

5   Related Work

Literature work demonstrates the importance of protein structures and theirs active sites for the discovering of protein functions. Hereafter we report some of the related work.

In [3], novel Recurrent Neural Networks for the detection of Protein secondary structures are proposed. These models exploit non-casual bidirectional dynamics to capture up-stream and down-stream information. In [5] we can see the first general approach to structure searches based on active site rather than exclusively on fold similarity. The authors showed that three-dimensional signature consisting of only a few functionally important residues can be diagnostic of membership in superfamily of enzymes which can represent a first step in the inference of some functional properties. This membership, results not only from fold similarity but also from the disposition of residues involved in a conserved function. It could be interesting to get a potential active site of a protein starting from its structure rather than get only an active site template from a known protein as the authors do in such work. In [14] a kernel-based approach is used to predict signal peptides and their cleavage sites from the primary sequence of proteins. In [15] the task of catalytic residue prediction is solved using 26 different classifiers from WEKA package. The authors show that the best performing algorithm is a Support Vector Machine. In this work structural properties are captured with linear features.

Many other approaches have been employed in different application areas of bioinformatics (functional genomics, protein bioinformatics, etc.) with success. Learning methods have been applied to face other biological tasks such as translation initiation site recognition in DNA genes [16], promoter region-based classification of genes [17], protein classification, protein-protein interaction [18], functional classification from microarray expression data [19], [20], [21], [22]. In such work SVMs and kernel methods (see [6] for a survey of kernels for structured data) are used as the main learning algorithm.

6   Conclusions

In this paper, we have studied the problem of the identification of protein functional sites. We have defined a novel computational representation based on biological and spatial considerations and several classes of linear and structural features.

The experiments with SVMs using polynomial and tree kernels and their combinations show that the highest F_1, i.e. 68%, is achieved with the combined model. Such finding is very important since it firstly shows the successful identification of catalytic sites of a very large family of catalytic proteins belonging to a broad class of enzymes. Moreover, our work highlights the importance of structural information in the detection of protein active sites. This result motivates the need of structural representations which we efficiently modeled by means of tree kernels.

Acknowledgements

The authors thank Dr. Sergio Ammendola for the valuable support regarding to the biological aspects of this work.

References

1. Cilia, E., Fabbri, A., Uriani, M., Scialdone, G.G., Ammendola, S.: The signature amidase from sulfolobus solfataricus belongs to the cx3c subgroup of enzymes cleaving both amides and nitriles: Ser195 and cys145 are predicted to be the active sites nucleophiles. The FEBS Journal 272, 4716–4724 (2005)
2. Tramontano, A.: The ten most wanted solutions in Protein Bioinformatics. Mathematical Biology and Medicine Series. Chapman & Hall/CRC (2005)
3. Brunak, S., Baldi, P., Frasconi, P., Pollastri, G., Soda, G.: Exploiting the past and the future in protein secondary structure prediction. Bioinformatics 15(11) (1999)
4. Berman, H.M., Westbrook, J., Feng, Z., Gilliland, G., Bhat, T.N., Weissig, H., Shindyalov, I.N., Bourne, P.E.: The protein data bank. Nucleic Acids Res. 28(1), 235–242 (2000)
5. Meng, E.C., Polacco, B.J., Babbitt, P.C.: Superfamily active site templates. PROTEINS: Structure, Function, and Bioinformatics 55, 962–976 (2004)
6. Gärtner, T.: A survey of kernels for structured data. Multi Relational Data Mining (MRDM) 5, 49–58 (2003)

7. Vapnik, V.: The Nature of Statistical Learning Theory. Springer, Heidelberg (1995)
8. Moschitti, A.: Efficient convolution kernels for dependency and constituent syntactic trees. In: Proceedings of The 17th European Conference on Machine Learning, Berlin, Germany (2006)
9. Collins, M., Duffy, N.: New ranking algorithms for parsing and tagging: Kernels over discrete structures, and the voted perceptron. In: ACL02 (2002)
10. Borgwardt, K.: Graph-based Functional Classification of Proteins using Kernel Methods. Ludwig Maximilians University of Monaco (2004)
11. Prim, R.C.: Shortest connection networks and some generalizations. Bell Syst. Tech. Journal 36, 1389–1401 (1957)
12. Moschitti, A.: A study on convolution kernel for shallow semantic parsing. In: ACL-2004. Proceedings of the 42th Conference on Association for Computational Linguistic, Barcelona, Spain (2004)
13. Joachims, T.: Making large-scale svm learning practical. In: Schölkopf, B., Burges, C., Smola, A. (eds.) Advances in Kernel Methods - Support Vector Learning (1999)
14. Yang, Z.R.: Orthogonal kernels machines for the prediction of functional sites in proteins. IEEE Trans. on Systems, Man and Cybernetics 35(1), 100–106 (2005)
15. Petrova, N.V., Wu, C.H.: Prediction of catalytic residues using support vector machine with selected protein sequence and structural properties. BMC Bionformatics (7), 312–324 (2006)
16. Zien, A., Rätsch, G., Mika, S., Schölkopf, B., Lengauer, T., Muller, K.R: Engineering support vector machine kernel that recognize translation initiation sites. Bioinformatics 16(9), 799–807 (2000)
17. Pavlidis, P., Furey, T.S., Liberto, M., Grundy, W.N.: Promoter region-based classification of genes. In: Proceedings of the Pacific Symposium on Biocomputing, pp. 151–163 (2001)
18. Bock, J.R., Gough, D.A.: Predicting protein-protein interactions from primary structure. Bionformatics 17(5), 455–460 (2001)
19. Brown, M.P.S., Grundy, W.N., Lin, D., Cristianini, N., Sugnet, C., Ares, M., Haussler, D.: Support vector machine classification of microarray expression data. In: UCSC-URL (1999)
20. Brown, M.P.S., Grundy, W.N., Lin, D., Cristianini, N., Sugnet, C., Furey, T.S., Ares, M., Haussler, D.: Knowledge-based analysis of microarray gene expression data by using support vector machine. PNAS 97(1), 262–267 (2000)
21. Furey, T.S., Duffy, N., Cristianini, N., Bednarski, D., Schummer, M., Haussler, D.: Support vector machine classification and validation of cancer tissue samples using microarray expression data. Bioinformatics 16(10), 906–914 (2000)
22. Pavlidis, P., Furey, T., Liberto, M., Grundy, W.N.: Learning gene functional classification from multiple data types. Journal of Computational Biology (2002)

A Genetic Approach to the Automatic Generation of Fuzzy Control Systems from Numerical Controllers

Giuseppe Della Penna[1], Francesca Fallucchi[3], Benedetto Intrigila[2], and Daniele Magazzeni[1]

[1] Department of Computer Science
University of L'Aquila, Italy
[2] Department of Mathematics
University of Roma "Tor Vergata", Italy
[3] DISP, University of Roma "Tor Vergata", Italy

Abstract. Control systems are small components that control the behavior of larger systems. In the last years, sophisticated controllers have been widely used in the hardware/software *embedded systems* contained in a growing number of everyday products and appliances. Therefore, the problem of the automatic synthesis of controllers is extremely important. To this aim, several techniques have been applied, like *cell-to-cell mapping*, *dynamic programming* and, more recently, *model checking*. The controllers generated using these techniques are typically *numerical controllers* that, however, often have a huge size and not enough robustness. In this paper we present an automatic iterative process, based on *genetic algorithms*, that can be used to compress the huge information contained in such numerical controllers into smaller and more robust *fuzzy control systems*.

1   Introduction

Control systems (or, shortly, *controllers*) are small hardware/software components that control the behavior of larger systems, the *plants*. A controller continuously analyzes the plant state (looking at its *state variables*) and possibly adjusts some of its parameters (called *control variables*) to keep the system in a condition called *setpoint*, which usually represents the *normal* or *correct* behavior of the system.

In the last years, the use of sophisticated controllers has become very common in robotics, critical systems and, in general, in the hardware/software *embedded systems* contained in a growing number of everyday products and appliances.

Therefore, the problem of the automatic synthesis of control systems starting from the plant model is extremely important. This problem is particulary difficult for *non-linear systems*, where the mathematical model of the plant is not analytically tractable. To this aim, several techniques have been developed, based on a more or less systematic exploration of the state space. One can mention, among others, *cell-to-cell mapping* techniques [1] and *dynamic programming* [2].

R. Basili and M.T. Pazienza (Eds.): AI*IA 2007, LNAI 4733, pp. 230–241, 2007.

Recently, *model checking* techniques have also been applied [3, 4] in the field of automatic controller generation. In particular, this approach can be actually considered as a *planning* technique. Indeed, a model checking-based controller generator does not simply look for good *local* actions towards the setpoint, but searches for *the best possible sequence of actions* to bring the plant to the setpoint. Therefore, with this technique it is possible to find an *optimal* solution to the control problem.

The controllers generated using all these techniques are typically *numerical controllers*, i.e. tables indexed by the plant states, whose entries are commands for the plant. These commands are used to set the control variables in order to reach the setpoint from the corresponding states. Namely, when the controller reads a state from the plant, it looks up the action described in the associated table entry and sends it to the plant. However, this kind of controllers can present two main problems.

The first problem is the *size* of the table, which for complex systems may contain millions of entries, since it should be embedded in the control system hardware that is usually very limited.

The second problem is the controller *robustness*. A controller is robust if it is able to handle all the possible plant states. Due to approximation of continuous variables, plants unavoidably present states that are not known to the controller, although they may be more or less *close* to some states in the table. In numerical controllers this problem is typically handled by interpolation techniques (e.g., see [2]). However, interpolation does not always work well [1]: table based control may also give a bumpy response as the controller jumps from one table value to another. Therefore, other approaches have been proposed (e.g. see [5, 6]).

A natural solution to these problems is to derive, from the huge numerical information contained in the table, a small *fuzzy control system*. This solution is natural since fuzzy rules are very flexible and can be adapted to cope with any kind of system. Moreover, there are a number of well-established techniques to guide the choice of fuzzy rules by statistical considerations, such as in Kosko space clustering method [7], or by abstracting them from a neural network [8]. In particular, the approach that we have adopted in the present paper is inspired by [1]. However, there are several substantial differences.

The crucial point is of course the algorithm to extract the fuzzy rules from the numerical controller table. We used *genetic algorithms* [9]. This choice is based on the following considerations:

- genetic algorithms are suitable to cope with very large state spaces [9]; this is particularly important when the starting point is the huge table generated by model checking techniques;
- the *crossover* mechanism ensures a fair average behavior of the system, avoiding irregularities;
- the *fitness function*, which is the core of any genetic algorithm, can be obtained in a rather direct way from the control table of the numerical controller;
- the genome coding can also be derived from the structure of the sought-for fuzzy system.

Therefore, the process is almost automatic. Only a few parameters, such as the number of fuzzy sets, have to be determined by hand. However, also the choice of such parameters can be automatized or at least supported by an automatic process. Indeed, the correctness of the resulting fuzzy controller can be verified [10], so in case of a poor behavior the parameters are changed and the process restarted. This automatic loop is stopped when the right values for the parameters are detected. Of course [11], it is possible that no such values exist, that is the system is so complex that the controller table turns out to be *incompressible*.

The paper is organized as follows. In Section 2 we present the numerical control systems and we summarize the methods for their synthesis, while in Section 3 we describe the fuzzy control systems. In Section 4 we give an overview of genetic algorithms and in section 5 we describe how we use them to automatically synthesize fuzzy controllers. In Section 6 we present a case study and experimental results. Section 7 concludes the paper.

2   Numerical Control Systems

As mentioned in the Introduction, a *numerical controller* is a table, indexed by the plant states, whose entries are commands for the plant.

The use of such kind of controller is very suitable (and often necessary) to cope with non-linear systems, which have a dynamics too complex to allow an analytical treatment [3, 4]. On the other hand, the table size of a numerical controller could be huge, especially when we are interested in the efficiency of controller and thus we use a high precision. In these cases, we could have tables containing millions of state-action pairs and if we are working with small embedded systems, the table size could be a potential issue.

2.1   Numerical Control System Synthesis

There are a number of well-established techniques for the synthesis of numerical control systems. For short, we mention only three of them: (1) dynamic programming, (2) cell mapping and (3) model checking.

The classical dynamic programming approach for the synthesis of controllers of a plant P (see [2] for details) is based on an optimal cost function J defined as follows:

$$J(x) =_{def} \inf_{\underline{u}} \left[\sum_{t=0}^{\infty} l(f(x, u_t), u_t) \right] \tag{1}$$

where $f(x, u)$ is the continuous dynamics of the plant, $l(x, u)$ is a continuous, positive definite *cost function* and $\underline{u}$ stands for a generic control sequence: $\underline{u} = \{u_0, u_1, u_2, \ldots\}$.

J is well defined (i.e. the infimum always exists in the region of interest) if and only if the plant P is controllable. So, assuming that J is well defined, then it satisfies the so-called *Bellman Equation*:

$$J(x) = \inf_u \left[l(x, u) \ + \ J(f(x, u)) \right] \tag{2}$$

and it can be computed by the following iterative method:

$$J_{T+1}(x) = \inf_u [l(x, u) + J_T(f(x, u))]$$
$$J_0 =_{def} 0, T \ \in \mathbf{Z}_0^+ \tag{3}$$

In the cell mapping method [1], the trajectories (i.e. sequences of state-control pairs) in the continuous space are converted to trajectories in the discrete cell state space. The discrete cells have rectangular shape and each point of the continuous space is represented with the center of the cell containing the point itself. Then, the dynamic $f(x, u)$ of the plant is transformed into a dynamic f_C in the discrete cell space. The image of a cell under f_C, can be determined as follows: for a given cell $z(k)$, first find the coordinates of its center $x(k)$. Under control action u, $x(k+1)$ is determined as the image of $x(k)$ by the plant dynamic, that is $x(k + 1) = f(x(k), u)$. If the cell corresponding to the point $x(k+1)$ is $z(k+1)$, then $z(k+1)$ is the image cell of the cell $z(k)$ and the control action u, that is we put $f_C(z(k), u) = z(k + 1)$.

Finally, we recall how model checking techniques can be applied for the synthesis of controllers. This kind of methodology allows to *automatically* synthesize *optimal* controllers starting from the plant description [3, 4]. The main idea is that, in order to build a controller for a plant P, a suitable discretization of the state space of P is considered, as well as of the control actions u.

The plant behavior, under the (discretized) control actions, gives rise to a transition graph $\mathcal{G}$, where the nodes are the reachable states and a transition between two nodes models an allowed control action between the corresponding states. In this setting, the problem of designing the optimal controller reduces to finding the minimum path in $\mathcal{G}$ between each state and the nearest *goal state* (a discretization of the setpoint). Clearly, a transition graph for complex, real-world systems could be often huge, due to the well-known *state explosion* problem. However, model checking techniques developed in the last decades have shown to be able to deal with very huge state spaces. In particular, in [3, 4] a model checking based methodology for the automatic synthesis of optimal controllers is presented, and it is also shown that the methodology can cope with very complex systems (e.g. the truck-trailer obstacles avoidance parking problem). Finally, the methodology presented in [3, 4] has been implemented in the CGMurphi tool [12] that, given a model of the plant, automatically generates a controller.

Note that, in the case study of this paper, we consider the numerical controller generated with the CGMurphi tool.

3   Fuzzy Control Systems

Fuzzy logic derives from the fuzzy set theory and is used to deal with approximate reasoning. In the fuzzy set theory, the set membership is expressed by a number usually ranging from 0 to 1, indicating different "membership degrees".

In other words, an element may have a partial membership in many different (and disjoint) fuzzy sets.

In the same way, in the fuzzy logic there are several degrees of truth and falsehood, and a fuzzy logic statement may be at the same time partially true and partially false. Indeed, there may be several conflicting fuzzy logic statements that are satisfied by the same conditions with a different "degree of truth".

As a typical application, fuzzy logic is used to deal with systems described by continuous variables (e.g., physical systems), where the density of the domain and the consequent approximation problems make it difficult to express the *certainty* required by the classical logic. Therefore, fuzzy logic is very suitable to be applied in the control theory, especially when dealing with *hybrid systems*, where the plant state is characterized by both continuous and discrete variables, and in general systems that are subject to control and actuation errors (e.g., mechanical systems) too complex to allow an analytical treatment [13].

Fuzzy control systems (FCS in the following) are based on qualitative fuzzy rules which have the form "**if** *condition* **then** *control action*", where both *condition* and *control action* are formulated making use of the so called "linguistic variables", which have a qualitative, non mathematical character [14].

In a FCS, the *crisp* input variables read from the plant state are mapped into the "linguistic variables" through the *fuzzification* process. The input variables' domains are divided in (possibly overlapping) subranges, and particular (fuzzy) membership functions are used to determine the degree of membership of each variable to all the subranges of the corresponding domain. Then, the controller makes its decision using the fuzzy rules on the fuzzified input values, and generates a set of fuzzy values for the output (control) variables, that are then converted back into crisp values and sent to the plant.

FCS are very effective in handling "uncertain" or "partially known" situations, and therefore may be used to build very robust controllers for such kind of complex systems. Moreover, FCS are well suited to low-cost implementations based on limited devices, since the fuzzy knowledge representation is usually very compact. Note that, in many cases, FCS can also be used to improve existing controller systems, for example by adding an extra layer of intelligence and robustness to the control algorithm.

The design of a FCS is usually accomplished by "translating" into fuzzy sets and inference rules the knowledge derived from human experts or mathematical models. Unfortunately, this process may be often difficult and error-prone. From this point of view, designing an effective controller at a reasonable cost is the real problem to deal with in the FCS field.

To this aim, different approaches have been studied to automatically generate a FCS by analyzing the plant specifications and/or behavior. As shown in [1], a FCS can be also generated from a numerical controller. These approaches are all based on some kind of automatic statistical analysis, which can be done using various techniques, including neural networks and genetic algorithms [15, 16, 17, 11]. In the present paper, we use genetic algorithms.

4   Genetic Algorithms

Genetic algorithms (GA) are used to find approximate solutions to optimization and search problems, using techniques inspired by evolutionary biology such as inheritance, mutation, selection, and crossover [9].

Generally speaking, in a GA a population of abstract representations of possible solutions (*individuals*) to a problem evolves to find better solutions. The information carried by each individual is called *genome*. The evolution develops through a sequence of steps (*generations*), usually starting from a population of randomly generated individuals. In each generation, the algorithm estimates the *fitness* of every individual in the population, which represents the quality of the problem solution encoded in its genome. If an individual fitness reaches the given threshold, the evolution ends and the corresponding solution is returned. Otherwise, some individuals are probabilistically selected from the current population, so that the higher is the their fitness, the higher is the probability of being selected. The genomes are recombined and possibly mutated to form the population of the next generation.

Therefore, a typical genetic algorithm requires a minimal startup information: a representation of the solution domain in terms of genomes and a fitness (quality) function of the solution domain

Note that no initialization data is usually required, and this makes GA very suitable for problems having no known approximate solutions.

GAs are often able to quickly locate good solutions, even in difficult search spaces. Moreover, such algorithms are very suitable to search irregular solution spaces, since they do not usually get trapped by *local optima*.

Therefore, GA may be a very effective good tool to automatically synthesize FCS. However, as with all machine learning processes, many parameters of a GA should be tuned to improve the overall efficiency. These parameters include the population size and the mutation/crossover probabilities. Moreover, a good implementation of the fitness function considerably affects the speed and efficiency of the algorithm. Due to the difficulty of tuning such parameters by hand, some systematic process of trial-and-error should be used, as mentioned in the Introduction. We plan to consider this aspect in a future work.

5   GA for Automatic Synthesis of the FCS

Many works in the literature use GA to generate part of a FCS. Usually, GA are applied to generate membership functions when inference rules are known [11]. However, when the system under control has several control variables and/or a complex dynamics, deciding the control setting to obtain a desired result may be difficult, even when working with the probabilistic approximation of fuzzy values. Therefore, an effective FCS generator should create both membership functions and inference rules.

The concrete implementation of the fitness function is determined by the kind of FCS that the GA should generate. Indeed, we may want to

1. create a FCS for the entire plant completely *from scratch*, or
2. create one or more FCS to assist a pre-existing plant controller in certain critical situations, or
3. create one or more FCS to encode the complete knowledge of a pre-existing controller.

The first task is very difficult to accomplish in a general setting, whereas the second and third are usually applied to add robustness to a given controller. The third kind of FCS has a further advantage: besides building a more robust controller, it may act as a *controller compressor*. Indeed, the knowledge encoding given by a FCS can greatly decrease the amount of memory needed to store the controller.

Moreover, in the first two cases above a plant simulator is needed to check the fitness of the generated FCS, whereas in the third case the fitness function can be simply derived from the the original controller.

Therefore, in the following we will discuss how GA can act on a numerical controller to transform it in a compact and robust FCS.

5.1   Implementation

To make the process almost automatic we have made some simplifications. In particular, we have supposed that the membership function is always triangular and it is coded by the position of its vertices. So, each fuzzy set is represented by 3 bytes as shown in Fig. 1.

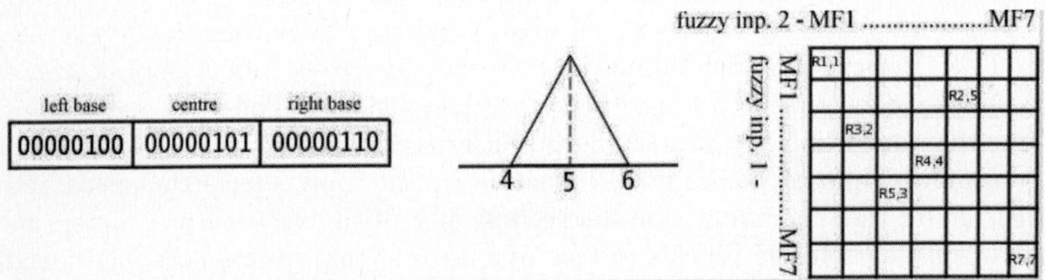

Fig. 1. Fuzzy sets and rules coding

As usual, a matrix codes the structure of the fuzzy rules [11] . An example is shown in Fig. 1.

The fuzzy sets and the fuzzy rules, encoded as described above, form the genome of any individual of the population, as shown in Fig. 2, where MF1... MF7 are the membership functions of a FCS.

Therefore, each individual of the population is a complete FCS. The individuals forming the first generation have a random initialization. Finally, the fitness function is defined as follows.

fuzzy inp. 1	fuzzy inp 2.	fuzzy out	rule base
MF1...MF7	MF1...MF7	MF1...MF7	R1,1 R7,7

Fig. 2. Genome of an individual of the population

First we partition the plant state space into smaller regions to make the learning process easier. In the following, by numerical controller we mean the numerical controller restricted to a given region R. Given a starting point p in R, we require the individuals to completely learn the trajectory of the numerical controller starting from p. To this aim, the fitness function is defined to be the distance between the trajectory generated by the individual and the trajectory stored in the numerical controller.

We repeat the GA for a sample set of points $p_1, ..., p_k \in R$, generating k FCSs, $F_1, ..., F_k$, where each F_i is able to drive the system from p_i to the setpoint. Then we analyze the capability of each F_i to perform well on the other points of R, and select the one who is able to drive all points of R to the setpoint in the most efficient way. If no one is able to cope with all points of the region, we can restart the process with other points. After a given number of negative outcomes, we conclude that the region R is too large to be compressed in the space given by the genome. Then, we may either split the region into smaller subregions or augment the number of fuzzy sets and fuzzy rules (so each individual can store more information), and restart the process.

```
void GAFuzzy(char * finput){
    ...
    GAAlleleSet<double> allele_x(inf_x-1, max_x);
    GAAlleleSet<double> allele_y(inf_y-1, max_y);
    GAAlleleSet<double> allele_o(inf_o-1, max_o);
    GAAlleleSet<double> allele_r(inf_r-1, max_r);
    GAAlleleSetArray<double> alleleArray;
    for (i=0; i< 3*n_x; i++) alleleArray.add(allele_x);
    for (i=0; i< 3*n_y; i++) alleleArray.add(allele_y);
    for (i=0; i< 3*n_o; i++) alleleArray.add(allele_o);
    for (i=0; i< n_r; i++) alleleArray.add(allele_r);
    GA1DArrayAlleleGenome<double> genome(alleleArray,objective);
    ...
}
```

Fig. 3. The genome representation in GAlib

To support the development of our GA technique, we used Galib, an efficient multiplatform open source library containing a set of C++ objects that implement several different kinds of genetic algorithms and genetic operations [18].

The GAlib library defines the main components of the genetic algorithm, but allows to freely choose the genome representation that best fits the problem to solve. In our case, the genome should contain the knowledge base of a fuzzy controller. In particular, we implemented our genome representation using the built-in Galib `GAAlleleSetArray` class. Each element of this array is a `GAAlleleSet` which represents the (range of) possible different values of a specific gene.

As an example, in the car parking fuzzy controller described in Section 6 we used four different kinds of `GAAlleleSet`: three to encode the membership functions (two input variables and one output variable), and one to encode the fuzzy rules. Each kind of `GAAlleleSet` define a specific range of values (see Fig. 3). The complete genome is a `GAAlleleSetArray` containing the genes required to encode the fuzzy sets of each variable ($3n_x + 3n_y + 3n_o$ genes, where n_x, n_y and n_o are the number of fuzzy sets for variables x, y and o, respectively) and the fuzzy rules (n_r genes). Each group of genes is created from the corresponding `GAAlleleSet`.

Finally, GAlib allows to define a fitness function and a terminator function. The latter is used to specify the terminating condition of the GA, which may be, e.g., a particular value of fitness.

6   A Case Study: The Car Parking Problem

To prove the effectiveness of our approach, in this section we show how it can be applied to the well-known car parking problem. After describing the problem setting, we consider the optimal control system generated with the CGMurphi tool, and finally we present experimental results related to the automatic synthesis of a fuzzy controller that compresses the optimal one.

6.1   Problem Definition

In the car parking problem, the goal is backing a car up to a parking place starting from any initial position in the parking lot [10, 7]. As shown in Fig. 4, we describe the car state with three real values:

- the abscissa and the ordinate of the car $x, y \in [0, 12]$, referred to the center of the rear wheels;
- the angle $\varphi \in [-90°, 270°]$ of the longitudinal axis of the car w.r.t. the horizontal axis of the coordinate system.

The objective is to move the car to a final position satisfying $x = 6, \varphi = 90°$. Note that, as in [7], we have no restrictions on the y coordinate, since we assume the initial position to be sufficiently far away from the parking place: if the final x position is reached, to move the car to the parking place it is sufficient to drive back without steering the wheels.

A controller for the car parking problem takes as input the car position and outputs a suitable steering wheels angle $\theta \in [-30°, 30°]$.

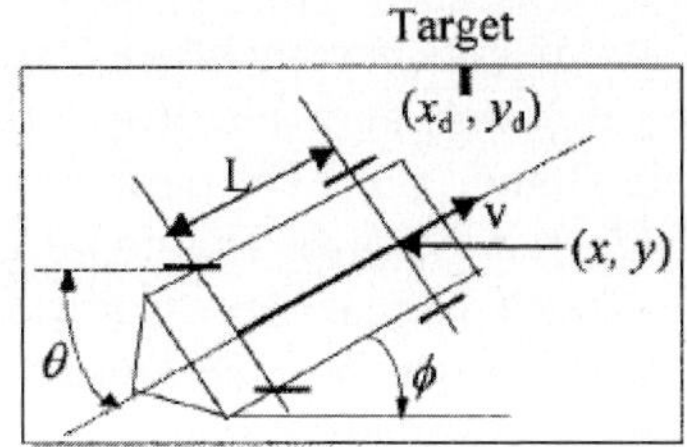

Fig. 4. The simulated car and parking lot

6.2 Experimental Setting and Results

To synthesize the FCS for the car-parking problem, we first partition the state space as follows:

- the abscissa and the ordinate of the car $x, y \in [0, 12]$, are partitioned into 4 regions: $[3i, 3(i+1)] \times [0, 12]$, $i = 0, \ldots, 3$;
- the angle φ of the longitudinal axis is partitioned into 8 adjacent regions of 45 degrees.

Therefore, the state space is partitioned into 32 regions. In each region R_i, we sample 10 points $p_1, \ldots, p_{10}$ and use the GA to synthesize a FCS for each point, using the following algorithm.

Given a starting point p_i, the task of any individual is to learn the set of control actions, stored in the numerical controller generated by the *CGMurphi* tool, which drives the car from p_i to the parking position. Recall that each individual codes a complete FCS. The fitness of a FCS is obtained by summing up the modula of the distances between the numerical controller actions and the corresponding fuzzy controller actions on the same trajectory. Therefore, the population evolution terminates when the fitness of some individual is zero (i.e., the FCS acts exactly as the numerical controller).

More formally, the evolution process has the following steps:

1. get from the controller table the trajectory from the stating point p_i to the goal; let this trajectory be composed of $k+1$ positions $p_{i1}, \ldots, p_{ik+1}$ and let $r_1, \ldots, r_k$ be the corresponding control actions;
2. WHILE (`fitness` > 0)
   (a) run the genetic algorithm to synthesize the fuzzy controller S;
   (b) determine the action r'_j of S in each position p_{ij};
   (c) calculate the fitness function: `fitness` $= \dfrac{\sum_{j=1}^{k}(||r_j - r'_j||)}{k}$;

The outcome of the previous process is, for each region R_i, a set of 10 FCS $F_{1,i}, \ldots, F_{10,i}$. Between these, we select the FCS that is able to drive the car to the parking position starting from *any* point in R_i.

To evaluate the performance of the FCS, we have considered all the trajectories starting from each state in the optimal controller table and we have compared the number of steps required to reach the setpoint.

Table 1 shows experimental results of comparison. Note that the FCS is able to cope with a larger number of states, and this proves the improvement in terms of robustness. On the other hand, the FCS performs worse than the optimal one with a degrade of 100%, but however this is an expected result since the CGMurphi-based controller has a tabular representation of *optimal* trajectories.

Moreover, Table 1 shows that with the FCS we obtain a compression of 90% in terms of memory occupation.

Table 1. Experimental comparison between fuzzy and optimal controller performance

Control System	Number of Controlled States	Average Number of Steps to Setpoint	Memory Occupation
FCS	46128	7.568	36608 bytes
CGMurphi	38256	3.614	382560 bytes

7 Conclusions

In this paper we have shown a genetic approach to the automatic generation of fuzzy control systems from preexisting numerical controllers.

Our methodology splits the problem state space in smaller ranges and iteratively uses a GA to synthesize a restricted FCS for each area. The fitness of a FCS is evaluated by comparing its behavior with the one of the numerical controller. The resulting controllers have an average size that is 1/10 of the corresponding numerical controllers, thus achieving a considerable compression ratio. Moreover, the FCS are inherently more robust than the numerical counterparts, so they actually encode a *larger* state space using a *smaller* memory size.

As a natural next step, we are studying how to merge the FCSs generated through our methodology in a single FCS that could be used to drive the system to the setpoint from any position of the state space. We feel that this merge could result in a further compression, since there may be knowledge redundancy between the single FCSs. Moreover, we are interested in finding algorithms for dynamically tuning the GA parameters (e.g., crossover and mutation ratio) in order to speed up the algorithm convergence.

References

1. Leu, M.C., Kim, T.Q.: Cell mapping based fuzzy control of car parking. In: ICRA, pp. 2494–2499 (1998)
2. Kreisselmeier, G., Birkholzer, T.: Numerical nonlinear regulator design. IEEE Transactions on Automatic Control 39(1), 33–46 (1994)
3. Della Penna, G., Intrigila, B., Magazzeni, D., Melatti, I., Tofani, A., Tronci, E.: Automatic generation of optimal controllers through model checking techniques (To be published in Informatics in Control, Automation and Robotics III, Springer-Verlag, Heidelberg) draft available at the `http://www.di.univaq.it/magazzeni/cgmurphi.php`

[4] Della Penna, G., Intrigila, B., Magazzeni, D., Melatti, I., Tofani, A., Tronci, E.: Automatic synthesis of robust numerical controllers (To appear in IEEE Proceedings of the Third International Conference on Autonomic and Autonomous Systems) (ICAS 2007), draft available at the `http://www.di.univaq.it/magazzeni/tr.php`

[5] Papa, M., Wood, J., Shenoi, S.: Evaluating controller robustness using cell mapping. Fuzzy Sets and Systems 121(1), 3–12 (2001)

[6] Kautz, H., Thomas, W., Vardi, M.Y.: 05241 executive summary – synthesis and planning. In: Kautz, H., Thomas, W., Vardi, M.Y. (eds.) Synthesis and Planning. Number 05241 in Dagstuhl Seminar Proceedings (2006)

[7] Kosko, B.: Neural Networks and Fuzzy Systems. Prentice-Hall, Englewood Cliffs (1992)

[8] Sekine, S., Imasaki, N., Tsunekazu, E.: Application of fuzzy neural network control to automatic train operation and tuning of its control rules. In: Proc. IEEE Int. Conf. on Fuzzy Systems 1993, pp. 1741–1746. IEEE Computer Society Press, Los Alamitos (1995)

[9] Mitchell, M.: An Introduction to Genetic Algorithms. MIT Press, Cambridge (1998)

[10] Intrigila, B., Magazzeni, D., Melatti, I., Tofani, A., Tronci, E.: A model checking technique for the verification of fuzzy control systems. In: CIMCA05. Proceedings of International Conference on Computational Intelligence for Modelling Control and Automation (2005)

[11] Tan, G.V., Hu, X.: More on design fuzzy controllers using genetic algorithms: Guided constrained optimization. In: Proc. IEEE Int. Conf. on Fuzzy Systems, pp. 497–502. IEEE Computer Society Press, Los Alamitos (1997)

[12] CGMurphi Web Page: `http://www.di.univaq.it/magazzeni/cgmurphi.php`

[13] Li, H., Gupta, M.: Fuzzy Logic and Intelligent Systems. Kluwer Academic Publishers, Boston, MA (1995)

[14] Jin, J.: Advanced Fuzzy Systems Design and Applications. Physica-Verlag (2003)

[15] Nelles, O., Fischer, M., Muller, B.: Fuzzy rule extraction by a genetic algorithm and constrained nonlinear optimization of membership functions. In: Proceedings of the Fifth IEEE International Conference on Fuzzy Systems, FUZZ–IEEE '96, vol. 1, pp. 213–219. IEEE Computer Society Press, Los Alamitos (1996)

[16] Jian Wang, L.S., Chao, J.F.: An efficient method of fuzzy rules generation. In: Intelligent Processing Systems. ICIPS '97, vol. 1, pp. 295–299 (1997)

[17] Homaifar, A., McCormick, E.: Simultaneous design of membership functions and rule sets for fuzzy controllers using genetic algorithms. In: IEEE Transactions Fuzzy Systems, vol. 3, pp. 129–139. IEEE Computer Society Press, Los Alamitos (1995)

[18] GAlib Web Page: `http://lancet.mit.edu/ga`

Trip Around the HMPerceptron Algorithm:
Empirical Findings and Theoretical Tenets

Roberto Esposito and Daniele P. Radicioni

Dipartimento di Informatica, Università di Torino
Corso Svizzera 185, 10149 - Torino
{esposito,radicion}@di.unito.it

Abstract. In a recent work we have carried out `CarpeDiem`, a novel algorithm for the fast evaluation of Supervised Sequential Learning (SSL) classifiers. In this paper we point out some interesting unexpected aspects of the learning behavior of the HMPerceptron algorithm that affect `CarpeDiem` performances. This observation is the starting point of an investigation about the internal working of the HMPerceptron, which unveils crucial details of the internal working of the HMPerceptron learning strategy. The understanding of these details, augment the comprehension of the algorithm meanwhile suggesting further enhancements.

1 Introduction: The SSL Task

In the supervised learning framework examples are assumed to be drawn independently and identically from some joint distribution $P(x, y)$. While this assumption is fulfilled in many application fields, there are many others where the classified data has a sequential structure (i.e., nearby x elements are likely to have correlated classifications) that must be exploited in order to obtain accurate classifiers. To analyse web logs, to recognize speech or handwriting, to understand music are all tasks where this correlation exists and is essential to the classification purposes.

Within the broader field of learning systems for sequential data, let us consider the *Supervised Sequential Learning* (SSL) task: in this particular problem, each observation in the sequence is associated with an individual label. The goal of SSL systems is to learn how to best predict the sequence of labels, given the sequence of observations. More formally, the SSL task can be specified as follows [1]:

Given: A set L of training examples of the form (X_m, Y_m), where each $X_m = (x_{m,1}, \ldots, x_{m,T_m})$ is a sequence of T_m feature vectors and each $Y_m = (y_{m,1}, \ldots, y_{m,T_m})$ is a corresponding sequence of class labels, $y \in \{1, ..., K\}$.

Find: A classifier H that, given a new sequence X of feature vectors, predicts the corresponding sequence of class labels $Y = H(X)$ accurately.

The SSL problem has been approached with many different techniques. Among others, we recall Sliding Windows [1], Hidden Markov Models [2], Maximum Entropy Markov Models [3], Conditional Random Fields [4], and the HMPerceptron algorithm [5].

R. Basili and M.T. Pazienza (Eds.): AI*IA 2007, LNAI 4733, pp. 242–253, 2007.

The HMPerceptron has been defined within the boolean features framework [3]. In this setting, the learnt classifier is built in terms of a linear combination of boolean features. Each feature reports about a salient aspect of the sequence to be labelled in a given time instant. More formally, given a time point t, a boolean feature is a 1/0-valued function of the whole sequence of feature vectors X, and of a restricted neighborhood of y_t. The function is meant to return 1 if the characteristics of the sequence X around time step t support the classifications given at and around y_t.

In general, the labeling of an entire sequence X may show dependences among labels which extend on the whole labeling. In this case, the labeling task must take into account every possible sequence of labels, thus resulting in a $\Theta(K^T)$ complexity. However in practice it is possible to evaluate H in polinomial time by making some simplifying assumption. In particular, assuming a *first order Markov property* allows evaluating H in quadratic time by means of the Viterbi algorithm [6]. The Viterbi algorithm is thereby crucial to many SSL systems, in that most state-of-the-art methods for dealing with the SSL task rely on the Viterbi algorithm for classifying and/or learning purposes.

Unfortunately even the drastic reduction in complexity achieved by Viterbi's algorithm is not always sufficient in many important application domains. In particular, when the number of possible labels is large (more than few tens) as in some web-logs related tasks [7] or in analyzing music [8], the classification times can grow prohibitively high. In order to allow sub-quadratic evaluation of sequential classifiers, we have recently proposed the `CarpeDiem` [9] algorithm, which returns the same results as Viterbi, meanwhile allowing for significant time savings.

In the present paper we provide an experimental assessment of its functioning and of its peculiarities. We start by expanding on the time saving that can be obtained when `CarpeDiem` is used instead of Viterbi in the HMPerceptron learning algorithm. We then recall the functioning of `CarpeDiem`, and introduce further experiments. The new experimentation shows that –to a good extent, unexpectedly– by increasing the size of the training set, and/or the number of learning iterations, we badly affect the classification time. The rest of the paper is devoted to investigate this phenomenon and to draw consequences about the way learning works.

2   Review of Past Results

The main idea underlying `CarpeDiem` stems from noting that in many application domains classifying an item at time t not always requires knowledge about both previous and current labels, y_{t-1}, y_t. On the contrary, very often the characteristics of the item are, by themselves, very relevant for predicting y_t. Then, we identify two kind of features: the *vertical* features that do not require to know the previously predicted label –and work, thus, under a zero-order Markov assumption–, and the *horizontal* features that do need it –thereby working under a first-order Markov assumption. For instance, in speech recognition the features that report about the current phoneme are what we refer to as *vertical* features.

By contrast, we call *horizontal* features those ones taking into consideration the previously predicted phoneme. For instance, one may want to discourage the prediction of phoneme /r/ after phoneme /s/. In such application vertical features provide much information about the classification: based on vertical features inspection, it may happen that phoneme /d/ is confused with /t/, but rarely this happens with /tʃ/. In other words, one would expect that after inspecting vertical information, the uncertainty about the correct label sensibly decreases until only few of the initial guesses are left as probable.

`CarpeDiem` works by exploiting vertical information to avoid evaluating the more costly horizontal features. In the best case, it scans only the most promising node for each layer (instead of all the nodes, like Viterbi). In such a case, the cost of the algorithm would be $\Theta(K \log(K)T)$, where the factor $K \log(K)$ is due to the time spent for sorting the nodes in each layer[1]. In the worst case (no vertical features), the algorithm has a complexity of K^2T, that is, the algorithm is never asymptotically worse than Viterbi algorithm[9].

In the following and throughout the paper, we will report and elaborate about experimental performances obtained on tonal harmony analysis. The task is briefly introduced in the following.

2.1   Test Domain: Harmony Analysis

Harmony analysis is arguably one of the most sophisticated tasks that musicians deal with, and a formidable challenge for Sequential Learning, in that: *i*) it can be naturally cast to a sequential problem; *ii*) an intuitively neat separation between horizontal (that refers to the musical flow) and vertical (that pertains simultaneous sounds) features exists; *iii*) K (the number of labels) is over one hundred, thereby pointing out a typical case where the Viterbi algorithm shows bad time performance.

Analyzing music harmony consists in associating a label to each *vertical* (that is, set of simultaneous notes) [11]. Such labels explain which harmony is sounding, by indicating a chord name through a fundamental note (*root*) and a *mode*, such as C minor. Given a score in MIDI format, we individuate sets of simultaneous notes (*verticals* or *events*), and associate to each vertical a *label* composed by ⟨fundamental note, mode⟩ (Fig. 1).

Music analysis task can be naturally represented as a Machine Learning classification problem, suitable to be solved by SSL techniques. In fact, by considering only the "vertical" aspects of musical structure, one would hardly produce reasonable analyses. Experimental evidences about human cognition reveal that in order to disambiguate unclear cases, composers and listeners refer to "horizontal" features of music as well: in these cases, context plays a fundamental role, and contextual cues can be useful to the analysis system. Moreover, harmony changes are well known to follow patterns where analysis must take into consideration the succession of chords (e.g., the case of *cadence*).

---

[1] In cases where the vertical rewards range over a limited interval, one could reduce the $K \log(K)$ factor to K by using standard techniques [10, Chap. 9]. However, in the present application, this amounts to trade space for speed.

Fig. 1. The tonal harmony analysis problem consists of indicating for each vertical which chord is currently sounding

Let us go back to the SSL definition: in the case of music analysis, each X_m corresponds to a particular piece of music; $x_{m,t}$ is the information associated to the event at time t; and $y_{m,t}$ corresponds to the chord label (i.e., the chord root and mode) associated to the event sounding at time t. The problem is, thus, to learn how to predict accurately the chord labels given the information about musical events.

By definition, a feature $\phi_s(X, y_t, y_{t-1})$ is a boolean function of the entire sequence and of labels y_t and y_{t-1}. Usually, it analyzes a small neighborhood of the current event, and returns 1 if there is evidence that the currently predicted label is correct. For the present application, the features have been engineered so that they take into account the prescriptions from Music Harmony Theory, a field where vertical and horizontal features naturally arise. *Vertical* features report about simultaneous sounds and their correlation with the currently predicted chord. *Horizontal* features capture metric patterns and chordal successions.

2.2 CarpeDiem's Performance Compared with Viterbi

We briefly recall some results of previous experimentation showing that we obtain significant running time improvements w.r.t. Viterbi. CarpeDiem has been embedded in a SSL system implementing the HMPerceptron learning algorithm [5]. The learning system has been trained iterating ten times on a data set composed of 30 chorales by J.S. Bach (1675-1750). The learnt weights have been then used to build two classifiers: one based on standard Viterbi, the other one based on CarpeDiem. The two classifiers have been fed with 42 testing sequences (chorales from the same author), their running time has been recorded and is reported in Figure 2 and in the following.

Needless to say, being equal their results, both algorithms provided the same accuracy results (on average, 79% accuracy rate). The Viterbi based HMPerceptron took 62,333 seconds of CPU time in order to complete the learning step. Performing the *learning task* with the CarpeDiem-based HMPerceptron took only 10,866 seconds, with a net saving of 82.56%. Figure 2 reports the time spent by both algorithms to analyze each sequence of the test set. On average, 79% of the *testing time* has been saved. In the best case CarpeDiem ran in 7 seconds instead of 77, thus saving 90% of the time. In the worst case it ran in 37 seconds instead of 118, thus saving 68.64% of the time. Also, the magnitude of the improvement

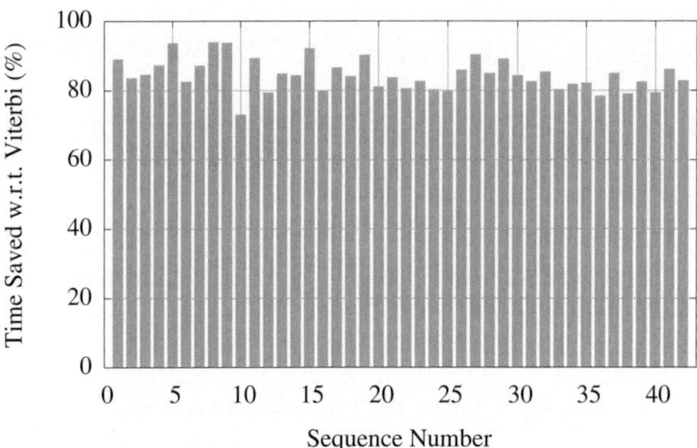

Fig. 2. Percentages of time saved by `CarpeDiem` w.r.t. Viterbi in analyzing the test set

does not show large variations depending on the sequences, thus encouraging the generalization of these results to new musical pieces.

`CarpeDiem` clearly improves on the Viterbi algorithm on all tested sequences. However, an interesting facet of the algorithm behavior is hidden in the reported graphs: the time spent in classifying varies according to the number of sequences and the number of iterations performed.

We therefore study how the performance of the algorithm varies as important learning parameters (the training set size and the number of iterations) change. As we will see, the `CarpeDiem` algorithm spends more time evaluating classifiers acquired on larger datasets or by allowing more iterations of the HMPerceptron.

3   The Growth of Classification Time

In order to corroborate our preliminary observations, we set up a systematic experimentation where we recorded the running time of `CarpeDiem`. Here, the classifiers were acquired on data sets of increasing size and using an increasing number of learning iterations. More specifically, we recorded the learning and classification times of a learning system based on `CarpeDiem` on *nine training sets* of size increasing from one to nine sequences. On each training set, we acquired ten classifiers by varying (from one to ten) the *number of iterations* of the HMPerceptron algorithm. We thereby obtain 90 classifiers. In each experiment, we recorded both the time needed for training the classifier and the time spent in classifying the independent test set, composed by the 42 sequences earlier mentioned (see Section 2.2).

In the following we will indicate each one of the 90 classifiers by using two digits separated by a colon: the first digit corresponds to the number of sequences in the training set, the second one indicates the number of iterations. For instance, the classifier 8:7 is trained on 8 sequences with 7 learning iterations, while the classifier 5:10 corresponds to the classifier acquired on 5 sequences with 10 iterations.

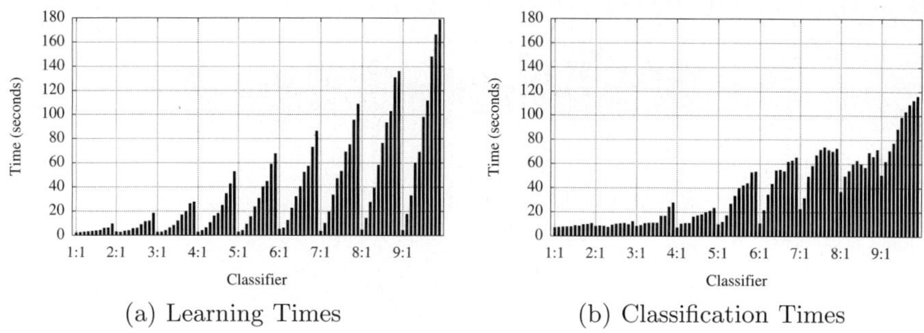

(a) Learning Times   (b) Classification Times

Fig. 3. Timings versus increasing training set size and increasing number of iterations

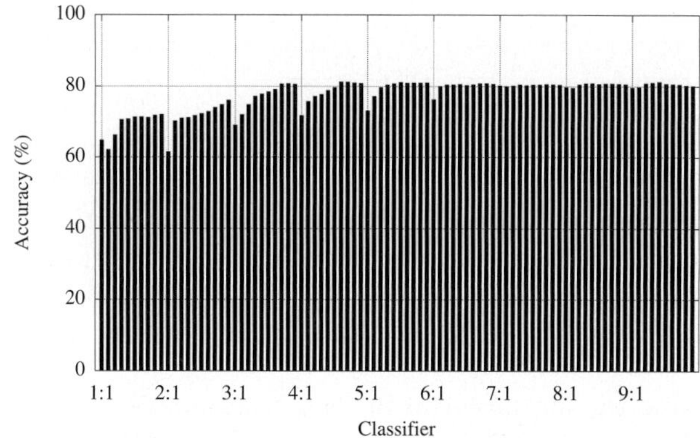

Fig. 4. Accuracies of the classification versus increasing training set size and increasing number of iterations

Figure 3 reports training and test times[2].

Let us consider the behavior of learning time first. The Figure 3(a) shows a largely anticipated pattern: classifiers $m{:}n$ take increasing time as m and n grow. Much more interesting is, on the contrary, the shape of the classification time. Since classification is performed on a dataset of fixed size (the dataset is the same for all classifiers), one would expect a roughly constant classification time. On the contrary, the observed pattern looks similar to the one observed for learning times. This not only comes as a surprise, but casts in a new light the interpretation of the former graph: likely, the increase in learning times should not have been as steep as the one observed. We remark that the reported growth of testing times are to be imputed to the weights used by the classifiers. Then, as the HMPerceptron learns, it somehow fiddles with the weights in a way that proves to be detrimental to the work of `CarpeDiem`. Moreover, if we take a look at Figure 4, we see that all this tinkering does not provide any significant benefit as regards as the classification accuracy.

---

[2] On a machine equipped with 2.16GHz Intel Core 2 Duo processor.

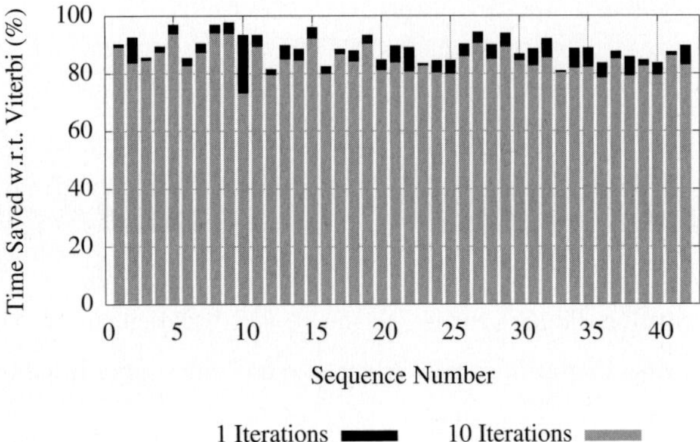

Fig. 5. Percentages of times saved over Viterbi by `CarpeDiem` (1 iteration) and `CarpeDiem` (10 iterations) in analyzing the test set

We implemented the above observation by re-running the above experiment and stopping the execution after the first iteration. Not only the results reveal a further improvement in the percentage of time saved by `CarpeDiem` (from 79% to 88%; see Figure 5), but also the generalization accuracy increases from 79% to 81.5%. Thus, it is preferable to stop the learning process much sooner than we did in [9].

Notwithstanding the improvement in the performances of the algorithm, we are still cue-less about why the internal working of the HMPerceptron impacts so crucially on the execution of `CarpeDiem`.

`CarpeDiem` is very efficient when two conditions are met: i) vertical features are sufficient to discriminate among labels (i.e., few distinguished labels have very high rewards), and/or ii) horizontal features do not provide significant cues (i.e., most transition weights are close to the sum of positive horizontal weights). Then, two parameters that are relevant to the performances of `CarpeDiem` are the sum of vertical weights, and the sum of positive horizontal weights. Figure 6 illustrates their evolution as more sequences/iterations are added.

One interesting facet of the reported graph is the distinguished pattern followed by horizontal and vertical weights. This is somehow surprising, since the weights are learnt by the HMPerceptron which is totally unaware of the distinction between horizontal and vertical weights. In a subtle though evident way, the HMPerceptron grasps the difference. In order to work out this unexpected behavior, we briefly recall few details about the learning strategy implemented by the HMPerceptron.

3.1   HMPerceptron Learning Strategy

The hypothesis acquired by the HMPerceptron has the form:

$$H(X) = \arg \max_{Y'=\{y'_1,\ldots,y'_T\}} \sum_t \sum_s w_s \phi_s(X, y_t, y'_{t-1}) \tag{1}$$

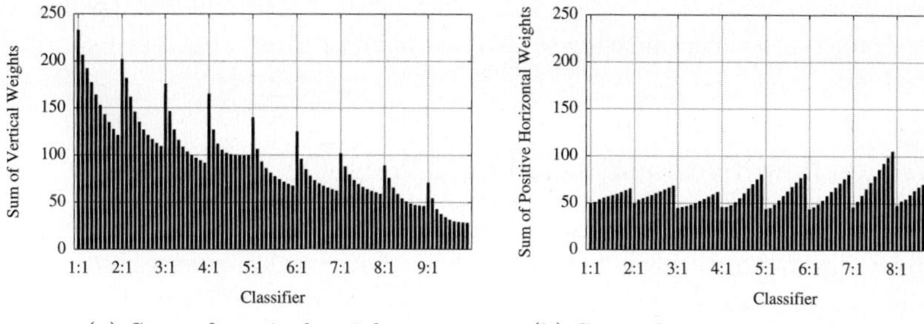

(a) Sum of vertical weights   (b) Sum of positive horizontal weights

Fig. 6. Evolution of learned weights for increasing number of sequences and number of iterations

where ϕ_s is a boolean feature and $\{w_s\} \overset{\text{def}}{=} W$ are the weights being estimated. The HMPerceptron applies a simple scheme to optimize w_s values: it iterates over the training set updating the weights so that features correlated to "correct" outputs receive larger values, and those correlated with "incorrect" ones receive smaller values.

This is the same kind of strategy adopted by Rosenblat's perceptron algorithm [12], the only real difference between the two algorithms is in the way the hypothesis is evaluated. In the classification problem faced by the perceptron algorithm, in fact, it is sufficient to enumerate all the possible labels and to pick the best one. In the case of the SSL problem, however, this cannot be done efficiently: the labelling of a single "example" is a sequence of T labels, the number of such labellings is thus exponential in T. To overcome this problem, the algorithm uses Viterbi decoding to pick the best labelling under a first order Markov assumption.

At the beginning W is initialized to the zero vector; then, for each example (X_m, Y_m) in the training set, $H(X)$ is evaluated using the current W. Two situations may occur: the sequence of labels predicted by H is identical to Y_m or this is not the case, and a number of errors are committed. In the first case, nothing is done for that example, and the algorithm simply jumps to the following one. In the second case, the weight vector is updated by means of the following update rule

$$w_s = w_s + \sum_{t=1}^{T} \phi_s(X, y'_t, y'_{t-1})(I_{y'_t=y_t} - I_{y'_t \neq y_t})$$

where ϕ_s represents a feature, y_t represent the t-th "correct label", y'_t denotes currently predicted t-th label, and I_P represents the function that returns 1 in case P is verified and 0 otherwise. By noticing that (we omit the arguments of ϕ_s for brevity):

$$\phi_s \cdot (I_{y'_t=y_t} - I_{y'_t \neq y_t}) = \begin{cases} +1 & \text{if } \phi_s = 1 \wedge y'_t = y_t \\ -1 & \text{if } \phi_s = 1 \wedge y'_t \neq y_t \\ 0 & \text{if } \phi_s = 0 \end{cases}$$

it is immediate to verify that the rule emphasizes features ϕ_s which are positively correlated with good classification and de-emphasize those that are negatively correlated with it.

3.2 Trends in Vertical and Horizontal Weights

We now come back to the problem of interpreting Figure 6. In building the `CarpeDiem` algorithm we have been guided by the intuition that vertical information is indeed very discriminative. Let us focus on an informative vertical feature $\phi_\bullet$ and consider the first iteration of the HMPerceptron on a sequence having length T. Just to give a bit of concreteness to our example, we assume $T = 100$, that $\phi_\bullet$ is asserted 60 times, and that it votes for the correct label 50 times out of 60. This example may seem very unrealistic, but it is not[3]. Since at the first iteration on the first sequence all labels are chosen at random, the vast majority of them will be incorrectly predicted, thus implying a large number of updates. If all the labels for which $\phi_\bullet$ is asserted are actually mislabelled, due to the way the update rule acts, the weight associated to $\phi_\bullet$ will be increased by 40 in this step. This large increase occurs all at once at the end of the first iteration on the first sequence, it is likely to overestimate the "true" weight of $\phi_\bullet$, and the HMPerceptron will spend the rest of learning trying to compensate for this overestimation. However, subsequent updates will be of smaller magnitude. In fact, the following predicted labeling will not be randomly guessed, thus implying a reduced number of updates. By summarizing, very predictive features have their weights initially set to very large values; such weights slowly decrease in the following. The behavior described clearly emerges in Figure 7, where the individual weights of vertical features are plotted as the updates occur. Some of the features have moderately highly negative weights. Since higher vertical weights are expected to improve the performances of `CarpeDiem`, one wonders if there is any means of increasing that weights without hindering the classification accuracy. To these ends, by building on the *boolean* nature of the features we propose a technique that we call the "inversion trick".

The assertion of a positive boolean feature can be naturally interpreted as a way to indicate which candidate labels are good. By converse, if we invert the weight of the feature and we swap its answers, the resulting feature indicates bad candidates instead of good ones. The meaning and the contribution of the feature do not change, what changes is only the way they interact with the system. Unfortunately, the inversion trick does not work with vertical features. Let us introduce the following bits of notation, and consider the inequality tested by `CarpeDiem` when cutting the search [9]. We denote with $\omega_{y'_{t-1}}$ the best path found until label y' at time $t - 1$; with $\Sigma^1_{\bar{y}_t, y'_{t-1}}$ the sum of horizontal weights of features that vote in favour of the transition between $\bar{y}_t$ (our best candidate so far) and y'_{t-1} the best previous label; $\Sigma^0_{\bar{y}_t}$ the sum of vertical features that vote

---

[3] Some of the high level features we plugged in our Musical Analysis system work in a similar setting (for instance, this could be the case for the feature that votes for the chord that has exactly 3 notes asserted in the current event).

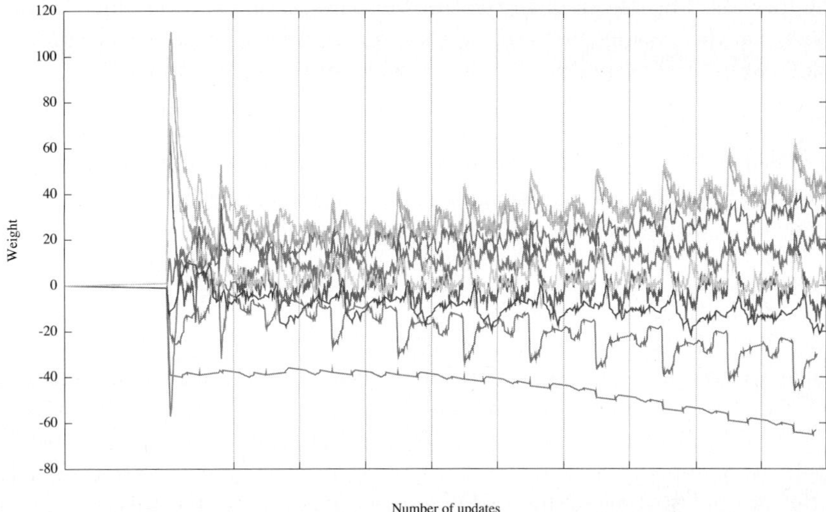

Fig. 7. Evolution of vertical weights throughout learning. Each line corresponds to an individual vertical feature; vertical lines correspond to the beginning of new iterations.

for $\bar{y}_t$; with ω^*_{t-1} the best of all paths to time $t-1$; and with Σ^{1*} the sum of positive horizontal features. The inequality tested by `CarpeDiem` in order to cut the search is:

$$\omega_{y'_{t-1}} + \Sigma^1_{\bar{y}_t, y'_{t-1}} + \Sigma^0_{\bar{y}_t} > \omega^*_{t-1} + \Sigma^{1*} + \Sigma^0_{y''_t}.$$

Since vertical weights appear on both ends of the inequality, the improvement on one side (i.e., on $\Sigma^0_{\bar{y}_t}$) is likely to be counterbalanced by an improvement on the other side (i.e., on $\Sigma^0_{y''_t}$). Interestingly enough, however, this does not hold for horizontal features. If we succeed in decreasing the weight of the vertical features it may happen that the decrease in Σ^{1*} is not counteracted by a decrease in $\Sigma^1_{\bar{y}_t, y'_{t-1}}$ [4]. Guided by this intuition we tried a preliminar experiment in which we tinkered with the horizontal weights so that all positive horizontal weights were inverted, thus obtaining $\Sigma^{1*} = 0$. With our great surprise, a large decrease in `CarpeDiem` time performance was observed.

We are still unaware about why this happens, but the system seems to behave in a chaotic way: little changes with the inversion trick produce large variations in the running times. However, solid evidence advocates for the possibility of overcoming the mentioned issues by means of the inversion trick. First and foremost, the results we obtained so far show that the inversion trick on horizontal features indeed produces relevant changes in the running time of the algorithm without changing the learnt hypothesis. Secondly, we are currently using 30 different features in our system, resulting in about 1 billion of possible inversions

---

[4] This can actually happen, but the effect is likely to be less systematic since on one hand we have the single horizontal weight $\Sigma^1_{\bar{y}_t, y'_{t-1}}$, on the other hand there is the sum of *all* positive horizontal weights.

configurations. The design of the features in our system has been done by focusing more on their cognitive meaning than on whether they were appropriate to the ends of improving performances by means of the inversion trick.

Basing on purely statistical accounts, one would then expect that a configuration of inversions exists that further enhances the performances of our algorithm. To efficiently find the correct inversions involves solving a new optimization problem in the space of inversions. Heuristics and algorithms for searching in this space are problems that we leave open for future work.

4   Conclusion

In this paper we have discussed previous relevant results, raising interesting issues about the performances of a recently proposed algorithm which improves on the Viterbi algorithm. By starting from an unexpected correlation between CarpeDiem running times and the overall amount of learning allowed, we delved into the internal working of the HMPerceptron. We showed that this phenomenon is connected with the evolution of vertical and horizontal weights as learning proceeds. In particular, vertical weights seem to be doomed to decrease while horizontal weights slightly grow. We have then approached the evolution of the vertical weights. We confirmed our hypothesis about their relevance to sequential learning. To enhance the time performances of the HMPerceptron, we have considered adjusting both vertical and horizontal weights, by means of what we called inversion trick. This is influential to the run-time performances of CarpeDiem and does not affect the accuracy of the HMPerceptron. The trick is arguably relevant to improve even more CarpeDiem performances. However, it also emerged that finding the optimal configuration for (the inversions of) the features leads to a novel, difficult, optimization problem.

References

1. Dietterich, T.: Machine Learning for Sequential Data: A Review. In: Caelli, T.M., Amin, A., Duin, R.P.W., Kamel, M.S., de Ridder, D. (eds.) SPR 2002 and SSPR 2002. LNCS, vol. 2396, pp. 15–30. Springer, Heidelberg (2002)
2. Rabiner, L.R.: A tutorial on Hidden Markov Models and Selected Applications in Speech Recognition. In: Proceedings of the IEEE, vol. 77, pp. 267–296. Morgan Kaufmann Publishers Inc, San Francisco, CA, USA (1989)
3. McCallum, A., Freitag, D., Pereira, F.: Maximum entropy Markov models for information extraction and segmentation. In: Proc. 17th International Conf. on Machine Learning, pp. 591–598. Morgan Kaufmann, San Francisco, CA (2000)
4. Lafferty, J., Pereira, F.: Conditional random fields: Probabilistic models for segmenting and labeling sequence data. In: Proceedings of the Eighteenth International Conference on Machine Learning, pp. 282–289. Morgan Kaufmann, San Francisco, CA (2001)
5. Collins, M.: Discriminative training methods for hidden markov models: Theory and experiments with perceptron algorithms. In: Proceedings of the Conference on Empirical Methods in Natural Language Processing (2002)

6. Viterbi, A.J.: Error Bounds for Convolutional Codes and an Asymptotically Optimum Decoding Algorithm. In: IEEE Transactions on Information Theory, vol. 13, pp. 260–269. IEEE Computer Society Press, Los Alamitos (1967)
7. Felzenszwalb, P.F., Huttenlocher, D.P., Kleinberg, J.M.: Fast Algorithms for Large-State-Space HMMs with Applications to Web Usage Analysis. In: Advances in Neural Information Processing System (2003)
8. Radicioni, D.P., Esposito, R.: Tonal Harmony Analysis: a Supervised Sequential Learning Approach. In: Pazienza, M.T., Basili, R. (eds.) AI*IA 2007. Advances in Artificial Intelligence, 10th Congress of the Italian Association for Artificial Intelligence, Springer, Heidelberg (2007)
9. Esposito, R., Radicioni, D.P.: CarpeDiem: an Algorithm for the Fast Evaluation of SSL Classifiers. In: ICML 2007. Proceedings of the 24th Annual International Conference on Machine Learning (2007)
10. Cormen, T.H., Leiserson, C.E., Rivest, R.L.: Introduction to Algorithms. MIT Press, Cambridge, MASS (1990)
11. Pardo, B., Birmingham, W.P.: Algorithms for chordal analysis. Computer Music Journal 26, 27–49 (2002)
12. Rosenblatt, F.: The perceptron: A probabilistic model for information storage and organization in the brain (Reprinted in Neurocomputing (MIT Press, 1998)). Psychological Review 65, 386–408 (1958)

Instance-Based Query Answering with Semantic Knowledge Bases

Nicola Fanizzi, Claudia d'Amato, and Floriana Esposito

Dipartimento di Informatica, Università degli Studi di Bari
Campus Universitario, Via Orabona 4, 70125 Bari, Italy
{fanizzi,claudia.damato,esposito}@di.uniba.it

Abstract. A procedure founded in *instance-based learning* is presented, for performing a form of analogical reasoning on knowledge bases expressed in a wide range of ontology languages. The procedure exploits a novel semi-distance measure for individuals, that is based on their semantics w.r.t. a number of dimensions corresponding to a committee of features represented by concept descriptions. The procedure can answer by analogy to class'membership queries on the grounds of the classification of a number of training instances (the nearest ones w.r.t. the semi-distance measure). Particularly, it may also predict assertions that are not logically entailed by the knowledge base. In the experimentation, where we compare the procedure to a logical reasoner, we show that it can be quite accurate and augment the scope of its applicability, outperforming previous prototypes that adopted other semantic measures.

1   Introduction

In the perspective of knowledge sharing and reuse of the *social* vision of the Semantic Web, new services are required aiming at noise-tolerant and efficient forms of reasoning. From this perspective, instance-based inductive methods applied to multi-relational domains appear particularly well suited. Indeed, they are known to be both very efficient and noise-tolerant and noise is always harmful in contexts where knowledge is to be acquired from distributed sources.

A relational instance-based framework for the Semantic Web context has been devised (based on a similarity measure) to derive (by analogy) both consistent consequences from the knowledge base and, possibly, also new assertions which were not previously logically derivable. The main idea is that similar individuals, by analogy, should likely belong to similar concepts. Specifically, we derive a classification procedure that constitutes a relational form of the *Nearest Neighbor* algorithm (*NN*, henceforth) [5], a well-known approach to *lazy learning*.

These algorithms are efficient because no explicit hypothesis has to be learned. Rather, the workload is shifted towards the classification phase when knowledge concerning the training instances is used to classify new ones. Particularly, this only requires checking the assertions for a limited set of instances training on such concepts and making a decision (classification) for new query instances.

From a technical viewpoint, upgrading NN algorithms to work on multi-relational representations [5], like the concept languages used in the Semantic

R. Basili and M.T. Pazienza (Eds.): AI*IA 2007, LNAI 4733, pp. 254–265, 2007.

Web [4], required novel similarity measures that are suitable for such representations. This adaptation could not be straightforward. In particular, a theoretical problem has been posed by the *Open World Assumption* (OWA) that is generally made in the target context, differently from typical the machine learning settings where the *Closed World Assumption* (CWA) is the standard. Besides, in the standard NN multi-class setting, different concept are assumed to be disjoint, which typically cannot hold in a Semantic Web context. As pointed out in [2], most of the existing measures focus on the similarity of atomic concepts within hierarchies or simple ontologies. Moreover they have been conceived for assessing *concept* similarity. On the other hand, for our purposes, a notion of similarity between *individuals* is required.

Recently, dissimilarity measures for specific description logics concept descriptions have been proposed [3]. Although they turned out to be quite effective for the inductive tasks of interest [4], they were still partly based on structural criteria (a notion of normal form) which determine their main weakness: they are hardly scalable to deal with standard languages, such as OWL-DL, commonly used for knowledge bases.

In this paper we introduce a new semantic dissimilarity measure which can overcome these limitations. Following some ideas introduced in [6], we present a new family of measures that is suitable a wide range of ontology languages (RDF through OWL) since it is merely based on the discernibility of the input individuals with respect to a fixed set of features represented by concept definitions (hypotheses). As such the new measures are not absolute, yet they depend on the knowledge base they are applied to.

The measure and the NN procedure have been integrated in a system that allowed for an extended experimentation the method on performing instance retrieval with real ontologies drawn from public repositories comparing its predictions to the assertions that were logically derived by a standard reasoner. These experiments show that the novel measure considerably increases the effectiveness of the method with respect to the past experiments where the same procedure was integrated with other structural/semantic dissimilarity measures [4]. Moreover, as expected, an increase of accuracy was observed with the increase of the dimensions employed for the measure, which proposes further lines of development for the presented measure.

The paper is organized as follows. The basics of the instance-based approach applied to ontology representations are recalled in Sect. 2. The next Sect. 3 presents the novel semantic similarity measure adopted with the inductive procedure. Successively, Sect. 4 reports the outcomes of experiments performed with its implementation. Possible developments are finally examined in Sect. 5.

2   A Nearest Neighbor Approach to Instance-Checking

In the following, we assume that concept descriptions are defined in terms of a generic ontology language that may be mapped to some description logic with the standard model-theoretic semantics (see the handbook [1] for a thorough reference).

A *knowledge base* $\mathcal{K} = \langle \mathcal{T}, \mathcal{A} \rangle$ contains a *TBox* $\mathcal{T}$ and an *ABox* $\mathcal{A}$. $\mathcal{T}$ is a set of concept definitions. $\mathcal{A}$ contains assertions (facts, data) concerning the world state. Moreover, normally the *unique names assumption* is made on the ABox individuals. The set of the individuals occurring in $\mathcal{A}$ will be denoted with $\mathsf{Ind}(\mathcal{A})$. As regards the inference services, like all other instance-based methods, our procedure may require performing *instance-checking*, which amounts to determining whether an individual, say a, belongs to a concept extension, i.e. whether $C(a)$ holds for a certain concept C.

Given an ontology, a classification method can employed for predicting the concepts to which a new individual it is likely to belong. These individuals are supposed to be described by assertions in the knowledge base. Such an classification procedure may also suggest new assertions about such an individual which cannot not be inferred by deduction, in analogy with the class-membership of other similar instances.

We review the basics of the k-Nearest Neighbor method in the semantic web context [4] and propose how to exploit this classification procedure for inductive instance checking and query answering. It is ascribed to the category of lazy learning, since the learning phase is reduced to memorizing instances of the target concepts pre-classified by an expert. Then, during the classification phase, a notion of similarity over the instance space is employed to classify a new instance in analogy with its neighbors.

The objective is to induce an approximation for a discrete-valued target function $h : IS \mapsto V$ from a space of instances IS to a set of values $V = \{v_1, \ldots, v_s\}$ standing for the classes (concepts) that have to be predicted.

Let x_q be the query instance whose class-membership is to be checked. Using a dissimilarity measure, the set of the k nearest (pre-classified) training instances w.r.t. x_q is selected: $NN(x_q) = \{x_i \mid i = 1, \ldots, k\}$. In its simplest setting, the k-NN algorithm approximates h for classifying x_q on the grounds of the value that h is known to assume for the training instances in $NN(x_q)$, i.e. the k closest instances to x_q in terms of a dissimilarity measure. Precisely, the value is decided by means of a majority voting procedure: it is simply the most *voted* value by the instances in $NN(x_q)$.

A problem with this formulation is that it takes into account similarity only when selecting those instance to be included in the neighborhood. Therefore a modified setting is generally adopted, that is based on weighting the vote according to the distance of the query instance from the training instances:

$$\hat{h}(x_q) := \operatorname*{argmax}_{v \in V} \sum_{i=1}^{k} w_i \delta(v, h(x_i)) \tag{1}$$

where δ is a function that returns 1 in case of matching arguments and 0 otherwise, and, given a distance measure d, the weights are determined by $w_i = 1/d(x_i, x_q)$ or $w_i = 1/d(x_i, x_q)^2$.

Note that the hypothesis function $\hat{h}$ is defined only extensionally, since the basic k-NN method does not return an intensional classification model (a function or a concept definition), it merely gives an answer for the query instances to be classified.

It should be also observed that a strong assumption of this setting is that it can be employed to assign the query instance to the concept from a set of pairwise disjoint concepts (those corresponding to the value set V). This is an assumption that cannot be always made. In our setting, indeed, an individual might be an instance of more than one concept. In a more general setting that does not assume the pairwise disjointness of the concepts, given a query concept Q, the membership of an instance x_q may be checked through a NN classification procedure, transforming the multi-class problem into a binary one. Therefore, a simple binary value set $V = \{-1, +1\}$ may be employed. Then, a hypothesis h_Q is computed for performing inductive query answering:

$$\hat{h}_Q(x_q) := \operatorname*{argmax}_{v \in V} \sum_{i=1}^{k} \frac{\delta(v, h_Q(x_i))}{d(x_q, x_i)^2} \tag{2}$$

where the value of h_Q for the training instances x_i is simply determined to the occurrence $(+1)$ or absence (-1) of the corresponding assertion $Q(x_i)$ in the ABox. Alternately, Q may return $+1$ when $Q(x_i)$ can be inferred[1] from the knowledge base $(\mathcal{K} \models Q(x_i))$, and -1 otherwise.

The problem with non-explicitly disjoint concepts is also related to the CWA usually made in the knowledge discovery context. To deal with the OWA, the absence of information on whether a certain training instance x is likely to belong to the extension of the query concept Q should not be interpreted negatively, as in the standard machine learning settings which adopt the CWA. Rather, it should count as neutral information. Thus, another value set has to be adopted for the classification of the neighboring training instances, namely $V = \{-1, +1, 0\}$, where the three values denote, respectively, occurrence of the assertion, occurrence of the opposite assertion and absence of both:

$$Q(x) = \begin{cases} +1 & \mathcal{K} \models Q(x) \\ -1 & \mathcal{K} \models \neg Q(x) \\ 0 & otherwise \end{cases}$$

Occurrence can be easily computed with a look-up in the ABox, therefore the overall complexity of the procedure depends on the number $k \ll |\mathsf{Ind}(\mathcal{A})|$, that is the number of times the distance measure is needed.

Note that, being based on a majority vote of the individuals in the neighborhood, this procedure is less error-prone in case of noise in the data (i.e. incorrect assertions in the ABox), therefore it may be able to give a correct classification even in case of (partially) inconsistent knowledge bases.

Again, a more complex procedure may be devised by simply substituting the notion of occurrence (absence) of assertions in (from) the ABox with the one of derivability (non-derivability) from the whole knowledge base, i.e. $\mathcal{K} \models Q(x)$, $\mathcal{K} \models \neg Q(x)$ and neither of the previous relations, respectively. Although this

---

[1] In the following $\models$ will denote entailment, as computed through a reasoner.

may exploit more information and turn out to be more accurate, it is also much more computationally expensive, since the simple look-up in the ABox must be replaced with a logical inference (instance checking). However much of the computation can be performed in advance w.r.t. to the classification phase and the number of inferences needed is bounded by k.

It should be noted that the inductive inference made by the procedure shown above is not guaranteed to be deductively valid. Indeed, inductive inference naturally yields a certain degree of uncertainty. In order to measure the likelihood of the decision made by the procedure (individual x_q belongs to the concept denoted by value v maximizing the argmax argument in Eq. (2)), given the nearest training individuals in $NN(x_q)$, the quantity that determined the decision should be normalized by dividing it by the sum of such arguments over the (three) possible values:

$$l(class(x_q) = v|NN(x_q)) = \frac{\sum_{i=1}^{k} w_i \cdot \delta(v, h_Q(x_i))}{\sum_{v' \in V} \sum_{i=1}^{k} w_i \cdot \delta(v', h_Q(x_i))} \tag{3}$$

3   A Semantic Semi-distance for Individuals

As mentioned in the first section, various attempts to define semantic similarity (or dissimilarity) measures for concept languages have been made, yet they have still a limited applicability to simple languages [2] or they are not completely semantic depending also on the structure of the descriptions [3]. Moreover, for our purposes, we need a function for measuring the similarity of individuals rather than concepts. It can be observed that individuals do not have a syntactic structure that can be compared. This has led to lifting them to the concept description level before comparing them (recurring to the notion of the *most specific concept* of an individual w.r.t. the ABox [1].

For the nearest-neighbor classification procedure recalled in Sect. 2, we have developed a new measure with a definition that totally depends on semantic aspects of the individuals in the knowledge base.

3.1   The Measure

On a semantic level, similar individuals should behave similarly with respect to the same concepts. We introduce a novel measure for assessing the similarity of individuals in a knowledge base, which is based on the idea of comparing their semantics along a number of dimensions represented by a committee of concept descriptions. Following the ideas borrowed from [6], we can define totally semantic distance measures for individuals in the context of a knowledge base.

The rationale of the new measure is to compare them on the grounds of their behavior w.r.t. a given set of hypotheses, that is a collection of concept descriptions, say $\mathsf{F} = \{F_1, F_2, \ldots, F_m\}$, which stands as a group of discriminating *features* expressed in the language taken into account.

In its simple formulation, a family of distance functions for individuals inspired to Minkowski's distances can be defined as follows:

Definition 3.1 (family of measures). *Let* $\mathcal{K} = \langle \mathcal{T}, \mathcal{A} \rangle$ *be a knowledge base. Given set of concept descriptions* $\mathsf{F} = \{F_1, F_2, \ldots, F_m\}$, *a family of dissimilarity functions* $d_p^{\mathsf{F}} : \mathsf{Ind}(\mathcal{A}) \times \mathsf{Ind}(\mathcal{A}) \mapsto \mathbb{R}$ *defined as follows:*

$$\forall a, b \in \mathsf{Ind}(\mathcal{A}) \quad d_p^{\mathsf{F}}(a, b) := \frac{1}{m} \left[\sum_{i=1}^{m} \mid \pi_i(a) - \pi_i(b) \mid^p \right]^{1/p}$$

where $p > 0$ *and* $\forall i \in \{1, \ldots, m\}$ *the* projection function π_i *is defined by:*

$$\forall a \in \mathsf{Ind}(\mathcal{A}) \quad \pi_i(a) = \begin{cases} 1 & F_i(x) \in \mathcal{A} \\ 0 & \neg F_i(x) \in \mathcal{A} \\ \frac{1}{2} & \textit{otherwise} \end{cases}$$

The superscript F will be omitted when the set of hypotheses is fixed.

As an alternative, like in the definition of the hypothesis function for the NN procedure, the definition of the measures can be made more accurate by considering entailment rather than the simple ABox look-up, when determining the values of the projection functions:

$$\forall a \in \mathsf{Ind}(\mathcal{A}) \quad \pi_i(a) = \begin{cases} 1 & \mathcal{K} \models F_i(x) \\ 0 & \mathcal{K} \models \neg F_i(x) \\ \frac{1}{2} & \textit{otherwise} \end{cases}$$

In particular, we will consider the following measures:

$$\forall a, b \in \mathsf{Ind}(\mathcal{A}) \quad d_1(a, b) := \frac{1}{m} \sum_{i=1}^{m} \mid \pi_i(a) - \pi_i(b) \mid$$

or:

$$\forall a, b \in \mathsf{Ind}(\mathcal{A}) \quad d_2(a, b) := \frac{1}{m} \sqrt{\sum_{i=1}^{m} (\pi_i(a) - \pi_i(b))^2}$$

3.2 Discussion

It is easy to prove that these functions have the standard properties for semi-distances:

Proposition 3.1 (semi-distance). *For a fixed hypothesis set and* $p > 0$, *given any three instances* $a, b, c \in \mathsf{Ind}(\mathcal{A})$. *it holds that:*

1. $d_p(a, b) > 0$
2. $d_p(a, b) = d_p(b, a)$
3. $d_p(a, c) \leq d_p(a, b) + d_p(b, c)$

Proof.

1. *trivial*
2. *trivial*
3. *Noted that*

$$(d_p(a,c))^p = \left(\frac{1}{m}\right)^p \sum_{i=1}^{m} \mid \pi_i(a) - \pi_i(c) \mid^p =$$

$$= \left(\frac{1}{m}\right)^p \sum_{i=1}^{m} \mid \pi_i(a) - \pi_i(b) + \pi_i(b) - \pi_i(c) \mid^p \leq$$

$$\leq \left(\frac{1}{m}\right)^p \sum_{i=1}^{m} \mid \pi_i(a) - \pi_i(b) \mid^p + \left(\frac{1}{m}\right)^p \sum_{i=1}^{m} \mid \pi_i(b) - \pi_i(c) \mid^p \leq$$

$$\leq (d_p(a,b))^p + (d_p(b,c))^p \leq (d_p(a,b) + d_p(b,c))^p$$

then the property follows for the monotonicity of the power function.

It cannot be proved that $d_p(a,b) = 0$ iff $a = b$. This is the case of *indiscernible* individuals with respect to the given set of hypotheses F.

Compared to other proposed distance (or dissimilarity) measures [2], the presented function does not depend on the constructors of a specific language, rather it requires only retrieval or instance-checking service used for deciding whether an individual is asserted in the knowledge base to belong to a concept extension (or, alternatively, if this could be derived as a logical consequence).

Note that the π_i functions ($\forall i = 1, \ldots, m$) for the training instances, that contribute to determine the measure with respect to new ones, can be computed in advance thus determining a speed-up in the actual computation of the measure. This is very important for the measure integration in algorithms which massively use this distance, such as all instance-based methods.

The underlying idea for the measure is that similar individuals should exhibit the same behavior w.r.t. the concepts in F. Here, we make the assumption that the feature-set F represents a sufficient number of (possibly redundant) features that are able to discriminate really different individuals. The choice of the concepts to be included – *feature selection* – is beyond the scope of this work. Experimentally, we could obtain good results by using the very set of both primitive and defined concepts found in the ontology.

4   Experiments

4.1   Experimental Setting

In order to test the inductive instance-checking NN procedure proposed in Sect. 2, integrated with the new dissimilarity measure, we have applied it to a number of retrieval problems. To these purposes, we selected a number of different ontologies represented in OWL, namely: FSM, SURFACE-WATER-MODEL, SCIENCE and NEWTESTAMENTNAMES from the Protégé library[2], the FINANCIAL ontology[3] employed as a testbed for the PELLET reasoner. Table 1 summarizes important details concerning the ontologies employed in the experimentation.

---

[2] http://protege.stanford.edu/plugins/owl/owl-library
[3] http://www.cs.put.poznan.pl/alawrynowicz/financial.owl

Table 1. Ontologies employed in the experiments

ontology	DL	#concepts	#obj. prop	#data prop	#individuals
FSM	$\mathcal{SOF}(D)$	20	10	7	37
S.-W.-M.	$\mathcal{ALCOF}(D)$	19	9	1	115
Science	$\mathcal{ALCIF}(D)$	74	70	40	331
Financial	$\mathcal{ALCIF}$	60	17	0	652
NTN	$\mathcal{SHIF}(D)$	47	27	8	676

The FSM ontology describes the domain of *finite state machines* using the $\mathcal{SOF}(D)$ language. It is made up of 20 (primitive and defined) concepts (some of them are explicitly declared to be disjoint), 10 object properties, 7 datatype properties, 37 distinct individual names. About half of the individuals are asserted as instances of a single concept and are not involved in any role (object property) assertion. SURFACE-WATER-MODEL is an $\mathcal{ALCOF}(D)$ ontology describing the domain of the surface water and the water quality models. It is made up of 19 concepts (both primitive and defined) with no specification about their disjointness, 9 object properties, 115 distinct individual names; each of them is an instance of a single class and only some of them are involved in object properties. The SCIENCE ontology describes scientific facts in $\mathcal{ALCIF}(D)$. It is made up of 74 concepts, 70 object properties, 331 individual names. FINANCIAL is an $\mathcal{ALCIF}$ ontology that describes the domain of eBanking. It is made up of 60 (primitive and defined) concepts (some of them are declared to be disjoint), 17 object properties, and no datatype property. It contains 17941 distinct individual names. From the original ABox, we randomly extracted assertions for 652 individuals. NEWTESTAMENTNAMES (developed for the *Semantic Bible* Project) describes facts related to the New Testament. It contains of 47 concepts, 27 object properties, 676 individual names.

The experiment was quite intensive involving the classification of all the individuals in each ontology; namely, the individuals were checked through the inductive procedure to assess wether they were to be retrieved as instances of a query concept. Therefore, 15 queries were randomly generated by conjunction/disjunction of primitive or defined concepts of each ontology. The performance was evaluated comparing its responses to those returned by a standard reasoner[4] as a baseline.

The experiment has been repeated twice adopting different procedures according to the size of the corresponding ABox (measured by $|\mathsf{Ind}(\mathcal{A})|$): a leave-one-out cross validation for the smaller ontologies (FSM and S.-W.-M.) and a ten-fold cross validation one for the larger ones Applying the k-NN method, we chose $\sqrt{|\mathsf{Ind}(\mathcal{A})|}$, as a value for k, as advised in the instance-based learning literature. Yet we found experimentally that much smaller values could be chosen, resulting in the same classification. We employed the simpler version of the distance (d_1) utilizing all the concepts in the ontology for determining the set F.

---

[4] We employed PELLET: `http://pellet.owldl.com`

Table 2. Results (average±std-dev.) of the experiments with the method employing the new semantic measure

	match rate	*commission rate*	*omission rate*	*induction rate*
FSM	97.7 ± 3.00	2.30 ± 3.00	0.00 ± 0.00	0.00 ± 0.00
S.-W.-M.	99.9 ± 0.20	0.00 ± 0.00	0.10 ± 0.20	0.00 ± 0.00
SCIENCE	99.8 ± 0.50	0.00 ± 0.00	0.20 ± 0.10	0.00 ± 0.00
FINANCIAL	90.4 ± 24.6	9.40 ± 24.5	0.10 ± 0.10	0.10 ± 0.20
NTN	99.9 ± 0.10	0.00 ± 7.60	0.10 ± 0.00	0.00 ± 0.10

For each concept in the ontology, we measured the following parameters for the evaluation:

- *match rate*: number of cases of individuals that got exactly the same classification by both classifiers with respect to the overall number of individuals;
- *omission error rate*: amount of unlabeled individuals (our method could not determine whether it was an instance or not) while it was to be classified as an instance of that concept;
- *commission error rate*: amount of individuals (analogically) labeled as instances of a concept, while they (logically) belong to that concept or vice-versa
- *induction rate*: amount of individuals that were found to belong to a concept or its negation, while this information is not logically derivable from the knowledge base

We report the average rates obtained over all the concepts in each ontology and also their standard deviation.

4.2   Retrieval Employing the New Measure in the NN Procedure

By looking at Tab. 2 reporting the experimental outcomes (mean values and standard deviations), preliminarily it is important to note that, for every ontology, the commission error was low. This means that the procedure is quite accurate: it did not make critical mistakes i.e. cases when an individual is deemed as an instance of a concept while it really is an instance of another disjoint concept.

If we compare these outcomes with those reported in previous papers [4], where the average accuracy on the same was slightly higher than 80%, we find a significant increase of the performance due to the accuracy of the new measure. Also the elapsed time (not reported here) was lowered because, once the values for the π's functions are pre-computed, the efficiency of the classification, which depends a lot on the computation of the dissimilarity, gains a lot of speed-up.

The usage of all concepts for the set F made the measure quite accurate, which is the reason why the procedure resulted quite conservative as regards inducing new assertions. It rather matched faithfully the reasoner decisions. A noteworthy difference was observed for the case of the FINANCIAL ontology for which we find

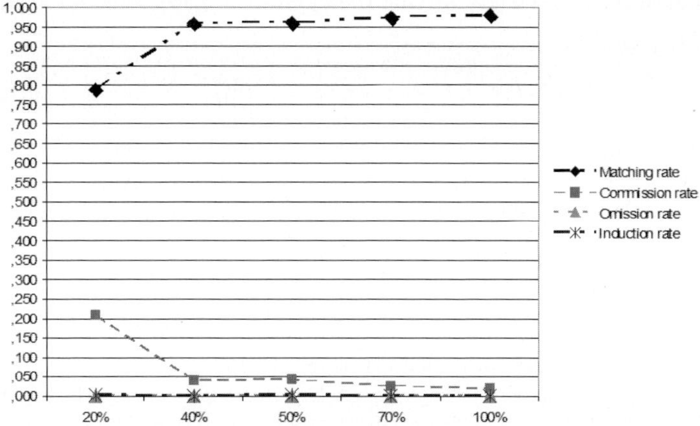

Fig. 1. Average results varying the number of hypotheses in the set F

the lowest match rate and the highest variability in the results over the various concepts. On a careful examination of the experimentation with this ontology, we found that the average results were lowered by a concept whose assertions, having been poorly sampled from the initial ontology, could not constitute enough evidence to our inductive method for determining the correct classification. The same problem, to a lesser extent, were found also with the FSM ontology which was the one with the least number of assertions. This shows that the weaker side of any instance-based procedure is really when data are too sparse or non evenly distributed.

As mentioned, we found also that a lower value for k could have been chosen, for in many cases the decision on the correct classification was easy to make even on account of a few (the closest) neighbor instances. This yields also the likelihood of the inference made (see Eq. (3)) turned out quite high.

4.3   Varying the Hypothesis Set

In the previous experiments all concepts involved in an ontology were used for inclusion in the hypothesis set F. We sensed that the inherent redundancy helped a lot the measure accuracy. Yet larger sets yield more effort to be made for computing the measures. Nevertheless, it is well known that the NN approach suffers when lots of further irrelevant attributes for describing the instances are added. Thus, we have tested also how the variation of hypotheses (concept descriptions) belonging to the set F could affect the performance of the measure. We expected that with an increasing number of hypotheses considered in F, the accuracy of the measure would increase accordingly.

To test this claim experimentally, one of the ontologies considered the previous experiment was considered. We performed repeatedly (three times) a leave-one-out cross validation with an increasing percentage of concepts randomly selected for F w.r.t. the overall number of primitive or defined concept names in the

Table 3. Average results varying the number of hypotheses in the set F

% of concepts	match rate	commission rate	omission rate	Induction rate
20%	79.1	20.7	0.00	0.20
40%	96.1	03.9	0.00	0.00
50%	97.2	02.8	0.00	0.00
70%	97.4	02.6	0.00	0.00
100%	98.0	02.0	0.00	0.00

ontology. The average results returned by the system are depicted in Fig. 1. Numerical details of such outcomes are given in Table 3.

As expected, it is possible to see that the accuracy of the decisions (*match rate*) is positively correlated with the number of concepts included in F. The same outcomes were obtained by repeating similar experiments with other ontologies. It should be observed that in some cases the concepts randomly selected for inclusion in F actually turned out to be a little redundant (by subsumption or because of a simple overlap between their extension) This suggest a line of further investigation that will concern finding minimal subsets of concepts to be used for the measure.

5   Conclusions and Future Work

This paper explored the application of an instance-based learning procedure for analogical reasoning applied to concept representations adopted in the Semantic Web context. We defined a novel semantic similarity measure that has a wide scope of application to methods which require the assessment of the semantic (dis)ssimilarity of individuals. Particularly, in this paper we employed it integrated in an instance-based instance-checking procedure in the task of instance retrieval (predicting class-membership) which can be effective even in the presence of missing (or noisy) information in the knowledge bases.

The experiments made on various ontologies showed that the method is quite effective, and, as expected, its performance depends on the number (and distribution) of the available training instances. Besides, the procedure is robust to noise since it seldom made commission errors in the experiments that have been carried out so far.

Various developments for the measure can be foreseen as concerns its definition. Namely, since it is very dependant on the concepts included in the committee of features, two immediate lines of research arise: 1) reducing the number of concepts saving those concepts which are endowed of a real discriminating power; 2) learning optimal sets of discriminating features, by allowing also their composition employing the specific constructors made available by the representation language of choice. Both these objectives can be accomplished by means of machine learning techniques especially when ontologies with a large set of individuals are available. Namely, part of the entire data can be drawn in order to learn optimal feature sets, in advance with respect to the successive usage.

As mentioned, the measure is applicable to other instance-based tasks which can be approached through machine learning techniques. The next step will be plugging the measure in a hierarchical clustering algorithm where clusters would be formed grouping instances on the grounds of their similarity assessed through the measure.

References

[1] Baader, F., Calvanese, D., McGuinness, D., Nardi, D., Patel-Schneider, P. (eds.): The Description Logic Handbook. Cambridge University Press, Cambridge (2003)

[2] Borgida, A., Walsh, T., Hirsh, H.: Towards measuring similarity in description logics. In: Horrocks, I., Sattler, U., Wolter, F. (eds.) Working Notes of the International Description Logics Workshop. CEUR Workshop Proceedings, Edinburgh, UK, vol. 147 (2005)

[3] d'Amato, C., Fanizzi, N., Esposito, F.: A dissimilarity measure for ALC concept descriptions. In: Proceedings of the 21st Annual ACM Symposium of Applied Computing, SAC 2006, Dijon, France, 2006, vol. 2, pp. 1695–1699. ACM, New York (2006)

[4] d'Amato, C., Fanizzi, N., Esposito, F.: Reasoning by analogy in description logics through instance-based learning. In: Tummarello, G., Bouquet, P., Signore, O. (eds.) Proceedings of Semantic Web Applications and Perspectives, 3rd Italian Semantic Web Workshop, SWAP2006. CEUR Workshop Proceedings, Pisa, Italy, vol. 201 (2006)

[5] Emde, W., Wettschereck, D.: Relational instance-based learning. In: Saitta, L. (ed.) Proceedings of the 13th International Conference on Machine Learning, ICML96, pp. 122–130. Morgan Kaufmann, San Francisco (1996)

[6] Sebag, M.: Distance induction in first order logic. In: Džeroski, S., Lavrač, N. (eds.) Inductive Logic Programming. LNCS, vol. 1297, pp. 264–272. Springer, Heidelberg (1997)

A Hierarchical Clustering Procedure for Semantically Annotated Resources

Nicola Fanizzi, Claudia d'Amato, and Floriana Esposito

Dipartimento di Informatica – Università degli Studi di Bari
Campus Universitario, Via Orabona 4, 70125 Bari, Italy
{fanizzi,claudia.damato,esposito}@di.uniba.it

Abstract. A clustering method is presented which can be applied to relational knowledge bases. It can be used to discover interesting groupings of resources through their (semantic) annotations expressed in the standard languages employed for modeling concepts in the Semantic Web. The method exploits a simple (yet effective and language-independent) semi-distance measure for individuals, that is based on the resource semantics w.r.t. a number of dimensions corresponding to a committee of features represented by a group of concept descriptions (discriminating features). The algorithm is an fusion of the classic BISECTING k-MEANS with approaches based on medoids since they are intended to be applied to relational representations. We discuss its complexity and the potential applications to a variety of important tasks.

1   Learning Methods for Concept Languages

In the inherently distributed applications related to the Semantic Web (henceforth SW) there is an extreme need of automatizing those activities which are more burdensome for the knowledge engineer, such as ontology construction, matching and evolution. Such an automatization may be assisted by crafting supervised or unsupervised methods for the specific representations of the SW field (RDF through OWL).

In this work, we investigate on unsupervised learning for knowledge bases expressed in such standard concept languages. In particular, we focus on the problem of conceptual clustering of semantically annotated resources. The benefits of *conceptual clustering* [17] in the context of semantically annotated knowledge bases are manifold:

- *concept formation*: clustering annotated resources enables the definition of new emerging concepts on the grounds of the primitive concepts asserted in a knowledge base;
- *evolution*: supervised methods can exploit these clusters to induce new concept definitions or to refining existing ones;
- *discovery and ranking*: intensionally defined groupings may speed-up the task of search and discovery; a hierarchical clustering also suggests criteria for ranking the retrieved resources.

R. Basili and M.T. Pazienza (Eds.): AI*IA 2007, LNAI 4733, pp. 266–277, 2007.

Essentially, many existing clustering methods are based on the application of similarity (or density) measures defined over a fixed set of attributes of the domain objects. Classes of objects are taken as collections that exhibit low interclass similarity (density) and high intraclass similarity (density). Often these methods cannot into account any form of *background knowledge* that could characterize object configurations by means of global concepts and semantic relationship. This hinders the interpretation of the outcomes of these methods which is crucial in the SW perspective which foresees sharing and reusing the produced knowledge in order to enable forms of semantic interoperability.

Thus, early conceptual clustering methods aimed at defining groups of objects through conjunctive descriptions based on selected attributes [17]. In the perspective, the expressiveness of the language adopted for describing objects and clusters (concepts) is equally important. Alternative approaches, particularly suitable to concept languages and terminological representations, have pursued a different way for attacking the problem, devising logic-based methods [12,7]. Yet it has been pointed out that these methods may suffer from noise in the data.

This motivates our investigation on similarity-based clustering methods which can be more noise-tolerant, still saving the advantages of conceptual clustering. Specifically we propose a multi-relational extension of effective clustering techniques, which is tailored for the SW context. It is intended for grouping similar resources w.r.t. a semantic dissimilarity measure which allows for discovering new concepts. Specifically, our relational method derives from the *Bisecting k-means* algorithm [10], a well-known partitional clustering method.

From a technical viewpoint, upgrading existing algorithms to work on multi-relational representations, like the concept languages used in the SW, required novel similarity measures that are suitable for such representations. In particular, as for the original method, one may fix a given number k of clusters of interest, yet this may be hard when scarce knowledge about the domain is available. As an alternative, a partitional method may be employed up to reaching a minimal threshold value for cluster *quality* (many measures have been proposed in the literature [9]) which makes any further bisections useless.

In this setting, the notion of means that characterizes the algorithms descending from *k-means* and *EM* [10] developed for numeric (or just ordinal) features. In our case we recur to the notion of *medoids* (like in algorithm *PAM* [11]) as central individuals in a cluster. Another theoretical problem is posed by the *Open World Assumption* (OWA) that is generally made in the target context, differently from the *Closed World Assumption* (CWA) which is often made when performing machine learning or query-answering tasks.

The notion of similarity to be employed has to deal with the rich representations of semantically annotated resources. Therefore we developed a measure which could be used specifically for the SW standard representations (see below). As pointed out in a seminal paper [3] on similarity measures for DLs, most of the existing measures focus on the similarity of atomic concepts within hierarchies or simple ontologies. Moreover, they have been conceived for assessing *concept* similarity, whereas, for our purposes, a notion of similarity between *individuals* is required.

Recently, dissimilarity measures for specific DLs have been proposed [4]. Although they turned out to be quite effective for the inductive tasks, they are still partly based on structural criteria which determine their main weakness: they are hardly scalable to deal with standard languages used in the current knowledge management frameworks. Therefore, we have devised a family of dissimilarity measures for semantically annotated resources, which can overcome the aforementioned limitations. Following some ideas introduced in [16], we present a new family of measures that is suitable for a wide range of ontology languages since it is merely based on the discernibility of the input individuals with respect to a fixed set of features represented by concept definitions (features). As such the new measures are not absolute, yet they depend on the knowledge base they are applied to.

The remainder of the paper is organized as follows. Sect. 2 presents the basics representation and the novel semantic similarity measure adopted with the clustering algorithm. This algorithm is presented and discussed in Sect. 3. After Sect. 4 concerning the related work, possible developments are finally examined in Sect. 5.

2   Semantic Distance Measures

2.1   Preliminaries on the Reference Representation

One of the strong points of our method is that it does not rely on a particular language for semantic annotations. Hence, in the following, we assume that resources, concepts and their relationship may be defined in terms of a generic ontology language that may be mapped to some DL language with the standard model-theoretic semantics (see the handbook [1] for a thorough reference).

In this context, a *knowledge base* $\mathcal{K} = \langle \mathcal{T}, \mathcal{A} \rangle$ contains a *TBox* $\mathcal{T}$ and an *ABox* $\mathcal{A}$. $\mathcal{T}$ is a set of concept definitions. $\mathcal{A}$ contains assertions (facts, data) concerning the world state. Moreover, normally the *unique names assumption* is made on the ABox individuals[1] therein. The set of the individuals occurring in $\mathcal{A}$ will be denoted with $\mathsf{Ind}(\mathcal{A})$.

As regards the inference services, like all other instance-based methods, our procedure may require performing *instance-checking*, which amounts to determining whether an individual, say a, belongs to a concept extension, i.e. whether $C(a)$ holds for a certain concept C.

2.2   A Semantic Semi-distance for Individuals

Moreover, for our purposes, we need a function for measuring the similarity of individuals rather than concepts. It can be observed that individuals do not have a syntactic structure that can be compared. This has led to lifting them to the concept description level before comparing them (recurring to the approximation of the *most specific concept* of an individual w.r.t. the ABox).

---

[1] Individuals can be assumed to be identified by their own URI.

For the clustering procedure specified in Sect. 3, we have developed a new measure with a definition that totally depends on semantic aspects of the individuals in the knowledge base.

On a semantic level, similar individuals should behave similarly with respect to the same concepts. We introduce a novel measure for assessing the similarity of individuals in a knowledge base, which is based on the idea of comparing their semantics along a number of dimensions represented by a committee of concept descriptions. Following the ideas borrowed from ILP [16] and *multi-dimensional scaling*, we propose the definition of totally semantic distance measures for individuals in the context of a knowledge base.

The rationale of the new measure is to compare them on the grounds of their behavior w.r.t. a given set of hypotheses, that is a collection of concept descriptions, say $\mathsf{F} = \{F_1, F_2, \ldots, F_m\}$, which stands as a group of discriminating *features* expressed in the language taken into account.

In its simple formulation, a family of distance functions for individuals inspired to Minkowski's distances can be defined as follows:

Definition 2.1 (family of measures). *Let* $\mathcal{K} = \langle \mathcal{T}, \mathcal{A} \rangle$ *be a knowledge base. Given set of concept descriptions* $\mathsf{F} = \{F_1, F_2, \ldots, F_m\}$, *a family of functions*

$$d_p^{\mathsf{F}} : \mathsf{Ind}(\mathcal{A}) \times \mathsf{Ind}(\mathcal{A}) \mapsto \mathbb{R}$$

defined as follows:

$$\forall a, b \in \mathsf{Ind}(\mathcal{A}) \quad d_p^{\mathsf{F}}(a, b) := \frac{1}{m} \left[\sum_{i=1}^{m} \mid \pi_i(a) - \pi_i(b) \mid^p \right]^{1/p}$$

where $p > 0$ *and* $\forall i \in \{1, \ldots, m\}$ *the* projection function π_i *is defined by:*

$$\forall a \in \mathsf{Ind}(\mathcal{A}) \quad \pi_i(a) = \begin{cases} 1 & F_i(x) \in \mathcal{A} \\ 0 & \neg F_i(x) \in \mathcal{A} \\ 1/2 & otherwise \end{cases}$$

The superscript F will be omitted when the set of hypotheses is fixed.

As an alternative, the definition of the measures can be made more accurate by considering entailment rather than the simple ABox look-up, when determining the values of the projection functions:

$$\forall a \in \mathsf{Ind}(\mathcal{A}) \quad \pi_i(a) = \begin{cases} 1 & \mathcal{K} \models F_i(x) \\ 0 & \mathcal{K} \models \neg F_i(x) \\ 1/2 & otherwise \end{cases}$$

In particular, for the sake of saving computational resources, we have considered the following measures in the experiments: $\forall a, b \in \mathsf{Ind}(\mathcal{A})$

$$d_1(a, b) := \frac{1}{m} \sum_{i=1}^{m} \mid \pi_i(a) - \pi_i(b) \mid \quad \text{or} \quad d_2(a, b) := \frac{1}{m} \sqrt{\sum_{i=1}^{m} (\pi_i(a) - \pi_i(b))^2}$$

In order to clarify the application of the presented measures the following example is considered.

Example 2.1. Let us consider the knowledge base $\mathcal{K} = \langle \mathcal{T}, \mathcal{A} \rangle$ reported below.
Primitive Concepts: $N_C = \{$Female, Male, Human$\}$.
Primitive Roles: $N_R = \{$HasChild, HasParent, HasGrandParent, HasUncle$\}$.

T-Box: $\mathcal{T} = \{$ Woman $\equiv$ Human $\sqcap$ Female, Man $\equiv$ Human $\sqcap$ Male
Parent $\equiv$ Human $\sqcap$ $\exists$HasChild.Human, Mother $\equiv$ Woman $\sqcap$ Parent $\exists$HasChild.Human
Father $\equiv$ Man $\sqcap$ Parent, Child $\equiv$ Human $\sqcap$ $\exists$HasParent.Parent,
Grandparent $\equiv$ Parent $\sqcap$ $\exists$HasChild.($\exists$ HasChild.Human),
Sibling $\equiv$ Child $\sqcap$ $\exists$HasParent.($\exists$ HasChild $\geq$ 2),
Niece $\equiv$ Human $\sqcap$ $\exists$HasGrandParent.Parent $\sqcup$ $\exists$HasUncle.Uncle,
Cousin $\equiv$ Niece $\sqcap$ $\exists$HasUncle.($\exists$ HasChild.Human) $\}$.

A-Box: $\mathcal{A} = \{$Woman(Claudia), Woman(Tiziana), Father(Leonardo), Father(Antonio),
Father(AntonioB), Mother(Maria), Mother(Giovanna), Child(Valentina), Sibling(Martina),
Sibling(Vito), Mother(Tiziana), HasParent(Claudia,Giovanna), HasParent(Leonardo,AntonioB),
HasParent(Martina,Maria), HasParent(Giovanna,Antonio), HasParent(Vito,AntonioB),
HasParent(Tiziana,Giovanna), HasParent(Tiziana,Leonardo), HasParent(Valentina,Maria),
HasParent(Maria,Antonio), HasSibling(Leonardo,Vito), HasSibling(Martina,Valentina),
HasSibling(Giovanna,Maria), HasSibling(Vito,Leonardo), HasSibling(Tiziana,Claudia),
HasSibling(Valentina,Martina), HasChild(Leonardo,Tiziana), HasChild(Antonio,Giovanna),
HasChild(Antonio,Maria), HasChild(Giovanna,Tiziana), HasChild(Giovanna,Claudia),
HasChild(AntonioB,Vito), HasChild(AntonioB,Leonardo), HasChild(Maria,Valentina),
HasUncle(Martina,Giovanna), HasUncle(Valentina,Giovanna) $\}$

Considered this knowledge base and a feature set F $= \{$Woman, Man, Parent, Sibling, Child$\}$ it is possible to compute the similarity value between the individuals: Claudia and Tiziana as:

$$d_1(\text{Claudia}, \text{Tiziana}) := \frac{1}{5} \sum_{i=1}^{5} \mid \pi_i(\text{Claudia}) - \pi_i(\text{Tiziana}) \mid =$$

$$= \frac{1}{5} \cdot (\mid 1 - 1 \mid + \mid 0 - 0 \mid + \mid 0 - 1 \mid + \mid 1 - 1 \mid + \mid 1 - 1 \mid) = \frac{1}{5} = 0.2$$

2.3   Discussion

It is easy to prove that these functions have the standard properties for semi-distances:

Proposition 2.1 (semi-distance). *For a fixed feature set and $p > 0$, given any three instances $a, b, c \in$ Ind$(\mathcal{A})$. it holds that:*

1. $d_p(a, b) > 0$
2. $d_p(a, b) = d_p(b, a)$
3. $d_p(a, c) \leq d_p(a, b) + d_p(b, c)$

Proof.

1. trivial

2. *trivial*

3. *Noted that*

$$(d_p(a,c))^p = \frac{1}{m^p} \sum_{i=1}^{m} \mid \pi_i(a) - \pi_i(c) \mid^p$$

$$= \frac{1}{m^p} \sum_{i=1}^{m} \mid \pi_i(a) - \pi_i(b) + \pi_i(b) - \pi_i(c) \mid^p$$

$$\leq \frac{1}{m^p} \sum_{i=1}^{m} \mid \pi_i(a) - \pi_i(b) \mid^p + \frac{1}{m^p} \sum_{i=1}^{m} \mid \pi_i(b) - \pi_i(c) \mid^p$$

$$\leq (d_p(a,b))^p + (d_p(b,c))^p \leq (d_p(a,b) + d_p(b,c))^p$$

then the property follows for the monotonicity of the power function.

It cannot be proved that $d_p(a,b) = 0$ iff $a = b$. This is the case of *indiscernible* individuals with respect to the given set of hypotheses F.

Compared to other proposed distance (or dissimilarity) measures [3], the presented function does not depend on the constructors of a specific language, rather it requires only retrieval or instance-checking service used for deciding whether an individual is asserted in the knowledge base to belong to a concept extension (or, alternatively, if this could be derived as a logical consequence).

Note that the π_i functions ($\forall i = 1, \ldots, m$) for the training instances, that contribute to determine the measure with respect to new ones, can be computed in advance thus determining a speed-up in the actual computation of the measure. This is very important for the measure integration in algorithms which massively use this distance, such as all instance-based methods.

The underlying idea for the measure is that similar individuals should exhibit the same behavior w.r.t. the concepts in F. Here, we make the assumption that the feature-set F represents a sufficient number of (possibly redundant) features that are able to discriminate really different individuals. Experimentally, we could obtain good results by using the very set of both primitive and defined concepts found in the ontology. The choice of the concepts to be included – *feature selection* – may be crucial. We have devised a specific optimization algorithms founded in *genetic programming* and *simulated annealing* (whose presentation goes beyond the scope of this work) which are able to find optimal choices of discriminating concept committees.

3   Grouping Individuals by Hierarchical Clustering

The conceptual clustering procedure implemented in our method works top-down, starting with one universal cluster grouping all instances. Then it iteratively finds two clusters bisecting an existing one up to the desired number of clusters is reached. This algorithm can be thought as producing a dendrogram levelwise: the number of levels coincides with the number of clusters. It can be very fast.

3.1   The Algorithm

In particular our algorithm can be ascribed to the category of the heuristic partitioning algorithms such as K-MEANS and EM [9,10]. Each cluster is represented by the center of the cluster. In our setting we will consider the notion of medoid as a notion of cluster center since our distance measure works on a categorical feature-space. In particular it can be seen as a hierarchical extension of the PAM algorithm (*Partition Around Medoids* [11]): each cluster is represented by one of the individuals in the cluster, the medoid, i.e., in our case, the one with the lowest average distance w.r.t. all the others individuals in the cluster. The bi-partition is repeated level-wise producing a dendrogram.

Fig. 1 reports a sketch of our algorithm. It essentially consists of two nested loops: the outer one computes a new level of the resulting dendrogram and it is repeated until the desired number of clusters is obtained (which corresponds to the latest level; the inner loop consists of a run of the PAM algorithm at the current level.

Per each level, the next worst cluster is selected (*selectWorstCluster*() function) on the grounds of its quality, e.g. the one endowed with the least average inner similarity (or cohesiveness [17]). This cluster is candidate to being parted in two. The partition is constructed around two medoids initially chosen (*selectMostDissimilar*() function) as the most dissimilar elements in the cluster and then iteratively adjusted in the inner loop. In the end, the candidate cluster is replaced by the newly found parts at the next level of the dendrogram.

The inner loop basically resembles to a 2-means (or EM) algorithm, where medoids are considered instead of means which can hardly be defined in symbolic computations. Then, the classical two steps are performed in an iteration:

E step. given the current medoids, the first distributes the other individuals in one of the two partitions under construction on the grounds of their similarity w.r.t. either medoid;

M step. given the bipartition obtained by *distribute*(), this second step computes the new medoids for either cluster. These tend to change on each iteration until eventually they converge to a stable couple (or when a maximum number of iteration have been performed).

The medoid of a group of individuals is the individual that has the lowest distance w.r.t. the others. Formally. given a cluster $C = \{a_1, a_2, \ldots, a_n\}$, the medoid is defined:

$$m = \mathrm{medoid}(C) = \operatorname*{argmin}_{a \in C} \sum_{j=1}^{n} d(a, a_j)$$

Each node of the tree (a cluster) may be labeled with an intensional concept definition which characterizes the individuals in the given cluster while discriminating those in the twin cluster at the same level. Labeling the tree-nodes with concepts can be regarded as a number of supervised learning problems in the specific multi-relational representation targeted in our setting. As such it deserves specific solutions that are suitable for the DL languages employed.

```
input    allIndividuals: set of individuals
         k: number of clusters;
         maxIterations: max number of inner iterations;
output clusterVector: array [1..k] of sets of clusters

level := 0;
clusterVector[1] := allIndividuals;
repeat
         ++level;
         cluster2split := selectWorstCluster(clusterVector[level]);
         iterCount := 0;
         stableConfiguration := false;
         (newMedoid1,newMedoid2) := selectMostDissimilar(cluster2split);
         repeat
             ++iterCount;
             // E step
             (medoid1,medoid2) := (newMedoid1,newMedoid2);
             (cluster1,cluster2) := distribute(cluster2split,medoid1,medoid2);
             // M step
             newMedoid1 := medoid(cluster1);
             newMedoid2 := medoid(cluster2);
             stableConfiguration := (medoid1 = newMedoid1) ∧ (medoid2 = newMedoid2);
         until stableConfiguration ∨ (iterCount = maxIterations);
         clusterVector[level+1] := replace(cluster2split,cluster1,cluster2,clusterVector[level]);
until (level = k);
```

Fig. 1. The HIERARCHICAL BISECTING AROUND MEDOIDS Algorithm

A straightforward solution may be found, for DLs that allow for the computation of (an approximation of) the *most specific concept* (msc) and *least common subsumer* (lcs) [2] (such as $\mathcal{ALC}$). This may involve the following steps: given a cluster of individuals $node_j$

- **for each** individual $a_i \in node_j$ **do**
      compute $M_i := msc(a_i)$ w.r.t. $\mathcal{A}$;
- **let** $MSCs_j := \{M_i \mid a_i \in node_j\}$;
- **return** $lcs(MSCs_j)$

As an alternative, algorithms for learning concept descriptions expressed in DLs may be employed [5]. Indeed, concept formation can be cast as a supervised learning problem: once the two clusters at a certain level have been found, where the members of a cluster are considered as positive examples and the members of the dual cluster as negative ones. Then any concept learning method which can deal with this representation may be utilized for this new task.

3.2   Discussion

The representation of centers by means of medoids has two advantages. First, it presents no limitations on attributes types, and, second, the choice of medoids is dictated by the location of a predominant fraction of points inside a cluster and, therefore, it is lesser sensitive to the presence of outliers. In K-MEANS case a cluster is represented by its centroid, which is a mean (usually weighted average) of points within a cluster. This works conveniently only with numerical attributes and can be negatively affected by a single outlier.

A PAM algorithm has several favorable properties. Since it performs clustering with respect to any specified metric, it allows a flexible definition of similarity. This flexibility is particularly important in biological applications where researchers may be interested, for example, in grouping correlated or possibly also anti-correlated elements. Many clustering algorithms do not allow for a flexible definition of similarity, but allow only Euclidean distance in current implementations. In addition to allowing a flexible distance metric, a PAM algorithm has the advantage of identifying clusters by the medoids. Medoids are robust representations of the cluster centers that are less sensitive to outliers than other cluster profiles, such as the cluster means of K-MEANS. This robustness is particularly important in the common context that many elements do not belong exactly to any cluster, which may be the case of the membership in DL knowledge bases, which may be not ascertained given the OWA.

4   Related Work

The unsupervised learning setting presented in this paper is mainly is based on two factors: the semantic similarity measure and the clustering method. In the following, we briefly discuss sources of inspiration and related approaches.

4.1   Semantic Similarity Measures

As mentioned in the first section, various attempts to define semantic similarity (or dissimilarity) measures for concept languages have been made, yet they have still a limited applicability to simple languages [3] or they are not completely semantic depending also on the structure of the descriptions [4].

Our measure is mainly based on Minkowski's measure and on a method for distance induction developed by Sebag [16] in the context of machine learning (and *inductive logic programming*). It is shown that the induced measure could be accurate when employed for classification tasks even though set of features (hypotheses) to be used were not the optimal ones (or they were redundant).

A source of inspiration was also *rough sets* theory [15] which aims at the formal definition of vague sets by means of their approximations determined by an indiscernibility relationship. Hopefully, these methods developed in this context will help solving the open points of our framework (see the next section) and suggest new ways to treat uncertainty.

Another related metric was defined [14] for the Herbrand interpretations of logic clauses as induced from a metric on ground atoms. Specifically, it may be employed to assess the dissimilarity of individuals by deriving a related *most specific concept* description (MSC) [1] accounting for them.

4.2   Clustering Procedures

Our algorithm adapts to the specific representations devised for the SW context a combination of BISECTING K-MEANS clustering and the approaches based on medoids. Specifically, in K-MEDOIDS methods each cluster is represented by one of its points. Two early versions of K-MEDOID approach are the algorithms PAM (*Partitioning Around Medoids*) and CLARA (*Clustering LARge Applications*) [11]. PAM is an iterative optimization method that combines relocation of points between perspective clusters with re-nominating the points as potential medoids. The guiding principle for the process is the effect on an objective function, which, obviously, is a costly strategy. CLARA uses several samples of points, which are subjected to PAM. The whole dataset is assigned to resulting medoids, the objective function is computed, and the best system of medoids is retained.

CLARANS algorithm (*Clustering Large Applications based upon RANdomized Search*) [13] was introduced in the context of spatial databases. A graph is considered whose nodes are sets of k medoids and an edge connects two nodes if they differ by exactly one medoid. While CLARA compares very few neighbors corresponding to a fixed small sample, CLARANS uses random search to generate neighbors by starting with an arbitrary node and randomly checking maxneighbor neighbors. If a neighbor represents a better partition, the process continues with this new node. Otherwise a local minimum is found, and the algorithm restarts until a certain number of local minima is found. The best node (i.e. a set of medoids) is returned for the formation of a resulting partition. The complexity of CLARANS is $O(N^2)$ in terms of number of points. Ester et al. [6] extended CLARANS to very large spatial databases. Our algorithm may be considered an extension of the simpler forms of K-MEDOIDS to a hierarchical case. This allows also do determine a good estimate of the number of clusters

Further comparable clustering methods are those based on an indiscernibility relationship [8]. While in our method this idea is embedded in the semi-distance measure (and the choice of the committee of concepts), these algorithms are based on an iterative refinement of an equivalence relationship which induces clusters as equivalence classes.

5   Conclusions and Future Work

This work has presented a clustering for (multi-)relational representations which are standard in the SW field. Namely, it can be used to discover interesting groupings of semantically annotated resources in a wide range of concept languages. The method exploits a novel dissimilarity measure, that is based on the resource semantics w.r.t. a number of dimensions corresponding to a committee of features represented by a group of concept descriptions (discriminating features). The algorithm, is an adaptation of the classic bisecting k-means to complex representations typical of the ontology in the SW. We have discussed its complexity and the potential applications to a variety of important tasks.

In order to exploit the method, the underlying application needs only to model the knowledge base according to this ontology language, thus, for instance, a

SW service registry may be searched provided that services are described in the standard representations defined on top of OWL (e.g. OWL-S or WSML).

Ongoing work concerns the mentioned feature selection task. Namely, we aim at inducing an optimal set of concepts for the distance measure by means of randomized algorithms based on genetic programming and simulated annealing. Furthermore, also the clustering process itself may be carried out by means of a randomized method based on the same approaches.

References

1. Baader, F., Calvanese, D., McGuinness, D., Nardi, D., Patel-Schneider, P. (eds.): The Description Logic Handbook. Cambridge University Press, Cambridge (2003)
2. Baader, F., Küsters, R.: Non-standard inferences in description logics: The story so far. In: Gabbay, D., Goncharov, S.S., Zakharyaschev, M. (eds.) Mathematical Problems from Applied Logic. New Logics for the XXIst Century. International Mathematical Series, vol. 4, Plenum Publishers, New York (2005)
3. Borgida, A., Walsh, T., Hirsh, H.: Towards measuring similarity in description logics. In: Horrocks, I., Sattler, U., Wolter, F. (eds.) Working Notes of the International Description Logics Workshop, Edinburgh, UK. CEUR Workshop Proceedings, vol. 147 (2005)
4. d'Amato, C., Fanizzi, N., Esposito, F.: Reasoning by analogy in description logics through instance-based learning. In: Tummarello, G., Bouquet, P., Signore, O. (eds.) Proceedings of Semantic Web Applications and Perspectives, 3rd Italian Semantic Web Workshop, SWAP2006. CEUR Workshop Proceedings, Pisa, Italy, vol. 201 (2006)
5. Esposito, F., Fanizzi, N., Iannone, L., Palmisano, I., Semeraro, G.: Knowledge-intensive induction of terminologies from metadata. In: McIlraith, S.A., Plexousakis, D., van Harmelen, F. (eds.) ISWC 2004. LNCS, vol. 3298, pp. 441–455. Springer, Heidelberg (2004)
6. Ester, M., Kriegel, H.-P., Sander, J., Xu, X.: A density-based algorithm for discovering clusters in large spatial databases. In: Proceedings of the 2nd Conference of ACM SIGKDD, pp. 226–231. ACM Press, New York (1996)
7. Fanizzi, N., Iannone, L., Palmisano, I., Semeraro, G.: Concept formation in expressive description logics. In: Boulicaut, J.-F., Esposito, F., Giannotti, F., Pedreschi, D. (eds.) ECML 2004. LNCS (LNAI), vol. 3201, pp. 99–113. Springer, Heidelberg (2004)
8. Hirano, S., Tsumoto, S.: An indiscernibility-based clustering method. In: Hu, X., Liu, Q., Skowron, A., Lin, T.Y., Yager, R., Zhang, B. (eds.) 2005 IEEE International Conference on Granular Computing, pp. 468–473. IEEE Computer Society Press, Los Alamitos (2005)
9. Jain, A., Dubes, R.: Algorithms for Clustering Data. Prentice-Hall, Englewood Cliffs, NJ (1988)
10. Jain, A., Murty, M., Flynn, P.: Data clustering: A review. ACM Computing Surveys 31(3), 264–323 (1999)
11. Kaufman, L., Rousseeuw, P.J.: Finding Groups in Data: an Introduction to Cluster Analysis. John Wiley & Sons, England (1990)
12. Kietz, J.-U., Morik, K.: A polynomial approach to the constructive induction of structural knowledge. Machine Learning 14(2), 193–218 (1994)

13. Ng, R., Han, J.: Efficient and effective clustering method for spatial data mining. In: VLDB94. Proceedings of the 20th Conference on Very Large Databases, pp. 144–155 (1994)
14. Nienhuys-Cheng, S.-H.: Distances and limits on herbrand interpretations. In: Page, D.L. (ed.) Inductive Logic Programming. LNCS, vol. 1446, pp. 250–260. Springer, Heidelberg (1998)
15. Pawlak, Z.: Rough Sets: Theoretical Aspects of Reasoning About Data. Kluwer Academic Publishers, Boston, MA (1991)
16. Sebag, M.: Distance induction in first order logic. In: Džeroski, S., Lavrač, N. (eds.) Inductive Logic Programming. LNCS, vol. 1297, pp. 264–272. Springer, Heidelberg (1997)
17. Stepp, R.E., Michalski, R.S.: Conceptual clustering of structured objects: A goal-oriented approach. Artificial Intelligence 28(1), 43–69 (1986)

Similarity-Guided Clause Generalization

S. Ferilli, T.M.A. Basile, N. Di Mauro, M. Biba, and F. Esposito

Dipartimento di Informatica
Università di Bari
via E. Orabona, 4 - 70125 Bari - Italia
{ferilli, basile, ndm, biba, esposito}@di.uniba.it

Abstract. Few works are available in the literature to define similarity criteria between First-Order Logic formulæ, where the presence of relations causes various portions of one description to be possibly mapped in different ways onto another description, which poses serious computational problems. Hence, the need for a set of general criteria that are able to support the comparison between formulæ. This could have many applications; this paper tackles the case of two descriptions (e.g., a definition and an observation) to be generalized, where the similarity criteria could help in focussing on the subparts of the descriptions that are more similar and hence more likely to correspond to each other, based only on their syntactic structure. Experiments on real-world datasets prove the effectiveness of the proposal, and the efficiency of the corresponding implementation in a generalization procedure.

1   Introduction

First-order logic (*FOL* for short) is a powerful formalism, that is able to express relations between objects and hence can overcome the limitations shown by propositional or attribute-value representations. However, the presence of relations causes various portions of one description to be possibly mapped in different ways onto another description, which poses problems of computational effort when two descriptions have to be compared to each other. Hence, the availability of techniques for the comparison between FOL (sub-)descriptions could have many applications, particularly in the Artificial Intelligence community: helping a subsumption procedure to converge quickly, assessing a degree of similarity between two formulæ, implementing a *flexible matching* procedure, supporting instance-based classification techniques or *conceptual clustering*.

As to supervised learning, many systems generalize definitions against observations, and a similarity function could help the procedure in focussing on the components that are more similar and hence more likely to correspond to each other. Clearly, this concerns the semantic aspects of the domain, and hence there is no precise (i.e., algorithmic) way for recognizing the correct (sub-)formulæ. Thus, the problem must be attacked heuristically, by developing some method that can hypothesize which part of a description refers to which part of the other, based only on their syntactic structure. To these aims, partial similarities among description components must be searched for.

R. Basili and M.T. Pazienza (Eds.): AI*IA 2007, LNAI 4733, pp. 278–289, 2007.

Specifically, many first-order Machine Learning systems infer theories in the form of Logic Programs, a restriction of FOL to sets of *Horn clauses*, i.e. logical formulæ of the form $l_1 \wedge \cdots \wedge l_n \Rightarrow l_0$ where the l_i's are *atoms*, usually represented in Prolog style as $l_0 :\text{-} l_1, \ldots, l_n$ to be interpreted as "l_0 (called *head* of the clause) is true, provided that l_1 and ... and l_n (called *body* of the clause) are all true". Without loss of generality [9], we will deal with the case of linked Datalog clauses.

In the following sections, some criteria and a formula on which basing similarity considerations between first-order logic clauses will be presented, that are intended to represent a good tradeoff between significance, effectiveness and expressiveness on one side, and computational efficiency on the other. Then, Section 5 will show how the proposed formula and criteria, are able to effectively guide a clause generalization procedure. Lastly, Section 4 will deal with related work, while 6 will conclude the paper and outline future work directions.

2   Similarity Formula

Intuitively, the evaluation of similarity between two items i' and i'' might be based both on the presence of common features, which should concur in a positive way to the similarity evaluation, and on the features of each item that are not owned by the other (defined as the *residual* of the former with respect to the latter), which should concur negatively to the whole similarity value assigned to them [6]. Thus, plausible similarity parameters are:

n , the number of features owned by i' but not by i'' (*residual* of i' wrt i'');
l , the number of features owned both by i' and by i'';
m , the number of features owned by i'' but not by i' (*residual* of i'' wrt i').

We developed a novel similarity function that expresses the degree of similarity between i' and i'' based on the above parameters:

$$sf(i', i'') = \mathrm{sf}(n, l, m) = 0.5 \frac{l+1}{l+n+2} + 0.5 \frac{l+1}{l+m+2} \tag{1}$$

It takes values in $]0, 1[$, which resembles the theory of probability and hence can help human interpretation of resulting value. A complete overlapping of the model onto the observation tends to the limit of 1 as long as the number of common features grows. The full-similarity value 1 is never reached, which is consistent with the intuition that the only case in which this should happen is the exact identification of items, i.e. $i' = i''$ (in the following, we assume $i' \neq i''$). Conversely, in case of no overlapping the function will tend to 0 as long as the number of non-shared features grows. This is consistent with the intuition that there is no limit to the number of different features owned by the two descriptions, which contribute to make them ever different. Moreover, in case of no features at all in two descriptions ($n = l = m = 0$, e.g., two objects with no characteristics associated) the function evaluates to $1/2$, which can be considered intuitively correct for a case of maximum uncertainty. For instance, one such case is when a model includes an object for which there are no properties to be fulfilled: when comparing it to an observed object without properties as well, one cannot know if the overlapping is actually total because in fact both descriptions have no property at all to be fulfilled, or it just happens that previous generalizations have dropped from the model all the features that it previously owned. Note that each of the two terms refers specifically to one of the two clauses under comparison, and hence a weight could be introduced to give different importance to either of the two.

This formula was developed to overcome some limitations of other formulæ in the literature (e.g., Tverski's, Dice's and Jaccard's); however, the main contribution of this paper is in the exploitation of the formula in various combinations that can assign a similarity degree to the different clause constituents.

3   Similarity Criteria

In FOL formulæ, terms represent specific objects; unary predicates generally represent term properties and n-ary predicates express relationships. Hence, two levels of similarity can be defined for pairs of first-order descriptions: the *object* level, concerning similarities between terms in the descriptions, and the *structure* one, referring to how the nets of relationships in the descriptions overlap.

Example 1. Let us consider, as a running example throughout the paper, the following two clauses (in this case, a rule C and a classified observation E):

$$C : h(X) :\!\text{-}\ p(X,Y), p(X,Z), p(W,X), r(Y,U), o(Y,Z), q(W,W), s(U,V),$$
$$\pi(X), \phi(X), \rho(X), \pi(Y), \sigma(Y), \tau(Y), \phi(Z), \sigma(W), \tau(W), \pi(U), \phi(U).$$
$$E : h(a) :\!\text{-}\ p(a,b), p(a,c), p(d,a), r(b,f), o(b,c), q(d,e), t(f,g),$$
$$\pi(a), \phi(a), \sigma(a), \tau(a), \sigma(b), \tau(b), \phi(b), \tau(d), \rho(d), \pi(f), \phi(f), \sigma(f).$$

3.1   Object Similarity

Consider two clauses C' and C''. Call $A' = \{a'_1, \ldots, a'_n\}$ the set of terms in C', and $A'' = \{a''_1, \ldots, a''_m\}$ the set of terms in C''. When comparing a pair $(a', a'') \in A' \times A''$, i.e. an object taken from C' and one taken from C'', respectively, two kinds of object features can be distinguished: the properties they own as expressed by unary predicates (*characteristic features*), and the ways in which they relate to other objects according to n-ary predicates (*relational features*). More precisely, relational features are defined by the position the object holds among the n-ary predicate arguments, since different positions actually refer to different roles played by the objects. In the following, we will refer to a *role* as a couple $R = (predicate, position)$ (written compactly as $R = predicate/arity.position$). For instance, characteristic features could be `male(X)` or `tall(X)`, while relational features could be expressed by predicates such as `parent(X,Y)`, where specifically the first argument position identifies the 'parent' role ($parent/2.1$), and the second one represents the 'child' role ($parent/2.2$).

Two corresponding similarity values can be associated to a' and a'': a *characteristic similarity*, where (1) is applied to values related to the characteristic features, and a *relational similarity*, based on how many times the two objects play the same or different roles in the n-ary predicates.

The characteristic similarity between a' and a'', $\mathrm{sf}_c(a', a'')$, can be computed, by considering the set P' of properties related to a' and the set P'' of properties related to a'', as $\mathrm{sf}(n_c, l_c, m_c)$ for the following parameters:

$n_c = |P' \setminus P''|$ is the number of properties owned by the object represented by term a' in C' but not by the object represented by term a'' in C'' (*characteristic residual* of a' wrt a'');

$l_c = |P' \cap P''|$ is the number of common properties between the object represented by term a' in C' and the object represented by term a'' in C'';

$m_c = |P'' \setminus P'|$ is the number of properties owned by the object represented by term a'' in C'' but not by the object represented by term a' in C' (*characteristic residual* of a'' wrt a').

A similar technique can be applied to compute the relational similarity between a' and a''. In this case, due to the possibility that one object plays multiple times the same role in different relations (e.g., a parent of many children), we have to consider the *multisets* R' and R'' of roles played by a' and a'', respectively. Hence, the relational similarity between a' and a'', $\mathrm{sf}_r(a', a'')$, can be computed as $\mathrm{sf}(n_r, l_r, m_r)$ for the following parameters:

$n_r = |R' \setminus R''|$ expresses how many times a' plays in C' role(s) that a'' does not play in C'' (*relational residual* of a' wrt a'');

$l_r = |R' \cap R''|$ is the number of times that both a' in C' and a'' in C'' play the same role(s);

$m_r = |R'' \setminus R'|$ expresses how many times a'' plays in C'' role(s) that a' does not play in C' (*relational residual* of a'' wrt a').

Overall, we can define the *object similarity* between two terms as $\mathrm{sf}_o(a', a'') = \mathrm{sf}_c(a', a'') + \mathrm{sf}_r(a', a'')$.

Example 2. The properties and roles for some terms in C and E, and the comparison for some of the possible pairs, are reported in Table 1.

3.2   Structural Similarity

When checking for the structural similarity of two formulæ, many objects can be involved, and hence their mutual relationships represent a constraint on how each of them in the former formula can be mapped onto another in the latter. Differently from the case of objects, what defines the structure of a formula is the set of n-ary predicates, and specifically the way in which they are applied to the various objects to relate them (a predicate, applied to a number of terms equal to its arity, is called an *atom*). This is the most difficult part, since relations are specific to the first-order setting and are the cause of indeterminacy in mapping (parts of) a formula into (parts of) another one. In the following, we will call *compatible* two FOL (sub-)formulæ that can be mapped onto each

Table 1. Object Similarity

C			E		
t'	P'	R'	t''	P''	R''
X	$\{\pi,\phi,\rho\}$	$\{p/2.1,p/2.1,p/2.2\}$	a	$\{\pi,\phi,\sigma,\tau\}$	$\{p/2.1,p/2.1,p/2.2\}$
Y	$\{\pi,\sigma,\tau\}$	$\{p/2.2,r/2.1,o/2.1\}$	b	$\{\sigma,\tau\}$	$\{p/2.2,r/2.1,o/2.1\}$
Z	$\{\phi\}$	$\{p/2.2,o/2.2\}$	c	$\{\phi\}$	$\{p/2.2,o/2.2\}$
W	$\{\sigma,\tau\}$	$\{p/2.1,p/2.1,p/2.2\}$	d	$\{\tau,\rho\}$	$\{p/2.1,p/2.1\}$
U	$\{\pi,\phi\}$	$\{r/2.2,s/2.1\}$	f	$\{\pi,\phi,\sigma\}$	$\{r/2.2,t/2.1\}$

t'/t''	$(P'\setminus P''),(P'\cap P''),(P''\setminus P')$		$(R'\setminus R''),(R'\cap R''),(R''\setminus R')$		$\mathrm{sf}_o(t',t'')$
X/a	$\{\rho\},\{\pi,\phi\},\{\sigma,\tau\}$	$(1,2,2)$	$\emptyset,\{p/2.1,p/2.1,p/2.2\},\emptyset$	$(0,3,0)$	1.35
Y/b	$\{\pi\},\{\sigma,\tau\},\emptyset$	$(1,2,0)$	$\emptyset,\{p/2.2,r/2.1,o/2.1\},\emptyset$	$(0,4,0)$	1.46
Y/c	$\{\pi,\sigma,\tau\},\emptyset,\{\phi\}$	$(3,0,1)$	$\{r/2.1,o/2.1\},\{p/2.2\},\{o/2.2\}$	$(2,1,1)$	0.72
Z/b	$\{\phi\},\emptyset,\{\sigma,\tau\}$	$(1,0,2)$	$\{o/2.2\},\{p/2.2\},\{r/2.1,o/2.1\}$	$(1,1,2)$	0.74
Z/c	$\emptyset,\{\phi\},\emptyset$	$(0,1,0)$	$\emptyset,\{p/2.2,o/2.2\},\emptyset$	$(0,2,0)$	1.42
W/d	$\{\sigma\},\{\tau\},\{\rho\}$	$(1,1,1)$	$\{p/2.2\},\{p/2.1,p/2.1\},\emptyset$	$(1,2,0)$	1.18
U/f	$\emptyset,\{\pi,\phi\},\{\sigma\}$	$(0,2,1)$	$\{s/2.1\},\{r/2.2\},\{t/2.1\}$	$(1,1,1)$	1.18

other without yielding inconsistent term associations (i.e., a term in one formula cannot correspond to different terms in the other formula).

Given an n-ary literal, we define its *star* as the multiset of n-ary predicates corresponding to the literals linked to it by some common term (a predicate can appear in multiple instantiations among these literals). Intuitively, it depicts 'in breadth' how it relates to the rest of the formula. The *star similarity* $\mathrm{sf}_s(l',l'')$ between two compatible n-ary literals l' and l'' having stars S' and S'', respectively, can be computed as $\mathrm{sf}(n_s,l_s,m_s)$ for the following parameters:

$n_s = |S'\setminus S''|$ expresses how many more relations l' has in C' than l'' has in C'' (*star residual* of l' wrt l'');

$l_s = |S'\cap S''|$ is the number of relations that both l' in C' and l'' in C'' have in common;

$m_s = |S''\setminus S'|$ expresses how many more relations l'' has in C'' than l' has in C' (*star residual* of l'' wrt l').

Overall, a more adequate evaluation of similarity between l' and l'' can be obtained by adding to the above result the characteristic and relational similarity values for all pair of their arguments in corresponding positions:

$$\mathrm{sf}_s(l',l'') = \mathrm{sf}(n_s,l_s,m_s) + \Sigma_{t'/t''\in\theta}\mathrm{sf}_o(t',t'')$$

where θ is the set of term associations that map l' onto l''.

Then, any first-order logic formula can be represented as a graph in which atoms are the nodes, and edges connect two nodes *iff* they are related in some way. It follows that a comparison between two formulæ to assess their structural similarity corresponds to the computation of (sub-)graph homomorphisms, a problem known to be *NP*-hard in general, due to the possibility of mapping a (sub-)graph onto another in many different ways. As a consequence, we are interested in heuristics that can give significant hints on the structure overlapping

---

Algorithm 1. Construction of the graph associated to C

Require: $C = l_0 : -l_1, \ldots, l_n$: Clause
  $i \leftarrow 0$; $Level_0 \leftarrow \{l_0\}$; $E \leftarrow \emptyset$; $Atoms \leftarrow \{l_1, \ldots, l_n\}$
  while $Atoms \neq \emptyset$ **do**
    $i \leftarrow i + 1$
    $Level_i \leftarrow \{l \in Atoms \mid \exists l' \in Level_{i-1} s.t. terms(l) \cap terms(l') \neq \emptyset\}$
    $E \leftarrow E \cup \{(l', l'') \mid l' \in Level_{i-1}, l'' \in Level_i, terms(l') \cap terms(l'') \neq \emptyset\}$
    $Atoms \leftarrow Atoms \setminus Level_i$
  end while
  return $G = (\bigcup_i Level_i, E)$: graph associated to C

---

between two formulæ with little computational effort. Indeed, leveraging on the fact that clauses are made up by just a single atom in the head and a conjunction of atoms in the body, we can exploit a graph representation that is easier than that for general formulæ, as described in the following. In particular, we will deal with *linked* clauses only (i.e. clauses whose associated graph is connected), and will build the graph based on a simple (as to the details it expresses about the fomula), yet powerful (as regards the information it conveys) feature, that is term sharing between couples of atoms. Given a clause C, we define its *associated graph* as $G_C = (V, E)$ with

- $V = \{l_0\} \cup \{l_i | i \in \{1, \ldots, n\}, l_i$ built on k-ary predicate, $k > 1\}$ and
- $E \subseteq \{(a_1, a_2) \in V \times V \mid terms(a_1) \cap terms(a_2) \neq \emptyset\}$

where $terms(a)$ denotes the set of terms that appear as arguments of atom a. The strategy for choosing the edges to be represented, summarized in Algorithm 1, leverages on the presence of a single atom in the head to have both a starting point and precise directions for traversing the graph in order to choose a unique and well-defined perspective on the clause structure among the many possible. More precisely, we build a Directed Acyclic Graph (DAG), *stratified* (i.e., with the set of nodes partitioned) in such a way that the head is the only node at level 0 (first element of the partition) and each successive level (element of the partition) is made up by new nodes (not yet reached by edges) that have at least one term in common with nodes in the previous level. In particular, each node in the new level is linked by an incoming edge to each node in the previous level having among its arguments at least one term in common with it.

Example 3. Let us build the graph G_C. The head represents the 0-level of the stratification. Then directed edges may be introduced from $h(X)$ to $p(X, Y)$, $p(X, Z)$ and $p(W, X)$, that are the only atoms having X as an argument, which yields level 1 of the term stratification. Now the next level can be built, adding directed edges from atoms in level 1 to the atoms not yet considered that share a variable with them: $r(Y, U)$ – end of an edge starting from $p(X, Y)$ –, $o(Y, Z)$ – end of edges starting from $p(X, Y)$ and $p(X, Z)$ – and $q(W, W)$ – end of an edge starting from $p(W, X)$. The third and last level of the graph includes the only remaining atom, $s(U, V)$ – having an incoming edge from $r(Y, U)$.

Table 2. Star Similarity

C		E	
l'	S'	l''	S''
$p(X,Y)$	$\{p/2, p/2, r/2, o/2\}$	$p(a,b)$	$\{p/2, p/2, r/2, o/2\}$
$p(X,Z)$	$\{p/2, p/2, o/2\}$	$p(a,c)$	$\{p/2, p/2, o/2\}$
$r(Y,U)$	$\{p/2, o/2, s/2\}$	$r(b,f)$	$\{p/2, o/2, t/2\}$

l'	l''	$(S' \setminus S''), (S' \cap S''), (S'' \setminus S')$	$\mathrm{sf}_s(l', l'')$
$p(X,Y)$	$p(a,b)$	$\emptyset, \{p/2, p/2, r/2, o/2\}, \emptyset \; (0,4,0)$	3.52
$p(X,Y)$	$p(a,c)$	$\{r/2\}, \{p/2, p/2, o/2\}, \emptyset \; (1,3,0)$	2.80
$p(X,Z)$	$p(a,c)$	$\emptyset, \{p/2, p/2, o/2\}, \emptyset \quad (0,3,0)$	3.57
$p(X,Z)$	$p(a,b)$	$\emptyset, \{p/2, p/2, o/2\}, \{r/2\} \; (0,3,1)$	2.82
$r(Y,U)$	$r(b,f)$	$\{s/2\}, \{p/2, o/2\}, \{t/2\} \; (1,2,1)$	3.24

Now, all possible paths starting from the head and reaching *leaf* nodes (those with no outcoming edges) can be interpreted as the basic components of the overall structure of the clause. Being such paths univocally determined reduces the amount of indeterminacy in the comparison. Intuitively, a path depicts 'in depth' a portion of the relations described in the clause. Given two clauses C' and C'', we define the *intersection* between two paths $p' = < l'_1, \ldots, l'_{n'} >$ in $G_{C'}$ and $p'' = < l''_1, \ldots, l''_{n''} >$ in $G_{C''}$ as the pair of longest compatible initial subsequences of p' and p'':

$$p' \cap p'' = (p_1, p_2) = (< l'_1, \ldots, l'_k >, < l''_1, \ldots, l''_k >) \text{ s.t.}$$
$$\forall i = 1, \ldots, k : l'_1, \ldots, l'_i \text{ compatible with } l''_1, \ldots, l''_i \wedge$$
$$(k = n' \vee k = n'' \vee l'_1, \ldots, l'_{k+1} \text{ incompatible with } l''_1, \ldots, l''_{k+1})$$

and the two residuals as the incompatible trailing parts:

$$p' \setminus p'' = < l'_{k+1}, \ldots, l'_{n'} >, p'' \setminus p' = < l''_{k+1}, \ldots, l''_{n''} >)$$

Hence, the *path similarity* between p' and p'', $\mathrm{sf}_s(p', p'')$, can be computed by applying (1) to the following parameters:

$n_p = |p' \setminus p''| = n' - k$ is the length of the trail incompatible sequence of p' wrt p'' (*path residual* of p' wrt p'');

$l_p = |p_1| = |p_2| = k$ is the length of the maximum compatible initial sequence of p' and p'';

$m_p = |p'' \setminus p'| = n'' - k$ is the length of the trail incompatible sequence of p'' wrt p' (*path residual* of p'' wrt p').

plus the star similarity of all couples of literals in the initial sequences:

$$\mathrm{sf}_p(p', p'') = \mathrm{sf}(n_p, l_p, m_p) + \Sigma_{i=1,\ldots,k} \mathrm{sf}_s(l'_i, l''_i)$$

Example 4. Since the head is unique (and hence can be uniquely matched), in the following we will deal only with the body literals for structural criteria. Table 2 reports the star comparisons for a sample of literals in C and E, while Table 3 shows some path comparisons.

Note that no single criterion is by itself neatly discriminant, but their cooperation succeeds in distributing the similarity values and in making the difference ever clearer as long as they are composed one ontop the previous ones.

Table 3. Path Similarity

Path No.	C	E
1.	$< p(X,Y), r(Y,U), s(U,V) >$	$< p(a,b), r(b,f), t(f,g) >$
2.	$< p(X,Y), o(Y,Z) >$	$< p(a,b), o(b,c) >$
3.	$< p(X,Z), o(Y,Z) >$	$< p(a,c), o(b,c) >$
4.	$< p(W,X), q(W,W) >$	$< p(d,a), q(d,e) >$

p' p''	$p' \cap p''$	$p' \setminus p''$ $p'' \setminus p'$	$\theta_{p' \cap p''}$	$(n,l,m)_p$ $\mathrm{sf}_p(p',p'')$
C.1 E.1	$< p(X,Y), r(Y,U) >$ $< p(a,b), r(b,f) >$	$< s(U,V) >$ $< t(f,g) >$	$\{X/a, Y/b, U/f\}$	$(1,2,1)$ 7.36
C.1 E.2	$< p(X,Y) >$ $< p(a,b) >$	$< r(Y,U), s(U,V) >$ $< o(b,c) >$	$\{X/a, Y/b\}$	$(2,1,1)$ 3.97
C.2 E.1	$< p(X,Y) >$ $< p(a,b) >$	$< o(Y,Z) >$ $< r(b,f), t(f,g) >$	$\{X/a, Y/b\}$	$(1,1,2)$ 3.97
C.2 E.2	$< p(X,Y), o(Y,Z) >$ $< p(a,b), o(b,c) >$	$<>$ $<>$	$\{X/a, Y/b, Z/c\}$	$(0,2,0)$ 7.95

Algorithm 2. Similarity-based generalization

Require: C: Rule; E: Example
  $P_C \leftarrow paths(C)$; $P_E \leftarrow paths(E)$;
  $P \leftarrow \{(p_C, p_E) \in P_C \times P_E | p_C \cap p_E \neq (<>, <>)\}$;
  $G \leftarrow \emptyset$; $\theta \leftarrow \emptyset$
  while $P \neq \emptyset$ **do**
    $(\overline{p}_C, \overline{p}_E) \leftarrow \mathrm{argmax}_{(p_C, p_E) \in P}(sf(p_C, p_E))$
    $P \leftarrow P \setminus \{(\overline{p}_C, \overline{p}_E)\}$
    $(\overline{q}_C, \overline{q}_E) \leftarrow p_C \cap p_E$
    $\theta_q \leftarrow$ substitution s.t. $q_C = q_E$
    if θ_q compatible with θ **then**
      $G \leftarrow G \cup q_C$; $\theta \leftarrow \theta \cup \theta_q$
    end if
  end while
  return G: generalization between C and E

Now, a generalization can be computed considering the path intersections by decreasing similarity, adding to the partial generalization generated thus far the common literals of each pair whenever they are compatible (see Algorithm 2). Further generalizations can then be obtained through backtracking. This optionally allows to cut the generalization when some length threshold is reached, ensuring that only the less significant similarities are dropped.

Example 5. The path intersection with highest similarity value is C.3/E.3, and hence the first partial generalization becomes $\{p(X,Z), o(Y,Z)\}$, with associations $\{X/a, Y/b, Z/c\}$. Then C.2/E.2 is considered, whose associations are compatible with the current ones, so it contributes with $\{p(X,Y)\}$ to the generalization (there are no new associations). Then comes C.1/E.1, that being compatible extends the generalization by adding $\{r(Y,U)\}$ and the association with $\{U/f\}$. It is the turn of C.1/E.2 and then of C.2/E.1, that are compatible but redundand, and hence do not add anything to the current generalization (nor to the associations). Then C.4/E.4 is considered, that is compatible and extends with $\{p(W,X)\}$ and $\{W/d\}$ the current generalization and associations, respectively. Lastly C.3/E.2, C.2/E.3, C.3/E.1 and C.1/E.3 are considered, but discarded because of their associations being incompatible.

4   Related Works

Despite of many distance measures developed for attribute-value representations [5], few works faced the definition of similarity or distance measures for first-order descriptions. [4] proposes a distance measure based on probability theory applied to the formula components. Compared to that, our function does not require the assumptions and simplifying hypotheses (statistical independence, mutual exclusion) to ease the probability handling, and no *a-priori* knowledge of the representation language is required (such as the type domains). It does not require the user to set weights on the predicates' importance, and is not based on the presence of 'mandatory' relations, like for the $G1$ subclause in [4].

Many supervised learning systems prove the importance of a distance measure. For instance, KGB [1] uses a similarity function, parameterized by the user, to guide generalization; our ideas of characteristic and relational similarity are very close to those, but the similarity computation is more straightforward. While KGB cannot handle negative information in the clauses, our approach can be easily extended to do that. The k-Nearest Neighbor classifier $RIBL$ [2] is based on a modified version of the function proposed in [1]. The basic idea is that object similarity depends on the similarity of their attributes' values and, recursively, on the similarity of the objects related to them. Such a propagation poses the problem of indeterminacy in associations, that our technique avoids thanks to the different structural approach.

[10] presents an approach for the induction of a distance on FOL examples, that depends on the pattern discriminating the target concepts. k clauses are choosen and the truth values of whether each clause covers the example or not are used as k features for a distance on the space $\{0,1\}^k$ between the examples. [7] organizes terms in an importance-related hierarchy, and proposes a distance between terms based on interpretations and a level mapping function that maps every simple expression on a natural number. [8] presents a distance function

Table 4. Experimental results

		Ratio	Time (sec.)	Cl	Gen	Exc$^+$	Spec$^+$	Spec$^-$	Exc$^-$	Acc
Classification	SF	90.52	579	8	47(+0)	0	2	0	0	0.94
	I	70.22	137	7	33(+100)	0	1	1	1	0.97
	S80	73.63	206	7	33(+13)	0	0	1	1	0.97
Labelling	SF	91.09	22220	36	180(+0)	0	8	3	3	0.89
	I	68.85	33060	39	137(+5808)	0	15	11	12	0.93
	S80	71.75	15941	54	172(+220)	0	14	8	2	0.93

between atoms based on the difference with their lgg, and uses it to compute distances between clauses. It consists of a pair: the first component extends the distance in [7] and is based on the differences between the functors on both terms, while the second component is based on the differences in occurrences of variables and allows to differentiate cases where the first component cannot.

5   Experiments

The similarity-driven generalization procedure was compared to a previous non-guided procedure, embedded in the learning system INTHELEX [3]. The system was set so that, whenever the first generalization returned by the guided procedure was not consistent with all past negative examples, the system could search for more specific ones on backtracking[1]. 10-fold cross-validation was exploited to assess predictive accuracy.

A first comparison on the classical ILP Mutagenesis dataset revealed a slightly better predictive accuracy (87%) than the non-guided version (86%) exploiting only 30% runtime (4035 seconds instead of 13720). Noteworthy, the first generalization found was always correct, and thus no backtracking was ever required to search for other alternatives, whereas the non-guided version computed 5815 additional generalizations to takle cases in which the first generalization found was inconsistent with past examples. This confirmed that the similarity criteria, strategy and formula are able to lead the correct identification of corresponding sub-parts of the compounds descriptions, and convinced us to investigate more deeply on the system behaviour. Other experiments were run on a dataset[2] containing 122 descriptions of scientific papers first page layout, belonging to 4 different classes and corresponding to 488 positive/negative examples for learning document classification rules plus 1488 examples for learning rules to identify 12 kinds of significant logical roles document components (e.g., title, author, abstract). Results are reported in Table 4.

The first question concerns whether the proposed similarity function is actually able to lead towards the identification of the proper sub-parts to be put in correspondence in the two descriptions under comparison. Since the 'correct' association is not known, this can be evaluated only indirectly. A way for doing this is evaluating the 'compression' factor of the guided generalization, i.e., the portion of literals in the clauses to be generalized that is preserved by the generalization. Indeed, since each generalization in INTHELEX must be a subset of either clause to be generalized (because of the Object Identity assumption), the more literals the generalization preserves from these clause, the less general it is. More formally, we evaluate the compression as the ratio between the length of the generalization and that of the shortest clause to be generalized: the

---

[1] In order to avoid the system to waste too much time on difficult generalizations, it was set so to try to generalize another clause (if any) whenever 500 redundant (sub-)generalizations were found on backtracking, or 50 new iconsistent ones were computed, which happened first.

[2] http://lacam.di.uniba.it:8000/systems/inthelex/index.htm#datasets

higher such a value, the more confident one can be that the correct associations were provided by the similarity criteria and formula. Of course, the more the difference in length between the two clauses to be generalized, the more indeterminacy is present, and hence the more difficult it is to identify the proper corresponding parts between them. Interestingly, on the document dataset the similarity-driven generalization (SF) preserved on average more than 90% literals of the shortest clause, with a maximum of 99,48% (193 literals out of 194, against an example of 247) and just 0,006 variance. As a consequence, one woud expect that the produced generalizations are least general ones or nearly so. To check this, instead of computing the actual least general generalization for each performed generalization and compare it to that returned by the guided procedure, that would have been computationally heavy and would require modifying the system behaviour, we counted how many backtrackings the system had to perform in order to reach a more specific one. The outcome was that no more specific generalization was ever found within the given limit, which suggests that the first generalization found is likely to be very near to (and indeed it often is just) the least general one. Note that application of Tverski's similarity formula [11] (a state-of-the-art one in the current literature) to the same setting always returned shortest generalizations than those obtained by using our formula.

However, being such generalizations very specific, they show lower predictive accuracy than the non-guided INTHELEX algorithm (I), probably due to the need of more examples for converging to more predictive definitions or to overfitting. For this reason, the similarity-driven generalization was bound to discard at least 20% literals of the shortest original clause (S80): this led to the same predictive accuracy as I, and dramatically reduced runtime with respect to the unbound version (and also to I on the labelling task). The number of generalizations also decreases, although at the cost of more specialization effort (also by means of negative literals, that are handled as suggested in the previous section), that is in any case more effective than in I (particularly as regards negative exceptions). In the classification task the number of clauses slightly decreases, while in the labelling task it increases of 15, but balanced by 10 negative exceptions less. Noteworthy, the generalizations found are still very tight to the examples, since in the classification experiment only 13 more specific generalizations (of which only 1 correct) were found (and tested for correctness) by backtracking, whereas I found 100, of which 6 correct. In the labelling task, $S80$ found 220 additional candidate generalizations (of which 6 correct) against 5808 (of which 39 correct) of I. This means that one could even avoid backtracking with small loss in $S80$, but not in I.

Another important parameter for comparison is runtime. Table 4 reveals that, on the labelling task, using the similarity function leads to savings that range from 1/3 up to 1/2 of the time, in the order of hours, also on this dataset. The performance on the classification task is in any case comparable (difference in the order of tens of seconds), and can probably be explained with the fact that such a task is easier, so there is little space for improvement and the time needed for computing the formula nullifies the savings.

6   Conclusions

Relations in First-Order Logic lead to indeterminacy in mapping portions of a description onto another one. In this paper we identify a set of criteria and a formula for clause comparison, and exploit it to guide a generalization procedure by indicating the subparts of the descriptions that are more likely to correspond to each other, based only on their syntactic structure. According to the experimental outcomes, the similarity-based generalization is able to capture the correct associations, and can get the same predictive accuracy as the non-guided version, but yielding 'cleaner' theories and dramatically reducing the amount of time required to converge (interestingly, time savings increase as long as the problem complexity grows). Future work will concern fine-tuning of the similarity computation methodology, and its application to other problems, such as flexible matching, conceptual clustering and instance-based learning.

References

[1] Bisson, G.: Learning in FOL with a similarity measure. In: Swartout, W.R. (ed.) Proc. of AAAI-92, pp. 82–87 (1992)

[2] Emde, W., Wettschereck, D.: Relational instance based learning. In: Saitta, L. (ed.) Proc. of ICML-96, pp. 122–130 (1996)

[3] Esposito, F., Ferilli, S., Fanizzi, N., Basile, T., Di Mauro, N.: Incremental multistrategy learning for document processing. Applied Artificial Intelligence Journal 17(8/9), 859–883 (2003)

[4] Esposito, F., Malerba, D., Semeraro, G.: Classification in noisy environments using a distance measure between structural symbolic descriptions. IEEE Transactions on PAMI 14(3), 390–402 (1992)

[5] Li, M., Chen, X., Li, X., Ma, B., Vitanyi, P.: The similarity metric (2003)

[6] Lin, D.: An information-theoretic definition of similarity. In: Proc. 15th International Conf. on Machine Learning, pp. 296–304. Morgan Kaufmann, San Francisco, CA (1998)

[7] Nienhuys-Cheng, S.: Distances and limits on herbrand interpretations. In: Page, D.L. (ed.) Inductive Logic Programming. LNCS, vol. 1446, pp. 250–260. Springer, Heidelberg (1998)

[8] Ramon, J.: Clustering and instance based learning in first order logic. PhD thesis, Dept. of Computer Science, K.U.Leuven, Belgium (2002)

[9] Rouveirol, C.: Extensions of inversion of resolution applied to theory completion. In: Inductive Logic Programming, pp. 64–90. Academic Press, London (1992)

[10] Sebag, M.: Distance induction in first order logic. In: Džeroski, S., Lavrač, N. (eds.) Inductive Logic Programming. LNCS, vol. 1297, pp. 264–272. Springer, Heidelberg (1997)

[11] Tversky, A.: Features of similarity. Psychological Review 84(4), 327–352 (1977)

Structured Hidden Markov Model: A General Framework for Modeling Complex Sequences

Ugo Galassi, Attilio Giordana, and Lorenza Saitta

Dipartimento di Informatica, Università Amedeo Avogadro
Via Bellini 25G, Alessandria, Italy

Abstract. Structured Hidden Markov Model (S-HMM) is a variant of Hierarchical Hidden Markov Model that shows interesting capabilities of extracting knowledge from symbolic sequences. In fact, the S-HMM structure provides an abstraction mechanism allowing a high level symbolic description of the knowledge embedded in S-HMM to be easily obtained. The paper provides a theoretical analysis of the complexity of the matching and training algorithms on S-HMMs. More specifically, it is shown that Baum-Welch algorithm benefits from the so called locality property, which allows specific components to be modified and retrained, without doing so for the full model. The problem of modeling duration and of extracting (embedding) readable knowledge from (into) a S-HMM is also discussed.

1 Introduction

Since their introduction, Hidden Markov Models (HMMs) proved to be a fundamental tool in solving real-world pattern recognition problems, notably speech recognition [14] and DNA analysis [4]. However, HMMs are stochastic models including a potentially high number of parameters; hence, many research efforts have been devoted to constrain their structure in such a way to reduce the complexity of the parameter estimation task. To this aim have been proposed, for instance, the *hierarchical* HMM [5,12] and the *factorial* HMM [8],

In this paper we aim at reducing the generality of the HMM's structure as well, but with an additional goal with respect to previous works: in fact, not only parameter estimation must be efficiently performed, but also the model itself should offer a high level, interpretable description of the knowledge it encodes, in a way understandable by a human user. In several application domains (*e.g.*, Molecular Biology [4]), this requirement is of primary concern when evaluation of the model has to be done by humans. Moreover, in this way, domain knowledge provided by an expert could be easily integrated, as well.

More specifically, this paper investigates a variant of HMM called *structured* HMM [7] (S-HMM in the following). An S-HMM is a graph built up, according to precise composition rules, with several "independent" sub-graphs (sub-models).

After a brief introduction of the S-HMM, its properties are formally analyzed: first of all it will be shown how an S-HMM can be locally trained using the classical Baum-Welch algorithm, considering only a subset of the sub-models

R. Basili and M.T. Pazienza (Eds.): AI*IA 2007, LNAI 4733, pp. 290–301, 2007.

occurring in the compound one. A nice consequence of this property is that an S-HMM can be constructed and trained incrementally, by adding new sub-models or revising existing ones as new information comes in. A newly added sub-model may have different origins: for instance, it may be provided by an expert as a-priori knowledge, or it can be produced by an independent learning process. An interesting property of an S-HMM is that sub-models may also correspond to *gaps* in the observed sequences, *i.e.*, to not meaningful or not interesting regions. This ability elegantly solves the problem of building models of complex and *sparse* patterns. Finally, S-HMM is compared to other existing approaches such HHMM [5].

2   The Structured HMM

The basic assumption underlying an S-HMM (see Bouchaffra and Tan [3]) is that a sequence $O = \{o_1, o_2, o_3, ..., o_T\}$ of observations could be segmented into a set of subsequences $O_1, O_2, ..., O_N$, each one generated by a sub-process with only weak interactions with its neighbors. This assumption is realistic in many practical applications, such as, for instance, speech recognition [14,15], and DNA analysis [4]. In speech recognition, regions are phonetic segments, like syllables, corresponding to recurrent structures in the language. In DNA, they may be biologically significant segments (*motifs*) interleaved with non-coding segments (such as *junk-DNA*). S-HMMs aim exactly at modeling such kind of processes, and, hence, they are represented as directed graphs, structured into sub-graphs (*blocks*), each one modeling a specific kind of sub-sequences.

Informally, a block consists of a set of states, only two of which (the *initial* and the *end* state) are allowed to be connected to other blocks. As an S-HMM is itself a block, a nesting mechanism is immediate to define.

2.1   Structure of a Block

In this section, a formal definition of S-HMM will be provided. Adopting the notation used in [14], O will denote a sequence of observations $\{o_1, o_2, ..., o_T\}$, where every observation o_t is a symbol v_k chosen from an alphabet V. An HMM is a stochastic automaton characterized by a set of states Q, an alphabet V, and a triple $\lambda = \langle A, B, \pi \rangle$, being:

- $A : Q \times Q \to [0,1]$ a probability distribution, a_{ij}, governing the transition from state q_i to state q_j;
- $B : Q \times V \to [0,1]$ a probability distribution, $b_i(v_k)$, governing the emission of symbols in each state $q_i \in Q$;
- $\pi : Q \to [0,1]$ a distribution assigning to each state $q_i \in Q$ the probability of being the start state.

A state q_i will be said a *silent* state if $\forall v_k \in V : b_i(v_k) = 0$, *i.e.*, q_i does not emit any observable symbol. When entering a silent state, the time counter must not be incremented.

292 U. Galassi, A. Giordana, and L. Saitta

Definition 1. *A basic block of an S-HMM is a 4-tuple $\lambda = \langle A, B, I, E \rangle$, where $I, E \in Q$ are silent states such that: $\pi(I) = 1$, $\forall q_i \in Q : a_{iI} = 0$, and $\forall q_i \in Q : a_{Ei} = 0$.*

In other words, I and E are the input and the output states, respectively. Therefore, a composite block can be defined by connecting, through a transition network, the input and output states of a set of blocks.

Definition 2. *Given an ordered set of blocks $\Lambda = \{\lambda_i | 1 \leq i \leq N\}$, a composite block is a 4-tuple $\lambda = \langle A_I, A_E, I, E \rangle$, where:*

- *$A_I : \mathbf{E} \times \mathbf{I} \to [0, 1]$, $A_E : \mathbf{I} \times \mathbf{E} \to [0, 1]$ are probability distributions governing the transitions from the output states $\mathbf{E}$ to the input states $\mathbf{I}$, and from the input states $\mathbf{I}$ to the output states $\mathbf{E}$ of the component blocks Λ, respectively.*
- *For all pairs $\langle E_i, I_j \rangle$ the transition probability $a_{E_i I_j} = 0$ if $j \leq i$.*
- *$I \equiv I_1$ and $E \equiv E_N$ are the input and output states of the composite block, respectively.*

According to Definition 2 the components of a composite block can be either basic blocks or, in turn, composite blocks. In other words, composite blocks can be arbitrarily nested. Moreover, we will keep the notation S-HMM to designate non-basic blocks only.

As a special case, a block can degenerate to the *null block*, which consists of the start and end states only, connected by an edge with probability $a_{IE} = 1$. The *null block* is useful to provide a dummy input state I or a dummy output state E, when no one of the component block is suited to this purpose.

An example of S-HMM structured into three blocks λ_1, λ_2, λ_3, and two *null blocks* λ_0, λ_4, providing the start and the end states, is described in Figure 1.

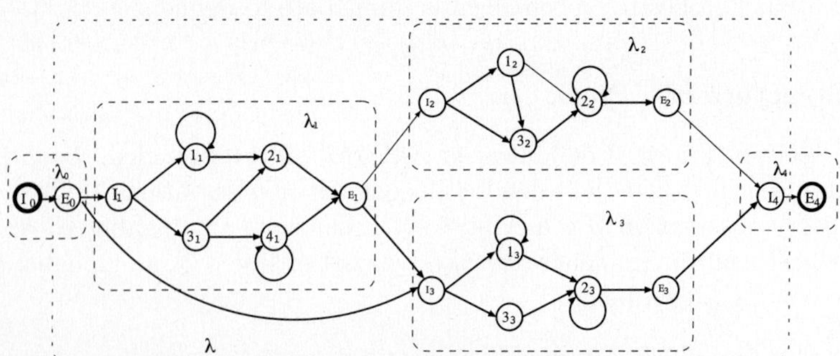

Fig. 1. Example of Structured Hidden Markov Model composed of three interconnected blocks, plus two *null blocks*, λ_0 and λ_4, providing the start and end states. Distribution A is non-null only for explicitly represented arcs.

2.2 Estimating Probabilities in S-HMM

As formally stated in [14], three problems are associated with the HMM approach:

1. given a model λ and a sequence of observations O, compute the probability $P(O|\lambda)$;
2. given a model λ and a sequence of observations O, assumed to be generated by λ, compute the most likely sequence of states in λ;
3. given a model λ and a sequence of observations O (or a set of sequences [15]), estimate the parameters in λ in order to maximize $P(O|\lambda)$.

The classical solution to Problem 1 and 3 relies on two functions α and β, plus other auxiliary functions γ and ξ, defined on α and β. The classical solution to Problem 2 relies on Viterbi algorithm [6], which implements a function computationally analogous to α. In the following we will extend α and β to S-HMMs in order to prove some properties to be exploited by an incremental learning algorithm.

Given a sequence of observations $O = \{o_1, o_2, ..., o_t, .., o_T\}$ and a model λ, the function $\alpha_t(i)$ computes, for every time t $(1 \leq t \leq T)$, the joint probability of being in state q_i and observing the symbols from o_1 to o_t.

Let us consider an S-HMM λ containing N blocks. We want to define the recursive equations allowing α to be computed. In order to do this, we have to extend the standard definition in order to include silent states: when leaving a silent state, the time counter is not incremented. When entering the block $\lambda_k = \langle A_k, B_k, I_k, E_k \rangle$ with N_k states, at time r $(1 \leq r \leq T)$, the following equations are to be used:

$$
\begin{aligned}
\alpha_r(I_k) &= P(o_1, ..., o_r, q_r = I_k) \\
\alpha_t(j) &= \alpha_{t-1}(I_k)a_{I_k j}^{(k)}b_j^{(k)}(o_t) + \sum_{i=1}^{N_k} \alpha_{t-1}(i)a_{ij}^{(k)}b_j^{(k)}(o_t) \\
&\quad (r+1 \leq t \leq T, 1 \leq j \leq N_k, q_j \neq I_k, q_j \neq E_k) \\
\alpha_t(E_k) &= \alpha_t(I_k) + \sum_{i=1}^{N_k} \alpha_t(i)a_{jE_k}^{(k)}
\end{aligned}
\tag{1}
$$

Notice that the above equations only depends upon external states through the values of $\alpha_r(I_k)$ $(1 \leq r \leq T)$ computed for the input state; moreover, the block propagates $\alpha_t(E_k)$ $(1 \leq t \leq T)$ to the following blocks only through the output state. Finally, $\alpha_1(I_1) = 1$ and $\alpha_T(E_N) = P(O|\lambda)$.

Funtion $\beta_t(i)$ is complementary to $\alpha_t(i)$, and computes the probability of observing the symbols $o_{t+1}, o_{t+2}, ... , o_T$, given that q_i is the state at time t. For β a backward recursive definition can be given:

$$
\begin{aligned}
\beta_r(E_k) &= P(o_{r+1}, ..., o_T | q_r = E_k) \\
\beta_t(i) &= \beta_{t+1}(E_k)a_{iE_k}^{(k)} + \sum_{j=1}^{N_k} \beta_{t+1}(j)b_j^{(k)}(o_{t+1})a_{ij}^{(k)} \\
&\quad (1 \leq t \leq r-1, 1 \leq i \leq N_k, q_i \neq E_k, q_i \neq I_k) \\
\beta_t(I_k) &= \beta_t(E_k) + \sum_{j=1}^{N_k} \beta_t(j)a_{I_k j}^{(k)}
\end{aligned}
\tag{2}
$$

From equations (2), it follows that $P(O|\lambda) = \beta_1(I_1)$.

Definition 3. *An S-HMM is said a forward S-HMM when for all non-basic blocks the matrix A_I and A_E define a directed acyclic graph.*

For a forward S-HMM it is easy to prove the following theorem.

Theorem 1. *In a forward S-HMM, the complexity of computing functions α and β is:*

$$C \leq T\left(\sum_{h=1}^{N_C} N_h^2 + M \sum_{k=1}^{N} N_k^2\right)$$

being N_h the dimension of matrix $A_I^{(h)}$ of the $h-th$ block, M the cardinality of the alphabet, N_C the number of composite blocks, and N the number of basic blocks.

Proof. Notice that the second summation in the right-hand side of the formula corresponds to the computation of α and β inside the basic blocks, whereas the first summation is due to the block interconnection. Following the block recursive nesting and starting from the basic blocks, we observe that, in absence of any hypothesis on distribution A, each basic block is an HMM, whose complexity for computing α and β is upperbounded by $N_k^2 MT$ [14]. As the global network interconnecing the basic blocks is a directed forward graph, every basic block needs to be evaluated only once.

Let us consider now a composite block; the interconnecting structure is an oriented forward graph, by definition, and, then, equations (1) and (2) must be evaluated only once on the input (output) of every internal block S-HMM$_h$. As a conclusion, the complexity for this step in upperbounded by TN_h^2.

3   S-HMMs Are Locally Trainable

The classical algorithm for estimating the probability distributions governing state transitions and observations are estimated by means of the Baum-Welch algorithm [2,14], which relies on the functions α and β defined in the previous section. In the following we will briefly review the algorithm in order to adapt it to S-HMMs. The algorithm uses two functions, ξ and γ, defined through α and β. Function $\xi_t(i,j)$ computes the probability of the transition between states q_i (at time t) and q_j (at time $t+1$), assuming that the observation O has been generated by model λ:

$$\xi_t(i,j) = \frac{\alpha_t(i)a_{ij}b_j(O_{t+1})\beta_{t+1}(j)}{P(O|\lambda)} \tag{3}$$

Function $\gamma_t(i)$ computes the probability of being in state q_i at time t, assuming that the observation O has been generated by model λ, and can be written as:

$$\gamma_t(i) = \frac{\alpha_t(i)\beta_t(i)}{P(O|\lambda)} \tag{4}$$

The sum of $\xi_t(i,j)$ over t estimates the number of times transition $q_i \rightarrow q_j$ occurs when λ generates the sequence O. In an analogous way, by summing $\gamma_t(i)$ over t, an estimate of the number of times state q_i has been visited is obtained. Then a_{ij} can be re-estimated (a-posteriori, after seeing O) as the ratio of the sum over time of $\xi_t(i,j)$ and $\gamma_t(i)$:

$$\bar{a}_{ij} = \frac{\sum_{t=1}^{T-1} \alpha_t(i)a_{ij}b_j(O_{t+1})\beta_{t+1}(j)}{\sum_{t=1}^{T-1} \alpha_t(i)\beta_t(i)} \tag{5}$$

With a similar reasoning it is possible to obtain an a-posteriori estimate of the probability of observing $o = v_k$ when the model is in state q_j. The estimate is provided by the ratio between the number of times state q_j has been visited and symbol v_k has been observed, and the total number of times q_j has been visited:

$$\bar{b}_j(k) = \frac{\sum_{t=1_{o_t=v_k}}^{T-1} \alpha_t(j)\beta_t(j)}{\sum_{t=1}^{T-1} \alpha_t(j)\beta_t(j)} \tag{6}$$

From (1) and (2) it appears that, inside basic block λ_k, equations (5) and (6) are immediately applicable. Then the Baum-Welch algorithm can be used without any change to learn the probability distributions inside basic blocks.

On the contrary, equation (5) must be modified in order to adapt it to re-estimate transition probabilities between output and input states of the blocks, which are silent states. As there is no emission, α and β propagate through transitions without time change; then, equation (5) must be modified as in the following:

$$\bar{a}_{E_i I_j} = \frac{\sum_{t=1}^{T-1} \alpha_t(E_i)a_{E_i I_j}\beta_t(I_j)}{\sum_{t=1}^{T-1} \alpha_t(E_i)\beta_t(I_j)} \tag{7}$$

It is worth noticing that functions α and β depend upon the states in other blocks only through the value of $\alpha_t(I_k)$ and $\beta_t(E_k)$, respectively. This means that, in block λ_k, given the vectors $\alpha_1(I_k), \alpha_2(I_k), ...\alpha_T(I_k)$ and $\beta_1(E_k), \beta_2(E_k), ...\beta_T(E_k)$, Baum-Welch algorithm can be iterated inside a block without the need of recomputing α and β in the external blocks. We will call this a *locality property*. The practical implication of the locality property is that a block can be modified and trained without any impact on the other components of an S-HMM.

4   Applying S-HMM to Real World Tasks

Most HMM applications can be reduced to classification (instances of *Problem 1*) or interpretation (instances of *Problem 2*) tasks. Word recognition and user/process profiling are typical classification tasks. Sequence tagging and knowledge extraction, as done in DNA analysis, are typical interpretation tasks. In this section we will focus on the problem of knowledge extraction, but most of the proposed solutions also hold for classification tasks.

A model for interpreting a sequence is a *global* model, able to identify interesting patterns (*i.e.*, *motifs*, adopting Bio-Informatics terminology), which occur with significant regularity, as well as *gaps, i.e.*, regions where no regularities are found. Having a global model of the sequence is important, because it allows inter-dependencies among motifs to be detected. Nevertheless, a global model must account for the distribution of the observations on the entire sequence, and hence it could become intractable. We tame this problem by introducing special basic blocks, designed to keep low the complexity of modeling the irrelevant parts of sequences.

In the following we address the following issues: (a) how to construct basic blocks modeling motifs; (b) how to construct models of gaps between motifs; (c) how to segment a sequence detecting the instances of the basic blocks; (d) how to extract a readable interpretation from a sequence.

4.1   Motif Modeling

A motif is a subsequence frequently occurring in a reference sequence set. Motif occurrences may be different from one to another, provided that an assigned equivalence relation be satisfied. In the specific case, the equivalence relation is encoded through a basic block of an S-HMM. Many proposals exist for HMM architectures oriented to capture specific patterns. Here, we will consider the Profile HMM (PHMM), a model developed in Bio-Informatics [4], which well fits the needs of providing a readable interpretation of a sequence. The basic assumption underlying PHMM is that the different instances of a motif originate from a canonical form, but are subject to insertion, deletion and substitution errors.

As described in Figure 2, a PHMM has a left-to-right structure with a very restricted number of arcs. Moreover, it makes use of *typed* states: *Match* states, where the observation corresponds to the expectation, *Delete* states (silent states) modeling deletion errors, and *Insert* states modeling insertion errors supposedly due to random noise. According to this assumption, the observation distribution in all insert states is the same, and it can be estimated just once.

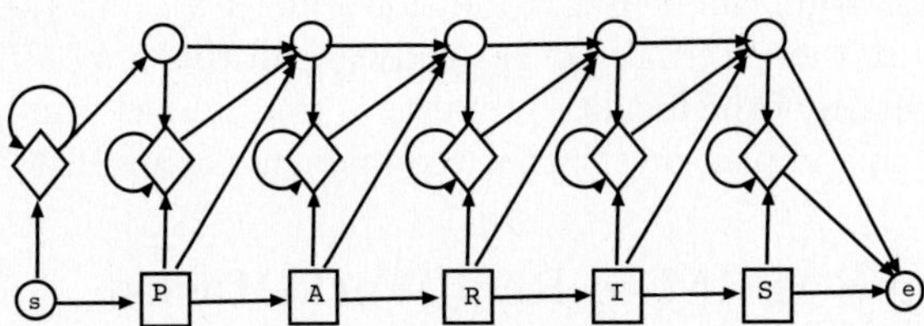

Fig. 2. Example of Profile Hidden Markov Model. Circles denote states with *no-observable* emission, rectangles denote *match states*, and diamond denote *insert states*.

After training, the canonical form can be easily extracted from a PHMM, by collecting the maximum likelihood observation sequence from the match states.

4.2   Modeling Duration and Gaps

The problem of modeling durations arises when the time span covered by an observation or the interval length between two observations is important. In the HMM framework, this problem has been principally faced in Speech Recognition and in Bio-informatics. However, the problem setting is slightly different in the two fields, and consequently the dominant approach tends to be different. In speech recognition, the input is a continuous signal, which, after several steps of signal processing, is segmented into variable length intervals each one labeled with a symbol. Then, the obtained symbolic sequence is fed into a set of HMMs, which accomplish the recognition of long range structure, such as syllables or words, requiring thus to deal with interval durations [11]. In Bio-informatics the major application for HMMs is the analysis of DNA strands [4]. Here, the input sequence is a string of equal length symbols. The need of modeling duration comes from the presence of gaps, *i.e.*, substrings where no coding information is present. The gap duration is often a critical cues to interpret the entire sequence.

The approach first developed in Speech Recognition is to use Hidden Semi-Markov Models (HSMM), which are HMMs augmented with probability distributions over the state permanence [11,10,13,17,16]. An alternative approach is the so called *Expanded HMM* [10]. Every state, where it is required to model duration, is expanded into a network of states, properly interconnected. In this way, the duration of the permanence in the original state is modeled by a sequence of transitions through the new state network in which the observation remain constant. The advantage of this method is that the markovian nature of the HMM is preserved. Nevertheless, the complexity increases according to the number of new states generated by expansion.

A similar solution is found in Bio-Informatics for modeling long gaps. In this case, the granularity of the sequence is given, and so there is no expansion. However, the resulting model of the gap duration is similar to the one mentioned above. A Profile HMM [4], naturally models the duration of observations

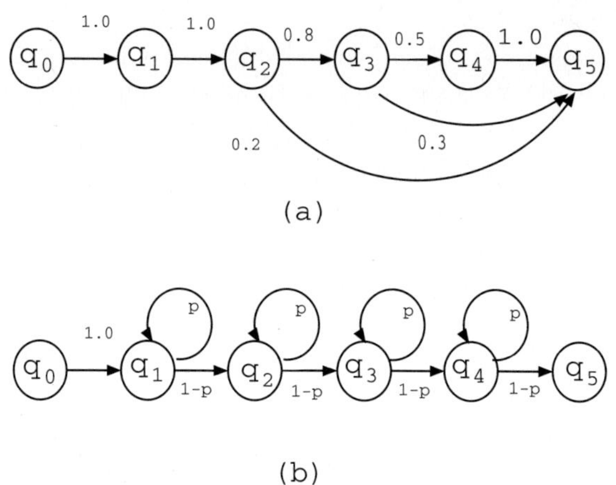

Fig. 3. Possible HMMs for modeling duration

according to the expansion technique, but it is only able to model short gaps inside a motif, attributed to random noise controlled by a Poisson statistics. Nevertheless, single insertion states do not correctly model long gaps occurring in between two motifs. The most appropriate probability distribution for this kind of gaps may vary from case to case, but it is never the exponential decay defined by an insert state with a self-loop.

Two HMM topologies, suitable for modeling gaps, are reported in Figure 3. The architecture in Figure 3(a) can be used to model any duration distribution over a finite and discrete interval. However, the drawback of this model is the potentially large number of parameters to estimate. In all cases, the observation is supposed to be produced by random noise. Model in Figure 3(b) exhibits an Erlang's distribution, when the Forward-Backward algorithm is used. Unfortunately, the distribution of the most likely duration computed by Viterbi algorithm still follows an exponential law. Therefore, this model, which is more compact with respect to the previous one, is not useful for the task of segmenting and tagging sequences by means of Viterbi algorithm.

4.3   Sequence Segmentation

In the S-HMM framework, sequence segmentation means detecting where boundaries between blocks are most likely located. Segmentation provides a probabilistic interpretation of a sequence model, and plays a fundamental role when an S-HMM is used for knowledge extraction.

Two methods exist for accomplishing this task. The classical one is based on Viterbi algorithm in order to find the most likely path in the state space of the model. Then, for every pair of blocks λ_r, λ_s on the path, the most likely time instant for the transition from the output state of λ_r to the input state of λ_s is chosen as the boundary between the two blocks. In this way a unique, non ambiguous segmentation is obtained, with a complexity which is the same as for computing α and β.

The second method, also described in [14], consists in finding the maximum likelihood time for the transition from λ_r to λ_s by computing:

$$\tau_{rs} = argmax_t \left(\frac{\xi_t(E_r, I_s)}{\gamma_t(E_r)} \right) \tag{8}$$

Computing boundaries by means of (8) requires a complexity $O(T)$ for every boundary that has to be located, in addition to the complexity for computing one α and β.

The advantage of this method is that it can provide alternative segmentations by considering also blocks that do not ly on the maximum likelihood path. Moreover, it is compatible with the use of gap models of the type described in Figure 3(c), because it does not use Viterbi algorithm.

4.4   Knowledge Transfer

When a tool is used in a knowledge extraction task, two important features are desirable: (a) the extracted knowledge should be readable for a human user; (b) a human user should be able to elicit chunks of knowledge, which the tool will exploit during the extraction process.

The basic HMM does not have such properties, whereas task oriented HMMs, such as Profile HMM, may provide such properties to a limited extent. On the contrary, the S-HMM structure naturally supports high level logical descriptions. An example of how an S-HMM can be described in symbolic form is provided

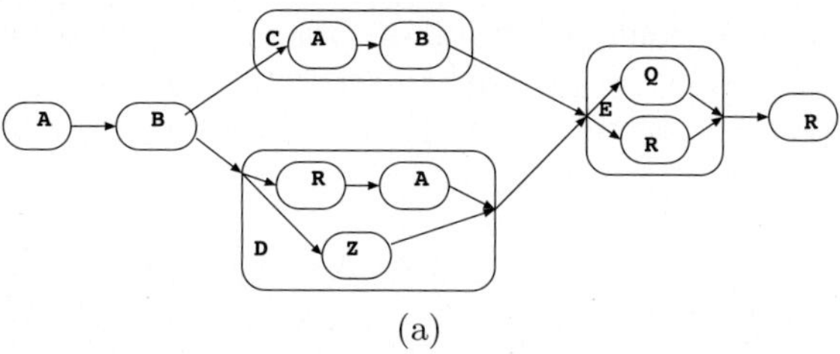

(a)

(b) Basic block description:

$motif(x) \wedge MLS(x,"ctgaac") \wedge AvDev(x,0.15) \rightarrow A(x)$
$motif(x) \wedge MLS(x,"cctctaaa") \wedge AvDev(x,0.15) \rightarrow R(x)$
$motif(x) \wedge MLS(x,"tatacgc") \wedge AvDev(x,0.15) \rightarrow Q(x)$
$gap(x) \wedge AvDr(x,11.3) \wedge MnDr(x,8) \wedge MxDr(x,14) \rightarrow B(x)$
$gap(x) \wedge AvDr(x,15.6 \wedge MnDr(x,12) \wedge MxDr(x,19) \rightarrow Z(x)$

(c) Block structure logical description:

$A(x) \wedge B(y) \wedge follow(x,y) \rightarrow C([x,y])$
$R(x) \wedge A(y) \wedge follow(x,y) \rightarrow D([x,y])$
$Z(x) \rightarrow D(x), \quad Q(x) \rightarrow E(x), \quad R(x) \rightarrow E(x)$
$B(x) \wedge C(y) \wedge follow(x,y) \rightarrow G([x,y]$
$B(x) \wedge D(y) \wedge follow(x,y) \rightarrow G([x,y]$
$A(x) \wedge G(y) \wedge E(z) \wedge R(w) \wedge follow(x,y) \wedge$
$\qquad \wedge follow(y,z) \wedge follow(z,w) \rightarrow MySEQ([x,y,z,w)]$

(d) Block structure as a regular expression:

A (B (AB — (RA — Z)))(Q—R) R

Fig. 4. Structured HMMs are easy to translate into an approximate logic description

in Figure 4. Basic blocks and composite blocks must be described in different
ways. Basic blocks are either HMMs (modeling subsequences), or gap models. In
both cases, a precise description of the underlying automaton will be complex,
without providing readable information to the user. Instead, an approximate description, characterizing at an abstract level the knowledge captured by a block,
is more useful. For instance, blocks corresponding to regularities like *motifs* can
be characterized by providing the maximum likelihood sequence (MLS) as the
nominal form of the sequence, and the average deviation (AvDv) from the nominal form. Instead, gaps can be characterized by suppling the average duration
(AvDr), and the minimum (MnDr) and maximum (MxDr) duration.

On the contrary, the model's composite structure is easy to describe by means
of a logic language. As an example, Figure 4(c) provides the translation into Horn
clauses, whereas Figure 4(d) provides the translation into regular expressions. In
both cases, richer representations can be obtained by annotating the expressions
with numeric attributes.

By using a logic description language, or regular expressions, a user can also
provide the specification of an S-HMM structure, or part of it, which will be
completed and trained by a learning algorithm. Logic formulas as in Figure 4(c)
can be immediately translated into the structure of composite blocks. Nevertheless, also an approximate specification for basic blocks, as described in Figure
4, can be mapped to block models when the model scheme is given. For instance, suppose that motifs are described by Profile HMMs, and gaps by the
scheme of Figure 3(a) or (b). Then, the maximum likelihood sequence provided
in the logic description implicitly sets the number of match states and, together
with the average deviation, provides the prior for an initial distribution on the

observations. In an analogous way, minimum, maximum and average values specified for the gap duration can be used to set the number of states and a prior on the initial probability distribution. Then, a training algorithm can tune the model parameters.

5 Conclusive Remarks

In the previous sections we have formally defined an S-HMM, showing how it can be used to model complex patterns in symbolic sequences. S-HMMs are an attempt to unify in a formal framework previous attempts, which we briefly review in this section.

First of all it is worth noticing that S-HMMs derive from Hierarchical HMMs (HHMM)[5], in that both construct a hierarchy of HMMs. The difference is that a block in an S-HMM can be reached from only one state in a block at higher level, whereas in a generalized HHMM, many ancestors may exists. For this reason, an HHMM is not easy to handle for the purposes addressed in this paper; in fact, re-structuring or compiling an HHMM into a single level HMM poses non trivial problems. S-HMMs addresses this point by means of silent states and of further constraints on the structure. In this way, the same structure can be considered at the desired abstraction level without needing any reformulation of the HMMs. The most important property of an S-HMM is *locality*, which can be exploited for incrementally constructing very complex models.

A similar proposal was put forward by Bouchaffra and Tan [3], who proposed Structural HMMs (SHMM in the following). The initial goal of SHMMs was analogous to the one that inspired S-HMM, *i.e.*, to capture in an HMM local regularities in the observation sequences. However, SHMMs have been developed primarily for segmentation problems, setting the emphasis on data structure, while the structure of the model remains somehow implicit. S-HMMs explicitly put the emphasis on the model structure and on its compositional properties. Then, quite different formalizations have been obtained. Nevertheless, the relations between the two models deserve further investigations.

Another relevant point concerns modeling duration; many authors tend to handle this aspect by using continuous time distributions on the state permanence. We only considered modeling duration through the expanded state approach, which is made possible because of the low complexity inherent to an S-HMM. Modeling durations with continuous distributions over the time does not seem the right way to go, because it will dramatically increase the complexity, being then not suitable to exploit the S-HMM structure.

References

1. Bailey, T., Elkan, C.: Fitting a mixture model by expectation maximization to discover motifs in biopolymers. In: Proceedings of the Second International Conference on Intelligent Systems for Molecular Biology, pp. 28–36. AAAI Press, Menlo Park, California (1994)

2. Baum, L.E., Petrie, T., Soules, G., Weiss, N.: A maximisation techniques occurring in the statistical analysis of probabilistic functions of markov chains. The Annals of Mathematical Statistics 41(1), 164–171 (1970)
3. Bouchaffra, D., Tan, J.: Structural hidden markov models using a relation of equivalence: Application to automotive designs. Data Mining and Knowledge Discovery 12, 79–96 (2006)
4. Durbin, R., Eddy, S., Krogh, A., Mitchison, G.: Biological sequence analysis. Cambridge University Press, Cambridge (1998)
5. Fine, S., Singer, Y., Tishby, N.: The hierarchical hidden markov model: Analysis and applications. Machine Learning 32, 41–62 (1998)
6. Forney, G.D.: The viterbi algorithm. Proceedings of IEEE 61, 268–278 (1973)
7. Galassi, U., Giordana, A., Saitta, L.: Incremental construction of structured hidden markov models. In: proceedings IJCAI-2007, pp. 2222–2227 (2007)
8. Ghahramani, Z., Jordan, M.: Factorial hidden markov models. Machine Learning 2, 1–31 (1997)
9. Grundy, N.W., Bailey, T., Elkan, C., Baker, M.: Meta-meme: Motif-based hidden markov models of biological sequences. Computer Applications in the Biosciences 13(4), 397–406 (1997)
10. Josep, A.B.: Duration modeling with expanded hmm applied to speech recognition
11. Levinson, S.: Continuous variable duration hidden markov models for automatic speech recognition. Computer Speech and Language 1, 29–45 (1986)
12. Murphy, K., Paskin, M.: Linear time inference in hierarchical hmms. In: Advances in Neural Information Processing Systems (NIPS-01), vol. 14 (2001)
13. Pylkknen, J., Kurimo, M.: Using phone durations in finnish large vocabulary continuous speech recognition (2004)
14. Rabiner, L.R.: A tutorial on hidden markov models and selected applications in speech recognition. Proceedings of IEEE 77(2), 257–286 (1989)
15. Rabiner, L., Juang, B.: Fundamentals of Speech Recognition. Prentice Hall, Englewood Cliffs, NY (1993)
16. Tweed, D., Fisher, R., Bins, J., List, T.: Efficient hidden semi-markov model inference for structured video sequences. In: Proc. 2nd Joint IEEE Int. Workshop on VSPETS, Beijing, China, pp. 247–254. IEEE Computer Society Press, Los Alamitos (2005)
17. Yu, S.-Z., Kobashi, H.: An efficient forward-backward algorithm for an explicit duration hidden markov model. IEEE Signal Processing Letters 10(1) (2003)

Nearest Local Hyperplane Rules
for Pattern Classification

Gábor Takács and Béla Pataki

Budapest University of Technology and Economics,
Department of Measurement and Information Systems,
Magyar Tudósok körútja 2., 1117 Budapest, Hungary
{gtakacs, pataki}@mit.bme.hu

Abstract. Predicting the class of an observation from its nearest neighbors is one of the earliest approaches in pattern recognition. In addition to their simplicity, nearest neighbor rules have appealing theoretical properties, e.g. the asymptotic error probability of the plain 1-nearest-neighbor (NN) rule is at most twice the Bayes bound, which means zero asymptotic risk in the separable case. But given only a finite number of training examples, NN classifiers are often outperformed in practice. A possible modification of the NN rule to handle separable problems better is the nearest local hyperplane (NLH) approach. In this paper we introduce a new way of NLH classification that has two advantages over the original NLH algorithm. First, our method preserves the zero asymptotic risk property of NN classifiers in the separable case. Second, it usually provides better finite sample performance.

1 Introduction

Organizing things into categories is an everyday act of human mind. There are many situations however, in which the category cannot be measured directly, but only some low-level attributes of the entities can be observed. Learning the relationship between the high-level category and the low-level features is a characteristic ability of intelligence, therefore *classification* (*pattern recognition* or *discrimination*) has always been an inspiring research area.

In the probabilistic formalization of the problem, labeled observations are modeled with an (X, Y) random pair, where $X \in \mathcal{R}^d$ denotes the *observation* and $Y \in \mathcal{C}$, $\mathcal{C} = \{c_1, c_2, \ldots, c_M\}$ its corresponding *class label*. The joint distribution of (X, Y) describes the frequency of encountering particular pairs in practice. The goal is to predict the true class of unseen examples, which is done by a function $g(x) : \mathcal{R}^d \mapsto \mathcal{C}$ called *classifier*. An *error* occurs if $g(X) \neq Y$, and the probability of error for classifier g is

$$R(g) = \mathbf{P}\{g(X) \neq Y\}. \tag{1}$$

The best possible classifier g^* is defined as

$$g^* = \underset{g:\mathcal{R}^d \mapsto \mathcal{C}}{\arg\min}\, \mathbf{P}\{g(X) \neq Y\}. \tag{2}$$

R. Basili and M.T. Pazienza (Eds.): AI*IA 2007, LNAI 4733, pp. 302–313, 2007.

The problem of finding g^* is a *Bayes problem*, and the classifier g^* is called the *Bayes classifier*. The minimal probability of error is called the *Bayes error* (*Bayes risk*) and is denoted by $R^* = R(g^*)$. In most cases, the distribution of (X, Y), and hence g^* and R^* are all unknown.

In practice we usually have a finite sequence of observation - label pairs from the past. We assume that these pairs were drawn independently from the unknown distribution of (X, Y), thus the *training set* can be modeled as an i.i.d. random sample $T_n = ((X_1, Y_1), (X_2, Y_2), \dots, (X_n, Y_n))$. If we would like to emphasize that the classifier was built up via learning from the data, then we denote it by $g_n(x, t_n) : \mathcal{R}^d \times (\mathcal{R}^d \times \mathcal{C})^n \mapsto \mathcal{C}$. This description incorporates the recipe for constructing the decision function from the concrete training set realization t_n. A complete *classification algorithm* (*rule*) deals with arbitrary sample size, thus it can be represented with a sequence of functions $\{g_n, n \geq 1\}$.

A natural question is how to create good classification rules. Theory says that no pattern recognition algorithm can be inherently superior to any other in terms of generalization performance [1]. For any fixed n, if g_n outperforms h_n for a specific problem, then there necessarily exists another distribution for which h_n has lower error probability. However an engineer would surely count the first rule more useful than the second, if it performed better for real-life problems and worse for pathological ones like separating rational numbers from irrationals. The existence of "practically good rules" is possible, but finding them is a somewhat heuristic issue, because nobody can formalize which distributions are typical in practice. Our point of view is that distribution-free properties (e.g. universal consistence, asymptotic complexity) are valuable guiding principles at designing classification algorithms, but empirical comparison is important too.

Among the many possible ways of constructing $\{g_n\}$ an interesting one is the *local hyperplane* approach, that was introduced by Vincent and Bengio in 2002 [2]. Their rule is a modification of the well known nearest neighbor (NN) method. It is similar in spirit to *tangent distance* [3], but with invariances inferred from the local neighborhood rather than prior knowledge. Their rule addresses the pattern recognition problem from the heuristic side, and tries to improve the finite sample generalization performance of NN classifiers in the zero Bayes error case. Vincent and Bengio's algorithm was applied by Okun to the problem of protein-fold recognition [4].

In this paper we introduce a new way of local hyperplane classification that has two advantages over Vincent and Bengio's original approach. The first is that our method inherits the asymptotic optimality of NN classifiers in the zero Bayes error case. Secondly, it usually provides better finite sample performance.

The rest of this paper is organized as follows. In the next section we discuss the derivation of the local hyperplane approach, and somehow locate it on the map of classification algorithms. In section 3 we present our modifications in the way of defining the local hyperplanes, and propose a novel algorithm for computing them. In section 4 we prove an asymptotic error bound theorem for our classification rule, while in section 5 we analyze the finite sample behavior. Section 6 presents experiments with real-world datasets. Finally, section 7 concludes.

2   The Local Hyperplane Approach

The concept of *margin* (distance between the decision surface and the closest training point) proved to be a useful approach in machine learning, and led to new classification algorithms that have good generalization capabilities. The most famous ones are support vector machines (SVMs) ([5], first introduced in [6]) that produce a linear decision surface with *maximal* margin for linearly separable problems. For the non-linearly separable case SVMs map the input into a higher (possibly infinite) dimensional *feature space* with some non-linear transformation and build a maximal margin hyperplane there. The trick is that this mapping is not computed directly but is implicitly induced by a kernel function. While non-linear SVMs can solve any separable classification problems with zero training error, the large margin in the feature space does not necessarily translate into a large margin in the input space [7].

A natural idea is to try and build a decision surface with large margin directly in the input space. But allowing an arbitrary decision function we have too much freedom, and the problem intrinsically reduces to the appropriate separation of the closest pair. To avoid this we can introduce the notion of *local margin* as the distance between a given point on the decision surface and the closest training point. Would it be possible to find an algorithm that produces a non-linear decision boundary which correctly separates the classes, such that the input space local margin is maximal everywhere along its surface? Surprisingly the plain old 1-nearest-neighbor (NN) algorithm does precisely this.

Besides NN is an amazingly simple, non-parametric rule, it has appealing theoretical properties. The Cover-Hart inequality ([8], proved more generally in [9]) states for the asymptotic probability of error R in the 2-class case that

$$R \leq 2R^*(1 - R^*), \tag{3}$$

independent of the distance metric used. As a weaker but more illustrative consequence, the asymptotic risk is at most twice the Bayes bound. This still means asymptotic optimality for separable problems.

But given only a finite number of training examples, NN classifiers are often outperformed in practice, e.g. by SVMs. The typical explanation of this phenomenon is that NNs have too much capacity (VC-dimension). The decision surface built by NNs is too complex compared to the number of available training examples, therefore maximizing the local margin in the input space can easily lead to poor generalization performance (Fig. 1).

A more reasonable goal is trying to obtain a large (not maximal) local margin in the input space, while trying to keep the separating surface simple. A possible way to improve the generalization capability of NN classifiers in the separable case is to somehow fantasize the "missing" training points based on the local linear approximation of the support of each class [2]. This is what we call the *local hyperplane approach* (Fig. 2, 3). In this approach classification goes schematically as the following. First the local hyperplanes are determined for each class at the input point. Then the category of the input is decided from the nearest local hyperplane instead of the nearest training example.

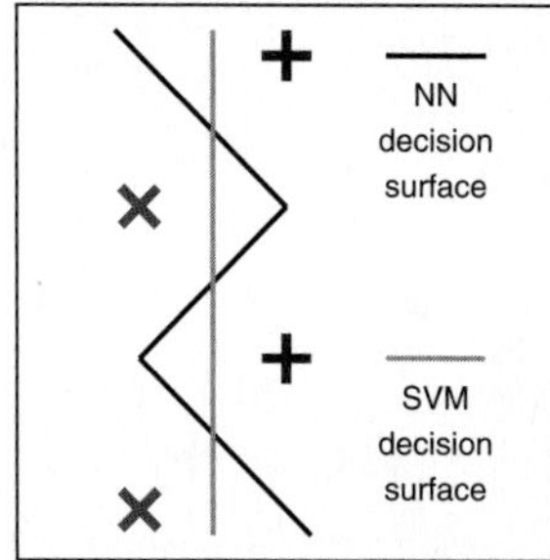

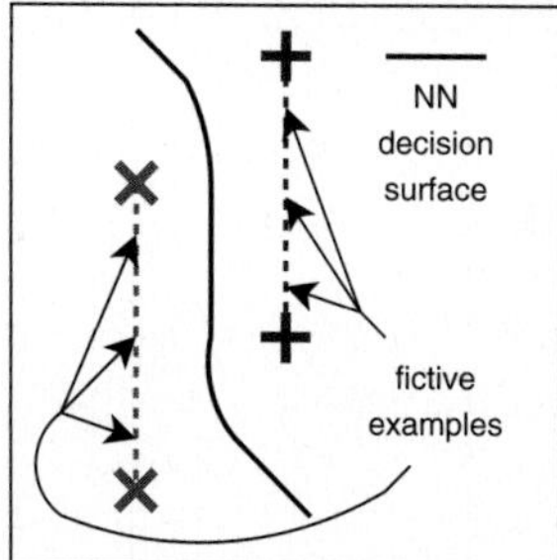

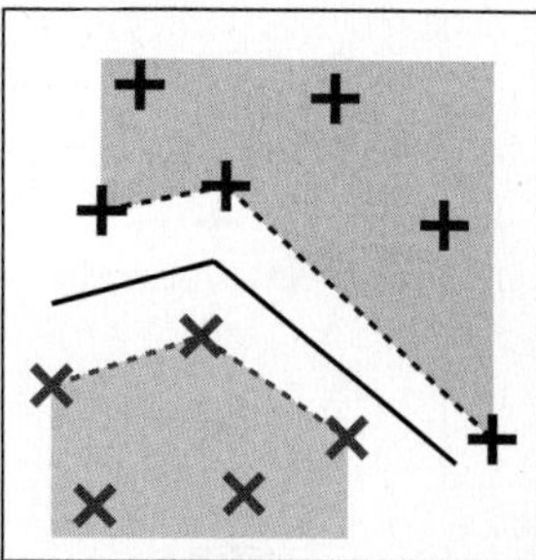

Fig. 1. (NN vs SVM) The decision surface built by the NN classifier is more complex than that of the SVM. This often leads to worse generalization, especially in the separable case.

Fig. 2. (The LH approach) The decision of NN can be made smoother, if we virtually enrich the training set with fictive examples, by linearly combining real ones located close to each other

Fig. 3. (LH vs SVM in the nonlinearly separable case.) There exist nonlinearly seprable problems, for which the LH approach finds a better solution than the nonlinear SVM

3 Defining the Local Hyperplanes

Given a test point $\mathbf{x}$, a straightforward way to define the local hyperplane for class c is to take the affine subspace of the K training points from c whose Euclidean distance to $\mathbf{x}$ is the smallest. Unfortunately this simple definition (introduced in [2]) has both a theoretical and a practical flaw.

Taking per-class nearest neighbors means that we often choose points that are very far from $\mathbf{x}$ indeed (Fig. 4). For certain distributions this remains true even if the number of training patterns tends to infinity. The decision of the classifier can be influenced by far examples, which is theoretically undesirable. This phenomenon causes that we cannot *guarantee* anything for the asymptotic performance of the classification rule. Of course one can imagine distributions, for which the probability of this bad event asymptotically tends to zero. But things get worse, if we allow using approximate nearest neighbor search [10,11] instead of exact one for computational efficiency reasons.

To illustrate the practical flaw, consider a test point near the decision boundary. Taking its nearest neighbors from class c does not necessarily mean to pick the closest surface segment from the support of class c, because the training examples are usually located irregularly in practice (Fig. 5).

A solution for removing the theoretical flaw is the following: Take the L nearest neighbors of $\mathbf{x}$ first globally, regardless of class labels. Then compute the K per-class nearest neighbors for each class among these L points (it can happen that the number of examples belonging to class c is less than K). This is our first modification in the local hyperplane definition. It eliminates the theoretical flaw but does little against the practical one.

Such exact removal of the practical flaw seems impossible, because it is hard to formalize precisely what actually we want. We have seen that it intuitively looks bad to take simply the K nearest neighbors of $\mathbf{x}$ from class c as the generator

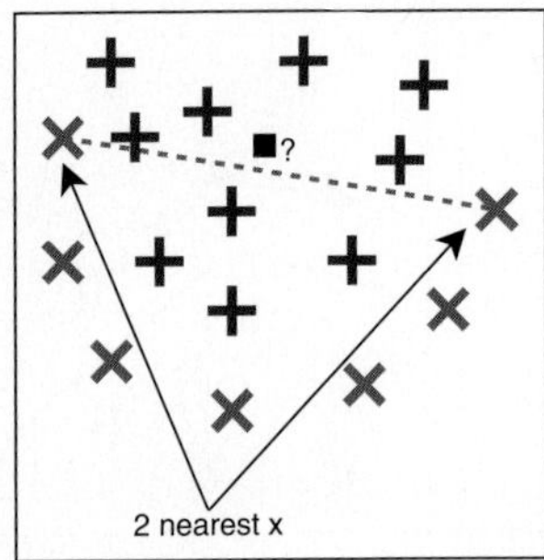

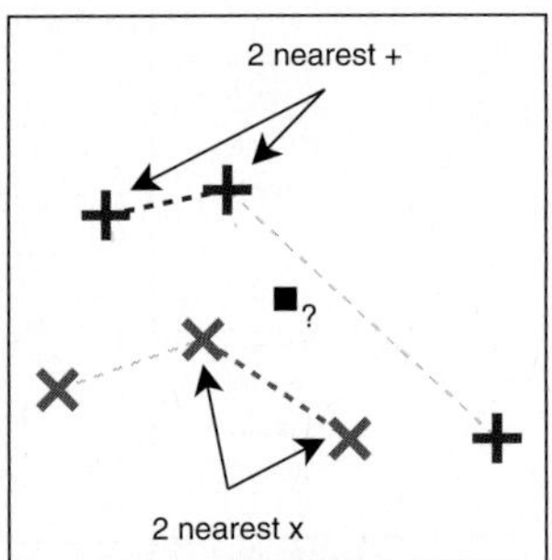

Fig. 4. (The theoretical flaw) Taking the nearest neighbors per-class separately causes that far examples can affect the answer of the classifier. This may lead to errors even in the middle of the classes.

Fig. 5. (The practical flaw) The usefulness of defining local hyperplane simply by the K nearest neighbors from class c is questionable, because the training points are often located irregularly

points of the local hyperplane. We might try to enforce locality by considering a larger $(K+l)$-sized neighborhood, and selecting the hyperplane closest to $\mathbf{x}$ from the $\binom{K+l}{K}$ possible choices. But doing so we can easily walk into the pitfall of untruthfulness, which means that we do not fantasize missing training examples any more, but generate fake ones. *Locality* and *truthfulness* are contradictionary requirements. Our second modification in the local hyperplane definition is an algorithm that tries to find a reasonable trade-off between them.

- **Input:** a test point $\mathbf{x} \in \mathcal{R}^d$, a class label $c \in \mathcal{C}$, the training set plus three integer parameters L (neighborhood size), K (hyperplane dimension, $K \leq d$) and l (number of steps).
- **Output:** the generator points of the local hyperplane for class c.

- **Step 1:** Compute the label-independent L-neighborhood of $\mathbf{x}$ among the training examples. Any further steps work only with the elements of this L-neighborhood, therefore the remaining part of the training set can be dropped here. Denote the number of elements belonging to class c in the L-neighborhood with N_c. If $N_c = 0$, then return NULL.
- **Step 2:** Initialize the generator points of the actual local hyperplane with the $K' = \min\{K, N_c\}$ training examples with class label c that are closest to $\mathbf{x}$. Arrange the generator points into a d-by-K' matrix. $(\mathbf{H} = [\mathbf{x}_{(1)}^{(c)}, \mathbf{x}_{(2)}^{(c)}, \ldots, \mathbf{x}_{(K')}^{(c)}], K' \leq K \leq d)$
- **Step 3:** Compute the nearest point to $\mathbf{x}$ on the actual local hyperplane by solving a constrained optimization problem. $(\mathbf{p} = \mathbf{H}\mathbf{t}, \text{ where } \mathbf{t} = \arg\min_{\mathbf{s}:\sum s_i = 1} \|\mathbf{H}\mathbf{s} - \mathbf{x}\|)$
- **Step 4:** Stop if the nearest point is located inside the convex hull of the generator points (if $\forall i : t_i \geq 0$ then return $\mathbf{H}$).
- **Step 5:** Compute the location where the line connecting the center-of-gravity and nearest point exits the convex hull. $(\mathbf{p}_{\text{exit}} = \bar{\mathbf{h}} + (\mathbf{p} - \bar{\mathbf{h}})/(1 - K't_{\min})$, where $\bar{\mathbf{h}} = \frac{1}{K'}\sum \mathbf{x}_i$ and $t_{\min} = \min_i t_i)$

- **Step 6:** Replace the generator point corresponding to the most violating t_i with the next closest training point from class c. $(\mathbf{x}_{\min}^{(c)} = \mathbf{x}_{(\text{next})}^{(c)})$
- **Step 7:** If the iteration count is less than or equal to l, then go to *step 3*. Otherwise return the hyperplane whose exit point was closest to $\mathbf{x}$.

The critical part of the algorithm is the constrained optimization problem, encountered in *step 3*. The standard way of computing $\mathbf{p}$ is eliminating the constraint and solving a linear system of equations in $K - 1$ variables (see [2]). But if we also wanted to know the barycentric representation of the nearest point $(\mathbf{t})$, then we would have to compute it from the Cartesian representation $\mathbf{p}$ by solving another system of equations. Therefore we applied a small trick here. Our idea is to try and solve the constrained optimization problem directly, so that the convex hull containment question can be decided easily in *step 4*.

We show now that the minimization can be performed with gradient descent method without breaking the constraint. The partial derivatives of the objective function are the following:

$$\frac{\partial}{\partial s_i} \|\mathbf{Hs} - \mathbf{x}\|^2 = 2\mathbf{x}_i^T (\mathbf{Hs} - \mathbf{x}).$$ (4)

Thus the sum of the components in $\mathbf{s}^{(\text{new})}$ after a step into gradient-direction is

$$\sum_{i=1}^{K} s_i^{(\text{new})} = \left(\sum_{i=i}^{K} s_i \right) + \alpha \left(\sum_{i=i}^{K} \mathbf{x}_i^T \right) (\mathbf{Hs} - \mathbf{x}).$$ (5)

We initialize $\mathbf{s}$ such that the constraint holds $(\sum s_i = 1)$. If the generator points are origin-centered $(\sum \mathbf{x}_i = \mathbf{0})$, then gradient-directed steps will never violate the constraint. This can be assured by an initial translation of the problem.

If the algorithm stops in *step 7*, then it would be problematic to build upon the exact distance between $\mathbf{x}$ and the local hyperplane in the decision making, because the linear approximation is valid only in a small neighborhood of the generator points. It is more reasonable to use the distance between $\mathbf{x}$ and the exit point.

4   Asymptotic Behavior

Theorem 1. *Let (X, Y) be a random pair, representing a 2-class classification problem $(Y \in \{0, 1\})$. If either X is discrete or X is continuous such that the conditional density functions $f_{X|Y=0}$ and $f_{X|Y=1}$ are almost everywhere continuous, then for the infinite sample risk of the proposed local hyperplane classifier*

$$R \le 1 - (R^*)^{L+1} - (1 - R^*)^{L+1}.$$ (6)

Proof. The proof is very similar to Cover and Hart's one for the nearest neighbor rule [8], but we write it down for completeness. Given an input point x the answer of the Bayes classifier is

$$g^*(x) = \arg\max_{y \in \{0,1\}} \mathbf{P}\{Y = y | X = x\}.$$ (7)

Thus the conditional Bayes risk $r^*(x)$ can be expressed with the regression function $\eta(x) = \mathbf{E}[Y|X = x]$ as the following

$$r^*(x) = \mathbf{P}\{g^*(x) \neq Y|X = x\} = \min\{\eta(x), 1 - \eta(x)\}. \tag{8}$$

Note that if X is a continuous random variable with continuous conditional density functions $f_{X|Y=0}$ and $f_{X|Y=1}$, then η is a continuous function of x. The Bayes error R^* can be obtained from r^* via expectation

$$R^* = \mathbf{E}[r^*(X)]. \tag{9}$$

Now we bound the finite sample conditional risk $r_n(X, O_n)$ of the proposed classifier from above. Denote the ith nearest neighbor of the input X among the training observations O_n with $X_{(i)} = X_{(i)}(X, n)$, with respect to an arbitrary distance metric. Denote the class label of $X_{(i)}$ with $Y_{(i)}$. We can exploit the fact that no error occurs, if each pattern from the L-neighborhood of X has the same class label as the true label of X. Thus with probability one

$$\begin{aligned} r_n(X, O_n) &= \mathbf{P}\{g_n(X, T_n) \neq Y|X, O_n\} \\ &\leq 1 - \mathbf{P}\{Y = Y_{(1)} = Y_{(2)} = \ldots = Y_{(L)}|X, X_{(1)}, X_{(2)}, \ldots, X_{(L)}\} \\ &= 1 - \eta(X) \prod_{i=1}^{L} \eta(X_{(i)}) - (1 - \eta(X)) \prod_{i=1}^{L} (1 - \eta(X_{(i)})). \end{aligned} \tag{10}$$

We use a simple lemma (proved in [8]) to kill $X_{(i)}$-s from the bound.

Lemma 1 (Convergence of the nearest neighbors)
For any fixed i, $\lim_{n\to\infty} X_{(i)}(X, n) = X$ with probability one, independent of the distance metric used.

Corollary 1. *If X is discrete, or X is continuous such that the conditional density functions $f_{X|Y=0}$ and $f_{X|Y=1}$ are almost everywhere continuous, then with probability one $\lim_{n\to\infty} \eta(X_{(i)}(X, n)) = \eta(X)$.*

Hence for the asymptotic conditional risk $r(X)$ with probability one

$$\begin{aligned} r(X) &= \lim_{n\to\infty} r_n(X, O_n) \leq 1 - \eta(X)^{L+1} - (1 - \eta(X))^{L+1} \\ &\leq 1 - r^*(X)^{L+1} - (1 - r^*(X))^{L+1} \quad \text{(by symmetry)}. \end{aligned} \tag{11}$$

Putting all together the asymptotic risk R can be bounded as follows:

$$\begin{aligned} R = \lim_{n\to\infty} R_n &= \lim_{n\to\infty} \mathbf{E}[r_n(X, O_n)] = \mathbf{E}[\lim_{n\to\infty} r_n(X, O_n)] \\ &\text{(the last step by the dominated convergence theorem)} \\ &= \mathbf{E}[r(X)] \leq \mathbf{E}[1 - r^*(X)^{L+1} - (1 - r^*(X))^{L+1}] \\ &\leq 1 - (R^*)^{L+1} - (1 - R^*)^{L+1} \quad \text{(by Jensen's inequality)} \end{aligned} \tag{12}$$

$$\qquad\qquad\qquad\qquad\qquad\qquad\qquad\qquad\qquad\qquad\qquad\qquad\qquad\qquad\qquad\Box$$

If the problem is separable, then the proposed rule is asymptotically optimal. In other cases the bound is quite pessimistic, because the proof counts every situation an error, in which the L-neighborhood of the input contains instances from both classes. We note that the theorem remains valid if approximate nearest neighbor search [10,11] is used instead of exact one in the local hyperplane finding algorithm. However, this would affect finite sample performance. In the special case $L = 1$ we recover the Cover-Hart inequality (3). All conditions on the distribution of (X, Y) could be dropped, if we followed the more powerful but less intuitive way of the standard book [9].

5   Finite Sample Behavior

In this section we consider only the separable case, because the local hyperplane approach is designed for this situation. We only deal with 2-class problems to keep things simple.

It may feel comfortable to know that our classification rule reaches optimal accuracy with infinite training examples. But this sounds quite artificial for an engineer who has to live with finite datasets. The zero asymptotic risk property is a good guiding principle but worth nothing in practice if the convergence is too slow.

It is known that no universal (distribution-free) rate of convergence exists for the asymptotic risk of classification rules [9]. This remains true if we restrict ourselves to the separable case. The distribution-free analysis is impossible, but we can compare for example the convergence rate of some rules for a given class of problems.

Consider a separable problem (X, Y). Suppose that the Bayes decision partitions the support of X such that the points located at decision boundaries form a continuous surface. This implies that X has to be a continuous random variable but otherwise the assumption is admissible in many real-world situations. If the Bayes decision boundary is not a fractal-like nightmare, but is a smooth surface with bounded curvature, then its small segments can be approximated linearly. If we go further and also suppose that the density function f_X is smooth, then the distribution of X can be treated as uniform in the neighborhood of sufficiently small surface segments.

These ideas lead towards the investigation of a simple artificial problem, in which X is a uniform random variable over a hypercube such that the two classes partition this hypercube into two identical hyperrectangles. Beyond a certain training set size n the generalization performance of neighborhood-based rules depends only on how can they get along with this "layered cake" test.

Therefore we empirically compared the finite sample performance of three classification rules for different variants of the "layered cake" problem. The parameters were the input dimension d and the training set size n. Given a configuration (d, n) we made 100 experiments independently, in each of which we generated a d-dimensional n-sized training and a 1024-sized testing set and measured the number of (test) errors. Then we could compute the average error rate $\hat{R}_n$ of the 100 experiments. The first rule in the comparison was the simple nearest neighbor

(NN) method. The second was a specific representant of Vincent and Bengio's original local hyperplane approach, called HKNN [2]. The third was our nearest local hyperplane (NLH) rule. Note that HKNN is not a neighborhood-based classification algorithm in its original form. Therefore we considered a HKNN variant, in which our first modification on the local hyperplane definition was applied. The parametric rules needed to be adjusted for different d values. We used the following reasonable recipe: NLH($L = 4d$, $K = d$, $l = d$), HKNN($L = 4d$, $K = d$, $\lambda = 10$). The summary of the results of can be seen in Fig. 5.

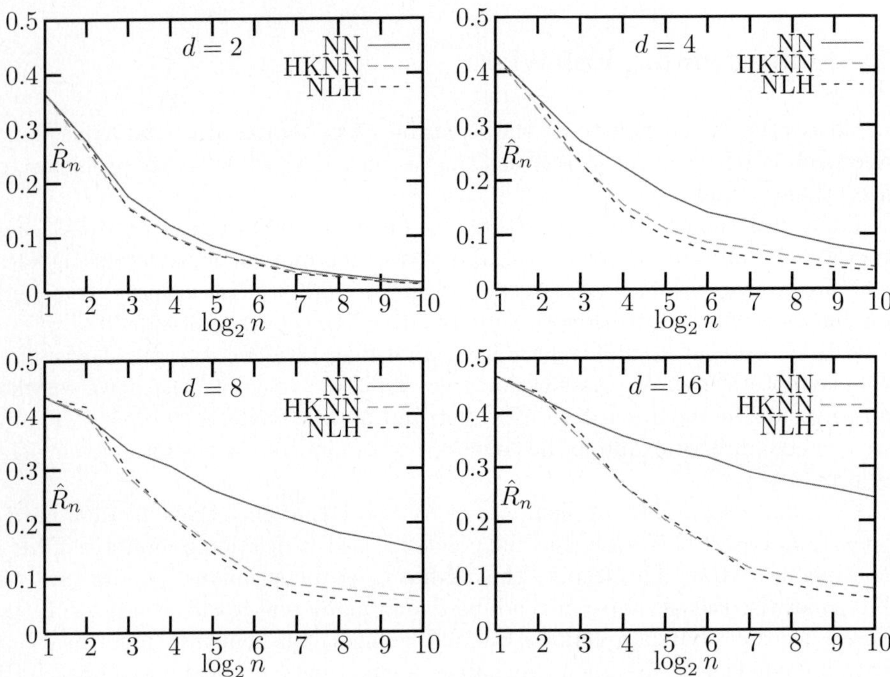

Fig. 6. The above plots show results of the "layered cake" test in many configurations. Typically the lowest average error rate was achieved by the proposed NLH classifier and the second by Vincent and Bengio's HKNN. The plain NN method could slightly outperform the others at very small training set sizes in high dimensions.

The results suggest that for a large family of separable problems HKNN and NLH can really mean a significant improvement over NN. The difference between NN and the other methods increases with the input dimension d. Among HKNN and NLH the proposed NLH method achieved slightly better results.

6   Experimental Results

We tested the new classification rule with 4 real-world datasets, originating from the UCI Machine Learning Repository [12] and the MNIST Database of

Table 1. Experimental results with real-world datasets

Dataset	Algorithm	Test Error	Parameters Used
Iris	NN	4.00 %	—
	SVM	**2.67** %	$\mathcal{K}(\mathbf{x}, \mathbf{x}_i) = \exp(-0.25\|\mathbf{x} - \mathbf{x}_i\|^2), C = 1$
	HKNN	4.00 %	$L = 12, K = 3, \lambda = 10$
	NLH	3.33 %	$L = 12, K = 3, l = 3$
Votes	NN	6.67 %	—
	SVM	**3.45** %	$\mathcal{K}(\mathbf{x}, \mathbf{x}_i) = \exp(-0.06\|\mathbf{x} - \mathbf{x}_i\|^2), C = 5$
	HKNN	4.60 %	$L = 16, K = 4, \lambda = 10$
	NLH	4.83 %	$L = 20, K = 5, l = 5$
Wisconsin	NN	4.10 %	—
	SVM	2.78 %	$\mathcal{K}(\mathbf{x}, \mathbf{x}_i) = \exp(-0.11\|\mathbf{x} - \mathbf{x}_i\|^2), C = 5$
	HKNN	2.78 %	$L = 28, K = 7, \lambda = 10$
	NLH	**2.64** %	$L = 28, K = 7, l = 7$
MNIST*	NN	4.42 %	—
	SVM	3.07 %	$\mathcal{K}(\mathbf{x}, \mathbf{x}_i) = (0.005\mathbf{x}^T\mathbf{x}_i + 1)^{15}, C = 10$
	HKNN	3.09 %	$L = 300, K = 15, \lambda = 10$
	NLH	**2.27** %	$L = 300, K = 15, l = 30$

Handwritten Digits [13]. The local hyperplane approach is designed for the separable (or mostly separable) case, therefore we chose problems on which other pattern recognizers had achieved good performance. If the observations contain discrete attributes, then there is another criterion of applicability too, since the interpolation between such training points is not always meaningful. Suppose that the possible values of the discrete attribute are encoded as numbers. The criterion is that the difference between two codes must express the dissimilarity between the corresponding attribute values. The following real-world problems fulfil all these requirements:

- **Iris:** This dataset consists of $d = 4$ measurements made on each of 150 iris plants of $M = 3$ species. This database, originating from Fisher's classical article [14], is probably the oldest and best known one in the pattern recognition literature.
- **Votes:** This dataset includes votes for each of the U.S. House of Representatives Congressmen on the $d = 16$ key votes identified by the Congressional Quarterly Almanac. The dataset consists of 435 instances and $M = 2$ classes (democrat and republican).
- **Wisconsin:** This breast cancer database was obtained from the University of Wisconsin Hospital. The task is to decide benignness or malignancy ($M = 2$) of tumors based on $d = 9$ attributes. After removing instances with missing attribute values the number of examples is 683.
- **MNIST*:** This dataset was extracted from the MNIST handwritten digit recognition database [13]. The reduced dataset contains 20000 instances from $M = 10$ classes. The images were resized from 28×28 to 14×14 pixels, so the number of attributes is $d = 196$.

In our experiments we compared the performance of NN, SVM, HKNN and the proposed NLH method. The first three datasets contain relatively few examples therefore we evaluated the classifiers with leave-one-out cross validation. In the *MNIST** problem we used 10000 examples for training and the remaining 10000 for testing.

Note that while NN, HKNN and NLH handle multiclass problems in a natural way, pure SVM is a 2-class classifier. We implemented multiclass SVM by all-pairs decomposition, using identically parameterized 2-class SVMs for the subproblems.

We can see from Table 1 that the worst performance was delivered by NN in each problem. For *Iris* and *Votes* we measured the best results with SVM. For *Wisconsin* and *MNIST** the proposed NLH classifier was the best. NLH was better than HKNN in 3 out of 4 cases.

7   Conclusions

We have presented a new way of local hyperplane classification in this paper. The main contributions are the following: First we made a minor modification in the definition of the local hyperplanes. It eliminates errors far from the (Bayes) decision boundary and makes it possible to prove zero asymptotic risk for separable problems. Second we made another change in the definition that contains a novel algorithm for computing the local hyperplanes. It improves the accuracy near the decision boundary in many practical situations. Third we compared the finite sample near-boundary performance of the new rule with the nearest neighbor and the original local hyperplane approach. Finally we tested our classification rule on real-world datasets.

References

1. Schaffer, C.: A Conservation Law for Generalization Performance. In: Proc. of the 11th International Conference on Machine Learning, pp. 259–265 (1994)
2. Vincent, P., Bengio, Y.: K-Local Hyperplane and Convex Distance Nearest Neighbor Algorithms. In: Advances in Neural Information Processing Systems 14, pp. 985–992. MIT Press, Cambridge, MA (2002)
3. Simard, P., LeCun, Y., Denker, J., Victorri, B.: Transformation Invariance in Pattern Recognition – Tangent Distance and Tangent Propagation. In: Orr, G.B., Müller, K.-R. (eds.) Neural Networks: Tricks of the Trade. LNCS, vol. 1524, pp. 239–274. Springer, Heidelberg (1998)
4. Okun, O.: Protein Fold Recognition with K-Local Hyperplane Distance Nearest Neighbor Algorithm. In: Proc. of the 2nd European Workshop on Data Mining and Text Mining in Bioinformatics, pp. 47–53 (2004)
5. Burges, C.: A Tutorial on Support Vector Machines for Pattern Recognition. Data Mining and Knowledge Discovery 2(2), 121–167 (1998)
6. Boser, B., Guyon, I., Vapnik, V.: A Training Algorithm for Optimal Margin Classifiers. In: Proc. of the Fifth Annual Workshop on Computational Learning Theory, pp. 144–152 (1992)

7. Akaho, S.: SVM Maximizing Margin in the Input Space. In: Proc. of the 9th International Conference on Neural Information Processing, vol. 2, pp. 1069–1073 (2002)
8. Cover, T., Hart, P.: Nearest Neighbor Pattern Classification. IEEE Transactions on Information Theory 13(1), 21–27 (1967)
9. Devroye, L., Györfi, L., Lugosi, G.: A Probabilistic Theory of Pattern Recognition. Springer, New York (1996)
10. Kleinberg, J.: Two Algorithms for Nearest-Neighbor Search in High Dimensions. In: Proc. of the 29th Annual ACM Symposium on Theory of Computing, pp. 599–608. ACM Press, New York (1997)
11. Arya, S., Mount, D., Netanyahu, N., Silverman, R., Wu, A.: An Optimal Algorithm for Approximate Nearest Neighbor Searching in Fixed Dimensions. Journal of the ACM 45(6), 891–923 (1998)
12. Newman, D., Hettich, S., Blake, C., Merz, C.: UCI Repository of Machine Learning Databases. University of California, Irvine, CA,
    http://www.ics.uci.edu/~mlearn/MLRepository.html
13. LeCun, Y.: The MNIST Database of Handwritten Digits.
    http://yann.lecun.com/exdb/mnist/
14. Fisher, R.: The Use of Multiple Measurements in Taxonomic Problems. Annals of Eugenics 7, 179–188 (1936)

The JIGSAW Algorithm for
Word Sense Disambiguation and
Semantic Indexing of Documents

P. Basile, M. Degemmis, A.L. Gentile, P. Lops, and G. Semeraro

Dipartimento di Informatica
Università di Bari
Via E. Orabona, 4 - 70125 Bari - Italia
{basilepp,degemmis,al.gentile,lops,semeraro}@di.uniba.it

Abstract. Word Sense Disambiguation (WSD) is traditionally considered an AI-hard problem. In fact, a breakthrough in this field would have a significant impact on many relevant fields, such as information retrieval and information extraction. This paper describes JIGSAW, a knowledge-based WSD algorithm that attemps to disambiguate all words in a text by exploiting WordNet[1] senses. The main assumption is that a Part-Of-Speech (POS)-dependent strategy to WSD can turn out to be more effective than a unique strategy. Semantics provided by WSD gives an added value to applications centred on humans as users. Two empirical evaluations are described in the paper. First, we evaluated the accuracy of JIGSAW on Task 1 of SEMEVAL-1 competition[2]. This task measures the effectiveness of a WSD algorithm in an Information Retrieval System. For the second evaluation, we used semantically indexed documents obtained through a WSD process in order to train a naïve Bayes learner that infers semantic *sense-based* user profiles as binary text classifiers. The goal of the second empirical evaluation has been to measure the accuracy of the user profiles in selecting relevant documents to be recommended within a document collection.

Keywords: Word Sense Disambiguation, WordNet, Information Retrieval and Extraction, Search, User Profiling.

1 Introduction

The task of word sense disambiguation (WSD) consists in assigning the most appropriate meaning to a polysemous word within a given context. Applications such as machine translation, knowledge acquisition, common sense reasoning, and others, require knowledge about word meanings, and word sense disambiguation is considered important for all these applications. Most of the efforts in solving this problem were concentrated so far towards targeted supervised learning, where each sense tagged occurrence of a particular word is transformed into

---

[1] wordnet.princeton.edu/
[2] www.senseval.org

R. Basili and M.T. Pazienza (Eds.): AI*IA 2007, LNAI 4733, pp. 314–325, 2007.

a feature vector, which is then used in an automatic learning process. The applicability of such supervised algorithms is however limited to those few words for which sense tagged data are available, and their accuracy is strongly connected to the amount of labeled data available at hand. Instead, methods that address all words in unrestricted text have received significantly less attention. While the performance of such methods is usually exceeded by their supervised lexical-sample alternatives, they have the advantage of providing larger coverage. In this paper, we present a method for solving the semantic ambiguity of all words contained in a text. The method is implemented into a knowledge-based word sense disambiguation algorithm, called JIGSAW. It does not use any dataset for training, but it exploits an external knowledge source, WordNet [8], in order to assign the most appropriate meaning to each word. JIGSAW differs from other similar algorithms because it uses a different approach for each Part Of Speech (POS) in order to improve the disambiguation accuracy.

The paper is organized as follows: After a brief discussion about the main works related to our research, Section 3 describes our WSD strategy, while Section 4 presents the formal model we adopted for semantic indexing of documents, which exploits WordNet senses. An experimental session was carried out in order to evaluate the proposed approach and results are presented in Section 5. Conclusions and future work are discussed in Section 6.

2   Related Work

For some natural language processing tasks, such as part of speech tagging or named entity recognition, regardless of the approach considered, there is a consensus on what makes a successful algorithm. Instead, no such consensus has been reached yet for the task of word sense disambiguation, and previous work has considered a range of knowledge sources, such as local collocational clues, common membership in semantically or topically related word classes, semantic density, and others. In recent SENSEVAL-3 evaluations[3], the most successful approaches for *all words* word sense disambiguation relied on information drawn from annotated corpora. The system developed by Decadt [2] uses two cascaded memory-based classifiers, combined with the use of a genetic algorithm for joint parameter optimization and feature selection. A separate word expert is learned for each ambiguous word, using a concatenated corpus of English sense tagged texts, including SemCor, SENSEVAL datasets, and a corpus built from WordNet examples. The performance of this system on the SENSEVAL-3 English all words dataset was evaluated at 65.2%. Another top ranked system is the one developed by Yuret [14], which combines two Naïve Bayes statistical models, one based on surrounding collocations and another one based on a bag of words around the target word. The statistical models are built based on SemCor and WordNet, for an overall disambiguation accuracy of 64.1%. All previous systems use supervised methods. These methods have some limitations because they need a tagged corpus for training data: This is a strong requirement in a context such

---

3 http://www.senseval.org

as the web. On the other hand, the knowledge-based approaches show a lower accuracy than superivised methods, but they do not need any training data. Furthermore, the increasing availability of large-scale rich lexical knowledge resources seems to provide new challanges to knowledge-based approaches. Two interesting works in this direction are proposed by Navigli and Velardi [9] and Mihalcea [7]. In the remainder of the paper, we propose a detailed description of our knowledge-based algorithm and provide detailed experimental results.

3 The JIGSAW Algorithm for WSD and Semantic Indexing of Documents

The goal of a WSD algorithm consists in assigning a word w_i occurring in a document d with its appropriate meaning or sense s, by exploiting the *context* C in which w_i is found. The context C for w_i is defined as a set of words that precede and follow w_i. The sense s is selected from a predefined set of possibilities, usually known as *sense inventory*. In the proposed algorithm, the sense inventory is obtained from WordNet. JIGSAW is a WSD algorithm based on the idea of combining three different strategies to disambiguate nouns, verbs, adjectives and adverbs. The main motivation behind our approach is that the effectiveness of a WSD algorithm is strongly influenced by the POS tag of the target word. An adaptation of Lesk dictionary-based WSD algorithm has been used to disambiguate adjectives and adverbs [1], an adaptation of the Resnik algorithm has been used to disambiguate nouns [10], while the algorithm we developed for disambiguating verbs exploits the nouns in the *context* of the verb as well as the nouns both in the glosses and in the phrases that WordNet utilizes to describe the usage of a verb. JIGSAW takes as input a document $d = [w_1, w_2, \ldots, w_h]$ encoded as a list of words in order of their appearance, and returns a list of WordNet synsets $X = [s_1, s_2, \ldots, s_k]$ $(k \leq h)$, in which each element s_j is obtained by disambiguating the *target word* w_i based on the information obtained from WordNet about a few immediately surrounding words. Notice that $(k \leq h)$ because some words could not be found in WordNet, such as proper names, or because of bigram recognition. More details for each one of the above mentioned procedures follow.

3.1 *JIGSAW$_{nouns}$*

The procedure is obtained by making some variations to the algorithm designed by Resnik [10] for disambiguating noun groups.

Given a set of nouns $W = \{w_1, w_2, \ldots, w_n\}$, obtained from document d, with each w_i having an associated sense inventory $S_i = \{s_{i1}, s_{i2}, \ldots, s_{ik}\}$ of possible senses, the goal is assigning each w_i with the most appropriate sense $s_{ih} \in S_i$, according to the *similarity* of w_i with the other words in W (the context for w_i). The idea is to define a function $\varphi(w_i, s_{ij})$, $w_i \in W$, $s_{ij} \in S_i$, that computes a value in $[0, 1]$ representing the confidence with which word w_i can be assigned to sense s_{ij}.

The intuition behind this algorithm is essentially the same exploited by Lesk [5] and other authors: The most plausible assignment of senses to multiple co-occurring words is the one that maximizes *relatedness* of meanings among the chosen senses. $JIGSAW_{nouns}$ differs from the original algorithm by Resnik [10] in the similarity measure used to compute relatedness of two senses. We adopted the Leacock-Chodorow measure [4], which is based on the length of the path between concepts in an IS-A hierarchy. The idea behind this measure is that similarity between two synsets, s_1 and s_2, is inversely proportional to their distance in the WordNet IS-A hierarchy. The distance is computed by finding the *most specific subsumer* (MSS) between s_1 and s_2 (each ancestor of both s_1 and s_2 in the Word-Net hierarchy is a subsumer, the MSS is the one at the lowest level) and counting the number of nodes in the path between s_1 and s_2 that traverses their MSS. We extended this measure by introducing a parameter k that limits the search for the MSS to k ancestors (i.e. that climbs the WordNet IS-A hierarchy until either it finds the MSS or $k + 1$ ancestors of both s_1 and s_2 have been explored). This guarantees that "too abstract" (i.e. "less informative") MSSs will be ignored.

In addition to the semantic similarity function, $JIGSAW_{nouns}$ differs from the Resnik algorithm in the use of:

1. a Gaussian factor G, which takes into account the distance between the words in the text to be disambiguated;
2. a factor R, which gives more importance to the synsets that are more common than others, according to the frequency score in WordNet;
3. a *parametrized* search for the MSS between two concepts (the search is limited to a certain number of ancestors).

Algorithm 1 describes the complete procedure for the disambiguation of nouns. This algorithm considers the words in W pairwise. For each pair (w_i,w_j), the most specific subsumer MSS_{ij} is identified, by reducing the search to $depth1$ ancestors at most. Then, the similarity $sim(w_i, w_j, depth2)$ between the two words is computed, by reducing the search for the MSS to $depth2$ ancestors at most. MSS_{ij} is considered *as supporting evidence* for those synsets s_{ik} in S_i and s_{jh} in S_j that are descendants of MSS_{ij}. The MSS search is computed choosing the nearest MSS in all pairs of synsets s_{ik}, s_{jh}. Likewise, the similarity for (w_i,w_j) is the max similarity computed in all pairs of s_{ik}, s_{jh} and is weighted by a gaussian factor that takes into account the position of w_i and w_j in W (the shorter is the distance between the words, the higher is the weight). The value $\varphi(i, k)$ assigned to each candidate synset s_{ik} for the word w_i is the sum of two elements. The first one is the proportion of support it received, out of the support possible, computed as $support_{ik}/normalization_i$ in Algorithm 1. The other element that contributes to $\varphi(i, k)$ is a factor $R(k)$ that takes into account the rank of s_{ik} in WordNet, i.e. how common is the sense s_{ik} for the word w_i. $R(k)$ is computed as:

$$R(k) = 1 - 0.8 * \frac{k}{n - 1} \tag{1}$$

where n is the cardinality of the sense inventory S_i for w_i, and k is the rank of s_{ik} in S_i, starting from 0.

Algorithm 1. The procedure for disambiguating nouns derived from the algorithm by Resnik

---

1: **procedure** $JIGSAW_{nouns}(W, depth1, depth2)$ ▷ finds the proper synset for each polysemous noun in the set $W = \{w_1, w_2, \ldots, w_n\}$, $depth1$ and $depth2$ are used in the computation of MSS
2:     **for all** $w_i, w_j \in W$ **do**
3:         **if** $i < j$ **then**
4:             $sim \leftarrow sim(w_i, w_j, depth1) * G(pos(w_i), pos(w_j))$ ▷ $G(x, y)$ is a Gaussian function which takes into account the difference between the positions of w_i and w_j
5:             $MSS_{ij} \leftarrow MSS(w_i, w_j, depth2)$ ▷ MSS_{ij} is the most specific subsumer between w_i and w_j, search for MSS restricted to $depth2$ ancestors
6:                 **for all** $s_{ik} \in S_i$ **do**
7:                     **if** is-ancestor(MSS_{ij}, s_{ik}) **then**   ▷ if MSS_{ij} is an ancestor of s_{ik}
8:                         $support_{ik} \leftarrow support_{ik} + sim$
9:                     **end if**
10:                 **end for**
11:                 **for all** $s_{jh} \in S_j$ **do**
12:                     **if** is-ancestor(MSS_{ij}, s_{jh}) **then**
13:                         $support_{jh} \leftarrow support_{jh} + sim$
14:                     **end if**
15:                 **end for**
16:                 $normalization_i \leftarrow normalization_i + sim$
17:                 $normalization_j \leftarrow normalization_j + sim$
18:         **end if**
19:     **end for**
20:     **for all** $w_i \in W$ **do**
21:         **for all** $s_{ik} \in S_i$ **do**
22:             **if** $normalization_i > 0$ **then**
23:                 $\varphi(i, k) \leftarrow \alpha * support_{ik}/normalization_i + \beta * R(k)$
24:             **else**
25:                 $\varphi(i, k) \leftarrow \alpha/|S_i| + \beta * R(k)$
26:             **end if**
27:         **end for**
28:     **end for**
29: **end procedure**

Finally, both elements are weighted by two parameters: α, which controls the contribution given to $\varphi(i, k)$ by the normalized support, and β, which controls the contribution given by the rank of s_{ik}. We set $\alpha = 0.7$ and $\beta = 0.3$. The synset assigned to each word in W is the one with the highest φ value. Notice that we used two different parameters, $depth1$ and $depth2$ for setting the maximum depth for the search of the MSS: $depth1$ limits the search for the MSS computed in the similarity function, while $depth2$ limits the computation of the MSS used for assigning support to candidate synsets. We set $depth1 = 6$ and $depth2 = 3$.

3.2 $JIGSAW_{verbs}$

Before describing the $JIGSAW_{verbs}$ procedure, the *description* of a synset must be defined. It is the string obtained by concatenating the gloss and the sentences that WordNet uses to explain the usage of a word.

First, $JIGSAW_{verbs}$ includes, in the context C for the target verb w_i, all the nouns in the window of $2n$ words surrounding w_i. For each candidate synset s_{ik} of w_i, the algorithm computes $nouns(i, k)$, that is the set of nouns in the description for s_{ik}. Then, for each w_j in C and each synset s_{ik}, the following value is computed:

$$max_{jk} = max_{w_l \in nouns(i,k)} \left\{ \mathtt{sim}(w_j, w_l, depth) \right\} \tag{2}$$

where $\mathtt{sim}(w_j, w_l, depth)$ is defined as in $JIGSAW_{nouns}$. In other words, max_{jk} is the highest similarity value for w_j wrt the nouns related to the k-th sense for w_i. Finally, an overall similarity score among s_{ik} and the whole context C is computed:

$$\varphi(i, k) = R(k) \cdot \frac{\sum_{w_j \in C} G(pos(w_i), pos(w_j)) \cdot max_{jk}}{\sum_h G(pos(w_i), pos(w_h))} \tag{3}$$

where $R(k)$ is defined as in Equation 1 with a different constant factor (0.9) and $G(pos(w_i), pos(w_j))$ is the same Gaussian factor used in $JIGSAW_{nouns}$, that gives a higher weight to words closer to the target word. The synset assigned to w_i is the one with the highest φ value. Algorithm 2 provides a detailed description of the procedure.

3.3 $JIGSAW_{others}$

This procedure is based on the WSD algorithm proposed by Banerjee and Pedersen [1]. The idea is to compare the glosses of each candidate sense for the target word to the glosses of all the words in its context.

Let W_i be the sense inventory for the target word w_i. For each $s_{ik} \in W_i$, $JIGSAW_{others}$ computes the string $targetGloss_{ik}$ that contains the words in the gloss of s_{ik}. Then, the procedure computes the string $contextGloss_i$, which contains the words in the glosses of all the synsets corresponding to each word in the context for w_i. Finally, the procedure computes the *overlap* between $contextGloss_i$ and $targetGloss_{ik}$, and assigns the synset with the highest overlap score to w_i. This score is computed by counting the words that occur both in $targetGloss_{ik}$ and in $contextGloss_i$. If ties occur, the most common synset in WordNet is chosen.

4 Keyword-Based and Synset-Based Document Representation

The WSD procedure described in the previous section is adopted to obtain a synset-based vector space representation that we called *bag-of-synsets* (BOS).

Algorithm 2. The procedure for the disambiguation of verbs

1: **procedure** $JIGSAW_{verbs}(w_i, d, depth)$ ▷ finds the proper synset of a polysemous verb w_i in document d
2:     $C \leftarrow \{w_1, ..., w_n\}$ ▷ C is the context for w_i. For example, $C = \{w_1, w_2, w_4, w_5\}$, if the sequence of words $\{w_1, w_2, w_3, w_4, w_5\}$ occurs in d, w_3 being the target verb, w_j being nouns, $j \neq 3$
3:     $S_i \leftarrow \{s_{i1}, ... s_{im}\}$ ▷ S_i is the sense inventory for w_i, that is the set of all candidate synsets for w_i returned by WordNet
4:     $s \leftarrow null$ ▷ s is the synset to be returned
5:     $score \leftarrow -MAXDOUBLE$ ▷ $score$ is the similarity score assigned to s
6:     $p \leftarrow 1$ ▷ p is the position of the synsets for w_i
7:     **for all** $s_{ik} \in S_i$ **do**
8:         $max \leftarrow \{max_{1k}, ..., max_{nk}\}$
9:         $nouns(i, k) \leftarrow \{noun_1, ..., noun_z\}$ ▷ $nouns(i, k)$ is the set of all nouns in the description of s_{ik}
10:        $sumGauss \leftarrow 0$
11:        $sumTot \leftarrow 0$
12:        **for all** $w_j \in C$ **do** ▷ computation of the similarity between C and s_{ik}
13:            $max_{jk} \leftarrow 0$ ▷ max_{jk} is the highest similarity value for w_j, wrt the nouns related to the k-th sense for w_i.
14:            $sumGauss \leftarrow G(pos(w_i), pos(w_j))$ ▷ Gaussian function which takes into account the difference between the positions of the nouns in d
15:            **for all** $noun_l \in nouns(i, k)$ **do**
16:                $sim \leftarrow sim(w_j, noun_l, depth)$ ▷ sim is the similarity between the j-th noun in C and l-th noun in $nouns(i, k)$
17:                **if** $sim > max_{jk}$ **then**
18:                    $max_{jk} \leftarrow sim$
19:                **end if**
20:            **end for**
21:        **end for**
22:        **for all** $w_j \in C$ **do**
23:            $sumTot \leftarrow sumTot + G(pos(w_i), pos(w_j)) * max_{jk}$
24:        **end for**
25:        $sumTot \leftarrow sumTot/sumGauss$
26:        $\varphi(i, k) \leftarrow R(k) * sumTot$ ▷ $R(k)$ is defined as in $JIGSAW_{nouns}$
27:        **if** $\varphi(i, k) > score$ **then**
28:            $score \leftarrow \varphi(i, k)$
29:            $p \leftarrow k$
30:        **end if**
31:    **end for**
32:    $s \leftarrow s_{ip}$
33:    **return** s
34: **end procedure**

In this model, a synset vector instead of a word vector represents a document. Another key feature of the approach is that each document is represented by a set of M *slots*, where each slot is a textual field corresponding to a specific feature of the document, in an attempt to take also into account the document structure. According to the BOS model, the text in each slot is represented by counting separately the occurrences of a synset in the slots in which it occurs. An example of BOW-represented document is depicted following: More formally, assume that we have a collection of N documents. Let m be the index of the slot, for $n = 1, 2, \ldots, N$, the n-th document d_n is reduced to M bags of synsets, one for each slot:

$$d_n^m = \langle t_{n1}^m, t_{n2}^m, \ldots, t_{nD_{nm}}^m \rangle, \ m=1, 2, \ldots, M$$

where t_{nk}^m is the k-th synset in slot s_m of document d_n and D_{nm} is the total number of synsets appearing in the m-th slot of document d_n. For all n, k and m, $t_{nk}^m \in V_m$, which is the vocabulary for the slot s_m (the set of all different synsets found in slot s_m). Document d_n is finally represented in the vector space by M synset-frequency vectors:

$$f_n^m = \langle w_{n1}^m, w_{n2}^m, \ldots, w_{nD_{nm}}^m \rangle$$

where w_{nk}^m is the weight of the synset t_k in the slot s_m of document d_n, and can be computed in different ways: It can be simply the number of times synset t_k appears in slot s_m, as we used in our experiments, or a more complex TF-IDF score. The difference with respect to keyword-based model is that synset unique identifiers replace words. JIGSAW algorithm has been used within our content-based profiling system ITem Recommender (ITR) to obtain semantic user profiles. In ITR we consider the problem of learning user profiles as a binary text categorization task: Each document has to be classified as interesting or not wrt the user preferences. Therefore, the set of categories is $C = \{c_+, c_-\}$, where c_+ is the positive class, user-likes, and c_- the negative one, user-dislikes. There are several ways in which documents can be represented in order to be used as a basis for the learning component and there exists a variety of machine learning methods that could be used for inferring user profiles. The adopted strategy consists of two steps. In the first one, the JIGSAW WSD algorithm is used to build a BOS representation of documents. In the second step, a naïve Bayes approach learns sense-based user profiles as binary text classifiers from disambiguated documents. More details about ITR are in [12].

5   Experiments

We performed two experiments. In the first one, we evaluated the accuracy of JIGSAW on Task 1 of SEMEVAL-1 competition. This task is an application-driven one, where the application is a fixed Cross-Lingual Information Retrieval (CLIR) system. Participants must disambiguate text by assigning WordNet synsets, then the CLIR system must perform both the expansion to other languages and the indexing of the expanded documents; the final step is the retrieval (in batch) for all the languages. The retrieval results are taken as a measure of the disambiguation accuracy.

For the second evaluation, we adopted JIGSAW for the semantic indexing of documents: The algorithm exploits the WordNet lexical database to select, among all the possible meanings (*senses*) of a polysemous word, the correct one. Semantically indexed documents are then used to train a naïve Bayes learner that infers semantic, *sense-based* user profiles as binary text classifiers (user-likes and user-dislikes). The goal of the second experimental session was to evaluate whether the new synset-based version (BOS) of user profiles learned by ITR actually improved the performance wrt the keyword-based version (BOW) of the profiles. Synset-based profiles learned by ITR were formerly evaluated in a content-collaborative recommender system [3,6].

5.1   SEMEVAL-1 Task 1 Experiment

We performed the experiment following the instructions for SEMEVAL-1 Task 1. *JIGSAW* is implemented in JAVA, by using JWNL library[4] in order to access the WordNet dictionary. The dataset consists of 29,681 documents, including 300 topics (short text). Results are reported in Table 1. Besides the two systems (JIGSAW and PART-B) that partecipated to SEMEVAL-1 Task 1 competition, a third system (ORGANIZERS), developed by the organizers themselves, was included in the competition. The systems were scored according to standard IR/CLIR measures as implemented in the TREC evaluation package[5].

Table 1. SEMEVAL-1 Task1 Results

system	*IR documents*	*IR topics*	*CLIR*
no expansion	0.3599		0.1446
full expansion	0.1610	0.1410	0.2676
1st sense	0.2862	0.1172	0.2637
ORGANIZERS	0.2886	0.1587	0.2664
JIGSAW	0.3030	0.1521	0.1373
PART-B	0.3036	0.1482	0.1734

All systems showed similar results in IR tasks, while their behaviour was extremely different on CLIR task. Probably, the negative results of JIGSAW in CLIR task depends on complex interaction of WSD, expansion and indexing. Contrarily to other tasks, the task organizers do not plan to provide a ranking of systems on SEMEVAL-1 Task 1. As a consequence, the goal of this task - what is the best WSD system in the context of a CLIR system? - is still open.

WSD results are reported in Table 2. These results refer to the all-word task. In this case, the dataset consists of approximately 5000 words of coherent Penn Treebank[6] text with WordNet tags. All the predicating words and the head words of their arguments, as well as many adjectives and adverbs, are tagged. This task is useful to evaluate the ability of the WSD algorithm to disambiguate all words in a text. These results are encouraging as regards precision, considering

---

[4] http://sourceforge.net/projects/jwordnet
[5] http://trec.nist.gov/
[6] http://www.cis.upenn.edu/ treebank/

Table 2. WSD results on the all-words task

system	precision	recall	attempted
SENSEVAL-2			
ORGANIZERS	0.584	0.577	93.61%
JIGSAW	0.498	0.375	75.39%
PART-B	0.388	0.240	61.92%
SENSEVAL-3			
ORGANIZERS	0.591	0.566	95.76%
JIGSAW	0.484	0.338	69.98%
PART-B	0.334	0.186	55.68%

that our system exploits only WordNet as knowledge base, while the system
ORGANIZERS implements a supervised method that exploits SemCor to train
a k-NN classifier.

5.2 ITR Experiment

The goal of this evaluation was to compare the performance of keyword-based
profiles to that of synset-based profiles. Experiments were carried out on a collection of 100 papers (42 papers accepted to ISWC 2002, 58 papers accepted
to ISWC 2003) rated by 11 real users, that we called *ISWC dataset*. Papers
are rated on a 5-point scale mapped linearly to the interval [0,1]. Tokenization,
stopword elimination and stemming have been applied to index the documents
according to the BOW model.

Keyword-based profiles were learned from BOW-represented documents, while
synset-based profiles were inferred from BOS-represented documents. We measured both the classification accuracy and the effectiveness of the ranking set
by the two different kinds of profile on documents to be recommended. Classification effectiveness was evaluated by the classical measures *precision*, *recall*
and *F1* [11]. We adopted the Normalized Distance-based Performance Measure
(NDPM) [13] to compute the distance between the ranking set on papers by the
user ratings and the ranking predicted by ITR. Each run consisted in:

1. selecting the documents and the corresponding ratings given by the user;
2. splitting the selected data into a training set Tr and a test set Ts;
3. using Tr for learning the corresponding user profile;
4. evaluating the predictive accuracy of the induced profile on Ts, using the
   aforementioned measures.

The methodology adopted for obtaining Tr and Ts was the 5-fold cross validation. Table 3 shows the results reported over all 11 users.

From the results reported in Table 3, we notice an improvement both in
precision (+1%) and recall (+2%). Precision improves for 4 users out of 11, while
a more significant improvement (8 users out of 11) is obtained for recall. The
BOS model outperforms the BOW one specifically for users 7 and 10, for whom
we observe an increased precision, and in the worst case the same recall. The

Table 3. Performance of the BOW - BOS profiles

Id User	Precision		Recall		NDPM	
	BOW	BOS	BOW	BOS	BOW	BOS
1	0.57	0.55	0.47	0.50	0.60	0.56
2	0.73	0.55	0.70	0.83	0.43	0.46
3	0.60	0.57	0.35	0.35	0.55	0.59
4	0.60	0.53	0.30	0.43	0.47	0.47
5	0.58	0.67	0.65	0.53	0.39	0.59
6	0.93	0.96	0.83	0.83	0.46	0.36
7	0.55	0.90	0.60	0.60	0.45	0.48
8	0.74	0.65	0.63	0.62	0.37	0.33
9	0.60	0.54	0.63	0.73	0.31	0.27
10	0.50	0.70	0.37	0.50	0.51	0.48
11	0.55	0.45	0.83	0.70	0.38	0.33
Mean	0.63	0.64	0.58	0.60	0.45	0.45

rating style of these users has been thoroughly analyzed, and we observed that they provided a well balanced number of positive and negative ratings (positive examples not exceeding 60% of Tr). Moreover, they had a very clean rating style: They tend to assign the score 1 to not interesting papers, and the score 5 to interesting ones. We also observed the effect of the WSD on the training set of these users: If a polysemous word occurs both in positive and negative examples, the system is unlikely to be able to detect the discriminatory power of that feature for the classification, because the conditional probabilities of the word are almost the same for the two classes $\{C_+, C_-\}$. It could be noted from the NDPM values that the relevant/not relevant classification is improved without improving the ranking. A possible explanation of this result is that the BOS document representation has improved the classification of items whose scores are close to the relevant / not relevant threshold. A Wilcoxon signed ranked test, requiring a significance level $p < 0.05$, confirms that there is a statistically significant difference in favor of the BOS model as regards recall.

6   Conclusions and Future Work

In this paper, we presented a WSD algorithm that exploits WordNet as knowledge base and uses three different methods for each part-of-speech. Our hypothesis is that replacing words with synsets in the indexing phase produces a more accurate document representation that could be successfully exploited in more than one user-centric application. We ran experiments in two different applications, a CLIR System and a Recommender System based on user profiles. In the first application, we notice some negative results that probably depend on the expansion method used into the CLIR system. This was a first attempt to evaluate our WSD algorithm in this kind of application. In the second one, results confirm the effectiveness of the proposed approach. As a future work, we plan to exploit not only the WordNet hierarchy, but also domain ontologies in order to realize a more powerful document indexing. Furthermore, we intend to investigate if semantic information about terms can be employed in the matching phase (in addition to indexing one).

References

1. Banerjee, S., Pedersen, T.: An adapted lesk algorithm for word sense disambiguation using wordnet. In: Gelbukh, A. (ed.) CICLing 2002. LNCS, vol. 2276, pp. 136–145. Springer, Heidelberg (2002)
2. Decadt, B., Hoste, V., Daelemans, W., Van den Bosch, A.: Gambl, genetic algorithm optimization of memory-based wsd. In: Senseval-3: 3th International Workshop on the Evaluation of Systems for the Semantic Analysis of Text (2002)
3. Degemmis, M., Lops, P., Semeraro, G.: A content-collaborative recommender that exploits wordnet-based user profiles for neighborhood formation. User Modeling and User-Adapted Interaction: The Journal of Personalization Research (UMUAI) , 1573–1391 (2007) ISSN: 0924-1868 (print) 1573-1391 (online) (in press)
4. Leacock, C., Chodorow, M.: Combining local context and wordnet similarity for word sense identification. In: Fellbaum, C. (ed.) WordNet: An Electronic Lexical Database, MIT Press, Cambridge (1998)
5. Lesk, M.: Automatic sense disambiguation using machine readable dictionaries: how to tell a pine cone from an ice cream cone. In: Proc. of the 1986 SIGDOC Conf., pp. 20–29 (1986)
6. Lops, P., Degemmis, M., Semeraro, G.: Improving social filtering techniques through wordnet-based user profiles. In: McCoy, K., Conati, C., Paliouras, G. (eds.) UM 2007, Greece, June 25-29. LNCS (LNAI), vol. 4511, pp. 278–287. Springer, Heidelberg (2007)
7. Mihalcea, R.: Unsupervised large-vocabulary word sense disambiguation with graph-based algorithms for sequence data labeling. In: Proc. of the Joint Conf. on HLT/EMNLP (2005)
8. Miller, G.: Wordnet: An on-line lexical database. International Journal of Lexicography 3(4) (1990) (special issue)
9. Navigli, R., Velardi, P.: Structural semantic interconnections: A knowledge-based approach to word sense disambiguation. IEEE Transactions on Pattern Analysis and Machine Intelligence 27(7), 1075–1086 (2005)
10. Resnik, P.: Disambiguating noun groupings with respect to WordNet senses. In: Proc. of the 3th Workshop on Very Large Corpora, pp. 54–68. ACL (1995)
11. Sebastiani, F.: Machine learning in automated text categorization. ACM Computing Surveys 34(1), 1–47 (2002)
12. Semeraro, G., Degemmis, M., Lops, P., Basile, P.: Combining learning and word sense disambiguation for intelligent user profiling. In: IJCAI-07. Proceedings of the Twentieth International Joint Conference on Artificial Intelligence, pp. 2856–2861. M. Kaufmann, San Francisco, California (2007)
13. Yao, Y.Y.: Measuring retrieval effectiveness based on user preference of documents. Journal of the American Society for Information Science 46(2), 133–145 (1995)
14. Yuret, D.: Some experiments with a naive bayes wsd system. In: Senseval-3: 3th Internat. Workshop on the Evaluation of Systems for the Semantic Analysis of Text (2004)

Data-Driven Dialogue for Interactive Question Answering

Roberto Basili, Diego De Cao, Cristina Giannone, and Paolo Marocco

University of Rome Tor Vergata,
Department of Computer Science, Systems and Production,
00133 Roma (Italy)
`{basili,decao,giannone,marocco}@info.uniroma2.it`

Abstract. In this paper, a light framework for dialogue based interactive question answering is presented. The resulting architecture is called *REQUIRE (Robust Empirical QUestion answering for Intelligent Retrieval)*, and represents a flexible and adaptive platform for domain specific dialogue. REQUIRE characterizes as a domain-driven dialogue system, whose aim is to support the specific tasks evoked by interactive question answering scenarios. Among its benefits it should be mentioned its *modularity* and *portability* across different domains, its *robustness* through adaptive models of speech act recognition and planning and its adherence of knowledge representation standard. The framework will be exemplified through its application within a sexual health information service tailored to young people.

1   Introduction

In the recent years, the distinctions between the Question Answering (QA) and Dialogue technologies are increasingly narrowing and the number of overlaps increases accordingly. In general, QA aims to provide precise answers. In an interactive QA system, the inefficiency of an Information Retrieval engine is supplied by the ability of posing questions in natural language in order to get feedback from the user and detect the proper and useful answer(s). In other words, the system must not only comprehend the meaning of the user requests, but it has to negotiate interactively with him to achieve the evidence he was not able to fully express at the beginning. A dialogue management system is thus needed as a kind of wrapper for the QA engine able to upgrade the system information through its conversational ability. Here the processing of utterances and the management of the user attitudes have to be dynamically combined with the information returned by the underlying retrieval engine. *REQUIRE* makes use of a frame-based model for information seeking in support of interactive QA tasks. The aim is to limit the complexity for the user against cases where multiple and diverging answers are possible according to the retrieved documents. The conversation helps the user to converge to the most useful answer(s) with the minimum number of interactions (turns). In fact, it is able to build a plan

R. Basili and M.T. Pazienza (Eds.): AI*IA 2007, LNAI 4733, pp. 326–338, 2007.

according to the current *"Question Answering"* problem (the initial user question) and across the whole session. At the same time, questions may also refer to terms or concepts introduced during the dialogue itself so that the user can also improve his level of knowledge about the target argument. From this point of view, *REQUIRE* is not just characterizable as a QA support system but it realizes a wider notion of information seeking, where dialogue enables a paradigm for both access and acquisition of knowledge newer to the user evoked during a session, just like in a human-to-human conversation.

In order to deal with the complexity of the involved information, *REQUIRE* makes an explicit use of the knowledge regarding the domain and the QA task. In order to minimize the burden due to the interaction, a *plan* should include the minimal number of user turns needed to select the best answer. A static model of these interactions (i.e. turns) can be defined as during a session a limited set of dialogue acts can be foreseen. The dialogue management task can thus be mapped to a form of navigation through these finite set, as described in Section 3. The system manages all the speech acts related to interactive QA and provides a conversational interface through natural language dialogue. REQUIRE has been applied to a domain specific interactive QA system aiming to provide sexual health information to communities of young people. An agent prototype has been designed and developed according to the principles of the REQUIRE platform and its evaluation is in progress. This application, financed by the *Ministero delle Attivita' Produttive*[1], is applied in scenarios of mobile computing. In the Section 2 an overview of the system architecture is presented while Section 3 describes the dialogue management system and the planning functionalities. Finally, section 4 presents the results of experimental evaluation.

2   The REQUIRE Architecture

The main purpose of REQUIRE is to provide a dialogue management platform that supports a flexible design of portable *Interactive Question Answering* applications across different domains. It is thus designed according to *modularity* principles. The support to answer retrieval and planning dialogue management is organized into a pool of software components some of which are distributed servers. Two types of subsystems are foreseen: *external* and *internal* components. The main idea is that the *external* modules are strictly tight to *application domain* and can be easily substituted or extended when a new domain is targeted. As the REQUIRE components are compliant to current communication and knowledge representation standards (i.e. RDF/OWL), flexibility and porting constitute some of its strong advantages.

The *internal modules* are almost fully independent from the specific application and constitute a general framework for dialogue-based QA systems. Figure 1 shows the overall architecture of the REQUIRE platform. The central component in REQUIRE is the *Dialogue Manager* that controls the activation and

---

[1] The MIND project has been funded in 2005 by the Italian Governement and it will conclude at the end of 2007.

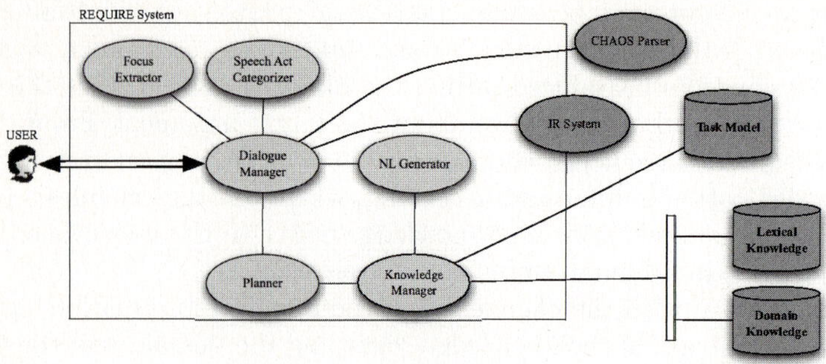

Fig. 1. System Architecture

the flow of information across individual components. During the coordination activities, the *Dialogue Manager* controls the dialogue evolution by storing the intermediate information (e.g. the focus of current turns) and activating the suitable state transitions according to the *dialogue model.*

In order to manage the user input in form of natural language utterances, two levels of analysis are applied: *Speech Act Recognition* and *Focus Detection.* Speech Act Recognition (SAR) supports the classification of the user utterances into the major Speech Act classes. This reduces the huge variety of rules required to recognize acts from the user input. The SAR is accomplished by a data-driven supervised model called *Speech Act Classifier.* More in details, the Speech Act Recognizer uses linguistic features on different levels (lexical, morpho-syntactic and semantic) adopting an unsupervised method. An utterance emitted by the user during a turn of dialogue is parsed, producing a network of nodes representing grammatical categories and morphological-syntactic (dependency) relationships. From this network we take out a list of features (lexical, morpho-syntactic etc.), by means of these we are able to map the turn's phrases into a structure, in order to put in evidence both syntactic structure of an utterance and the meaning of intentions of the user. The goal of the Speech Act Classifier is integrate lexical and syntatic information into an extended Vector Space, through Latent Semantic Analysis methods [1,2], and then use proximity for detecting the canonical act involved.

According to the latter inference, when the topic is not explicitly mentioned by a user, the *Focus Extractor* is triggered. This component recognizes the intended *focus* by analyzing the grammatical structure of the user utterance produced by the *CHAOS* syntactic parser [3].

The generation of the natural language output is under the responsibility of the *NL Generator* module. The NL generation is based on textual grammars, i.e. *NL Templates* [4]. Given the dialogue status, the proper system responses are detected and templates allow to efficiently compile the output according to the context (e.g. the user focus). The mechanism used to find the correct response at a given step requires a *plan* of the interactions. This *plan* is based on the initial user question in general characterized by multiple answers. The *Planner* computes the best plan according to a probabilistic model.

The interpretation of the user input and the planning depends on the available knowledge of the domain of application. An ontology infrastructure is available to the system where the domain and the task are represented. The *Task Model* represents the answers and their corresponding concepts organized into a hierarchy. This repository is accessed by the external *Information Retrieval System*, that initially retrieves all the candidate answers to the user question. No constraint is posed to the IR engine except the requirement of deriving a relevance score associated to each candidate answer in the ranked list (The IR engine has been implemented using the package Lucene [5]).

The *Domain Model* represents the conceptual information related to the application domain, i.e. concepts organized in an ontology and their definitions. In order to manage the gap between domain expert expressions and common linguistic expressions, the domain model is linked to a semantic lexicon, i.e. *Lexical Knowledge* in Fig. 1. The integration of the two resources allows to deal consistently with user utterances even when ontological reasoning is required. The *Knowledge Manager* is a component in charge of supplying the abstract interface to all the different ontological (i.e. the task and domain model) and lexical resources. In more technical details, the Domain Model and its encyclopedic knowledge is represented by MeSH [6], a large scale medical taxonomy created by the National Library of Medicine. The RDF/OWL version of MeSH includes definitions, hierarchical relations and other relations between concepts including aliases or synonyms. The employed lexicon is Wordnet [7] which expresses word senses and the major lexical semantic relations. An integration between MeSH and Wordnet has been obtained according to the method discussed in [8]. In the integrated lexicon special OWL properties are defined to map ontological concepts into the corresponding word senses. The adoption of standards in the knowledge infrastructure designed in REQUIRE increases its flexibility and interoperability. Automatic mapping methods also support its portability toward other domains [8].

Finally, the REQUIRE System, has been implemented in order to evaluate his performance, as we put in relevance in in Section 4.

3   The Dialogue Management in REQUIRE

In a IQA system, the role of the dialogue is to aid the user to reach the desired information, through a natural interaction like in a help desk or an information office. The most important problems are the required understanding of the user intention, that should be captured from his utterances and the elaboration of the better response. To guide the user toward the suitable answer, the REQUIRE dialogue manager makes a dynamic plan that evolves at every dialogue turn. The plan, based on the user input utterance and on the dialogue history, allows the agent to interact with the user through two main initiatives, i.e. system dialogue acts [9].

In **Clarification** steps, the Dialogue Manager asks the user about a topic as "a request of information about something". Positive user answers to clarification questions allow to trigger some refinement steps until a single answer is selected.

U$_1$: *Can you tell me the cost of the morning-after pill?*
A$_1$: *Are you interested to speak about the pill?* (Clarification)
U$_2$: *No, I'm interested to the morning-after one.*
A$_2$: *The morning-after pill costs roughly 15 Euro.* (Exit with Success)

Fig. 2. Dialogue example with the system in clarification state

Negative replies allow to eliminate a topic (and all of its subtopics) from the future interaction: the plan is thus pruned. In Figure 2 one such example is shown.

The plan is thus made by the set of clarifications about some topics that provide to detect the precise answer with a minimal involvement of the user. Negative replies to clarification questions reduce incrementally the candidate answers until a single one is left and it is output to the user.

During clarifications, the system may introduce concepts that are unknown or ambiguous for the user. In this case, the user may request about them, and the plan must be adapted accordingly. Every nested request activates an **Explanation** initiative where the system helps the user to disambiguate previously introduced terms and then come back to the preceding plan state. An example of this is reported in Figure 3. Finally, if the user redirects his attention (focus) on newly encountered concepts (i.e. those that have never been met during the current dialogue context), the system needs to restart a search phase as a new question answering session. A special case of Explanation is activated when the user focus is ambiguous: a specific speech act, **Disambiguation**, is defined in this case. When a referred concept is ambiguous for the system knowledge, as for example the word *venom*, that can be either a chemical compound or the natural substance produced by snakes, the agent inquiries the user for the alternatives (definitions as available from the knowledge resources). The user feedback allows to select the intended alternative and let the system go back to an explanation state.

U$_1$: *How can I use a long term effect contraceptive methods?*
A$_1$: *Are you interested to artificial contraceptive methods?* (Clarification)
U$_2$: *Yes, I am.*
A$_2$: *Do you want to speak about under-skin implants and about its prescription, in particular?*
U$_3$: *What is an under-skin implant?* (Explanation)
A$_3$: *The under-skin implants are a long effect contraceptive methods. They are plastic capsule to insert under the skin, through a cut.*
U$_4$: *Why not?*
A$_4$: *A doctor, or a sanitary assistant, have to insert and remove the under-skin implant.*
(Exit with Success)

Fig. 3. Dialogue example with the system in explanation state

3.1   Finite State Technology for Dialogue Management

The speech acts discussed up to now originate from a limited set of dialogue states. They can be thus assimilated to a finite state (i.e. a Mealy) machine: every dialogue act is performed by the system according to a specific state and a user focus. A Mealy machine is defined as an ordered sextuple $A = (S, I, O, \delta, \lambda, s_0)$ where

- S, I and O are the sets of states, input and output symbols, respectively
- $\delta : S \times I \rightarrow S$ and $\lambda : S \times I \rightarrow O$ are the *transition* and the *output function*, respectively
- $s_0 \in S$ is the specific *initial state*

In a generic state $s \in S$, the automaton (1) detects the actual speech act characterizing the last user input, (2) changes its state according to the δ function and (3) outputs a symbol according to the output function λ. Output here includes the current topics (see the next section on planning) and a dialogue act (e.g. clarification) used to trigger the NL generation component. In REQUIRE, the transition function is also influenced by the current plan (see next Section): given a state and the speech act characterizing the user reply, it produces the suitable next state. For example, clarifications may follow other clarifications in general, according to the next topics foreseen in the plan.

The set of states Q in REQUIRE includes the previously introduced states, i.e. clarification, explanation and disambiguation. Other specific states are the following:

- The s_0 state, *Start*, where the retrieval process is triggered by the initial question, as seen in section 2.
- The exit states that distinguish situations where the best individual answer has been found (*Exit whit Success, EWS*), a switch of attention has been manifested by the user and a new question answering session is to be run (*Change Focus, CF*) or no answer can be found after some clarification steps (*Unsuccessful Exit, UE*).

The transitions between intermediate states are shown in the state transition diagram of Figure 4.

It is worth noticing that intermediate states reflect the speech act characterizing each system initiative. The speech acts characterizing the user utterances express instead user intentions. They play here the role of input symbols. The

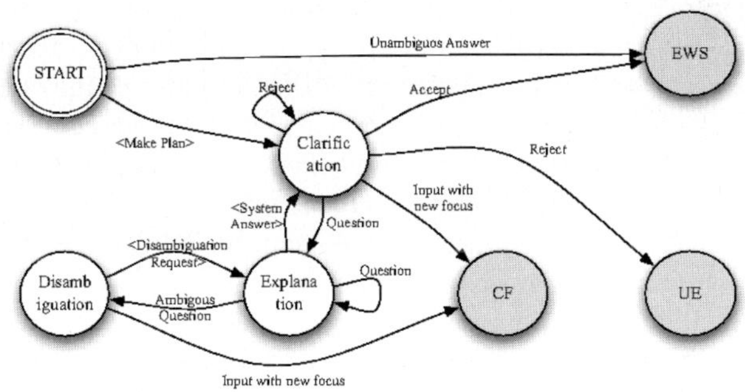

Fig. 4. State Diagram for Dialogue Control

user utterances can be mainly partitioned into *agreements* and *questions*. In the state transition diagram of Fig. 4, the two different types of agreement are shown: *acceptance* and *rejection*. These types apply to the current focus of the discourse as they may refer to the focus agreed between the user and the system or to a newly introduced focus.

The speech act recognition is a critical stage of the above finite state technology. Early and basic approaches, like the input-reaction rules adopted in A.L.I.C.E.-like agents (i.e. AIML expressions, as defined in [10]), require extensive compilation of pattern matching rules, acting on the input utterances.

3.2   Planning Dialogue Turns

Planning is the activity of deciding how the dialogue will proceed during a session triggered by the initial user question. As many candidate answers are returned by the IR engine (they form the answer list AL), the plan must decide which interactions are useful to focus on the subset of relevant ones. The dialogue in fact aims to fully prune out the irrelevant responses. The goal of the *Planner* component is to design the proper sequence of interactions to reach the correct response(s) minimizing the burden for the user.

The *Planner* can exploit a structured organization of the domain topics, called task model. The task model is a hierarchy, where individual nodes represent topics and (possibly) associated answers. Every answer in the AL set is thus associated to one node in the *Task Model*. In this way, the hierarchy defines topically coherent subsets of the AL members: each subset is a topic and their grouping is a partition $P(AL)$ of the original AL. A partial order relation results in $P(AL)$ from the dominance in the Task Model. Each set in $P(AL)$ is defined by the most specific node in the hierarchy that dominates some answers in AL. Notice that the different sets in $P(AL)$ include nodes (and the corresponding answers) characterized by different relevance scores after the retrieval process. A static visit impacts on the perceived naturally of a conversation: it would proceed independently by the initial user answer and without accounting for the quality and coherence of the obtained responses. A much better model can be obtained as a function of the relevance scores obtained for the individual answers. The approach adopted in REQUIRE formulates a probabilistic model of the initial $P(AL)$ and derives the navigation strategy that find a correct response in a minimum number of steps. The basic idea is that each clarification step acquires information about a node and this allows to concentrate on specific subsets in $P(AL)$ and prune other ones. The amount of available information increases at each step according to the pruning of members of the $P(AL)$. In this perspectives clarification questions that are more informative amount to a richer pruning steps. A probabilistic way to measure the *informative power* of a node (or of its subtree) can be defined. Every clarification question about a topic T, provides negative (in case of rejection) or positive (in case of acceptance) evidence about T. In case of acceptance, every node in $P(AL)$ that is not accessible from T should be discarded. Every user answer reduces the uncertainty, as reduces the number of possible candidates responses in AL. The

search strategy is therefore heuristic and proceeds through successive approximations. Given the initial state of $P(AL)$, i.e. the set of relevance scores for its
topics/subsets, a probabilistic model of the correct answers can be obtained: every node will be characterized by a probability of being relevant proportional to
its relevance score. The amount of uncertainty depends on the resulting probability distribution and a good measure of it is its *entropy*. Every clarification step
about a topic T reduces the overall uncertainty as it prunes some of the members
from the $P(AL)$. This reflects in a different probability distribution associated
to the remaining members that results in a lower overall entropy. The amount of
reduction in the entropy due to a single clarification step is an effective indicator
of the role of a topic T in a good dialogue, i.e. a sequence of questions short
enough to converge quickly to the relevant answers in AL.

4   Evaluation

Evaluation of dialogue systems is problematic as it deals with a large set of
factors, all of them strictly depending on specific applications. Moreover, such
systems are usually designed as composition of rather complex components that
critically influence the whole system performance. In this section, we will try to
design general evaluation criteria that can be reasonably applied for comparative analysis against previous approaches. Specific as well as general metrics have
been defined. The primary goal of the experiments was to set-up baselines for
various subtasks useful to assess individual components and enable comparisons
with future versions of REQUIRE. Metrics that have been proposed for evaluate dialogue systems can be grouped into three main classes: *user satisfaction,
dialogue-dependent costs* and *task-based success* based measures. Previous studies have provided ways to combine these different measures as for example the
PARADISE paradigm (PARAdigm for DIalogue System Evaluation, [11]). This
framework is strictly dependent on an *attribute value matrix* (AVM) representation of the target dialogue task, it consists in the information exchanged between
the agent and the user, expressed as a set of ordered attribute-value pairs. In
our case, i.e. information seeking within a specific domain through vaguely defined questions, the target AVM representation was inapplicable. As discussed
in 1, REQUIRE is a hybrid system with mixed initiative and several aspects
must be taken into account. It deals in fact with the traditionally underspecified
relevance issue of Information Retrieval. Most questions do not have a specific
answer and the role of dialogue is also to guide the user to better understanding his needs, or increase his level of acquaintance of the domain by providing
information initially unknown to the user (e.g. definition of tecnical concepts in
a domain). Moreover, tasks depend on the nature of questions, that may be targeted to different kinds of concepts. We distinguished four different information
needs, i.e. request types:

- Questions about *diseases*, like *How can I contract AIDS ?)*
- Questions about *contraception methods*, as in *How to get the morning after
  pill without being adviced by a doctor?)*

- Questions about *anatomy, body parts*, like *What are the ovaries ?)*
- General inquiries about *sexuality*, as *At what age do boys and girls start to get sexual feelings?)*

In order to evaluate different aspects of the system we thus designed an evaluation that is sensible to all the above different types. The aim here is not to directly compare our system with previous ones, but rather to set-up an evaluation scheme able to detect sources of weakness in REQUIRE and support incremental comparative evaluation against its future releases.

4.1   Experimental Setup

The targeted domain was sexual health consultancy, where a closed set of answers were certified by psychologists and professional doctors (due to the critical social implications of the domain). The set includes 703 different answers that are organized into a topical taxonomy of about $1,089$ concepts. The user initial question triggers a retrieval process from the answers repository: each question retrieves usually a large number of answers, as these are made of short sentences (average length is 15 words) and are relatively very similar as they focus on a very specialized domain. As a result, the application of a standard IR engine (Lucene [5]) achieves an F measure[2] of about 0.15.

We collected user satisfaction metrics through a Web-based survey based on a questionnaire compiled by the users: they were asked to fill out the questionnaire immediately after the completion of a dialogue session. A community of 35 users have been studied and the overall number of sessions is 118. Although some users provided few sessions , they are representative of a large variety of attitudes and criteria, that makes this evaluation more realistic. The adopted subjective criteria for evaluation suggested by the questionnaire were the following

- *Topic understanding*: the ability of the system in recognizing the main focus of the originating question
- *Meaningful interaction*: the quality of the system behaviour according to the utility of each generated turn
- *Topic coverage*: the user perception of how good is the system knowledge about the target topic
- *Contextual Appropriateness*: the ability to produce clear turns consistent with the dialogue progress [12]
- *Interaction/Dialogue quality*: the overall quality of the system generated sentences. It captures mainly the grammatical correctness of the NL generation
- *Ease of use*: the usability of the system, that is the system friendliness perceived by the user
- *Overall Effectiveness*: the user comprehensive judgment about the system usefulness

---

[2] The F measure is the harmonic mean between *recall* and *precision*, but given the assumption that each question has only one valid answer associated it also corresponds to *accuracy*.

All the above criteria were scored by the users according to a 1 to 5 scale (where 5 means full satisfaction and 1 disappointment, respectively) and are declared by a user with respect the entire dialogue session. Only *Contextual Appropriateness* is declared on a per turn basis, and it is reported as average across the full set of turns (i.e. micro-average).

4.2   Results: Objective Measures

A good measure of retrieval (i.e. dialogue) complexity is the average number of concepts in the topic taxonomy related to at least one of the answers retrieved by Lucene. The initial system plan starts from these concepts and is thus more complex whenever a larger number of answers are returned. In our case, we have found a non trivial number of questions with a very large number of retrieved answers (e.g. between 60 and 90). In general, we found more nodes than answers inasmuch as specific answers are found in different branches of the topic taxonomy. Therefore they require some generalization. This complexity is not trivial and confirms the realistic information seeking task employed in the evaluation.

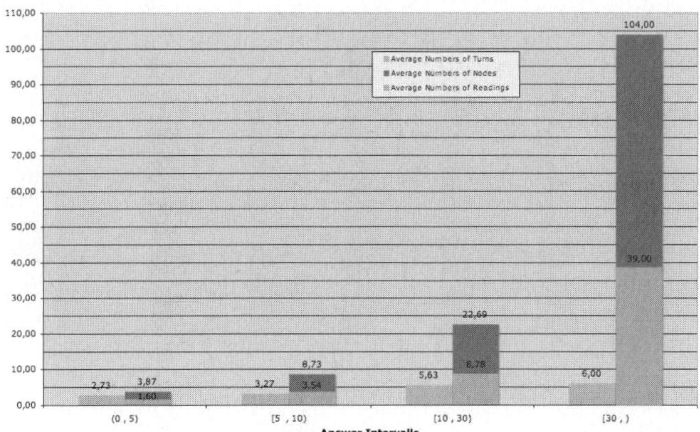

Fig. 5. Impact of the dialogue on the retrieval effectiveness

It is to be noticed that, given the low precision of the information retrieval stage, a user needs to read (and reject) a large number of wrong retrieval hits (false positives) before getting to the precise answer (in the cases he/she is able to recognize it). On average, the number of this readings is 6.12. The core objective of REQUIRE is to strictly reduce this score. In Figure 5, we report the turns, answers and activated nodes coresponding to questions of increasing complexity: four question classes are reported for different numbers of retrieved answers. In Fig. 5, we also report the average number of readings needed by the user to select the proper answer. As we see, different classes are characterized by different readings on average. Comparing the number of turns that REQUIRE needs to converge, we notice that for questions of minimal complexity (< 5) the dialogue is not effective. However, when the number of false positives increase (in line with the behaviour of most IR engines), the impact of REQUIRE is very high: for the most complex cases we reach a compression rate (number of average readings vs. number of observed turns) of about 8.7. The overall number of successfully concluded sessions is 76, that is the 64.4% of the tests. Given the relatively low quality of the retrieval system and the full automation of the dialogue capabilities of the system, this result is very attractive for a large number of applications. REQUIRE in fact does not rely on complex hand coded knowledge and can be tailored easily to new domains. An analysis of mistakes revealed that in most cases the wrong behaviour is due to generic questions, where the correct answer was not available to the system (out of domain tests), or no answer could be retrieved by the IR engine.

4.3   Results over Questionnaires

Figure 6 reports the subjectives scores according to the different question types.

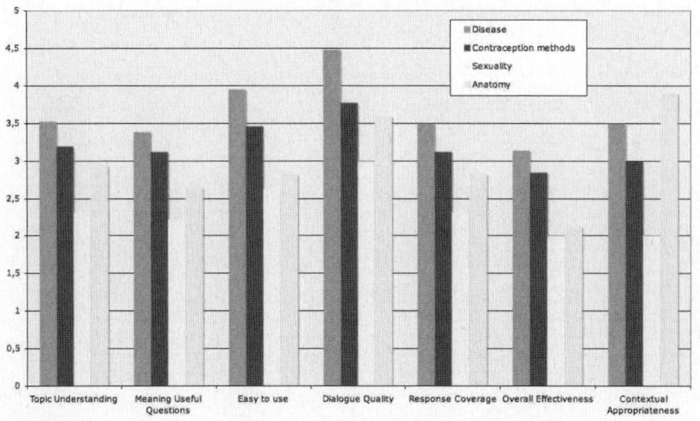

Fig. 6. Perceived Accuracy by the user according to different question types

At first glance, the class *disease*, i.e. a well-specified topic, has the better scores across the different criteria. Notice how this was the starting point of the domain modeling, as the service was targeted to provide information and consultancy about possible sexual problems and diseases, largely unknown among young people. On the contrary, the class *sexuality* has the lowest values in all cases. Basically, this is due to the inherent vagueness and ambiguity of this class that usually is populated by confused and unclear questions from the user.

It is interesting to notice that the best values for all classses are generated by the *Dialogue Quality* measure, that emphasizes the good perceived quality of the *NL-Generator* component. Another useful metric is the *Contextual Appropriateness* that is derived from scores assigned by the user on every individual turn. Here, the best value is achieved for the *anatomy* topic and not for *disease*s, that is the best class with respect to the other metrics. Notice also that for *anatomy* the system has a rather low *Response coverage*. This suggests that although the final response is not very good, individual turns across a whole dialogue session still keep the interactions within acceptable levels of quality and consistency: the average accuracy of the several individual turns is in line with user expectations of a naturally flowing comunication.

5   Conclusion and Future Works

Although experiments for measuring the accuracy and usability of the REQUIRE technology are still in progress, the presented dialogue platform for *domain-specific* Interactive Question Answering represents a solid implementation of a robust technology. The rich set of functionalities defines an adaptive framework for domain-specific dialogue. The major benefits are its adherence to standards for knowledge representation, the adaptivity, based on state-of-art classification methods, for speech act recognition. The flexibility of the system is enforced by the high level of architectural modularity, where some specific components are domain independent and can be fully reused (e.g. the planner).

Methods for automatic adaptation of the domain knowledge, as in the case of the automatic mapping between the world model and a general purpose lexicon, are foreseen in the framework. They make directly available the lexical knowledge necessary to support typical dialogue inferences like focus detection in an inexpensive and semiautomatic way. The results of the large scale testing, as this actually used by a wider user communities, will provide sufficient evidence for depeer quantitative evaluation and quality assessment.

References

1. Landauer, T., Dumais, S.: A solution to plato's problem: The latent semantic analysis theory of acquisition, induction, and representation of knowledge. Psychological Review 104, 211–240 (1997)
2. Serafin, R., Di Eugenio, B.: Flsa: Extending latent semantic analysis with features for dialogue act classification. In: ACL'04. Proceedings of the 42nd Meeting of the Association for Computational Linguistics, Main Volume, Barcelona, Spain, pp. 692–699 (2004)
3. Basili, R., Zanzotto, F.M.: Parsing engineering and empirical robusteness. Journal of Language Engineering 8 (2/3) (2002)
4. Stent, A., Dowding, J., Gawron, J., Bratt, E.O., Moore, R.: The commandtalk spoken dialogue system. In: Proceedings of ACL'99 (1999)
5. Goetz, B.: The Lucene search engine (v. 2.2): Powerful, flexible, and free (June 2007), http://lucene.apache.org/
6. MeSH: http://www.nlm.nih.gov/mesh/
7. Fellbaum, C.: WordNet, an electronic lexical database. MIT Press, Cambridge (1998)
8. Basili, R., Vindigni, M., Zanzotto, F.M.: Integrating ontological and linguistic knowledge for conceptual information extraction. In: Proceedings of the IEEE/WIC WI2003 Conference on Web Intelligence (2003)

9. Bunt, H.C.: Context and dialogue control. THINK Quarterly 3, 19–31 (1994)
10. Bush, N.: AIML Intelligence Markup Language (AIML) Version 1.0.1. A.L.I.C.E. AI Foundation (2005)
11. Walker, M.A., Litman, D.J., Kamm, C.A., Abella, A.: PARADISE: A framework for evaluating spoken dialogue agents. In: Cohen, P.R., Wahlster, W. (eds.) Proceedings of the Thirty-Fifth Annual Meeting of the Association for Computational Linguistics and Eighth Conference of the European Chapter of the Association for Computational Linguistics, Somerset, New Jersey, pp. 271–280. Association for Computational Linguistics (1997)
12. Danieli, M., Gerbino, E.: Metrics for evaluating dialogue strategies in a spoken language system. In: Working Notes of the AAAI Spring Symposium on Empirical Methods in Discourse Interpretation and Generation (1995)

GlossExtractor: A Web Application to Automatically Create a Domain Glossary

Roberto Navigli and Paola Velardi

Dipartimento di Informatica, Università di Roma "La Sapienza",
via Salaria 113, Roma
{navigli,velardi}@di.uniroma1.it

Abstract. We describe a web application, *GlossExtractor*, that receives in input the output of a terminology extraction web application, *TermExtractor*, or a user-provided terminology, and then searches several repositories (on-line glossaries, web documents, user-specified web pages) for sentences that are candidate definitions for each of the input terms. Candidate definitions are then filtered using statistical indicators and machine-learned regular patterns. Finally, the user can inspect the acquired definitions and perform an individual or group validation. The validated glossary is then downloaded in one of several formats.

1 Introduction

Navigli and Velardi (2004) presented a technique, named *OntoLearn*, to automatically learn a domain ontology from the documents shared by the members of a web community. This technique is based on three learning steps, each followed by manual validation: terminology extraction, glossary extraction, and finally, ontology enrichment. The OntoLearn methodology has been enhanced, and experimented in the context of a European project, INTEROP (Velardi et al. 2007). Recently, we started to develop web applications to make freely available each of the steps of the OntoLearn methodology. The first web application, *TermExtractor* (Sclano and Velardi, 2007), was made available on http://lcl.uniroma1.it about one year ago. We here describe GlossExtractor, a tool that receives in input a terminology T, i.e. a list of relevant domain terms, and automatically extracts from web documents one or more definitions for each term in T.

2 Summary of the Gloss Extraction Algorithm

Figure 1 shows the basic steps of the glossary extraction algorithm. The input to the system a list T of terms, for which a glossary has to be learned. Possibly, this list is the result of a previous terminology extraction process.

The first phase is <u>candidate extraction</u>: for each term, definition sentences are searched first, in on-line glossaries, then, in on-line documents. Simple, manually defined regular expressions are used to extract the candidate definition sentences.

R. Basili and M.T. Pazienza (Eds.): AI*IA 2007, LNAI 4733, pp. 339–349, 2007.

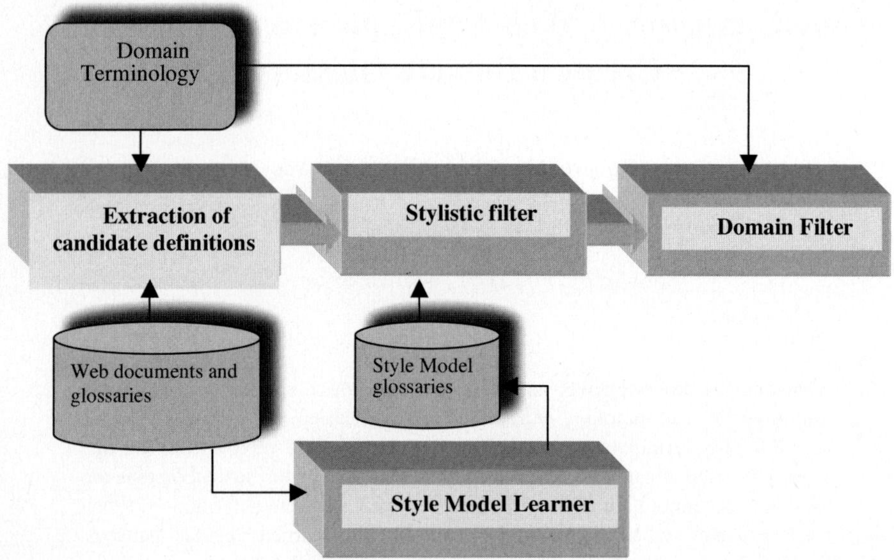

Fig. 1. The glossary extraction algorithm

Figure 2 shows an example of html page of a web glossary including definitions. To extract the relevant information (highlighted with arrows in Figure 2) it is necessary to perform layout and syntactic analysis of the html pages, in order to prune the noise. Similarly, Figure 3 shows an example of definition embedded in a web document. Here, not only graphical and irrelevant information has to be pruned, but also some simple regular expression must be defined to determine whether the sentence including a term $t \in T$ is a candidate definition. Examples of simple filtering patterns are: *(("<term> is a ")|("<term> are the ")) (("<term> defines ")|("<term> refers to ")) (("<term> concerns ")|("<term> is the ") (("<term> is any ")|("<term> is an ")) (("<term> is a kind of ") (("<term> is defined (to|as) "))* etc. These patterns (inspired by Hearst (1992) and subsequent works) are intentionally very simple, to reduce search time over the web.

The web-search step described above usually produces a large number of hits, including a considerable amount of noise. Noise is generated by two factors:

First, a sentence matching one of the above simple regular expressions is likely not to be a definition, e.g.: *"**Knowledge management** <u>is a</u> contradiction in terms, being a hangover from an industrial era when control modes of thinking."*

Second, the sentence could indeed be a definition, but not pertinent to the domain, e.g: *A **model** is a person who acts as a human prop for purposes of art, fashion, advertising, etc.* that would not be pertinent to, e.g. a "software engineering" domain, but rather to a "fashion" domain. The two subsequent steps of the glossary extraction methodology are conceived in order to eliminate these two sources of noise.

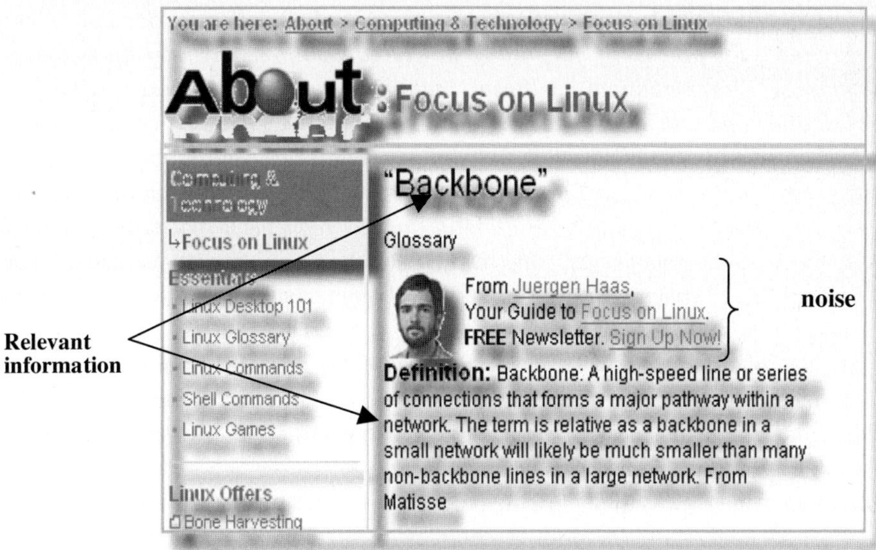

Fig. 2. Example of a definition in a web glossary page

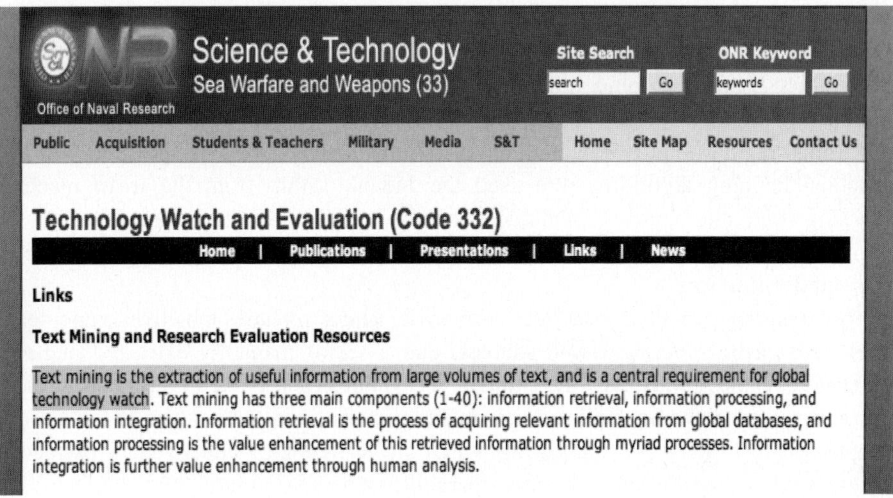

Fig. 3. Example of a definition embedded in a web document

2.1 Application of a Stylistic Filter

The objective of the stylistic filter is to select *"well-formed"* definitions, i.e. definitions expressed in term of *genus* (the *kind* a concept belongs to) and *differentia* (what specializes the concept with respect to its kind), e.g. *"enterprise information integration is* **the process** *of integrating structured data from any relevant source for the purpose of presenting an intelligent, real-time view of the business to a business analyst or an operational application."* In this definition, the phrase that identifies the genus is marked in bold. Not all definitions are well-formed in the above mentioned sense, e.g. *"component integration is obtained by composing the component's refinement structures together, resulting in (larger) refinement structures which can be further used as components"*, and many sentences being not well-formed are non-definitions, e.g. *"component integration has been recently proposed to provide a solution for those issues"*

Stylistic filtering is a novel criterion with respect to related literature on definition extraction, and has several advantages: i) to prefer definitions adhering to a uniform style, commonly adopted by professional lexicographers; ii) to distinguish definitions from non-definitions (especially when candidate definitions are extracted from free texts, rather than glossaries); iii) to be able to extract from definitions a *kind-of* information, used to arrange terms taxonomically.

To verify well-formedness, we use regular expressions that impose constraints on a sentence structure at the lexical, part-of-speech and syntactic level. Part of speech and syntactic elements are identified using an available parser, the TreeTagger[1]. Figure 4 shows an example of sentence tagged with part of speech (POS) and segmented (chunked) according to syntactic categories. For example, DT and NN are POS for determiners (e.g. *the*) and nouns (e.g. *process*), respectively, while the sentence chunk *"The process"* is tagged with NC (noun phrase).

"Style" regular expressions have been automatically learned using a decision tree machine learning algorithm. We used the J48 algorithm from the *weka* machine learning web site (www.cs.waikato.ac.nz/ml/weka/).   As input features for the algorithm, we used the first 5 POS/chunk tags pairs. Figure 5 shows an example of learned decision tree.

The *training set* (TS) used to learn style filters includes positive example of definitions from several on-line sources, and a set of manually extracted negative examples. Table 1 illustrates the training set composition. Notice that most negative examples come from evaluation experiments performed in the context of the already mentioned INTEROP project, during which our terminology and glossary extraction tools have been used to create an interoperability glossary (Velardi et al. 2007).

<NC> The DT process NN </NC><PC> of IN <VC> achieving VVG </VC></PC><NC> the DT objectives NNS </NC><PC> of IN <NC> the DT business NN organization NN </NC></PC><PC> by IN <VC> bringing VVG </VC></PC><ADVC> together RB </ADVC><NC> some DT resources NNS </NC>. SENT

Fig. 4. Example of a sentence annotated with part of speech and syntactic tags (TreeTagger)

---

[1] TreeTagger is available at http://www.ims.unistuttgarrt.de/projekte/corplex/ TreeTagger/ Decision/TreeTagger.html

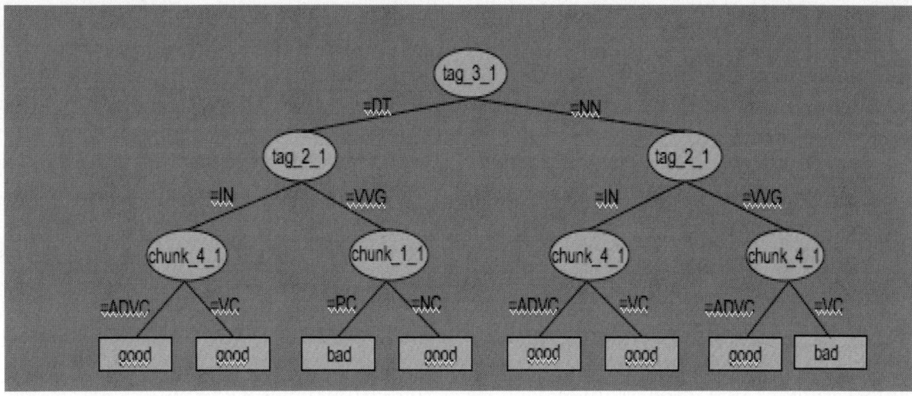

Fig. 5. A style decision tree learned with J48 machine learning algorithm

Table 1. Training Set used to learn a style filter for definition sentences

Examples	Art (AT&T[2], WordNet[3])	Tourism (WordNet+STB[4])	Computer Network (Geek.com[5])	Interoperability (Interop glossary)
Positive	310+415	270+270	450	215+1220
Negative	80	60	50	2032

2.2 Application of a Domain Filter

The domain filter is used to prune candidate definitions that are not pertinent with the domain. A probabilistic model of the domain is obtained by analyzing the domain terminology. As explained in the introduction, the input to the glossary extraction algorithm is a terminology T, e.g. a flat list of single and multi-word terms.

From the set of word *components* forming the terminology T, a *probabilistic model of the domain* is learned, assigning a probability of occurrence to each word component. More precisely, let T be the lexicon of extracted terms, LT the set of singleton word components appearing in T, and let :

$$E(P(w)) = \frac{freq(w)}{\sum_{w_i \in LT} freq(w_i)}$$

be the estimated probability of w in D, where $w \in LT$ and the frequencies are computed in T. For example, if $T = [$*distributed system integration, integration method*$]$ then $LT=[$*distributed, system, integration, method*$]$ and $E(P(integration))=2/5$, since over 5 singleton words in T, integration appears twice.

---

[2] www.getty.edu/research/conducting_research/vocabularies/aat/
[3] wordnet.princeton.com
[4] http://app.stb.com.sg/asp/tou/tou08.asp
[5] www.geek.com/glossary/

We then define and measure the <u>domain pertinence</u> of each extracted definition, as follows: let W_t be the set of words in def(t), a candidate definition of t. Let $W'_t \subseteq W_t$ be the subset of words in *def(t)* belonging to *LT*. Compute:

$$weight(def(t)) = \sum_{w \in W'_t, w \in LT} E(P(w)) \log(N_t / n_t^w) + \alpha \sum_{w \in LT, w \in t} E(P(w))$$

where N_t is the number of definitions extracted for the term t, and n_t^w is the number of such definitions including the word w. The log factor, called *inverse document frequency* in information retrieval literature, reduces the weight of words that have a very high probability of occurrence in any definition, regardless of the domain (e.g. *"system"*). The additional sum in this formula assigns a higher weight to those sentences including some of the components of the term *t* to be defined, e.g. *"Schema integration* is [the process by which *schemata* from heterogeneous databases are conceptually *integrated* into a single cohesive *schema*.]"

The domain pertinence is applied over definitions that are classified as such by the decision-tree classifier mentioned in previous section. An adjustable threshold ϑ is applied to every definition, in order to select only definitions for which $weight(def) \geq \vartheta$.

2.3 Evaluation of the Glossary Extraction Algorithm

We defined a novel validation policy: we extracted a set of non-definition sentences (yet matching the simple regular patterns of section 2) and we immersed definitions from on-line glossaries (not used during the style-learning phase) into the set of non-definition. We then computed precision and recall of the glossary filtering methodology. First, we created a test set of glossary and web definitions, as detailed in Table 2. To obtain examples of "good" definitions, we first extracted definitions from professional glossaries on the web (partially from the same sources as for the learning set, but different definitions), then, we searched the web for definitions of the same terms as in the glossaries, and finally we compared the glossary definitions with those extracted from web documents, to decide whether they were good definitions or not. The bad definitions were used as negative examples.

Since "good" definitions are professionally created, the test set can be considered what is usually called a *"gold standard"*. Notice that, in the literature, bad and good definitions are evaluated using the *"2-3 judges with adjudication"* policy, a technique that suffers from subjectivity: it is not very robust, and the judges often are not expert lexicographers (usually, the authors of the publication).

Table 2 shows that the test set included definitions also from domains that were not in the training set (compare with Table 1). This was decided to better test the generality of the style filter.

On this test set, we ran several experiments, to evaluate:

1. The ability of the system at correctly classifying good and bad definitions, when definitions are extracted only from glossaries;
2. The ability of the system at correctly classifying good and bad definitions, when these are extracted only from web documents;
3. The ability of the system at pruning out definitions which are good, but not pertinent with the selected domain (domain filter).

Table 2. Sources used to create the test sets

Domain	Glossary definitions	Web Definitions
Art	AT&T	-
Economy	Michigan University glossary[6] and Wikipedia[7]	Web definitions for the same terms
Medicine	University of Maryland glossary[8]	Web definitions for the same terms
Interoperability	Interop. glossary	-
Computer networks	-	Web definitions for the same terms
Tourism	WordNet and STB	-

Table 3 shows the result of experiment 1, and table 4 the results of experiment 2. Both have been obtained using *10-fold cross validation* technique. The evaluation measures are *accuracy, precision, recall* and *f-measure*, which are standard measures in the *Information Retrieval* and *Machine Learning* literature.

Table 3. Performance of the algorithm searching only web glossaries and Google's define

Set	#	Accuracy	Precision	Recall	F-Measure
Training (TR)	2105	0,863	0,831	0,935	0,880
Test (TS)	1978	0,862	0,897	0,889	0,893
TR+TS	4083	0,874	0,880	0,911	0,895

Table 4. Performance of the algorithm searching only web documents

Set	#	Accuracy	Precision	Recall	F-Measure
Training (TR)	402	0,864	0,854	0,859	0,857
Test (TS)	359	0,851	0,925	0,810	0,864
TR+TS	4371	0,874	0,876	0,860	0,868

Both tables highlight good results, even in comparison with the few available data in literature. The only performance data available in literature concern a task similar to glossary extraction, i.e. in the Question Answering TREC context, the sub-task *"answering what-is questions"*.

To evaluate the performance of the domain filter in isolation (experiment 3), we created a test set composed by 1000 economy definitions and 250 medicine definitions (extracted both from web documents and glossaries). We then ordered the set of definitions, based only on the domain pertinence, computed on the economy

---

[6] www.umich.edu/alandear/glossary
[7] www.wikipedia,org
[8] www.umm.edu/glossary

terminology. The first non-pertinent definition is found in position 571, and only 72 economy definitions appear in positions from 571 to 1000. Therefore the domain filter seems to be rather effective. Of course, with an appropriate selection of the threshold, it is possible to balance precision and recall at best: we stress that, in certain new domains, a high recall could be preferable to high precision.

Table 3 and 4 provide an "objective" evaluation of the system, since "good" examples come from professional glossaries, or have been compared with professional definitions. However, the experiments are, in a sense, "canned", since the system is asked to analyze a pre-defined set of candidate definitions, and to classify them as good or bad using the style and domain filters.

To obtain an evaluation more close to the reality of system's intended use, we performed another experiment, in which the validation is performed manually by the contributors of this paper, using their intuition. To exploit the evaluator's experience, we used the interoperability domain. We repeated the experiment on a medical domain, since expertise in this domain was also available. Table 5 shows the results.

Notice that in this experiment the system was provided only with a set of terms, and all returned definitions were actually found on the web, either in glossaries or in documents. The table shows that, overall, the performance of the system is similar to that measured on the predefined test set (Tables 3 and 4). However, in this case we could not measure the "real" Recall, but only the Recall over the total number of extracted candidates, before pruning with the style and domain filters.

Notice that performance is similar across the two domains, but the coverage is considerably lower for interoperability terms, as expected: for new, or relatively recent domains, it is more difficult to find definitions, both in glossaries or in web documents.

Table 5. Performance of the extraction algorithm when using a "live" search with post-evaluation

	Interoperability	Medicine
Total number of submitted terms (T)	100	100
Total number of extracted sentences (from all sources) (E)	774	1137
Sentences over the threshold ϑ^9 (C)	517	948
Accepted by evaluators(A)	448	802
Precision (A/C)	81,27%	80,73%
Recall on positive (A/E)	86,65%	84,59%
F-measure	83,87	82,61
Terms with at least one positive definition (N)	51	96
Coverage (N/T)	51%	96%

---

[9] The threshold is selected computing the average difference between the two consecutive definitions , when definitions are ordered by weight.

3   The Web Application

We here describe the web application that encapsulates the methodology described so far, named GlossExtractor, available on http://lcl.uniroma1.it/glossextractor.

The user login and either accepts the default options or selects the Options button. In the option window, the user can first select the sources from which a glossary has to be extracted: i) web glossaries searched by the system or suggested by the user itself; ii) the Google's "define" feature, and iii) documents on the web, searched by GlossExtractor as described in previous sections. The user can also set the relevance threshold ϑ and select a single-user validation or group validation. In the group validation, a coordinator selects the initial and final date of the validation campaign, and then (s)he selects the list of user's e-mail (all users must –freely- subscribe to use the application). The other members of the validation team receive an e-mail to announce starting and ending dates.

Figure 6 is a screen-dump showing the subsequent steps of the workflow. In step 2, the user uploads the terminology T, or (s)he can run a demo session, where only one term is specified. In the demo session, the user can select the domain from a list of existing terminologies, but, if the term does not belong to any of these domains, (s)he will be presented with a list of selected definitions where only the style filter has been applied.

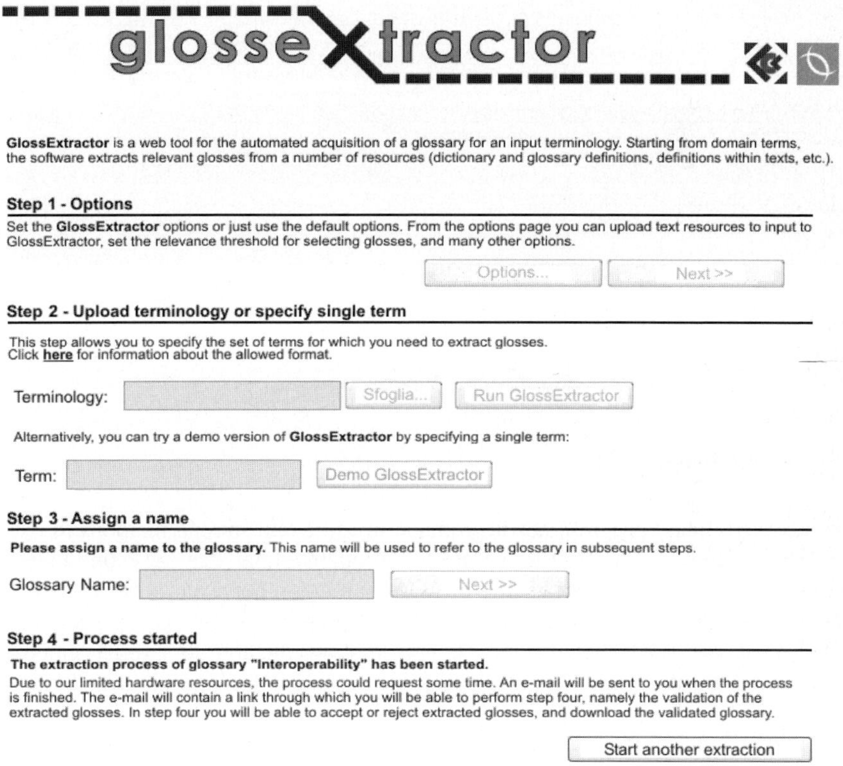

Fig. 6. A Screen-dump of a GlossExtractor session

348   R. Navigli and P. Velardi

Finally, in step 3 a name is assigned to the glossary extraction task, and in step 4 the user is disconnected.

When the glossary extraction process is terminated, the user receives an e-mail and is directed to the validation page. Figure 7 shows a screen-dump of a multiple users validation page. For each definition, the page shows the computed weight and the source type from which the definition has been extracted (web glossary, Google's define feature, web document). By clicking on the pencil icon to the left of each gloss, the user can modify the text of a definition if the definition is judged good, but not fully satisfactory. Manual changes are tracked by the system.

The coordinator has a different view, in which he can inspect the global votes received by each definition.

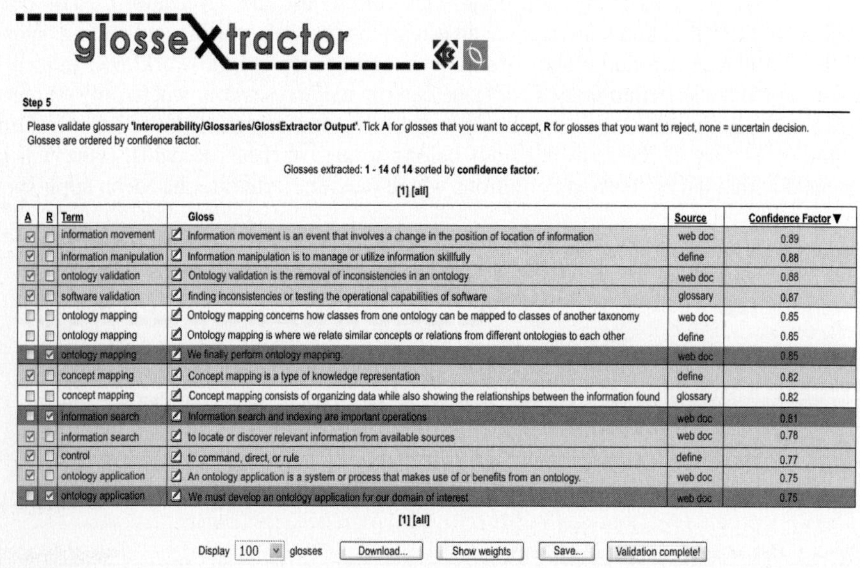

A	R	Term	Gloss	Source	Confidence Factor ▼
☑	☐	information movement	Information movement is an event that involves a change in the position of location of information	web doc	0.89
☑	☐	information manipulation	Information manipulation is to manage or utilize information skillfully	define	0.88
☑	☐	ontology validation	Ontology validation is the removal of inconsistencies in an ontology	web doc	0.88
☑	☐	software validation	finding inconsistencies or testing the operational capabilities of software	glossary	0.87
☐	☐	ontology mapping	Ontology mapping concerns how classes from one ontology can be mapped to classes of another taxonomy	web doc	0.85
☐	☐	ontology mapping	Ontology mapping is where we relate similar concepts or relations from different ontologies to each other	define	0.85
☐	☑	ontology mapping	We finally perform ontology mapping.	web doc	0.85
☑	☐	concept mapping	Concept mapping is a type of knowledge representation	define	0.82
☐	☐	concept mapping	Concept mapping consists of organizing data while also showing the relationships between the information found	glossary	0.82
☐	☑	information search	Information search and indexing are important operations	web doc	0.81
☑	☐	information search	to locate or discover relevant information from available sources	web doc	0.78
☑	☐	control	to command, direct, or rule	define	0.77
☑	☐	ontology application	An ontology application is a system or process that makes use of or benefits from an ontology.	web doc	0.75
☐	☑	ontology application	We must develop an ontology application for our domain of interest	web doc	0.75

Fig. 7. Group Validation session

4   Related Work

Recently, significant progress has been made in using text mining methods to extract information from the web, for a variety of applications that rely on document meaning. The literature on automatic glossary extraction however is not very rich. In (Klavans and Muresan, 2001), and in other subsequent works by the same authors, it is described the DEFINDER system, a text mining method to extract embedded definitions in on-line texts. The system is based on pattern matching at the lexical level, guided by cue phrases as "is called" "is defined as" etc.. However, the application of lexical patterns on unrestricted documents (e.g. the web) may produce poor results in terms of precision and recall, especially the relevant but noisy "is a" pattern. A problem closely related to glossary extraction is that of answering *"what is x?"* questions in open domain question answering (QA). Many approaches presented in QA literature, especially those evaluated in TREC conferences[10], require the availability of training data, e.g. large collection of sentences tagged as "definitions" or "non-definitions". The majority of methods are fully supervised e.g. (Miliaraki and Androutsopoulos, 2004) and (Ng et al. 2001). In (Androutsopoulos and Galanis, 2005) a weakly supervised approach is proposed, in which feature vectors associated to each candidate definition are augmented with automatically learned patterns. Patterns are sequences of *n words* (*n-grams*) occurring before or after the term for which a definition has to be found. This approach is more realistic, but the application of contextual patterns only at the lexical (word) level might not suffice to identify definitions in texts. In TREC conferences, the target is to mediate at best between precision and recall, whereas when the objective is to typify an emerging domain, recall is the most relevant performance figure. For certain novel concepts very few or possibly just one definition might be available, and the target is to capture the majority of them.

With reference to the literature, the work described in this paper has several novel features: i) the evaluation is rather more objective than standard thee-judges with adjudication; ii) the extraction process is more sophisticated and fully general, since the supervised learning phase is non-domain dependent; iii) it has been fully implemented as a web application, which allows to extract not only individual definitions, but a complete domain glossary, and furthermore it supports a group validation. Finally, the method has been applied and validated with success in the "real" context of a research community on enterprise interoperability, as discussed in (Velardi et al. 2007).

References

Androutsopoulos, I., Galanis, D.: A practically unupervised learning method to identify single-snippets answers to definition questions on the web. In: HLT-EMNLP 2005. Proc. of the Human Language Technology Conference, Vancouver, Canada (2005)

Hearst, M.A.: Automatic acquisition of hyponyms from large text corpora. In: Proceedings of the 14th conference on Computational linguistics, Nantes, France (1992)

Klavans, J., Muresan, S.: Text Mining Techniques for fully automatic Glossary Construction. In: Proc. of the HTL2001 Conference, San Diego, CA (2001)

Miliaraki, S., Androutsopoulos, I.: Learning to identify single-snippet answers to definition questions. In: Proceedings of COLING-2004, pp. 1360–1366 (2004)

Ng, H.T., Kwan, J.L.P., Xia, Y.: Question answering using a large text database: A machine learning approach. In: Proceedings of EMNLP-2001, Pittsburgh, PA, pp. 67–73 (2001)

Navigli, R., Velardi, P.: Learning Domain Ontologies from Document Warehouses and Dedicated Web Sites. Computational Linguistics 50(2) (2004)

Sclano, F., Velardi, P.: TermExtractor: a Web Application to Learn the Shared Terminology of Emergent Web Communities. In: Proc. of 3rd I-ESA '07, Madeira, March 28-30 (2007)

Velardi, P., Cucchiarelli, A., Pétit, M.: A Taxonomy Learning Method and its Application to Characterize a Scientific Web Community. IEEE Transaction on Data and Knowledge Engineering (TDKE) 19(2), 180–191 (2007)

---

[10] The Question Answering track page of TREC is http://trec.nist.gov /data/qa.html

A Tree Kernel-Based Shallow Semantic Parser for Thematic Role Extraction

Daniele Pighin[1,2] and Alessandro Moschitti[1]

[1] University of Trento, DIT
[2] FBK-irst - Trento, Italy

Abstract. We present a simple, two-steps supervised strategy for the identification and classification of thematic roles in natural language texts. We employ no external source of information but automatic parse trees of the input sentences. We use a few attribute-value features and tree kernel functions applied to specialized structured features. Different configurations of our thematic role labeling system took part in 2 tasks of the SemEval 2007 evaluation campaign, namely the closed tasks on semantic role labeling for the English and the Arabic languages. In this paper we present and discuss the system configuration that participated in the English semantic role labeling task and present new results obtained after the end of the evaluation campaign.

1   Introduction

The availability of large scale data sets of manually annotated predicate argument structures has recently favored the use of Machine Learning approaches to the design of automated Semantic Role Labeling (SRL) systems.

Research in this area is largely focused in two directions, namely the decomposition of the SRL task in a proper set of possibly disjoint problems and the selection and design of the features that can provide an effective and accurate model for the above learning problems. Though many different task decompositions have been attempted with more or less success, it is largely agreed that full syntactic information about the input free text sentences provides relevant clues about the position of an argument and the role it plays with respect to the predicate [1].

In this paper we present a system for the labeling of semantic roles that produces VerbNet [2] like annotations of free text sentences using only full syntactic parses of the input sentences. The labeling process is modeled as a cascade of two distinct classification steps: (1) boundary detection (BD), in which the word sequences that encode a thematic role for a given predicate are recognized, and (2) role classification (RC), in which the thematic role label is assigned with respect to the predicate. In order to be consistent with the underlying linguistic model, at the end of the process a set of simple heuristics are applied to ensure that only well formed annotations are output.

We use Support Vector Machines (SVMs) as our learning algorithm, and combine 2 different views of the incoming syntactic data: a) an explicit representation of a few relevant features in the form of attribute-value pairs, evaluated by

R. Basili and M.T. Pazienza (Eds.): AI*IA 2007, LNAI 4733, pp. 350–361, 2007.

a polynomial kernel, and b) structural features derived by applying canonical transformations to the sentence parse trees, evaluated by a tree kernel function.

All of this aspects will be discussed top-down in the remainder of this paper: Section 2 describes the architecture of our labeling system; Section 3 discusses the kernel function that we employ for the learning task; Section 4 discusses the linear and structural features that we use to represent the classifier examples; Section 5 describes the experimental setting and reports the accuracy of the system on the SemEval2007 closed task on semantic role labeling, along with the evaluation of different system configurations carried out after the end of the challenge; finally, Section 6 discusses the results that we obtained and presents our conclusions.

2   System Description

Given a target predicate word in a natural language sentence, a SRL system is meant to correctly identify all the arguments of the predicate. This problem is usually divided in two sub-tasks:

- the detection of the boundaries (i. e. the word span) of each argument, and
- the classification of the argument type, e.g. *Arg0* or *ArgM* in PropBank or *Agent* and *Goal* in FrameNet or VerbNet.

The standard approach to learn both the detection and the classification of predicate arguments is summarized by the following steps:

1. Given a sentence from the *training-set*, generate a full syntactic parse-tree;
2. let $\mathcal{P}$ and $\mathcal{A}$ be the set of predicates and the set of parse-tree nodes (i.e. the potential arguments), respectively;
3. for each pair $\langle p, a \rangle \in \mathcal{P} \times \mathcal{A}$:
    - extract the feature representation set, $F_{p,a}$;
    - if the sub-tree rooted in a covers exactly the words of one argument of p, put $F_{p,a}$ in T^+ (positive examples), otherwise put it in T^- (negative examples).

For instance, in Figure 2.a, for each combination of the predicate *approve* with any other tree node a that do not overlap with the predicate, a classifier example $F_{approve,a}$ is generated. If a exactly covers one of the predicate arguments (in this case: *The charter*, *by the EC Commission* or *on Sept. 21*) it is regarded as a positive instance, otherwise it will be a negative one, e. g. $F_{approve,(\text{NN charter})}$.

The T^+ and T^- sets are used to train the boundary classifier (BC). To train the role multi-class classifier (RM), T^+ can be reorganized as positive $T^+_{\text{arg}_i}$ and negative $T^-_{\text{arg}_i}$ examples for each argument i. In this way, an individual One-vs-All classifier for each argument i can be trained. We adopted this solution, according to [3], since it is simple and effective. In the classification phase, given an unseen sentence, all its $F_{p,a}$ are generated and classified by each individual role classifier. The role label associated with the maximum among the scores provided by the individual classifiers is eventually selected.

To make the annotations consistent with the underlying linguistic model, we employ a few simple heuristics to resolve the overlap situations that may occur, e. g. both *charter* and *the charter* in Figure 2 may be assigned a role:

- if more than two nodes are involved, i. e. a node d and two or more of its descendants n_i are classified as arguments, then assume that d is not an argument. This choice is justified by previous studies [4] showing that the accuracy of classification is higher for nodes located lower in the tree;
- if only two nodes are involved, i. e. they dominate each other, then keep the one with the highest classification score.

More complex, and generally more accurate, solutions can be adopted to improve the accuracy of the final annotation output by a SRL system[1]. Among other interesting strategies, [6] used a probabilistic joint evaluation over the whole predicate argument structure in order to establish a global relation between the local decisions of the role classifiers; [7] described a method based on Levenshtein-distance to *correct* the inconsistencies in the output sequence of role labels; [8] used a voting mechanism over multiple syntactic views in order to reduce the effect of parsing errors on the labeling accuracy.

Many supervised learning algorithms have more or less successfully been employed for SRL. We chose to use Support Vector Machines (SVMs) as our learning algorithm as they provide both a state-of-the-art learning model (in terms of accuracy) and the possibility of using kernel functions [9]. The kernels that we employ are described in the next section, whereas Section 4 presents the linear and structural features that we use to characterize the learning problem.

3   Kernel Functions for Semantic Role Labeling

In this study we adopted Support Vector Machines (SVMs) to exploit our new kernel functions. SVMs are learning algorithms which take training examples labeled with the class information as input and generate classification models. Each example e_i is represented in the feature space as a vector $\boldsymbol{x_i} \in \Re^n$ by means of a feature function

$$\phi : \mathcal{E} \to \Re^n \ ,$$

where $\mathcal{E}$ is the set of examples.

The generated model is a hyperplane $H(\boldsymbol{x}) = \boldsymbol{w} \cdot \boldsymbol{x} + b = 0$ which separates positive from negative examples, where $\boldsymbol{w} \in \Re^n$ and $b \in \Re$ are parameters learned from data by applying the *Structural Risk Minimization principle* [9]. An example e_i is categorized in the target class only if $H(\boldsymbol{x}_i) \geq 0$.

The kernel trick allows the evaluation of the similarity between example pairs, $K(e_1, e_2)$, to be carried out without an explicit representation of the whole feature space, i.e. $K(e_1, e_2) = \phi(e_1) \cdot \phi(e_2) = \boldsymbol{x_1} \cdot \boldsymbol{x_2}$.

---

[1] Indeed, previous versions of our SRL system sported a joint-inference model and a re-ranker mechanism based on tree kernels, as described in [5], which is currently offline due to changes in the interface of our feature extraction software module.

A traditional example is given by the polynomial kernel:

$$K_P(e_i, e_j) = (c + \boldsymbol{x}_i \cdot \boldsymbol{x}_j)^d \,, \tag{1}$$

where c is a constant and d is the degree of the polynomial. This kernel generates the space of all conjunctions of feature groups up to d elements.

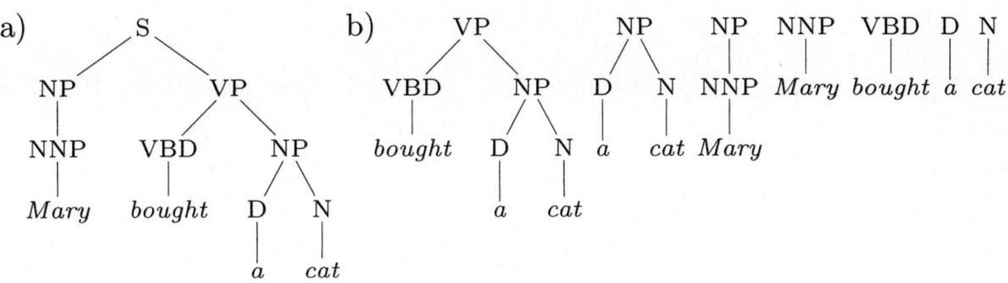

Fig. 1. Fragment space generated by an ST (b) and an SST (c) kernel from an example sub-tree (a)

A more abstract class of kernel functions evaluate the similarity between two discrete structures in terms of their overlap, generally measured as a function of the number of common substructures [10]. The kernels that we consider here represent trees in terms of their substructures (fragments). The kernel function detects if a tree sub-part (common to both trees) belongs to the feature space that we intend to generate. For such purpose, the desired fragments need to be described. As we consider syntactic parse trees, each node with its children is associated with a grammar production rule, where the symbol at the left-hand side corresponds to the parent and the symbols at the right-hand side are associated with the children. The terminal symbols of the grammar are always associated with tree leaves.

We define a SubTree (ST) [11] as a tree rooted in any non-terminal node along with all its descendants. For example, Figure 1 shows the parse tree of the sentence *Mary brought a cat* (a) together with its 7 STs (b). A SubSet Tree (SST) [10] is a more general structure since its leaves can be non-terminal symbols. Figure 1(c) shows some of the SSTs for the same example sentence. The SSTs satisfy the constraint that grammatical rules cannot be broken. For example, [VP [V NP]] is an SST which has two non-terminal symbols, V and NP, as leaves. On the contrary, [VP [V]] is not an SST as it violates the production VP→V NP.

The main idea underlying tree kernels is to compute the number of common substructures between two trees t_1 and t_2 without explicitly considering the whole fragment space. Let $\{f_1, f_2, ..\} = \mathcal{F}$ be the set of fragments and let the indicator function $I_i(n)$ be equal to 1 if the target f_i is rooted at node n and 0 otherwise. A tree kernel function $K_T(\cdot)$ over two trees is defined as:

$$K_T(t_1, t_2) = \sum_{n_1 \in N_{t_1}} \sum_{n_2 \in N_{t_2}} \Delta(n_1, n_2) \tag{2}$$

where N_{t_1} and N_{t_2} are the sets of nodes of t_1 and t_2, respectively. The function $\Delta(\cdot)$ evaluates the number of common fragments rooted in n_1 and n_2:

$$\Delta(n_1, n_2) = \sum_{i=1}^{|\mathcal{F}|} I_i(n_1) I_i(n_2) \tag{3}$$

We can compute Δ as follows:

1. if the productions at n_1 and n_2 are different then $\Delta(n_1, n_2) = 0$;
2. if the productions at n_1 and n_2 are the same, and n_1 and n_2 have only leaf children (i.e. they are pre-terminal symbols) then $\Delta(n_1, n_2) = 1$;
3. if the productions at n_1 and n_2 are the same, and n_1 and n_2 are not pre-terminals then

$$\Delta(n_1, n_2) = \prod_{j=1}^{nc(n_1)} (\sigma + \Delta(c_{n_1}^j, c_{n_2}^j)) \tag{4}$$

where $\sigma \in \{0, 1\}$, $nc(n_1)$ is the number of the children of n_1 and c_n^j is the j-th child of node n. Note that, since the productions are the same, $nc(n_1) = nc(n_2)$.

When $\sigma = 0$, $\Delta(n_1, n_2)$ is equal to 1 only if $\forall j \quad \Delta(c_{n_1}^j, c_{n_2}^j) = 1$, i.e. all the productions associated with the children are identical. By recursively applying this property, it follows that the sub-trees in n_1 and n_2 are identical. Thus, Eq. 2 evaluates the subtree (ST) kernel. When $\sigma = 1$, $\Delta(n_1, n_2)$ evaluates the number of SSTs common to n_1 and n_2 as shown in [10].

In our case, each classifier example e_i is represented by a set of attribute-value features $\mathcal{L}_i$ and a structural feature t_i. The similarity between to examples e_i and e_j is evaluated by applying a polynomial kernel $K_P(\cdot)$ of degree $d = 3$ to the attribute-value features and an SST kernel $K_{SST}(\cdot)$ to the structured representation of the examples. The contribution of each kernel function is individually normalized and the tree kernel output is weighted by the w_k factor, which is set to 0.3. The resulting kernel function is the following:

$$K(e_i, e_j) = \frac{K_P(\mathcal{L}_i, \mathcal{L}_j)}{\|K_P(\mathcal{L}_j, \mathcal{L}_j)\|} + w_k \times \frac{K_{SST}(t_i, t_j)}{\|K_{SST}(t_i, t_j)\|}, \tag{5}$$

where

$$\|K_{SST}(t_i, t_j)\| = \sqrt{K_{SST}(t_i, t_i) \times K_{SST}(t_j, t_j)},$$

$$\|K_P(\mathcal{L}_j, \mathcal{L}_j)\| = \sqrt{K_P(\mathcal{L}_j, \mathcal{L}_j) \times K_P(\mathcal{L}_j, \mathcal{L}_j)}.$$

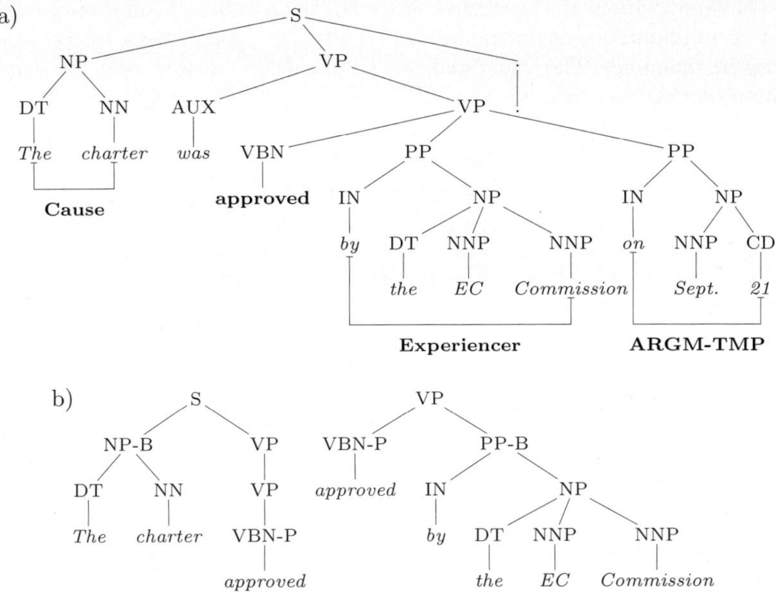

Fig. 2. A sentence parse tree (a) and two example AST_1^m structures relative to the predicate *approve* (b)

4   Features for Semantic Role Labeling

We explicitly represent as attribute-value pairs the following features of each $F_{p,a}$ pair:

- *Phrase Type, Predicate Word, Head Word, Position* and *Voice* as defined in [12];
- *Partial Path, No Direction Path, Head Word POS, First and Last Word/POS in Constituent* and *SubCategorization* as proposed in [3];
- *Syntactic Frame* as designed in [13].

We also employ structured features derived by the full parses in an attempt to capture relevant aspects that may not be emphasized by the explicit feature representation.

We indicate with structured features the basic syntactic structures extracted or derived from the sentence-parse tree by means of some canonical transformation. [14] and [4] defined several classes of structured features that were successfully employed with tree kernels for the different stages of an SRL process. Figure 2 shows an example of the AST_1^m structures that we used for both the boundary detection and the argument classification stages.

Table 1. Composition of the dataset in terms of: number of annotations (Props); number of candidate argument nodes (T); positive (T^+) and negative (T^-) boundary classifier examples. The annotated test set has been released after the end of the evaluation period.

Set	Props	T	T^+	T^-
Train	15,838	793,104	45,157	747,947
Dev	1,606	75,302	4,291	71,011
Train - Dev	14,232	717,802	40,866	676,936
Test	3,094	144,965	6,931	138,034

5   Experiments

In this section we discuss the setup and the results of the experiments carried out on the dataset of the SemEval2007 closed task on SRL.

5.1   Setup

The training set comprises 15,838[2] training annotations organized on a per-verb basis. In order to build a development set (Dev), we sampled about one tenth, i. e. 1,606 annotations, of the original training set. For the final evaluation on the test set (Test), consisting of 3,094 annotations, we trained our classifiers on the whole training data. Statistics on the dataset composition are shown in Table 1.

The evaluations were carried out with the SVMLight-TK[3] software [15] which extends the SVMLight[4] package [16] with tree kernel functions. We used the default polynomial kernel (degree=3) for the linear features and a SubSet Tree (SST) kernel [10] for the comparison of AST_1^m structured features. The kernels are normalized and summed by assigning a weight of 0.3 to the TK, as explained in Section 3.

5.2   SemEval2007 Evaluation

The configuration presented at the SemEval2007 closed task on SRL comprised 50 boundary classifiers (BC), and 619 distinct role classifiers combined into 50 role multi-classifiers (RM) with an One-vs-All strategy, i. e. one BC and a RM per predicate word. The whole training took about 4 hours on a 64 bits machine (2.2GHz, 1GB RAM)[5].

All the evaluations were carried out using the CoNLL2005 evaluator tool available at `http://www.lsi.upc.es/~srlconll/soft.html`.

---

[2] A bunch of unaligned annotations were removed from the dataset.

[3] `http://ai-nlp.info.uniroma2.it/moschitti/`

[4] `http://svmlight.joachims.org/`

[5] In order to have a faster development cycle, we limited to 60 thousands the training examples of the boundary classifier for the verb *say*. The accuracy on this relation is still very high, as we measured an overall F_1 of 87.18 on the development set and of 85.13 on the test set.

Table 2. SRL accuracy on the development test for the boundary detection (BD) and the complete SRL task (BD+RC) using the polynomial kernel alone (poly) or combined with a tree kernel function (poly + TK)

Task	Kernel(s)	Precision	Recall	$F_{\beta=1}$
BD	poly	94.34%	71.26%	81.19
	poly + TK	92.89%	76.09%	83.65
BD + RC	poly	88.72%	68.76%	77.47
	poly + TK	86.60%	72.40%	78.86

Table 2 shows the aggregate results on boundary detection (BD) and the complete SRL task (BD+RC) on the development set using the polynomial kernel alone (poly) or in conjunction with the tree kernel and structured features (poly+TK). For both tasks, tree kernel functions do trigger automatic feature selection and improve the polynomial kernel by 2.46 and 1.39 F_1 points, respectively.

The SRL accuracy for each of the 47 distinct role labels is shown in Table 3 under Column *Split*. Column *#TI* lists the number of instances of each role in the test set. Many roles have very few positive examples both in the training and the test sets, and therefore have little or no impact on the overall accuracy which is dominated by the few roles which are very frequent, such as *Theme*, *Agent*, *Topic* and *ARGM-TMP* which account for almost 80% of all the test roles.

Table 4 shows the results of the two systems that participated in the SemEval 2007 closed task on English SRL. The winning system (labeled *UBC-UPC*, [17]) uses a sequential approach to role labeling and unlike our own exploits a) verb-sense information to restrict the possibile sequences of output roles, and b) WordNet-based selectional preferences on the potential arguments. The result is a much more accurate SRL system, i. e. 83.66 vs 75.44 F1 points in the official evaluation.

5.3   Further Evaluation

After the official evaluation was over we run another series of experiments in order to evaluate the effect of different configurations of the SRL system. We did not change any parameter in the setup of the SVMs but used the poly+TK kernel to compare different strategies for training the BC and the RM. These strategies are:

- training both the BC and the RM by splitting the data on a per-predicate basis, i. e. the configuration that participated in the SemEval evaluation;
- training a monolithic BC and an RM for each predicate, i.e. BC is trained with the data of all predicates;
- training a split BC and a monolithic RM, i.e. the latter classifier is trained putting together all different predicates. This means that there is only one classifier for each role type. For example, the *Agent* role classifier will be unique for all predicates.
- Using both a monolithic BC and a monolithic RM.

Table 3. Evaluation of the semantic role labeling accuracy on the SemEval2007 - Task 17 test set. Column *#TI* reports the number of instances of each role label in the test set. The results under Column *Split* are relative to the configuration that participated in the official evaluation (one BC and one RM per predicate word); the results under Column *Monolithic* are those of the most accurate configuration that we tried (one BC, one RM).

Role	#TI	Split			Monolithic		
		Precision	Recall	$F_{\beta=1}$	Precision	Recall	$F_{\beta=1}$
Overall	6931	81.58%	70.16%	75.44	81.25%	74.42%	77.69
ARG2	4	100.00%	25.00%	40.00	50.00%	25.00%	33.33
ARG3	17	61.11%	64.71%	62.86	52.63%	58.82%	55.56
ARG4	4	0.00%	0.00%	0.00	0.00%	0.00%	0.00
ARGM-ADV	188	55.14%	31.38%	40.00	52.45%	39.89%	45.32
ARGM-CAU	13	50.00%	23.08%	31.58	66.67%	30.77%	42.11
ARGM-DIR	4	100.00%	25.00%	40.00	100.00%	25.00%	40.00
ARGM-EXT	3	0.00%	0.00%	0.00	0.00%	0.00%	0.00
ARGM-LOC	151	51.66%	51.66%	51.66	59.12%	62.25%	60.65
ARGM-MNR	85	41.94%	15.29%	22.41	46.81%	25.88%	33.33
ARGM-PNC	28	38.46%	17.86%	24.39	53.33%	28.57%	37.21
ARGM-PRD	9	83.33%	55.56%	66.67	83.33%	55.56%	66.67
ARGM-REC	1	0.00%	0.00%	0.00	0.00%	0.00%	0.00
ARGM-TMP	386	55.65%	35.75%	43.53	64.79%	59.59%	62.08
Actor1	12	85.71%	50.00%	63.16	90.91%	83.33%	86.96
Actor2	1	100.00%	100.00%	100.00	100.00%	100.00%	100.00
Agent	2551	91.38%	77.34%	83.78	90.42%	81.81%	85.90
Asset	21	42.42%	66.67%	51.85	48.39%	71.43%	57.69
Attribute	17	60.00%	70.59%	64.86	63.16%	70.59%	66.67
Beneficiary	24	65.00%	54.17%	59.09	66.67%	50.00%	57.14
Cause	48	75.56%	70.83%	73.12	71.11%	66.67%	68.82
Experiencer	132	86.49%	72.73%	79.01	83.33%	68.18%	75.00
Location	12	83.33%	41.67%	55.56	80.00%	33.33%	47.06
Material	7	100.00%	14.29%	25.00	100.00%	28.57%	44.44
Patient	37	76.67%	62.16%	68.66	88.89%	64.86%	75.00
Patient1	20	72.73%	40.00%	51.61	78.57%	55.00%	64.71
Predicate	181	63.75%	56.35%	59.82	64.12%	60.22%	62.11
Product	106	70.79%	59.43%	64.62	69.79%	63.21%	66.34
R-ARGM-LOC	2	0.00%	0.00%	0.00	0.00%	0.00%	0.00
R-ARGM-MNR	2	0.00%	0.00%	0.00	0.00%	0.00%	0.00
R-ARGM-TMP	4	0.00%	0.00%	0.00	0.00%	0.00%	0.00
R-Agent	74	70.15%	63.51%	66.67	65.93%	81.08%	72.73
R-Experiencer	5	100.00%	20.00%	33.33	0.00%	0.00%	0.00
R-Patient	2	0.00%	0.00%	0.00	0.00%	0.00%	0.00
R-Predicate	1	0.00%	0.00%	0.00	0.00%	0.00%	0.00
R-Product	2	0.00%	0.00%	0.00	0.00%	0.00%	0.00
R-Recipient	8	100.00%	87.50%	93.33	100.00%	87.50%	93.33
R-Theme	7	75.00%	42.86%	54.55	42.86%	42.86%	42.86
R-Theme1	7	100.00%	85.71%	92.31	100.00%	85.71%	92.31
R-Theme2	1	50.00%	100.00%	66.67	0.00%	0.00%	0.00
R-Topic	14	66.67%	42.86%	52.17	70.00%	50.00%	58.33
Recipient	48	75.51%	77.08%	76.29	76.00%	79.17%	77.55
Source	25	65.22%	60.00%	62.50	62.50%	60.00%	61.22
Stimulus	21	33.33%	19.05%	24.24	46.67%	33.33%	38.89
Theme	650	79.22%	68.62%	73.54	79.04%	70.77%	74.68
Theme1	69	77.42%	69.57%	73.28	81.36%	69.57%	75.00
Theme2	60	74.55%	68.33%	71.30	76.47%	65.00%	70.27
Topic	1867	84.26%	82.27%	83.25	84.12%	82.59%	83.35

The whole training set was used to learn the models and the evaluation was carried out on the test set. Training the monolithic BC and role classifiers took almost one week on the same hardware platform. Table 5 shows the results of this comparison with respect to the boundary detection (BD) and the complete

Table 4. Results of the two teams that took part in the closed task on English SRL. Our system (labeled *RTV*) ranked second out of two.

Rank	Team	P	R	$F_{\beta=1}$
1	UBC-UPC	85.31%	82.08%	83.66
2	RTV	81.58%	70.16%	75.44

Table 5. Accuracy comparison between the split (s) and the monolithic (m) boundary (bnd) and role (role) classifiers on the boundary detection (BD) and the complete SRL task (BD + RC) on the test set. Of course, no role classifier is employed for the boundary detection task.

Task	Classifier bnd	role	Precision	Recall	$F_{\beta=1}$
BD	s	–	87.09%	72.96%	79.40
	m	–	87.42%	77.36%	82.09
BD + RC	s	s	81.58%	70.16%	75.44
	s	m	81.72%	70.57%	75.74
	m	s	81.05%	73.64%	77.17
	m	m	81.25%	74.42%	77.69

SRL task. The flags "s" and "m" in column 2 and 3 indicate the strategy ("split" or "monolithic") employed to train the BC and the RM, respectively.

For the boundary detection task, the data show that the accuracy of the monolithic approach is much higher than the split one, i. e. 82.09 vs 79.40. While the precision is almost the same, the monolithic BC improves by almost 4.5 percent points, i. e. 77.36% vs 72.96%, the recall over the split configuration. A similar trend can be observed on the complete SRL task. Here the overall accuracy improves by 2.25 F_1 points if an all-monolithic configuration is used instead of an all-split configuration. And also in this case, while there is little or no difference in terms of precision (the precision values measured for the four combinations range from 81.05% to 81.72%), the recall of the RM improves by 3-4 percent points when a monolithic boundary classifier is used, i. e. 73.64% vs 70.16% and 74.42% vs 70.57% for the split and the monolithic RM, respectively. The right side of Table 3 (Column *Monolithic*) details the accuracy of the all-monolithic configuration on the classification of each thematic role label from the SemEval test set.

6   Final Remarks

In this paper we presented a system that employs tree kernels and a basic set of flat features for the classification of thematic roles.

The basic approach that we adopted is meant to be as general and fast as possible. The issue of generality is addressed by training the boundary and role classifiers on a per-predicate basis and by employing tree kernels and structured features in the learning algorithm. The resulting architecture can also be used to learn the classification of roles of non-verbal predicates since the automatic feature selection triggered by the tree kernel compensate for the lack of *ad-hoc*, well established explicit features for some classes of non-verbal predicates, such as adverbial or prepositional ones.

Splitting the learning problem also has the clear advantage of noticeably improving the efficiency of the classifiers, thus reducing training and classification time. On the other hand, this split results in some classifiers having too few training instances and therefore being very inaccurate. This is especially true for the boundary classifiers, which conversely need to be very accurate in order to positively support the following stages of the SRL process. The solution of a monolithic boundary classifier that we previously employed [4] is noticeably more accurate though much less efficient, especially for training.

Indeed, after the SemEval2007 evaluation period was over, we ran another series of experiments comparing the split and the monolithic approaches both for boundary detection and the complete SRL task. The results show that the monolithic approach always outperforms the split one, especially for cases like this in which the training instances of some split may be too few and too sparse to generalize properly. In particular, the monolithic boundary classifier grants a noticeable improvement in accuracy, both for the boundary detection and the complete labeling task. Nevertheless, training and classification time with the split configuration is much lower. This issue should be taken into account when we need to: (a) carry out an extensive experimentation with different feature sets; (b) design time-constrained applications, e. g. on-line services; or (c) annotate very large datasets.

Although it was provided as part of both the training and test data, we chose not to use the verb sense information. This choice is motivated by our intention to depend on as less external resources as possible in order to be able to port our SRL system to other linguistic models and languages, for which such resources may not exist. Still, identifying the predicate sense is a key issue especially for role classification, as the argument structure of a predicate is largely determined by its sense. Indeed, the results of the UBC-UPC system clearly show that semantic information can boost the accuracy of SRL, and that it should be employed when dealing with languages, domains or tasks for which it is available and dependable. In the near feature we plan to use larger structured features, i. e. spanning all the potential arguments of a predicate, to improve the accuracy of our role classifiers. We also plan to reintroduce the joint-model evaluation and the TK-based re-ranking mechanism that we presented in [5], which is currently offline due to changes in our feature extraction software component.

References

1. Carreras, X., Màrquez, L.: Introduction to the CoNLL-2005 Shared Task: Semantic Role Labeling. In: Proceedings of CoNLL-2005 (2005)
2. Kipper, K., Dang, H.T., Palmer, M.: Class-based construction of a verb lexicon. In: Proceedings of AAAI-2000 Seventeenth National Conference on Artificial Intelligence, Austin, TX (2000)

3. Pradhan, S., Hacioglu, K., Krugler, V., Ward, W., Martin, J.H., Jurafsky, D.: Support vector learning for semantic argument classification (2005) (to appear in Machine Learning Journal)
4. Moschitti, A., Pighin, D., Basili, R.: Tree kernel engineering in semantic role labeling systems. In: EACL 2006. Proceedings of the Workshop on Learning Structured Information in Natural Language Applications, Trento, Italy, pp. 49–56. European Chapter of the Association for Computational Linguistics (2006)
5. Moschitti, A., Pighin, D., Basili, R.: Tree kernel engineering for proposition reranking. In: ECML/PKDD 2006. Proceedings of the International Workshop on Mining and Learning with Graphs (2006)
6. Toutanova, K., Haghighi, A., Manning, C.: Joint learning improves semantic role labeling. In: ACL'05. Proceedings of the 43rd Annual Meeting of the Association for Computational Linguistics, Ann Arbor, Michigan, pp. 589–596. Association for Computational Linguistics (2005)
7. Sang, E.T.K., Canisius, S., van den Bosch, A., Bogers, T.: Applying spelling error correction techniques for improving semantic role labelling. In: CoNLL-2005. Proceedings of the Ninth Conference on Natural Language Learning, Ann Arbor, MI (2005)
8. Punyakanok, V., Koomen, P., Roth, D., Yih, W.t: Generalized inference with multiple semantic role labeling systems. In: CoNLL-2005. Proceedings of the Ninth Conference on Computational Natural Language Learning, Ann Arbor, Michigan, pp. 181–184. Association for Computational Linguistics (2005)
9. Vapnik, V.N.: Statistical Learning Theory. John Wiley and Sons, England (1998)
10. Collins, M., Duffy, N.: New ranking algorithms for parsing and tagging: Kernels over discrete structures, and the voted perceptron. In: ACL02 (2002)
11. Vishwanathan, S., Smola, A.: Fast kernels on strings and trees. In: Proceedings of Neural Information Processing Systems (2002)
12. Gildea, D., Jurasfky, D.: Automatic labeling of semantic roles. Computational Linguistic 28(3), 496–530 (2002)
13. Xue, N., Palmer, M.: Calibrating features for semantic role labeling. In: Proceedings of EMNLP 2004, Barcelona, Spain, pp. 88–94 (2004)
14. Moschitti, A., Pighin, D., Basili, R.: Semantic role labeling via tree kernel joint inference. In: Proceedings of the Tenth Conference on Computational Natural Language Learning, CoNLL-X (2006)
15. Moschitti, A.: A study on convolution kernel for shallow semantic parsing. In: proceedings of ACL-2004, Barcelona, Spain (2004)
16. Joachims, T.: Making large-scale SVM learning practical. In: Schölkopf, B., Burges, C., Smola, A. (eds.) Advances in Kernel Methods - Support Vector Learning (1999)
17. Zapirain, B., Agirre, E., Márquez, L.: UBC-UPC: Sequential SRL Using Selectional Preferences. An approach with Maximum Entropy Markov Models. In: Proceedings of the Fourth International Workshop on Semantic Evaluations (SemEval 2007), Prague, Czech Republic, Association for Computational Linguistics (2007)

Inferring Coreferences Among Person Names in a Large Corpus of News Collections

Octavian Popescu and Bernardo Magnini

FBK-irst, Fondazione Bruno Kessler, Trento, Italy
{popescu, magnini}@itc.it

Abstract. We present a probabilistic framework for inferring coreference relations among person names in a news collection. The approach does not assume any prior knowledge about persons (e.g. an ontology) mentioned in the collection and requires basic linguistic processing (named entity recognition) and resources (a dictionary of person names). The system parameters have been estimated on a 5K corpus of Italian news documents. Evaluation, over a sample of four days news documents, shows that the error rate of the system (1.4%) is above a baseline (5.4%) for the task. Finally, we discuss alternative approaches for evaluation.

Keywords: Named Entities, Coreference, Ontology Population.

1 Introduction

Finding information about people is likely to be one of the principal interests of someone reading a newspaper. In the web space, person search is a very popular task and, as a person is primarily identified by her/his name, usually it is the name that is the key of the search. However, as names are very ambiguous (Artiles et al. 2007), it is a big challenge for automatic systems to cluster name occurrences in a corpus according to the persons they refer to.

The input of a coreference system is a document collection where person names are already identified; the output is a set of clusters of person names, where each cluster represents a different person.

Person coreference has been addressed in previous work (e.g. Baga and Baldwin 1998, Pederson et al. 2006) building vector-based representations of persons' names which use lists of named entities (e.g. person, locations, organizations) associated with person names (i.e. the *association set* of a person). The underlying idea is that a person can be identified by the events he/she is associated with, and that such event can be conveniently represented by the list of the named entities mentioned in a particular document. However, all person names have been assumed to behave equally.

The approach we propose is based on two main working hypotheses[1]. The first one is that establishing coreference is an iterative process, where at each cycle the system attempts at establishing new coreferences, taking advantage of the coreferences

---

[1] This work has been partially supported by the Ontotext Project.

R. Basili and M.T. Pazienza (Eds.): AI*IA 2007, LNAI 4733, pp. 362–373, 2007.
© Springer-Verlag Berlin Heidelberg 2007

established in previous cycles. When no new coreferences are realized, the algorithm stops. The second consideration that has motivated our work is that we think that the full potential of names has not been exploited yet. First, it is useful to distinguish between first and last names. They behave differently with respect to coreference (three times less perplexity for last names than for first names) and, as there are items that could be both first and last names, making the distinction helps in reducing false coreference. Secondly, we can identify rare names for which the probability of different persons carrying them is very low and therefore their coreference may be realized by loosening the conditions on the number of named entities in common.

The paper is structured as follows. In Section 2 we present the architecture of our system, introducing the three main modules. Sections 3, 4, and 5 are dedicated to detailed descriptions of the algorithms we have implemented for Name Splitter, Local Coreference and Global Coreference respectively. In Section 6 we discuss the evaluation methodology and report the results we have obtained. Section 7 presents our future goals and interests.

2   System Architecture

The input of the coreference system is a list of named entities (i.e. *Person Names*, PNs) of type Person, Location, Organization[2], automatically recognized by a Named Entity Recognition (NER) system within a document collection. The output of the system is a number of clusters of the named entities of type Person, where each cluster is interpreted as the set of PNs that refer to the same person.

The system has three main modules corresponding to three steps: Person Name Splitter, Local Coreference module and Global Coreference module.

- The *Person Name Splitter* splits the Person Names into first_name and last_name. The motivation is that first_name and last_name are used differently in mentioning persons and play different roles in coreference.
- The *Local Coreference module* establishes which of the PNs occurring within a single document corefer. We use a probabilistic approach, estimating, inside each document, the joint probability of occurrence of any pair formed by two free names (either first or last names) and a certain complete name (first and last name). For each cluster of coreferred PNs, we choose a representing name, which we call *cluster name*. The set of cluster names is the output of this module.
- The *Global Coreference module* establishes the coreference among all the cluster names of the collection based on their association set (the set of named entities they are associated with) and on the probability that the same PN refers to two different persons (common vs. uncommon names).

Three resources are accessed, and dynamically enriched, during the coreference process: the Name Dictionary, the Entity Ontology and the Topic Ontology.

- The *Name Dictionary* is a list of first_names and last_names. We start with a Name Dictionary of Italian names which contains 68,654 last_names and 3,230 first_names. There are 1267 ambiguous names, which can be both first and last names.

---

[2] The Named Entities we are using are defined according to the ACE standard. However, for our purposes, the GPE entities have been considered as Location entities.

- The *Entity Ontology* contains all the known entities. We start with an empty Entity Ontology, which, at the end of the coreference process, will contain all the person entities identified in the corpus.
- The *Topic Ontology* is a resource specific for the news domain, where each document of the collection is classified under a limited number of topics. The idea is that PNs that occur in the same topic tend to increase their probability to corefer. We start with a fix set of topics, which are actually the newspaper sections.

3   Person Name Splitter

This module identifies first_names and last_names in a sequence of tokens composing a PN and selects the most representative token, i.e. the one with the highest probability to be used for identifying the person. For instance, given the PN "Luca Cordero di Montezemolo", the module recognizes that "Luca" is a first_name, that "Cordero" and "di_Montezemolo" are last_names and that "di_Montezemolo" is the most representative one. There are at least two relevant issues that make the task challenging: (i) the high proportion of tokens that are ambiguous (i.e. that can be used both as first and last names), which makes their classification difficult. For instance, in Italian, the name "Viola" can be used both as first_name and as last_name; (ii) the presence of first_names of famous people, such as "Michelangelo", that are actually used as last_names.   This phenomenon makes the identification of the most representative token difficult.

The Person Name Splitter is based on a multi layer perceptron which, for each token in a PN, assigns a score corresponding to the probability of the token to be a last_name. The perceptron has four input nodes and three hidden nodes (Figure 1).

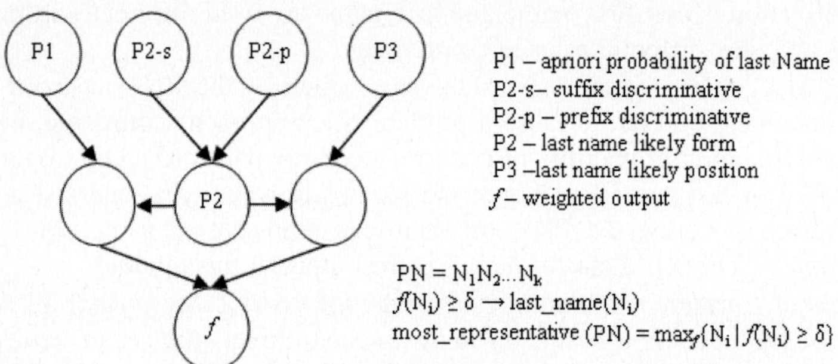

$$PN = N_1N_2...N_k$$
$$f(N_i) \geq \delta \rightarrow last\_name(N_i)$$
$$most\_representative\ (PN) = \max_f\{N_i \mid f(N_i) \geq \delta\}$$

Fig. 1. Last_Name Perceptron

The parameters considered for the input nodes of the perceptron are:

- *P1*: the prior probability of a token of being either first_name or last _name;
- *P2*: the prior probability of the prefix and suffix of a token to signal a last_name;
- *P3*: the prior probability that a last_name occupies the rightmost position in a PN.

The perceptron has been trained on the set of PNs present in the Name Dictionary (see Section 2) in order to determine the weights for each parameter and the threshold.

If a token $f(N_i) \geq \delta$ then N_i is considered a last_name. If a PN contains more than one last_name, the one with the highest score is chosen as the most representative one. All the tokens, belonging to a PN which has at least one last name, which did not pass the threshold are considered first_names. For example, given the PN "Tommaso Padoa Schioppa", the Person Name Splitter correctly classifies "Padoa" and Schioppa" as last_names with "Padoa" as the most representative token and "Tommaso" as first_name. If none of the tokens of a PN passes the threshold and at least one is ambiguous, no label is assigned and the names are considered unknown_names. The information needed to resolve these cases may come at the next levels (see section 4 and 5). The three parameters of the perceptron have been empirically estimated using available resources.

For estimating *P1*, the prior probability of a token of being either a first_name or a last_name, we used the Web. First, we extracted from the corpus (I-CAB, see section 6) the names that collocate with known names (existing in the Name Dictionary), from which we obtained a list of some 15,000 unknown names. From a public webpage[3] we extracted the list of the top twenty frequent first and last names. Then, we used the Google API interface to see how many times each unknown name appears with one of the twenty last_names and we computed the average frequency μ without considering the highest two values. We take this caution in order to reduce the risk of considering a name frequent just because it happens that a famous person carries it. Nevertheless, we include also the highest values if they are within a standard deviation interval from μ. The probabilities estimated over the Web are finally weighed according to a number of parameters obtained by normalizing corpus data: how many times a certain token occurs by itself, how many times it occurs as first and last name and how many times it occurs on the left and on the right of other names.

The parameter *P2* encodes the intuition that generally last_names have a distinct form, which is predictable by observing both prefixes and suffixes carried by names. For example, in Italian, "-ni', "-olli", "-ucci", "ellini" are typical last_names suffixes. We have derived a list of prefixes and suffixes which discriminate first_names from last_names comparing the last and first names included in the Name Dictionary. We have considered only those suffixes and prefixes which are discriminative in more than 90% of the cases and have more than 100 occurrences. The fact that *P2* is a reliable indicator can be seen from the fact that the great majority of suffixes and prefixes which score over 90%, scores also over 98%. For example, there are 255 suffixes respecting the above conditions out of which 154 are 100% discriminative and 203 score better than 98%.

The third parameter, *P3*, takes into account that, generally, if a PN has a last_name, then usually it is the rightmost token. A more precise estimation on a corpus of 200 unambiguous PNs (two tokens each, both of them unambiguously either first or last name) is that the general rule is not obeyed in 7.5% of the cases, with a 95% confidence of being in the interval (7.5-5.15, 7.5+5.15) = (2.35, 12.65). Assuming that *P3* has a Poisson distribution with $\mu = 7.52$, we can determine whether an unknown name is a first or last name solely on its position, even if its accompanying names are unknown. For example, the probability of a token to be a last_name, given that it

---

[3]http://europa.tiscali.it/futuro/speciali/200210/nomi_home.html

appears only three times in a corpus, two times at the left of other names and one time by itself, is only 0.015 (1.5%).

4 Local Coreference

This module addresses coreference among PNs within a single document. The input is made of all the PNs of the document, tagged by the Name Splitter as described in Section 3, while the output of the module is a set of clusters of PNs, where each cluster refers to a different person mentioned in a document.

Our major assumption for local coreference is the One Entity per Document (OED) hypothesis, according to which all the occurrences of the same PN in a document refer to the same person. In order to explain the conditions under which the coreference of two different PNs takes place we need to introduce *incomplete names*, which fall into two types: (i) PNs which are just first_names (e.g. "Silvio") or just last_names (e.g. "Berlusconi"); (ii) pseudo complete PNs, which are made out of a first and last name, that are strictly included into one or more PNs.

An incomplete PN can be coreferred with another, different, PN. In the case of incomplete PN, the coreference is seen as a completion: for a free name we find its complementary name (the complement of a first free name is a last name and vice versa) and for a pseudo complete PN we choose one PN from all the PNs that includes it. To each incomplete name we associate a list of coreference candidates: for a free name the list of candidates is made of all complementary names and for a pseudo complete PN the list of coreference candidates is made out of all PNs that include it. For an incomplete name we find the most probable completion. The completion is a probabilistic event, modelled by the following random variables: first name (l), last name (L), first_last name (l_L) and topic (t). For example, finding the most probable last_name for a free_first_name is finding the value of L which maximizes the following joint probability:

$$max_L \, p(l \, , L \, , l\_L \, , t) = max_L \, p(t) \, p(L \mid t) \, p(l \mid L, t) \, p(l\_L \mid l \, , L \, , t) \tag{1}$$

where:

- $p(t)$, is an independent constant, it does not count in the computation of (1).
- $p(L \mid t)$, the probability that a last_name is in that news document, shows the connection between a topic and a last_name and may be computed in two ways: (i) by taking values in {60/100, 29/100, 10/100, 1/100} corresponding to "very frequent", "frequent", "less frequent" and "no clue" respectively. (ii) by using the Bayes theorem, and keeping in mind that p(t) does not count, we have p(L | t) = p(t | L) p(L). Let $p(L)$, which represents the probability that a certain last_name is in the newspapers, be computed as a ratio. The probability p(t | L) is normalized as above.
- $p(l \mid L, t)$ is the probability that a certain person is referred to by first_name in a news document. If nothing is known we consider it 1/2. Otherwise, with evidence from corpus, we compute a yes/no function, considering whether it is more probable for that person to be called by first_name than not, and consequently, a quantity is added/subtracted from 1/2.

- $p(l\_L \mid l, L, t)$ is the probability that a person's name is made out of a first_name and a last_name. If there is a known link between l_L and t, like "very frequent", or "frequent", then we approximate the p(l_L | l, L, t) with the probability p(L | t). When this strong evidence is not present, we approximate it as {80/100, 20/100, 0} considering the probability that the last_name is indeed a last_name. "0" value means that we have unmatched abbreviations.

All the above probabilities have been calculated over the whole document collection. The reason to normalize each of the probabilities in (1) is twofold. Firstly, the probabilities in the right hand side can be very low and we are unable to correctly set a probabilistic space (the sum of marginal probabilities to be 1). Secondly, the number of occurrences of a collocation, such as last_name and topic, or first_name and last_name, is relevant once a certain threshold is passed. We cannot say that one person is more a politician than another once we know that both are, nor can we say that a legal name is more legal than another.

Suppose we have a news document where the next PNs are present: *"G.W.B."*, *"Silvio"*, *"George"*, *"Bush"*, *"Michelangelo"*, *"Silvio"*, *"Bush"*, *"Berlusconi"*. From the Name splitter we know that *"Silvio"*, *"George"*, *"Michelangelo"* are first names and *"Bush"*, *"Berlusconi"* are last names. The two *"Silvio"* corefer by OED. Statistically, *"Bush"* and *"Berlusconi"* represent a valid collocation, but the fact that both are free_last_names correctly prevents their coreference. Rather, *"Silvio"* is coreferred with *"Berlusconi"* and *"George"* with *"Bush"* by using (1). "Michelangelo" is not coreferred with any of them. By OED, *"G.W.B."* is also coreferred with *"George Bush"*.

The set of PNs that corefer represent a cluster. To each cluster we associate a name, which we call cluster name. This name represents the name of one person and all the PNs inside the respective cluster are (different) ways to refer to that person. To this name a set of NEs is associated and this information will be used further by the Global Coreference Module. The global coreference regards only the cluster names, not directly the PNs inside the clusters. The name of the cluster is the longest name we build out of different names inside the same cluster. As the local coreference module may corefer a free_first_name with a (free) last name, the resulting cluster name could be a name which is not a PN in the text. For example, in a news document in which we find *"G.W.B."*, *"George Bush"* and *"Bush"* we create the cluster name *"George W. Bush"*, a name which is not found as such in the respective news document.

5   Global Coreference

Given our probabilistic approach to coreference, the fundamental question addressed by the global coreference module is to estimate the probability of two PNs that have the same form to refer to different persons in the world. For any PN, we are interested in estimating the probability that different persons share it (compare, for instance, the probability of a person being called by two extremely common names like *"Paolo Rossi"* vs. *"Roldano Not"* which very probably will identify a person uniquely)

A first intuition is that the probability above is correlated to the frequency of the PNs: for a rare name it will be almost impossible that two different persons having that name, made it into the newspaper. According to this intuition we have divided the PNs in the corpus into five categories: extremely uncommon (less than 10), uncommon (less than 100), common (less than 300), very common (less than 700), extremely common (more than 700). In Table 1 we show the figures and percentiles of the five categories computed on the Adige corpus.

Table 1. PN Categories clustered according to their frequency

# Name Category	# First name	#Last Name
extremely uncommon	4 834 (7.21%)	14 319 (13.44%)
Uncommon	6 294 (9.38%)	16 079 (15.09%)
Common	52 167 (77.80%)	73 886(69.38%)
very common	2 634(3.92%)	1 485(1.39%)
extremely common	1 116 (1.66%)	717 (0.6%)
Total	**67 045**	**106 486**

Since the probability of a person in the world carrying a "common" name to be mentioned in a newspaper is relatively low, we can assume that the probability of two different persons having the same "common name" is very small. In addition, even if they do appear in the newspaper, it is very probable that they are not related to the same entities, such as organizations and locations. Therefore, a common name appearing in two different news documents that also have in common at least one specific entity may refer to the same person with a high probability.

The same line of reasoning applies for "very common" or "extremely common" PNs as well. Even if the probability for an "extremely common" name to refer to different persons is high, it decreases exponentially once we also consider the entities it occurs with. Consider, for instance, a trigram formed by an "extremely common" PN, an organization and a location, from the same news document, like in ("*Fabrizio*", "*Vertical Shop*", "*Arco*"). The probability that this trigram appears for different persons is very low, indeed negligible, even if "*Fabrizio*" by itself is an extremely common name. Therefore, its re-occurrence is, reliably, an indicator that the respective name refers to the same person.

We represent contextual entities (i.e. organizations and locations as recognized by the named entities recognizer) co-occurring with a given PN within a single document in the *association set* of the PN. Association sets that have common entities (two for extremely common PNs) are held to identify a unique person.

In addition to shared entities, the topic of a news document may be a strong evidence for global coreference among PNs. According to this intuition the topic is an element of the association set which scores negatively if different. The rule we use is that a very common name refers to different persons if the topic is distinct and the association sets have less than three entities in common.

We consider that the order in which we corefer the local heads is important. Once two local heads are coreferred the association set of this person includes all the entities present in their association sets. Initial errors in coreference are amplified further and to reduce probability of false coreference we start from the surest cases.

The global coreference module works according to the algorithm described in Figure 2.

```
for each name category clustered according to frequency
        compute the association set (topic considered)
        corefer surest cases (freq category and association set)
        update Name Ontology, Entity Ontology
    endfor
    repeat
        compute the association set (topic and no topic considered)
        corefer based on freq category and common entities
        individuate free names without completion (nicknames)
        update Name Ontology and Entity Ontology
    until no update is made
```

Fig. 2. Global Coreference Algorithm

The output of the Global Coreference Module is a set of persons which are added to the Entity Ontology.

6 Experiments and Evaluation

The coreference algorithm has been applied to the Adige corpus, a collection of 586,017 news documents (having 20,199,441 Name Entities mentions) appeared in the Italian newspaper "L'Adige" over a period of seven years. The three modules of the system have been independently evaluated on the ICAB benchmark.

Dataset

The Adige corpus has been tokenized and then passed to a SVM based Named Entity Recognition system (Zanoli and Pianta 2006), which was trained on the ICAB benchmark (Magnini et al. 2006), a four days portion of the Adige collection. There are 5,559,314 person named entities, out of which 558,352 are unique, which corresponds to an average of ten occurrences for each PN. We show in Table 2 that the distribution is far from being uniform: as it can be seen, the number of PNs having just one occurrence represents more than half of the unique names (second column in Table 2).

Apriori we may assume that the most difficult cases for coreference will be the ones in which the number of occurrences is relatively small. We expect such cases to be concentrated in, but not restricted to, the ones with numbers of occurrences in the interval [6-20], which represents around 12% of all names. However, a newspaper is in a certain sense a hall of fame. If a full name is mentioned frequently into a newspaper, it is very probable that that name refers just to one person. Consequently, the distribution of frequency of unique names is biased on the extremes: either many names are mentioned just once or there are many mentions of a few names. The names appearing more than 100 times, representing 1.14% of all names, cover more than 56% of all PNs (Table 2).

Table 2. Person name distribution in the Adige corpus

#occurrences	#unique names	#PNs
1	306 473	306 473
2 – 5	160 455	451 358
6 – 20	74 780	688 920
21 – 100	25 518	1 052 636
101 – 1000	7 321	1 941 375
1001 – 5000	573	1 023 236
5001 –	22	193 606
1 – 30811	**558 352**	**5 559 314**

I-CAB is a four days news corpus completely annotated and all the entity mentions manually coreferred. Table 3 shows the figures for I-CAB relevant for our evaluation: the number of occurrences of Person Mentions (second column) with, within parentheses, the proportion of mentions containing a certain attribute; the number of names correctly recognised by the NER system (third column); the number of distinct names (fourth column); the number of distinct persons carrying them (fifth column). Additional details on the I-CAB corpus, relevant for estimating the difficulty of coreference task, are reported in (Popescu et al. 2006, Magnini et al. 2006b).

Table 3. I-CAB: figures of interest for evaluating name coreference

#attribute	#occ in ICAB	#correct NER	#distinct	#persons
FIRST_NAME	2299 (31%)	2283	676	1592
MIDDLE_NAME	110 (1%)	104	67	74
LAST_NAME	4173 (57%)	4157	1906	2191
NICKNAME	73 (1%)	54	44	41

The coverage of the dictionary with respect to the document collection is 47.68%. Therefore, for more than half of the names we meet in the corpus we are unable to tell whether they are first or last names.

Baselines

We use the "all for one" baseline: all equal PNs stand for the same person. Partial_names are completed with the most frequent complete name that includes them (for instance, the free_firt_name "Silvio" is completed with "Silvio Berlusconi"). The rightmost token in a PN is considered the last name.

Evaluation of the Name Splitter

The Name Dictionary covers 87.3% of first names and 91.8% of last names occurring in the I-CAB corpus. There are 245 ambiguous names, out of which 9 are actually ambiguously used in ICAB, and there are 13 ambiguous abbreviations.

The Name Splitter Module performs quite well. We report a 96.73% precision for first_name and 98.17% precision for last_name, considering the figures from third column of Table 3. In total the module has 97.45% accuracy. The errors most likely do not influence the coreference results as they occur just one time. The base line goes at 89.13%.

In I-CAB there are 248 occurrences of free first name and 2119 occurrences of free last names. They represent 10.71% and 50.76% of the PNs respectively (Table 3, column 2). It is interesting to look at names also, not only at their occurrence. There are 127 unique free_names and 1064 unique free last names which actually represent 18.78% and 55.82% of names (Table 3, column 4). Comparing these figures with the one reported in Table 2 we can draw a preliminary conclusion: in a four day period time the average number of reoccurrence of last names is low. The consequence of this fact will be discussed at the end of this section.

Evaluation of Local Coreference

The baseline for local coreference is very high: only 29 errors. That is, there are only 29 cases in which the coreference is not trivial, or the most frequent collocation is not the correct answer. Our algorithm scores better: it saves 11 cases out of these 29 cases.

It is relevant to discuss performance in terms of ratios. There are 6633 PNs in ICAB and 2976 local coreferences, which means an average of 2.22 PNs per name referent. Our algorithm, which for the first run behaves like the baseline algorithm, has found 1,039,203 local coreferences out of 5,559,314 PNs, which means a 5.34 average, which is almost twice. At the end, the local coreference module outputs 1,748,212 local coreferred PNs, with an average of 3.17, which is probably closer to the true value.

Evaluation of Global Coreference

The Global Coreference module is evaluated for those cases where the name appears at least two times in ICAB. For all complete names the baseline goes wrong in 24 cases. It means that there are 24 cases in four days where the same complete name does not refer to the same person. Our algorithm performs a little better – it keeps them correctly separated in 17 cases. However, there are 10 coreferred names which our algorithm does not realize. As far as partial names are concerned, there are 91 last_names which do not have a first name and refer to different persons. The system scores 87 while the baseline scores 0. (i.e. it always finds a first name). There are 45 first names referring to different persons, yet without having the last name mentioned. Our algorithm realizes correctly in 34 cases that the respective names should remain free and distinct.

We would like to refer again, informatively, to the figures for the whole corpus, where we count 558,352 distinct PNs. Our algorithm finds 630,613 persons while the baseline indicates 495,129 persons. The analysis above suggests that numbers do not tell the whole story by themselves. As seen above, not in all cases where the baseline is wrong do we succeed in having the correct answer. The reverse is also true. In Table 4 we summarize the figures of this section, comparing the error rate of the system and of the baseline.

Table 4. System and Baseline error rate

Module	#System errors	#Baseline errors
Name Category Recognizer	151 (2.65%)	603 (10.97%)
Local Coreference	11 (0.4%)	29 (0.8%)
Global Coreference	31 (1.46%)	150 (5.49%)

A second evaluation of the proposed system comes indirectly from a more or less independent task. A variant of the coreference algorithm has been used in the Semeval 2007 Web People Search task (Artiles et al. 2007) where it performed quite well, ranking second against sixteen participants.

7 Conclusion and Further Work

We have presented a probabilistic framework for Person Name Coreference. The system is divided in three modules: firstly, the first and last name of a person name are recognized, then the coreference among a single document is established and finally the coreference at the level of the whole collection is addressed. Each module has been evaluated against a corpus of manually annotated documents.

Our analysis suggests that generally good results can be achieved. There is still a long way to go before perfection. The principal bottleneck is, in our opinion, the fact that names may have different distributions from corpus to corpus, and besides, many times there is no explicit evidence in the corpus for their coreference.

There are open issues in the Name Coreference tasks. The exact coreference is guaranteed only by ontological facts, but we are unable to extract this information out of news documents. We approximate uniqueness by computing the probability of occurrence considering that it is a rare event that different persons have the same names and/or share partially the same set of NEs.

We have used only Named Entities for clustering. However, many times there is no sufficient evidence to realize the coreference. For the same person the algorithm produces clusters that have nothing in common and consequently incorrect persons are invented. We hope the analysis of the full text may be used to bridge these gaps. Nevertheless, there are many practical difficulties that must be overcome in order to do that. From our point of view, the most important thing is to be able to extract additional specifications for each name, such as, for instance, professions, and to be able to make connections to an existing ontology. We think this goal is a realistic one and we have already started working on it.

The evaluation of our system has been carried out on I-CAB, which is only a continuous four day period of news documents. As the mentions of the same person may span over a long discontinuous period of time, the baseline algorithm may score much lower in reality. An evaluation corpus made out of some of these cases may be more informative about the performances of different algorithms. We plan to find a solution for building such an evaluation corpus.

References

1. Gonzalo, J., Sekine, S.: Establishing a benchmark for the Web People Search Task: The Semeval 2007 WePS Track. In: Proceedings of Semeval 2007. Association for Computational Linguistics (2007)
2. Bagga, A., Baldwin, B.: Entity-based cross-document co-referencing using the vector space model. In: Proceedings of the 17th international conference on Computational linguistics, pp. 75–85 (1998)
3. Magnini, B., Pianta, E., Girardi, C., Negri, M., Romano, L., Speranza, M., Bartalesi Lenzi, V., Sprugnoli, R.: I-CAB: the Italian Content Annotation Bank. In: Proceedings of LREC-2006, Genova, Italy (2006)
4. Pedersen, T., Purandare, A., Kulkarni, A.: Name Discrimination by Clustering Similar Contexts. In: Proceedings of the World Wide Web Conference (2006)
5. Popescu, O., Magnini, B., Pianta, E., Serafini, L., Speranza, M., Tamilin, A.: From Mentions to Ontology: A Pilot Study. In: Proceedings SWAP06, Pisa, Italy (2006)
6. Zanoli, R., Pianta, E.: SVM based NER, Technical Report, Trento, Italy (2006)
7. Magnini, B., Pianta, E., Popescu, O., Speranza, M.: Ontology Population from Textual Mentions: Task Definition and Benchmark. In: Proceedings of the OLP2 workshop on Ontology Population and Learning, Sidney, Australia (2006) (Joint with ACL/Coling 2006)

Dependency Tree Semantics:
Branching Quantification in Underspecification

Livio Robaldo

Department of Computer Science - University of Turin
C.so Svizzera 185, 10149, Torino, Italy
robaldo@di.unito.it

Abstract. Dependency Tree Semantics (DTS) is a formalism that allows to underspecify quantifier scope ambiguities. This paper provides an introduction of DTS and highlights its linguistic and computational advantages. From a linguistics point of view, DTS is able to represent the so-called Branching Quantifier readings, i.e. those readings in which two or more quantifiers have to be evaluated in parallel. From a computational point of view, DTS features an easy syntax–semantics interface wrt a Dependency Grammar and allows for incremental disambiguations.

1   Introduction

Dependency Tree Semantics (DTS) is an underspecified[1] formalism for dealing with quantifier scope ambiguities. DTS has a straightforward syntax-semantics interface with a Dependency Grammar, just as Quasi Logical Form (QLF) has (see [14] and [1]), and allows for monotonically adding constraints to take partial disambiguations into account, just as in Underspecified Discourse Representation Theory (UDRT) [27], Minimal Recursion Semantics (MRS) [7], Hole Semantics (HS) [3] or Constraint Language for Lambda Structures (CLLS) [10].

The main advantage of DTS, however, is the possibility to represent the so-called Branching Quantifier (BQ) readings (see [13], [2], [30], and [31]). In DTS, all NPs are taken to be referential rather than quantificational, i.e. as having semantic type e rather than $((e, t), t)$. Quantifier scope is specified by inserting further dependencies between NP denotations in order to allow a certain set of entities to vary depending on the entities belonging to another one.

In other words, DTS aims at importing in NL Semantics the same ideas lying behind the well-known Skolem theorem, defined in standard First Order Logic.

Several similar attempts have already been made in the literature; see [34], [12], [24], [36], [11], [37], and, recently, [32]. Analogously, [26] and [35] suggested the use of Choice Functions in place of the Skolem ones.

Nevertheless, all these proposals devolve the generation of all available scopings upon the combinatorics of the syntax, while in DTS quantifier scope ambiguities and their relatives are seen as instances of underspecified meaning that can

---

[1] A full overview of goals and techniques recently proposed in Underspecification may be found in [6]. See also [9] for a comparison among existing underspecified formalisms, their expressivity, and their computational complexity.

R. Basili and M.T. Pazienza (Eds.): AI*IA 2007, LNAI 4733, pp. 374–385, 2007.

adopt a more restricted sense depending on the world-knowledge, the syntactic structure, the topic\focus distinction and so forth.

Well-formed structures in DTS are based on a simple graph G that represents the predicate-argument relations, without any quantification. The nodes of G are either predicates or discourse referents; each arc connects a predicate with a discourse referent and is labelled with the number of the argument position. Each discourse referent is also related to a *quantifier*, via a function quant from discourse referents to quantifiers, and to a *restriction*, via a function restr from discourse referents to subgraphs of G. In (1), a first simple example is shown

(1) Two students study three theorems

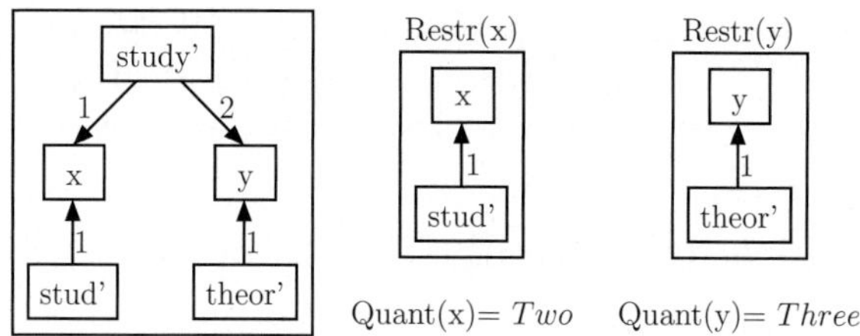

The structure in (1) is ambiguous, since it does not specify how the quantifiers relate to each other. In order to make explicit the dependencies among quantifiers, additional dotted arcs between discourse referents are inserted. Fig.1 shows the three possible disambiguations of (1)

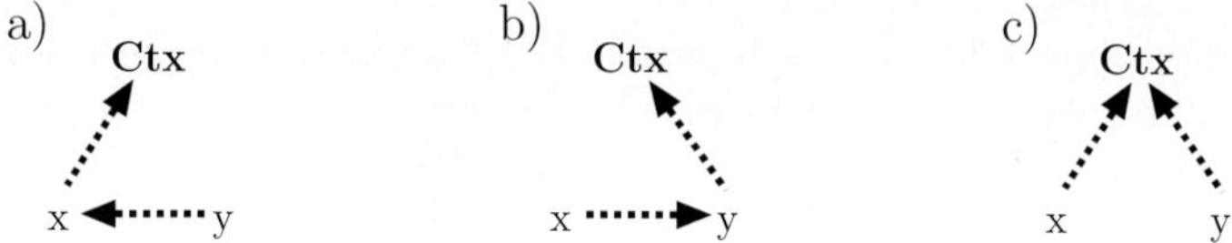

Fig. 1. The three readings of sentence (1)

Fig.1.a shows the reading in which 'three' depends on (is outscoped by) 'two'. Hence, this structure is true only in those models in which there are two students each of who studies three (potentially different) theorems. On the contrary, in fig.1.b, the arc linking x to y specifies that the two students depend on the theorems; in this case, a model satisfies the reading only if it contains a triple of theorems studied each by two (potentially different) students. Finally, fig.1.c depicts the BQ reading of (1): this reading is true in those models in which there are two students studying three *same* theorems. In all readings, the widest-scope quantifiers are linked to a new node called Ctx. Ctx refers to the context, i.e. the domain of individuals wrt which the representation will be evaluated. Clearly, discourse referents directly linked to Ctx correspond, in standard logics, to Skolem constants, while the other ones to Skolem functions having as argument the discourse referents reachable from them via a path of dotted arcs. A more complex example is shown in (2):

(2) Most boys ate a portion of every course.

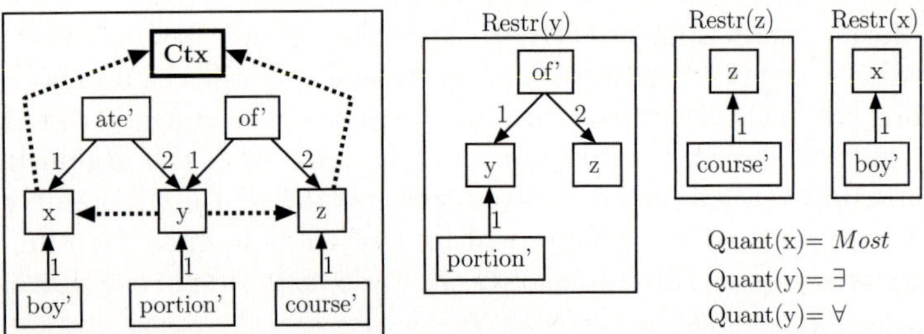

Quant(x)= *Most*
Quant(y)= ∃
Quant(y)= ∀

The representation yields the preferred reading of the sentence; note that y depends on both x and z, that are in BQ to each other; in fact, the sentence describes a situation where there is a different portion for each pair ⟨*boy, course*⟩.

2   Are BQ Readings Really Available in NL?

Although, to my knowledge, there are no works in NL semantics that explicitly state the unavailability of BQ readings in NL, their coverage has been, by and large, neglected in the literature. In fact, it can be argued that they can be pragmatically inferred from other available readings; for example, it is easy to see that the set of models satisfying the BQ reading in fig.1.c is the intersection of the sets of models satisfying the readings in fig.1.a and fig.1.b. Therefore, it seems that BQ readings are just subcases of their linear counterparts.

This section shows evidence in favour of BQ readings and argues that, instead, they should be taken into account in NL semantics.

First at all, it may be shown (see [29], §6) that BQ readings are not always logical subcases of the other ones. Roughly speaking, this logical entailment does not hold when non-upwards monotone quantifiers are involved.

Second at all, BQ is not the only logical construction leading to interpretations that can be inferred from other ones. This may be also found rather often when existential and\or universal quantifiers are involved; nevertheless, in such cases, all possible scopings are standardly considered as autonomous readings.

Finally, it can be argued that although it seems difficult to interpret a sentence taken in isolation via a BQ reading, there are many real cases in which the speaker, wrt contextual information, intends to refer to fixed sets of entities.

For instance, consider sentences in (3)

(3)   a. <u>Two</u> students of mine have seen <u>three</u> drug-dealers in front of the school.
      b. <u>Most</u> men noticed that <u>few</u> children left the room.
      c. The director suggested the failure of <u>two</u> students (of this class) to <u>most</u> of the teachers.

Concerning sentence (3.a), world knowledge seems to render the reading featuring a BQ between the quantifiers *two* and *three* the most salient; in fact, (3.a) appears to involve just two students and just three drug-dealers, i.e. there are two students who have seen three *same* drug-dealers.

Analogously, (3.b) refers to a set of most men and a set of few children such that each men in the former notices that each child in the latter left the room.

Finally, (3.c) is saying that the director has two specific persons in mind and suggested their respective failure to any teacher he contacted in some way (such that the sum of these teachers are "most teacher"). Again, a BQ between *two* and *most* should be preferred.

To conclude, my opinion is that BQ readings must be licensed because what is really important for a NL semantic formalism is the ability to restrict, as much as possible, the set of models in which a sentence is true. Instead, it does not matter if this set is also included in the set of models satisfying other readings. In other words, since NL provides ways that allow the speaker to identify a restrict meaning, it seems that there is no reason to set up a representation referring to a more general one.

3   Easy Interface with a Dependency Grammar

As the name *Dependency Tree Semantics* suggests, DTS features a strong closeness with a Dependency Grammar (see [22] and [15]). The dependency structures we refer to during the ongoing research on DTS are being used at the University of Torino in a number of projects, including the development of a Treebank for Italian [4] and the implementation of a rule-based dependency parser [20]. More details on the labelling scheme can be found in [5]. It has also been applied to English and its relations with the Paninian scheme are currently under study.

The DTS syntax-semantics interface just deals with predicate-argument relations, while the disambiguation task (see below) is completely devolved upon a subsequent module. Since a Dependency Tree already provides a description of the predicate-argument relations carried by the sentence, it is easy to see that, in order to obtain the corresponding DTS representation, it is sufficient to associate each determiner d with a discourse referent x, and insert x as argument of all predicates denoted by the lemmas related to d via some grammatical functions in the Dependency Tree. This process can be automatically accomplished via a set of (monotinic) if-then rules as shown in [29], §3.

For instance, the two underspecified DTS structures in (1) and (2) can be obtained starting from the Dependencies Trees shown in fig.2.

Starting from the Dependency Tree in fig.2 on the right, we associate y to the quantifier '*a*' and insert y as argument of the predicates *ate′*, *portion′* and *of′*. In fact, these predicates are respectively denoted by the lemmas '*ate*', '*portion*' and '*of*' that, in the Dependency Tree, are related to '*a*': the object of '*ate*' is the subtree having '*a*' as root, '*portion*' is the only complement of '*a*', and '*of*' is an adjunct of this complement.

The last ingredient needed to build the DTS underspecified representation is a criterion to set the value of the function $\mathsf{restr}(x)$, for each discourse referent

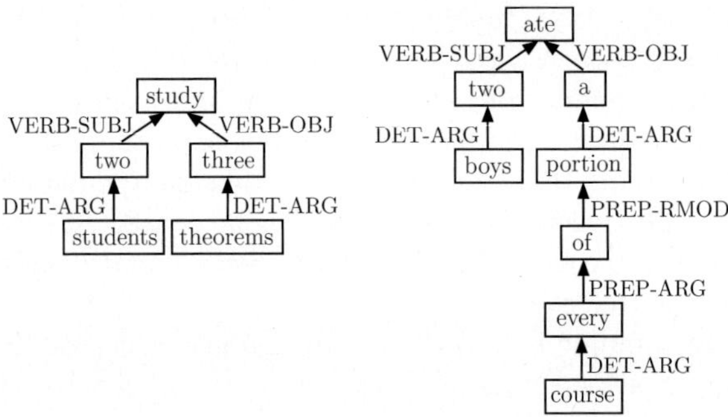

Fig. 2. Dependency Trees for (1) and (2)

x in the graph. $\mathsf{restr}(x)$ is simply set to the subgraph of all predicate-argument relations $R(x_1, \ldots, x_n)$ such that:

- $R(x_1, \ldots, x_n)$ arises from the subtree having the determiner associated with x as root.
- x is one of the $x_1, \ldots, x_n$

This seems to be consistent with the ideas lying behind the architecture of a Dependency Tree; in fact, in a dependency relation between a word head and a word dependent, the latter plays a role of "completion" of the former, in the sense that it circumscribes\restricts the head meaning by acting as its parameter. However, it has been pointed out that not only the dependent is involved in this completion, but the whole subtree having the dependent as root.

With respect to the syntax-semantic interface, DTS is rather close to approches as QLF [1]. For instance, consider the fully underspecified QLF formula shown in (4). This formula contains terms in the form $<q \; v \; r>$, where q is a quantifier, v the variable on which q ranges on and r, i.e. the restriction, another QLF formula. These terms are called *qterms* and enclose quantifier scope ambiguities. The QLF disambiguation mechanism (described in details in [23]) acts on these complex terms to enumerate all readings.

(4) $ate'(<Most \; x \; boy'(x) >, <\exists \; y \; portion'(y) \wedge of'(y, <\forall \; z \; course'(z) >)>)$

A fully underspecified QLF formula reflects the architecture of a Dependency Tree as DTS does. For instance, in order to obtain (4) from the Dependency Tree in fig.2 on the right, it is sufficient to start from the root and, when a determiner is met, create a qterm $<q \; v \; r>$ where q is the involved quantifier, and v a new variable. Finally, the value of r is obtained by recursively applying this procedure on the subtree having the quantifier as root.

On the contrary, building a UDRT or a MRS fully underspecified representation starting from the syntactic stucture is basically harder in that it is necessary to manage, besides the predicate-argument relations, also initial scope constraints. For example, consider the MRS fully underspecified representation built via the syntax-semantic interface proposed in [18][2], i.e.

(5)

$$\{\, l_1{:}Most_x(h_{11}, h_{12}),\ l_2{:}\exists_y(h_{21}, h_{22}),\ l_3{:}\forall_z(h_{31}, h_{32}),\ l_6{:}course'(z),\ l_4{:}boy'(x),$$
$$l_{51}{:}portion'(y),\ l_{52}{:}of'(y, z),\ l_7{:}ate'(x, y)\},\ \{\, l_4 \leq h_{11}, l_6 \leq h_{31}, l_{51} \leq h_{21},$$
$$\mathbf{l_7 \leq h_{12},\ l_7 \leq h_{22},\ l_7 \leq h_{32},\ l_{52} \leq h_{32},\ l_{52} \leq h_{21}}\,\}$$

This representation is made up by two sets: a set of labelled pieces of formula containing particular variables named holes (e.g. h_{11}, h_{12}, etc.) and a set of dominance constraints between holes and labels. The latter imposes constraints on how the labels can be plugged into the holes to trigger the final available readings. A dominance constraint is in the form $l \leq h$ and specifies that the piece of formula labelled by l will fill h either direcly or transitively, i.e. h will be filled either by it or by a larger fragment containing it.

Six of these initial dominance relations (marked in boldface) constrain the membership of some predicates to the *bodies* of the three quantifiers, rather than to their restrictions. The syntax-semantic interface also has to manage these constraints besides the ones that, together with the labelled formulae, describe the predicate-argument relations carried by the sentence.

Furthermore, as pointed out in [19], in order to avoid unexpected interpretations when the sentence contains a syntactic Nested Quantification, as in the phrase [*a portion of* [*every course*]], the basic constraint-based mechanisms have to be augmented with additional ad-hoc constructs, whose management is again devolved upon the syntax-semantics interface. For example, [19] introduces further constructs and constraints in the syntax-semantics interface from LTAG to MRS, previously proposed in [18]. In particular, MRS basic formulae are augmented with an ad-hoc mechanism based on quantifier sets, and a particular LTAG derivation, called 'flexible composition', is imposed.

In QLF there is no need to assert similar initial scope constraints, because the order imposed on the resolution of the complex terms already provides a proper treatment of Nested Quantification and prevents the occurrence of free variables in the final representation. In other words, in QLF the prevention of unavailable readings of this kind is up to the disambiguation process rather than to the syntax-semantic interface. Consequently, the latter turns out to be simpler. Although it may seem that this simply delays work that must be done in any case, it has been observed by [25] that formal constraints on binding at a level of logical form, as those implemented in [14], can be expressed as constraints on the derivation of possible meanings. Therefore, it seems that the correct strategy to block the generation of such unavailable readings is the one adopted in the QLF and related approaches. This has been adopted in DTS too, where an account of Nested Quantification has been proposed in terms of constraints on possible disambiguations, based on logical grounds.

---

[2] This interface is defined with respect to LTAG [17]. A syntax-semantic interface that allows to obtain a formula in a constraint-based underspecified formalism (CLLS) starting from a Dependency Grammar has been defined in [8].

4 DTS Partial and Full Disambiguations

Constraint-based formalisms like UDRT, HS o MRS feature an important advantage with respect to QLF: they naturally achieve partial disambiguations, and allow for a suitable management of partial knowledge. This is very important for an underspecified formalism, because, in real-life scenarios, the knowledge needed to disambiguate normally does not become available simultaneously.

A constraint-based framework allows to *incrementally* perform disambiguation, in that dominance relations can be asserted one by one, independently of each other[3]. Instead, formalisms like QLF *intrinsically* prevent partial disambiguations. This has been claimed by [28] in the light of examples as

(6) Every$_x$body believed that many a$_y$ problem about the environment preoccupied most$_z$ politicians.

As is well known, quantifiers are (with some exceptions) clause bounded; concerning sentence (6), this amounts to saying that both *Many a$_y$* and *Most$_z$* must have narrow scope with respect to *Every$_x$* (in symbols, *Many a$_y$* $\leq$ *Every$_x$* and *Most$_z$* $\leq$ *Every$_x$*). In QLF, it is impossible to specify this partial scoping. In fact, once we fix the relative scope between two quantifiers, for instance *Many a$_y$* $\leq$ *Every$_x$*, it is only possible to specify the scope of *Most$_z$* wrt them both, whereas we cannot independently assert a weaker constraint *Most$_z$* $\leq$ *Every$_x$*.

On the contrary, this may be easily done in HS or UDRT, since each dominance constraint indicates that a certain piece of formula must be inserted into another one, but still it leaves underpecified whether this insertion is achieved directly or rather transitively, via other pieces.

It should be clear, then, that in order to perform monotonic disambiguation, the underspecified logic must enable *partial* scope orderings. However, it is not clear how this could be achieved in terms of semantic dependencies. For instance, consider again sentence (6); in DTS, in order to represent that *Many a$_y$* and *Most$_z$* have narrow scope wrt *Every$_x$*, it seems that the dotted arcs should be instantiated as in fig.3.a. Nevertheless, fig.3.a already describes a *final* ordering for (6): it specifies that *Many a$_y$* and *Most$_z$* must be in BQ between them.

In other words, *each* of the three representations in fig.3 is a possible final configurations having *Many a$_y$* and *Most$_z$* with narrow scope wrt *Every$_z$*.

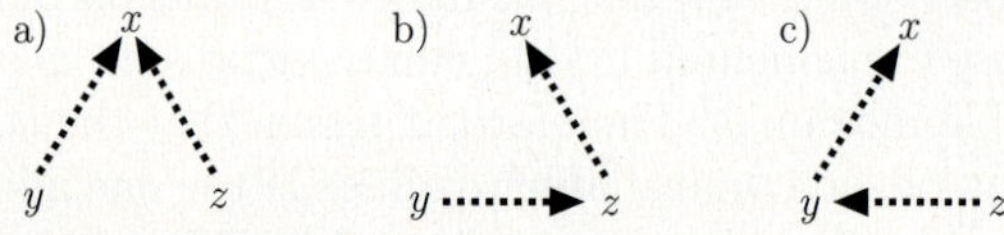

Fig. 3. Three readings for (6)

---

[3] It must be pointed out that some translation processes from QLF and QLF-like approaches to constraint-based ones have been proposed. Their aim is to combine the advantages of both by obtaining a QLF formula from the syntactic representation, then translating it into a constraint based one. See [33] and [21]

Therefore, as in MRS, it is necessary to distinguish between partial and fully specified representations. In order to get this result, I distinguish between two types of arc, respectively called *SkDep* and *SemDep* arcs. The former denotes partial dependencies, while the latter denotes the final ones. The discourse referents $\{x_1, x_2, ..., x_n\}$ reachable from the discourse referent x via the *SkDep* arcs are always a subset of those reachable from x via *SemDep* arcs.

In other words, the *SkDep* arcs express all known dependencies, so that the absence of an arc from y to z implies that it is not known whether y depends on z, or viceversa, or no dependence does exist (unless a dependence can be inferred from the existing ones via transitivity). Conversely, *SemDep* arcs are such that the absence of an arc implies that neither of the two nodes precedes the other.

With this distinction, we can now use the *SkDep* in fig.4 to underspecify the three *SemDep* in fig.3 (*SkDep* arcs are shown by means of thinner dotted arcs). It should now be clear that, even if *SemDep* and *SkDep* may have the

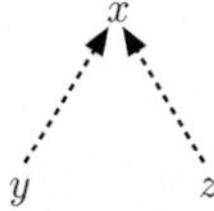

Fig. 4. Underspecified reading for (6)

same values, they describe different things. *SkDep* in fig.4 just asserts that, for each person in the set X (i.e. the set of all "believers"), there is both a set Y of problems about the environment and a set Z of politicians. There are three choices for these sets: either Y may be a set of *many a* problems about the environment and Z a set of *most* politicians, as in fig.3.a, or Y may be a set of *many a* problems about the environment and Z the union of $|Y|$ sets of *most* politicians (one for each $y \in Y$), as in fig.3.b, or Z may be a set of *most* politicians and Y the union of $|Z|$ sets of *many a* problems about the environment (one for each $z \in Z$), as in fig.3.c. Now, the interpretation process proceeds as follows: we add *SkDep* arcs in the representation according to the constraints coming from the context; each new *SkDep* arc provides a new piece of information, that further constrains the scope of the quantifiers and the set of possible models satisfying the graph. When the disambiguation is complete, the set of *SkDep* arcs is "frozen" and converted into a set of *SemDep* arcs. Now, the model-theoretic interpretation of the SDG can be given, according to the semantics provided in [29].

5   Formalisation: Syntax of DTS

This section formally defines DTS well-formed structures in the light of what has been discussed so far. There are two kinds of well-formed structures: Scoped Dependency Graph (SDG) and Underspecified Scoped Dependency Graph (USDG). The former is a model-theoretically interpretable representation referring to a non-ambiguous reading of the sentence, while the latter is an underspecified representation describing a partial disambiguation.

Both structures refer to a third common structure, called Flat Dependency Graph, which conveys all predicate-argument relations carried by the sentence.

As in standard semantics, the definitions below are stated in terms of three sets: a set of predicates pred, a set of constants name and a set of variables D called *discourse referents* as in DRT [16]. Moreover, I write $P^1 \subseteq$ pred for the unary predicates, $P^2 \subseteq$ pred for the binary ones and $\iota_{name} \subseteq P^1$ for those obtained by applying the ι-operator to a constant in name[4].

Definition 1. *[Flat Dependency Graphs (FDG)]*
A FDG is a tuple $\langle N, L, A, Dom, f \rangle$ s.t.:

- *N is a set of nodes $\{n_1, \dots, n_k\}$.*
- *L is a set of labels; in fig.1, $L \equiv \{1, 2\}$.*
- *$Dom \equiv$ pred $\cup\, D$ is a set domain objects: predicates and discourse referents.*
- *f is a function $f : N \mapsto Dom$, specifying the domain object with which the node is associated. If $f(n) \in$ pred, we will say that node n is of type pred, else we say it is of type D.*
- *A is a set of arcs. An arc is a triple $\langle n_s, n_d, l \rangle$, where $n_s, n_d \in N$, n_s is of type pred, n_d is of type D and $l \in L$.*

Definition 2. *[Underspecified Scoped Dependency Graph (USDG)]*
A USDG is a tuple $\langle G_f, $ Ctx, Q, quant, restr, SkDep$\rangle$ s.t.:

- *$G_f = \langle N, L, A, Dom, f \rangle$ is an FDG.*
- *Ctx is a special element called "the context".*
- *Q is a set of standard Generalized Quantifiers as every, most, two, ...*
- *quant is a total function $N_D \mapsto Q$, where $N_D \subseteq N$ are the nodes of type D.*
- *restr is a total function assigning to each $d \in N_D$ a subgraph of G_f.*
- *SkDep is a total function $N_D \mapsto \wp(N_D) \cup \{Ctx\}$, where $\wp(N_D)$ is the power set of N_D, satisfying constraints in def.4.*

Definition 3. *[Scoped Dependency Graph (SDG)]*
A SDG is a tuple $\langle G_f, $ Ctx, Q, quant, restr, SemDep$\rangle$ s.t.:

- *G_f, Ctx, Q, quant and restr are defined as in def.2*
- *SemDep is a total function $N_D \mapsto \wp(N_D) \cup \{Ctx\}$ satisfying def.4*

Without going into further details, I stipulate that an FDG is a connected acyclic graph s.t. each node of type pred has one exiting arc for each of its argument place. Note that there can be two nodes n_u and n_v s.t. $f(n_u)=f(n_v)$, i.e. the nodes in N can be seen as *occurrences* of symbols from Dom. The constraints mentioned in the two definitions above are defined as in def.4. These constraints exclude certain dependency relations that are 'logically impossible', and make sure that, for example, sentence (2) does not get a reading in which 'a' depends on 'every' and 'every' depends on 'most'.

---

[4] The ι-operator has the standard semantics: if α is a constant, $\iota\alpha$ is a unary predicate which is true only for α.

Definition 4. *[Constraints on $SkDep\backslash SemDep$]*

- SkDep\SemDep *implements a partial order on discourse referents and* Ctx, *with* Ctx *as its maximal element.*
- *Let d be a discourse referent, and let $R(d)$ be the smallest set that contains d, and for which it holds that if d' is in $R(d)$ and d'' occurs in the restriction of d', then also $d'' \in D$. Then*
    - *If $d_1 \in R(d)$, $d_2 \notin R(d)$, and d_1 depends on d_2, then also d depends on d_2.*
    - *If $d_1 \in R(d)$, $d_2 \notin R(d)$, and d_2 depends on d_1, then also d depends on d_1.*

The $SkDep\backslash SemDep$ arc introduced is just a compact graphical representation of the SkDep\SemDep function. If we take into account the transitive closure of $SkDep$, i.e. $SkDep*$, we have that n_1 $SkDep*$ n_2 iff $n_2 \in$ SkDep (n_1).

Finally, the last definition allows to transform a USDG into a SDG, after the disambiguation is complete. The SDG in which a USDG is "frozen" features a SemDep function having the same values of the SkDep function of the latter.

Definition 5. *[Freezing]*
A SDG $\langle SG_f, \text{Ctx}_1, Q_1, \text{quant}_1, \text{restr}_1, \text{SemDep} \rangle$ is a freezing of the USDG $\langle USG_f, \text{Ctx}_2, Q_2, \text{quant}_2, \text{restr}_2, \text{SkDep} \rangle$ iff:

- $SG_f = USG_f$, $\text{Ctx}_1 = \text{Ctx}_2$, $Q_1 = Q_2$, $\text{quant}_1 = \text{quant}_2$, $\text{restr}_1 = \text{restr}_2$
- $\forall(n) \text{SemDep}(n) = \text{SkDep}(n)$.

6   Conclusion

In this paper, a new approach to NL semantic underspecification has been proposed and implemented into a formalism called Dependency Tree Semantics (DTS). In this approach, disambiguation of quantifier scope is achieved by explicitly asserting dependencies between involved quantifiers, as is done by the well-known Skolem theorem in First Order Logics. To my knowledge, no other attempt to import in Underspecification the ideas lying behind the Skolem theory has been proposed in the literature.

DTS then represents an intermediate solution between the proposals based on referential interpretation of NPs and the current literature on Underspecification. It seems that this solution is able to combine the advantages of both approaches to the problem of quantifier scope ambiguities.

As the former, it is possible to represent the so-called Branching Quantifier readings. In contrast, current underspecified formalisms do not take them into account because they consider BQ as a special case of standard linear quantification. The motivations for considering them as autonomous readings, worth an explicit representation, have been investigated in section 2.

As the latter, DTS provides some computational benefits that seem hard to reconcile in the former.

- In underspecification, the logical form is, by definition, language-independent, as certain intuitions also seem to suggest. This feature clearly leads to a uniform account for the semantics of all languages, in which the Underspecified representation acts as a reasonable interlingua.

- An underspecified formula allows to store all available readings in a compact way, and to achieve disambiguation as the contextual knowledge becomes available.
- It is possible to incorporate weak inference rules in order to enable partial reasoning even on ambiguous knowledge, as is done in [27], and [28]. This is very important for NLP\NLU real systems, in that often the choice of a particular scope ordering on quantifiers is either non-relevant or marginal with respect to what the speaker actually intends to communicate.

Finally, DTS features an easy syntax-semantic interface and allows for incremental disambiguation. These two features are usually in trade-off in other approaches to Underspecification, while DTS appears to be immune from it.

References

1. Alshawi, H.: The Core Language Engine, pp. 32–39. Mit Press, Cambridge, UK (1992)
2. Barwise, J.: On branching quantifiers in English. The Journal of Philosophical Logic 8, 47–80 (1979)
3. Bos, J.: Predicate Logic Unplugged. In: Proc. Of the 10th Amsterdam Colloquium, Amsterdam, pp. 133–142 (1996)
4. Bosco, C.: A grammatical relation system for treebank annotation. PhD thesis, University of Turin (2004)
5. Bosco, C., Lombardo, V.: A relation schema for treebank annotation. In: Cappelli, A., Turini, F. (eds.) AI*IA 2003. LNCS (LNAI), vol. 2829, pp. 462–473. Springer, Heidelberg (2003)
6. Bunt, H.: Underspecification in Semantic Representations: Which Technique for What Purpose? In: Proc. of the 5th Workshop on Computational Semantics, Tilburg, The Netherlands, pp. 37–54 (2003)
7. Copestake, A., Flickinger, D., Sag, I.A.: Minimal Recursion Semantics. An introduction. Manuscript, Stanford University (1999)
8. Debusmann, R.: Extensible Dependency Grammar: A Modular Grammar Formalism Based On Multigraph Description. PhD thesis, Saarland University (2006)
9. Ebert, C.: Formal Investigations of Underspecified Representations. PhD thesis, Department of Computer Science, King's College London (2005)
10. Egg, M., Koller, A., Niehren, J.: The Constraint Language for Lambda Structures. Journal of Logic, Language and Information 10, 457–485 (2001)
11. Farkas, D.: Dependent Indefinites and Direct Scope. In: Condoravdi, C., Renardel, G. (eds.) Logical Perspectives on Language and Information, Stanford. CSLI Lecture Notes, pp. 41–72 (2001)
12. Fodor, J., Sag, I.: Referential and quantificational indefinites. Linguistics and Philosophy 5, 355–398 (1982)
13. Hintikka, J.: Quantifiers vs Quantification Theory. Dialectica 27, 329–358 (1973)
14. Hobbs, J.R., Shieber, S.: An Algorithm for Generating Quantifier Scoping. Computational Linguistics 13, 47–63 (1987)
15. Hudson, R.: English word grammar. Basil Blackwell, Oxford, Cambridge (1990)
16. Kamp, H., Reyle, U.: From Discourse to Logic. Kluwer Academic Publishers, Dordrecht (1993)

17. Joshi, A.K., Schabes, Y.: Tree-Adjoining Grammars. In: Rozenberg, G., Salomaa, A. (eds.) Handbook of Formal Languages, pp. 69–123. Springer, Heidelberg (1997)
18. Joshi, A.K., Kallmeyer, L.: Factoring Predicate Argument and Scope Semantics: Underspecified Semantics with LTAG. Research on Language and Computation 1, 3–58 (2003)
19. Joshi, A.K., Kallmeyer, L., Romero, M.: Flexible Composition in LTAG: Quantifier Scope and Inverse Linking. In: Musken, R., Bunt, H. (eds.) Computing Meaning, vol. 3, Kluwer, Dordrecht (2003)
20. Lesmo, L., Lombardo, V.: Transformed Subcategorization Frames in Chunk Parsing. In: LREC 2002. Proc. of the 3rd Int. Conf. on Language Resources and Evaluation, Las Palmas, pp. 512–519 (2002)
21. Lev, I.: Decoupling Scope Resolution from Semantic Composition. In: Proc. 6th Workshop on Computational Semantics, Tilburg, the Netherlands, pp. 139–150 (2005)
22. Mel'cuk, I.: Dependency syntax: theory and practice. SUNY University Press (1988)
23. Moran, D.B.: Quantifier scoping in the SRI core language engine. In: Proc. of the 26th annual meeting on ACL, Buffalo, New York, pp. 33–40 (1988)
24. Park, J.: A Lexical Theory of Quantification in Ambiguous Query Interpretation. PhD thesis, University of Pennsylvania, USA (1996)
25. Pereira, F.: A calculus for semantic composition and scoping. In: Proc. of the 27th annual meeting on ACL, Vancouver, Canada, pp. 152–160 (1988)
26. Reinhart, T.: Quantifier-Scope: How labor is divided between QR and choice functions. Linguistics and Philosophy 20, 335–397 (1997)
27. Reyle, U.: Dealing with ambiguities by Underspecification: Construction, Representation and Deduction. Journal of Semantics, 123–179 (1993)
28. Reyle, U.: Co-Indexing Labelled DRSs to Represent and Reason with Ambiguities. In: Peters, S., van Deemter, K. (eds.) Semantic Ambiguity and Underspecification, Stanford, pp. 239–268 (1996)
29. Robaldo, L.: Dependency Tree Semantics. PhD thesis, University of Turin, Italy (2007)
30. Sher, G.: Ways of branching quantifiers. Linguistics and Philosophy 13, 393–422 (1990)
31. Sher, G.: Partially-ordered (branching) generalized quantifiers: a general definition. The Journal of Philosophical Logic 26, 1–43 (1997)
32. Steedman, M.: Surface-Compositional Scope-Alternation Without Existential Quantifiers. Draft 5.1, for comments (2006)
33. van Genabith, J., Crouch, R.: F-Structures, QLFs and UDRSs. In: Proc. of the the 1st Int1. Conference on LFG, pp. 190–205. CSLI Publications, Stanford, CA (1996)
34. Webber, B. L.: A Formal Approach to Discourse Anaphora PhD thesis, Harvard University, USA (1999)
35. Winter, Y.: Choice Functions and the Scopal Semantics of Indefinites. Linguistics and Philosophy 20(4), 399–467 (1997)
36. Winter, Y.: Distributivity and Dependency. Natural Language Semantics 8, 27–69 (2000)
37. Winter, Y.: Functional Quantification. Research on Language and Computation 2, 331–363 (2004)

User Modelling for Personalized
Question Answering

Silvia Quarteroni and Suresh Manandhar

The University of York, York YO10 5DD, United Kingdom
{silvia,suresh}@cs.york.ac.uk

Abstract. In this paper, we address the problem of personalization in
question answering (QA). We describe the personalization component of
YourQA, our web-based QA system, which creates individual models of
users based on their reading level and interests.

First, we explain how user models are dynamically created, saved and
updated to filter and re-rank the answers. Then, we focus on how the
user's interests are used in YourQA. Finally, we introduce a methodology for user-centered evaluation of personalized QA. Our results show a
significant improvement in the user's satisfaction when their profiles are
used to personalize answers.

1 Introduction

Question answering (QA) can be seen as a form of information retrieval (IR)
where the aim is to respond to queries in natural language with actual answers
rather than relevant documents. A common problem in QA and IR (especially
when web-based) is information overload and consequently the low relevance
of results with respect to the user's needs [1]. While the need for personalized
(or profile-based) IR has been addressed by the IR community for a long time
[1,2], no extensive effort has yet been carried out in the QA community in this
direction. Indeed, personalization has been advocated in the main QA evaluation
campaign, TREC-QA (http://trec.nist.gov), but expeditiously solved by
assuming a fixed "average news reader" profile [3].

In this paper, we explain how the user's characteristics can be represented
in a QA system via a user model. We argue that personalization is a key issue
to make QA closer to the user's actual information requirements, and plays an
important role among the current directions for improving QA technology.

Sections 2 – 4 discuss how our QA system, YourQA [8], dynamically creates,
saves and updates user models. Sections 5 – 6 focus on how the user's interests
are used to achieve personalization. Sections 7 – 8 introduce and report the
results of an evaluation methodology for personalized QA. Section 9 concludes
on the application of user modelling to QA and discusses further work.

2 A Personalized Question Answering System

YourQA [8] is a web-based question answering system designed with the purpose
of supporting web search. As in the majority of QA systems [4,3], question

R. Basili and M.T. Pazienza (Eds.): AI*IA 2007, LNAI 4733, pp. 386–397, 2007.
© Springer-Verlag Berlin Heidelberg 2007

answering in YourQA is organized into three main phases: 1) question processing, where the user's question is analyzed to estimate the expected answer type; 2) document retrieval, where an IR engine is used to retrieve web documents relevant to the query; 3) answer extraction, where such documents are analyzed to extract answers which are eventually returned to the user in a ranked list.

However, YourQA aims at moving beyond traditional approaches to QA by targeting the answers to individual users based on their information needs. For this purpose, YourQA applies a user model to filter the documents during the retrieval phase and to re-rank its candidate answers during answer extraction.

2.1   The User Model

The user model (UM) in YourQA is designed to represent students searching for information on the web. The model is composed of three modules:

- age range, $a \in \{7 - 10, 11 - 16, adult\}$;
- reading level, $r \in \{basic, medium, advanced\}$;
- profile, p, a set of documents and/or web pages of interest.

The user's age range corresponds to the primary school, secondary school and adult age range in Britain. Although the reading level can be modelled separately from the age range, for simplicity we here assume that these are paired.

Although currently basic, such model may be extended in the future with additional modules encompassing different aspects of the user.

Analogous UM components can be found in the SeAn [5] and SiteIF [6] news recommender systems, where information such as age and browsing history, respectively are part of the user model. More generally, our approach is similar to that of personalized search systems such as [7], which constructs user models based on the user's documents and web pages of interest.

In previous work [8], we assumed a fixed user model with an empty profile component to illustrate how the reading level parameter is applied to answer filtering, efficiently contributing to improving the users' perceived readability of answers. In this paper, we focus on how user *profiles* can be dynamically created, saved and updated in YourQA. Section 3 reports how YourQA creates the user profile and how the latter is used to achieve personalization.

3   A Dynamic User Profile

This section illustrates the life cycle of the UM profile parameter in YourQA.

3.1   Profile Creation

When accessing YourQA, the user has three options (see Figure 1.(a)):

A) Create a new profile from documents of interest and/or browser bookmarks; in this case, keyphrase extraction is used to obtain a list of keyphrases from the text documents or bookmarked web pages;

B) Load a previously saved profile; in this case, the list of keyphrases contained in the loaded user profile are obtained;

C) Decide not to use a profile; in this case, no keyphrases are extracted.

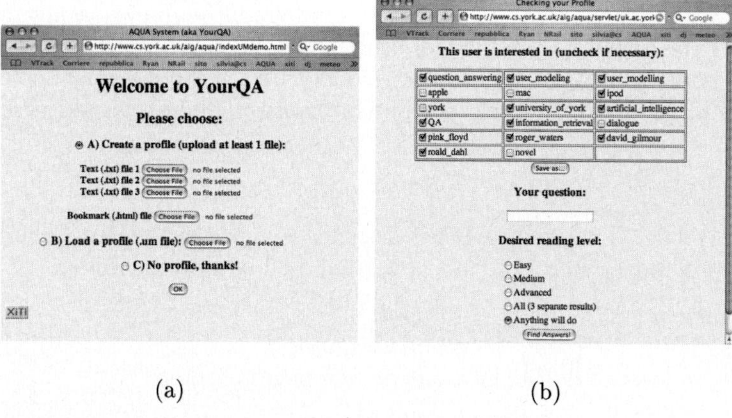

(a)   (b)

(c)

Fig. 1. Profile creation/reload (a), profile modification and save, query submission (b), first answer to the question: "What is *Ginger and Fred?*" (c)

Keyphrase extraction plays an important role in the representation of the user's profile: for this, we use the Naïve Bayes based Kea extractor [9]. Kea takes two attributes to classify a phrase p as a keyphrase or a non-keyphrase: its $TF \times IDF$ score within the set of retrieved documents[1] (in short, T), and the index of p's first appearance in the document. Based on these, Kea outputs for each document a list of phrases, ordered by decreasing relevance, among which the top k (currently $k=6$) are selected as keyphrases.

3.2   Profile Confirmation, Update and Save

In cases A) and B), the keyphrases corresponding to the user's profile are shown to him/her, who can then exclude those he/she finds unsuitable or incorrect (see Figure 1.(b)). The profile resulting from the remaining keyphrases is the base

---

[1] Given a document d in a corpus C, the salience of p to d can be measured as:
$TF \times IDF(p, d) = P(p \in d) \cdot -log P(p \in [C/d])$

for all the subsequent QA activity: any question the user will submit to YourQA will be answered by taking such profile into account.

Providing documents of interest is a way to solve the cold start problem of creating a profile from a previously unseen user [10]. While defining a complete profile can be time consuming for the user, simply asking for web pages of interest or mining his/her bookmarks folder appears to be a fairly unobtrusive and effortless way to collect initial information.

The user can click on the "Save as..." button (see Figure 1.(b)) in order to remember a newly created profile or the current updates (i.e. selected/deselected keyphrases) and reload the profile in the future. Enabling the user to modify and save a profile, in addition to the implicit updates consisting in the user's evolving bookmarks and documents of interest, makes the UM component dynamic.

3.3   From the Query to Answers

Once a profile has been chosen, the QA session can start. The user enters a question and optionally chooses to filter the answers based on one of the reading levels specified in the UM (or each one separately, see Figure 1.(b)). By default, YourQA performs no filtering based on reading levels.

Section 4 illustrates the core question answering phases; the effects of the user's profile on the results are described in Section 5.

4   Core Question Answering Phase

The core question answering phaseis organized as follows in YourQA:

1. The query's expected answer type is estimated using SNoW [11] according to a coarse-grained 11-class taxonomy.
2. The 20 top documents retrieved for the query using Google[2] are obtained;
3. Their reading levels are estimated using unigram language models (see [8]);
4. Keyphrases are extracted from these documents using Kea (see Section 3.1);
5. Documents having an incompatible reading level with the user are discarded;
6. On the remaining documents, different lexical, syntactic and semantic criteria (based on the query's expected answer type) are applied to compute the similarity between each sentence in the document and the query (see [8]);
7. One passage is created for each document, containing the most similar sentence to the query, preceded and followed by up to 2 adjacent sentences (depending on the structure of the original text);
8. Passages are ranked based on the similarity of their top sentence to the query. In case of a tie, passages from documents having a higher Google rank are given priority in the YourQA ranking.

Figure 1.(c) shows the format of a sample answer in YourQA: this consists of a header containing information about the original document (title, URL, . . .),

---

[2] http://www.google.com

followed by a short passage where the most similar sentence to the query is in boldface. Useful terms such as the question keywords are highlighted.

Up to this point, the system's behaviour is completely independent of the profile parameter of the user model. Section 5 explains how the profile is used to determine the final answer ranking.

5 Profile-Based Answer Re-ranking

As illustrated in Step 8 of the algorithm above, in the standard version of YourQA the primary answer ranking criterion is the similarity to the question (Step 6), and the secondary criterion is the Google rank of the document from which the passage has been extracted. The personalized version of YourQA applies an additional answer ranking criterion giving priority to answers from documents having common keyphrases with the user's profile documents, as shown below.

5.1 Document Relevance Computation

For each document composing the UM profile set and the retrieved document set, a ranked list of keyphrases is available from the previous steps. Both keyphrase sets are represented by the user modelling component of YourQA as arrays, where each row corresponds to one document and each column corresponds to the rank within such document of the keyphrase in the corresponding cell.

A basic example profile, created from two documents about Italian cuisine and a the animation picture "Akira", respectively, might result in the array: $P =$`{{pizza, lasagne, tiramisu},{akira, anime, film}}`.

We name P and $Retr$ the arrays of UM profile keyphrases and of retrieved document keyphrases, respectively. We call $Retr_i$ the document represented in the i-th row in $Retr$ and P_n the one represented in the n-th row of P^3.

We define $w(k_{ij}, P_n)$, i.e. the relevance of k_{ij} (the j-th keyphrase extracted from $Retr_i$) with respect to P_n (the n-th document in P), as:

$$w(k_{ij}, P_n) = \begin{cases} \frac{|Retr_i|-j}{|Retr_i|}, & k_{ij} \in P_n \\ 0, & otherwise \end{cases} \qquad (1)$$

The total relevance of $Retr_i$ with respect to P, $w_P(Retr_i)$, is defined as the maximal sum of the relevance of its keyphrases, obtained for all the rows in P^4:

$$w_P(Retr_i) = max_{n \in P} \sum_{k_{ij} \in Retr_i} w(k_{ij}, P_n). \qquad (2)$$

---

[3] While column index reflects a ranking based on the relevance of a keyphrase to its source document, row index only depends on the name of such document.

[4] Keeping the relevance computation separated across the single documents (rows) in the profile prevents errors: we want to avoid a profile about programming and Greek islands to result in a high weight for a document about the Java island.

5.2   Final Answer Ranking

Having computed a relevance score for each document retrieved for the query, the personalized version of YourQA uses the following answer ranking criteria:
1. Similarity of the answer passage to the question;
2. Relevance of the passage's source document with respect to the UM profile;
3. Google rank of the source document.

In Figure 1.(c) for instance, the answer is targeted at a user interested in architecture, hence the high relevance of a result about a building.

Table 1 compares the results of the query: "UM conference" when no profile is used and when a profile containing the keyphrase "user modelling" is active. In the second case, the profile keyphrases disambiguate the query and contribute to a higher ranking of answers related to user modelling (potentially more interesting to the user). Considering that in a QA system the list of answers is rarely supposed to include more than five results, filtering based on the UM can dramatically improve the relatedness of answers to the user profile.

Table 1. Meaning of "UM" in the 10 top answers to: "UM conference"

Rank	Profile OFF	Profile ON	Rank	Profile OFF	Profile ON
1	Uni. Miami	**User Modelling**	6	Uni. Michigan	Utd Methodism
2	Uni. Montana	**User Modelling**	7	Uni. Michigan	Uni. Michigan
3	undetermined	Uni. Miami	8	Uni. Michigan	Uni. Miami
4	Utd Methodism	Uni. Montana	9	**User Modelling**	Uni. Michigan
5	Uni. Miami	undetermined	10	**User Modelling**	Uni. Michigan

6   Discussion and Related Work

Although as explained in Section 1, the intuition behind the above approach is not new [12], this paper describes to our knowledge the first fully implemented and evaluated application of user modelling for QA.

As in standard IR, a key issue in pursuing personalization is that this must not be at the cost of objectivity. We believe that this is the case in our approach for two main reasons: first, due to the limited number of keyphrases extracted from documents, when common keyphrases are found between one document in the UM set and one in the $Retr$ set, it appears worthwhile to point out to the user that such document is very relevant to his/her profile.

Second, the compatibility of a given document with respect to a given user model is always a secondary ranking criterion to the semantic similarity to the query; profile match is only considered in case of a tie between candidate answers.

6.1   User Modelling as a Form of Implicit Relevance Feedback

Our approach to user modelling can be seen as a form of implicit (or quasi-implicit) relevance feedback, i.e. feedback not explicitly obtained from the user but inferred from latent information in the user's documents.

Indeed, we take inspiration from Teevan et al.'s approach for personalized search [7], computing the relevance of unseen documents (such as those retrieved for a query) as a function of the presence and frequency of the same terms in a second set of documents on whose relevance the user has provided feedback.

More specifically, for each of the N documents retrieved for a query, and for each term $t_i \in N$, the number of documents $\in N$ containing t_i, n_i, is computed. The relevance of term t_i with respect to the current user is then: $w(t_i) = log\frac{(r_i+1/2)(N-n_i+1/2)}{(n_i+1/2)(R-r_i+1/2)}$, where R is the number of documents for which relevance feedback has been provided (i.e. documents which have been indexed), and r_i is the number of documents which contain t_i among the R examined.

We interpret R as the set of documents composing the user model profile, while N evidently corresponds to the set of documents retrieved by YourQA during document retrieval. Moreover, instead of handling all the terms contained in the user's documents (which can be costly and introduce noise), we use the information deriving from keyphrase extraction and only analyse the terms contained in the keyphrase arrays P and $Retr$.

Relevance based on profile keyphrases. Teevan's relevance formula accounts for the frequency of a term within the document it is contained in and across the documents in the set, computing the log product between $\rho_i = \frac{(r_i+1/2)}{(R-r_i+1/2)}$ and $\nu_i = \frac{(N-n_i+1/2)}{(n_i+1/2)}$. This product can be seen as a $TF \times IDF$ measure, as ρ_i accounts for term frequency in documents for which relevance feedback has been given, and ν_i accounts for inverse document frequency.

In YourQA, this frequency-related information is already available from keyphrase extraction: Kea classifies a term as a keyphrase for a document if it occurs frequently in such document (high TF) and not too frequently in the other documents under exam (low DF). We can assume that if a term t_i is a keyphrase for some document in P, then $\rho_i \approx \frac{1}{R}$. Similarly, $\nu_i \approx N$ if t_i is a keyphrase for some document in $Retr$. Hence, when $t_i \in P$, $w(t_i) \approx \omega = log\frac{N}{R}$, i.e. we can approach $w(t_i)$ by a constant. This yields: $w(t_i) = \begin{cases} \omega, t_i \in P \\ 0, otherwise \end{cases}$.
The final relevance formula in (1) is a refined version of the former where the relevance is normalized and sensitive to keyphrase rank.

7   Evaluating Personalized Question Answering

In designing an evaluation method for personalized QA, our aim was to assess whether user-adaptive answer filtering would be positive in terms of answer usefulness and, in any case, whether it would be perceived at all.

Since to our knowledge there is no published work on the evaluation of user-adaptive QA, we drew our evaluation guidelines from general work on user-adaptive system evaluation [13] and from the closest domain to QA for which this exists: personalized search [12].

As personalized search is a form of IR, its typical evaluation metrics are precision and recall, where precision is measured in terms of user satisfaction.

An example of such evaluation is the one for UCAIR [14], a search engine plugin which re-orders the list of results with respect to the user's information need model (this is based on his/her browsing actions). Here, the baseline system for evaluation is the underlying search engine, and the application's performance metric is result precision at different recall levels.

In our evaluation, we tested the impact of the YourQA user modelling component by using as a baseline the default version of YourQA where such component is inactive, as exposed in Section 7.1.

7.1   Evaluation Methodology

Our evaluation experiment was taken by twelve adult participants from different backgrounds and occupations. The experiment involved the following two phases.

First phase: profile design. In the first phase, participants were invited to explore the Yahoo! Directory (`http://dir.yahoo.com`) and provide 2-3 categories of their interest. Moreover, they were invited to brainstorm as many keyphrases as they wanted relating to each of their chosen categories.

Keyphrases were used to create offline individual profiles to be loaded into memory in the following phase. For each profile domain, related queries were elaborated in such a way that the system's answers would be different when the UM-based filtering component was active (to ensure that the final answer ranking would be affected by the use of the profile), and entered in one set.

Second phase: QA. Participants were then assigned an instruction sheet with three tasks. Each task started with one of three fixed queries to be typed in YourQA, chosen from the previously compiled query set with specific criteria:

$Q_\mathbf{A}$: related to one of his/her interest domains, answered using his/her profile;
$Q_\mathbf{B}$: related to a different interest domain of the same user, answered using a baseline QA (i.e. YourQA *without* user modelling);
$Q_\mathbf{C}$: related to another user's profile, with no overlap with the current user's profile; answered using the baseline QA system[5].

Q_A tests YourQA's personalization abilities; hence it was chosen for each user so that the final list of answers would be affected by the UM component.

Q_B represents the baseline QA system: its role is to compare YourQA to a state-of-the art system under the same experimental conditions.

Q_C is an additional, "control" baseline query whose role is to check if there is a bias in the user towards questions relevant to his/her profile. Also, since the same queries were used as Q_A and Q_C for different users, we could compare the answers given to each query when the UM profile was active and when not.

For each query, the top five answers were computed in real time by the QA system by switching off reading level filtering to minimize biases.

---

[5] Since by construction there is no common keyphrase between the current profile and the retrieved documents, by (1) *the output is the same as if the profile was used.*

Questionnaire. As soon as each query's results were available, the users had to answer the following four questions on the instruction sheet. First, for each of the five results separately:

TEST1: *This result is useful in answering the question*: Yes / No
TEST2: *This result is related to my profile*: Yes / No

Finally, for the five results taken as a whole:

TEST3: *Finding the information I wanted in the result page took*:
   (1) Too long, (2) Quite long, (3) Not too long, (4) Quite little, (5) Very little
TEST4: *For this query, the system results were sensitive to my profile*:
   Yes / No / Don't know

The questionnaire provides a qualitative assessment of the effects of user modelling, which are tested at user level to eliminate the nuisance introduced by cross-user evaluation [13]. Each question relates to a separate factor:

TEST1 measures the perceived usefulness of each result in answering the corresponding query. This measurement corresponds to the standard user-centered precision metric applied by other personalized IR applications, such as [14]. TEST2 measures the perceived relatedness of the answer content with respect to the profile. TEST3 measures the user's satisfaction with respect to the time taken browsing results, while TEST4 measures the perceived profile sensitivity in answering the query overall (i.e. not with respect to the individual answers).

Interaction logs. Users interacted with YourQA on a workstation equipped with $MORAE^{TM}$ (www.techsmith.com/morae), a commercial, non-intrusive software able to record the user's activity while carrying on a task. Interaction logs were recorded to measure the time taken to find information and to complete and understand user comments and questionnaire answers.

8   Evaluation Results

Answer usefulness (TEST1). Table 2 reports the average and standard deviation of the number of answers judged useful for each query (answers to TEST1). These were compared by carrying out a one-way analysis of variance (ANOVA) and performing the Fischer test using the usefulness as factor (with the three queries as levels) at a 95% level of confidence. This revealed a significant difference in the specific contrast between Q_A and Q_C (linear F= 5.86, degrees of freedom = 1,11, $p = 0.034$), suggesting that users are positively biased towards questions related to their own profile when it comes to perceived utility.

However, we did not find a significant difference overall, hence not between Q_A and Q_B, therefore we cannot prove that there is a significant impact in utility when the UM is active. We believe that this may be due to the fact that our study involved a limited number of users and that their judgments may have been "distracted" by other aspects of the system, such as the response time.

To further investigate perceived utility, we counted *for each query q* the number of answers judged useful by the user to which q had role Q_A (i.e. was addressed by the personalized QA system). We counted the occurrences of the same answers in the list of results to the user for which q had role Q_C (i.e. when results were not affected by personalization). The paired t-test showed a statistically significant difference ($p = 0.006$), so we can say that for the same questions, useful answers are more likely to occur when profile filtering is active.

As a final remark, the number of users finding each single answer to Q_A useful started high for the first result and tended to decrease with the answer rank, as visible in Figure 2.(a). In contrast, the usefulness of answers to Q_B and Q_C exhibited a more random allure. However, when we performed the Friedman test on these values, we did not find a significant difference, probably because the data came from five measurements (i.e. ranks) only. In the future, we will elicit Likert scale answers instead of Yes/No answers for a more fine-grained analysis.

Answer relatedness (TEST2). To analyze the answers to TEST2, which measured the perceived relatedness of each answer to the current profile, we computed the ANOVA table on the data in Table 2, row 2. We used the number of answers judged as related as the independent variable and the three queries as factors. This time, the results showed an overall significant difference (F= 11.9, d.f. = 1,11, $p < 0.001$). These results confirm that answers obtained without using the users' profile were perceived as significantly less related to those obtained using their own profile, i.e. there is a significant difference between Q_A and Q_B. As expected, the difference between Q_A and Q_C (where the question is unrelated to the profile) is even more significant.

Once again, we observed that the perceived relatedness of the results to Q_A tended to be higher for the first ranked answers and to slightly decrease with the answer rank (see Figure 2.(b)). For Q_B, the result relatedness was generally lower and seemed to follow a more irregular pattern; this makes sense as the profile ranking was not active. For Q_C, the result relatedness was much lower and again did not exhibit a descending pattern across the rank as the relatedness for Q_A did. However, from Friedman's ANOVA we can only call Q_A's descending pattern a trend, as $0.05 < p = .098 < 0.1$ (F=8.2, d.f.=4).

Time spent looking for answers (TEST3). In formulating TEST3, we assumed that profile-based QA would help users find interesting information more quickly. However, the time question proved problematic: we noticed from user comments and MORAE logs that such time was often mistaken with the perceived duration of the document retrieval phase. Another factor making time difficult to interpret is the fact that the system was previously unknown, hence examining the results to the first query took longer than the following ones.

Furthermore, several users mistook the time spent looking for information with the time spent actively browsing the result page and clicking on the result links to read interesting information; to these users, a longer browsing time probably meant better fitness of the answers to the profile. Hence, we decided to discard time as a source of information in the current study and plan to re-formulate the TEST3 in the future.

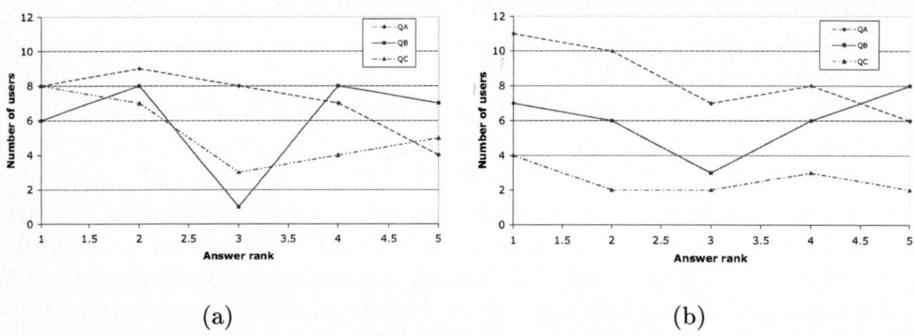

(a)   (b)

Fig. 2. Answer usefulness (a) and relatedness to profile (b): number of users vs rank

Table 2. Perceived answer usefulness and relatedness to the user profile

Measurement	Q_A	Q_B	Q_C
Perceived usefulness	0.6±1.42	0.5±1.57	0.45±0.29
Perceived relatedness	0.7±1.38	0.5±1.98	0.22±1.88

Profile sensitivity (TEST4). One surprising result from the questionnaire was that although for each user Q_C was selected to be as unrelated as possible to his/her categories, the latter did not always realize that their profile had no role in answering such query (perhaps the wording "the system's answers were sensitive to my profile" was ambiguous).

In any case, the perceived relatedness to the user's profile of the answers as a whole, i.e. the profile sensitivity of the system in answering the query altogether, was sensibly higher for Q_A (0.92±0.27) than for Q_B (0.5±0.52) and Q_C (0.28±0.47). We computed the ANOVA table using as a variable the number of users agreeing that the system had been sensitive to their profile in answering the current query and the three queries as factors. This gave a significant difference between each query (F= 22, d.f.=1,11, $p < 0.001$), confirming that users perceived the sensitivity of the system to their own profile when the UM component was active.

9   Conclusions and Further Work

We present an efficient and light-weight method to personalize the results of a web-based question answering system based on a user model. We show how individual users' interests can be extracted automatically from their documents and how they can be used to filter and re-rank the answers to their queries.

We introduce a user-centered evaluation methodology for personalized QA and report the results of an actual evaluation, where we found a statistically significant improvement when filtering answers based on the users' profile in terms of both perceived answer usefulness and profile relatedness.

Our future work will further integrate the user modelling component and the core QA component of YourQA to allow dynamic updates of the UM based on previous information-seeking history.

Acknowledgements. We are indebted to Prof. Helen Petrie for her advice on user model evaluation, as well as for contributing resources to our user experiments.

References

1. Belkin, N.J., Croft, W.: Information filtering and information retrieval: Two sides of the same coin? Communications of the ACM 35, 29–38 (1992)
2. Kobsa, A.: Generic user modeling systems. User Modeling and User-Adapted Interaction 11, 49–63 (2001)
3. Voorhees, E.M.: Overview of the TREC 2003 Question Answering Track. In: Proceedings of TREC (2003)
4. Kwok, C.T., Etzioni, O., Weld, D.S.: Scaling question answering to the web. In: Proceedings of WWW (2001)
5. Ardissono, L., Console, L., Torre, I.: An adaptive system for the personalized access to news. AI Commun. 14, 129–147 (2001)
6. Magnini, B., Strapparava, C.: Improving user modelling with content-based techniques. In: Bauer, M., Gmytrasiewicz, P.J., Vassileva, J. (eds.) UM 2001. LNCS (LNAI), vol. 2109, Springer, Heidelberg (2001)
7. Teevan, J., Dumais, S.T., Horvitz, E.: Personalizing search via automated analysis of interests and activities. In: Proceedings of SIGIR '05, pp. 449–456. ACM Press, New York, NY, USA (2005)
8. Quarteroni, S., Manandhar, S.: Incorporating user models in question answering to improve readability. In: Proceedings of KRAQ'06 (2006)
9. Witten, I.H., Paynter, G.W., Frank, E., Gutwin, C., Nevill-Manning, C.G.: KEA: Practical automatic keyphrase extraction. In: ACM DL, pp. 254–255. ACM Press, New York (1999)
10. Lashkari, Y., Metral, M., Maes, P.: Collaborative interface agents. In: Proceedings of AAAI'94 (1994)
11. Li, X., Roth, D.: Learning question classifiers. In: Proceedings of ACL'02 (2002)
12. Brusilovsky, P., Tasso, C.: User modeling for web information retrieval. Special issue of User Modeling and User-Adapted Interaction 14 (2004)
13. Chin, D.N.: Empirical evaluation of user models and user-adapted systems. User Modeling and User-Adapted Interaction 11, 181–194 (2001)
14. Shen, X., Tan, B., Zhai, C.: Implicit user modeling for personalized search. In: Proceedings of CIKM '05, pp. 824–831. ACM Press, New York, NY, USA (2005)

A Comparison of Genetic Algorithms for Optimizing Linguistically Informed IR in Question Answering

Jörg Tiedemann

University of Groningen, Alfa Informatica,
P.O. Box 716, 9700 AS Groningen, The Netherlands
j.tiedemann@rug.nl

Abstract. In this paper we compare four selection strategies in evolutionary optimization of information retrieval (IR) in a question answering setting. The IR index has been augmented by linguistic features to improve the retrieval performance of potential answer passages using queries generated from natural language questions. We use a genetic algorithm to optimize the selection of features and their weights when querying the IR database. With our experiments, we can show that the genetic algorithm applied is robust to strategy changes used for selecting individuals. All experiments yield query settings with improved retrieval performance when applied to unseen data. However, we can observe significant runtime differences when applying the various selection approaches which should be considered when choosing one of these approaches.

1   Introduction

Information retrieval (IR) techniques are used in question answering (QA) to select relevant passages from large document collections that may contain answers to a given natural language question. Spotting answers in large collections is expensive and the purpose of IR is to reduce the search space for the answer selection modules. There are two main strategies: (1) a two-step strategy with a retrieval of documents first and a passage selection thereafter (see for instance [1], and, (2) a one-step strategy of directly retrieving passages instead of documents (see [2] for a comparison of different approaches). Our approach implements the second strategy and we will refer to it as *passage retrieval* in remaining parts of the paper.

Passage retrieval in QA is different to common IR in at least two points: First of all, the segmentation size of the document collection is different (passages instead of documents). However, we assume that standard IR techniques work well also on units smaller than documents which is also supported by our experiments. A passage in our case is a well-defined paragraph marked as such in the document collection. Secondly, passage retrieval relies on queries *generated* from a natural language question instead of a user-defined keyword query as it is in

R. Basili and M.T. Pazienza (Eds.): AI*IA 2007, LNAI 4733, pp. 398–409, 2007.

ordinary IR. Today's users of IR engines (such as Google) are trained to tune their keyword queries to get close to the desired result whereas a QA system does not get more information than a well-formed natural language question. The consequence of this is that the passage retrieval module in a QA system has to maximize the use of all linguistic clues in the given question not only the lexical ones. In our approach we apply robust syntactic parsing to obtain additional linguistic features to facilitate the retrieval component in matching questions with relevant paragraphs. More details will be discussed in section 2.

Important for the success of passage retrieval extended with linguistic features is a careful selection and combination of clues that help to improve retrieval performance [3]. A brute-force selection of all features would make a query too specific in many cases. Hence, retrieval performance may even go below the baseline. However, selecting and weighting appropriate features is far from straightforward considering the enormous feature space defined in our module (see section 2). Hence, an automatic optimization process is needed to fit query parameters in such a way that they produce an optimal retrieval performance. For this, we apply a genetic algorithm (GA) that runs the passage retrieval for a given training set of questions (and their answers) with various settings. The success (fitness) is measured in terms of mean reciprocal ranks which is taken to be the objective function to be optimized. Genetic algorithms can be seen as an umbrella term for several stochastic optimization procedures. A lot of variants have been proposed with various parameters to be specified. One of the important operations in GAs is the *selection of individuals* to be considered in producing the next generation. In this paper we focus on the comparison of four different selection strategies applied to our task. Section 3 provides details about the implementation of our GA. Section 4 describes our experiments and, finally, section 5 includes discussion and conclusions.

2   Linguistically Informed IR for QA

Our work is focused on Dutch open-domain question answering. There are two strategies implemented in our QA system [4], one using previously extracted fact databases and a look-up strategy and the other using passage retrieval and "on-line" answer extraction from unrestricted text. We are only interested in the latter where passage retrieval is crucial. All our experiments are carried with data from the QA tasks at the Cross-Language Evaluation Forum (CLEF).

In our QA system we make heavy use of deep syntactic analysis in all modules of the system. The entire Dutch document collection used in CLEF (about 80 million words) has been parsed off-line using the wide-coverage dependency parser Alpino [5]. This enables us to use various linguistic features provided by the parser when building the IR index. Alpino produces not only syntactic dependency relations but also adds part-of-speech tags, named entity labels and lexical roots. It also detects certain multi-word units and splits compounds. From this we extract various features and feature combinations to be included in the IR index. Each feature type is stored in a separate index field using Lucene as our IR engine [6]. In the current settings we define the following 14 feature types: text (plain text tokens as used in standard IR including a Dutch stemmer and stop word filtering), root (lexical root forms), RootPos (root forms together with their part-of-speech labels), RootHead (root form bigrams of syntactic head-dependent pairs), RootRelHead (the same as RootHead but together with the name of the relation between head and dependent), RootRel (the root form of a word and the relation type to its head), compound (compounds in concatenated and split form), mwu (multi-word units), ne (words labeled as any named entity), nePER (words labeled as person name), neLOC (location names), neORG (organization names) and neTypes (named entity labels occurring in the paragraph). All paragraphs from the CLEF corpus are indexed along these dimensions.

Querying such an extended IR index can now be done in various ways. Each index field can be queried independently but also combined in a boolean or disjunctive way. Naturally, each question has to be analyzed first in the same way as the corpus in order to obtain the same features to be matched with the index. Using an analyzed questions we can define further constraints to make a fine-grained selection of keywords to generate a query that will be passed on to the IR engine. For example, we may restrict RootHead keywords taken from a question to such words only that have been labeled as nouns. Such restrictions give us a wide variety of query parameters in terms of feature type selection and feature constraints. Furthermore, each keyword in a query can be weighted individually using Lucene's query language. In this way, they can be balanced according to their importance. They can also be marked as required. In our module we define one weight per feature type and feature constraint. Furthermore, the Lucene query language includes proximity restrictions as well. Queries can be constructed where certain keywords have to appear in a given window of items in matching documents. Here, the window size can be variated. In our module we include one window size parameter per constrained feature type for which proximity queries are feasible[1]. In order to reduce the number of parameters we define a small sub-set of constraints to be used in keyword selection. Finally, we also define another parameter with regards to the question type. The QA system analyses the question before running IR and, hence, we know its question type which can be mapped to an expected answer type. In many cases, this corresponds to a named entity of a certain type. In such cases we can include a named entity label corresponding to the question type as additional keyword querying the *neTypes* field. Obviously, this keyword can also be weighted in the same way as other keywords. The following list summarizes the query parameters in our system:

feature type: one of 14 fields in the IR index + question type keywords
selection constraint: keyword selection constraints: part-of-speech (name, noun, verb, adjective); relation type (direct object, modifier, apposition,

---

[1] Feature type fields such as compounds, MWUs and named entities contain only selected tokens from each paragraph without position information. Therefore it makes no sense to query these fields with token window restrictions.

subject); all combinations of constraints and feature types are considered discarding only those that do not produce any keyword in the entire training set of questions

keyword weights: one weight per feature type + keyword constraint (for instance the weight for *root* keywords restricted to nouns in a question is a different parameter to *root* keywords restricted to words in an object relation)

window sizes: one size per feature type + keyword constraint (in the same way as for keyword weights)

Queries are constructed by disjunction of sub-queries corresponding to one of the index fields. Proximity queries are separate sub-queries. Some query parameters will refer to the same keywords corresponding to the same index field. We apply simple preference rules in these cases in order to create sub-queries with such overlaps. We define that more specific parameters overwrite less specific ones. More specific parameters refer to the ones with stronger constraints. Here, we define that relation type constraints are stronger than part-of-speech constraints.

3   A Genetic Algorithm for Query Optimization

As described in the previous section, there is a large variety of possible queries that can be constructed from a given question using the features provided by the parser. There are 292 open parameters (weights and window sizes) to be considered using our limited set of part-of-speech and relation type constraints and after filtering out keyword constraints which are not instantiated in the training data. Thus, the search space is huge and interactions between the various parameters are unknown. A brute-force search is not feasible and individual optimization of the various parameters cannot be successful because of the dependencies between them. Genetic algorithms on the other hand provide efficient stochastic search strategies for optimizing a target in large spaces with unknown landscapes. They have been applied before in information retrieval for ranking optimization and relevance feedback among others [7,8,9,10,11,12,13,14,15]. In GAs, the optimization criterion can be rather indirect in form of a fitness function defined over individuals in a population representing settings in the application under consideration.

In our implementation we use the following general setup:

Representation of individuals: Parameters settings are directly encoded in individuals without mapping them into binary genetic sequences. Each query parameter can be seen as a gene. Not all parameters have to be present (which corresponds to a weight of 0)

Fitness: We use mean reciprocal ranks of paragraphs returned by the IR engine for questions in a given training corpus. We retrieve 20 paragraphs per question and use simple string matching to check if an accepted answer is included in a paragraph.

Population size: 100 individuals

Initialization: The initial population consists of 100 unique individuals created from scratch by mutation operations.

Mutation: Several mutation operations with fixed probabilities have been defined: adding a parameter to the current settings (probability of 0.2), remove a parameter (probability 0.1), change the weight/window size of one randomly selected parameter (probability 0.2) and set the required marker (probability of 0.01).

Crossover: Select 20% of the current population to survive. The remaining part will be replaced by new offspring created using crossover. Individuals are selected from the current population to be parents of new offspring to fill the next generation. Crossover in our setup works as follows: One offspring is created by merging parameter settings of two parents. Here, we compute the arithmetic mean of weights and window sizes. Required markers overwrite weights. Mutation operations are applied to each new offspring with the probabilities specified above.

Termination: The genetic algorithm is stopped after 5 generations without any improvements observed.

The settings above are fixed. There is still one important operation missing in defining the genetic algorithm: The selection strategy. Several strategies have been proposed and the following are implemented in our module:

Roulette: Probabilistically select individuals according to their fitness. The likelihood to be selected is defined as follows:

$$P(I_i) = \frac{fitness(I_i)}{\sum_{j=1}^{p} fitness(I_j)}$$

Unique Roulette: Same as roulette selection but with the additional constraint that selected individuals have to be unique (do not select one individual twice).

Tournament: Uniformly select 2 individuals from the current population and select the one with the higher fitness.

Top-N/uniform: (deterministically) select N individuals from the current population with the highest fitness scores. From this selection uniformly select parents to create new offspring.

In the first three strategies pairs of parents are taken in the same order they are selected. The crucial difference in the last strategy is that individuals below a certain threshold are never selected whereas in the other strategies all individuals have a chance to produce new offspring. Another difference of the top-N selection strategy is that it is not necessary to wait for an entire new generation to perform the selection because it is probabilistic among all living individuals. Hence, new offspring can be produced at any time by randomly selecting parents from the top N individuals. Our implementation makes use of this feature by adding a new offspring at each time a fitness score for another individual in the current population is computed. In other words, we always fill empty slots as soon as an IR run is finished. This also implies a slight change in the termination criterion. The optimization process stops now after a sequence of 500 individuals (corresponding 5 generations) for which no improvement has been found with regards to the currently highest fitness score.

The impact of the four selection strategy on the optimization procedure is described in the next section using experiments with the CLEF data.

4   Experiments

4.1   Comparing Selection Strategies

In our experiments we used data from the Dutch question answering track at CLEF from the previous years. The CLEF corpus has been indexed using the techniques described earlier. For training (measuring fitness in the genetic algorithm) we used 577 questions from the QA tasks in 2003 and 2005 and for evaluation we used 200 questions from 2004. All the data is annotated with the correct answer strings which we use to judge retrieved paragraphs.

One of the advantages of genetic algorithms is that they can easily be parallelized, i.e. new offspring can "develop" in parallel to build up a new generation. Taking advantage of this feature we made use of the HPC cluster with its 200 nodes provided by the High Performance Computing Center of the University of Groningen. The jobs running IR with various settings are distributed among the nodes and a server process collects the results in terms of fitness scores and creates new generations.

In order to illustrate the differences in using various selection strategies we collected the intermediate results after each 10 individuals tested. We ran the optimization process four times for each selection strategy in order to compare their runtime behavior and their impact on the final result. Figure 1 shows the plots of the top fitness scores[2] on *training data* for the four strategies implemented.

The evolutionary algorithm optimizes the IR settings in all cases with fitness scores significantly above the baseline scores (standard plain text IR, see table 1). Due to the randomized search each run is unique and produces a different output after termination. However, the development of the fitness scores is rather similar for all experiments. Top-N optimizations seem to be a bit smoother than the other approaches due to a larger number of improvement steps. It also reaches the highest overall score (0.628) and produces the "fittest" individual on average (see table 1). Despite their strict selection strategy top-N optimization processes run on average longer than the others exploring the search space well. An exception is one experiment which terminates extremely early indicating the strong impact of the initial population on this approach. The other experiments using

---

[2] The overall highest scores are used disregarding whether the corresponding individual is still part of the current population or not. However, in top-N it is always part of the population by definition.

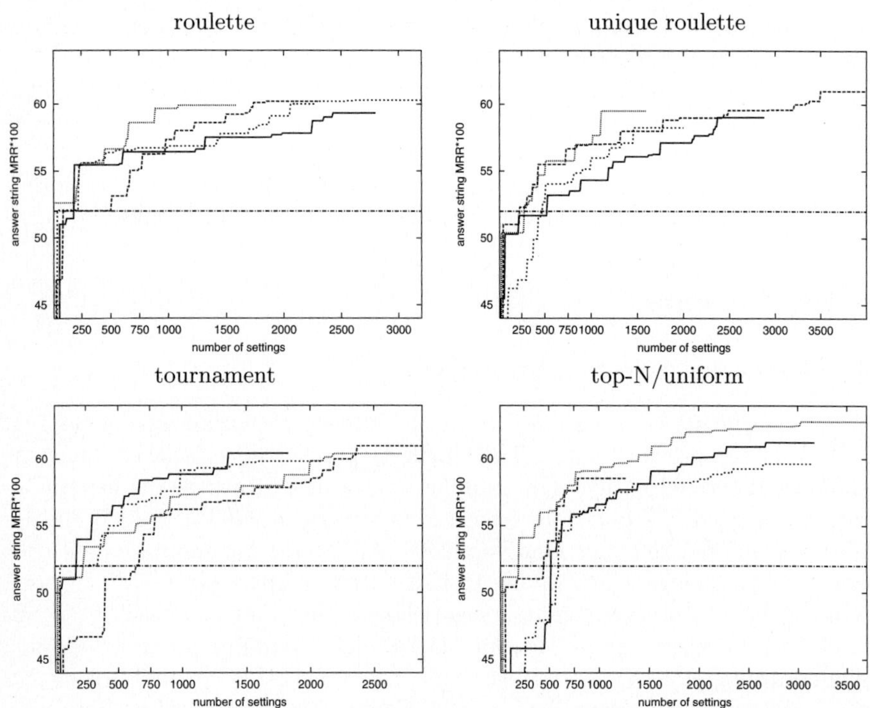

Fig. 1. Training with different selection strategies

probabilistic selection strategies on the other hand seem to develop a bit slower than the top-N approach which often causes an early termination.

Let us now look at the corresponding fitness scores measured on unseen *evaluation data*. In figure 2 top fitness scores are plotted in the same way as above using the optimized settings found on training data but applied to our test set.

Obviously, the picture on evaluation data is much more blurred. The fitness scores do not improve monotonically but nevertheless the main tendency is an iterative increase even on unseen data. All experiments using the four different selection strategies produce improved settings for the passage retrieval component in our question answering task with MRR scores above the baseline in all runs.

There are several differences between the individual experiments that can be observed. First of all, the development of the fitness scores in the top-N selection strategy is much more consistent than for the other approaches and improves in a rather similar way in all four experiments we ran. This is due to the strict selection method dismissing all individuals below a certain threshold. In the top-N strategy only the best individuals are used and new offspring are based on their settings which makes the optimization process more deterministic. The other probabilistic selection strategies give individuals with lower fitness scores a chance to survive. This results in a larger variation and, usually, a slower optimization process. To illustrate these differences, the fitness scores of

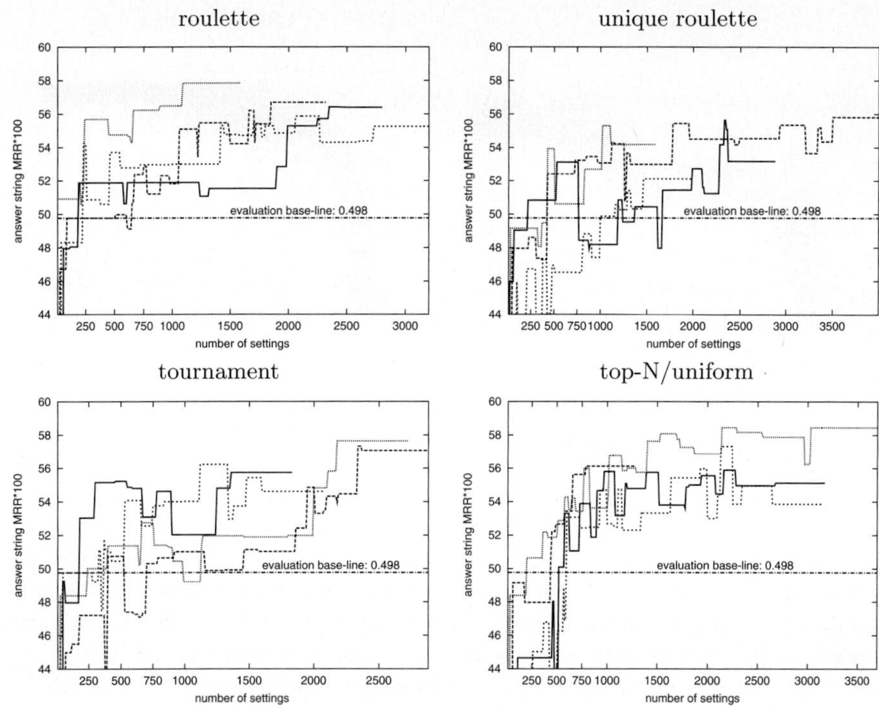

Fig. 2. Different selection strategies on evaluation data

all individuals tested during two experiments are plotted in figure 3, one using the roulette selection strategy and the other one using top-N/uniform selection.

As we can see in figure 3, the development of the population is less monotonic when applying the roulette selection strategy than for the top-N strategy because of the larger influence of individuals with lower fitness on the creation of new generations.

Despite the fact that the selection of individuals in top-N is very strict its parent selection is very liberal. All "living" individuals have the same chance to be selected which reduces the effect of *crowding*, in which certain individuals dominate a population because of their superior fitness. Crowding often has a negative effect on a genetic algorithm causing the process to get stuck in a local maximum early. The liberal parent selection might be the reason why this effect does not seem to appear as much in the top-N selection approach as it would be expected considering the deterministic selection of individuals. In fact, top-N optimization processes run on average longer than the other experiments we carried out. Furthermore, the overall best setting according to MRR scores on evaluation data is again found by the top-N approach (0.585). It can also be noticed that the probabilistic selection approaches seem to struggle more with overfitting problems compared to the top-N approach. Especially in the tournament and in the unique roulette approach we can observe dramatical

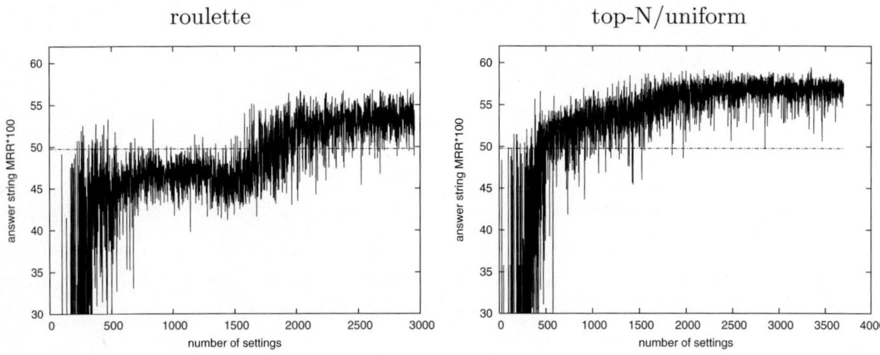

Fig. 3. Individual fitness scores on evaluation data

drops in fitness during the optimization process when measured on evaluation data. The selectional restrictions in top-N seem to prevent this to a large extent.

It also has to be noted that all experiments yield different settings and do not clearly converge to a global optimum. In fact, final settings might differ very much from each other even though their scores are rather similar. This is partly due to the nature of our IR parameters which often have very little impact on the overall retrieval performance. Many of them overlap with each other and have little influence on the construction of the actual queries. Hence, various parameters can be selected without changing the retrieval performance significantly.

4.2   Further Experiments

Family Check. As we discussed in the previous section, crowding can be a serious problem in genetic algorithms. Certain individuals may dominate the population so much that new generations are not diverse enough to enable further development. The tournament selection provides a solution by uniformly selecting pairs among all individuals and keeping the winner of each pair. However, in our experiments no improvement could be observed. On the contrary, experiments using this approach terminated on average even earlier than the other experiments which came as a surprise.

Another possibility to avoid crowding is to integrate another restriction to the selection of parents which we call a *family check*: Crossover is only allowed for parents who are not "related", i.e. they do not share any parents and they are not children nor grand children of each other. In that way, we expect to produce a larger variety of settings within each population when performing crossover with probabilistically selected parents. In contrast to this, we do not expect an improvement in the top-N strategy using the additional family constraint. On the contrary, it might even decrease the variety within a population because we restrict the uniform parent selection which should produce the largest variation possible. In order to validate our expectations we applied the family check to two selection strategies: the unique roulette and the top-N/uniform selection.

Due to time constraints we could only run one experiment for each setting. The final results are shown in table 1. Unfortunately, it is not possible to draw general conclusions from a single experiment. However, there seems to be only little effect of the family check on the unique roulette approach. The final scores are comparable to the ones without it. However, we could observe less problems with overfitting in this particular run. Surprisingly, the impact of the family check on the top-N approach seems to be stronger. Our experiment runs significantly longer than the average of the other runs without the additional constraints. It also jumps to a high fitness already at the beginning (above 0.59 on training data after only 630 individuals) probably due to a "lucky guess".

Changing Environment. Another (general) problem in optimization is the effect of overfitting: improvements on training data may lead to decreasing performance on evaluation data as we could see in our previous experiments. One way to address this problem is to stop early before overfitting starts to happen. The main difficulty is to determine the right moment. Validation data could be used for that purpose. Another strategy that can be used in genetic algorithms is to slightly change the *environment* in order to prefer individuals with a flexible nature (assuming that this corresponds to a stronger generalization). We did an experiment with random environment changes in terms of a variable fitness function: For each individual 80% of the training data is randomly selected to determine fitness. This means that individuals with identical settings may score differently depending on the current training data selected. Table 1 lists the final scores of our experiments again using unique roulette and top-N as the basic selection strategies. Unfortunately, the results are very disappointing. We expected to see less overfitting and, hence, better scores on evaluation data for the final settings when applying variable environments. However, the scores are actually decreased in both experiment. Fitness measured on training data is comparable to our experiments with fixed fitness scores but on evaluation data it is much below their scores. This actually suggests that the new approach overfits even more which is indeed very unexpected. Further experiments have to be carried out to verify these observations.

Combination and Summary. Finally, we also combined family check and variable environments to see their overall effect. The outcome is given in table 1. Again, the results are disappointing which was to be expected considering the experiments described above. No improvement can be seen, neither in terms of overfitting nor retrieval performance.

To sum up, table 1 lists all results obtained in our experiments. All of them yield results that are above the two baselines. Baseline 1 refers to the best-performing single index field (which also corresponds to standard IR) and baseline 2 refers to queries that use all index fields with identical weights. The results compared to the second baseline show that careful selection and weighting is important to improve passage retrieval results. Simply taking all keyword types and weighting them uniformly does not yield any considerable improvement as we can see in the scores on evaluation data.

Table 1. Summary of all experiments (MRR scores * 100)

	training	evaluation	#individuals
baseline 1 (text)	52.02	49.77	n.a.
baseline 2 (all)	55.64	49.80	n.a.
roulette	$59.94_{\pm 0.37}$	$56.55_{\pm 0.92}$	$2478_{\pm 600}$
unique roulette	$59.45_{\pm 0.99}$	$54.18_{\pm 1.36}$	$2618_{\pm 924}$
tournament	$60.38_{\pm 0.41}$	$56.26_{\pm 1.17}$	$2215_{\pm 397}$
top N/uniform	$60.55_{\pm 1.60}$	$55.89_{\pm 1.68}$	$2825_{\pm 918}$
unique roulette			
+ family check	59.16	55.17	3040
+ variable fitness	58.56	50.72	2480
+ family check, variable fitness	61.01	52.63	2640
top N/uniform			
+ family check	60.22	54.43	4240
+ variable fitness	61.66	53.58	4070
+ family check, variable fitness	60.93	54.81	3040

5   Discussion and Conclusions

In this paper we compared four selection strategies for a genetic algorithm applied to the optimization of passage retrieval in question answering. All approaches yield performance improvements compared to a baseline of standard plain text retrieval. We could also show that the appropriate weighting and selection of keywords is important to improve retrieval with linguistic features. Simply using all features does not immediately produce any improvements in passage retrieval.

According to our experiments changing the selection strategy does not result in significantly different results in terms of retrieval performance of the final settings. However, we could observe several interesting runtime differences between the four approaches tested. Selection strategies based on probabilistic selection tend to converge early whereas a deterministic top-N selection with uniform parent selection runs longer on average resulting in an increased fitness score. We also investigated the impact of family checking and environment changes (in terms of variable fitness scores) on the optimization procedure in order to reduce the effect of crowding and overfitting. However, we could not see any improvements using these techniques. This has to be investigated further in future work.

References

1. Tellex, S., Katz, B., Lin, J., Fernandes, A., Marton, G.: Quantitative evaluation of passage retrieval algorithms for question answering. In: Proceedings of the SIGIR conference on Research and development in information retrieval, pp. 41–47. ACM Press, New York (2003)
2. Roberts, I., Gaizauskas, R.: Evaluating passage retrieval approaches for question answering. In: Proceedings of 26th European Conference on Information Retrieval (2004)

3. Katz, B., Lin, J.: Selectively using relations to improve precision in question answering. In: Proceedings of the EACL-2003 Workshop on Natural Language Processing for Question Answering (2003)
4. Bouma, G., Mur, J., van Noord, G., van der Plas, L., Tiedemann, J.: Linguistic knowledge and question answering (Special Issue on Question Answering Systems). Traitement Automatique des Langues 46(3), 15–39 (2005)
5. Bouma, G., Van Noord, G., Malouf, R.: Alpino: Wide coverage computational analysis of Dutch. In: Computational Linguistics in the Netherlands CLIN, 2000, Rodopi (2001)
6. Apache: Lucene - a high-performance, full-featured text search engine library (2004), http://lucene.apache.org/java/docs/index.html
7. Chen, H.: Machine learning for information retrieval: Neural networks, symbolic learning, and genetic algorithms. Journal of the American Society for Information Science 46(3), 194–216 (1995)
8. Fan, W., Gordon, M.D., Pathak, P.: A generic ranking function discovery framework by genetic programming for information retrieval. Inf. Process. Manage. 40(4), 587–602 (2004)
9. Horng, J.-T., Yeh, C.-C.: Applying genetic algorithms to query optimization in document retrieval. Information Processing and Management 36(5), 737–759 (2000)
10. Boughanem, M., Chrisment, C., Tamine, L.: On using genetic algorithms for multimodal relevance optimization in information retrieval. Journal of the American Society for Information Science and Technology 53(11), 934–942 (2002)
11. Billhardt, H., Borrajo, D., Maojo, V.: Learning retrieval expert combinations with genetic algorithms. International Journal of Uncertainty, Fuzziness and Knowledge-Based Systems 11(1), 87–113 (2003)
12. Trotman, A.: Choosing document structure weights. Information Processing and Management 41(2), 243–264 (2005)
13. López-Pujalte, C., Bote, V.P.G., de Moya Anegón, F.: A test of genetic algorithms in relevance feedback. Inf. Process. Manage. 38(6), 793–805 (2002)
14. Cordón, O., Moya, F., Zarco, C.: A new evolutionary algorithm combining simulated annealing and genetic programming for relevante in fuzzy information retrieval systems. Soft Computing 6, 308–319 (2002)
15. López-Pujalte, C., Guerrero-Bote, V.P., de Moya-Anegón, F.: Genetic algorithms in relevance feedback: a second test and new contributions. Inf. Process. Manage. 39(5), 669–687 (2003)

A Variant of N-Gram Based Language Classification

Andrija Tomović[1] and Predrag Janičić[2]

[1] Friedrich Miescher Institute for Biomedical Research
Part of the Novartis Research Foundation
Maulbeerstrasse 66, CH-4058 Basel, Switzerland
andrija.tomovic@fmi.ch
[2] Faculty of Mathematics, University of Belgrade,
Studentski trg 16,11000 Belgrade, Serbia
janicic@matf.bg.ac.yu

Abstract. Rapid classification of documents is of high-importance in many multilingual settings (such as international institutions or Internet search engines). This has been, for years, a well-known problem, addressed by different techniques, with excellent results. We address this problem by a simple n-grams based technique, a variation of techniques of this family. Our n-grams-based classification is very robust and successful, even for 20-fold classification, and even for short text strings. We give a detailed study for different lengths of strings and size of n-grams and we explore what classification parameters give the best performance. There is no requirement for vocabularies, but only for a few training documents. As a main corpus, we used a EU set of documents in 20 languages. Experimental comparison shows that our approach gives better results than four other popular approaches.

1 Introduction

The problems of similarities and dissimilarities between different languages and classification of multi-language documents have many everyday applications. One of them is automated classification of web pages, required, for instance, for restricting search only to documents written in a given language. Multilingual institutions, like EU, handle documents in more than twenty languages and rapid processing of such data is absolutely vital[1]. Automated classification of multi-language text has been studied for years and a variety of techniques give very good results.

In this paper we present a new variant of classification of multi-language documents based on n-grams. N-grams have been successfully used for a long time in a wide variety of problems and domains, including text compression, spelling

---

[1] There are 3400 people employed on translation and publications tasks in the European Commission. The annual budget for translations (between 23 languages) tasks is one billion Euros.

R. Basili and M.T. Pazienza (Eds.): AI*IA 2007, LNAI 4733, pp. 410–421, 2007.

error detection and correction, information retrieval, automatic text categorization, authorship attribution, finding topical similarity between documents, but also in domains not related to language processing such as music representation, computational immunology, analysis of whole-genome protein sequences, protein classification and phylogenetic tree reconstruction (for more details and references see [14]).There are n-gram based techniques for distinguishing between documents written in different languages related to the work presented in this paper [3, 11]. Experimental comparison shows that our variation of n-grams-based classification is better than four other successful approaches to the language classification.

Overview of the paper. In Section 2 we give some basic definition and preliminary information. In Section 3 we describe our methodology for classification of multi-language documents, and the data we used for our analyses. In Section 4 we present and discuss our experimental results. In Section 5 we briefly discuss related work, and in Section 6 we present experimental comparison between our system and four other language classification tools. In Section 7 we draw final conclusions.

2   Preliminaries

In this section we give a brief overview of the notion of n-grams, of classification, and some algorithms for addressing this problem.

N-grams
Given a sequence of tokens $S = (s_1, s_2, ..., s_{N+(n-1)})$ over the token alphabet $\mathcal{A}$, where N and n are positive integers, an *n-gram* of the sequence S is any n-long subsequence of consecutive tokens. The ith n-gram of S is the sequence $(s_i, s_{i+1}, ..., s_{i+n-1})$ [13]. Note that there are N such n-grams in S. There are $|\mathcal{A}|^n$ different n-grams over the alphabet $\mathcal{A}$ (where $|\mathcal{A}|$ is the size of $\mathcal{A}$).

For example, if $\mathcal{A}$ is the English alphabet, and l a string over the alphabet $\mathcal{A}$, $l = $ `life_is_a_miracle`, then 1-grams are: `l`, `i`, `f`, `e`, `_`, `i`, `s`, `a`, `m`, `r`, `c`; 2-grams are: `li`, `if`, `fe`, `e_`, `_i`, `is`, `s_`, `_a`, ...; 3-grams are: `lif`, `ife`, `fe_`, `e_i`, ... ; 4-grams are: `life`, `ife_`, `fe_i`, ... and so on.

When used in processing natural-language documents, n-grams show some of its good features:

- robustness: relatively insensitive to spelling variations/errors;
- completeness: token alphabet known in advance;
- domain independence: language and topic independent;
- efficiency: one pass processing;
- simplicity: no linguistic knowledge is required.

The problem with using n-grams is exponential combinatorial explosion. If A is the Latin alphabet with the space delimiter, then $|A| = 27$. If one distinguishes between upper and lower case letters, and also uses numerical digits, then $|A| = 63$. It is clear that many of algorithms with n-grams are computationally too expensive even for $n = 5$ or $n = 6$ (for instance, $63^5 \approx 10^9$).

Dissimilarity measures

Dissimilarity measure d is a function on two sets of texts $\mathcal{P}_1$ and $\mathcal{P}_2$ (defining specific *profiles*) and it should reflect the dissimilarity between these two. In the following text, by *(dis)similarity of texts* we denote a measure of (dis)similarity of two n-gram distributions.

In [2], some pioneer methods for the authorship attribution problem[2] and dissimilarity measures were discussed. For a range of language processing problems there were proposed techniques based on n-grams. For the authorship attribution problem, the bigram letter statistic was used: two texts are compared for the same authorship, using the dissimilarity formula:

$$d(M, N) = \sum_{I,J} [M(I,J) - E(I,J)] \cdot [N(I,J) - E(I,J)] \tag{1}$$

where I and J are indices over the range $\{1, 2, \ldots, 26\}$, i.e., all letters of the English alphabet; M and N are two texts written in the English alphabet; $M(I,J)$ and $N(I,J)$ are normalized character bigram frequencies for these texts and $E(I,J)$ is the same normalized frequency for "standard English". The technique is based on the following idea: the smaller $d(M, N)$, the more likely is that the author of the text N is the same as the author of the text M. As the bigram frequencies of "standard English" are obviously language-dependent parameters, another dissimilarity measure is given:

$$d(M, N) = \sum_{I,J} [M(I,J) - N(I,J)]^2 \ . \tag{2}$$

Following the ideas from [2, 8], a wide range of new dissimilarity functions were introduced and tested in [14]. The following functions performed best on different sets of problems:

$$d'(\mathcal{P}_1, \mathcal{P}_2) = \sum_{n \in profile} \frac{|f_1(n) - f_2(n)|}{\sqrt{f_1(n) \cdot f_2(n)} + 1} \tag{3}$$

$$d''(\mathcal{P}_1, \mathcal{P}_2) = \sqrt{\sum_{n \in profile} (f_1(n) - f_2(n))^2} \tag{4}$$

where *profile* is a set of all n-grams appearing in $\mathcal{P}_1$ or $\mathcal{P}_2$ and $f_i(n)$ is a normalized frequency for n-gram n in the set $\mathcal{P}_i$. While the function d'' is widely used, as far as we know, the dissimilarity function d'' was introduced recently in [14].

Classification

Given a set of objects, which is partitioned into a finite set of classes, *classification* is the task of automatically determining the class of an unseen object, based

---

[2] The authorship attribution problem is as follows: given texts written by authors A_1, $A_2, \ldots A_n$, and one additional piece of text, guess who of the given authors wrote that piece of text.

typically on a model trained on a set of objects with known class memberships. Classification is a *supervised* process, in a sense that it typically requires labelled training data to train a classifier.

We use the following simple classification method based on n-grams [14]: for a given set of families $\mathcal{P}_i$, $i = 1, 2, \ldots, k$ and the given object e, compute the dissimilarity measures $d(\{e\}, \mathcal{P}_i)$, $i = 1, 2, \ldots, k$. If the value $d(\{e\}, \mathcal{P}_s)$ is the smallest one, then the guess is that e belongs to the family $\mathcal{P}_s$. Thus, the classification algorithm is simple and its quality completely relies on the appropriateness of the dissimilarity measure used. This is essentially the well-known k Nearest Neighbours (kNN) classification method, with $k = 1$ [6].

3   Methodology and Data

For classification, we use the algorithm described in Section 2. For dissimilarity measure, we use the functions d' and d'' (as given by the equations (3) and (4)).

Our corpus is made out of documents in 20 European languages available from the EU web site[3]. For each language we took 20 documents for the corpus[4]. These are not necessarily translations of the same texts. Table 1 shows the list of these 20 languages and their codes.[5]

Table 1. Language codes

code	language	code	language
cs	Czech	lt	Lithuanian
da	Danish	hu	Hungarian
de	German	mt	Maltese
et	Estonian	nl	Dutch
el	Greek	pl	Polish
en	English	pt	Portuguese
es	Spanish	sk	Slovakian
fr	French	sl	Slovenian
it	Italian	fi	Finish
lv	Latvian	sv	Swedish

We consider the classification in the following way: for each language we randomly take 15 (out of 20) documents as a training corpus, for building n-gram language profiles. Then we classify the remaining 20×5 documents[6] and count a percentage of correct guesses. The variant of this classification task is as follows:

---

[3] http://europa.eu/

[4] The whole corpus is available from:
http://www.fmi.ch/members/andrija.tomovic/corpus-all.zip.

[5] Complete Unicode table of language codes can be found at:
http://unicode.org/onlinedat/languages.html

[6] Test documents are available from:
http://www.fmi.ch/members/andrija.tomovic/test.zip.

from the test documents (20×5 of them) we produce all subsequences of length
L (L=$10, 20, 30, \ldots$) and apply the classification algorithm to these sequences.
The motivation for this experiment is exploring the lower limits in length of
documents for reliable classification.

The algorithm is implemented using Visual C# (Visual Studio 2003) within
a wider application[7]. The application offers a range of functionalities concerning classification and clustering algorithms and the user can choose between a
number of dissimilarity functions [14].

4   Experimental Results

The basic classification task (classification of 20×5 documents) is performed
in the way described in Section 3. Table 2 shows success rates for dissimilarity
functions d' and d''.[8] It can be seen that the success rate for both functions
is perfect 100% for small values of n. The quality of the results is very high,
especially taking into account that the classification is 20-fold (i.e., each test
document was supposed to be classified into one of 20 categories). As expected,
the success rate decreases as n increases (after some value). Indeed, long (e.g.,
10 characters long) n-grams do not have high frequencies, so the classification
results cannot be very stable. Despite that, success rate for d' remain 99% for
$n = 8, 9, 10$, with only one error (one document in the Slovakian language classified as being in the Czech language). As observed for different domains in [14],
the function d' performed better than d'', proving its quality in classification
problems.

Table 2. Success rates for dissimilarity functions d' and d'' in classification of multi-
language documents

n	1	2	3	4	5	6	7	8	9	10
d'	100%	100%	100%	100%	100%	100%	100%	99%	99%	99%
d''	100%	100%	100%	100%	100%	99%	92%	88%	84%	28%

The above results show excellent success rate for classification of whole documents. The question is whether shorter texts would also be successfully classified.
Of course, very short strings (e.g., up to 20 characters) are very unlikely to be
classified with high success rate (since n-gram frequencies in one short string can
be very different than frequencies in the whole of the language). It is interesting
to explore what string length is sufficient for obtaining high (say, more than
99%) success rate in classification. The following experiment is aimed at answering this question. As in the previous experiment, for each language we take 15

---

[7] The application is available from:
   `http://www.fmi.ch/members/andrija.tomovic/NgramsApplication.zip`
[8] All training data and the detailed experimental results can be obtained upon request
   from the first author.

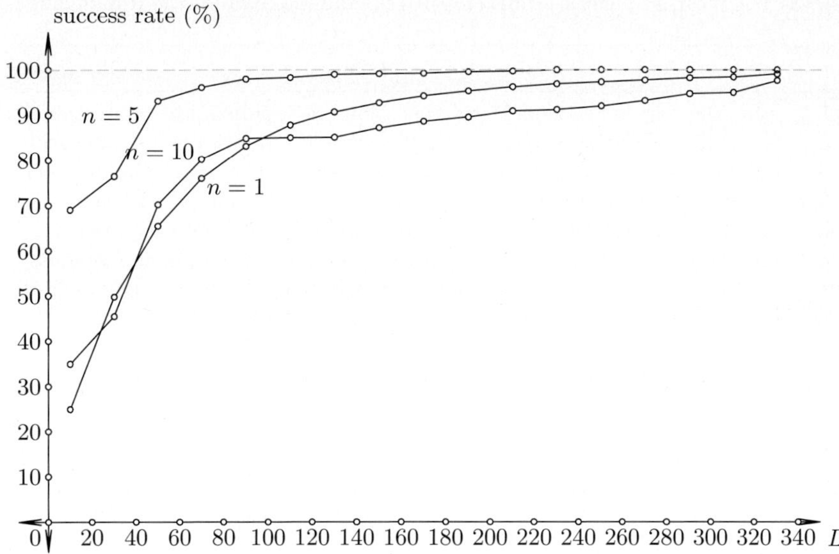

Fig. 1. Success rate for classification of strings of length L, by using n-grams with different values of n

(out of 20) documents as a training corpus, for building the n-gram language profile. Then we construct *all* L-substrings (L-grams) from the remaining 20×5 documents and count a percentage of correct guesses for these L-grams, as for strings to be classified. For classification of these strings, we used n-grams for different values of n. Figure 1 shows the results for n=1, 5, 10, for L=10, 30, ... For all values of n, almost perfect success rate is reached for L as small as 300. For all values of L the success rate was best for n= 5. For n=5, 93% success rate is reached for L as small as 50, and 99% success rate is reached for L equal 150. The value n=5 gives the best results because:

- Short n-grams cannot distinguish different languages easily. Namely, different languages with similar alphabets can have similar frequencies for some n-grams, and hence, a short test text, with non-representative distribution of n-grams (non-representative w.r.t. the language it belongs to), can be wrongly classified.
- Long n-grams have lower and lower frequencies and become more and more language- and string-specific. Table 3 and Table 4 show the first 10 most frequent n-grams in training data set for Italian and English. It can be seen that with higher n, n-grams become highly dependent on the training set. Long n-grams make better distinguishing between different languages, but on the other hand, text from the same language which is not from the same domain as the training data set is difficult to be recognized (this is well-known *over-fitting problem*).

Table 3. The most frequent n-grams (top 10) in training data for the Italian language

n=1	n=2	n=3	n=4	n=5	n=6	n=7	n=8	n=9	n=10
_	e_	_de	_di_	ione_	zione_	azione_	zione_de	ommission	ommissione
i	i_	_di	ione	azion	azione	zione_d	azione_d	mmissione	_Commissio
e	a_	ion	zion	zione	ione_d	ione_de	ione_del	_Commissi	Commission
a	_d	re_	one_	ation	e_dell	_della_	missione	Commissio	a_Commissi
o	o_	di_	_del	_dell	mento_	_europe	mmission	zione_del	mmissione_
t	on	one	azio	_che_	one_de	amento_	ommissio	a_Commiss	la_Commiss
r	re	ne_	che_	e_del	amento	_delle_	Commissi	missione_	zione_dell
n	ti	to_	dell	e_di_	sione_	one_del	_Commiss	ione_dell	azione_del
l	_c	zio	_con	_del_	_della	ssione_	_deputat	azione_de	terrorismo
s	er	_co	_la_	_del_	della_	issione	a_Commis	_terroris	_terrorism

Table 4. The most frequent n-grams (top 10) in training data for the English language

n=1	n=2	n=3	n=4	n=5	n=6	n=7	n=8	n=9	n=10
_	e_	_th	_the	_the_	n_the_	_of_the	_of_the_	European_	_European_
e	_t	the	_of_	_and_	_of_th	of_the_	European	_European	Parliament
t	th	he_	_to_	tion_	of_the	_Europe	uropean_	arliament	Commission
o	_a	ion	and_	ation	_that_	uropean	_on_the_	Parliamen	arliament_
a	he	on_	_and	n_the	f_the_	Europea	_Europea	_terroris	_Commissio
i	s_	_to	tion	_of_t	ation_	_on_the	rliament	ommission	e_European
n	n_	to_	ing_	_for_	Europe	ropean_	arliamen	Commissio	e_Commissi
r	d_	_of	ion_	of_th	_Europ	on_the_	_in_the_	rliament_	he_Commiss
s	in	of_	ment	f_the	_the_E	in_the_	Parliame	_Commissi	_Parliamen
h	on	_an	_in_	that_	uropea	_in_the	terroris	e_Europea	he_Europea

The results shown in Figure 1 also suggest a general classification strategy: if the string that is to be classified is shorter than 350, apply the classification procedure with n=5, otherwise apply the classification procedure with n=1 (because the success rates are almost equal for n=5 and n=1, and the classification for larger n is more time-consuming).

In order to make a system more efficient, the option is to take into account only a certain number of most frequent n-grams (instead of considering all occurring n-grams). However, in that case, classification with the functions d' and d'' is not perfect for all values of n. The results of classification performed using the first 100 most frequent n-grams are given in Table 5. For 1-grams results are the same (perfect 100%) like in Table 2 because there are no more than 100 1-grams. For 2-grams, 3-grams, 4-grams results are good, because first 100 most frequent n-grams (n=2,3,4) represents a significant portion of the set of all 2,3,4-grams. In these cases, the result of the training phase is a set of only $20 \times 100 \times n$ characters, yielding a knowledge sufficient for perfect identification of 20 languages.

We can conclude that our n-grams based technique gives excellent results, even for 20-fold classification of documents in different languages, and even for short strings. For this sort of classification, there is no need for vocabularies,

Table 5. Success rates for dissimilarity functions d' and d'' in classification of multi-language documents using only the first 100 most frequent n-grams

n	1	2	3	4	5	6	7	8	9	10
d'	100%	100%	100%	100%	90%	68%	54%	35%	35%	27%
d''	100%	100%	100%	100%	94%	76%	69%	59%	54%	51%

but only for a very small amount of training data. For training data we used only 15, rather short documents for each of 20 languages. For instance, training data for English had a total size of only 52Kb and around 2000 different words (including different forms).

It is interesting to report on the dissimilarities (based on the given functions) between profiles for different languages. To a somewhat surprise, these dissimilarities are not in accordance with the traditional clustering of languages — for instance, the English language is closer to the Italic languages than to the Germanic languages (this is true for both dissimilarity functions, for all values of n, and for the variant with 100 most frequent n-grams used). A possible explanation for this could be that written languages and distributions of their n-grams do not reflect deeper relationships between spoken languages.

5   Related Work

Automated classification has been studied for years and there is a number of methods for these problem. Also, there are many techniques for classification of documents in different languages and many of them give excellent results. However, some of them use some language-specific knowledge, some are applied to specific corpora, some are applied over specific sets of languages, and so it is not easy to make a direct, relevant comparison between different approaches. In [12] there is a good overview of different approaches to this problem, including approaches based on the presence of specific characters, on the presence of specific letter combinations, on the presence of specific words, on distribution of n-grams, etc.

The technique presented in [3] is based on using an ad hoc rank order statistic to compare the prevalence of n-grams. The test and training texts are first tokenized in order to avoid sequences which straddle two words. Comparison between test and training profiles was based on comparing rankings of the most frequent n-grams. There are results for 8-fold classification (over 8 languages), and for test strings long 300 characters or more.

A n-gram-based Bayesian classifier is described in [7]. The technique is domain independent and does not require tokenization. There are results only for 2-fold classification (over English and Spanish). As expected, classification success rate is higher with longer training data and longer test data, and generally better results are obtained for bigrams and trigrams. For 50Kb of training sets and for 20 bytes of input string, the success rate was 92%, while for 500 bytes of input string, the success rate was even 99.9%.

Approach based on n-grams, described in [10], uses simple information theoretic principles (perplexity and entropy) in combination with Bayesian decision theory. That technique has been evaluated on four different languages and four different text categorization problems.

The technique presented in this paper is similar to the one from [12], but based on different dissimilarity functions. The technique from [12] is applied to 18-fold language classification and it performs well even with short training and test data, it is simple and easy to implement. The success rate goes from 78.2% for 1-grams, for 200 lines of training data, and 1 line of test data, up to 100% for 2-grams, 2000 lines of training data, and 20 lines of test data.

In a recent paper [9], the problem of identifying language in web documents is addressed, for which the authors claim that it is more difficult variant of the problem. The authors use n-grams and several dissimilarity measures and reach around 91% success rates for 12-fold language classification.

There is another recent paper [4], addressing the problem of language identification and some of its hard variants: including distinguishing between European and Brazilian variants of Portuguese and identifying small tourists advertisements. The proposed, n-gram based, approach was also used for the standard language identification problem: the system was trained by 235 documents written in 19 European languages, and tested by 290 new test samples — once of size at least 6 lines (with 100% success rate) and once of size 4 lines (with 98.9% success rate). The system was also tested for identifying European and Brazilian variants of Portuguese (with 200 training documents and 369 test documents), reaching 98.37% success rate.

6   Experimental Comparison to Other Tools

We performed the experimental comparison between our system and several well-known tools:

Xerox language identifier is based on [1]. The algorithm performs the classification by calculating probabilities, based on n-gram probabilities for each language from a training data set. It has support for 47 languages.

Unknown language identification [9] is based on the algorithm described in [5]. The method uses a vector with frequencies of all n-grams for training profiles. The distance function is defined as cosine function of the angle between the sample text vector and each of text vector from the library. It has support for 66 languages.

TextCat is an implementation of the text categorization method described in [3]. This algorithm is similar to the algorithm proposed here. A preprocessing of the input text is performed, and digits and punctation are discarded. In order to generate a profile, the method uses all n-grams for n=1,2,3,4,5 on preprocessed text. Then the first 300 most frequent n-grams are used by different methods for comparing n-gram profiles. It has support for 77 languages.

---

[9] http://complingone.georgetown.edu/~langid/

SILC [10] uses Bayesian decision theory and classic Noisy Channel statical approach. This approach is different from our method and uses only 1-grams and 3-grams. It has support for 39 languages.

Table 6. Experimental results of four language classification tools

Tool	success rate	comment
XEROX	99.00% (99/100)	
ULI	98.75% (79/80)	no support for el,mt,sl,sk
TextCat	97.89% (93/95)	no support for mt
SILC	97.33% (73/75)	no support for lt,lv,mt,sk,sl

We used the corpus and the test data described in Section 3.[11] For testing the above tools, we used the set of 100 documents that we used as a test set for our system, so — all systems were ran on the same documents. Some of the above four tools do not have support for some languages, so the total of available tests was lower for some tools. Table 6 shows the experimental results. As it can be seen, all the tools performed in an excellent way, however none of them reached perfect success, unlike our approach (see the results in Table 2 and Table 5). Despite the fact that the above tools have support for more languages than our system, the given results are still relevant and fair. Namely, almost all wrong (5 out of 6) classifications made by the tested tools pointed to the languages that our system also has support for(with one exception for SCI). The most frequent error (4 out of 6) was wrongly classifying czech documents as slovakian and vice versa.

For further evaluation of our method we also used one chapter of the Bible like in work [10]. In that work authors used translation of one chapter into 6 different languages and achieved 100% accuracy. We used one chapter (Ruth) in 10 different languages. We have used fist two subchapter for the training data set and the rest for test data. Our approach has achieved 100% accuracy for all size n-grams.

7 Conclusions

We presented a new variant of a language classification algorithm based on n-grams (using the dissimilarity function recently introduced in [14]). We

---

[10] `http://rali.iro.umontreal.ca/`

[11] Unfortunately, for most of approaches described in Section 5, data sets and software which authors used are not publicly, freely available. This makes it difficult to perform a fair comparison between different existing tools and further evaluation of the presented method. Trying to promote another practice, we provide all data and tools which we used publicly availably. A good practice is also using rich sources of freely available multilingual corpora (and specifying used subsets), such as the one we use in this paper (`http://europa.eu/`, `http://eur-lex.europa.eu/`), or collections of translations of the Bible (`http://bibledatabase.net/`, `http://www.biblegateway.com/`).

analyzed its performance on the test documents written in 20 languages. The results are very good, and they reach perfect 100% success rate for our corpus of integral documents (for small size of n-grams). There is also high success rate for very short fragments of test text, reaching 99%, while longer fragments were classified with 100% success rate. These are very good results, especially taking into account that the classification is 20-fold. This sort of classification does not require massive vocabularies, but only very few training documents in different languages. We made an experimental comparison of our tool with four other language classification tools, and it gave the best performance. Our classification mechanism is fast, robust, and does not require any knowledge of the different languages. We believe it can be used in different contexts, like in multi-lingual institutions, and in Internet search engines.

References

[1] Beesley, K.R.: Language Identifier: A Computer Program for Automatic Natural-Language Identification of On-Line Text. In: Languages at Crossroads: Proceeding of the 29 th Annual Conference of the American Translator Association, pp. 47–54 (1988)

[2] Bennett, W.R.: Scientific and engineering problem-solving with the computer. Prentice-Hall, Inc., Englewood Cliffs, New Jersey (1976)

[3] Cavnar, W.B., Trenkle, J.M.: N-gram-based text categorization. In: Proceedings of the 1994 Symposium On Document Analysis and Information Retrieval, University of Nevada, Las Vegas (April 1994)

[4] da Silva, J.F., Lopes, G.P.: Identification of document language is not yet a completely solved problem. In: CIMCA. International Conference on Computational Intelligence for Modeling, Control & Automation, IEEE Computer Society Press, Los Alamitos (2006)

[5] Damashek, M.: Gauging similarity with n-grams: Language independent categorization of text. Science 267, 843–848 (1995)

[6] Dunham, M.H.: Data Mining Introduction and Advanced Topics. Southern Methodist University, Pearson Education Inc., New Jersey (2003)

[7] Dunning, T.: Statistical Identification of Language. Technical Report Technical report. CRL MCCS-94-273, Computing Research Lab, New Mexico State University (1994)

[8] Kešelj, V., Peng, F., Cercone, N., Thomas, C.: N-gram-based author profiles for authorship attribution. In: PACLING'03. Proceedings of the Conference Pacific Association for Computational Linguistics, August 2003, Dalhousie University, Halifax, Nova Scotia, Canada (2003)

[9] Martins, B., Silva, M.J.: Language identification in web pages. In: Proceedings of the 2005 ACM symposium on Applied computing, ACM Press, New York (2006)

[10] Pegn, F., Schuurmans, D., Wang, S.: Language and Task Independent Text Categorization with Simple Language Models. In: Proceedings of Human Language Technology Conference, pp. 110–117 (2003)

[11] Schmitt, J.: Trigram-based method of language identification. U.S. Patent number: 5062143 (October 1991)

[12] Sibun, P., Reynar, J.C.: Language identification: Examining the issues. In: Proceedings of 5th Symposium on Document Analysis and Information Retrieval (1996)

[13] Tauritz, D.: Application of n-grams. Department of Computer Science, University of Missouri-Rolla

[14] Tomović, A., Janičić, P., Kešelj, V.: n-Gram-based classification and unsupervised hierarchical clustering of genome sequences. Computer Methods and Programs in Biomedicine 81(2), 137–153 (2006)

SAT-Based Planning with Minimal-#actions Plans and "soft" Goals

Enrico Giunchiglia and Marco Maratea

DIST, University of Genova, Viale F. Causa 15, Genova, Italy
{enrico,marco}@dist.unige.it

Abstract. Planning as Satisfiability (SAT) is the best approach for optimally solving classical planning problems. The SAT-based planner SAT-PLAN has been the winner in the deterministic track for optimal planners in the 4th International Planning Competition (IPC-4) and the co-winner in the last 5th IPC (together with another SAT-based planner). Given a planning problem Π, SATPLAN works by (i) generating a SAT formula Π_n with a fixed "makespan" n, and (ii) checking Π_n for satisfiability. The algorithm stops if Π_n is satisfiable, and thus a plan has been found, otherwise n is increased.

Despite its efficiency, and the optimality of the makespan, SATPLAN has significant deficiency related in particular to "plan quality", e.g., the number of actions in the returned plan, and the possibility to express and reason on "soft" goals.

In this paper, we present SATPLAN$^\prec$, a system, modification of SAT-PLAN, which makes a significant step towards the elimination of SAT-PLAN's limitations. Given the optimal makespan, SATPLAN$^\prec$ returns plans with minimal number of actions and maximal number of satisfied "soft" goals, with respect to both cardinality and subset inclusions. We selected several benchmarks from different domains from all the IPCs: on these benchmarks we show that the plan quality returned by SATPLAN$^\prec$ is often significantly higher than the one returned by SATPLAN.

Quite surprisingly, this is often achieved without sacrificing efficiency while obtaining results that are competitive with the winning system of the "SimplePreferences" domain in the satisfying track of the last IPC.

1 Introduction

Planning as Satisfiability (SAT) [1] is the best approach for optimally solving classical planning problems. The SAT-based planner SATPLAN [2,3] has been the winner in the deterministic track for optimal planners in the 4th International Planning Competition (IPC-4) [4] and the co-winner in the recent IPC-5 (together with another SAT-based planner, MAXPLAN [5]). Given a planning problem Π, SATPLAN works by (i) generating a SAT formula Π_n with a fixed "makespan" n, and (ii) checking Π_n for satisfiability. The algorithm stops if Π_n is satisfiable, and thus the plan has been found, otherwise n is increased.

Despite its efficiency, and the optimality of the makespan, SATPLAN has significant deficiency related in particular to "plan quality", e.g., the number of

R. Basili and M.T. Pazienza (Eds.): AI*IA 2007, LNAI 4733, pp. 422–433, 2007.

actions in the returned plan, and the possibility to express and reason on "soft" goals. The issues are related with the following facts: in SATPLAN, when solving the propositional formula Π_n, there is no indication of what propositional variables correspond to actions, and the SAT solver does not perform any kind of optimization on the number of actions in the plan, treating each propositional variable in the same way, independently from what it indicates. The makespan is fixed, but multiple, mutually exclusive (mutex) actions can take place simultaneously, even if often not all actions are relevant to reach the goal. On the other hand, "soft" goals arise in planning problems when there is no possibility to satisfy simultaneously all the goals, and/or when it is sufficient (from the view point of the user) that only some of them are satisfied.

In this paper, we present SATPLAN$^\prec$, a system, modification of SATPLAN [3], which makes a significant step towards the elimination of SATPLAN's limitations. Given the optimal makespan, SATPLAN$^\prec$ returns plans with the minimal number of actions and maximal number of the satisfied "soft" goals, with respect to both cardinality and subset inclusions. This is achieved by integrating the OPTSAT solver in SATPLAN. OPTSAT [6,7] is a tool for solving SAT related optimization problems based on the state-of-the-art SAT solver MINISAT. Besides other features, given a SAT formula Π_n and a subset S of the variables in Π_n, OPTSAT returns an "optimal" solution, i.e., a satisfying assignment that minimize/maximize the atom in S assigned to TRUE.

We selected several domains of benchmarks from all the IPCs: on these benchmarks we show that the plan quality returned by SATPLAN$^\prec$ is often significantly higher than the one of SATPLAN using both SIEGE and MINISAT. In particular

- SATPLAN$^\prec$ is usually able to satisfy a number of soft goals which is much higher than the one of SATPLAN, e.g., there are instances with several soft goals where SATPLAN$^\prec$ satisfy all (or almost all) soft goals while SATPLAN is able to satisfy just a few of them.
- SATPLAN$^\prec$ usually returns plans with fewer number of actions than SATPLAN.

Quite surprisingly, this results are often achieved without sacrificing efficiency while the obtained results are competitive with the winning system of the "SimplePreferences" domain in the satisfying track of the last IPC, i.e., SGPLAN [8], as shown in [11]. Moreover, a closer look at the performance in terms of metrics for which SATPLAN$^\prec$ is optimized, i.e., makespan and number of actions in the plan, in comparison to both SATPLAN and SGPLAN, on benchmarks where each of the solvers satisfies all the soft goals, reveals that (i) SATPLAN and SATPLAN$^\prec$ often return plans with a much better makespan than SGPLAN; (ii) on some benchmarks the reduction in terms of number of actions in the plan returned by SATPLAN$^\prec$ is very significant; but also that (iii) there are particular instances in which SGPLAN returns plans with fewer actions. Because this is due to the non-optimal makespan returned, (iii) suggests that is could be useful, in order to further improve SATPLAN$^\prec$'s performance, to "trade-off" between optimality of the makespan and optimality of the plan quality.

The paper is structured as follows. In Sec 2 some basic preliminaries about planning (as satisfiability) are presented. Sec. 3 is devoted to the details on how the new features of SATPLAN$^{\prec}$ are implemented. In Sec. 4 is then shown how to use SATPLAN$^{\prec}$, its command line and options. Sec. 5 shows the results we have obtained with SATPLAN$^{\prec}$, and finally Sec. 6 draws some conclusions and possible topics for future research.

2 Preliminaries

Let $\mathcal{F}$ and $\mathcal{A}$ be the set of *fluents* and *actions*, respectively. A *state* is an interpretation of the fluent signature. A *complex action* is an interpretation of the action signature. Intuitively, a complex action α models the concurrent execution of the actions satisfied by α.

A *planning problem* is a triple $\langle I, tr, G \rangle$ where
- I is a Boolean formula over $\mathcal{F}$ and represents the set of *initial states*;
- tr is a Boolean formula over $\mathcal{F} \cup \mathcal{A} \cup \mathcal{F}'$ where $\mathcal{F}' = \{f' : f \in \mathcal{F}\}$ is a copy of the fluent signature and represents the *transition relation* of the automaton describing how (complex) actions affect states (we assume $\mathcal{F} \cap \mathcal{F}' = \emptyset$);
- G is a Boolean formula over $\mathcal{F}$ and represents the set of *goal states*.

The above definition of planning problem differs from the traditional ones in which the description of actions' effects on a state is described in an high-level action language like STRIPS or PDDL. We preferred this formulation because the techniques we are going to describe are largely independent of the action language used, at least from a theoretical point of view. The only assumption that we make is that the description is deterministic: there is only one state satisfying I and the execution of a (complex) action α in a state s can lead to at most one state s'. More formally, for each state s and complex action α there is at most one interpretation extending $s \cup \alpha$ and satisfying tr. Consider a planning problem $\Pi = \langle I, tr, G \rangle$. In the following, for any integer i
- if F is a formula in the fluent signature, F_i is obtained from F by substituting each $f \in \mathcal{F}$ with f_i,
- tr_i is the formula obtained from tr by substituting each symbol $p \in \mathcal{F} \cup \mathcal{A}$ with p_{i-1} and each $f \in \mathcal{F}'$ with f_i.

If n is an integer, the *planning problem Π with makespan n* is the Boolean formula Π_n defined as

$$I_0 \wedge \wedge_{i=1}^{n} tr_i \wedge G_n \qquad (n \geq 0) \tag{1}$$

and a *plan for Π_n* is an interpretation satisfying (1). For example, considering the planning problem of going to work from home. Assuming that we can use the car or the bus or the bike, this scenario can be easily formalized using a single fluent variable *AtWork* and three action variables *Car*, *Bus* and *Bike* with the obvious meaning. The problem with makespan 1 can be expressed by the conjunction of the formulas:

$$\neg AtWork_0,$$
$$AtWork_1 \equiv \neg AtWork_0 \equiv (Car_0 \vee Bus_0 \vee Bike_0), \tag{2}$$
$$AtWork_1,$$

in which the first formula corresponds to the initial state, the second to the transition relation, and the third to the goal state. (2) has 7 plans (i.e., satisfying interpretations), each corresponding to a non-empty subset of $\{Car_0, Bus_0, Bike_0\}$. For instance, in the plan corresponding to $\{Car_0, Bus_0\}$ both the car and the bike are used to get to work. If we want to avoid any two actions in $\{Car_0, Bus_0, Bike_0\}$ to occur in parallel, the following mutex axioms are to be added as part of the formulas encoding the transition relation

$$\neg(Car_0 \wedge Bus_0), \neg(Car_0 \wedge Bike_0), \neg(Bus_0 \wedge Bike_0).$$

3   SATPLAN$^{\preceq}$ Implementation

SATPLAN$^{\preceq}$ is a modification of the SATPLAN system. When constructing the SAT formula Π_n, a number of information are added to the formula (which in SATPLAN is specified in CNF format), in order to cope with the specific problem. If minimization on the number of actions in the Π is considered, the total number of actions and the list of the propositional variables corresponding to actions are specified in the comment lines of (the CNF file related to) Π_n. The comment lines also specify if the minimization has to be computed under cardinality or subset inclusion.

Otherwise, if we are dealing with maximization of the number of "soft" goals to be satisfied, some of the clauses in Π_n have to be modified, resulting in a new formula Π'_n. Each clause $C \in \Pi_n$ that represents the i-th goal is modified by adding a "goal selectors" s_i, i.e., by substituting C with $C' := \overline{s}_i \cup C$. Intuitively, the clause selectors tell us how many soft goals are satisfied, i.e., assuming C' is satisfied, if s_i is assigned by TRUE this means that clause C' is satisfied by C, thus the related soft goal holds; otherwise, if s_i is assigned by FALSE, this means that it could be the case that C' is only satisfied by the clause selector. For the soft goals, in the command line it is only needed to specify the problem, and the type of minimality.

Now we explain how optimality is obtained. Consider the set of atoms S to be the set that should be optimized, i.e., the set of actions in Π_n or the set of the goal selectors. If the optimality is to be performed under subset inclusion, it suffices to "preferentially" splits on the atom in S, and assign it to FALSE (resp. TRUE). The resulting satisfying assignment μ of Π_n (resp. Π'_n) is guaranteed to contain the minimal number of atoms assigned by TRUE (resp. the maximal number of goal selectors assigned by TRUE), thus resulting in a plan with the minimal number of actions (resp. the maximal number of soft goals satisfied).

On the other hand, if the minimality is by cardinality, we have to compute an auxiliary boolean encoding $Bool(S)$ of S whose implementation depends on whether we rely on (a) a binary or (b) a unary encoding. For any satisfying assignment μ of Π_n, there exists a unique interpretation μ' to the variables in $\Pi_n \wedge Bool(S)$ such that μ' extends μ and satisfies $\Pi_n \wedge Bool(S)$. Given an atom p, consider that $\mu(p)$ is 1 if μ assigns p to true, and is 0 otherwise. $Bool(S)$ contains k new variables $b_{k-1}, \ldots, b_0$ such that

(a) if $k = \lceil log_2(|S| + 1) \rceil$, $\sum_{p \in S} \mu(p) = \sum_{i=0}^{k-1} \mu(b_i) \times 2^i$, or

(b) if $k = |S|$, $\sum_{p \in S} \mu(p) = \sum_{i=0}^{k-1} \mu(b_i)$.

Intuitively, the goal of points (a) and (b) is to encode an optimization function (in our case related to the cardinality $|S|$ of the atoms p in S assigned to TRUE) as a boolean formula $Bool(S)$ which contains a set of atoms $b_{k-1}, \ldots, b_0$ that "characterize" the optimization function.

We considered Warners' [9] and Bailleux and Boufkhad's [10] encodings of $Bool(S)$, denoted with W-encoding and B-encoding respectively, as representative encodings for (a) and (b), respectively.

1. Warners. It uses a binary representation of integers. This is a linear time and space encoding, that relies on sums via adder circuits and works directly with objective functions with weights. In OPTSAT, and thus in SATPLAN$^{\prec}$, the encoding is optimized for the non-weighted case, and the size of the encoding is approximately halved.

   Example 1. Consider $S = \{p_1, p_2, p_3\}$. $Bool(S)$ is the set of clauses corresponding to the sum of three variables, i.e., $\{\{p_7, p_4, \neg p_1\}, \{p_7, \neg p_4, p_1\},$ $\{\neg p_7, \neg p_4, \neg p_1\}, \{\neg p_7, p_4, p_1\}, \{p_6, \neg p_4, \neg p_1\}, \{\neg p_6, p_4\}, \{\neg p_6, p_1\}, \{p_8, p_5, \neg p_6\},$ $\{p_8, \neg p_5, p_6\}, \{\neg p_8, \neg p_5, \neg p_6\}, \{\neg p_8, p_5, p_6\}, \{p_4, p_2, \neg p_3\}, \{p_4, \neg p_2, p_3\},$ $\{\neg p_4, \neg p_2, \neg p_3\}, \{\neg p_4, p_2, p_3\}, \{p_5, \neg p_2, \neg p_3\}, \{\neg p_5, p_2\}, \{\neg p_5, p_3\}\}$.

   The b_i variables are p_7 and p_8, and this corresponds to $\sum_{i=1}^{3} \mu(p_i) = 2^1 \mu(p_8) + 2^0 \mu(p_7)$, while p_4, p_5 and p_6 are added by the encoding.

2. Bailleux/Boufkhad (B). In this encoding a unary representation of integers is used: an integer x s.t. $0 \leq x \leq z$ is represented using z propositional variables $\{p_1, \ldots, p_z\}$ with (the first) "x" variables assigned to 1 (TRUE), and the others to 0 (FALSE). This representation has the property that when a variable p_j has value TRUE, all the variables p_w with $1 \leq w < j$, are TRUE as well; and similarly if p_k has value FALSE. The encoding is efficient with respect to unit-propagation but it adds a quadratic number of new clauses.

   Example 2. Consider the same Example used in 1, $Bool(S)$ is now $\{\{\neg p_6, p_1, p_4\},$ $\{p_6, \neg p_4\}, \{\neg p_7, p_1, p_5\}, \{p_7, \neg p_5\}, \{\neg p_8, p_1\}, \{p_6, \neg p_1\}, \{\neg p_7, p_4\}, \{p_7, \neg p_1, \neg p_4\},$ $\{\neg p_8, p_5\}, \{p_8, \neg p_1, \neg p_5\}, \{\neg p_4, p_2, p_3\}, \{p_4, \neg p_3\}, \{\neg p_5, p_2\}, \{p_4, \neg p_2\}, \{\neg p_5, p_3\},$ $\{p_5, \neg p_2, \neg p_3\}\}$, in which the b_i variables are p_6, p_7 and p_8, $\sum_{i=1}^{3} \mu(p_i) = \mu(p_6) + \mu(p_7) + \mu(p_8)$, with p_8 being the most significant variable (i.e., b_2), while p_4 and p_5 are introduced by the encoding.

We also exploited a further alternative, modification of the B-encoding, leveraging on its representation. We noticed that the encoding does not take into full account the relations among the resulting b_i variables, e.g., it is safe to enforce that when b_i is assigned to FALSE (resp. TRUE), also b_{i+1} (resp. b_{i-1}) is assigned to FALSE (resp. TRUE) by unit propagation. This is easily done by adding the clauses $\{b_i, \neg b_{i+1}\}$, $i = 0, \ldots, v - 1$ to the above encoding. Given that this modification did not show significant enhancement over B-encoding, we will not consider it in the design of SATPLAN$^\prec$ and in the experimental evaluation.

Despite the difference in the size of the encodings, the B-encoding has better computational properties and it has been consistently reported in the literature to lead to good results [10,12].

Given $b_{k-1}, \ldots, b_0$, preferentially and in-order splitting from b_{k-1} to b_0 and assign it with the "needed" value (i.e., the one resulting from the combination of optimization and minimality, following the schema of assignment we used when dealing with a subset inclusion minimality) leads to an "optimal" solution (see [7] for more details).

As we noticed before, this is achieved by using the OPTSAT system, instead of invoking a basic SAT solver, like MINISAT or SIEGE.

A final, important consideration has to be made. We have seen that in the last IPC-5 SATPLAN was the winner together with MAXPLAN. The question is whether the new features we have proposed can be simply integrated into MAXPLAN. MAXPLAN works by firstly estimating an upper bound n of the optimal makespan, and than (i) generating a SAT formula Π_n for the fixed makespan n, and (ii) checking Π_n for satisfiability, by using a modified version of MINISAT. The algorithm stops if Π_n is unsatisfiable, otherwise n is decreased. Given this, it should be relatively easy to integrate the new features of SATPLAN$^\prec$ into MAXPLAN.

4   SATPLAN$^\prec$ Command Line and Options

SATPLAN$^\prec$ has to be invoked as follows:

./SATPLAN$^\prec$ -solver <> -opt <> -minimality <> -enc <> -problem <> -domain <>

The command line of SATPLAN$^\prec$ is thus very similar to the one of SATPLAN. Indeed, SATPLAN$^\prec$ accepts all the options of SATPLAN (here we report only the mandatories "-problem" and "-domain"), and adds new options in order to deal with the new features of SATPLAN$^\prec$.

Going in more details,

    -solver: indicates the solver to be used for solving the SAT problem. Among others, the most important are OPTSAT, MINISAT and SIEGE ("optsat1.0", "minisat1.14" and "siege" are the specific strings to be specified in place of <>). If the goal is to use the new features of SATPLAN$^\prec$, it is mandatory to rely on OPTSAT, otherwise all the modifications explained in the Section above are ignored, and SATPLAN$^\prec$ behaves like the standard SATPLAN.

    -opt: specifies if the optimization is related to the number of actions, or to "soft" goals ("action" or "goal").

    -minimality: specifies the type of optimization, i.e., if the optimization is subject to cardinality or subset inclusion ("card" or "subset").

    -enc: if minimality is by cardinality, this option specifies what encoding has to be used ("w" or "b")

-problem: is the planning problem in (propositional) STRIPS format
-domain: is the domain specification in (propositional) STRIPS format

It should be noted that only the last two options are mandatory, i.e., if only the problem and domain parameters are specified the other options are set by default to their first choice ("optsat1.0", "action", "card", and "w" respectively). Otherwise, a command line like the following:

```
./SATPLAN≺ -opt goal -minimality subset -problem log.pddl -domain domain-log.pddl
```

specifies that a logistic planning problem is subject to a maximization (under subset inclusion) of the "soft" goals to be satisfied. Given that no encoding is involved, the related specification (i.e., "-enc") is in this case useless. The OPTSAT system is used as a back-end solver for SATPLAN≺.

5   Experimental Evaluation

We remind that SATPLAN can only handle propositional STRIPS domains, and, among them, we considered the pipesworld, satellite, airport, promela philosophers and optical, psr, depots, driverLog, zenoTravel, freeCell, logistic, blocks, mprime and mistery domains from the first 4 IPCs, and pathway, storage, tpp and trucks from IPC-5 (notice that we do not consider the domains in the "simple preferences" track in IPC-5 because they are not handled by SATPLAN). These are standard planning problems in which the goal corresponds to a set G of goals and without soft goals. We modified these problems in order to interpret all the goals in G as soft goals, following what is explained in Section 3 for SATPLAN≺ about goal selectors, and by encoding the problems in the language PDDL3 [13] for SG-PLAN. Note that our proposed modification exactly encodes the fact that the goals in G are now "soft" in the sense that it is desirable but not necessary to achieve them. Since there are no "hard" goals, the various versions of SATPLAN/SATPLAN≺ would always find a valid plan, even when the makespan n is 0 (in which case the returned plan would be the empty one). In order to avoid this situation, we added a constraint stating that at time n at least one of the soft goals has to be satisfied. Because of this, we discarded the problems whose original version has only one goal because they would have no soft goal.[1] In the following, we use SATPLAN≺(s), SATPLAN≺(w) and SATPLAN≺(b) to denote SATPLAN≺ when is subject to subset inclusion optimality, and to cardinality (with W-encoding and B-encoding, respectively). We also use SATPLAN and SATPLAN(m) to denote basic SATPLAN employing SIEGE and MINISAT respectively. We considered both SAT solvers because (i) SIEGE is the default solver for SATPLAN, but (ii) MINISAT is used in SATPLAN≺ and OPTSAT because SIEGE's code is not available, and, most importantly, MINISAT is the winner of the last SAT Competition, in 2005,[2] together with the SAT/CNF minimizer SATELITE, and the winner of the SAT race 2006.[3] In any case, in our

---

[1] Note that also SGPLAN does not accept problems with only one goal.
[2] http://www.satcompetition.org/2005/
[3] http://fmv.jku.at/sat-race-2006/

experiments, we have seen no significant differences in SATPLAN's performances when employing the two solvers.

In [11] we showed that SATPLAN$^\prec$ is competitive with respect to SGPLAN in terms of both metric (in this case the number of soft goals satisfied), and number of problem solved, i.e., with respect to the first two parameters used to evaluate planning systems in the "SimplePreferences"-track of the last IPC-5. Moreover, in the same paper, it is shown that this is achieved without sacrificing efficiency, i.e., that only in a small fraction of the hundreds of problems analyzed SATPLAN$^\prec$ (with the W-encoding in case of optimality by cardinality) can have performances significantly worse than SATPLAN when minimizing the number of actions in the plan.

On the contrary, in this paper we focus on:

- the reduction in the number of actions in the plan returned by SATPLAN$^\prec$ over SATPLAN (and SGPLAN);
- the number of soft goals satisfied in the plan of SATPLAN$^\prec$ over SATPLAN;
- a comparison between SATPLAN$^\prec$, SATPLAN and SGPLAN on the makespan returned, on problem instances in which all the systems satisfy all soft goals.

Even if the real contribution of the analysis we will be showing is over SATPLAN, we decided also to include SGPLAN as a reference, taking into account that it uses a different approach, and that it is not targeted for optimizing the number of actions and makespan in the returned plan. All the tests have been run on a Linux box equipped with a Pentium IV 2.4GHz processor and 512MB of RAM. The timeout has been set to 300s for each problem instance. In the plots, a point is missed if a system runs out of time or memory in the given problem instance.

The first results are shown in Figure 1. The left plot shows the performances of SATPLAN, SATPLAN(m), SATPLAN$^\prec$(w) and SATPLAN$^\prec$(s) on the problems considered, ordered according to SATPLAN's performances. The plot shows the number of soft goals each planner does not satisfy. This way of presenting the data has the feature that results about the same problem are not lost, i.e., the results for all the systems at a given x-coordinate refer to the same problem.

As expected SATPLAN does not satisfy many of the soft goals, in particular when using MINISAT, while SATPLAN$^\prec$(w)/(s) manage to satisfy all of them in many cases. Interestingly, the number of soft goals not satisfied by SATPLAN(w)/(s) are in most cases equal, while in theory this is not necessary the case. In the plot, for sake of readability, we have not included SATPLAN$^\prec$(b): its plot would be exactly the same to the one of SATPLAN$^\prec$(w), given that they manage to solve all the benchmarks presented, and with similar performances. Moreover, the performances of SATPLAN$^\prec$(w)/(b) are very similar to the ones of SATPLAN$^\prec$(s), SATPLAN and SATPLAN(m). The explanation for the CPU performances of SATPLAN$^\prec$(w)/(b) is that all the problems considered have at most 30 soft goals and the burden introduced by the Boolean encodings is negligible. We will see that, when considering minimal #actions-plan, this is no longer the case. Another interesting observation can be drawn from the use of the SAT solvers in SATPLAN: MINISAT manages to always satisfy very few soft goals (almost always

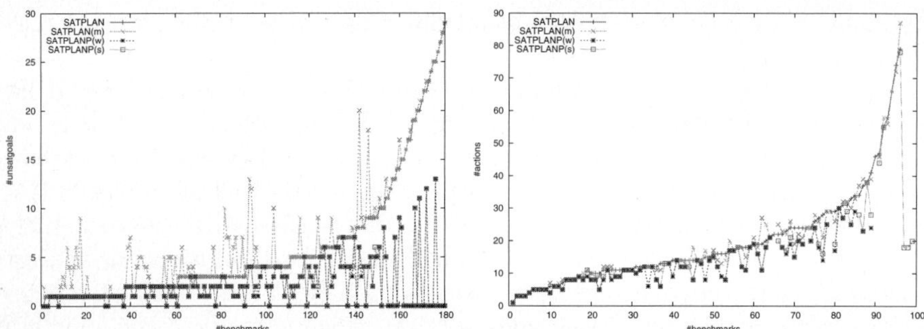

Fig. 1. Left: Number of unsatisfied soft goals by SATPLAN, SATPLAN(m), and SATPLAN$^{\prec}$(w)/(s). Right: Number of actions in the returned plan for SATPLAN, SATPLAN(m), and SATPLAN$^{\prec}$(w)/(s).

one). Given this, and given that SATPLAN$^{\prec}$ is based on MINISAT, the results on SATPLAN$^{\prec}$ are made even stronger by this point.

Considering the "quality" of the plan returned in terms of number of actions, the results are in Figure 1, right plot. The results are again ordered according to SATPLAN's performances.

In the plot, for sake of readability, we do not show the results for the airport, promela philosophers and optical, and psr domains: for each problem in these domains SATPLAN, SATPLAN(m) and SATPLAN$^{\prec}$/(w)/(b)/(s) return plans with the same length. Similarly to the case of soft goals, the quality of the plan returned by SATPLAN(s) is in most cases equal to that of SATPLAN(w), and in many cases both return plans of better quality than SATPLAN. Again, in the plot we do not include results for SATPLAN$^{\prec}$(b): when it manages to solve a problem, it obviously returns a plan of the same quality of SATPLAN$^{\prec}$(w), but in several cases it runs out of time or memory when problems are big. Thus, its representative line would be exactly the same of SATPLAN$^{\prec}$(w), but with a significant portion of the line missing.

We remind that in [11] we showed that SATPLAN$^{\prec}$ is competitive with respect to SGPLAN in terms of both number of soft goals satisfied and number of problem solved, i.e., with respect to the first two parameters used to evaluate planning systems in the "SimplePreferences"-track of the last IPC-5, without sacrificing efficiency.

Now, we want to evaluate what is the behavior, and the relative performance, of SGPLAN with respect to SATPLAN$^{\prec}$ on the metrics for which SATPLAN$^{\prec}$ is optimized, i.e., number of actions and makespan of the returned plan.

This analysis is performed on those instances in which all the systems satisfy all the soft goals (when greater than one),[4] i.e., we posed SGPLAN and all the versions of SATPLAN/SATPLAN$^{\prec}$ on the same conditions. Table 1 shows the

---

[4] We also could not consider some domains, e.g., promela philosophers, because SG-PLAN time outs or returns segmentation faults on all instances, the latter due to the high number of grounded operators in the problems. The last information is a personal communication with the authors.

Table 1. Number of actions and makespan for SATPLAN, SATPLAN$^{\prec}$ and SGPLAN

PB	#actions					Makespan	
	SATPLAN	SATPLAN(m)	SATPLAN$^{\prec}$(w)	SATPLAN$^{\prec}$(s)	SGPLAN	SATPLAN[$^{\prec}$]	SGPLAN
log4-0	24	24	20	20	20	9	20
log4-1	24	26	19	21	19	9	19
log4-2	24	19	15	15	15	9	15
log5-0	31	32	27	27	31	9	31
log5-1	29	26	17	19	17	9	17
log6-0	33	30	25	25	26	9	26
log6-1	28	21	14	16	15	9	15
log6-9	41	39	24	28	28	11	28
block4-2	6	6	6	6	6	6	6
block5-2	16	16	16	16	26	16	26
block6-0	12	12	12	12	12	12	12
block6-1	10	10	10	10	16	10	16
block6-2	20	20	–	20	32	20	32
stor5	11	9	9	9	8	6	8
stor6	11	9	9	9	10	6	10
stor7	14	14	14	14	14	14	14
stor8	16	14	12	12	13	8	13
stor9	14	14	12	12	11	7	11
stor10	–	–	–	18	18	18	18
stor11	–	–	–	18	17	11	17
stor12	22	25	–	20	17	9	17
sat1	9	9	9	9	9	8	9
sat2	13	–	–	13	13	12	13
psr15	10	10	10	10	10	8	10
psr19	25	25	25	25	31	15	31
psr25	9	9	–	9	9	9	9
psr33	21	21	21	21	21	16	21
psr40	20	20	20	–	20	15	20
psr42	30	30	30	30	30	16	30
driv1	14	18	8	8	7	6	7
zeno2	6	7	6	6	8	5	8
zeno3	13	11	6	6	6	5	6
zeno4	11	11	11	11	13	5	13
zeno5	15	14	14	14	11	5	11
zeno6	14	13	12	12	13	5	13
zeno8	16	17	15	15	12	5	12
zeno9	29	29	–	–	23	6	23
free1	9	11	9	11	10	5	10
free2	18	18	–	18	14	8	14
free3	21	21	21	21	19	7	19
tpp4	14	14	14	14	14	5	14
tpp5	19	21	19	19	19	7	19
air7	41	41	41	41	41	21	41
air9	71	71	–	71	73	27	73
air12	39	39	39	39	39	21	39

results obtained and is structured as follows: the first column contains the specific instance (where sat, air, driv, zeno, free, log, block, and stor stay for satellite, airport, driverLog, zenoTravel, freeCell, logistics, blocks-world and storage domain, respectively); columns 2-6 contain the number of actions in the returned plan for SATPLAN, SATPLAN(m), SATPLAN$^{\prec}$(w), SATPLAN$^{\prec}$(s) and SGPLAN, respectively, while the last two columns contain the makespan for all the modification of SATPLAN/SATPLAN$^{\prec}$ and SGPLAN, respectively. An "–"

indicates that the corresponding instance has not been solved in the given time limit of memory limit. The results suggest the following considerations:

- The makespan returned by SGPLAN if often significantly higher than the one returned by the various versions of SATPLAN and SATPLAN$^\prec$, up to a factor of 4 (zeno9 instance). Nonetheless, there are also (even if just a few) cases in which SGPLAN returns the same, optimal makespan (namely psr25, block4-2, block6-0, stor4 and stor10).

- When a reduction on the number of action is possible (i.e., given the fixed makespan and the "structure" of the planning instance) SATPLAN$^\prec$ can return plans with a significant lower number of actions, with respect to both SATPLAN and SGPLAN: many of the logistics and blocks-world instances better underline this behavior. Interestingly, there are also instances where SGPLAN returns plans with fewer actions than SATPLAN/SATPLAN$^\prec$, e.g., driv1, zeno5, free2, and stor11). This is due to the usual non-optimal makespan returned by SGPLAN, and from the intuitive consideration that on some instances, with a longer makespan actions can be easily better "serialazable", thus producing a plan with fewer actions. In fact, finally note how in the instances where this happen, SGPLAN returns a much higher makespan than SATPLAN/SATPLAN$^\prec$ (but driv1).

The last point opens the way to an interesting research issue, suggesting a possible extension of SATPLAN$^\prec$ in order to further improve its plan quality. The idea would be to "trade-off" between optimality of the makespan and number of actions in the plan. We have seen that, on some instances, it is possible to compute plans of better quality by do not stop the search when the (first) plan is found, but going ahead and increase the makespan. It is interesting to note how the same trade-off could also help when trying to maximize the number of soft goals satisfied.

6   Conclusions

In this paper we have presented a system, SATPLAN$^\prec$, which makes a significant step toward the elimination of same deficiency of SATPLAN related to plan quality, i.e., the number of actions and the satisfied soft goals in the returned plan. We have considered a wide number of benchmarks from all previous IPCs, and experimentally shown that significant gain can be obtained with SATPLAN$^\prec$. Interestingly, this is often achieved without sacrificing efficiency, and being competitive with SGPLAN, the winner of the "SimplePreferences"-track of the last IPC-5. As a future work, we plan to analyze if the results reported in this paper can be further strengthened by not considering a bounded horizon, and what is the corresponding lost in the efficiency of the system.

7   Availability of the System and SGPLAN Benchmarks

The binary executable of SATPLAN$^\prec$, together with the benchmarks used adapted to the PDDL3 format in order to be processed by SGPLAN, are available at
`http://www.star.dist.unige.it/~marco/SATPLANP/`.

References

1. Kautz, H., Selman, B.: Planning as satisfiability. In: Proc. ECAI-92, pp. 359–363 (1992)
2. Kautz, H., Selman, B.: Unifying SAT-based and graph-based planning. In: Proc. IJCAI-99, pp. 318–325. Morgan-Kaufmann, San Francisco (1999)
3. Kautz, H., Selman, B.: SATPLAN04: Planning as satisfiability. In: ICAPS-06. Proc. of 5th International Planning Competition, Internation Conference on Automated Planning and Scheduling, pp. 45–47 (2006)
4. Hoffmann, J., Edelkamp, S.: The deterministic part of IPC-4: An overview. Journal of Artificial Intelligence Research (JAIR) 24, 519–579 (2005)
5. Xing, Z., Chen, Y., Zhang, W.: MaxPlan: Optimal planning by decomposed satisfiability and backward reduction. In: ICAPS-06. Proc. of 5th International Planning Competition, Internation Conference on Automated Planning and Scheduling, pp. 53–55 (2006)
6. Giunchiglia, E., Maratea, M.: OPTSAT: A Tool for Solving SAT related optimization problems. In: Fisher, M., van der Hoek, W., Konev, B., Lisitsa, A. (eds.) JELIA 2006. LNCS (LNAI), vol. 4160, pp. 485–489. Springer, Heidelberg (2006)
7. Giunchiglia, E., Maratea, M.: Solving Optimization Problems with DLL. In: ECAI. Proc. of the 17th European Conference on Artificial Intelligence, pp. 377–381. IOS Press, Amsterdam (2006)
8. Hsu, C., Wah, B., Huang, R., Chen, Y.: Constraint Partitioning for Solving Planning Problems with Trajectory Constraints and Goal Preferences. In: Proc. IJCAI, pp. 1924–1929 (2007)
9. Warners, J.P.: A linear-time transformation of linear inequalities into CNF. Information Processing Letters 68(2), 63–69 (1998)
10. Bailleux, O., Boufkhad, Y.: Efficient CNF Encoding of Boolean Cardinality Constraints. In: Rossi, F. (ed.) CP 2003. LNCS, vol. 2833, Springer, Heidelberg (2003)
11. Giunchiglia, E., Maratea, M.: Planning as Satisfiability with Preferences. In: AAAI. Proc. of 22th National Conference of the American Association for Artificial Intelligence (2007) (to appear)
12. Büttner, M., Rintanen, J.: Satisfiability planning with constraints on the number of actions. In: Proc. ICAPS, pp. 292–299 (2005)
13. Gerevini, A., Long, D.: Plan constraints and preferences in PDDL3. In: ICAPS-06. Proc. of 5th International Planning Competition, Internation Conference on Automated Planning and Scheduling, pp. 7–13 (2006)

Plan Diagnosis and Agent Diagnosis
in Multi-agent Systems

Roberto Micalizio and Pietro Torasso

Università di Torino, corso Svizzera 187, Torino, Italy
{micalizio,torasso}@di.unito.it

Abstract. The paper discusses a distributed approach for monitoring
and diagnosing the execution of a plan where concurrent actions are
performed by a team of cooperating agents.

The paper extends the notion of plan diagnosis(introduced by Roos
et al. for the execution of a multi-agent plan) with the notion of agent
diagnosis. While plan diagnosis is able to capture the distinction between
primary and secondary failures, the agent diagnosis makes apparent the
actual health status of the agents.

The paper presents a mechanism of failure propagation which captures
the interplay between agent diagnosis and plan diagnosis; this mechanism
plays a critical role in the understanding at what extent a fault affecting
the functionalities of an agent affects the global plan too. A relational
formalism is adopted for modeling both the nominal and the abnormal
execution of the actions.

1   Introduction

While the problem of cooperation in multi-agent systems has received a lot of
attention in the last years, not so much attention has been paid to the problem
of supervising the execution of *multi-agent plans*, i.e., plans where actions are
executed concurrently by a team of cooperating agents. In this scenario, one of
the problems we have to consider is that the actual execution of a (multi-agent)
plan can be *threatened* [1] by the occurrence of unexpected events such as faults
in the agents functionalities or harmful interactions, which arise when many
agents try to use the same resources. The occurrence of plan threats does not
necessarily imply that the plan goal can no longer be achieved. In many cases,
in fact, the plan goal can still be achieved but the plan may need to be adjusted
(i.e. a recovery process is required). In order to repair a multi-agent plan, one
has to know not only which actions are failed (*primary failures*), but also how
the rest of the plan has been affected by these failures (*secondary failures*). In
other words, the execution of a multi-agent plan needs to be *on-line monitored*
and *diagnosed* to take into account possible anomalous evolutions during the
execution of the plan.

While monitoring and diagnosis of dynamic component-based systems have
received a significant amount of attention (see e.g., [2,3]), only recently some
works have addressed the issues of monitoring and diagnosing the execution of
a multi-agent plan (see e.g., [4,5]).

R. Basili and M.T. Pazienza (Eds.): AI*IA 2007, LNAI 4733, pp. 434–446, 2007.

In particular, Roos et al. [6] have introduced the notion of plan diagnosis as the minimal set of actions which have to be assumed failed to explain the anomalous behavior of the system. Moreover, by exploiting a set of (precompiled) causal rules, this notion of plan diagnosis is used to determine how the failure of an action propagates in the plan and causes the failure of other actions even assigned to different agents.

In this paper we discuss and formalize a novel model-based methodology to solve the problems of monitoring and diagnosing the execution of a multi-agent plan. In particular, we propose a distributed approach, where the global multi-agent plan is decomposed into sub-plans, each of which is assigned to a specific agent of the team. Every agent is responsible for monitoring and diagnosing the sub-plan it executes. We assume that actions are atomic and we model them as relations, for capturing their non deterministic effects due to the possible occurrence of faults.

A first contribution of the paper consists in extending the Roos's framework by complementing the notion of *plan diagnosis* (which highlights primary and secondary failures) with the notion of agent diagnosis which makes apparent the actual health status of the agents. It is worth noting that the agent diagnosis is an important piece of information which can be exploited for determining the set of recovery actions an agent is able to execute. A second relevant contribution of the paper is represented by a mechanism of failure propagation which captures the interplay between agent diagnosis and plan diagnosis; this mechanism plays a critical role in the understanding at what extent a fault affecting the functionalities of an agent affects the global plan.

The paper is organized as follows. The basic concepts of the proposed approach are introduced in sections 2 and 3; while the former describes the distributed framework, the latter addresses the notions of global and local plans to be supervised. In section 4 we present two important concepts, namely, the *agent status* and the *action outcome*; these concepts will result to be essential for the formalization of the supervision process, in section 5, which includes the definitions of plan and agent diagnosis. The paper closes with some remarks on the use of plan and agent diagnosis for the plan recovery purpose.

2   Setting the Framework

In the present paper we propose a distributed approach to the problem of supervising the execution of a given multi-agent plan P. While a formal definition of the multi-agent plan is reported in the next section, for the time being it is sufficient to consider that P is a completely instantiated partial-order plan (POP), where each action a is assigned to a specific agent i of the team $\mathcal{T}$, and where a is modeled in a STRIPS-like language, i.e., in terms of preconditions and direct effects.

The class of systems we deal with is referred to as *synchronous transition systems* [3]. In these systems the time is a discrete sequence of instants, the actions are executed synchronously by the agents in the team and each action in

Table 1. The preconditions and the effects of the actions in the plan of Figure 1

MOVE(A, P1, P2)	LOAD_S(A, OBJ, P)	LOAD_L(A, OBJ, P)
ASMT: MOBILITY(OK) PWR(HIGH)	**ASMT**: HANDLING(OK)	**ASMT**: HANDLING(OK) PWR(HIGH)
PRE: AT(A, P1) FREE(P2)	**PRE**: AT(A, P), AT(OBJ,P) SMALL(OBJ), EMPTY(A)	**PRE**: AT(A, P), AT(OBJ,P) LARGE(OBJ, EMPTY(A))
EFF: ∼AT(A, P1) ∼FREE(P2), AT(A,P2) FREE(P1)	**EFF**: ∼EMPTY(A) ∼AT(OBJ,P), LOADED(A,OBJ) HALF-LOADED(A)	**EFF**: ∼EMPTY(A) ∼AT(OBJ,P), LOADED(A,OBJ) FULL-LOADED(A)

P takes a time unit to be executed (this is a common assumption, see e. g. [6]); finally, at each instant some observations are available (typically the system is just partially observable).

The problem of supervising the execution of P is decomposed into a set of sub-problems: the global plan P is decomposed in as many sub-plans as the agents in the team $\mathcal{T}$; each sub-plan P_i is assigned to agent i, which is responsible for executing and supervising the actions in P_i.

At each time instant t, an agent i receives a set of observations obs_t^i relevant for the status of agent i itself. Although in general the observations obs_t^i are not sufficient for precisely inferring the status of agent i, we assume that they are sufficient to evaluate: 1) the effects of action a_t^i agent i has executed at time t; 2) the preconditions of the next action a_{t+1}^i the agent i has to execute.

The partitioning of activities among agents described above does not guarantee that the sub-problems are completely independent of one another. In fact, we deal with the case where the agents in $\mathcal{T}$ cooperate to achieve a common global goal G. The cooperation among agents consists in the exchange of services, as will be formalized in the next section. Such a cooperative behavior among agents introduces causal dependencies among the actions the agents have to execute; therefore, when an action failure occurs in the sub-plan P_i (i.e., a *primary failure* occurs), the failure may affect the sub-plans of other agents, namely, the failure may propagate not only in P_i, but even in the global plan P. According to the traditional terminology (see e.g., [2]), the actions which fail as a direct or indirect consequence of a primary failure are called *secondary failures*.

Albeit the supervision of the execution of plan P is decomposed into a set of sub-problems, these sub-problems can not be solved independently of one another. In fact, the agents need to communicate during the supervision process, in order to determine, in a distributed way, a plan diagnosis which highlights the distinction between primary and secondary failures. In the following of the paper we point out when the agents have to communicate and which sort of data they exchange one another. Moreover, we formalize the relation between primary failures and agent diagnoses and show the critical role played by the agent diagnosis to determine the set of primary failures.

3   The Global Plan and the Local Plans

In this section we introduce a formal definition of the multi-agent plan P we have to monitor.

Atomic actions. As mentioned above, we assume that each action a in P is an atomic action, modeled in a STRIPS-like language by means of $PRE(a)$ (which denotes the set of atoms encoding the preconditions of action a) and $EFF(a)$ (the set of atoms representing the effects of the execution of a). The action model is supplemented by $ASMT(a)$: a set of assumptions on the health status of the functionalities required to complete a. In other words, the assumptions in $ASMT(a)$ indicates under which health conditions an agent is able to execute the action a. To exemplify this concept consider the action models showed in Table 1. These action models have been defined assuming that a team of agents have to operate in a blocks world domain; for example the action MOVE(A,P1,P2), requires that agent A moves from its current position P1 to the target position P2. To this end, the preconditions of the action requires that A is located in P1 and P2 must be *free* (i.e., no agent is located in $P2$). The effects of the action state that, after the execution of the MOVE, A is located in P2, which is no longer free, and P1 is now free. The set of assumptions state that the MOVE action is successfully executed by A when both the power and the mobility functionalities of A are in their nominal mode, i.e. *high* and *ok* respectively. These conditions of the health status are assumptions since in general there is no way of directly observing the actual health status of an agent. Conversely, the anomalous behavior of the action, when either mobility or power (or even both) are not nominal, is not modeled. Observe that the action model showed in Table 1 can be used by a planner to synthesize the global plan P.

Multi-agent plan. A partial order plan is traditionally defined (see e.g., [7]) as a directed acyclic graph POP=$\langle ACTS, E, C \rangle$, where $ACTS$ is the set of nodes representing the action instances the agents have to execute; E is a set of precedence links between actions, a precedence link $a \prec a'$ in E indicates that the action a must precede the execution of the action a'; C is a set of causal links of the form $l : a \xrightarrow{q} a'$; the link l indicates that the action a provides the action a' with the service q, where q is an atom occurring in the preconditions of a'. The class of multi-agent plans we deal with in the present paper is a subclass of the POP defined above. In fact, as in the POP case, we define P as the DAG $\langle ACTS, E, C \rangle$, where $ACTS$, E and C have the same meanings, but we introduce the following requirements:

  - Every action instance $a \in ACTS$ is assigned to a specific agent $i \in \mathcal{T}$.
  - All the actions assigned to the same agent i are totally ordered, i.e., for any pair of actions a and a' assigned to i, either a precedes a' or a' precedes a.
  - The access to the resources is ruled by causal links, where the offered service consists in relinquishing the resources.

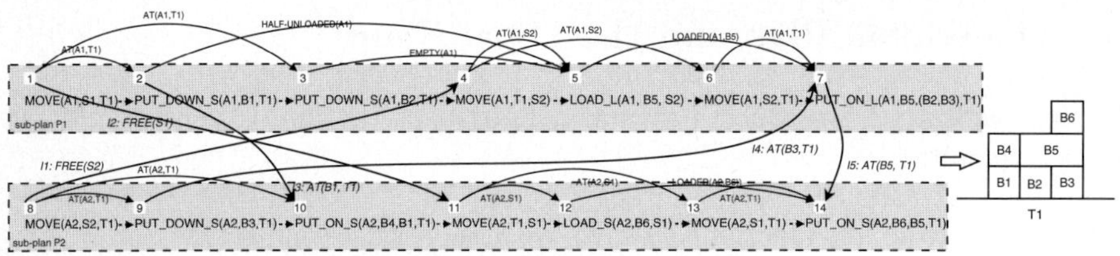

Fig. 1. The plan built by a POMP-like planner

A plan instance P, satisfying the above characteristics, can be synthesized by exploiting a planner similar to the POMP proposed by Boutilier et al. in [8].

Local Plans. The decomposition of the plan instance P is an easy task, which involves just the selection from P of all the actions an agent has to execute; formally, the sub-plan for agent i is the tuple $P_i = \langle\ ACTS_i, <_i, C_i, X_i^{in}, X_i^{out}\ \rangle$ where: $ACTS_i$ is the subset of actions in $ACTS$ that agent i has to execute; $<_i$ is a total order relation defined over the actions in $ACTS_i$; C_i is a set of causal links $a \xrightarrow{q} a'$ where both a and a' belong to $ACTS_i$; X_i^{in} is a set of *incoming* causal links where $a' \in ACTS_i$ and $a \in ACTS_j$ (i.e., a is assigned to another agent j); finally, X_i^{out} is a set of *outgoing* causal links (i.e., a belongs to $ACTS_i$ and a' to $ACTS_j$).

It is worth noting that the communication between two agents i and j is ruled by the presence of causal links defined between actions in P_i and P_j. More precisely, for each causal link $l \in X_i^{out}$, $l : a \xrightarrow{q} a'$ (where $a \in ACTS_i$ and $a' \in ACTS_j$), the agent i must communicate to j whether the service q has been achieved or not. Conversely, for every incoming causal link $l' \in X_i^{in}$, $l' : a' \xrightarrow{q} a$, the agent i has to wait a message from j conveying the successful (or unsuccessful) execution of a', and agent i is able to execute action a only when all the incoming services have been provided.

Therefore, although the supervision task is distributed among the agents, we limit the amount of communication by exploiting the structure of the global plan P. In fact the amount of messages the agents have to exchange is limited by the number of causal links; moreover, the agents need to inform one another just about the achievement or the failure of a service.

Running Example. In the paper we will use the following, simple example from the blocks world. Let us consider two agents $A1$ and $A2$, which have to cooperate to build a "wall" in a target position $T1$ (see right part of Figure 1; to this end the two agents can move a number of blocks initially located in two source positions $S1$ and $S2$. We distinguish between two type of blocks: *small* and *large*. In its nominal behavior each agent can carry at most two small blocks or a large one. The access to the source locations is constrained since just one agent at a time can load (unload) a block within them, on the contrary the access to the target $T1$ is not constrained, hence the two agents can be located simultaneously in $T1$. Table 1 reports the STRIPS-like definition of a sub-set of actions the agents can execute (for lack of space the definitions of the other actions are omitted).

Let us assume that at the initial time instant agent $A1$, located in $S1$, is loaded with B1 and B2; and agent $A2$, located in $S2$, is loaded with B3 and B4. Figure 1 shows the global plan produced by a POMP-like planner for achieving the goal (introduced above) of building the wall. The plan is a DAG where nodes correspond to actions and edges correspond to precedence (dashed) or causal (solid) links. The causal links are labeled with the services an action provides to another one, for example the causal link between actions $a5$ and $a7$ is labeled with the service LOADED(A1,B5), which is both one of the effects of the action $a5$ and one of the preconditions for the execution of action $a7$. The information associated with the causal link play a critical role in evaluating the effect of a failure: in fact, when the action $a5$ fails the action $a7$ fails too since one of its preconditions is not satisfied.

The dashed rectangles highlight the sub-plans assigned to the agents. It is easy to see that the sub-plans P_1 and P_2 have causal dependent actions; thereby a failure in P_1 (P_2) may have harmful effects in P_2 (P_1). To point out this fact let's assume that action $a1$ fails (primary failure) as a consequence of a fault. It is easy to see that this failure affects the whole plan since many actions, even assigned to agent $A2$, can no longer be executed (secondary failures).

4   Agent Status and Action Outcome

Since each agent i has to supervise the actions it is responsible for, agent i has to determine, at each time t, the outcome of the action a_t^i (i.e the action executed by i at time t), and its own health status after the execution of a_t^i.

Agent Status. The status of agent i is expressed in terms of a set of status variables VAR^i; in particular, this set of variables is partitioned into two subsets: OBS^i denotes the set of observable status variables (e.g., the agent *position*) and $NOBS^i$ represents the set of not observable status variables; to keep the discussion simple, we consider that a not observable status variable concerns the health status of an agent functionality (e.g., mobility or power), therefore in following the set $NOBS^i$ will be referred to as $HEALTH^i$.

Since agent i receives just partial observations about the changes occurring in the system, it is in general unable to precisely determine its own status; rather i can determine just a set of states after the execution of a_t^i, this set is known in literature as *belief state* and will be denoted as $\mathcal{B}_t^i$.

Extended Action Model. As mentioned above, the synthesis of the plan P can be performed by exploiting STRIPS-like action models, which consider only the nominal behavior of the actions. However, in order to supervise the execution of the actions in P_i, the agent i must have at disposal extended action templates, which model not only the nominal behavior of the actions, but also the actions behavior when faults occur. For such a modeling task we adopt a relational representation, which has been proved to be useful for the on-line monitoring and diagnosis of multi-agent systems (see [9]). In particular, this formalism is able to capture non deterministic effects of the action execution.

The extended model of an action a_t^i is a transition relation $\Delta(a_t^i)$, where every tuple $d \in \Delta(a_t^i)$ models a possible change in the status of agent i, which may occur while i is executing a_t^i. More precisely, each tuple d has the form $d = \langle s_{t-1}, fault, s_t \rangle$; where s_{t-1} and s_t represent two agent states at time $t-1$ and t respectively, each state is a complete assignment of values to the status variables VAR^i of agent i; $fault$ denotes the fault which occurs to cause a change of status from s_{t-1} to s_t (of course, in the transitions which model the nominal behavior $fault$ is empty). As commonly assumed in approaches to the diagnosis of Discrete Events Systems (see e.g. [2]), we assume that two faults can not occur simultaneously on the functionalities of the same agent. It follows, that an agent i can be struck by only one fault per time instant, however it can be affected by more than one faults over the time; moreover, the assumption allows the simultaneous occurrence of faults on different agents.

Table 2 shows the extended model of a MOVE action from a location $P1$ to a location $P2$; due to space reasons we show just a subsets of tuples of the transition relation $\Delta(\text{MOVE})$. Moreover, for sake of readability, the agent states are expressed just in the subset of status variables directly affected by the MOVE action, in particular they are: *position*, the position of the agent; *carried* the amount of load carried by the agent, this variable assumes values in the set *empty*, *half-loaded* and *full-loaded*; *pwr*, the power of the agent's battery, which can be *high* (the nominal mode) or *low* (a degraded mode) and *mobility*, the health status of the agent's mobility functionality which can be *ok* (nominal) or *bk* (i.e., broken, a faulty mode). Observe that, while the STRIPS model of the MOVE action just represents the nominal behavior of the MOVE action, assuming that both power and mobility are in their nominal mode; the corresponding extended model represents also how the MOVE action behaves in any combination of power and mobility modes, included the faulty ones.

The nominal behavior of the MOVE action is modeled by transition 1, the $*$ symbol (don't care) indicates that, when the agent's functionalities behave nominally, the actual carried load does not impact the outcome of the action. In our example the MOVE action can fail as a consequence of two types of faults: f-BRY and f-MOB. f-BRY affects the battery by reducing the level of power from the nominal *high* to the degraded *low*. An agent can complete a move action with battery power *low* iff the agent is not carrying any block or the agent is carrying a small block, the action fails otherwise (see transitions 2, 3 and 4). f-MOB affects the health status of the mobility functionality, which changes from the nominal *ok* to the anomalous *bk* (broken); under this health status there is no way to complete the move action (see transition 5).

Action Outcome. Since the actual execution of an action is threatened by the occurrence of unexpected events (e.g., faults), the outcome of an action may be not nominal. To keep the discussion simple we assume that each agent i observes, at each time instant t, the status variables in OBS^i; relying on these observations, the agent i can always determine the outcome of the last executed action a_t^i. This assumption can be relaxed, as we have shown in [10], by dealing with cases where the outcome of some actions cannot be univocally determined.

Table 2. The extended model of action `MOVE(A,P1,P2)`

| | s_{t-1} | | | | $fault$ | s_t | | | |
| | observables | | health variables | | | observables | | health variables | |
	position	carried	power	mobility		position	carried	power	mobility
1	P1	*	High	OK	null	P2	*	High	OK
2	P1	EMPTY	High	OK	f-BRY	P2	EMPTY	Low	OK
3	P1	HALF	High	OK	f-BRY	P2	HALF	Low	OK
4	P1	FULL	High	OK	f-BRY	P1	FULL	Low	OK
5	P1	*	High	OK	f-MOB	P1	*	High	BK

The outcome of an action is *succeeded* when all the effects of the action have been achieved, or *failed* otherwise. Since at each time instant t we may have to deal with an ambiguous belief states $\mathcal{B}_t^i$, we consider the action a_t^i as succeeded only when all the expected effects of action a_t^i hold in every state s included in $\mathcal{B}_t^i$; more formally.

Definition 1. *The outcome of the action a_t^i, executed by i at time t, is* succeeded *iff* $\forall q \in EFF(a_t^i)$, $\forall s \in \mathcal{B}_t^i$, $s \models q$; *i.e., iff all the atoms q in $EFF(a_t^i)$ are satisfied in every state s in $\mathcal{B}_t^i$.*

Of course, when we can not assert that action a_t^i is succeeded we assume that the action is failed.

5   On-Line Supervision of Plan Execution

Belief State estimation. In order to determine the outcome of action a_t^i, the agent i has to infer its own belief state $\mathcal{B}_t^i$. Essentially, inferring $\mathcal{B}_t^i$ corresponds to a prediction process, which can be formalized in terms of the Relational Algebra operators. In fact, besides the action model $\Delta(a_t^i)$, also the belief state $\mathcal{B}_t^i$ can be viewed as a relation where each tuple of $\mathcal{B}_t^i$ is a complete assignment of values to the status variables in VAR^i.

Definition 2. *Let $\mathcal{B}_{t-1}^i$ be the belief state of agent i at time $t-1$, and let $\Delta(a_t^i)$ be the action model of action a_t^i executed by i at time t; the belief state of agent i at time t is estimated as* $\mathcal{B}_t^i = \pi_{VAR_t^i}(\sigma_{obs_t^i}(\mathcal{B}_{t-1}^i \bowtie \Delta(a_t^i)))$

The join operator represents the prediction step: $\mathcal{B}_{t-1}^i \bowtie \Delta(a_t^i)$ has the effect of predicting all the possible states assumed by agent i after the execution of action a_t^i. This set of predictions is filtered out w.r.t. the observations agent i receives at time t by means of the selection $\sigma_{obs_t^i}$. Finally, the belief state at time t is obtained by means of the relational projection $\pi_{VAR_t^i}$, which captures all the status variables labeled with the current time t. Of course, the belief state $\mathcal{B}_0^i$ for agent i at time 0 is an input of the supervision task.

Agent Diagnosis. Once the agent belief state $\mathcal{B}_t^i$ has been estimated, agent i can determine the outcome of action a_t^i according to Definition 1. In case the outcome of a_t^i is failed, agent i has to infer a set of possible explanations for such an action failure; i.e., an agent diagnosis. Intuitively, the agent diagnosis for i is an assignment of values to the status variables in $HEALTH^i$. In the relational framework we propose, the agent diagnosis D_t^i for agent i, at time t, is defined as follows:

Definition 3. *Let $\mathcal{B}_t^i$ be the belief state of agent i at time t, the agent diagnosis D_t^i is $\pi_{HEALTH_t^i}(\mathcal{B}_t^i)$.*

Every tuple $d \in D_t^i$ is an assignment of values to the variables in $HEALTH^i$, moreover, according to Definition 2, every assignment d is consistent with the observations obs_t^i; hence, every tuple d is a possible explanation for the failure of action a_t^i.

Observe that the occurrence of at most one fault per agent at each time instant does not imply that the agent diagnosis $\mathcal{D}_t^i$ contains just one possible explanation: in fact, D_t^i includes in general more than one tuple since the variables in $HEALTH^i$ can not be directly observed and, as a consequence, the actual fault f occurred at time t may not be univocally determined.

In the following we denote as $\overline{d}$ the preferred explanation extracted from D_t^i. In this paper we assume that by exploiting the rank (see [11] for details on ranks) associated with the occurrence of faults, $\overline{d}$ can be univocally determined.

Plan Diagnosis. So far we have discussed how an agent is able to supervise the actions it executes and, in particular, how it can infer the health status of its own functionalities. The agent diagnosis is an important piece of information which can be exploited for anticipating the failure of other actions even if assigned to other agents. In fact the presence of causal links between actions introduces dependencies among sub-plans; therefore, the occurrence of a (primary) failure may cause the occurrence of other (secondary) failures. In our framework the set of primary failures is defined as:

Definition 4. *Given the failure of action a_t^i executed by agent i, we define the primary failures as*
$$primaryFailedActs_i = \{a \in ACTS_i | (a_t^i < a \lor a = a_t^i) \land ASMT(a) \cup \overline{d} \vdash \perp\}$$

where $\overline{d}$ is the preferred explanation extracted from D_t^i, and $ASMT(a)$ is the set of (nominal) health status assumptions for the functionalities used by agent i during the execution of action a.

Definition 4 states that the primary failures are, besides the failed action a_t^i, all those actions a that agent i has to execute in the future ($a_t^i < a$), and that can no longer be executed. In fact, in the preferred diagnosis $\overline{d}$, at least one functionality of agent i is not in the nominal health status required by $ASMT(a)$. Secondary failures are defined by taking into consideration the causal links in the plan according to the following definition.

Definition 5. *Given the global plan $P = \langle ACTS, E, C \rangle$ and the set primaryFailedActs$_i$ determined by agent i, the set of secondary failures secondaryFailedActs$_i = \{a \in ACTS$ such that*

$\exists$ *a causal link $l' : a' \xrightarrow{q'} a$, where $l' \in C$ and $a' \in primaryFailedActs_i$ or*

$\exists$ *a causal link $l'' : a'' \xrightarrow{q''} a$, where $l'' \in C$ and $a'' \in secondaryFailedActs_i\}$

Observe that, in order to single out the secondary failures in whole plan, the agents in the team have to cooperate. In particular, the propagation of a failure in the global plan is an iterative process during which the agents communicate one another the set of services which can longer not be provided.

In definitions 4 and 5 we have introduced the notion of plan diagnosis w.r.t. an agent i; however, these definitions can be extended to the more general case where the plan diagnosis considers all the agents in the team $\mathcal{T}$. More precisely, given the global plan P, it is possible to demonstrate that the plan diagnosis for P can be computed in distributed way as the pair $\langle primaryFailedActs, secondaryFailedActs \rangle$ where:

- $primaryFailedActs = \bigcup_{i \in \mathcal{T}} primaryFailedActs_i$
- $secondaryFailedActs = \bigcup_{i \in \mathcal{T}} secondaryFailedActs_i$.

Algorithm. Figure 2 shows the high-level algorithm agent i performs for supervising the execution of its own sub-plan P_i. The algorithm consists of a while cycle; at each iteration, which corresponds to a new time instant, agent i supervises the execution of action a_t^i, which is started only when the set $PRE(a_t^i)$ are satisfied. The process for estimating $\mathcal{B}_t^i$ has been represented in relational terms (line 07). The outcome of a_t^i is determined according to Definition 1 by the function **EvaluateOutcome** (line 09); to this end the conditions expressed in $EFF(a_t^i)$ must be expressed as a relation by the function **translate** (line 08). If the action outcome is *succeeded* the agent propagates the positive effects (line 11) by marking as succeeded all the causal links outgoing from a_t^i. This step may require that agent i notifies some other agents the successful completion of a_t^i. Conversely, when a_t^i fails, agent i infers the agent diagnosis D_t^i (line 11) and propagates the effects of the preferred diagnosis $\bar{d}$ to determine the set $primaryFailedActs_i$ according to Definition 4 (line 13). The set of secondary failures is determined by function **PropagateNegativeEffects** (line 14), which marks as failed all the causal links outgoing from a_t^i; possibly, during this step, the agent i notifies other agents about the failure of action a_t^i. Finally, the agent i invokes a **LocalRecovery** module, which is has to recover (if possible) the nominal execution of the local plan P_i from the failure of action a_t^i (see [12] for details on the local recovery process).

Concerning the correctness of the algorithm, the most critical point regards the process for estimating the current belief state $\mathcal{B}_t^i$. It is possible to demonstrate that the following property holds.

Property 1. At each time t, the belief state $\mathcal{B}_t^i$ estimated according to Definition 2 satisfies the following characteristics:

- $\mathcal{B}_t^i$ is consistent with the observations obs_t^i
- $\mathcal{B}_t^i$ is consistent with the belief state $\mathcal{B}_{t-1}^i$ previously estimated and with the extended model of action a_t^i
- $\mathcal{B}_t^i$ always contains the actual status of agent i at time t even after the occurrence of faults.

Due to space reasons the proof is omitted. Since Property 1 guarantees that the actual status of the agent i is always included in $\mathcal{B}_t^i$, we can conclude that the

```
PlanExecutionSupervision(B₀ⁱ, Pᵢ) {
  01 t = 0;
  02 while (true){   t = t + 1;
  03      aₜⁱ = ⟨get next action from Pᵢ⟩;
  04      if ( PRE(aₜⁱ) are not satisfied in Bₜ₋₁ⁱ) ⟨ execute WaitAction ⟩;
  05      else {  ⟨execute aₜⁱ⟩;
  06        obsₜⁱ = ⟨get current observations for agent i⟩;
  07        Bₜⁱ=Π_VARₜⁱ(σ_obsₜⁱ(Bₜ₋₁⋈Δ(aₜⁱ)));
  08        actionGoals=translate(EFF(aₜⁱ));
  09        outcome=EvaluateOutcome(Bₜⁱ, actionGoals);
  10        if (outcome is succeeded)PropagatePositiveEffects(Pᵢ, aₜⁱ);
  11        else{  Dₜⁱ=Π_HEALTHₜⁱ(Bₜⁱ);
  12          d̄=ExtractPreferredDiagnosis(Dₜⁱ);
  13          primaryFailedActsᵢ=PropagateDiagnosis(Pᵢ, d̄);
  14          secondaryFailedActsᵢ=PropagateNegativeEffects(Pᵢ, primaryFailedActsᵢ); } }
  15      if (primaryFailedActsᵢ ≠ ∅) ∨ (secondaryFailedActsᵢ ≠ ∅)
  16        LocalRecovery(Dₜⁱ, primaryFailedActsᵢ, secondaryFailedActsᵢ);    } }
```

Fig. 2. The algorithm agent i performs for supervising the execution of sub-plan P_i

agent diagnosis, extracted from B_t^i according to Definition 3, always includes the actual health status of agent i at time t: the algorithm does not lose solutions.

Regarding the computational analysis it is possible to demonstrate that, without considering the sizes of the involved relations, the computational complexity of a single iteration is polynomial in the number of operations (included the functions for propagating the positive and negative effects of an action outcome and the diagnoses). However, the complexity of some operations critically depends on the sizes of the involved relations (see e.g., the belief estimation step at line 07). In order to cope with this issue, in [9] we have shown that the monitoring and the diagnostic processes can be efficiently implemented by exploiting the symbolic formalism of the Ordered Binary Decision Diagrams (OBDDs); the experimental results reported in [9] show that the space and time complexities of the approach actually allow to perform on-line the supervision task.

Running example. Now let's go back to the blocks world example and let's assume that the action $a1$ (assigned to agent $A1$) fails. According to the formalization we have introduced, agent $A1$ infers, at time 1, the local diagnosis $D_1^{A1}=\{mobility=\ bk\ \lor\ power=low\}$ (see Table 2). Let's assume that the preferred explanation is $\bar{d}=\{power=low\}$ by taking into account the qualitative probabilities of faults encoded as ranks; in particular the occurrence of **F-BRY** is qualitatively more probable than the occurrence of **F-MOB** (a severe fault blocking of the mobility). Given $\bar{d}$, agent $A1$ determines the set of primary failures $primaryFailedActs_{A1}=\{a1,\ a4,\ a5,\ a6,\ a7\}$, in fact all these actions are directly affected by the preferred diagnosis $\bar{d}$ (in fact, the nominal behavior of these actions require that $power=high$, see the action models in Table 1). Finally, agent $A1$ infers the set of secondary failures $secondaryFailedActs_{A1}=\{a2,\ a3,\ a11,\ a12,\ a13,\ a14\}$. Observe that the set $secondaryFailedActs_{A1}$ is computed by means of a cooperation with agent $A2$.

Exploiting Diagnosis for Recovery. It is worth noting that the agent diagnosis and plan diagnosis are important pieces of information, which can be exploited for reducing the harmful effects of the failure of an action a_t^i. For example, the preferred explanation for the failure of action 1 is $\bar{d}=\{power=low\}$; i.e., the move action fails because agent $A1$ is *full loaded* and the power of its battery is *low*. However, such a fault does not prevent completely agent $A1$ from moving: in fact, the extended model of *move* states that agent $A1$ can move even if *power=low* and *carried* is *half loaded*. Therefore agent $A1$ can synthesize a recovery sub-plan involving two different travels: first $A1$ moves the small block B1 from S1 to T1 and then moves B2 in a subsequent step.

6   Discussion and Conclusion

While the supervision of dynamic component-based systems have been extensively investigated and a number of solutions have been developed (see e.g., [2,3]), just a few approaches have been proposed in the multi-agent scenario.

Kalech et al. [5] address the task of explaining the disagreements emerging in a team of cooperating agents in terms of *social diagnosis*. The approach presented in this paper is similar to the one described in [6], where Roos et al. propose a distributed approach for monitoring and diagnosing the execution of a multi-agent plan.

The solutions discussed in [6] are interesting but they rely on some simplifying assumptions. First of all, the actions are modeled as functions of their nominal behavior only, whereas the faulty action behaviors are unknown. As a consequence the monitoring of the plan execution is only partial: in fact, whenever an action fails, the monitoring is unable to predict the status of a portion of the system. Moreover, the notion of plan diagnosis, based just on the minimal set of failed actions, does not make evident the actual health status of the agents, i.e., an agent diagnosis.

In this paper, we propose an extension of the works by Roos et al., by introducing an extended model of the actions for capturing both the nominal and the anomalous action execution. Thereby the monitoring process we propose is complete since the status of the system is estimated even after the occurrence of a fault. Moreover, we have complemented the notion of plan diagnosis with the notion of agent diagnosis and we have pointed how the notion of agent diagnosis plays an important role in predicting which actions in the plan won't be executable as a consequence of the detected fault.

References

1. Birnbaum, L., Collins, G., Freed, M., Krulwich, B.: Model-based diagnosis of planning failures. In: Proc. AAAI90, pp. 318–323 (1990)
2. Pencolé, Y., Cordier, M.: A formal framework for the decentralised diagnosis of large scale discrete event systems and its application to telecommunication networks. Artificial Intelligence 164, 121–170 (2005)

3. Kurien, J., Nayak, P.: Back to the future for consistency-based trajectory tracking. In: Proc. AAAI00, pp. 370–377 (2000)
4. Carver, N., Lesser, V.: Domain monotonicity and the performance of local solutions strategies for cdps-based distributed sensor interpretation and distributed diagnosis. Journal of Autonomous Agents and Multi-Agent Systems 6, 35–76 (2003)
5. Kalech, M., Kaminka, G.: Diagnosing a team of agents: Scaling up. In: Proc. International Conference AAMAS05, pp. 249–255 (2005)
6. Roos, N., Witteveen, C.: Diagnosis of plan execution and the executing agent. In: Furbach, U. (ed.) KI 2005. LNCS (LNAI), vol. 3698, pp. 357–366. Springer, Heidelberg (2005)
7. Kambhampati, S.: Refinement planning as a unifying framework for plan synthesis. AI Magazine 18(2), 67–97 (1997)
8. Boutilier, C., Brafman, R.I.: Partial-order planning with concurrent interacting actions. Journal of Artificial Intelligence Research 14, 105–136 (2001)
9. Micalizio, R., Torasso, P., Torta, G.: On-line monitoring and diagnosis of a team of service robots: a model-based approach. AI Communications 19(4), 313–349 (2006)
10. Micalizio, R., Torasso, P.: Diagnosis of multi-agent plans under partial observability. In: Proc. 18th Int. Work. on Principles of Diagnosis (DX07), pp. 346–353 (2007)
11. Goldszmidt, M., Pearl, J.: Rank-based systems: a simple approach to belief revision, belief update, and reasoning about evidence and actions. In: Proc. KR92, pp. 661–672 (1992)
12. Micalizio, R., Torasso, P., Torta, G.: Intelligent supervision of plan execution in multi-agent systems. Int. Tran. on Systems Science and App. 1(3), 259–267 (2006)

Boosting the Performance of Iterative Flattening Search

Angelo Oddi[1], Nicola Policella[2], Amedeo Cesta[1], and Stephen F. Smith[3]

[1] ISTC-CNR, Rome, Italy
{name.surname}@istc.cnr.it
[2] European Space Agency, Darmstadt, Germany
nicola.policella@esa.int
[3] The Robotics Institute, Carnegie Mellon University, USA
sfs@cs.cmu.edu

Abstract. Iterative Flattening search is a local search schema introduced for solving scheduling problems with a makespan minimization objective. It is an iterative two-step procedure, where on each cycle of the search a subset of ordering decisions on the critical path in the current solution are randomly retracted and then recomputed to produce a new solution. Since its introduction, other variations have been explored and shown to yield substantial performance improvement over the original formulation. In this spirit, we propose and experimentally evaluate further improvements to this basic local search schema. Specifically, we examine the utility of operating with a more flexible solution representation, and of integrating iterative-flattening search with a complementary tabu search procedure. We evaluate these extensions on large benchmark instances of the Multi-Capacity Job-Shop Scheduling Problem (MCJSSP) which have been used in previous studies of iterative flattening search procedures.

1   Introduction

The integration of local search and heuristic procedures has produced interesting and efficient approaches to several complex scheduling problems. One such example is the *iterative flattening* (or IFLAT) algorithm proposed in [1] for solving scheduling problems with a makespan minimization objective. IFLAT consists of an iterative, two-step local search schema. Within each cycle of the search, a *relaxation step* is first applied to remove some search decisions from the current solution and create a partial solution. In this context, search decisions correspond to precedence constraints that must be added between pairs of activities to resolve resource conflicts, and the relaxation step limits its attention to those constraints residing on the solution's *critical path*. Starting from this new partial solution, the second *flattening step* then incrementally adds back new precedence constraints to regain a feasible solution. In the original work, IFLAT was shown to produce high-quality solutions in reasonable time on a challenging set of large Multi-Capacity Job-Shop Scheduling Problem MCJSSP benchmarks.

R. Basili and M.T. Pazienza (Eds.): AI*IA 2007, LNAI 4733, pp. 447–458, 2007.

More recently two works [2,3] have extended the results of the original paper through refinement of the basic IFLAT search schema. [2] identified an anomaly in IFLAT search and proposed a simple extension, which dramatically improved the quality of its schedules while preserving its computational efficiency. The key idea was to iterate the relaxation step multiple times, hence the name IFLATRELAX used in what follows. Additional improvements were obtained by [3] with an approach which follows the same schema of IFLAT but using different engines for both the flattening and the relaxation steps.

In the same spirit, this paper proposes and evaluates further extensions to the iterative flattening search. We focus specifically on two potential shortcomings of the basic approach: (1) the lack of temporal flexibility in the solutions that are manipulated by IFLAT and (2) the inability to perform a fine-grained neighborhood search in the vicinity of near-optimal solutions. To cope with the first issue, we explore the use of partial order schedules [4] as an underlying solution representation. To address the second issue, we introduce a complementary *tabu-seach* procedure to refine solutions found by IFLAT and propose two meta-heuristic search schemas for integrating the two procedures to achieve an appropriate interplay of diversification (exploration) and intensification (exploitation) in the overall search process. Eventually we evaluate these extensions against well-known MCJSSP benchmark sets and discuss further opportunities to extend and enhance the basic iterative.

2   The Iterative Flattening Schema

Before describing the iterative flattening approach it is necessary to introduce the modeling perspective on which this schema is based. In this a schedule S is represented as a directed graph $G_S(A, E)$. A is the set of activities specified in MCJSSP, plus a fictitious a_{source} activity temporally constrained to occur before all others and a fictitious a_{sink} activity temporally constrained to occur after all others. E is the set of precedence constraints defined between activities in A. Following a *Precedence Constraint Posting* (PCP) approach, the set E can be partitioned in two subsets, $E = E_{prob} \cup E_{post}$, where E_{prob} is the set of precedence constraints originating from the problem definition, and E_{post} is the set of precedence constraints posted to resolve resource conflicts. In general the directed graph $G_S(A, E)$ represents a set of temporal solutions. The set E_{post} is added in order to guarantee that at least one of those temporal solutions is also resource feasible. Given this description of the solution model, the Iterative Flattening search procedure [1] iterates the following two steps:

Relaxation step: first, a feasible schedule is relaxed into a possibly resource infeasible, but precedence feasible, schedule by removing some search decisions represented as precedence constraints between pair of activities;

Flattening step: second, a sufficient set of new precedence constraints is posted to re-establish a feasible schedule.

These two steps are executed until a better solution is found or a maximal number of iterations is executed. Figure 1 shows the *iterative flattening* algorithm in

iFlatRelax$(S, p_r, MaxFail, MaxRlxs)$
1. $S_{best} \leftarrow S$
2. $counter \leftarrow 0$
3. **while** $(counter \leq MaxFail)$ **do**
4.   Relax$(S, p_r, MaxRlxs)$
5. $Sol \leftarrow$ Flatten(S)
6.   **if** Mk$(Sol) <$ Mk(S_{best}) **then**
7. $S_{best} \leftarrow S$
8.   counter $\leftarrow 0$
9.   **else**
10.   counter $\leftarrow$ counter $+ 1$
11. **return** (S_{best})

Relax$(S, p_r, MaxRlxs)$
1. **for** 1 **to** $MaxRlxs$
2.   **forall** $(a_i, a_j) \in$ CP$(S) \cap E_{post}$
3.   **if** random$(0,1) < p_r$
4. $S \leftarrow S \setminus (a_i, a_j)$

Fig. 1. The iFlatRelax algorithm and the Relax procedure

detail. iFlatRelax takes as input four elements: (1) a starting solution S; (2) a value $p_r \in [0, 1]$ designating the percentage of precedence constraints $pc_i \in E_{post}$ on the critical path to be removed; (3) a positive integer $MaxFail$ which specifies the maximum number of non-makespan-improving moves that the algorithm will tolerate before terminating; and (4) a positive integer $MaxRlxs$ which specifies the maximum number of relax iterations to be performed in the relaxation step. Note that it is the value of this last parameter that distinguishes between the approaches taken in [1] and [2] respectively (see below). Returning to the algorithm iFlatRelax described in Figure 1, after initialization (Steps 1-2), a solution is repeatedly modified within the while loop (Steps 3-10) by the application of the Relax and Flatten procedures. In the case that a better makespan solution is found (at Step 6), the new solution is stored in S_{best} and the *counter* is reset to 0. Otherwise, if no improvement is found in $MaxFail$ moves, the algorithm terminates and returns the best solution found. The rest of this section describes the relaxation and the flattening steps in more detail.

Relaxation. The relaxation step is based on the concept of *critical path*. A *path* in $G_S(A, E)$ is a sequence of activities $a_1, a_2, \ldots, a_k$, such that, $(a_i, a_{i+1}) \in E$ with $i = 1, 2, \ldots, (k-1)$. The length of a path is the sum of the activities processing times and a *critical path* is a path from a_{source} to a_{sink} which determines the solution's makespan. Any improvement in makespan will necessarily require change to some subset of precedence constraints situated on the *critical path*, since these constraints collectively determine the solution's current makespan. Following this observation, the relaxation step introduced in [1] is designed to retract some number of posted precedence constraints on the solution's critical path. Figure 1 shows also the Relax procedure. Steps 2-4 consider the set of posted precedence constraints $(pc_i \in E_{post})$, which belong to the current critical path $CP(S)$. A subset of these constraints is randomly selected and then removed from the current solution. Step 1 represents the crucial difference between the approaches of [1] and [2]. In the former approach Steps 2-4 are performed only once (i.e., $MaxRlxs = 1$), whereas in [2] these steps are iterated several times (from 2 to 6). In practice the new critical path of S is computed at each iteration. Notice that this path can be completely different from the previous one. This allows the relaxation step to also take into account those paths that have a length very close to the critical path one.

Flattening. The flattening step used in [1] is inspired by prior work on the Earliest Start Time Algorithm (ESTA) from [5]. ESTA was designed to address more general, multi-capacity scheduling problems with generalized precedence relations between activities (i.e., corresponding to metric separation constraints with minimum and maximum time lags). This algorithm is a variant of a class of PCP scheduling procedures, characterized by a two-phase, solution generation process. First step is *to construct an infinite capacity solution*. The current problem is formulated as an STP [6] temporal constraint network[1] where temporal constraints are modeled and satisfied (via constraint propagation) but resource constraints are ignored, yielding a time feasible solution that assumes infinite resource capacity. The second phase consists instead in *leveling resource demand by posting precedence*. Resource constraints are super-imposed by projecting "resource demand profiles" over time. Detected resource conflicts are then resolved by iteratively posting simple precedence constraints between pairs of competing activities. For further details on the flattening procedure the reader should refer to the original references.

3   Extensions to Iterative Flattening Search

The concept of Iterative Flattening introduced in [1] is quite general and provided an interesting new basis for designing more sophisticated and effective local search procedures for scheduling optimization. The IFLATRELAX procedure proposed in [2] is a nice example of an IFLAT extension which obtains substantial improvements over its original version. This section describes further extensions to the iterative flattening search schema based on two possible *drawbacks*.

A first potential shortcoming is the lack of temporal flexibility in the initial solution provided to seed IFLATRELAX. Previous work has used ESTA as an initial solution generator and, as indicated earlier, ESTA only guarantees that the earliest start time solution (ESS) is resource feasible. In fact, the effectiveness of the IFLATRELAX procedure relies on finding new orderings of activities such that an increasingly more compact solution is found on each cycle. The greater the flexibility, the higher the probability that new start times for relaxed activities can be found on a given *relax-and-flatten* cycle that reduce the overall makespan. A second possible drawback is the lack of an ability to conduct a *fine-grained* search when a near-optimal solution is generated by IFLAT. In fact, due to its

---

[1] In a STP (Simple Temporal Problem) network we make the following representational assumptions: temporal variables (or time-points) represent the start and end of each activity, and the beginning and end of the overall temporal horizon; distance constraints represent the duration of each activity and separation constraints between activities including simple precedences.

random behavior, the procedure is unlikely to be able to explore *close* neighbors of a near-optimal solution, in order to further improve it. In the following subsections we propose two extensions to address each of these two potential limitations.

3.1   Introducing Partial Order Schedules

The first extension of the search schema, aimed at increasing the temporal flexibility of solutions generated during the flattening step, is to substitute the use of Partial Order Schedules (POS) [5,4] for the solutions produced by ESTA. Both types of the solutions are based on a graph representation. The difference is that while ESTA solutions guarantee that at least one of the temporal solutions they represent is also resource feasible, a POS guarantees that *all* delineated temporal solutions are also resource feasible. The use of a POS in general increases the possibilities for rearranging relaxed activities.

The common thread underlying a POS is the characteristic that activities which require the same resource units are linked via precedence constraints into precedence *chains*. Given this structure, each constraint becomes more than just a simple precedence. It also represents a *producer-consumer* relation, allowing each activity to know the precise set of predecessors that will supply the units of resource it requires for execution. In this way, the resulting network of chains can be interpreted as a flow of resource units through the schedule; each time an activity terminates its execution, it passes its resource unit(s) on to its successors. It is clear that this representation is flexible if and only if there is temporal slack that allows chained activities to move "back and forth". Polynomial methods for producing a POS from an input solution represented as a precedence graph (or equivalently as a set of start times) have been introduced in [5,4]. Given an input solution, a transformation method, named *chaining*, is defined that proceeds to create sets of chains of activities. This operation is accomplished over three steps: (1) all the previously posted leveling constraints are removed form the input partial order; (2) the activities are sorted by increasing activity earliest start times; (3) for each resource and for each activity a_i (according to the increasing order of start times), one or more predecessors a_j are chosen, which supplies the units of resource required by a_i – a precedence constraint (a_i, a_j) is posted for each predecessor a_j. The last step is iterated until all the activities are linked by precedence chains.

Having a flexible solution is not the only benefit in considering the use of partial order schedules. A second property that appears to be relevant is the reduction in the number of additional precedence constraints that must be posted to obtain a solution: Given a problem with n activities to be scheduled, the number of constraints appearing in the solution is always $O(n)$. This because the chaining procedure creates POSs with only the "necessary" precedence constraints, and eliminates all "redundant" constraints. The removal of redundant precedence constraints tends to intensify the effect of the IFLAT relaxation step in the IFLAT procedure. More solutions are accessible at each flattening cycle, because the removal of redundant constraints increases possibilities for rearranging relaxed activities.

This intuition is confirmed in the experimental section of the paper, where we see how the use of partial order schedules as input allows the iterative flattening search to find better quality solutions in comparison to the procedure proposed in [2]. It is worth noting that although [3] uses the concept of POS, it uses them solely to overcome the natural lack of flexibility of fixed time solutions and to apply a large neighborhood search schema.

3.2 Meta-heuristics for Fine-Grained Exploration

A second potential drawback of the basic IFLATRELAX procedure is its lack of an ability to conduct a *fine-grained* search when a near-optimal solution is generated. In fact, due to its random behavior, the procedure is actually unlikely to explore *close* neighbors of a near-optimal solution, and hence will miss opportunities to further improve it before moving on to another region of the space. In this section we describe a complementary extension to designed to overcome this structural drawback of IFLATRELAX. Inspired by the well-known principle in local search that advocates interleaved *diversification* and *intensification* of the search over time (e.g., see [7]), we propose a meta-heuristic search strategy that couples the IFLATRELAX procedure with a complementary *tabu-search* procedure. By its nature, IFLATRELAX tends to promote diversification, emphasizing exploration of different subspaces of the search on successive cycles. Introduction of the tabu search procedure, alternatively, provides a mechanism for exploitation of good solutions found by IFLATRELAX, intensifying the search in the neighborhood of such solutions and maximizing the chances of reaching local optima in this particular subspace. To enable integration the tabu search procedure is designed to operate, like IFLATRELAX, with a POS solution representation. We refer to this meta-heuristic search schema for coupling IFLATRELAX and tabu search as METAFLAT. In the subsections below, we first describe the tabu search procedure that we have developed for this purpose and then summarize the ways in which these two components have been integrated.

A Tabu Search Procedure on Partial Order Schedules. To complement IFLATRELAX's randomized search behavior, we combine it, in a larger meta-schema, with a tabu search algorithm to enable fine-grained exploration in the neighborhood of near-optimal solutions discovered by IFLAT. In brief, tabu search is a local search procedure that proceeds by iteratively moving from a given current solution S to a new solution S' in the neighborhood of S, until some stopping criterion has been satisfied. For any current solution S, a set of moves m are applied to S to define the neighborhood of S of interest, and then the neighbor S_i with the best objective value (in our case the S_i with the smallest makespan) is selected as the new solution S'. The move leading to the best neighbor is then performed, and a new neighborhood is then calculated and searched to find a new best neighbor S_{i+1}. To hedge against getting trapped in local optima, the procedure modifies its neighborhood structure as the search progresses. This is accomplished by maintaining the set of most recently visited solutions in a *tabu list*, and forbidding selection of a neighbor that has been visited within the past $MaxSt$ moves (where $MaxSt$ is the length of the tabu-list).

The tabu search procedure we have developed can be seen as an extension of the algorithm first proposed in [8] for Job Shop Scheduling Problems (JSSP). The tabu search procedure is designed to operate on the directed graph $G(A, E)$ representation of a solution (schedule), with analogous definitions of *path, length* of a path and *critical path* assumed in the previous sections. In particular, we consider a POS form for the input solutions, such that for each resource r_k with capacity c_k, we assume the activities partitioned in a set of c_k different chains $chain_1, chain_2, \ldots, chain_k$.

Our *tabu search* algorithm interleaves two types of moves in searching for a minimum makespan solution: *vertical moves* and *horizontal moves* (see Fig. 2). A *vertical move* on a resource r_k is defined as the movement of an activity a_m on a *critical path* from one $chain_i$ to another $chain_j$ (Fig. 2(a)). We use a heuristic criterion to determine where in $chain_j$ to insert a_m. For each pair of consecutive activities (a_i, a_{i+1}) in $chain_j$, we compute a penalty function which estimates the increase in the solution's makespan if a_m is inserted between a_i and a_{i+1}, and the insertion point with the minimum penalty

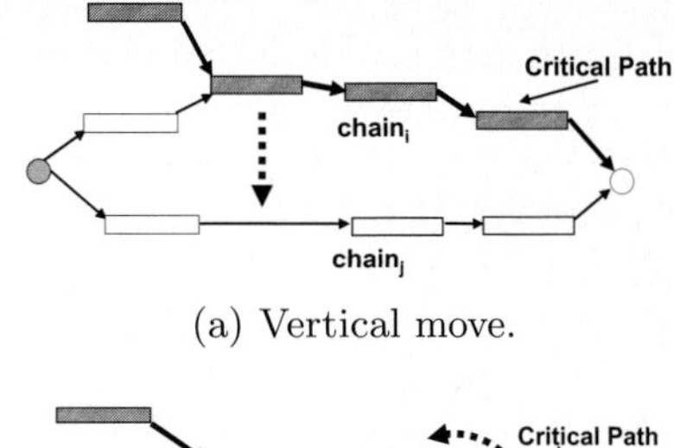

(a) Vertical move.

(b) Horizontal move.

Fig. 2. Tabu search moves

is chosen. Alternatively, a *horizontal move* on a resource r_k is defined as the swap of the execution order of a pair of consecutive activities (a_i, a_j) belonging to the same chain and *critical path* (Fig. 2(b)). Our implementation of horizontal moves directly exploits the results introduced in [8] concerning neighborhood definition in the case of unit capacity problems. It is worth noting that by applying the two types of move to a POS we still obtain a partial order schedule. Hence, the POS-form for a solution is crucial to preserving solution feasibility after a move.

The tabu search algorithm takes as input the initial type of move from which to start (*init-move*), the *tabu-list* length $MaxSt$ and two integer parameters: max_{intrlv} and max_{iter}. These parameters respectively designate the maximum number of interleaving steps between moves of each type without makespan improvements and the maximum number of move steps of a given move type without further makespan improvement. In practice, the algorithm alternates the use of the two types of moves and each time it changes type, restarts from the best solution found with the previous type of move.

Interleaving Iterative Flattening and Tabu Search. We have defined two possible alternatives for interleaving the IFLATRELAX method and the tabu search procedure . A first approach, called *serial integration*, simply executes IFLATRELAX and tabu search algorithms in sequence, submitting the best solution found in the first step to a tabu-search session for further improvement. In this case the tabu search procedure works as a classical *intensification* step within a meta-heuristic schema by focusing more intently on a region close to the best solution found by the previous IFLATRELAX step. A second approach, called *loop integration*, iteratively applies the following two steps until a termination condition is met:

1. the IFLATRELAX procedure takes as input a solution S (the initial solution or the output of the tabu search): with probability p it returns the last solution found S_{last}; with probability $(1 - p)$ the best solution found S^*;
2. the output of the previous step becomes the input of the tabu search procedure: with probability p it returns the last solution found in the local search procedure; with probability $(1 - p)$ the best solution found.

The probability p works as a *noise* mechanism, to avoid the circumstance where a near optimal solution *circulates* in the loop without any improvement. In fact, it is possible that a solution S cannot be improved either by the IFLAT algorithm or by the tabu search algorithm. When we compose the two basic strategies (IFLAT and Tabu Search) in loop integration, by default each strategy returns the best solution found. As the makespan decreases, the probability that a component returns the input solution, as the best one, becomes increasingly higher. The noise p promotes restarting from different solutions and thus controls the interplay between search intensification and diversification. In fact, when both component strategies return the best solution found, the search tends to be more localized in a subregion of the search space (intensification). Whereas, in the case one of the two components returns last solution found, the search tends to move toward another region of the search space (diversification).

4   The MCJSSP Scheduling Problem and Test Sets

We consider the Multi-Capacity Job-Shop Scheduling Problem, MCJSSP, as a basis for evaluating the performance of our search procedures. This problem involves synchronizing the use of a set of resources $R = \{r_1 \ldots r_m\}$ to perform a set of jobs $J = \{j_1 \ldots j_n\}$ over time. The processing of a job j_i requires the execution of a sequence of m activities $\{a_{i_1} \ldots a_{i_m}\}$, each a_{ij} has a constant processing time p_{ij} and requires the use of a single unit of resource $r_{a_{ij}}$ for its entire duration. Each resource r_j is required only once in a job and can process at most c_j activities at the same time ($c_j \geq 1$). A *feasible solution* to a MCJSSP is any temporally consistent assignment to the activities' start times which does not violate resource capacity constraints. An *optimal solution* is a feasible solution with minimal overall duration or makespan. Generally speaking, MCJSSP has the same structure as JSSP but involves multi-capacitated resources instead of unit-capacity resources. For our analysis, we use the benchmarks introduced in [9]. They consist of four sets of problems which are derived from the 40 Lawrence's job-shop scheduling problems LA1-LA40 [10] by increasing the number of activities and the capacity of the resources.

Set A: *LA1-10x2x3* (problems from LA1 to LA10, with resource capacity duplicated and triplicated). 5 problems each of sizes[2] 20x5(2), 30x5(3), 30x5(2),
45x5(3).

Set B: *LA11-20x2x3.* 5 problems each of sizes 40x5(2), 60x5(3), 20x10(2),
30x10(3).

Set C: *LA21-30x2x3.* 5 problems each of sizes 30x10(2), 45x10(3), 40x10(2),
60x10(3).

Set D: *LA31-40x2x3.* 5 problems each of sizes 60x10(2), 90x10(3), 30x15(2),
45x15(3).

We observe that the proposed benchmark set still represents a challenging benchmark for comparing algorithms. In fact, (a) in relatively few instances they cover
a wide range of problem sizes; (b) they also provide a direct basis for comparative
evaluation. In fact, as noted in [9], one consequence of the problem generation
method is that the optimal makespan for the original JSSP is also a tight upper
bound for the corresponding MCJSSP (Lawrence upper bounds). Hence, even if
for many instances there are known better solutions, distance from these upper-
bound solutions can provide a useful measure of solution quality.

5   Experimental Results

The evaluation has been performed in two phases. A first, explorative, phase
evaluates the effect of the *components* described in the previous sections. In this
phase we work only with the Set C benchmark. This set is a representative subset of instances ranging from 300 to 600 activities. A second phase then compares
the best performing procedures from the first phase with current best MCJSSP
benchmark results in a more CPU intensive test. All algorithms are implemented
in Allegro Common Lisp, and all experiments were run on a P4 processor 1.8
GHz under Windows XP.

Explorative comparison. We have defined a progression of extended strategies with respect to the previous best IFLATRELAX [2]. In particular they are
defined as follows:

1. IFLATRELAX-pos: this variant augments IFLATRELAX with a POS representation of the input solution;
2. METAFLAT-serial: in this configuration, the best solution found by IFLA-
   TRELAX-pos is serialized with the tabu search algorithm;
3. METAFLAT-loop: this variant interleaves IFLATRELAX-pos-tl with the tabu
   search procedure in a loop integration mode.

In running the first phase experiments, the following settings were used for IFLA-
TRELAX: $p_r = 0.2$, $MaxFail = 400$, $MaxRlxs = 6$. The Tabu Search parameters were set as follows: *tabu-list*'s length $MaxSt = 9$, *init-move= 'vertical'*,

---

[2] Using the notation #jobs × #resources (resource capacity).

$max_{intrlv} = 1$ and $max_{iter} = 50$. The noise value for the strategy METAFLAT-loop was set to $p = 0.2$. We finally imposed a timeout of 1000 seconds for each instance of the Set C and for each composite strategy. It is worth noting how we have implemented the previous three strategies in order to met the imposed CPU bounds. In the case of the strategy METAFLAT-loop, the procedure executes the loop until the time bound is reached. For the other three strategies, we adopt the same restarting schema used in previous works [1,2]. In the case a first run finishes before the imposed time limit, the random procedure restarts from the initial solution until the time bound is reached. At the end, the best solution found is returned.

Table 1 compares on the Set C the basic IFLATRELAX with the alternative strategies described above. The column *Algorithm* represents the algorithmic variant, the column $\Delta LWU_\%$ represents the average percentage deviation from the

Table 1. Comparative performance on Set C

Algorithm	$\Delta LWU_\%$	$\Delta iFlat_\%$
IFLATRELAX	4.01	0.0
IFLATRELAX-pos	3.61	0.37
METAFLAT-serial	2.99	0.97
METAFLAT-loop	2.80	1.16

Lawrence upper bound [10], and finally, the column $\Delta iFlat_\%$, represents the percentage improvement over the original IFLATRELAX algorithm. The results shown in Table 1 give a first empirical evidence to the hypotheses described in the previous sections. In fact, the results show that all methods improve on the base IFLATRELAX algorithm. In particular, the simple use of a partial order schedule (POS) as input solution for IFLATRELAX, improves the previous approach described in [2] from 4.01% to 3.61%. This is because a partial order schedule entails a reduced number of redundant precedence constraints in the input precedence graph with respect to the one produced by ESTA. This different shape of the solution tends to intensify the effect of the relaxation step within the IFLATRELAX procedure and increases the degrees of freedom in rearranging the relaxed activities. Note also that the introduction of the tabu search procedure, also produces a rather interesting further improvement to 2.99%. Finally, as might be expected, the best performance (2.80%) is obtained with the METAFLAT-loop. This result confirms the general principle adopted in meta-heuristic search to interleave diversification and intensification. For this reason this variant was selected for the intensive experiments of the next phase.

Intensive evaluation. In the second phase of the experiments, we compared IFLATRELAX-pos, METAFLAT-loop, and the *STRand* algorithm introduced in [3], which has obtained the best current results on these benchmark problems. In this phase, the following settings were adopted for the IFLATRELAX procedure: $p_r = 0.2$, $MaxFail = 1000$, $MaxRlxs = 6$ and a timeout of 8000 seconds for each instance. For the tabu search procedure we preserved the same parameters as before. It is worth remarking that the selection of the values of these parameters was not random, but rather the result of a set of preliminary exploratory runs.

Table 2. $\Delta LWU_\%$ values on the complete benchmark

Algorithm	Set A	Set B	Set C	Set D	All
IFLATRELAX-pos	-0.06	-1.38	1.19	0.52	0.07
METAFLAT-loop	-0.07	-1.68	0.69	0.26	-0.2
STRand	-0.28	-2.04	-0.71	-0.22	-0.81

Table 2 shows the figures of the intensive evaluation. For each algorithm we present the $\Delta LUW_\%$ values obtained for all four benchmarks and the cumulative results. The results in the table show that both extended methods introduced, IFLATRELAX-pos and METAFLAT-loop, outperform the original procedure. In fact, although in [2] the authors use a more intensive search, the average $\Delta LWU_\%$ is only about 1%, which is significantly higher than the -0.2% obtained with our extensions. In comparison to the *STRand* procedure, neither IFLATRELAX-pos and METAFLAT-loop achieve the level of performance of the STRand procedure [3], which currently maintains the best performance on the MCJSSP benchmarks. However in this case it is worth again noting that while this approach shares the same search schema of IFLATRELAX it uses different components to implement the flattening and the relaxation steps. Additional analysis is needed to assess the real difference between METAFLAT-loop and STRand, given that the results of the latter are from the original paper and take advantage of an implementation built on top of the ILOG suite. One of our next steps will be to implement STRand algorithm within our algorithmic framework (written in Common Lisp), in particular to compare the performance of the SetTimes algorithm – a description of this algorithm can be found in [3] – used in place of ESTA within STRrand. Moreover we expect that the STRand procedure may benefit from one or more of the same extensions that we have introduced into METAFLAT-loop.

6   Conclusions and Future Work

In this paper we have explored a set of extensions to the IFLAT search procedure. IFLAT is a local search procedure for solving large-scale scheduling problems with a makespan minimization objective criterion [1,2]. The extensions presented were motivated by two potential limitations in the IFLAT algorithm: (1) the lack of flexibility in the initial seed solution, and (2) the inability of IFLAT procedure to explore the close neighborhood of a near-optimal solution for purposes of further improvement. The proposed extensions were found to significantly improve the performance of the reference strategies on MCJSSP benchmark problems, and these results give first experimental evidence of the effectiveness of coupling tabu search concepts and procedures with iterative flattening search. Further study will be necessary to clearly understand the effectiveness of the algorithms proposed, especially with regard to the best results available in the current literature and given by STRand [3]. However, we believe that the proposed extensions are quite general and can be also usefully used within the STRand algorithm. There are further directions for future research. One particular interest will be the exploration of alternative approaches to integrating iterative flattening and tabu search. In this regard, we believe a Back Jumping Tracking schema [8], where search is restarted from promising solutions accumulated during the search, holds particular promise.

Acknowledgments. Amedeo Cesta, Angelo Oddi and Nicola Policella's work is partially supported by MIUR (Italian Ministry for Education, University and Research) under the project VINCOLI E PREFERENZE (PRIN). Stephen F. Smith's work is supported in part by the National Science Foundation under contract #9900298, by the Department of Defense Advanced Research Projects Agency under contract # FA8750-05-C-0033 and by the CMU Robotics Institute.

References

1. Cesta, A., Oddi, A., Smith, S.F.: Iterative Flattening: A Scalable Method for Solving Multi-Capacity Scheduling Problems. In: AAAI/IAAI, 17th National Conference on Artificial Intelligence, pp. 742–747 (2000)
2. Michel, L., Van Hentenryck, P.: Iterative Relaxations for Iterative Flattening in Cumulative Scheduling. In: ICAPS'04. Proceedings of the 14th International Conference on Automated Planning & Scheduling, pp. 200–208 (2004)
3. Godard, D., Laborie, P., Nuitjen, W.: Randomized Large Neighborhood Search for Cumulative Scheduling. In: ICAPS'05. Proceedings of the 15th International Conference on Automated Planning & Scheduling, pp. 81–89 (2005)
4. Policella, N., Smith, S.F., Cesta, A., Oddi, A.: Generating Robust Schedules through Temporal Flexibility. In: ICAPS'04. Proceedings of the 14th International Conference on Automated Planning & Scheduling, pp. 209–218 (2004)
5. Cesta, A., Oddi, A., Smith, S.: Profile Based Algorithms to Solve Multiple Capacitated Metric Scheduling Problems. In: AIPS-98. Proceedings of the 4th International Conference on Artificial Intelligence Planning Systems, pp. 214–223 (1998)
6. Dechter, R., Meiri, I., Pearl, J.: Temporal constraint networks. Artificial Intelligence 49, 61–95 (1991)
7. Blum, C., Roli, A.: Metaheuristics in combinatorial optimization: Overview and conceptual comparison. ACM Comput. Surv. 35(3), 268–308 (2003)
8. Nowicki, E., Smutnicki, C.: A Fast Taboo Search Algorithm for the Job Shop Problem. Management Science 42, 797–813 (1996)
9. Nuijten, W., Aarts, E.: A Computational Study of Constraint Satisfaction for Multiple Capacitated Job Shop Scheduling. European Journal of Operational Research 90(2), 269–284 (1996)
10. Lawrence, S.: Resource Constrained Project Scheduling: An Experimental Investigation of Heuristic Scheduling Techniques (Supplement). Technical report, Graduate School of Industrial Administration, Carnegie Mellon University (1984)

Real-Time Trajectory Generation for Mobile Robots

Alireza Sahraei[1], Mohammad Taghi Manzuri[1], Mohammad Reza Razvan[2],
Masoud Tajfard[1], and Saman Khoshbakht[1]

[1] Department of Computer Engineering, Sharif University of Technology
[2] Department of Mathematical Sciences, Sharif University of Technology

Abstract. This paper presents a computationally effective trajectory generation algorithm for omni-directional mobile robots. This method uses the Voronoi diagram to find a sketchy path that keeps away from obstacles and then smooths this path with a novel use of Bezier curves. This method determines velocity magnitude of a robot along the curved path to meet optimality conditions and dynamic constrains using Newton method. The proposed algorithm has been implemented on real robots, and experimental results in different environments are presented.

1   Introduction

The path planning problem is as old as mobile robotics, but does not have a universal solution yet. Path planning is the process of calculating a path for a mobile robot which is usually required in real time applications. The problem of fast generating a trajectory for a mobile robot is usually required in robotic applications such as Robocup or other robot soccer games. In these applications the generated trajectory should meet some dynamic constraints of the robot and make the robot to reach the destination in the shortest possible time. The robot should avoid obstacles as well as satisfying dynamic constraints.

Many theoretical researchers worked on this problem under different criteria such as minimum Euclidean distance [2], Manhattan distance [3], link distance (number of rotations) [5], and many other distance metrics. A variety of problems such as path planning for pursuing a moving target (see [6] and [7]), parking a car-like robot [2], and etc. were also examined.

Mobile robots could be built car-like, differential, omni-directional, and in many other models. For each kind, many algorithms have been developed [2]. This paper solves the problem of motion planning for omni-directional mobile robots. This kind of vehicles provides superior maneuvering capability compared to the car-like or differential ones. They are able to move in any direction and spin as they move. An omni-directional mobile robot usually consists of three sets of wheel assemblies equally placed at 120 degrees from one another. Each of these wheels transfers the motor force in one direction and move freely in the orthogonal direction.

Practical motion planning usually deals with velocities, accelerations, and dynamic constraints. Trajectory planning is the extension of path planning to

R. Basili and M.T. Pazienza (Eds.): AI*IA 2007, LNAI 4733, pp. 459–470, 2007.

consider velocity. The trajectory control builds a geometric path and then uses feedback control to track the path. The two main goals in most robotic applications are time optimality and obstacle avoidance of generated trajectories. Reaching to the goal without collisions is usually much more important than time optimality. For this purpose dynamic capabilities of the robot must be considered (see [1], [8], [9] and [10]).

Motion planning requires real-time algorithm in dynamic environments; therefore many real-time approaches developed in this field. The potential field method is widely used for autonomous mobile robot path planning due to its elegant mathematical analysis and simplicity. The potential field is a function whose gradient is used to calculate a torque applied to the robot motors, enforcing it to reach its goal while avoiding obstacles. This function depends on the destination position and the geometry of the obstacles around the robot (see [15], [16] and [17]).

Most researches have been focused on solving motion planning problems considering time optimality or obstacle avoidance, separately. This paper proposes a new algorithm for motion planning of mobile robots which avoids obstacles and also satisfies time optimality. The resulting trajectory keeps the robot as far away from obstacles as possible to eliminate the probability of obstacle collision. This algorithm is designed to work real-time in dynamic environments. However most motion planning algorithms have time complexities as a function of obstacles complexity (i.e. number of vertices of all obstacles), the proposed algorithm runs in the time complexity of $O(N \log N)$ where N is the number of obstacles. Apparently N is much less than complexity of obstacles. Section 2 describes dynamic constraints of an omni-directional vehicle. In section 3 a new algorithm is presented to generate a near optimal trajectory. Some details in implementation of the proposed algorithm are presented in section 4. Section 5 shows the experimental result in different environments. Finally conclusions are reached in section 6.

2   Dynamic Constrains

Generally, the optimal control problem for vehicles is considered with either velocity bound or acceleration bound, not both. Kalmar-Nagy et al. described an accurate model that relates the amount of torque available for acceleration to the speed of a three wheeled omni-directional vehicle in [1]. This section is based on the results of [1]. Fig. 1 shows the bottom view of a three wheeled mobile robot.

Reference [1] shows that in such a vehicle the motor velocities are linear functions of the velocity and the angular velocity of the robot.

$$\begin{pmatrix} v_1 \\ v_2 \\ v_3 \end{pmatrix} = \begin{pmatrix} -\sin\theta & \cos\theta & L \\ -\sin(\pi/3 - \theta) & -\cos(\pi/3 - \theta) & L \\ \sin(\pi/3 + \theta) & -\cos(\pi/3 + \theta) & L \end{pmatrix} \begin{pmatrix} \dot{x} \\ \dot{y} \\ \dot{\theta} \end{pmatrix} \tag{1}$$

where L is the distance of the drive unit from the robot center of mass and θ is the angle of rotation illustrated in Fig. 2. This model describes our vehicle dynamic restriction as follows:

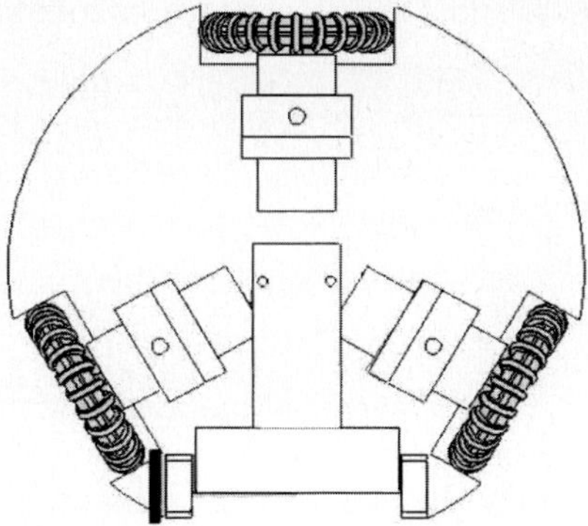

Fig. 1. Bottom view of a three wheeled omni-directional vehicle

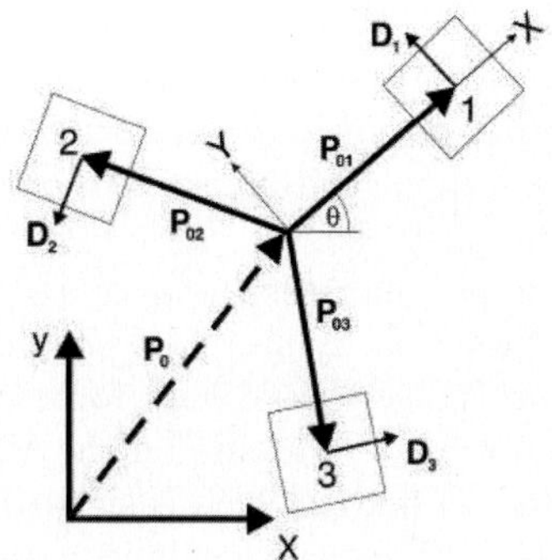

Fig. 2. Geometry of the omni-directional vehicle from [1]

$$q_x(t)^2 + q_y(t)^2 \leq 1, \tag{2}$$

where

$$q_x(t) = \dot{x} + \ddot{x} \tag{3}$$

$$q_y(t) = \dot{y} + \ddot{y}. \tag{4}$$

The x, y and t are normalized and non-dimensional quantities. we consider x and y as functions of time, t. In fact these equations show the relation of robot's acceleration to its velocity.

It is shown in [4] that time optimality achieves when equality condition holds in (2) for all possible quantities of t; therefore we can formulate optimality condition in (5). Reference [1] solves the problem of time optimal motion trajectory by ensuring the equality, but no obstacles are considered.

$$q_x(t)^2 + q_y(t)^2 = 1 \tag{5}$$

Normalized variables x, y, and t are determined as follow

$$x = \frac{x_r}{\Psi}, \quad y = \frac{y_r}{\Psi}, \quad t = \frac{t_r}{T}. \tag{6}$$

The length and time scales are

$$\Psi = \frac{4\alpha m U_{max}}{9\beta^2}, T = \frac{2m}{3\beta}. \tag{7}$$

In these equations x_r, y_r, and t_r are real quantities with their standard units. U_{max} is the maximum voltage applied to the motors and the constants α and β characterize the dc motors of the mobile robot. Finally m shows the mass of the robot.

3   Proposed Algorithm

The proposed algorithm constructs a curve that satisfies obstacle avoidance and then adjusts velocity of the robot to meet the dynamic constraints and optimality condition formulated in (5). This algorithm is based on results of [1] to meet time optimality while considering obstacles.

Due to dynamic constraints, shortest distance path is not always shortest time path. In shortest distance path the robot should stop on vertices of the path which is waste of time, so we should look for a curved path to guarantee obstacle avoidance and smoothness. Walking on the Voronoi diagram results in a path away from obstacles; so finding such a shortest path and then smooth the path with Bezier curve method will result in a smooth path which avoids obstacles and partially holds the distance optimality. We apply velocities to this curve in order to meet optimality conditions. First assume that our robot is just a point and later we will generalize this assumption to deal with real robots.

3.1   Voronoi Diagram

Voronoi diagram of P (a set of n distinct points in the plane which are called sites) is defined as the subdivision of the plane into n cells, one for each site in P, with the property that a point q lies in the cell corresponding to a site p_i if and only if the distance of q to p_i is less than the distance of q to any other sites. We denote the Voronoi diagram of P by $Vor(P)$.

Reference [11] shows that if all the sites are collinear then $Vor(P)$ consists of $n-1$ parallel lines. Otherwise, $Vor(P)$ is connected and its edges are either segments or half lines. In this paper we assume all sites do not lie on a line (we could avoid this case with a small perturbation). Fig. 3 shows an example of a Voronoi diagram for 9 sites.

Since obstacles may have various sizes we use a weighted Voronoi diagram with obstacles radii as their weights. In the weighted Voronoi problem the distance of a site to a point is the Euclidean distance, plus its additive weight. Reference [12] provides an algorithm to find weighted Voronoi diagrams in $O(N \log N)$.

First we construct a Voronoi graph with this algorithm and then add s and t, start and target points, to this graph with corresponding edges which connect these two points to their cells vertices (we do not consider edges that collide with obstacles). After constructing the graph we run Dijkstra's shortest path algorithm. The resulting path is the shortest path whose edges are in the Voronoi diagram; therefore this path is away enough from obstacles and satisfies obstacle avoidance. Reference [11] shows that this graph has $O(N)$ edges and vertices; so the Dijkstra's algorithm would run in $O(N \log N)$ on this graph (see [18]). In this algorithm N is the number of obstacles not the complexity of obstacles (i.e. number of vertices of all obstacles). Fig. 3 shows a shortest path on the graph obtained from a Voronoi diagram.

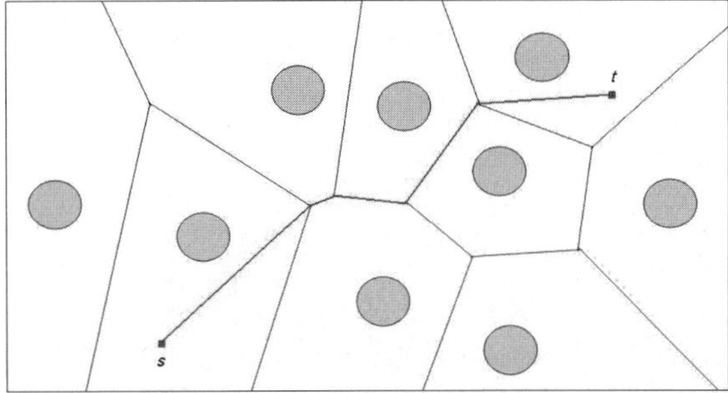

Fig. 3. A Voronoi diagram and a shortest path in the corresponding graph

3.2   Bezier Curves

a Bezier curve is a kind of spline important in computer graphics. These curves were developed independently by de Casteljau and Bezier in 1959 and 1962, respectively. Bezier curves were the result of demand by the automobile industry to develop modern curved shapes for cars (see [13]).

A Bezier curve of degree n is specified by $n + 1$ control points, $p_0, p_1, \ldots, p_n$. The curve passes through the first and last points, and is pulled toward the intermediate control points according to the Bernstein-Bezier equation

$$P(t) = \sum_{i=0}^{n} \binom{n}{i} (1 - t)^{n-i} t^i p_i, \tag{8}$$

where t is a parameter that varies from 0 to 1 along the curve.

We are to find a smooth path near the result of section 3.1 with regards to initial and final conditions. If we use the shortest path vertices as control points of a Bezier curve, initial position constraint will be satisfied but initial velocity may not be satisfied. Hence we use two Bezier curves to meet these conditions.

Let $p_0, p_1, \ldots, p_n$ are vertices of the shortest path resulting from previous step and p_0, and p_n are s and t respectively. We also know initial velocity v_0. First we find a Bezier curve for $p_1, \ldots, p_n$. Considering initial slope of this Bezier curve in p_1 and initial velocity, v_0, which define the slope in p_0, we introduce two new control points q and r to construct another Bezier curve with control points p_0, q, r, and p_1 to satisfy initial velocity constraint and also continuity of curve and its slope in p_1. We deal with slope (direction of first derivative) not with first derivative, because later in section 3.3 we will adjust velocity magnitudes (magnitude of first derivative). Following equations describe curves and boundary conditions.

$$P_a(t) = p_0(1 - t)^3 + 3qt(1 - t)^2 + 3rt^2(1 - t) + p_1 t^3 \tag{9}$$

$$P_b(t) = \sum_{i=0}^{n-1} \binom{n-1}{i} (1 - t)^{n-i-1} t^i p_{i+1} \tag{10}$$

$$\frac{\dot{P}_a(0)}{\left|\dot{P}_a(0)\right|} = \frac{v_0}{|v_0|} \tag{11}$$

$$\frac{\dot{P}_a(1)}{\left|\dot{P}_a(1)\right|} = \frac{\dot{P}_b(0)}{\left|\dot{P}_b(0)\right|} \tag{12}$$

Bezier curves P_a and P_b are connected at p_1. Equation (11) satisfies the initial velocity constraint and equation (12) shows the continuity of first derivative at p_1.
   Reference [13] shows that if $B(t)$ is a Bezier curve of degree k, then

$$\dot{B}(0) = k(p_1 - p_0) \quad and \tag{13}$$

$$\dot{B}(1) = k(p_k - p_{k-1}). \tag{14}$$

From equations (11, 12, 13, 14) we can conclude that vectors p_0q and v_0 and also vectors rp_1 and p_1p_2 should be in the same direction. If q and r are farther from p_0 and p_1 respectively, the robot may move with lower acceleration and therefore with higher velocity. Since the Bezier curves are always in the circumferential convex polygon of its control points, we could make q and r as far away from p_0 and p_1 as the circumferential convex polygon of p_0, q, r, and p_1 would not collide with any obstacle to ensure that the Bezier curve satisfies obstacle avoidance. Fig. 4 shows two Bezier curves constructed for the shortest path between s and t.

3.3   Adjusting Velocities

Finally we assign velocity magnitude to each point on the generated curve in previous section which satisfies obstacle avoidance and smoothness. In this step we deal with dynamic constraints and also time optimality. In section 3.2 a Bezier curve $C(X(t), Y(t))$ is produced where X and Y are Bernstein polynomials and $t \in [0, 1]$. In this section we are to find a function $\alpha : [0, \tau] \to [0, 1]$ that $X(\alpha(s))$ and $Y(\alpha(s))$ satisfy the following equation. Finding such a function means adjusting velocity magnitude for all points on the given curve.

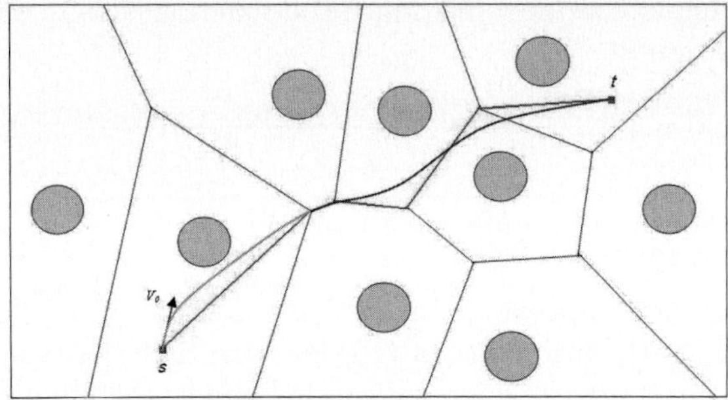

Fig. 4. A smooth path resulted from two Bezier curves. The first Bezier curve is illustrated in green and the second one is shown in blue.

For the sake of optimality we want the left-side of the inequality (15) to approach 1. Note that this inequality is applicable to normalized values which are scaled by equation (6); hence the first step in this section is transforming the real values to normalized values. At last the results of this section will be transformed back to real values.

$$(\dot{X} + \ddot{X})^2 + (\dot{Y} + \ddot{Y})^2 \leq 1 \tag{15}$$

We divide the interval $[0, \tau]$ to sections with length h and use α_n instead of $\alpha(nh)$ for simplicity. To find α_n values for all n's we could use the equation (15) and some approximations for derivatives.

We use derivative approximations to rewrite the inequality (15) as follow

$$\left(\frac{X(\alpha_{n+1}) - X(\alpha_{n-1})}{2h} + \frac{X(\alpha_{n+1}) + X(\alpha_{n-1}) - 2X(\alpha_n)}{h^2} \right)^2$$
$$+ \left(\frac{Y(\alpha_{n+1}) - Y(\alpha_{n-1})}{2h} + \frac{Y(\alpha_{n+1}) + Y(\alpha_{n-1}) - 2Y(\alpha_n)}{h^2} \right)^2 \leq 1 - \epsilon, \tag{16}$$

where

$$\frac{X(\alpha_{n+1}) - X(\alpha_{n-1})}{2h} = \dot{X}(\alpha_{n+1}) + \frac{h^2}{6} X^{(3)}(\xi_1)$$

$$\frac{X(\alpha_{n+1}) + X(\alpha_{n-1}) - 2X(\alpha_n)}{h^2} = \ddot{X}(\alpha_{n+1}) + \frac{h^2}{12} X^{(4)}(\xi_2) \tag{17}$$

and so forth for Y.

We use $1 - \epsilon$ instead of 1 in the inequality (16) because of approximation errors. This guarantees that the inequality (15) holds. α_{n+1} is easy to calculate based on α_{n-1} and α_n by Newton method in order to make the left-side of inequality (16) close to 1. Newton method is a root finding algorithm in which a sequence x_n is produced by the following recursive formula. This sequence converges to the function root:

$$x_{n+1} = x_n - \frac{f(x_n)}{\dot{f}(x_n)} \tag{18}$$

To use Newton method we first introduce the function f that we want to find its root. The function is

$$f(\lambda) = \left(\frac{X(\lambda)-X(\alpha_{n-1})}{2h} + \frac{X(\lambda)+X(\alpha_{n-1})-2X(\alpha_n)}{h^2} \right)^2$$
$$+ \left(\frac{Y(\lambda)-Y(\alpha_{n-1})}{2h} + \frac{Y(\lambda)+Y(\alpha_{n-1})-2Y(\alpha_n)}{h^2} \right)^2 \tag{19}$$
$$-1 + \epsilon + \epsilon_n.$$

The positive constant ϵ_n is used to ensure that the result of the Newton method will make left side of the inequality of (16) less than but close to $1 - \epsilon$. Assume that M_3 and M_4 are third and forth derivative bounds; therefore error terms for function X would be $\frac{h^2}{6}M_3$ and $\frac{h^2}{12}M_4$. Considering Y and the power of 2, the total error is approximately as follow.

$$\epsilon = \frac{h^2}{6} \left(M_1 M_4 + 2M_2 M_3 + N_1 N_4 + 2N_2 N_3 \right) \tag{20}$$

Where M_i and N_i are the ith-order derivative of X and Y bounds respectively. Since X and Y are Bernstein polynomials, their ith-order derivative bounds are $cn(n-1)\ldots(n-i+1)$ where c is a bound for coordinates of the points in the plane. So we rewrite the equation (20) as

$$\epsilon \leq \frac{h^2}{6}(cn^5 + 2cn^5 + cn^5 + 2cn^5) \Rightarrow \epsilon \leq h^2 cn^5. \tag{21}$$

To attain a small error, ϵ, it is sufficient to choose $h = \frac{1}{cn^3}$ and the error would be less than $h = \frac{1}{cn}$. Determining a suitable value for h is a key point in this section. In fact the less value we assign to h, the nearer trajectory to the optimal one is attained but the more computation time is needed as well which draws a trade-off between optimality and computational time.

In this method we need two previous values of α to attain α_{n+1} so at the first step we should calculate α_0 and α_1. Note that $\alpha_0 = 0$ and therefore it is sufficient to calculate α_1. We use the given initial velocity to find α_1. We approximate the position of the robot before initial time and introduce a hypothetical α_{-1}. First derivative approximation in the initial point of the curve as shown below, relates α_{-1}, α_0, and the initial velocity.

$$\frac{X(\alpha_0) - X(\alpha_{-1})}{h} = \dot{X}(\alpha_0) + \frac{h}{2}\ddot{X}(\xi) \approx v_{0x} \tag{22}$$

From equation (22), we determine α_{-1}. Note that the similar equation for the y-coordinate holds because the ratio of the y and x coordinates derivative is the same as v_0 coordinates (this condition considered in section 3.2). Now it is easy to find α_1 by applying equation (16) and using α_{-1} and α_0. In section 3.2 we introduced a curve which satisfied the given initial velocity direction condition and here we adjust the velocity in the initial point of the curve to meet the initial velocity magnitude condition.

In this section an iterative method for finding the function α is introduced. When the α_n reaches 1 the procedure ends because the purpose is to find the function α which ranges over $[0, 1]$.

4   Implementation Details

The following assumptions and simplifications were made for implementation:

- Robots are treated as a circles; therefore we enlarged obstacles proportional to robots radius and consider robots as points. We enlarge obstacles a little more to prevent paths passing through narrow passages.
- If two obstacles collide after enlargement, we merge them and consider them as one obstacle.
- For each obstacle the center of its circumferential circle would produce a site and the radius of this circle defines this site's weight.

5   Experimental Results

The presented algorithm is developed in C++ programming language and tested in Linux environment. It was used for motion planning of soccer playing robots: Robocup small size league. The field is a 4.9 by 3.4 meter rectangle covered with a green carpet. Each team consists of five robots with diameters no more than $18cm$ and height no more than $15cm$ and uses one or more cameras mounted 4 meters above the field.

Experiments were performed in simulation and on real robots using a Pentium IV 2400MHz computer. The robots were custom built, omni-directional drive, and equipped with wireless transmission devices to communicate with central computer [14]. Their maximum velocity and acceleration were $2.2m/s$ and $3.0m/s^2$ respectively.

We have compared the proposed algorithm with other motion planning algorithms used previously in Robocup competitions in simulation (Illustrated in Fig. 5 and 6). In this comparison we examined this algorithm and two other algorithms: potential field and shortest path using bang-bang method [1]. This comparison was performed on more than one thousand of possible situations in a robot soccer competition.

Artificial potential fields, originally developed in [15], are a quite popular approach in robot motion planning, because of their capability to act in continuous domains in real-time. This method has some disadvantages such as producing non-smooth paths and blockage in local minima. Previously we used the potential field method and for smoothing the resulted path we performed Exponential Weighted Moving Average method. We also added some random moves to this algorithm to avoid getting stuck in local minima.

Another path planner that we have examined is shortest path planner featuring bang-bang method. This path planner first finds the shortest path in the environment and then uses bang-bang approach to move on the path in a time optimal manner. Robots moving on shortest paths are likely to collide with obstacles because shortest paths are tangent to obstacles.

Fig. 6 shows the results of discussed algorithms and also time optimal paths. Apparently finding a time optimal path requires searching a large space and could not be accomplished real-time. It is not practical to produce a time optimal path in real-time but we mentioned it just for comparison. Fig. 5 illustrates how much the results of the presented algorithm and two other discussed algorithms approximate the time optimal path. This comparison to the time optimal path is experimented in two different environments: highly cluttered and moderately cluttered. We use about five obstacles in moderately cluttered environments and ten obstacles in highly cluttered ones. This figure shows outstanding results of the presented algorithm in both environments. There is a considerable difference between highly cluttered and moderately cluttered results for two other algorithms. The potential field method works weak in highly cluttered environments because the resulting path is much fluctuated and it is more likely to get stuck in local minima in comparison to moderately cluttered environments. The shortest path method produces a path with more vertices in highly cluttered environments which enforce the robot to have more stops and therefore less average speed. Although shortest path method performs well in moderately cluttered environments, it suffers from high probability of obstacle collision.

In experiments on real robots the average computational time for calculating the trajectory was about $0.3ms$ that includes constructing the Voronoi diagram, finding shortest path based on the diagram, calculating Bezier curves, and assigning velocities by using Newton method. This experiment was performed on a Pentium IV 2400MHz computer. In these experiments we used five iteration for Newton method and considered $h = 0.01$ to make the errors introduced in section 3.3 negligible.

Total latency of our system which includes image processing, planning, network and wireless delays, motion planning, and robot hardware delay, was about $120ms$; therefore this algorithm is only produce less than 0.25 percent of the total delay.

This experiments show that proposed algorithm is suitable for our application since it provides obstacle avoidance, near time optimal trajectory, and low computational time which meets our real time constraints.

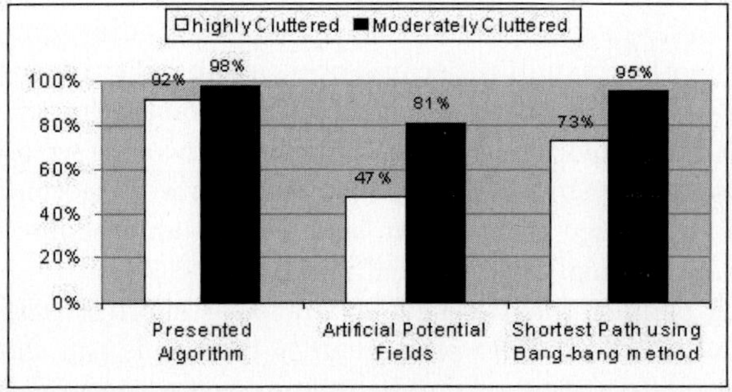

Fig. 5. Three different path planner's results (time to complete the path) in two different environments are compared to optimal paths

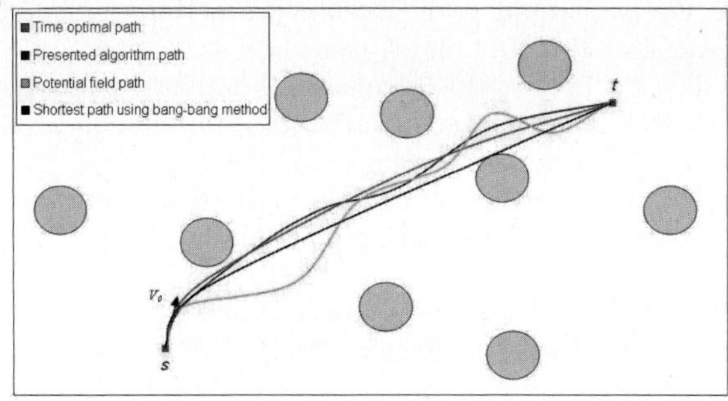

Fig. 6. Paths produced by different path planners with starting point s, ending point t, and initial velocity v_0

6 Conclusion

This paper presented an algorithm to find a near time-optimal dynamic trajectory for mobile robots. We represent the environment as a Voronoi diagram, and use Dijkstra's algorithm to find a shortest distant path in Voronoi diagram as a sketch. Then, with a novel use of Bezier curves we smooth the resulting shortest path. We satisfy the time-optimality condition with appropriate velocity assignments along the curve.

Due to low time complexity of the proposed algorithm, it is suitable to be used in real-time and dynamic applications. This algorithm can generate near time-optimal trajectories for real robots, as shown in experimental results.

References

1. Kalmar-Nagy, T., D'Andrea, R., Ganguly, P.: Near-optimal dynamic trajectory generation and control of an omnidirectional vehicle. Robotics and Autonomous Systems 46, 47–64 (2004)
2. Lavalle, S.M.: Planning Algorithms. Available Online
3. Latombe, J.C.: Robot Motion Planning. Kluwer Academic Publishers, Dordrecht (1991)
4. Athans, M., Falb, P.L.: Optimal Control: An Introduction to the Theory and its Applications. McGraw-Hill, New York (1966)
5. Mitchell, J.S.B., Rote, G., Woeginger, G.J.: Minimum-Link Paths Among Obstacles in the Plane. Algorithmica 8, 431–459 (1992)
6. LaValle, S.M., Gonzalez-Banos, H.H., Becker, C., Latombe, J.C.: Motion strategies for maintaining visibility of a moving target. In: Proc. IEEE Int'l Conf. on Robotics and Automation, pp. 731–736. IEEE Computer Society Press, Los Alamitos (1997)
7. Guibas, L.J., Latombe, J.C., LaValle, S.M., Lin, D., Motwani, R.: A visibility-based pursuit-evasion problem. International Journal of Computational Geometry and Applications 9, 471–494 (1999)
8. He, Z., Lin, L., Ma, X.: Design, modeling and trajectory generation of a kind of four wheeled omni-directional vehicle. IEEE International Conference on Systems, Man and Cybernetics 7, 6125–6130 (2004)

9. Bobrow, J.E.: Optimal robot path planning using the minimum-time criterion. IEEE Transactions on Robotics and Automation 4, 443–450 (1988)
10. Fiorini, P., Shiller, Z.: Time optimal trajectory planning in dynamic environments. IEEE International Conference on Robotics and Automation 2, 1553–1558 (1996)
11. de Berg, M., van Krefeld, M., Overmars, M., Schwarzkopf, O.: Computational Geometry Algorithms and Applications. Springer, Heidelberg (2000)
12. Fortune, S.J.: A sweepline algorithm for Voronoi diagrams. Algorithmica 2, 153–174 (1987)
13. Buss, S.R.: 3D Computer Graphics A Mathematical Introduction with OpenGL. Cambridge University Press, Cambridge (2003)
14. Manzuri, M.T., Sahraei, A., Miremadi, S., Khoshbakht, S., Tajfard, M.: Team Description paper of the robocup small-size league sharif CESR (2005)
15. Khatib, O.: Real-time obstacle avoidance for manipulators and mobile robots. International Journal of Robotics Research 5, 90–98 (1986)
16. Feder, H.J.S., Slotine, J.J.E.: Real-time path planning using harmonic potentials in dynamic environments. IEEE International Conference on Robotics and Automation 1, 874–881 (1997)
17. Khatib, M., Chatila, R.: An extended potential field approach for mobile robot sensor-based motions. In: Proc. Int. Conf. on Intelligent Autonomous Systems, pp. 490–496 (1995)
18. Cormen, T.H., Leiserson, C.E., Rivest, R.L., Stein, C.: Introduction to Algorithms. McGraw-Hill, New York (2001)

Curricula Modeling and Checking

Matteo Baldoni, Cristina Baroglio, and Elisa Marengo

Dipartimento di Informatica — Università degli Studi di Torino
C.so Svizzera, 185 — I-10149 Torino (Italy)
{baldoni,baroglio}@di.unito.it, elisa.mrng@gmail.com

Abstract. In this work, we present a constrained-based representation for specifying the goals of "course design", that we call curricula model, and introduce a graphical language, grounded into Linear Time Logic, to design curricula models which include knowledge of proficiency levels. Based on this representation, we show how model checking techniques can be used to verify that the user's learning goal is supplied by a curriculum, that a curriculum is compliant to a curricula model, and that competence gaps are avoided.

1 Introduction and Motivations

As recently underlined by other authors, there is a strong relationship between the development of peer-to-peer, (web) service technologies and e-learning technologies [17]. The more learning resources are freely available through the Web, the more modern e-learning management systems (LMSs) should be able to take advantage from this richness: LMSs should offer the means for easily retrieving and assembling e-learning resources so to satisfy specific users' learning goals, similarly to how (web) services are retrieved and composed [12]. As in a composition of web services it is necessary to verify that, at every point, all the information necessary to the subsequent invocation will be available, in a learning domain, it is important to verify that all the *competencies*, i.e. the *knowledge*, necessary to fully understand a learning resource are introduced or available before that learning resource is accessed. The composition of learning resources, a curriculum, does not have to show any *competence gap*. Unfortunately, this verification, as stated in [10], is usually performed *manually* by the learning designer, with hardly any guidelines or support.

A recent proposal for automatizing the competence gap verification is done in [17] where an analysis of pre- and post-requisite annotations of the Learning Objects (LO), representing the learning resources, is proposed. A logic based validation engine can use these annotations in order to validate the curriculum/LO composition. Melia and Pahl's proposal is inspired by the CocoA system [8], that allows to perform the analysis and the consistency check of static web-based courses. Competence gaps are checked by a prerequisite checker for *linear courses*, simulating the process of teaching with an overlay student model. Pre- and post-requisites are represented as "concepts".

R. Basili and M.T. Pazienza (Eds.): AI*IA 2007, LNAI 4733, pp. 471–482, 2007.
© Springer-Verlag Berlin Heidelberg 2007

Together with the verification of consistence gaps, there are other kinds of verification. Brusilovsky and Vassileva [8] sketch some of them. In our opinion, two are particularly important: (a) verifying that the curriculum allows to achieve the users' *learning goals*, i.e. that the user will acquire the desired knowledge, and (b) verifying that the curriculum is compliant against the *course design goals*. Manually or automatically supplied curricula, developed to reach a learning goal, should match the "design document", a *curricula model*, specified by the institution that offers the possibility of personalizing curricula. Curricula models specify general rules for designing sequences of learning resources (courses). We interpret them as *constraints*, that are expressed in terms of concepts and, in general, are not directly associated to learning resources, as instead is done for pre-requisites. They constrain the process of acquisition of concepts, independently from the resources.

More specifically, in this paper we present a constraint-based representation of curricula models. Constraints are expressed as formulas in a temporal logic (LTL, linear temporal logic [11]) represented by means of a simple graphical language that we call DCML (*Declarative Curricula Model Language*). This logic allows the verification of properties of interest for all the possible executions of a model, which in our case corresponds to the specific curriculum. Curricula are represented as *activity diagrams* [1]. We translate an activity diagram, that represents a curriculum, in a *Promela* program [16] and we check, by means of the well-known SPIN Model Checker [16], that it respect the model by verifying that the set of LTL formulas are satisfied by the Promela program. Moreover, we check that learning goals are achieved, and that the curriculum does not contain competence gaps. As in [10], we distinguish between *competency* and *competence*, where by the first term we denote a concept (or skill) while by the second we denote a competency plus the level of proficiency at which it is learnt or known or supplied. So far, we do not yet tackle with "contexts", as defined in the competence model proposed in [10], which will be part of future work.

This approach differs from previous work [5], where we presented an adaptive tutoring system, that exploits *reasoning about actions and changes* to plan and verify curricula. The approach was based on abstract representations, capturing the *structure* of a curriculum, and implemented by means of prolog-like logic clauses. Such representations were applied a procedure-driven form of planning, in order to build personalized curricula. In this context, we proposed also some forms of verification, of competence gaps, of learning goal achievement, and of whether a curriculum, given by a user, is compliant to the "course design" goals. The use of procedure clauses is, however, limiting because they, besides having a *prescriptive* nature, pose very strong constraints on the sequencing of learning resources. In particular, clauses represent what is "legal" and whatever sequence is not foreseen by the clauses is "illegal". However, in an open environment where resources are extremely various, they are added/removed dynamically, and their number is huge, this approach becomes unfeasible: the clauses would be too complex, it would be impossible to consider all the alternatives and the clauses should change along time.

For this reason we considered as appropriate to take another perspective and represent only those constraints which are strictly necessary, in a way that is inspired by the so called *social approach* proposed by Singh for multi-agent and service-oriented communication protocols [18,19]. In this approach only the *obligations* are represented. In our application context, obligations capture relations among the times at which different competencies are to be acquired. The advantage of this representation is that we do not have to represent all that is legal but only those *necessary conditions* that characterize a legal solution. To make an example, by means of constraints we can request that a certain knowledge is acquired before some other knowledge, without expressing what else is to be done in between. If we used the clause-based approach, instead, we should have described also what can legally be contained between the two times at which the two pieces of knowledge are acquired. Generally, the constraints-based approach is more flexible and more suitable to an open environment.

2   DCML: A Declarative Curricula Model Language

In this section we describe the *Declarative Curricula Model Language* (DCML, for short), a graphical language to represent the specification of a curricula model (the course design goals). The advantage of a graphical language is that drawing, rather than writing, constraints facilitates the user, who needs to represent curricula models, allowing a general overview of the relations which exist between concepts. DCML is inspired by DecSerFlow, the Declarative Service Flow Language to specify, enact, and monitor web service flows by van der Aalst and Pesic [21]. DCML, as well as DecSerFlow, is grounded in Linear Temporal Logic [11] and allows a curricula model to be described in an easy way maintaining at the same time a rigorous and precise meaning given by the logic representation. LTL includes temporal operators such as next-time ($\bigcirc \varphi$, the formula φ holds in the immediately following state of the run), eventually ($\Diamond \varphi$, φ is guaranteed to eventually become true), always ($\Box \varphi$, the formula φ remains invariably true throughout a run), until ($\alpha \ \mathsf{U} \ \beta$, the formula α remains true until β), see also [16, Chapter 6]. The set of LTL formulas obtained for a curricula model are, then, used to verify whether a curriculum will respect it [4]. As an example, Fig. 1 shows a curricula model expressed in DCML. Every box contains at least one competence. Boxes/competences are related by arrows, which represent (mainly) temporal constraints among the times at which they are to be acquired. Altogether the constraints describe a curricula model.

2.1   Competence, Competency, and Basic Constraints

The terms *competence* and *competency* are used, in the literature concerning professional curricula and e-learning, to denote the "effective performance within a domain at some level of proficiency" and "any form of knowledge, skill, attitude, ability or learning objective that can be described in a context of learning, education or training". In the following, we extend a previous proposal [4,7] so

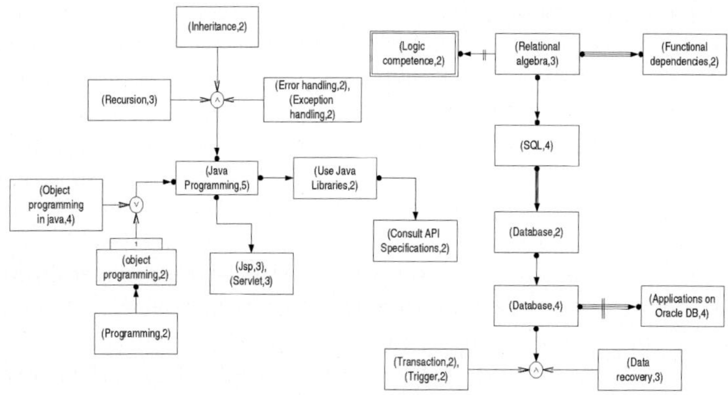

Fig. 1. An example of curricula model in DCML

as to include a representation of the *proficiency level* at which a competency is owned or supplied. To this aim, we associate to each competency a variable k, having the same name as the competency, which can be assigned natural numbers as values. The value of k denotes the proficiency level; zero means absence of knowledge. Therefore, k encodes a *competence*, Fig. 2(a). On competences, we can define three basic *constraints*.

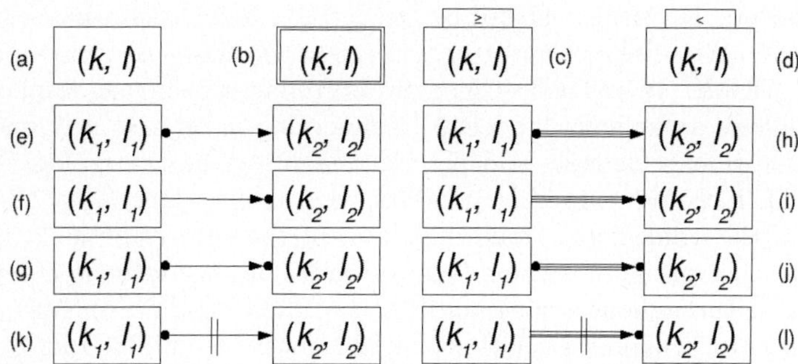

Fig. 2. Competences (a) and basic constraints (b), (c), and (d). Relations among competences: (a) implication, (b) before, (c) succession, (d) immediate implication, (e) immediate before, (f) immediate succession, (g) not implication, (h) not immediate before.

The *"level of competence"* constraint, Fig. 2(c), imposes that a certain competency k must be acquired at least at level l. It is represented by the LTL formula $\Diamond(k \geq l)$. Similarly, a course designer can impose that a competency must never appear in a curriculum with a proficiency level higher than l. This is possible by means of the *"always less than level"* constraint, shown in Fig. 2(d). The LTL formula $\Box(k < l)$ expresses this fact (it is the negation of the previous one). As a special case, when the level l is one $(\Box(k < 1))$, the competency k must never appear in a curriculum.

The third constraint, represented by a double box, see Fig. 2 (b), specifies that k must belong to the initial knowledge with, at least, level l. In other words, the simple logic formula $(k \geq l)$ must hold in the initial state.

To specify relations among concepts, other elements are needed. In particular, in DCML it is possible to represent *Disjunctive Normal Form* (DNF) formulas as *conjunctions* and *disjunctions* of concepts. For lack of space, we do not describe the notation here, however, an example can be seen in Fig. 1.

2.2   Positive and Negative Relations Among Competences

Besides the representation of competences and of constraints on competences, DCML allows to represent *relations* among competences. For simplicity, in the following presentations we will always relate simple competences, it is, however, of course possible to connect DNF formulas. We will denote by (k, l) the fact that competence k is required to have at least level l (i.e. $k \geq l$) and by $\neg(k, l)$ the fact that k is required to be less than l.

Arrows ending with a little-ball, Fig. 2(f), express the *before* temporal constraint between two competences, that amount to require that (k_1, l_1) holds *before* (k_2, l_2). This constraint can be used to express that to understand some topic, some proficiency of another is required as precondition. It is important to underline that if the antecedent never becomes true, also the consequent must be invariably false; this is expressed by the LTL formula $\neg(k_2, l_2) \text{ U } (k_1, l_1)$, i.e. $(k_2 < l_2) \text{ U } (k_1 \geq l_1)$. It is also possible to express that a competence must be acquired *immediate before* some other. This is represented by means of a triple line arrow that ends with a little-ball, see Fig. 2(i). The constraint (k_1, l_1) *immediate before* (k_2, l_2) imposes that (k_1, l_1) holds before (k_2, l_2) and the latter either is true in the next state w.r.t. the one in which (k_1, l_1) becomes true or k_2 *never* reaches the level l_2. The difference w.r.t the *before* constraint is that it imposes that the two competences are acquired *in sequence*. The corresponding LTL formula is "(k_1, l_1) *before* (k_2, l_2)" $\wedge \Box((k_1, l_1) \supset (\bigcirc(k_2, l_2) \vee \Box\neg(k_2, l_2)))$.

Both of the two previous relations represent temporal constraints between competences. The *implication* relation (Fig. 2(e)) specifies, instead, that if a competency k_1 holds at least at the level l_1, some other competency k_2 must be acquired sooner or later at least at the level l_2. The main characteristic of the implication, is that the acquisition of the consequent is imposed by the truth value of the antecedent, but, in case this one is true, it does not specify when the consequent must be achieved (it could be before, after or in the same state of the antecedent). This is expressed by the LTL formula $\Diamond(k_1, l_1) \supset \Diamond(k_2, l_2)$. The *immediate implication* (Fig. 2(h)), instead, specifies that the consequent must *hold* in the state right after the one in which the antecedent is acquired. Note that, this does not mean that it must be *acquired* in that state, but only that it cannot be acquired after. This is expressed by the LTL implication formula in conjunction with the constraint that whenever $k_1 \geq l_1$ holds, $k_2 \geq l_2$ holds in the next state: $\Diamond(k_1, l_1) \supset \Diamond(k_2, l_2) \wedge \Box((k_1, l_1) \supset \bigcirc(k_2, l_2))$.

The last two kinds of temporal constraint are *succession* (Fig. 2(g)) and *immediate succession* (Fig. 2(j)). The *succession* relation specifies that if (k_1, l_1) is acquired, afterwards (k_2, l_2) is also achieved; otherwise, the level of k_2 is not important. This is a difference w.r.t. the *before* constraint where, when the antecedent is never acquired, the consequent must be invariably false. Indeed, the *succession* specifies a condition of the kind *if $k_1 \geq l_1$ then $k_2 \geq l_2$*, while *before* represents a constraint without any conditional premise. Instead, the fact that the consequent must be acquired after the antecedent is what differentiates *implication* from *succession*. Succession constraint is expressed by the LTL formula $\Diamond(k_1, l_1) \supset (\Diamond(k_2, l_2) \wedge (\neg(k_2, l_2) \ \mathsf{U} \ (k_1, l_1)))$. In the same way, the *immediate succession* imposes that the consequent either is acquired in the same state as the antecedent or in the state immediately after (not before nor later). The immediate succession LTL formula is "(k_1, l_1) *succession* (k_2, l_2)" $\wedge\Box((k_1, l_1) \supset \bigcirc(k_2, l_2))$.

After the "positive relations" among competences, let us now introduce the graphical notations for "negative relations". The graphical representation is very intuitive: two vertical lines break the arrow that represents the constraint, see Fig. 2(k)-(l). (k_1, l_1) *not before* (k_2, l_2) specifies that k_1 cannot be acquired up to level l_1 before or in the same state when (k_2, l_2) is acquired. The corresponding LTL formula is $\neg(k_1, l_1) \ \mathsf{U} \ ((k_2, l_2) \wedge \neg(k_1, l_1))$. Notice that this is not obtained by simply negating the before relation but it is weaker; the negation of *before* would *impose the acquisition* of the concepts specified as consequents (in fact, the formula would contain a strong until instead of a weak until), the *not before* does not. The *not immediate before* is translated exactly in the same way as the *not before*. Indeed, it is a special case because our domain is monotonic, that is a competency acquired at a certain level cannot be forgotten.

(k_1, l_1) *not implies* (k_2, l_2) expresses that if (k_1, l_1) is acquired k_2 cannot be acquired at level l_2; as an LTL formula: $\Diamond(k_1, l_1) \supset \Box\neg(k_2, l_2)$. Again, we choose to use a weaker formula than the natural negation of the implication relation because the simple negation of formulas would impose the presence of certain concepts. (k_1, l_1) *not immediate implies* (k_2, l_2) imposes that when (k_1, l_1) holds in a state, $k_2 \geq l_2$ must be false in the immediately subsequent state. Afterwards, the proficiency level of k_2 does not matter. The corresponding LTL formula is $\Diamond(k_1, l_1) \supset (\Box\neg(k_2, l_2) \vee \Diamond((k_1, l_1) \wedge \bigcirc\neg(k_2, l_2)))$, that is weaker than the "classical negation" of the *immediate implies*.

The last relations are *not succession*, and *not immediate succession*. The first imposes that a certain competence cannot be acquired after another, (either it was acquired before, or it will never be acquired). As LTL formula, it is $\Diamond(k_1, l_1) \supset (\Box\neg(k_2, l_2)\vee$ "(k_1, l_1) *not before* (k_2, l_2)"). The second imposes that if a competence is acquired in a certain state, in the state that follows, another competence must be false, that is $\Diamond(k_1, l_1) \supset (\Box\neg(k_2, l_2)\vee$ "(k_1, l_1) *not before* (k_2, l_2)" $\vee\Diamond((k_1, l_1) \wedge \bigcirc\neg(k_2, l_2)))$.

3   Representing Curricula as Activity Diagrams

Let us now consider specific curricula. In the line of [5,3,4], we represent curricula as sequences of courses/resources, taking the abstraction of courses as simple actions. Any action can be executed given that a set of preconditions holds; by executing it, a set of post-conditions, the effects, will become true. In our case, we represent courses as actions for acquiring some concepts (*effects*) if the user owns some competences (*preconditions*). So, a curriculum is seen as a sequence of actions that causes *transitions* from the initial set of competences (possibly empty) of a user up to a final state that will contain all the competences owned by the user in the end. We assume that concepts can only be added to states and competence level can only grow by executing the actions of attending courses (or more in general reading a learning material). The intuition behind this assumption is that no new course erases from the students memory the concepts acquired in previous courses, thus knowledge grows incrementally. We represent

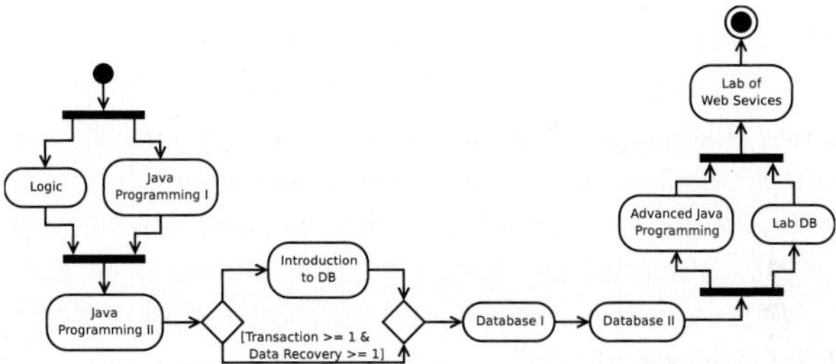

Fig. 3. Activity diagram representing a set of eight different curricula. Notice that *Logic* and *Java Programming I* can be attended in any order (even in parallel), as well as *Advanced Java Programming* and *Lab DB*, while *Introduction to DB* will be considered only if the guard *Transaction* and *Data Recovery* is false.

curricula as *activity diagrams* [1], normally used for representing *business processes*. We decided to do so, because they allow to capture in a natural way the simple sequencing of courses as well as the possibility of attending courses in *parallel* or in possibly conditioned *alternatives*. An example is reported in Fig. 3. Besides the initial and the final nodes, the graphical elements used in an activity diagram are: *activity nodes* (rounded rectangle) that represent activities (attending courses) that occur; *flow/edge* (arrows) that represent activity flows; *fork* (black bar with one incoming edge and several outgoing edges) and *join nodes* (black bar with several incoming edges and one outgoing edge) to denote parallel activities; and *decision* (diamonds with one incoming edge and several outgoing edges) and *merge nodes* (diamonds with several incoming edges and one outgoing edge) to choose between alternative flows.

In the modeling of *learning processes*, we use activities to represent attending courses (or reading learning resources). For example, by fork and join nodes we represent the fact that two (or more) courses or sub-curricula are not related and, it is possible for the student to attend them in parallel. This is the case of *Java Programming I* and *Logic*, as well as *Advanced Java Programming* and *Lab. of DB* showed in Fig. 3. Till all parallel branches have not been attended successfully, the student cannot attend other courses, even if some of the parallel branches have been completed. Parallel branches can also be used when we want to express that the order among courses of different branches does not matter.

Decision and merge nodes can be used to represent alternative paths. The student will choose only one of these. Alternative paths can also be conditioned, in this case a *guard*, a boolean condition, is added at the beginning of the branch. Guards should be mutually exclusive. In our domain, the conditions are expressed in terms of concepts that must hold, otherwise a branch is not accessible. If no guards are present, the student can choose one (and only one) of the possible paths. In the example in Fig. 3, the guard consists of two copetences: *Transaction* and *Data Recovery*. If one of these does not hold the student has to attend the course *Introduction to DB*, otherwise does not.

4   Verifying Curricula by Means of SPIN Model Checker

In this section we discuss how to validate a curriculum. As explained, three kinds of verifications have to be performed: (1) verifying that a curriculum does not have competence gaps, (2) verifying that a curriculum supplies the user's learning goals, and (3) verifying that a curriculum satisfies the course design goals, i.e. the constraints imposed by the curricula model. To do this, we use *model checking techniques* [9].

By means of a *model checker*, it is possible to generate and analyze all the possible states of a program exhaustively to verify whether no execution path satisfies a certain property, usually expressed by a temporal logic, such as LTL. When a model checker refuses the negation of a property, it produces a *counterexample* that shows the violation. SPIN, by G. J. Holzmann [16], is the most representative tool of this kind. Our idea is to translate the activity diagram, that represents a set of curricula, in a Promela (the language used by SPIN) program, and, then to verify whether it satisfies the LTL formulas that represents the curricula model.

In the literature, we can find some proposals to translate UML activity diagrams into Promela programs, such as [13,14]. However, these proposals have a different purpose than ours and they cannot be used to perform the translation that we need to perform the verifications we list above. Generally, their aim is debugging UML designs, by helping UML designers to write sound diagrams. The translation proposed in the following, instead, aims to simulate, by a Promela program the acquisition of competencies by attending courses contained into the curricula represented by an activity diagram.

Given a curriculum as an activity diagram, we represent all the competences involved by its courses as *integer variables*. In the beginning, only those variables that represent the initial knowledge owned by the student are set to a value greater than zero. *Courses* are represented as actions that can modify the value of such variables. Since our application domain is monotonic, the value of a variable can only grow.

The Promela program consists of two main processes: one is called *Curriculum Verification* and the other *UpdateState*. While the former contains the actual translation of the activity diagram and simulates the acquisition of the competences for *all* curricula represented by the translated activity diagram, the latter contains the code for updating the state, i.e. the competences achieved so far, according to the definition in terms of preconditions and effects of each course. The processes *Curriculum Verification* and *UpdateState* communicate by means of the channel *attend*. The notation *attend!courseName* represents the fact that the course with name "courseName" is to be attended. On the other hand, the notation *attend?courseName* represents the possibility for a process of receiving a message. For example, the process *Curriculum Verification* for the activity diagram of Fig. 3 is defined as follows:

```
proctype CurriculumVerification()
{ activity_forkjoin_1();
  course_java_programming_II();
  activity_decisionmerge_1();
  course_database_I();
  course_database_II();
  activity_forkjoin_2();
  course_lab_of_web_services();
  attend!stop; }
```

If the simulation of all its possible executions end, then, there are no competence gaps; *attend!stop* communicates this fact and starts the verification of user's learning goal, that, if passed, ends the process. Each *course* is represented by its preconditions and its effects. For example, the course "Laboratory of Web Services" is as follows:

```
inline preconditions_course_lab_of_web_services()
{ assert(N_tier_architectures >= 4 && sql >= 2); }
inline effects_course_lab_of_web_services()
{ SetCompetenceState(jsp, 4); [...]
  SetCompetenceState(markup_language, 5); }
inline course_lab_of_web_services()
{ attend!lab_of_web_services; }
```

assert verifies the truth value of its condition, which in our case is the precondition to the course. If violated, SPIN interrupts its execution and reports about it. *SetCompetenceState* increases the level of the passed competence if its current level is lower than the second parameter. If all the curricula represented by the translated activity diagram have *no competence gaps*, no assertion violation will be detected. Otherwise, a counterexample will be returned that corresponds to an effective sequence of courses leading to the violation, giving a precise feedback to the student/teacher/course designer of the submitted set of curricula.

The *fork/join nodes* are simulated by activating as many parallel processes as their branches. Each process translates recursively the corresponding sub-activity diagram. Thus, SPIN simulates and verifies *all possible interleavings* of the courses (we can say that the curriculum is only one but it has different executions). The join nodes are translated by means of the synchronization message *done* that each activated process must send to the father process when it finishes its activity:

```
proctype activity_joinfork_11()
{ course_java_programming_I(); joinfork_11!done; }
proctype activity_joinfork_12()
{ course_logic(); joinfork_12!done; }
inline activity_joinfork_1()
{ run activity_joinfork_11(); run activity_joinfork_12();
  joinfork_11?done; joinfork_12?done; }
```

Finally, *decision and merge nodes* are encoded by either conditioned or non-deterministic *if*. Each such *if* statement refers to a set of alternative sub-activity diagrams (sub-curricula). Only one will be effectively attended but all of them will be verified:

```
inline activity_decisionmerge_11()
{ course_introduction_to_database(); }
inline activity_decisionmerge_12() { skip; }
inline activity_decisionmerge_1()
{ if
  :: (transaction >= 1 && data_recovery >= 1) ->
       activity_decisionmerge_12();
  :: else -> activity_decisionmerge_11();
  fi }
```

On the other hand, the process *UpdateState*, after setting the initial competences, checks if the preconditions of the courses communicated by *Curriculum Verification* hold in the current state. If a course is applicable it also updates the state. The test of the preconditions and the update of the state are performed as an atomic operation. In the end if everything is right it sends a feedback to *Curriculum Verification* (*feedback!done*):

```
proctype UpdateState() { SetInitialSituation();
  do [ ... ]
  :: attend?lab_of_web_services -> atomic {
       preconditions_course_lab_of_web_services();
       effects_course_lab_of_web_services(); }
  :: attend?stop -> LearningGoal(); break;
  od }
```

When *attend?stop* (see above) is received, the check of the user's learning goal is performed. This just corresponds to a test on the knowledge in the ending state:

```
inline LearningGoal()
{ assert(advanced_java_programming>=5 && N_tier_architectures
         >= 4 && relational_algebra>=2 && ER_language>=2); }
```

To check if the curriculum complies to a curricula model, we check if every possibly sequence of execution of the Promela program satisfies the LTL formulas, now transformed into *never claims* directly by SPIN. For example, the curriculum shown in Fig. 3 respects all the constraints imposed by the curricula model described in Fig. 1, taking into account the description of the courses supplied at the URL above. The assertion verification takes very few seconds on an old notebook; the automaton generated from the Promela program on that example has more than four-hundred states, indeed, it is very tractable. Also the verification of the temporal constraints is not hard if we check the constraints one at the time. The above example is available for download at the URL `http://www.di.unito.it/~baldoni/DCML/AIIA07`.

5   Conclusions

In this paper we have introduced a graphical language to describe curricula models as temporal constraints posed on the acquisition of competences (supplied by courses), therefore, taking into account both the concepts supplied/required and the proficiency level. We have also shown how model checking techniques can be used to verify that a curriculum complies to a curricula model, and also that a curriculum both allows the achievement of the user's learning goals and that it has no competence gaps. This use of model checking is inspired by [21], where LTL formulas are used to describe and verify the properties of a composition of Web Services. Another recent work, though in a different setting, that inspired this proposal is [20], where medical guidelines, represented by means of the GLARE graphical language, are translated in a Promela program, whose properties are verified by using SPIN. Similarly to [20], the use of SPIN, gives an *automa-based semantics* to a curriculum (the automaton generated by SPIN from the Promela program) and gives a declarative, formal, representation of curricula models (the set of temporal constraints) in terms of a LTL theory that enables other forms of reasoning. In fact, as for all logical theories, we can use an inference engine to derive other theorems or to discovery inconsistencies in the theory itself.

The presented proposal is an evolution of earlier works [6,3,5], where we applied semantic annotations to learning objects, with the aim of building compositions of new learning objects, based on the user's learning goals and exploiting planning techniques. That proposal was based on a different approach that relied on the experience of the authors in the use of techniques for reasoning about actions and changes which, however, suffers of the limitations discussed in the introduction. We are currently working on the automatic translation from a textual representation of DCML curricula models into the corresponding set of LTL formulas and from a textual representation of an activity diagram, that describes a curriculum (comprehensive of the description of all courses involved with their preconditions and effects), into the corresponding Promela program. We are also going to realize a graphical tool to define curricula models by means of DCML. We think to use the Eclipse framework, by IBM, to do this. In [2], we discuss the integration into the Personal Reader Framework [15] of a web service that implements an earlier version of the techniques explained here, which does not include proficiency levels.

Acknowledgements. The authors would like to thank Viviana Patti for the helpful discussions. This research has partially been funded by the 6th Framework Programme project REWERSE number 506779 and by the Italian MIUR PRIN 2005.

References

1. Unified Modeling Language: Superstructure, version 2.1.1. OMG (February 2007)
2. Baldoni, M., Baroglio, C., Brunkhorst, I., Marengo, E., Patti, V.: Curriculum Sequencing and Validation: Integration in a Service-Oriented Architecture. In: Proc. of EC-TEL'07. LNCS, Springer, Heidelberg (2007)
3. Baldoni, M., Baroglio, C., Henze, N.: Personalization for the Semantic Web. In: Eisinger, N., Małuszyński, J. (eds.) Reasoning Web. LNCS, vol. 3564, pp. 173–212. Springer, Heidelberg (2005)
4. Baldoni, M., Baroglio, C., Martelli, A., Patti, V., Torasso, L.: Verifying the compliance of personalized curricula to curricula models in the semantic web. In: Proc. of Int.l Workshop SWP'06, at ESWC'06, pp. 53–62 (2006)
5. Baldoni, M., Baroglio, C., Patti, V.: Web-based adaptive tutoring: an approach based on logic agents and reasoning about actions. Artificial Intelligence Review 22(1), 3–39 (2004)
6. Baldoni, M., Baroglio, C., Patti, V., Torasso, L.: Reasoning about learning object metadata for adapting SCORM courseware. In: Proc. of Int.l Workshop EAW'04, at AH 2004, Eindhoven, The Netherlands, August 2004, pp. 4–13 (2004)
7. Baldoni, M., Marengo, E.: Curricula model checking: declarative representation and verification of properties. In: Proc. of EC-TEL'07. LNCS, Springer, Heidelberg (2007)
8. Brusilovsky, P., Vassileva, J.: Course sequencing techniques for large-scale web-based education. Int. J. Cont. Engineering Education and Lifelong learning 13(1/2), 75–94 (2003)
9. Clarke, O.E.M., Peled, D.: Model checking. MIT Press, Cambridge (2001)
10. De Coi, J.L., Herder, E., Koesling, A., Lofi, C., Olmedilla, D., Papapetrou, O., Sibershi, W.: A model for competence gap analysis. In: Proc. of WEBIST 2007 (2007)
11. Emerson, E.A.: Temporal and model logic. In: Handbook of Theoretical Computer Science, vol. B, pp. 997–1072. Elsevier, Amsterdam (1990)
12. Farrell, R., Liburd, S.D., Thomas, J.C.: Dynamic assebly of learning objects. In: Proc. of WWW 2004, New York, USA (May 2004)
13. del Mar Gallardo, M., Merino, P., Pimentel, E.: Debugging UML Designs with Model Checking. Journal of Object Technology 1(2), 101–117 (2002)
14. Guelfi, N., Mammar, A.: A Formal Semantics of Timed Activity Diagrams and its PROMELA Translation. In: Proc. of APSEC'05, pp. 283–290 (2005)
15. Henze, N., Krause, D.: Personalized access to web services in the semantic web. In: The 3rd Int.l Workshop SWUI, at ISWC 2006 (2006)
16. Holzmann, G.J.: The SPIN Model Checker. Addison-Wesley, Reading (2003)
17. Melia, M., Pahl, C.: Automatic Validation of Learning Object Compositions. In: Proc. of IT&T'2005: Doctoral Symposium, Carlow, Ireland (2006)
18. Singh, M.P.: Agent communication languages: Rethinking the principles. IEEE Computer 31(12), 40–47 (1998)
19. Singh, M.P.: A social semantics for agent communication languages. In: Dignum, F.P.M., Greaves, M. (eds.) Issues in Agent Communication. LNCS, vol. 1916, pp. 31–45. Springer, Heidelberg (2000)
20. Terenziani, P., Giordano, L., Bottrighi, A., Montani, S., Donzella, L.: SPIN Model Checking for the Verification of Clinical Guidelines. In: Proc. of ECAI 2006 Workshop on AI techniques in healthcare, Riva del Garda (August 2006)
21. van der Aalst, W.M.P., Pesic, M.: DecSerFlow: Towards a Truly Declarative Service Flow Language. In: Bravetti, M., Núñez, M., Zavattaro, G. (eds.) WS-FM 2006. LNCS, vol. 4184, Springer, Heidelberg (2006)

Case–Based Support to Small–Medium Enterprises: The Symphony Project

Stefania Bandini[1], Paolo Mereghetti[1], Esther Merino[2], and Fabio Sartori[1]

[1] Research Center for Complex Systems and Artificial Intelligence (CSAI)
University of Milan - Bicocca
via Bicocca degli Arcimboldi, 8
20126 Milan, Italy
Ph.: +39 02 64487857 - Fax: +39 02 64487839
{bandini, mere, sartori}@disco.unimib.it
[2] Le Réseau CCSO Centre Directeur
Route du Jura, 37
Ph.: +41 (26) 347 48 48 - Fax: +41 (26) 347 48 49
1706 FRIBOURG, Switzerland
esther.merino@ccso.ch

Abstract. This paper presents Symphony, an IMS (Intelligent Manufacturing System) developed in the context of an interregional project supported by the European Commission. Symphony was a three year project that aimed at the development of an integrated set of tools for management of enterprizes, in order facilitate the continuous creation, exploration and exploitation of business opportunities through strategic networking. In particular, Symphony is devoted to support human resource managers of Small–Medium Enterprises in their decision making process about the looking for newcomers and/or assigning people to jobs. About this topic, the paper focuses on SymMemory, a case–based module of the main system that has been developed to identify what features are necessary to evaluate a person, aggregate them into a suitable case–structure representing a person or job profile and comparing profiles according to a specific similarity algorithm.

1 Introduction

The knowledge era has seen the emergence of information–intensive markets, some of whose key characteristics are the abundance of information available to companies and customers, information–intensive products, increased product application domains, and more demanding customers. These markets become more and more dynamic and unpredictable. Business opportunities only reveal themselves as vague trends and with a very short notice.

In such a turbulent environment, especially "high–tech or service oriented companies with high-information part in their value chain" have to cope with the enormous challenge of sustaining their competitive advantage. In order to take up this challenge, they have to be knowledge–based and adaptive. This means facing with higher complexity management [2].

R. Basili and M.T. Pazienza (Eds.): AI*IA 2007, LNAI 4733, pp. 483–494, 2007.

In this paper we present Symphony [13], an Intelligent Management System that focuses on this complexity by taking into account the specific management situation of three dedicated target groups of organizations, all belonging to the category of high–tech or service oriented companies with high information part in their value chain: Small–Medium Enterprises (SMEs), modular units of bigger companies and start–up companies.

The overall vision/objective of Symphony is to supply this target group of companies a dynamic management methodology with modular and integrated methods and tools supporting them in their key management activities. By doing so, Symphony aims at supporting two major management concerns: the *management of responsiveness and adaptation* in a turbulent environment and the *management of growth and leveraging of capabilities*.

In particular, the paper focuses on the SymMemory module of Symphony, a case–based reasoning [1] (CBR) system supporting decision making processes involved in human resource recruitment and competencies' management. The CBR paradigm has been chosen due to its suitability to deal with domains which have not been fully understood and modelled, like e.g. finance [7], weather forecasting [9], chemical product design and manufacturing [5].

SymMemory is part of the SymResources component of Symphony, a collection of Knowledge–Based tools to represent, use and share knowledge involved in human resources decisional processes: The SymMemory system has been designed to be used in a network of SMEs, where jobs and person profiles change quite often. The human resource manager problem solving activity consists in comparing the new job profile with person profiles in order to find out similarities (which, in this case, are considered as indicators of suitability of the person to the job position).

In such an environment it becomes more and more crucial to describe correctly job and person profiles, in order to be able to assign the most suited person to that new job. In the Symphony context both the kind of job and person profiles are described in terms of *competencies*: competencies are the features on which the case structure of the SymMemory module has been defined. Section 2 is devoted to further explain this concept.

Section 3 describes the case structure and the retrieval algorithm developed in SymMemory. The attributes of the case description and solution have been defined starting from competencies and arranged into a hierarchical structure (see e.g. [12] and [3]), to make the problem and solution representation more flexible. Moreover, the similarity algorithm, that is based on the k–nearest algorithm [8] gets benefits from this choice.

Then (see Section 4), a brief description of the architecture of SymMemory will be given, in order to clarify how it fits with the component–based approach [10] in order to manage competencies and retrieve cases from the case memory, presenting outputs to the user.

Finally, Section 5 will make some considerations about results and future works.

2   The Domain and Scope of Symphony: Job and Person Description

As the previous Section has briefly introduced, in the Symphony context both job and person profiles have been described in terms of competencies.

Competence management is one of the basic factors determining the economic performance of a company. Indeed, the global performance of the firm depends more and more upon individual performance, especially in SMEs. One of the aims of Symphony project is to support competence management in SMEs. Actually, the approach based on cognitive competencies seems particularly suited to the situation of adaptable SMEs, since it can be suitably supported by Information and Communication Technology (ICT) instruments which can be designed and implemented in an effective and straightforward way.

The term competence assumes a number of different meanings. Actually, competence can be approached alternatively from the perspective of knowledge of the professional behavior to be adopted, or the re–use of experience. The main idea is to translate actions into mental activities, i.e. to analyze them in terms of problem solving strategies, and to codify them according to four criteria (*mental approach, reference knowledge, relation to time and space,* and *interaction with others*).

These criteria allow the codification of competencies in order to manage them. This in turn allows to: codify the competencies related to present and future employments; analyze the competencies of individual persons; compare competencies as a support to human resources decision making (recruitment, evaluation, mobility and career management); form the competencies necessary for action (education, orientation, and so on).

The methodology [14] that has been applied in the Symphony project is named COROM[1] and it is based on a very prosaic definition of competence: *it is the capacity to solve problems efficiently in a given context.* This means that efficiency does not exist by itself, but it is determined by its context, among other factors.

The cognitive approach proposes four criteria for qualifying *mental activity* in the course of an action (for simplicity it will be used the term *activity* instead of *mental activity*):

- what kind of *Mental Approach* (MA) (i.e. successions of mental actions required to solve a problem) is needed to carry out the activity;
- which is the *Critical Knowledge Area* (CKA) (i.e. a knowledge repertory whose content is indispensable for success in a given profession) where the knowledge to carry out the activity can be found;
- what kind of *Interaction With Others* (IO) (i.e. the type and nature of the interactions that is required to solve a problem) the person must have in order to carry out the activity;

---

[1] The COROM methodology has been developed by CEGOS, Paris. http://www.cegos.fr/uk/

– what level of *Complexity in Time and Space* (CTS) (the former is the temporal perspective in which one situates oneself in the framework of the problem solving approach; the latter is the amount of information that has to be taken into account in the framework of the problem solving approach) is related to the activity.

It is now possible to define an *activity* starting from the above described dimensions. An activity is a set of instances belonging to the four dimensions and, more in details, it has the following structure: from *one* to *two* instances of the MA dimension (the first one is mandatory, the second is optional); from *one* to *four* instances of the CKA (also in this case it is mandatory to define the first instance, the others are optional); *one* mandatory instance of the IO dimension; *one* mandatory instance of the CTS dimension. The *job and person profiles* (see

Activity	MA 1	MA 2	CKA 1	CKA 2	CKA 3	CKA 4	IO	CTS
Activity 1								
Activity 2								
Activity 3								
Activity n								
Synthesis								

Fig. 1. The SymMemory Job and Person Profile Structure

Figure 1) can be now described in terms of a ranked list of *activity* elements (usually from four to seven), defining in the former case the activities necessary to perform in order to carry out a job and, in the latter case the activities that a person has (successfully) performed in the past.

It must be noticed that an advantage of this approach is the possibility to describe jobs and persons using the same structure and elements. At the bottom of Figure 1 there is a "special" activity called *synthesis*, that is a sort of summary of the activities defined in the profile. It is used by the human resources' manager since it allows to compare profiles with different number of activities defined.

3   SymMemory Case Structure and Retrieval

The definition of an opportune case structure for the problem is a critical activity in the design of a CBR system: the choice of significant attributes is essential for the definition of a suitable similarity function among cases. A problem is usually viewed as a n–tuple of features. This structure may be fixed or variable [6], depending on the complexity of the involved knowledge. During the SymMemory development it has been pointed out that the *synthesis* (i.e. a summary of all the other activities) is used by the human resources (HR) manager to compare profiles, which means that the synthesis description corresponds to the problem part of a case description. In Figure 1 the synthesis and every other activity are

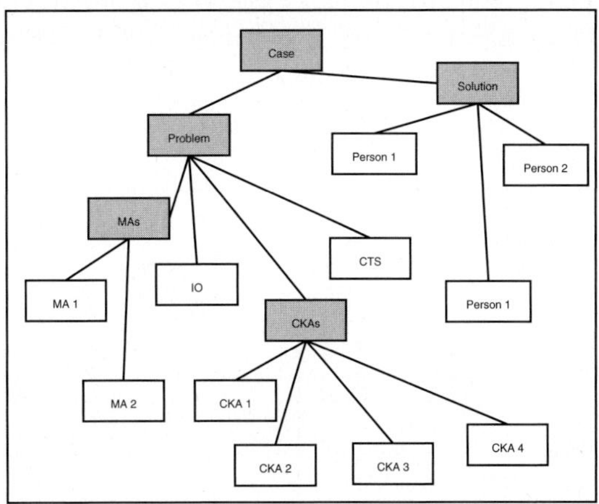

Fig. 2. The SymMemory Case Problem Structure

described by a small number of features. This consideration leads to consider the adoption of a flat case representation, as a vector. Actually, this is probably not the best choice since the number of features to be considered is not fixed: In fact, the number of MA and CKA features may vary from description to description.

For this reason a hierarchical structure (see Figure 2) for the problem description has been adopted that combines the advantages to have a flexible case structure with the simplicity of using a traditional *k–nearest neighbor* algorithm in the retrieval phase: A tree inner node, named *category* (i.e. gray filled boxes), represents a collection of *attributes*, which are drawn as tree leaves (i.e. white filled boxes). A category can be made up of other categories too.

It must be pointed out that the *outcome* [11] component in the SymMemory case structure is not defined: this decision has been taken because experts haven't yet defined a detailed measurement of the success of a performed activity. However, thanks to the adopted choice to represent and manage cases, their structure could easily integrate the outcome part once the description will be available. The solution part is simply constituted by a list of people that have performed the job.

One of the main steps in a CBR system is the retrieval phase, whose result is a subset of the case–base. Its elements are cases whose problem description is considered to compute their *similarity* to the new problem. In designing the

488   S. Bandini et al.

retrieval phase, it has been decided to exploit the following solution approach:
For each category *cat* defined in the case structure it has been designed a function
$f_{cat}(v_1, v_2, \ldots, v_n)$ to compute the value of *cat* starting from the values of the
children. In particular

$$f_{MA}(MA_1, MA_2)$$

and

$$f_{CKA}(CKA_1, CKA_2, CKA_3, CKA_4)$$

functions have been designed to compare cases with different number of instances
belonging to those categories. Since the value for the two categories can be
selected from a finite set of string values, the function defined is the same for
both.

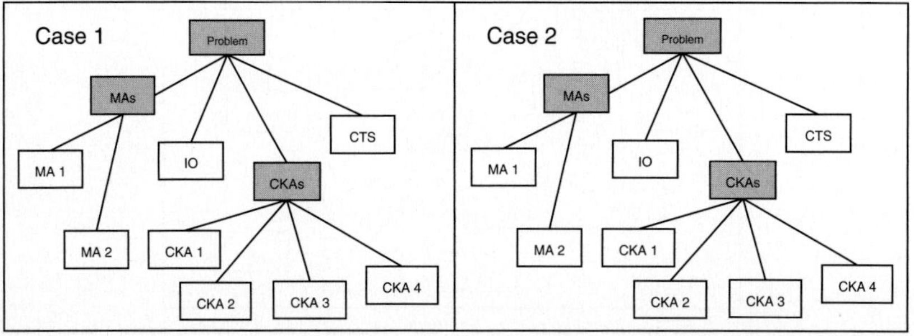

Fig. 3. Similarity between cases having the same structures

Given n the number of category children, given $V = \{v_1, v_2, \ldots, v_n\}$ the set
of values the category *cat* may assume and $W = \{w_1, w_2, \ldots, w_n\}$ the related
set of weights,

$$f_{cat} : \{V\}^n \to V$$

$$\forall v_i, w_i : i = \{1..n\}$$

Finally, by defining

$$f_{v_i} = \sum_{j=1}^{m} w_i \cdot \begin{cases} 1 & \text{if } v_j = v_i \\ 0 & \text{otherwise} \end{cases}$$

the value of f_{cat} is

$$f_{cat}(v_1, v_2, \ldots, v_n) = v_k \mid k, i \in \{1..n\}, \; i \neq k, \; f_{v_k} \geq f_{v_i}$$

These functions allow the adoption of the traditional k–nearest neighbor algorithm for comparing cases with the *same* or *different* structures.

In the former situation (see Figure 3) the cases to be compared have exactly the same structure, those the same number of features. The k–nearest neighbor algorithm can be used without the need to compute categories' values.

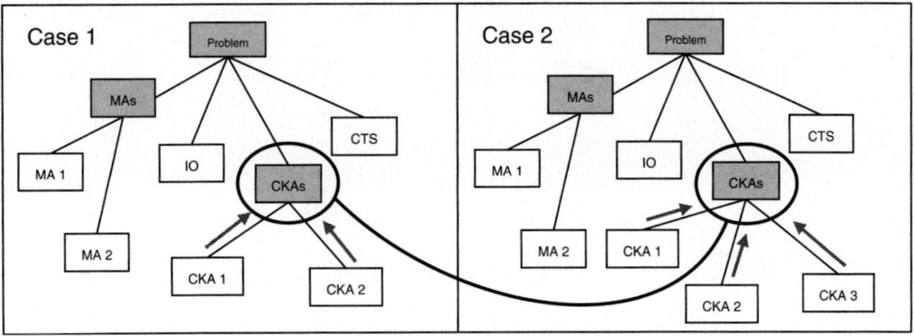

Fig. 4. Similarity between cases having different structures

In the latter situation, cases have a different case structure, for example, due to a different number of children for a category. The example in Figure 4 shows that the CKA category has two children in Case 1 problem description and three in Case 2. Before applying the similarity algorithm the CKA category value is computed, then it is used in the comparison as a feature.

An order of importance among attributes and categories has been identified. For a complete definition of the *similarity function*, in addition to weights, for each node of the tree case structure, a function indicating how to calculate the distance between two analogous elements must be specified. Thus, the rate of similarity of a past case to the current one is recursively calculated starting from the root of the structure: for each category the rate of similarity is obtained aggregating the contribute of each sub–node. When a sub–node is an attribute, the evaluation of the similarity consists in a comparison function working on attribute values.

4   SymMemory Architecture

The architecture of the SymMemory system reflects the component–based approach [4] shown in Figure 5. While the SymMemory *Data Tier* is quite simple, the *Application Tier* is split into a *Data Management Tier* and an *Application Specific Tier*: The latter is devoted to the implementation of mechanisms and strategies provided by the previously described CBR approach, the former provides a uniform access module to data sources. In order to provide this kind of abstraction level, data stored and details on related access mechanisms are described through XML files. Referring to *Presentation Tier* of SymMemory allows to show the CBR solution to the user from different point of views.

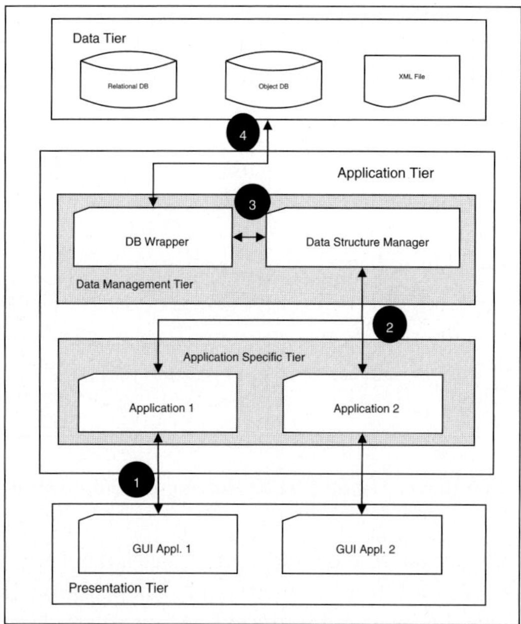

Fig. 5. The SymMemory three–tier architecture

4.1   SymMemory Data Tier

The Data Tier represents the place where data are stored. Since the focus of this work is the support of Organizations, it can be supposed that the data stored in this tier belong to the same organization or network of organizations. Moreover, in nowadays organization, data are not necessary stored in the same place, which means that data can be stored in different *data sources*. The term data source is related to a software component that supplies data storage and management facility, allowing the data storage, access, modification, deletion, and so on. Different data sources stand for data sources that are based on different technology or that are located (physically or logically) in different departments or functions of the organization. Data sources components are mainly: Data Base Management Systems (DBMS) and Structured files.

Both DBMS and structured files can be based on different approaches.

4.2   SymMemory Application Tier

Data Management Tier. As it has been previously briefly introduced, the Data Management tier can be considered as a glue placed between applications and data, allowing the former to access the Data tier in a transparent and uniform way. This tier is made up by two main software components: Data Base Wrapper (*DBWrapper*) and Data Structure Manager (*DSManager*).

On one hand the DSManager provides every application belonging to the Application Specific tier with a set of functionalities to work on data (e.g. access, visualization, updating) granting actual data structure transparency.

On the other hand the DBWrapper, instructed by the DSManager, interacts with the data sources in order to retrieve data. The DBWrapper allows transparency on the specific mechanisms for accessing data to the DSManager. In other words the DSManager does not need to explicitly know how a specific data source can be accessed (e.g. which driver must be used), it needs only to know the type of the data source.

The mechanism that allows data structure transparency to applications and data access to the Data Management tier components is mainly based on the use of the *hierarchical structure* previously discussed.

Application Specific Tier. This tier represents the implementation of concepts, mechanisms and strategies that were introduced in Section 3, through the suitable definition of data structures and algorithms for accomplishing services. In particular SymMemory mainly provides three different functionalities: comparing a job to jobs; assign a person to a given job (comparing a job profile with person profiles); find out a job for a person profile (comparing a given person profile with available jobs).

Since the job and person profiles description are exactly the same, the same logic can be used to compute similarities.

The presence of intermediate entities such as the DB Wrapper and the Data Structure Manager allows to abstract away from the actual representation of the information exploited by this module, and focus on the needs and requirements of the application level. With reference to a case, which for SymMemory has a tree–structure, the adopted representation provides a single root, identifying the case, which can contain a set of categories, which in turn may be made up of other sub–categories of attributes. These are the leafs of this tree structure, and must conform to basic services specification that an attribute must supply.

4.3   SymMemory Presentation Tier

The basic function of the Presentation Tier is to implement an interface to the user that is able to efficiently present information and receive commands and indications. Since it has been identified only one role in system user, the SymMemory Presentation Tier provides only one modules devoted to granting access to application to the human resources manager of the company.

SymMemory exploits the presentation approaches in order to show data and results related to three different functionalities provided: comparing a job to jobs, assign a job to a person and find out jobs suitable for a person profile. Since, as it has previously said, the logic to compute similarities between problems is the same, also the results can be structured in the same way.

Figure 6 shows an example of SymMemory Output: given the description of the person in terms of COROM features described in Section 2, it is compared with the categorization of the wanted person. In the example, the user is looking

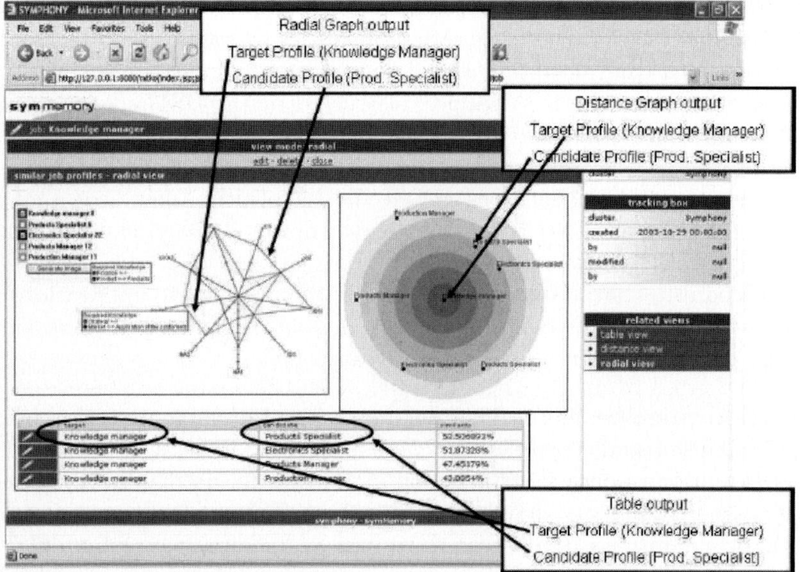

Fig. 6. Comparing job profiles: the three types of output

for a *Knowledge Manager* (i.e. the *target profile*) and the most similar profile retrieved by system is a *Product Specialist* (i.e. the *candidate profile*). The output can be visualized in the form of a *table*, a *radial graph* or a *distance graph*. The radial graph representation is the most complete, since it shows how much the characterization of the candidate profile is different from the requested one feature by feature. Tabular representation returns only the similarity value between the target profile and the candidate one. Finally, distance graph gives an immediate and more qualitative visualization of the retrieval result representing profiles as "arrows" in a sort of "dart target" with the required profile in the center and candidates distributed on it according to similarity values.

5   Conclusions and Future Work

This paper has presented a work developed in the context of Symphony, a three year project funded by European Commission[2] that aimed to build innovative methodologies and tools for supporting human resources experts of Small–Medium Enterprises in their daily activities of looking for new employers and assigning jobs to people. The project started on december 2001 and ended on november 2004.

In this context, we have paid particular attention in describing SymMemory, a CBR system that allow to retrieve people profiles form a case memory

---

[2] Symphony IST Project No 2000–61206.

according to a similarity function that works on a collection of significant featured defined by the COROM methodology. The adoption of CBR paradigm in the development of SymMemory has allowed to build an effective and efficient tool to aggregate competencies suggested by the COROM methodology and use them to support human resources manager in their daily activities. SymMemory is part of the Symphony component named SymResources.

We can say that since the end of the Symphony project, we have achieved a number of successful applications of the methodology and use, as a support, the software SymResources.

By now, the SymResources methodology has been applied in many cases and different contexts. In the industry, we mainly use this approach to support the identification of emergent jobs in fast growing sectors and subsequently to compare the required competences (jobs profiles) with the current resources. The SymResources software platform efficiently supports this process of analysis and matching and is particularly useful to enlighten the gap between the needs and the existing competences of a company. Based on these results, a competences development roadmap can easily be deployed and customised in relation to each individual's needs and competences profile and aligned with the company's goals.

For instance, a case has been achieved during the year 2006 in a Swiss SME, where the entire organisation and the relative jobs have been redefined in order to enable the company to achieve its strategy. This drastic shift has been carried out with the whole support of the SymResources kit (methods and tools). At the end of the year, the SME was able to stand on an organisation fitting with its strategy requirements, with well formalised processes and customised jobs. The annual employees' assessment has been directly realised with SymResources (SW), allowing comparing each individual's competences profile with the new jobs profiles.

Therefore, we can draw the conclusions that the methodology is fully validated and applicable in an SME as well as that the SymResources software platform is by now usable by a HR expert. But this pilot phase has shown that the software still needs to be refined, particularly regarding some details about the access right module and the matching process in order to be accessible by all the employees of an SME. Moreover, the latest applications show that once the customers have understood the SymResources methods, the SymResources software platform is easy to use and its functioning is quickly acquired by the users.

Besides, a Swiss company, Harmony Solutions SA[3], is actually successfully exploiting the Symphony project's results in different sectors like biotech companies (because they are the fastest growing industry in developed economies and they are knowledge based) and health sectors (particularly in hospitals, which are evolving very quickly and need to be more adaptive and efficient).

The approach adopted in its design and implementation is general enough to be applied in a number of similar contexts: Future works are devoted to explore this possibility thanks to the start of a couple of similar projects.

---

[3] http://www.harmony-solutions.net

References

1. Aamodt, A., Plaza, E.: Case–Based Reasoning: Foundational Issues, Methodological Variations, and System Approaches. AI Communications 7(1), 39–59 (1994)
2. Affolter, I., Merino, E., Sciboz, L.: Competences Management for Dynamic Collaborative Value-creating Networks[IMS Symphony project]. In: International IMS Forum 2004, Global Challenges in Manufacturing, Cernobbio, Italy, 17-19 May 2004, pp. 17–19 (2004)
3. Bandini, S., Colombo, E., Sartori, F., Vizzari, G.: Case Based Reasoning and Production Process Design: the Case of P-Truck Curing. In: Funk, P., González Calero, P.A. (eds.) ECCBR 2004. LNCS (LNAI), vol. 3155, pp. 504–517. Springer, Heidelberg (2004)
4. Bandini, S., Colombo, E., Mereghetti, P., Sartori, F.: A General Framework for Knowledge Management System Design. In: Proceedings of ISDA04 – 4th IEEE International Conference on Intelligent Systems Design and Application, Budapest, pp. 61–66 (August 2004)
5. Bandini, S., Manzoni, S., Sartori, F.: An Approach to Knowledge Management, Sharing and Maintenance: the Case of the P-Truck Project. In: Cappelli, A.,Turini, F. (eds.) AI*IA 2003. LNCS (LNAI), vol. 2829, pp. 489–510. Springer, Heidelberg (2003)
6. Bergmann, R., Stahl, A.: Similarity Measures for Object–Oriented Case Representations. In: Smyth, B., Cunningham, P. (eds.) EWCBR 1998. LNCS (LNAI), vol. 1488, pp. 25–36. Springer, Heidelberg (1998)
7. Bonissone, P.P., Cheetham, W.: Financial Application of Fuzzy Case-Based Reasoning to Residential Property Valuation. In: Proceedings of the 6th IEEE International Conference on Fuzzy Systems, vol. 1, pp. 37–44. IEEE Computer Society Press, Los Alamitos (1997)
8. Finnie, G., Sun, Z.: Similarity and Metrics in Case-based Reasoning. Intelligent Systems 17(3), 273–285 (2002)
9. Hansen, B.K., Riordan, D.: Weather Prediction Using Case-Based Reasoning and Fuzzy Set Theory. In: Aha, D.W., Watson, I. (eds.) ICCBR 2001. LNCS (LNAI), vol. 2080, Springer, Heidelberg (2001)
10. Herzum, P., Sims, O.: Business Component Factory. OMG Press (2000)
11. Kolodner, J.: Case-Based Reasoning. Morgan Kaufmann, San Mateo (CA) (1993)
12. Manzoni, S., Mereghetti, P.: A Tree Structured Case Base for the System P-Truck Tuning. In: Proceedings of UK CBR workshop at ES 2002, Cambridge (December 10, 2002)
13. Merino, E., Mereghetti, P., et al.: Conceptual data design and architecture document and platform description, Deliverable 4.1 Symphony project (January 2003), http://www.simphony-village.com
14. Michel, S., Ledru, M.: Capital Compétence dans l'entreprise. ESF, Paris (1991)

Synthesizing Proactive Assistance
with Heterogeneous Agents

Amedeo Cesta, Gabriella Cortellessa, Federico Pecora, and Riccardo Rasconi

ISTC-CNR, Institute for Cognitive Science and Technology
Italian National Research Council, Rome, Italy
`name.surname@istc.cnr.it`

Abstract. This paper describes outcome from a project aimed at creating an instance of integrated environment endowed with heterogeneous software and robotic agents to actively assist an elderly person at home. Specifically, a proactive environment for continuous daily activity monitoring has been created in which an autonomous robot acts as the main interactor with the person. This paper describes how the synergy of different technologies guarantees an overall intelligent behavior capable of personalized and contextualized interaction with the assisted person.

1   Goal: A Context-Aware Intelligent Assistant

The use of intelligent technology for supporting elderly people at home has been addressed in various research projects in the last years, e.g., PEAT [1], PEARL [2,3], I.L.S.A. [4]. Increasing attention is also given to the synthesis of Cognitive Systems to produce aids that enhance human cognition capabilities. As an example, the project CALO [5] has as its primary goal the development of cognitive systems which integrate multiple intelligent capabilities for the complex task of contextual support to humans. The ROBOCARE project shares several of the challenges with those projects. More specifically its objective was to build a distributed multi-agent system to provide assistive services for elderly users at home, the agents being a heterogeneous collection of fixed and mobile robotic, sensory and problem solving components. As a target domain a prototypical home environment was chosen where the presence of an intelligent robotic assistant could be of potential help in the daily life of a cognitively impaired user. The important capabilities of such an intelligent assistant concern the ability to (a) maintain *continuity of behavior*, such as ensuring continuous monitoring of what happens in the environment (the state of the assisted elder and of his/her domestic context), (b) create a *context* at the knowledge level around the actions that the assisted elder performs (routinely, exceptionally, etc.), and (c) provide contextualized interaction services with the assisted elder aimed at *proactive assistance*. Our system employs AI-based scheduling technology to support daily activity management, vision-based sensory components to sense symbolic information on the whereabouts and actions of the assisted person, a mobile robot with verbal interaction capabilities as a primary interface with the assisted person, and a multi-agent coordination infrastructure based on Distributed Constraint Reasoning (DCR) for service integration.

R. Basili and M.T. Pazienza (Eds.): AI*IA 2007, LNAI 4733, pp. 495–506, 2007.

This article describes how contextualized and proactive cognitive services are obtained in such an environment. The main contributions described are: (1) the use of a distributed constraint optimization algorithm for coordination of the multiple agents involved in activity monitoring; (2) the use of a constraint based scheduling system to continuous monitor for providing appropriate alerts and warnings in the face of constraint violations; (3) the generation of relevant explanations from these constraint violations to be presented to the users in the form of verbal interaction instances. The paper specifically focuses on the aspects related to the system's context-awareness and interaction capabilities. In particular, we describe how the constraint-based scheduling technology is used to maintain a knowledge repository aimed at supporting on-demand specific interactions as well as enabling autonomous system initiative.

2   Separate Intelligent Capabilities

The main "actor" in our smart home environment is a robotic agent with verbal interaction capabilities. The robot acts as a "mediator" through which the assisted person receives advice/warnings and can query the environment. As shown in Figure 1, the robot is composed of two distinct modules. The mobile robotic platform provides advanced mobility functionalities (referred to as "robot motion skills" in the figure[1]). A second module creates an additional level of competence for the robot, referred to as "interactive skills" in Figure 1(a). Indeed this capability groups and provides access to the functionalities of the overall intelligent system. Figure 1(b) shows how the interaction skills use (a) a simplified Interaction Manager, (b) a front-end for the interaction module consisting in a Talking Head and a Speech Recognition subsystem taken as external off-the-shelf modules, (c) a key component called Intelligent Activity Monitor whose role is very relevant for the situated interaction capability of the system.

The Activity Monitor is a separate module which integrates a constraint-based scheduler with additional features for knowledge engineering, in particular for problem modeling. Particular attention has been given to the definition of "user-oriented terminologies" in order to easily synthesize both the basic elements of a target domain as well as different problem instances in the particular domain (i.e., in the form of activities and constraints among activities). For example, it allows the definition of "home domain activities" like *breakfast, lunch, go-for-walk,* and also temporal/causal links among activities like *meal-bound-medication* to express rules like "aspirin cannot be taken before eating". Through this high level language an external user (a doctor, a relative of the assisted person, etc.) may define a network of activities, a *schedule,* that the observed person is supposed to carry out in the home environment during the day. This schedule is

---

[1] The robotic platform, developed by colleagues from University of Rome "La Sapienza", consists of a Pioneer 2 integrated with a Sick laser scanner for localization. Additional work has been required to both integrate advanced SLAM algorithms and obtain robust navigation abilities which are suited for the domestic environment. Details are outside the scope of the paper.

dispatched for execution and monitored using the underlying schedule execution technology.

The key step for carrying schedule execution is to integrate information coming from *sensors*. In particular, we used stereo cameras distributed over the apartment and endowed with specific software for people localization and tracking developed by our colleagues from "La Sapienza". Even if human activity recognition is outside the scope of the project, it is worth highlighting how the sequence of observations from the artificial vision sensors allows to follow the evolution of the activities of the observed person (e.g., if and when she took a pill, when she had lunch, etc.). The key focus of this paper is on the generation of a comprehensive assistive task from the combination of all these separate intelligent components. This is made possible by three features, namely the original use of a DCR-based multi-agent coordination algorithm, the specialized use of the activity monitor, and through the generation of speech acts for active interaction based on constraint violations.

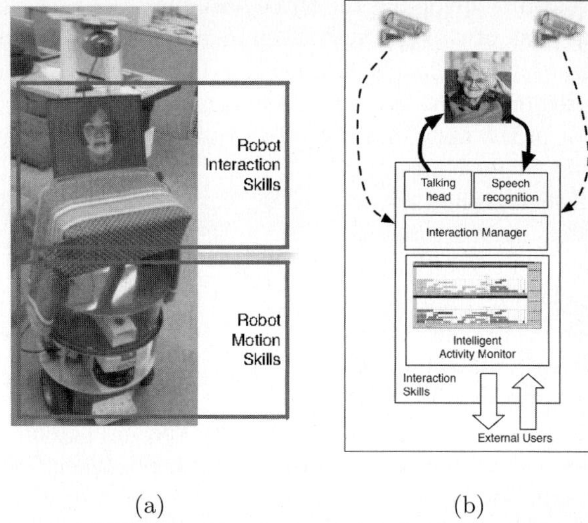

(a)   (b)

Fig. 1. (a) the robotic assistant for user interaction, and (b) a sketch of "proactive interactor" behind the robot

3   The Coordination Subproblem

Coordination of multiple services is achieved by solving a Multi-Agent Coordination problem. This problem is cast as a Distributed Constraint Optimization Problem (DCOP), and solved by ADOPT-N [6], an extension of the ADOPT (Asynchronous Distributed Optimization) algorithm [7] for dealing with n-ary constraints. Figure 2 gives an intuition of the chosen approach. We call $Application_i$ the generic intelligent subsystem that is to be integrated in the overall multi-agent system, and Var_j one out of a set $\mathcal{V}$ of variables in terms of which the coordination problem is defined. Each variable has an associated domain of Values D_j. Variables are bound by constraints like in regular Constraint Satisfaction Problems (CSP). Conversely, while constraints in CSP evaluate to *satisfied* or *unsatisfied*, in the optimization case constraints evaluate to costs, and can thus express what are often referred to as "soft constraints". Such constraints are useful for modeling preferences, and in general requirements which have a "degree of satisfiability". Constraints may involve an arbitrary subset of the variables (n-ary constraints): a constraint among the set $C \subset V$ of k variables is expressed as a function in the form $f_C : D_1 \times \ldots \times D_k \to \mathbb{N}$. For instance, a constraint involving the three variables $\{Var_1, Var_3, Var_7\}$ may prescribe that the cost of a particular assignment of values to these variables amounts to c, e.g., $f_{Var_1, Var_3, Var_7}(0, 3, 1) = c$. The objective of a constraint optimization algorithm is to calculate an assignment $\mathcal{A}$ of values to variables minimizing the cost of the assignment $\sum_{C \in \mathcal{C}} f_C(\mathcal{A})$, where each f_C is of arity $|C|$.

In RoboCare, the soft constraints are decided in order to orient the solution of the DCOP toward preferred world situations (broadly speaking those situations in which

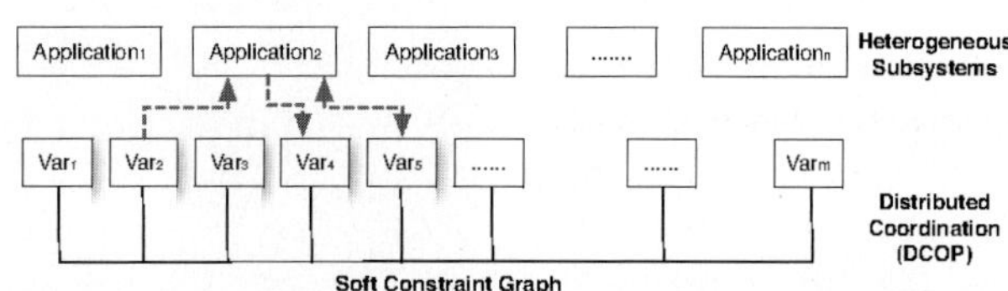

Fig. 2. DCOP to maintain distributed coherence

the person is maximally helped by the intelligent system). The system is composed of a number of heterogeneous applications: (a) an activity monitor, (b) the interaction manager plus the speech I/O modules, (c) the robot mobile platform, (d) one application for each of the cameras, each of them with the appropriate software for people localization and tracking.

Each application manages one or more of the variables which are part of the DCOP. A variable may represent (a part of) the input to an application, its output, or both (see the dashed lines in Figure 2 as an example). When the DCOP resolution algorithm (Adopt-N) is called into play, the values of the application-output variables are taken into account in the distributed resolution. When resolution reaches a fixed-point, the input variables will reflect an updated input for the applications. The correspondence between the applications' output at the i-th iteration and their input at iteration $i + 1$ is a result of the propagation rules specified in the DCOP. Overall the decisions of the applications constitute the input for the subsequent iteration of the cycle ⟨*DCOP-resolution; read-variable; application-decision; write-variable*⟩. The complete iterative procedure is depicted in Algorithm 1, which constitutes the core of the continuous operation requirement of the smart home.

Algorithm 1. Synchronization schema followed by each application *app*.

---

1. $\quad$ iter $\leftarrow 0$; $S_\text{iter} \leftarrow$ getSensoryInput(V_in^{app})
2. $\quad$ **while** true **do**
3. $\quad\quad$ $S_\text{iter-1} \leftarrow S_\text{iter}$
4. $\quad\quad$ **while** $(S_\text{iter} = S_\text{iter-1}) \wedge (\text{iter} \geq app'.\text{iter}, \forall app' \neq app)$ **do**
5. $\quad\quad\quad$ $S_\text{iter} \leftarrow$ getSensoryInput(V_in^{app})
6. $\quad\quad$ iter $\leftarrow$ iter $+ 1$
7. $\quad\quad$ **forall** $v \in V_\text{in}^{app} \cup V_\text{out}^{app}$ **do**
8. $\quad\quad\quad$ resetVarAssignment()
9. $\quad\quad$ $\mathcal{A}|_{V_\text{out}^{app}} \leftarrow$ runAdopt() $\quad$ /** Adopt-N termination **/
10. $\quad\quad$ triggerBehavior$(\mathcal{A}|_{V_\text{out}^{app}})$

Specifically, let the situation, i.e., the state of the environment, of the assisted person, and of the services themselves, at time t be S_t. The DCOP formulation of the coordination problem represents the desired behavior of the system in function of the possible states of the environment and of the assisted person. Therefore, if $S_t \neq S_{t-1}$, the agents must trigger an "instance of coordination" so as to decide the assignment $\mathcal{A}$ which represents the desired enactment of services. The strong difference in nature between the various components of the multi-agent system reflects heavily on the coordination mechanism because of the uncertainty connected to the time employed by services to update the symbolic information which is passed on to the agents. For instance, the system contains devices which are driven by artificial stereo-vision algorithms, the convergence of which is strongly affected by a variety of factors. This problem also affects other components of the smart home, such as the activity monitor (described later in this article) which must propagate sensor-derived information on the temporal representation of the assisted person's daily schedule. As a consequence, it is in general impossible to have strict guarantees on the responsiveness of the agents. For this reason the albeit asynchronous solving procedure needs to be iterated synchronously. More specifically, the agents continuously monitor the current situation and execute the ADOPT-N algorithm whenever a difference with the previous situation is found. The getSensoryInput() method in the pseudo-code samples the state of the environment which is represented by agent *app*'s input variables V_{in}^{app}. All agents concurrently initiate the ADOPT-N algorithm whenever the state changes or another agent has initiated the solving iteration. Thus, when an agent senses a difference in its input variables, its decision to run the coordination algorithm is cascaded to all other agents in the priority tree (see the condition in the internal while loop above). Since ADOPT-N does not rely on synchronous communication between agents, it natively supports message transfer with random (but finite) delay. This made it possible to employ ADOPT-N within the smart home scenario without modifying the algorithm internally. Furthermore, while most distributed reasoning algorithms are employed in practice as concurrent threads on a single machine (a situation in which network reliability is rather high), the asynchronous quality of ADOPT-N strongly facilitated the step towards "real" distribution, where delays in message passing increase in magnitude as well as randomness.

4   Continuous Monitoring of the Assisted Person

The ability to detect and follow the actions of the assisted person is one of the important features of the assistant. In this context we employed scheduling technology as a specific knowledge component. In fact, the Activity Monitor plays the role of activity *supervisor* and continuously tries to maintain situation awareness by updating the representation of the set of activities that the assisted person performs in the environment. As mentioned above, the desired behavior the assisted person should adhere to is initially decided by a caregiver (a doctor, or a family member) in terms of a set of activities to be monitored, i.e., the *schedule.* Activities in the schedule are bound to one another through potentially complex temporal relationships.

An important role of the intelligent assistant in this context is played by the management of all the temporal constraints present in the schedule. As the environment sensing cycle commences, the system periodically checks the state of the monitored area, trying to detect and recognize the execution state of all the activities. Regardless of the prescribed behavior in the baseline schedule, the assisted person is obviously free to act as she likes: this basically means that at each detection cycle, the system is called to precisely assess the possible differences between the actual and desired state. While monitoring the person's behavior, the system takes note of the evolution of the environment, continuously keeping an updated internal representation of the latter, and possibly reacting to some significant events, if deemed necessary. The monitoring efforts will therefore focus upon: (1) keeping the internal representation of the real world consistent with the behavioral decisions of the assisted person at all times, and (2) performing the necessary rescheduling actions so as to satisfy a maximum number of temporal constraints originally imposed by the caregiver.

An example. To be more concrete, let us consider a behavioral pattern described by a schedule composed of 6 different activities (*breakfast, lunch, dinner,* as well as taking one of three different medicines). Due to medical requirements, let us also suppose that such activities must satisfy certain temporal requirements, such as "dinner should not begin before 7:30 PM, nor should it occur less than 5 hours after lunch" and "aspirin should only be taken after dinner, but no later than 20 minutes after", and so on.

An "ideal schedule", i.e., an enactment of these activities which does not violate any temporal constraint, is shown in Fig. 3. Broadly speaking, the objective of the Activity Monitor is to recognize deviations from

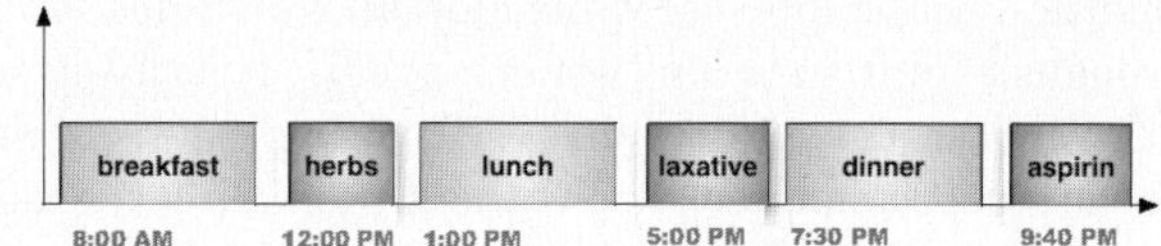

Fig. 3. Example of desired behavior specified by the care giver for the assisted person in form of a *schedule*

this ideal situation. Specifically, the system should assess the extent to which the elder user's behavior deviates from this situation. This equates to assessing which temporal constraints are progressively violated during the day. In a nutshell, system interventions are driven by constraint violations: warnings, alarms and suggestions result from violated constraints, which are processed by the interactive subsystem on board the robotic mediator.

The execution monitoring algorithm. Once the monitoring starts, the sensors are periodically queried and the nominal schedule is adjusted in accordance with the assisted person's detected behavior. At each detection cycle, the execution status of each activity is checked: among the possible cases, some activities may be reported as under execution before their nominal start time, the execution of other activities may be reported as delayed, the duration of some activities may

---

Algorithm 2. The Execution Monitoring Algorithm.

```
1.   while true do
2.       Events_t ← S_t
3.       if Events_t ≠ ∅ then
4.           C_{r,t} ← removeConstraints()
5.           insertContingencies(Events_t)
6.           K_t ← ∅
7.           while C_{r,t} ≠ ∅ do
8.               c_j ← chooseConstraint(C_{r,t})
9.               if ¬ re-insertConstraint(c_j) then
10.                  K_t ← K_t ∪ c_j
```

---

exceed the nominal value, and so on; each deviation from the nominal schedule may entail a conflict which has to be reacted upon.

As an example (see figure 3), let us suppose that the patient, after having dinner, sits on the sofa and starts watching TV: at each new sensor detection cycle, the system assesses the situation and delays the *aspirin-taking* activity. But since, according to the medical requirements, the aspirin should be taken no later than twenty minutes after dinner, delaying the aspirin activity beyond the prescribed time will eventually determine a time constraint insertion conflict in the data base of constraints; upon the occurrence of this conflict, the intelligent assistant will possibly respond by issuing a warning to the patient as a reminder for the forgotten action. Algorithm 2 shows the execution monitoring algorithm we employ. As shown, an "environment sensing" action is periodically performed (line 2). This occurs by accessing the symbolic representation of the current situation (S_t), that is obtained by reading the DCOP variable described previously. As a result, the set $Events_t$ of the occurred events is periodically acquired. By *event* we mean any mismatch between the expected situation, according to the caregiver's prescriptions, and the actual situation (i.e., a planned action which fails to be executed, is considered as an event). If events are detected, the first action is to remove all the active constraints present in the schedule (line 4). By *active* constraints, we mean those which do not completely belong to the past, with respect to the actual time of execution t_E.[2] All constraints that are not idle are active. Obviously, idle constraints do not take part in the analysis because they will not play any role in the evolution of the future states of the world. In the next step (line 5) all the detected contingencies, properly modeled as further constraints, are inserted in the plan. This is the step where the system updates the internal representation of the schedule in order to preserve consistency with the world's true state. Lines 7–10 implement the constraint re-insertion cycle, where the algorithm tries to restore as many caregiver requirements as possible given the current situation. Notice in fact that it is probable that not all the original constraints will be accepted at this point: the occurrence of the contingencies might in fact have changed the

---

[2] More formally, given an execution instant t_E and a constraint c_k binding two time points t_a and t_b, c_k is considered *idle* if and only if $(t_a < t_E) \wedge (t_b < t_E)$.

temporal network constrainedness, so as to make impossible the complete re-insertion of the constraints removed at the previous step. During the cycle, all the constraints which are rejected are stored in the set K_t. Constraints insertion (and rejection) is an extremely delicate issue, for many reasons:

- System reaction may consist in verbal suggestions or warning. The information conveyed by these messages strongly depends on the contents of the set K_t. As we will show, the analysis of all the rejected constraints quantitatively and qualitatively determines the system's response. Given a temporal network TN underlying the current schedule, the set $K_t = \{k_{t,1}, k_{t,2}, ..., k_{t,r}\}$ must be such that: (1) the insertion of each $k_{t,j}$ in TN causes a propagation failure; (2) the cardinality of K_t is maximum. Condition (1) ensures that every constraint in K_t plays a role in determining system's reaction, ruling out false-positive situations; condition (2) ensures that no contingency escapes system's attention.
- The acceptance of each constraint c_j (and complementarily, the contents of K_t), is generally dependent on the particular order chosen for re-insertion. In general, a number of different choice heuristics (chooseConstraint() method) can be envisaged, leading to different approaches for contingency management. To clarify this issue, let us consider a temporal network TN and two constraints c_1 and c_2 such that the attempt of posting both of them in TN would determine an inconsistency: in this case, if the insertion order is $\{c_1, c_2\}$, then c_2 is going to be rejected; if the opposite order is used, c_1 is rejected. Since in this context it is essential that the reaction be related to the closest contingency with respect to execution time t_E, the particular heuristic employed for re-insertion is backward-chronological. The result of this choice is that the rejected constraints will be the ones which are temporally closer to the actual instant of execution, therefore meeting the condition of reaction urgency. In other terms, the monitoring system is oriented towards synthesizing a suggestion regarding the primary cause of a violation, rather than forming one based on a distant effect of the assisted person's behavior. The constraints are chronologically ordered taking into account the values of the time point pairs they are connected to. More formally, given a set of constraints $\{c_1(t_{1,s}, t_{1,e}), c_2(t_{2,s}, t_{2,e}), \ldots, c_n(t_{n,s}, t_{n,e})\}$, where each $c_i(t_{i,s}, t_{i,e})$ connects the time points $t_{i,s}$ and $t_{i,e}$, the constraint $c_i(t_{i,s}, t_{i,e})$ chronologically precedes the constraint $c_j(t_{j,s}, t_{j,e})$, if $min(t_{i,s}, t_{i,e}) < min(t_{j,s}, t_{j,e})$.

5   Managing Assistant/Assisted Interaction

As already mentioned, interaction relies here on the embodied robotic assistant as the focal point between the user and the system. Communication between the user and the robotic mediator occurs verbally. We distinguish two form of interaction based on *who takes the initiative* to start a dialogue:

On-Demand interaction in which the user takes the initiative first. The assisted person commences interaction, for instance, by querying the system's knowledge base: "have I taken my pills?", or "can I make an appointment for tomorrow at 5 PM?".

Proactive interaction in which the intelligent environment commences interaction guided by its internal reasoning. In this project constraint violations have been considered as a *trigger* for the system to take the initiative and perform some actions: issue an alarm in case of illness, or verbalize warnings and suggestions.

All interaction services rely on the Interaction Manager. This module essentially consists in a rule-based system that fires *situation-action* rules. In other words, it continuously assesses the situation and activates a particular submodule as an action. We categorize as *On-Demand* interaction the "Question-Answer" category of dialogues. This activity is triggered by a speech input from the assisted person. The generation of the answer is managed mostly internally to the manager that has information on the activities' history and/or on the current state of the environment, to answer questions like "Have I had lunch?" or "What time is it?", etc. Instances of *Proactive* interaction are "Danger" and "Warning" scenarios. Undoubtedly, one of the important tasks for assistance is to recognize emergencies for the monitored person. The emergency trigger is fired by particular combinations of the input provided by the sensors that monitor the environment and the assisted person. As an example we can discriminate as a dangerous situation the case in which a person is "laying down in the kitchen floor" or "laying down in bed half and hour after usual wake up" as a danger, rather than "laying down in bed within a given period" which is recognized as a regular situation. The danger trigger is dealt with by a specific behavior of the multi-agent system that interrupts the usual flow of activities and undertakes an action: the robot is sent to the assisted person, a specific dialogue is attempted, and if no answer from the assisted person is obtained, an *Alarm* is immediately fired to the external world (call to a relative, to an emergency help desk, etc.). A warning scenario in one in which constraint violations are detected by the Activity Monitor. Broadly speaking, the monitor decides the values for the variables that are used by the interaction manager to trigger a proactive dialogue with the assisted person. The content of the dialog is synthesized on the basis of the monitor's internal knowledge. Overall the Interaction Manager is a quite simple planner that supervises the initiative of the "interactor" towards the assisted person. It is worth underscoring how the combination of this manager and the activity monitor endows the whole assistive environment with capabilities of proactive participation in a mixed-initiative interaction.

6   From Scheduler Knowledge to Interaction

The main issue here is how to translate constraint violation information into semantically meaningful verbalizations that the user may immediately understand. First, we present the building blocks of this semantic analysis. At this level, all semantic inference will have to be derived exclusively from the analysis of information of temporal nature; the second step is to integrate temporal data with different types of environmental information.

Each element in the violated constraints set K_t is either a *minimum* or a *maximum* constraint. *Duration* constraints are defined through both a minimum and a maximum constraint insisting between the start and end time points of an activity and representing, respectively, the minimum and the maximum duration allowed. At a basic level, the violation of each constraint is immediately given a semantic interpretation: (a) violation of the minimum constraint c_{min}^{ij} between activities A_i and A_j (where A_i is the *SOURCE* activity), directly involves the following interpretation: "*A_j is taking place too soon.*"; similarly, violation of the maximum constraint c_{max}^{ji} between activities A_j and A_i (where A_i is the *SOURCE* activity), enables the possible semantics interpretation: "*A_j is being delayed too much.*". Duration constraints undergo a slightly different analysis: in fact, a violation of a duration constraint on activity A_i might either entail the violation of the minimum or of the maximum constraints involved. In the first case, we imply the semantics: "*A_i was too brief.*"; in the second case, "*A_i is lasting too long.*".

Given these building blocks for higher level interpretation of the events related to constraint violation, can employ other kinds of information to improve semantic precision. Again, the meaning of the violation of the constraint c_{min}^{ij} might take a different interpretation depending on the execution status of activity A_i. In fact, in case A_i has not yet been executed, it is easy to see that the violation of c_{min}^{ij} directly implies that the activities A_i and A_j have been temporally swapped, against the caregiver's prescriptions. Therefore, a general verbalization consistent with the situation is: "*Shouldn't A_i be performed first?*". Obviously, in case A_i has been executed, a more realistic verbalization is: "*Shouldn't you wait a little longer before performing A_j?*". Regarding the maximum constraints c_{max}^{ji}, a different interpretation might be given depending if activity A_i is the *SOURCE* or not. When $A_i = SOURCE$, we are describing an *absolute* time limit which involves the start time of A_i; in the opposite case, the time constraint is *relative* to the end time of A_j. This difference might influence the verbalization related to c_{max}^{ji} violation: in the first case, "*Expedite the execution of A_i.*" might suffice; in the second case, "*Too much time is passing between A_i and A_j.*" is more appropriate.

Another source of information that is used to enhance verbalization meaningfulness is related to the causal domain theory. In other words, information about casual links between direct neighbors of the activities involved in a constraint violations can be exploited to deliver explanations. An example is given in figure 4 (a): in this case, the delay on A_2 involves also a delay on A_3, as both activities are causally linked; as shown, two maximum constraints might be simultaneously violated, and causal link analysis can interpret the situation according to the following semantics: "*Commence A_2, as it cannot be executed too late with respect to A_1, and A_3 cannot begin later than a certain hour.*". Figure 4 (b) shows another example: A_1 is currently under execution and the causal link between A_1 and A_2 eventually gets the maximum constraint between A_2 and A_3 violated. Again, the deduced verbalization would be: "*Stop A_1, as A_2 must be immediately executed because it cannot be performed too late with respect to A_3.*".

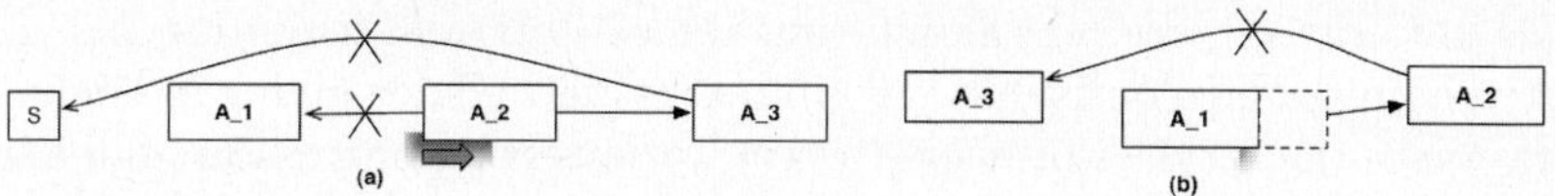

Fig. 4. Exploiting causal information for meaningful semantic deduction

7   Assessment of System Performance

There are two meaningful measures with respect to the performance of the overall system: (1) the *application responsiveness*, i.e., the time t_{A^i} between a physical change in the environment and the recognition of the change in the input variable(s) of application A_i; (2) the *coordination responsiveness*, i.e., the time t_{iter} it takes for a complete iteration of Algorithm 1 to terminate. The overall responsiveness of the system is therefore represented by $t_{\text{iter}} + \max_{A^i}(t_{A^i})$. The former measure is affected by the uncertainty connected to the time employed by services to update the symbolic information which they are responsible for deducing. For instance, the People Localization and Tracking service is realized through an artificial stereo-vision algorithm the convergence of which is strongly affected by a variety of factors (for instance, object tracking is difficult when many similar objects move in the same space, when the environment and the agents cannot be adequately structured, and when moving observers are used for monitoring large environments). A similar problem affects also the activity monitor, which must propagate sensor-derived information on the temporal representation of the behavioral constraints. This may require a combination of simple temporal propagation, re-scheduling, as well as other complex procedures (e.g., deciding which of the violated constraints are meaningful with respect to verbal warnings and suggestions). Dually, the responsiveness of coordination can be affected by two factors, namely network load and number of variables involved in the coordination (specifically, the complexity of the ADOPT family of DCOP algorithms is exponential in the number of variables). In practice, coordination responsiveness in the environment is mostly affected by the network load (which becomes high when services such as streaming video are activated). Qualitative observations have shown that application responsiveness can vary between about 1 and 10 seconds. In normal conditions (i.e., if no streaming video service is active) coordination responsiveness varies in the same order of magnitude of application responsiveness. The overall responsiveness of the system (e.g., the delay between an emergency situation occurring and the system activating the contingency plan) varies typically between about 5 and 30 seconds.

8   Conclusions

The ROBOCARE project has addressed one of the open challenges in AI, namely that of integrating diversified intelligent capabilities to create a proactive assistant for everyday life in a domestic environment. Our effort to integrate diverse intelligent components has allowed us to develop a system prototype which is capable not only of passively monitoring the execution of activities, but also of proactively initiating consistent and contextualized advice-giving dialogue. The integration of the services provided by the various components through DCOP-based coordination provided the necessary "functional glue" to demonstrate an overall intelligent and proactive behavior, improving on previous preliminary versions of the integrated system (e.g., as described in [8]). A key feature of our assistive environment is the ability to intervene proactively and contextually in the assisted person's daily activity management. Specifically, this is achieved through the use of a continuous schedule monitoring functionality which provides appropriate alerts and warnings through the robotic mediator. The generation of relevant explanations stems from constraint violations from which verbal messages are synthesized and presented to the user. This particular use of the internal knowledge of a constraint-based scheduler is to the best of our knowledge quite novel, as constraint violations directly determine both *when* the system has to interact and the interpretation of the violation contributes to determine *how* to interact with the user.

Acknowledgements. Special thanks to the colleagues of the Dept. of Computer and Systems Science (DIS) of the University of Rome "La Sapienza" for joint work on the ROBOCARE intelligent environment. This research has been partially supported by MIUR (Italian Ministry of Education, University and Research) under project ROBOCARE: http://robocare.istc.cnr.it.

References

1. Levinson, R.: PEAT - The Planning and Execution Assistant and Trainer. Journal of Head Trauma Rehabilitation (1997)
2. Pineau, J., Montemerlo, M., Pollack, M., Roy, N., Thrun, S.: Towards Robotic Assistants in Nursing Homes: Challenges and Results. Robotics and Autonomous Systems 42, 271–281 (2003)
3. Pollack, M.: Intelligent Technology for an Aging Population:The Use of AI to Assist Elders with Cognitive Impairment. AI Magazine 26, 9–24 (2005)
4. Haigh, H.Z., Kiff, L.M., Ho, G.: The Independent Lifestyle Assistant (I.L.S.A.): Lessons Learned. Assistive Technology 18 (2006)
5. Myers, K.: CALO: Building an intelligent personal assistant. Invited Talk. In: AAAI-06. The Twenty-First National Conference on Artificial Intelligence and the Eighteenth Innovative Applications of Artificial Intelligence Conference (2006)
6. Pecora, F., Modi, P., Scerri, P.: Reasoning About and Dynamically Posting n-ary Constraints in ADOPT. In: Proceedings of 7th Int. Workshop on Distributed Constraint Reasoning (DCR-06), at AAMAS'06 (2006)
7. Modi, P., Shen, W., Tambe, M., Yokoo, M.: Adopt: Asynchronous distributed constraint optimization with quality guarantees. Artificial Intelligence 161, 149–180 (2005)
8. Bahadori, S., Cesta, A., Iocchi, L., Leone, G., Nardi, D., Pecora, F., Rasconi, R., Scozzafava, L.: Towards Ambient Intelligence for the Domestic Care of the Elderly. In: Remagnino, P., Foresti, G., Ellis, T. (eds.) Ambient Intelligence: A Novel Paradigm, Springer, Heidelberg (2005)

Robust Color-Based Skin Detection for an Interactive Robot

Alvise Lastra, Alberto Pretto, Stefano Tonello, and Emanuele Menegatti

Department of Information Engineering
via Gradenigo 6/b, 35131 Padova, Italy
`lastraal@dei.unipd.it`

Abstract. Detection of human skin in an arbitrary image is generally hard. Most color-based skin detection algorithms are based on a static color model of the skin. However, a static model cannot cope with the huge variability of scenes, illuminants and skin types. This is not suitable for an interacting robot that has to find people in different rooms with its camera and without any a priori knowledge about the environment nor of the lighting.

In this paper we present a new color-based algorithm called VR filter. The core of the algorithm is based on a statistical model of the colors of the pixels that generates a dynamic boundary for the skin pixels in the color space. The motivation beyond the development of the algorithm was to be able to correctly classify skin pixels in low definition images with moving objects, as the images grabbed by the omnidirectional camera mounted on the robot. However, our algorithm was designed to correctly recognizes skin pixels with any type of camera and without exploiting any information on the camera.

In the paper we present the advantages and the limitations of our algorithm and we compare its performances with the principal existing skin detection algorithms on standard perspective images.

1 Introduction

The identification of people represented into images or videos is a challenging problem addressed since many years. The applications of a reliable and robust algorithm for people detection in any kind of images can be virtually unlimited. Techniques and theoretical assertions were presented, but most of them give reliable results only with structured settings or with "a priori" fixed imaging conditions. Moreover, the most reliable solutions require specific and expensive hardware-software resources. The aim of this work is a general technique that correctly recognizes skin pixels independently on the different ethnic groups, under varying illumination conditions in whatever complex environment, only using chromatic informations. The result is the development of a new complex, but fast end efficient to compute filter, we called it VR Filter.

This work was motivated by the creation of a robust and reliable skin detection algorithm to be used as main input for the "people finding module" of the

R. Basili and M.T. Pazienza (Eds.): AI*IA 2007, LNAI 4733, pp. 507–518, 2007.

software architecture controlling the robot in Fig. 1. This work is the result of the meeting of Robotics and Art. This is an interactive robotic sculpture conceived and realized by the artist Albano Guatti. The robotic part was totally developed by people at the IAS-lab and at IT+Robotics according to Guatti's concept. The robot's main sensor is an omnidirectional camera (well integrated with the artistic appearance of the statue). The omnidirectional camera is used to detect the persons in the environment, thanks to the skin detection algorithm described in this paper. The omnidirectional visual perception is coupled to an omnidirectional range sensor realized with a ring of Polaroid sonar sensors.

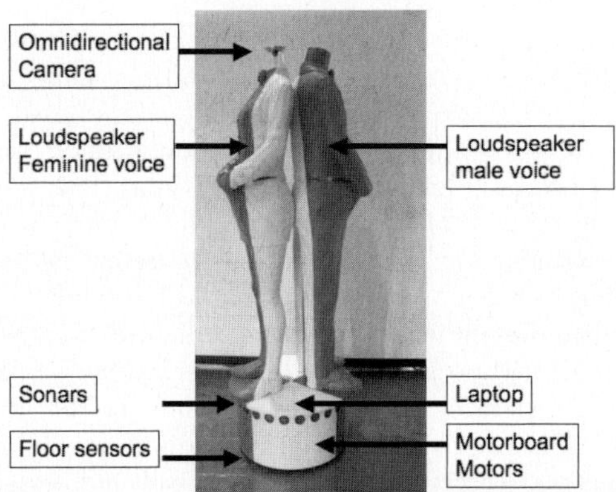

Fig. 1. The interactive robotic sculpture by Albano Guatti

2   The Skin Detection Problem

2.1   Definition of Problem

First of all we shall formalize the skin detection problem as generally as possible Let be P the following problem we are going to solve: P:

Given I(R,G,B), in the following simply I, an arbitrary image we don't know anything about it (which are its contents, type of source and the environment conditions when it has been generated), we want to identify all the regions and only the regions Ω of I where human skin is present.

In particular, we want to be able to successfully process low definition images with moving objects in very complex scenarios as usually are the omnidirectional images grabbed by mobile robots.

2.2   Related Work

As mentioned in the introduction, the skin detection problem is still a very investigated problem; many authors have proposed techniques to solve it by fixing one or more parameters of the problem, but a solution of P considering all of them has never been given. Soriano et al. [1] showed a camera-specific color-based method ables to recognize skin in different light conditions and proposed a database of camera behaviors to complete it. The use of a normalized color space, in this case the **rg** normalized color space, is interesting because it allow to isolate skin locus with simple quadratic functions. Also for [2], [3], [4], [5] a normalized color space, the **rg** normalized color space again (in the following simply **rg**), is the most effective to extract with success a skin locus. This is because it is as little as possible dependent on the illuminant. In addition, Albiol et al. [6] affirmed that an optimum filter for skin detection will have the same performance even working in different color spaces. Other authors suggested to solve the P problem proposing a union of different techniques to improve the results of a single color-based method and its defects; Kruppa et al. [7] and Tomaz et al. [4] used, for example, a color-based filtering with a shape identification obtaining good result for face detection. In [4] again and also in [8] a static prefilter on RGB space is used too: with this last kind of filters it is easier and more natural to remove zones that surely are non-skin areas (pixels too inclined to black, to green or to blue etc). At last we mention Lee et al. [9] who proposed an elliptical boundary for skin locus using a gaussian model and six chromatic spaces and Sebe et al. [10] who proposed a Bayesian network approach instead.

2.3   The VR Filter

As stated, the P problem is too wide, we need to insert some limitations. We need to introduce two constraints (that anyway do not compromise the generality of method itself):

$\mathbf{V}_1$ *The image I has to represent a scene not too obscure nor too saturated*
$\mathbf{V}_2$ *The source of I has to ensure that its calibration is not strongly unbalanced*

V_1 excludes from P all images captured in illumination conditions near to darkness or saturation, while V_2 excludes from P all images that have chromatic features too altered (e.g., images with a very high contrast).

From now on, P will be the initial problem, restricted by V_1 and V_2, and I will be an image satisfying V_1 and V_2.

In brief, the strategy of our method is the sequence of two distinct color-based techniques and could be called "catch and clean the skin locus". The first

(a)   (b)   (c)   (d)

Fig. 2. Example images: (a) satisfies V_1, (b) does not satisfies V_1, (c) satisfies V_2, (d) does not satisfies V_2

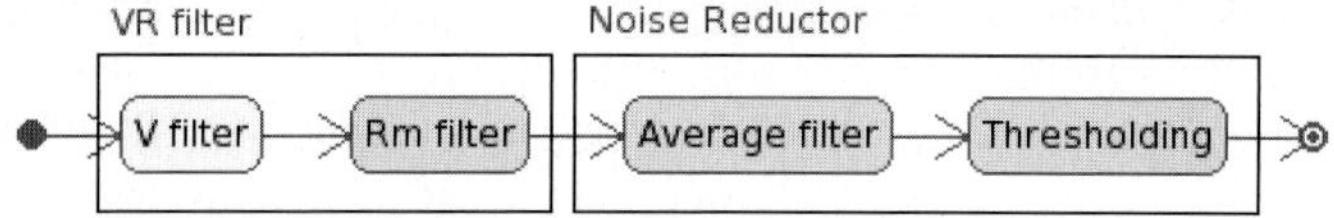

Fig. 3. UML flow of the algorithm implementing the VR filter

filter "catches" the skin locus, even capturing spurious pixels, while the second "cleans" possible false positive pixels selected by the first one. We chose this approach, because we experimentally obtained a dynamic region, depending on the statistics of first and second order of the image, ables to intercept the skin locus; the formal and mathematical expression of this region is the core of our work. So, our filter, called VR filter, is a cascade of two filters that we called V filter and Rm filter, respectively.

V Filter. The V filter is a dynamic filter based on the definition of a 2D region of a color space that we called V region (Ω_V). Ω_V depends on the statistics of first and second order of I: let be **xy** a generic two-dimensional color space and let be f_x and f_y the distributions of I with respect to **x** and **y**, respectively. f_x and f_y can be considered as mass distributions of two discrete aleatory variables x and y. Thus, we can compute the expectation m (1) and the positive radix of the second order central moment σ (2):

$$m_x = \sum_{\alpha \in A_x} \alpha f_x(\alpha), \quad m_y = \sum_{\alpha \in A_y} \alpha f_y(\alpha) \tag{1}$$

$$\sigma_x = \left[\sum_{\alpha \in A_x} (\alpha - m_x)^2 f_x(\alpha) \right]^{\frac{1}{2}}, \sigma_y = \left[\sum_{\alpha \in A_y} (\alpha - m_y)^2 f_y(\alpha) \right]^{\frac{1}{2}} \tag{2}$$

where in (2) A_x and A_y are the alphabets of the two aleatory variables x, y

Let's now define a set, we called V_{bone} (γ_V), that will be helpful to understand the meaning of Ω_V:

$$\gamma_V = \left\{ (x, y) : x < m_x, \, y = m_y, \, x \in \mathbf{x}, \, y \in \mathbf{y} \right\}$$

$$\bigcup \tag{3}$$

$$\left\{ (x, y) : y = \frac{\sigma_y}{\sigma_x} (x - m_x) + m_y, \, y < m_y, \, x \in \mathbf{x}, \, y \in \mathbf{y} \right\}$$

γ_V is the union of two half-rays of $\mathbb{R}^2$ with origin in (m_x, m_y) the first with angular factor equals to zero, the second with a non-negative one. Finally we define Ω_V as the union of two half-stripes described by the following formulas:

$$\Omega_V = \big\{ (x,y): \ x < m_x, \ |y - m_y| < \sigma_y, \ x \in \mathbf{x}, \ y \in \mathbf{y} \big\}$$

$$\bigcup \tag{4}$$

$$\left\{ (x,y): \left| y - \frac{\sigma_y}{\sigma_x}(x - m_x) - m_y \right| < \sigma_y, \ y < m_y + \sigma_y, \ x \in \mathbf{x}, \ y \in \mathbf{y} \right\}$$

Intuitively, Ω_V appears, in the generic $\mathbf{xy}$ plane, as a "V" rotated counterclockwise of about $\pi/2$. In Fig. 4, we plot three examples of γ_V (blue lines) with corresponding Ω_V (red areas) in a generic $\mathbf{xy}$ normalized color space generated by three different images.

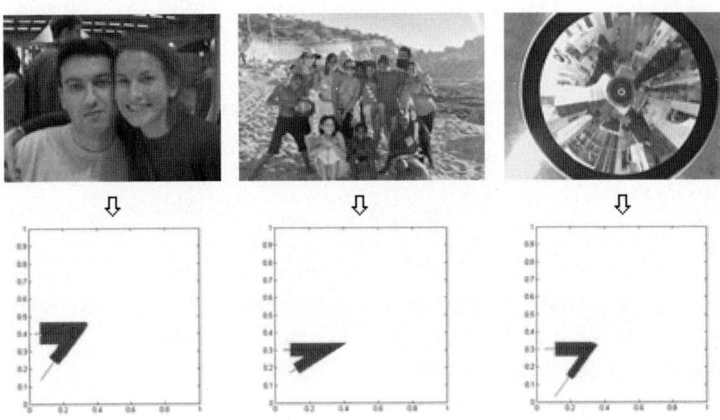

Fig. 4. Examples of different γ_V and Ω_V

Both γ_V and Ω_V can be create in any 2D-space, but their usefulness for our goal is that we have experimentally verified that *if the 2D-space $\mathbf{xy}$ is the bg normalized color space, the γ_V intercepts the skin locus for each I of P. Therefore, in the $\mathbf{bg}$ normalized color space, Ω_V contains at least a part of the skin locus for each I of P.*

Thus, V filter works in the $\mathbf{bg}$ normalized color space; we recall that the $\mathbf{bg}$ normalized color space is defined from the $\mathbf{RGB}$ color space as:

$$b = \frac{B}{R+G+B}, \quad g = \frac{G}{R+G+B} \tag{5}$$

so defined w and h as the width and the height of I, respectively, the V filter can be defined by:

$$V(i,j) = \begin{cases} 1 & \text{if } \mathbf{bg}(i,j) \in \Omega_V \\ 0 & \text{otherwise} \end{cases} \quad \text{with } 0 < i \leqslant w, \ 0 < j \leqslant h$$

Rm Filter. The Rm filter is a static filter. It works in the RGB color space and has been designed to remove regions of the color space that the V filter might has selected and that with high probability not belong to the skin locus. Rm filter is simply defined as:

$$Rm(\mathrm{R},\mathrm{G},\mathrm{B}) = \begin{cases} 1 & \text{if } \mathrm{G} < k_G \text{ AND } \mathrm{G} < \mathrm{R} - k_{RG} \text{ AND} \\ & m_R\mathrm{R} < \mathrm{G} < M_R\mathrm{R} \text{ AND } \mathrm{B} < \frac{\mathrm{R+G}}{k_B} \\ 0 & \text{otherwise} \end{cases} \tag{6}$$

The equations in 6 have been designed to remove, in this order, color tones that have too much green, too much green with respect to red and too much blue with respect to green and red.

To set the five constant parameters in (6) a directed reinforcement learning technique, called Counter-based with decay [11], has been used. As learning patterns, we have considered 25 images with different subjects and lighting conditions. The target of this technique was to maximize the test score we will define in (10).

So the optimal values for the parameters have been resulted the following: $k_G = 166$; $k_{RG} = 25$; $m_R = 0.563$; $M_R = 0.808$; $k_B = 2.0$;

Finally we can define our VR filter as this mask:

$$VR = V \text{ AND } Rm \tag{7}$$

After VR (7) an average filter and a thresholding operation are applied to the output of VR, to stabilize the results and to remove noise around the selected regions; so, they appear more regular and are easier to process by any subsequent image processing algorithm (see Fig. 3).

3   Tests and Results

The tests are been executed on a dataset of over 950 images of different generic sources (pictures taken form omnidirectional cameras, the Internet, perspective cameras and videoframes) but also from all the "Georgia Tech Image Database" [12]. To better catalog all the images, they have been divided into seven categories:

Cat A: Subject in foreground with simple background
Cat B: Subjects in foreground with complex background
Cat C: Night indoor/outdoor environments with artificial lights
Cat D: Daily outdoor environment with difficult scene or lighting conditions
Cat E: Different ethnic groups
Cat F: Complex omnidirectional images
Cat G: Complex omnidirectional images with moving subjects

3.1   Test Metrics Definition

To test and to measure the perform of our filter we have design some formal rules.

Let's consider two B&W images, the first generated by the VR Filter as the mask of the filtered output and the second that represents the mask of the skin pixels manually extracted from the original image. Let be M_{VR} and M_{HR} respectively. Both these images are in binary encoding: for M_{HR}, as example, $M_{HR}(x,y) = 1$ if the pixel (x,y) is considered a skin pixel, $M_{HR}(x,y) = 0$ otherwise. From M_{VR} and M_{HR} is computed a new image T:

$$T = M_{HR} - M_{VR} \tag{8}$$

Each pixel of T can assume only three values:

-1 if the pixel is a non-skin pixel recognized as a skin pixel (false positive [FP])
 0 if the pixel, either skin or non-skin, is correctly recognized (recognized [OK])
 1 if the pixel is a skin pixel not recognized (miss [MS])

From T are successively computed three parameters:

$$k_{OK} = \#(0) \text{ in T}; \ k_{FP} = \#(\text{-1}) \text{ in T}; \ k_{MS} = \#(1) \text{ in T}$$

Finally, defined $N = w \cdot h$ where w and h are the same defined in 2.3 and $k_{M_{HR}} = \#(1)$ in M_{HR}, we compute the following result test values:

$$p_{OK} = \frac{k_{OK}}{N}, p_{MS} = \frac{k_{MS}}{k_{M_{HR}}}, p_{FP} = \frac{k_{FP}}{N - k_{M_{HR}}} \tag{9}$$

and a resume test score as:

$$S = 2p_{OK} - 5p_{MS} - p_{FP} \tag{10}$$

With the values defined in (9) a strict test conclusion can be given as reported in Table I, so a test results a positive match, if and only if, at least the 75% of pixels are correctly recognized, and the each of the percentages of the skin pixel and of the non-skin pixels that have been correctly recognized is over 80 % and 90 % respectively.

Table 1. Test result based on values of (9) with $p_{OK} \geqslant 0.75\%$. All tests having $p_{OK} < 0.75\%$. are labeled as Miss.

$p_{OK} \geqslant 0.75$	$p_{FP} < 0.10$	$p_{FP} \geqslant 0.10$
$p_{MS} < 0.20$	Correct match	Correct match with too false positives
$p_{MS} \geqslant 0.20$	Miss	Miss

In Figure 5 we show an example of visual test result.

3.2   Algorithm Performance and Statistical Results

All operations executed by the VR filter are linear in the image dimensions; thus, its computational complexity is $\Theta(w \cdot h)$.

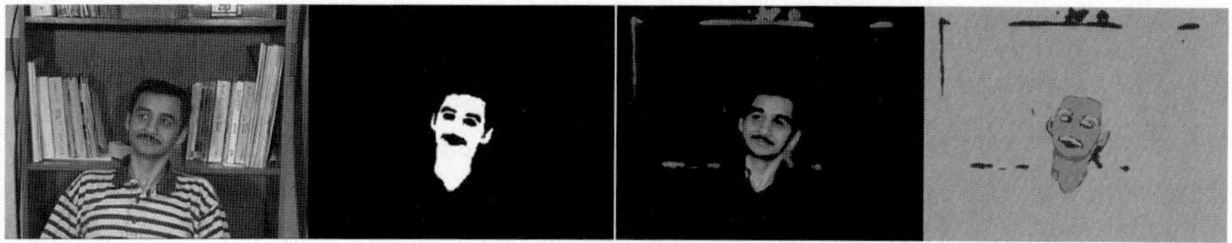

Fig. 5. From left to right: original image (s13/13.jpg of [12]), manually extracted skin mask, VR filter output and graphical output of the test. In this last image the skin and the non-skin pixels correctly recognized are respectively green and lime, the FP pixels are blue and the MS pixels are red. For this image we have: OK = 92.62%; MS = 14.67% and FP = 2.87%; S = 1.56.

Table 2. Summary of test result's percentage by category

Cat	Positive match	Positive match with too false positives	Miss cases
A	87.23 %	9.04 %	3.73 %
B	88.00 %	10.00 %	2.00 %
C	86.00 %	8.00 %	6.00 %
D	82.00 %	12.00 %	6.00 %
E	85.18 %	9.08 %	5.74 %
F	90.00 %	8.00 %	2.00 %
G	88.00 %	8.00 %	4.00 %
Total	**86.63 %**	**9.16 %**	**4.21 %**

In Table II we reported the statistical test results by apply the VR filter on the dataset of images, while Table III shows the processing time spent by our algorithm in a C/C++ implementation.

The percentage of hit is very high on images with normal lighting conditions, even if there are complex scenes, and is lower, but still good, on night images. Using a resolution of 800x600 is possible to compute up to 2.5 frame per second; this rate is not very high, however is higher then most alternative techniques proposed in the literature. To speed-up the computation of a sequence of video frames, the VR filter can be used to create a look-up table (LUT) containing the 3D region of the RGB color space that contains the skin locus of the first frame; the subsequent frames can be processed accessing the LUT to check if the pixels

Table 3. Computation time - test on Pentium M 1.5GHz

Image resolution	C/C++ kpxlps	fps	Image resolution	C/C++ kpxlps	fps
320x240	1182	15.36	1024x76	1311	1.67
640x480	1258	4.07	1280x1024	1327	1.22
800x600	1280	2.67	1600x1200	1319	0.69

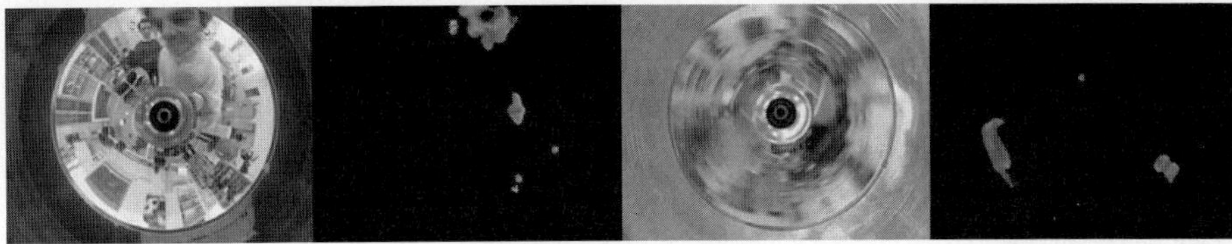

Fig. 6. On the left, an example of Cat. F: positive match 90.00 %. Picture grabbed by the interactive robotic sculpture of Figure 1 and an example of Cat. G: positive match 88.00 %, on the right.

Fig. 7. On the left, an example of Cat. A: positive match 87.23 % (this example refers to the image s03/04.jpg of [12]) and, on the right, two examples of Cat. B: positive match 88.00 %.

belong to the skin locus or not. The LUT needs to be updated by VR filter only if the lighting conditions change in time.

Fig. 8. Top: Examples of Cat. D: positive match 82.00 %; Bottom: Examples of Cat. E: positive match 85.18 %.

3.3 Some Tests on Generic Images

In this section we present the results of our skin detector on some images grabbed with the omnidirectional camera of our robot (Fig. 6), generic images grabbed with a digital camera (top-left of Fig. 8) and obtained from the Internet (other images). Figures have been organized into categories as explained in Section 3.

Comparison 1. Soriano et al. technique [1] vs VR filter:

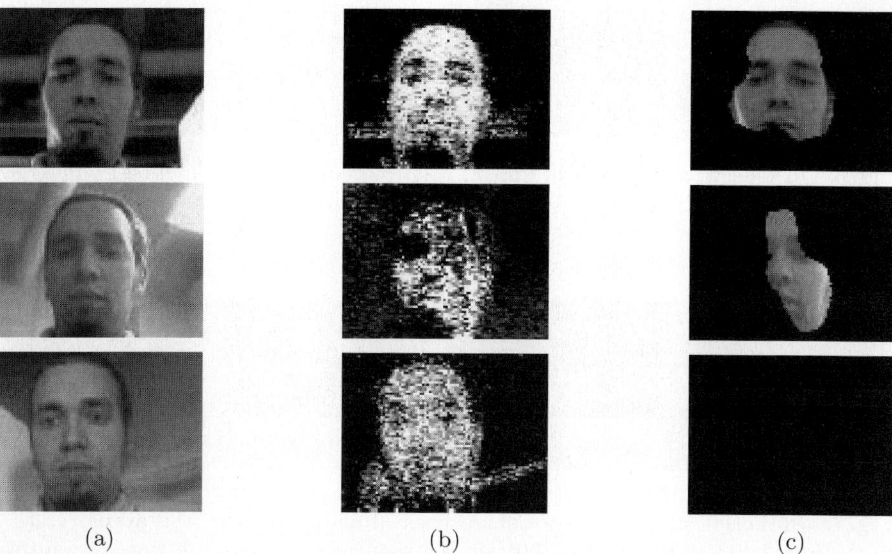

(a)   (b)   (c)

Fig. 9. Original images (a), Soriano filter (b) and VR filter (c). Soriano's camera-specific technique is able to correctly recognize skin pixels under incandescent and fluorescent lamps, while VR filter is camera independent and less sensitive to noise, but misses the face under fluorescent light.

Comparison 2. Tomaz et al. technique [4] vs VR filter:

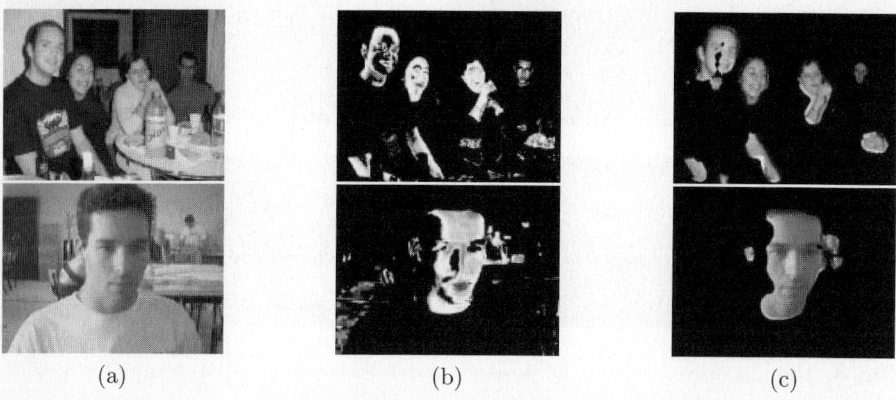

(a)   (b)   (c)

Fig. 10. Original images (a), Tomaz filter (b) and VR filter (c). VR filter is more robust to highlights (first row) and to background noise (second row), in addition Tomaz el al. method also needs an initial camera calibration.

Finally we report a comparison between our VR filter with some skin detector proposed by other authors (Fig. 9–11). We used the original images extracted by the cited papers.

Comparison 3. Kruppa et al. technique [7] vs VR filter:

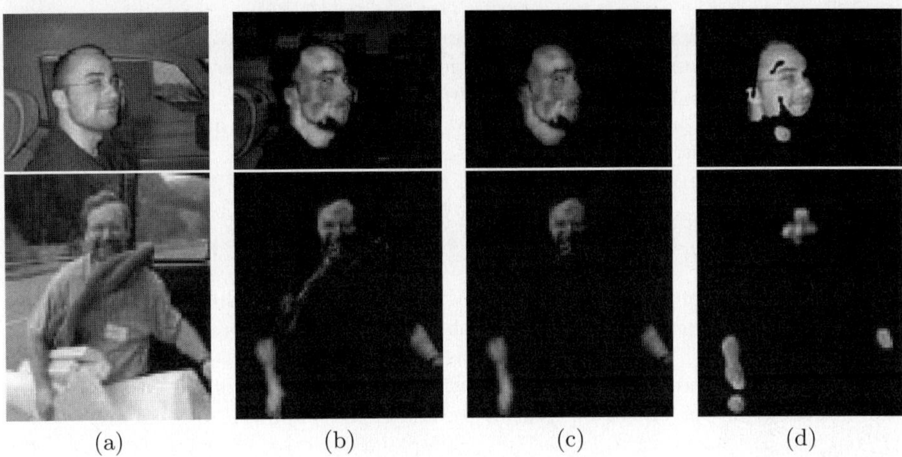

(a)   (b)   (c)   (d)

Fig. 11. Original images (a), Kruppa color-based filter (b), Kruppa color+shape filter (c) and VR filter (d). VR filter and Kruppa's color+shape algorithm results are similar; comparing the performance of the two algorithms, VR performs better.

4   Conclusions and Future Works

A new color-based skin detection algorithm has been presented. Our approach gives a solution for the skin detection problem, in conditions as generic as possible and it uses only chromatic information as input. As reported in the literature, the use of one color space is not enough for arbitrary images and a combined solution is needed. The result of our work is the VR filter; it is composed of a cascade of two filters: the V filter and Rm filter. The first is a dynamic filter working in the bg normalized color space. The latter is a static filter working in the RGB color space. This technique is robust and reliable, if the input image satisfies two constraints V_1 and V_2 (that anyway do not compromise the generality of method itself).

We compared the performance of the VR filter with various skin detector (color-based and not) and our method gave comparable or better results, even if it uses a simpler and faster technique; it also works correctly with a larger range of images.

The proposed VR filter has been successfully used in several exhibitions of the interactive robotic sculpture of Fig. 1. The robot run for five days at SMAU 2005 (the biggest Information Technology fair in Italy) moving around among hundreds of persons. At MART (Museum of Modern Art, Rovereto (TN) Italy the robot run for two days in the cafeteria and in the museum hall.

Future works will be aimed at relaxing the assumption V_1 and V_2, in order to be able to correctly process any images. For this scope we are working to remove the static numerical parameters of the filter, by making the Rm filter dynamic.

References

1. Soriano, M., Huovinen, S., Martinkauppi, B., Laaksonen, M.: Skin detection in video under changing illumination conditions. In: 15th International Conference on Pattern Recognition, vol. 1, pp. 839–842 (2000)
2. Martinkauppi, B.: Face colour under varying illumination - analysis and applications. PhD thesis, University of Oulu (2002)
3. Schwerdt, K., Crowley, J.: Robust face tracking using color (2000)
4. Tomaz, F., Candeias, T., Shahbazkia, H.: Improved automatic skin detection in color images. In: 7th Digital Image Computing: Techniques and Applications, pp. 419–427 (2003)
5. Wilhelm, T., Böhme, H.J., Gross, H.M.: A multi-modal system for tracking and analyzing faces on a mobile robot. Robotics and Autonomous Systems 48, 31–40 (2004)
6. Albiol, A., Torres, L., Delp, E.J.: Optimum color spaces for skin detection. In: International Conference on Image Processing, vol. 1, pp. 122–124 (2001)
7. Kruppa, H., Bauer, M.A., Schiele, B.: Skin patch detection in real-world images. In: Van Gool, L. (ed.) Pattern Recognition. LNCS, vol. 2449, pp. 109–117. Springer, Heidelberg (2002)
8. Kjeldsen, R., Kender, J.: Finding skin in color images. In: 2nd International Conference on Automatic Face and Gesture Recognition, pp. 312–317 (1996)
9. Lee, Y.J., Yoo, I.S.: An elliptical boundary model for skin color detection. In: International Conference on Imaging Science, Systems, and Technology, pp. 472–479
10. Sebe, N., Cohen, I., Huang, T.S., Gevers, T.: Skin detection: A bayesian network approach
11. Thrun, S.B.: Efficient exploration in reinforcement learning. Technical Report CMU-CS-92-102, Pittsburgh, Pennsylvania (1992)
12. Georgia Tech Laboratories: Georgia Tech Face Database, `ftp://ftp.ee.gatech.edu/pub/users/hayes/facedb/`

Building Quality-Based Views of the Web

Enrico Triolo[1], Nicola Polettini[1,2], Diego Sona[1], and Paolo Avesani[1]

[1] Fondazione Bruno Kessler (FBK-IRST), 38050, Trento - Italy
[2] DIT, University of Trento, 38050, Trento - Italy

Abstract. Due to the fast growing of the information available on the Web, the retrieval of relevant content is increasingly hard. The complexity of the task is concerned both with the semantics of contents and with the filtering of quality-based sources. A recent strategy addressing the overwhelming amount of information is to focus the search on a snapshot of internet, namely a Web view. In this paper, we present a system supporting the creation of a quality-based view of the Web. We give a brief overview of the software and of its functional architecture. More emphasis is on the role of AI in supporting the organization of Web resources in a hierarchical structure of categories. We survey our recent works on document classifiers dealing with a twofold challenge. On one side, the task is to recommend classifications of Web resources when the taxonomy does not provide examples of classification, which usually happens when taxonomies are built from scratch. On the other side, even when taxonomies are populated, classifiers are trained with few examples since usually when a category achieves a certain amount of Web resources the organization policy suggests a refinement of the taxonomy. The paper includes a short description of a couple of case studies where the system has been deployed for real world applications.

1   Introduction

The tremendous dimension of the Web offers previously unseen amounts of easily accessible information. We know that Web retrieval has received a big improvement in the last few years, and many Web search engines provide reliable results for many queries. On the other side, the growth of contents published on the Web is weakening the notion of relevance. Dealing with increasing amount of information requires combining the notion of relevance with the notion of quality. The issue of quality is not new since the notion of authority has been one of the key factors of the success of Google's search engine. Nevertheless it has been proved [1] that the computational models for authority can be easily biased by malicious users. The assessment of quality-based Web resources is still an open issue in the research agenda.

The notion of quality is a hill-defined concept that still needs to be managed manually. According to this view, one of the recent strategies dealing with the search engine challenge is to focus the retrieval process on a snapshot of the Web. The intuitive idea is that, the reduction of information noise is obtainable seeding search engines with a collection of topic-centered Web resources, filtered

R. Basili and M.T. Pazienza (Eds.): AI*IA 2007, LNAI 4733, pp. 519–530, 2007.

according to quality criteria. The assessment of quality is currently in charge of a user.

The idea of organized collections of Web resources is not new. Web directories are probably the most representative example of the effort in this direction. Bookmarking is another attempt trying to implement the notion of personal view of the Web. Nevertheless, in the past the purpose of Web directories was mainly to support the browsing of an end-user.

The latest trend is to provide a different way to exploit a thematic collection of Web resources. Recently both Google and Yahoo! deployed a new service allowing custom search engines on given Web views (Google with CSE[1] and Yahoo! with Rollyo[2]). The idea is very simple: delivering a search engine on a predefined topic-driven portion of the Web selected according to criteria of quality. The working assumption is that, if a Web view is well defined, the search engine can achieve a better trade-off between precision and recall of the retrieval process.

From these experiences, it turns out that a situation where an editorial staff organizes the Web resources for better access is conceivable with the ultimate goal of capturing a high quality view of the Web. However, as valuable as these efforts are, they cannot cover more than a small part of the Web. This because, to guarantee a quality standard, these efforts need to be done by hand, with obvious costs in terms of money and time resources.

It is now evident that there is a demand of new supporting tools improving the efficiency of this editorial activity. In this paper, we present QuIEW, a system specifically designed to help editors to create and manage repositories of reviewed and certified Web resources. This system incorporates many features that help editorial staff to retrieve, collect, organize, and review Web sources of information.

In Section 2 we will provide a background on the most adopted approaches to make the Web resources easily accessible by consumers and we will describe the basic hypothesis for the construction of the system. In Section 3 a description of the QuIEW system with its basic and most interesting functionalities/services is given. Section 4 will describe one of the most interesting features of the system, solved with artificial intelligence models. Finally, in Sections 5 and 6 a description of two case studies and concluding remarks are drawn.

2   Background

The retrieval of pertinent and qualitative Web resources is a problem particularly perceived nowadays, due to the huge amount of useless information unavoidable by standard search engines. One way to solve this problem is to create restricted views of the Web where someone filters, classifies and, in case, reviews the Web sites according to some policy. Within this perspective there are two main approaches that we refer to as *top-down* and *bottom-up* strategies.

---

[1] CSE stands for Custom Search Engine. http://www.google.com/coop/cse/
[2] http://www.rollyo.com/

In the *top-down* strategy, the underling hypothesis is that the Web resources are categorized according to a number of classes. In this scenario, the editorial committee can work in two ways. One is to decide and fix in advance the interesting categories for the specific domain. All the retrieved resources are then classified in one or many of these categories. The other approach is to let the set of categories change in time. This allows for adaptation of the categorical system to the rapid changes of the Web. Nonetheless, also in the second approach the editorial committee mediates the change of the categorical system.

Topic hierarchies are usually used to simplify the management of many categories. In this schema, the most general topic is divided into sub-topics, and these divisions continue until the classes represent sufficiently fine-grain concepts. Web directories are the most common scenario of classification of Web sites into topic hierarchies. One of the most famous examples of Web directory is the *Open Directory Project*[3] supported by Google, where a collaborative activity of Web sites reviewing is performed by a community of Web consumers.

A problem with the taxonomic classification schemes is that the Web tends to change rapidly and it does not like very much the hierarchical arrangements of categories. The main reason is that many classification schemes are too restrictive and they have high inertia, i.e., their change is too slow with respect to the Web evolution. This is a reason for the emerging trend in the categorization of Web resources referred to as *bottom-up* strategy. This approach allows for a more complex categorization structure, where sets of free-form keywords are applied to the information providing a sort of open categorization scheme. The idea is to build categories from the bottom: instead of maintaining lists of documents by category, the categories construct themselves from free *tags* associated to document sources.

It follows that information producer and consumers are largely adopting collaborative tagging systems as powerful tools to organize, browse, and share collections of resources. This aggregation of user metadata is often referred to as a folksonomy, a user-generated classification emerging through bottom-up consensus while users assign free-form keywords to online resources for personal or social benefit. Well known examples of Web-based collaborative systems are Del.icio.us and Furl for social bookmarking, Technorati for blogs browsing, and Flickr for photo sharing[4].

There has been a big debate on which of the two approaches is the best. Until now however, there is not any clear answer to this question. As usual, there are promoters in both sides; in fact the answer strongly depends on both the application domain and the addressed community of users. It is clear for example, that the librarian community can only accept taxonomies, while social tagging is the perfect solution in the blogging community.

Our idea is that the two approaches can easily cohabit by taking advantage from each other. This is why we are now presenting a system that manages the

---

[3] http://dmoz.org

[4] Del.icio.us - http://del.icio.us/, Furl - http://www.furl.net/, Technorati - http://www.technorati.com/, Flickr - http://www.flickr.com/

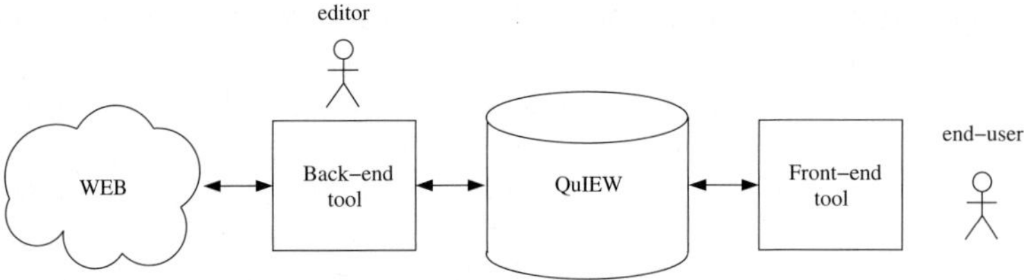

Fig. 1. The QuIEW System mainly focuses the back-end module

Web resources allowing for both *top-down* and *bottom-up* approaches. It is matter of the user then to make use of any of the two or both. The system provides the concept of *quiew* that is conceived as a taxonomic classification system. In our system, the taxonomy is mainly defined by two components: a set of categories either unrelated or (partially) related by a hierarchical relationships, and a collection of classified and tagged Web resources.

3   The QuIEW System

Our application focuses in being an aid to editors that want to create thematic views of the Web. This tool helps to discover Web resources, to build and manage thematic views of the Web, and to review the retrieved resources. We consider this instrument as a back-end tool used by one or more editors (the editorial staff) allowing to take care of the above tasks. The result of its usage generates what we refer to as a *quiew* (Quality-based Web View), i.e., an indexed and organized repository of Web resources. This *quiew* can then be exploited by any suitable front-end interface, which can be implemented either as a simple search engine or as a browsing system. Figure 1 depicts this scenario.

A *quiew* is a collection of Web sources of information regarding a particular theme or argument, filtered by quality criteria and organized into a taxonomic structure, namely the *workspace*. Each node in the taxonomy is a category and represents a classification concept. An edge between two nodes represents a hierarchical relationship between the two concepts. The creation of a *quiew* is a filtering process that takes the Web as input and generates a set of classifications for a set of collected documents.

Each document is indexed in the taxonomy along with its content and title, and it is furthermore enriched with additional meta-data, such as user provided reviews, user ratings, and tags. The set of meta-data can be easily extended to support other type of information. QuIEW can handle different file formats, such as html, pdf, Microsoft Office documents and rss feeds. Other formats can be added to the system by means of plugins.

3.1   Architectural View

Since QuIEW is primarily a tool for building Web views, it focuses mainly on the editorial job, and as such, it implements a back-end module that can help

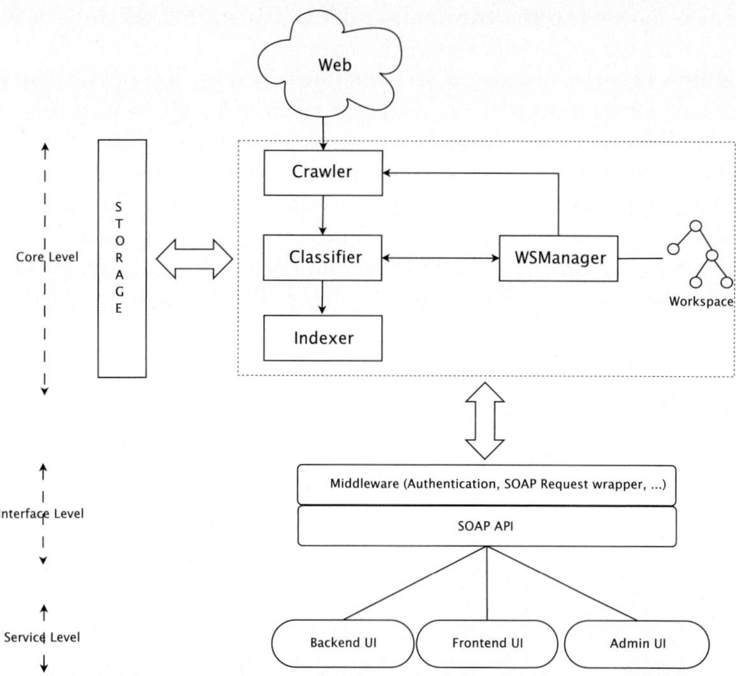

Fig. 2. High level QuIEW architecture

editors discover and categorize Web resources. The resulting Web view can then
be exploited in many scenarios, for example in a front-end system giving access
to a thematic search engine. From an architectural point of view, the application implements a service-oriented architecture (SOA[5]), composed of many
autonomous and loosely coupled components that communicate with each other
through standard interfaces. An overall architectural sketch is presented in Figure 2. As shown, the architecture is layered in three main levels:

The Core level. is the main component of the application and is composed of
many modules that perform the core activities: crawling, automatic classification, and indexing of the Web. The WSManager is merely a management
interface for the taxonomy structure, while the Storage module handles resource storage for all of the core modules and maintains data consistency.

The Interface level. allows for the interaction between the core functionalities
and the exposed services by means of an API. Through this interface we
achieved a highly extensible architecture, so that even third party developers
can implement independent and autonomous services.

The Middleware is the internal endpoint of the core modules and it implements many functions such as the Authentication module. It also allows for
wrapping of external method calls to internal ones. The SOAP API is the

---

⁵ http://www.oasis-open.org/committees/tc_home.php?wg_abbrev=soa-rm

interface exposed to the external services. Using a SOAP[6] interface enables loosely coupling of services from the core level.

The Service level. contains all services developed on top of the core application. This allows the creation of ad-hoc services for different case studies, as long as the possibility for the implementation of third party services.

One of the most important services is the *back-end User Interface* (UI), as it defines interfaces for helping editors in their classification job. The *front-end UI* implements a potential end-user service, that exploits the Web view created by an editorial staff through the back-end UI. In its basic form, it can simply expose a focused search engine. Finally, the *Administration UI* defines interfaces for the administration of the application.

3.2 Functional View

The application exposes many functionalities that can guide an editor in the process of building his own quiew: from the discovery of the interesting Web resources, to their indexing, from their semi-automatic classification to their annotation. One of the distinguishing features of our solution is the ability to perform full text searches on the document space, thus simplifying the browsing and the management of acquired resources.

QuIEW exposes the user interfaces and the functions through a Web application compatible with most modern browsers. While the back-end UI is quite complete and functional, currently we only developed a basic front-end UI that provides read only access to available quiews as a full text search engine. As stated previously indeed, our main goal was to implement the functions needed to build Web views. The exploitation of the resulting quiews depends on the specific case study. In any case, the administration UI allows for the creation of many independent Web views associated with potentially different editorial staffs. Each user in the group can be an editor of different views.

The back-end allows for editing and modification of the taxonomy by adding, updating, or removing both categories at any level in the hierarchy and relations between them. The taxonomy has no limits both on depth and on dimension. A category is defined by specifying a title and a brief description (these information will be afterward used by the automatic classifier module to suggest potential classifications). Whole sub-trees can be moved from a node to another in the hierarchy.

The system provides different methods for the discovery of resources; documents can in fact be added to the quiew in many ways, both automatically or manually. For example, after the creation of a new category, the application tries to bootstrap it by retrieving potentially meaningful documents. This is achieved by automatically starting a *meta-search* process, which queries some popular search engines using the category's title and description as search terms. The user can also explicitly request a meta-search on a specific category at any time.

Resources can also be manually added to the system using bookmarklets, i.e., simple JavaScript applications that can be stored as Urls within a bookmark in

---

[6] http://www.w3.org/TR/soap12-part0/

a Web browser. The idea is that while browsing an interesting Web page, the editor can instruct the application to retrieve and classify it by simply clicking on the bookmarklet. A pop-up window will open with the title and the Url of the page already filled. The user can then tag the resource in place. The application also suggests matching tags as the user starts typing. At this point, the system downloads the resource, which is then parsed and sent to the classifier that tries to identify the relevant categories. Finally, the application takes care of storing and indexing the resource in a full text index.

When a resource is in the system, it can be manually classified either by accepting the system's recommendations or by explicitly assigning it to other relevant categories. The user can furthermore enrich the resource with additional meta-data. For example, the editor can write his own review, assign a numerical rating, or add further tags.

As already referred in Sec. 2, the exploration of the quiews can be performed using the hierarchical structure of the taxonomy (the *top-down* approach), or "transversely" using a dynamically built tag cloud (the *bottom-up* method). While browsing the categories, potentially meaningful documents for the current class are automatically suggested by the system. The user can decide to accept a suggestion (in which case the resource will be added to the list of the classified ones), or reject it. On the other hand, when browsing the quiew by tags, the system tries to discover new meaningful resources by querying del.icio.us and retrieving the most popular resources tagged with the current tag. The editor can easily accept the suggestion and instruct the system to retrieve the desired documents. Figure 3 gives a snapshot of the application and shows some of its features.

3.3   AI Contributions

Recent trends in artificial intelligence and especially in knowledge management and machine learning highlight the interest on the organization of documents or other sources of knowledge into hierarchies of concepts. In this context, document classification is a typical task. We approached it using machine learning techniques, developing algorithms that allow our system to "learn" from resources added, certified or rejected by editors.

As stated in Sec. 2, literature distinguishes between two major types of classification schemes: the *top-down* and the *bottom-up* approaches. In our system, the AI contribution is twofold; in fact we consider both the situation of a hierarchical document classification following the *top-down* fashion and the *bottom-up* situation of recommendation of new categories.

In the *bottom-up* approach, each document can be retrieved through a simple set of keywords (i.e., tags), collaboratively introduced by editors (and in case end-users) to describe and categorize the documents. This is very much like in a keyword-based search process in which descriptive terms can be used to get a set of applicable items. In Sec. 6 we will describe how we arranged the *bottom-up* classification approach in our system.

In the classical *top-down* hierarchical classification scheme (i.e., where a taxonomy is given) all classification information is completely represented by the

Fig. 3. Snapshot of the back-end UI while browsing a quiew. The system allows the exploration of the resources by tag, and exposes a full-text search engine on the documents.

nodes of the tree. In this scheme, a child node inherits all characteristics of its parent node. These two aspects stress the importance of an appropriate organization of the categories in the tree. Much effort has to be put into the definition of the tree structure as well as in assigning documents to the correct nodes.

Unlike pre-built taxonomies, our system allows for a manual creation of a taxonomy that can be very specific to an organization, its objectives, and culture. The editor has control over the selection of terminology to make sure it reflects the understanding and needs of an intended audience, as well as the range of content to which it is applied.

Analyzing hierarchical document classification literature, we note that hierarchical indexes are usually treated as discrimination trees, where the intermediate nodes do not necessarily refer to a specific category. Contrary to most previous works[2,3], where documents are only classified on the leaves of the concept hierarchy, we consider every node in the concept hierarchy as a valid class. We are considering the Web directories framework, the most common scenario that adopts taxonomic structures, where even interior nodes in the hierarchies refer to specific concepts.

4   Hierarchical Recommender of Documents

The main purpose of the QuIEW classification module is to address a document classification task where taxonomies are playing an important role. This can be performed by a process that exploits the taxonomic structure to improve the quality of the classifier, approaching both the semi-supervised and the supervised problem. We can divide this process into **three** main phases.

In the first phase the system starts with no categories. The editorial staff starts defining the taxonomy structure where each new class is defined by linguistic meta-data. While the hierarchical structure is growing up, sets of documents are crawled and downloaded by the system. In this situation, we are in the middle of a semi-supervised learning phase, where predetermined categories exist, but no documents are certified or rejected by editors. In this case, the taxonomy is mainly defined by two components: the hierarchy of categories and a collection of unlabeled documents. The categories are described both by linguistic labels that denote the "meaning" of the nodes, and by the hierarchical relationships with other categories.

In this framework, the goal can be conceived as the activity of finding a classification hypothesis just using the knowledge encoded in the taxonomy. We can find this scenario in literature referred to as "bootstrapping process" [4,2], a process that takes as input a structured organization of classes and a set of documents and produces as output a labeling hypothesis for the given examples. The goal of the bootstrapping task is the creation of a premise for the successful training of a supervised classifier.

There are many existing classifiers that ignore the structured organization of classes in which documents are classified. The main idea of the classifiers developed for QuIEW instead is to exploit the prior knowledge encoded in the structured organization of classes.

To solve this unsupervised task we designed a clustering model referred to as Taxonomic Self-Organizing Maps (TaxSOM) [4]. This neural model organizes data according to a given taxonomy using information coming both from node labels and their topological organization. The unsupervised training algorithm takes into account this taxonomic structure and both the documents similarity and the constraints determined by the labels and the relationships. This model has been also generalized for multi-classification tasks[5].

We observed that TaxSOM is significantly better than other keyword-matching and centroid-based models. In a further analysis [6] we provided experimental results as evidence that using a shrinkage concept (propagation of knowledge driven by class relationships) significantly improves the accuracy of existing standard models that usually do not use the relational knowledge such as EM and k-means. With this preliminary work, we provided evidence that relational knowledge can improve the models performance increasing the robustness of estimators when there are too few examples. However, we also observed that more or less for all the given models the quality of results depends on the starting learning parameters.

We also proposed an alternative unsupervised probabilistic solution [7,8], a generative Hierarchical Dirichlet model for the documents in the corpus, that derives an unsupervised classification method to classify a set of text documents into a given concept hierarchy. This model formally encodes our intuition about the relationships between neighboring nodes in the hierarchy by means of hierarchically dependent Dirichlet priors for the class parameter vectors. Under this model, we derived formulae to estimate the parameters in a supervised as well as an unsupervised setting. We have seen that under this model the parameter estimates closely resemble the shrinkage estimates used in statistics. The advantage of this model with respect to the previously exposed one is that it is formally derived from starting hypotheses, and there are not learning parameters that can influence the quality of classification. The main drawback of this algorithm however is its computational complexity.

In a second phase, the editor can analyse the preliminary hypothesis formulated by the system for the candidate documents, and can therefore confirm or reject the classification hypothesis. He/she can also suggest new classifications or totally discard current ones. We consider this intermediate step still a semi-supervised task, where however we start having some labeled examples. This then creates a situation in which some categories have a small number of positive examples and an overwhelming number of negative ones.

At the end, considering benefits and drawbacks of all proposed models, in QuIEW we decided to use a simple hierarchical centroid based classifier for these two classification phases, able to manage the transition situation of a taxonomy continuously changing and to exploit the few documents certified by the editor. This simple model (a variation of the "baseline" algorithm proposed in [4]), thanks to the low computational complexity, is able to give a hypothesis location in the taxonomy for a document in real time. This is very important to satisfy usability needs.

The third and last phase arrives when a "proper" number of labeled documents is available for a supervised learning model. In this supervised classification task we have a set of training examples, which are known to belong to one or more categories and the aim is to learn the underling classification hypothesis. The artificial intelligence community has partially addressed this problem by developing hierarchical supervised classifiers that help people categorize new resources within given hierarchies. The worst problem of hierarchical supervised classifiers, however, is their high demand in terms of labeled examples. The number of examples required is related to the number of topics in the taxonomy. In a real situation, we instead have a lot of categories with few labeled examples and we have to manage possible empty categories. Furthermore in our case, the hierarchical structure can continuously change in time and the editors of the taxonomy usually prefer to split a category with many positive labeled examples into other "smaller" categories.

To solve this problem we analyzed many existing supervised algorithms (Neural Networks [9], SVMs and Hierarchical SVMs [10,11,3], Probabilistic Models [12], Association Rules [13]). At the end we decided to devise our solution which is based on artificial neural networks (a relational model derived from the recurrent cascade-correlation model). This model is able to deal with taxonomic or graph structures and overall able to manage situations where the learning process must be performed on dynamic taxonomic structures with few or no certified documents per node, thus obtaining a better precision thanks to the exploited supervision.

5 Case Studies

As for now, two main case studies have been conducted in two very different contexts. The first tries to explore the potentialities of the main idea behind QuIEW in a scholastic context. This study proposes a tool and a methodology to help students write drafts for thematic reports. Students are required not only to write reports on the proposed argument, but they also have to provide a bibliography of the sources they use. Each source should furthermore be annotated and classified in a taxonomy defined by the student himself. Our system adapted very well to this context with minimal modification from the original idea. Currently, 29 thematic reports have been completed on different themes, with a total of 40 students and 4 teachers involved. All reports are publicly available for consultation on the QuIEW Web site[7].

The goal of the second case study is to build a mountain encyclopedia referencing online resources on the argument. In this case, we provided only the backend application, while the frontend exploiting the resulting Web view was developed by a third party company. This case study exactly fits our starting hypothesis and requirements, so it was used as a testbed for our use cases. Users are using the system on a daily basis and are very pleased with it, both from a functional and usability point of view. Currently, the editorial staff is composed of 9 users and has built a taxonomy with 122 categories. About 1400 resources are indexed and classified. While the QuIEW backend access is restricted to authenticated users, the frontend[8] is public, although yet in beta stage.

6 Conclusions and Future Work

For future improvements we would like to further analyze the advantages deriving from browsing the resources by tag clouds and, in case, exploiting it. This would allow to effectively realize the *bottom-up* approach in the taxonomy construction. In this perspective we could obtain hierarchical relationships between tags. This achievement can be very useful for browsing the new obtained taxonomy, for searching words inside a category, and for improving classifier accuracy. This new functionality will eventually show how the two approaches (*top-down, bottom-up*) can cohabit and especially take advantage from each other.

Furthermore, we want to improve our supervised classifiers, exploiting the information given by the editor of the taxonomy especially when he removes a document classification for a specific category (i.e. learning from false positives).

---

[7] http://quiew.itc.it/mete/
[8] http://anguana.imont.gov.it

Acknowledgement

This work is funded by Fondo Progetti PAT, QUIEW (Quality-based indexing of the Web), art. 9, Legge Provinciale 3/2000, DGP n. 1587 dd. 09/07/04.

References

1. Gori, M., Witten, I.: The bubble of web visibility. Communications of ACM 48(3), 115–117 (2005)
2. McCallum, A., Nigam, K.: Text classification by bootstrapping with keywords, EM and shrinkage. In: Proc. of ACL-99 Workshop for Unsupervised Learning in Natural Language Processing, pp. 52–58
3. Cesa-Bianchi, N., Gentile, C., Zaniboni, L.: Hierarchical classification: combining bayes with svm. In: Proc. of 23rd International Conference on Machine Learning ICML, pp. 177–184 (2006)
4. Adami, G., Avesani, P., Sona, D.: Clustering documents into a web directory for bootstrapping a supervised classification. Journal of Data and Knowledge Engineering 54(1), 301–325 (2005)
5. Sona, D., Avesani, P., Moskovitch, R.: Multi-classification of clinical guidelines in concept hierarchies. In: IDAMAP. Proc. of Workshop on Intelligent Data Analysis in Medicine and Pharmacology, pp. 256–263 (2005)
6. Sona, D., Veeramachaneni, S., Avesani, P., Polettini, N.: Clustering with propagation for hierarchical document classification. In: ECML-04 Workshop on Statistical Approaches to Web Mining, pp. 50–61 (2004)
7. Veeramachaneni, S., Sona, D., Avesani, P.: Hierarchical dirichlet model for document classification. In: ICML. Proc. of Int. Conf. on Machine Learning, pp. 928–935 (2005)
8. Sona, D., Veeramachaneni, S., Polettini, N., Avesani, P.: Regularization for unsupervised classification on taxonomies. In: Esposito, F., Raś, Z.W., Malerba, D., Semeraro, G. (eds.) ISMIS 2006. LNCS (LNAI), vol. 4203, pp. 691–696. Springer, Heidelberg (2006)
9. Ruiz, M, Srinivasan, P.: Hierarchical text categorization using neural networks. Journal of Information Retrieval 5(1), 87–118 (2002)
10. Dumais, S., Chen, H.: Hierarchical classification of web document. In: Proc. of SIGIR-00, 23rd ACM Int. Conf. on Research and Development in Information Retrieval, pp. 256–263. ACM Press, New York (2000)
11. Hofmann, T., Caiand, L., Ciaramita, M.: Learning with taxonomies: Classifying documents and words. In: Proc. of Workshop on Syntax, Semantics, and Statistics, at NIPS'03 (2003)
12. Ceci, M., Malerba, D.: Web-pages classification into a hierarchy of categories. In: Sebastiani, F. (ed.) ECIR 2003. LNCS, vol. 2633, pp. 57–72. Springer, Heidelberg (2003)
13. Wang, K., Zhou, S., Liew, S.: Building hierarchical classifiers using class proximity. In: Proc. of the 25th VLDB Conference (1999)

Reinforcement Learning
in Complex Environments
Through Multiple Adaptive Partitions

Andrea Bonarini, Alessandro Lazaric, and Marcello Restelli

Artificial Intelligence and Robotics Laboratory
Department of Electronics and Information
Politecnico di Milano
Piazza Leonardo da Vinci 32, I-20133 Milan, Italy
{bonarini, lazaric, restelli}@elet.polimi.it

Abstract. The application of Reinforcement Learning (RL) algorithms to learn tasks for robots is often limited by the large dimension of the state space, which may make prohibitive its application on a tabular model. In this paper, we describe LEAP (Learning Entities Adaptive Partitioning), a model-free learning algorithm that uses overlapping partitions which are dynamically modified to learn near-optimal policies with a small number of parameters. Starting from a coarse aggregation of the state space, LEAP generates refined partitions whenever it detects an *incoherence* between the current action values and the actual rewards from the environment. Since in highly stochastic problems the adaptive process can lead to over-refinement, we introduce a mechanism that *prunes* the macrostates without affecting the learned policy. Through refinement and pruning, LEAP builds a multi-resolution state representation specialized only where it is actually needed. In the last section, we present some experimental evaluation on a grid world and a complex simulated robotic soccer task.

1 Introduction

Most of the RL algorithms [12] represent the action-value function as a look-up table. While this approach has strong theoretical foundations and is very effective in many applications, it is a severe limitation when applied to problems characterized by large state and action spaces (*curse of dimensionality* [12]), such as robotic problems. Several approaches try to overcome this problem by applying function approximation so as to approximate the action-value function with few parameters.

State aggregation is one of the most-studied function approximators. Several algorithms use multiple overlapping partitions of the state space so that the value function is approximated by a linear combination of the values in each partition. Many learning algorithms [4,1] are based on a *multigrid* approach that uses partitions with different resolutions to speed-up the learning process. Multiple overlapping partitions (*tilings*) are also used in *CMAC* (or *tile coding*)

R. Basili and M.T. Pazienza (Eds.): AI*IA 2007, LNAI 4733, pp. 531–542, 2007.

[11]. Finally, Singh et al. introduced *soft-state aggregations*, in which states are soft clustered [9].

All the above mentioned approaches exploit the multiple partitions structure with different levels of resolution to improve generalization capabilities of the learning algorithm, but they require the partitions to be defined in advance. Since defining partitions may be difficult and imposes an arbitrary fixed limit to the learning capabilities of the system, several algorithms automatically adapt the structure of the function approximator. Most of them (e.g., [7]) rely on a single initial partition that is split according to heuristic criteria. A complete analysis about different splitting criteria when variable resolution discretization is adopted in deterministic environments is reported in [6]. In particular, they remark how, in stochastic environments, the partition may be over-refined because of the difficulty to distinguish between the uncertainty introduced by state aggregation and the stochasticity of the environment. Therefore, although adaptive algorithms can change the structure of the approximator according to the complexity of the problem, the use of only one partition and the over-refinement in stochastic environments often leads to highly inefficient solutions.

In this paper, we present LEAP (Learning Entities Adaptive Partitioning) [2], a model-free RL algorithm that uses both a multi-partition scheme and an adaptive process that changes the function approximator structure on-line, according to the rewards received from the environment. Furthermore, we introduce a mechanism that deal with the problem of over-refinement by removing macrostates that are not necessary for the current policy.

In the next section, we introduce the basic notation and discuss the issues related to state aggregation. Section 3 describes the framework of LEAP. The adaptive process is introduced in Section 4. Section 5 shows the results in experiments proposed to the community as a reference [13,10].

2   Reinforcement Learning and State Aggregation

In RL, the interaction between the agent and the environment is defined as a Markov Decision Process (MDP), which is characterized by a tuple $\langle \mathcal{S}, \mathcal{A}, P, \mathcal{R} \rangle$, i.e., the states of the environment, the actions available to the agent, the transaction model and the reward function. At each time step, the agent acts according to a policy $\pi(s, a)$, that is the probability to take action a in state s. The performance of a policy π is measured as the expected discounted reward collected in time, $E_\pi \left[\sum_{k=0}^{\infty} \gamma^k r_{t+1+k} \right]$, where $\gamma \in [0, 1)$ is the *discount factor* that weights the relevance of future rewards with respect to recent ones. The action-value function $Q^\pi(s, a)$ is defined as the expected reward by taking action a in state s and following π thereafter. For any MDP, there exists at least one deterministic optimal policy (π^*) that maximizes the expected discounted reward and whose corresponding action-value function $Q^*(s, a)$ can be computed as:

$$Q^*(s, a) = R(s, a) + \gamma \sum_{s'} P(s, a, s') \max_{a'} Q^*(s', a') \tag{1}$$

The action-value function is often approximated using a linear function approximator:

$$\widehat{Q}(s, a) = \phi(s)\Theta(a) = \sum_{i=1}^{n} x_i w_i \tag{2}$$

where $\phi : \mathcal{S} \to \mathcal{X}$ is the input mapping from the state space to a feature space, $\Theta : \mathcal{A} \to \mathcal{W}$ maps each action to a set of parameters that are adjusted during the learning process, x_i is the i-th element of the feature vector $\phi(s)$, and w_i is the i-th element of the parameter vector $\Theta(a)$.

The most simple function approximator is state aggregation, based on the idea that wide regions, where either the policy or the action-value function is homogeneous, can be aggregated into macrostates.

Definition 1. *A macrostate m is a subset of the state space $\mathcal{S}$: $m \subseteq \mathcal{S}$. A partition P is a set of non-overlapping macrostates. The macrostate mapping function $\mu : \mathcal{S} \to P$, maps state s to the macrostate $m = \mu(s)$ such that $s \in m$, where $m \in P$.*

When the approximator contains only one partition, in each state only one macrostate is active and it can be useful to define a macrostate action-value function $Q(m, a)$ as the approximation $\widehat{Q}(s, a)$, for all the states such that $\mu(s) = m$. Given a fixed policy π, it is possible [6,9] to compute the action-value function $Q(m, a)$ using either a Bellman-like equation or a Q-Learning update rule:

$$Q^{\pi}(m, a) = (1 - \alpha)Q^{\pi}(m, a) + \alpha \left(R(s, a) + \gamma \max_{a'} Q^{\pi}(m', a') \right),$$

where s is in macrostate m and $m' = \mu(s')$.

Many algorithms use an approximator obtained by multiple overlapping partitions of the state space. Given M partitions, only one macrostate is active for each partition on state s. Thus, the input mapping function is non-zero in M elements corresponding to the active macrostates:

$$\widehat{Q}(s, a) = \sum_{i=1}^{n} x_i w_i = \sum_{j=1}^{M} \overline{x}_j \overline{w}_j, \tag{3}$$

where n is the total number of macrostates, $\overline{x}_j$ is the j-th non zero element in $\phi(s)$ and $\overline{w}_j$ is the action value of j-th active macrostate in state s for action a. As it can be noticed from the previous equation, weights x_i may significantly affect the accuracy of the approximation. In particular, in LEAP, the variance of the parameters is used to weight the parameters. Thus, the less a parameter is variable the more it is relevant in the computation of the approximation. Similarly to $Q(m, a)$, when a fixed policy π is used, the variance $\sigma(m, a)$ can be computed on-line as:

$$\sigma_{\pi}^{2}(m, a) = (1 - \beta)\sigma_{\pi}^{2}(m, a) + \beta \left(Q^{\pi}(m, a) - T(s, a, s') \right)^{2}, \tag{4}$$

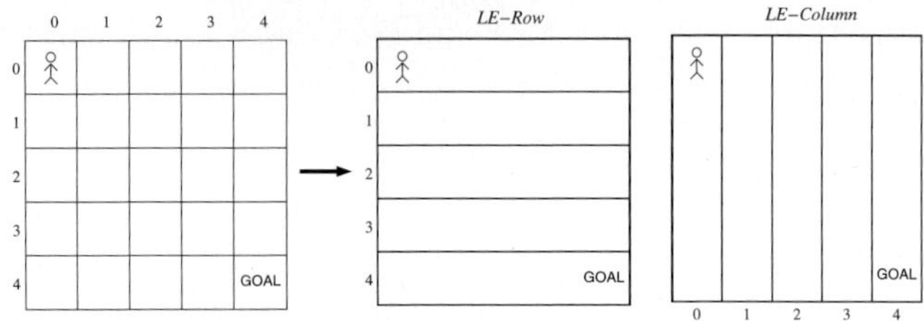

Fig. 1. A simple 5x5 single-agent grid world environment and the initial partitioning in two LEs

where $\beta \in [0,1]$ is a learning rate and $T(s,a,s') = R(s,a) + \gamma \max_{a'} Q^\pi(m',a')$ is the *target value*. Each weight is set to the inverse of the variance $\overline{x}_i = \frac{1}{\sigma^2(m_i,a)}$ and the resulting approximation is:

$$\widehat{Q}(s,a) = \sum_{i=1}^{M} \overline{x}'_i Q_i(m_i,a), \tag{5}$$

where $\overline{x}'_i$ is the normalized weight and $Q_i(m_i,a)$ is the action value function for the i-th partition.

As it will be discussed in Section 4, the variance is also used in the heuristic criterion defined in LEAP that identifies regions in which the resolution of the approximator must be increased. While in the learning process the parameters are changed to minimize the approximation error given the structure of the approximator, LEAP introduces a second level of adaptivity whose goal is to modify the partitions in order to increase the resolution of the approximator in the regions where its initial structure is not sufficient to achieve a good approximation.

3   LEAP

At the beginning of the learning process, LEAP uses a set of Learning Entities (LEs) $\mathcal{L} = \{LE_1, LE_2, ..., LE_M\}$. A generic LE_i is related to a partition P_i of the state space $\mathcal{S}$. Since the initial structure cannot be aggregated further during the learning process, it is convenient to use coarse partitions of the state space. In factored state spaces, the initial configuration is obtained by creating one LE (i.e., partition) for each variable. Thus, each LE considers only the value of its state variable, and ignores the others.

An example of the initial configuration of LEs in a grid-world environment is reported in Figure 1. The environment is characterized by two discrete state variables, *row* and *column*. The initial set $\mathcal{L}$ contains two LEs: *LE-Row* (associated to the *row* variable) and *LE-Column* (associated to the *column* variable). While a tabular approach uses 25 rows in the Q-table, the decomposition in LEAP uses only 10 rows (5 rows for each LE).

The action selection and the way the action values from different LEs are merged together are derived from the function approximation in Equation 5. At each time step, the set $\mathcal{L}(s)$ of active LEs in state s is computed (see Section 4.2) and the *merged action value* $\overline{Q}(s, a)$ is obtained as the mean of the action values for each LE, weighted by the inverse of their variances:

$$\overline{Q}(s, a) = \sum_{LE_i \in \mathcal{L}} \left(\frac{1}{\sigma'_{LE_i}(m_i, a)^2} Q_{LE_i}(m_i, a) \right), \tag{6}$$

where $m_i = \mu_{LE_i}(s)$ and $\sigma'_{LE_i}(m_i, a)$ is the normalized standard deviation. It is interesting to notice that, since each LE is related to one variable in the environment, in state s only the variables of the LEs whose standard deviation is low are relevant to the computation of the final action values, while the others are actually ignored. Similarly to the computation of the merged action values, it is possible to compute the merge standard deviation (used in the incoherence criterion in Section 4.1):

$$\overline{\sigma}(s, a) = \left(\sum_{LE_i \in \mathcal{L}} \frac{1}{\sigma_{LE_i}(m_i, a)^2} \right)^{-\frac{1}{2}}. \tag{7}$$

Once an action is selected and executed, the action values of the LEs are updated according to the reward received from the environment and to the expected future reward:

$$Q_i(m_i, a) = Q_i(m_i, a) + \alpha \left[R(s, a) + \gamma \max_{a' \in A} \overline{Q}(s', a') - Q_i(m_i, a) \right]. \tag{8}$$

While many adaptive algorithms update the values of the approximator according to the update rule derived from the Least Mean Square Error (LMS), Equation 8 is obtained from the approximation error of the *linear averagers* [5]. Unlike many of the LMS-based algorithms, this class of function approximators are guaranteed not to diverge and at least to converge to a region [5]. Furthermore, as pointed out in [8], since each parameter gives an accurate approximation of the desired output and can be used independently from the approximator, averagers are suitable for adaptive systems in which changes to the structure of the approximator do not directly affect the value of the parameters.

4   Adaptive State Space Representation

In general, a function approximator with fixed structure may lead to poor performance because of a coarse resolution. On the other hand, when the resolution is too fine, the approximator is not able to generalize and the learning process is slow. Since it is often needed to perform a long hand-tuning to find the best structure, it is better to adapt the resolution of the approximator starting from an initial coarse representation. LEAP changes its structure according to a heuristic criterion based on the comparison between the target values and the merged action values and their variability.

4.1   The Incoherence Criterion

The criterion is two-fold. The first part detects when the action executed in the previous step, assumed to be *optimal* (*sub-optimal*), obtains a target value that is *less* (*greater*) than the expected action value for *a sub-optimal* (*the optimal*) action. The test compares the target value $T(s, a, s')$ with the expected return for the best action $(\overline{Q}(s, a^*))$ and for the second best action $(\overline{Q}(s, a^+))$. Depending on the result of this test, two different kinds of incoherence may be detected:

- *improvement*, the executed action a is suboptimal but the target value is greater than the expected return for the greedy action $(a \neq a^*)$:

$$T(s, a, s') > \overline{Q}(s, a^*)$$

- *worsening*, the executed action is greedy, but the target value is lower than the expected return for the second best action $(a = a^*)$:

$$T(s, a, s') < \overline{Q}(m, a^+)$$

Thus, state s is detected as incoherent whenever the target value *contradicts* the current policy.

The second part of the criterion uses the standard deviations to measure the compliance of the target value to the expected action value. A state is detected as incoherent whenever the difference between the target value and the action value is relevant with respect to the standard deviation:

$$\left|\overline{Q}(s, a) - T(s, a, s')\right| > h\overline{\sigma}(s, a),$$

where h is the tolerance on the difference. The value of h is a key factor for regulating the tolerance on the refinement process. Since the standard deviation is partially determined by the intrinsic stochasticity of the environment, low values for h can cause the incoherence criterion to identify many incoherent states and to over-refine the partitions. At the opposite, high values can prevent the criterion from identifying incoherent macrostates, thus making the agent unable to learn the optimal policy. Generally, it is desirable to use low h (within [1..3]), since the pruning mechanism (Section 4.3) is able to remove some of the macrostates that are not useful for the learned policy.

4.2   Refining the State Representation

Once a state s is detected as incoherent, the state aggregation is modified to reduce its incoherence. Unlike most of the adaptive algorithms, the incoherent state is not extracted from the macrostates and no split takes place, but the multiple overlapping partitions structure is exploited. The incoherence in state s is guaranteed to be solved only when the single state is extracted from the macrostates, but this would lead to over-refinement for highly incoherent regions, while often it is possible to solve the incoherence and to keep a high level of

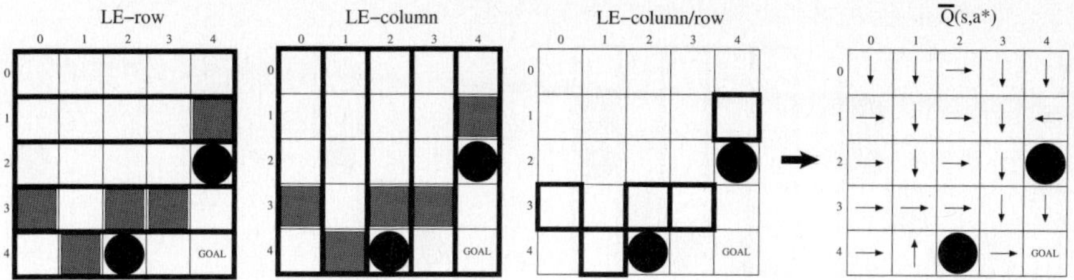

Fig. 2. An example of structure in a 5x5 grid world problem (black rounds are additional walls)

generalization at the same time. Thus, the refinement of the state representation is carried out by the creation of a more specialized, but general, macrostate obtained by the intersection of only two macrostates and entrusted to a Joint Learning Entity (JLE).

The LEs whose macrostates are used to generate the new macrostate m_{JLE}, are chosen according to a measure of the relevance of their contribution to the computation of the incoherence of the state. The incoherence degree ρ_{LE_i} is computed as the difference between the merged action value and the clamped action value $\widetilde{Q}_{-i}(s, a)$, obtained by removing the i-th LE from the set $\mathcal{L}(s)$ of active LEs. According to the type of incoherence, $\overline{Q}(s, \cdot)$ is computed as:

$$\rho_{LE_i} = \begin{cases} \widetilde{Q}_{-i}(s, a) - \overline{Q}(s, a) & \text{for } \textit{improvement} \text{ incoherence} \\ \overline{Q}(s, a) - \widetilde{Q}_{-i}(s, a) & \text{for } \textit{worsening} \text{ incoherence} \end{cases}$$

A positive ρ_{LE_i} means that a LE is a relevant cause of the incoherence. The two LEs with highest incoherence degree are used to generate the new macrostate.

The partition of the JLE is obtained by aggregating all the state variables but those entrusted to the two selected LEs. Once created, the partition contains only the macrostate m_{JLE}. The generation of JLEs leads to the definition of a hierarchy of LEs and of a multi-resolution representation of the state space. At the lowest level of the hierarchy there are the LEs created at the beginning, at higher levels there are JLEs. The higher the level of a LE, the more detailed is its view of the state space.

When a macrostate of a JLE is active, all the LEs at a lower level in the hierarchy become *inactive*, and perform neither action selection nor update.

Definition 2. *Given the set of the current LEs $\mathcal{L}$, the set of active LEs $\mathcal{L}(s)$ is defined as:*

$$LE_i \in \mathcal{L}(s) \Leftrightarrow \mu_i(s) \neq \emptyset \wedge \neg \exists LE_j \in \mathcal{L}(s) : \mu_j(s) \subset \mu_i(s).$$

Figure 2 shows a configuration in which five states are detected as incoherent and a JLE (*LE-Column/Row*) is created. Although the partition of the JLE covers the entire state space, it contains only the incoherent states (cells with thicker border). The two basic LEs (*LE-Row* and *LE-Column*) are deactivated in states covered by the JLE (cells in dark gray).

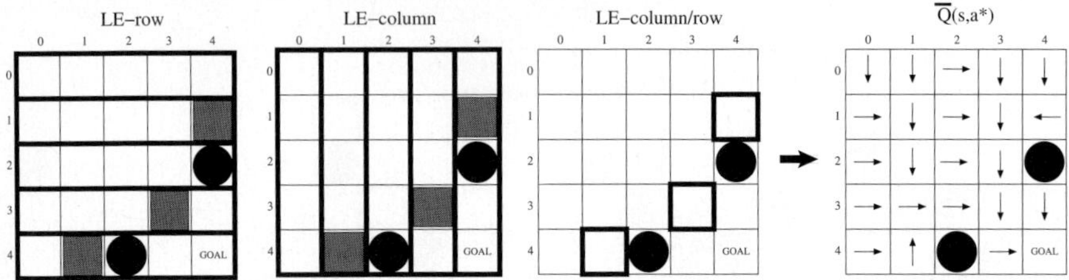

Fig. 3. The effects of pruning in a 5x5 grid world problem

4.3 Pruning of the JLE Hierarchy

Most of the adaptive algorithms [7,6] suffer from over-refinement in stochastic environments. Unless to consider single state values (i.e., tabular approach) or histories of the interaction with the environment [3], it is not possible to distinguish between the stochasticity of the transition model and the one induced by the aggregation. Since the refinement process of LEAP is heuristic, it may happen that some JLEs are generated even if they are actually useless for learning an optimal or near-optimal policy. Therefore, we have defined an on-line mechanism able to identify when a macrostate m can be removed from the partition of a JLE without modifying the learned policy. As a consequence, the set of active LEs $\mathcal{L}(s)$ in all the states in m changes and some LEs can be *restored*. When, after the pruning of a macrostate the mapping function $\mu_{JLE}(s)$ is empty for each state (i.e., no macrostate left in the partition), the JLE itself is removed from the hierarchy. In general, when a macrostate is removed and the set $\mathcal{L}(s)$ is computed, the policy changes and the performance can worsen. Therefore, before a pruning can take place, it is necessary to compute the policy that would result from the deletion of the macrostate. After the update phase, in state s the pruning merged action values $\widehat{Q}_{-i}(s, a)$ is computed on the set $\mathcal{L}'(s)$ obtained by removing macrostate m_i from the active list $\mathcal{L}(s)$ and restoring all the deactivated LEs. Macrostate m_i can be pruned from the state space of the JLE when no change on the current policy occurs ($arg\max_a \overline{Q}(s, a) = arg\max_a \widehat{Q}_{-i}(s, a)$).

The introduction of the pruning mechanism brings two important advantages: it *reduces the number of states* and, at the same time, it leads to a *better generalization* over the state space. The result of the pruning mechanism over the configuration in Figure 2 is reported in Figure 3, where two states are removed from the partition of *LE-column/row*.

5 Experiments

In this section, we present some results obtained by LEAP on a grid-world problem and a simulated robotic task. These experiments aim at studying the properties of LEAP in stochastic problems in terms of macrostates generated and learning performance. In all the experiments, the ϵ - *greedy* soft policy exploration strategy is adopted.

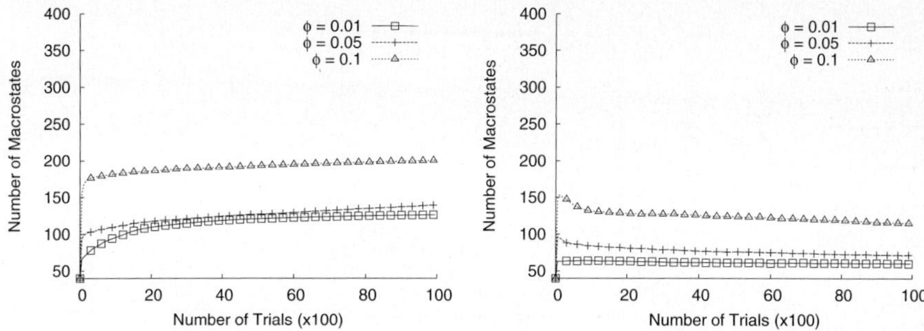

Fig. 4. Macrostates generated in the Grid World without and with pruning

5.1   Grid World

A grid-world environment is characterized by two continuous state variables (*Row* and *Column*), whose values range on $[0, 1]$. There are four actions $\{right, down, up, left\}$, each action moves the robot a step of 0.05 along the chosen direction. Each step is affected by a Gaussian noise with zero mean and a standard deviation φ. The robot receives a reward of -1 except for the goal region (the bottom right corner). Each variable is discretized in 20 uniform intervals. The results are averaged over 30 runs with $\alpha = 0.2$, an ϵ-greedy exploration ($\epsilon = 0.05$) and a tolerance $h = 2.0$.

First, we analyze the effect of the pruning mechanism in reducing the number of macrostates with respect to the stochasticity of the environment. Figure 4 shows the number of macrostates generated by LEAP with and without the pruning mechanism with three different values for the standard deviation of the noise: $\varphi = 0.01, 0.05, 0.1$. In Figure 4−*left*, notice that the number of macrostates continuously increases over time and that the more stochastic the environment is the more LEAP detects incoherent states and generates new macrostates. On the other hand, the pruning mechanism (Figure 4−*right*) leads to a dramatic reduction of the number of macrostates (an average reduction of 47.8%). Therefore, while the incoherence criterion tends to over-refine the state representation, the pruning mechanism reduces the number of macrostates without affecting the performance.

Graphs in Figure 5 compare the performance of LEAP, with and without pruning, and Q-Learning in terms of average reward in each learning episode. With low stochasticity ($\varphi = 0.01$), LEAP learns a good policy with slightly worse performance than Q-Learning with only 60 ± 11.3 macrostates with respect to the 400 states used by Q-Learning. When the environment is more stochastic ($\varphi = 0.1$), LEAP generates few more macrostates (115 ± 16.38), but obtains better results than Q-Learning. Furthermore, these results show that the pruning mechanism does not affect the performance and that it increases the generalization capabilities of the algorithm and its convergence rate.

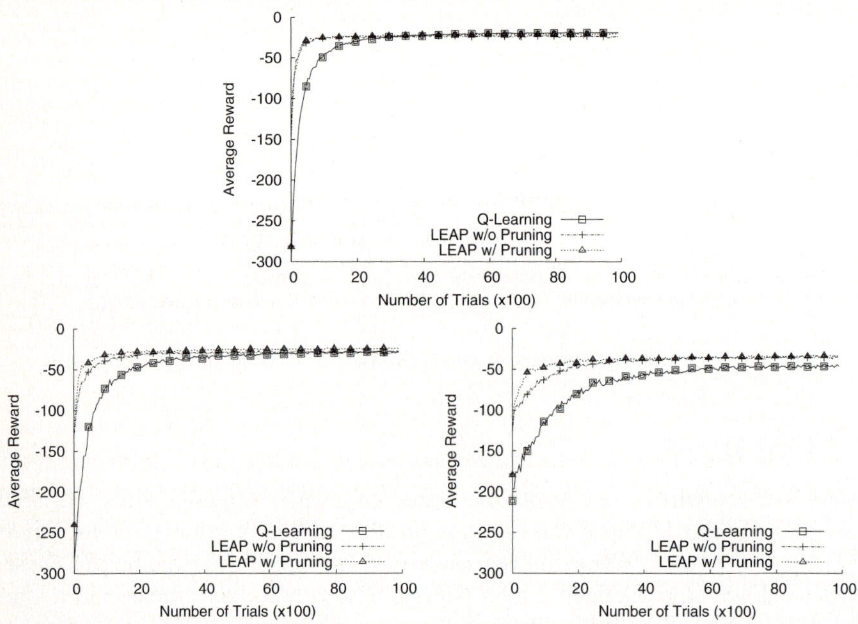

Fig. 5. Average reward for Q-Learning, LEAP with and without pruning with different stochasticity ($\varphi = \{0.01, 0.05, 0.1\}$)

5.2 RoboCup Keepaway

In this section, we report the results of LEAP in the Keepaway task. Keepaway is a sub-task of the RoboCup soccer in which one team (i.e., *the keepers*) tries to keep the possession of the ball as long as possible, and another team (i.e., *the takers*) tries to intercept the ball. All the players are placed into a limited region of the soccer field and an episode finishes when either the takers catch the ball or the ball goes outside the field. This experiment has been set up using the Keepaway testbed [10] that provides a framework in which the keepers should try to learn the best sequence of passages to maximize the length of each episode. All the low-level skills (i.e., *GoToBall*, *GetOpen*) are hand-coded and each keeper has two available actions: *HoldBall*, that is stand still and keep the ball possesion, *PassBall(k)*, that is pass the ball to k-th keeper. The reward function proposed in the framework is such that when a keeper receives the ball she gets a reward equal to the elapsed time from the last time she had the ball possesion. The Keepaway environment is also highly stochastic because both the player actuators and sensors are affected by noise. In particular, the outcome of the player's actions (e.g. dash, turn, kick) can be significantly different with respect to what expected because of noise and inertia. The same is for the movement of the ball that can slightly change its trajectory when moving. Furthermore, the visual sensor of each player is perfect only in a bounded region and the precision degrades with the distance.

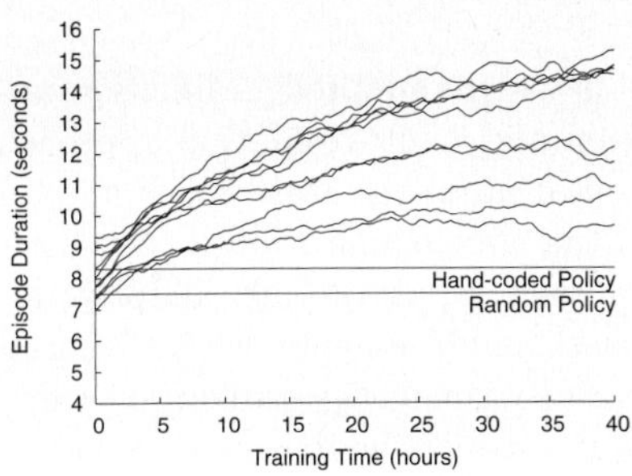

Fig. 6. Possesion time in 10 runs on the 3v2 Keepaway task

Table 1. Parameters used in the Keepaway domain

Parameter	Value
Discount Factor (γ)	0.99
Learning Rate (α)	0.5
Learning Rate Decreasing Rate (δ_α)	0.001
Exploration Constant (ϵ)	1.0
Exploration Decreasing Rate (δ_ϵ)	0.01
Certainty Degree Threshold (τ)	0.9

For all these parameters we used the default settings of the RoboCup server (*ball rand* = 0.05, *player rand* = 0.1 and *visible distance* = 3). Our experiment is focused on the 3v2 Keepaway task (3 keepers against 2 takers) in a $20m \times 20m$, region and the results are compared to the random policy and the hand-coded policy defined in the framework. In the experiment, we used the set of 5 state variables suggested in [10]: 1) $dist(K_1, T_1)$ 2) $\min(dist(K_2, T_1), dist(K_2, T_2))$ 3) $\min(dist(K_3, T_1), dist(K_3, T_2))$ 4) $\min(ang(K_2, K_1, T_1), ang(K_2, K_1, T_2))$ 5) $\min(ang(K_3, K_1, T_1), ang(K_3, K_1, T_2))$, where K_1 is the keeper with the ball, K_2 and K_3 are the other two keepers ordered by distance, T_1 and T_2 are the takers ordered by distance. State variables have been discretized in 7 intervals for angles (the discretization is finer for small angles) and in 14 intervals for the distances (the discretization is finer for small distances), so that the joint state-space contains $134,456$ states.

In Figure 6, we report the results of 10 independent runs, in which the 3 keepers concurrently learn their policy using LEAP with the parameters reported in Table 1. The average possesion time, after 40 hours of training, is $12.99s\pm2.14s$ and outperforms both the random and the hand-coded policies ($7.5s \pm 3.7s$ and $8.3s \pm 4.7s$ respectively). At the same time, it is worth noting that, starting from an initial configuration with 76 states, the system refines the state space partition by creating new Joint Learning Entities up to an average number of 1705 ± 122 states. Furthermore, LEAP succeeds in obtaining a better result with respect to the experiments with 5 variables reported in [10] where CMAC with SARSA is adopted. The reason is that, while CMAC exploits a fixed generalization breadth, LEAP can adaptively generate smaller macrostates specialized only over specific, and relevant situations. For instance, when the nearest taker is quite far from the ball keeper, the LE whose state space is $dist(K_1, T_1)$ is enough, since the action *HoldBall* is effective independently from all other state variables values. On the other hand, when the nearest taker is close to the keeper with the ball and it covers the trajectory to farest keeper, a JLE is needed to handle the situation and to propose a passage to the other keeper.

6   Conclusion

In Reinforcement Learning, state aggregation is widely adopted as function approximator. LEAP unifies the multiple-partition and multi-resolution approach used in many algorithms with a static representation of the state space and an adaptive process that changes the structure of the approximator until the target values in a macrostate are not sufficiently coherent. Since on-line, adaptive algorithms suffer from over-refinement in stochastic environments, we introduced a pruning mechanism, which removes macrostates whenever possible (i.e., when the policy is expected not to change). Finally, the use of the linear averager update rule allows to reduce the effect of the adaptive process on the action values of the macrostates of the LEs. The experiments show that LEAP succeeds in achieving very high performance using a small number of macrostates even in highly stochastic environments.

Further work will focus on a deeper theoretical analysis of the interaction between incoherence criterion and pruning mechanism and on the extension of the adaptive process to the action space for problems with multiple actuators. We are also running experiments with real robots, and an extensive report on the experimental results will be available in a next paper.

References

1. Anderson, C., Crawford-Hines, S.: Multigrid q-learning. Technical Report CS-94-121, Colorado State University, Fort Collins (1994)
2. Bonarini, A., Lazaric, A., Restelli, M.: Learning in complex environments through multiple adaptive partitions. In: Proceedings of the ECAI'06 workshop PLMUDW, pp. 7–12 (2006)
3. Chapman, D., Kaelbling, L.P.: Input generalization in delayed reinfrocement learning: an algorithm and performance comparisons. In: Proc. of IJCAI (1991)
4. Dayan, P., Hinton, G.E.: Feudal reinforcement learning. In: NIPS, vol. 5 (1993)
5. Gordon, G.J.: Reinforcement learning with function approximation converges to a region. In: NIPS, vol. 12 (2000)
6. Munos, R., Moore, A.: Variable resolution discretization in optimal control. Machine Learning 49(2/3), 291–323 (2002)
7. Reynolds, S.I.: Decision boundary partitioning: Variable resolution model-free reinforcement learning. In: Proceedings of ICML, pp. 783–790 (2000)
8. Reynolds, S.I.: Reinforcement Learning with Exploration. PhD thesis, University of Birmingham (2002)
9. Singh, S.P., Jaakkola, T., Jordan, M.I.: Reinforcement learning with soft state aggregation. In: NIPS, vol. 7 (1995)
10. Stone, P., Sutton, R.S., Kuhlmann, G.: Reinforcement learning for RoboCup-soccer keepaway. Adaptive Behavior (13), 165–188 (2005)
11. Sutton, R.S.: Generalization in reinfrocement learning: Successful examples using sparse coarse coding. In: NIPS, vol. 8 (1995)
12. Sutton, R.S., Barto, A.G.: Reinforcement Learning: An Introduction. MIT Press, Cambridge (1998)
13. Sutton, R.S., White, A., Lee, M.: UofA Reinforcement Learning Library. University of Alberta, Department of Computing Science (2005)

Uses of Contextual Knowledge in Mobile Robots

D. Calisi, A. Farinelli, G. Grisetti, L. Iocchi,
D. Nardi, S. Pellegrini, D. Tipaldi, and V.A. Ziparo

Dipartimento di Informatica e Sistemistica,
Sapienza Università di Roma
`lastname@dis.uniroma1.it`

Abstract. In this paper, we analyze work on mobile robotics with the goal of highlighting the uses of contextual knowledge aiming at a flexible and robust performance of the system. In particular, we analyze different robotic tasks, ranging from robot behavior to perception, and then propose to characterize "contextualization" as a design pattern. As a result, we argue that many different tasks indeed can exploit contextual information and, therefore, a single explicit representation of knowledge about context may lead to significant advantages both in the design and in the performance of mobile robots.

1   Introduction

The requirement that robotic systems are flexible and robust to the uncertainties of the environment are becoming more and more compelling, as new applications of robotics in daily life are envisioned. A promising approach to meet this kind of requirements is to organize the system in such a way that some of the processes, that run on the robot, can be specialized based on knowledge that is not typically handled by the processes themselves. Roughly speaking, one could argue that several tasks that are typical of mobile robots can take advantage of knowledge about context.

The notion of *context* has been deeply investigated both from cognitive standpoint (see for example [1]) and from an AI perspective (see for example [24]). In the former case, the study is more focussed on the principles that underlie human uses of contextual knowledge; in the latter case, the main point is how to provide a formal account of deductive systems supporting context representation and contextual reasoning. The interest for contexts in robotics is clear; according to Turner [31]:

> A *context* is any identifiable configuration of environmental, mission-related, and agent-related features that has predictive power for behavior.

In this work, we are interested in discussing to what extent and how the use of contextual knowledge has been advocated in mobile robot design. While Turner's definition captures our general intuition about context, we take a bottom-up approach, which relies on a rough intuitive notion of context, without providing

R. Basili and M.T. Pazienza (Eds.): AI*IA 2007, LNAI 4733, pp. 543–554, 2007.

either a technical definition or a specific representation, and look at specific instances. For example, we are interested in finding systems that can improve the map construction process, by knowing that the robot is currently moving in the corridor of an office building. Sometimes, the term "semantic" is used to characterize this type of knowledge [14], but we will adopt nevertheless the term context.

More precisely, we are interested in a design pattern, where the process, needed in the realization of a mobile robot, is accomplished with general methods, that can be specialized (thus becoming more effective) by taking into account knowledge that is specific to the situation the robot is facing and is acquired and represented "outside" the process itself. This design pattern is often regarded as a *hierarchical architecture* [6], where different layers correspond to different levels of abstraction. There are indeed a variety of approaches concerning layered architectures; however, our main concern is to find interesting instances of the pattern, rather then specific architectural organizations. We call this design pattern *contextualization*, despite the differences with respect to the above cited studies in cognitive science and AI on context.

Consequently, we look at various tasks that are required in mobile robot design and try to provide concrete examples of contextualization. In particular, we first look at contextualization of behaviors (Section 2), navigation and strategic decisions, such as exploration (Section 3). We then look at SLAM (Section 4), where there are already several proposals of contextualization, and other perception tasks (Section 5).

The result of our analysis is that contextualization can be effectively used in each of the tasks addressed (Section 6). It seems therefore very appropriate, from an engineering perspective, to build and maintain a single representation of the knowledge that can be contextualized in many different processes.

2   Behaviors

The behavior of intelligent agents, as for humans and animals, is strongly dependent on context. For example, when driving a car, if we realize that there is some fog we automatically reduce our speed and switch to more careful behaviors. Or, consider the case where you would like to call the attention of a friend who is on the other side of a room. If you are attending a talk at a conference, you would never choose to call him loudly, while this could be a good choice, if you where in a gym playing basketball.

It is broadly agreed that context driven choices are fundamental in robotic scenarios for adapting the behavior of robots to the different situations, which they may encounter during execution. Historically, this has been implemented in robotic systems as plan selection, that is a mechanism, which selects at run-time plans from a library based on the current context. The idea of plan selection is very common, and indeed plan selection is a basic solution to the classical AI planning problem [9,12,11]. For example, Turner [31] defines a plan selection approach which clearly separates context and plan representation. The context is represented as contextual schemas (c-schemas), a frame-like knowledge structure. C-schemas are represented by slots (or roles), which are features of what is being represented, and fillers, which are a description of the value of the feature. Each c-schema represents a particular context, that is, a particular class of problem-solving situations.

In contrast to c-schemas, which are a context representation specific to plan selection, we argue that context could be represented in a general way, leading to a common representation for all modules composing the robotic system. Indeed, the contextual knowledge could be clearly acquired and represented "outside" the process to control. The control (i.e. contextual knowledge) and the controlled processes are loosely coupled. In particular, the controlled system could perceive a context change as a change of its parameters or, more generally, of its strategy. In plan selection, and hierarchical approaches to planning (see also [29]), however, both contextual knowledge and plans are represented in symbolic form. The use of context to adapt basic behaviors, that is concerned with the interface between a symbolic and numerical representation of knowledge, is more interesting for our purposes.

Fig. 1. A S.P.Q.R Legged robot grabbing a ball

Typically, basic behaviors require fine tuning of many parameters, which could be adjusted according to contextual knowledge. For example, in a robotic soccer scenario for the 4-Legged RoboCup[1] competition, consider an AIBO robot, which has to grab a ball with its head (see Figure 1) during a soccer game [15]. The set of parameters controlling the speed (and thus the accuracy) of the behavior depend on whether there are opponents nearby, the ball is near the field sideline and so on. We have experienced that instead of having a proliferation of behaviors for several specific situations, the contextualization of one general behavior is an effective design approach. The characterization of contexts can also be combined with learning techniques and it provides a useful approach to structuring the design/learning of behaviors.

---

[1] www.robocup.org

Fig. 2. Two different contexts that need different navigation strategies: on the left a "Lurkers" robot of Rescue Robots Freiburg facing a ramp, on the right together with an SPQR robot forming a group exploring an open space

The use of contextual knowledge for behavior specialization is also suggested in Beets & al. [2]. Here context is determined using sampling-based inference methods for probabilistic state estimation to deal with noisy and unreliable perceptions. By adopting a probabilistic representation of contextual knowledge it is possible to allow for a smooth transitions between behaviors. Recently, much work has been devoted to mobility issues through terrain classification. In particular, knowing the type of terrain a robot has to traverse provides a context for navigation tasks. Triebel *et al.* [28] use multi-level surface maps to estimate and classify terrain on their traversability level (traversable, non-traversable and wall). Kim *et al.* [17] describe an on-line learning method to predict the traversability properties of complex terrain, exploiting the robot's experience in navigating the environment. In a similar perspective, notable mobility results have been achieved using behavior maps [8]. These maps are a classification of the environment, extracted from an elevation map, based on the type of mobility challenge of the area. This behavior map is then used to adapt navigation capabilities the context such as ramps or open stairs (see Figure 2). In such cases, the contextual knowledge is specific to the type of task, while in this work our goal is to design a general mechanism identified by a "design pattern".

3   Search and Exploration

In this section we focus on the uses of contextual knowledge in a specific robotic task, such as search and exploration. The aim of this task is to build a representation of an unknown environment, while at the same time gathering mission relevant information. An instance of this problem can be a rescue mission in which a robot has to explore a post-disaster scenario, looking for human victims and interesting features such as fires, chemical agents and so on. In order to describe how context knowledge can be used, we will focus on the two major processes in which a generic search and exploration strategy can be divided: *target selection* and *navigation*.

In target selection, contextual knowledge can be used in several ways. Since the search and exploration task is a multi-objective task, requiring a choice among, often conflicting, sub-goals (e.g. exploring unknown areas and looking for features in known areas, see for example [4]), contextual knowledge can change the relative importance of one kind of sub-goal with respect to the other ones. For example, when the robot is exploring a dangerous area (e.g. if contextual knowledge shows that the building is about to collapse or there are fires), the mission strategy may increase the bias to explore as much environment as possible instead of losing time for a deep investigation in areas that have a low probability to contain interesting features.

Although navigation has been studied for decades, there is no general solution, because the problem is computationally very hard and usually involves many degrees of freedom (there are several surveys on this topic, see for example [19,20,21]). This means that it is hard to find a single navigation algorithm that can perform well in all the situations that the robot can find during its exploration task. Consequently, either the specialization of general techniques, or the design of ad-hoc methods, are typically embedded into specific applications. The ability to dynamically adapt navigation based on contextual knowledge could be very effective.

The adaptation of the navigation strategy should take into consideration contextual knowledge like openness/clutterness, roughness, if the robot is moving on a skewed plane or in an indoor environment (see Figure 2), etc., and adjust the motion algorithm accordingly. There is no need of an accurate motion planner in wide spaces where the robot is far from obstacles and other complex terrain challenges. For instance, the robot can move quickly in areas that are already been explored and searched for features, while it needs to proceed slowly when it is looking for features (due, for example, to the computational time needed by classification algorithms). Besides the speed, the algorithm can take advantage also of different obstacle configurations. For example, it can be coarse and quick in easy situations and perform a precise motion planning, though computationally heavier, in cluttered areas. Moreover, the coarse method can try to avoid those situations that can be critical for navigation (e.g. narrow passages, going near obstacles, etc.). However, such situations usually have to be faced when searching for interesting features.

Some work exists in this direction. For example, Coelho Jr. *et al.* [16] try to learn the most efficient navigation policies together with context classification, by inferring context classification from system dynamics in response to robot motion actions.

These issues can be extended to multi-robot systems deployed in a search and exploration task. The coordination method may be modified (i.e. it may be tuned accordingly) taking into account contextual knowledge: i.e. the kind of environment the robots are going to explore (e.g. a chemical factory, an office, a collapsed building, etc.). For example, in [30] the coordination algorithm takes into account contextual knowledge related to places in the environment. In particular, the authors show that in an indoor environment long corridors with doors are interesting places to be explored. In fact, sending at least one robot to explore the whole corridor increases the overall performance, because it discovers quickly the structure of the environment and thus it can coordinate better the other robots.

Contextualization in multi-robot coordination is still in a preliminary stage. One main reason, is the difficulty to share a common high-level environment representation among the robots.

4   SLAM

The problem of Robot Mapping, or the more general problem of Simultaneous Localization and Mapping, is one of the most important and deeply studied aspect of modern robotics. This problem has been addressed from a geometrical and numerical point of view, focusing on the underlying estimation process. While general solutions have been proposed, and several working implementations have been developed, the use of contextual knowledge within the mapping process has received limited attention.

Generally speaking, contextual knowledge in robot mapping can be classified according to the level of abstraction in the following way (from higher to lower):

- Environment Knowledge,
- Process Contextual Knowledge.

In the following, we will explain, for each class, the information it provides and its possible use. It is worth to notice, here, that the first class can be viewed as *human understandable*, in the sense that it can be mainly used in Human Robot Interfaces, as it represents typical knowledge of human being. The second class can be viewed as *robot understandable*, in the sense that it can be mainly used to tune the robot mapping process for efficacy and efficiency purposes.

4.1   Environment Knowledge

In high level spatial reasoning, as well as for Human-Robot communication, knowledge regarding the abstract structure of the environment are very useful. Generic concepts, like rooms and corridors, or more specific ones, like Diego's office, can be used by a human user to give easy commands to the robot ("go to Room A" is easier than "go to point 34.5, 42.79").

Up to now, this kind of contextual information is the most studied one. Several approaches extend metric maps with this kind of semantic information. Martinez Mozos *et al.* [23] extracts a semantic topological maps from a metric one using AdaBoost. In a work by Galindo *et al.* [10], a topological map, extracted with fuzzy morphological operators, is augmented by semantic information using anchoring. Diosi *et al.* [7] use an interactive procedure and a watershed segmentation to create a semantic topological map. [18] introduces the paradigm of Human Augmented Mapping, where a human user interacts with the robot by means of natural language processing.

In our RoboCare project [5], aimed at having an intelligent system to take care of the elderly, some contextual information about the environment have been used. The metric map of the environment has been enriched by semantic labels for the rooms and the objects therein. Those labels were used to monitor the elder during his daily activities and to assist him in tasks like bringing water or food. However, the augmented map was not built autonomously or in a guided tour, but the labeling was done by a human operator.

The contextual knowledge extracted from these representations are mainly used when robotic systems have to be deployed in domestic environment (see Figure 3). The Incremental Mapping of [7] or the Human Augmented Mapping of [18] represent valid applications of such knowledge.

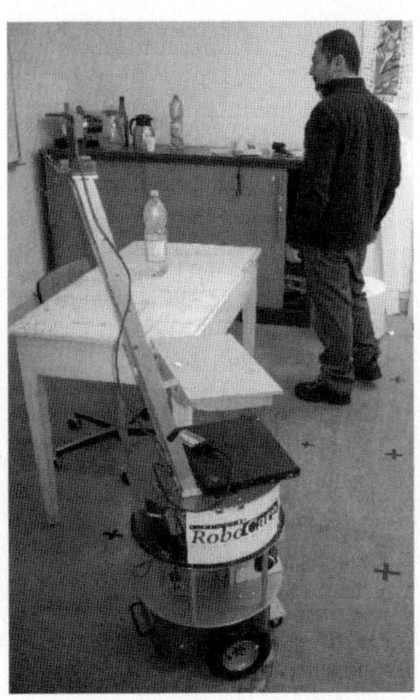

Fig. 3. Our robot deployed in a domestic environment

Another source of contextual knowledge comes from the nature of the environment being mapped. However, this knowledge is currently mainly used by the human operator, who selects the right algorithm on the mobile platform. No adaptive systems, which detects, for example, indoor or outdoor environments and switch to different SLAM algorithms, have been developed.

4.2   Process Context

On the lower level, contextual knowledge about the mapping process can be extracted and used to improve the robustness and the speed of current SLAM algorithms. This contextual information arises from different aspect of the embedded estimation algorithm. It is well known that the uncertainty of the robot position and the map increase when the robot is exploring new areas, while this uncertainty drastically decreases when the robot reenters previously known areas. Moreover, it is not clear yet when the robot can stop doing mapping and start to simple localize itself. To the best of our knowledge, only two works exploit this knowledge explicitly.

In [26], two different algorithms are used for incremental mapping and loop closure. Efficient and incremental 3D scan matching is used when mapping open loop situations, while a vision based system detects possible loop closures. The two algorithms are integrated within an EKF filter with a delayed-state map representation.

In [13], three different phases in robot mapping algorithms are defined, namely *exploration, localization* and *loop closure.* The proposed method detects those phases and tunes the computation accordingly. By exploiting this knowledge it is shown that it is possible to drastically speed up classical mapping algorithm in grid maps. Figure 4 shows the map of MIT Killian Court computed by using this approach.

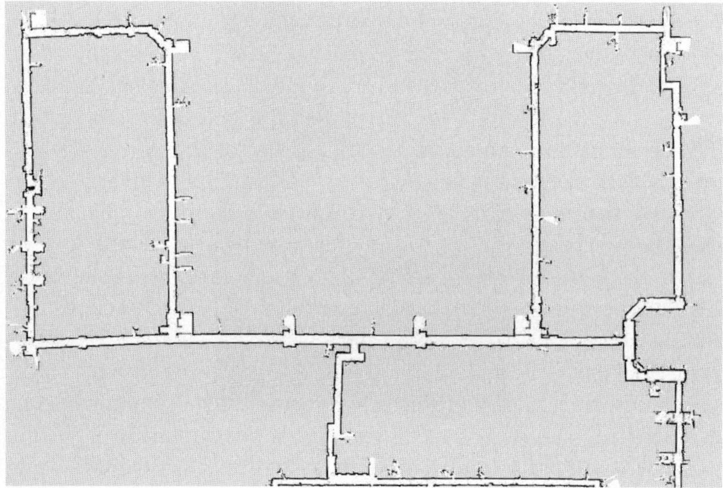

Fig. 4. Map of the MIT Killian Court computed using the algorithm of [13]. The robot computed a path of about 3Km in about 2.5h. The algorithm took about 40 minutes to correct the data, while standard techniques need about 5h.

5   Perception

Robot Perception can significantly benefit from contextual knowledge. It is important to notice that when we talk about Perception, we are dealing with sensing modalities. This means not only that it is possible to exploit contextual knowledge to achieve the goal in a specific Perception task, but also that one can use these modalities to achieve knowledge about the context. In Robot Perception, normally, an iterative knowledge process occurs: a top-down analysis, in which the contribution given by the context helps the perception of features and objects in the scene; a bottom-up analysis, in which scene understanding

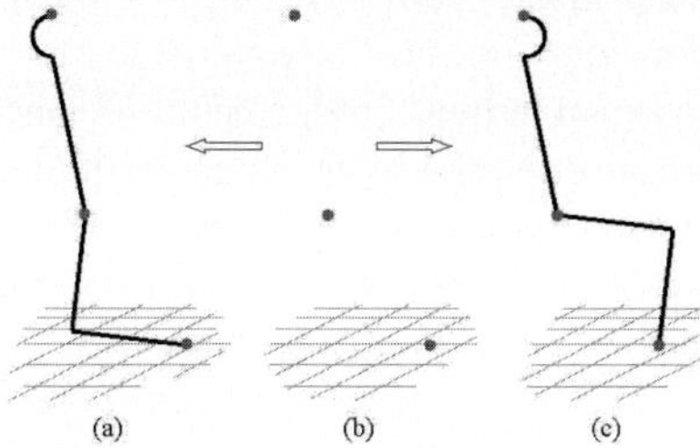

Fig. 5. The posture recognition application procedure is based on the extraction of the position of three "principal" points (head, pelvis and feet point of contact with the ground). In some cases, two different postures are characterized by the same set of points, making an ambiguity arise. Contextual knowledge would help solving this problem.

increases the knowledge about the context. This highlights the difficulty in precisely distinguishing contextual knowledge from the knowledge that is directly addressed by the application. We will focus on the contribution given by the context in extracting useful knowledge from the scene, (i.e. the top-down flux), and we will consider only the visual modality.

As pointed out by an earlier paper [3], the concept of contextual knowledge is not fully described by the a priori knowledge about the environment, but one might consider the robot's goal as a part of the context. Indeed, a robot might save computational load if the algorithm used for perception is choosen according to its goal (i.e. "there is little use in applying a bridge detection module when the images are acquired in an office setting, and the goal is to locate a telephone on the desk." [3]). Though these considerations are usually commonly agreed upon, in practice they are rarely exploited, as the lack of example in the literature clearly shows.

One task in which the Robot Vision is crucial is navigation. In [22] the objective is to detect the road pixels on an input camera. In this case the contextual knowledge is the knowledge about the direction the car is heading to, that is, straight, left or right. The use of such knowledge is translated in the choice of the opportune template to be used for the road-segmentation task. Here, Robot Vision is also used to retrieve contextual knowledge. What it really matters though, is the design of the system that clearly separates the contribution coming from the main procedure from the contribution given by the contextual knowledge.

Human Robot Interaction offers a variety of applications that make use of contextual knowledge. Even though these kinds of applications are usually conceived with fixed cameras, in some cases the extension to a mobile robot is easy. For instance, in a posture recognition application [27], it is suggested to make use of contextual knowledge such as the kind of environment represented in the scene (i.e, office rather than a gym) to extend the classifier with an a-priori distribution over the postures that might help solving ambiguous situations (see for example 5). More specifically, a Hidden Markov Model is used to filter the state (i.e. posture) transition probability. The values of the (posture) state transition matrix can be tuned taking into account the same kind of contextual knowledge as above, or otherwise considering details specific to the person.

Another interesting case in which integration of the contextual knowledge leads to a higher performance, is the work done by [25]. In this application, an ECA (Embodied Conversational Agent) talks with a user, while it tries to detect his/her head gesture, that is, to detect the nod and the shaking of the head. This recognition is based on the integration of the visual input and the lexical features, the punctuation features and the timing features in the sentence proposed by the ECA. The results clearly show the improvement in the performance of the classification task when using contextual knowledge.

6   Conclusions

In this paper we have proposed a notion of contextualization, which is based on a simple intuition about the context of operation and captures a design pattern that can be found in several robotics applications. The idea is to make systems more adaptive by exploiting information about the environment or its internal processes in order to improve some of the basic tasks that are typical of mobile robots. In particular, we focussed on behaviors and plans, search and exploration strategies, SLAM and perception in general.

The results of our analysis (not meant to be exhaustive) suggest that there are indeed a few systems, where one can find instances of contextualization. As it turns out, the suggested design pattern is often applicable, while it is not so common to find, because the information extracted from context are often not represented explicitly, but hard coded in the specific techniques.

It seems natural, at this stage, to build a single representation of this kind of information, pulling it out from various system components. A uniform and shared representation of context can lead to two types of advantages: first an improvement in the acquisition and management of contextual information; second, an increased ability of the system to analyze its internal status and recover from malfunctioning that often block the robot operation in the face of unexpected circumstances.

References

1. Context web, http://www.context-web.org/
2. Beetz, M., Arbuckle, T., Bennewitz, M., Burgard, W., Cremers, A., Fox, D., Grosskreutz, H., Hahnel, D., Schulz, D.: Integrated plan-based control of autonomous service robots in human environments (2001)
3. Brown, F.M., Agah, A., Gauch, J.M., Schreiber, T., Speer, S.R.: Ambiguity Resolution in Natural Language Understanding, Active Vision, Memory Retrieval, and Robot Reasoning and Actuation. In: SMC '99. Proceedings of the IEEE International Conference on Systems, Man, and Cybernetics, Tokyo, October 1999, IEEE Computer Society Press, Los Alamitos (1999)
4. Calisi, D., Farinelli, A., Iocchi, L., Nardi, D., Pucci, F.: Multi-objective autonomous exploration in a rescue environment. In: SSRR. Proceedings of IEEE International Workshop on Safety, Security and Rescue Robotics, Gaithersburg, MD, USA (2006)

5. Cesta, A., Cortellessa, G., Giuliani, M.V., Iocchi, L., Leone, R.G., Nardi, D., Pecora, F., Rasconi, R., Scopelliti, M., Tiberio, L.: The robocare assistive home robot. Autonomous Robots (2007) (to appear)
6. Coste-Manière, È., Simmons, R.G.: Architecture, the backbone of robotic systems. In: ICRA. Proc. of the IEEE Int. Conf. on Robotics & Automation, San Francisco, CA, USA, pp. 67–72. IEEE Computer Society Press, Los Alamitos (2000)
7. Diosi, A., Taylor, G., Kleeman, L.: Interactive slam using laser and advanced sonar. In: ICRA. Proc. of the IEEE Int. Conf. on Robotics & Automation, Barcelona, Spain, pp. 1103–1108. IEEE Computer Society Press, Los Alamitos (2005)
8. Dornhege, C., Kleiner, A.: Behavior maps for online planning of obstacle negotiation and climbing on rough terrain. Technical Report 233, University of Freiburg (2007)
9. Firby, R.J.: Adaptive Execution in Complex Dynamic Worlds. PhD thesis, Yale (1989)
10. Galindo, C., Saffiotti, A., Coradeschi, S., Buschka, P., Fernández-Madrigal, J.A., González, J.: Multi-hierarchical semantic maps for mobile robotics. In: IROS. Proc. of the IEEE/RSJ Intl. Conf. on Intelligent Robots and Systems, Edmonton, CA, pp. 3492–3497 (2005), Online at http://www.aass.oru.se/~asaffio/
11. Gat, E.: Esl: A language for supporting robust plan execution in embedded autonomous agents. In: Proceedings of the IEEE Aerospace Conference, IEEE Computer Society Press, Los Alamitos (1997)
12. Georgeff, M.P., Lansky, A.L.: Procedural knowledge. Proceedings of the IEEE Special Issue on Knowledge Representation 74, 1383–1398 (1986)
13. Grisetti, G., Tipaldi, G.D., Stachniss, C., Burgard, W., Nardi, D.: Speeding up rao blackwellized slam. In: ICRA. Proc. of the IEEE Int. Conf. on Robotics & Automation, Orlando, FL, USA, pp. 442–447. IEEE Computer Society Press, Los Alamitos (2006)
14. ICRA 2007 Workshop on Semantic Information in Robotics (ICRA-SIR 2007), Rome, Italy (April 2007)
15. Iocchi, L., Nardi, D., Marchetti, L., Ziparo, V.A.: S.P.Q.R. Legged Team Description Paper (2006)
16. Coelho, Jr., J.A., Araujo, E., Huber, M., Grupen, R.: Contextual control policy selection (1998)
17. Kim, D., Sun, J., Oh, S.M., Rehg, J.M, Bobick, A.: Traversability classification using unsupervised on-line visual learning for outdoor robot navigation. In: ICRA. Proc. of the IEEE Int. Conf. on Robotics & Automation, Orlando, FL, USA, IEEE Computer Society Press, Los Alamitos (2006)
18. Kruijff, G.-J.M., Zender, H., Jensfelt, P., Christensen, H.I.: Clarification dialogues in human-augmented mapping. In: Geert-Jan, M. (ed.) HRI'06. Proc. of the 1st Annual Conference on Human-Robot Interaction, Salt Lake City, UT (March 2006)
19. Latombe, J.C.: Robot Motion Planning. Kluwer Academic Publishers, Dordrecht (1991)
20. LaValle, S.M.: Planning Algorithms. Cambridge University Press (2006), Also available at http://msl.cs.uiuc.edu/planning/
21. Lindemann, S.R., LaValle, S.M.: Current issues in sampling-based motion planning. In: Proceedings of the International Symposium of Robotics Research (2003)
22. Lombardi, P., Zavidovique, B., Talbert, M.: On the importance of being contextual. Computer 39(12), 57–61 (2006)

23. Martínez Mozos, O., Burgard, W.: Supervised learning of topological maps using semantic information extracted from range data. In: IROS. Proc. of the IEEE/RSJ International Conference on Intelligent Robots and Systems, Beijing, China, pp. 2772–2777 (2006)
24. McCarthy, J., Buvač,: Formalizing context (expanded notes). In: Buvač, S., Iwańska, (eds.) Working Papers of the AAAI Fall Symposium on Context in Knowledge Representation and Natural Language, Menlo Park, California, pp. 99–135. American Association for Artificial Intelligence (1997)
25. Morency, L.-P., Sidner, C., Lee, C., Darrell, T.: Contextual recognition of head gestures. In: ICMI '05: Proceedings of the 7th international conference on Multimodal interfaces, pp. 18–24. ACM Press, New York (2005)
26. Newman, P., Cole, D., Ho, K.: Outdoor slam using visual appearance and laser ranging. In: ICRA. Proc. of the IEEE Int. Conf. on Robotics & Automation, Orlando, FL, USA, pp. 1180–1187. IEEE Computer Society Press, Los Alamitos (2006)
27. Pellegrini, S., Iocchi, L.: Human posture tracking and classification through stereo vision. In: VISAPP. Proc. of Int. Conf. on Computer Vision Theory and Applications, pp. 261–269 (2006)
28. Triebel, R., Pfaff, P., Burgard, W.: Multi-level surface maps for outdoor terrain mapping and loop closing. In: IROS. Proc. of the IEEE/RSJ Int. Conf. on Intelligent Robots and Systems, Beijing, China (2006)
29. Simmons, R., Apfelbaum, D.: A task description language for robot control. In: Proceedings Conference on Intelligent Robotics and Systems (October 1998)
30. Stachniss, C., Martínez-Mozos, O., Burgard, W.: Speeding-up multi-robot exploration by considering semantic place information. In: ICRA. Proc. of the IEEE Int. Conf. on Robotics & Automation, Orlando, FL, USA, pp. 1692–1697. IEEE Computer Society Press, Los Alamitos (2006)
31. Turner, M.R.: Context-mediated behavior for intelligent agents. International Journal of Human-Computer Studies 48(3), 307–330 (1998)

Natural Landmark Detection for Visually-Guided Robot Navigation

Enric Celaya, Jose-Luis Albarral, Pablo Jiménez, and Carme Torras

Institut de Robòtica i Informàtica Industrial (CSIC-UPC). Barcelona, Spain
{celaya, albarral, jimenez, torras}@iri.upc.edu

Abstract. The main difficulty to attain fully autonomous robot navigation outdoors is the fast detection of reliable visual references, and their subsequent characterization as landmarks for immediate and unambiguous recognition. Aimed at speed, our strategy has been to track salient regions along image streams by just performing on-line pixel sampling. Persistent regions are considered good candidates for landmarks, which are then characterized by a set of subregions with given color and normalized shape. They are stored in a database for posterior recognition during the navigation process. Some experimental results showing landmark-based navigation of the legged robot Lauron III in an outdoor setting are provided.

1 Introduction

Indoor robot navigation has received a great deal of attention, and many of the proposed approaches are now successfully used in industrial settings and other specific applications like hospital couriers or museum guides. Such applications are often strongly dependent on known structured features present in each specific environment [1]. Currently the research interest is rapidly shifting towards service robots able to work in cooperation with humans in more general situations not especially well suited for robot operation. Often, robots are required to navigate in unknown and unstructured outdoor environments, where little assumptions can be made about the kind of objects or structures that can be used for robot guidance.

In such outdoor applications, partly teleoperated robots able to reach autonomously a destination marked by a human operator on the image as seen by the robot are agreed to be very handy. Then, updating the target as the robot advances, permits long-range journeys. Our visually-guided navigation approach provides this performance by relying on natural landmarks.

Most related works use point-based visual features, leading to large landmark databases and high numbers of lookups to attain localization. These drawbacks are palliated by recurring to more involved feature detectors, such as the scale-invariant feature transform (SIFT) [2], and by selecting a maximally-informative subset of landmarks [3]. We explore the alternative approach of relying on only a few region-based features, similarly to [4,5]. The former of these previous works builds an environmental model incrementally by using color and stereo range

R. Basili and M.T. Pazienza (Eds.): AI*IA 2007, LNAI 4733, pp. 555–566, 2007.
© Springer-Verlag Berlin Heidelberg 2007

information, while the latter uses a multi-resolution visual attention mechanism to extract image regions most salient in terms of color contrast.

Saliency detection in our system is also based on color, but instead of processing entire static frames, our algorithm can be applied directly to the dynamic image stream acquired while the robot moves. Thus, it can be thought as implementing a form of visual memory that replicates the phenomenon of the persistence of images in the retina of the animals' eyes. Salient regions are used as a filter for the search of visual landmarks in the image.

The paper is structured as follows: Section 2 describes our visually-guided navigation context in which the landmark detection system is to be used. Section 3 introduces our approach to natural landmark detection and identification, showing some results for real images taken by a mobile robot in an outdoor setting. Finally, some conclusions and future work are pointed out in Section 4.

2   An Approach to Visually-Guided Navigation

We developed a visually-guided navigation system [6] in which a user controls the robot by signaling the navigation target in the images received from a camera transported by the robot. This form of navigation control is convenient for exploration purposes or when there is no previous map of the environment, situations in which systems like GPS, even if available, become useless and can be discarded. The user can decide the next target for the robot and change it as new views of the environment become available.

Fig. 1 shows the two main windows of the navigation interface: The *Camera Window* and the *Robot Control Interface*. In the Camera Window, the user can see the images taken from the camera of the robot and control its gaze direction to observe the environment. The user may select the current navigation target by clicking on the image with the mouse.

One of the problems we had to face while designing our visually-guided navigation system was how to specify the navigation target. Ideally, what we wanted is to allow the user to select any object in sight and use it as the current target.

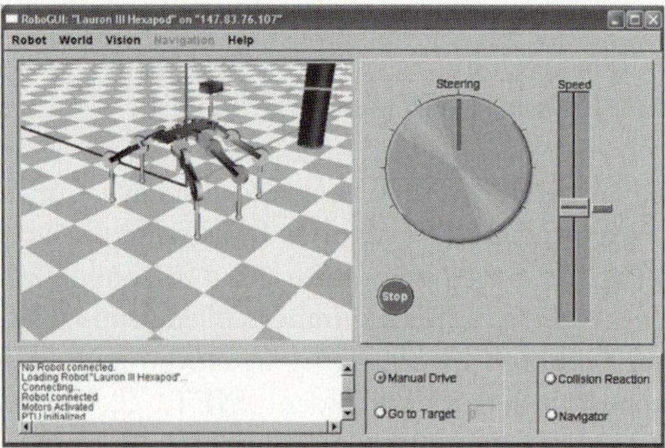

Fig. 1. Camera window and Robot Control Interface

The problem with this approach is that, what can be a clearly identifiable object for the user, may not be easily recognized by an artificial vision system, so that it can be lost very soon. Another difficulty that appears with the definition of the target by pointing at it consists in determining what exact area of the image has to be considered as the target object. Our strategy to solve these problems consists in limiting the selection of possible targets to those that the robot is able to identify with its visual recognition system. Thus, it is the system that first shows to the user the set of available landmarks, and the user may select one of them as the target.

Additionally, landmarks detected by the visual system can be used by a landmark-based navigation system (like e.g., that of [7]) to plan a feasible path to the goal in those cases in which obstacles in the way to the goal do not allow a direct approach to it.

3   Natural Landmarks

We relied on the assumption that useful landmarks must be salient, i.e., they must constitute distinctive regions in the image, so that its repeated detection and identification is facilitated. The saliency of a region is not determined by the absolute value of any intrinsic magnitude, but rather by the contrast or difference of this value with respect to the value of the same magnitude in the surroundings [8]. This is also known as *opponency* [9].

Many variables can be used to define the saliency of a region, like color components, intensity, or feature orientation. Works like [10] compute saliency as a combination of the opponency values of these three variables. In what follows, we present a very simple approach that just considers RGB color values, but the same idea could be used with more informative features.

3.1   Detecting Salient Regions

We take an approach to image processing that is inspired in the visual system of living organisms. A key difference between natural eyes and artificial vision systems is that in the eye, individual light receptors fire asynchronously, giving rise to a continuous image flow that can not be naturally decomposed into separate individual image shots. In contrast, artificial systems work in a strictly sequential way taking one frame after another, each involving all individual receptors updated at fixed frequency. Our approach emulates the asynchronous process of the eye by taking pixels at random from the image with a frequency which is not related with that of frame acquisition. Thus, the input image is treated as a continuously varying source of information with no distinction between successive frames.

One advantage of this approach is that the process is independent of the frame rate of the acquisition system, which can be safely ignored in the image processing task. This avoids any need of synchronization between image acquisition and image processing. Another advantage is that the processing cost is independent of image resolution: the same number of pixels per second will be processed whatever the number of pixels of the image is. Image size or resolution affects only the probability that a given pixel is examined in a given period of time.

To detect saliency, the information of individual pixels is used only statistically and stored in local units that cover different regions of the image. This approach allows us to implement a form of visual memory that replicates the phenomenon of the persistence of images in the retina: Units can persist as long as new pixels keep them active, decreasing in strength until disappearing if they are not fed enough by appropriate inputs. The system is robust to sporadic noisy frames, since most units will not be substantially perturbed by noisy pixel values and will keep the essential information through the next uncorrupted frame.

Units have elliptic receptive fields in the image plane, which adapt through successive updates to cover regions whose pixels have similar colors. These ellipses arise naturally from considering normal distributions for pixels taken at random from each region: the center $\mathbf{U}_{xy} = (U_x, U_y)$ of the ellipse corresponds to the mean value of the pixels' positions, whereas its dimensions (the major and the minor axis) and orientation are determined by the covariances. Each unit also has a spherical receptive field in the RGB color space with a fixed radius, which is a parameter of the system, and whose center adapts to approach the average color value of the input pixels to which the unit responded.

Each unit U is defined with the following attributes:

- Center vector $\mathbf{U}_{xy}$ and covariance matrix Σ_{XY} in the image plane,
- Center vector $\mathbf{U}_{rgb}$ in the color space,
- Contrast C_U, a scalar that measures saliency, as explained in point 2) below,
- Creation date $Creac_U$, to record the time from which the unit exists,
- Counter $Updates_U$ for the number of times a unit has been updated,
- Counter $Inside_U$ for the number of times an input pixel has fallen inside the receptive field of the unit in the image plane, and
- Strength S_U, a scalar that estimates the current proportion between the number of pixels to which the unit responds and those lying into the unit's receptive field in the image plane.

Description of the Saliency Detection Algorithm. In the main loop of the algorithm, a random input pixel I is selected and, for each unit U, its Mahalanobis distance in the image coordinates and Euclidean distance in color space are computed as:

$$Mdist_{xy}(U, I) = \sqrt{(\mathbf{I}_{xy} - \mathbf{U}_{xy})^\top \Sigma_{XY}^{-1} (\mathbf{I}_{xy} - \mathbf{U}_{xy})}, \tag{1}$$

where Σ_{XY} is the covariance matrix of unit U, and

$$Edist_{RGB}^2(U, I) = \sum_i (\mathbf{I}_i - \mathbf{U}_i)^2, \qquad \text{with } i \in \{r, g, b\}. \tag{2}$$

The Mahalanobis distance is used in image space instead of the Euclidean one in order have a geometric proximity measure taking into account the shape of the spatial distribution.

If these distances are below given thresholds (MAXDISTXY and MAXDIS-TRGB, respectively), then the unit is said to respond to the input pixel. Among the units that respond, the one which is closest in the image space, is considered as the *winner*.

1) Updating the winner unit
The winner is updated according to the following rules:

- **Center position.** The unit is approached to the pixel, in the image plane as well as in color space:

$$\mathbf{d}_i = \mathbf{I}_i - \mathbf{U}_i \qquad (3)$$
$$\mathbf{U}_i \leftarrow \mathbf{U}_i + \gamma \mathbf{d}_i \qquad (4)$$

where $i \in \{x, y, r, g, b\}$ and $0 < \gamma < 1$

- **Covariances in image space.** The update of the covariances can be viewed as a simultaneous update of the dimensions and the orientation of the ellipse that represents the unit. The updating of covariances is straightforward:

$$\sigma_{ij} \leftarrow \sigma_{ij} + \gamma(\mathbf{d}_i\mathbf{d}_j - \sigma_{ij}), \quad \text{where } i,j \in \{x,y\}. \qquad (5)$$

- **Counter of updates**

$$Updates_U \leftarrow Updates_U + 1 \qquad (6)$$

2) Updating other units
If the Mahalanobis distance from the input pixel to a non-winner unit is below three times the MAXDISTXY value, the pixel is considered to lay in the unit's neighborhood, and the pixel color is used to update the unit contrast. The update rule is:

$$C_U \leftarrow \alpha C_U + (1 - \alpha)\sqrt{\sum_{i \in \{r,g,b\}} (\mathbf{I}_i - \mathbf{U}_i)^2}, \qquad 0 < \alpha < 1 \qquad (7)$$

i.e., increasing or decreasing according to the Euclidean distance in the color space between the input pixel and the unit.

The updating of the strength S_U and $Inside_U$ is done for all units for which the Mahalanobis distance of the input pixel is below the MAXDISTXY value, i.e., the pixel is in the receptive field of the unit. While $Inside_U$ is simply incremented by one, the strength is increased when the unit responds to the input (i.e., also chromatically) according to:

$$S_U \leftarrow \beta S_U + (1 - \beta), \quad \text{with } 0 < \beta < 1. \qquad (8)$$

If the unit does not respond to the input color, S_U is decreased according to:

$$S_U \leftarrow \beta S_U \qquad (9)$$

3) Reallocation of units

To avoid a proliferation of useless units, the maximum number of them is limited by a parameter of the system, which may be adjusted depending on image complexity and the intended level of detail of the result. When the maximum number of units is reached, in order to allow the creation of new ones corresponding to interesting regions not yet captured by any unit, older ones must be removed. When this is the case, the less useful unit is selected according to the following criteria: First, the unit with the lowest strength value is sought. If its strength is below a certain value, it is assumed that the region it is representing is no longer there, and the unit can be reallocated for the new input. If no low-strength unit is found, the reallocation will only take place provided a contrast estimation of the unit to be created is above that of the lowest-contrast unit. Such contrast estimation is given by the distance in color space of the input pixel to its spatially closest unit.

New units are initialized with center vectors given by the values of the input pixel, with a circular shape in the image plane, and a radius equal to its distance to the closest unit.

4) Merging of units

When two units respond to a given pixel, they are probably representing different parts of the same region and have to be merged together. For the merged unit, the center values and covariances are computed as a weighted sum of those of the original units. The weights are proportional to the respective area and strength, thus roughly corresponding to the "mass", or number of pixels each unit responds to:

$$Weight(U) = Area(U)S_U \tag{10}$$

The area is computed from the covariances as

$$Area(U) = \sqrt{((\sigma_{xx} + \sigma_{yy} + \Delta) \cdot (\sigma_{xx} + \sigma_{yy} - \Delta))} \tag{11}$$

$$\text{where } \Delta = \sqrt{(\sigma_{xx} - \sigma_{yy})^2 + 4\sigma_{xy}^2}$$

The contrast of the merged unit is set to the highest contrast value of the two original ones, and for the strength, the weighted sum of the strengths is made, this time using the respective values of $Updates_U$ as weights.

5) Output of the system

As for the output of the system, less relevant units are filtered out before being output as salient regions. To this end, units covering too large regions of the image are discarded, as they usually capture the background and are not useful for navigation. Regions that are too small are also discarded to remove isolated pixels or noise. Finally, units that have not been updated a minimum number of times are not considered, since they are still not reliable enough. From the remaining units, those with contrast values above a given threshold are selected for output as corresponding to salient regions.

3.2   Landmark Characterization

Salient regions are not considered as landmarks by themselves, but as easily recognizable pointers potentially denoting the presence of a landmark, which usually will present a richer structure than a single uniform region. We define a landmark as a set of uniform color regions, each of them with a characteristic color and shape.

Each region R composing a landmark L is defined with the following attributes:

- Center vector $\mathbf{R}_{rgb}$ in the color space,
- Geometrical central moments μ_{20}, μ_{11} and μ_{02} of the region,
- Squared patch $\mathbf{R}_{patch}$ to store a normalized version of the region's mask.

With a desired frequency, the current image frame is analyzed in order to characterize the landmark associated with the salient region defined by each unit U, according to the following steps:

1) Region mask determination
Every pixel I in the image for which the unit responds is included into the salient region's mask.

$$mask_U(I) = 1 \Leftrightarrow \begin{cases} Mdist_{xy}(U, I) \leq MAXDISTXY \\ Edist_{RGB}(U, I) \leq MAXDISTRGB \end{cases} \qquad (12)$$

In a second step, the region mask is expanded, possibly beyond the limits of the ellipse, by a growing process that includes those pixels connected to the mask that also satisfy the color constraint.

2) Landmark layout
Once the region mask is obtained, we define the landmark layout as the convex hull of the mask. This allows to include regions of different colors into the landmark, and not only the single color region that was found as salient.

3) Extraction of relevant regions of the landmark
The landmark layout is subject to a non-exhaustive segmentation process which tries to obtain its most relevant regions. The goal is to obtain a description of the landmark consisting in a small number of significant regions that cover the most part of the area, excluding too small regions from the description. This is obtained by a process of color-based region growing initiated at successive randomly chosen seeds within the landmark layout. The process stops as soon as at least 80% of the landmark area has been segmented, or after a given number of seeds, determined in proportion to the region size, has been used.

During the growing process the region's color is updated as new pixels are included in the region's mask $\mathbf{R}_{mask}$:

$$\mathbf{d}_i = \mathbf{I}_i - \mathbf{R}_i \qquad (13)$$

$$\mathbf{R}_i \leftarrow \mathbf{R}_i + \gamma \mathbf{d}_i \qquad \text{with } i \in \{r, g, b\} \tag{14}$$

$$\gamma = \frac{1}{R_{weight}+1} \tag{15}$$

$$R_{weight} \leftarrow R_{weight} + 1 \tag{16}$$

4) Region merging

In order to make the segmentation more robust to initial seed selection, a post-process of merging is done, which joins those neighboring regions whose colors are similar enough. The result of merging two regions R^a and R^b is a new region R^c obtained as follows:

$$\mathbf{R}^c_{mask} = \mathbf{R}^a_{mask} \cup \mathbf{R}^b_{mask} \tag{17}$$

$$R^c_{weight} = R^a_{weight} + R^b_{weight}, \tag{18}$$

$$\mathbf{R}^c_i = \frac{R^a_{weight}\mathbf{R}^a_i + R^b_{weight}\mathbf{R}^b_i}{R^c_{weight}} \qquad \text{with } i \in \{r, g, b\} \tag{19}$$

After this, regions representing a too small fraction of the landmark area are removed.

5) Region normalization

Each region is normalized to a patch of 40x40 pixels to make its description invariant to changes in scale and moderate perspective deformations. For this, the geometric central moments of order 2 are computed, from which the equivalent ellipse axes are found providing a rotation angle to align the region, and scale factors for the x and y dimensions.

The geometrical moments are computed as:

$$m_{ij} = \sum_x \sum_y x^i y^j \mathbf{R}_{mask}(x, y) \tag{20}$$

$$\mu_{ij} = \sum_x \sum_y (x - \bar{x})^i (y - \bar{y})^j \mathbf{R}_{mask}(x, y) \tag{21}$$

$$\text{where} \qquad \bar{x} = \frac{m_{10}}{m_{00}}, \qquad \bar{y} = \frac{m_{01}}{m_{00}}$$

from which the equivalent ellipse orientation and axes are obtained:

$$\theta = \tfrac{1}{2} arctan\left(\frac{2\mu_{11}}{\mu_{20} - \mu_{02}}\right), \tag{22}$$

$$w = \sqrt{\frac{\mu_{20} + \mu_{02} + \Delta}{2m_{00}}} \quad \text{and} \quad h = \sqrt{\frac{\mu_{20} + \mu_{02} - \Delta}{2m_{00}}}, \tag{23}$$

$$\text{where} \quad \Delta = \sqrt{(\mu_{20} - \mu_{02})^2 + 4\mu_{11}^2}.$$

The region mask normalization (translation, rotation and scaling) into a square patch $\mathbf{R}_{patch}$ is done in the following way:

$$\mathbf{R}_{patch}(x', y') = \mathbf{R}_{mask}(x, y) \tag{24}$$

$$(x', y')^t = M * (x, y)^t + b \tag{25}$$

$$M = \begin{bmatrix} s_x cos(\theta) & s_x sin(\theta) \\ -s_y sin(\theta) & s_y cos(\theta) \end{bmatrix}, \quad b = \begin{bmatrix} t_x s_x cos(\theta) + t_y s_x sin(\theta) \\ -t_x s_y sin(\theta) + t_y s_y cos(\theta) \end{bmatrix} \tag{26}$$

$$\text{where:} \quad t_x = -\bar{x} \qquad t_y = -\bar{y} \qquad s_x = \frac{40}{2w} \qquad s_y = \frac{40}{2h}$$

Fig. 2. The six-legged robot Lauron III used in the experiments

Finally, a landmark description is stored as a set of regions, each defined by its characteristic color, its geometric moments and the normalized 40x40 region mask.

3.3   Landmark Identification

In order to identify previously encountered landmarks and update their description with the new view, each newly found landmark is compared against all landmarks currently in the landmark database. The comparison between two landmarks is done by trying to match the regions that form each landmark. Each region of the new landmark is compared with all regions of the stored landmark. Region comparison is performed according to two features: color and shape. The color match is simpler to test and is made first so as to act as a filter for the second test. Regions passing the color match filter are tested for shape similarity by computing the normalized cross-correlation NCC of the corresponding normalized masks:

$$NCC = \frac{\sum_x \sum_y \mathbf{R}^a_{patch}(x,y)\mathbf{R}^b_{patch}(x,y)}{\sqrt{\sum_x \sum_y (\mathbf{R}^a_{patch}(x,y))^2 \sum_x \sum_y (\mathbf{R}^b_{patch}(x,y))^2}} \tag{27}$$

If the shape similarity of two regions is higher than a threshold (defined as 85%), the correspondence between the two regions is added to a list of correspondences. This list may contain multiple matches for each landmark region, leaving the disambiguation of the correct matches for a later process of global coherence. A new landmark is identified with a landmark stored in the database if the percentage of matching regions is above 50%.

Non identified landmarks are added to the landmark database as new detected landmarks, so that they can be identified in later stages of the navigation process.

Fig. 3. Landmark detection and identification in an image sequence

3.4   Experimental Results

The landmark detection and identification system was tested on real images taken during the navigation of a legged robot Lauron III (Figure 2). The Salience Detection algorithm was executed on the whole video sequence, while the processes of Landmark Characterization and Landmark Identification were only performed on the six isolated frames shown in Figure 3.

Superimposed on the video images are the ellipses corresponding to the regions detected as salient by the Saliency Detection algorithm. Next to each image, the regions obtained for each landmark by the Landmark Characterization algorithm are shown. Arrows between frames indicate the landmark correspondences found by the Landmark Identification module. It can be observed that the blue bag and the two bright objects are consistently detected as relevant all the time the robot is approaching them. Other objects like the windows or the stairs are also found relevant most of the time they appear in the visual field. Other regions are eventually detected as salient, but not in a systematic way.

In the experiment, landmark correspondences are sought only between the landmarks of each frame with those of the previous one. As can be seen in the pictures, all detected landmarks that appear in two consecutive frames are correctly identified, except for the windows appearing in frames 1 and 2, which are only partially visible, and the bag in frame 5, which is largely out of view and can not be matched against the fully visible one of frame 4.

4   Conclusions and Future Work

We have presented a system for landmark detection, characterization and posterior identification, able to automatically select and track natural landmarks in arbitrary, non-structured environments. At the current stage, the system has shown the ability to reliably identify landmarks appearing in different views of the scene, taken at different stages of a navigation process performed by a legged robot. The new approach to detect and track salient regions provides an attention mechanism that serves as a filter of specific parts of the image, which can be further analyzed in detail to identify landmarks, thus allowing a real-time visual processing suitable for landmark-based navigation.

Further work is needed to make the landmark characterization more robust to large differences in the viewpoint and illumination conditions that may be expected during the travel of the robot in outdoor environments. As a future enhancement, a landmark could be represented by a collection of views taken form different locations at different stages of the navigation, thus coping with the problem of the appearance/disappearance of regions when changing the point of view. Another improvement concerns the algorithm for landmark matching: when the number of matched regions between two landmarks is not enough to assess a landmark identification, the missing regions could be actively sought in the landmark to confirm the correctness of the match.

Acknowledgements. This work has been supported by the Spanish *Ministerio de Ciencia y Tecnología* and FEDER under the project SIRVENT (DPI2003-05193-C02-01).

References

1. DeSouza, G., Kak, A.: Vision for mobile robot navigation: a survey. PAMI 24(2), 237–267 (2002)
2. Lowe, D.: Distinctive Image Features from Scale-Invariant Keypoints. International Journal of Computer Vision 60, 91–110 (2004)
3. Sala, P., Sim, R., Shokoufandeh, A., Dickinson, S.: Landmark Selection for Vision-Based Navigation. IEEE Trans. on Robotics 22(2), 334–349 (2006)
4. Murrieta-Cid, R., Parra, C., Devy, M.: Visual navigation in natural environments: from range and color data to a landmark-based model. Autonomous Robots 13(2), 143–168 (2002)
5. Todt, E., Torras, C.: Detecting Salient Cues Through Illumination-Invariant Color Ratios. Robotics and Autonomous Systems 48(2-3), 111–130 (2004)
6. Celaya, E., Albarral, J-L., Jiménez, P., Torras, C.: Visually-Guided Robot Navigation: From Artificial To Natural Landmarks. In: 6th International Conference on Field and Service Robotics, Chamonix, France (July 2007)
7. Busquets, D., Sierra, C., de Màntaras, R.L.: A multi-agent approach to qualitative landmark-based navigation. Autonomous Robots 15, 129–153 (2003)
8. Nothdurft, H.-C.: Saliency from Feature Contrast: Additivity Across Dimensions. Vision Research 40, 1183–1201 (2000)
9. Todt, E., Torras, C.: Detection of natural landmarks through multiscale opponent features. In: 15th International Conference on Pattern Recognition, Barcelona, Spain, pp. 976–979 (2000)
10. Itti, L., Koch, C., Niebur, E.: A Model of Saliency-based visual Attention for Rapid Scene Analysis. IEEE Transactions on Pattern Analysis and Machine Intelligence 20(11), 1254–1259 (1998)

Real-Time Visual Grasp Synthesis Using Genetic Algorithms and Neural Networks

Antonio Chella, Haris Dindo, Francesco Matraxia, and Roberto Pirrone

Department of Informatics Engineering, University of Palermo, Viale delle Scienze, 90128 Palermo, Italy

Abstract. This paper addresses the problem of automatic grasp synthesis of unknown planar objects. In other words, we must compute points on the object's boundary to be reached by the robotic fingers such that the resulting grasp, among infinite possibilities, optimizes some given criteria. Objects to be grasped are represented as superellipses, a family of deformable 2D parametric functions. They can model a large variety of shapes occurring often in practice by changing a small number of parameters. The space of possible grasp configurations is analyzed using genetic algorithms. Several quality criteria from existing literature together with kinematical and mechanical considerations are considered. However, genetic algorithms are not suitable to applications where time is a critical issue. In order to achieve real-time characteristics of the algorithm, neural networks are used: a huge training-set is collected off-line using genetic algorithms, and a feedforward network is trained on these values. We will demonstrate the usefulness of this approach in the process of grasp synthesis, and show the results achieved on an anthropomorphic arm/hand robot.

1 Introduction and Related Work

Despite the construction of human-hand-like robotic effectors, much work is still to be done in order to gave robots the capability to grasp and manipulate objects. Most applications are concerned with structured environments, in which the deterministic allocation and geometric description of elements that form the work-cell is essential to achieve acceptable results. In addition, the variety of object shapes and different object dimensions, makes the choice of the most appropriate grasp strategy a particularly difficult and complex task.

The problem of automatic grasp synthesis is a classical one in the robotics literature. Many works are inspired on the nature of human grasps [1,2]. Works in [3,4,5,6,7] provide a good starting point for the study of robotic grasping and manipulation. A particularly important concept in grasping are *force-closure* and *form-closure* properties of a grasp which deal about how well a grasped object resist to external disturbance [8]. We are interested in force-closure grasps: a grasp achieves force-closure when it can resist arbitrary forces and torques, and the grasped object is fully constrained by the contact forces. It is possible to devise necessary and sufficient conditions for force closure grasps [9].

R. Basili and M.T. Pazienza (Eds.): AI*IA 2007, LNAI 4733, pp. 567–578, 2007.

For a given hand and object, there are usually a large number of grasps which will satisfy the some closure criteria. To select a "good" or an "optimal" grasp, it is necessary to develop *measures of grasp quality* and a means of searching the space of possible grasps. Several criteria for evaluating the quality of 2D grasps are given in [10,11]. A simplified version of some quality criteria and a computationally efficient algorithm for evaluating the force closure property of a grasp is presented in [9]. In [12] the problem of grasp synthesis is tackled using a biologically-inspired approach based on genetic algorithms. However, the algorithm has been tested in simulation only.

Determining a "good" grasp depends on the nature of the effector involved. The goal is to automatically perform the grasp synthesis on unknown planar objects described as superellipses, a family of parametric curves, and extracted from the input images using machine vision techniques. In other words, we must compute points on the object's surface to be reached by the robotic fingers (*contact points*) such that the resulting grasp, among infinite possibilities, optimizes some given criteria. Methods for computing the quality of a particular grasp have been taken from the huge literature on the subject. The space of possible configurations is analyzed using genetic algorithms. However, genetic algorithms are well suited to off-line computations, while ability to perform grasp analysis and synthesis in real time is critical for many robotic applications. To this aim neural networks are used: a huge training-set is collected off-line using genetic algorithms, and the network is trained on these values. We will demonstrate the usefulness of this approach in the process of grasp synthesis, and show some results achieved on our robotic platform composed of a four-fingered anthropomorphic hand and the PUMA200 industrial manipulator.

2   Superellipses

Superellipses are a flexible representation that naturally generalize ellipses. They were first introduced by the French mathematician Gabriel Lamé in the beginning of the nineteenth century. Superellipses can model a large variety of natural shapes, including ellipse, rectangles, parallelograms, by changing a small number of parameters, and are useful for modelling in the fields of computer graphics and computer vision. Regular objects are represented using the size parameters $\{a_x, a_y\}$ which define the lengths of the semi axes, and the squareness parameter ϵ specifies the global shape of the curve in the 2-D plane. All quantities are expressed in a superellipse (or object) centered coordinate system, which we will denote S. To model or to recover superellipses from image data we must represent them in general position, which requires 3 additional parameters for expressing the translation and rotation of the superellipse relative to the center of the world coordinate system W, x_c, y_c, and θ, relative to the world coordinate system.

However, the power of superellipses lies not in its ability to model perfect geometric shapes, but in its ability to model deformed geometric shapes through global deformations. The deformations used in this work are *linear tapering* and *circular bending* along axis x and y. These transformations are described with parameters *tap*, $bend_x$, and $bend_y$. Thus, each point on the superellipse is a function of superellipse parameters, and a sampling parameter $\omega \in [0, 1]$. Several optimization approaches for fitting superellipse to intensity or range images are described in [13,14].

3   Genetic Algorithms

Genetic algorithms, introduced in [15] have been inspired by the *natural selection mechanism* introduced by Darwin. They apply certain *operators* (reproduction, crossover and mutation) to a population of solutions of the problem at hand, in such a way that the new population is improved compared with the previous one according to a given criterion function, called *fitness*. The possibility to "survive" is proportional to the fitness value of a particular individual. This procedure is applied for a preselected number of iterations. So, the genetic algorithm transforms a *population* of *individuals*, each one with an associated fitness value, into a new *generation*. The fitness function depends on n parameters, or variables, that are called *genes*; genes constitute a *genome*.

Each individual in the population represents a possible solution to a given problem. Genetic algorithms search across huge population for a good solution to the problem, represented by an individual in the last population, or the best individual across several generations. They fit well to situations in which it is hard, or even impossible, to analytically express the function to optimize. This is particularly true in our case. In the next sections we will see that the evaluation of how good a particular grasp is on an object is given by a set of quality criteria on force-closure, stability and other properties. These can be express as functions of the position of the contact points on the surface of the grasped object, and properties of the object itself. However, seldom it is not possible to find a closed form of these relations. Another difficulty arising in grasping synthesis, is that the function to maximize/minimize is a non-convex one. This make the choice of genetic algorithms a natural one: the sum of diverse quality criteria constitutes our fitness function, and the genetic algorithm will figure out what the best configuration is.

4   Measures for Assesting Grasp Quality

In order to apply genetic algorithms to the problem of grasp synthesis, we must decide what each gene of a genome represent, and how to assign it a fitness measure. We will denote with I, II, III, thumb, index and middle fingers respectively. Suppose for the moment that each individual codes the three contact points of the robotic hand on the object surface. These points are expressed in an object-centered reference system, and may, or not, respect the kinematics constraints imposed by the robot's morphology. Hence, each gene codes the 2D position of the respective finger which may be expressed as a function of the superellipse sampling parameter $\omega \in [0,1]$. Thus, the genome is a three-dimensional real valued vector $\omega = [\omega_I, \omega_{II}, \omega_{III}]^T$. The initial population is obtained by randomly sampling three points lying on the superellipse's boundary for N individuals in the generation.

In order to be selected for the reproduction, a grasp **must** satisfy the force-closure property. The algorithm to compute and verify the force-closure property for a given grasp is described in [9] and will not be further analyzed here. Fitness function measures the qualities of each grasp. We use five quality criteria, and each criteria is normalized. The lower is the score, the better is the resulting grasp configuration. The fitness will be a sum of these scores, and the genetic algorithm will be used to seek for the configuration that minimizes the fitness. If the grasp is not force-closure, the associated individual will be assigned an arbitrarily high fitness with the effect of minimizing its probability of being selected for the reproduction.

Triangle Area (TA). It can be stated that the larger the area of the grasping triangle, the more stable a grasp is ([16,17]). This criteria has an intuitive explanation: the further the forces, the higher the torques they are able to resist. The area of the grasping triangle is represented Fig. 1. The quality value is computed as the normalized area of the triangle in order to obtain values in the range [0,1]. Let denote the area of superellipse as AS, and the area of the triangle formed by three contact points as AT. The criterion may be expressed as:

$$score = \frac{(AS - AT)}{AS} \tag{1}$$

Equilateral Triangle (ET). A grasp is more reliable in terms of stability, sliding avoidance and force equilibrium when the grasping triangle given by the contact points is closer to an ideal equilateral grasp [16]. Each three finger grasp is then given a score which measures the similarity of its grasping triangle to an equilateral one.

In the most obvious implementation of this criteria, each angle is compared to a $60 \deg(\frac{\pi}{3} rad)$ angle. We denote α_I, α_{II}, and α_{III} the angles of the grasp triangle formed by thumb, index, and middle fingers respectively (see Fig. 1a). For each grasp, the criterion assigns a measure as:

$$score = \frac{|\alpha_{thumb} - \frac{\pi}{3}| - |\alpha_{index} - \frac{\pi}{3}| - |\alpha_{middle} - \frac{\pi}{3}|}{\frac{4}{3}\pi} \tag{2}$$

Denominator acts as a normalization factor in order to obtain values in the range $[0, 1]$. The minimum possible value is 0 for a perfect equilateral triangle, while the maximum is $\frac{4}{3}\pi$ for a triangle having two angles close to 0 and the third being nearly π.

Triangle Center (TC). This criterion is designed to obtain stable grips with respect to wrenches generated by gravitational and inertial forces. These wrenches are minimum when the center of the grip is closest to the mass center of the object, which can be reliably computed as the centroid of the two-dimensional contour ([11]). The criterion calculates the Euclidean distance between the center of the grasp, TC, and the superellipse's center, SC (see Fig. 1b). The distance is normalized in order to obtain values included in the range $[0, 1]$:

$$score = \frac{D(SC, TC)}{max(a_x, a_y)} \qquad (3)$$

where $D(x, y)$ denotes the Euclidean distance between points x and y, and a_x and a_y are the superellipse's axes (see Section 2).

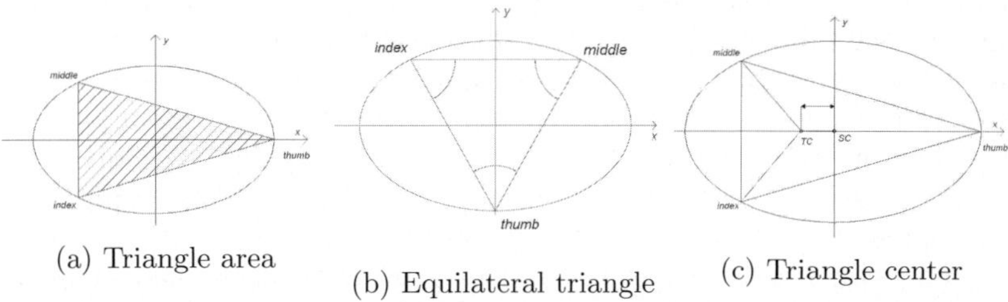

(a) Triangle area   (b) Equilateral triangle   (c) Triangle center

Fig. 1. Triangle area, equilateral triangle and triangle center criteria

Curvature. Humans prefer concave surfaces when grasping objects. Thus, a criterion that takes into account the curvature of the object contact points is a desirable in synthesizing good grasps. Furthermore, [18] showed that grasps tend to be more stable when contacts are made on concave surfaces.

The concave/convex property of an object may be as its *curvature* at the contact point. The curvature may be computed using the notion of *circulum osculans* (osculating circle) introduced by Leibniz, which is a circle that closely touches the curve at the given point. It can be defined as the circle passing through the point P, and other two arbitrary points on the object's boundary. The curvature of an object at the three contact points is computed as:

$$\rho_i = \frac{1}{R_i} \qquad \text{with i=I,II,III} \qquad (4)$$

where R_i is the radius of the obscuring circle at the contact point. ρ_i assumes positive values if the contact point lies in a concave region, negative if the contact point lies in convex region, and zero for perfectly flat surfaces. Empirical studies show that the curvature for typical objects is in the range $[-2.50, 2.50]$. The criterion assigns the following curvature measure to a grasp:

$$score = \frac{N_c - \rho_I - \rho_{II} - \rho_{III}}{2 * N_c} \qquad (5)$$

with the normalization factor, N_c being 7.50. The score is in the range $[0, 1]$.

5 Genome

The correct choice of the genome is fundamental for the success of the genetic algorithm. It codes the solution to the problem, and the genetic algorithm outputs the individual with the best fitness value in the population. Each gene in the genome is a quantity we wish to estimate. Up to now we have considered a three degrees-of-freedom genome for the purposes of the grasp synthesis: contact points at the boundary of the object expressed as functions of the superllipse's parameter ω (see section 4). However, in real-world robotic applications, this choice is inappropriate for two reasons:(1) Genetic algorithm may output contact points which do not respect the kinematics of the robotic system;(2) Inverse kinematics for a redundant hand/arm robotic system must *a posterior* be solved.

Our approach takes into account the kinematic constraints of the real robot in that it encodes the *final configuration of joint angles* which the robot should assume in order to successfully perform a three-fingered grasp of an object. Limits on the extension of joint angles of the robot, as imposed by mechanical design, are easily expressed as the admissible range of variation of each gene representing such quantities. Furthermore, our solution implicitly solves the inverse kinematics for the robotic hand. This choice makes the problem more challenging given the increased search-space of the possible solution. Recall that our robotic system has 22 degrees-of-freedom: 6 DOFs for the PUMA arm and 4 DOFs for each finger of the robotic hand. Next sections depicts several reasonable assumptions, whose adoption makes the grasp synthesis problem tractable.

5.1 Robotic Arm and Hand Assumptions

We are interested the most suitable position and orientation of the robot's end-effector in order to grasp an object. This information can be expressed relatively to the position of the object to be grasped which significantly reduces the variability of the input arguments. Since we deal with planar grasp, some degrees-of-freedom may be set beforehand. We assume that each object is grasped in a similar fashion by approaching it from above. By analogy with human grasps, we may set the *pitch* and *yaw* angles of the robot's end-effector to some reasonable values, and allow only the *roll* angle to change. We have empirically found that $pitch = 0$ and $yaw = 25$ are reasonable choices for planar grasps. Information about the position and orientation of the arm's end-effector is coded in the genome as the position of the frame attached to the end-effector expressed in the object-centered coordinate system (X, Y, Z) and the roll angle of the end-effector frame (θ).

Our robotic hand has four identical fingers, with index, middle and ring fingers in opposition to the thumb finger. Each finger has four degrees-of-freedom corresponding to tendon driven rotational joints. The structure of the robotic hand appears to be similar to the human hand. This inspired us to adopt some biomechanical constraints in order to reduce the search space for the genetic algorithm. The constraints are of two types: *static*(limit the range of finger motion), and *dynamic* (describe relationships between some finger joints) [19]. We are particularly interested in dynamic constraints. The most commonly used constraint is the one which relates proximal interphalangeal (q_{PIP}) and distal interphalangeal (q_{DIP}) joints of each finger except the thumb. Since these two joints are driven by the same tendon it can be stated that: $q_{DIP} = \frac{2}{3}q_{PIP}$. This relation may be used to further reduce the dimensionality of our genome, since for index and middle fingers of the robotic hand it provides an acceptable approximation. The genes $q_{1:4}^{I}$, $q_{1:3}^{II}$ and $q_{1:3}^{III}$ encode the joint angles of the thumb, index and middle fingers respectively (fourth joint angle for index and middle is computed using the dynamic constraint). Since we deal with three-fingered grasps only, we do not consider the fourth, ring, finger of the robotic hand.

5.2   How Does the Genome Encode the Contact Points?

Quality criteria explained in section 4 need an information about contact points on the grasped object. Since we are encoding the position and orientation of the end-effector (robotic hand) and joint angles of each finger, we need to compute Cartesian position of each contact point in a object-centered reference system. However, the choice of the genome allows us to perform this by simple direct kinematics calculations.

An articulated object is made up of rigid bodies, called links, connected by joints. Each link has its own coordinate frame in the kinematic model, and pairs of link frames are connected by coordinate transformations. A coordinate transform from frame i to frame j, $^{j}T_{i}$, is specified by a rotation matrix $^{j}R_{i} \in \Re^{3x3}$ and translation vector $^{j}t_{i} \in \Re^{3x1}$, arranged in a 4x4 homogeneous transformation matrix. The most important reference frames in this work are depicted in Fig. 2. Given the direct kinematics function of each finger, $^{PALM}T_{TIP}(\mathbf{q})$, which relates the position and orientation of the fingers' end-effector (fingertip) to the frame attached to the hand's palm, and the position and orientation of the hand's palm, $^{SE}T_{PALM}(X, Y, Z, \theta)$, with respect to the object-centered reference system, the frame for each finger's end-effector can be computed by the following expression in homogeneous coordinates (see Fig. 2):

$$^{SE}T_{TIP}(X, Y, Z, \theta, \mathbf{q}) =^{SE} T_{PALM}(X, Y, Z, \theta) *^{PALM} T_{TIP}(\mathbf{q}) \qquad (6)$$

Admissible Values for Each Gene. As explained in the previous sections, our genome is composed of 14 genes. The first three genes constitute the (X, Y, Z) coordinates of the base of the palm $(PALM)$ in the object-centered reference system (SE). The fourth gene constitutes the rotation about the Z axis of the palm base relative to the object-centered reference system, θ. There follows four genes encoding the thumb joint angles, and six genes representing the joint angles of the index and middle fingers. Figure 2b shows admissible values for each gene[1]. These ranges take into account the mechanical properties of the robotic hand,

---

[1] Linear measures are in cm, while angular ones are in rad. Δ is the discrete step of variation of each gene. I, II, and III denote thumb, index and middle fingers respectively.

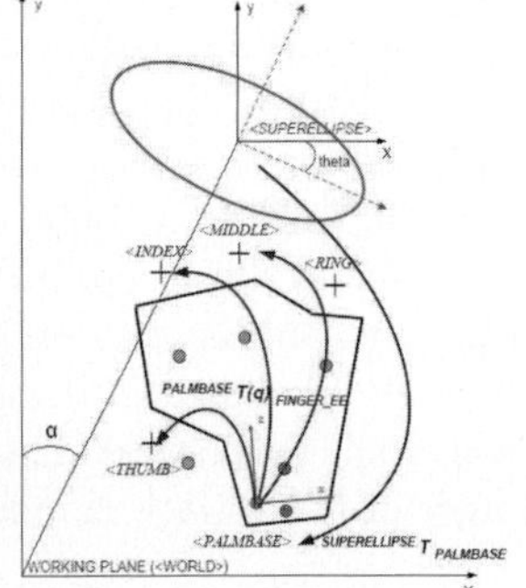

(a) Reference systems used to compute the points of contact

Gene	Min	Max	Δ
X	$-2 * max\{a_x, a_y\}$	$2 * max\{a_x, a_y\}$	0.1
Y	$-2 * max\{a_x, a_y\}$	$2 * max\{a_x, a_y\}$	0.1
Z	7	15	0.1
θ	$\alpha - \pi/4$	$alpha + \pi/4$	$\pi/36$
q_1^I	0	$\pi/2$	$\pi/36$
$q_{2:4}^I$	0	$\pi/2$	$\pi/36$
q_1^{II}, q_1^{III}	$-\pi/12$	$\pi/12$	$\pi/36$
$q_{2:3}^{II}, q_{2:3}^{III}$	0	$\pi/2$	$\pi/36$

(b) Range of variation for each gene in the genome

Fig. 2. Reference systems and range of variation for each gene in the genome

as well as empirical values depending on the characteristics of the object being grasped. Furthermore, each gene is allowed to take values from a discrete set, instead of a continuous one. This choice is justified by the minimum resolution of the robot's sensors and actuators, without sacrificing the precision of the final grasp.

6   Fitness Computation

The fitness function assigns a score to each individual (genome) in the population. Genomes with greater score will have greater possibility to be copied in the new generation, or to be selected for the reproduction. Appropriate choice of the fitness function represents a crucial factor in using genetic algorithms. Given the genome, the coordinates $\mathbf{F}^i = [F_x^i, F_x^i, F_z^i]^T$ of each fingertip (where $i = \{I, II, III\}$) can be obtained through the direct kinematics calculations (section 5.2). Due to a high dimensionality of the search space, several individuals in the population may lead to configurations which are too far from the object's boundary in order to perform a grasp. If the fingertips are near enough to the object's boundary (i.e. below a fixed threshold, σ), the algorithm checks if they respect the force-closure property. In this case the fitness value is the sum of grasp quality criteria (section 4. Otherwise, a penalty fitness value, proportional to the sum of the distances between each fingertip from the boundary, is assigned to the individual. The distance of each fingertip $\mathbf{F}^i$ from the object may be computed as the Euclidean distance between the fingertip $[\mathbf{F}$ and the nearest point on the object's boundary $\mathbf{Obj}^i = [Obj_x^i, Obj_x, 0]^T$. This distance will be denoted as $D(\mathbf{F}, \mathbf{Obj})$. It worths noting that force-closure algorithm and quality criteria work only with the contact points, without checking the actual direction of forces acting on the object. It may happen, for example, that the robotic finger crosses the object, thus creating an undesirable torque. An additional criterion, *force direction*, checks if the computed grasp could be physically achieved. For each finger, i, we compute the direction of its last link, $\overrightarrow{q_3^i q_4^i}$, and check if it points towards the object. In this case we set force direction as VALID, otherwise it is set to INVALID. Table 1 depicts our algorithm for assigning a fitness value to each genome. Proportional factors a, and b are empirically tuned until satisfactory results are obtained.

Table 1. Fitness algorithm

For each genome $[X, Y, Z, \theta, q_1^I, \ldots, q_4^I, q_1^{II}, \ldots, q_3^{II}, q_1^{III}, \ldots, q_3^{III}]$ obtain the Cartesian position of the robotic hand fingertip, $\mathbf{F}^i$, and the nearest postion on the superellipse boundary, $\mathbf{Obj}^i$,
$\forall i \in [I, II, III]$,

    IF $D(\mathbf{F^i}, \mathbf{Obj^i}) \leq \sigma$ AND force direction for the ith finger is VALID,
        IF force-closure property is satisfied
        THEN $score = \sum_{i=I}^{III} \sum_{j=1}^{4} j^{th}$ quality criteria,
        where j={triangle area, equilateral triangle, curvature and triangle center}
        ELSE $score = b * \sum_{i=I}^{III} \|\mathbf{F}^i - \text{center of grasping triangle}\|$
    ELSE $score = a * \sum_{i=I}^{III} D(\mathbf{F}^i, \mathbf{Obj}^i)$

7 Neural Networks for Grasping

Genetic algorithms work well for off-line function optimization. Due to time-to-converge requirements of a typical genetic algorithm, they are generally not suitable for real-time applications. This is especially true in our case. As will be shown in the experimental section, the grasp for an unknown object is synthesis ed in an average time of 2-3 minutes, with the variance of 2 minutes. Obviously, not what is intended for real-time behavior. We would like to have a grasp being computed in orders of seconds, instead of minutes. This is mostly due to the huge search space of the problem, and hard requirements we have imposed to a solution. Several individuals simply get assigned a huge fitness because the grasps they generate are too far from the object's boundary, or do not respect the force-closure property. That means that only a small number of individuals are allowed to be reproduced across generations, which drastically slows down the algorithm. However, if the initial population was generated from a sufficiently good approximation of the actual solution, genetic algorithms would converge in slightly less time.

These observations led us to adopt a neuro-genetic approach to the problem of three-finger grasp synthesis of planar objects. Genetic algorithms are used to create a huge training-set of good grasps on randomly created objects. During the creation of the training-set we imposed some reasonable constraints on the shape, dimensions and positions of objects in the workspace, in order to reproduce situations commonly encountered in practice. A feedforward neural network is then trained on these values, having object parameters as input (i.e. superellipse's parameters), and genomes as output. The neural network approximates the non-linear manifold in the solution space. Inputs to the neural network are the object's shape information (arctan $\frac{y_{SE}}{x_{SE}}$, $a_x, a_y, \epsilon, tap, bend_x, bend_y$), together with its orientation, θ, in the SUPERELLIPSE reference system, and the angle α which encodes the displacement of the object relative to the base of the robotic system (see Fig. 2). The output is the genome, as described in section 5.

At real-time, the object is extracted from the background and superellipse's parameters (position, orientation, shape, and deformation values) are obtained from the fitting process. Trained neural network outputs a rough approximation of the grasp (in terms of a genome, G), which is used to create the initial population for the genetic algotihm by sampling from a multivariate Gaussian with mean value G, and covariance matrix Σ (which are empirically set). This **restricts** the search space, and allows to set the population size, as well as the the maximum number of generations to smaller values, thus improving the overall computational time. The genetic algorithm then outputs the improved solution in terms of grasp quality.

8   Experimental Results

We have tested our algorithm on a variety of shapes obtained by varying the superellipses' parameters. Tests have been performed both in simulation and on the real robotic platform with excellent results. Main features used in our gentic algorithm and neural network are depicted in the figure Fig. 3. With these settings, an average time of 2-3 minutes is needed to obtain a solution. The trained neural network is a feedforward network with one hidden layer. Input and output layers have 8 and 14 neurons respectively, while the hidden layer is composed of 50 neural units. The mean-square error is shown in Fig. 4.

Type	Steady-state
Population size	4000
Reproduction operator	Tournament
Crossover(%)	Uniform(40%)
Mutation(%)	Swap(5%)

(a) GA characteristics

Training (test) set size	4500 (500)
Learning rate	0.7
Training algorithm	Backprop.
Training epochs	2000
Training (test) set MSE	0.89 (0.92)

(b) NN characteristics

Fig. 3. Characteristics of the genetic algorithm and neural network used in the experimental section

In practice, objects are segmented from the background and the fitting of superellipses is performed. Neural network outputs an approximation of the grasp, which is then used as input to the genetic algorithm, which refines the grasp. The algorithm operates in 2-3 sec which is acceptable for most applications. During this time interval the robot may perform the reaching and pre-grasp operations, without affecting the performances of the overall robot control system. Figure 5 shows some successful grasps obtained with our algorithm. Tables depict values assumed by the quality criteria for the best individual, number of generations needed

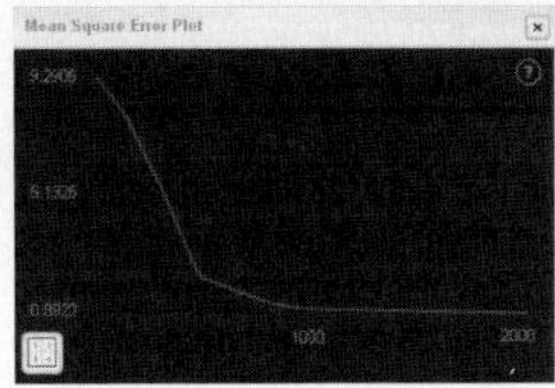

Fig. 4. Mean square error during neural network training

Feature	Value
TA	0.685
TC	0.126
Curv.	1.03
ET	0.165
Tot.	2.006
Generations	31
Time	3.2 sec

(a) GA summary

(b) Contact points

(c) Successful grasp

Feature	Value
TA	0.787
TC	0.072
Curv.	0.997
ET	0.043
Tot	1.899
Generations	15
Time	1.5 sec

(d) GA summary

(e) Contact points

(f) Successful grasp

(g) Grasping a rectangular object

(h) Grasping a spherical object

Fig. 5. Some successful grasps performed in simulation and on real robotic system

to converge, and the total time on our hardware[2]. Contact points for robotic hand fingers are depicted in green for thumb, red for index, and blue for middle. The position of the palm base and its orientation with respect to the object is shown in black. Some examples of grasps on the real robotic platform are also shown.

---

[2] 2GHz CPU, 2GB RAM, Linux OS; software is written in C++ programming language.

References

1. Cutkosky, M., Howe, R.: Human grasp choice and robotic grasp analysis. Dextrous robot hands table of contents, 5–31 (1990)
2. Iberall, T., Mackenzie, C.: Opposition space and human prehension. Dextrous robot hands table of contents, 32–54 (1990)
3. Bicchi, A., Kumar, V.: Robotic grasping and contact: a review. In: Proceedings IEEE International Conference on Robotics and Automation ICRA'00, vol. 1, IEEE Computer Society Press, Los Alamitos (2000)
4. Shimoga, K.: Robot grasp synthesis algorithms: a survey. International Journal of Robotics Research 15(3), 230–266 (1996)
5. Li, Z., Sastry, S.: Issues in dextrous robot hands. Dextrous robot hands table of contents, 154–186 (1990)
6. Yoshikawa, T., Nagai, K.: Analysis of multi-fingered grasping and manipulation. Dextrous robot hands, 187–208 (1990)
7. Yamada, T., Ooba, T., Yamamoto, T., Mimura, N., Funahashi, Y.: Grasp Stability Analysis of Two Objects in Two Dimensions. In: Proceedings 2005 IEEE International Conference on Robotics and Automation, pp. 760–765. IEEE Computer Society Press, Los Alamitos (2005)
8. Bicchi, A.: On the closure properties of robotic grasping. The International Journal of Robotics Research 14(4), 319–334 (1995)
9. Li, J., Jin, M., Liu, H.: A new algorithm for three-finger force-closure grasp of polygonal objects. In: Proceedings IEEE International Conference on Robotics and Automation ICRA'03, IEEE Computer Society Press, Los Alamitos (2003)
10. Park, Y., Starr, G.: Optimal grasping using a multifingered robot hand. In: Proceedings IEEE International Conference on Robotics and Automation, pp. 689–694. IEEE Computer Society Press, Los Alamitos (1990)
11. Morales, A., Sanz, P., del Pobil, A.: Vision-based computation of three-finger grasps on unknown planar objects. In: IEEE/RSJ International Conference on Intelligent Robots and System, 2002, vol. 2 (2002)
12. Fernandez, J., Walker, I., Inc, M., Houston, T.: Biologically inspired robot grasping using genetic programming. In: Proc. IEEE International Conference on Robotics and Automation, vol. 4, IEEE Computer Society Press, Los Alamitos (1998)
13. Rosin, P.: Fitting superellipses. IEEE Transactions on Pattern Analysis and Machine Intelligence 22(7), 726–732 (2000)
14. Jaklic, A., Leonardis, A., Solina, F.: Segmentation and recovery of superquadrics. Kluwer Academic Publishers, Boston, Mass (2000)
15. Holland, J.: Adaption in Natural and Artificial Systems. MIT Press, Cambridge (1975)
16. Mirtich, B., Canny, J.: Easily computable optimum grasps in 2-D and 3-D. In: Proc. IEEE Intl. Conference Robotics Automation, Piscataway, NJ,USA, pp. 739–747. IEEE Computer Society Press, Los Alamitos (1994)
17. Xiong, C., Li, Y., Ding, H., Xiong, Y.: The International Journal of Robotics Research. On the Dynamic Stability of Grasping 18(9), 951 (1999)
18. Montana, D., Beranek, B., Inc, N., Cambridge, M.: Contact stability for two-fingered grasps. IEEE Transactions on Robotics and Automation 8(4), 421–430 (1992)
19. Wu, Y., Lin, J.Y., Huang, T.S.: Modelling Human Hand Constraints. In: Proceedings of the Workshop on Human Motion (Humo2000) (2000)

Attention-Based Environment Perception in Autonomous Robotics

Antonio Chella, Irene Macaluso, and Lorenzo Riano

Università degli studi di Palermo, Dipartimento di Ingegneria Informatica,
Viale delle Scienze ed. 6

Abstract. This paper describes a robotic architecture that uses visual attention mechanisms for autonomous navigation in unknown indoor environments. A foveation mechanism based on classical bottom-up gaze shifts allows the robot to autonomously select landmarks, defined as salient points in the camera images. Landmarks are memorized in a behavioral fashion, coupling sensing and acting to achieve a representation view and scale independent. Selected landmarks are stored in a topological map; during the navigation a top-down mechanism controls the attention system to achieve robot localization. Experiments and results show that our system is robust to noise and odometric errors, being at the same time adaptable to different environments and acting conditions.

1   Introduction

Navigation in unknown environments is one of the most fundamental subject in mobile robotic research. Recent works tend to provide the robot with abilities to autonomously navigate without relying on *a priori* environment knowledge. For the purpose of localization and navigation, the robot must construct a representation of the world, or a map, (for example see [1]). Occupancy grid map [2] is an usually adopted approach, which produces accurate results but requires large amount of memory. Other common approaches include: i) appearance based navigation [3], which uses a sequence of frontal views in a route (memorized during the learning phase) for matching and recognition; ii) landmark-based navigation, which uses static recognizable sensor patterns to build a coarse map (for a review of robotic mapping and localization see [4]). In our work we adopted a landmark-based approach, using an *absolute diktiometric map*; instead of giving the robot a pre-defined set of landmarks, our system should be able to choose them by itself. To define what a landmark is for the robot, we relied on the visual attention mechanisms present in biological systems.

One of the most studied aspect of biological vision is the shift of visual attention to direct our gaze towards parts of scene meaningful for the being [5,6]. This is accomplished by a small part of the eye, called fovea, which contains the major density of photo-receptors. By moving the fovea (foveating) we can shift our focus of attention, allowing to cut off the complexity of analyzing all the information that crosses the optic nerve. It is generally accepted that the attention system is guided by two main components acting in parallel: the bottom-up

R. Basili and M.T. Pazienza (Eds.): AI*IA 2007, LNAI 4733, pp. 579–590, 2007.

gaze shifts controlled by low-level features of the image and the top-down ones controlled by cognitive tasks (for a review, see [7]). One of the first computational model of the bottom-up attention system has been described in [8]. Their hypothesis was that a centralized two-dimensional map, called *saliency map*, was the basis for the control of attention shift. Such map was built from several pre-attentive layers, each of them tuned to detect features like colors, contrast, intensity, orientations, junctions and so on. The output of the layers is combined in the saliency map. Its greatest value is chosen for the next foveation in a winner-take-all fashion. After a foveation a mechanism of inhibition of return [9] prevents the fovea from remaining in the same position. There are distinct ways to define top-down attention: from a physiological point of view, top-down neural signals go from the higher sensory areas to the lower ones, in an anatomical hierarchy [10]; from a psychological point of view, the task being performed modulates the low-level stimuli, enhancing the ones meaningful for the task itself [11].

The proposed system uses a classical model of biological inspired attention mechanism [12] to select salient locations from the whole input image. Moreover, we adopted a foveation mechanism [13] based on classical bottom-up gaze shifts allowing the robot to autonomously select as landmark those regions which yield a sufficiently complex local descriptor. Following this approach, which introduces an interesting concept of sensory-motor coupling, we gained a landmark representation robust to noise and scale-invariant. To solve the obvious problems related to recognition in the case of viewpoint changes, we extended the single view approach of [13] to a multi-view representation by memorizing different snapshots of the same landmark along with the related viewpoint. To control the shift of attention, we focused on the task role, i.e. looking for a landmark in a scene or finding information about a landmark itself.

2   An Overview of the Proposed Architecture

The proposed architecture is depicted in figure 1. The two main components are the memorizing system, concerned with landmarks selection and representation, and the recognizing one, related to robot localization. All these operations are carried out while navigating (in autonomous or controlled way) in a static environment. The two systems share a memory, where all the information about landmarks is stored.

During the memorization phase the robot observes the scene in front of it, while the bottom-up attention system is active. It will find some places with saliency value strong enough to attract its attention, and among them will choose one. This place (which is not necessarily an object or a location with a semantic value) is a candidate landmark L. Once discovered L, the robot starts memorizing information about it: the position relative to the robot and a series of small foveations as in [13]. The number of different foveations is the criterion by which to accept or reject a landmark: if the number of foveations is over a threshold (currently set to 4), the landmark is accepted, otherwise it is rejected and the robot will continue navigating and looking for another salient place. Once accepted, the landmark is placed in a topological map, and the robot starts to move around it to gather some snapshots from different viewpoints. Each snapshot is stored in the memory referring to the same landmark L. Once the track system fails to recognize the landmark, the robot will resume its task until a new location is discovered (see section 2.1).

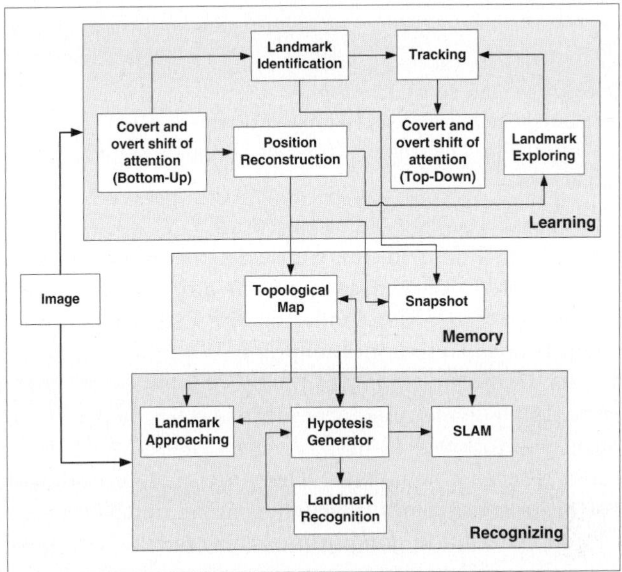

Fig. 1. The schema of the proposed architecture

During the recognition phase the robot uses the landmarks memory to make hypotheses about its position. The nearest landmark in the topological map is selected and the robot approach it. Pan-tilt unit is controlled to center the image with respect to the estimated position of L . When the robot is near enough to L, the snapshot indexed by the current angle between the robot and L is selected for matching. If such a match succeeds the robot's estimated position is nearly correct and it can continue navigating. Otherwise other hypotheses have to be considered, including trying other orientations or moving around to get rid of occlusions. If none of these tries succeed, the memory entry of that landmark is deleted and the robot will start a new memorize process.

The algorithm 1 summarizes the above description. Further details will be given in next sections.

2.1   The Topological Map

In our approach the topological map is an *absolute diktiometric map* ([14,15,16]) represented as an unoriented graph (see figure 2): each node stores information

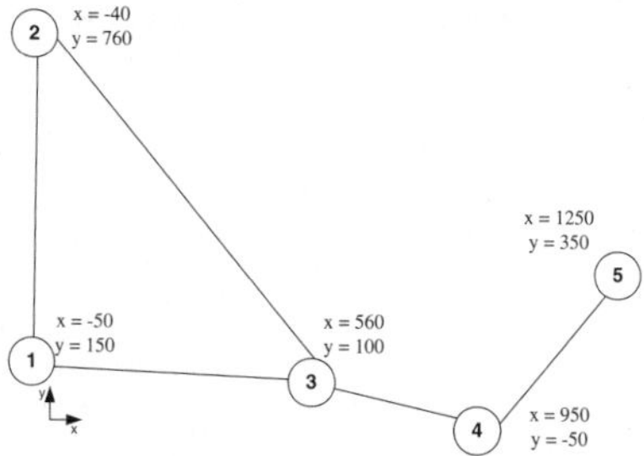

Fig. 2. The topological map constructed after recognizing five nodes (landmarks). For each node is associated the position as estimated by the odometer and the map-position correction algorithm ([14]). The frame of reference origin is placed at the starting robot position and orientation.

about the landmark position, while an edge exists between two landmarks l_i and l_j if the robot discovered the landmark j right after the landmark i (either in memorization mode or recognition mode) or *vice-versa*. The topological map is used by the robot to localization and mapping.

The localization procedure computes the robot position in an absolute frame of reference as in [16]. The mapping procedure is concerned with nodes creation and correction in the topological map. A new node is added to the graph as soon as the robot reaches a new place. There are many criterions to determine when the robot has reached a new place, depending on the sensors the robot is equipped with and the kind of computations involved. The robot will look for a new landmark when the distance from the previous one is above a threshold (currently it is set to three meters in a straight line) or the similarity between subsequent images is too low. We applied a block matching motion compensation algorithm [17] to estimate the similarity between the current image I_{t_0+t} and the reference image I_{t_0}, acquired as soon as a landmark memorization process ends. The difference between I_{t_0+t} and I_{t_0+t-1} is computed as:

$$\epsilon = \sum_j e_j \tag{1}$$

where e_j is the mean squared difference between the block $b_j \in I_{t_0+t}$ and the matching block in I_{t_0+t-1}. The similarity between I_{t_0+t} and I_{t_0} is computed as:

$$E_t = \sum_k \epsilon_{t_0+k} \tag{2}$$

In the current implementation, as the robot moves it tracks its position using odometry, accumulating errors due to wheel slippage and floor irregularities. If during navigation the robot is near enough to a known landmark, the recognition process is activated. This allows to correct both robot position and map. If the

---

Algorithm 1. The system main loop

- If no known landmark is near enough, start the memorization process:
  1. Look for a landmark L1 using the attention system of [12]. Once found, calculate its position and store it in the topological map.
  2. Detect basic and context edges as in [13].
  3. Memorize the edges in a scale-translation-rotation invariant frame of reference.
  4. If there are unvisited context edges, move the fovea along them and go to step 2.
  5. If there are not enough foveations, roll back the topological map changes and go to step 1.
  6. Insert a snapshot in L1 node containing all the fovea movements and edges and index it with the angle between the robot and L1
  7. Move the robot around L1 while tracking it.
  8. If there are not enough snapshot get a new one returning to step 2.
  9. Suppress the memorization process and the recognition process, until the robot is far enough from L1.
- If the robot is near enough to a known landmark L2, start the recognition process:
  1. Move the camera to center the known L2 position.
  2. Try to recognize L2 using the snapshot indexed by the current angle between the robot and L2 by reproducing the memorized fovea movements.
  3. If the recognition succeeds, calculate the new L2 position and update the node in the topological map. Next suppress the recognition process.
  4. Otherwise, use all the stored snapshots (i.e. all the other angles) to recognize L2, go to step 2.
  5. If L2 is not recognized, delete the corresponding node in the topological map and start the memorization process.

---

recognition succeeds the landmark position is updated using an average of the previous position x_{t-1} and the current one x_t with innovation factor α:

$$x_t \leftarrow \alpha x_t + (1-\alpha)x_{t-1}, 0 \leq \alpha \leq 1 \tag{3}$$

For similar approaches see [18] and [14]. We did not choose to update the nodes offline (as in [19]), because our main purpose is not a perfect metric representation of the environment, but rather a study of the use of biological inspired attention systems in robotic.

2.2   The Landmark

The fovea movements have the purpose of focusing the attention on the most informative part of an image. Looking at an object may be seen as moving the fovea around it, recording the movements done and the parts of the object foveated. This way there is strong coupling between the 'passive' vision, i.e. detecting features like edges or contrast, and 'active' vision, i.e. memorizing the possible interactions with an object in a behavioral fashion.

For the purpose of our system, which is unable to interact with the world apart from seeing it and moving inside it, we adopted the approach proposed

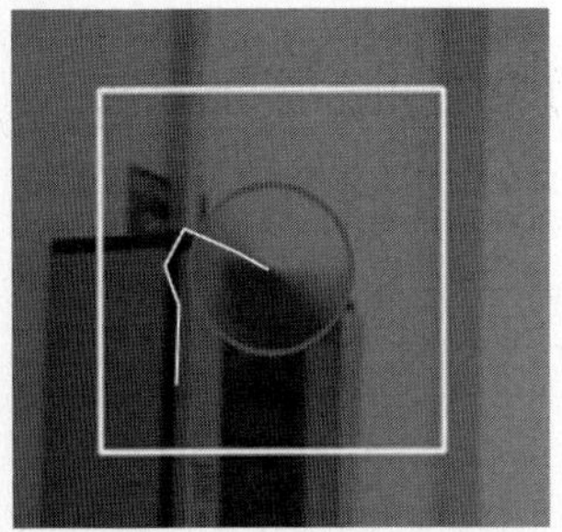

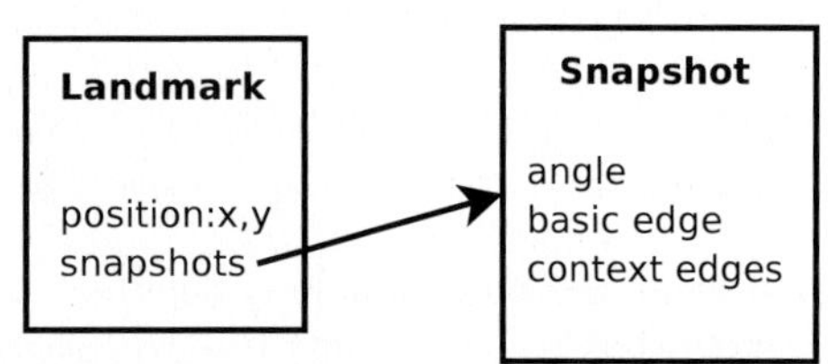

(a) Figure 6(a) zoomed inside the white rectangle. Here the Gaussian pyramid effect may be seen.

(b) The landmark memory structure.

Fig. 3.

in [13]. We define a landmark as a collection of snapshots of a static pattern, each of them being a series of sequential foveation. In particular, a landmark is memorized with:

- its position in the topological map;
- a set of n snapshots from n different viewpoints, each of them storing:
  - the angle between the robot and the landmark itself;
  - a basic edge;
  - one or more context edges;

A schematic representation of the landmark memory is depicted in figure 3(b). Each snapshot is indexed by the angle between the robot and the landmark. Such angle is computed using the estimated robot position and the landmark position in the topological map.

During the memorization process a landmark is initially perceived as a salient point in the camera image, detected using the model of [12] tuned to give the orientation channel more weight. Fovea movements are restricted to a square region centered in the saliency point and with a side of about $\frac{1}{4 \times I_h}$, where I_h is the image height[1]. In such square (referred as R) we identify a circular area, named *Attention Window*, which diameter is about $\frac{1}{2}$ the length of R side. A recursive Gaussian-like convolution ([20]) is applied to obtain a decrease in resolution from the center to the surrounding. The central point (named *the fixation point*) is surrounded by three concentric circles, with a resolution ranging from full in the center (the fovea) to $\frac{1}{2^2}$ in the outer circle (see figure 3(a)). The feature detector mimics some functions similar to the ones in the primary visual cortex orientationally selective neurons. Edge detection is dependent on the circle resolution the edge is inside and it is performed by the neural network described in [21]. Such network uses competitive dynamics to reach a steady state where only one neuron is firing, in which case an edge is found with orientation equal

---

[1] If the square falls outside the image, the pan-tilt is rotated to center such point.

to the one the firing neuron is tuned to, or no neurons are firing, in which case no edge is present.

According to [13], in the Attention Window we distinguish two kind of edges: the basic edge, located in the center of the fovea, and context edges. The basic edge orientation (in an absolute frame of reference) will be the basis for a new relative frame of reference where all the context edges may be expressed. The parameters of such frame of reference may be plotted on three toroidal surfaces, achieving a representation of the image features invariant to shift, rotation and scale. The three surfaces are next used to train a classical Hopfield neural network for recognition of images under the Attention Window, and compose the 'what' memory of a pattern. Once the edges are found in R the fixation point is chosen from all the detected edges in a winner-take-all fashion using the formula:

$$A_k = a_1 z_k + a_2 \lambda_k + a_3 \eta_{ij}(t) + a_4 \chi_{ij} \tag{4}$$

where, referring to context edge k, A_k is the 'importance' level, z_k is the activation level, λ_k is its distance from the fovea center, $\eta_{ij}(t)$ is an inhibition of return function and χ_{ij} is a 'semantic' value associated with an image to introduce a top-down control in the attention process. While in [13] such a value was used to push the fovea along pre-defined meaningful image regions (for example eyes or mouth), we used it to obtain the pattern shown in figure 4. This way the fovea is forced to get away from the same vertical edge after few foveations because vertical edges are prevailing in indoor environment and they are not distinctive. The coefficients a_1, a_2, a_3, a_4 are found experimentally. Once the context edges importance levels are computed, the Attention Window is centered on the maximum one, starting a new context edges memorization procedure. All the movements are recorded using the same relative frame of reference described above, achieving a scale translation rotation invariant 'where' memory of all the fovea movements used to memorize a landmark (see figure 6(a) and 6(b) for examples of fovea movements). The fovea movements are terminated when a previous selected edge is selected again.

During the recognition process the robot places itself in a position in the environment with a known angle θ between the landmark and itself, centers the camera over it, and starts doing the memorized fovea movements to recognize the landmark. The recognition starts from the image center and uses the snapshot correspondent to the angle θ. However the recognition may fail: if this happens,

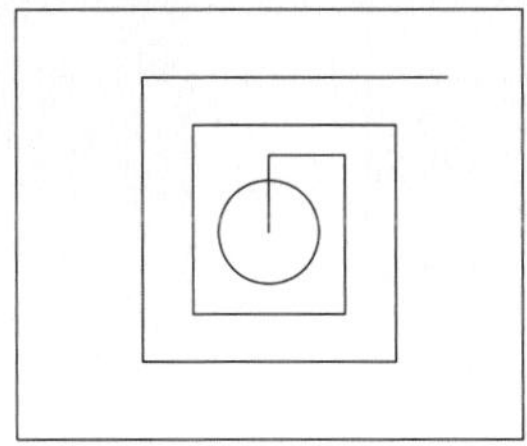

Fig. 4. The spiral-like pattern used to look for the first landmark foveation

the search will be done in the entire image in a spiral-like pattern, thus moving away from the image center, as in figure 4. If this search process fails too, the robot will try to move to another position and start again the search process, this time querying the entire snapshots memory. If the researched landmark is found, then the topological map (including the robot position) is updated using the new information, otherwise the robot suppose it lost itself and will begin a new memorization process.

2.3 Controlling the Robot

Let suppose that the landmark L has been identified in the right image; in order to reconstruct its position, the fovea intensity in the initial position is matched along the direction of the related epipolar line in the left image. Once the correspondence has been determined, the landmark 3D position, computed by triangulation, is stored in the Topological Map and used to compute the next points of view. To this aim, a tangential potential field is generated forcing the robot to move along a circle centered in the current landmark. Such field is obtained by computing the direction θ of a repulsive potential field centered in L and therefore by setting $\theta \leftarrow \theta \pm 90$. The resulting vector points in the direction of the tangent to the circle centered in L. The sign of the new θ (clockwise or counterclockwise) is chosen according to the current robot heading. During robot motion, pan-tilt movements are performed to keep L in the image center. However, due to odometry errors, the landmark could not be at the predicted location, so a Kalman filter [22] has been adopted to track L in the image sequence. The next point of view is selected as the effective landmark position in the image is outside of a central region (its width is one third of the camera image width and its height is about half of the camera image, see figure 5), or the distance from the last viewpoint is greater than a threshold, which is directly proportional to the robot-landmark distance. The landmark exploration procedure stops when the robot can not follow its trajectory anymore (i.e. due to the presence of some obstacle) or when the landmark is not visible anymore from the current robot position.

The robot is provided with a set of low-level behaviors (i.e. wall-following) allowing it to explore its environment. The environment exploration strategy

(a) Landmark loss   (b) Re-centering the landmark

Fig. 5. The tracking. In the left image, the landmark (depicted as white cross) gets out of the white central region, triggering the camera re-centering (right image)

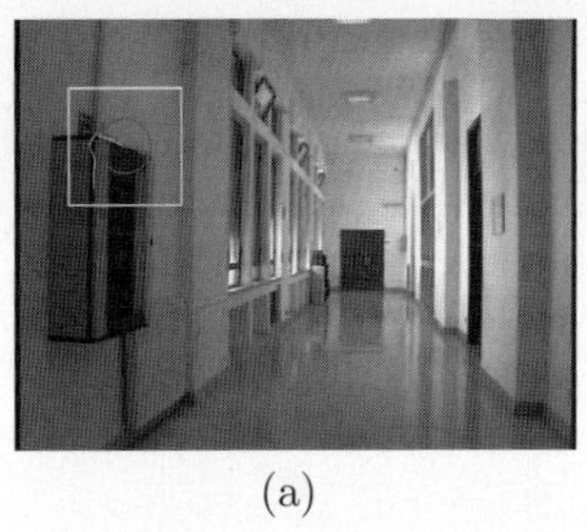 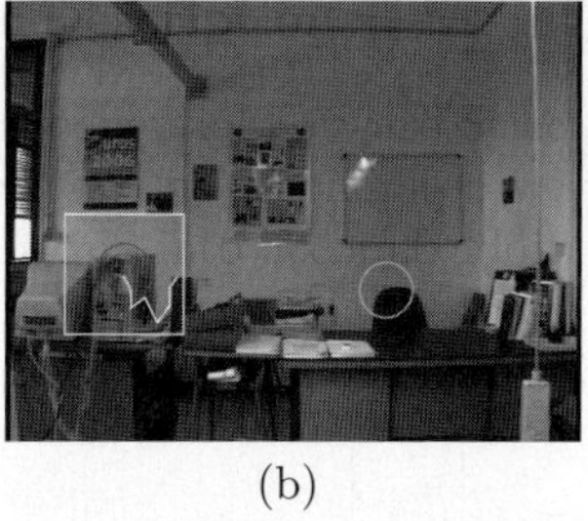

(a)   (b)

Fig. 6. a) The first landmark recognized by the robot. The red circle is the first fovea placing, while along the white line there are the subsequent movements. The large white square is the image region inside which fovea movements are allowed during the landmark memorization. b) The two landmarks detected in the lab near the corridor. The robot at first detected the salient point to the right, discarded it (see text) and memorized the second landmark to the left.

consists of turning towards an open direction and selecting a low-level behavior to be activated.

3   Experiments and Results

The proposed system has been tested on a Real World Interface RWI-B21 robot, equipped with a pan-tilt stereo head, laser rangefinder and sonars. The tests were performed in an indoor static environment composed by three laboratories and a corridor. For the purpose of landmark identification and during the bottom-up attention process, only one of the two images captured by the calibrated stereo rig has been used; the stereo procedures are activated after the landmark identification to compute its 3D position. In figure 6(a) the robot was placed at the start of the corridor and was carrying the memorization process (the topological map was empty). The bottom-up subsystem detected a salient point (the red circle), a region around that point was selected (the white square) and a sequence of foveating movements was performed in this region (the white line). In this situation the number of fixation points was 8, and the points set was accepted as a valid landmark (our threshold was 4). Its 3D position was computed and stored in the topological map as node 1 (see figure 2). It should be pointed out that a landmark could be rejected if its 3D position can not be accurately determined (i.e. it is farther than 3 meters away). Finally the move around behavior started. As soon as the landmark position moved outside the image center, a new snapshot was taken, the robot centered its camera on the landmark and the snapshot procedure started again (figure 5). The robot movements during the move around behavior are depicted in figure 7(b). After the robot circled the first landmark, the tracker lost it and a standard navigation procedure restarted (in this experiment a simple wall-following behavior). The next candidate landmark was a large door at the end of the corridor, but it did not receive enough foveations and was discarded. The bottom-up attention

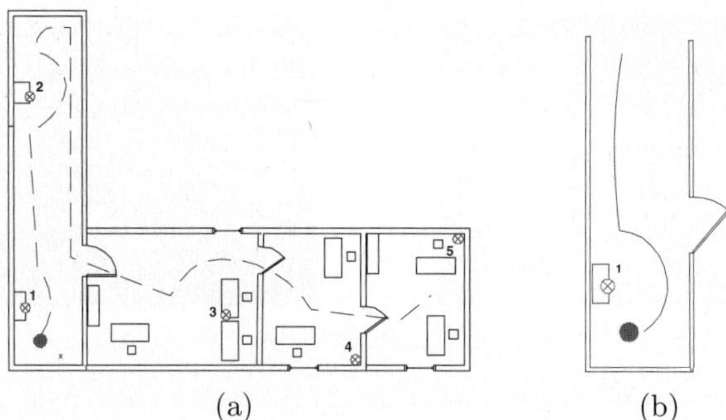

(a)   (b)

Fig. 7. Figure (a) shows the complete path made by the robot during the memorization process. We omitted the circling paths and the error paths for figure clarity. Figure (b) shows the move around behavior during the snapshotting procedure of landmark 1.

subsystem chose a coffee machine as new landmark, it received 5 foveations and was memorized as landmark 2. The wall-following behavior made the robot turn ahead, going down the corridor. During such traveling it discovered again the first landmark, recognized it and went across the open door on its left. After the robot moved from the corridor to a lab, it had gone for more than 3 meters, so it started to look for a new landmark. The first candidate (the green circle on the right in figure 6(b)) was rejected because only 3 foveations happened around it. The next candidate (the red circle on the left in the same figure) received 7 foveations, so it was accepted as a new landmark numbered 3. The memorization procedure started again, together with moving around and snapshooting. It should be pointed out that the selected landmark was not an object, but only a salient region of the image. Furthermore the robot was unable to take rear snapshot of the landmark, because of occlusions (there was a monitor on its left). The robot went on in the other two labs memorizing the landmarks and gaining a complete topological map of its environment (see figure 2) The whole robot path during the memorization phase is displayed in figure 7(a).

We carried out experiments to evaluate our model. We tested the system performances on 20 trials in the previously learned map under different conditions. For each landmark (identified by its number) we reported the recognition success

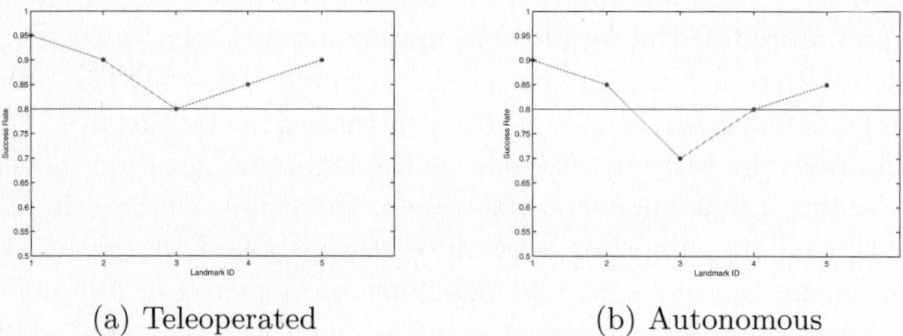

(a) Teleoperated   (b) Autonomous

Fig. 8. Landmark recognition rate over 20 trials. Two different conditions were tested. The x-axis shows the landmark ID, while the y-axis shows the ratio of correct recognitions. The red line is an acceptability threshold of 80%.

ratio, fixing an acceptability threshold of 80%. Figure 8 summarizes the results of these experiments. In figure 8(a) the robot was teleoperated (i.e. odometric errors were absent), and the recognition rate was very high. In figure 8(b) the robot was autonomously controlled as described in our model; as pointed above the third landmark was the most difficult one to recognize, and it obtained only a 70% success rate.

4   Conclusions

In this paper we proposed a robot navigation system based on a biological inspired attention mechanism. The robot is able to recognize landmarks in its environment, memorize them in a topological map and use them for navigation and localization. A particular care has been dedicated to the attentive systems: we put together bottom-up and top-down attention, reacting to salient part of images when necessary and stepping to a controlled search in the visual input when the robot 'knows' what and where to look for. Following this guideline, we allowed the robot to detect by itself the landmarks, defined as salient points in the images taken from the camera. A landmark is memorized in a behavioral fashion, using a mixture of fovea movements and robot movements to grasp its shape and features.

References

1. Thrun, S.: Learning metric-topological for indoor mobile robot navigation. Artificial Intelligence 99(1), 21–71 (1999)
2. Moravec, H., Elfes, A.: High resolution maps from wide angular sensors. In: ICRA-85. Proceedings of the IEEE International Conference On Robotics and Automation, pp. 116–121. IEEE Computer Society Press, Los Alamitos (1985)
3. Matumoto, Y., Sakai, K., Inaba, M., Inoue, H.: View-based approach to robot navigation. In: Proceedings of the 2000 IEEE/RSJ International Intelligent Robots and Systems, pp. 1702–1708. IEEE Press, NJ, New York (2000)
4. Meyer, J., Filliat, D.: Map-based navigation in mobile robots: I. a review of map learning and path-planning strategies. Elsevier Science, Amsterdam (2003)
5. Treisman, A.M., Gelade, G.: A feature-integration theory of attention. Cognitive Psychology 12, 97–136 (1980)
6. Braun, J., Sagi, D.: Vision outside the focus of attention. Perception Psychophys 48, 45–58 (1990)
7. Itti, L., Koch, C.: Computational modelling of visual attention. Nature reviews in neurscience 2 (2001)
8. Koch, C., Ullman, S.: Shift in selective visual attention: towards the undelying neural circuitry. Human Neurobiology 4, 219–227 (1985)
9. Klein, R.M.: Inhibition of return. Trends in Cognitive Science 4, 138–147 (2000)
10. Felleman, D.J., Essen, D.C.V.: Distributed hierarchical processing in the primate cerebral cortex. cerebral cortex 1, 1–47 (1991)
11. Driver, J., Frith, C.D.: Shifting baselines in attention research. Nature reviews in neurscience 1, 147–148 (2000)

12. Itti, L., Koch, C., Niebur, E.: A model of saliency-based visual attention for rapid scene analysis. IEEE Transaction on Pattern analysis and Machine Inteligence 20(11), 1254–1259 (1998)
13. Rybak, I., Gusakova, V.I., Golovan, A.V., Podladchikova, L., Shevtsova, N.: A model of attention-guided visual perception and recognition. Vision Research 38, 2387–2400 (1998)
14. Nehmzow, U., Owen, C.: Robot navigation in the real world: experiments with manchester's fortytwo in unmodified, large environments. Robotics and Autonomous Systems 33(4), 223–242 (2000)
15. Engelson, S.P., McDermott, D.V.: Error correction in mobile robot map-learning. In: ICRA-92. Proceedings of the international conference on robotics and automation, pp. 2555–2560. IEEE Press, NJ, New York (1992)
16. Yamauchi, B., Beer, R.: Spatial learning for navigation in dynamic environments. IEEE Transactions on Systems, Man and Cybernetics-Part B. 26(3), 496–505 (1996) (Special Issue on Learning Autonomous Robots)
17. Jain, J., Jain, A.: Displacement Measurement and Its Application in Interframe Image Coding. Communications, IEEE Transactions on [legacy, pre-1988] 29(12), 1799–1808 (1981)
18. Ducket, G., Nehmzow, U.: Experiments in evidence based localization for a mobile robot. In: Proceedings of the AISB 97 workshop on spatial reasoning in animals and robots, Springer, Heidelberg (1997)
19. Ducket, T., Marsland, S., Shapiro, J.: Learning globally consistent maps by relaxation. In: ICRA-2000. Proceedings of the international conference on robotics and automation, pp. 3841–3846. IEEE Press, NJ, New York (2000)
20. Burt, P.J.: Smart sensing within a pyramid vision machine. Proceedings of the IEEE 76 (1988)
21. Grossberg, S., Mingolla, E., Todorovic, D.: A neural network architecture for preattentive vision. IEEE Transactions on Biomedical Engeneering 36, 65–84 (1989)
22. Maybeck, P.S.: Sthocastic models estimation and control, vol. 1. Academic Press, New York (1979)

A 3D Virtual Model of the Knee Driven by EMG Signals

Massimo Sartori[1], Gaetano Chemello[2], and Enrico Pagello[3]

[1] Department of Information Engineering, University of Padua,
Via Gradenigo 6/B, 35131, Padova, Italy
gdesus@gmail.com
[2] ISIB-CNR, Corso Stati Uniti, 4, 35127 Padova, Italy
gaetano.chemello@isib.cnr.it
[3] Department of Information Engineering, University of Padua and ISIB-CNR
epv@dei.unipd.it

Abstract. A 3D virtual model of the human lower extremity has been developed for the purpose of examining how the neuromuscular system controls the muscles and generates the desired movement. Our virtual knee currently incorporates the major muscles spanning the knee joint and it is used to estimate the knee joint moment. Beside that we developed a graphical interface that allows the user to visualize the skeletal geometry and the movements imparted to it. The purpose of this paper is to describe the design objectives and the implementation of our EMG-driven virtual knee. We finally compared the virtual knee behavior with the torque performed by the test subject in order to obtain a qualitative validation of our model. Within the next future our aim is to develop a real-time EMG-driven exoskeleton for knee rehabilitation.

Index Terms - EMG signals, human knee, exoskeleton, simulation.

1 Introduction

Muscles and tendons actuate movements by developing and transmitting forces to the skeleton [20]. We investigate how individual muscles are activated to generate joint moments and movements, and to produce coordinated knee torques. This knowledge is instrumental to design a robotic exoskeleton suitable to support a neurologically injured human knee and to provide the proper rehabilitative treatment to the patient. Since exoskeletons necessitate of great amount of resources to be developed, the availability of realistic simulators to be used in testing different situations of rehabilitation is a must. Furthermore, from a mechanical point of view, exoskeletons are becoming more and more cost effective and reliable. On the other hand, the increasing availability of small computing devices with considerable embedded computational power makes now possible to endow exoskeletons with more and more intelligence and autonomy. Following our former research experiences with service robotics and humanoids, we are now investigating how more intelligence can be brought on-board exoskeletons. We

R. Basili and M.T. Pazienza (Eds.): AI*IA 2007, LNAI 4733, pp. 591–601, 2007.

particularly wish to develop control systems capable of learning a specific motor gait and independently move the robotic orthosis when the injured patient can't.

The virtual knee presented in this manuscript is actually a three-dimensional graphical representation of a human knee which moves in response to electromyographic activity pre-recorded from the legs of different test subjects as they perform time varying knee flexion and extension tasks. Our virtual knee is suitable for the study of the neural control mechanisms involved in the transition between two knee postures.

2   Initial Observations

We mainly focused on the study of the knee torsion. In order to keep simple the structure of the model (see Sect. 5), we decided to limit to a number of two the EMG signals to acquire for the control of the virtual knee. Adding more muscles, already in this first experimentation, would have indeed leaded to a complex model very hard to handle. We chose to record the contractile activity of the *biceps femoris* because, among all the flexor muscles, it has the highest *Physiological Cross-sectional Area* (PCA) [22], therefore its contribution to the total force generated at the knee articulation will be the highest one [13,14,15,16]. Among the extensor muscles we chose the *rectus femoris* because of its proximity to the skin surface. For this reason it's possible to record its activity without experiencing too much *cross-talk* interferences [10,12].

3   Graphical Interface

The Fig. 1 depicts the virtual leg which is driven by the biomechanical model according to the pre-recorded electromyograms. The 3D Human Lower Extremity has been developed at the Department of Anatomy of the University of Brussels (ULB) and it is anatomically correct. The original 3D image was a *.msf file. By using the *Data Manager* program, also developed at the University of Brussels, we exported every single part of the lower extremity in the *.wrl format. Successively we wrote a VRML program in order to put all the exported parts together again and to form the image shown in the Fig. 1. We chose to adopt VRML for rendering the 3D knee, mainly because it makes the communication with the MATLAB Simulink biomechanical model easier to set up [5].

The 3D model of the human skeleton developed at the University of Brussels (ULB) is available online [2].

4   A Forward Dynamics Approach

We have used a forward dynamic approach in the study of the human movement (Fig. 1). This choice has been encouraged by the results obtained by Buchanan *et al.* [8,19]. A detailed description of the phases involved in the control of the virtual knee will be offered in the following subsections.

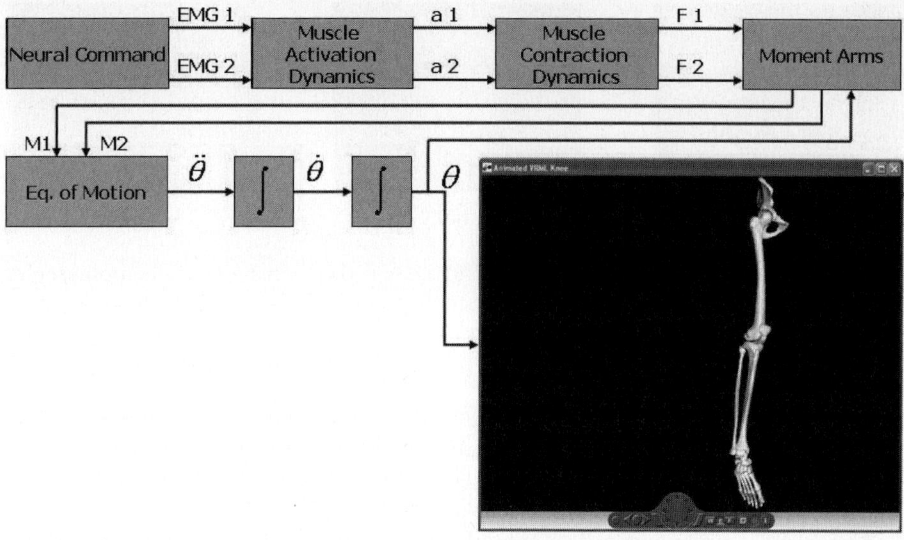

Fig. 1. The Forward Dynamics Approach and the Graphical Interface. The flowchart depicts the neural commands and forces for two muscles and moments and the joint angle used to control the virtual human lower extremity.

4.1   Signal Acquisition and Muscle Activation

The acquisition stage comprises the sampling and the processing of the EMG signals while the subject executes flexions and extensions of his leg. The signals have been sampled at 1 kHz while the BIOPAC MP35 data acquisition unit [1] was connected to a personal computer with an Intel Centrino processor and a 512 MB RAM memory. The disposable differential surface electrodes have been placed as shown by the Fig. 2. We retrieved information on how to correctly place the electrodes and on how to adequately prepare the skin tissue from the SENIAM Project web site [3]. During the acquisition stage the signals have been amplified (gain of $1000\frac{V}{V}$) on both channels and successively bandpass filtered from 20 to 450 Hz [4,11]. In software, the resulting signals have been full wave rectified and normalized to approximate the *activation* of the muscles, $a_i(t)$.

4.2   Muscle Force

We now want to obtain some kind of measure of the force, starting from the muscle activation, $a_i(t)$, previously computed. We can theoretically express the muscular force, $F_i(t)$, as a function of $a_i(t)$:

$$F_i(t) = f(a_i(t)) \tag{1}$$

We approximated it with the following formula:

$$f(t) = \frac{1}{T} \int_{t-T}^{t} |a(t)|\, dt \tag{2}$$

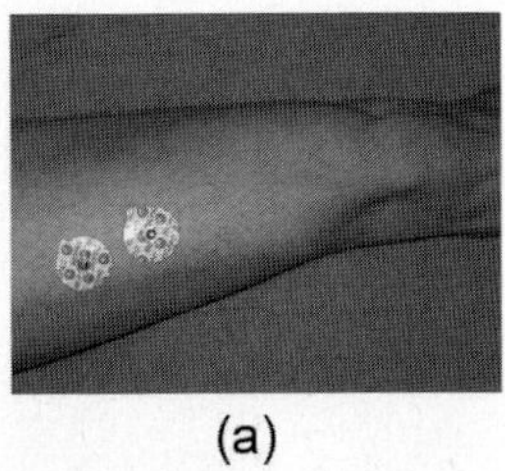
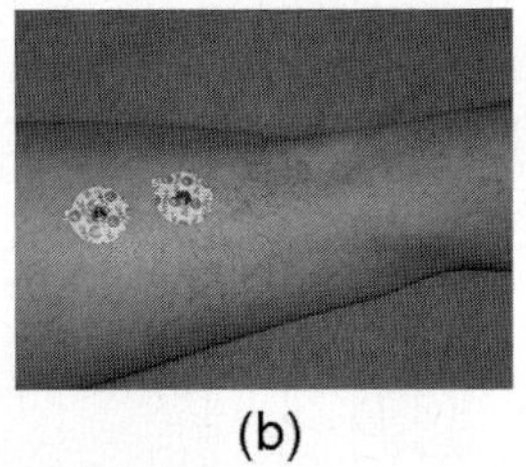
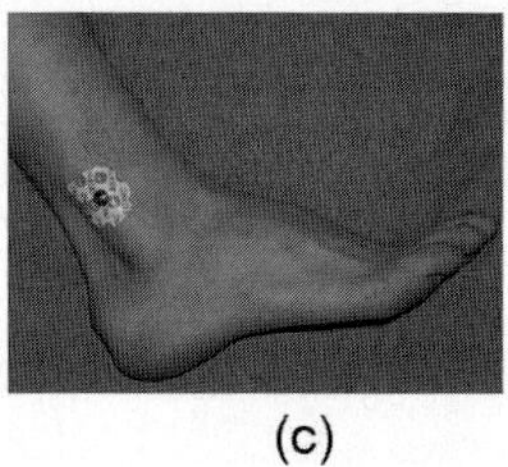

(a)   (b)   (c)

Fig. 2. Electrodes placed in the correspondence of: the rectus femoris neuromuscular junction (a), the biceps femoris neuromuscular junction (b) and the ankle intended as a neutral area (c)

where T is a temporal window specifying the dimension of the interval during which the calculation of every sample is executed. The equation (2) is actually a very rough approximation of the muscular force. However, we should keep in mind that our aim is not performing a careful clinical analysis of the muscles behavior. For our purposes it's enough understanding the time interval during which the muscles are active along with the intensity of contraction. Refer to Sect. 6 to see how our approximations did not negatively affect our simulations.

4.3   Driving the Virtual Knee

Once all the muscle forces are calculated, it is important to compute the corresponding contribution to the joint moment. This requires knowledge of the muscle's moment arms. We evaluated them as follow:

$$r_i(\theta) = b_0 + b_1 \cdot \theta + b_2 \cdot \theta^2 + b_3 \cdot \theta^3 + b_4 \cdot \theta^4 \tag{3}$$

where θ is the knee joint angle expressed in degrees, while b_0, b_1, b_2, b_3, b_4 are coefficients related to the i-th muscle (see [18] for more details). The corresponding joint moment M can now be estimated:

$$M(\theta, t) = \sum_{i=1}^{m} (r_i(\theta) \cdot F_i(t)). \tag{4}$$

The muscle's force $F_i(t)$ is obtained from (2). In this case the index i has been introduced, and it corresponds to a particular muscle. The joint moment, in turn, will cause the movements. The knee angular acceleration and the related command signal are calculated directly from the computed joint moment as shown in the following section.

5   The Biomechanical Model

5.1   Modeling the Human Lower Extremity

The human lower extremity has been modeled as a rigid body swinging between $0°$ and $130°$ (Fig. 3). Our software mainly simulates the action of the gravity

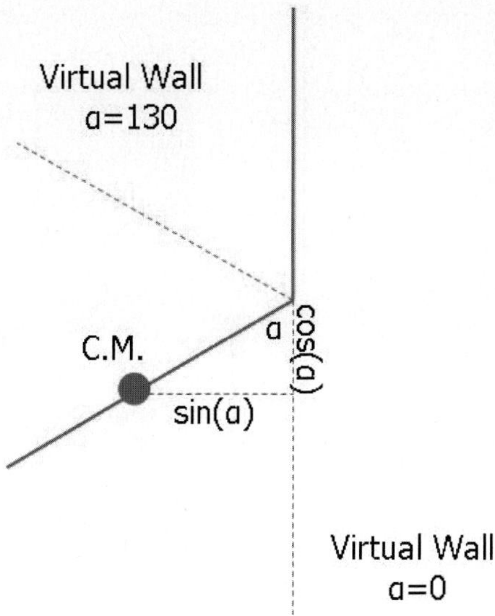

Fig. 3. The human lower extremity has been modeled as a rigid body capable of swinging in the interval of $0° < \alpha < 130°$

force affecting the rigid body during its movement, the action of the extensor muscle force and the action of the flexor muscle force. It also simulates the force that takes place when the leg is extended until reaching the angular position $\alpha = 0°$. At this point an impulsive force is generated in order to stop the motion of the leg preventing it from extending beyond the threshold $\alpha = 0°$. As soon as the leg is blocked, the effect of the force fades away and the leg is free again to flex itself under the action of the successive contraction. The anthropometric data for modeling the rigid body has been taken from [9]. We particularly considered a centre of mass of the rigid body placed at 21.67 cm from the knee joint and with a weigh of 3.805 Kg.

5.2 The Structure of the Model

The Fig. 4 shows the structure of the biomechanical model which evaluates a prediction of the torque executed by the subject. In the first stage the muscular forces, along with the gravity, are coupled with their respective moment arms (according to the formula 4). The net knee joint moment, M, is then combined with the inertial coefficient and the resulting acceleration $\ddot{\vartheta}$ is composed with the action of the Virtual Walls placed at $\alpha = 0°$ and at $\alpha = 130°$. The resulting signal is integrated twice to obtain the angular position ϑ used as a command signal for the virtual knee depicted in the Fig. 1.

5.3 The Virtual Walls

As already explained in the Sect. 5.1, the Virtual Walls generate an impulsive force that stops the motion of the leg before it reaches undesired positions. The

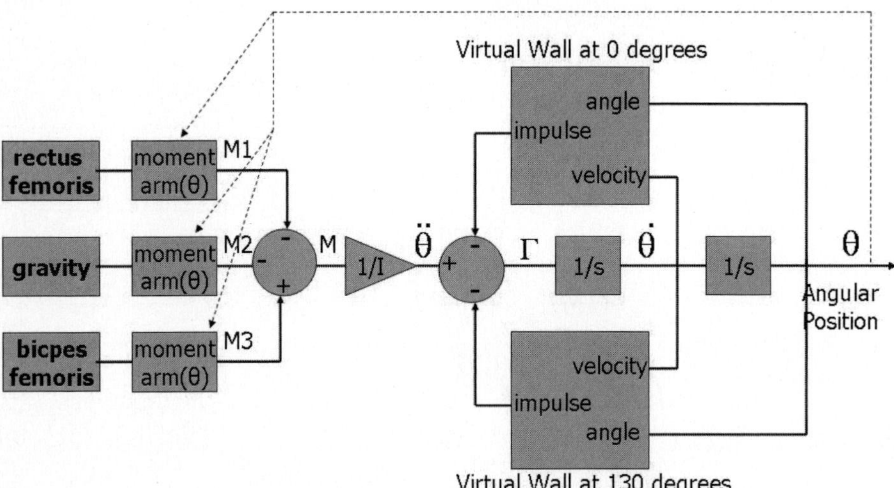

Fig. 4. Biomechanical Model. It calculates the command signal starting from the pre-recorded electromyograms. The original biomechanical model has been developed using MATLAB Simulink. The diagram here depicted is to show the general structure of the control system.

force must be impulsive and it has to be generated only in the correspondence of the temporal instants in which α gets equal to $0°$ (*critical instants*). In the Fig. 5 is depicted the structure of the Simulink block implementing the Virtual Wall placed at $\alpha = 0°$. We will omit the explanation of the Virtual Wall placed at $\alpha = 130°$ because its organization is highly similar to the one we are about to describe now. We will just say that the Virtual Wall at $\alpha = 130°$ is to simulate the restriction of motion caused by an hypothetical exoskeleton wore by a subject. The Virtual Wall at $\alpha = 0°$ constantly checks the current angular position and as soon as it gets negative (critical instant) an unitary impulse is generated and multiplied by the scalar value of the velocity in the correspondence of the critical instant (Fig. 5). The outgoing slowing down impulse train (Fig. 6) is thus composed by a series of impulses that are centered in the critical instants and multiplied by the related scalar value of the velocity. In order to stop the motion of the leg in the correspondence of the critical instant we must set to zero the velocity of the leg in those instants. To achieve this we subtract the impulse train to the acceleration signal, $\ddot{\vartheta}(t)$, as follow:

$$\Gamma(t) = \ddot{\vartheta}(t) - \sum_c \delta(t - t_c) \tag{5}$$

where $\delta(t - t_c)$ is an impulse centered in the critical instant t_c. $\Gamma(t)$ is then integrated as follow:

$$\int_{t_{start}}^{t_{stop}} \Gamma(t)dt = \dot{\vartheta}(t) - \sum_c \Im(t - t_c) \tag{6}$$

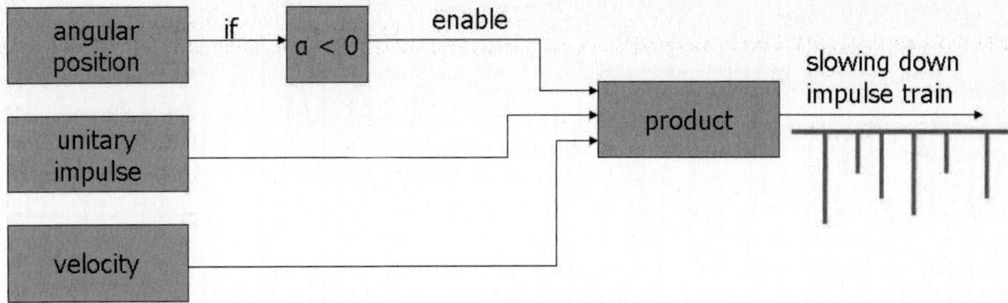

Fig. 5. Virtual Wall placed at $\alpha = 0°$

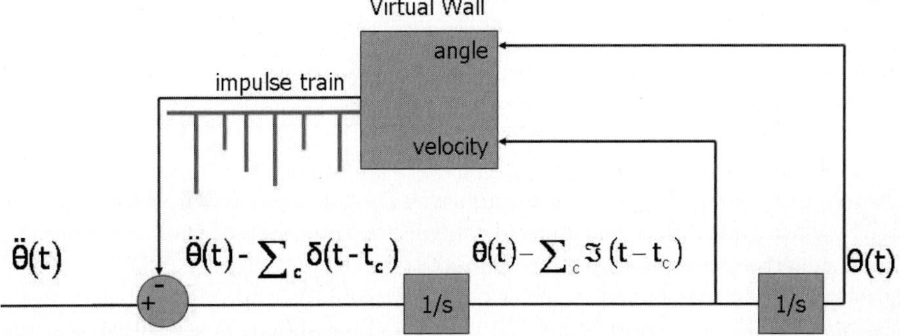

Fig. 6. The acceleration is combined with the action of the Virtual Wall and the resulting signal is double integrated

where t_{start} and t_{stop} indicate, respectively, the starting and stopping time of the simulation, while $\sum_c \Im(t-t_c)$ is a step train (resulting from the integration of the impulse train) whose steps are centered in the critical instants. What happens is that the velocity signal $\dot{\vartheta}(t)$ is set to zero by the action of the integrated impulse train exactly in the correspondence of the critical instants.

6 Test and Simulation

To verify the accuracy of our simulator in predicting the human movement, we performed two tests. In both tests the command signal, and therefore the number of knee torsions reproduced by the virtual knee, are compared with the muscle forces from which it is possible to understand how many torsions the subject actually performed. In this way it is possible to have an idea about the precision of the simulation.

6.1 The First Test

The first test has been done by recording the contractile activity of the flexor muscle only. The subject was supposed to flex his leg until reaching the position

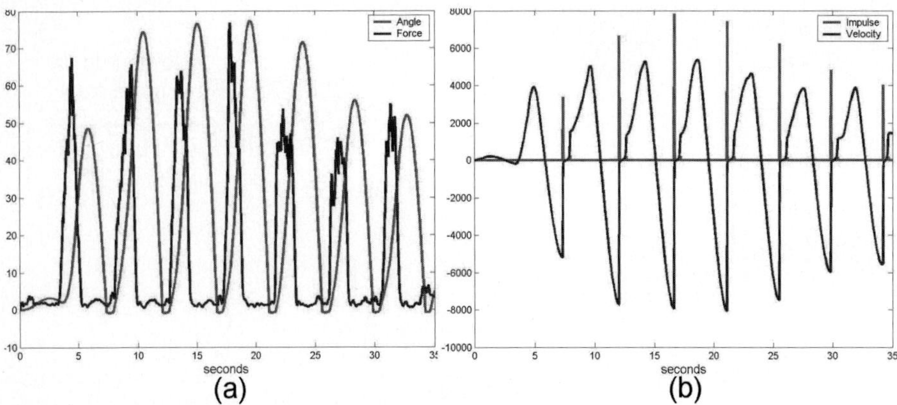

Fig. 7. First test. Biceps femoris force and command signal (a). Angular velocity and impulse train (b).

of $\alpha = 90°$ and successively to let the leg fall down under the action of the gravity. The test has lasted 35.456 seconds and seven torsions have been performed. The Fig. 7a shows that after every muscle contraction (blue signal) the biomechanical model generates an appropriate command signal (red signal). The command signal will drive the virtual knee which will correctly reproduce all the seven torsions. The Fig. 7b shows that the velocity (blue signal) is set to zero, in the correspondence of every critical instant, after the generation of an impulse (red signal).

6.2   The Second Test

The second test has been done by recording the contractile activity of both the flexor and extensor muscles. The test has lasted 51.078 seconds and four torsions have been performed. The Fig. 8a shows that after every flexor muscle contraction (green signal) and after every extensor muscle contraction (blue signal) the biomechanical model generates the command signal (red signal) that drives the virtual knee which will reproduce all four torsions. However, note that between torsions there are some small oscillations that should not occur. These undesired movements are mainly due to *cross-talk* interferences between the recorded electromyograms. The noise can be eliminated by improving the processing of the EMG's. The Fig. 8b shows that the velocity (blue signal) is set to zero, in the correspondence of every critical instant, after the generation of an impulse (red signal).

6.3   Medical Problems

During the development of our simulator we have been working together with Dr. Giovannini (Head of the Department of Rehabilitation, Sant'Antonio Hospital, Padua). We believe that putting together our knowledge about Engineering and

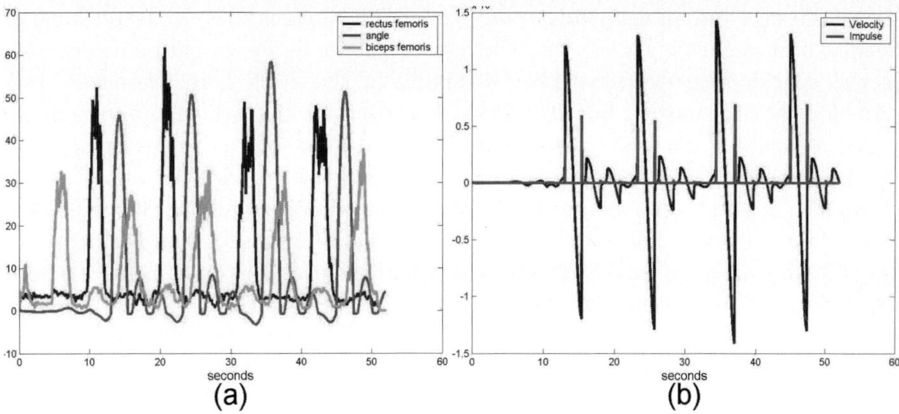

Fig. 8. Second test. Biceps femoris and rectus femoris force overlying the angular position (a). Angular velocity and impulse train (b).

Computer Science along with the experience of doctors will lead us toward the development of efficient robotic devices capable of supporting the patient safely and to provide a valid aid for the therapist during his or her supervision. We are actually trying to answer to a set of questions; how can *neuroplasticity* be stimulated in a patient? We know that neuroplasticity is the key element lying at the basis of every motor relearning [6,7,17,21]. How should an exoskeleton behave in order to support a paralyzed patient? Answering to this question will give us hints on how to design an appropriate control system to properly drive the device. Those are only some of the questions that emerge when dealing with *neurorehabilitation* mediated by robots. We believe that an organized cooperation between doctors and engineers is the only way to carry real progresses out.

7   Discussion and Future Work

Since the here-shown simulator is a prototype, there are still many improvements to do. First of all we need to extend the biomechanical model to include at least two extensor and two flexor muscles, otherwise the torque prediction in the knee joint could be inaccurate depending on the movement. At the present state our simulator only uses the *rectus femoris* extensor muscle that is mainly active during low force movements. This means that when the subject performs higher force extensions the evaluated prediction might be imprecise.

Several studies show that the *EMG-to-force* relationship strongly depends on the muscle's length. A non inclusion of such a relationship may lead to predictions off by 50% or more, depending on the joint angle [8,14,19]. We therefore want to include a *geometry model* that takes into account the *force-length* relationship of muscles.

We have noticed that the resulting knee joint torque (which is converted into acceleration, velocity and finally in position) is an overlay of the torque produced by the muscles and all *external contact forces*. This means that the latter have to be measured accurately, otherwise the movement prediction might be inaccurate. In the specific case we have been studying in the work here presented, this problem does not occur, but it will as soon as we will start with experiments involving walking. For this reason, we will start to use sensors to detect physical signals as the pressure force between the foot and the ground.

We also intend to endow our model with a real-time controller. This will allow us to apply our biomechanical model directly on a real exoskeleton. Furthermore our software will be used to test the reaction of the exoskeleton to EMG's before its application on patients preventing dangerous situations.

In order to focus on the design of good rehabilitative tools, we will keep the co-operation with rehabilitation practitioners.

8   Conclusions

In this paper, we sketched the direction of building a model of a human leg. More precisely, we focused on the knee articulation. First, we studied the major muscles spanning the knee joint and the equations that govern the knee articulation movement in an adult human subject. Then we developed a biomechanical model capable of evaluating a torque prediction starting from the pre-recorded electromyograms. We then performed two experimentations to test the accuracy of our simulator. Our aim is to develop robotic orthosis capable of learning a specific motor gait and supporting the patient in his or her movement. Finally, we discussed our work and presented our future research direction.

Acknowledgements

We thank Christian Fleischer for his help in developing the leg model and the Institute of Biomedical Engineering of the National Research Council (ISIB-CNR) of Padua for supporting this work. We express gratitude to Dr. Giovannini for his help and his guidance across the medical problems. We finally thank Prof. Toffolo for placing at our disposal the BIOPAC System MP35 and the Biomedical Laboratory of the Department of Information Engineering at the University of Padua.

References

1. BIOPAC Systems Inc., `http://www.biopac.com/`
2. Department of Anatomy of the University of Brussels. The ULB Virtual Human, `http://homepages.ulb.ac.be/~anatemb/the_ulb_virtual_man.htm`
3. The SENIAM Project, `http://www.seniam.org/`
4. Surface Electromyograms. Slovenian Ministry of Education, Science, and Sport. European Shared Cost Project Neuromuscular Assessment in the Elderly Worker (NEW), `http://www.storm.uni-mb.si/semg/index.htm`
5. The MathWorks Inc, `http://www.mathworks.com`

6. Neuroanatomy and Neuropathology on the Internet (2005), `http://www.neuropat.dote.hu/`
7. Banala, S.K., Agrawal, S.K.: Gait Rehabilitation with an Active Leg Othosis. In: Proceedings of IDETC/CIE 2005, ASME 2005, International Design Engineering Technical Conferences and Computers and Information in Engineering, Long Beach, California, USA, September 24–28 2005, vol. 74, pp. 102–108 (2005)
8. Buchanan, T.S., Lloyd, D.G., Manal, K., Besier, T.F.: Neuromusculoskeletal Modeling: Estimation of Muscle Forces and Joint Moments and Movements from Measurements from Neural Command. Journal of Applied Biomechanics 20, 367–395 (2004)
9. Clauser, C.E., McConville, J.T., Young, J.W.: Volume and Center of Mass of Segments of the Human Body. Ohio (August 1969). Aerospace Medical Research Laboratory, Aerospace Medical Division, Air Force System Command.
10. Cluss, M., Laws, K., Martin, N., Nowicki, T.S.: The Indirect Measurement of Biomechanical Forces in the Moving Human Body. American Journal of Physics 74, 102–108 (2006)
11. Day, S.: Important Factors in urface EMG Measurement. Bortec Biomedical Ltd., `www.bortec.ca/Images/pdf/EMG%20measurement%20and%20recording.pdf`
12. Delp, S.L., Loan, J.P., Hoy, M.G., Zajac, F.E., Topp, E.L., Rosen, J.M.: An Interactive Graphics-Based Model of the Lower Extremity to Study Orthopedic Surgical Procedures. IEEE Transactions on Biomedical Engineering 32, 757–767 (1990)
13. Fleischer, C., Hommel, G.: Embedded Control System for a Powered Leg Exoskeleton. In: Proc. 7th Intern. Workshop Embedded Systems-Modeling, Technology and Applications, Berlin, pp. 177–185. Springer, Heidelberg (2006)
14. Fleischer, Ch., Hommel, G.: Calibration of an EMG-Based Body Model with Six Muscles to Control a Leg Exoskeleton. In: ICRA'07. IEEE International Conference on Robotics and Automation, Roma, Italy, April 10–14 2007, IEEE Computer Society Press, Los Alamitos (2007)
15. Fleischer, Ch., Kondak, K., Reinicke, Ch., Hommel, G.: Online Calibration of the EMG to Force Relationship. In: Proc. IROS 2004, Sendai, Japan, vol. 20, pp. 1305–1310. IEEE Robotics and Automation Society (2004)
16. Fleischer, Ch., Reinicke, Ch., Hommel, G.: Predicting the Intended Motion with EMG-Signals for an Exoskeleton Orthosis Controller . In: IROS. Proc. of the 2005 IEEE/RSJ Int. Conf. On Intelligent Robots and Systems, Edmonton, Alberta, Canada, 02.-06.08.2005, pp. 3449–3454 (2005)
17. Harwin, W.S., Patton, J.L., Edgerton, V.R.: Challenges and Opportunities for Robot-Mediated Neurorehabilitation. Proceedings of the IEEE 94, 1717–1726 (2006)
18. Herzog, W., Read, L.J.: Lines of Action and Moment Arms of the Major Force-Carrying Structures Crossing the Human Knee Joint. Journal of Anatomy 182, 213–220 (1992)
19. Manal, K., Gonzalez, R.V., Lloyd, D.G., Buchanan, T.S.: A Real-Time EMG Driven Virtual Arm. Comp. Biol. Med. 32, 25–36 (2002)
20. Pasqualino, A., Panattoni, G.L.: Anatomia Umana. In: UTET (2002)
21. Patton, J.L., Wei, Y., Scharver, C., Kenyon, R.V., Scheidt, R.: Motivating Rehabilitation by Distorting Reality. In: The first IEEE / RAS-EMBS International Conference on Biomedical Robotics and Biomechatronics (BioRob 2006), Pisa, Italy, 20–22 February 2006, IEEE Robotics and Automation Society (2006)
22. Yamaguchi, G.T., Sawa, A.G., Moran, D.W., Fessler, M.J., Winters, J.M.: A Survey of Human Musculotendon Actuator Parameters. In: Winters, J., Woo, S.L.-Y. (eds.) Multiple Muscle Systems: Biomechanics and Movement Organization, pp. 717–773. Springer, Heidelberg (1990)

'O Francesca, ma che sei grulla?' Emotions and Irony in Persuasion Dialogues

Irene Mazzotta, Nicole Novielli, Vincenzo Silvestri, and Fiorella de Rosis

Intelligent Interfaces, Department of Informatics, University of Bari
Via Orabona 4, 70126 Bari, Italy
{mazzotta, novielli, silvestri, derosis}@di.uniba.it

Abstract. In this paper we investigate the interaction between emotional and non-emotional aspects of persuasion dialogues, from the viewpoint of both the system (the Persuader), when reasoning on the persuasion attempt, and the user (the Receiver), when reacting to it. We are working on an Embodied Conversational Agent (ECA) which applies natural argumentation techniques to persuade users to improve their behaviour in the healthy eating domain. The ECA observes the user's attitude during the dialogue, so as to select an appropriate persuasion strategy or to respond intelligently to user's reactions to suggestions received. We grounded our work on the analysis of two corpora: a corpus of 'natural' persuasion examples and a corpus of user's reactions to persuasion attempts.

1 Introduction

We are working at an Embodied Conversational Agent (ECA) which applies natural argumentation techniques to persuade users to improve their behaviour in a given domain. Observing of the users' attitude during the dialogue is crucial to select an appropriate persuasion strategy and to respond intelligently to their reactions to suggestions received. The ECA plays the role of the Persuader (P), the user the role of the Receiver (R) of the argumentation message.

With 'natural' argumentation, we mean integrating rational arguments with the common sense, friendly style and emotional ingredients that are used in human-human communication. With 'observing the user', we mean two kinds of tasks:

a. to prudently wait to get knowledge about the user's attitudes (values, interests, goals etc) before planning the persuasion strategy to adopt, so as to select the presumably strongest arguments in the given circumstance;
b. to observe the user's reaction to the received suggestion, so as to understand whether and how to correct inappropriate choices and integrate the information provided with other data that might increase the user's level of persuasion.

Among the various aspects that are considered in designing an ECA, we are interested in verbal rather than nonverbal communication forms. We therefore focus our study on both generating the natural language persuasion message (planning its content and how to render it) and recognizing and interpreting the user's reactions. Two aspects of the users' reaction are of particular relevance in this kind of dialogues: their

R. Basili and M.T. Pazienza (Eds.): AI*IA 2007, LNAI 4733, pp. 602–613, 2007.
© Springer-Verlag Berlin Heidelberg 2007

level of engagement, which proved to influence considerably the success of the dialogue itself (see, e.g. Bickmore and Cassel, 2005) and the way they react to the information item or the suggestion received.

In addition to the theories about argumentation and persuasion (Walton 1992; O'Keefe, 2002; Fogg, 2002), we grounded our work on two corpora (in Italian): a corpus of 'natural' persuasion examples that we collected from subjects with various backgrounds (de Rosis et al, 2006a) and a corpus of user's reactions to the ECA's suggestions, that we collected with a Wizard of Oz (WoZ) study (de Rosis et al, 2006b)

In this paper we describe the results of the analysis of the first corpus in the light of theories about persuasion and show the role played by 'a-rational' persuasion strategies (Miceli et al, 2006). We then briefly describe how knowledge acquired with the cited theories and the experimental corpus may be represented into a knowledge base, which enables selecting the appropriate strategy in a given context. The highlight of this work is in the choice of a formalism that allows representing uncertainty and gradualness in building an image of the message Receiver, which are typical of any persuasion process. From the analysis of the second corpus, we formulated a method to recognize the level of engagement of users in the dialogue and their reaction to the information or the suggestion received. We adopt, in this case, a method which integrates Latent Semantic Analysis (Landauer, 1997) with Bayesian classification (de Rosis et al., 2007). Although the application domain we considered so far is advice-giving about healthy dietary behaviour, the methods described are domain independent.

2　Background Theories

O'Keefe (2002) suggests defining persuasion as *"human communication designed to influence others by modifying their beliefs, values or attitudes"*. By influencing others, one may intend attempting to modify either their beliefs or their intentions, and may name 'argumentation' and 'persuasion' the respective communication processes. In both cases, influencing is not a direct and rough suggestion, but is supported by a careful selection of the target beliefs, values or attitudes and of the methods to activate or strengthen them. Factors related to the Receiver, the context in which the persuasion dialogue occurs and the source of information provided are considered, by O'Keefe (2002) to be of primary importance for the success of a persuasion attempt. To Fogg (2002), computer tools may increase the persuasion power by providing tailored information or by leading people through a selected process. O'Keefe claims the importance of source credibility, liking and physical attractiveness: this suggest a thoughtful choice of the ECA' s aspect, of the language adopted and of its 'scientific credibility'. These requirements are achieved by demonstrating awareness of the peculiarities of the Receiver with which the ECA interacts. If not purely rational persuasion strategics are adopted, another key factor is the role the ECA pretends to play: a 'scientific' consultant or a competent but also friendly persona. However, users are not necessarily inclined to establish a friendly relationship with an artificial agent: they may rather prefer to see them as animated versions of a scientific advice-giving website. A good persuading ECA should therefore observe the user's reactions during the dialogue, to decide whether to put itself in the shoes of a traditional therapist or to recur to artifices of various kinds (such as irony, colloquial language, admitting its knowledge limits and so on) to reciprocate the social attitude of the user.

The last ten years witnessed a flourishing of contributions on how an argumentation (or persuasion) message may be formulated, given a goal to achieve. Walton reflected, in particular, on the relationship between the phases of 'reasoning' and of 'argumentation'; in the first one, P performs a what-if kind of reasoning on R's mind to select the most promising strategy to adopt; in the second one, this strategy is translated into an appropriately formulated message (Walton, 1990). The same author cooperated with other researchers to define a set of 'argumentation schemes' to formalize the structure of argumentation messages (premises that must hold for the scheme to be applied and conclusions) and the 'critical questions' (CQs) that Receivers may formulate in their attempts to argue in their turn. With some exceptions, these are schemes adopting rational arguments, such as pointing out the positive or negative consequences of (respectively) performing or omitting the suggested action. Other authors suggested an extension of these schemes, to enable formalizing, as well, a-rational aspects of persuasion (Miceli et al, 2006; Mazzotta and de Rosis, 2006). In this case, enthymemes (that is, omissions from the message of some of the premises that P considered in his reasoning: Walton, 2001) are not limited to the facts the two interlocutors are presumed to share but are aimed at hiding emotional considerations which, if expressed in the message, would compromise its efficacy.

3   Two Corpora

In this Section we describe more in detail the two corpora on which we designed and tested the methods that will be outlined in the next one. In both cases, the application domain is that of advice giving about healthy eating.

3.1   Corpus 1: 'Common Sense' Persuasion Messages

To study the strategies our ECA should apply in attempting to persuade the users to adopt a 'correct' eating behaviour, we performed a web-based experiment. Two versions of a scenario describing the situation in which the subjects involved (taking the role of P) should imagine to be, were presented randomly: one of them was formulated in a 'positive framing' (positive consequences of a diet rich in vegetables), the other one in a 'negative framing' (negative consequences of a diet poor in vegetables) (Levin et al, 1998). We collected, overall, *thirty-two messages* from Italian subjects with various backgrounds (psychologists, philosophers, computer scientists, epidemiologists, health care providers), aged between 23 and 63, of both genders (all examples in this paper will be translated into English). We factored every message into 'discourse segments', each including one or more utterances with a given communicative goal. To test the framing effect of the scenario on the valence of arguments employed by the subjects, we categorized every discourse segment as 'negative' or 'positive'. To test the effect of the rational formulation of the scenario on the arguments employed by the subjects, we classified a discourse segment as 'emotional' when it included one of the techniques mentioned in (Miceli et al, 2006): 'appeal to the goal to feel an emotion', 'emotional activation of a goal', expression of emotion in the language style or display of some form of empathy. The following are the main findings of our experiment:

- independently of the framing scenarios, *the subjects tended to combine negative with positive arguments* but *preferred positive arguments to negative ones.*
- *Rational and a-rational arguments* were usually combined in the messages, with a *prevalence of emotional arguments*, both in the negative and the positive framing conditions. Some examples of emotional hints:
  - in the *desirability of the goal* and its *activation*: "Just think Mary, how much more beautiful and healthy you would be if you ate more fruit and vegetables!";
  - in the *proofs that conditions existed for making the activity*: "you are a really good cook!"
  - in introducing *high-order values* that the activity might contribute to achieve: "You wouldn't be hurting anyone and you'd be helping the biological farmers to live better"or "With vegetables you can prepare gorgeous, very light meals";
  - in making more or less explicit *appeal to emotions*: "Here lies the wisdom of a mature woman: you have creative intelligence on your side *(pride)*, "If you insist on not eating fruit and vegetables, you show that you don't care about yourself" *(self-esteem).*
- The recommendation of the behaviour to follow was usually introduced at the beginning of texts which were prevalently rational, only subsequently in more emotional ones, after preparing the subject to receive the suggestion. In some cases, this section was substituted with the description of some tempting consequences of the activity. This recommendation was supported with a *combination of different strategies*: by attempting to increase the desirability of the outcome, by reminding information about activity-outcome relationship or by proving that conditions hold to make the activity. E.g.: "A meal based on vegetables can be tasty: with just a little imagination you can prepare a first-rate dinner for your friends!". Other segments were aimed specifically at evoking the *cognitive dissonance* in R's mind (Festinger, 1957).

3.2   Corpus 2: WoZ Dialogues

To study the kind of response the users might display when interacting with our ECA (a female, young character implemented with a wrapper to Haptek and Loquendo: see de Rosis et al, 2006b), we performed a Wizard of Oz study. In this study, we collected *thirty* text-based and *thirty* speech-based dialogues (with 1600 moves overall) from subjects aged between 21 and 28, equidistributed by gender and background (in computer science or in humanities). The ECA's moves available to the wizard included a set of sentences responding to several communicative goals: to Assess the situation and collect information about the subject, to Provide suggestions about healthy eating, to Persuade the subject to follow these suggestions in case of doubt, and others. The subjects were left totally free in answering to the ECA's dialogue move. A log of the dialogues was collected, to analyse the factors affecting dialogue and move length, level of initiative of the subjects and language features (as described in Section 4.2).

4 PORTIA: A Persuasion Dialogue Simulator

PORTIA[1] is a speech-based mixed-initiative dialogue system based on the Information-State architecture (Traum and Larsson, 2003). In this system, the ECA plays the role of the Persuader, the user the role of the Receiver. The system includes a *user model* to represent the presumed characteristics of R that are acquired and updated during the dialogue both explicitly (that is, through direct questions) and implicitly (that is, through the interpretation of user moves). The User Model includes a *specific knowledge* (facts acquired during the dialogue) and a *generic knowledge* (criteria to infer the user's attitudes in conditions of uncertainty). These components are restricted to the aspects that are relevant for the persuasion process: behaviour and beliefs in the domain of the dialogue, goal and values of R, 'social' attitude of R towards the ECA. Both a system's 'persuasion attempt' and its subsequent replies to the user's reaction are based on a sequencing of *'reasoning'* and *'planning'*: P first reasons on R's mind to select a promising persuasion strategy or an appropriate response to the user's reaction and then translates the selected strategy into a rhetorically coherent NL message.

4.1 Generating a Persuasion Attempt

In the reasoning process, PORTIA (Mazzotta et al, in press) simulates the presumed effect of different persuasion strategies on its image of R's mind: *appeal to the consequences* based on the presumed goal and values of R ("Just think how satisfied you would feel after adopting a correct eating pattern!"), *appeal to cognitive dissonance* to encourage R to a more consistent behaviour ("Are you silly Francesca? -'O Francesca, ma che sei grulla?'- You do sport, look after yourself with regular medical check-ups and then you almost excludes vegetables from your diet!") and others. Dynamic Bayesian Networks (implemented by Hugin's OOBN) are used to represent uncertainty and progressiveness in building and updating the image of R's mind. After reasoning on R's mind to select the attitudes on which to ground persuasion, an argument is constructed to express the selected strategy. The strategy is translated into a 'discourse plan' by combining, if necessary, fragments of different plans and pruning them out to avoid too complex messages. Message plans represent Walton's argumentation schemes as XML files. We extended these schemes to formalize a-rational aspects of persuasion (Miceli et al, 2006; Mazzotta and de Rosis, 2006).

To demonstrate the functioning of this module, let us consider the following case: R (Francesca) declared, during the dialogue, that she does sport and regular medical check-ups. At the same time, her diet seems to be poor in fruit and vegetables. PORTIA propagates in its model of Francesca the available knowledge: it infers that being in good health is probably an important goal to her, selects a 'rational' persuasion strategy focused on the goal of 'being in good health' and translates it into a discourse plan (Fig. 1). In formulating its persuasion message in natural language, various techniques are combined to express the message in positive terms, to employ

---

[1] From the famous character of The Merchant of Venice, who was skilled in argumentation.

a 'friendly' language, to reinforce Francesca's awareness of the positive effects of eating vegetables and finally to appeal to cognitive dissonance. The following is the message produced: "Are you silly, Francesca? You do sport, look after yourself with regular medical check-ups and then you almost excludes vegetables from your diet! Perhaps you don't know the benefits that a diet rich in vegetables can have on your health". Fig. 1 shows the complex discourse plan used to build this message: this plan is built by instantiating and combining the elementary plans of 'PersuasionFromConsequences' and 'ArgumentFromEvidence'.

```
========================================================
<plan name="Persuade&JustifyAboutGoodHealth" action="EatVeg"
  goal="GoodHealth">
    <RR name="Motivation">
        <RR name="Joint">

          ...............................................
          <RR name="Evidence">
              <RR name="Joint">
                  <c_act type="Remind" term="MakeSport(R)"/>
                  <c_act type="Remind" term="MakeCheckUps(R)"/>
              </RR>
              <c_act type="Claim" term="Like(R,g)"/>
          </RR>

          ...............................................
          <c_act type="Inform" term="Implies(a,g)"/>
        </RR>
        <RR name="Enablement">
            <c_act type="Suggest" term="Do(R,a)"/>
            <c_act type="Claim" term="CanDo(R,a)"/>
        </RR>
      </RR>
    </plan>
========================================================
```

Fig. 1. An example of complex discourse plan

4.2 Observing the User's Reaction

In adapting its answer, the ECA should be equipped to recognize two main aspects of the users' reaction: their social attitude towards the ECA and their reaction to its suggestion.

a. Social attitude displayed
To distinguish warm from cold social attitude, we refer to Andersen and Guerrero's definition of interpersonal warmth (1998) as *"the pleasant, contented, intimate feeling that occurs during positive interactions with friends, family, colleagues and romantic partners...[and]... can be conceptualized as... a type of relational experience, and a dimension that underlines many positive experiences"*. According to this definition, users display their social attitude towards the agent through various 'signs' in the language employed (table 1), that is by introducing colloquial style, friendly greetings, farewells or humour as 'offers of sympathy', questions about the agent's 'private life' and self-disclosure to establish a common ground, positive or negative comments as a demonstration of interest in the dialogue.

b.   Reaction to a suggestion

If the dialogue is natural in its developing, users tend to not accept a-critically the system's suggestions. We found, in our WoZ corpus, several examples of perplexity, requests of more information, provision of information about their own situation, or clear objections. We grounded our analysis of the user's reaction to a persuasion attempt on Walton's argumentation schemes and their later interpretations and refinements (Verheij 2003, Gordon 2005). Argumentation schemes are common types of defeasible arguments, evaluated by a set of related critical questions (Walton and Godden, 2005). The majority of them are focused on 'persuading to believe' (Argument from Evidence, Argument from Expert Opinion, Argument From Position to Know). Among the few of them which are aimed at 'persuading to do', the most commonly applied are the Argument from Consequences and the Practical Reasoning. Critical questions can be seen as 'representing additional relevant factors that might cause an argument to default' (Walton and Reed, 2003). They are used in everyday conversational arguments *'when a user is confronted with the problem of replying to an argument or making some assessment of what the argument is worth and whether to accept it'* (Walton and Gordon, 2005). From the viewpoint of the Receiver, CQs are questions that inquire about the conditions or circumstances that tend to challenge premises of a suggestion or the suggestion itself. We started from analysis of the critical questions of these schemes to define a markup language which enables us to define a method to recognize the User's reaction to the System's suggestions.

c.   Markup language

We asked three independent raters (PhD students) to annotate dialog pairs (System move–User move), after segmenting complex moves into individual communicative acts. Two markup languages were employed to annotate the subjects' moves according to the two kinds of features mentioned above.

The first language is described in Table 1: this table shows that two sets of signs were defined, to be recognized respectively from language and from prosodic features.

Although the ECA adopted, in the Wizard of Oz study, a purely rational persuasion strategy, subjects introduced various a-rational elements in their reactions. The following are some examples of subjects' responses to the following ECA's suggestion: "International research demonstrated the importance of fruits and vegetables in a correct diet. It recommends a daily assumption of a portion of row and a portion of cooked vegetables and two or three portions of fruits. Precooked food helps in controlling the portions".

U1: uhm… but I don't like fresh fruits: how may I substitute them?
U2: But I know fresh food is better than precooked products.
U3: But… a sin of gluttony is better than any healthy and balanced diet!
U4: I can't eat vegetables because I suffer of colitis
U5: Are you sure that precooked food is not dangerous for health?

Table 2 describes the language that was defined to annotate the subjects' reactions to a persuasion attempt: as we are still in the process of defining a recognition method for these features, we do not include recall and precision data in this table.

Table 1. Our markup language for signs of social attitude

Linguistic signs		Recall	Precision
Friendly self-introduction: The subjects introduce themselves with a friendly attitude (e.g. by giving her name or by explaining the reasons why they are participating in the dialogue)		99.5	37.5
Colloquial style: The subject employs a current language, dialectal forms, proverbs etc		75.9	11.7
Talks about self: The subject provides more personal information about self than requested by the agent		78.5	48.9
Personal questions to the agent: The subject tries to know something about the agent preferences, lifestyle etc, or to give it suggestions in the domain.		85.2	30.9
Positive or negative comments: The subjects comment the agent behavior in the dialogue: its experience, its domain knowledge etc.	Pos	4.3	66.7
	Neg	48.4	94.9
Friendly farewell: This may consist in using a friendly farewell form or in asking to carry-on the dialogue.		99.5	38.9
Neutral: No signs of social attitude.		48.4	94.9
Humor and irony: The subjects make some kind of verbal joke in their move		-	-
Acoustic signs			
Agreement: The dialogue segment displays an intonation of agreement with the system		47.1	21.4
Friendly intonation: The dialogue segment displays a friendly intonation		24.5	20.9
Laughter: The dialogue segment displays a smile or laughter		44.7	23.8
Neutral: The dialogue segment does not display any affective intonation		32.6	58.8
Negative intonation: The dialogue segment displays a negative intonation		19.6	12.4
I'm thinking: The dialogue segment displays, in its intonation, a reflection attitude		57.5	62.4

5   User Move Recognition Methods

Several studies investigated how to recognize emotions from written or spoken language, by combining prosodic information with language features (Litman and Forbes-Riley, 2003; Devillers and Vidrascu, 2006. By working on WoZ data, Batliner et al (2003) demonstrated that the combination of prosodic with linguistic and conversational data yielded better results than the use of prosody only, for recognizing the beginning of emotionally critical phases in a dialogue. To our knowledge, our work is the first one in the domain of recognition of social attitude from language. All the mentioned methods show some common steps: *a.* defining a markup language and tagging of the corpus by independent raters; *b.* evaluating the markup language and classifying units of annotation to create a training dataset; *c.* applying learning methods to the training corpus, to subsequently verify the method's accuracy by applying it to a test database.

5.1   Detecting Signs of Social Attitude

To recognize the linguistic signs of social attitude listed in Table 1, we applied a Bayesian classifier in which an input text is categorized as 'showing a particular sign of social attitude' if it includes some word sequences belonging to *semantic categories* which are defined as 'salient' for the considered sign. Bayesian classification enables associating with every string (segment or full move) a value of a-posteriori probability for every sign of social attitude (de Rosis et al., in press).

Table 2. Markup language for the subject's reaction to a System's suggestion

Comm. Act	Purpose	Examples
UNCERTAIN	R nods without expressing any clear opinion	mmm
ASKIF	R ask the truth value of a fact	Do you think my diet is correct?
ASKINFO	R asks for more information about some topic	How could I substitute fruits?
ASKJUSTIFY	R asks the system to justify its statement	And how do you know it?
INFORM	R provides some evidence about his/her attitudes or behaviour	I eat meat, fish, vegetables, lots of fruits…
CONFIRM	R declares to agree with the evidence provided by the system	Right, I agree
DISCONFIRM	R declares to disagree with the evidence provided by the system	No, you're wrong. I don't agree
I-REBUTTAL	R presents an exception that falsifies the system argument	I love unbridled life, with light aversion towards healthy food.
OBJECT	R argues about the truth value of a premise of the suggestion	Are you joking? So you mean I have to bring a fruit bag with me, at work?
ACCEPT	R declares to agree with the received suggestion	Understood! So I should try to do it?
COMMIT	R commits him/herself to apply the received suggestion	Ok, I will do it
CHALLENGE	R declares to not be persuaded by the suggestion	So many portions of fruits? I've heard contrary theories on this topic
REJECT	R refuses the suggestion	But… a sin of gluttony is better than any healthy and balanced diet!
S-REBUTTAL	R presents an exception that falsifies the suggestion	I don't want to avoid sweets at all

The last two columns of Table 1 show the level of accuracy of the method in terms of recall and precision. We did not attempt to recognize irony, because of the low frequency of moves displaying this sign. The table shows that Positive and Negative comments are the most difficult signs to recognize, while the recall for the other signs is quite good. Selecting a cutoff point that insures a good compromise between recall and precision is not an easy task: by changing the cutoff values, and checking the effect of this change by means of ROC analysis (Zweig and Campbell, 1993) one may get a different balancing between the two measures. This decision is not a technical one, but depends on the consequences of identifying a sign which was not actually expressed in a move or missing a sign that was expressed. In the maximize recall strategy, the ECA will risk to respond with a 'warm' social attitude to a 'neutral' or 'cold' behaviour of the user. In the maximize precision strategy, the inverse will occur. A 'good for all cases' solution does not exist but depends on the application domain and the goals one aims to achieve: we therefore applied the cutoff points suggested by ROC analysis in order to build a 'reasonably social' ECA (not too cold but not too warm either). More details about the method and its results may be found in (de Rosis et al., in press).

When language analysis is integrated with prosodic one (a work we are performing in cooperation with the University of Erlangen), a good recognition accuracy of the social attitude of users is obtained. In this case, *linguistic analysis* is aimed at recognizing in a user move the signs that may be employed to adapt the next system move. At the same time, as far as the dialogue goes on, linguistic signs discovered in the dialogue history contribute to build an overall, dynamic image of the social attitude of the user towards the advice-giving ECA (de Rosis et al, 2006b). *Acoustic analysis* is aimed at enriching the linguistic connotation of moves with information about their intonation. When the segment corresponds to an entire move, acoustic parameters just refine the linguistic description. When several acoustically different segments are isolated in a single move, the variation of prosody within a move may help in interpreting its meaning and reducing the risk of errors. In table 3, the 8x6 combinations of linguistic and acoustic labels are compacted into a lower number of categories, defined according to adaptation purposes ('negative', 'neutral' or -light or strong- 'warm' attitude of the user). We processed this dataset with the K2 learning algorithm (k-fold cross validation, with k=number of segments with WEKA) and got a 90.05 % of recall.

Table 3. Confusion matrix for the combination of acoustic and linguistic features

	Negative	Neutral	Light-warm	Warm	Recall	Precision
Negative	232 (94 %)	11 (4 %)	1 (.5 %)	4 (1.5 %)	.94	.94
Neutral	2 (1 %)	174 (95 %)	8 (4 %)	0	.95	.84
Light-warm	10 (3 %)	23 (6 %)	317 (85 %)	21 (6 %)	.85	.92
Warm	3 (1 %)	0	19 (9 %)	201 (90 %)	.90	.89

5.2 Understanding the User's Reaction to a System' s Move

As we said, this part of the research project is still ongoing. Data in our corpus are very sparse: therefore, we cannot rely only on machine learning techniques to automatically infer communicative acts during the dialogue but we also need to refer to the context (previous system move). Latent Semantic Analysis (Landauer and Dumais, 1997) has been already employed to extract the semantics of students' dialogue turns (Graesser et al., 2000) and might help us in recognizing the communicative act. According to the results of our markup experiment (majority agreement among raters), the complete range of possible users' reactions will be represented in a 'documents by terms' matrix. In this multidimensional representation, documents are the single communicative acts while the choice of features to include as 'terms' is still an open problem. A possibility is to build a lexicon based on the language used in the database of user's reactions. In general, a simple word based approach demonstrated to be not powerful enough (de Rosis and Novielli, 2007) and the accuracy of text-based methods may be improved by introducing rules based on the observation of context based-features, such as the target of the communicative act or the contextual role of words.

6 Conclusion

In this paper we investigated the interaction between emotional and non-emotional aspects of persuasion, from the viewpoint of both the system, when reasoning on the persuasion attempt, and the user, when reacting to it. We grounded our work on the analysis of two corpora: a corpus of 'natural' persuasion examples and a corpus of dialogues with an ECA. With analysis of the first one, we singled out the a-rational persuasion strategies adopted by our subjects; from the analysis of the second corpus, we formulated a set of criteria and a method to recognize the users' level of engagement and their reaction to the received suggestion. The preliminary results of our study proved that purely rational strategies were employed very infrequently and that emotional elements could be found everywhere and in various forms (first corpus). Similarly, in the second corpus we could find several forms of rational but also a-rational user's reactions, which go beyond the formalization of critical questions proposed by Walton. We are working at the speech-based, mixed initiative dialogue system PORTIA which applies 'natural' argumentation techniques to persuade users to improve their behavior in the health promotion domain. According to the analysis exposed so far, PORTIA should be equipped to recognize the user's reaction in terms of social attitude and level of acceptance of the suggestion received. We defined a Bayesian classifier which analyses the users moves linguistically to extract a social attitude value. Future work will focus on implementing a module which combines LSA with decision rules based on context to recognize the users' reaction.

Acknowledgements. This work was financed, in part, by HUMAINE, the European Human-Machine Interaction Network on Emotion (EC Contract 507422).

References

Andersen, P.A., Guerrero, L.K.: Handbook of Communication and Emotions. Research, theory, applications and contexts. Academic Press, Research (1998)

Batliner, A., Fisher, K., Huber, R., Spilker, J., Nöth, E.: How to find trouble in communication. Speech Communication 40(1-2), 117–143 (2003)

Bickmore, T., Cassell, J.: Social Dialogue with Embodied Conversational Agents. In: van Kuppevelt, J., Dybkjaer, L., Bernsen, N. (eds.) Advances in Natural, Multimodal Dialogue Systems, Kluwer Academic, New York (2005)

de Rosis, F., Batliner, A., Novielli, N., Steidl, S.: You are sooo cool, Valentina. In: Recognizing social attitude in speech-based dialogues with an ECA (2007) (in press)

de Rosis, F., Mazzotta, I., Miceli, M., Poggi, I.: Persuasion artifices to promote wellbeing. In: IJsselsteijn, W., de Kort, Y., Midden, C., Eggen, B., van den Hoven, E. (eds.) PERSUASIVE 2006. LNCS, vol. 3962, pp. 84–95. Springer, Heidelberg (2006a)

de Rosis, F., Novielli, N.: From Language to Thoughts: Inferring Opinions And Beliefs From Verbal Behavior. In: Proceedings of AISB '07 (2007)

de Rosis, F., Novielli, N., Carofiglio, V., Cavalluzzi, A., De Carolis, B.: User modeling and adaptation in health promotion dialogs with an animated character. Journal of Biomedical Informatics, Special Issue on Dialog systems for health communications 39(5), 514–531 (2006b)

Devillers, L., Vidrascu, L.: Real-life emotions detection with lexical and paralinguistic cues on human-human call center dialogs. In: INTERSPEECH-2006, pp. 1636-Tue1A30.3 (2006)

Festinger, L.: A theory of cognitive dissonance. Stanford University Press (1957)

Fogg, B.J: Persuasive Technology: Using Computers to Change What we Think and Do. Morgan Kaufmann, San Francisco (2002)

Gordon, T.F.: A computational model of argument for legal reasoning support systems. In: Dunne, P.E., Bench-Capon, T. (eds.) Argumentation in Artificial Intelligence and Law. IAAIL Workshop Series, pp. 53–64. Wolf Legal Publishers (2005)

Graesser, A., Wiemer-Hastings, P., Wiemer-Hastings, K., Harter, D., Person, N.: Using Latent Semantic Analysis to Evaluate the Contributions of Students in AutoTutor. Interactive Learning Environments 8, 128–148 (2000)

Landauer, T.K., Dumais, S.T.: A solution to Plato's problem: The Latent Semantic Analysis theory of the acquisition, induction, and representation of knowledge. Psychological Review 104, 211–240 (1997)

Levin, I.P., Schneider, S.L., Gaeth, G.J.: All frames are not created equal: a typology and critical analysis of framing effects. Organizational Behaviour and Human Decision Processes 76(2), 149–188 (1998)

Litman, D., Forbes-Riley, K., Silliman, S.: Towards emotion prediction in spoken tutoring dialogues. In: HLT/NAACL, pp. 52–54 (2003)

Mazzotta, I., de Rosis, F.: Artifices for persuading to improve eating habits. In: AAAI Spring Symposium on Argumentation for consumers of health care, Stanford, USA (2006)

Mazzotta, I., de Rosis, F., Carofiglio, V.: PORTIA: A User-Adapted Persuasion System in the Healthy Eating Domain. IEEE Intelligent Systems, Special Issue on Argumentation Technology (2007) (in press)

Miceli, M., de Rosis, F., Poggi, I.: Emotional and non emotional persuasion. Applied Artificial Intelligence: an International Journal 20(10), 849–880 (2006)

O'Keefe, D.J.: Persuasion: Theory and Research, 2nd edn. Sage Publications Inc, Thousand Oaks, CA (2002)

Traum, D., Larsson, S.: The information state approach to dialogue management. In: Smith, R., van Kuppevelt, J. (eds.) Current and New Directions in Discourse and Dialogue, pp. 325–353. Kluwer Academic Publishers, Dordrecht (2003)

Verheij, B.: Dialectical argumentation with argumentation schemes: An approach to legal logic. Artificial Intelligence and Law 11(2-3), 167–195 (2003)

Walton, D.N.: What is reasoning? What is an argument? The Journal of Philosophy 87(8), 399–419 (1990)

Walton, D.N.: The place of emotion in argument. Pennsylvania State University Press, University Park (1992)

Walton, D.N.: Enthymemes, Common Knowledge, and Plausible Inference. Philosophy and Rhetoric 34(2), 93–112 (2001)

Walton, D., Godden, D.: The Nature and Status of Critical Questions in Argumentation Schemes, The Uses of Argument. In: Hitchcock, D., Farr, D. (eds.) The Uses of Argument, pp. 423–432. OSSA, Hamilton (2005)

Walton, D., Gordon, T.S.: Critical Questions in Computational Models of Legal Argument. In: Dunne, P.E., Bench-Capon, T. (eds.) IAAIL Workshop Series, pp. 103–111. Wolf Legal Publishers, Nijmegen (2005)

Walton, D., Reed, C.: Diagramming, Argumentation Schemes and Critical Questions. In: van Eemeren, F.H., et al. (eds.) Anyone Who Has a View: Theoretical Contributions to the Study of Argumentation, pp. 195–211. Kluwer, Dordrecht (2003)

Zweig, H.H., Campbell, G.: Receiver Operating Characteristic (ROC) plots: a fundamental evolution tool in medicine. Clinical Chemistry 39, 561–577 (1993)

Music Expression Understanding Based on a Joint Semantic Space

Luca Mion and Giovanni De Poli

Department of Information Engineering
University of Padova
Via Gradenigo 6/a, 35131 Padova, Italy
{luca.mion,depoli}@dei.unipd.it

Abstract. A paradigm for music expression understanding based on a joint semantic space, described by both affective and sensorial adjectives, is presented. Machine learning techniques were employed to select and validate relevant low level features, and an interpretation of the clustered organization based on action and physical analogy is proposed.

Keywords: Expression, Music Performance, Semantic Expressive Space.

1   Introduction

Human mind is embodied, that is to understand the world we live in, we humans mediate the environmental information by the body in such a way to provide compact and abstract representations. Cognitive sciences indeed focus on how humans interact with their environment, searching the connection between perception and action to bridge the semantic gap that humans experience in their everyday life: as sound and music are linked to their physical energy, the meaning/content of the auditory information has to be linked to meaningful actions that we can use to access the encoded high-level information. To face this gap problem we pursue the idea that the human mind is embodied, so the relation between meaning and physical energy is mediated by the human body. This embodiment viewpoint can also lead to a different way to think about ICT, creating machine-embodied knowledge for the understanding of high-level contents. This consequence is linked to the development of machine-embedded knowledge supplied, for instance, by machine-learning techniques: such methods can provide useful bridges between information technology and cognitive sciences and neurosciences, which are particularly relevant disciplines for research in music technology and for the specific design of techniques for signal processing related to artificial intelligence.

In verbal and non-verbal communication, both research and technology spent big efforts to understand explicit messages represented by the text or the musical score, but implicit messages are not understood just as well. Understanding the expressive intentions is one of the key tasks associated with this implicit channel, and in the context of music we are interested in comprehending the expressive intentions from the performers side regarding what the music should

R. Basili and M.T. Pazienza (Eds.): AI*IA 2007, LNAI 4733, pp. 614–625, 2007.

express to the listeners. In particular, we are interested in actions and feedback mechanisms that, at different processing levels, allow for creating the missing link from actions to perceived expressions: within such multi-sensorial scenario, machine-learning techniques can supply the necessary information to comprehend the main lines of the phenomena. In the context of artificial intelligence, we can adapt this theory in order to embody expressive knowledge in machines and to adapt the communication to the basic forms of human behavior. From this perspective, the comprehension of the mechanisms of expressive communication by a music performer can help us designing systems to retrieve expressive content on audio data, and then to design a next generation of search engines for Music Information Retrieval (MIR). The music performance paradigm can indeed be very useful, since musicians can act on their playing to communicate different expressive intentions, resulting in deviations of acoustic parameters from a performance played in a scholastic way. Beyond the potential applications to the MIR field, other application fields can be forecast for virtual expressive environments [1] and artistic applications [2].

In this paper we present a paradigm for music expression understanding based on a joint semantic space, described by both affective and sensorial adjectives in order to embody in machines the knowledge for music expression understanding. We aim to two different goals: from one side, we want to recognize the expressive content in audio data by using machine learning techniques; also, we want to see how these descriptors organize within a joint space where adjectives from both spaces are taken into account: since our audio descriptors can be specifically related to qualitative descriptions of the sound by physical metaphors, we can establish a correspondence among different semantic levels. In such a way we can speculate on the usefulness of our descriptors as support to machine-embedded knowledge for the understanding of expressive content on audio data.

2   An Experiment to Embed Expressive Knowledge

Up to now, many empirical studies have demonstrated that moods and emotions can be conceptualized both by labelling emotions as discrete categories and by mapping emotions as points on multi-dimensional space, distinguished by their relative position. Also, the relation between music and emotions has been addressed by various studies. From the categorical viewpoint, Gabrielsson and Juslin [3] concluded that there is no universally accepted set of adjectives for classifying music according to emotion, while on the other side dimensional models were proposed demonstrating that the valence-activity organization of Russell's circumplex model of affect [4] is confirmed in the music domain [5]. Other spaces were derived by using physical descriptors of the dimensions; in [6], a kinematics-energy space for expressive representation of music performances was conceptualized.

Moreover, interesting approaches on emotion representations have been proposed as in [7], where a hierarchical framework was investigated considering independence and bipolarity views as respectively structured at low and high levels. Following this hierarchical approach, our research focuses on a model for the automated analysis of music expression by linking the hierarchy of representations to the embodied description of emotions, using the physical descriptions as metaphors. This approach can help bridging the semantic gap between the physical level and the affective domain, since it allows for approaching the analysis of music expression at an intermediate level, between music intended as a structured language, and sound at a more physical level [8].

Most models for analysis of expression are based on modelling the measured deviations in human performances [9]. These works are based on the knowledge of the score, but it is not advisable in practical applications since it excludes musical improvisation or many non-western musical forms and score following is difficult. A few attempts tried to describe expression without the reference to a score. In [10], a system to predict which emotion the performer is trying to convey was developed, while other approaches used machine learning and data mining algorithms: in [11] the aim was oriented to the extraction of regularities and to recognize performance styles. In [12], a model based on Bayesian networks was proposed to automatically recognize the expressive content of MIDI piano improvisations, and in [13], a hierarchical framework was proposed to detect the mood in a music clip by means of intensity, timbre, and rhythm features.

Expression is conveyed at different level of musical structural complexity. However, it was demonstrated [14] that emotions in music performance can be estimated from excerpts of few notes: this means that high level structural factor are not necessary for expression recognition and that performer uses cues at different level to convey expression. It may be argued that expression can be recognized only considering features which are independent from the score. In order to better understand the expressiveness it is advisable to study all the levels with an integrated approach: thus our choice on the material to use in our experiments included simple notes, structured patterns and music excerpts.

2.1   Our Approach and Domains

By means of significant cases we want to find which are the most suitable labels to be suggested to performers. These significant cases derive from the Valence Arousal space (affective space) and to the Kinematics Energy space (sensorial space), respectively conceptualized in [4] and [6] (Fig. 1). These spaces were extensively used in previous researches on music expression, and they were confirmed in many experiments to be robust. Inspired by these spaces, different antinomies were used to label the dimensions, thus we choose the adjectives well representing these antinomies. Within each space, we investigated musical expressions represented by labels situated at the opposite sides of the axis. Regarding the affective space, the categories *Happy-Sad* (High and Low Valence), *Angry-Calm* (High and Low Arousal) represent the bipolarity induced by independent dimensions valence and arousal; for the sensorial space, we have the correspondences *Hard-Soft* (High and Low energy) and *Light-Heavy* (High and Low Kinematics). In this way each adjectives has its opposite in order to deliberately induce contrasting performances by the musician. Beyond the pair of

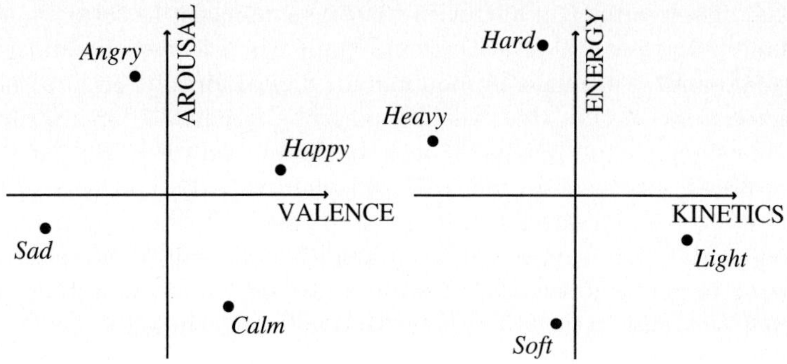

Fig. 1. The Valence-Arousal space (left) and the Kinematics-Energy space (right), respectively adapted from [4] and [6]

adjectives representing the bipolarities of the spaces, we considered a neutral performance as well, which listeners placed between the pair of opposite adjectives [6]. By "neutral" we intend a human performance without any specific expressive intention and stylistic choice.

The experiment starts with the extraction of audio features from a set of expressive performances played by professional musicians on various instruments. Then we employed two feature selection procedures: in a first step, we applied Sequential Forward Selection (SFS) with reference to a Naive Bayesian classifier to rank and select a set of features; as second step, to overcome limitations due to nesting effect we made the Principal Component Analysis (PCA) on the performance data by taking into account additional cues. We derived a set of features for a general description of the expressions and a set of descriptors specific for each instrument. To test the selected features we measured the effectiveness by the leave-one-out cross validation.

2.2   Audio Cues Extraction

Professional performers of violin, flute and guitar were invited to play musical performances inspired by different expressive intentions, described by the adjectives that lies on the affective space (happy, sad, angry and calm), and on the sensorial space (light, heavy, soft and hard). Moreover, we asked to record a neutral performance for each excerpt. We recorded six pieces to cover three levels of structural complexity: two sets of repeated notes with different fixed pitches G4 and D5 (simple musical gestures), a G major scales (simple patterns, structured musical gestures), and some excerpts from the classical and traditional repertoire (performance based on score, structured musical gestures): Twinkle Twinkle Little Star (traditional), theme from Handel's Sonata in E minor (Adagio), Frère Jacques (traditional). These excerpts were selected among simple traditional melodies in order to induce few artistic ambitions to the performers, so that they felt free to play also with extreme emphasis. In total we collected 324 examples (6 pieces x 9 adjectives x 2 emphasis x 3 instruments) resulting in about 190 minutes of music in monophonic digital form at 16 bits, 44.1 kHz. We extracted a set of cues that were found to be important for discriminating emotions in listening experiments [5], and that were used to classify the style [11] and the expressive content in musical performances [10]. Two sets of features were computed: we extracted a first set of 10 audio features by using 46 ms-length non overlapping frames, and additional 7 audio features (related to note events) using larger windows with 4 s duration and 3.5 s overlapping. In total we collected 17 audio features on about 9700 different windows:

Roughness (R) is considered to be a sensory process highly related to sound texture perception, and a good method to compute this feature is based on Leman's Synchronization Index Model [15]. Spectral Centroid (C) is a quantification of spectral energy distribution and it is related to perceptual timbre attribute of brightness. Spectral Ratios SRa, SRm, SRh, are computed by splitting the frequency range in two ways: by splitting below and above a frequency close to 1000 Hz we derive features SRa and SRb, while features SRl, SRm and SRh are given by the separation of the frequencies into three regions below 534 Hz, from 534 Hz to 1805 Hz, and over 1805 Hz. These bands are derived from the actual frequencies separation of the cochlear filter-bank used for the roughness computation. Features SRb and SRl were not used because they can be derived directly from the other spectral features. Residual Energy $REa, Reb, REl, REm, REh)$ describe the stochastic residual of the audio signal, obtained by removing the deterministic (harmonic) sinusoidal components. The computation of the residual energy on various bands of the spectrum can give information on the quality of the perceived effort [17]. We extracted the residual over different frequency regions by removing the sinusoidal component, and we characterize such residual by opportune ratios within the same subbands used for spectral ratios, yielding audio descriptors indicated with $RE_{sb} = \sum_{j \in sb} |X_R(j)|^2 / \sum_{k=1}^{N/2-1} |X(k)|^2$, where sb indexes each subband and X_R is the spectrum of the residual component of the signal.

Additional 7 audio features were computed inside the 4 s long windows and they are related to the audio events. These features were computed after segmentation of the signal by onset detection, based both on the derivative of the spectral magnitude and on pitch-tracking approach (the offset instant was detected when the temporal envelope $RMS(t)$ falls by the 60% from its previous maximal value): Notes per Second (NPS) is the number of notes that occur in one second. Note Duration (D) is the measure of time between note-onset and note-offset. Inter-Onset-Interval (IOI) is the measure of time between two consecutive note-onsets. Attack time (A) is the time required to reach the $RMS(t)$ peak, starting from the onset instant. Articulation or Legato Degree (L) defined as D/IOI. Peak Sound Level $PSL = \max[RMS(t)]$ directly derived from the $RMS(t)$ temporal envelope. Sound Level Range $SLR = \max[RMS(t)] - \min[RMS(t)]$ derived from the $RMS(t)$ temporal envelope.

2.3   Features for General and Specific Description

We applied two feature selection procedures: Sequential Forward Selection (SFS) with reference to a Naive Bayesian classifier, and as second step we made the PCA analysis on the performance data by taking into account additional cues. The SFS method [16] starts the search with an empty variable subset and consists of successively building up a feature subset by adding one feature at a time. During one step, SFS considers for selection all the features that have not yet been selected, by adding the locally best feature that provides the highest objective function. In our experiment the objective function was assumed as the highest F-measure score, i.e. the harmonic mean between precision and recall indicators obtained by the classifier. After the PCA analysis, we finally selected the features with significant factor loadings. We call General descriptors the features selected from the whole data set, while we call Specific descriptors the features selected from data of each instrument separately. This analysis allowed us to collect the set of features suitable for recognizing expressions in case of knowledge of the instrument. Once the features for each instrument were selected, we trained a Naive Bayesian classifier in order to test the features using leave-one-out cross validations, and we identified and removed the most correlated features via PCA analysis avoiding misleading results. Bayesian classifiers have been used in previous works for the analysis of style [11] and expressive content in musical audio [12].

SFS started from the 17 features of pieces played according to 8 intentions plus a neutral performance by violin, flute and guitar. Analysis led to a best set of features from each performance by the leave one out method, and the average dimension of the optimal feature vector was 4.15, yielding an average value of maximal F-measure equal to 64.97% of correct classifications. We proceeded by taking into account the set of features formed by NPS, PSL, A, and R, which in our experiment represented the most frequently selected features for reaching the maximal number of correct classifications. We call $\mathcal{G}$ this set of features.

Then, via PCA analysis we derived two dimensions for each space, leading to the following cumulative explained variance: 56.19% and 99.01% in the sensorial space, 71.33% and 98.69% in the affective space. We found large magnitude of factor loadings of features NPS, PSL, A, and R along the principal components (Fig. 2). Other features appeared correlated (such as L to A) and other features had minor magnitude, due to the contribution of the various instrument. We argued that much of the expressive information is carried on by features of set $\mathcal{G}$ (General descriptors), confirming the results from previous SFS analysis.

More specific analysis were also conducted on the data from instruments separately: for violin performances, PCA analysis on cues selected via SFS revealed that both spaces are characterized by high relevance of $\mathcal{G}$. An interesting aspect is given by Roughness, which is an important feature for discriminating expressions along the Energy dimension and along the Arousal dimension. Regarding features selected by considering flute performances only, SFS led to a set of 5 features: A, SRa, NPS, R, REh. As expected, flute has less dynamic capabilities

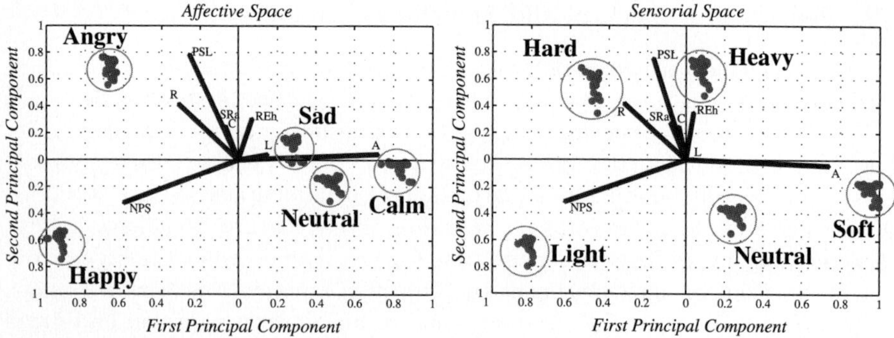

Fig. 2. Principal Component Analysis on the whole recorded audio from three instruments, according to affective adjectives (left) and sensorial adjectives (right). The factor loadings of each feature contribution are shown.

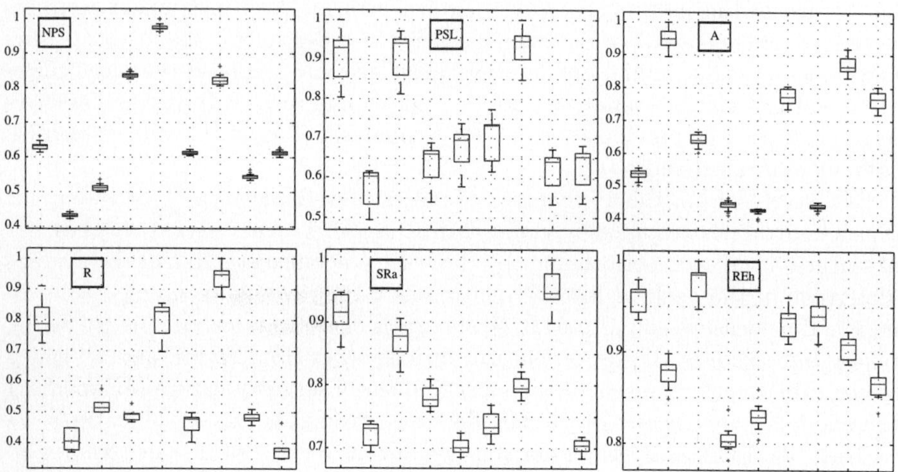

Fig. 3. Middle 50% of the data, median and extreme points. Nine adjectives played by three instruments are considered: from left to right respectively hard, soft, heavy, light, happy, sad, angry, calm, neutral.

with respect to violin, resulting in lower dynamic range: in fact, PSL was not selected. Via PCA we finally selected the set of features A, SRa, NPS, R, REh.

Concerning guitar, SFS led to select 8 features, reaching 86.93% of correct classifications: $NPS, L, PSL, R, D, REb, SRh, REc$. In spite of this high number of features, PCA analysis revealed many correlations and low magnitude of factor loadings from several audio features, and we finally selected the set $\mathcal{G}$ for guitar. We found that expressions from violin and guitar can be described by the same group of features $\mathcal{G}$. In addiction, for violin the additional feature REh related to residual energy was selected. Moreover, the flute due to dynamic limitations, showed less dependance to PSL but the feature SRa has to be taken into account. In fact, the bowing fluctuations in the violin and the blowing of the flutist are expressive means used by the performers to convey expressions. Figure 3 shows the middle 50% of the data, the median, and the extreme points for features G and additional specific features REh and SRa are taken into account.

We trained a Naive Bayesian classifier with the following sets of features, using leave-one-out cross validations: i) General descriptors, selected by taking into account the whole data set from three instruments, in order to test the cues in the general case when the instrument is not known; ii) Common descriptors (i.e. General plus Specific descriptors), in order to test whether by adding descriptors that are specific for each instrument we improve the detection; iii) Specific descriptors, to test the features in case of instrument knowledge. In this case we classified data from each instrument separately.

We trained the classifier with all data, excluding each time one piece which was used for testing. We found that the average classification accuracy using the General set of features is 64.58%, greater than the accuracy when using the Common descriptors (Average = 62.68%), supporting the choice of General descriptors. Concerning the confusion matrices, we found that opposite expressions (e.g. Hard/Soft) are never confused. Some misclassifications arose for the expression Calm: for flute and for guitar it is classified as Sad, while violin present significant percentages of misclassifications. Moreover, better recognition rates were achieved for expressions Heavy and Happy in particular.

3   Description of the Joint Space

In this experiment we used machine learning techniques to select the most relevant low level features allowing to recognize different expressive intentions both in the emotional and sensory domain. Then we explored the organization of adjectives in the feature space and their relation with the intended expression. The PCA analysis shows two 2D projections of the features space (Fig. 2). We can see that the positions of emotional and sensory adjectives are in good agreement with their positions in the corresponding perceptual space (Fig. 1). We now want to investigate how these features are projected by PCA within the joint space, taking into account all the performances related to both spaces (Fig. 4). We want to see whether the organization of the selected features, in this joint space, gives us information about the association between sensorial and affective labels. Normally emotional and sensorial adjectives are studied separately, to avoid problems associated with subjective evaluation and comparison of different psychological functions. However our feature space allows us to directly compare different level adjectives in a mathematical way. Thus we exploited the significance of the selected features in order to see how all the adjectives are jointly organized in the feature space, and to explain the found relations relating the space to a semantic interpretation.

By comparing the two axis, we can observe that performances are projected in a way that allows us to relate the descriptors to the dimensions Energy/Kinetics and Valence/Arousal. In particular, we can see that the adjectives from the two spaces

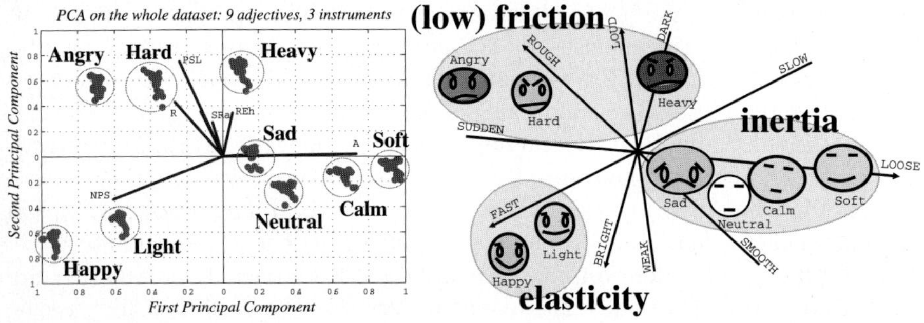

Fig. 4. Principal Component Analysis on the whole recorded audio from three instruments, according to adjectives from both affective and sensorial spaces (left), and representations of adjectives with their physical descriptions (right)

Table 1. Qualitative description of adjectives

Physical analogy	Adjectives	Tempo + fast - slow	Intensity + loud - weak	Attack + loose - sudden	Texture + rough - smooth	Brightness + bright - dark	Effort + strong - weak
friction	Hard, Heavy – Angry	-	+++	-	++	- - -	++
elasticity	Happy – Light	+++	- -	- -	-	+	- -
inertia	Sad, Calm – Soft	- - -	- - -	+++	- -	++	-

are placed along the projections of the General descriptors PSL, NPS, A, R: Hard-Soft and Angry-Calm are mainly differentiated along the descriptors PSL and R; Light-Heavy and Happy-Sad mainly along the descriptors NPS and A.

A qualitative physical description of the expressive intentions by means of the selected features can be derived as well from Fig. 2 and 4. Tab. 1 summarizes the qualitative contributions to the expression description. NPS, PSL, A are directly related to physical properties of the signal, and they can easily be mapped into physical description such as fast/slow, loud/weak, sudden/loose respectively. Moreover, roughness R is considered to be a sensory process highly related to texture perception, thus we can think of texture-related properties of expressions explained by the physical metaphor of rough/smooth. Feature SRa is related to the amount of energy in the frequency region below 1000 Hz. Thus, expressions characterized by low values of SRa reveal high energy in the higher bands, and this can be translated into the Brightness property, and then the adjectives can be described by means of bright/dark description. Finally, feature REh is related to the quality of the perceived effort, and it can be associated with physical metaphor of strong/weak. We can also notice that the position of the neutral performance, that in perceptual experiments subjects normally tend to place it near the center of the semantic space, in our feature space it is still in a central position but it tends to cluster with sad/calm/soft adjectives. Probably performers choose to play with an inertial character, as opposed to the other two cluster which present a strong or sudden reaction to a cause.

We can compare our projection with the results of an experiment by Bigand et al. [14] which consisted in requiring participants to group pieces according to superficial similarities: multidimensional scaling analysis of such task leaded to very similar grouping of our feature space. These findings support the idea that, during expressive intention communication, the expressive musical structures, used for expression communication both at structural and performance level are strongly associated with some superficial cues.

Moreover psychological functions (as perception, cognition and emotion) overlap each other and distinctions are relative, not absolute. We can observe that sensorial adjectives may have an emotional quality. Words as hard, light or heavy are used in many different contexts with a variety of meanings, including emotional meanings and are adequate for describing the behavioral aspects of emotions as anger, happiness and sadness, respectively. This possible semantic relation is reflected in our space, where these couples of sensorial and emotional adjectives are placed in the same region. On the other hand experiments on the time course of musical emotion e.g. [18,14] showed that very short music excerpt (containing even a single tone) are quite sufficient to generate consistent, and emotionally relevant, categorizations in listeners. This implies that performance and timbre cues are often adequate to induce or recognize a specific emotion.

This relation between cues and expression encourages us to proceed with the interpretation of positions in the joint feature space. Another important aspect arises by observing this diagram, we can notice that the audio features split in three clusters. The expressive labels belonging to each cluster reflect the intuitive correspondence of Light with Happy, Sad with Calm and Soft, Hard with Heavy and Angry. After having proposed an interpretation of the dimensional organization of the two categories of adjectives based on linguistic analogy and human behavior, we suggest an interpretation of the clusters based on action and physical analogy [8]. In fact, actions can be considered as an intermediate level of representation between the semantic and superficial feature levels. Moreover in many domains, and especially in music, expressive contents are conveyed by actions and gestures, which are essentially physical and dynamic events. Therefore, direct or indirect reference to human physical behavior can be a common denominator to all the multi-modal expressive actions and it can yield a suitable representation. As an example, consider a pianist or a dancer who wants to communicate, during a performance, an intention labelled as soft. Each performer will translate this intention into modifications of his action in order to render it softer, e.g. by taking into account the attack time of single events (such as notes or steps). The actions will therefore be more "elastic" or "weightless". These and other overall properties (like inertia or viscosity), together with energy (used as a scale factor), will be taken into account to define the mid-level description.

When using the physical analogy, force is often subjectively considered as the cause and movement (velocity or position) as the effect. The cause-effect relationship is represented by the *admittance Y* which mathematically describes the dynamic mapping and the qualitative behavior from force to velocity by an integral-differential equation. We can distinguish three kinds of basic behaviors: friction, which determines the amount of effect and thus scales the energy; elasticity, which opposes changes in force; inertia, which opposes changes in movement. In friction velocity is proportional to applied force, in elasticity velocity is proportional to the derivative of the force, and in inertia velocity is proportional to the integral of the force: their behavior in the frequency domain is all-pass, high-pass and low-pass respectively. This allows us the associate an interpretation to the three clusters shown in tab. 1: the heavy/hard/angry cluster can be related to the concept of energy and (low) *friction*, the cluster happy/light to *elasticity*, and the cluster sad/calm/soft to *inertia*.

There is finally a potential link between this analogy and the natural language processing. According to Ortony, Clore and Collins [19], emotion theory defines emotions as valenced reactions to events, or objects with their particular nature being determined by the way in which the eliciting situation is construed. Thus, emotions result the outcome of an evaluation of the extent to which one's goals are being met in interaction with the environment, from cognitive interpretation of some emotion eliciting situation. Authors propose a mechanism for converting eliciting situations into cognitive emotions, but not much is done for converting eliciting situations into expressions: our interpretation of music expressions by means of physical analogy can be helpful to find a mechanism for converting eliciting situations such as events or objects into cognitive expressions, even in practical applications e.g. to disambiguate language expressions in a movie, through understanding the musical expressions that may accompany them.

4   Conclusions

In this experiment we used machine learning techniques to select the most relevant low level features allowing to recognize different expressive intentions both in the emotional and sensory domain. Then we explored the organization of adjectives in the feature space and their relation with the intended expression. Since our audio descriptors can be directly mapped to physical properties of the sound, we could establish a correspondence among these properties and higher semantic levels. In this way, the expression can be embodied in machines by means of physical metaphors based on a low-level descriptors rather than musical attributes.

Acknowledgments. This research was supported by the EU FP6 Network of Excellence "Enactive Interfaces" IST-1-002114, and the FET Coordination Action "Sound to Sense, Sense to Sound (S2S2)" IST-2004-03773.

References

1. Mion, L., D'Incà, G.: Analysis of expression in simple musical gestures to enhance audio in interfaces. Virtual Reality 10(1), 62–70 (2006)
2. Camurri, A., De Poli, G., Leman, M., Volpe, G.: Communicating expressiveness and affect in multimodal interactive systems. IEEE Multimedia 12(1), 43–53 (2005)

3. Gabrielsson, A., Juslin, P.N.: Emotional expression in music. In: Davidson, R.J., Scherer, K.R., Goldsmith, H.H. (eds.) Handbook of Affective Sciences, pp. 503–534. Oxford University Press, Oxford (2002)
4. Russell, J.A.: A circumplex model of affect. Journal of Personality and Social Psychology 39, 1161–1178 (1980)
5. Juslin, P.N., Sloboda, J.A.: Music and Emotion: Theory and Research. Oxford University Press, Oxford (2001)
6. Canazza, S., De Poli, G., Rodà, A., Vidolin, A.: An abstract control space for communication of sensory expressive intentions in music performance. Journal of the New Music Research 32(3), 281–294 (2003)
7. Tellegen, A., Watson, D., Clark, L.A.: On the dimensional and hierarchical structure of affect. Psychological Science 10(4), 297–303 (1999)
8. De Poli, G., Avanzini, F., Rodà, A., Mion, L., D'Incà, G., Trestino, C., Pirrò, D., Luciani, A., Castagne, N.: Towards a multi-layer architecture for multi-modal rendering of expressive actions. In: Proc. 2nd Int. Conf. on Enactive Interfaces (2005)
9. De Poli, G.: Methodologies for Expressiveness Modelling of and for Music Performance. Journal of New Music Research 33(3), 189–202 (2004)
10. Friberg, A., Schoonderwaldt, E., Juslin, P., Bresin, R.: Automatic real-time extraction of musical expression. In: Proc. ICMC02, pp. 365–367 (2002)
11. Dannenberg, R., Thom, B., Watson, D.: A machine learning approach to musical style recognition. In: Proc. ICMC97, pp. 344–347 (1997)
12. Mion, L.: Application of bayesian networks to automatic recognition of expressive content of piano improvisations. In: Proc. Stockholm Music Acoustics Conf.(SMAC'03), pp. 557–560 (2003)
13. Lu, L., Liu, D., Zhang, H.J.: Automatic mood detection and tracking of music audio signals. IEEE Trans. on Audio, Speech and Language Processing 14(1), 5–18 (2006)
14. Bigand, E., Vieillard, S., Madurell, F., Marozeau, J., Dacquet, A.: Multidimensional scaling of emotional responses to music: The effect of musical expertise and of the duration of the excerpts. Cognition and Emotion 19(8), 1113–1139 (2005)
15. Leman, M.: Visualization and calculation of roughness of acoustical musical signals using the synchronization index model (SIM). In: Proc. Int. Conf. on Digital Audio Effects (DAFX-00), pp. 125–130 (2000)
16. Whitney, A.W.: A direct method of nonparametric measurement selection. IEEE Trans. Comput. 20, 1100–1103 (1971)
17. Laurenti, N., De Poli, G., Montagner, D.: A nonlinear method for stochastic spectrum estimation in the modeling of musical sounds. IEEE Trans. on Audio, Speech and Language Processing 15(2), 531–541 (2007)
18. Peretz, I.: Listen to the brain: a biological perspective on music and emotion. In: Juslin, P.N., Sloboda, J.A. (eds.) Music and Emotion: Theory and Research, pp. 105–135. Oxford University Press, New York (2001)
19. Ortony, A., Clore, G.L., Collins, A.: The Cognitive Structure of Emotions. Cambridge University Press, Cambridge (1988)

Towards Automated Game Design

Mark J. Nelson[1] and Michael Mateas[2]

[1] College of Computing
Georgia Institute of Technology
Atlanta, Georgia, USA
mnelson@cc.gatech.edu
[2] Computer Science Department
University of California—Santa Cruz
Santa Cruz, California, USA
michaelm@cs.ucsc.edu

Abstract. Game generation systems perform automated, intelligent design of games (*i.e.* videogames, boardgames), reasoning about both the abstract rule system of the game and the visual realization of these rules. Although, as an instance of the problem of creative design, game generation shares some common research themes with other creative AI systems such as story and art generators, game generation extends such work by having to reason about *dynamic, playable* artifacts. Like AI work on creativity in other domains, work on game generation sheds light on the human game design process, offering opportunities to make explicit the tacit knowledge involved in game design and test game design theories. Finally, game generation enables new game genres which are radically customized to specific players or situations; notable examples are cell phone games customized for particular users and newsgames providing commentary on current events. We describe an approach to formalizing game mechanics and generating games using those mechanics, using WordNet and ConceptNet to assist in performing common-sense reasoning about game verbs and nouns. Finally, we demonstrate and describe in detail a prototype that designs micro-games in the style of Nintendo's *WarioWare* series.

1   Introduction

Game generation systems perform automated, intelligent design of games, reasoning about both the abstract rule system of the game and the visual realization of these rules. While procedural content generation focuses on the generation of assets such as textures, meshes, animations, sounds, and the physical layout of levels, game generation involves the entire game design process, including generating the game rules themselves, the game mechanics that describe how the game state evolves over time, how player action influences the game state, and the audio-visual realization of the game.

The goal of our research is not to replace human designers, but rather to: facilitate formal game analysis through the computational expression of game

R. Basili and M.T. Pazienza (Eds.): AI*IA 2007, LNAI 4733, pp. 626–637, 2007.

rules, mechanics, and representations; enable new game mechanics and game genres where the game dynamically changes as a function of player interaction; move human design up the abstraction hierarchy to the meta-authorship of generative processes that generate games; and enable intelligent game design tools to support human game designers.

Game designers and scholars have discussed the need for a game design language, noting that there is no unified vocabulary for describing existing games and thinking through the design of new ones. While some semi-formal analysis languages are being developed [1], game design has not been described at the level of detail and formality necessary to support automatic generation. Automatic game generators can serve as highly detailed theories of both game structure and game design expressed operationally as a program. In the same way that AI-based story generators have, over the years, served as operational models of both narrative and the story generation process, and thus served to expose the strengths and weaknesses of different models of narrative, so too can game generation facilitate the development of a design science for games.

In addition to shedding light on the game design process, dynamic generation enables new game mechanics and game genres where the game dynamically changes (or is generated from scratch) as a function of player input or other exogenous events. Newsgames are one such category of game—micro-games that provide commentary on a news item, much like political cartoons. Unlike political cartoons, however, newsgames provide their commentary through gameplay: the point is made through interaction on the part of the player. Some well-known newsgames include *Madrid*,[1] a memorial game released shortly after the Madrid train bombings on March 11, 2004, and *Bacteria Salad*,[2] a game about the fall 2006 *E. coli* infections spread by spinach in the United States. To offer timely commentary on a news item, newsgames must be created rapidly, motivating the need for automatic (or at least AI-assisted) game design. Newsgames tend to be relatively small micro-games, making automated generation tractable, even in the short term.

In the rest of the paper, we describe our view of game design as a problem-solving activity comprising four major aspects of games, and describe a prototype system that generates games in the style of Nintendo's *WarioWare* games—short games that typically last several seconds, come in rapid sequence, and ask the player to do a single thing, such as dodging a car or shooting a duck.

2   Game Design as a Problem-Solving Activity

To understand game design as a problem-solving activity, we factor it into four interacting domains (or aspects): abstract game mechanics, concrete game representation, thematic content, and control mapping. A game design space (the space of possible games the design system can reason about) is defined by the

---

[1] http://www.newsgaming.com/games/madrid/

[2] http://www.persuasivegames.com/games/game.aspx?game=arcadewireecoli

knowledge given to the system for each of these domains. Though the domains interact, we hope to support the modular mixing and matching of different knowledge sources for each domain, thus supporting the rapid specification of new design spaces.

We'll use the 1983 arcade game *Tapper* as an example. *Tapper* is a nice example because is it well known within the game-design community, and small enough to allow formal analysis yet large enough to clearly exhibit all four knowledge domains. In *Tapper*, the player is a bartender who fills up mugs of beer and serves customers by sliding the beers down one of several bars. The customers move along the bars towards the bartender; serving a customer pushes him back towards the door. The goal is to push the customers out of the bar without letting any reach the bartender. Effective *Tapper* play is an exercise in rapid time management.

A game's *abstract game mechanics* specify an abstract game state and how this state evolves over time, both autonomously and in response to player interaction. In *Tapper*, the abstract mechanics are those of an order-fulfillment game: There are requesters (customers) who want certain items (beers) within time limits, sources for the player to get those items (taps), and a means for the player to ferry the items from the sources to the requesters (sliding them down the bar). The space of order-fulfillment mechanics is defined by general knowledge about requesters, sources, requested objects, the progression of time, and the relationships between each; the mechanics in *Tapper* are one instance, making commitments to specific design decisions in this space. Chess likewise makes concrete design commitments within the space of symmetric, 2D, tile-based games [2]. In *WarioWare* games, the abstract mechanics are usually a single rule, such as "avoid being hit for five seconds".

Concrete game representation specifies how the abstract mechanics are instantiated and represented to the player in a concrete game world, that is, the audio-visual representation of the abstract game state. In *Tapper*, the abstract time limit within which an order request must be serviced is represented concretely by the customer's position along the bar; in other games, an abstract time limit might be represented by a literal on-screen clock, through a slowly emptying bar graph, etc. In *WarioWare*, one concrete representation of the "avoid being hit for five seconds" abstract mechanic is a dodging game in which the player has to move around in a 2d top-down view and avoid getting hit. General knowledge about representational strategies for different types of abstract game states (and state transitions) constitutes a visual design space. Holding the abstract mechanics domain constant while changing the game representation domain results in a new overall design space, such as 3D, first-person order-fulfillment games (*Tapper* is a 2D, third-person game).

Thematic content comprises the real-world references expressed by the game. For example, *Tapper* takes place in a bar, with beer glasses, customers, and so on; *Diablo* takes place in a fantasy world with swords and monsters; *The Sims* takes place in a suburban house; and a *WarioWare* dodging game might have a person on a road dodging cars. The thematic knowledge domain comprises the common-sense knowledge about the real-world domain being expressed in the game. Holding the other domains constant while changing the thematic content domain results in a new overall design space, such as the design space of 2D order-fulfillment games set in fast-food restaurants.

Finally, *control mapping* describes the relationships between the physical player input, such as button presses and joystick movement, and modification of abstract game state. In *Tapper*, pressing a button at the tap begins filling a mug, while releasing the button stops filling and, if the mug is full, automatically slides it down the bar. Possible alternative mappings for filling the beer include repeatedly pumping the joystick back and forth, repeatedly hitting a button, holding the joystick down for a specified period of time, etc. (to say nothing of alternate physical control mechanisms such as dancepads or gestural controllers).

It might be tempting to see these four game-design aspects as a pipelined process: Come up with an abstract game, represent it concretely, add a "skin" of thematic content, and finally set up control mappings. That approach may work for some types of games, but we feel that enabling non-pipelined interactions between these aspects is likely to lead to more interesting and creative game designs. Even something as seemingly straightforward as setting up the control mappings is not a one-way street; for example, a game written for a computer with keyboard and mouse might call for different game mechanics and representations than one written for the Nintendo Wii, with its physical gestural controller (indeed, the idea that an interesting control scheme can lead to interesting game design is one of the core market hypotheses of the Wii).

Thematic knowledge should also ideally be more than a "skin" chosen according to the constraints of an already-designed abstract mechanic; instead, it should suggest gameplay opportunities as well. For example, thematic knowledge from a bar theme might lead a system to reason that as people drink they become drunk and that drunk people move erratically, suggesting that drunk customers might serve as obstacles for the player as they serve drinks, but only if the player is a cocktail server moving between tables. This movement from theme to mechanics and representation is particularly important for the generation of newsgames and other games dealing with real-world events, where much of the rhetorical force of the game depends on the appropriate incorporation of thematic elements into the gameplay—rather than merely skinning an off-the-shelf game with the faces of politicians or something equally superficial.

Of course, it is not a requirement that all games equally emphasize all aspects. In chess the thematic content and concrete realization are of minimal importance; design of interesting chess variants would focus on the abstract game mechanics. A first-person shooter, on the other hand, puts large emphasis on the game's concrete representation (3D graphics and physics); design of first-person shooters would focus on this aspect. Our goal is to have all these aspects available for interesting interaction when desired.

Like any problem-solving activity, game design is driven by goal achievement. These may be internal goals such as "maximize the variety in a collection of generated games" or "design an interesting game", where internal notions of variety and interestingness guide design; or external goals to create games with specific properties for one or more aspects of the design, or specific properties relative to a player model. For example, one might ask for a symmetric chess-like game with a certain locality of movement [2] (here abstract mechanics would be the guiding aspect of the design process), or an order-fulfillment game with a desired visual complexity in terms of the number of simultaneously moving objects on screen (here concrete representation would be the guiding aspect). For our *WarioWare*-style generator, we chose to focus on theme as the guiding aspect. Design goals are specified in terms of nouns and verbs; the generator's job is to create micro-games that are "about" the verb and/or noun. Since a micro-game instantiates a single, atomic game mechanic, and maps real-world referents onto this mechanic, such games are a nice vehicle for exploring the common-sense reasoning issues that arise in the thematic aspect of game design.

3   Generating *WarioWare*-Style Games

Although *WarioWare*-style micro-games are quite simple structurally, usually containing one or two pieces of abstract mechanics and lasting for no more than a few seconds, they are an example of a game style that actual game designers work on and release commercially (rather than an artificial toy domain), with a design space that touches on a wide cross-section of issues in game design [3]. Their abstract simplicity allows us to focus on the thematic elements of game generation, and the fact that they are lightweight games that are easy and quick to play meshes well with a number of potential applications, such as web-distributed casual games and customized cell-phone games.

3.1   Common-Sense Thematic Content

Since our initial focus is on the thematic aspect of game generation, we have the user direct the system by specifying a verb and/or noun to describe a desired theme (e.g. a game about "shooting" and "ducks"). Generating a game that fulfills the request is now a combination of two common-sense problems: The game should "make sense" in terms of the roles its thematic elements are playing, and it should be "reasonably close" to what the user requested.

To address both problems, we use a combination of the ConceptNet [4] and WordNet [5] knowledge bases. ConceptNet is a graph-structured common-sense knowledge base mined from OpenMind [6], a collection of semi-structured English sentences expressing common-sense facts gathered from online volunteers. ConceptNet's nodes are English words or phrases, and links between them express semantic relationships such as (`CapableOf "person" "play video game"`). Compared to more formally specified common-sense knowledge bases such as Cyc [7] and ThoughtTreasure [8], ConceptNet uses natural language and informal semantics. This is nice for ease of use and interfacing with text, but has drawbacks when it comes to ambiguity and inability to usefully respond to complex queries; nonetheless, it has been useful for a number of applications [9], and we have found it useful as well.

A second drawback of ConceptNet is that its coverage is somewhat weak: it knows that a duck can be shot, but not that a pheasant can be shot. Fortunately, combining it with data from WordNet mitigates this problem to a very large extent. WordNet is a similarly graph-structured knowledge base (ConceptNet's structure was based on WordNet's), but it positions itself as a dictionary rather than as a semantic knowledge base. Nonetheless, it contains semantic information in the form of word hierarchies, where a word below another one in the hierarchy is a specialization of the higher-up one (the higher word is a "hypernym", and the lower one a "hyponym" if a noun, or "troponym" if a verb). This information allows us to add inheritance to ConceptNet queries: If something is true of animals in general, then it is true for specific kinds of animals as well. Since ConceptNet knows that an animal can be shot, WordNet-based inheritance lets us figure out that a pheasant, as a specific kind of animal, can also be shot.

In addition to using WordNet to extend ConceptNet's coverage, we use its hypernymy relationships to determine simple attributes, such as whether a noun is animate (if it is, it will be below "animate thing" in the hierarchy). This is only possible for attributes deemed primary by WordNet—although we might say "money" is conceptually a type of "valuable thing", that isn't a sufficiently primary attribute for WordNet. Finally, we use distances between nouns and verbs in WordNet and ConceptNet, respectively, as simple measures of similarity. We use WordNet for nouns due to its fairly comprehensive taxonomy, and ConceptNet for verbs since this captures more complex notions of similarity such as "can operate on the same object". While link distance is a simple notion of similarity, it has worked well as a first approximation; in the future we plan to explore more complex measures [10].

3.2   Decomposing *WarioWare*

To facilitate generation, we abstract a number of styles of *WarioWare* games into abstract game types; currently the system knows about three of them. An *Avoid* game is one in which one entity, the "avoider", must avoid (for the duration of the game) one or more other entities, the "attackers", which may attack the avoider either directly or via other objects. The player can play either role. An *Acquire* game is one in which the player must find an object within a time limit. A *Fill* game is one in which the player must fill a meter within a time limit. These abstract game types capture the abstract mechanics the system currently knows about.

These game types can be implemented via several stock sets of concrete game mechanics, represented in a mixable J2ME (Java mobile platform) class library. A *Dodger* game is a 2d top-down game in which one object, the "dodger", tries to avoid one or more other entities, the "attackers"; it is used to implement some Avoid games and some Acquire games. A *Shooter* game is a 2d side-view game in which objects move across the screen, and can be shot by aiming crosshairs and firing; it is used to implement some Avoid games. A *Pick-Up* game is a 2d top-down game with a player and an object for them to pick up, usually through some obstacle such as a maze; it is used to implement some Acquire games. A

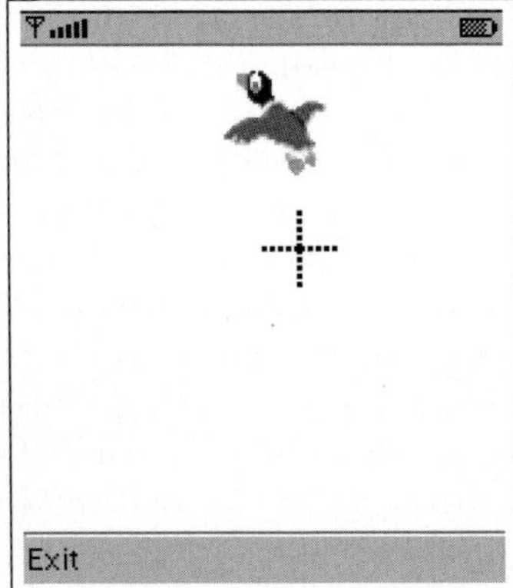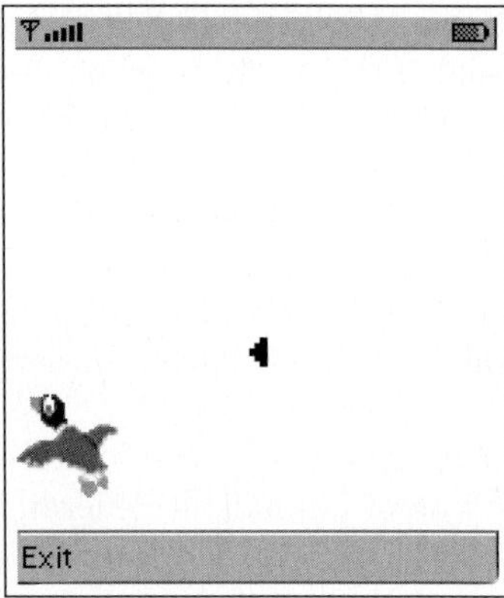

Fig. 1. Two games generated for the noun "pheasant" and verb "shoot". A duck is in both since it is the closest noun to "pheasant" for which the generator has a sprite. Both are Avoid games with Attacker-verb "shoot", Avoider-noun "duck", and Attacker-noun "bullet". The left game is implemented by the Shooter concrete mechanic and has the player trying to shoot the duck; the right game is implemented by the Dodger concrete mechanic and has the player, as the duck, trying to avoid bullets.

Pump game has a reservoir of some sort that needs to be filled up; it is used to implement some Fill games. A *Move* game has a player moving some distance; it is used to implement some Fill games.

Each of the five types of game mechanics can then be matched with composable movement managers that determine how the non-player-controlled objects will move, based on some common-sense reasoning about the thematic representation they've been assigned (see next section). For example, attackers in a Dodger game where the player plays the dodging side might chase the player (if animate) or travel in a straight line (if not). The interface mappings are currently bundled with the objects in the concrete game mechanics: If the player plays the dodging side in a Dodger game, then the controls will be arrow-keys to move. These concrete game mechanics capture the concrete representations and control mappings the system currently knows about. Finally, we have a stock set of sprites, each attached to a noun describing them, that can be used as the graphical representation of any of the objects in any of the games.

The end result of the generation process is a recipe for building a game. The game is then built out of the composable classes corresponding to the five sets of stock concrete mechanics (plus input and movement-control classes) to produce a running game. Screenshots of the realizations of two generated games are shown in Figure 1.

3.3 Common-Sense *WarioWare* Generation

In response to a request, we generate a number of games meeting a set of constraints on what games "make sense" in each of the three types of abstract games, and score them according to a heuristic measure of how "reasonably close" they are to the player's actual request. These games are then built and fed to the player in rapid-fire sequence, much as in Nintendo's original *WarioWare*, with the games growing increasingly distant from the original request as the system has to stretch further to find games satisfying the thematic request that it hasn't yet used.

We start by defining prototype verbs that specify some canonical ways of describing the action in each game. For example, an Avoid game from the perspective of the attacker has prototype verbs "attack", "injure", "shoot", and several more. If the user requests a verb, we compare it with a set of prototype verbs via ConceptNet distance (with closer verbs making for higher-scored games), to determine if the verb can be mapped onto one of the abstract game types. The original verb, not the prototype, is then used to determine which nouns can be mapped into the game.

Filling in a game's nouns is where the meat of common-sense reasoning comes in; the process varies per game type, but can usually be done to reasonable accuracy with surprisingly simple constraints once the basic logic of the game type is teased apart. We choose nouns from those for which we have sprites that meet the constraints of the game and are close to what the player requested. The methods we use for each of the three game types are described below. In addition to selecting the abstract game type, the specifics of the semantic relationships discovered between the noun and verb are also used to select the concrete realization (*e.g.* deciding to implement *Acquire* using *Dodger* with the player playing the attacker).

Avoid. The relationship of nouns and verbs in an Avoid game can follow two patterns: "Avoider-noun Avoids-verb being Attack-verbed by Attacker-noun"; or "Avoider-noun Avoids-verb an Attacker-noun Attacker-verbed by Instigator-noun". In the first case, an attacker directly attacks the avoider (*e.g.*, "person avoids being hit by car"), while in the second, an attacker is a projectile being used by some other noun (the instigator) to attack the avoider (*e.g.*, "pheasant avoids a bullet shot by gun"). Although both types of games make sense, it is important not to confuse one for the other, lest we end up with a gun shooting a pheasant by moving across the screen towards it instead of firing bullets at it. Since many of the same nouns could conceivably function in either type of game, we decide between these two phrases by testing the verb. We say that a game is of the projectile sort if the Attacker-verb is a type of verb that acts on devices; that is, whether for some noun that is a hyponym of "device", that noun is `CapableOfReceivingAction` the Attacker-verb.[3]

In either version, the Avoider-noun must be `CapableOfReceivingAction` the Attacker-verb, and furthermore must be an "animate thing". The

---

[3] We use "device" rather than "projectile" because some non-hyponyms of "projectile" can be used as projectiles, such as "baseball" and "hammer". There are also devices that would be awkward to use as projectiles, but with the semantic information in ConceptNet and WordNet they are difficult to avoid, so for now we admit some— hopefully amusing—games with unlikely projectiles.

Attacker-noun's constraints depend on whether this is a projectile or non-projectile Avoid game. In a projectile game, the Attacker-noun is a device being acted upon by the Attacker-verb, so it must be `CapableOfReceivingAction` the Attacker-verb and must be a "device". In a non-projectile game, the Attacker-noun is doing the attacking itself, so it must be `CapableOf` the Attacker-verb.

The player can be assigned to play either side. If assigned to play the Avoider-noun, the game is implemented by the Dodger concrete game mechanic. If the game is a projectile type game, then the Attacker-noun will be duplicated into multiple copies that move via a "move in a straight line" movement manager. If the game is a non-projectile type, then there will be a single Attacker-noun, controlled by a "chase the player" movement manager.

If the player is assigned to play the attacking side, the specifics depend on whether this is a projectile or non-projectile type game. In a projectile game, the player plays the Instigator-noun, and the game is implemented by the Shooter concrete game mechanic, with the player firing Attacker-noun projectiles. In a non-projectile game, the game is implemented by a Dodger game in which the player plays the Attacker-noun, and the Avoider-noun has a movement manager that runs away from the player.

Acquire. In an Acquire game, the situation is somewhat simpler. There is an Acquirer-noun, which the player always plays, and it is trying to acquire a Target-noun. The Target-noun must be a `DesireOf` the Acquirer-noun (for example, a squirrel may want to acquire a nut). The game is usually implemented by the Pick-Up concrete game mechanic, but if the Target-noun is an "animate thing", then it may also be implemented by the Dodger mechanic, with the player playing the attacker. In either case, a non-animate Target-noun will have a movement manager that causes it to sit still, while an animate Target-noun will run away from the player.

Fill. In a Fill game, the player is a Filler-noun trying to fill an abstract reservoir, which can be represented as a literal reservoir via the Pump concrete mechanic, or metaphorically by distance across the screen with the Move mechanic; there are prototype verbs for both. Once we've chosen a verb, we require that the Filler-noun be `CapableOf` the verb. If the verb is a troponym of "move", we generate a Move game; otherwise, we generate a Pump game with a Thing-To-Fill-noun that is `CapableOfReceivingAction` the verb.

4   Related Work

The earliest automatic game-generation system we're aware of is the component of METAGAMER [2] that generates "symmetric chess-like" games. METAGAMER itself is a general game player for such games: It takes a formal description of a particular game written in a grammar that can represent a class of games, and tries to figure out how to play it well. Given a class of games specified by a grammar, new games can be generated at random by following production rules in the grammar. To generate games that would test specific aspects of METAGAMER, Pell parameterized the generator along four axes so it could, via some heuristics, generate games with greater or lesser rule complexity, decision complexity, search complexity, and movement locality. Although the primary purpose of the generator was to provide games with which to test METAGAMER, Pell notes that it nonetheless generated some interesting games. From of our view of game generation, METAGAMER tackles the portion of game design involving the abstract gameplay mechanics.

EGGG [11], on the other hand, takes a formally specified game as its *input*, and from that generates a graphical, playable game. The formal specification gives the abstract mechanics for a specific game from one of several classes of games (chess-like games, card games, etc.), and also partly specifies the concrete game representation (*e.g.* whether the abstract rules should be represented as operating on cards or board pieces). EGGG itself then tackles the process of fleshing out the on-screen representation, assigning input mappings, and "compiling" this all into a final product. For two-player games it also generates an AI opponent, which could be seen as generating abstract game mechanics to flesh out the one-human-player version of the game.

Another body of work, mostly in the game industry and graphics field, aims to procedurally generate graphics, animations, terrain, and levels [12,13,14,15]. Though only a subset of the game design problem, procedural content generation would be a useful component of an automated game-design system, allowing it to generate custom content on demand rather than relying on libraries of canned content.

Holm, Jukka, & Arrasvuori [16] propose games that customize themselves to music, for example by synchronizing movement in the game to the music's beat. This is similar to our goal of customizing games, but it is not game generation *per se*, since the games are programmed explicitly to respond to music as input, rather than adapted on the fly by a process that explicitly reasons about the game's design.

Insofar as we're exploring an expressive domain at least partly in order to better understand the potential for computer creativity within it, there are similarities with work in automated story generation [17,18], art generation [19], music composition [20,21], and film generation [22]. The main difference is that in story generation the product is an interactive artifact, rather than text, art, music, or film, and so involves mechanics and dynamics as well as content.[4] A particularly interesting parallel is with MAKEBELIEVE [23], a demo that produces very short stories about a requested subject by querying OpenMind for plausible things the subject might do and stringing them together. Our prototype might be viewed as the interactive analog, generating micro-games that tell plausible stories about the noun and/or verb the user requests.

---

[4] It's worth noting that several of these systems [22,21] are themselves highly interactive, but they don't *generate* interactive systems.

5   Conclusions and Future Work

Automated game generation is a little-explored area of research that we feel holds great potential, both as a technique that would enable the development of new types of games, and as a research agenda that tackles the problem of machine creativity from the perspective of the generation of highly interactive artifacts. We described a general framework for viewing this problem, and a prototype system that generates games in the style of *WarioWare* about user-requested subjects, while respecting common-sense expectations about the roles of verbs and nouns in those games.

There are a large number of avenues for future work on this subject. In the short term, we plan to scale up our prototype to generate a wider variety of *WarioWare*-style games and gain feedback from users on the perceived strengths and weaknesses of the system to guide future improvements. We will also explore the use of the system to generate newsgames, using biased summaries of news stories as a starting point for generation. In the longer term, we'd like a more iterative blackboard approach to generation, in which different components of the generator revise a design-in-progress, allowing design failures in various aspects of the design to force revision of other aspects. To allow such a system to perform complex analysis of its design-in-progress, we envision a more formal representation of a game, perhaps as a high-level game simulation defined by logical assertions; in such a system, a more formal database of common-sense knowledge along the lines of Cyc might be a good fit.

Acknowledgments

We would like to thank Nuri Amanatullah, Thib Guicherd-Callin, Jeremy Hay, and Ian Paris-Salb (UC Santa Cruz) for developing a package to implement *WarioWare*-like games in J2ME; Ian Bogost (Georgia Tech) for useful discussions on various aspects of the project; and Chaim Gingold (Maxis) for suggesting *WarioWare* as an interesting game-generation domain. Thanks also to support from Intel and from the National Science Foundation's Graduate Research Fellowship Program.

References

1. Zagal, J.P., Mateas, M., Fernández-Vara, C., Hochhalter, B., Lichti, N.: Towards an ontological language for game analysis. In: DiGRA. Proceedings of the 2005 Digital Games Research Association Conference (2005)
2. Pell, B.: Metagame in symmetric, chess-like games. In: Allis, L.V., van den Herik, H.J. (eds.) Heuristic Programming in Artificial Intelligence 3: The Third Computer Olympiad, Ellis Horwood (1992)
3. Gingold, C.: What WarioWare can teach us about game design. Game Studies 5(1) (2005)
4. Liu, H., Singh, P.: ConceptNet: A practical commonsense reasoning toolkit. BT Technology Journal 22(4) (2004)

5. Fellbaum, C. (ed.): WordNet: An Electronic Lexical Database. MIT Press, Washington (1998)
6. Singh, P.: The public acquisition of commonsense knowledge. In: Proceedings of the AAAI Spring Symposium on Acquiring (and Using) Linguistic (and World) Knowledge for Information Access (2002)
7. Lenat, D.B.: CYC: A large-scale investment in knowledge infrastructure. Communications of the ACM 38(11), 33–38 (1995)
8. Mueller, E.T.: Natural Language Processing with ThoughtTreasure. Signiform, Online (1998), http://www.signiform.com/tt/book/
9. Lieberman, H., Liu, H., Singh, P., Barry, B.: Beating common sense into interactive applications. AI Magazine 25(4), 63–76 (2004)
10. Pedersen, T., Patwardhan, S., Michelizzi, J.: WordNet:Similarity: Measuring the relatedness of concepts. In: AAAI. Proceedings of the 19th National Conference on Artificial Intelligence (2004)
11. Orwant, J.: EGGG: Automated programming for game generation. IBM Systems Journal 39(3–4), 782–794 (2000)
12. Wright, W.: The future of content. Keynote address, 2005 Game Developers Conference (2005),
    Recording: http://www.gamasutra.com/features/20050525/wright_01.shtml
13. Roden, T., Parberry, I.: Procedural level generation. In: Pallister, K. (ed.) Game Programming Gems, vol. 5, pp. 579–588. Charles River Media (2005)
14. Compton, K., Mateas, M.: Procedural level design for platform games. In: AIIDE. Proceedings of the 2nd Artificial Intelligence and Interactive Digital Entertainment Conference (2006)
15. Zhou, H., Sun, J., Turk, G., Rehg, J.M.: Terrain synthesis from digital elevation models. IEEE Transactions on Visualization and Computer Graphics 13(4), 834–848 (2007)
16. Holm, J., Arrasvuori, J., Havukainen, K.: Using MIDI to modify video game content. In: NIME. Proceedings of the 2006 International Conference on New Interfaces for Musical Expression, pp. 65–70 (2006)
17. Meehan, J.: TALE-SPIN. In: Schank, R.C., Riesbeck, C. (eds.) Inside Computer Understanding: Five Programs Plus Miniatures, pp. 197–258. Lawrence Erlbaum, Mahwah (1981)
18. Turner, S.R.: The Creative Process: A Computer Model of Storytelling. Lawrence Erlbaum, Mahwah (1994)
19. Cohen, H.: What is an image? In: IJCAI. Proceedings of the 6th International Joint Conference on Artificial Intelligence (1979)
20. Cope, D.: Virtual Music: Computer Synthesis of Musical Style. MIT Press, Cambridge (2001)
21. Thom, B.: Interactive improvisational music companionship: A user-modeling approach. User Modeling and User-Adapted Interaction 13(1–2), 133–177 (2003)
22. Mateas, M., Vanouse, P., Domike, S.: Generation of ideologically-biased historical documentaries. In: AAAI. Proceedings of the 17th National Conference on Artificial Intelligence, pp. 36–42 (2000)
23. Liu, H., Singh, P.: MAKEBELIEVE: Using commonsense knowledge to generate stories. In: AAAI. Proceedings of the 18th National Conference on Artificial Intelligence, pp. 957–958 (2002)

Tonal Harmony Analysis:
A Supervised Sequential Learning Approach

Daniele P. Radicioni and Roberto Esposito

Dipartimento di Informatica, Università di Torino
{radicion,esposito}@di.unito.it
Corso Svizzera 185, 10149 - Torino

Abstract. We have recently presented `CarpeDiem`, an algorithm that can be used for speeding up the evaluation of Supervised Sequential Learning (SSL) classifiers. `CarpeDiem` provides impressive time performance gain over the state-of-art Viterbi algorithm when applied to the tonal harmony analysis task. Along with interesting computational features, the algorithm reveals some properties that are of some interest to Cognitive Science and Computer Music. To explore the question whether and to what extent the implemented system is suitable for cognitive modeling, we first elaborate about its design principles, and then assess the quality of the analyses produced. A threefold experimentation reviews the learned weights, the classification errors, and the search space in comparison to the actual problem space; data about these points are reported and discussed.

Keyword: AI in Art and Music; Cognitive Modeling; Machine learning; Music Analysis.

1   Introduction

Musical domain always exerted a strong fascination on researchers from very different fields; in the last few years a wealth of research has been invested in attempting to analyze music, under a twofold academic and industrial pressure. Not only music investigation is interesting *per se*, but it is also required by the novel forms of music e-commerce, e.g. to devise systems for recommendation, algorithmic playlist generation, and music summarization. Recent technological advances significantly enhanced the way automatic environments compose music [1], expressively perform it [2], accompany human musicians [3], and the way music is sold by web stores like iTunes, as well [4].

Music *analysis* is a necessary step for composing, performing and –ultimately– understanding music, for both human beings and artificial environments (see, e.g., the works in [5] and [6]). Within the broader area of music analysis, we single out the task of *tonal harmony* analysis. This is a challenging problem for music students, that spend considerable amounts of time in learning tonal harmony, as well as for automatic systems. In Western tonal music at each time point of the musical flow (or *vertical*) one can determine which chord is sounding:

R. Basili and M.T. Pazienza (Eds.): AI*IA 2007, LNAI 4733, pp. 638–649, 2007.

harmonic analysis mainly consists in indicating the fundamental note (or *root*) and the mode of the chord.

We have designed a system for tonal analysis, BREVE, where the analysis task is cast to a supervised sequential learning (SSL) problem [7]. From a methodological viewpoint, it transports to the musical domain the state-of-art machine learning *conditioned models* paradigm, originally devised for the part-of-speech (POS) tagging problem [8]. A set of *features* has been devised mimicking the main cues used by human experts to analyze music. Intuitively, the analysis of a musical piece can be computed by finding the optimum path in a layered graph (with T layers, one for each vertical) where a node represents one of the possible K labels. The most widely used algorithm to solve this problem is the Viterbi, a dynamic programming algorithm having $\Theta(TK^2)$ time complexity [9]. To overcome the quadratic dependence on K, we designed a novel algorithm, `CarpeDiem`, which finds the *optimal* path in $O(TK\log(K))$ time in the best case, degrading to Viterbi complexity in the worst case [10]. Further computational considerations about `CarpeDiem` have been carried out in [11].

In this paper we provide an assessment of the system for tonal harmony analysis. Since our approach puts together various insights from the fields of Machine Learning, Cognitive Science and Computer Music in an interdisciplinary fashion, several aspects are considered. We discuss experiments along three main lines: we elaborate on the meaning of the learned knowledge; we expand on committed errors; and analyze how the search strategy of `CarpeDiem` allows considering a reduced set of meaningful labels. One major strength lies in the attempt to discuss on the same table strengths and weaknesses of the two cooperating systems: BREVE and `CarpeDiem`. Yet, an interesting finding is that both accuracies and time performances reveal deep cognitive roots.

2   Tonal Harmony Analysis Problem

We define the problem of harmonic analysis as follows. In Western tonal music, at each time point of the musical flow one can determine which chord is sounding. A *chord* is a set of (three or more) notes sounding at the same time. Harmonic analysis consists in indicating the fundamental note (or *root*) and the *mode* of the chord, e.g., *C-Maj* or *F-min*, at each time point of the musical flow (Figure 1). Given a score, we individuate sets of simultaneous notes (*verticals*), and associate to each vertical a *label* ⟨*fundamental note, mode*⟩. We individuate added notes that can enrich the basic harmony: namely, the cases of seventh, sixth and fourth. This approach to the harmonic structure analysis directly compares, e.g., with that of [12]. However, an higher level *functional* analysis approach exists that aims at individuating harmonic functions in chords. We'll address the latter in future work.

To analyze the harmonic structure of a piece is a sequential task, where contextual cues play a fundamental role. We start by considering two main musical dimensions: vertical and horizontal information. The former grasps the simultaneity of sounds, whereas the latter applies to successions.

Fig. 1. The tonal harmony analysis problem consists of indicating for each vertical which chord is currently sounding. Excerpt from Beethoven's Piano Sonata Op.10 n.1.

Tonal harmony theory encodes how to build chords, that is which sets of pitches can be played simultaneously. For example, three main kinds or *modes* of chords are defined, and specifically they are *major*, *minor* and *diminished* chords. Optionally, these basic patterns can be enriched with added notes. This is an example of what we refer to as "vertical" information. Furthermore, tonal harmony theory encodes how to concatenate chords, that is which successions are acceptable: for example, after a *C-Maj* chord one could expect *F-Maj* or *G-Maj*, rather than *C♯-Maj*. This is an example of what we refer to as "horizontal" information.

To complicate things for music analysts, music can be incompletely stated (i.e., we could find only one or two elements of a major triad), or it can be stated by *arpeggio* (i.e., one note at a time); moreover, *passing tones*, *retards*, etc., can make the correct identification a less trivial task. In addition, one has to handle ambiguous cases, where composer's strategies aim at violating listener's expectation: intuitively, this corresponds to breaking "grammatical" rules. To disambiguate unclear cases, analysts refer to horizontal features of music as well. Hence, tonal harmony analysis can be represented as a sequential problem, where both vertical and horizontal aspects prove to be notably influential.

3   HMPerceptron Algorithm Grounded on `CarpeDiem`

The SSL task can be specified as follows [13]:

Given: A set L of training examples of the form (X_m, Y_m), where each $X_m = (x_{m,1}, \ldots, x_{m,T_m})$ is a sequence of T_m feature vectors and each $Y_m = (y_{m,1}, \ldots, y_{m,T_m})$ is a corresponding sequence of class labels, $y \in \{1, ..., K\}$.

Find: A classifier H that, given a new sequence X of feature vectors, predicts the corresponding sequence of class labels $Y = H(X)$ accurately.

Presently, X_m corresponds to a particular piece of music; $x_{m,t}$ is the information associated to the event at time t; $y_{m,t}$ is the chord label (i.e., the chord root and mode) associated to the event sounding at time t. The problem is, thus, to learn how to predict the sequence of chord labels given the musical events information.

The SSL problem can be solved with several techniques, such as Sliding Windows, Hidden Markov Models, Maximum Entropy Markov Models [14], Conditional Random Fields [15], and Collin's adaptation of the Perceptron algorithm to sequential problems [8] (henceforth, HMPerceptron).

BREVE is implemented by the HMPerceptron algorithm. Although not grounded on a solid probabilistic framework as some of the cited algorithms, the HMPerceptron is reportedly as accurate as other state of the art learning tools, with the advantage of faster learning times. The hypothesis acquired by the HMPerceptron has the form

$$H(X) = \arg\max_{\overline{Y}=\{\overline{y}_1\cdots\overline{y}_T\}} \sum_t \sum_s w_s \phi_s(X, \overline{y}_t, \overline{y}_{t-1}) \tag{1}$$

where ϕ_s is a *boolean* function of the sequence of events X and of the previous and current labels. The ϕ_s functions are called *features*: they are used by the algorithm to collect information about the salient aspects of the sequence being analyzed. The w_s weights are the parameters that need to be estimated by the HMPerceptron. This is done by iterating over the training set and updating the weights so that features correlated to correct outputs are emphasized, whilst those correlated with incorrect ones are penalized. We first introduce the features, and then focus on how the HMPerceptron works.

3.1   Features Design

In general, features are used to provide discriminative power to the learning system. They are evaluated at each time point t in order to compute an informed prediction about the label to be associated with the event. The present features analyze a small neighborhood of the current event, and return 1 if it contains evidence that the predicted label is correct. Formal definitions cannot be reported here for space reasons. We distinguish among *vertical* features, that do not require knowledge about the previously predicted label, and *horizontal* features, that make use of the surrounding context information: both classes are outlined in the following, where $x_{\cdot,t}$ denotes the current event, and y_t denotes the currently predicted label.

Vertical features. typically report about the presence (or absence) of some note in a given event, thus providing a proof for (or against) a given label. For example, the feature *Chord-root-is-asserted* informs about whether the root note of label y_t is present in event $x_{\cdot,t}$. This feature can provide a precious cue, since the root note is the most salient sound in any chord. Other features providing similar cues are *Fully-stated-chord*, *Asserted-added-note* and *Root-asserted-in-next-event*. Altogether, they form the class of features *Asserted-degrees*.

Features named *v-chord-notes-asserted* are triggered when exactly v notes of y_t are present in $x_{\cdot,t}$. In principle, the smaller is v, the lesser evidence exists for y_t.

It is relevant to point out that our features allow learning classifiers that naturally *generalize* to unseen chords. For instance, *Fully-stated-chord* will fire any time all the notes of label y_t are present in $x_{\cdot,t}$, regardless of whether y_t was present in the training set or not. Such generalization capabilities characterize all features we implemented, and are a major aspect of BREVE.

Horizontal features. can be arranged into two classes. One reports about how *meter and harmonic changes* relate. The other one reports about transitions relevant in tonal harmony theory. *Chord-changes-on-metrical-pattern* features account for the correlation of label changes and the *beat level* of a neighborhood of $x_{\cdot,t}$. We have two kinds of beat (accented, unaccented). In analyzing event $x_{\cdot,t}$, we consider events $x_{\cdot,t-1}$ and $x_{\cdot,t+1}$, too. We denote with triplets of 1 and 0 the eight possible metrical patterns. For instance, *010* denotes an accented event surrounded by two weak beats. The associated feature returns 1 if $y_{t-1} \neq y_t$ in correspondence of such a pattern.

Human analysts are known to refer to a reduced set of transitions frequent in tonal music. *Chord-transition-pattern* features are used to model them, as a way for biasing the system to behave accordingly. We represent a transition as a pattern composed by *i*) a starting mode and added note; *ii*) a distance between root notes, expressed in number of half-tones; *iii*) an ending mode and added note. For instance, the notation (*Maj7, 5, Maj*) refers to a transition from a major chord with added seventh to a major chord with no added note, whose roots are five half-tones apart (e.g., from *FMaj7* to *B♭Maj*).

Finally, both *Chord-changes-on-metrical-pattern* and *Chord-transition-pattern* features can be used to capture musical aspects that are deeply ingrained with musical style. On one side, this implies that restrictive constraints are posed to the stylistic homogeneity between training and testing sets. On the other one, such style sensitivity grasps valuable 'linguistic' aspects that characterize musical language.

3.2   Learning Strategy

As mentioned, to find the best sequence of chord labels for an excerpt can be seen as finding a path in a graph. An example of such a graph for the music analysis problem is reported in Fig. 2.

As a main difference w.r.t. non sequential classification tasks, to classify a sequence implies considering an exponential number of possible label sequences. For instance, in music analysis over 150 different chord labels exist, so that in principle 150^{200} possible labelings need to be examined in analysing an excerpt containing 200 events. In order to tame the complexity, a (kind of) *first order Markov assumption* can be made: this amounts to assume that observing any given label y_t does not depend on labels preceding $t-1$. Given the above assumption, Viterbi decoding can be used to decide about the best possible sequence of labels.

The HMPerceptron algorithm uses Viterbi decoding to evaluate H (see Equation 1) and estimates the weights associated to the features so to maximize H accuracy over the training set. Briefly stated, the algorithm works as follows. The weights vector is initially set to **0**. Then, for each example (a music excerpt) in the training set, H is evaluated using the current set of weights. If H correctly labels the entire sequence, nothing is done and the algorithm simply jumps to the following sequence. Otherwise, the weights vector is updated so to increment the weights of features that would have contributed to a correct classification, and to decrement the ones that caused a wrong classification.

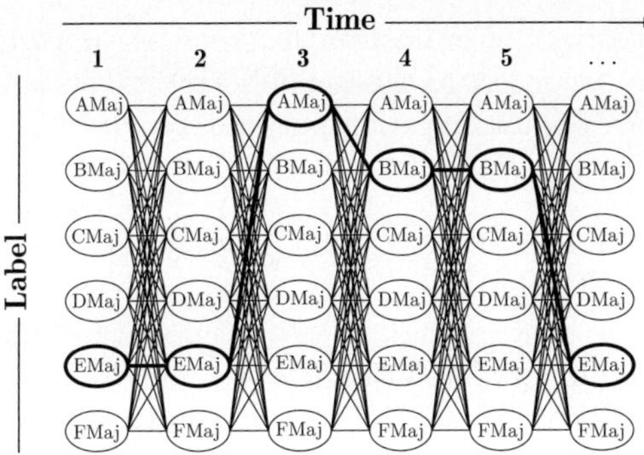

Fig. 2. Graphical representation of the labelling problem for $K{=}6$

3.3   `CarpeDiem` **Algorithm**

As mentioned, it is reasonable to assume that human analysts mainly exploit vertical information, resorting to horizontal cues primarily to resolve ambiguities [16,17]. This is to say that to label a given vertical, one *first* looks at information provided by the current event; *then* one uses surrounding context to make a decision if still in doubt. Relatedly, vertical information restricts the number of possibilities faced by the analyst, allowing human beings to only consider a subset of possible labeling alternatives.

`CarpeDiem` implements the described strategy: it uses vertical information over horizontal information, aiming at reducing the number of nodes considered per layer. To provide an intuitive description of the algorithm, it is worth recalling that Viterbi algorithm [9] spends most computational resources to evaluate the formula:

$$\max_{y_t, y_{t-1}} \left[\overbrace{\omega_{y_{t-1}}}^{\text{weight of the best path to } y_{t-1}} + \overbrace{\sum_s w_s \phi_s(X, y_t, y_{t-1}, t)}^{\text{weight for transition } y_{t-1}, y_t} \right] \qquad (2)$$

where $\omega_{y_{t-1}}$ denotes the weight of the best path to label y_{t-1}.

If we partition the set $\{1, 2, \ldots p\}$ of all feature *indexes* into the two sets Φ^0 and Φ^1, corresponding to indexes of vertical and horizontal features respectively, then the equation (2) can be rewritten into:

$$\max_{y_t} \left[\sum_{s \in \Phi^0} w_s \phi_s(X, y_t, t) + \max_{y_{t-1}} \left[\omega_{y_{t-1}} + \sum_{s \in \Phi^1} w_s \phi_s(X, y_t, y_{t-1}, t) \right] \right] \qquad (3)$$

Equation (3) is equivalent to Equation (2); in addition, it emphasizes how features in Φ^0 need to be evaluated only once per y_t label, and not once for each y_t, y_{t-1} pair. It is then obvious (and in accord with the intuition) that whenever $\Phi^1 = \emptyset$ the cost of the Viterbi algorithm can be reduced to be linear in the number of labels. The core idea underlying `CarpeDiem` is to exploit vertical information for avoiding the evaluation of the inner maximization as long as possible. In this way, we resort to the use of horizontal features only in case this is really necessary for the classification purposes.

4   Experimentation

In previous works we showed that BREVE accuracy is 81.5% on a corpus of Bach chorales; this figure lowers to 73.8% over a much less homogeneous dataset (namely, the Kostka-Payne corpus [18]). Also, `CarpeDiem` saves over 88% of classification time w.r.t. Viterbi [11]. Here we are concerned with the *quality* of its outcomes and, specifically, we explore *i*) whether the learned rules are meaningful, based on musical accounts; *ii*) whether the error analysis can shed any light or suggest any improvement to the set of features or to the classification strategy, and *iii*) whether the labels actually considered through the search process are to some extent similar to the 'reduced set' of labels considered by humans.

The system has been trained on a data set composed of 30 4-parts harmonized chorales by J.S. Bach. A different set of 42 chorales from the same author has been used for testing.

i) **Did we learn anything musically meaningful?** In Figure 3 we present the learned weights arranged into the four classes introduced above.

The highest positive weights involve vertical features (see for instance *Chord-root-is-asserted* (Fig. 3(a)) and *v-chord-notes-asserted* (Fig. 3(b))): as expected, information about which notes are currently sounding prevails over contextual information. In other terms BREVE, like human analysts, puts much emphasis on vertical information[1]. In considering *v-chord-notes-asserted* features (Fig. 3(a)), we see that the case *v=3* received more emphasis with respect to the case *v=4*. In the examined corpus events with 4 or more notes are likely to contain passing tones which mislead the *4-chord-notes-asserted* feature. Furthermore, the lower frequency with which the feature is asserted influences the magnitude of the learned weight as well.

In cases *v=1* and *v=2* we note how the features are used to report about evidence *against* a given label, rather than supporting it. We also note how the feature with *v=1* received a penalty heavier than the feature with *v=2*. This in spite of the fact that seeing one single asserted note provides, in principle, much more evidence against a given label w.r.t. seeing two of them. To understand this surprising fact, one needs to recall that the HMPerceptron changes the weight of a given feature when the predicted labeling is wrong. In particular, the algorithm decreases the weight of the features that voted for the wrong class, and increases the weight of features that voted for the correct one. *1-chord-notes-asserted* feature fires when harmony is only loosely stated. If, in the meanwhile, the correct label does contain exactly one of the sounding notes, then the feature

---

[1] It is also interesting to study the musical and cognitive effects of weights' evolution in a dynamic fashion, as learning proceeds. The surprising computational impact of weights evolution on classification times has been investigated in [11].

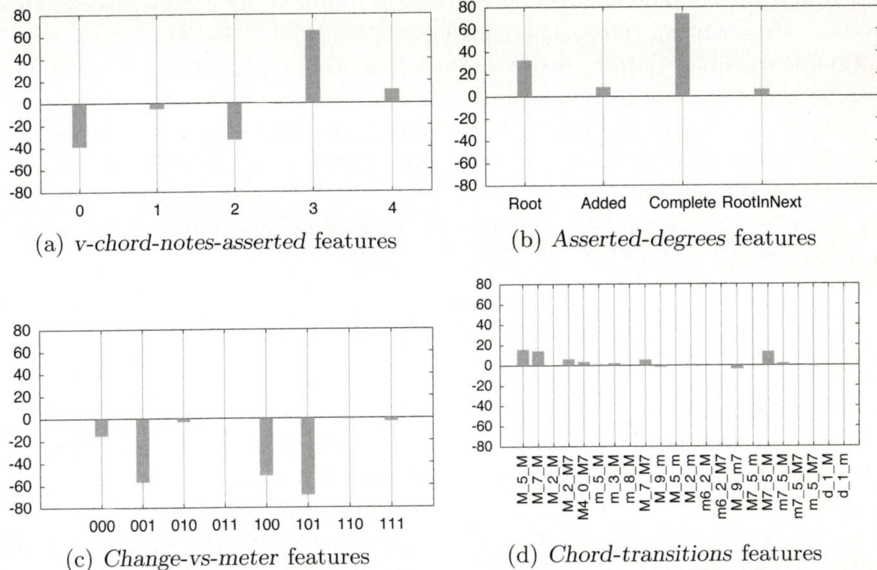

(a) *v-chord-notes-asserted* features (b) *Asserted-degrees* features

(c) *Change-vs-meter* features (d) *Chord-transitions* features

Fig. 3. Weights learned on a training set composed by 30 4-parts harmonized chorales by J.S. Bach. Graphics in the first row present weights obtained by vertical features, whilst in the second row the weights obtained by horizontal features are presented.

correlates with exact classification and its weight is augmented. On the contrary, when more notes are present and the classification is wrong, the label predicted by HMPerceptron probably contains more than a single note in common with the current vertical. Thus, the feature for *v=1* is not to be deemed responsible for the error and its weight is not decremented. The same explanation, with inverted arguments holds for $v = 2$, since this feature is the most likely to fire in correspondence of wrong labelings.

By looking at the *Asserted-degrees* features class (Fig. 3(b)), we observe that the features *Fully-stated-chord*, *Chord-root-is-asserted*, and *(2|3)-chord-notes--asserted* necessarily fire simultaneously. In such situations, the 'amount of evidence' in favour of y_t is overwhelming and BREVE will probably investigate only few alternative labels.

Let us now consider horizontal features (Figure 3(c) and 3(d)). Weights associated to harmony changes in correspondence with weak beats (*?0?* patterns) receive the highest penalty among all features. While harmony change is globally discouraged, the system clearly exhibits a preference for changing harmony on accented beats. The preference for chord transitions in correspondence with accented events substantially fits to experimental evidences and analytical strategies known in music cognition literature, e.g., the *Strong beat rule* proposed by [16], and experimentally verified by Temperley [17]. Interestingly, the speed of harmony changes is deeply ingrained with musical style: these features result in a rough way of modeling the harmonic rhythm and, as a consequence, they provide important indications about style.

Chord-transition-pattern features do not provide highly discriminative contributions to the classification process; they rather constitute refinement criteria when classification is ambiguous. This fact is somehow surprising, as in Bach chorales one would expect to find few, well-distinguished transition patterns. However, each and every transition in the *cadence* have been identified[2]. In fact, the following five best scoring features are those needed to build cadences.

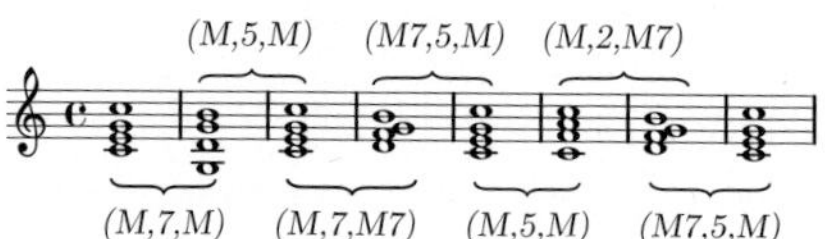

This fact would suggest that (at least for dealing with Bach chorales), it is possible to reduce the *Chord-transition-pattern* features to those involved in the cadence, in that all the other ones are mainly used for fine tuning purposes. A new experimentation with the *Chord-transition-pattern* features reduced to the five mentioned still obtains a 79.44% classification accuracy (2% less than with the full block).

ii) Do errors shed any light on the system's functioning, or suggest any improvement? As mentioned, BREVE is incorrect in the 18.5% of cases. A closer look at the errors shows some identifiable error classes. First, in about 30% of errors, we obtain completely wrong labelings. In these cases BREVE classifies with wrong root, wrong mode and wrong added note: i.e., situations where the system is totally mislead. In many cases the system is caught in interpretative nuances that are hardly avoided given the simplified input representation (e.g., the system cannot consider inversions, chord substitutions, nor tonality). In other cases, the resistance to chord changes forces the system to inherit by mistake previously attributed labels (this is especially true for chord changes on weak beats).

Among other mistakes, few errors appear execrable from the viewpoint of harmony theory. For instance, those due to confusing chord modes such as major with minor chords or viceversa. This is an error never committed by human analysts, and seldom committed by BREVE: only 5% of the overall error rate falls in this class. One may argue that a lager context is needed to improve on this issue.

The errors due to confusion between relative keys amount to 15% of the total. Relative keys are intrinsically related tones (in that they share the same *key signature* while having different roots), and to confuse between them is considered venial from a musical perspective.

Many errors (namely the 23.2%) are due to wrong added note (root and mode being correct). In these cases the chord is analyzed in a substantially correct

---

[2] Cadence is a sequence of chords comprising the close of a musical phrase, which is commonly acknowledged to be a sort of "cradle" of tonal language.

fashion. In some cases, it is again the resistance to chord changes that causes this kind of mistake. For example, in the case of succession F-$Maj{\rightarrow}F$-$Maj{\rightarrow}B\flat$-Maj let us consider the case that the added seventh of F-Maj is stated in correspondence of the second *unaccented* F-Maj chord. This case can be controversial even for human analysts, in that both F-Maj and F-$Maj7$ can be considered correct labelings for the second vertical. In summary, there is evidence that the system makes errors that are either venial, or justifiable on musical accounts, or due to information lacking in the input representation.

***iii*) Which labels are considered.** On average, BREVE inspects only a fraction of all possible labels. This datum, which grasps a kind of "computational effort" measure, correlates (though only mildly) with the classification error. In fact, if we consider the correctly predicted labels, BREVE inspects 48% of them; this figure raises to 62.5% in case of wrong predictions. In other words, to analyze difficult events a larger effort is required. We now show that inspecting few/more labels obeys a musically reasonable strategy.

Let us examine the behavior of BREVE in action as it analyses the first few measures from the chorale presented in the top part of Figure 4. We consider this toy example (many more labels are usually present) suitable to provide some insight on BREVE's inner mechanisms. At the bottom of the Figure we report three pictures showing the state of the analysis (i.e., nodes just inspected (opened), nodes yet to be opened, and nodes opened in previous steps), at the time points $t = 7, 8, 9$.

BREVE always inspects all nodes of the first vertical: only for the first time step this is a cheap operation that through a preliminary reconnaissance provides solid ground for subsequent investigation. In the subsequent steps, BREVE exploits vertical information to inspect only few labels.

Figure 4 points out a that counterintuitive fact occurs at $t = 8$. Even though ambiguities arise at time step 8, to solve them the algorithm inspects 16 labels for event 7, and only 3 for event 8. At $t = 8$ we have a passing note on a weak beat; notes sounding at $t = 8$ $\langle F\sharp,D,A,C\rangle$, make labels D-Maj, D-$Maj7$ and $F\sharp$-dim plausible. It is then necessary to find the best ancestors for those nodes in the 7th layer, thus considering their 'true' horizontal contribution to the maximization strategy (see [10]). Among the possible ancestors considered at time step 7 there are some that are not completely justifiable on musical accounts. BREVE often succeeds in reducing the search space by exploiting a bound on the maximal horizontal score. Instead, in the present case the bound is not sufficient to cut the search and the algorithm forcefully inspects even less musically justifiable alternatives like B-Maj. It is somehow ironic that, after all the efforts spent in analyzing this layer, metric considerations override any other criterion and prevent harmony from changing. Though correct, this is amazing, in that D-$Maj7$ chord is fully asserted, and it is remarkable how much horizontal features contribute to tune the classification towards meaningful labelings.

Fig. 4. The starting measures of the chorale *BWV 206* by J.S. Bach (top), along with three dumps of the analysis graph when dealing with the events at times $t = 7, 8, 9$ (bottom). *Gray* chord labels indicate nodes yet to be inspected (closed), while *black* labels stand for open nodes; *white* labels on a gray background indicate nodes that have been opened at the last step; finally, *underlined* labels indicate the correct label.

5   Conclusions

This paper addressed the issue of tonal harmony analysis, which is at the ridge of AI, Cognitive Science and Computer Music. After surveying the learning principles of the HMPerceptron algorithm, we have pointed out that music harmony is an appropriate test-bed for SSL classifiers. The classifiers designed for tonal analysis greatly benefit from working in conjunction with `CarpeDiem`. In addition to computational gain w.r.t. to the Viterbi algorithm, we argued that `CarpeDiem` performs analyses that are also more justifiable on cognitive grounds. Results have been presented about a threefold experimentation discussing *i*) the meaning of the learned weights –interpretable as high-level rules–; *ii*) which errors were committed –along with some arguments on causes and solutions–; and *iii*) the part of the search space actually explored.

Few final remarks about the future extensions of the work are in order. First, we will focus on extending the music representation to allow taking into account inversions, chords substitutions and functional analysis. Moreover, we are devising an extension of `CarpeDiem` that allows for the exploitation of higher order Markovian hypotheses.

References

1. Cope, D.: A Musical Learning Algorithm. Comput. Music J. 28(3), 12–27 (2004)
2. Grachten, M., Arcos, J.-L., López de Mantaras, R.: A Case Based Approach to Expressivity-Aware Tempo Transformation. Mach. Learn. 65(2–3), 411–437 (2006)
3. Raphael, C.: A Hybrid Graphical Model for Rhytmic Parsing. Artif. Intell. 137(1-2), 217–238 (2002)
4. Freeman, J.: Fast generation of audio signatures to describe iTunes libraries. Journal of New Music Research 35(1), 51–61 (2006)
5. Widmer, G.: Discovering Simple Rules in Complex Data: A Meta-learning Algorithm and Some Surprising Musical Discoveries. Artif. Intell. 146, 129–148 (2001)
6. López de Mantaras, R., Arcos, J.: AI and Music: From Composition to Expressive Performance. AI Magazine 23, 43–57 (2002)
7. Radicioni, D.P., Esposito, R.: A Conditional Model for Tonal Analysis. In: Esposito, F., Raś, Z.W., Malerba, D., Semeraro, G. (eds.) ISMIS 2006. LNCS (LNAI), vol. 4203, pp. 652–661. Springer, Heidelberg (2006)
8. Collins, M.: Discriminative Training Methods for Hidden Markov Models: Theory and Experiments with Perceptron Algorithms. In: Proceedings of the Conference on Empirical Methods in Natural Language Processing (2002)
9. Viterbi, A.J.: Error Bounds for Convolutional Codes and an Asymptotically Optimum Decoding Algorithm. In: IEEE Transactions on Information Theory, vol. 13, pp. 260–269. IEEE Computer Society Press, Los Alamitos (1967)
10. Esposito, R., Radicioni, D.P.: `CarpeDiem`: an Algorithm for the Fast Evaluation of SSL Classifiers. In: ICML 2007. Proceedings of the 24th Annual International Conference on Machine Learning (2007)
11. Esposito, R., Radicioni, D.P.: Trip Around the HMPerceptron Algorithm: Empirical Findings and Theoretical Tenets. In: Pazienza, M.T., Basili, R. (eds.) AI*IA 2007. LNCS, vol. 4733, pp. 242–253. Springer, Heidelberg (2007)
12. Pardo, B., Birmingham, W.P.: Algorithms for chordal analysis. Comput. Music J. 26, 27–49 (2002)
13. Dietterich, T.G., Ashenfelter, A., Bulatov, Y.: Training conditional random fields via gradient tree boosting. In: ICML '04. Twenty-first international conference on Machine learning, ACM Press, New York, NY, USA (2004)
14. McCallum, A., Freitag, D., Pereira, F.: Maximum entropy Markov models for information extraction and segmentation. In: Proc. 17th International Conf. on Machine Learning, pp. 591–598. Morgan Kaufmann, San Francisco, CA (2000)
15. Lafferty, J., Pereira, F.: Conditional random fields: Probabilistic models for segmenting and labeling sequence data. In: Procs. of the 18th International Conference on Machine Learning, pp. 282–289. Morgan Kaufmann, San Francisco, CA (2001)
16. Lerdahl, F., Jackendoff, R.: A Generative Theory of Tonal Music. MIT Press, Cambridge, MA (1983)
17. Temperley, D.: The Cognition of Basic Musical Structures. MIT, Cambridge, MASS (2001)
18. Kostka, S., Payne, D.: Tonal Harmony. McGraw-Hill, New York, NY (1984)

Words Not Cast in Stone

Carlo Strapparava, Alessandro Valitutti, and Oliviero Stock

FBK-irst, I-38050, Povo, Trento, Italy
{strappa, alvalitu, stock}@itc.it

Abstract. An advertising message induces in the recipient a positive (or negative) attitude toward the subject to advertise, for example through the evocation of a appropriate emotion. This paper is about the use of text processing techniques for proposing solutions to advertising professionals, opening up the way to a full automatization of the whole process. The system has two steps: (i) the creative variation of familiar expressions, taking into account the affective content of the produced text, (ii) the automatic animation (semantically consistent with the affective text content) of the resulting headline, using kinetic typography techniques.

1   Introduction

Variating familiar expressions (proverbs, movie titles, famous citations, etc.) in an evocative way has been an effective technique in advertising for a long time [1]. A lot of efforts by professionals in the field go into producing ever novel catchy expressions. Indeed it is common of "creatives" to be recruited in pairs formed by a copywriter and an art director. They work in a creative partnership to conceive, develop and produce effective advertisement. While the copywriter is mostly responsible for the textual content of the creative product, the art director focalizes efforts on the graphical presentation of the message. Advertising messages tend to be quite short but, at the same time, rich of emotional meaning and persuasive power.

We combined some computational functionalities for the semiautomatic creation of advertising messages. In particular, we implemented a strategy for the creative variation of familiar expressions. This strategy is articulated in two steps. The first consists in the selection and creative variation of familiar or common sense expressions. The second step consists in the presentation of the headline through automated text animation, and it is based on the use of kinetic typography.

1.1   Advertising Messages and Optimal Innovation

An advertising message induces in the recipient a positive (or negative) attitude toward the subject to advertise, for example through the evocation of an appropriate emotion. Another mandatory characteristic of an advertisement is its memorizability. These two aspects of an ads increase the probability to induce some wanted behaviours, for example the purchase of some product, the choice

R. Basili and M.T. Pazienza (Eds.): AI*IA 2007, LNAI 4733, pp. 650–661, 2007.

of a specific brand, or the click on some specific web link. In the last case, it is crucial to make the recipient curious about the subject referred by the URL. The best way to realize within an ads both attitude induction and memorizability is the generation of surprise, generally based on creative constraints.

In order to develop a strategy for surprise induction, we considered an interesting property of pleasurable creative communication that was named by Rachel Giora as the *optimal innovation hypothesis* ([2]). According to this assumption, when the novelty is in a complementary relation to salience (familiarity), it is "optimal" in the sense that it has an aesthetics value and "induce the most pleasing effect".

Therefore the simultaneous presence of novelty and familiarity makes the message potentially surprising, because this combination allows the recipient's mind to oscillate between what is known and what is different from usual. For this reason, an advertising message must be original but, at the same time, connected to what is familiar [1]. Familiarity causes expectations, while novelty violates them, and finally surprise arises.

1.2   Familiar Expression Variation

With "familiar expression variation" we indicate an expression (sentence or phrase) that is obtained through a linguistic change (e.g. substitution of a word, morphological or phonetic variation, etc.) of an expression recognized as familiar by recipients (e.g. selected by some collection of proverbs, famous movie titles, etc.). In this work we limited the variation to the word substitution.

Moreover, a headline should have a semantic connection with some concept of the target topic. At the same time, it has to be semantically related with some emotion of a prefixed valence (e.g. positive emotion as `joy` or negative emotion as `fear`).

We combined all these constraints in a compatible way with the optimal innovation hypothesis. The "innovation" is provided by the semantic similarity with the target topic and the emotion, and the "optimality" is guaranteed by the assonance (i.e. the old and the new word have to be assonant, e.g. rhymed).

We were inspired in this process by some works in computational humor (e.g. [3,4,5]) and mainly by our recent approach in this field [6], in which incongruity theory is exploited to produce funny variations of given acronyms. In this work we extend this approach, focussing on the affective load of lexicon for the variation production and generating automatically typographical animations that are coherent with the emotions we want to communicate.

The paper is structured as follows. In Section 2 we introduce the resources used in the system, in particular (i) WORDNET-AFFECT, an extension of the WordNet database in which some affective labels are assigned to a number of synsets; (ii) an affective semantic similarity, based on a Latent Semantic Analysis, which gives us an indication of the affective weight of generic terms; (iii) databases of familiar expressions and assonance tools; and (iv) a kinetic typography scripting language used for the final sentence animation. Section 3 describes the algorithm to variate familiar expressions and Section 4 displays some examples. Conclusions and future works are reported in Section 5.

2   Resources

2.1   Affective Semantic Similarity

All words can potentially convey affective meaning. Each of them, even those more apparently neutral, can evoke pleasant or painful experiences, because of their semantic relation with emotional concepts. While some words have emotional meaning with respect to the individual story, for many others the affective power is part of the collective imagination (e.g. words "mum", "ghost", "war" etc.).

We are interested in this second group, because their affective meaning is part of common sense knowledge and can be detected in the linguistic usage. For this reason, we studied the use of words in textual productions, and in particular their co-occurrences with the words in which the affective meaning is explicit. As claimed by Ortony et al. [7], we have to distinguish between words directly referring to emotional states (e.g. "fear", "cheerful") and those having only an indirect reference that depends on the context (e.g. words that indicate possible emotional causes as "killer" or emotional responses as "cry"). We call the former *direct affective words* and the latter *indirect affective words* [8].

In order to manage affective lexical meaning, we (i) organized the direct affective words and synsets inside WORDNET-AFFECT, an affective lexical resource based on an extension of WORDNET, and (ii) implemented a selection function (named *affective weight*) based on a semantic similarity mechanism automatically acquired in an unsupervised way from a large corpus of texts (100 millions of words), in order to individuate the indirect affective lexicon[1].

Applied to a concept (e.g. a WORDNET synset) and an emotional category, this function returns a value representing the semantic affinity with that emotion. In this way it is possible to assign a value to the concept with respect to each emotional category, and eventually select the emotion with the highest value. Applied to a set of concepts that are semantically similar, this function selects subsets characterized by some given affective constraints (e.g. referring to a particular emotional category or valence).

As we will see, we are able to focus selectively on positive, negative, ambiguous or neutral types of emotions. For example, given "difficulty" as input term, the system suggests as related emotions: IDENTIFICATION, NEGATIVE-CONCERN, AMBIGUOUS-EXPECTATION, APATHY. Moreover, given an input word (e.g. "university") and the indication of an emotional valence (e.g. positive), the system suggests a set of related words through some positive emotional category (e.g. "professor" "scholarship" "achievement") found through the emotions ENTHUSIASM, SYMPATHY, DEVOTION, ENCOURAGEMENT.

This fine-grained affective lexicon selection can open up new possibilities in many applications that exploit verbal communication of emotions. For example,

---

[1] In particular, we used the British National Corpus, a very large (over 100 million words) corpus of modern English, both spoken and written (see `http://www.hcu.ox.ac.uk/bnc/`). Of course, it is possible to add and/or consider specific corpora to get a more domain oriented similarity.

[9] exploited the semantic connection between a generic word and an emotion for the generation of affective evaluative predicates and sentences.

WORDNET-AFFECT *and the Emotional Categories.* WORDNET-AFFECT is an extension of the WordNet database [10], including a subset of synsets suitable to represent affective concepts. Similarly to what was done for domain labels [11], one or more affective labels (*a-labels*) are assigned to a number of WordNet synsets. In particular, the affective concepts representing an emotional state are individuated by synsets marked with the a-label EMOTION. There are also other a-labels for those concepts representing moods, situations eliciting emotions, or emotional responses. WORDNET-AFFECT is freely available for research purpose at `http://wndomains.itc.it`. See [12] for a complete description of the resource.

Table 1. Number of elements in the emotional hierarchy

	# Synsets	*# Words*	*# Senses*
Nouns	280	539	564
Adjectives	342	601	951
Verbs	142	294	430
Adverbs	154	203	270
Total	918	1637	2215

We extended WORDNET-AFFECT with a set of additional a-labels (i.e. the *emotional categories*), hierarchically organized, in order to specialize synsets with a-label EMOTION. In a second stage, we introduced some modifications, in order to distinguish synsets according to emotional valence. We defined four additional a-labels: POSITIVE, NEGATIVE, AMBIGUOUS, NEUTRAL. The first one corresponds to "positive emotions", defined as emotional states characterized by the presence of positive edonic signals (or pleasure). It includes synsets such as `joy#1` or `enthusiasm#1`. Similarly the NEGATIVE a-label identifies "negative emotions" characterized by negative edonic signals (or pain), for example `anger#1` or `sadness#1`. Synsets representing affective states whose valence depends on semantic context (e.g. `surprise#1`) were marked with the tag AMBIGUOUS. Finally, synsets referring to mental states that are generally considered affective but are not characterized by valence, were marked with the tag NEUTRAL.

Computing Lexical Affective Semantic Similarity. There is an active research direction in the NLP field about sentiment analysis and recognition of semantic orientation from texts (e.g. [13,14,15]). In our opinion, a crucial issue is to have a mechanism for evaluating the semantic similarity among generic terms and affective lexical concepts. To this aim we estimated term similarity from a large scale corpus (i.e. the BNC in our case). In particular we implemented a variation of Latent Semantic Analysis (LSA). LSA yields a vector space model that allows for a *homogeneous* representation (and hence comparison) of words, word sets, sentences and texts. For representing word sets and texts by means of a LSA vector, we used a variation of the *pseudo-document* methodology described in [16]. This variation takes into account also a *tf-idf* weighting schema (see [17] for more details). In practice, each document can be represented in the LSA space by summing up the normalized LSA vectors of all the terms contained in it. Also a synset in WORDNET (and then an emotional category) can be represented in the LSA space, performing the pseudo-document technique on all the words contained in the synset. Thus it is possible to have a vectorial representation of each emotional category in the LSA space (i.e. the *emotional vectors*), and consequently we can compute a similarity measure among terms and affective categories. We defined the *affective weight* [9] as the similarity value between an emotional vector and an input term vector (e.g. we can check how a generic term is similar to a given emotion).

For example, the noun "gift" is highly related to the emotional categories: LOVE (with positive valence), COMPASSION (with negative valence), SURPRISE (with ambiguous valence), and INDIFFERENCE (with neutral valence).

In summary, the vectorial representation in the Latent Semantic Space allows us to represent, in a *uniform* way, emotional categories, generic terms and concepts (synsets), and eventually full sentences.

2.2   Database of Familiar Expressions

The base for the strategy of "familiar expression variation" is the availability of a set of expressions that are recognized as familiar by English speakers.

We considered three types of familiar expressions: proverbs, movie titles, clichés. We collected 1836 familiar expressions from the Web, organized in three types: common use proverbs (628), famous movie titles (290), and clichés (918). Proverbs were retrieved in some of many web sites in which they are grouped (e.g. `http://www.francesfarmersrevenge.com/ stuff/proverbs.htm` or `www. manythings.org /proverbs`). We considered only proverbs of common use. In a similar way we collected clichés, that are sentences whose overuse often makes them humorous (e.g. home sweet home, I am playing my own game). Finally, movie titles were selected from the Internet Movie Database (`www.imdb.com`). In particular, we considered the list of the best movies in all sorts of categories based on votes from users.

The list of familiar expressions is composed mostly of sentences (in particular, proverbs and clichés), but part of them are phrases (in particular, movie title list includes a significant number of noun phrases)

2.3   Assonance Tool

To cope with this aspect we got and reorganized the CMU pronouncing dictionary (`http://www.speech.cs.cmu.edu/cgi-bin/cmudict`) with a suitable indexing. The CMU Pronouncing Dictionary is a machine-readable pronunciation dictionary for North American English that contains over 125,000 words and their transcriptions.

Its format is particularly useful for speech recognition and synthesis, as it has mappings from words to their pronunciations in the given phoneme set. The current phoneme set contains 39 phonemes; vowels may carry lexical stress.

2.4   Kinetic Typography Scripting Language

Kinetic typography is the technology of text animation, i.e. text that uses movement or other changes over time. The advantage of kinetic typography consists in a further communicative dimension, combining verbal and visual communication, and providing opportunities to enrich the expressiveness of static texts. According to [18], kinetic typography can be used for three different communicative goals: capturing and directing attention of recipients, creating characters, and expressing emotions. A possible way of animating a text is mimicking the typical movement of humans when they express the content of the text (e.g. "Hi" with a jumping motion mimics exaggerated body motion of humans when they are really glad).

Taking Kinetic Typography Engine (KTE), a Java package developed at the Design School of Carnegie Mellon University [18], as a starting point, we first realized a development environment for the creation and the visualization of text animations. Our model for the animation representation is a bit simpler than the KTE model. The central assumption consists of the representation of the animation as a composition of elementary animations (e.g. linear, sinusoidal or exponential variation). In particular, we consider only one operator for the identification of elementary animations (K-BASE) and three composition operators: kinetic addition (K-ADD), kinetic concatenation (K-JOIN), and kinetic loop (K-LOOP).

The K-BASE operator selects an elementary animation (named *elementary kinetic behavior*) as a temporal variation of some kinetic property. Elementary kinetic behaviors correspond to a subset of dynamic variations implemented in KTE, for example linear variation (*linear*), sinusoidal variation (*oscillate*), and exponential variation (*exponential*).

The kinetic addition (K-ADD) of two animations with the same start time is obtained by adding, for each kinetic property of text, the corresponding

Table 2. Some elementary kinetic behaviors

linear	linear variation
oscillate	sinusoidal variation
pulse	impulse
jitter	sort of "chaotic" vibration
curve	parabolic variation
hop	parabolic variation with small impulses at the endpoints
hop-secondary	derivative of hop, used as secondary effect to simulate elastic movements

dynamical variation of each single animation. The kinetic concatenation (K-JOIN) consists in the temporal shifting of the second animation, so that the ending time of the first is the starting time of the second. The kinetic loop (K-LOOP) concatenates an animation with itself a fixed number of times. In the development environment it is possible to freely apply these operators for the real time building of new animations. Compositional structure of animations can be represented in XML format and then easily exported. Finally, an interpreter allows us to generate in real time the animation starting from its structural representation.

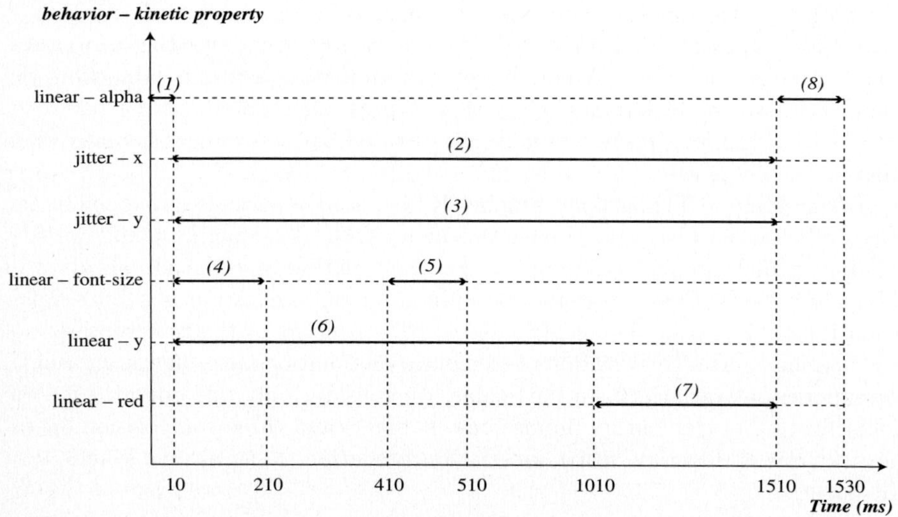

Fig. 1. Kinetic behavior description for "anger" emotion

Fig. 2. Jittering *anger*

After building the development tool, we selected a set of emotional categories and, for each of them, we created the corresponding text animations.

In particular, we focused on five emotional categories: joy, fear, surprise, anger, sadness (i.e. a subset of Ekman emotions [19]).

The kinetic animation to associate to a fixed emotion can be realized imitating either emotional and physiological rensponses (*analogous motion* technique), or tone of voice. We consider only animations of the first type, i.e. we represent each emotion with an animation that simulates a particular emotional behavior. In particular, JOY is represented with a sequence of hops, FEAR with palpitations, ANGER with a strong tremble and blush, SURPRISE with a sudden swelling of text, and finally SADNESS with text deflaction and getting squashed. Thus we annotated the corresponding emotional categories in WORDNET-AFFECT with these kinematic properties.

Figure 1 displays in detail the behavior of the anger emotion, showing the time-dependent composition graph of the basic animations. The string appears (1) and disappears (8) with a linear variation of the alpha property (that defines the transparency of a color and can be represented by a float value). The animation is contained between these two intervals and its duration is 1500 ms. The first component is a tiny random variation of the position (2) (3), represented by x and y kinetic properties, with jitter behavior. The second component consists of an expansion of the string (4) and a subsequent compression (5). The third component is given by a slow rise up (6). The last component, before disappearing, is a color change to red (7). The whole behavior is then described and implemented using the scripting language introduced above.

As it is difficult to enjoy the animations on *static* paper, please visit the web page `http://tcc.itc.it/people/strapparava/affective-KT` where some downloadable short movies are available.

3   Algorithm

In this section, we describe the algorithm developed to perform the creative variation of an existing familiar expression.

1. **Insertion of an input concept.** The first step of the procedure consists of the insertion of an input concept. This is represented by one or more words, a set of synonyms, or a WordNet synset. In the latter case, it is individuated through a word, the part of speech (noun, adjective, verb, or adverb), and the sense number, and it corresponds to a set of synonyms. Using the pseudo-document representation technique described above, the input concept is represented as a vector in the LSA vectorial space. For example, say that a cruise vacation agency seeks to produce a catchy message on the topics "vacation" and "beach".

2. **Generation of the target-list.** A list (named *target-list*) including terms that are semantically connected (in the LSA space) with the input concept(s) is generated. This target list represents a semantic domain that includes the input concept(s).For example, given the vector representing "vacation", "beach", the LSA returns a list "sea", "hotel", "bay", "excursion", etc.

3. **Association of assonant words.** For each word of the target-list one or more possible *assonant words* are associated. Then a list of word pairs (named *variation-pairs*) is created. The list of variation-pairs is filtered according to some constraints. The first one is syntactic (elements of each pair must have the same part of speech). The second one is semantic (i.e. the second element of each pair must not be included in the target-list), and its function is to realize a semantic opposition between the elements of a variation pair. Finally, to each variation pair an *emotion-label* (representing

the emotional category most similar to the substituting word) is provided with the corresponding affective weight. Some possible assonant pairs for the example above are: *(bay, day)*, *(bay, hay)*, *(hotel, farewell)*, etc.

4. **Creative variation of familiar expressions.** In this step, the algorithm gets in input a set of familiar expressions (in particular, proverbs and movie titles) and, for each of them, generates all possible variations. The list of variated expressions is ordered according to the global affective weight.

Following the example, a resulting ad is *Tomorrow is Another Bay* as a variation of the familiar expression *Tomorrow is Another Day*. Note that still for moment, the final choice among the best resulting expressions proposed by system is left to human selection.

At this point, the variated expression is animated with kinetic typography, as explained in the above section. In particular, words are animated according to the underlying emotion to emphasize the affective connotation.

4   Examples

In this section we want to show some additional examples of the creative variations.

Using the affective weight function, it is possible to select a variation according to the valence (e.g. the substitution of the word *bad*, detected as negative, with *glad*, recognized as positive) or to push some affective direction.

Table 3 shows how word substitution may propagate the change of connotation at the level of the entire expressionIn particular, we observed that the semantic opposition, determined by switching affective polarity, generates another more complex semantic opposition at phrase (or sentence) level. In a possible scenario in which the creative user interacts with the system to generate creative headlines, the human recognition of high level humorous effects may be part of the creative interaction. The system proposes a list of possible candidates and the user makes the ultimate decision, selecting the creative variations that seem more meaningful.

Table 3. Some variations on proverbs

Original	Variation	Category
when all else fails, read the instructions	when all else fails, *dread* the instructions	Fear
children and fools tell the truth	children and fools *repel* the truth	Repugnance
divide and rule	divide and *cool*	Coolness
a guilty conscience feels continual fear	a guilty conscience feels continual *cheer*	Cheerfulness

In Table 4 there are some examples of automatically generated advertising expressions from movie titles. The creative variation has a semantic connection with a target topic and it is suitable for advertising purposes. In the first example, the original word *park* is substituted by the work *dark*, that have high semantic similarity with a target topic (*clothes*) and has a negative affective weight. The global expression communicate the idea that the colours for the new fashion must be light and the dark clothes are old fashioned. The second example shows the substitution of the original word *night* with the word *fright* , that is semantically similar to the target topic *crash* and has a negative affective weight. The entire phrase can be used to warn young drivers about alcool related driving accidents. The third example could be an ad for caution towards the risk of aesthetic surgery (note the similarity between "surgery" and "suture"), while the fourth one could be proposed for a campaign against internet frauds.

Table 4. Variations for advertising headlines

Original	Variation	Category
Jurassic Park	Jurassic *Dark*	Gloom
Saturday Night Fever	Saturday *Fright* Fever	Fear
Back to the Future	Back to the *Suture*	Apprehension
The Silence of the Lambs	The Silence of the *Scams*	Distress

5   Discussion

From an application point of view we think the world of advertisement has a great potential for the adoption of AI techniques.

Investments are important, we are talking about a relevant economical sector. For instance in the UK alone in 2002 about 28,000 million euro were spent in advertisement (source Ac Nielsen and IPA). Media used for getting the message across to the public is quite conservative at present. For instance in Italy in 2004 the large Italian companies (the first 200 investors) aimed 74% of their investments towards TV commercials. For the total market TV commercials got about 56%, while radio 5%. So we can say that media based on some technology prevails, and also that within technology images have the lion's share. If we look at printed advertisement we observe that 21% advertisement investments went with newspapers, 14% with magazines and 2.4% with posters. So, it seems it is not just a matter of image but also that the market favors being bound to recent news. Of course internet appears as a fundamental medium already now. Internet advertising was about 9.4 billion $ (8,000 million euro) in 2004 according to Kagan Research LLC. And growth is very fast: Google advertisement revenues went from 0 to 3,400 million euro in five years according to Business Week.

The future will probably include two important factors: a) reduction in time to market and extension of possible occasions for advertisement; b) more attention to the wearing out of the message and for the need for planning variants and connected messages across time and space; c) contextual personalisation, on the basis of audience profile and perhaps information about the situation. Leaving alone questions of privacy as far as this paper is concerned (but of course advertisement and promotion can be for a good cause and for social values!), all three cases call for a strong role for computer-based intelligent technology for producing novel appropriate advertisements.

In this paper, exploiting some state-of-the-art natural language processing techniques, we described a system that produces creative variations of familiar expressions and animates them accordingly to the affective content. The creative textual variations are based on lexical semantics techniques such as affective similarity, while the animation makes use of a kinetic typography dynamic scripting language.

From an applied point of view, we believe that a thorough environment for proposing solutions to advertising professionals can be a practical development of this work, for the moment leaving the last word to the human professional. In the future, the potential of fully automatic production of advertisements will have a special role if linked to an evolving context, such as incoming news, or changing of audience location and tailored to the specific audience characteristics.

Acknowledgments

This work was developed in the context of HUMAINE Network of Excellence.

References

1. Pricken, M.: Creative Advertising. Thames & Hudson (2002)
2. Giora, R.: On Our Mind: Salience, Context and Figurative Language. Oxford University Press, New York (2003)
3. Masterman, M.: Computerized haiku. In: Reichardt, J. (ed.) Cybernetics, art and ideas, Studio Vista, London (1971)
4. Binsted, K., Ritchie, G.: Computational rules for punning riddles. Humor 10(1) (1997)
5. Binsted, K., Takizawa, O.: BOKE: A japanese punning riddle generator. The Journal of the Japanese Society for Artificial Intelligence 13, 920–927 (1998)
6. Stock, O., Strapparava, C.: Getting serious about the development of computational humour. In: IJCAI-03. Proceedings of the 18th International Joint Conference on Artificial Intelligence, Acapulco, Mexico (August 2003)
7. Ortony, A., Clore, G.L., Foss, M.A.: The psychological foundations of the affective lexicon. Journal of Personality and Social Psychology 53, 751–766 (1987)
8. Strapparava, C., Valitutti, A., Stock, O.: The affective weight of lexicon. In: LREC 2006. Proceedings of the Fifth International Conference on Language Resources and Evaluation, Genoa, Italy (May 2006)
9. Valitutti, A., Strapparava, C., Stock, O.: Lexical resources and semantic similarity for affective evaluative expressions generation. In: Tao, J., Tan, T., Picard, R.W. (eds.) ACII 2005. LNCS, vol. 3784, Springer, Heidelberg (2005)
10. Fellbaum, C.: WordNet. An Electronic Lexical Database. The MIT Press, Cambridge (1998)
11. Magnini, B., Cavaglià, G.: Integrating subject field codes into wordnet. In: LREC2000. Proc. of the 2nd International Conference on Language Resources and Evaluation, Athens, Greece (2000)

12. Strapparava, C., Valitutti, A.: WordNet-Affect: an affective extension of WordNet. In: LREC 2004. Proc. of 4th International Conference on Language Resources and Evaluation, Lisbon (May 2004)
13. Turney, P., Littman, M.: Measuring praise and criticism: Inference of semantic orientation from association. ACM Transactions on Information Systems (TOIS) 21(4), 315–346 (2003)
14. Liu, H., Lieberman, H., Selker, T.: A model of textual affect sensing using real-world knowledge. In: IUI 2003. Proc. of the Seventh International Conference on Intelligent User Interfaces, Miami (2003)
15. Mihalcea, R., Liu, H.: A corpus-based approach to finding happiness. In: Proc. of Computational approaches for analysis of weblogs, AAAI Spring Symposium 2006, Stanford (March 2006)
16. Berry, M.: Large-scale sparse singular value computations. International Journal of Supercomputer Applications 6(1), 13–49 (1992)
17. Gliozzo, A., Strapparava, C.: Domains kernels for text categorization. In: CoNLL-2005. Proc. of the Ninth Conference on Computational Natural Language Learning, Ann Arbor (June 2005)
18. Lee, J., Forlizzi, J., Hudson, S.: The kinetic typography engine: An extensible system for animating expressive text. In: Proc. of ACM UIST 2002 Conference, ACM Press, New York (2002)
19. Ekman, P.: Biological and cultural contributions to body and facial movement. In: Blacking, J. (ed.) Anthropology of the Body, pp. 34–84. Academic Press, London (1977)

Annotations as a Tool for Disclosing Hidden Relationships Between Illuminated Manuscripts

Maristella Agosti, Nicola Ferro, and Nicola Orio

Department of Information Engineering, University of Padua, Italy
{agosti, ferro, orio}@dei.unipd.it

Abstract. Image digital archives of illuminated manuscripts can become a useful tool for researchers in different disciplines. To this aim, it is proposed to provide them with tools for annotating images to disclose hidden relationships between illustrations belonging to different works. Relationships can be modeled as typed links, which induce an hypertext over the archive. In this paper we present a formal model for annotations, which is the basis to build methods for automatically processing existing relationships among link types and exploiting the properties of the graph which models the hypertext.

1   Introduction

The ideas and concepts reported in this paper build upon our experience on the analysis of the user requirements, the design of a methodology, the development of a prototype system, and the analysis of the feedback from real users of a digital archive of historical material. The archive aims at the study and research on *illuminated manuscripts*, which are books, usually handwritten, that include illustrations and, in the past centuries, were manually and artistically decorated. Illuminated manuscripts are still the subject of scientific research in different areas, namely history of arts and history of science, and all the disciplines that are related to the subject of the book – e.g., botany, astronomy, medicine. Before the invention of photography, illuminated manuscripts have been the main mean for the dissemination of the scientific culture, and to this end play a major role as witness of the cultural heritage of different cultures, in Europe, Asia, and in the countries under the influence of the Arabic culture. The particular application to the cultural heritage domain poses interesting problems and challenges as reported in [5].

According to reached results [1,2] and a deep study about annotations [3,4], the use of annotations has been proposed as a useful way of accessing a digital archive, sharing knowledge in a collaborative environment of researchers, disseminating research results to students, automatically analysing user's annotations, with the aim of highlighting inconsistencies and suggesting new relationships among the images of the digital archive. The use of annotations as a research tool in the humanities has been reported also in [6].

The prototype digital archive of illuminated manuscripts that has been developed within our research activities has been called IPSA (Imaginum Patavinae

R. Basili and M.T. Pazienza (Eds.): AI*IA 2007, LNAI 4733, pp. 662–673, 2007.

Scientiae Archivum, archive of images of the Paduan science) [1,2], because the main focus of our initial project was to provide a tool for the analysis of the role of the Paduan school during the Middle Ages and the Renaissance for the spread of the new scientific method in difference sciences, from medicine to astronomy. IPSA is a case study for our research on methodologies and tools for researchers and scholars working on the study, the preservation and the dissemination of the cultural heritage. In this paper we focus on the modelling of additional functionalities that will be developed in the next release of the prototype.

The paper is structured as follows. In Section 2 we introduce the motivations and objectives of our work. The formal model for annotations of the content of a digital archive is presented in Section 3, and the methods exploited for automatic suggestions are presented in Section 4. Conclusions are drawn in Section 5.

2   Motivations and Objectives

Even if the primary goal of images in illuminated manuscripts was to represent the reality, during the Middle Ages authors of drawings were more interested on aesthetics than on realism and the primary role of illuminated manuscripts as a tool for scientists was lost. Images were often copied from or inspired by existing manuscripts, while the resulting drawings became increasingly different from the subjects they should represent. For researchers, it is of primary importance to state if drawings of a illuminated manuscripts are copied from previous manuscripts or if they are directly inspired by the nature. The disclosure of a link between two images belonging to two independent manuscripts, because one was the source for creating the other, allows to draw connections between the art of natural representations through the years and across the countries.

This is one of the main reasons why illuminated manuscripts are still the subject of research, for which a digital archive such as IPSA has to provide support for a number of particular users' needs.

In the following we discuss the major outcomes highlighted by the user requirements.

2.1   Disclosure of Relationships Among Manuscripts

As mentioned, it is of primary importance for researchers to discover if illustrations have been copied from images of other manuscripts, if they have been merely inspired by previous works, or if they are directly inspired by nature. A major requirement thus regards the possibility of enriching the digital archive by highlighting explicit relationships that have been discovered by a researcher. In particular, a research user should be able to create *links* that connect one image to another that it is related to, in some way. The analysis of user requirements on link management highlighted a number of advisable features that could be implemented.

- **Link authorship:** The creation of a link between two or more images depends on the scientific results of a researcher, who owns the intellectual rights to the disclosure of a new relationship between images; for this reason the author of each new link has to be recorded by the system.

- **Link typology:** Since two images can be related for a number of different reasons, the kind of relationship should be explicit. Different typologies of links are envisaged to express the possibility that an image is the progenitor of a set of other images, or that two images are a copy of one another, and so on.
- **Paths:** Links may form *historical paths* among images, because images in a manuscript can be copies of another one which in turn are copies themselves of previous illustrations; hence two images may not be directly linked, because there is no direct relationship between them, but it could be possible to follow a path from one to the other by exploiting existing links.

It can be useful to clarify the notion of historical paths among images. A concept that has been introduced by researchers in the field of illuminated manuscripts is the one of *chains of derivation* among images. Each chain has a *progenitor*, which is an image that has been created through a direct examination of nature (i.e., a plant or a part of the human body). Other authors, who accessed the manuscript containing that image, may have directly *copied* or may have been simply *inspired* by that image. These new images may in turn be copied or be the source of inspiration of other authors and so on, creating a chain of references to previous works. Clearly, it may have happened that a same progenitor gave rise to more than one chain.

This requirement suggests the use of typed annotations that connects two manuscripts, two images, or even two parts of different images. These annotations, that have been called *linking annotations* need to have a type, which describes the kind of relationship between the two objects and provides a semantic to the link.

2.2   Dynamic Records and Intellectual Rights

Almost every digital archive dynamically changes over the years, mainly because of new acquisitions that increase the number of documents. This is also true for a digital archive of illuminated manuscripts, but there are other reasons that produce changes on the archive over time. The creation of records describing the documents and the images in a illuminated manuscript, as for any collection of historical works, is part of the scientific research itself. Some examples of changes to records are, for instance, that new relationships with other works have been discovered, or that the attribution to a given author became less certain.

Because creating a new record or modifying an existing one is part of the scientific work of researchers, the data management has to deal with intellectual rights. A researcher may prefer that some of the newly created records are not accessible by other users, at least until the results of his research have been published and his work have been acknowledged. This situation implies that users may decide which information can be shared with other users and which can not.

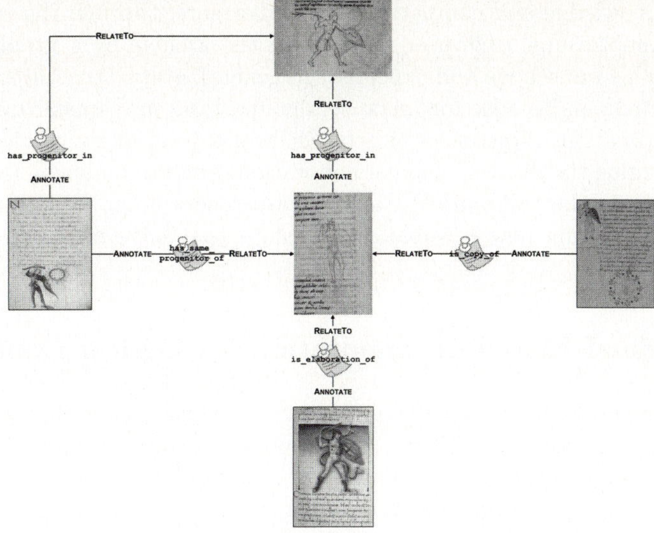

Fig. 1. Example of a personalized view on some linked images

This novel information, which is due to original results, should be stored in the digital archive at a different level than the information that is based on a general consensus. To this end, the use of annotations, both classical textual annotations and the proposed linking annotations, can be a viable tool providing that a user may state which annotations can be shared with the community or with his research group, and which ones has to remain private. Such a mechanism allows researchers for both using the digital archive as an advanced research tool and protecting their intellectual rights. Moreover, linking annotations add an hypertextual structure to the archive, which is different for each user and reflects his personal knowledge on the field, as shown in Figure 1.

2.3 Collaborative Environment

The study of illuminated manuscripts involves a number of researchers from different fields. In fact, illuminated manuscripts are of interest for both the historian of art and the historian of science, but at the same time, a herbal is of interest for the botanist because they represent plants and their possible variations through the centuries, a codex is useful for researchers on the evolution of civil and penal laws, an astrological book may give insights to researchers in medicine on the way stars where perceived to influence the health of people and to astronomers on how constellations where seen and represented. Hence, the scientific research on illuminated manuscripts involves a number of persons with different expertise, which should be able to cooperate in order to share their different knowledge and background.

As already mentioned, annotations that can be shared among researchers of different disciplines can provide an environment for collaboration and for the sharing of knowledge and competencies. Furthermore, through the exploitation of linking annotations, each user may enrich the archive by a graph structure that reflects his knowledge and expertise. In general, graph structures may differ among researchers, because for instance a connection may appear evident for a botanist and not for a historian of arts. Sharing the set of connection, through tools for merging the different linking annotations and for analyzing the resulting graph, may ease the collaboration among researchers by pointing out inconsistencies or suggesting new possible relationships that have not been discovered yet.

3   A Formal Model of Annotations of Digital Content

As underlined in the previous section, the analysis of user requirements suggested that annotations, both in the form of text and in the form of typed links, can be a useful tool for a digital archive. This section presents the model of annotations that we are developing, aimed at a formal approach to annotations.

Digital Object Sets. An archive of illuminated manuscripts has to deal with different kinds of *Digital Objects* (DO). A preliminary user study highlighted that the objects that are studied by researchers are of three kinds: *manuscripts*, *pages* within a given manuscript, and *details* of pages, which usually are hand drawn images. We call them *Digital Contents* (DC), because they carry the information content that is the subject of scientific research.

The user study highlighted that a fourth DO has to be added to the digital archive: the *annotation* on digital content. Annotations are authored by researchers, and they may be either a tool for studying the collection of manuscripts – e.g., a way to highlight some interesting relationships that need to be further investigated – or the results itself of scientific research – the disclosure of new information about the DC in the archive. The following definition formalizes the different sets of DOs we need to deal with.

Definition 1. *Let us define the following sets:*

- *M is a **set of manuscripts** and $m \in M$ is a generic manuscript.*
- *P is a **set of pages** and $p \in P$ is a generic page. We define a function $\mathrm{mp} : M \to 2^P$ which maps a manuscript to the pages contained in it. The following constraints must be adhered to: $\forall m \in M$, $\mathrm{mp}(m) \neq \varnothing$ and $\forall m_1, m_2 \in M$, $\mathrm{mp}(m_1) \cap \mathrm{mp}(m_2) = \varnothing$, that is each manuscript must contain, at least, one page and pages cannot be shared among manuscripts.*
- *D is a **set of details** and $d \in D$ is a generic detail. We define a function $\mathrm{pd} : P \to 2^D$ which maps a page to the details contained in it. The following constraint must be adhered to: $\forall p_1, p_2 \in P$, $\mathrm{pd}(p_1) \cap \mathrm{pd}(p_2) = \varnothing$, that is details cannot be shared among pages.*
- *$DC = M \cup P \cup D$ is a **set of digital contents** and $dc \in DC$ is a generic digital content.*
- *A is a **set of annotations** and $a \in A$ is a generic **annotation**.*

- $DO = DC \cup A$ is a **set of digital objects** and $do \in DO$ is a generic digital object.

Note that DO (capital italic letters) is the set of defined digital objects, DO (capital letters) is the acronym for Digital Object and do (lowercase italic letters) is a digital object $do \in DO$. Similar considerations apply to digital contents and to annotations.

Each DO is uniquely identified by means of an *handle*.

Definition 2. *H is a **set of handles** such that $|H| = |DO|$ and $h \in H$ is a generic handle. We define a bijective function* $\mathrm{h} : H \to DO$ *which maps a handle to the DO identified by it*[1]: *$\forall\, do \in DO, \exists!\, h \in H \mid \mathrm{h}(h) = do \Rightarrow \mathrm{h}^{-1}(do) = h$.*

We will explicitly indicate when a handle identifies an annotation with the notation h_a, for the generic handle, and with $H_a \subseteq H$ for the subset of annotations handles.

Author and Group of Authors. Each DO has an author who creates it. In the particular case of a digital archive of historical manuscripts, the author of a DC cannot interact with the present archive, because he lived centuries ago. On the other hand, nowadays researchers do not author manuscripts, pages, or details. For these reasons, we refer as *author* to only the users of the present archive that create annotations and that cannot create DCs. In our application scenario, groups of authors correspond to research groups, in which different researchers cooperate; a researcher may collaborate with different research groups.

Definition 3. *Let us define the following sets:*

- *AU is a **set of authors** and $au \in AU$ is a generic author. We define a function* $\mathrm{au} : AU \to 2^{H_a}$ *which maps an author to the handles of the annotations authored by him.*
- *$GR \subseteq 2^{AU}$ is a **set of groups of authors** and $G \in GR$ is a generic group of authors. We define a function* $\mathrm{gr} : AU \to 2^{GR}$ *which maps an author to groups of authors he belongs to. The following constraint must be adhered to $\forall\, au \in AU, \mathrm{gr}(au) \neq \varnothing$, that is each author in AU must belong to, at least, one group of authors.*

Types of Annotation. The type of annotation represents part of the semantics of an annotation. The following definition formalizes the notion of type of annotation.

Definition 4. *T is a **set of types of annotation**, and $t \in T$ is a generic type of annotation.*

*The **types graph** is a labeled directed graph (G_T, l_T), where $G_T = (T, E_T \subseteq T \times T)$, T set of vertices, E_T set of edges, and $\mathrm{l}_T : E_T \to L_T$ with L_T set of labels.*

---

[1] $\exists!$ is the *unique existential quantifier*, and it is read "there exists a unique ... such that ...".

The goal of the types graph is to provide some sort of structure and hierarchy among the types of annotation in order to navigate and browse through them.

As we discussed in the previous section, we need the possibility to express a relationship between DCs in the archive through the use of a *linking annotation* and the definition of the type gives us such possibility. Linking annotations are divided in two groups, that is the types graph can be partitioned in two disjoint subgraphs, which express a *hierarchical* or a *relatedness* relationship respectively between DCs of the same set – M, P, or D.

Scope of Annotation. An annotation can have different scopes, i.e. it can be *private*, *shared*, or *public*.

Definition 5. *Let $S = \{Private, Shared, Public\}$ be a **set of scopes** and $s \in S$ is a scope. Let us define the following relations:*

- **equality relation** $=: \{(s, s) \in S \times S \mid s \in S\}$
- **strict ordering relation** $\prec$:
  $\{(Private, Shared), (Private, Public), (Shared, Public)\}$
- **ordering relation** $\preceq \{(s_1, s_2) \in S \times S \mid s_1 = s_2 \vee s_1 \prec s_2\}$

We assume that each annotation can have only one of the three scopes listed above. Note that $(S, \preceq)$ is a *totally ordered set*. The choice of three levels of scopes is motivated by the fact that, an annotation can either be: of general interest, that is the consolidated results of past scientific research (public); a tool for exchanging information on a research work carried out by a group of researchers (shared); a way to highlight an interesting aspect that needs further investigation before being submitted to other researchers (private).

Annotation. Now we can introduce a formal definition of annotation.

Definition 6. *An **annotation** $a \in A$ is a tuple:*

$$a = \left(h_a \in H_a, au_a \in AU, G_a \in 2^{GR}, s_a \in S, t_a \in T \right)$$

where:

- *h_a is the unique handle of the annotation a, i.e. $h(h_a) = a$;*
- *au_a is the author of the annotation a, i.e. $h_a \in au(au_a)$;*
- *G_a are the groups of authors which can access the annotation, such that $G_a \subseteq gr(au_a)$;*
- *s_a is the scope of the annotation a – Private, Shared, or Public;*
- *t_a is the type of the annotation a.*

Annotation-Based Hypertext. Given that each type of annotations that is taken into account expresses a relationship between two DCs in the form of a typed link, we consider that existing DCs and user's annotations constitute a hypertext.

Definition 7. *The* annotation-based hypertext *is a labeled directed multigraph:*

$$(\mathcal{H} = (DC, A), \text{annotate})$$

where:

- *DC is the set of vertices;*
- *A is the set of edges;*
- annotate $: A \rightarrow DC \times DC$ *is the edge-function, which puts an edge between two DCs dc_1 and dc_2 if and only if there is a relationship between them, which is expressed by the annotation a.*

The following constraints must be adhered to:

1. *a $dc \in DC$ cannot be put in relationship with itself, that is $dc_1 \neq dc_2$;*
2. *the two DCs connected by an annotation must be of the same type, that is $dc_1, dc_2 \in M \vee dc_1, dc_2 \in P \vee dc_1, dc_2 \in D$.*

The annotation-based hypertext is built by putting an edge between two DCs vertices, if an annotation between that two DCs exists. Note that edges can be put only between DCs and not between annotations: this means that an annotation cannot connect other annotations. The two constraints on the annotation-based hypertext are based on a study carried out on the user requirements of the researchers that will access and annotate the digital archive: annotations do not have to express a relationship of a DC with itself, or with DCs of different kind. Since there are no constraints on the number of annotations that connect a pair of vertices, we deal with a multigraph. The existence of multiple edges between the same pair of vertices allows us to express different kinds of relationships between two DCs. In this way, we take into account both the possibility of different interpretations of the same contents given by independent authors, and the partial results of a same author, who is studying a particular subset of the digital content and expresses alternative relationships that need further investigations. Users are not expected to access the whole annotation-based hypertext, because annotations have scopes that are related to user's access rights. Thus, the following definition introduces an operator suitable for choosing the subset of the annotation-based hypertext that can be accessed by a user.

Definition 8. *Given an annotation-based hypertext $\mathcal{H}$, we introduce a **projection operator** that can have the forms:*

- *$\mathcal{H}^\pi = \pi\left(\mathcal{H}, AU_\pi, S_\pi, T_\pi\right)$, with $AU_\pi \subseteq AU$, $S_\pi \subseteq S$, $T_\pi \subseteq T$, constructs a new annotation-based hypertext $\mathcal{H}^\pi \subseteq \mathcal{H}$ such that:*

$$\begin{cases} A^\pi = \{a \in A \mid au_a \in AU_\pi \wedge s_a \in S_\pi \wedge t_a \in T_\pi\} \\ DC^\pi = DC \end{cases}$$

- *$\mathcal{H}^\pi = \pi\left(\mathcal{H}, GR_\pi, S_\pi, T_\pi\right)$, with $GR_\pi \subseteq GR$, $S_\pi \subseteq S$, $T_\pi \subseteq T$, constructs a new annotation-based hypertext $\mathcal{H}^\pi \subseteq \mathcal{H}$ such that:*

$$\begin{cases} A^\pi = \{a \in A \mid G_a \in GR_\pi \wedge s_a \in S_\pi \wedge t_a \in T_\pi\} \\ DC^\pi = DC \end{cases}$$

Both operators have a generalized version, where the $\star$ symbol can be replaced to an input parameter in order to express that the whole set has to be used.

For example $\pi\left(\mathcal{H}, AU_\pi, S_\pi, \star\right) = \pi\left(\mathcal{H}, AU_\pi, S_\pi, T\right)$.

This operator provides us with a personalized view for the user of the annotation-based hypertext $\mathcal{H}$. The first form allows us to select edges on the basis of author(s), scope(s) and type(s) of the annotation, while the second form utilizes groups of authors instead of authors as selection criterion. This operator is quite flexible, if combined with the previous definitions. For example, if, given an author $au \in AU$, we want to extract the subgraph with all the public annotations (edges) inserted by authors that belong to the same groups of au, we can use $\mathcal{H}^\pi = \pi\left(\mathcal{H}, \mathrm{gr}(au), \mathrm{Public}, \star\right)$. Finally, the expressive power of this operator can be further enriched by using also the usual union, intersection, and difference set operators. The projection operator represents the standard way for a user to perceive the annotation-based hypertext, because a user is not allowed to access all the edges of the hypertext but he can access only the public ones, those belonging to him, and the ones shared with groups of authors the user belongs to.

Definition 9. *Let us define the **annotation compatibility set** $C \subseteq A \times A \times [0, 1]$ that expresses the degree of compatibility of the types of annotation among given pairs of annotations, where 0 means no compatibility at all and 1 means full compatibility. Let us define the **compatibility score** $\mathrm{c}(C, a_1, a_2) = c \in [0, 1]$ between two annotations given an annotation compatibility set C, which returns the compatibility c between two annotations if $\exists\,(a_1, a_2, c) \in C$.*

The actual value that c assumes for different pairs of annotation types is part of previous knowledge about the semantic of the annotation types and on their organization in the types graph. We assume this value is given by specialists in the field of illuminated manuscripts.

Definition 10. *Given an annotation-based hypertext $\mathcal{H}$, a set T of annotation types, and a types graph G_T, we introduce a **pair-wise compatibility operator** $\xi\left(\mathcal{H}, T, G_T, dc_1, dc_2\right) = C_\xi$ that $\forall a_1, a_2 \in A \mid \mathrm{annotate}(a_1) = (dc_1, dc_2) = \mathrm{annotate}(a_2)$ returns a compatibility score for the annotations connecting dc_1 and dc_2.*

*Given an annotation-based hypertext $\mathcal{H}$, a set T of annotation types, and a types graph G_T, we introduce a **path-wise compatibility operator** $\xi\left(\mathcal{H}, T, G_T, dc_1, dc_2, dc_3\right) = C_\xi$ that $\forall a_1, a_2 \in A \mid \mathrm{annotate}(a_1) = (dc_1, dc_2) \wedge \mathrm{annotate}(a_2) = (dc_2, dc_3)$ returns a compatibility score for the annotations connecting dc_1 and dc_2 with respect to the annotations connecting dc_2 and dc_3.*

Both forms of the compatibility operator make use of the types graph, which expresses the relationships among the different types of annotation, in order to determine the degree at which the type of two different annotations is compatible. Note that the annotation compatibility set C can be used to produce a ranking among the annotations connecting different DCs in order of severity of compatibility problems.

4   Automatic Suggestions of Relationships Among DCs

The introduced model and operators can be exploited to create tools for helping the user of a digital archive to perform scientific research on its content. In particular, the annotation-based hypertext can be automatically analyzed to highlight possible inconsistencies among the annotations – e.g., two DCs are annotated with typed annotations that have different and possibly contrasting semantics – as well as to extract new information about possible relationships – e.g., two DCs are not annotated but the surrounding set of edges suggest the possibility of a relationship among them. It has to be stressed that the automatic analysis of the graph can only provide the user with *suggestions* on possible new or different annotations. The final choice of which annotations are to be added or modified is made by the research user who, from his cultural and scientific background, can take the final decision on relationships among digital content. Moreover, the research on illuminated manuscripts is an ongoing work, for which temporary inconsistency and incompleteness are normal events. Yet, the automatic analysis may help the researcher by suggesting the creation of new annotations, because the task of accepting to author an automatic annotation is expected to be simpler than creating an annotation from scratch.

4.1   Suggestions of Possible Inconsistencies

As previously explained, the model allows for multiple annotations of the same pair of digital contents. This means that public annotations of different authors may be different, or that for a given author, public annotations may differ from private ones, or even that there can be different private annotations. These inconsistencies may be made on purpose, but may also be the result of an erroneous interaction with the system, or to changes in the view of the DC relationships over the years. In any case, the analysis of the graph may pinpoint particular relationships that need to be carefully checked by the user.

Definition 11. *Given an annotation-based hypertext $\mathcal{H}$, a set T of annotation types, a types graph G_T, a subset of authors $AU_\psi \subseteq AU$ and a subset of scopes $S_\psi \subseteq S$, the **pair-wise inconsistency finder operator** $\psi(\mathcal{H}, T, G_T, AU_\psi, S_\psi)$ $= C_\psi$ firstly computes $\mathcal{H}^\pi = \pi(\mathcal{H}, AU_\psi, S_\psi, T)$ and secondly computes*

$$C_\psi = \bigcup_{\substack{dc_1, dc_2 \in DC^\pi \mid \exists a \in A^\pi, \\ \mathrm{annotate}(a) = (dc_1, dc_2)}} \xi(\mathcal{H}^\pi, T, G_T, dc_1, dc_2)$$

*The **path-wise inconsistency finder operator** $\psi(\mathcal{H}, T, G_T, AU_\psi, S_\psi) = C_\psi$ firstly computes $\mathcal{H}^\pi = \pi(\mathcal{H}, AU_\psi, S_\psi, T)$ and secondly computes*

$$C_\psi = \bigcup_{\substack{dc_1, dc_2, dc_3 \in DC^\pi \mid \\ \exists a_1, a_2 \in A^\pi, \\ \mathrm{annotate}(a_1) = (dc_1, dc_2) \wedge \\ \mathrm{annotate}(a_2) = (dc_2, dc_3)}} \xi(\mathcal{H}^\pi, T, G_T, dc_1, dc_2, dc_3)$$

Once that either the pair-wise or the path-wise operator is applied, from the set C_ψ it is possible to extract all the compatibility scores related to annotations made by authors AU_ψ (possibly belonging to the same group) with scopes S_ψ. It is then possible to apply a threshold function on the set of compatibility scores, in order to provide the user with all the annotations that may be inconsistent or even contradictory. The degree by which two annotations are inconsistent depends on the semantics that the users give to the annotation types and to the types graph. The approach is general enough to support different definitions of the compatibility score, which are based on the knowledge of the application domain. In the case of illuminated manuscripts, the compatibility scores are based on the particular kind of relationships that can express a hierarchical relationship or a relatedness (and non-hierarchical) one. Examples of inconsistencies are that the same two DCs could be annotated as in hierarchical and non-hierarchical relationship at the same time, or that a dc_1 has been set as an ancestor of dc_2 by one author and viceversa for a different author. Suggestions of inconsistencies can be exploited in different way: as placeholders for highlighting unclear relationships between DCs that a user is interested in investigating in detail; as an indication of the more debated relationships in the archive.

4.2   Suggestions of New Relationships

The analysis of the annotation-based graph can highlight that two DCs are not annotated, yet there is a path that connects them. Moreover, since DCs are made of different sets which are organized hierarchically, the annotation of two manuscripts may suggest a similar annotation between two details, and viceversa. Also in this case, the existence of similar relationships may only suggest the presence of new relationships, which must be validated by the research user. Yet it can be considered that the presence of suggestions would ease the user in creating the network of annotations of the digital archive. Of course, there is also the possibility that the automatic analysis of the graph will disclose new relationships, at least for non expert users.

Definition 12. *Given an annotation-based hypertext $\mathcal{H}$, a set T of annotation types, a types graph G_T, a subset of authors $AU_\psi \subseteq AU$ and a subset of scopes $S_\psi \subseteq S$ we introduce a **relationship finder operator** $\rho\left(\mathcal{H}, T, G_T, AU_\rho, S_\rho\right) = C_\psi$ that functions as follow:*

1. *compute $\mathcal{H}^\pi = \pi(\mathcal{H}, AU_\rho, S_\rho, T)$*
2. *compute the transitive closure $\mathcal{H}^{\pi+}$ of $\mathcal{H}^\pi$*
3. *$\forall dc_1, dc_2 \in \mathcal{H}^{\pi+} \mid \nexists a \in A^\pi, \text{annotate}(a) = (dc_1, dc_2)$, that is all of the DCs among which exists a path but are not directly connected, for each path $P = dc_1 a_1 \ldots dc_m a_h dc_n \ldots a_k dc_2$ connecting dc_1 to dc_2, compute $C_{\rho,P} = \bigcup_{dc_{i_1}, dc_{i_2}, dc_{i_3} \in P} \xi\left(\mathcal{H}, T, G_T, dc_{i_1}, dc_{i_2}, dc_{i_3}\right)$*
4. *if exists a path P such that $\sum_{a_1, a_2 \in C_{\rho,P}} c(C_{\rho,P}, a_1, a_2) > T_\rho$ (alternatively $\prod_{a_1, a_2 \in C_{\rho,P}} c(C_{\rho,P}, a_1, a_2) > T_\rho$), with T_ρ given threshold, than it suggests the existence of a possible relationship between dc_1 and dc_2.*

5   Conclusions

This paper describes an approach to the development of models and tools for a digital archive of illuminated manuscripts. We carried out an analysis of the user requirements for the use of the archive as a tool for scientific research. According to the user requirements, annotations have been suggested as the main functionality to be added to a digital archive.

We have proposed a formal model of annotations that introduces the notion of annotation-based hypertext and explores some of its properties, in order to automatically extract some relevant information about the relationships among digital contents and provide users with suggestions about possible inconsistencies between different results, and suggest the existence of new relationships.

References

1. Agosti, M., Ferro, N., Orio, N.: Annotating Illuminated Manuscripts: an Effective Tool for Research and Education. In: JCDL 2005. Proc. 5th ACM/IEEE-CS Joint Conference on Digital Libraries, pp. 121–130. ACM Press, New York, USA (2005)
2. Agosti, M., Ferro, N., Orio, N.: Graph-based Automatic Suggestion of Relationships among Images of Illuminated Manuscripts. In: SAC 2006. Proc. 21st ACM Symposium on Applied Computing, pp. 1063–1067. ACM Press, New York, USA (2006)
3. Agosti, M., Bonfiglio-Dosio, G., Ferro, N.: A Historical and Contemporary Study on Annotations to Derive Key Features for Systems Design. International Journal on Digital Libraries (2007), http://dx.doi.org/10.1007/s00799-007-0010-0
4. Agosti, M., Ferro, N.: A Formal Model of Annotations of Digital Content. ACM Transactions on Information Systems (TOIS) 26, 1–55 (2008) (to appear)
5. Crane, G.: Cultural heritage digital libraries: Needs and components. In: Agosti, M., Thanos, C. (eds.) ECDL 2002. LNCS, vol. 2458, pp. 626–637. Springer, Heidelberg (2002)
6. Frommholz, I., Brocks, H., Thiel, U., Neuhold, E., Iannone, L., Semeraro, G., Berardi, M., Ceci, M.: Document-Centered Collaboration for Scholars in the Humanities – The COLLATE System. In: Koch, T., Sølvberg, I.T. (eds.) ECDL 2003. LNCS, vol. 2769, pp. 434–445. Springer, Heidelberg (2003)

Mining Web Data for Image Semantic Annotation

Roberto Basili[1], Riccardo Petitti[2], and Dario Saracino[2]

[1] University of Rome "Tor Vergata",
Department of Computer Science, Systems and Production, Roma, Italy
[2] Exprivia S.p.A, Via Cristoforo Colombo 456, 00145, Roma, Italy

Abstract. In this paper, an unsupervised image classification technique combining features from different media levels is proposed. In particular geometrical models of visual features are here integrated with textual descriptions derived through Information Extraction processes from Web pages. While the higher expressivity of the combined individual descriptions increases the complexity of the adopted clustering algorithms, methods for dimensionality reduction (i.e. LSA) are applied effectively. The evaluation on an image classification task confirms that the proposed Web mining model outperforms other methods acting on the individual levels for cost-effective annotation.

1   Introduction

The increasing importance of the World Wide Web has driven the creation of various digital formats for the storage and sharing of multimedia contents. Search engines which represent important achievements for text *Information Retrieval* (*IR*), require adaptation to deal with multimedia properties. Early approaches provide either keyword-based SQL interfaces or image-based queries in query-by-example settings. This strict separation between the textual and visual dimension is unsatisfactory. Better methods for retrieving semantic information from multimedia content are thus needed to support search, classification and knowledge extraction from visual data.

The critical problem in these scenarios has been defined as the "semantic gap" between descriptions obtained from different media levels ([8]). The gap is the "*lack of coincidence between the information that one can extract from the visual data and the interpretation that the same data have for a user in a given situation*" [8]. Advancements in content-based retrieval is critically tight to the filling of this *semantic gap*, as the meaning of an image is rarely self-evident. The major methodological position behind these conclusions is that much of the interesting work in attempting to bridge the semantic gap automatically is tackling the gap between low-level descriptors and linguistic labels as effective surrogates of the full visual semantics. This is even strengthened by the fact that queries to multimedia data are typically formulated with respect to their semantics, via more or less complex linguistic descriptors.

R. Basili and M.T. Pazienza (Eds.): AI*IA 2007, LNAI 4733, pp. 674–685, 2007.
© Springer-Verlag Berlin Heidelberg 2007

Linking visual properties to image semantics is strictly connected with an *annotation* task, i.e. the selection of proper symbolic labels able to express the concepts underlying visual properties. As noticed by [4], the discrete nature of symbolic labels rigidly assigned to images provides a too strict semantic position. Deciding the appropriateness of a label during annotation is a discretization problem, much prone to fallacies. *Hard* annotation techniques are prone to these errors. The so-called *soft* approach has been recently introduced as a solution [4] making a better use of the geometrical modeling of image properties. A vector space is introduced where visual properties, i.e. low level descriptors, *live with* textual properties, i.e. terms or keywords. This *duality* property characterizes latent semantic spaces. In this view, annotations are no longer rigid descriptors but *clouds* of terms "*close*" enough to the corresponding visual properties. Viceversa, some visual properties can be seen as expressions of concepts expressed by keywords "*close*" enough in the space. A set of terms is more expressive than single keywords as the inherent linguistic ambiguities characterizing a single word disappear in a larger context. These sets provide a natural notion of *class* as widely studied in automatic text classification. As in [4], we produce vector representations for images including both visual and textual (i.e. symbolic) properties. Quantitative measures of similarity in this vector space capture flexible properties and imply a more effective notion of annotation.

The focus of this work is a specific problem: how can we classify and index multimedia information throughout automatic content annotation, in an accurate and cost-effective way? The paper presents a Web based image classification methodology, its experimental evaluation and the results achievable by the semi-supervised learning approach with respect to a realistic image classification task. Section 2 describes how multimediality is managed by the combined evidence of visual and textual properties. In Section 3, the learning methods are presented, resulting in a general architecture for the Image Classification. In Section 4, the evaluation of the experimental results is presented.

2   Extracting Multimedia Features in the Web

Web documents including both texts and images are widely distributed in the Web and can be used as source evidence to manage the visual domain, in line with current approaches to text indexing. The most difficult task here is the representation of the visual information coming from images, i.e. the design of descriptions to be indexed, able to reduce the unavoidable semantic loss. A possible approach is to learn the relationships between low level image features and the words observable in texts *as an emerging property of available data*, even when the latter are unlabeled. The semantic information brought by the observable language facts about images is thus exploited to improve the design efficiency and the usability in a range of multimedia indexing problems.

The multimediality in the work presented here is addressed by the combination of the two abstraction levels, visual and textual information. The aim is both improving the precision of the semantic annotations and recognizing correlations between the visual features and the image textual descriptions. The proposed analysis is based on an initial separation of the visual and textual domains by preserving the reference to the originating context (e.g. a Web page). Images and texts are here processed according to different modalities acting over the same similarity model, i.e. Latent Semantic Analysis [3]. The resulting geometrical models are then combined to obtain a unique final space, able to represent both of them and support the application of a unique similarity measure. The features used in the classification are both visual and textual properties as they are observed over images and texts in the target Web pages.

Textual features include *POS tagged individual terms* (e.g. *grass, fields, airport*), as well as *terminological* (i.e. multiword) *expressions* and proper nouns (e.g. *civil airport, air traffic, Rome Fiumicino,* or *Golden Gate Bridge*). In line with the traditional weighting schemes adopted in vector space models (VSM, [7]), each term receives a weight depending on its distribution in the local document and global collection. Terms are selected by statistical filters on their relevance for the collection, while single terms above 5 occurrences in the corpus are retained in the vocabulary. No other feature selection filter is applied. Textual features are extracted from the experimental corpus by the Deep Knowledge[1], (DK), system. DK carries out the following tasks from the pages properly retrieved from the Web: *Indexing,* that generates unique references to the source images and pages; *Morphological recognition*; *Terminology extraction* that produces the seed term vocabulary of the system; *Segmentation,* that split pages into data units in which the coexistence of one image and some text is represented[2] The *visual features* refer to three major classes: *chromatic features, textures* and *transformations.* Chromatic features express the color properties of the image. Textures emphasize the background properties and their composition. Transformations are also modeled in order to take into account possible shapes that are invariant according to some geometrical transformations. These features should allow to compute similarities of the depicted discrete objects independently from their position in the images. Images are analyzed through LTI-lib, [6], an object-oriented open source library with dedicated algorithms and data structures for image processing. It has been developed at the Aachen University of Technology and is frequently used in image processing and computer vision tasks.

Each feature is expressed through a real valued number, defining its weight. A geometrical space is thus derived by juxtaposing the dimensions generated by individual (textual and visual) features. However, some issues specific to our problem arise as image annotation is different from the typical IR case, where the dimensionality is high but the feature types are homogeneous (i.e. they are all originating from words). Different sampling and models are required to make the different feature types comparable. Distributions are also very different as the variance across individual domains can significantly differ.

---

[1] *Deep Knowledge,* a text mining platform produced and commercialized by Exprivia S.p.A, URL:www.exprivia.it

[2] When more than one image is found into a single segment, multiple data units are generated, with different images and the same segment text.

The aim of our model is to derive a rich geometrical space where the distinguishing features can suggest useful relations between the visual and textual dimensions: for example, terms like *grass* or *fields* should be represented "close" enough to high levels of the green band for the RGB chromatic representation. We aim thus to capture correlations among the subdomains of visual and textual propreties, as they can be found with a significant regularity in the data collected from the Web.

3   Mining the Visual and Textual Features

It has been often noticed that traditional vector space models in IR ([7]) do not capture correlations among terms that are by definition independent dimensions. While term-based vector space models assume term independence, natural languages are characterized by strong associations between terms, so that this assumption is never satisfied. Correlations can be captured via Latent Semantic Analysis methods [3] that attempt to capture such dependencies using the purely automatic matrix decomposition process, called *Singular Value Decomposition (SVD)*. The original term-by-document matrix M describing the traditional term-based document space is transformed in the product of three new matrices: T, S, and D such that their product $TSD^T = M$. They capture the same statistical information than M in a lower k-dimensional space: each dimension represents one of the derived LSA features (or concepts), thought of as an artificial concept i.e. an emerging meaning component from words and documents [3]. S is a diagonal matrix whose non zero values (called "singular values") express the decreasing significance of the k LSA factors. Therefore, the least important factors can be easily neglected by truncating matrices T, S, and D. The first k columns are called the LSA factors. The usual number of dimensions k needed for effective performances obviously depends on the collection and the task.

When multimedia properties are targeted, the ability to decompose the original matrix (with mixed visual and textual features) and map it into an LSA space enables the detection of specific correlations between multimedia features and Web images. Closeness in the resulting space should be able to suggest latent semantic relationships between terms (like *green*, *fields* or *vegetation*) and visual properties dominating some images (e.g. color as the green band in an RGB chromatic representation).

In our approach, LSA is applied in a structured fashion. First, it is run separately over the vectorial representations of visual and textual features. In this way two independent k-dimensional LSA spaces are derived. These spaces express correlations among features lying in the individual domains, i.e. the visual domains and the linguistic one. Correlations among words like *green, fields* or *vegetation* are obtained at this stage due to the topical association imposed by LSA. In a second phase a $2k$-dimensional space is obtained by juxtaposing the two k-dimensional vectors of the same objects. On the resulting LSA space, another SVD step is applied to gather the final unified k-dimensional representation. The final latent semantic space should integrate in k-dimensions all the original multimedia properties and should explicitate the useful correlations: these emerge from the comparable k-dimensional vectors derived through the double SVD step. Cosine similarity in the resulting space is a distance metrics useful for capturing the suitable notion of similarity helpful to cluster objects and features. Notice how individual vectors in the final space represent groups of visual or textual features in the original space: clustering over this space exploit a large body of evidence derived from the previous independent LSA analysis.

3.1   An Architecture for Multimedia Semantic Retrieval and Classification

In an unsupervised approach to image classification we aim to exploit the inherent redundancy of features observable in Web pages as well as the combination of different learning methods this including Latent Semantic Analysis, unsupervised clustering and automatic image classification, i.e. Support Vector Machine (SVM) learning. This leads to a complex architecture for image classification. The overall data flow is shown in Figure 1 where the four major phases are sketched: *Web mining, Feature Engineering, Unsupervised Learning* and *Supervised Image Classification.*

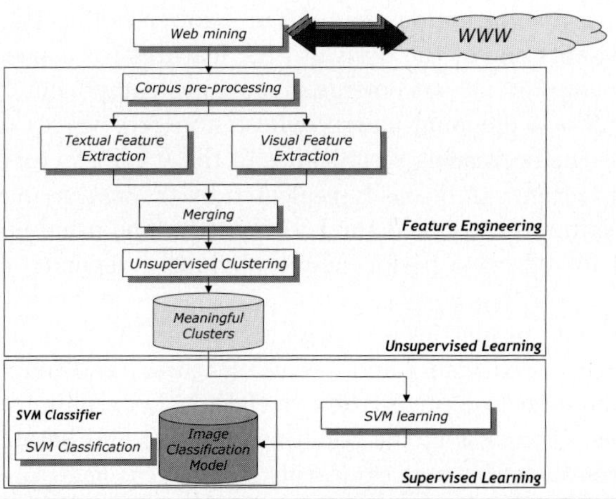

Fig. 1. The general architecture of the Image classification system

The cascade of processing steps works as follows. First, Web is searched for pages related to the types of interesting images. During this phase images and their surrounding text in the page layout is derived through the DK engine. In this phase the major extraction process relates the detection of interesting HTML material, the pruning of irrelevant mark-up and the feeding of an internal DB with all the potentially relevant Web data.

Then a *Corpus pre-processing* phase is applied to build the vector representations of the target images including visual as well textual descriptions. In this phase the role of DK is to segment individual pages into significant parts. This is done in the following steps:

- First, segments are derived according to the DK technology able to retrieve meaningful information units that include texts and images. Textual information is then processed by DK to derive the proper vocabulary and map segments into an internal real-valued vector representation. DK generates the term vocabulary and computes the term and document weighting. Complex terms are automatically detected (and POS tagged) so that jargon or technical expressions (e.g. *remote sensing* or *Very High Resolution Radiometer*) are given independent and specific weights. This provides a traditional space vector model [7] enriched with linguistic information that is very specific to the target information gathered. Visual properties are also extracted in this phase.
- Dimensionality reduction is then imposed via Latent Semantic Analysis (LSA), [3]. Two independent LSA processes are carried out separately for textual features and visual properties, respectively, as they obey to different laws and are characterized by quite different domains and distributions. The pseudovectors obtained by the SVD transformation (dimension k as in the order of the applied SVD) are then representing one data item (a segment) according to two independent vectors: text and visual pseudovectors are separate but they refer to the same Web segment.
- Finally, *Merging* of the two k-dimensional representations in the LSA spaces is carried out, where a single $2k$-dimensional vector is obtained by juxtaposing the original ones. In this phase, several merging methods have been experimented. The best results reported in section 4 have been obtained by applying a second LSA stage to the combined $2k$-dimensional vectors: during this stage correlations across textual and visual features are computed again in order to derive a single synthetic k-dimensional vector. In some configuration (e.g., the two-step LSA strategy, described below in Section 4), this further dimensionality reduction is not applied as the two original k-dimensional vectors are used separately in the remaining stages.

Unsupervised Learning is applied by clustering the derived vectorial data with all the available multimedia properties. In this phase, an efficient agglomerative clustering algorithm (i.e. k-mean [1]) is applied. The results are groups of images (and segments) that are similar according to their textual or visual properties (or both). Figure 2 reports clusters of images of *bridges* as they have been derived from different feature sets. Textual features are meaningful but still do not fully characterize the target concepts: in Fig. 2.(A) some images report design plots and not real bridges so that they are erroneous example of *bridge* images. Analogously, in Fig. 2.(B) bridges and airplane are confused in the shown cluster based only on visual features.

A cluster C (and its centroid) is usually close enough to *terminological expressions* and visual features (i.e. those typical for its members). Linguistic expressions justify C on a more abstract level and better capture the cluster's semantics. As it is shown in Fig. 2.(C), the combination of textual and visual

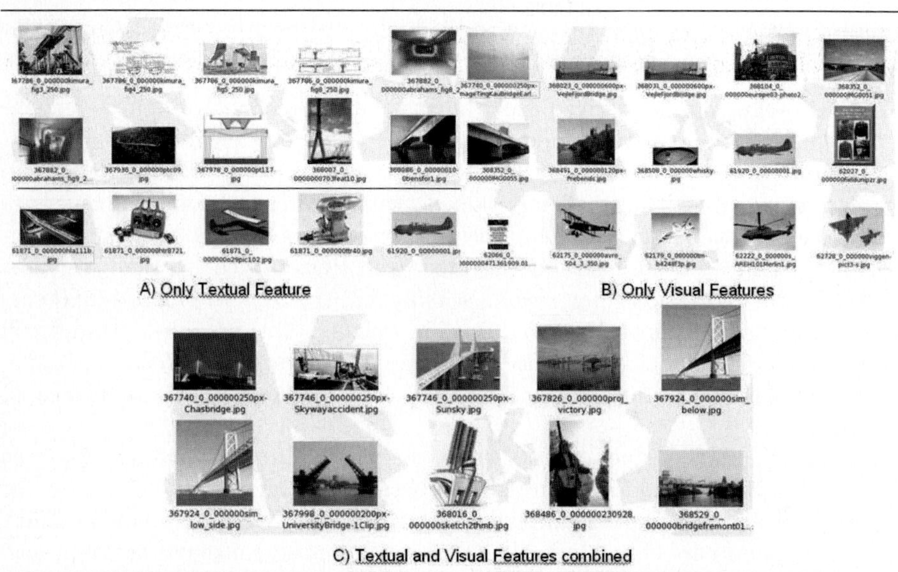

Fig. 2. Clusters derived according to different feature sets

features obtains usually the best result: the example is an accurate cluster representing *bridges* in different shapes and positions.

Supervised Classification. Given the quality of clusters derived automatically, a supervised image classification approach can be flexibly applied. In fact, the different clusters can be more easily annotated by looking only at the best cluster instances and to their terminological descriptions. Labeling one cluster provides, as a side effect, the availability of many examples so that the overall scalability of the supervised approach increases. Every cluster member is an individual example for a supervised image classification model. Several members are thus collectively labeled, by the unique label assigned at cluster level. In the last phase, clusters are thus used as training seeds for a supervised classifier. In all our experiments, we applied Support Vector Machines ([9], [2]) as a learning paradigm: we thus call these stages *SVM training* and *SVM classification*, respectively. During training an SVM develops (according to the risk minimization principle, [9]) the best image classification model able to separate negative from positive examples of one class. Different SVMs are trained for the different classes relying on separate models. The ensamble of these models is called *Image Classification Model* in Fig. 1. During classification, the different SVMs run on a new example in a binary fashion: they can accept or reject the example as valid member of each class. A final combination of the individual decisions selects the best global class. The integration of the *Image Classification Model* with the combined set of SVMs realizes the overall SVM classifier shown in Fig. 1.

Notice how the improvement over an image classification task is just one of the outcome of the proposed methodology. In fact, clusters with their relevant (centroid) properties define protypical ways of referring and describing a target category: the best features (e.g. most important terms characterizing the cluster centroid) can be thus seen as typical ways of querying a class of visual objects. This supports the learning of linguistic ways of referring to categories useful for searching images by NL queries.

4   Evaluation

The objective of the experiments was to validate the idea of enabling fast and accurate image classification via the combination of heterogeneous media properties and the adoption of clustering as a semisupervised learning process. In this perspective, at least three dimensions of the proposed approach should be explored. The *level of granularity* is the possibility of training over individual clusters rather than images. The *type of annotation* establish the ability of annotating clusters or individual images. Different *training evidence* is also made available by different media levels, i.e. text vs. visual properties.

The corpus adopted for the experiment has been obtained by Web spidering. It includes Web pages related to two target concepts *bridges* and *airplanes* as well as a large portion of errors (like banners or other advertising pictures). Segments of the pages include one picture and a corresponding text, from which all the features are derived. Table 1 describes the main aspects of the corpus.

Table 1. Description of the Web corpus used in the experiments

Number of target categories	2 + 1 (*Others*)
Number of HTML pages	23,520
Number of sections derived	1,527
Number of images	3,959
Number of selected terms	53,251
Number of words (types)	121,545
Number of Annotated images	867
Number of images in the Test Set	432
Number of images in the Training Set	3,527

The experiments in automatic image classification have been targeted to three classes, i.e. *bridges, airplanes* and *other*, the latter being used to recognize pictures irrelevant for the task. In the experiments clustering is applied in an unsupervised fashion over the training corpus and then used to feed an SVM classifier[3]. LSA has been applied first separately over the textual and visual properties and then for merging. The order k of the decomposition was 100 in all steps.

Two major experiments have been carried out. *Experiment 1* measures the ability of a supervised classifier to rebuild the clusters obtained from the first

---

[3] The SVM implementation called SMO made available by the WEKA machine learning platform [10] has been applied in all the experiments.

learning stage. *Experiment 2* has been designed to measure the effectiveness of the semi-supervised learning approach on the image categorization task. In this case, we compared the use of unsupervised clustering to train an SVM classifier with a traditional (i.e. fully supervised) use of the SVM. In the unsupervised case, the annotations of automatically derived clusters are used to gather positive and negative class instances (classified images plus their text) and then train the SVM. The reference supervised model makes no use of clusters and it is trained directly on hand-annotated images. The evaluation has been done in all cases by computing the *accuracy* measure, that is the percentage of correct classification decisions in the different tests.

4.1   Experiment 1: Validating the Acquired Image Clusters

Experiment 1 is the attempt to measure the ability of a supervised classifier to rebuild the clusters derivable from the first learning stage, i.e. *Unsupervised Learning*. First, clustering of the entire corpus of 3,959 images was run according to a set of properties and strategies as discussed in Section 3.1. On the derived final representation, a split of 70% (*training*) vs. 30% (*testing*) was applied and one SVM has been trained for each cluster. The accuracy of the SVM to re-assign the original cluster to each individual test object was then measured. The SVM decision here is correct if the data object is classified into the cluster it was also assigned during unsupervised clustering. Notice that this test is *cluster based*. We can thus assess here only the generalization power of the SVM.

   The best results of Experiment 1 is obtained when only visual features are employed, i.e. 96.8% acuracy. However, good levels of performances can be reached by almost all models: visual features only achieve 87.1% while the combination of both features results in a 89.1% accuracy. This suggests that exploiting clustering ability of an unsupervised system is a viable approach to large scale image classification. As expected textual features are the best predictors and provide more consistent results. This is in line with the original observation that texts are the best carriers of multimedia semantics and terms are thus the best candidates to express it in indexing and querying. Moreover, clusters give rise to good generalizations that can be better understood by users, instead of drowning in hundreds of indvidual images. Although feature combination is not achieving the best performance, it also does not produce a significant accuracy drop. However, adopting only the textual features is not best choice for image classification, as we will see in Experiment 2.

4.2   Experiment 2: Evaluating the Classification Accuracy

Experiment 2 aims to measure the effectiveness of the semi-supervised learning approach on the image categorization task by comparing it with a fully supervised training process. As it is possible that a cluster gathering mainly images of a class (e.g. *bridges*) includes also irrelevant examples (i.e. class=*other*), the evaluation aims to measure the impact of this potential noise sources on the reachable SVM accuracy. Obviously, the supervised learning scheme of the SVM constitutes an upper-bound for the accuracy of the semi-supervised setting.

The semi-supervised approach proceeds as follows:

1. Given the entire training set, we labeled some images so that each of the three classes is equally rapresented (e.g 20 aircrafts, 20 bridges and 20 other). Images are randomly chosen although they are selected so that each class is equally represented (about 289 images for each class). The derived test set is balanced and the baseline is around 33%. Portions of the labeled data are used as *seeds* of the training process.
2. We apply the clustering algorithm to the entire training set obtaining a set of clusters, some of them including annotated images.
3. A majority policy is used to assign a unique class to the entire cluster: the class suggested by the majority of labeled images in the cluster is selected.
4. Using such an extended set of labeled images, we trained an SVM and evaluate its performance over the test images, kept out from the seeding and labeling process.

As the number of seed (i.e. labeled) images is critical to the quality of the semisupervised learning, we compared the performance over sets of seed images of growing size.

Hand annotation has been applied by a small team of three experts in the different experiments with very high annotation agreement scores (over 95%). An annotation was accepted if proposed by at least two annotators. The annotators working on a cluster basis (i.e. by annotating all images of a cluster with the single decision over the entire cluster) were concluding their job 12 times faster than those labeling images individually. A training-test split of about 90% vs. 10% was applied for the training of the SVM.

Table 2. Semisupervised labeling rates based on textual features only

Percentage of Seeding images	Number of seed images	Number of labeled clusters	Number of labeled images	Annotation rate
1.22%	43	9	1262	29.21
3.67%	130	23	962	7.42
6.12%	216	27	1321	6.11
8.57%	302	36	1446	4.78

In Tables 2 and 3 we report the results of the automatic semisupervised labeling process in which training images (Column 4) are derived from the seed images. In the first table we use only the textual feature, while in the second one we show results from the combination of both kinds of features. This tables shows the *Number of seed images*, the *labeled clusters*, i.e. the number of automatically tagged clusters and *the number of labeled images* that is the number of automatically labeled images added to the SVM training set. Columns 5 reports

Table 3. Semisupervised labeling rates using combined textual and visual features

Percentage of Seeding images	Number of seed images	Number of labeled clusters	Number of labeled images	Annotation rate
1.22%	43	23	1840	42.59
3.67%	130	39	2140	16.51
6.12%	216	47	2324	10.76
8.57%	302	58	2447	8.09

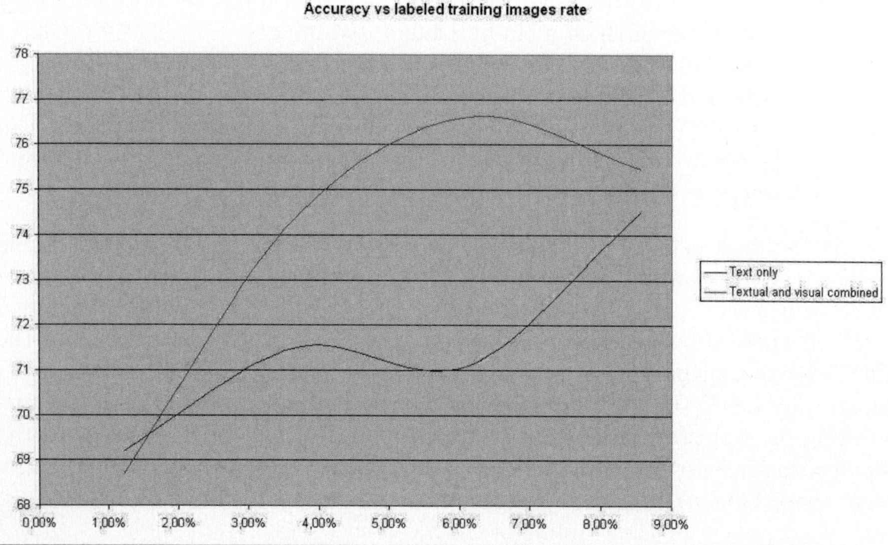

Fig. 3. Learning curves of different classifiers in Experiment 2

the *annotation rate*, i.e. the ratio between the resulting labeled images and the seeding images.

Accuracy measures for Experiment 2 are reported in Figure 3. Good accuracy values (greater than 60%) are obtained even when very small seeding sets are employed (about 1% of the entire training set, and about 5% of the annotated images). This suggests that the employed feature spaces are very effective also given the noisy neature of the source Web data. The plots in figure 3 shows that the classification accuracy grows monotonically with size, even if noisy semi-supervised image annotation is applied. The exceptions are given by small gaps (1% in the *text only* case) probably due to the random process of seed image selection. The best perfomance levels are provided by the second system: It corresponds to a semi-supervised model, characterized by a combination of all features and a training over about 6% of the training images (about 50% of the seeeding labeled data). It is about 14% below the performance of the fully supervised SVM that achieves 96.4%. This result is also interesting given that the estimated speed-up in annotation times is 12 (4 hours vs. 20 minutes for about 1,000 images).

5   Conclusions

A robust and accurate semi-supervised approach to image categorization has been here proposed. We shown that the use of SVD, a purely automatic matrix decomposition process, constitutes a very promising track to fill the semantic gap in multimedia analysis. The approach also supports image search via keyword-based queries, thanks to the integration of texts and visual features. Our method is particularly close to that in [4], although this latter is a pure image annotation task. The major difference is the adoption of a fully automatic approach to data collection, that in our case correspond to downloaded pages from the Web. As in [5], LSA seems a very effective way to capitalize the available heterogeneous features in image classification and annotation.

References

1. Alsabti, K., Ranka, S., Singh, V.: An efficient k-means clustering algorithm. In: First Workshop High Performance Data Mining (1998)
2. Basili, R., Moschitti, A.: Automatic Text Categorization: from Information Retrieval to Support Vector Learning. Aracne (2005)
3. Deerwester, S., Dumais, S., Furnas, G., Harshman, R., Landauer, T.: Indexing by latent semantic analysis. Journal of the American Society for Information Science 41(6), 391–407 (1990)
4. Hare, J.S., Lewis, P.H., Enser, P.G.B., Sandom, C.J.: Mind the gap: Another look at the problem of the semantic gap in image retrieval. In: Proceedings of Multimedia Content Analysis, Management and Retrieval 2006 SPIE (2006)
5. Monay, F., Gatica-Perez, D.: On image auto-annotation with latent space models. In: Proceedings of the 11th annual ACM international conference on Multimedia, ACM Press, New York (2003)
6. RWTH. Lti-lib - computer vision library. Website, Settembre, Universit di Aachen (2006)
7. Salton, G.: Automatic Text Processing–The Transformation, Analysis, and Retrieval of Information by Computer. Addison-Wesley, Reading, Massachusetts (1989)
8. Smeulders, A.W.M., Worring, M., Santini, S., Gupta, A., Jain, R.: Content-based image retrieval at the end of the early years. IEEE Transactions on Pattern Analysis and Machine Intelligence 12(22), 1349–1380 (2000)
9. Vapnik, V.: The Nature of Statistical Learning Theory. Springer, Heidelberg (1995)
10. Witten, I.H., Frank, E.: Data Mining: Practical machine learning tools and techniques. Morgan Kaufmann, San Francisco (2005)

Content Aware Image Enhancement

Gianluigi Ciocca, Claudio Cusano, Francesca Gasparini,
and Raimondo Schettini

DISCo (Dipartimento di Informatica, Sistemistica e Comunicazione)
Università degli Studi di Milano-Bicocca
Via Bicocca degli Arcimboldi 8, 20126 Milano, Italy
{ciocca, cusano, gasparini, schettini}disco.unimib.it

Abstract. We present our approach, integrating imaging and vision, for
content-aware enhancement and processing of digital photographs. The
overall quality of images is improved by a modular procedure automatically driven by the image class and content.

1   Introduction

The quality of real-world photographs can often be considerably improved by digital image processing. Since interactive processes may prove difficult and tedious,
especially for amateur users, an automatic image tool would be most desirable.
There are a number of techniques for image enhancement and processing, including global and local correction for color balancing, [1,2,3], contrast enhancement
[4,5] and edge sharpening [6,7]. Other techniques merge color and contrast corrections, such as all the Retinex like algorithms [8,9,10,11]. Rarely, traditional
enhancement algorithms available in the literature are driven by the content of
images [12].

Our interest is related to the design of content-aware image enhancement
for amateur digital photographs. The underlying idea is that global and/or local
image classification makes it possible to set the most appropriate image enhancement strategy according to the content of the photograph. To this end, we have
pragmatically designed a modular enhancing procedure integrating imaging and
vision techniques. Each module can be considered as an autonomous element,
related to color, contrast, sharpness and defect removal. These modules can be
combined in a complete unsupervised manner to improve the overall quality,
according to image and defect categories. The proposed method is modular so
that each step can be replaced with a more efficient one in future work, without changing the main structure. Also, the method can be improved by simply
inserting new modules. The initial global image classification makes it possible
to further refine the localization of the color regions requiring different types
of color and sharpness corrections. The following color, contrast, and edge enhancement modules may exploit image annotation, together with further image
analysis statistics (in same cases locally adaptive as well). As a final step we also
propose a self-adaptive image cropping module exploiting both visual and semantic information. This module can be useful for users looking at photographs

R. Basili and M.T. Pazienza (Eds.): AI*IA 2007, LNAI 4733, pp. 686–697, 2007.

on small displays that require a quick preview of the relevant image area. Figure 1 shows the overall schema of our content aware image enhancement and processing strategy. Processing blocks responsible for the image content annotation are at the left of the dashed line while those driven by it are at the right of the line. The single modules are described in the following sections.

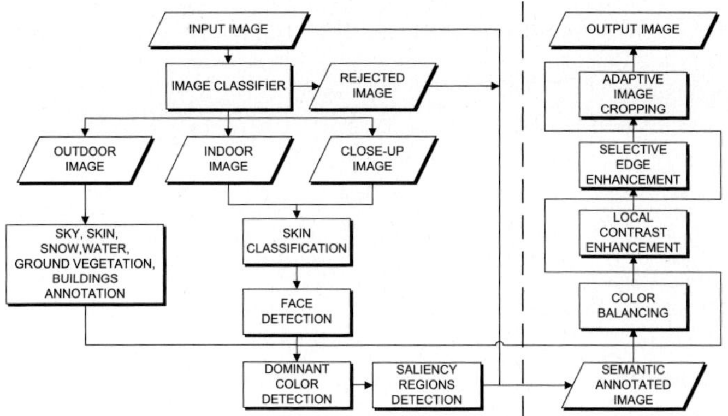

Fig. 1. The processing blocks on the left of the dashed line identify the content of the input image and produce a semantically annotated image. The blocks on the right perform several processing steps exploiting the given annotation.

2   Semantic Image Classification

Automatic image classification allows for the application of the most appropriate enhancement strategy according to the content of the photograph. To this end we designed an image classification strategy [13] based on the analysis of low-level features that can be automatically computed without any prior knowledge of the content of the image. We considered the classes outdoor, indoor, and close-up which correspond to categories of images that may require different enhancement approaches. The indoor class includes photographs of rooms, groups of people, and details in which the context indicates that the photograph was taken inside. The outdoor class includes natural landscapes, buildings, city shots and details in which the context indicates that the photograph was taken outside. The close-up class includes portraits and photos of people and objects in which the context provides little or no information in regards to where the photo was taken. The features we used are related to color (moments of inertia of the color channels in the HSV color space, and skin color distribution), texture and edge (statistics on wavelets decomposition and on edge and texture distributions), and composition of the image (in terms of fragmentation and symmetry).

We used the CART methodology [14] to train tree classifiers. Briefly, tree classifiers are produced by recursively partitioning the space of the features which describe the images. Each split is formed by conditions related to the values of the features. Once a tree has been constructed, a class is assigned to each of the terminal nodes, and when a new case is processed by the tree, its predicted class is the class associated with the terminal node into which the case finally moves on the basis of the values of the features. The construction process is based on a training set of cases of known class. A function of impurity of the nodes, $i(t)$, is introduced, and the decrease in its value produced by a split is taken as a measure of the goodness of the split itself. For each node, all the possible splits on all the features are considered and the split which minimizes the average impurity of the two subnodes is selected. The function of node impurity we have used is the Gini diversity index:

$$i(t) = 1 - \sum_{c=1}^{C} p(c|t)^2, \tag{1}$$

where $p(c|t)$ is the resubstitution estimate of the conditional probability of class c $(c = 1, \cdots, C)$ in node t, that is, the probability that a case found in node t is a case of class c. When the difference in impurity between a node and best subnodes is below a threshold, the node is considered as terminal. The class assigned to a terminal node t is the class c^* for which:

$$p(c^*|t) = \max_{c=1,\cdots,C} p(c|t). \tag{2}$$

In CART methodology the size of a tree is treated as a tuning parameter, and the optimal size is adaptively chosen from the data. A very large tree is grown and then pruned, using a cost-complexity criterion which governs the tradeoff between size and accuracy. Decision forests can be used to overcome the instability of the decision trees improving, at the same time, generalization accuracy. The trees of a decision forest are generated by running the training process on boostrap replicates of the training set. The classification results produced by the single trees are combined applying a majority vote. Each decision tree has been trained on bootstrap replicates of a training set composed of about 4500 photographs manually annotated with the correct class.

Evaluating the decision forest on a test set of 4500 images, we obtained a classification accuracy of about 89%. To further improve the accuracy of the classifier and to avoid doubtful decisions, we introduced an ambiguity rejection option in the classification process: an image is "rejected" if the confidence on the classification result is below a tunable threshold. For instance, setting the threshold in such a way that 30% of the test set was rejected, we obtained a classification accuracy of about 96% on the remaining images.

3 Image Content Annotation Using Intermediate Features

3.1 Outdoor Image Annotation

For the detection of semantically meaningful regions in outdoor photographs, we designed a strategy for the automatic segmentation of images. Segmented regions are assigned to seven classes: sky, skin, vegetation, snow, water, ground, and buildings [15]. The process works as follows: for each pixel, a fixed number of partially overlapping image subdivisions (tiles) that contain it is considered. Each tile is described by a joint histogram which combines color distribution with gradient statistics. Histograms are classified by seven Support Vector Machine (SVM) [16]. The $i-$th SVM defines a discrimination function $f_i(\mathrm{x})$ trained to distinguish between the tiles of class i and those of the other six classes:

$$f_i(\mathrm{x}) = \left(b_i + \sum_{j=1}^{N} k(\mathrm{x}, \mathrm{x}_j) \right) \left(\sum_{j=1}^{N} \sum_{k=1}^{N} \alpha_{ij} \alpha_{ik} k(\mathrm{x}_j, \mathrm{x}_k) \right)^{-\frac{1}{2}}, \tag{3}$$

where x_j, $(j = 1, \cdots, N)$ are the training patterns. The parameters b_i, α_{ij} are estimated by solving a suitable optimization problem. The discrimination function which assumes the maximum value determines the class assigned to a tile. In our method we used a Gaussian kernel function k:

$$k(\mathrm{x}_1, \mathrm{x}_2) = \exp(-p\|\mathrm{x}_1 - \mathrm{x}_2\|_2^2). \tag{4}$$

The final label assigned to a pixel is determined by a majority vote on the classification results obtained on the tiles which contain the pixel. When the majority vote is below a tunable threshold, the class of the pixel is considered as "unknown".

Our strategy achieved a classification accuracy of about 90% on a test set of 10500 tiles (1500 per class) randomly extracted from 200 images.

3.2   Indoor and Close-Ups Image Annotation by Skin Detection

Many different methods for discriminating between skin pixels and non-skin pixels are available. The simplest and most often applied method is to build an "explicit skin cluster" which expressly defines the boundaries of the skin cluster in certain color spaces. The underlying hypothesis of methods based on explicit skin clustering is that skin pixels exhibit similar color coordinates in a properly chosen color space. This type of binary method is very popular since it is easy to implement and does not require a training phase. The main difficulty in achieving high skin recognition rates, and producing the smallest possible number of false positive pixels, is that of defining accurate cluster boundaries through simple, often heuristically chosen, decision rules. We approached the problem of determining the boundaries of the skin clusters in multiple color spaces by applying a genetic algorithm.

A good classifier should have high recall and high precision, but typically, as recall increases, precision decreases. Consequently, we adopted a weighed sum of precision and recall as the fitness of the genetic algorithm. Keeping in mind that different applications can have sharply different requirements, the weighing coefficients can be chosen to offer high recall or high precision or to satisfy a reasonable trade-off between these two scores according to application demands

[17]. In the following applications addressing image enhancement, we adopted the boundaries evaluated for recall oriented strategies, leading to a recall of about 89% and a precision of about 40%.

3.3   Indoor and Close-Ups Image Annotation by Face Detection

Face detection in a single image is a challenging task because the overall appearance of faces ranges widely in scale, location, orientation and pose, as well as in facial expressions and lighting conditions [18,19]. Our objective therefore was not to determine whether or not there are any faces, but instead to evaluate the possibility of having a facial region. To do so, we have trained an auto-associative neural network [20] to output a score map reflecting the confidence of the presence of faces in the input image. It is a three layer linear network, where each pattern of the training set is presented to both the input and the output layers, and the whole network has been trained by a back-propagation sum square error criterion, on a training set of more than 150 images, considering not only face images (frontal faces), but non-face images as well. The network processes only the intensity image, so that the results are color independent. To locate faces of different sizes, the input image is repeatedly scaled down by a factor of 15%, generating a pyramid of sub-sampled images. The performance of the face detector is 95% of true positive and 27% of false positive.

4   Image Content Annotation Using Low Level Features

4.1   Saliency Regions Detection

Visual attention models simulate the human vision system to process and analyze images in order to identify conspicuous regions within the images themselves. These regions (ROIs) can be used to guide the analysis of the images. In the follows we describe the Itti and Koch model [21] that is inspired by the behavior and the neuronal architecture of the early primate visual system.

Input is provided in the form of a color image. Nine images with descending spatial scale are created from the original image using dyadic Gaussian pyramids which progressively low-pass filter and sub-sample the input images. Each feature to be extracted is computed with a set of linear "center-surround" operations akin to visual receptive fields, where visual neurons are most sensitive in a small region of the visual space (center), while stimuli presented in a broader region concentric to the center (surround) inhibit the neuronal response. The difference between images at fine (center) and coarse (surround) scales is used to mimic this behavior. A set of features maps are obtained by varying the scale. Three visual features are exploited: color, intensity and orientation. In the follows Θ indicates the center-surround difference operation between a center image c and a surround image s. A feature map for the intensity feature is computed as:

$$I(c, s) = |I(c)\Theta I(s)|. \tag{5}$$

The second set of maps are computed for the two channel pairs Red/Green and Blue/Yellow as follow:

$$RG(c, s) = |(R(c) - G(c))\Theta(G(s) - R(s))|, \tag{6}$$

$$BY(c, s) = |(B(c) - Y(c))\Theta(B(s) - Y(s))|. \tag{7}$$

Gabor pyramids $O(\sigma, \theta)$, with σ representing the scale and θ representing the orientation, are used to compute the orientation maps.

$$O(c, s, \theta) = |O(c, \theta)\Theta O(s, \theta)|. \tag{8}$$

In total 42 feature maps are computed: 6 for the intensity, 12 for color and 24 for orientation. Before computing the final saliency map, the feature maps are normalized in order to globally promote maps in which a small number of strong peaks of activity (conspicuous locations) are present, while globally suppress maps which contain numerous comparable peak responses. After the normalization process, all the sets of the normalized maps are combined and averaged into the final saliency map S.

4.2   Image Dominant Color Detection and Classification

The basic idea of our solution is that by analyzing the color distribution of the image in a suitable color space with simple statistical tools, it is possible not only to evaluate whether or not a dominant color is present, but also to classify it. The color gamut of the image is first mapped in the CIELab color space, where the chromatic components and lightness are separate. Intuitively, the 2-dimensional color histogram $F(a, b)$ depends on color properties of the image: for a multicolor image without cast this histogram will show several peaks distributed over the whole ab-plane, while for a single color image, it will present a single peak, or few peaks in a limited region. The more concentrated the histogram and the farther from the neutral axis, the more intense the cast. To study the histogram distribution we use the, respectively the mean values (μ_a, μ_b) and the variances (σ_a^2, σ_b^2) of the histogram projections along the two chromatic axes a, b.

We can now associate with each histogram an *Equivalent Circle* (EC) with its center in $C = (\mu_a, \mu_b)$ and a radius of $\sigma = \sqrt{\sigma_a^2 + \sigma_b^2}$, defining in this way a distance $D : D = \mu - \sigma$, where $\mu = \sqrt{\mu_a^2 + \mu_b^2}$, a measure of how far the whole histogram (identified by its equivalent circle) lies from the neutral axis $(a = 0, b = 0)$. To characterize the EC quantitatively, we introduce the ratio $D_\sigma = D/\sigma$, as a useful parameter for measuring the intensity of the cast: the greater the D_σ, the stronger the cast. The cast detection step first analyzes the color histogram distribution in the ab chromatic plane, examining its EC and evaluating the statistical values σ, μ, and D_σ. If the histogram is concentrated (small value of σ) and far from the neutral axis (high value of μ and D_σ), the colors of the image are confined to a small region. This means that there is either a strong cast (to be removed), or what we have called an intrinsic cast (to be preserved). The latter is usually found in the presence of widespread areas of vegetation, skin, sky, or sea.

To distinguish between true cast and predominant color, a statistical classifier exploiting both color and spatial information is used to identify regions that probably correspond to skin, sky, sea, or vegetation [22]. If the classifier considers one of these regions significant, an intrinsic cast is likely, and the image is not subjected to cast removal. Otherwise, the image is identified as a cast image, and processed for color correction. All images without a clearly concentrated color histogram are analyzed with a following procedure based on the criterion that a cast has a greater influence on a neutral region than on objects with colors of high chroma. The color distribution of what we call Near Neutral Objects (NNO) [23,24] is studied with the same statistical tools described above. A pixel of the image belongs to the NNO region if its chroma is less than an initial fixed value and if it is not isolated, but has some neighbors that present similar chromatic characteristics. If the percentage of pixels that satisfies these requisites is less than a predefined percentage of the whole image, the minimum radius of the neutral region is extended, and the region recursively evaluated.

When there is a cast, we may expect the NNO color histogram to show a single small spot, or at most a few spots in a limited region. NNO colors spread around the neutral axis, or distributed in several distinct spots indicate instead that there is no cast. The statistical analysis that we have performed on the whole histogram is now applied to the NNO histogram, allowing us to distinguish among three cases: cast images, no cast images, and ambiguous ones. If we define, with obvious meaning, σ_{NNO}, μ_{NNO}, and $D_{\sigma NNO}$, NNO histograms that are well defined and concentrated far from the neutral axis will have a positive $D_{\sigma NNO}$: the image has a cast. With negative values of $D_{\sigma NNO}$ the histogram presents an almost uniform spread distribution around the neutral axis, indicating no cast. Exploiting the experience of a large number of images we set as thresholds $D_{\sigma NNO} = 0.5$ for cast images and $D_{\sigma NNO} = -0.5$ for no cast images. Cases falling in the interval between -0.5 and 0.5 are considered ambiguous.

5   Image Processing and Enhancement

5.1   Color Balancing

To recover the original appearance of the scene, under different lighting and display conditions, the measured RGB values must be transformed. Many algorithms have been developed for color balancing based on the Von Kries assumption that each sensor channel is transformed independently. The gray world, and the white balance, which correspond respectively to average-to-gray and normalize-to-white, are perhaps the most commonly used [3,25].

The gray world algorithm assumes that, given an image with a sufficient amount of color variations, the mean value of the R, G, B components of the image will average out to a common gray value. Once we have chosen the common gray value, each color component is scaled by the averages of the three RGB channels. There are several versions of the white balance algorithm: the basic concept is to set at white a point or a region that appears reasonably white in the real scene. Once it has been set, each color component is scaled by the averages of the three RGB channels in this region. However, when one of these color balance adjustments is performed automatically, with no knowledge of the image source, the mood of the original scene is often altered in the output image.

The cast removal method we propose is applied only to those images classified as having a clear cast, or an ambiguous cast in order to avoid problems such as the mistaken removal of predominant color, or the distortion of the image's chromatic balance. The main peculiarity of the method lies in how it determines the White Balance (WB) region, which also depends on the strength of the cast. To avoid the mistaken removal of an intrinsic color, regions previously identified by the cast detector as probably corresponding to skin, sky, sea or vegetation, are temporarily removed from the analyzed image. At this point the algorithm differentiates between images with a clear cast and images with a low, or ambiguous one.

This color balance algorithm can be considered a mixture of the white balance and gray world procedures. The WB region is formed by several objects of different colors, which are set at white not singularly, but as an average. This prevents the chromatic distortion that follows on the wrong choice of the region to be whitened. When there is a clear cast, the colors of all the objects in the image suffer the same shift due to that specific cast. If we consider the average over several objects, introducing a kind of gray world assumption, only that shift survives and will be removed. Note that for images where the WB region consists of a single object, such as is usually the case of images with a strong cast, our method tends to correspond to the conventional white balance algorithm, while for images where the WB region includes more objects (as in images with a softer cast), the method tends to the gray world algorithm.

We have compared our results on 746 cast images, with those obtained with conventional white patch and gray world algorithms. We collected the majority opinion of the five experts. This analysis, gives our algorithm as consistently better than the gray world with the exception of only a few cases (10), when it is judged equal. In comparison with the white patch algorithm, our method is judged better in 40% of the cases, while in the rest it is judged equal. In the great majority of the experimented cases, the processed image was held to be superior to the original; only in less than 2% of the 746 images processed was the output judged worse than the original.

5.2   Local Contrast Enhancement

The original dynamic range of a scene is generally constrained into the smaller dynamic range of the acquisition system. This makes it difficult to design a global tone correction that is able to enhance both shadow and highlight details. Several methods for adjusting image contrast, [4,5,9,10,11], have been developed in the field of image processing for image enhancement. In general, it is possible to discriminate between two classes of contrast corrections: global and local corrections. With global contrast corrections it is difficult to accommodate both lowlight and highlight details. The advantage of local contrast corrections is that it provides a method to map one input value to many different output values, depending on the values of the neighboring pixels and this allows for simultaneous shadow and highlight adjustments.

Our contrast enhancement method is based on a local and image dependent exponential correction [26]. The simplest exponential correction, better known as gamma correction, is common in the image processing field, and consists in elaborating the input image through a constant power function. This correction gives good results for totally underexposed or overexposed images. However, when both underexposed and overexposed regions are simultaneously present in an image, this correction is not satisfactory. As we are interested in a local correction, the exponent of the gamma correction used by our algorithm is not a constant. Instead, it is chosen as a function that depends on the point to be corrected, on its neighboring pixels and on the global characteristics of the image. This function is also chosen to be edge preserving to eliminate halo artifacts. Usually it happens, especially for low quality images with compression artefacts, that the noise in the darker zones is enhanced. To overcome this undesirable loss in the image quality, a further step of contrast enhancement was added. This step consists of a stretching and clipping procedure, and an algorithm to increase the saturation.

5.3   Selective Edge Enhancement

The key idea is to process the image locally according to topographic maps obtained by a neurodynamical model of visual attention, overcoming the tradeoff between smoothing and sharpening typical of the traditional approaches. In fact, only high frequencies corresponding to regions that are non-significant to our visual system are smoothed while significant details are sharpened.

In our algorithm, the enhanced image $f_e(x,y)$ is obtained correcting the original $f(x,y)$ by subtracting non-salient high frequencies $f_{hNS}(x,y)$, which produces a smoothing effect, and adding salient high frequencies, $f_{hS}(x,y)$, with a consequent edge sharpening. In formula:

$$f_e(x,y) = f(x,y) - \lambda f_{hNS}(x,y) + \lambda f_{hS}(x,y). \tag{9}$$

Salient high frequencies, $f_{hS}(x,y)$ are obtained weighting all the image high frequencies through a topographic map corresponding to visually salient regions, obtained by the neurodynamical model of visual attention described in Section 4.1. This permits to enhance the edges differently without enhancing the perceived noise. On the other hand, non-salient high frequencies, $f_{hNS}(x,y)$ are simply obtained weighing all the high frequencies through the complement of the same topographic map, causing an adaptive smoothing. In our implementation, the high frequencies $f_h(x,y)$ of Equation 9 are evaluated using the Laplacian, which is the simplest isotropic derivative operator. It should be noted that our enhancement method is actually independent from the high-pass filter used.

5.4   Adaptive Image Cropping

Some of the efforts that have been put on image adaptation are related to the ROI coding scheme introduced in JPEG 2000 [27]. Most of the approaches for adapting images only focused on compressing the whole image in order to reduce the data transmitted. Few other methods use an auto-cropping technique to reduce the size of the image transmitted [28,29]. These methods decompose the image into a set of spatial information elements (saliency regions) which are then displayed serially to help users' browsing or searching through the whole image. These methods are heavily based on a visual attention model technique that is used to identify the saliency regions to be cropped. We designed a self-adaptive image cropping algorithm exploiting both visual and semantic information [30]. Visual information is obtained by a visual attention model, while semantic information relates to the automatically assigned image genre and to the detection of face and skin regions. The processing steps of the algorithm are firstly driven by the classification phase and then further specialized with respect to the annotated face and skin regions.

The classification of the images to be cropped allows us to build a cropping strategy specific for each image class. The efficacy of the strategy is maximized by taking into account the properties of the image and focusing our attention to some objects in the image instead of others. A landscape image, for example, due to its lack of specific focus elements, is not processed at all: the image is regarded as being wholly relevant. A close up image, generally, shows only a single object or subject in the foreground, and thus, the cropping region should take into account only this discarding any region that can be considered as background. In case of an image belonging to the other class, we are concerned in whether it contains people or not. In the first case, the cropping strategy should prioritize the selection of regions containing most of the people. To perform this, we first analyze the images in order to detect candidate face regions. These regions are then validated by checking the amount of skin present and those that have a given amount of skin are selected as true face regions. Regions detected by the visual attention model, skin regions, and face regions are then combined together to detect the final relevant regions to be cropped. Here we focus our interest in checking the presence of people, but the analysis can be further specialized for the identification of other objects. Images without people are processed with a pipeline similar to the one for the close up images. The main difference lays in the fact that more than one cropping region can be returned by the algorithm.

Although the visual attention model is used in all the different cropping strategies, it requires a tuning of several parameters that influence the results depending on the image content. The image classification phase allows us to heuristically tune these parameters at the best. The last phase in the adaptive image cropping aims at adjusting the cropping region such that the overall information is maximized and all the space in the output display is used. The region is rotated if the orientation of the region differs from the normal orientation of the display. Further, the region is enlarged and/or trimmed in order to retain the display's aspect ratio maintaining the cropped region centered. Finally, the cropped image is resized to the size of the display.

To evaluate the goodness of the proposed image cropping strategy, we collected the judgments of a panel of five nonprofessional photographers which can be summarized as follows: about 7% of the output images were judged worse than the original image scaled to fit the small screen display; about 40% were judged equivalent (the great majority of landscape images are correctly classified and since they are not cropped according to our procedure they are equivalent to the resized original), while the remaining 53% of the images were judged better. Without considering landscapes, the percentage of images judged better increases. The worst results are mostly due to the errors introduced by the face detector. Most of the misclassified images by the CART algorithm are still cropped acceptably.

6   Conclusions

The main objective of image enhancement is to compensate image degradations by altering local and global image features. We strongly believe that the most appropriate enhancement strategy can be safely and effectively applied only if the image to be processed is semantically annotated. To this end we have designed a modular, fully automatic, content-aware enhancement procedure. The modular structure adopted will make it possible to easily replace any of the implemented algorithms with a more efficient/effective one in the future. Also, the overall procedure can be improved by simply inserting new modules for other image artifacts.

References

1. Buchsbaum, G.: A spatial processor model for object color perception. Journal of Franklin Institute 310, 1–26 (1980)
2. Cardei, V., Funt, B., Barnard, K.: White Point Estimation for Uncalibrated Images. In: Proc. of the IS&T/SID Seventh Color Imaging Conference, pp. 97–100 (1999)
3. Barnard, K., Cardei, V., Funt, B.: Comparison of Computational Color Constancy Algorithms-Part I: Methodology and Experiments with Synthesized Data. IEEE Transactions on Image Processing 11(9), 972–983 (2002)
4. Tomasi, C., Manduchi, R.: Bilateral filtering for gray and color images. In: Proc. IEEE Int. Conf. on Computer Vision, pp. 836–846. IEEE Computer Society Press, Los Alamitos (1998)
5. Moroney, N.: Local colour correction using non-linear masking. In: Proc. IS&T/SID Eighth Color Imaging Conference, pp. 108–111 (2000)
6. Kashyap, R.L.: A robust variable length nonlinear filter for edge enhancement and noise smoothing. In: Proc. of the Int. Conf. on Signal Processing, pp. 143–145 (1994)
7. Polesel, A., Ramponi, G., Mathews, V.J.: Image Enhancement Via Adaptive Unsharp Masking. IEEE Transactions on Image Processing 9(3), 505–510 (2000)
8. Land, E.: The Retinex Theory of Color Vision. Scientific American 237, 108–129 (1997)
9. Rahman, Z., Jobson, D., Woodell, G.: Retinex processing for automatic image enhancement. Journal of Electronic Imaging 13(1), 100–110 (2004)
10. Rizzi, A., Gatta, C., Marini, D.: A new algorithm for unsupervised global and local color correction. Pattern Recognition Letters 24, 1663–1677 (2003)

11. Meylan, L., Susstrunk, S.: Bio-inspired image enhancement for natural color images. Proc. IS&T/SPIE Electronic Imaging 5292, 46–56 (2004)
12. Naccari, F., Battiato, S., Bruna, A., Capra, A., Castorina, A.: Natural Scene Classification for Color Enhancement. IEEE Trans. on Consumer Electronics 5(1), 234–239 (2005)
13. Schettini, R., Brambilla, C., Cusano, C., Ciocca, G.: Automatic classification of digital photographs based on decision forests. Int. Journal of Pattern Recognition and Artificial Intelligence 18(5), 819–845 (2004)
14. Breiman, L., Friedman, J.H., Olshen, R.A., Stone, C.J.: Classification and Regression Trees, Wadsworth and Brooks/Cole (1984)
15. Cusano, C., Gasparini, F., Schettini, R.: Image annotation for adaptive enhancement of uncalibrated color images. In: Bres, S., Laurini, R. (eds.) VISUAL 2005. LNCS, vol. 3736, pp. 216–225. Springer, Heidelberg (2006)
16. Cortes, C., Vapnik, V.: Support-Vector Networks. Machine Learning 20(3), 273–297
17. Gasparini, F., Schettini, R.: Skin segmentation using multiple thresholding. In: Santini, S., Schettini, R., Gevers, T. (eds.) Proc. Internet Imaging VII, vol. 6061, pp. 1–8 (2006)
18. Rowley, H., Baluja, S., Kanade, T.: Neural Network-Based Face Detection. IEEE Trans. on Pattern Analysis and Machine Intelligence 20(1), 23–28 (1998)
19. Yang, M.H, Kriegman, D.J., Ahuja, N.: Detecting Faces in Images: A Survey. IEEE Trans. on Pattern Analysis and Machine Intelligence 24(1), 34–58 (2002)
20. Gasparini, F., Schettini, R.: Automatic redeye removal for smart enhancement of photos of unknown origin. In: Bres, S., Laurini, R. (eds.) VISUAL 2005. LNCS, vol. 3736, pp. 226–233. Springer, Heidelberg (2006)
21. Itti, L., Koch, C.: A model of saliency based visual attention of rapid scene analysis. IEEE Trans. on Pattern Analysis and Machine Intelligence 20, 1254–1259 (1998)
22. Ciocca, G., Cusano, C., Schettini, R.: Image annotation using SVM. In: Santini, S., Schettini, R. (eds.) Proc Internet imaging V SPIE, vol. 5304, pp. 330–338 (2004)
23. Cooper, T.: A Novel Approach to Color Cast Detection and Removal in digital Images. In: Proc. SPIE, vol. 3963, pp. 167–175 (2000)
24. Cooper, T.: Color Segmentation as an Aid to White Balancing for Digital Still Cameras. In: Proc. SPIE, vol. 4300, pp. 164–171 (2001)
25. Barnard, K., Cardei, V., Funt, B.: A Comparison of Computational Color Constancy Algorithms-Part I: Experiments with Image Data. IEEE Transaction On Image Processing 11(9) (2002)
26. Capra, A., Corchs, S., Gasparini, F., Schettini, R.: Dynamic Range Optimization by Local Contrast Correction and Histogram Image Analysis. In: ICCE 2006. Proc. IEEE International Conference on Consumer Electronics, pp. 309–310 (2006)
27. Christopoulos, C., Skodras, A., Ebrahimi, T.: The JPEG2000 still image coding system: an overview. IEEE Trans. Consumer Electronic 46(4), 1103–1127 (2000)
28. Chen, L., Xie, X., Fan, X., Ma, W., Zhang, H., Zhou, H.: A visual attention model for adapting images on small displays. Multimedia Systems 9, 353–364 (2003)
29. Suh, B., Ling, H., Bederson, B.B., Jacobs, D.W.: Automatic Thumbnail Cropping and its Effectiveness. In: Proc. UIST'03, pp. 95–104 (2003)
30. Ciocca, G., Cusano, C., Gasparini, F., Schettini, R.: Self Adaptive Image Cropping for Small Displays. In: ICCE. Proc. IEEE Int. Conf. on Consumer Electronics, pp. 10–14. IEEE Computer Society Press, Los Alamitos (2007)

Semantic Annotation of Complex Human Scenes for Multimedia Surveillance

Carles Fernández[1], Pau Baiget[1], Xavier Roca[1], and Jordi Gonzàlez[2]

[1] Computer Vision Centre, Edifici O. Campus UAB, 08193, Bellaterra, Spain
[2] Institut de Robòtica i Informàtica Ind. UPC, 08028, Barcelona, Spain
{perno,pbaiget,xroca,poal}@cvc.uab.es

Abstract. A Multimedia Surveillance System (MSS) is considered for automatically retrieving semantic content from complex outdoor scenes, involving both human behavior and traffic domains. To characterize the dynamic information attached to detected objects, we consider a deterministic modeling of spatio-temporal features based on abstraction processes towards fuzzy logic formalism. A situational analysis over conceptualized information will not only allow us to describe human actions within a scene, but also to suggest possible interpretations of the behaviors perceived, such as situations involving thefts or dangers of running over. Towards this end, the different levels of semantic knowledge implied throughout the process are also classified into a proposed taxonomy.

1 Introduction

The idea of *Multimedia Surveillance Systems* (MSS) is growing importance in various application fields concerning the automatic extraction and management of contents from large databases of media streams [5]. The term *multimedia* is related to systems which provide human end-users for accessing to or communicating with applications dealing with certain type of multimedia content. Applications for sports and surveillance domains, on the other hand, generate continuous streams of abundant data from real-time monitoring over controlled environments, thus requiring proper techniques for the evaluation of video and audio sequences and efficient storing of their significant content. An effective management of these documents depends in great measure on the availability of indexes, as stated in [12], and since manual techniques are not feasible for large audiovisual collections, systems for automatic management of such databases in a real-time context are very valuable in order to facilitate real-time reactivity.

The detection, understanding, and description of human motion patterns in video sequences has been a subject of increased interest over the last years. Motion analysis techniques are used to address the semantic classification of visually perceived information. Motion detection is required for the solution of many other complex tasks, such as image sequence analysis and understanding. Moeslund et al. have extensively reviewed recent advances in human motion capture and analysis in [8]. The extraction of content from image sequences is currently becoming a central focus of attention for many researchers, too [6].

R. Basili and M.T. Pazienza (Eds.): AI*IA 2007, LNAI 4733, pp. 698–709, 2007.

Most efforts in semantic annotation and video indexing have been devoted so far to classification techniques for particular, definite domains, such as sports, movies, or news. Assfalg et al. have discussed approaches for the retrieval of visual information and semantic annotation of its contents [2]. They encourage the use of low-level visual primitives to capture semantic content at a higher level of significance, in specific domains such as news or sports. Also, Smeulders et al. discussed the content extraction and analysis in image retrieval systems [11].

Here, we focus on the automatic, real-time extraction of semantic content from video recordings obtained in outdoor surveillance environments. We aim to evaluate complex behaviors involving both humans and vehicles, detecting the significant events developed, and providing semantic-oriented outputs which are more easily handleable for indexing, search, and retrieval purposes, such as annotated video streams, small sets of content-expressing images, or summaries of occurrences. An important objective is also the temporal characterization of the structure of a recording from this semantic perspective. Although a single video modality is implemented so far, the designed outline pursues the eventual integration of knowledge sources having intrinsically different natures. For this purpose, a taxonomy has been conceived for ensuring a future effective collaboration among knowledge derived from agent, body, and face motion.

This paper is organized as follows: first, our proposal of taxonomy for classifying the different types of knowledge involved in MSS is presented in Section 2. In Section 3, the automatic acquisition of visual features is introduced, which provides structural information over time. Section 4 discusses how a subsequent abstraction step converts this knowledge into a logic-deductive form, thus expressing it by means of semantic predicates. Section 5 presents the high-level analysis of the contextualized situations to generate a set of thematic descriptors. Experimental results in Section 6 describe the main relevant happenings in a particular outdoor scene, resulting in the division of the temporal structure of the recording into content-based intervals. Finally, Section 7 concludes the paper and presents future lines of work.

2   Human Motion Taxonomy

When considering systems for the annotation of content, it becomes laborious – and sometimes uncertain– to accurately classify the concepts related to the field of evaluation, and to establish proper relationships among them. The reason for such a statement comes from thinking of the great generality of the situations to be considered. Upon this, a question arises: which kind of information needs to be represented for properly evaluating human behavior?

Although a specific problem domain has been chosen in this paper, a MSS needs to cope with a wide range of occurrences. The temporal dimension of a video sequence determines the nature of the semantic content to be extracted, thus suggesting that the use of mechanisms for a proper characterization should be based on motion detection. Additionally, the most difficult issues to solve are obviously related to human behaviors, so the proposed classification scheme is

Table 1. A knowledge-based classification of human motion representations. This *human motion taxonomy*, which includes several levels of representation, will guide the process of interpretation.

	Description	Examples for:		
		Agent	Body	Face
Pose Vector	Array of Static Configurations over time	trajectory of locations	sequence of postures, gestures	sequence of expressions
Event	Dynamic interpretaton of static elements	*stopped: sitting? / standing?*	*stand, move head up and down*	*serious expr.: worry? / concentration?*
Contextualized Event	Disambiguation using information from other levels	*standing in front of a scene object*	*nod? / search for something?*	*attention (staring at scene object)*
Interpreted Behavior	Hypothesis of interpretation using complete scene knowledge	*"A person is searching for information on the timetables of the subway station"*		

conceived in terms of human motion. Literature already contains some suggested classification criteria based on different models of taxonomy. The current taxonomy enhances the proposal of Gonzàlez [6], which in turn unifies the taxonomies of Bobick [4] and Nagel [9]. Our classification proposes four hierarchical levels of semantics, see Table 1:

- First of all, *Status Vectors* are collections of detected static configurations for the tracked elements. This includes positions, orientations or velocities for the agents for each time-step, and other spatial information over time such as postures, gestures, or expressions, but no interpretation at all. Semantics is present in form of structural information.
- The analysis of these collections over time allow to detect *Events*, i.e. basic dynamic interpretations of a predefined set of static configurations for a local environment. Patterns which are shared in common with a sequence of temporal status are identified and classified according to predefined models. Some examples include to detect that a pedestrian is running or turning, and that a car is accelerating or braking.
- Next level is suggested to be a *Contextualized Event*, this is, a concretion or disambiguation of the possible interpretations for an event. An event will be fenalyzed with respect to other detected elements within the scene. The interrelation among results from different tracking domains plays an important role in the process of contextualizing an event, e.g. 'sit down'–'bus stop', 'wave hand'–'open mouth', or 'tired expression'–'climb stairs'.
- Finally, a conjecture for global understanding of a scene is suggested by an hypothesis of *Interpretation* for the detected behaviors. All the information

Table 2. Classification of some possible semantic descriptions using the proposed taxonomy. The ontology of terms is formed by a set of conceptual predicates, which are associated to agents (human or vehicular), objects, and events related to the detected occurrences within the scene. Higher semantic levels also incorporate a higher level of uncertainty for the inferences.

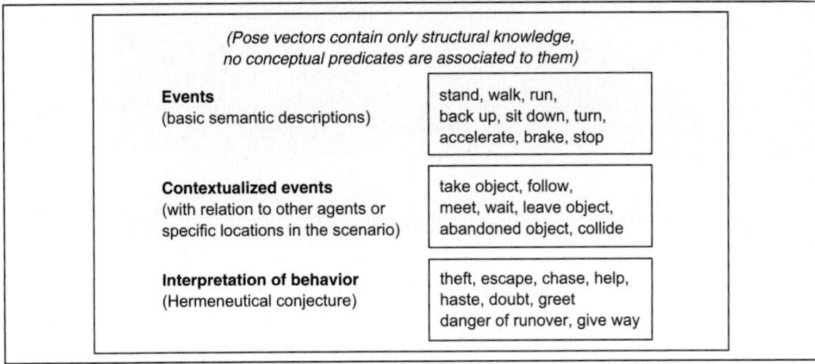

sources are considered at this point, including some domain-dependent bases of knowledge from the world. Interpretations include an important part of uncertainty, thus giving an impression of subjectiveness, which is founded on visual evidence and given models. This last level constitutes an actual process of *video hermeneutics* over the scene.

Table 2 applies this taxonomy to classify some of the targeted occurrences to be detected. In order to infer a complete interpretation of the scene, both sensory and semantic gaps need to be bridged. The last level of 'guided' uncertainty is included into the taxonomy towards this goal. It can be seen that this proposal takes into account all the considered levels of extraction of visual information –i.e. agent, body, face, and relation with other detected objects, agents, and events–, and also suggests a proper way of managing the different stages of knowledge. This categorization takes into account the relevance of the retrieved information, some hierarchical degrees of perspective, and also the level of subjectiveness required for a scene interpretation.

3   Extraction of Visual Information

There are many different tasks involved in the processes of acquisition of visual information from the video recordings. In the first place, a process of segmentation locates the significant information within the image data and considers it as a part of the foreground region by means of a background model. Next, tracking processes maintain the identification of the targets and recover from possible segmentation errors, principally derived from occlusions and illumination conditions. In this paper we use the segmentation and tracking processes presented in [3], which are far from the scope of this paper. As a result, information about the geometrical position of the agent in ground-plane coordinates at

Fig. 1. The Theft Scene

each time-step, and also his instantaneous velocity and orientation are achieved. This knowledge is enclosed in the so-called *Agent Status Vectors*.

Experimental results have been focused to be specialized to a single type of scenario in order to study the problems in-depth, rather attempting to come up with a supposedly generally applicable solution. A particular scene has been considered, which contains complex situations resulting from the interaction of pedestrians and vehicles in an outdoor environment. It consists of a crosswalk scene, in which some agents (pedestrians and cars) and objects appear and interact. This scene includes several behaviors by the agents, e.g. displacements, meetings, crossings, accelerations, object disposals, and more complex situations such as an abandoned object, a danger of running over, and a theft. The recording has been obtained using a distributed system of static cameras, and the scenario has been modeled a priori, see Fig. 1.

An algorithm has been applied for automatic segmentation of the scenario. The trajectories of the agents are sampled, interpolated, and finally a set of segments are defined for the scenario. More details about this process can be seen in [3]. Once the scenario has been automatically segmented in geometrical terms, the resulting locations need to be categorized according to their semantic properties. This way, different regions are enclosed into separate categories like *sideway_segment*, *road_segment*, *crosswalk*, *exit*, or *waiting_zone*, depending on which behaviors can be expected for an agent at the considered location. This step will enable further contextualization for the events of an agent. This process of categorization is done in a supervised manner at present.

4   Abstraction and Conceptual Manipulation

The acquisition of visual information produces an extensive amount of geometric data, considering that computer vision algorithms are applied continuously over the recordings. Such a large collection of results turns out to be increasingly difficult to handle. Thus, a process of abstraction is needed in order to extract and manage the relevant knowledge derived from the tracking processes. The question arises how these spatiotemporal developments should be represented in terms of significance, also allowing further semantic interpretations. Several requirements have to be accomplished towards this end [7]:

1. Generally, the detected scene developments are only valid for a certain time interval: the produced statements must be updated and time-delimited.
2. There is an intrinsic *uncertainty* derived from the estimation of quantities in image sequences (i.e. the sensory gap), due to the stochastic properties of the input signal, artifacts during the acquisition processes, undetected events from the scene, or false detections.
3. An abstraction step is necessary to obtain a formal representation of the visual information retrieved from the scene.
4. This representation has to allow different domains of human knowledge, e.g. analysis of human or vehicular agents, posture recognition, or expression analysis, for an eventual semantic interpretation.

Fuzzy Metric Temporal *Horn* Logic (FMTHL) has been conceived as a suitable mechanism to solve each of the aforementioned demands [10]. It is a rule-based inference engine in which conventional logic formalisms are extended by a temporal and a fuzzy component. This last one enables to cope with uncertain or partial information, by allowing variables to have degrees of truth or falsehood. The temporal component permits to represent and reason about propositions qualified in terms of time. These propositions are represented by means of *conceptual predicates*, whose validity is evaluated at each time-step.

All sources of knowledge are translated into this logic predicate formalism for the subsequent reasoning and inference stages. In the first place, agent status vectors are converted into `has_status` conceptual predicates:

$$t \ ! \ \texttt{has\_status (Agent, X, Y, Theta, V)} \tag{1}$$

These predicates hold information for a global identification of the agent ($Agent$), his spatial location in a ground-plane representation of the scenario (X, Y), and his instantaneous orientation ($Theta$) and velocity (V). A *has_status* predicate is generated at each time-step for each detected agent. In addition, certain predicates are generated for identifying the category of the agent, e.g. `pedestrian(Agent)` or `vehicle(Agent)`. Similarly, the segmented regions from the scenario are also converted into logic descriptors holding spatial characteristics, and the semantic categories are also included:

$$\texttt{point (14, 5, p42)}$$
$$\texttt{line (p42, p43, 142)}$$
$$\texttt{segment (131, 142, lseg\_31)}$$
$$\texttt{crosswalk\_segment (lseg\_31)} \tag{2}$$

The abstraction process is thus applied over the information obtained both from the scenario and from the agents, i.e. the categorized segments from the considered location and the agent status vectors generated. Quantitative values

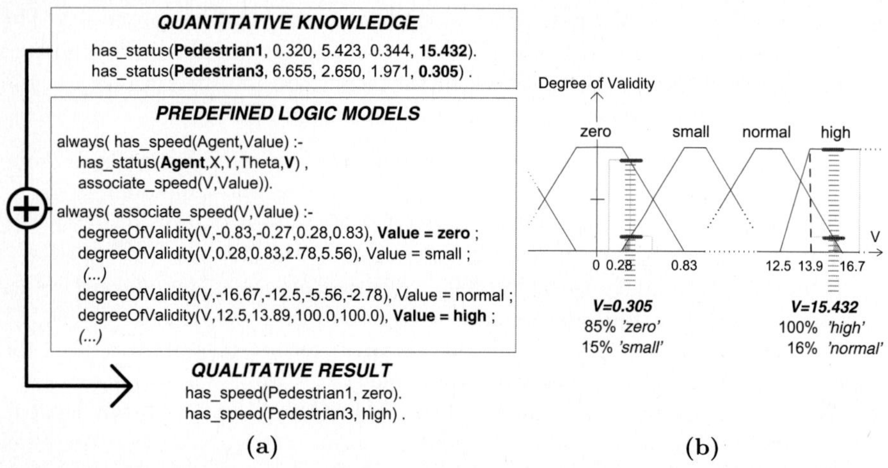

Fig. 2. Conversion from quantitative to qualitative values. (a) The input status vectors contain information for the agents. As a result, qualitative descriptions are represented logically. (b) FMTHL includes fuzzy mechanisms accepting more than one single interpretation, since it confers *degrees of validity* to values on uncertain ranges.

are converted into qualitative descriptions in form of conceptual predicates, by adding fuzzy semantic parameters such as *close*, *far*, *high*, *small*, *left*, or *right*. The addition of fuzzy degrees allows to deal with the uncertainty associated to visual acquisition processes, also stating the goodness of the conceptualization. Fig. 2 gives an example for the evaluation of a `has_speed` predicate from an asserted `has_status` fact. The conversion from quantitative to qualitative knowledge is accomplished by incorporating domain-related models to the reasoning system. Hence, new inferences can be performed over an instantaneous collection of conceptual facts, enabling the derivation of logical conclusions from the assumed evidence. Higher-level inferences progressively incorporate more contextual information, i.e. relations with other detected entities in the scenario. This spatiotemporal universe of basic conceptual relations supplies the dynamic interpretations which are necessary for detecting *events* within the scene, as described in the taxonomy.

5   Behavioral Analysis

An independent stage is implemented for achieving effective modeling of behaviors. The concurrence of hundreds of conceptual predicates makes necessary to think of a separate module for dealing with new semantic properties at a higher level: some guidelines are necessary to establish relations of cause, effect, precedence, grouping, interaction, and in general any reasoning performed with time-constrained information at multiple levels of analysis, i.e. the contextualization and interpretation levels as proposed in the taxonomy.

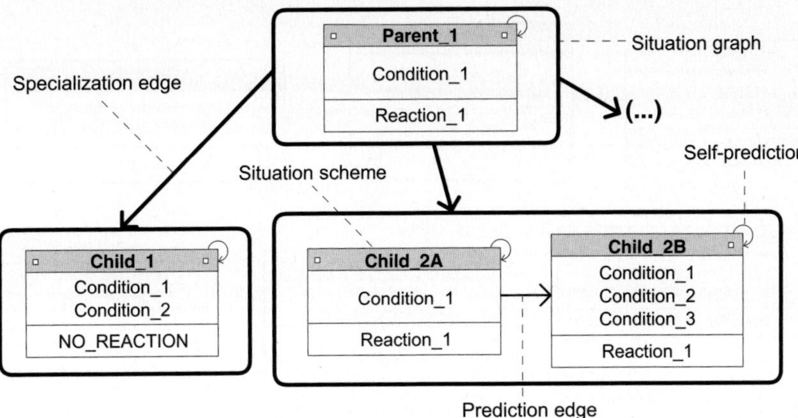

Fig. 3. General example of a Situation Graph Tree. Situation graphs are represented as rounded rectangles, situation schemes as normal ones. When the conditions of the parent situation scheme are asserted, the situation specializes in one of the possible situation graphs. Small rectangles to the left or to the right of the name of a situation scheme mark that scheme as a start- or end-situation.

The tool which has been chosen to enable behavior modeling is the Situation Graph Tree (SGT), see [1,6]. SGTs are hierarchical classification trees used to describe the behavior of the agents in terms of situations they can be in. These trees are based on deterministic models which explicitly represent and combine the specialization, temporal, and semantic relationships of the conceptual facts which have been asserted. A general example of a SGT is shown in Fig. 3.

The semantic knowledge related to any agent at a given point of time is contained in a *situation scheme*, which constitutes the basic component of a SGT. A situation scheme can be seen as a semantic function which evaluates an input consisting of a set of conditions –the so-called *state predicates*–, and generates logic outputs at a higher level –the *action predicates*– once all the conditions are asserted. Here, the action predicate is a `note` method which generates a semantic annotation in a language-oriented form, containing fields related to thematic roles such as *Agent, Patient, Object* or *Location*. Situations schemes representing different temporal episodes of the same situation are enclosed by situation graphs. The evolution over time is indicated by means of *prediction edges*, either between different situations or within a persistent state (self-prediction). On the other hand, SGTs also allow for conceptual or temporal particularizations of general situations, using *specialization edges*. Tree structures appear as a result of these specializations. A SGT has been designed for the Theft Scene: Fig. 4 shows a piece of it, which illustrates how the behavioral analysis is performed in order to identify situations such as an abandoned object or a theft. The whole SGT is transformed into FMTHL for automatic exploitation of its behavior schemes.

By selecting the conditions to incorporate into the set of state predicates, we both integrate asserted facts obtained from different sources and also establish

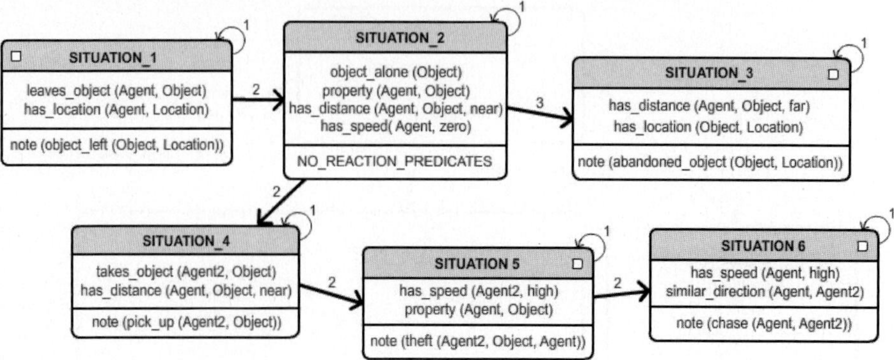

Fig. 4. Part of the SGT used for behavioral analysis of the Theft Scene. This situation graph is evaluated when the system detects that an object has been left by the pedestrian who owns it. The set of conditions are FMTHL predicates, the reaction predicate is a `note` command which generates a semantic tag.

certain attentional factors over the whole universe of occurrences. Thus, this first step accomplishes the *contextualization* stage included in the taxonomy. On the other hand, the generation of `note` action predicates can be understood as the *interpretation* of a line of behaviors, for a concrete domain and towards a concrete goal.

The results obtained from the behavioral level, i.e. the annotations generated by the situational analysis of an agent, can yet be considered as outputs of a process for *content detection*. From this point of view, a SGT would be the classified collection of all possible domain-related semantic tags to be assigned to a video sequence. In addition, the temporal segmentation of video is also achieved: since the semantic tags are temporally valid, a video sequence can be split in the time-intervals which define these tags. As a result, each video segment is associated to individual and cohesive conceptual information.

6   Experimental Results

Tests have been performed over recordings showing different behaviors. Fig. 5 gathers the collection of semantic annotations automatically generated for the *Theft Scene*. Experimental results show semantic shots generated at certain points of time, which allows to perform content-based time segmentation over the whole video sequence, by identifying remarkable occurrences and relating them to specific spaces of time[1]. The video sequence is thus split into significant time intervals, tagged with conceptual annotations, so the relevant content of a recording can be expressed as a collection of individual images and tags, such as the '*pick up*', '*theft*', and '*chase*' interpreted behaviors.

---

[1] The complete video sequence can be seen at `http://www.cvc.uab.es/ise`

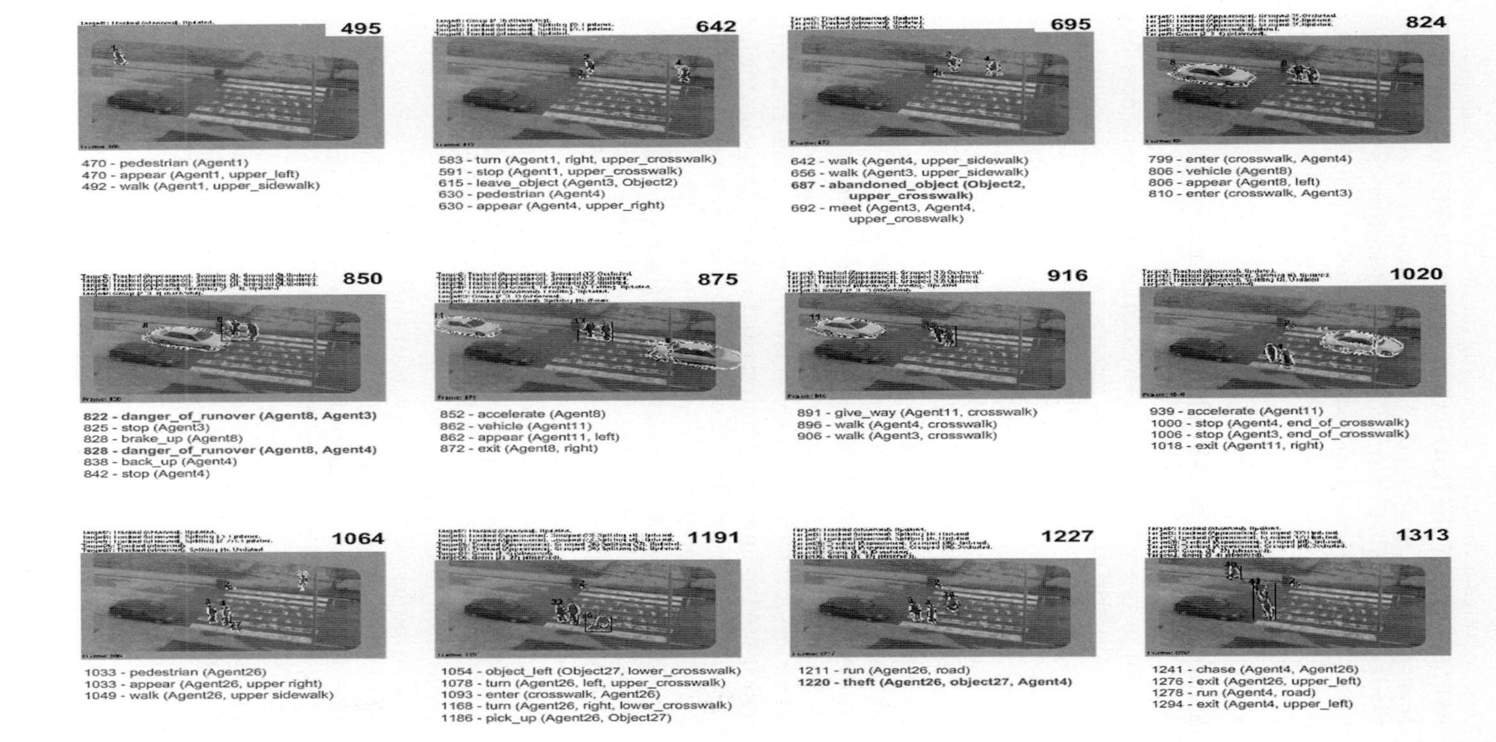

Fig. 5. Set of semantic annotations produced for the theft scene, which have been automatically generated for the fragment of recording comprised between frames 450 and 1301. Some captures showing the results after tracking processes have been provided, too, for illustration purposes. The number of frame appears in front of each produced annotation, and also in the upper-right corner of each capture. Detections of new agents within the scene have been marked in blue, annotations for activating predefined alerts have been emphasized in red.

Since the system operates differently depending on the concrete needs of a certain user, the level of detail for the descriptions can be established, concerning the amount of semantic shots generated. This adjustment is achieved by confronting a more extensive number of spatiotemporal descriptions with a more reduced number of logical inferences and interpretations (i.e. higher semantics involving greater uncertainty). Thus, subsequent search and retrieval algorithms can operate at different levels.

7   Conclusions and Future Work

The system presented in this paper (i) provides distilled video sequences from the monitored area, (ii) partitions these sequences into definite time-intervals depending on the associated content, and (iii) attaches semantic annotations in a real-time environment. It has allowed to automatically infer high-level reasonings and interpretations from geometrical results extracted by vision processes, and to generate semantic annotations abstracting these inferences. It identifies the targeted behaviors, by analyzing interactions among the different agents and objects involved in a scene. It also makes possible to ring alarms in the presence of certain defined complex situations, e.g. abandoned objects in the scenario, danger of imminent running over pedestrians or collision between vehicles, and detection of possible thefts. Since the conceptual stages of the system are deterministic, the accuracy of the results at these levels depend on the contextual and subjective models used to interpret occurrences. In those situations in which human agreement over the interpretation of events is low, no inferences are made.

New domains (e.g. sports) will be included for evaluation. The system needs to be extended regarding its multimedia capabilities. Further steps include processing of audio streams to detect sound and speech, and the evolution towards a multitracking system, which performs not only agent tracking, but also face expression and body analysis; towards this end, a set of PTZ (Pan, Tilt, Zoom) active cameras will be incorporated into the distributed camera system. All these steps can be naturally included into the proposed taxonomy, since it focus the interaction among different sources of knowledge. Only data conceptualizations and model extensions need to be considered.

Some tasks need to be improved regarding a better and more general performance: first, prior knowledge for the concrete scenario needs to be reduced as much as possible, to facilitate the characterization of content without excessive constraints. Refining the described stage for automatic modeling of common paths may be useful for this matter. In addition, the contextualization of events needs to be strengthened to facilitate knowledge acquisition by means of object relationships within the scene. Considering more complex behavioral patterns will include *group* and *crowd* detection. The impending addition of face and posture trackers will contribute a big leap towards this end, too.

Acknowledgements

This work has been supported by EC grant IST-027110 for the HERMES project and by the Spanish MEC under projects TIC-2003-08865 and DPI-2004-5414. Jordi Gonzàlez also acknowledges the support of a Juan de la Cierva Postdoctoral fellowship from the Spanish MEC.

References

1. Arens, M., Nagel, H.-H.: Behavioral Knowledge Representation for the Understanding and Creation of Video Sequences. In: Günter, A., Kruse, R., Neumann, B. (eds.) KI 2003. LNCS (LNAI), vol. 2821, pp. 149–163. Springer, Heidelberg (2003)
2. Assfalg, J., Bertini, M., Colombo, C., Bimbo, A.D.: Semantic Annotation of Sports Videos. Multimedia, IEEE 9(2), 52–60 (2002)
3. Baiget, P., Fernández, C., Roca, X., Gonzàlez, J.: Automatic Learning of Conceptual Knowledge for the Interpretation of Human Behavior in Video Sequences. In: Martí, J., Benedí, J.M., Mendonça, A.M., Serrat, J. (eds.) IbPRIA 2007. LNCS. vol. 4477, pp. 507–514. Springer, Heidelberg (2007)
4. Bobick, A.F.: Movement, Activity and Action: the Role of Knowledge in the Perception of Motion. Philosophical Transactions: Biological Sciences 352(1358), 1257–1265 (1997)
5. Cucchiara, R.: Multimedia Surveillance Systems. In: Proceedings of the third ACM international workshop on Video surveillance & sensor networks, pp. 3–10. ACM Press, New York (2005)
6. Gonzàlez, J.: Human Sequence Evaluation: The Key-Frame Approach. PhD thesis, Universitat Autònoma de Barcelona, Barcelona, Spain (2004)
7. Haag, M., Theilmann, W., Schäfer, K., Nagel, H.-H.: Integration of Image Sequence Evaluation and Fuzzy Metric Temporal Logic Programming, pp. 301–312. Springer, London, UK (1997)
8. Moeslund, T.B., Hilton, A., Kruger, V.: A Survey of Advances in Vision-based Human Motion Capture and Analysis. Computer Vision and Image Understanding 104, 90–126 (2006)
9. Nagel, H.-H.: From Image Sequences Towards Conceptual Descriptions. Image and Vision Computing 6(2), 59–74 (1988)
10. Schäfer, K., Brzoska, C.: F-Limette Fuzzy Logic Programming Integrating Metric Temporal Extensions. Journal of Symbolic Computation 22(5-6), 725–727 (1996)
11. Smeulders, A.W.M., Worring, M., Santini, S., Gupta, A., Jain, R.: Content-based Image Retrieval at the End of the Early Years. Pattern Analysis and Machine Intelligence, IEEE Transactions on 22(12), 1349–1380 (2000)
12. Snoek, C.G.M., Worring, M.: A Review on Multimodal Video Indexing. Multimedia and Expo, 2002. In: Proceedings of the ICME'02, vol. 2 (2002)

Synthesis of Hypermedia Using OWL and Jess

Alberto Machì and Antonino Lo Bue

Medialab Laboratory, ICAR-CNR Sezione di Palermo,
Via Ugo La Malfa 153
90146 Palermo, Italy
machi@pa.icar.cnr.it,
lobue@medialab.pa.icar.cnr.it

Abstract. An hypermedia is a spatio-temporal hypertext, namely a collection of media connected by synchronization and linking relations. HyperJessSyn is a tool which uses logic programming and Semantic Web technologies for synthesizing hypermedia according to descriptions of discourse structure and of presentation layout. A rule-based system in Jess applies inference rules to interpret from an OWL graph semantic and navigation relations among media instances, and production rules to turn media contents descriptions in XML/MPEG-7 format in an XMT-A/MPEG-4 hypermedia script via XSL transformations. The system has been used to produce an hyper-guide for virtual visiting a museum.

Keywords: Automatic Content Generation, Hypermedia, OWL, Jess, Ontologies, Rules.

1 Introduction

A huge unstructured collection of media and multimedia documents are now published on the Web and are then potentially available for reuse.

Semantic Web technologies allow to associate metadata to such media and to describe univocally their contents as well as relations among them, so opening the door to semantic media retrieval. Ontologies, for example, allow defining concepts, roles and individuals to represent knowledge in a number of domains and formally express semantics. Structure ontologies can be used to model knowledge about media contents and structure while representation ontologies to model multimedia organization. Creating well-designed multimedia presentations requires to understand the global discourse, the interaction structure and also the details of multimedia graphic design [1]. Semantic relations among media that compose the presentation are needed in the content generation process, relationships among domain concepts can influence layout and links in the presentation as well as knowledge about user can produce tailored presentation. Last, but not least, a platform description permits optimal use of the device.

Rule based expert systems have been used from decades for building knowledge bases (KB) connecting knowledge objects, assertions on them and rules which infer new knowledge objects from existing ones and perform consequent actions.

R. Basili and M.T. Pazienza (Eds.): AI*IA 2007, LNAI 4733, pp. 710–719, 2007.

Integration of expert systems with ontologies offer an enabling technology for intelligent semantic media retrieval and for smart reuse of retrieved contents in structured presentations like hypermedia.

An hypermedia is a spatio-temporal hypertext, namely a collection of media connected by synchronization and linking relations. Links express the discourse structure embodied in the hypermedia and allow coherent exploration of the media collection in a browser, while synchronizations maintain the semantic coherence of presentation during collection playback or navigation.

In the area of cultural heritage fruition, the usage of hypermedia has been proposed for smart navigation of museum collections using intelligent content-based search and browsing services. Hyvonen et als. [2] use ontological information and logical rules while Schreiber et als. [3] rely on semantic queries on annotated data, Prolog - algorithms and thesauri expressed in RDF/OWL.

A number of studies propose integration of logic programming and annotation technologies for automatic generation of multimedia. For instance, [4] proposes a high-level architecture (named Cuypers) for automatic generation of multimedia presentations. Cuypers makes use of inference rules, expressed in Prolog, to apply constraints to media retrieval and to dynamically rearrange the presentation layout. Similarly Little et als. [5] makes use of inference rules to define semantic relations among media objects annotated in DublinCore/RDF [6] for automatic adaptation of the presentation layout. In [7] Geurts et als. use ontological domain knowledge to select and organize the contents. The authors distinguish between three kinds of ontologies, the domain ontology which contains semantic metadata about the media, the discourse ontology which convey information about different document genres and the design ontology which contains knowledge about multimedia design. Using transformation rules, whose application is guided by the discourse and design ontologies, these systems generate real multimedia presentations from semantic graphs of document structure. Another approach for multimedia generation is taken in the Artequakt project [8] in which the systems automatically extracts knowledge about artist from the Web, and after populating a knowledge base, processes the data to obtain a tailored biography presentation in HTML. Presentation generation relies on composing pre-structured narrative templates with variable parts the system can fill in.

In this paper, we present a methodology and a Jess rule-based system, for automatic synthesis of hypermedia according to predefined layout templates described in OWL [9]. In section 2 we briefly introduce our methodology and the scenario of authoring a museum hyper-guide. Section 3 introduces an OWL design ontology defined for describing media contents and hypermedia structures. Finally in section 4 we discuss the operation of inference and production rules used by the rule-based system for actual hypermedia synthesis.

2 Authoring a Museum Hyper-guide

An expert hypermedia authoring platform is presently being developed at ICAR to assist the entire process of authoring, through a combination of logic programming and semantic web technologies.

Discussion of methodologies for coherent selection and composition of media items, according to templates of rhetoric structures, is outside the scope of the present work. Here we assume that, in the front-end of the authoring platform a description of media composition structure has been defined and we focus on the application of synchronization and layout constraints during the synthesis of the final hypermedia in the back-end of the authoring platform, namely the HyperJessSyn service.

For clarity of presentation we introduce here some terms used in the following sections while describing informally the scenario of building a hyper-guide for the virtual visit of an exhibition (e.g. a museum).

Let's suppose we have available a collection of images and videos containing views and shots (*media items*) representing works of art and places in a museum and that we want to arrange them in a museum hyper-guide. The guide could actively present works of art and collections in a temporal or topographical fashion (*guided tour metaphor*), or it could be navigated according to an exploration path chosen by the user (*virtual visit metaphor*). In the first case a story should semantically connect contents represented by media in a coherent sequence. In the second case taxonomy of navigable places (or topics) should constitute the *structure of the discourse* implicit in the net of hyperlinks, made available for navigating the media collection.

Narratologists divide narration into the *story* which is the basic description of the fundamentals events, and into the *discourse* which represents the techniques used to vary the presentation [8]. Media items constitute the pieces of information, which, like paragraphs in text, can be composed to create the *discourse* of the *story*. Media items can assume different roles in the *discourse* Some media items should be used as *indexe*s to introduce others, others selected to describe main discourse *subjects*, others to describe *details* or *related materials*. To activate media playback, links can be attached to spatial *anchors* as text areas or map regions as it happens in standard hypertexts or they can be attached to dynamic areas in videos corresponding to moving objects.

The layout of the rendered scene must to be addressed assigning windows to titles, maps, video-playback, captions, and controls, activated or hided according to a defined presentation policy.

Fig. 1 shows, as an example, snapshots from the navigation of a sample museum hyper-guide built according to a *virtual visit metaphor*: An *image* is used as an *index* and it hosts links to *audio-video segments* which present a dolly shot of a museum section (*subject*). The contour of an artefact is highlighted during *subject* playback to show a dynamic anchor to a new shots or image representing subject *details*. *Related materials* are reachable through static links in a separated, synchronized window.

The shot describing the *subject*, the video object showing the dynamic *anchor* and the shot presenting the *detail*, constitute a *narrative unit*, subject to synchronization constrains aimed to maintain semantic coherence of presentation. For instance playback of a *detail* suspends playback of its *subject* and selection of a new *subject* from the map halts the presentation of the whole *narrative unit*.

3   A Hypermedia Representation Ontology

The authoring platform describes concepts and roles concerning media composition in an custom Hypermedia Representation Ontology (HRO).The ontology make use

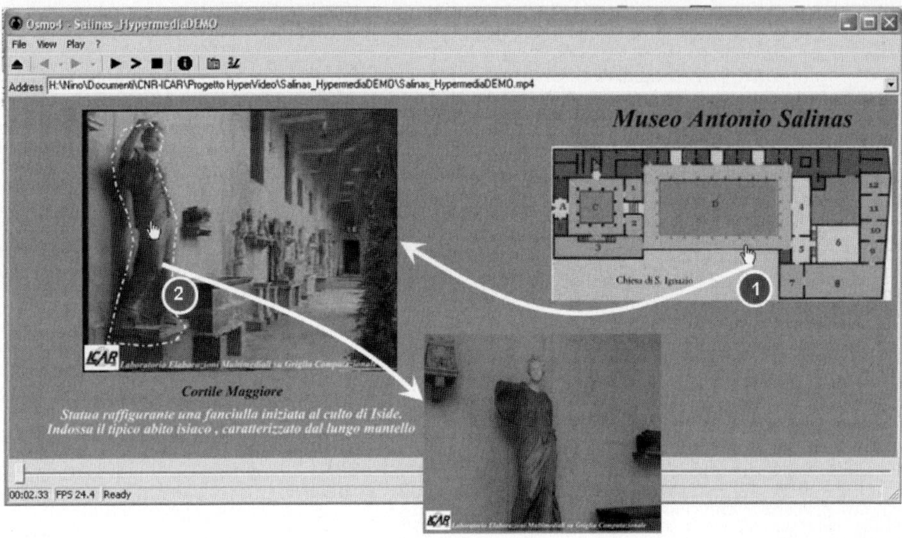

Fig. 1. Snapshots from navigation of the museum hyper-guide. Playback of a dolly shot of the museum major court is activated from a map of the museum ground floor used as an *index* (1) A possible focus of interest (*subject*) is suggested by highlighting the contour of a work of art hosting a dynamic *anchor* to a video segment describing it in detail (2).

of OWL DL semantics subset and defines classes of media segments at two levels of abstraction, one class of media relations and one class of media composition graphs.

The two media representation levels allow distinguishing structural and semantic features of media (like media types and formats and media content annotations) from composition features, relations and roles in their composition presentation, linking, and synchronization.

The Media Item Layer defines classes for media decomposition into reusable *media items* which corresponds media segments described by MPEG-7 Media Description Tools [10]. An index of relevant segments in a MPEG-7 metadata base is obtained by referencing in each `MediaItem` the URL and XPath of the MPEG-7 media segment descriptions.

The Hyper Semantic Object Layer defines classes of connectable `CompositionObjects` (like `Map,Image` and video regions hosting hyperlinks and `UserInterface` controls) as well as roles played in the composition (`index,subject,detail,relatedMaterial`).

The class `HypermediaRelations` defines the synchronization and linking relations among individuals of the Hyper Semantic Object Layer.

`CompositionObjects` and individuals of `HypermediaRelations` constitute nodes and arcs of the `CompositionGraph`. Fig. 2 shows classes and roles related to media of type `image`

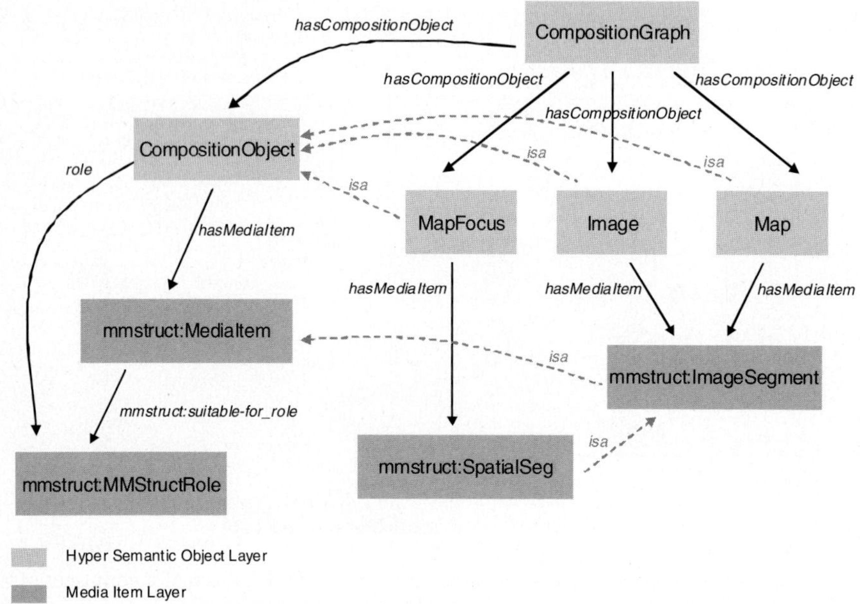

Fig. 2. Classes and roles related to media of type image. The *mmstruct* namespace marks concepts of the Media Item Layer . Relations in the CompositionGraph are omitted to simplify drawing.

3.1 The Hypermedia Composition Graph

The hypermedia *composition graph* (`CompositionGraph`) describes in OWL linking and synchronization relations among *composition objects* (`CompositionObjects`) to be rendered according to the *navigation metaphor.*

Each axiom defined in the OWL model as a restriction for a particular kind of *composition unit* (e.g. a *narrative unit,* an *index unit*) and any restriction on synchronizations required by a *navigation metaphor,* implies constraints on type and on cardinality of relations among `CompositionObjects`.

These constraints require that any linking property constituting a connection arc in the `CompositionGraph` must be labelled with facets expressing the effect of constrains (like *pause* or *play playstate* of source after activation of a destination object). Link and synchronization relations turn then from binary to multiple relations among two *composition objects* and their constrain values.

To express polyadic predicates in OWL we make use of the *n-ary relations* pattern (also known as *reified relations pattern*) [11].

According to this pattern, we define `HypermediaRelations` as classes of relations with two topological properties (`:FROM` and `:TO`), which have `CompositionObjects` as their domain and range.

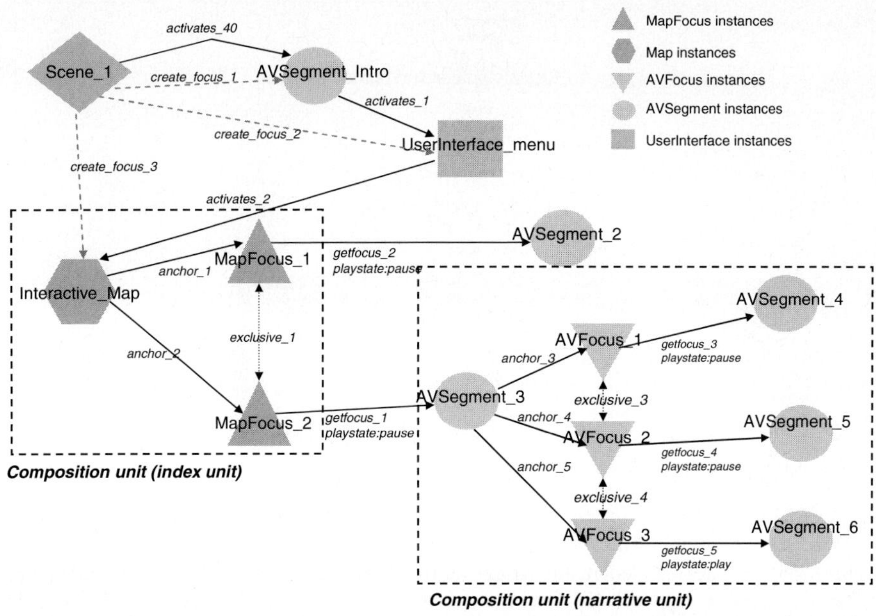

Fig. 3. A simplified `CompositionGraph` with two *composition units* outlined

Each relation is defined as a subclass with proper restrictions.

For instance we can fix the concept of a spatial hyperlink (a link originating from a static area in an image) or a spatio-temporal hyperlink (a link originating from a dynamic area in a video) by restricting the domain and range of the ANCHOR relation.

In the case of a spatial hyperlink, an image used as a map (`CompositionObjects` of type `Map`)) can contain as anchors just spatial active areas (`CompositionObjects` of type `MapFocus`) while in the case of a spatio-temporal link, a video-clip (`CompositionObjects` of type `AVSegment`) can contain just dynamic active areas as anchors (video objects represented as `CompositionObjects` of type `AVFocus`)

These restrictions are expressed in the HRO by following OWL axioms:

$$\text{ANCHOR} \subseteq \forall \; \text{:FROM} \; (\text{AVSegment} \cup \text{Map}). \tag{1}$$

$$\text{ANCHOR} \subseteq \forall \; \text{:TO} \; (\text{AVFocus} \cup \text{MapFocus}). \tag{2}$$

4 Operation of HyperJessSyn

The hypermedia `CompositionGraph` is built in the front-end service of the authoring platform and expresses semantic and navigation relations among media instances. HyperJessSyn applies a set of rules expressed in Jess to interpret the graph and to synthesize a hypermedia in the ISO standard XMT-A/MPEG-4 format [12] according to a custom presentation template.

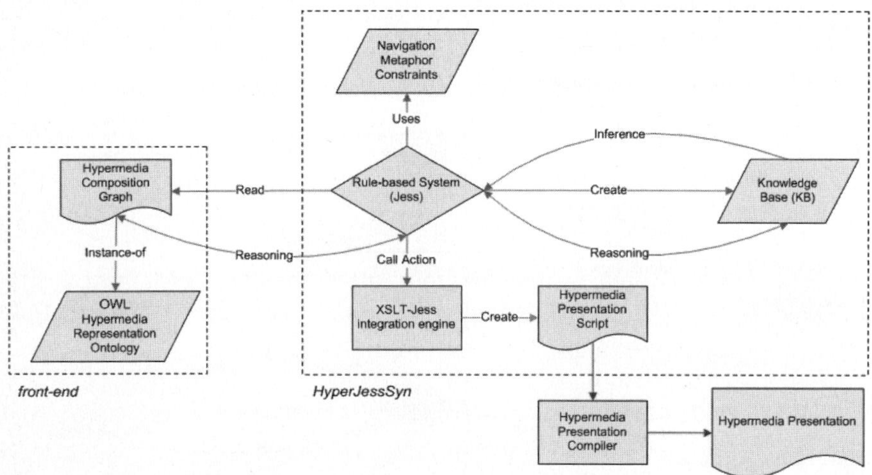

Fig. 4. Operation of HyperJessSyn: The authoring front-end service generates a hypermedia `CompositionGraph`. The Jess engine applies navigation metaphor constraints to *composition units* recognized in the graph and calls methods of the XSLT-Jess Integration engine to create a Hypermedia Presentation Script. Finally the Hypermedia Presentation Compiler produces the Hypermedia Presentation document.

The service implementation uses Protégé [13] as its knowledge ontology editor and knowledge acquisition system, Jess [14] as the inference engine and Saxon [15] as a XSLT processor for transforming OWL descriptions into XMT-A/MPEG-4 scripts.

4.1 Reasoning on the CompositionGraph

The rule-based system of HyperJessSyn applies three classes of rules on KB facts:

- ***Mapping rules*** between HRO and Jess KB facts.
- ***Inference rules*** on Jess KB which detects *composition units* (sub graphs) in the *composition graph* and assert the synchronization relations among CompositionObjects, required by the *navigation metaphor*.
- ***Production rules*** which activate external procedures like queries or transformations.

Once the *composition units* have been recognized, it is possible to apply to each media item the constraints required for the whole unit (e.g. overall unit duration) and to fill in variables in the appropriate composite template used to synthesize the presentation.

The input graph is parsed by the mapping rules and facts are declared in the KB which asserts the existence and typology of relations among *composition objects*.

For instance, the following code expresses in Jess a query on the OWL graph testing for `CompositionObjects` individuals belonging to list `?*ins2*` which are connected through an `ANCHOR` relation. In case of positive result, fact `Hyperlink I` is declared, and fact properties are set accordingly.

```
(foreach ?e ?*ins2*
 (do-for-all-instances ((?d ANCHOR))
   (eq (instance-name(slot-get ?d :FROM))
       (instance-name ?e)
    )
   (bind ?*ins3*
     (insert$ ?*ins3* 1
       (instance-name (slot-get ?d :TO))
    ))
   (assert
    (Hyperlink I source
        (instance-name (slot-get ?d :FROM))
         with-anchor
        (instance-name (slot-get ?d :TO))
      ))))
)
```

Once the KB has been populated with facts obtained during graph scan, inference rules may be applied to KB facts to detect the presence of presentation substructures.

As an example of such a kind of rules let's consider the rule set devoted to detect hypermedia *narrative units*, namely hyperlinks between video segments through spatio-temporal *anchors*.

A *narrative unit* sub graph contains a *composition object* of type `AVSegment` and one or more *composition objects* of type `AVSegment`, linked by relations through an `AVFocus` individual, as shown in fig. 3.

The following code expresses in SWRL [16] such an inference rule as a conjunction of atoms:

```
Hyperlink II(?a)^source(?a,?x)^

swrlb:equal(?x,AVSegment)^with-anchor(?a,?y)^

Hyperlink II(?b)^destination(?b,?z)  ^

with-anchor(?b,?y)

->

NarrativeUnit(?x)^Anchor(?x,?y)^Destination(?x,?z)
```

Inference rules grow rich the KB with consequent facts to reasoning on the ontology. These latter facts are used as "call parameters" of production rules.

Production rules call XSLT transformations which extract physical media attributes from the base of MPEG-7 metadata. Other XSL Transformations, using a predefined template generate in turn a Hypermedia Presentation Script in the chosen presentation language (presently XMT-A/MPEG-4) [17]. This latter script constitutes the hypermedia document corresponding to the input *composition graph* expressed in the HRO.

The following code, in Jess rule language, gives a simple example of such a production rule. For each *narrative unit* the rule calls the function `createNU` that activates through the API of the Saxon processor an XSL Transformation:

```
(defrule Rule1

  (NarrativeUnit ?x Anchor ?y Destination ?z )
    =>  (createNU ?y ?z)

)
```

5   Conclusions and Future Work

The paper has sketched the functionalities and some implementation choices of HyperJessSyn, a rule-based system for synthesizing hypermedia presentations.

We have shown how media items properties, hypermedia objects and their composition structure are described in an OWL hypermedia ontology. We have also shown how inference and production rules for integration of the hypermedia documents are described as Jess rules. Inference rules may also be expressed in SWRL to allow interoperability with other Semantic Web tools.

The integration of OWL with Jess allows separating the definition of hypermedia composition models from the definition of policies for hypermedia adaptability providing flexibility and scalability to the integration service.

Present service prototype implementation allows synthesizing hypermedia according to just one passive navigation metaphor, namely the *virtual visit* of a taxonomy of topics, but the chosen architecture is scalable to other metaphors augmenting the KB with appropriate sets of rules. Formalization of discourse models and sets of rules for active presentation metaphors is matter of current research.

The current target format for hypermedia encoding is XMT-A/MPEG-4. Adoption of the W3C SMIL [18] synchronization language is another topic of current activity.

References

1. Smeulders, A., Hardman, L., Schreiber, G., Geusebroek, J.-M.: An integrated multimedia approach to cultural heritage e-documents. In: 4th Intl. Workshop on Multimedia Information Retrieval, in conjunction with ACM Multimedia 2002 (2002)
2. Hyvonen, E., Junnila, M., Kettula, S., Makela, E., Saarela, S., Salminen, M., Syreeni, A., Valo, A., Viljanen, K.: MuseumFinland-Finnish Museums on the Semantic Web. User's perspective. In: Proceedings of Museums and the Web 2004 (2004)
3. Schreiber, G., Amin, A., van Assem, M., de Boer, V., Hardman, L., Hildebrand, M., Hollink, L., Huang, Z., van Kersen, J., de Niet, M., Omelayenjko, B., van Ossenbruggen, J., Siebes, R., Taekema, J., Wielemaker, J., Wielinga, B.: MultimediaN E-Culture Demonstrator. In: Cruz, I., Decker, S., Allemang, D., Preist, C., Schwabe, D., Mika, P., Uschold, M., Aroyo, L. (eds.) ISWC 2006. LNCS, vol. 4273, pp. 951–958. Springer, Heidelberg (2006)
4. van Ossenbruggen, J., Geurts, J., Cornelissen, F., Rutledge, L., Hardman, L.: Towards Second and Third Generation Web-Based Multimedia. In: The Tenth International World Wide Web Conference, Hong Kong, pp. 479–488 (2001)
5. Little, S., Geurts, J., Hunter, J.: Dynamic Generation of Intelligent Multimedia Presentations through Semantic Inferencing. In: Agosti, M., Thanos, C. (eds.) ECDL 2002. LNCS, vol. 2458, pp. 158–175. Springer, Heidelberg (2002)

6. Dublin Core Community.: Dublin Core Metadata Initiative (2001), http://purl.oclc.org/dc/

7. Geurts, J., Bocconi, S., van Ossenbruggen, J., Hardman, L.: Towards Ontology-driven Discourse: From Semantic Graphs to Multimedia Presentations. In: Fensel, D., Sycara, K.P., Mylopoulos, J. (eds.) ISWC 2003. LNCS, vol. 2870, pp. 597–612. Springer, Heidelberg (2003)

8. Alani, H., Kim, S., Millard, D.E., Weal, M.J., Hall, W., Lewis, P.H., Shadbolt, N.R.: Automatic ontology-based knowledge extraction and tailored biography generation from the web. IEEE Intelligent Systems, Special issue on Natural Language Processing 18(1), 14–22 (2003)

9. W3C.: OWL Web Ontology Language Overview, http://www.w3.org/TR/owl-features/

10. MPEG-7 Overview. ISO/IEC JTC1/SC29/ WG11/N6828 (October 2004) http://www.chiariglione.org/ mpeg/ standards/mpeg-7/mpeg-7.htm

11. W3C.: Defining N-ary Relations on the Semantic Web (2006), http://www.w3.org /TR/swbp-n-aryRelations/

12. MPEG-4 Overview. ISO/IEC JTC1/SC29/WG11 /N4668 (March 2002), http://www.chiariglione.org/mpeg/ standards/MPEG-4/mpeg-4.htm

13. Protégé Ontology Editor and Knowledge Acquisition System, http://protege.stanford.edu/

14. Friedman-Hill, E. J.: Jess in action: Java rule-based systems. Manning, Stockholm (2003)

15. Saxon SAXON XSLT Processor, http://saxon.sourceforge.net/

16. W3C.: Semantic Web Rule Language (2004), http://www.w3.org/Submission/SWRL/

17. Lo Bue, A.: Using Layout Profiles in MPEG-4 Hypervideo Presentation. In: Proceedings of 4th Eurographics Italian Chapter, Catania, Italy, pp. 273–277 (2006)

18. W3C.: Synchronized Multimedia Integration Language (2005), http://www.w3.org/AudioVideo/

NaviTexte, a Text Navigation Tool

Javier Couto[1] and Jean-Luc Minel[2]

[1] Universidad de la Republica, INCO. Herrera y Reissig 565 Montevideo, Uruguay
jcouto@fing.edu.uy
[2] MoDyCo, UMR 7114, CNRS-Université Paris X,
200 Avenue de la République 92 000 Nanterre, France
Jean-Luc Minel@u-paris10.fr

Abstract. In this paper, we describe NaviTexte, a software devoted to text navigation. First, we explain our conception of text navigation, which exploits linguistic information in texts to offer dynamic reading paths to a reader. Second, we describe a text representation specially defined to support our approach. Then we present a language for modeling navigation knowledge and its implementation framework. At last, two experimentations are presented: one aiming at teaching French at Danish students and the other one proposes text navigation as an alternative at the process of summarization based on sentences extraction.

Keywords: text navigation, text representation. navigation knowledge representation.

1 Introduction

Text navigation has several interpretations. Usually, this term is taken as a synonym of hypertext, i.e. the possibility to trigger a hyperlink, which moves the reading point from a text unit (source) to another one (target), this change being intra or inter-textual. From our point of view, this conception presents some limitations. First, the triggering of the hyperlink is not assisted. In other words, imprecise, poor or no information is provided to the reader before he triggers the link. Second, the reader doesn't know where the displacement will be carried out in the text (before or after the reading point or outside the text). Finally, hyperlinks are embedded in the hypertext. Consequently there is no distinction between text and navigation knowledge.

Different solutions have been proposed to address such problems. Adaptive hypertext [1] [2], relying on user model, proposes to modify the way the text is shown on the screen. Dynamic hypertext [3] computes the value of hyperlinks using several criteria such as text similarity or predefined relations. In this approach, a hyperlink is not defined as a pointer from a node (text unit) to another one but as a query returning a node (text unit) of the text.

Our conception of text navigation relies on this notion of computed query, but rather than taking into account criteria depending on the reader, the target is computed by exploiting linguistic information in texts. The remainder of this paper is organized as follows. In the next section, we discuss text navigation. The third

R. Basili and M.T. Pazienza (Eds.): AI*IA 2007, LNAI 4733, pp. 720–729, 2007.

section describes text representation and the fourth one a navigation knowledge modeling language named Sextant. The fifth section details the implementation framework of the text navigation. The final section describes several applications.

2   An Hybrid Approach of Text Navigation

Our conception of text navigation assumes as a hypothesis that navigating through texts is the expression of a cognitive process which relies on specific knowledge [4] [5] [6] [7]. To be more precise: a reader applies some knowledge to exploit text discursive markers. Furthermore, this knowledge may be defined in a declarative way (see section 4). The main difference between hypertext and our conception of navigation lies on the status of text and definition of knowledge navigation. In the case of hypertext, the visualization of text is unique and knowledge navigation is encoded (embedded) in the text. In our approach, there are several ways to visualize a text [6], each way called vue du texte (text view), and for each view, different navigation knowledge may be applied. As a consequence, the navigation is not guided by the author, compared to hypertext navigation where s/he has to determine links, but this is the result of an interpretation process relying on textual annotations.

Consequently, our conception of navigation [6] relies on four elements: i) a representation of text (see section 3); ii) a language, called Sextant, to design navigation knowledge (see section 4); iii) an agent (an individual, a software, etc.) for encoding such knowledge [7]; iv) a software, called NaviTexte, to interpret and apply knowledge to a specific text (see section 5).

3   Text Representation

The conceptual modeling is inspired by [8]: "A system for capturing documents structure should be flexible enough to accommodate the variations in structure that occur naturally" and improved by proposals from [9] [10]. As a consequence, our text model is based on typed units, which can be embedded. The description of a text is made up of two parts: the *Head* and the *Body*. In the *Body*, typed units (TU) are marked up using XML format and it is possible to embed them (cf. Fig.1).

Each unit has three attributes: "Type", "Nro" and, optionally, "Rang", the mix of them providing the TU key. Each TU may have an unlimited number of annotations tagged by the "Annotation" tag. Only innermost units in the hierarchy have an embedded tag, named "Chaine", which tags the string of character. Nevertheless, this kind of tagging has some well-known limitations: for example, the impossibility to tag overlapping or discontinuous units. Even though X-Link or Xpointer offer to solve such problems, their utilization by non expert users is far too complex. Consequently, in our approach it is possible to define new elements in the *Head*, composed with existing TU described in the *Body* part. To refer to an existing TU, the principle is to use a reference of the TU as it is defined in the *Body*. Four types of new elements can be created: *Set, Sequence, Reference* and *Graph*.

```
<TU Type="Proposition" Nro="1">
  <TU Type="SN" Nro="4">
    <Annotation Name="Type Referent">RD</Annotation>
    <Annotation Name="Index Referent">1</Annotation>
    <Chaine>le chef de l'Etat</Chaine>
  </TU>
  <TU Type="SV" Nro="1">
    <Annotation Name ="Modality">Valorisé¡/Annotation>
    <Annotation Name ="Polarity">Négative¡/Annotation>
    <Chaine>n'a pas su trouver un geste de rconfort ni un mot de
            compassion pour</Chaine>
  </TU>
</TU>
...
```

Fig. 1. Example of text annotations in the *Body* part of text

A *Set* is a collection of TU for which there exists an equivalence relation from the point of view of the annotator. For example, TU with different part of speech attributes can express a same topic (like verb and noun phrase), so a Set is the perfect structure to express that.

A *Sequence* is an ordered collection of TU for which a relation of syntactic or semantic cohesion exists. For example, in the *Body* it is not possible to tag as a unique structure, discontinuous enumeration, like "First, ...Second, ...". A *Sequence* allows to correctly tag such discontinuity (cf. Fig.2).

```
<Sequence Type="Enumeration" Nro="1">
  <TUP Type="Linear Integration Marker" Nro="15" >
  <TUP Type="Linear Integration Marker" Nro="25" >
  <TUP Type="Linear Integration Marker" Nro="35" >
</Sequence>
```

Fig. 2. Example of text annotations in the *Head* part of text

A *Reference* defines an oriented relation between two TU and one navigation operation is associated with this object. This operation goes from the referred to the referent. The representation of the link between a pronominal anaphora and its referent is a typical example of the utilization of a Reference.

At last, a *Graph* is used to build multiple relations between TU. This structure corresponds exactly to the mathematical notion of graph where nodes, which represent TU, are connected by oriented arcs, which represent relation between these TU. From our point of view, this complex structure could be very useful to represent complex discourse structures like coherence tracks or a thematic index like those put at the end of books.

4   Sextant Language

Conceptually, as in a hypertext approach, navigation is an operation, which links a text unit (TU) called *Source*, to another one, called *Target*. But, in our approach, it is possible to specify several *conditions* for the *Source* and for the *Target*, an *Orientation* and an *Order* (cf. Fig.3).

The *Orientation* parameter specifies the direction of the target search by using one of these pre-definite instructions: First, Last, Forward(i), Backward(i). First and Last indicate that the search of the target is absolute: the TU displayed will be the first (respectively the last) TU, in the specified span, that matched the conditions. Forward(i) and Backward(i) indicate that the search is carried out relatively to the source (before or after) and indexed by the integer i. For example, Forward(3) is interpreted as the search of the third TU located after the source, whose attributes match the conditions.

$$
\begin{array}{l}
\text{IF (Condition } TU_{Source}) \\
\text{THEN : DO SELECT CRITERIA (Orientation, Order)} \\
\qquad \text{WHERE } \{(\text{ condition } TU_{Target}) \\
\qquad\qquad\qquad \text{AND} \\
\qquad (\text{Relation } (TU_{Source}, TU_{Target}) \\
\qquad \} ; \\
\qquad : \text{DO DISPLAY (Operation label) ;}
\end{array}
$$

Fig. 3. Generic navigation operation

The *Order* parameter specifies an object *Sequence* and allows to search the target in a specific order of TU.

Before processing a navigation operation, conditions on properties of the source are checked. A basic condition expresses constraints on values of the annotations of TU (see section 3).

The conditions language is an important component of Sextant. For instance, we create a condition to indicate if a TU belongs to a view, to indicate on which TU a "Mise en relief" (enhancing) operation applies, or to specify the source and the target of a navigation operation.

The conditions language is composed by *basic conditions, TU elements existence conditions and hierarchical conditions.*

Basic conditions concern TU attributes and annotations. For this kind of conditions we use a notation close to the *pattern* notion. We define an operator named *TU*, having five operands that correspond to the following properties: *Type, Nro, Rang, Annotations* and *String*. With the three first operands and the fifth one, we denote constraints of equality, inequality, order, prefix, suffix and substring occurrence. The fourth operand is used to indicate the existence or not existence of annotations, whether it is an annotation name, a value or a name-value pair.

724   J. Couto and J.-L. Minel

For the TU elements existence conditions, we define an operator without operands (cf. Fig.4).

For the conditions that deals with the hierarchical relationship between different TU, a set of unary operators have been defined. These operators, showed in Fig.5, take as an argument a basic condition. We would like to draw attention to the fact that these operators allow to move through the entire hierarchy of TU from a starting TU [6] [7].

All conditions may be combined using the classic logic operators OR, AND and NOT.

existeAnnotations: checks if the TU set of annotations is empty
existeChaneLexicale: checks if the TU string is defined
existeTitre: checks if the TU has a title
existeParent: checks if the TU has a parent
existeFils: checks if the TU has children

Fig. 4. TU elements existence conditions

estParent: checks if a TU is the parent of another TU
estFils: checks if a TU is the parent of another TU
estFrère: checks if a TU is the sibling of another TU
estAscendant: checks if a TU is the ascendant of another TU
estDescendant: checks if a TU is one of the descendants of another TU
contientDansTitre: checks if a TU contains in its title a certain TU
estDansTitreDe: checks if a TU belongs to the title of another TU

Fig. 5. Hierarchical conditions

Figure 6 presents an example of a language expression that formulates the following condition: "TU of type SN and having an annotation named *Référent discursif*, for which it exists, among its descendants, a TU of type *Paragraphe* not having an annotation named *Étiquette Sémantique* whose value is *Conclusion*". This may be interpreted as: A nominal group being a discourse referent that doesn't occur in a concluding paragraph.

$$\text{TU}(\textit{Type} = \textit{SN},*,*,\{(\textit{Referent discursif},*)\},*)$$
$$\text{AND}$$
$$\text{estDescendant}(\text{TU}(\textit{Type} = \textit{Paragraphe},*,*,\{\nexists(\textit{Etiquette Conclusion})\},*))$$

Fig. 6. Example of condition: *nominal group being a discourse referent that doesn't occur in a concluding paragraph*

Lately, this first version has been upgraded with the possibility to express conditions on the relationship between the source and the target. A new tag

$< Relation - Source - Target >$ allows expressing only relations between the values of attributes. So far, operators equality($=$), difference ($!=$), contains ($\sim$) have been defined. With these extensions, all the operations on strings, described above, are replaced by one operation

5   NaviTexte

NaviTexte consists of several sub-systems [6] [7]. The first one builds a text representation $\{Ta\}$ from a text annotated by dedicated software [11] [12]. A second sub-system loads and compiles one or several cartridges, which describe the visualization and navigation knowledge (see section 4) as well as the form of the display (linear, structured, graphical, etc.).

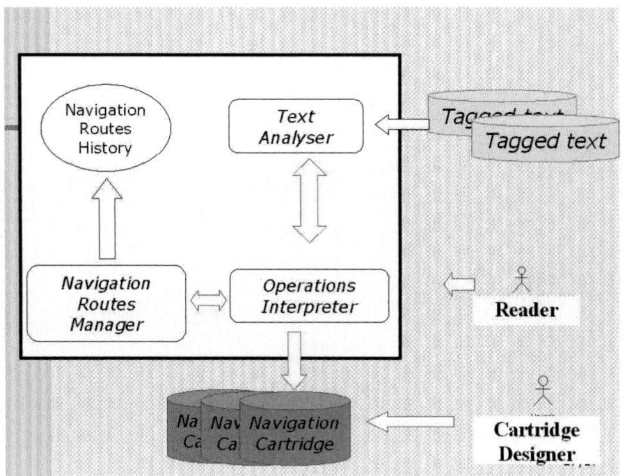

Fig. 7. General software organization

The result of this compilation is a graph of potential tracks. This graph is projected on the text $\{Ta\}$. A third sub-system displays the text on the screen by applying the semiotic forms chosen by the reader. It must be pointed out that the reader has the possibility to load another cartridge of reading knowledge at any time and that its compilation is dynamically computed.

6   Applications

6.1   NaviLire, Application in Text Linguistics

For the past thirty years, text linguistic researchers have worked on describing linguistic markers of textual coherence in order to bring out principles of text structuring [13]. A set of concepts and models of textual interpretation has been worked out, including for example, anaphora, connectors, mental spaces, etc. In particular, these studies have shown that even for languages apparently close like French and Danish, texts are not organized in the same way [14]. Consequently, text linguistics has important implications in foreign language teaching, especially from a contrastive point of view, when language pairs are analyzed through texts used in authentic communication situations. It seems that the teaching of text linguistics contributes to sharpen the attention of students towards the building of well-formed texts and to stimulate their own production of texts. Consequently, a tool that allows the student (reader) to perceive textual units that contribute to and maintain text coherence and to navigate between them in a text, can be supposed to be an outstanding didactic tool for teaching reading of foreign language texts, as well as producing written texts in the foreign language. In the reading process, the reader has to deal with two basic types of cognitive problems. First, the reader has to identify discourse referents in a text and choose the correct relations between the noun phrases that refer to them. Second, he has to identify the function and orientation intended by the sender.

Table 1. Comparison of *navilistes* and *papiristes* [15]

	Number of questions	Percentage
Navilistes better than *papiristes*	14	40
Navilistes the same as *papiristes*	16	45,7
Navilistes worse than *papiristes*	5	14,3
Total	35	100

So far, *NaviLire* has been put into practice on a small scale only, viz. in the teaching of French texts and text linguistics to Danish language students in the 4th year of Language and Communication studies at the Copenhagen Business School. A pilot experiment was carried out in order to evaluate the effects of using the program[1]. The first results are based on forty answers, of which 35 concern questions about the content of the text. These results show that the *navilistes* (people using NaviLire) have a better comprehension performance than the *papiristes* (people using paper and pencil) for 14 questions, an identical performance for 16 other questions, and a poorer performance for 5 questions (cf. Table 1).

6.2 Navigation as an Alternative to Automatic Summarization

Many automatic summarization systems have been proposed [5] [16]. All these systems, based on the principle of phrase, proposition or group extraction, have been confronted to two problems intrinsic to the extraction procedure.

The first problem is the rupture of text cohesion, like in cases of anaphora where the corresponding discourse referent is missing.

---

[1] See [15] for more details.

The second is the adaptation of the summary to a reader specific needs. Actually, there are no completely satisfying solutions to these problems. An alternative approach is to consider the summarizing process as a course belonging to the reader, more precisely a reading course [4] [17]. Thereby, instead of extracting text fragments, we propose specific reading courses. The reading courses specifications are based on proposition of [18] and on practice observations made in the frame of the automatic summarization system SERAPHIN evaluation [19] and the FilText framework [20].

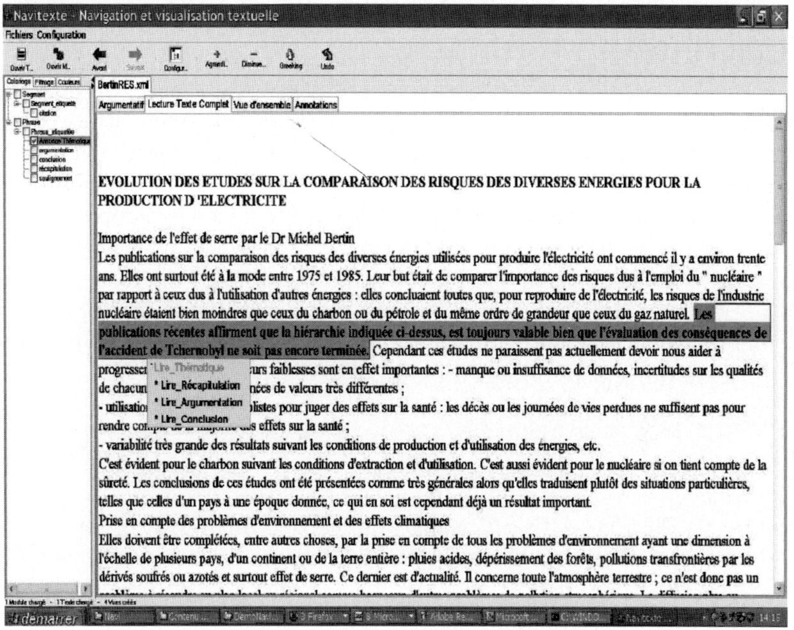

Fig. 8. Reading course example

These works showed that professional summarizers are interested by discourse categories that they retrieve by exploiting text organization and lexical markers. They also showed that these professionals navigate through texts using heuristics acquired by experience. For example, they begin by reading the conclusion, then they continue by looking, in the introduction, for nominal groups that occurred in the conclusion.

In consequence, a specific reading course specifies, on the one hand, the kind of discursive category searched by a reader (e.g. a conclusion, a definition, an argumentation, a hypothesis, etc.) and on the other hand, the course in which the segments that linguistically enunciate these categories (typically phrases) must be presented to the reader.

To carry out these reading courses, it is necessary to locate the discursive categories involved and mark them in the text. For this purpose, we used ContextO

[20]. A reading course example is presented in Fig.8. The reading point is positioned over the first TU, a phrase in this case, annotated "Annonce Thématique". When the user clicks over the TU, NaviTexte recommends him four navigation operations. The first one suggests bringing him to the following "Annonce Thématique". The others ones suggest going to the first "Conclusion", the first "Récapitulation" and the first "Argumentation".

Consequently, along his reading continuum, the reader is assisted by the display of a specific set of signs, and there is no rupture of cohesion because he is able to see all the text. [21].

7   Conclusion

In this paper, we have presented our approach to text navigation. We have defined it and explained the main differences with the traditional hypertext navigation approach. The four elements needed to implement our approach are described: the text representation, the navigation knowledge modeling language Sextant, the knowledge encoding agents (via applications) and the software that implements text navigation, the NaviTexte system. Two distinct applications of NaviTexte have been presented, showing the versatility of our approach. The quantitative results of our experimentation with Danish students learning French confirm the improvement obtained by using text navigation.

References

1. Mathe, N., Chen, J.: A User-Centered Approach to Adaptive Hypertext based on an Information Relevance Model. In: UM'94. 4th International Conference on User Modeling, pp. 107–114 (1994)
2. Brusilovsky, P.: Methods and techniques of adaptive hypermedia. User Modeling and User-Adapted Interaction 6(2-3), 87–129 (1996)
3. Bodner, R., Chignell, M.: Dynamic hypertext: querying and linking. ACM Computing Surveys 31(4), 120–132 (1999)
4. Minel, J.-L.: Filtrage sémantique de textes. Problèmes, conception et réalisation d'une plate-forme informatique. Habilitation à diriger des recherches, Université Paris-Sorbonne (2002)
5. Minel, J.-L.: Filtrage sémantique. Du résumé à la fouille de textes. Paris Hermès (2003)
6. Couto, J.: Modélisation des connaissances pour une navigation textuelle assistée. La plate-forme logicielle NaviTexte. PhD, Université Paris-Sorbonne (2006)
7. Couto, J., Minel, J.-L: Navigation textuelle: Représentation des textes et des connaissances. TAL 47/2, 29 (2007)
8. Clarke, L., Cormack, G.V, Burkowski, F.J.: An Algebra for Structured Text Search and a Framework for its Implementation. The Computer Journal 38(1) (1995)
9. Crispino, G.: Conception et réalisation d'un système informatique d'exploration contextuelle. Conception d'un langage de spécification de connaissances linguistiques, PhD Université Paris-Sorbonne, Paris (2003)
10. Text Encoding Initiative, http://www.tei-c.org

11. Cunningham, H., Maynard, D., Bontcheva, K., et al.: GATE: A Framework and Graphical Development Environment for Robust NLP Tools and Applications. In: ACL'02, pp. 168–175. ACM Press, Philadelphie, Pennsylvanie (2002)
12. Bilhaut, F., Ho-Dac, M., Borillo, A., Charnois, T., Enjalbert, P., Le Draoulec, A., Mathet, Y., Miguet, H., Pery-Woodley, M.P., Sarda, L.: Indexation discursive pour la navigation. intradocumentaire: cadres temporels et spatiaux dans l'information géographique. Actes de TALN, pp. 315–320 (2003)
13. Lundquist, L.: La cohérence textuelle, syntaxe, sémantique, pragmatique, Copenhagen, Nordisk Forlag (1980)
14. Lundquist, L.: Noms, verbes et anaphores (in)fidèles. Pourquoi les Danois sont plus fidèles que les Français. Langue française 145, 73–92 (2005)
15. Lundquist, L., Minel, J.L., Couto, J.: NaviLire, Teaching French by Navigating in Texts. In: IPMU'2006, Paris (2006)
16. Mani, I.: Automatic Summarization. John Benjamins Publishing Company, Amsterdam (2001)
17. Crispino, G., Couto, J.: Construction automatique de résumés. Une approche dynamique. TAL 45/1, 95–120 (2004)
18. Endres-Niggemeyer, B., Maier, E., Sigel, A.: How to implement a naturalistic model of abstracting: four core working steps of an expert abstractor. Information Processing et Management 31(5), 631–674 (1995)
19. Minel, J-L., Nugier, S., Piat, G.: How to appreciate the Quality of Automatic Text Summarization. In: EACL 97. Workshop Intelligent Scalable Text Summarization, Madrid, pp. 25–30 (1997)
20. Minel, J.-L, Cartier, E., Crispino, G., Desclés, J.P., Ben Hazez, S., Jackiewicz, A.: Résumé automatique par filtrage sémantique d'informations dans des textes, Présentation de la plate-forme FilText. Technique et Science Informatiques 3, 369–396 (2001)
21. Battistelli, D., Minel, J.-L.: Les systèmes de résumé automatique: comment assurer une continuité référentielle dans la lecture des textes. In: Sabah, G. (ed.) Compréhension des langues et interaction, pp. 295–330 (2006)

TV Genre Classification Using Multimodal Information and Multilayer Perceptrons

Maurizio Montagnuolo[1,*] and Alberto Messina[2]

[1] Università degli Studi di Torino, Dip. di Informatica, Torino, Italy
`montagnuolo@di.unito.it`
[2] RAI Centro Ricerche e Innovazione Tecnologica, Torino, Italy
`a.messina@rai.it`

Abstract. Multimedia content annotation is a key issue in the current convergence of audiovisual entertainment and information media. In this context, automatic genre classification (AGC) provides a simple and effective solution to describe video contents in a structured and well understandable way. In this paper a method for classifying the genre of TV broadcasted programmes is presented. In our approach, we consider four groups of features, which include both low-level visual descriptors and higher level semantic information. For each type of these features we derive a characteristic vector and use it as input data of a multilayer perceptron (MLP). Then, we use a linear combination of the outputs of the four MLPs to perform genre classification of TV programmes. The experimental results on more than 100 hours of broadcasted material showed the effectiveness of our approach, achieving a classification accuracy of $\sim 92\%$.

1 Introduction

Improvements in video compression, in conjunction with the availability of high capacity storage devices have made possible the production and distribution to users of digital multimedia content in a massive way. As large-scale multimedia collections come into view, efficient and cost-effective solutions for managing these vast amounts of data are needed. Current information and communication technologies provide the infrastructure to transport bits anywhere, but on the other hand, our current ability on user-oriented multimedia classification is not still mature enough, due to the lack of good automated semantic extraction and interpretation algorithms. The problem concerning the reduction of the "semantic gap" (i.e. combining and mapping low-level descriptors automatically extracted by machines to high-level concepts understandable by humans) is the main challenge of the Video Information Retrieval (VIR) research community. A critical review of the applicability of VIR technologies in real industrial scenarios in presented in [14].

In the television programme area, the classification of video content into different genres (e.g. documentary, sports, commercials, etc.) is an important topic

---

* PhD student, supported by EuriX S.r.l., Torino, Italy. – www.eurixgroup.com

R. Basili and M.T. Pazienza (Eds.): AI*IA 2007, LNAI 4733, pp. 730–741, 2007.

of VIR. Even if the definition of genre may depend on social, historical, cultural and subjective aspects, thus resulting in fuzzy boundaries between different genres, many common features characterise objects belonging to the same genre. Therefore, automatic genre classification provides a good way to capture semantic information about multimedia objects. For instance, in video production, genre is usually intended as a description of what type of content TV viewers expect to watch.

In this work, a solution for automatic genre classification is presented. In particular, we describe a framework that is able to discern between TV commercials, newscasts, weather forecasts, talk shows, music video clips, animated cartoons and football match videos. These genres are fairly representative of the programme formats that are currently produced and distributed either through the traditional distribution channels, such as broadcast, cable and satellite, or through new platforms like the Internet or mobile phones. The present approach is based on two foundations: (i) *Multimodal content analysis* to derive a compact numerical representation (here in after called *pattern vector* – PV) of the multimedia content; and (ii) *Neural Network training process* to produce a classification model from those pattern vectors. Neural networks are successfully used in pattern recognition and machine learning [21]. Our system uses four multilayer perceptrons to model both low-level and higher level properties of multimedia contents. The outputs of these MLPs are combined together to perform genre classification.

The remaining of the paper is organised as follows. The sets of extracted features are detailed in Section 2. The process of genre classification based on neural networks is described in Section 3. Experimental results are given in Section 4. Finally, conclusions and future work are outlined in Section 5.

2   Proposed Feature Sets

Multimodal information retrieval techniques combine audio, video and textual information to produce effective representations of multimedia contents [22]. Our system is multimodal in that it uses a pattern vector to represent the set of features extracted from all available media channels included in a multimedia object. These media channels are representative of modality information, structural-syntactic information and cognitive information. In the broadcast domain in which we operate, modality information concerns the physical properties of audiovisual content, as they can be perceived by users (e.g. colours, shapes, motion). Structural-syntactic information describes spatial-temporal layouts of programmes (e.g. relationships between frames, shots and scenes). Cognitive information is related to high-level semantic concepts inferable from the fruition of audiovisual content (e.g. genre, events, faces). An exhaustive analysis concerning the representation of multimedia information content of audiovisual material can be found in [16].

Starting from the basic media types introduced above, we derive the TV programme pattern vector $PV = (V_c, S, C, A)$. The pattern vector collects four sets of features that capture visual ($\boldsymbol{V_c}$), structural ($\boldsymbol{S}$), cognitive ($\boldsymbol{C}$) and aural ($\boldsymbol{A}$) properties of the video content. We have originally designed some of these features to reflect the criteria used by editors in the multimedia production process. For example, commercials are usually characterised by a rapid mix of both music and speech. On the other hand, the majority of talk shows present lengthy shots and have less music and more speech contribution. The physical architecture designed and implemented to calculate the pattern vector is presented in [15]. The four feature sets included in the pattern vector are detailed in the following subsections.

2.1 The Low-Level Visual Pattern Vector Component

The low-level visual pattern vector component includes seven features. Colours are represented by hue (H), saturation (S) and value (V) [23]. Luminance (Y) is represented in a grey scale in the range [16, 233], with black corresponding to the minimum value and white corresponding to the maximum value. Textures are described by contrast (C) and directionality (D) Tamura's features [24]. Temporal activity information (T) is based on the displaced frame difference (DFD) [26] for window size $t = 1$.

First, for each feature we compute a 65-bin histogram, where the last bin collects the number of pixels for which the computed value of the feature is undefined. The low-level visual features are originally computed on a frame by frame basis (e.g. there is one hue histogram for each frame). To provide a global characterisation of a TV programme, we use cumulative distributions of features over the number of frames within the programme. Then, we model each histogram by a 10-component Gaussian mixture, where each component is a Gaussian distribution represented by three parameters: weight, mean and standard deviation [27]. Finally, we concatenate these mixtures to obtain a 210-dimensional feature vector $\boldsymbol{V_c} = (\boldsymbol{H}, \boldsymbol{S}, \boldsymbol{V}, \boldsymbol{Y}, \boldsymbol{C}, \boldsymbol{D}, \boldsymbol{T})$.

2.2 The Structural Pattern Vector Component

The structural component of the pattern vector is constructed from the structural information extracted by a shot detection module. First, a TV programme is automatically segmented into camera shots. We define a shot as a sequence of contiguous frames characterised by similar visual properties. Then, we derive two features S_1 and $\boldsymbol{S_2}$, obtaining a 66-dimensional feature vector $\boldsymbol{S} = (S_1, \boldsymbol{S_2})$. S_1 captures information about the rhythm of the video:

$$S_1 = \frac{1}{F_r N_s} \sum_{i=1}^{N_s} \Delta s_i \tag{1}$$

where F_r is the frame rate of the video (i.e. 25 frames per second), N_s is the total number of shots in the video and Δs_i is the shot length, measured as the number of frames within the ith shot.

S_2 describes how shot lengths are distributed along the video. S_2 is represented by a 65-bin histogram. Bins 0 to 63 are uniformly distributed in the range $[0, 30s]$, and the 64th bin contains the number of shots whose length is greater than 30 seconds. All histograms are normalised by N_s, so that their area sums to one.

2.3   The Cognitive Pattern Vector Component

The cognitive component of the pattern vector is built by applying face detection techniques [5]. We use this information to derive the following three features:

$$C_1 = \frac{N_f}{D_p} \qquad (2)$$

where N_f is the total number of faces detected in the video and D_p is the total number of frames within the video.

The second feature (C_2) describes how faces are distributed along the video. C_2 is expressed by a 11-bin histogram. The ith $(i = 0, \ldots, 9)$ bin contains the number of frames that contain i faces. The 11th bin contains the number of frames that depict 10 or more faces.

The last feature (C_3) describes how faces are positioned along the video. C_3 is represented by a 9-bin histogram, where the ith bin represents the total number of faces in the ith position in the frame. Frame positions are defined in the following order: *top-left, top-right, bottom-left, bottom-right, left, left, top, bottom, centre*.

All histograms are normalised by N_f, so that their area sums to one. We concatenate C_1, C_2 and C_3, to produce a single 21-dimensional feature vector $C = (C_1, C_2, C_3)$.

2.4   The Aural Pattern Vector Component

The aural component of the pattern vector is derived by the audio analysis of a TV programme. We segment the audio signal into seven classes: *speech, silence, noise, music, pure speaker, speaker plus noise, speaker plus music*. These computed duration values, normalised by the total duration of the video, are stored in the feature vector A_1. In addition, we use a speech-to-text engine [2] to produce transcriptions of the speech content and to compute the average speech rate in the video (A_2). The aural component thus results in a 8-dimensional feature vector $A = (A_1, A_2)$.

3   Video Genre Classification

The process of video genre classification is shown in Figure 1. Let p be a TV programme to be classified and $\Omega = \{\omega_1, \omega_2, \ldots, \omega_{N_\omega}\}$ be the set of available genres. We firstly derive the pattern vector of p as described in Section 2. Each part of the pattern vector is the input of a neural network. We trained all networks by the iRPROP training algorithm described in [9]. The training process runs until the desired error ε is reached, or until the maximum number of steps MAX_S is exceeded.

In order to define the most suitable network architecture for each part of the pattern vector (i.e. the number of layers, neurons and connections), we considered the following two factors:

1. The *training efficiency* η, inspired by the F-measure used in Information Retrieval and expressed by Equation 3. The training efficiency combines the training *accuracy* (the ratio of correct items to the total number of items in the training set) and the training *quality* (the square error between the desired output of an output neuron and the actual output of the neuron, averaged by the total number of output neurons). The training efficiency, the accuracy and the quality are all included in the range [0,1].

$$\eta = \frac{2 \cdot accuracy \cdot (1 - quality)}{accuracy + (1 - quality)} \tag{3}$$

Figure 2 to Figure 5 show the training efficiency for each part of the pattern vector;

2. The *total number of hidden neurons* (HNs) and the *total number of hidden layers* (HLs).

For each NN we have an output vector $\boldsymbol{\Phi}^{(p,n)} = \{\phi_1^{(p,n)}, \ldots, \phi_{N_\omega}^{(p,n)}\}, n = 1, \ldots, 4$ whose element $\phi_i^{(p,n)}$ $(i = 1, \ldots, N_\omega)$ can be interpreted as the membership value of p to the genre i, according to the pattern vector part n. We then combine these outputs to produce an ensamble classifier [17], resulting in a vector $\boldsymbol{\Phi}^{(p)} = \{\phi_1^{(p)}, \ldots, \phi_{N_\omega}^{(p)}\}$, where:

$$\phi_i^{(p)} = \frac{1}{4} \sum_{n=1}^{4} \phi_i^{(p,n)} \tag{4}$$

We finally select the genre j corresponding to the maximum element of $\boldsymbol{\Phi}^{(p)}$ as the genre with which to classify p.

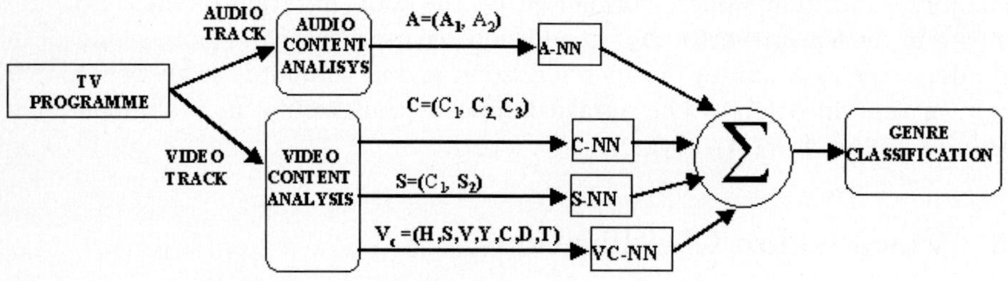

Fig. 1. The video genre classification process

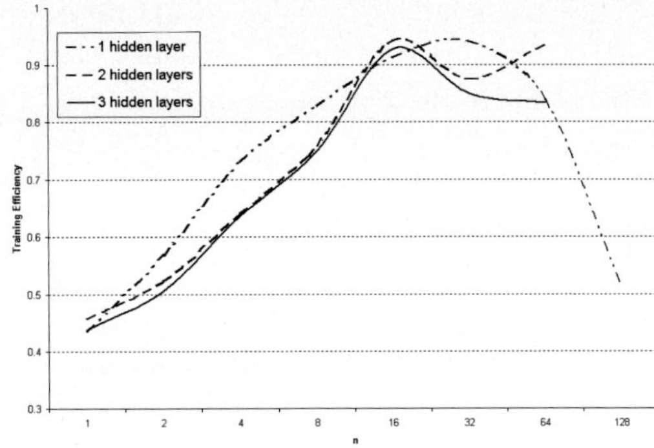

Fig. 2. Training efficiency versus the number of neurons per hidden layer (n) for the aural pattern vector component

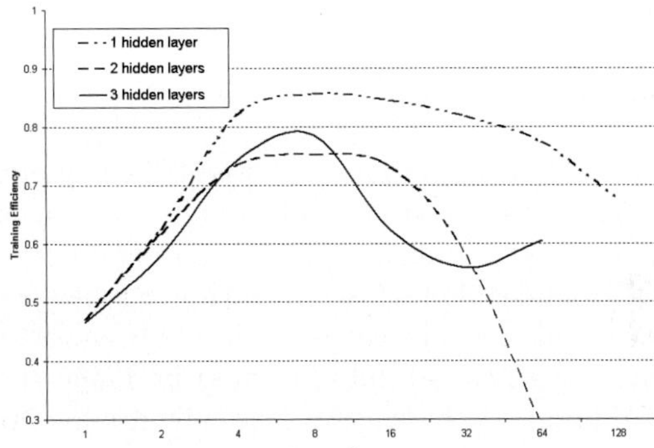

Fig. 3. Training efficiency versus the number of neurons per hidden layer (n) for the structural pattern vector component

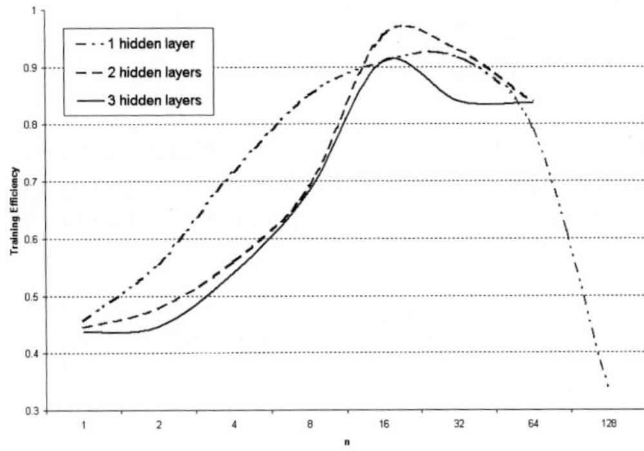

Fig. 4. Training efficiency versus the number of neurons per hidden layer (n) for the cognitive pattern vector component

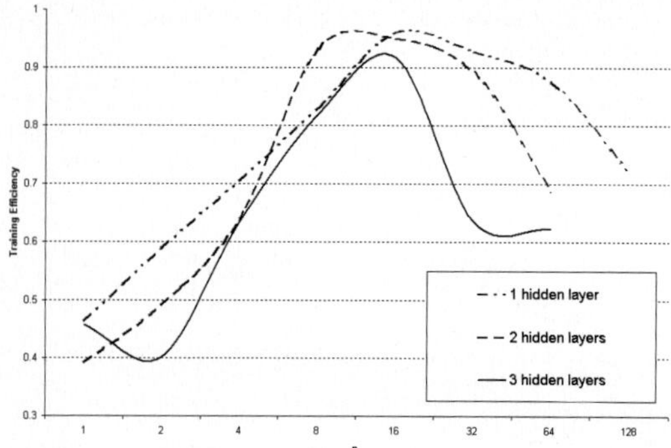

Fig. 5. Training efficiency versus the number of neurons per hidden layer (n) for the visual pattern vector component

4 Experimental Results

4.1 The Experimental Dataset

The experimental dataset collects about 110 hours of complete TV programmes from the daily programming of public and private broadcasters. We built the dataset so that to obtain seven uniformly (w.r.t. the number of occurrences of each genre in the TV programme schedules within a finite period of time) distributed genres: news, commercials, cartoons, football, music, weather forecasts and talk shows. This experimental dataset could be made available for use by researchers. Each TV programme was then manually pre-annotated as belonging to one of the previous genres. Finally, we randomly split the dataset into $K = 6$ disjointed and uniformly distributed (w.r.t. the occurrence of the seven genres in each sub-set) subsets of approximately equal size and used K-fold validation of data. Each subset was thus used once as test set and five times as training set, leading a more realistic estimation of classification accuracy.

4.2 Experimental Settings

In the experimental prototype we used the following libraries:

- The face detection task is performed using the RTFaceDetection library offered by Fraunhofer IIS.[1]
- The speech-to-text task is performed using an engine for the Italian language supplied by ITC-IRST (Centre for Scientific and Technological Research).[2]
- The neural network classifier is implemented using the Fast Artificial Neural Network (FANN) library.[3]

---

[1] http://www.iis.fraunhofer.de/bv/biometrie/tech/index.html
[2] http://www.itc.it/irst
[3] http://leenissen.dk/fann

Based on the selection criteria presented in Section 3, we chose the following
network architectures:

- All networks have one hidden layer and seven output neurons with sigmoid
  activation functions, whose outputs are in the range [0,1];
- All hidden neurons have symmetric sigmoid activation functions, whose outputs are in the range [-1,1];
- The Aural Neural Network (A-NN) has 8 input neurons and 32 hidden neurons;
- The Cognitive Neural Network (C-NN) has 21 input neurons and 32 hidden
  neurons;
- The Structural Neural Network (S-NN) has 65 input neurons and 8 hidden
  neurons;
- The Visual Neural Network (VC-NN) has 210 input neurons and 16 hidden
  neurons.

Finally, we set the desired error $\varepsilon = 10^{-4}$ and the maximum number of steps
$MAX_S = 10^4$.

4.3   Analysis of the Experimental Results

Table 1 reports the confusion matrix averaged on the six test sets. The obtained
classification accuracy is very good, with an average value of 92%. In some cases
the classification accuracy is greater than 95%. As expected, some news and talk
shows tend to be confused each other, due to their common cognitive and structural properties. Other false detection results may be due to the high percentage
of music with speech in the audio track of commercials, and thus misclassify-
ing some commercials as music clips. In addition, music genre shows the most
scattered results, due to its structural, visual and cognitive inhomogeneity.

Table 1. Confusion matrix for the task of TV genre recognition (Unit: 100%)

Genre	Talk Shows	Commercials	Music	Cartoons	Football	News	Weath.For.
Talk Shows	**91.7**	0	0	1.6	0	6.7	0
Commercials	1.5	**91**	4.5	0	0	1.5	1.5
Music	1.7	5	**86.7**	5	1.6	0	0
Cartoons	0	0	3.4	**94.9**	0	0	1.7
Football	0	0	0	0	**100**	0	0
News	11.1	0	0	1.6	0	**87.3**	0
Weath.For.	1.5	1.5	0	1.6	0	0	**95.4**

4.4   Comparisons with Other Works

During the recent years many attempts have been done at solving the task of TV
genre recognition, according to a number of genres from a reference taxonomy
[1,3,4,6,8,12,13,19,20,28,29]. A comparison between our approach and some other
classification methods is reported in Table 2. From the analysis of previous works,

several considerations can be made. First of all, the majority of past research focused on either few genres, or well distinguishable genres. The approaches in [1,6,8,20] led to focus on only one kind of genre (either cartoons or commercials). Roach et al [19] presented a method for the classification of videos into three genres (sports, cartoons and news). Dimitrova et al. [3] classified TV programmes according to four genres (commercials, news, sitcoms and soaps). Truong et al. [28] and Xu et al. [29] considered the same set of five genres, which includes cartoons, commercials, music, news and sports. Liu et al. [13] used weather forecasts instead of musics. Dinh et al. [4] split the music genre into two sub-genres (music shows and concerts), thus resulting in a six-genre classifier. As talk shows play an important role in the daily programming of TV channels, we considered the talk show genre in addition to the genres used in [12,13,28,29]. Our classifier can thus distinguish a greater number of genres.

Another common drawback of existing works is that only a restricted set of objects was used as representative of each genre. In fact, typical experimental datasets consisted of few minutes of randomly selected and aggregated audiovisual clips. We believe that this procedure is not applicable in real-world scenarios (e.g. broadcast archives), where users are usually interested in classifying and retrieving objects as whole and complete, rather than as fragments. To overcome this limitation we used complete broadcasted programmes (e.g. an entire talk show), thus limiting potential bias caused by authors in the clip selection phase. A comparison between our experimental dataset and those used in previous works is reported in Table 3. Notice that the total dimension (in minutes) of our experimental dataset increases by a factor of 37 w.r.t. the average dimension of the experimental datasets used in previous works.

A third problem deals with the kind of classifier employed. In many cases, classical statistical pattern recognition methods (i.e. crisp clustering algorithms [4], decision trees [4,28], support vector machines [4,8], Gaussian mixture models [19,29] and hidden Markow models [1,3,13]) were used. The biggest problem behind statistical pattern recognition classifiers is that their efficiency depends on the class-separability in the feature space used to represent the multimedia data (see [11] for details). We addressed this problem by using four parallel neural networks, each specialised in a particular aspect of multimedia contents, to produce more accurate classifications. In addition, neural networks do not require any *a priori* assumptions on the statistical distribution of the recognised genres, are robust to noisy data and provide fast evaluation of unknown data.

Another important factor in the development of a classification system is the choice of the data validation strategy [7]. Most of the earlier works used the hold-out validation (HOV) technique [3,4,12,13,28,29], whereby the experimental dataset is randomly split into two sub-sets for training and testing. The main drawback of this method is that the classification accuracy may significantly vary depending on which sub-sets are used. One approach used leave-one-out cross-validation (LOOCV) of data [19], which involves the recursive use of a single item from the experimental dataset for testing, and the remaining items for training. This method is time consuming and its classification accuracy may

Table 2. Classification accuracy compared between our work and some previous works

Authors	Recognised genres	Classifier type	Dataset Size [minutes]	Data Validation Strategy	Classification Accuracy
Dinh et al. [4]	6	k-NN	110	HOV	96%
Dinh et al. [4]	6	DT	110	HOV	91%
Dinh et al. [4]	6	SVM	110	HOV	90%
Xu et al. [29]	5	GMM	300	HOV	86%
Liu et al. [13]	5	HMM	100	HOV	85%
Truong et al. [28]	5	DT	480	HOV	83%
Liu et al. [12]	5	ANN	100	HOV	71%
Dimitrova et al. [3]	4	HMM	61	HOV	85%
Roach et al. [19]	3	GMM	15	LOOCV	94%
This work	**7**	**MLPs**	**6692**	**KFCV**	**92%**

be highly variable. In our system, we chose to use the K-fold cross-validation (KFCV) of data. This approach limits potential bias that could be introduced in the choice of training and testing data.

Finally, with regard to the accuracy of the experimental results, our approach shows better performance than those in [3,12,13,28,29]. In two cases our approach performs a bit worse [4,19].

Table 3. Details of some experimental databases used for the genre recognition task

Authors	Clip Duration [seconds]	Genre Duration [minutes]
Dinh et al. [4]	1	news (26), concerts (15), cartoons (19), commercials (18), music shows (11), motor racing games (21).
Xu et al. [29]	300	news (60), commercials (60), sports (60), music (60), cartoons (60).
Liu et al. [13]	1.5	news (20), commercials (20), football (20), basketball (20), weather forecasts (20).
Truong et al. [28]	60	news (96), music (96), sports (96), commercials (96), cartoons (96).
Dimitrova et al. [3]	60	training (26), testing (35).
Roach et al. [19]	30	news (1), cartoons (7), sports (7).
This work	**120 to 2640**	**music (233), commercials (209), cartoons (1126), football (1053), news (1301), talk shows (2650), weather forecasts (120).**

5   Conclusions and Future Work

In this paper we have presented an architecture for the video genre recognition task. Despite the number of existing efforts, the issue of classifying video genres has not been has not been satisfactory addressed yet. We have overcome the limitations of previous approaches by using *complete* TV programmes (instead of shot clips of content), and by defining a set of features that captures both low-level audiovisual descriptors and higher level semantic information. The greater number of genres considered (w.r.t. previous works), the quality of the experimental dataset built, the type of classifier employed and the data validation technique used makes us conclude that our approach significantly improves the state of the art in the investigated task. Future work will investigate the development of new features, the introduction of new classes (e.g. action movie, comedy, tennis, basketball) and the usefulness of new classifiers.

References

1. Albiol, A., Fullà, M.J.C., Albiol, A., Torres, L.: Commercials detection using HMMs. In: Proc. of the Int. Workshop on Image Analysis for Multimedia Interactive Services (2004)
2. Brugnara, F., Cettolo, M., Federico, M., Giuliani, D.: A system for the segmentation and transcription of Italian radio news. In: Proc. of RIAO, Content-Based Multimedia Information Access (2000)
3. Dimitrova, N., Agnihotri, L., Wei, G.: Video classification based on HMM using text and faces. In: Proc. of the European Conference on Signal Processing (2000)
4. Dinh, P.Q., Dorai, C., Venkatesh, S.: Video genre categorization using audio wavelet coefficients. In: Proc. of the 5th Asian Conference on Computer Vision (2002)
5. Fräba, B., Küblbeck, C.: Orientation Template Matching for Face Localization in Complex Visual Scenes. In: Proc. of the IEEE Int. Conf. on Image Processing, pp. 251–254. IEEE Computer Society Press, Los Alamitos (2000)
6. Glasberg, R., Samour, A., Elazouzi, K., Sikora, T.: Cartoon-Recognition using Video & Audio-Descriptors. In: Proc. of the 13th European Signal Processing Conference (2005)
7. Kohavi, R.: A study of cross-validation and bootstrap for accuracy estimation and model selection. In: Proc. of the Int. Conf. on Artificial Intelligence (1995)
8. Ianeva, T.I., de Vries, A.P., Rohrig, H.: Detecting cartoons: a case study in automatic video-genre classification. In: Int. Conf. on Multimedia and Expo. (2003)
9. Igel, C., Hüsken, M.: Improving the Rprop Learning Algorithm. In: Proc. of the 2nd Int. ICSC Symposium on Neural Computation (2000)
10. ISO/IEC 15398: Multimedia Content Description Interface (2001)
11. Jain, A.K., Duin, R.P.W., Mao, J.: Statistical Pattern Recognition: A Review. IEEE Trans. on Pattern Analysis and Machine Intelligence 22(1), 4–37
12. Liu, Z., Huang, J., Wang, Y., Chen, T.: Audio feature extraction and analysis for scene classification. In: IEEE Workshop on Multimedia Signal Processing, IEEE Computer Society Press, Los Alamitos (1997)
13. Liu, Z., Huang, J., Wang, Y.: Classification of TV programs based on audio information using Hidden Markov Model. In: Proc. of IEEE Workshop on Multimedia Signal Processing, IEEE Computer Society Press, Los Alamitos (1998)
14. Messina, A., Airola Gnota, D.: Automatic Archive Documentation Based on Content Analysis. IBC2005 Conference Pubblication

15. Messina, A., Montagnuolo, M., Sapino, M.L: Characterizing multimedia objects through multimodal content analysis and fuzzy fingerprints. In: IEEE Int. Conf. on Signal-Image Technology and Internet-Based Systems, IEEE Computer Society Press, Los Alamitos (2006)
16. Montagnuolo, M., Messina, A.: Multimedia Knowledge Representation for Automatic Annotation of Broadcast TV Archives. In: Proc. of the 4th Int. Workshop on Multimedia Semantics (2006)
17. Polikar, R.: Ensemble Based Systems in Decision Making. IEEE Circuits and Systems Magazine 6(3), 21–45 (2006)
18. Quinlan, J.R.: C4.5 - Programs for Machine Learning. Morgan Kaufmann, San Francisco (1993)
19. Roach, M.J., Mason, J.S.D., Pawlewski, M.: Video genre classification using dynamics. In: IEEE Int. Conf. on Acoustics, Speech, and Signal Processing, IEEE Computer Society Press, Los Alamitos (2001)
20. Sánchez, J.M., Binefa, X., Vitriá, J., Radeva, P.: Local Color Analysis for Scene Break Detection Applied to TV Commercials Recognition. In: Huijsmans, D.P., Smeulders, A.W.M. (eds.) VISUAL 1999. LNCS, vol. 1614, pp. 237–244. Springer, Heidelberg (1999)
21. Schwenker, F., Marinai, S.: Artificial Neural Networks in Pattern Recognition. In: Schwenker, F., Marinai, S. (eds.) ANNPR 2006. LNCS (LNAI), vol. 4087, Springer, Heidelberg (2006)
22. Snoek, C.G., Worring, M.: Multimodal video indexing: A review of the state-of-the-art. Multimedia Tools and Applications 25(1), 5–35 (2005)
23. Swain, M.J., Ballard, D.H.: Color indexing. Int. Journal of Computer Vision 7(1), 11–32 (1991)
24. Tamura, H., Mori, S., Yamawaki, T.: Texture features corresponding to visual perception. IEEE Trans. on Systems, Man and Cybernetics 8(6), 460–473 (1978)
25. Taylor, J.S., Cristianini, N.: Support Vector Machines and other kernel-based learning methods. Cambridge University Press, Cambridge (2000)
26. Tekalp, M.: Digital Video Processing. Prentice-Hall, Englewood Cliffs (1995)
27. Tomasi, C.: Estimating Gaussian Mixture Densities with EM – A Tutorial. Duke University (2005)
28. Truong, B.T., Dorai, C., Venkatesh, S.: Automatic Genre Identification for Content-Based Video Categorization. In: Proc. of the 15th IEEE Int. Conf. on Pattern Recognition, IEEE Computer Society Press, Los Alamitos (2000)
29. Xu, L.Q., Li, Y.: Video classification using spatial-temporal features and PCA. In: Proc. of the IEEE Int. Conf. on Multimedia and Expo, IEEE Computer Society Press, Los Alamitos (2003)

Hierarchical Text Categorization Through a Vertical Composition of Classifiers

Andrea Addis, Giuliano Armano, Francesco Mascia, and Eloisa Vargiu

University of Cagliari, Piazza d'Armi, I-09123, Cagliari, Italy
{addis,armano,f.mascia,vargiu}@diee.unica.it
http://iasc.diee.unica.it/

Abstract. In this paper we present a hierarchical approach to text categorization aimed at improving the performances of the corresponding tasks. The proposed approach is explicitly devoted to cope with the problem related to the unbalance between relevant and non relevant inputs. The technique has been implemented and tested by resorting to a multiagent system aimed at performing information retrieval tasks.

1   Introduction

Text categorization can be defined as the task of determining and assigning topical labels to content [10]. The more the amount of available data (e.g., in digital libraries), the greater the need for high-performance text categorization algorithms.

In the last years, text categorization has received attention also from the community that investigates ensembles of classifiers. In fact, there is strong theoretical and experimental evidence that combining multiple classifiers can actually boost the performance over a single classifier. Let us recall, here, (i) the work of Sebastiani [9] and of Schapire [8], which fall in the general category of boosting, (ii) the work of Larkey [5] and Yang et al. [11], aimed at assessing the impact of output combination techniques, and (iii) the work of Dong [3], where several input subsampling techniques (with heterogeneous classifiers) are experimented.

Furthermore, several researchers have recently investigated the use of hierarchies for text categorization, which is also the main focus of our work. To this end, we tackle the problem of text categorization by resorting to multiple classifiers derived from a suitable taxonomy able to represent topics deemed relevant to the domain being investigated. The proposed system is mainly devoted to take into account the problem that originates from an unbalance between relevant and non-relevant items studying the impact of a "vertical" composition of classifiers. In particular, each item to be classified undergoes progressive filtering by the pipelines of classifiers that originate from the adopted taxonomy. To assess the capabilities of a technique based on progressive filtering, we devised a multiagent system specifically tailored for a relevant task, i.e. news categorization. Tests have been performed on the RCV1-v2 [6] standard document collection.

R. Basili and M.T. Pazienza (Eds.): AI*IA 2007, LNAI 4733, pp. 742–748, 2007.

The remainder of the paper is organized as follows: Section 2 is focused on the proposed progressive filtering technique. Section 3 reports and discusses experimental results. In Section 4 conclusions are drawn and future work is pointed out.

2   Vertical Composition of Classifiers

A main issue in news categorization is how to deal, for each category, with an unbalance between relevant and non-relevant items. In particular, one may expect that most documents are non relevant to the user, the ratio between negative and positive examples being high (typical orders of magnitude are 10^2 - 10^3). Unfortunately, this aspect has a very negative impact on the precision of the system. With the aim of coping with this phenomenon, we propose a vertical composition of classifiers that exploits the ability of a pipeline of classifiers to progressively filter out non relevant information.

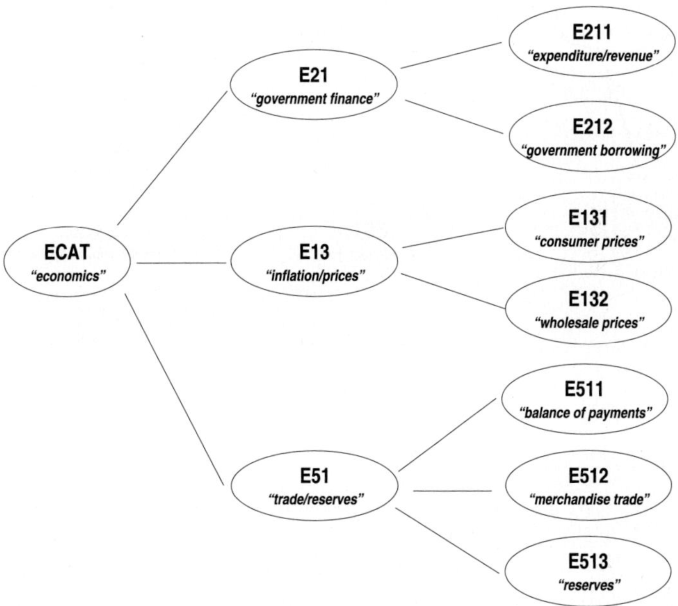

Fig. 1. A portion of the RCV1-taxonomy

2.1   The Proposed Approach

In the proposed approach, each item to be classified undergoes progressive filtering by the pipelines of classifiers that originate from the adopted taxonomy. To better illustrate it, let us consider the adopted taxonomy, i.e., the RCV1-taxonomy (Figure 1 reports part of the branch corresponding to the *economics* topic). Each node of the taxonomy represents a classifier entrusted with recognizing all corresponding relevant inputs. Any given input traverses the taxonomy as a "token", starting from the root (in the example in Figure, ECAT). If the current classifier recognizes the token as relevant, it passes it on to all its children (if any). The typical result consists of activating one or more pipelines of classifiers within the taxonomy. As an example, let us consider Figure 2 that illustrates the pipeline activated by an input document, which encompasses the categories economics (ECAT), government finance (E21), and expenditure/revenue (E211). This means that *all* involved classifiers recognize the input as relevant.

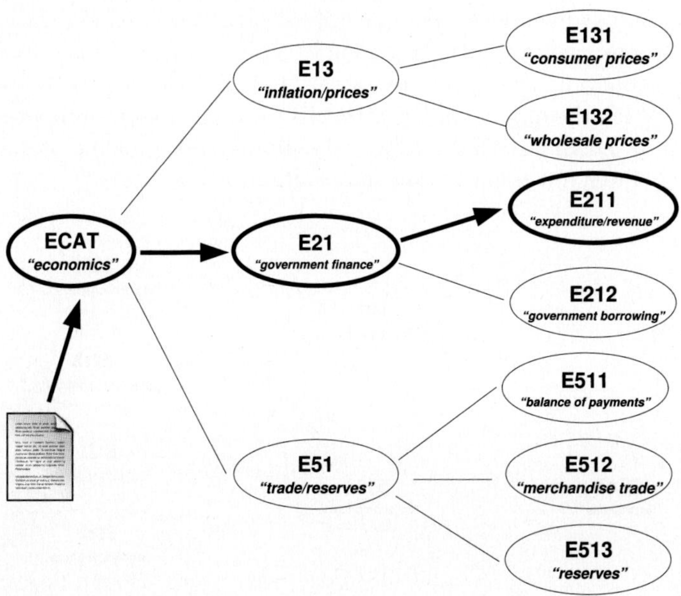

Fig. 2. An example of pipeline (highlighted in bold)

Let us point out in advance that particular care has been taken in using pipelines to limit the phenomenon of false negatives (FN), as a user may accept to be signaled about an article which is actually not relevant, but –on the other hand– would be disappointed in the event that the system disregards an input which is actually relevant. This behavior can be imposed in different ways, the simplest being lowering the threshold used to decide whether an input is relevant or not. In a typical text categorization system this operation typically has a negative impact on false positives (FP), i.e. augmenting their presence.

2.2   Theoretical Issues

From a theoretical point of view, if the set of inputs submitted to a classifier contains n_0 non relevant inputs and n_1 relevant inputs, the (expected) normalized confusion matrix associated with a classifier is:

$$\begin{vmatrix} n_0 \cdot c_{00} & n_0 \cdot c_{01} \\ n_1 \cdot c_{10} & n_1 \cdot c_{11} \end{vmatrix}$$

where the first and the second index represents the actual relevance of the input and the way it has been classified, respectively. For instance, c_{01} represents (an estimation of) the probability to classify as relevant (1) an input that is in fact non relevant (0). Hence:

$$\pi = \frac{TP}{TP + FP} = \left(1 + \frac{FP}{TP}\right)^{-1} = \left(1 + \frac{c_{01}}{c_{11}} \cdot \frac{n_0}{n_1}\right)^{-1} \tag{1}$$

$$\rho = \frac{TP}{TP + FN} = \left(1 + \frac{FN}{TP}\right)^{-1} = \left(1 + \frac{c_{10}}{c_{11}}\right)^{-1} \tag{2}$$

Having to deal with a pipeline of k classifiers linked by an *is-a* relationship, for the sake of simplicity let us assume that (i) each classifier in the pipeline has the same (normalized) confusion matrix and that (ii) classifiers are in fact independent.

It can be easily verified that the effect of using a pipeline of k classifiers on precision and recall is:

$$\pi^{(k)} = \frac{TP^{(k)}}{TP^{(k)} + FP^{(k)}} = \left(1 + \frac{FP^{(k)}}{TP^{(k)}}\right)^{-1} = \left(1 + \frac{c_{01}^k}{c_{11}^k} \cdot \frac{n_0}{n_1}\right)^{-1} \tag{3}$$

$$\rho^{(k)} = \frac{TP^{(k)}}{TP^{(k)} + FN^{(k)}} = \left(1 + \frac{FN^{(k)}}{TP^{(k)}}\right)^{-1} = \left(1 + \frac{c_{10}}{1 - c_{11}} \cdot \frac{1 - c_{11}^k}{c_{11}^k}\right)^{-1} \tag{4}$$

The equations above show that an unbalance of positive and negative examples (which is the usual case in text categorization problems) can be suitably counterbalanced with by keeping FN (i.e., c_{10}) low and by exploiting the filtering effect of classifiers in the pipeline. The former aspect affects the recall, whereas the latter allows to augment the precision according to the number of levels of the given taxonomy.

3 Experimental Results

To test the proposed approach, a multiagent system explicitly devised to perform information retrieval tasks has been implemented. From an architectural point of view, the system has been built using PACMAS (Personalized Adaptive and Cooperative MultiAgent System), a generic multiagent architecture aimed at retrieving, filtering, and organizing information according to the users' interests [1].

Tests have been performed using RCV1-v2, the standard document collection proposed in [6], which is composed of 103 classes organized in four hierarchical groups: CCAT (Corporate/Industrial), ECAT (Economics), GCAT (Government/Social), and MCAT (Markets).

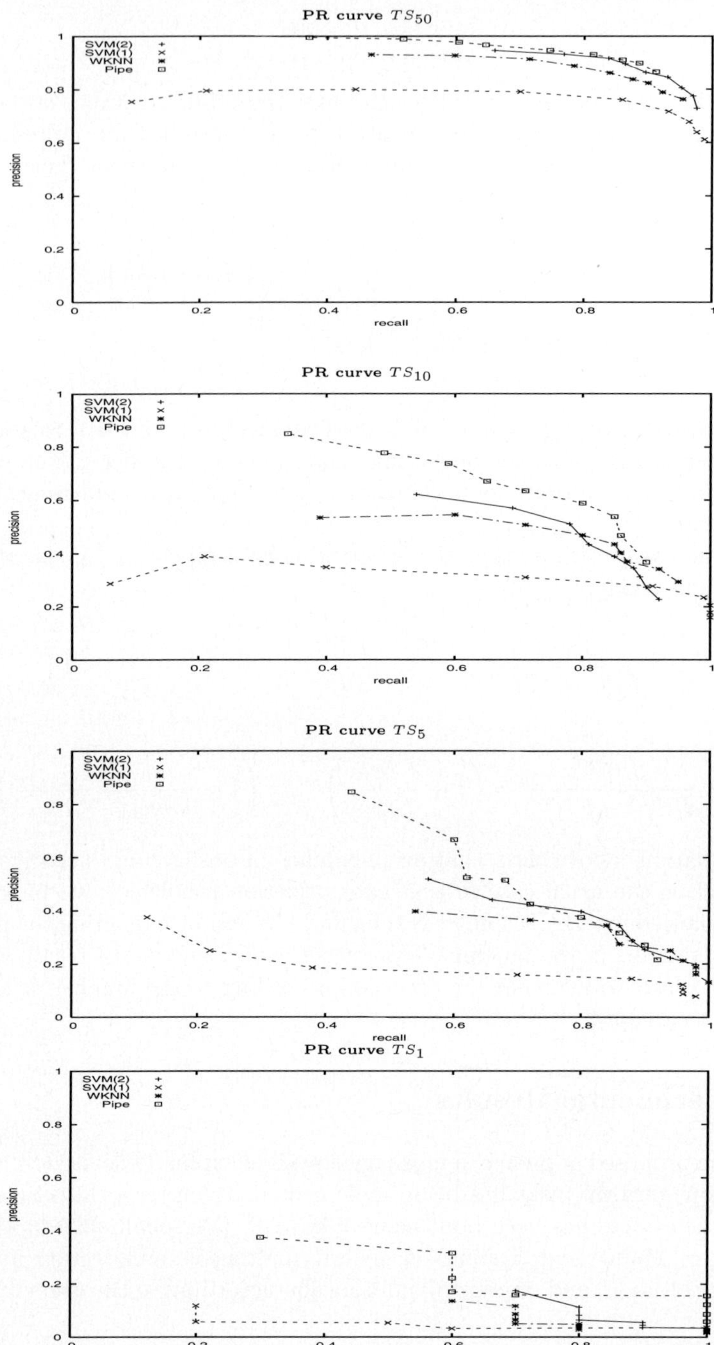

Fig. 3. Experimental results (PR curves) performed on a specific pipeline, i.e. [ECAT, E21, E211], reported together those obtained by running other classifiers on the flat –non hierarchical– model

Table 1. Micro- and macro-averaging

pos	f_1^{μ}WKNN	f_1^{M}WKNN	f_1^{μ}SVM^1	f_1^{M}SVM^1	f_1^{μ}SVM^2	f_1^{M}SVM^2	f_1^{μ}Pipe	f_1^{M}Pipe
50	0,883	0,883	0.831	0.832	0,898	0,897	0.905	0.905
10	0,646	0,647	0.507	0.521	0,719	0,722	0.721	0.720
5	0,513	0,514	0.412	0.428	0,535	0,543	0.683	0.682
1	0,165	0,169	0.169	0.190	0,344	0,349	0.412	0.431

To assess the capabilities of the proposed progressive filtering technique, 16 suitable pipelines, each one composed of three classifiers, have been selected. First, each node of the pipeline is trained with a balanced data set by using 200 features (TFIDF) selected according to the information gain method [7], being 200 the optimal number of features obtained experimentally. Then, for each node of the taxonomy, a learning set of 500 articles, with a balanced set of positive and negative examples, has been selected to train a classifier based on the wk-NN technology [2].

As for testing, different randomly selected sets of 1000 documents have been generated –characterized by a different ratio between relevant and non-relevant inputs. In particular, the ratio between positive and negative examples has been set to 1:2, 1:10, 1:20, and 1:100 (50%, 10%, 5%, and 1%), say TS_{50}, TS_{10}, TS_5, and TS_1, respectively. To study the impact of progressively filtering information with pipelines of wk-NN classifiers (denoted as PIPE), we tested with the above test sets some relevant pipelines, each concerning three nodes of the taxonomy ($k = 3$). Results have been compared with those obtained by running the same tests on three classifiers based on the following technologies: wk-NN (denoted as WKNN), [1] linear SVM (denoted as SVM^1), and RBF-SVM (denoted as SVM^2). As shown in Table 1, in all selected samples, the distributed solution based on multiple classifiers has reported better results than those obtained with flat models.

As for precision and recall, let us consider –for the sake of brevity– only one specific pipeline (taking into account, anyway, that it is representative of a typical behavioral pattern) composed of three classifiers. Figure 3 reports the curves PR, obtained by running on the selected tests: the pipeline (PIPE) corresponding to Figure 2, as well as the classifiers (WKNN, SVM^1, and SVM^2) trained to recognize as relevant only inputs belonging to the E211 category (which coincides with the "bottom" of the pipeline).

Experimental results show that in presence of unbalanced inputs, a pipeline of three classifiers is able to counteract an unbalance of up to 100 non relevant articles vs. one relevant article.

4   Conclusions and Future Work

In this paper an approach based on a vertical composition of classifiers aimed at improving the performances of text categorization tasks has been presented. The

---

[1] The technique based on wk-NN has been used both with the hierarchical classification (PIPE) and with the flat model (WKNN).

proposed approach, explicitly devoted to cope with the problem related to the unbalance between relevant and non relevant inputs, has been tested through a multiagent system aimed at performing information retrieval tasks. Experiments, performed on RCV1-v2, confirm that the adoption of a vertical composition of classifiers improve the overall performances of the involved classifiers.

As for the future work, we are planning to test our approach with different datasets, such as the OHSUMED corpus [4]. Furthermore, we are considering how to compare our results with the ones belonging to state-of-the-art systems that perform hierarchical text categorization.

References

1. Armano, G., Cherchi, G., Manconi, A., Vargiu, E.: PACMAS: A personalized, Adaptive, and Cooperative MultiAgent System Architecture. In: WOA 2005. Workshop dagli Oggetti agli Agenti, Simulazione e Analisi Formale di Sistemi Complessi, pp. 54–60 (2005)
2. Cost, W., Salzberg, S.: A weighted Nearest Neighbor Algorithm for Learning with Symbolic Features. Machine Learning 10, 57–78 (1993)
3. Dong, Y.-S., Han, K.-S.: A Comparison of Several Ensemble Methods for Text Categorization. In: IEEE SCC, pp. 419–422 (2004)
4. Hersh, W., Buckley, C., Leone, T.J., Hickam, D.: OHSUMED: an interactive retrieval evaluation and new large test collection for research. In: Croft, W.B., van Rijsbergen, C.J. (eds.) Proceedings of the 17th Annual international ACM SIGIR Conference on Research and Development in information Retrieval, Dublin, Ireland, July 03 - 06, 1994, pp. 192–201. Springer, New York (1994)
5. Larkey, L.S., Croft, W.B.: Combining classifiers in text categorization. In: Proceedings of the 19th Annual international ACM SIGIR Conference on Research and Development in information Retrieval, Zurich, Switzerland, August 18-22, 1996, pp. 289–297. ACM Press, New York (1996)
6. Lewis, D.D., Yand, Y., Rose, T., Li, F.: Rcv1: A New Benchmark Collection for Text Categorization Research. Journal of Machine Learning Research 5, 361–397 (2004)
7. Lewis, D.D.: An evaluation of phrasal and clustered representations on a text categorization task. In: Proceedings of SIGIR-92, 15th ACM International Conference on Research and Development in Information Retrieval, Kobenhavn, DK, pp. 37–50. ACM Press, New York (1992)
8. Schapire, R.E., Singer, Y., Singhal, A.: Boosting and Rocchio Applied to Text Filtering. In: Proceedings of the 21st Annual International ACM SIGIR Conference on Research and Development in Information Retrieval, pp. 215–223. ACM Press, New York (1998)
9. Sebastiani, F., Sperduti, A., Valdambrini, N.: An Improved Boosting Algorithm and its Application to Text Categorization. In: Proceedings of the Ninth international Conference on information and Knowledge Management, McLean, Virginia, United States, November 06-11, 2000, pp. 78–85. ACM Press, New York (2000)
10. Sebastiani, F.: Machine learning in automated text categorization. ACM Computing Surveys 34(1), 1–47 (2002)
11. Yang, Y., Ault, T., Pierce, T.: Combining multiple learning strategies for effective cross-validation. In: Proceedings of the 17th International Conference on Machine Learning, pp. 1167–1182 (2000)

Text Categorization in Non-linear Semantic Space

Claudio Biancalana and Alessandro Micarelli

Department of Computer Science and Automation
Artificial Intelligence Laboratory
Roma Tre University
Via della Vasca Navale, 79, 00146 Rome, Italy
{claudio.biancalana,micarel}@dia.uniroma3.it

Abstract. Automatic Text Categorization (TC) is a complex and useful task for many natural language applications, and is usually performed by using a set of manually classified documents, i.e. a training collection. Term-based representation of documents has found widespread use in TC. However, one of the main shortcomings of such methods is that they largely disregard lexical semantics and, as a consequence, are not sufficiently robust with respect to variations in word usage. In this paper we design, implement, and evaluate a new text classification technique. Our main idea consists in finding a series of projections of the training data by using a new, modified LSI algorithm, projecting all training instances to the low-dimensional subspace found in the previous step, and finally inducing a binary search on the projected low-dimensional data. Our conclusion is that, with all its simplicity and efficiency, our approach is comparable to SVM accuracy on classification.

1 Introduction

Text categorization consists in breaking down a textual document into one or more categories. The importance of this task is gaining significant attention as the volume of data becomes increasingly unmanageable due to the constant spreading of the World Wide Web and the rapid development of the Internet technology. In order to meet the challenges of this information boom, the demand for a high precision method that performs automatic text categorization inevitably increases. For example, it will help people find interesting Web pages efficiently, filter electronic mail messages, filter netnews [13], etc.

To date, various machine learning methods have been applied to text categorization. These include k-nearest-neighbor (kNN) [15], decision trees (DT), Naive-Bayes (NB) [6], ridge logistic regression [4]. Using a large number of words as features in these methods, which can potentially contribute to the overall task, is a challenge for machine learning approaches. More specifically, the difficulties in handling a large input space are twofold:

- How to design a learning algorithm with an effective use of large scale feature spaces [1][2].

R. Basili and M.T. Pazienza (Eds.): AI*IA 2007, LNAI 4733, pp. 749–756, 2007.
© Springer-Verlag Berlin Heidelberg 2007

- How to choose an appropriate subset of words for effective classification [3][5].

In this research we have developed learning machines with feature selection criteria because the suitable set of words greatly differs depending on the learning method. Latent Semantic Indexing (LSI) [14],[11] attempts to circumvent the problems of lexifcal matching approaches by using statistically derived conceptual indices rather than individual literal terms for categorization. LSI assumes that an underlying semantic structure of word usage exists in a document collection and uses this to estimate the semantic content of documents in the collection. This estimate is accomplished through a rank-reduced term by document space via the singular value decomposition (SVD). As a vector-space retrieval technique, LSI has outperformed the lexical searching techniques quite significantly. However, what is needed to improve the viability and versatility of current LSI implementation is a mechanism to incorporate *non-linear* perturbations to existing rank-reduced models, and this has been lacking. This paper is organized as follows. In section 2 we introduce the new Non-Linear-LSI technique. Section 3 presents a new algorithm for binary classification on the projected low-dimensional data processed by Non-Linear-LSI. Section 4 presents our experimental setup and gives a detailed description of the results. Finally, in Section 5 we illustrate our conclusions and outline some open questions.

2   Non-linear-LSI Implementation

The new LSI implementation proposed in this work is an updated LSI model equipped with a mechanism to incorporate *non-linear* perturbations to the existing rank-reduced model A_k. This new implementation provides an efficient information filtering technique. In LSI, all indexing terms and documents in a collection are represented as a vector in a rank-reduced term-by-document space. The documents are compared with the test document and then ranked according to their proximity to the test document. Due to the variability in word usage (e.g., polysemy) an LSI-based system may not always produce responses that accurately reflect the conceptual meaning of the test document. The new LSI implementation attempts to overcome these problems by performing appropriate *non-linear* perturbations to the existing term-by-document model A_k meaning that some term-document associations are changed and the corresponding term and document vectors are reconstructed and repositioned in the new perturbed rank-reduced term-by-document space.

For all the terms and documents in A_k, the matrix P determines the set of terms and the set of documents whose term-document associations are allowed to change (while other associations are fixed).

The perturbation matrix P can be constructed defining the splitting of A_k

$$A_k = A_k^F + A_k^C$$

where A_k^F defines the set of terms in A_k whose term-document associations are not allowed to change, and A_k^C is the complement of A_k^F, and

$$A_k v = D_v u \tau, \qquad u^T D_v u = 1, \tag{1}$$

$$A_k^T v = D_u v \tau, \qquad v^T D_u u = 1, \tag{2}$$

where the metrics D_u and D_v are defined by

$$D_v = diag(P diag(v) v),$$

$$D_u = diag(P^T diag(u) u).$$

For all the terms and documents in A_k, the matrix P determines the set of terms and the set of documents whose term-document associations are allowed to change (while other association are fixed). The perturbation matrix P can also be used to have more control in ranking the returned documents. Using an inverse iteration approach, a new algorithm (Non-Linear-LSI) for solving the new SVD problem (see (1) and (2)) is listed below:

Table 1. Pseudo-code of Non-Linear-LSI

Non-Linear-LSI Algorithm

$i = 0;$
Initialize $u^{(0)}$, $v^{(0)}$ and $\tau^{(0)}$
Compute matrices $D_u^{(0)}$ and $D_v^{(0)}$

While $(K \geq y)$ do
$i = i + 1;$
$x^{(i)} = \sum_k^{-1} V_k^T D_u^{(i-1)} v^{(i-1)} \tau^{(i-1)}$
$y^{(i)} = U_{m-k}^T u^{(i-1)}$
$u^{(i)} = U_k x^{(i)} + U_{m-k} y^{(i)}$
$s^{(i)} = \sum_k^{-1} U_k^T D_v^{(i-1)} u^{(i)} \tau^{(i-1)}$
$t^{(i)} = V_{n-k}^T v^{(i-1)}$
$v^{(i)} = V_k s^{(i)} + V_{n-k} t^{(i)}$
$\tau^{(i)} = u^{(i)T} A_k v^{(i)}$
$D_u^{(i)} = diag(P diag(v^{(i)}) v^{(i)})$
$D_v^{(i)} = diag(P^T diag(u^{(i)}) u^{(i)})$
$K = K + 1$

The perturbation Matrix P has a rectangular non-zero cluster with dimension $l \times w$. Compared to other concept-based approaches for information retrieval, our approach has several advantages. Firstly it uses an high dimensional space which better represents a wide range of semantic relations. Secondly, both terms and documents are explicitly represented in the same space. Thirdly, it retrieves documents from query terms directly, without interpreting the underlying dimensions as is the case of many factor-analytic applications. It only assumes that these factors represent one or more semantic relationship in the document collection.

3 OnLine Hyperplane

The last but fundamental module relates to the binary classification. Below the following training example is assumed:

$$z = ((x_1, y_1), \ldots, (x_m, y_m)) \in (\mathcal{X} \times \{-1, +1\})^m$$

of m dimension and a mapping function

$$\phi : \mathcal{X} \to \mathcal{K} \subseteq \mathcal{R}^n$$

in a vector space of n-dimensional $\mathcal{K}$. Our objective is to ascertain the $w \in \mathcal{K}$ parameters of the linear classifier

$$h_{w,b}(x) = sgn(f_{w,b}(x)) \qquad f_{w,b}(x) = \langle w, x \rangle + b$$

where $x = \phi(x)$ and $\langle \cdot, \cdot \rangle$, representing the internal product in $\mathcal{K}$. In a manner similar to algorithms concerned with the back-propagation of error, Online Hyperplane's final goal is error minimization on a training set furnished at point of entry. Given the procedure just outlined, let us fix the training set as follows:

$$D_m = (x_1, y_1), \ldots, (x_m, y_m)$$

and a $\mathcal{H}$ family threshold as $h : X \to \{-1, +1\}$. For sake of simplicity we also assume that we may initially fix d hidden conjunctions that are earmarked for inclusion in the final classifier f. What remains to be determined is the selection of the w coefficient and the method of incremental selection for the functions $h_1, \ldots, h_d$. Such selections will derive directly from the analysis of the f error on D_m. We remind that the f error or D_m is that fraction of elements of the training set which f classifies in a mistaken manner, that is

$$err_{D_m}(f) = \frac{1}{m}|\{1 \leq t \leq m : f(x_t) \neq y_t\} =$$

$$= \frac{1}{m}|\{1 \leq t \leq m : \sum_{i=d}^{d} w_i h_i(x_t) y_t \leq 0\}|$$

For the fixed training set D_m, functions $L_1, \ldots, L_d$ are defined as

$$L_i(t) = h_i(x_t) y_t$$

Note further that $L_i(t) \in \{-1, +1\}$ and $L_i(t) = 1$ if and only if $h_i(x_t) = y_t$. We have, therefore

$$err_{D_m}(f) = \frac{1}{m}|\{1 \leq t \leq m : \sum_{i=1}^{d} w_i L_i(t) \leq 0\}|$$

Hyperplane $w \cdot x + b = 0$ is called separator plane:

- w is the normal hyperplane
- $\frac{|b|}{\|w\|}$ is the orthogonal distance of the plane from the origin;
- $\|w\|$ represents the Euclidean norm of w;

$d_+(d_-)$ is defined as the minimum distance of the separator plane closest to the positive (negative) point. The separator plane's margin is defined as $d_+ + d_-$. In the event that points can be separated linearly many separator planes exist: all these points correctly classify the training set. As far as generalization capabilities are concerned, however, they are quite diverse. Online hyperplane seeks out a hyperplane that is not only correct in relation to the training set, but that manages to generalize as well. The chosen criterion consists in finding that hyperplane that maximizes the margin. The algorithm proceeds by determining whether the actual training set example $(x_i, y_i) \in z$ is correctly classified by the running classifier $(y_i(\langle w_t, x_i \rangle) + b_t) > C_z)$, or by otherwise updating the w_i vector. In this case the values of vector w_i and bias b_t are changed according to a loss function that extracts the generalization grade from the running solution by means of slack variables. For every training example the system gets the best kernel. Formally:

$$\texttt{minimize:} \quad V(\vec{w}, b, \xi) = \frac{1}{2}\|\vec{w}\|^2 + C_- \sum_i \xi_i + C_+ \sum_j \xi_j$$

$$\texttt{subject to:} \quad \forall k \quad y_k \cdot \texttt{Kernel}(\vec{w} \cdot \vec{x_k}) + b \geq 1 - \xi_k$$

By treating positive and negative examples our system obtains a definite robustness in order to compare the ensembles of examples of unmeasured learning. For it is well known how that when it comes to text categorization problems, it is far more important to correctly classify the positive examples as opposed to the negative ones since the latters differ from the formers by several orders of magnitude.

4 Experiments

To make the algorithm evaluation comparable to the most recently published results on TC, we chose three corpuses:

1. Reuters-21578 [1]
   - ModApte[10] split
   - ModApte[115] split
2. Reuters Corpus Volume 1, English language [2]
3. WebKB[3]

---

[1] http://www.daviddleis.com/testcollection/reuters21578
[2] http://about.reuters.com/researchandstandards/corpus/
[3] http://www.cs.cmu.edu/afs/cs/project/theo-20/www/data

All data are represented in Vector Space with TF-IDF technique. In keeping with some of the best system at TREC, our IDF for term t is $log(\frac{|D|}{|D_t|})$ where D is the document collection and $D_t \subseteq D$ is the set containing t. The term frequency $TF(d,t) = 1 + ln(1 + ln(n,(d,t)))$ where $n(d,t) > 0$ is the raw frequency of t in document d. d is represented as sparse vector with the l-th component being TF(d,t)IDF(t). Tables 2 and 3 show our results compared with the published results of other machine learning techniques on the same data collection.

4.1   Reuters-21578

The Reuters-21578 collection consists of 21578 newswire articles collected throughout 1987 from Reuters. Documents in Reuters deal with financial topics, and were classified in several sets of financial categories by personnel from Reuters Ltd. and Carneige Group Inc. There are five sets of categories: TOPICS, ORGANIZATIONS, EXCHANGES, PLACES, and PEOPLE. When a test collection is provided, it is customary to divide it into a training subset and test subset. Several partitions have been suggested for Reuters [9], among which we have opted for Modified Apte Split (ModApte).

ModApte[10]. In the ModApte[10] split, 75% of the stories (9603) are used as training documents to build the classifier and the remaining 25% (3299) to test the accuracy of our classifier. Note that the 92.6% BEP result over Reuters was established by Bekkerman [7] (table 3). With our system we found 93.0% micro F1-Measure.

ModApte[115]. Of the 135 potential topic categories only 115 for which there is at least one training example are used: ModApte[115]. In this case we found 87.5% F1-micro measure, despite a Weiss classifier (Boosting of Decision Tree) 87.8% BEP (table 3).

4.2   RCV1

The RCV1 corpus contains 806791 stories of the period going from 20 August 1996 to 19 August 1997. There are 103 categories organized hierarchically. We split the corpus into two sets of documents: training docs dated 14 April 1997 or earlier, test docs dated after 14 April 1997. The overall training and testing time over the entire corpus in the multi-label setting was about 288 hours (14 days). This kind of experimentation demonstrates large-scale domain applicability of our methodology.

4.3   WebKB

WebKB collection is a dataset of web pages made available by the CMU text-learning group; only classes, `course`, `faculty`, `project`, and `student` are used. The experiments with this small webKB corpus were accordingly less time-consuming.

Table 2. Categorization results of our system

Dataset	micro F1	macro Re	macro Pr
modApte[10]	93.0%	87.5%	74.4%
modApte[115]	87.5%	78.4%	79.4%
RCV1	69%	54%	63%
WebKB	91.5%	85.0%	78.7%

Table 3. Summary of related results

Authors	Dataset	Classifier	Result
Dumais et al. (1998)	**modApte[10]**	SVM + MI	92.0% micro F1
Bekkerman et al. (2003)	**modApte[10]**	SVM + IB	92.6% BEP
Joachims (1998)	modApte[90]	SVM	86.4% micro F1
Weiss et al. (1999)	modApte[95]	Boosting of Decision trees	87.8% BEP
Joachims (1998)	**WebKB**	SVM	79.1% micro F1

5   Conclusion

This article introduced a new classification technique for high-dimensional data such as text. Our approach is very fast, scaling linearly with input size, as opposed to SVM involving quadratic programming, which slows down following a quadratic scaling. It uses efficient sequential scans over the training data, unlike popular SVM implementation, which has less efficient disk and cache access patterns and a poorer locality of reference. This performance boost carries little or no penalty in terms of accuracy: we often beat SVM in the F_1 measure and closely match SVM in recall and precision. Let us conclude with some questions and directions for future research. Given a pool of two or more representation techniques and given a corpus, an interesting question is whether it is possible to combine them so as to compete with or even outperform the best technique in the pool. Another possibility is to try to combine the representation techniques by devising a specialized categorizer for each representation and then use ensemble techniques to aggregate decisions. Other sophisticated approaches such as *co-training* [8] may be considered too. In all our experiments we used the simple one-against-all decomposition technique. It would be interesting to study other decompositions.

References

1. Di Nunzio, G.M.: A bidimensional view of documents for text categorisation. In: McDonald, S., Tait, J. (eds.) ECIR 2004. LNCS, vol. 2997, pp. 112–126. Springer, Heidelberg (2004)

2. Di Nunzio, G.M., Micarelli, A.: Does a New Simple Gaussian Weighting Approach Perform Well in Text Categorization? In: Gottlob, G., Walsh, T. (eds.) IJCAI 2003. Proceedings of the 18th International Joint Conference of Artificial Intelligence, Acapulco, Mexico, August 2003, pp. 581–586. Morgan Kaufmann, San Francisco,CA, USA (2003)
3. Yang, Y., Pedersen, J.O.: A comparative study on feature selection in text categorization. In: ICML-97. Proceedings of the 14-th International Conference on Machine Learning, Nashville, Tennessee, US, pp. 412–420 (1997)
4. Zang, T., Oles, F.J.: Text categorization based on regularized linear classification methods. Information Retrieval 4(1), 5–31 (2001)
5. Forman, G.: An extensive empirical study of feature selection metrics for text classification. Journal of Machine Learning Research 3, 1289–1305 (2003)
6. Eyheramendy, S., Lewis, D.D., Madigan, D.: On the naive bayes model for text categorization. In: AISTATS-03. Proceedings of the 9-th International Workshop Artificial Intelligence and Statistics, Key West, Florida, US (January 2003)
7. Bekkerman, R., El-Yaniv, R., Tishby, N.: Distributional word clusters vs. words for text categorization. Journal of Machine Learning Research 3, 1183–1208 (2002)
8. Blum, A., Mitchell, T.: Combining labeled and unlabeled data with co-training. In (COLT): Proceedings of the Workshop on Computational Learning Theory, Morgan Kaufmann Publishers, San Francisco (1998)
9. Damerau, F., Apte, C., Weiss, S.W.: Automated learning of decision rules for text categorization. ACM Transactions on Information Systems 12(3), 233–251 (1994)
10. Deerwester, S.C., Dumais, S.T., Landauer, T.K., Furnas, G.W., Harshman, R.A.: Indexing by latent semantic analysis. Journal of the American Society of Information Science 41(6), 391–407 (1990)
11. Susan, T.D.: Using lsi for information filtering: Trec-3 experiments. The Third Text REtrieval Conferece (TREC3) NIST Special Publication, pp. 219–230 (1995)
12. Joachims, T.: Text categorization with support vector machines: learning with many relevant features. In: Nédellec, C., Rouveirol, C. (eds.) ECML 1998. LNCS, vol. 1398, pp. 137–142. Springer, Heidelberg (1998)
13. Lang, K.: Newsweeder: Learning to filter news. In: Proceedings of the 12th International Conference on Machine Learning, pp. 331–339 (1995)
14. O'Brien, G.W., Berry, M.W., Dumais, S.T.: Using linear algebra for intelligent information retrieval. SIAM Review 37(4), 177–196 (1995)
15. Yang, Y., Liu, X.: A re-examination of text categorization methods. In: 22nd Annual International SIGIR, Berkley, pp. 42–49 (August 1999)

A System Supporting Users of Cultural Resource Management Semantic Portals

Andrea Bonomi, Glauco Mantegari, Alessandro Mosca, Matteo Palmonari, and Giuseppe Vizzari

Department of Informatics, Systems and Communication (DISCo)
University of Milan - Bicocca, Via Bicocca degli Arcimboldi 8, 20126 Milano, Italy
{andrea.bonomi, glauco.mantegari, alessandro.mosca, matteo.palmonari, giuseppe.vizzari}@disco.unimib.it

Abstract. Cultural Resource Management (CRM) represents an interesting application domain for innovative approaches, models and technologies developed by computer science researchers. This paper presents NavEditOW, a system for the navigation, query and updating of ontologies through the web, as a tool providing suitable functionalities for the design and development of semantic portals in the CRM area. NavEditOW supports ontology maintainers, content editors, and end-users, that have little or no specific knowledge on Semantic Web technologies and on related formal tools. A description of the application of the tool to the representation and management of archaeological knowledge for the description of publications in an e-library is also provided.

1 Introduction

Cultural Resource Management (CRM) defines a complex process which essentially concerns the study, documentation, conservation and fruition of different kinds of cultural resources. Often equated with Cultural Heritage Management (CHM), it comprises both historical resources (Cultural Heritage – CH) and contemporary ones. During the years, the distinction between CRM and CHM has gradually shaded and the trend is nowadays to refer to CRM while dealing with cultural heritage [1,2]. CRM is a strongly multidisciplinary process which involves several disciplines which are not directly related with CH, such as sociology, economy and computer science. In fact computer science plays nowadays a central role in all the tasks involved in the process of CRM. While during the '80s computers were essentially used for the storage and management of data by means of databases and information systems and were thus employed mainly for documentation purposes, the scenario of ICT applications to CRM has hugely expanded during the last two decades. In particular, the availability of the Web and the related technologies has provided innovative possibilities ranging from simple informative pages up to systems targeted to specialistic research. Web applications have become crucial for CRM, although the results obtained by the different projects dealing specifically with this subject vary a lot. Moreover, there is a lack of systems which can really be useful for research: the Web is still

R. Basili and M.T. Pazienza (Eds.): AI*IA 2007, LNAI 4733, pp. 757–764, 2007.

often conceived as a toy and not as a potentially very powerful system which can substantially modify our approach to CRM.

In this framework, the Semantic Web community has already developed some relevant innovative proposals and applications for the Semantic Web to enhance CRM portals and information systems have been provided [1]. Nevertheless, besides domain specific applications, the interaction between end-users and semantic knowledge bases is still difficult due to the lack of tools supporting users in the different tasks related to this interaction; in particular we address navigation, editing and query of such knowledge bases.

NavEditOW (Navigating, Editing and query of Ontologies through the Web) is an environment for navigation, querying, and A-Box editing of OWL-based ontologies (up to OWL-DL) through a web-based interface [3]. The main aim of this paper is to present the application of NavEditOW to support both designers in the development of CRM web portals and users in the interaction with such portals. The system allows exploring the concepts and their relational dependencies as well as the instances by means of hyper-links. NavEditOW's functionalities have been developed especially to support ontology maintainers, content editors, and end-users, that have little or no specific knowledge on Semantic Web technologies and on the related formal tools (e.g. Description Logics, OWL-Lite, -DL and -Full languages, ontology editors, and query languages). In particular, this paper presents the new functionalities of the system, providing an annotation framework to support the visualization management and user-oriented support to query formulation. NavEditOW clearly separates the *Presentation Layer* from the *Semantic Framework Layer* through the implementation of suitable adapters, supporting the exploitation of different available Semantic Frameworks (in particular, *Sesame* and *Jena*).

In this paper we will describe the application of NavEditOW to the representation and management of ontological description of bibliographic entries in the e-Library of a portal dedicated to the archaeological research. In order to effectively describe contents beyond a keyword based approach, and thus in order to support effective forms of information retrieval and semantic navigation, human annotators must have a domain ontology, whose elements can be selected as relevant indicators of the topics treated in the described publication, at their disposal. NavEditOW provides a simple web-based access to this domain ontology to the different involved actors, from the editors and maintainers of the ontology itself, to the students that are involved in the insertion and description of the bibliographic entries, to the applications that exploit the ontology and the annotated data to provide semantic navigation schemes and semantic queries.

The remainder of this paper is organized as follows. Section 2 provides a description of the functionalities offered by NavEditOntOW, while in Section 3 we will describe the application of NavEditOW in a concrete case study in the CRM context. The paper will end with an outlook about some possible future extensions of the system and of the introduced application. A description of the system architecture is out of the scope of this paper and it can be found in [3].

---

[1] See, e.g., the MultimediaN N9C Eculture Project, http://e-culture.multimedian.nl/

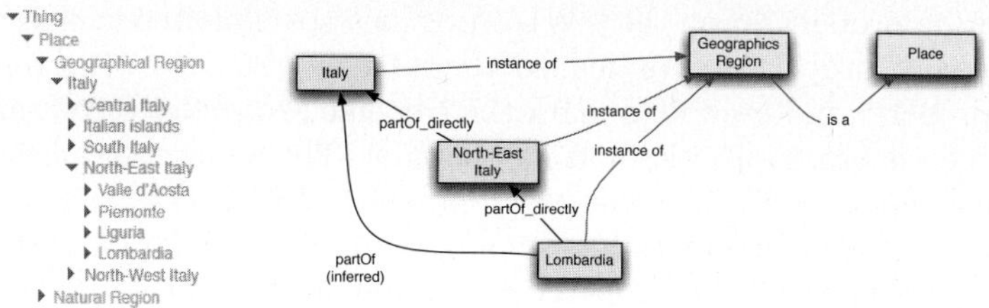

Fig. 1. Example of a navigation tree and the correspondent RDF graph

2   Functionalities of NavEditOW

NavEditOW is an environment for navigating, querying and A-Box editing of
OWL ontologies (up to OWL-DL) through a web-based interface. In the following
paragraphs, we presents more details about each of these tree basic functionalities supported by the application.

Navigation. By using the ontology navigation interface, users can view ontology
individuals and their properties and browse properties via hyperlinks. Browsing
the ontology is essential for the user in order to explore the available information
and it also helps non-expert users to refine their search requirements, when they
start with no specific requirement in mind [4]. The hierarchical organization of
the different concepts and individuals of the ontology is graphically represented
as a dynamic tree. The aim of the navigation tree is to explore the ontology,
view classes and instances, discover the relation between them. The tree does
not represent only the a hierarchy of classes connected with *isA* binary relations
(like the navigation tree of Protégé), but represents also also tree-like connections
of individuals for domain dependent classes of properties.

The root of the navigation tree is the OWL class *Thing*, and the rest of the
tree is organized as follows: under the root node, there are the top-level classes
(i.e. the classes that are only subclasses of Thing); under each class there is
its subclass hierarchy and the individual member of the class; individual-to-
individual tree connections are defined according to a number of selected tree-
like properties (e.g. *partOf*); finally if total order relations are selected, these
are exploited to order individuals within a same level of the tree. In order to
distinguish between classes and individuals, classes are represented in petrol
blue and individual in shocking pink. An example of a navigation tree and the
correspondent RDF graph is presented in the Figure 1.

From a formal point of view, ontological relations supporting tree-like visualization (tree-like properties) are those represented as not symmetric properties
whose inverse is functional (therefore identifying directed acyclic graphs). These
properties link directly an individual with its "father" and are particularly relevant with respect to mereological relations (e.g. *partOf, composedOf*), and to
relations defining hierarchical spatial and temporal structures (e.g. representing
the unfolding of historical periods). Another kind of relations exploited for the
visualization are those defining total orders on individuals (e.g. *isFollowedBy*).

Annotation properties[2] on the OWL ontologies are exploited in order to specify the tree-like properties. We defined the *navEditOW:isTreeLikeProperty* annotation property and used it to mark the tree-like properties (OWL allows annotations on classes, properties and individuals). The annotation phase is done with Protégé before loading the ontology into the NavEditOW.

An additional form of annotation property used by NavEditOW is the *navEditOW:isReifiedProperty*. This property is used to mark the classes that are reified relationships. A reified relationships is a class that connects a subject with an object, so that we could attach additional attributes to the relationship. For example, if we have a *isLocatedIn* property that connect an item to a place and we want to able to attach a time interval to this relationship, we can introduce a class (e.g. *ReifiedisLocatedIn*) to link the item, the place and the time interval. The instances of the classes annotated as *navEditOW:isReifiedProperty* are displayed in tabular form during the visualization of the subject and object instances (e.g. then the information about an item are visualized, a list of the places in which the item was located will be presented). To define which values are displayed in this table, the *navEditOW:viewTemplate* annotation is used. This annotation property allows to generate the summarized views of the individuals. Other annotation properties involved in the ontology visualization and navigation are the *navEditOW:order* which is used to order the individuals and the properties values in the visualization and the *navEditOW:hidden* which allows to hide classes, properties an individuals.

Editing. NavEditOW allows the users to define individuals and to assert properties about them. Users can create, edit and remove individuals of the ontology, their properties and, in particular, their labels. In fact, to ensure multi-languages support, it is possible to define several labels in different languages for every individual. The NavEditOW Web interface allows users to edit the properties values for each individual. Two types of properties are defined in OWL: *object property* is a binary relation between two individuals and *datatype property* is a binary relation between an individual and a literal (a primitive type, like string or number). For the object properties, the interface presents the user a tree for selecting the values; the individuals displayed in the tree are only those that are valid for the property range. For example, in an archeological ontology, the class *TypologyOfArchaeologicalObject* has the property *builtOf*. This property has no cardinality restriction (so it can have zero, one ore more values) but *Material* is specified as range (co-domain). For instance, *Sword* is an instance of *TypologyOfArchaeologicalObject* and has the property *builtOf Metal*, where *Metal* is an instance of *Material*. Datatype properties are edited with simple text input boxes. Users can create new individuals directly from the classes or they can also create new individuals related to an existent one by means of tree-like properties (e.g. *partOf*) (as shown in Figure 2): the new individuals are immediately displayed in the navigation tree under their "father".

---

[2] OWL allows classes, properties, individuals and the ontology itself to be annotated with meta-data. For example, the labels are annotations.

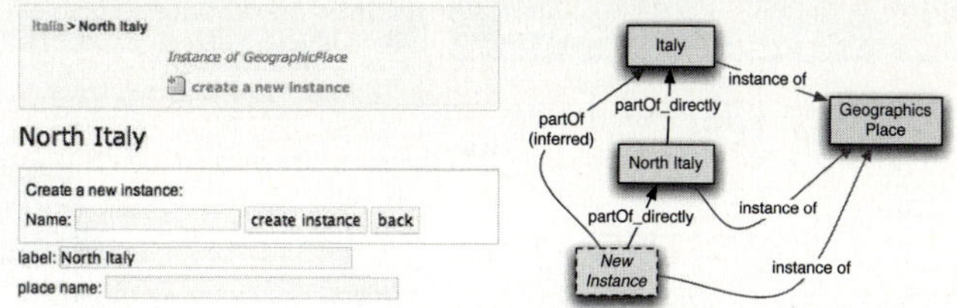

Fig. 2. Dialog box to create a new individual under North Italy and graphical representation of the graph after the creation of the new individual

Classes can be abstract, which means that they can not have direct instances. Abstract classes are identified by the *navEditOW:abstract* annotation. Another annotation property that impacts on the ontology editing is the *navEditOW:readOnly*: if a class, a individual or a property is marked with this property, the resource can not be edited by the users. In order to keep track of changes on the ontology, the Dublin Core metadata element set is used to associate the name of the user and the current date to the created or modified individual .

Querying. NavEditOW offers to the users two query interfaces: a SPARQL[3] free query form and an interface to perform queries based on templates. The first one is a query form in which users can write arbitrary query in the SPARQL language, display results in paginated tabular form and navigate through results via hyperlinks. This interface is very flexible because the users can write arbitrary queries but it is not suitable for end users. The second one is based on a predefined set of queries. This interface guides the user in the construction of a query by means of a wizard which enables the generation of query expressions. Every predefined query is composed of a description in natural language, a SPARQL query with (eventually) free parameters and a list of parameters. Every query parameter is constituted by a label, a type and eventually a restriction on the valid values (e.g. a parameter can be filled only with instances of a specific class). Initially the user is presented with a choice of different query description which provide the starting point for the query construction. Than the interfaces allows users filling the query parameters. Finally, the application composes the template and the parameters values, executes the query and generates the query result table. A future extension of this query mechanism may adapt the query with reference to the number of retrieved results.

3   Prototypal Application

In the course of 2005, the chair of Prehistory and Protohistory of the University of Milan, in collaboration with the Department of Informatics, Systems and

---

[3] SPARQL (SPARQL Protocol and RDF Query Language - its name is a recursive acronym) is an RDF query language standardized by the World Wide Web Consortium. More information could be found at http://www.w3.org/TR/rdf-sparql-query/

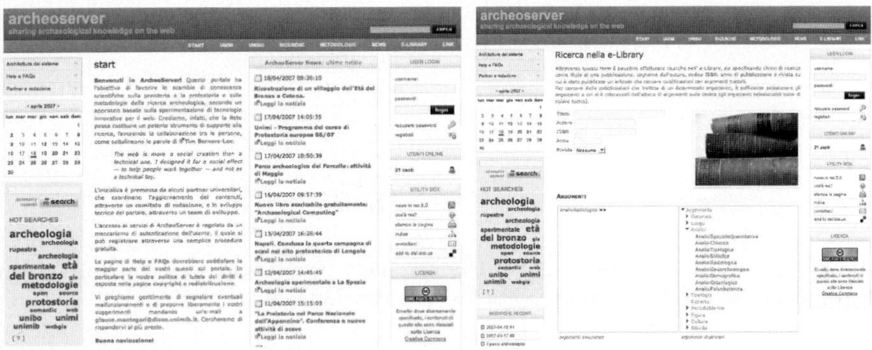

Fig. 3. Screenshots of the ArcheoServer Home and the e-Library search pages

Communication of the University of Milan-Bicocca and the Department of Archaeology of the University of Bologna, have started a long-term project for the creation of a set of Web-oriented services aimed at supporting the sharing of knowledge on prehistory and protohistory in Italy. The main objective of the project has been the creation of a Web portal, named ArcheoServer[4], which will provide a collaborative platform for the exchange of scientific information among the communities of Italian archaeology researchers.

In the ArcheoServer context, NavEditOW was used to develop the *e-Library*. This is a particularly relevant section of the portal which was devised to supply an effective mechanism for the retrieval of digital resources related to prehistory and protohistory, and in general to the archaeological research methodologies. In fact, even if there are a growing number of initiatives providing for the electronic publishing of scientific papers - as, for example, the digital archives of the Italian Institute for Prehistory and Protohistory[5] or the BibAr[6] project hosted at the University of Siena - archaeologists generally consider unsatisfactory the results of their indexing by means of traditional search engines. The main requirement of the *e-Library* (and the portal in general) is to give the community itself the possibility of autonomously managing the contents by means of simple editing tools. At this regard, we must keep in mind that, in most cases, archaeologists have just low-level technical competence and that the development of a complex editing system may result in the failure of the project. In our scenario there are two principal classes of editors. The first one is represented by the students of Archaeology of the Universities involved in the project, who are responsible of the content creation; the second one is represented by Archaeology professors or researchers that, beyond creating contents, supervise the work of students.

In order to fetch the *e-Library* contents, it may be interesting to describe, by means of a specific ontology, all the publications that will be archived in the e-Library section in order to provide advanced instruments for a more effective

---

[4] http://www.archeoserver.it/

[5] http://www.iipp.it/

[6] http://www.bibar.unisi.it/

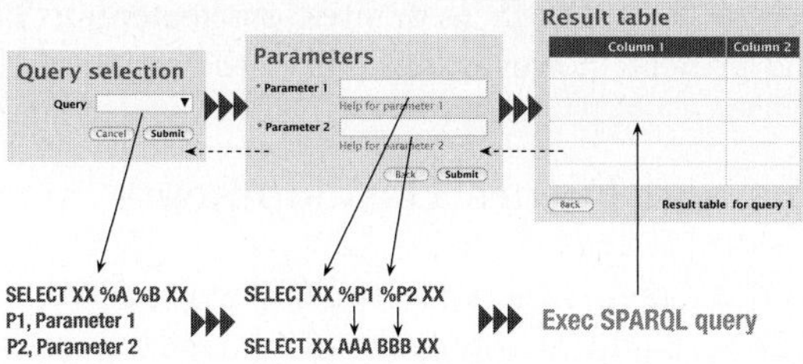

Fig. 4. A diagram showing the overall process of semantic query selection and specification of the required parameters

retrieval of the specific information a user is interested to. Moreover the system may even suggest relevant contents which are semantically related to the ones the user is actually viewing on the screen. Therefore, the e-Library must allow content editors to describe semantically all the publications in a collaborative and simple way, by adopting a simple web-based user interface. In particular this description will be performed manually by the students, while archaeology professors and researchers will supervise the work and will progressively refine/maintain the domain ontology. The above introduced functionalities of the NavEditOW system provided a suitable approach to the development of dynamic web pages supporting both the editing of the ontology A-Box, as well as ontology navigation and exploitation, supporting the description of newly introduced bibliographic

Since the users of the portals do not generally have experience with the SPARQL query language, the mainly used query interface is the one based on the predefined queries. The free SPARQL query interface is also available, but is generally used only by the portal developers. We have defined, with the help of an Archaeology researchers, an initial set of 15 predefined queries for searching the e-Library by specific topics. An example of a query is the following:

```
SELECT  ?publication ?topic ?material WHERE {
    ?publication archeoserver:hasTopic ?topic .
    ?topic rdf:type archeoserver:itemTypology .
    ?topic archeoserver:buildOf ?material .
    ?material rdfs:label ?x .
    FILTER regex(str(?x), "", "i")
} ORDER BY ?material
```

This query select all the publications that have as topic an item build of a specific material. For example, it the user write 'wood' as query parameter, NavEditOW founds one material (wood) which label match with the parameter, than select all the topic that are 'archeoserver:itemTypology' instances made of wood (e.g. 'bow', 'spoon') and returns to the users a list of all the publications about them.

It must be noted that this paper reports the first results of the project, but we also aim at adopting this approach to the ontological description of other contents of the portal, from images depicting findings and sites, to specific elements of interest in the webGIS (e.g. sites, settlements). The description of these aspects of the project, however, are out of the scope of this paper.

4   Conclusions and Future Developments

This paper discussed the main functionalities of NavEditOW, an environment to support the development and maintenance of semantic portals providing functionalities for navigation, querying, and A-Box editing of OWL-based ontologies through the Web. The main functionalities offered by the system, as well as its architecture, which supports the exploitation of different existing semantic frameworks (i.e. Jena, Sesame) and presents an innovative AJAX–based web interface, have been described. The system is presented as particularly useful for the CRM context since in this field users with little or no knowledge of formal languages need not only to navigate the knowledge base, but also to contribute to its enrichment. The paper also described a first NavEditOW application to the semantic description of e-library contents in a we web portal dedicated to archaeology.

Future works aim at performing a more though evaluation of the first version of the system, in order to identify additional requirements and improvements; in this line of work, NavEditOW will be used as the main tool for the editing of an ontology supporting a portal on archaeology and cultural resources of Central Asia. Moreover, NavEditOW does not currently support a complete revision control system because it does not enable the management of multiple revisions of the same unit of information. A future extension of the system will be focused on providing a mechanism to tackle this issue [5].

Acknowledgments. The authors would like to thank Stefania Bandini (CSAI Research Center - University of Milano-Bicocca), Bernardo Rondelli, Maurizio Cattani for their contribution and the useful suggestions.

References

1. King, T.F.: Cultural Resource Laws & Practice: An Introductory Guide. Altamira Press, Walnut Creek (1998)
2. King, T.F.: Thinking about Cultural Resource Management: Essays from the Edge. Altamira Press, Walnut Creek (2002)
3. Bonomi, A., Mosca, A., Palmonari, M., Vizzari, G.: NavEditOW - a System for Navigating, Editing and Querying Ontologies through the Web. In: Apollini, B., Howlett, R.J., Jain, L.C. (eds.) KES 2007. LNCS, vol. 4694, pp. 686–694. Springer, Heidelberg (2007)
4. Ram, S., Shankaranarayanan, G.: Modeling and Navigation of Large Information Spaces: a Semantics Based Approach. In: HICSS (1999)
5. Noy, N.F., Musen, M.A.: Ontology Versioning in an Ontology Management Framework. IEEE Intelligent Systems 19(4), 6–13 (2004)

Interactive Analysis of Time in Film Stories

Francesco Mele[1], Antonio Calabrese[1], and Roberta Marseglia[2]

[1] Istituto di Cibernetica Consiglio Nazionale delle Ricerche
[2] University of Naples Federico II
{a.calabrese, f.mele}@cib.na.cnr.it

Abstract. In this work we propose some principles that regulate temporal anchorages by means of which the spectator places the events of the story on the temporal axis of the fabula, the structure where the causality and the order of the events of a story are recorded. The approach adopted for the segmentation of the story of a film uses both syntactic elements, such as the scene and the sequence, and semantic elements, such as the events of the story, defined as actions that occur in a determined interval of time (diegetic). The base representation, chosen for the analysis of the time in a story, is a particular formulation of spectator beliefs, in which the time (explicit) is present both as the element that determines the variation of spectator beliefs during the vision of the film, and also as object of belief. In this paper, we propose also a system that supplies an interactive aid (as an example to a generic expert of cinema) in order to annotate the events of the story of a film. This system supplies in addition an aid in the analysis of the flashbacks, the forwards and the repetitions of events, and may apply temporal reasoning rules to order, both partially and totally, the events of the story.

Keywords: Film Analisys, Temporal Beliefs, Cognitive Agent Theories.

1 Introduction

One of the main activities of who watches a movie, or also of who reads or listens to a story, consists in the construction of the fabula, this activity brings the spectator to consider some aspects that regard the time. Starting from the plot, that is, from the "story as it is actually told, as it appears in surface, with its temporal dislocations, forward and backward jumps (predictions and flash-backs)", the spectator will construct the fabula, "the fundamental outline of the narration, the logic of actions and the syntax of characters, the course of temporarily arranged events. It may also be a sequence of human actions and may concern a series of events regarding inanimate objects, or also ideas" [1].

The construction of the fabula is a task that the spectator establishes to do (with or without awareness) since from the first sequence of the movie. All the clues that he has on hand, in order to construct the temporal arrangement of the events, are contained in the story. The fabula is *entirely* constructed by the spectator after the end of the film, in that only at that moment, he has at his disposal all plot elements needed to reconstruct the course of the events temporarily sorted.

R. Basili and M.T. Pazienza (Eds.): AI*IA 2007, LNAI 4733, pp. 765–772, 2007.

In cinematography there are several films with a complex plot (with respect to the temporal aspects). *The killing* by S. Kubrick [6] and *Pulp Fiction* by Q. Tarantino [4], are the forerunners of this category, but during the last few years many other films of the same typology have been proposed, among the other we mention *Memento* [5] and *21 Grams* [3]. Our analysis model adopts a formalism based on spectator beliefs. Such structures have two temporal references in explicit form. The representation of beliefs about story events is the following:

```
mEv(from_to([T1,T2]),bel(S, ev(Ec1,from_to([dT1,dT2]),Act1)))
```

In such formulation the spectator S in the interval `[T1, T2]` believes that the event `Ec1` of the story happened in the diegetic interval `[dT1, dT2]`.

2   Segmentation and Annotation of Filmic Events

In our representation we considered as indexing base elements the continuous scenes, also said shots (SC), that is a series of frames without camerawork interruptions. We have then introduced, as base analysis element, the diegetic event (that we will call simply event) which is an action that happens in the film story in a particular temporal modality: on a time interval (`from_to([T1,T2])`, after a certain interval of time (`after[T1,T2]`) starting from a certain time (`hap(T1)`) etc. In the adopted representation the filmic event is represented in the following way:

```
ev(eventcod, modality(d-interval), act(action))
```

that is, as a relation `ev` among a unique code, `eventcod`, that identifies the event, a temporal modality (from_to, after_to etc), a diegetic interval d-interval (interval of the story) and an action. As an example with

```
ev(ev8, from_to([dt17,dt18]), act(drink(mikei, bar))))
```

we represent a diegetic event `ev8` where a certain character (`mikei`) drinks at the bar `act (drink (mikei, bar))` between two temporal indices (diegetic) `dt17, dt18`. We point out that for a repeated diegetic event there will be two distinguished `eventcod` associates to the same action. A continuous scene SC is represented by means of the times of beginning vision and end vision (in the previous example `[dt17,dt18]`), they correspond to the indices of the starting and final frames of the scene. In our representation the continuous scene (or shot) therefore has been represented in the following way:

```
sc(sceneCod, sc-t-interval)
```

where `scenecod` is a code that identifies a filmic segment univocally and `sc-t-interval` corresponds to the vision intervals of the beginning and final scene. Similarly we represented a filmic sequence as a set of scenes identified by a unique code, a vision interval seq-t-interval of the entire sequence:

```
seq(seqCod, seq-t-interval, sceneList)
```

3 Temporal Plot-Fabula Diagrams

Continuous scene SC is a syntactic punctuation element of the film that can contain inside one or more filmic events. Therefore we have introduced a relation `sceenv` among filmic scenes and events `d-eventList` in order to represent such associations:

```
sceenv(sceneCod, d-eventList)
```

In our approach we associate the temporal indices that correspond to a continuous scene (indexing) to one or more diegetic events (events of the story) present (told) between such indices of vision. In such way we carry out an annotation that uses the events of the film story as semantic labels. In the analysis methodology that we propose the Time of Narration (TN) and Time of the Story (TS) diagrams play an important role (see fig.1).

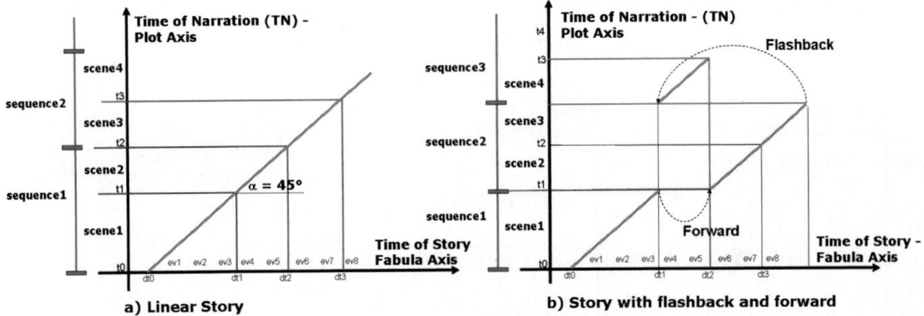

Fig. 1. TN-TS diagrams

In figure 1-a, as an example, in `scen2`, that happens in the narration interval [t1, t2], are present the story events `ev4` and `ev5`, that happen in the diegetic interval [dt1, dt2].

```
sc(scene2, [t1,t2]); sceenv(scene2, [ev4,ev5]).
```

In figure fig. 1-a is represented a story (linear) where the time of vision (time of narration TN) grows at the same speed of the time of fabula (the time of story TS). In the figure 1.b, instead, is displayed a story where are used a forward after the scene1 and a flashback after the scene2.

Through the proposed TN-TS diagrams it is possible to represent the main relationships between the time of the tale TR (time of vision) and the time of the story TS. Genette [2] has characterized the following 5 main relationships: (TN=n, TS=0), TN>TS, TN=TS, TN<TS and (TN=0, TS=n).

The pause (Fig. 2-a) consists in interrupting the presentation of the events of a story, where the diegetic time is idle. A pause is a digression of the story, and usually consists in a description of a character, an atmosphere, a framing of a detail or huge geographic areas.

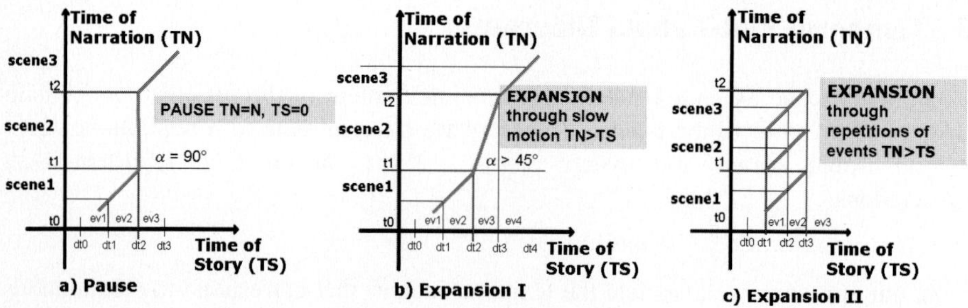

Fig. 2. Pause and Expansion

The expansion (Fig. 2-b, 2-c) occurs when the time of the narration is greater than the time of story (TR>TS). This happens when an action (slow motion $\alpha > 45°$) is slowed down or when a scene is repeated (or is shot from more points of view). The effect of a repetition (immediate) of an event that happens only once in the story determines an expansion of the time of the narration.

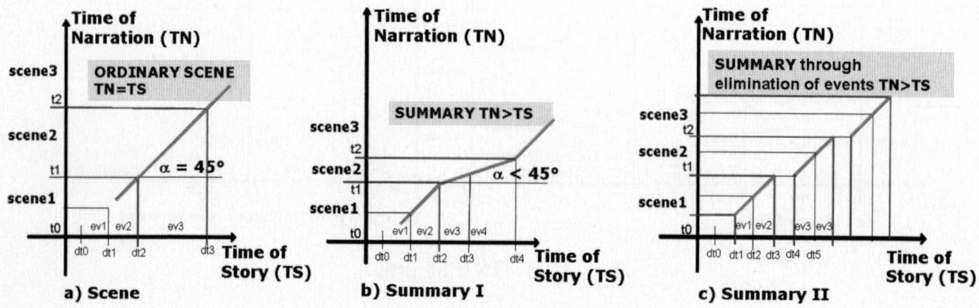

Fig. 3. Scene and Summary

In an ordinary scene (Fig. 3-a) the time of the vision is equal to the time of the story ($\alpha = 45°$). This condition can occur also when there are scenes that introduce discontinuities as in a dialog. The summary (Fig. 3-b) is a modality used in a film story in order to represent a chronological time that advances with great rapidity as in framings in which clock pointers turn very fast, sheets fall fast from a calendar, cigarette ends piles up, empty bottles of alcoholic accumulated, but also names that are magnified on billboards in order to represent the increase in time of the success of a character. The summary is represented in a plot-fabula diagram by a segment having an inclination $\alpha < 45$. Are labelled as summary-sequences those sequences composed only of significant events of a story, i.e. those sequences in which parts considered non essential have been removed (as an example, when a character does a phone call and the composition of the telephone number is not shown, but is only shown that he holds the receiver, or when are not presented scenes in order to describe how the character reached a determined place...).

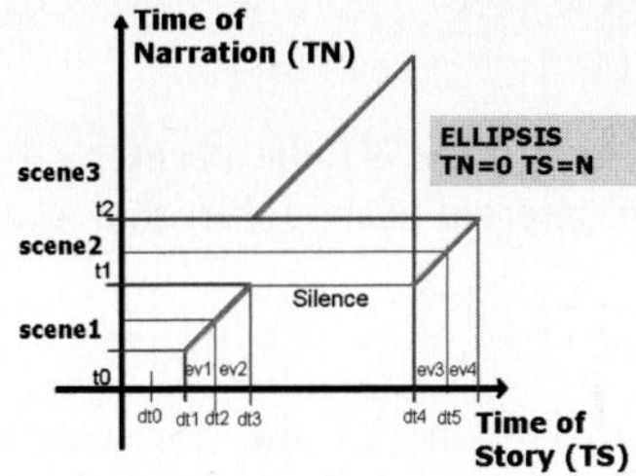

Fig. 4. Ellipsis

At last the ellipsis (Fig. 4) represents in a true sense a gap (omissions) of story events where there is a presentation silence, generally such gap is filled afterwards in the course of the story – it is a mental time where the spectator speculates about events that could be happened in such interval.

4   See Scenes and Believe to Taking Place of Events of the Story

The belief is the propositional attitude that we adopt in order to represent the changes of the cognitive states of the spectator in the time. The principle adopted (that we named perception principle) is the following:

```
mEv(hap(T2), bel(Spett, E1 and E2,.., and En)))  ←
    ev(eCod, from_to(T1,T2),see(Spett, Sx) and          (1)
    mEv(hap(T2), bel(Spett,sceenv(Sx,[E1,E2,..,En]))))
```

At the end of the vision of Sx the spectator, if believes that there is a correspondence between Sx and [E1,E2,..,En], executes a revision of its beliefs (starting from T2) relative to the conjunction of events E1 and E2,..., and En that it believes are happened in the context of the story after the vision of Sx.

5   Relations of Order on the Events of Stories

From the perception principle introduced above, the spectator records in its cognitive space beliefs of the following type:

```
hap(t1)bel(spett,ex)  or expressing the event
hap(t1)bel(spett,from([dt1,dt2])p(x)).
```

In the model proposed herein we have introduced two others typologies of beliefs that allow to represent from a cognitive point of view the order of the events. We consider that such order relation must be recorded in the space of beliefs of the spectator in that such relation changes during the vision of the story. Often both the scriptwriter and the director introduce filmic events in a way that induces the spectator to assume false beliefs on the order of the events. Beliefs that the spectator himself modifies as the events of the story reveal new developments. The representation of such belief is:

```
hap(T1)bel(spett,eq(E1,E2)) or
hap(T1)bel(spett,eq([T1,T2],[T3,T4]))
```

whose definition is: starting from time T1 the spectator beliefs that the E1 event is occurred in the same temporal interval of the E2 event. And

```
hap(T1)bel(A,prec(E1,E2))or
hap(T1)bel(spett,prec([T1,T2],[T3,T4]))
```

whose definition is: starting from time T1 the spectator believes that the event E1 precedes the event E2.

6   A Fundamental Rule About the Order of the Events

The following is a fundamental rule on the order of the events of a sequence:

```
mEv(hap(T2),bel(A,prec(E1,E2)))  ←
    ev(Ec1,until(T1),see(A, S1))          and
    mEv(hap(T1),bel(A,E1))                and
    ev(Ec2, until(T2), see(A, S2))        and           (2)
    mEv(hap(T2), bel(A, E2))              and
    T1<T2.
```

Inside a sequence if at time T1 the spectator A has finished to see S1 where he believes that E1 happened in the story, at time T2 A has finished to see S2, where he believes that E2 (with T1<T2) occurred in the story then the spectator A starting from T2 believes that E1 precedes E2. The principle 1) and the rule 2) suggested to add in TN-TS diagrams another axis that can help in the analysis of the time. On this axis it will be possible to record the beliefs of the spectator about the events of the story and about the order of the events.

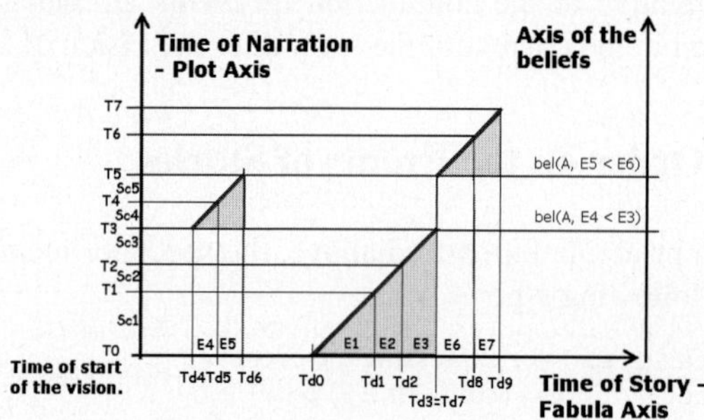

Fig. 5. Three axis of analysis

7   Forward, Flashback, Repetition and Temporal Anchorage

In our model of analysis both the forward and the flashback are supposed to be primitives. Therefore we will not add anything in relation to the techniques of implementation of these modalities for the presentation of stories, neither will formulate hypothesis on which are the cognitive processes activated by the spectator for their identification. Our attention and our analysis will be concentrated on the rules activated by the spectator, when it characterizes a flashback, a forward or a repetition of an event, in order to anchor on the temporal axis of the fabula the events of the story. The introduced notation is the following

```
flashback(e1,e2),   forward(e1,e2),   repeat(act1,act2)
flashback([t1,t2],[t3,t4])   forward([t1,t2],[t3,t4]).
```

Events e1 and e2 in the forward and the flashback are events that are introduced in correspondence of two consecutive scenes. On the contrary in the repetition e1, e2 are not in correspondence in consecutive scenes. The following three rules establish relations of temporal order on the events of the story and allow to temporarily anchor the scenes of the story to the events of the story:

```
mEv(hap(T2),bel(S,prec([dT3,dT4],[dT1,dT2])))   ←
  mEv(hap(T1),bel(S,ev(Ec1,from_to([dT1,dT2]),Act1))) and
  mEv(hap(T2),bel(S,ev(Ec2,from_to([dT3,dT4]),Act2))) and      (3)
  mEv(hap(T2),bel(S,ev(flashback([dT3,dT4],[dT1,dT2]))))).
```

```
mEv(hap(T2),bel(S,prec([dT1,dT2],[dT3,dT4])))   ←
  mEv(hap(T1),bel(S,ev(Ec1,from_to([dT1,dT2]),Act1))) and
  mEv(hap(T2),bel(S,ev(Ec2,from_to([dT3,dT4]),Act2))) and      (4)
  mEv(hap(T2),bel(S,ev(forward([dT3,dT4],[dT1, dT2])))).
```

```
mEv(hap(T2),bel(S,eq([dT1,dT2],[dT5,dT6]))) ←
  mEv(hap(T1),bel(S,ev(Ec1,from_to([dT1,dT2]),Act1)) and
  mEv(hap(T2),bel(S,ev(Ec2,from_to([dT5,dT6]),Act2)) and       (5)
  mEv(hap(T2),bel(S,ev(repeat(Act1,Act2)))).
```

Rule (3) states that if the spectator S has recorded among its beliefs that in the story the Ec1 event occurred and subsequently S records that a flashback for the Ec2 event is occurred then the time interval [dT3,dT4] of the Ec2 event precedes the temporal interval [dT1,dT2] of Ec1. The rule (4) expresses the analogous interpretation of the rule (3) for the forward. As far as rule (5) is concerned, if the spectator S records a repetition of a certain action (even if introduced from another point of view) this action will be positioned on the same interval. The repetition is a technique used often in movies and is commonly applied to connect the course of events of the story belonging to different episodes. It is also used in order to represent stories that introduce several alternative course of events, where are reported actions/events that are repeated but that are taken reference point for the beginning of different events. Examples of such stories are *Blind Chance* [9], *Lola Rennt* [8], *Sliding Doors* [7]. The repetition of events has been studied also by Genette [2], even if he does not supply any contribution about the mechanism of the temporal anchorage of the spectator.

8   An Aid System for Interactive Analysis of Film Stories

In this work we realized an aid system for time analysis of film stories. In fig. 8 the interface screen shot of the system is shown. The system user has also on hand some specific functions for the interactive analysis proposed in this work. As an example, the user has the possibility to examine the filmic segments on the basis of the contents of the story that is to execute an analysis of the film by means of the scenes and sequences contained on the plot and fabula axis. The user has also the possibility to annotate interactively the events (fig. 9), both the events of the story and the events of anchorage (flashback, forward or repetitions) and to use a special function that orders the story events considering the diegetic time.

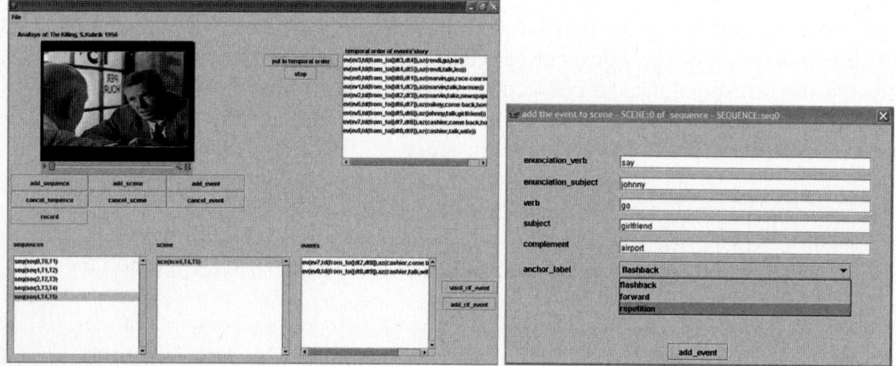

Fig. 6. Main layout of system   Fig. 7. Layout of annotation events

9   Conclusions

In this paper we proposed a methodology for time analysis of stories of films. Such methodology uses, as base representation, spectator beliefs about temporal relations of diegetic events. We also defined a formalism that allows to specify a set of rules of temporal anchorage that the spectator adopts, in presence of flashback, forward and repetition of events, when arranges on the temporal axis of the fabula. At last we proposed a system that helps an expert of cinema to annotate filmic events and to analyze temporal relations existing among events. In this system is also implemented an algorithm that allows to order automatically all the events of a story, helping the expert in carrying out further analysis on the temporal structure of the whole story.

References

1. Eco, U.: Lector in fabula, Bompiani, Milano (1979)
2. Genette G.: Figures III, Ediions du Seuil (1972)
3. Iñárritu, G.: 21 Grams, USA (2003)
4. Tarantino, Q.: Pulp Fiction, USA (1993)
5. Nolan, C.: Memento, USA (2000)
6. Kubrick, S.: The Killing, USA (1956)
7. Howitt, P.: Sliding doors (1998)
8. Tywer, T.: Lola Rennt (1998)
9. Kieslowsi, K.: Blind Chance, Il caso (1981)

Towards MKDA: A Knowledge Discovery Assistant for Researches in Medicine

Vincenzo Cannella, Giuseppe Russo, Daniele Peri, Roberto Pirrone,
and Edoardo Ardizzone

DINFO - University of Palermo
Viale delle Scienze 90128 Palermo, Italy
{cannella,russo,peri}@csai.unipa.it, {pirrone,ardizzon}@unipa.it

Abstract. Nowadays doctors are generating a huge amount of raw data.
These data, analyzed with data mining techniques, could be sources of
new knowledge. Unluckily such tasks need skilled data analysts, and not
so much researchers in Medicine are also data mining experts. In this
paper we present a web based system for knowledge discovery assistance
in Medicine able to advice a medical researcher in this kind of tasks. The
user must define only the experiment specifications in a formal language
we have defined. The system GUI helps users in their composition. Then
the system plans a Knowledge Discovery Process (KDP) on the basis
of rules in a knowledge base. Finally the system executes the KDP and
produces a model as result. The system works through the co-operation
of different web services specialized in different tasks. The system is still
under development.

Keywords: Knowledge Discovery in Databases, Data Mining, Workflow
Generation, Knowledge Discovery Assistant.

1   Introduction

In recent years the availability of huge medical data collections has sometimes
dramatically brought to light the (in)ability to analyze them. Medical centers
have huge databases containing therapies, diagnoses and personal data of their
patients. Moreover, the automatic devices of relevant data acquisition, such as
MRI and PET, are able to extract more and more accurate medical images of
patients. These images are produced in such a number and richness of detail that
they can only be analyzed with the help of complex systems. The investigation of
new knowledge could be usefully performed by medical researchers with suitable
tools. In this view a very important application field is the Knowledge Discovery
in Databases (KDD) that, according to [1], is defined as the *"non-trivial process of identifying valid novel, potentially useful and ultimately understandable
patterns in data"*. This task is brain-intensive and it is usually designed by a
human expert. Unluckily the use of the KDD techniques needs specific skills.
In this work we propose the Medical Knowledge Discover Assistant (MKDA).
The system receives a formal specification of the medical experiment research,

R. Basili and M.T. Pazienza (Eds.): AI*IA 2007, LNAI 4733, pp. 773–780, 2007.
© Springer-Verlag Berlin Heidelberg 2007

including goals and characteristics of inputs in terms of "what" users want, and not "how" to get it. The system must plan and execute a suitable Knowledge Discovery Process (KDP), designed according to the user's needs and the application domain. Finally, it returns results.

The rest of the paper is arranged as follows. The next paragraph describes the state of the art for Knowledge Discovery Assistants. The third paragraph introduces a new knowledge discovery workflow model. Then the language to describe the specifications of a medical experimental research is presented in the forth paragraph. The fifth one describes the knowledge base that helps the MKDA in construction of experiments. Functionalities of MKDA system followed by the system architecture are in the sixth and seventh paragraphs. Finally, conclusions and future works are reported.

2   State of the Art

In recent years many researches have been carried out in KDD, with the aim of developing a tool able to perform data analysis autonomously. The involved field is essentially a combination of some aspects of many research areas such as knowledge based systems, machine learning and statistics. Mlt-Consultant [3] was the first system where the selection of a machine learning method is made with the support of a knowledge-based system. Another approach is the meta-learning approach. MetaL [4] developed a prototype assistant system that supports users with model selection and method combination. NOEMON [5] is another meta-learned based system. It relies on a mapping between dataset characteristics and inducer performance to propose inducers for specific dataset steps. The most appropriate classifier for a dataset is suggested on the basis of the similarity with existing ones. Another approach is related to the possibility to build the entire process needed to achieve the goal. As an example the IDEA System [8] starts from characteristics of the data and of the desired mining result. Then it uses an ontology to search for and enumerate the data mining algorithms to produce the desired result from given data. Some commercial tool are also been developed such as IBM DB Intelligent Miner. Miner [6] integrates a relational database system, a Sybase SQL server, with a concept hierarchy module, and a set of knowledge discovery modules. Another commercial tool is Clementine [7]. In this system the user-guidance module uses a task/method decomposition to guide the user through a stepwise refinement of a high-level data mining process. It uses a limited model of operations to construct the best plan. Generated plans are compiled into scripts for execution. Important issues in this field are open source. Yale [9] is an environment for machine learning experiments and data mining. Yale uses Weka [10], a collection of Java implementations of machine learning algorithms. The preparation of data is supported in Yale by numerous feature selection and construction operators. However, Yale is applied to a single input data table. The Mining Mart software [12] can be used to combine data from several tables, or to prepare large data sets inside a relational database instead of main memory as in Yale.

3   Our KDD Workflow Model

Knowledge discovery in database can be planned as a process, that consists of a sequence of steps and that can be described with a workflow. We designed a general workflow model as synthesis of different workflows described by literature. Because most of them cover only partially the knowledge discovery process, we tried to redesign a more general workflow (see Fig. 1). Phases in the workflow must not be necessarily followed linearly. The workflow can be divided into main macro-phases, in their turns divided into sub-phases: problem analysis and specifications definition, choice of the tasks and their execution, results analysis.

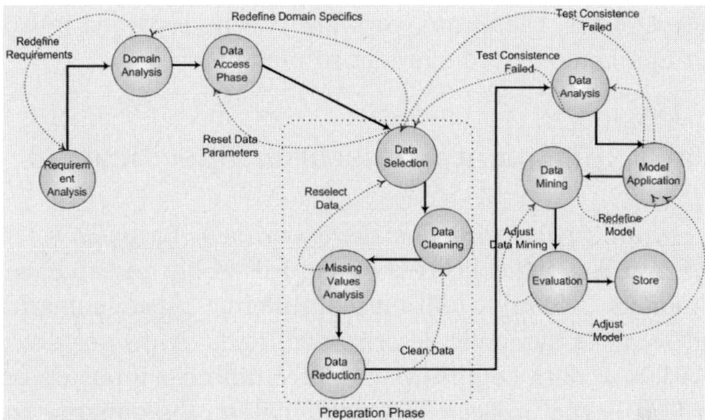

Fig. 1. The workflow steps

During the first phase, the analyst interacts with the user to understand her needs and expectations to build consequently effective experiments. To encompass problems related with this phase, we developed a particular problem definition language with the description of evaluation criteria too. On the basis of these criteria final results of the workflow can be evaluated to establish the satisfaction of user's needs. The second phase of the workflow deals with the definition of relevant knowledge on the application domain. This knowledge is used by the analyst to extract some domain-driven process choices. The data access phase often needs to consult different sources and bring together data in a common format with consistent definitions for fields and keys. Collected data could contain either too much, less or irrelevant information. These problems are solved during the preparation phase, before the application of the modeling and discovery techniques. Data transformation mainly is performed in two ways: horizontally (changing the dimensionality of the data) and vertically (changing the number of data items). The preparation phase can be split into four different sub-phases: data selection, data cleaning, missing values handling and data reduction. With data selection, a subset of data is taken to apply on it further evaluations. Through the data cleaning the problems due to the presence of noise in the data are solved. Data reduction phase deals with the transformations applied on complex data to get simpler ones, as shorter data vectors. The reduction can help to manage the effective number of variables under analysis. Data gained through the preparation phase are analyzed during the data exploration phase to assess the consistence of chosen data with requirements and with the problem domain. The next phase matches the goals expressed by the user and the selected data with the data mining methods. The application of data mining techniques requires parameters calibration to optimal values. Therefore, more than one data preparation and transformation step are often needed. After the model has been produced, it is converted in an autonomous application able to implement the model. The deployment phase deals with this task. The evaluation phase establishes how the model is suitable for user's needs according to the success and evaluation criteria specified in the first phase. If the system satisfies user's requests, the entire workflow can be recorded into a repository. In this way, it can be employed again in similar tasks.

4   Medical Experimental Research Specification

The medical researcher has to define the experiment formally, setting its specification. She has to list the collection of features of her research, as data, goals, metrics and models. The input data are of different types: numerical data, categorical data, complex symbolic descriptions, rules. A deeper differentiation of data is in relation to data composition. Three different input classes have been defined. The first is the object class: data matrix, dissimilarity matrix, single values, graphs are some possible examples. The second is the special input class, as, for instance, numerics, dates, therapy, diagnoses, diseases, patients, counts, IDs, binary data that are used for images or videos, texts and documents. The third class is the variable type class like internal variables, symmetric or asymmetric binary variables, discrete variables, continue variables, scaled variables.

The definition of possible goals drives the entire process of data discovery. Some users, for instance, prefer to get models that can be easily understood and evaluated. In this case the user wants to get a simple description of the domain to be able to make more analyses. So the system designs a workflow to generate symbolic models. Other users prefer to get more precise, even if not very understandable, models. In this case, the system produces black-box models, as neural networks. Some times the user needs a light model, quick but not precise. On the other hand, the user can desire a precise but not fast model. Due to complexity of processes many possible metrics have to be used. It's possible to distinguish them in terms of computation load, usefulness of new founded patterns, novelty. Measures are mostly related to particular data mining algorithms or tasks. In fact, they are in direct relation to goals that user wants to obtain. The same considerations are also valid for the set of possible task-dependent representations.

We have defined an XML-compliant experiment specification language, a suitable formal language to describe the inputs. Formally the defined language MESL (Medical Experiment Specification Language) is made up four elements $(\{D_i\}, \{G_i\}, \{M_i\}, R)$, where $\{D_i\}$ is the set of data useful to problem definition, $\{G_i\}$ is the set of user goals, $\{M_i\}$ is the set of metrics used to evaluate the process results and R is the representation used for results. Composing such a description could be too hard for a not expert user. To solve this problem, we have designed and implemented a very simple GUI interface.

5   The Knowledge Base

The Knowledge Base of the system supports the generation of a complete experiment starting from user requests. The knowledge base is built in a modular way and is organized in two main levels. In the high level there is the definition of concepts that are used for the experiments. The concepts have been grouped according to the roles they have in the KDP. The knowledge base is a composition of different aspects. An *experiment* is the composition of a *workflow*, a *model*, a set of *evaluations* about the model fitting with initial problem and a *representation* of the obtained model. A model is a formal and well defined specification of the result obtained from an experiment over some particular data. A model is obtained through a sequence of steps in a workflow. The workflow steps are essentially grouped in three aggregates: data pre-processing, data mining process and data post-processing. Also the composition rules have been added inside the knowledge bases. Rules define the workflow steps sequence and the choice method to select operators for a particular step. Some other relevant high level concepts have been defined: data, data descriptors, patterns, algorithms. Data are expressed and classified in formal terms to account their elementary structure. A composition of elementary data constitutes complex data. Data descriptors allows specifying data in terms of type of data, constraints on data or data aggregation. A pattern is a representation of data with an empirical law used to identify them. This type of concept is used to define the fitting of data on particular structures useful to comprehension for doctors such as the concepts like disease, patient. A data mining algorithm is a sequence of well defined steps that perform a possible operation about certain data. The low level of the Knowledge Base contains information about operators in terms of descriptions of applicability constraints, produced effects, types of inputs required and other particular characteristics. To define domain structure an OWL-Dl[14] ontology has been built. As previously seen, it is possible to split the ontology in different sub-ontologies. The links between the elements in the same sub-ontology are homogeneous and defines structural properties. The links through different sub-ontologies define the relations between different types of elements. We have used Jena [13], an ontology support tool able to query both RDF and OWL ontologies, to perform semantically enriched reasoning.

6   System Functionalities

The inputs of the system are the data, the preferences of the user and the domain knowledge regarding the problem treated with the experiment. The system has two outputs: the model describing the new knowledge mined from the data, and the workflow applied to get the model. The latter one can be recorded in a repository and re-used in new similar tasks. Initially the system must be able to analyze data evaluating the presence of problems like noise or missing data. The system must resolve these problems to get data that can be used for the construction of the model. It must reach a trade-off between the accuracy and the time cost. The characteristics of the produced model should be chosen by the user. The choices of the system are not mandatory. The user can change some parts of the workflow to get a different result. In other cases, the system can propose different possible workflows and the user chooses what she prefers. In these cases, the user can choose to try many different workflows to find the best one. The user can interact with the system in two different ways. As just said, we have defined the Medical Experiment Specification Language. An user can describe the experiment through this language. This functionality has been developed for expert users or repetitive processes. On the other hand, the system has a simple GUI which allows the user to define easily the problem and that compose automatically the description. The interaction process has been inspired to programmable interaction with users like in chatbot systems. Unlike such systems, our interaction is graphical. In particular, we refer to ALICE chatbot [11], a system that owns a repository composed of question-answer patterns called categories. They are defined in the Artificial Intelligence Markup Language, an XML-compliant language. The dialogue is based on algorithms for automatic detection of patterns in the statements. Our interaction process functionalities are developed in the same manner: the couple question-answer are categorized and through this mechanism is possible to have a tight interaction. This interaction allows the system to collects information about both tasks and needs of the users as explained in previous paragraphs.

7   System Architecture

MKDA system has been designed according to the well-known web service architecture in conjunction with the client-server three-tier one (see figure 2). The core application is executed on an HTTP server. The client connects to this server remotely. Through an intuitive GUI she composes the characteristics of the experiment. She specifies the data to manage, her preferences and needs. This task is executed graphically. The interface of the client has been developed using the AJAX technologies, which stands for Asynchronous JavaScript and XML. The interface dynamically composes the description of the request of the user in the language described previously. At this point the request is sent to the server. Afterwards, the request is sent to the workflow generator web service (WGWS), which analyzes this request, and constructs the correspondent knowledge discovery workflow. At this aim, it queries the knowledge base module. At the same time, it consults the Experiment Comparator Service, which, on the basis of a case-based reasoning, lists all past experiments in the repository matching the user's requests. Then it consults the data mining tasks catalogue managed by the tasks catalogue web service (TCWS). TCWS advertises the list of tasks that the system can employ. This list includes all operators of libraries

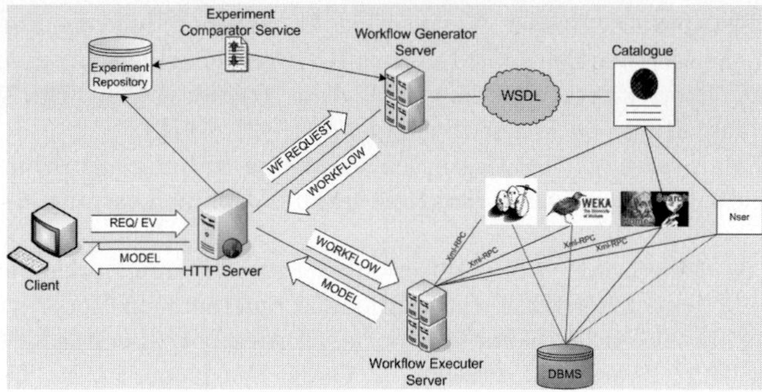

Fig. 2. The System Architecture

and systems as, for instance, Weka, Yale and Ptolemy. These three systems have
been embedded into web services, which make possible to use remotely their
functionalities. The tasks are advertised in WSDL. The data retrieved in this
way are inserted into the description of each step of the final workflow. During
the execution of the workflow, these data are used to know where each task has
to be executed. After the workflow has been generated, it is sent to the workflow
executor web service (WEWS). The model is returned by the WEWS to the application on the HTTP server and sent to the client as reply to its initial request.
The model together with the workflow can be recorded into the repository. The
collection of experiments can be consulted. In this way the user can eventually
re-employ a past workflow when she must work with a similar experiment.

8   Conclusion and Future Works

In this work we have proposed a new web based system to help knowledge discovery in Medicine for non expert users. We have described system architecture
and functionalities. The system is able to collect the characteristic of the treated
experiments in a very simple manner. Then a knowledge discovery worflow is generated according to the workflow model we have designed. Finally the system is
able to execute the workflow and produces a model as result. The user should
concentrate on the specification of the problem, while most of the implementation should be delegated to the system. The system is still under development.
The web infrastructure and the workflow model has been realized and future
work is focused on its whole development and test.

References

1. Fayyad, U.M., Haussler, D., Smith, P., Uthurusamy, R.: Advance in Knowledge
   Discovery and Data Mining. In: AKDDM, AAAI/MIT Press (1996)
2. Aleven, V., Koedinger, K.R.: An effective metacognitive strategy: Learning by
   doing and explaining with a computer-based cognitive tutor. Cognitice Science 26,
   147–179 (2002)

3. Craw, S., Sleeman, D., Graner, N., Rissakis, M., Sharma, S.: Consultant: Providing Advice for the Machine Learning Toolbox. In: Research and Development in Expert Systems IX: Proc. Expert Systems, 12th Ann. Technical Conf. British Computer Soc. Specialist Group on Expert Systems, pp. 5–23 (1992)
4. Brazdil, P.B., Scares, C., Da Costa, J.P.: Ranking learning algorithms: using IBL and meta-learning on accuracy and time results Machine Learning. 50(3), 251–277 (2003)
5. Kalousis, A., Hilario, M.: Model selection via meta-learning: a comparative study. In: ICTAI'0. Ictai 12th IEEE International Conference on Tools with Artificial Intelligence, p. 206. IEEE Computer Society Press, Los Alamitos (2000)
6. Jiawei, Fu, H.Y., Wang, W., Chiang, J., Gong, W., Koperski, K., Li, D., Lu, Y., Rajan, A., Stefanovic, N., Xia, B., Zaiane, O.R.: DBMiner: A System for Mining Knowledge in Large Relational Databases. In: KDD'96. Proc. 1996 Int'l Conf. on Data Mining and Knowledge Discovery, pp. 250–255 (1996)
7. Wirth, R., Shearer, C., Grimmer, U., Reinartz, T., Schlosser, J., Breitner, C., Engels, R., Lindner, G.: Towards Process-Oriented Tool Support for KDD. In: Komorowski, J., Żytkow, J.M. (eds.) PKDD 1997. LNCS, vol. 1263, pp. 55–64. Springer, Heidelberg (1997)
8. Bernstein, A., Provost, F., Hill, S.: Toward Intelligent Assistance for a Data Mining Process: An Ontology-Based Approach for Cost-Sensitive Classification. Proc. of IEEE Transactions on Knowledge and Data Engineering 17(4), 503–518 (2005)
9. Mierswa, I., Wurst, M., Klinkenberg, R., Scholz, M., Euler, T.: YALE: Rapid prototyping for complex data mining tasks. In: KDD 2006. Proc. of the ACM SIGKDD International Conference on Knowledge Discovery and Data Mining, ACM Press, New York (2006)
10. Witten, I.H., Frank, E.: Data mining: Practical machine learning tools and techniques with Java implementations. Morgan Kaufmann, San Francisco, CA, USA (2000)
11. (Alice), `http://www.alicebot.org/`
12. Euler, T.: Publishing Operational Models of Data Mining Case Studies. In: ICDM. Proc. of the Workshop on Data Mining Case Studies at the 5th IEEE International Conference on Data Mining, p. 99. IEEE Computer Society Press, Los Alamitos
13. Carroll, J.J., Dickinson, I., Dollin, C., Reynolds, D., Seaborne, A., Wilkinson, K.: Jena: Implementing the Semantic Web Recommendations. Tech. Rep. HPL-2003-146, HP Laboratories Bristol (2003)
14. Helfin, J. (eds.): Web Ontology Language (OWL): Use Cases and Requirements. W3C Recommendation (February 10, 2004)

Mobile Robots and Intelligent Environments

Francesco Capezio, Fulvio Mastrogiovanni,
Antonio Sgorbissa, and Renato Zaccaria

Laboratorium DIST, University of Genova, Italy
{francesco.capezio, fulvio.mastrogiovanni,
antonio.sgorbissa, renato.zaccaria}@unige.it

Abstract. This paper deals with a knowledge representation architecture for distributed systems. The aim is to adopt a common framework to deal with an "intelligent space", i.e., an ecosystem composed by artificial entities which cooperate to perform an intelligent multi-source data fusion. This information is used to coordinate the behavior of mobile robots and intelligent appliances. The experimental results discuss this interaction with respect to the fulfillment of complex service tasks.

1   Introduction

Recently, much research work focused on integrating different disciplines, e.g., intelligent surveillance [1] and knowledge representation [2], with Mobile Robotics. Two approaches are devised: (i) distributing intelligence within the environment by placing sensors and actuators where needed: the Ambient Intelligence (AmI) paradigm is aimed at designing *intelligent spaces*, i.e., distributed systems assigned to acquire information from the environment using networks of sensing devices, to manage coherent context patterns to be used in decision making, and to interact with end users through functional services; (ii) building autonomous agents, able to act in the real world, originally thought to be handy for humans. Both the approaches give rise to drawbacks which can not be underestimated.

Intelligent spaces require the evaluation and aggregation of possibly ambiguous information through data fusion. Information fusion must be supported by *a priori* knowledge guiding data interpretation, and it must cooperate with systems responsible for data acquisition. Current Robotics and AmI architectures address fusion of *numerical* or *sub-symbolic* information. In literature, data fusion is usually managed using bayesian [3][9] or sub-symbolic techniques [4]. On the other side, mobile robots are far from being used extensively in real-world scenarios such as human inhabited environments [5][8]. Even simple navigation tasks, such as interaction with doors, is focus of actual research [12].

In this paper we propose a distributed architecture which is able to coordinate the behavior of mobile robots and intelligent environments. We suggest that, with respect to autonomy, robustness and capability issues, the overall system is definitely improved by the introduction of a knowledge representation subsystem that - due to its distributed nature - we call "Knowledge Ecosystem". In Section II we introduce the main concepts related to our architectural approach. In

R. Basili and M.T. Pazienza (Eds.): AI*IA 2007, LNAI 4733, pp. 781–788, 2007.

Section III, we focus on its distributed data fusion capabilities. In Section IV we describe the representation at the symbolic level. Next, actual implementation and experimental results are presented and discussed. Conclusion follows.

2 An Ecosystem of Artificial Entities

An intelligent space can be modeled as an ecosystem where the *artificial* entities exchange information for the fulfillment of common goals. In our architecture, knowledge representation is a decentralized process which is managed by several cognitive-oriented entities. Each entity processes simple *pieces* of information, thus contributing to a "Knowledge Ecosystem".

An Artificial Ecosystem (henceforth referred to as Æ), is a set of m agents attending different tasks. An agent α is a 4-element vector, $\alpha = \langle \theta, \gamma, \iota, \omega \rangle$, where θ specifies the agent capabilities, γ is a set of goals that α can contribute to achieve, and ι and ω are operators returning, respectively, the set of data needed and produced by α. Agents can aggregate in more complex *niches*, characterized by common goals g. We define a goal g as the result of n cooperating agents. In particular, $g = \omega(A_g)$, where $A_g = \{\alpha_j : j = 1, ..., n\}$ is the niche of the involved agents, and ω is the previously introduced operator returning the *relevant* output data of A_g. With respect to a higher level of complexity, niches themselves can be modeled as agents and, as such, they are possibly part of larger niches. Therefore, we extend our definition of "agent" adopting a recursive definition such that $\alpha_k = A_g = \{\alpha_j : j = 1, ..., k - 1, k + 1, ..., n\}$.

Agents are assigned different roles. Device-related agents $\{\alpha^d\}$ manage physical devices (e.g., sensors for data acquisition or actuators), and are characterized by limited computational capabilities. Cognitive-related agents $\{\alpha^c\}$ are designed to perform data interpretation in order to guide the system behavior: in particular, they perform feature extraction, symbolic inferences, knowledge representation, data fusion and planning; because they process complex information, they require sophisticate capabilities in processing and exchanging data.

3 Distributed Niches of Agents

$\{\alpha\}$ agents are grouped in niches which are functionally autonomous. In our Æ we identify three main types of niches: Intelligent Spaces $Æ_{is}$, Mobile Robots $Æ_{mr}$ and Knowledge Ecosystems $Æ_{ke}$.

3.1 Intelligent Spaces

$Æ_{is}$ deals with the physical space provided with intelligent devices. It consists both of $\{\alpha^d\}$ and $\{\alpha^c\}$ agents. The former group controls either sensors like cameras, PIR (Passive Infra Red), smoke and temperature detectors, or actuators like controllers for automated doors or windows; the latter comprises cognitive behaviors. In particular, whilst a group of agents implements user tracking using probabilistic state estimation techniques, others manage either interfaces with users or other architectural modules, such as $Æ_{mr}$ or $Æ_{ke}$: these agents receive high level goals issued by $Æ_{ke}$, or to interact with $Æ_{mr}$ in order to fulfill complex goals in cooperation. Consider an user tracking system based on camera images. This task involves the fulfillment of the goal g_{bb}, i.e., to obtain bounding boxes from image data. This is achieved by instantiating the following agent $\alpha_{bbe} = A_{bbe} = \{\alpha_{cd}^d, \alpha_{be}^c\}$, where *bbe* stands for "bounding boxes extractor", α_{cd}^d is a camera device and α_{be}^c is an agent responsible for bounding box extraction.

3.2   Mobile Robots

$Æ_{mr}$ manages both the low-level and (part of) the cognitive activities for a mobile robot to operate. In our approach, a mobile robot is *situated* within an intelligent space. Whilst it can be considered a mobile *extension* to the $Æ_{is}$, $Æ_{is}$ *extends* the sensing/actuating capabilities of mobile robots, thus making them really *ubiquitous* as far as the device network is extended. For instance, a mobile robot could *sense* what is going on in areas far from its sensing scope, or it could *request* an elevator at its current floor without even being in front of it.

Analogously to $Æ_{is}$, complex behaviors are achieved through cooperation among device and cognitive oriented agents [5]. With respect to the interaction with other niches, specific interfaces exchange data with and receive commands from $Æ_{ke}$, and cooperate with $Æ_{is}$ to purposively interact with the environment: e.g., during a mission specified by $Æ_{ke}$, mobile robot subsystems can communicate with $Æ_{is}$ through a particular physical agent, α_{di}^p, where *di* stands for "device interface"; the communication is aimed requesting actions to be performed by $Æ_{is}$, e.g., to aid robot navigation (to open automated doors, to call an elevator for floor switching, etc.).

3.3   Knowledge Ecosystems

$Æ_{ke}$ is responsible for arranging information in patterns relating numerical data to symbols, i.e., the symbol grounding [6]. In our approach, symbolic knowledge representation and data fusion are managed by introducing α_{kb}^c, an agent dealing with knowledge bases represented using Description Logics (DLs). DLs consist of both a *Terminology Box* (TBox), modeling concepts, descriptions and relationships, and an *Assertional Box* (ABox), describing the actual scenario using the TBox ontology. α_{kb}^c allows symbolic data fusion and representation using two *layers*: (i) a model of the physical space to interact with and its related *information space*; (ii) the data fusion structure, responsible for the creation of meaningful concept instances (henceforth called "situations") from base predicates corresponding to sensor data. Furthermore, we assume the availability of niches providing α_{kb}^c with heterogeneous information (i.e., $Æ_{is}$ and $Æ_{mr}$).

Finally, planning activities are achieved by introducing another agent, namely α_p^c, where p stands for "planning". It receives a domain description and a problem formulation as input, and computes a course of action - if it exists - to be executed by agents belonging to $Æ_{is}$ and $Æ_{mr}$.

4   Knowledge Representation

Knowledge representation is concurrently performed by several cognitive agents, operating on symbols originating from sensor data. Æ_{ke} is organized in different layers: (i) representation of physical and information spaces; (ii) data fusion; (iii) situation modeling and assessment; (iv) planning and execution.

4.1   Representation of Physical and Information Spaces

Entity is a base concept for Object, User, Robot and Space. TBoxes maintain topological representations of environments: a Space is divided in Areas, containing instances of Object. Beside common objects (e.g., furniture and appliances), a particular group is Device. Their status is described by Predicates, which are regularly updated through information provided by $\{\alpha^d\}$ agents. Devices are classified in either Sensors (characterized by a *scope* within the environment, i.e., a collection of Areas) and Actuators.

User models users in the system. Space and Robot are used as abstract representations of Æ_{is} and Æ_{mr}. Each Entity performs Actions. These include: UserActions (e.g., ToBeSomewhere or ReadSomething), SpaceActions (i.e., executed by Æ_{is}, as RaiseTemperature) and RobotActions. The third class depends on the actual mobile robot capabilities: in our scenario, mobile robots are provided with specific domains of expertise, such as navigation (e.g., MoveFromTo, UseElevator), surveillance (e.g, PatrolArea, NotifySecurityStation), etc. Deliberative actions are mapped into sequences of actions which can be either predefined or planned on-the-fly according to the current Situations. Data is a basic concept for the data types exchanged within the system. DeviceAgent and CognitiveAgent are then introduced: the former uses an additional role specifying its controlled Device: for each Device, a corresponding DeviceAgent is introduced.

The ABox contains instances of the concepts Device, Entity, Area, Data, etc. Sensor data are mapped to specific instances of Data, and then in Predicates, thus updating predefined roles of Device instances. They are not given a semantic meaning: therefore, this layer does not suffer from the symbol grounding problem, because association between sensor data and symbols is *a priori* designed.

4.2   Symbolic Data Fusion

Inferences in DLs are performed through subsumption. Given two concepts, $\mathcal{C}_1$ and $\mathcal{C}_2$, we say that $\mathcal{C}_1$ is subsumed by $\mathcal{C}_2$ (and we write $\mathcal{C}_1 \sqsubseteq \mathcal{C}_2$) if $\mathcal{C}_2$ is more general than or equivalent to $\mathcal{C}_1$. Given a concept $\mathcal{C}$, we denote its description $\mathcal{D}$ as $\mathcal{D} = \delta\mathcal{C}$, and its instances $\mathcal{I}$ using $\mathcal{I} = \xi\mathcal{C}$.

Consider again user location tracking. We consider three sensors: one surveillance camera and two PIRs. A niche is arranged as follows. α_{cam}^d, α_{p1}^d and α_{p2}^d are introduced. α_{cam}^d provides raw images to a cognitive agent α_{bbe}^c. It extracts bounding boxes that are fed to another agent, α_{blob}^c, able to compute color blobs from the bounding boxes. These data are used to associate bounding boxes with users, whose dress colors are known in advance. α_{p1}^d and α_{p2}^d

can provide boolean information about the presence of someone in their surroundings, according to the sensor range and position. Within the Knowledge Base, `cameraDev` $= \xi$`Camera`, while `pirDev1, pirDev2` $= \xi$`PIR`. Together, α^c_{bbe} and α^c_{blob} are aimed at providing information about user identity, i.e., instances of `UserIdData` $\sqsubseteq$ `Data`. `pirDev1` and `pirDev2` are managed by `pirAgent`. Each `User` is described by a role `id` specifying its identity, such that $\forall$`id.UserIdData`, by a `Position` (i.e., a collection of areas), and by a dress color. This data fusion process is managed by α^c_{cul}, which checks subsumption between the `scope` of each `Device`. With `UserIdData` we identify the `User` whose location is to be computed. It is initialized to `cameraDev.scope` $=$ `area1` $\sqcap$ `area2` $\sqcap$ `area3`. If `dp1` $=$ δ`pirDev1.scope` $=$ `area2` $\sqcap$ `area3` and `dp2` $=$ δ`pirDev2.scope` $=$ `area2`, we have `d` $\sqsubseteq$ `dp1` $\sqsubseteq$ `dp2`. As a consequence, `dp2` $=$ `area2` is the new user location.

4.3   Situation Modeling and Assessment

Deliberative activities are carried out on the basis of the current `Situations`. These are collections of `Predicates`, stating facts about the current state of the entities. We model `UserSituations`, `SpaceSituations` and `RobotSituations`. The first class models the status of `Users`, using intermediate base concepts (e.g., `BeingSomewhere` or `ReadingSomething`), related to `Actions` like `ToBeSomewhere` or `ReadSomething`. Intelligent spaces model complex events occurring within the environment, such as `TemperatureTooHigh`, `SmokeInTheRoom`, etc. Mobile robots represent `RobotSituations` such as `BeingSomewhere`, `AtFloor`, `Patrolling`, etc. Specific situations can be used to represent specific robot actions: `WaitingForElevator`, `GoingToNextLandmark`, etc. For each `Entity`, its current state is inferred by considering the superimposition of the most recent instances of the `Situation` concept relating the `Entity` itself to each intermediate base concept introduced so far.

The hierarchical `Situation` structure proves to be effective in practice: (i) it is easily extensible: new branches can be added by creating new concepts, if the system is able to distinguish among different situations through (a combination of) sensor data; (ii) its creation can be automated through classification learning; (iii) using the subsumption, a system exploiting the tree for managing an *active* monitoring system can be easily implemented.

Once a symbolic structure $\mathcal{S}$ is updated, its description $\delta\mathcal{S}$ is added to all the involved situations `s`. For each branching concept of our `Situation` hierarchy, we must add a description $\delta\mathcal{S}$: if the resulting δ`s` is inconsistent, an alarm can be fired; otherwise, a new classification is in place. In principle, whenever a `Situation` has child concepts, the system can actively query the other agents to receive the necessary information to push further the classification.

5   Planning and Execution

$\text{\AE}_{ke}$ predicts the effects of the system behavior over users, intelligent spaces and mobile robots. Each `Device` is augmented with a description of its behavior modeled as a state machine, with the purpose of: (i) modeling each device as a *fluent*; (ii) determining expected state values given the actual device state and inputs. The behavior of intelligent spaces and mobile robots is represented as well. Once a deliberative process occurs, its effects (a sequence of `Actions` to be performed) are instantiated within the knowledge base before execution [7].

From Situations to Problems. Up-to-date information about the system status is provided by instances of `Situation` and `Predicates`. α_{kb}^c is provided with templates of problems to solve: a base `Problem` concept is introduced, characterized by roles specifying a *current* and a *goal* state, to be filled with instances of `Situation`. The goal state can be specified in different ways: by the system itself (as a consequence of previous inferences), by the user (after she has issued some command to the system), etc. We distinguish among specific `Problems`: e.g., for a mobile robot, we have `NavigationProblems`, `ManipulationsProblems`, etc. Corresponding current and goal states are classified, accordingly, using the corresponding as `Situations`: i.e., `NavigationSituations`, `ManipulationSituations`, etc.

From Problems to Plans. Once a `Problem` has been instantiated, α_{pi}^c (where *pi* stands for "planning interface") translates the required planning information in PDDL3, a format compatible with STRIPS-like planners. This step requires the translation of the required `Actions` and `Objects`. When dealing with specific problems (e.g., a `NavigationProblem`), only the corresponding actions are included (i.e., `NavigationActions`). This information is then sent to α_p^c. A solution, if it exists, is in the form of a `Plan`, i.e., a sequence of `Actions` that should be perfomed by various agents to reach the goal state is introduced in the ABox.

From Plans to Execution. At this point, we adopt a planning scheme in which there are high-level, generic `Actions` that, when executed, fire low-level, specific `Problems` to be instantiated and recursively solved by α_p^c, thus interleaving planning and execution. This approach proves to be robust with respect to unpredictabile changes in the environment, because we are allowed to disregard in the high level plan specific details about the environment, and to delay the acquisition of current information at the time of low-level planning or execution.

6   Implementation and Experimental Results

$\{\alpha^d\}$ agents exploit the Echelon LonWorks Fieldbus for distributed control. $\{\alpha^c\}$ agents, on the contrary, are implemented using ETHNOS, a distributed framework developed in C++. Knowledge bases are developed embedding in an ETHNOS agent Classic, a Description Logic which guarantees sound and complete subsumption inferences. Planning capabilities are achieved using SGPlan5 [11], a PDDL3 compatible planner.

The overall capabilities of our self-designed robot Staffetta have been previously presented in [5][7]. Here we report about some recent achievement about the cooperation of Æ_{is} and Æ_{mr}. Let's consider the following scenario, which describes a permanet set-up in our department. The Secretariat Office receives a package, to be forwarded to our laboratory. Through a web interface, which is managed by the α_{web}^c agent in Æ_{mr}, a new `TransportationProblem` is instantiated within α_{ke}^c, i.e., to go to the Secretariat Office and bring the package to the

Fig. 1. (Left) Staffetta entering the elevator; (Right) User tracking through cameras

Laboratorium. In cooperation with α_p^c, a new high level Plan is created as follows: 1) GoTo(SecretariatOffice); 2) LoadPackage; 3) GoTo(Laboratorium). Let's detail, e.g., the first high level Action. The execution of GoTo(SecretariatOffice) involves a complex navigation, possibly with floor switching. Assume that Staffetta is at the second floor, inside the Laboratorium. The execution of the first Action fires a new NavigationProblem: the precondition is atFloor(2)⊓in(Laboratorium), while the goal state is atFloor(0) ⊓ in(SecretariatOffice). Whilst the precondition list is determined by the actual Staffetta' Situations, the goal state is automatically derived by the high level Action. Again, the problem specification is submitted to α_p^c, which produces the corresponding NavigationPlan, constituted by a sequence of MoveFromTo to reach the elevator, followed by an UseElevator action, and then by another sequence of MoveFromTo to reach the SecretariatOffice. MoveFromTo actions are executed by retrieving in the knowledge base the Landmarks that the mobile robot should visit in sequence. This list is fed to the navigation subsystem of $Æ_{mr}$. Once all the landmarks are visited, the single MoveFromTo action is accomplished, and $Æ_{ke}$ continues the execution.

On the opposite, UseElevator requires a tight cooperation with $Æ_{is}$ (see Fig. 1 on the left). At each floor, near the elevator door, our intelligent space is provided with a device whose purpose is to manage mobile robot requests to use the elevator. We call this device "beacon", and we formally denote it as α_b^d. Through the α_{di}^c agent, $Æ_{mr}$ requests the presence of the elevator at the current floor. The information channel between the two agents is managed by an Infra Red channel, extension of the Echelon Fieldbus. This information is received by α_b^d, which notifies α_e^c (a cognitive agent managing the behavior of the elevator) about the request. α_e^c maintains a queue of all the requests, and notifies all the α_b^d agents distributed at different floors about the state of the elevator itself. Once the elevator is at the floor and the doors are opened, Staffetta is ready to reach a Landmark located inside the elevator itself. Thus, through the α_{di}^c interface, Staffetta extends its cognitive capabilities *observing* the behavior of the elevator. Once inside, Staffetta is continuously notified about the floor switching. We can model this process by assuming that the robot is provided with a virtual *floor sensor*: when the target floor is reached and the doors are opened, Staffetta can exit from the elevator reaching a predefined Landmark.

7 Conclusion

In this paper we presented a software architecture dealing with knowledge representation and data fusion for integrated Robotics and AmI applications. Despite its simple architecture, it is able to manage heterogeneous information at different levels, "closing the loop" between sensors and actuators. Whilst an intelligent space extends its capabilities through mobile robots, from the robot perspective its cognitive capabilites are augmented through intelligent space-mediated distributed sensing. The system is able to process both numerical and symbolic data. Based on the concept of an ecosystem of artificial entities, the system architecture has been thoroughly tested in simulation, and part of it has been used in a real set-up. Actual work is focused on expanding the data fusion capabilities through learning; moreover, the overall system is going to be tested at Istituto Figlie di N.S. della Misericordia, Savona, Italy, an assisted-living facility for elderly and disabled.

References

1. Kong, F.T., Chen, Y.-P., Xie, J.-M., Zhou, Z.-D.: Distributed Temperature Control System Based on Multi-sensor Data Fusion. In: Proc. of the 2005 Int. Conf. on Machine Learning and Cybernetics, China (August 2005)
2. Augusto, J.C., Nugent, C.D.: A New Architecture for Smart Homes Based on ADB and Temporal Reasoning. In: Proc. of ICOST-05, Canada (July 2005)
3. Al Dhaher, A.H.G., MacKesy, D.: Multi-sensor Data Fusion Architecture. In: Proc. of the 3rd IEEE HAVE Workshop, Ottawa, Canada, IEEE Computer Society Press, Los Alamitos (2004)
4. Hagras, H., Callaghan, V., Colley, M., Graham, C.: A Hierarchical Fuzzy-genetic Multi-agent Architecture for Intelligent Buildings Online Learning, Adaptation and Control. Journal of Information Sciences 150(1–2) (2003)
5. Sgorbissa, A., Zaccaria, R.: Robot Staffetta in its Natural Environment. In: Proc. of IAS-8, The Netherlands (March 2004)
6. Harnad, S.: The Symbol Grounding Problem. In: Physica D, vol. 42 (1990)
7. Mastrogiovanni, F., Sgorbissa, A., Zaccaria, R.: A System for Hierarchical Planning in Service Mobile Robotics. In: Proc. of IAS-8, The Netherlands (March 2004)
8. Kim, J.H., Kim, Y.D., Lee, K.H.: The Third Generation of Robotics: Ubiquitous Robot. In: Proc. of the 2nd Int. Conf. on Auton. Robots and Agents, NZ (2004)
9. Liao, L., Fox, D., Kautz, H.: Location-based Activity Recognition using Relational Markov Networks. In: Proc. of IJCAI-05, Edimburg, Scotland (2005)
10. Levesque, H.J., Branchman, R.J.: Expressiveness and Tractability in Knowledge Representation and Reasoning. Computational Intelligence 3(2) (1987)
11. Hsu, W., Wah, B.W., Huang, R., Chen, Y.X.: New Features in SGPlan for Handling Soft Constraints and Goal Preferences in PDDL3.0. In: Proc. of ICAPS-06, Cumbria, UK (June 2006)
12. Petrovskaya, A., Ng, A.Y.: Probabilistic Mobile Manipulation in Dynamic Environments with Application to Opening Doors. In: Proc. of IJCAI-07, Hyderabad, India (January 2007)

Multi-robot Interacting Through Wireless Sensor Networks

Antonio Chella, Giuseppe Lo Re, Irene Macaluso, Marco Ortolani,
and Daniele Peri

Department of Computer Engineering, University of Palermo
Viale delle Scienze, I-90128 Palermo, Italy
{chella, lore, macaluso, ortolani, peri}@unipa.it

Abstract. This paper addresses the issue of coordinating the operations
of multiple robots in an indoor environment. The framework presented
here uses a composite networking architecture, in which a hybrid wireless
network, composed by commonly available WiFi devices, and the more
recently developed wireless sensor networks. Such architecture grants
robots to enhance their perceptive capabilities and to exchange information so as to coordinate actions in order to achieve a global common goal.
The proposed framework is described with reference to an experimental
setup that extends a previously developed robotic tour guide application
in the context of a multi-robot application.

1   Introduction

Autonomous robots team engaged in complex mission, such as mines clearing,
surveillance, service applications (see [4] for a review), must be able to coordinate their actions in order to achieve a global common goal. To this purpose
an efficient network infrastructure must be put into place. Moreover, once a
proper communication channel is established, multiple robots may benefit from
the interaction with each other; for instance robots can exchange information
resulting from the collection of data from surrounding environment so as to
enhance individual robot perceptive capabilities.

Various classification of multi-robot systems have been proposed. Dudek, *et
al.* [6], for instance, have proposed a taxonomy on communication mechanism
and their cost to highlight that different multi-robot systems have very different capabilities. Some of the works presented in literature achieve coordination
among robots through distributed control, as in the case of the Alliance architecture [7]. On the other side, the MARTHA project [2] assumes a centralized
control to coordinate a team of autonomous robots for transport application in
structured environment.

Recently, the task of closely monitoring and also of localizing moving objects
in a structured environment has been tackled by employing the wireless sensor
network (WSN) technology [1]. Such networks have been successfully employed
in the design of an indoor localization system [10]. Such system may be employed
as support for robots localization. The synergy between wireless sensor networks

R. Basili and M.T. Pazienza (Eds.): AI*IA 2007, LNAI 4733, pp. 789–796, 2007.

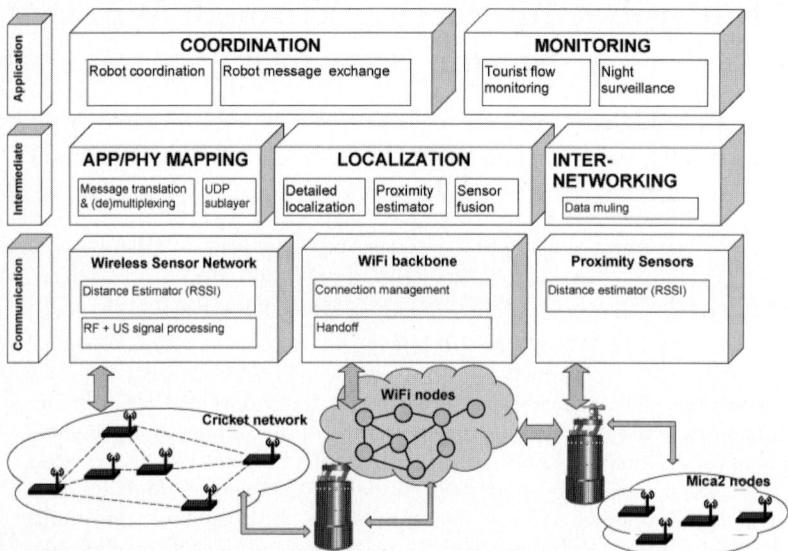

Fig. 1. The RoboNet architecture

and robotics has been analyzed for instance in [9], where the authors build a network of mobile sensors that can be controlled in order to collect samples of a distribution of interest, and also in [8], where some general design, cost and scalability issues are discussed.

This paper describes RoboNet, a networking framework that extends a previously developed robotic tour guide application [5] in the context of a multi-robot application; our system allows a team of robots to enhance their perceptive capabilities through coordination obtained via a hybrid communication network; moreover, the same infrastructure allows robots to exchange information so as to coordinate their actions in order to achieve a global common goal. Section 2 describes the underlying ideas and the motivation behind the proposed architecture, whose details are presented in Sections 3, 4, 5. A realistic application scenario is described in Section 6.

2   The RoboNet Framework

The design of the proposed framework has been mainly motivated by the experience developed in the context of the experiments conducted at the Archaeological Museum of Agrigento, Italy where findings from the close "Valley of the Temples", one of the UNESCO World Heritage Sites, are collected. The purpose of the framework is the coordination of a group of robots moving in a structured indoor environment in order to manage automatically guided museum tours. Museum managers would also like to be able to provide virtual visits. The quality of real visits, on the other hand, could be improved by careful planning, but this requires collection information and studying the tourist flows; moreover, it would be desirable to gather information also for surveillance purposes, so these are further *desiderata* for our framework. Finally, very tight requirements were posed by the museum board of directors regarding severe limitations on the deployment of any intrusive hardware devices on the museum premises.

Figure 1 shows the main components of the RoboNet framework. A 3-tier architecture has been devised to separate the main modules into functionally correlated layers, the lowest of which provides basic connectivity by means of two different network technologies; in the middle one data previously collected are aggregated to extract information useful for localization or event detection purposes, and finally the uppermost layer consists of an application layer protocol that defines message formatting and exchanging. The following sections will provide further details on each of the mentioned layers.

3   The Communication Layer

The lower layer includes the physical communication modules, that supervise the communications among robots and between a robot and the Central Coordination Unit (CCU). Moreover, this layer contains the modules necessary for the low-level functions of the localization and proximity networks. A wireless LAN will act as a backbone and provide connectivity to the robots, while limiting modifications to the environment to the deployment of few access points, with no cabling, in order to adhere to the previously mentioned requirements; robots will use the standard IEEE 802.11a (WiFi) protocol to communicate among themselves and with the CCU. A specialized wireless sensor network is thoroughly deployed to assist robots in their self-localization phase, according to the specifications of the Cricket project [10], this localization network is composed of Mica2 motes equipped with a CC1000 RF transceiver and an ultrasonic transmitter and receiver.

A few of those nodes are located at fixed positions in each sub-environment, while another one (named *listener*, in Cricket terminology) is carried by each moving robot. The same kind of nodes will also be carried by tourists, but, rather than acting as listeners, will only exploit their RF transceiver in order to provide proximity estimates. Proximity measures may still be used as an inexpensive means for the robots to approximately estimate how many tourists are "following" them and to plan the guided tour accordingly. Moreover, the same proximity sensors may be placed at specific spots in order to gather statistics about tourist flows by storing the IDs they sense over time for surveillance purposes. Since robots are also equipped with standard WiFi cards in order to communicate with the above mentioned backbone network, they are natural candidates for harvesting data from proximity sensor nodes.

4   The Intermediate Layer

Data originating from the different kinds of networks described above will be processed at the middle layer of the RoboNet architecture, in order to convert application-layer messages into physical-layer ones. Our framework achieves co-ordination among robots by a specifically designed application-layer protocol whose messages are carried by the WiFi backbone. Application-layer messages will travel over UDP, managed by a simple loss recovery mechanism implemented as a thin sub-layer. After a message is sent, an ACK is expected and, if a pre-defined timeout expires before the ACK is received, the sender tries a retrans-mission and waits for twice the timeout; in case of further failure, a loss is simply notified to the upper layer.

Localization is realized by combining data coming from the analysis of internal robots' parameters and from the Cricket infrastructure. As described in [3], the most recent version of the Cricket framework implements a Kalman filter to assist a moving device in tracking its position. Following the directions of [11], we provide each moving robot with an *active* localization device (the listener), so beacon nodes, whose location is known, estimate distances to the listener based on an active transmission from the listener itself. Since a mobile device in the active mobile architecture sends simultaneous distance estimates to multiple receivers, its performance is arguably better than with the passive mobile system in which the listener obtains only one distance estimate at a time and may have moved between successive estimates. As the listener is bolted to the robot whose movements are constrained in two dimensions, we modify the original EKF used to track the mobile device [11] considering a state vector composed by the two locations coordinates in the plane and the heading direction (θ). To take into account the information provided by the control data (i.e. the translational velocity v_t, and rotational velocity ω_t applied to control the robot), we adapted the prediction step of the EKF including a velocity motion model [13]. The state prediction at time t is:

$$\bar{\boldsymbol{\mu}}_t = \boldsymbol{\mu}_{t-1} + \begin{pmatrix} -\frac{\hat{v}_t}{\hat{\omega}_t}\sin(\theta) + \frac{\hat{v}_t}{\hat{\omega}_t}\sin(\theta + \hat{\omega}_t \Delta t) \\ \frac{\hat{v}_t}{\hat{\omega}_t}\cos(\theta) - \frac{\hat{v}_t}{\hat{\omega}_t}\cos(\theta + \hat{\omega}_t \Delta t) \\ \hat{\omega}_t \Delta t \end{pmatrix} \qquad (1)$$

where $\bar{\boldsymbol{\mu}}_t$ is the predicted state at time t and $\boldsymbol{\mu}_{t-1}$ is the state vector at time $t-1$; $\hat{v}_t$ and $\hat{\omega}_t$ are the translational velocity and the rotational velocity respectively, generated adding Gaussian noise to the motion control $\mathbf{u_t} = (v_t \ \omega_t)^T$. The estimated pose provided by the EKF is integrated with the one generated using the previously developed particle filter algorithm [5]. In particular the posterior distribution of the robot pose is computed as a weighted sum:

$$p(x_t|z_t, u_t) = w_{wsn,t}p(x_t|z_{wsn,t}, u_t) + w_{rs,t}p(x_t|z_{rs,t}, u_t) \qquad (2)$$

where $p(x_t|z_{wsn,t}, u_t)$ is the normal posterior distribution computed with the EKF taking into account measurements provided by the WSN ($z_{wsn,t}$) and $p(x_t|z_{rs,t}, u_t)$ is the posterior distribution computed by the particle filter given the robot sensors measurements ($z_{rs,t}$). The weights $w_{wsn,t}$ and $w_{rs,t}$ are a mea-sure of the uncertainty of the corresponding pose estimates. In particular $w_{wsn,t}$

Table 1. Message Types

Message Type	Description
SVC_SIG	used to signal the CCU about a new visit to be assigned .
SVC_REQ	used by CCU for starting the auction
SVC_REPLY	used by a robot to participate in the auction
TASK_ASS	used by CCU to assign a task to a robot
TASK_ACC	used by a robot to confirm acceptance of a task
SYNC_REQ	used by a robot to exchange its state with another robot
SYNC_REPLY	reply to SYNC_REQ

is the likelihood $p(z_{rs}|x_t)$ of the measurement model [13], while $w_{rs,t}$ is computed as the inverse of the trace of the covariance Σ_t of the posterior distribution estimated by the Kalman filter. The original localization algorithm may thus be customized to our scenario allowing better performance.

5   The Application Layer

For the purpose of the operations of the Central Coordination Unit (CCU), the environment is modeled as a topological map representing the connectivity and accessibility of the different regions in the environment. The environment is thus split into a collection of sub-environments connected by passages, and the relations of connectivity between the different sub-environment are captured by a connectivity graph representation: a node corresponds to a sub-environment; each sub-environment is univocally identified; an arc between two nodes exists if the corresponding sub-environments are connected.

The condition of accessibility for each robot is modeled by partitioning the connectivity graph and considering the subgraph representing regions reachable by the robot. A visit is described in the model by the sequence of sub-environments to be showed to visitors. For the reasons stated above, a visit generally needs to be split into a sequence of sub-visits each one guided by a robot. The CCU governs the assignment of sub-visits to robots by an auction mechanism. When a guiding service is needed the CCU is notified by either the ticket counter or a robot, with the former case happening only once at the beginning of a visit, while the latter may arise several times during the visit. When a robot decides to cease guiding the group, for instance because it cannot physically reach the next sub-environment, it communicates the remaining part of the visit to the CCU. In practice, a request from a robot guide that ceased a visit is identical to those issued by the ticket counter for a new visit and both are encoded with the same message kind in the protocol. When the CCU receives such a message it starts the auction by multicasting the request for a task to the robots able to reach the first sub-environment of the visit. The robots then reply to the CCU with their bid expressed as an estimate of the time needed to start the requested visit. This estimates accounts for the time to get to the starting point as well as the remaining time of the current visit, if any. The

CCU collects the bids and sends the robot with the best bid a task assignment message. Encoded in the message, beside the sequence of sub-environments to be shown, are the IDs of the visitors. The receiver can reply to accept the task thus ending the auction, otherwise another bidder must be chosen by the CCU.

5.1   The Message Exchange Protocol

We devised an application-layer protocol that allows the CCU to send and receive requests from robots and the robots to communicate with each other. CCU and the robots will thus be involved in a negotiation process, similarly to what happens in other works described in previous literature [12], where tasks are assigned to entities only after a preliminary message exchange through which entities with tasks to be executed select entities able to execute them. In our implementation, messages will travel on the WiFi network showing a fixed 4-bytes header followed by a variable length payload. The semantics of carried data depend on the specific message type that is specified in the 3-bit "Msg Type" field; this identifies one of the seven different types we are currently using for messages. The source of a message is indicated in the "Source ID" field as a 7-bit integer (the first bit is not used), whereas the next 8 bits carry the message destination information; this field is 8-bit long, with the 1st bit is reserved for multicast groups management. The "Destination ID" field contains the unique identifier of any addressable entity in the RoboNet framework, namely every individual robot or any predefined group of robots, with the address 0000000 reserved for identifying the CCU. Unique IDs are also assigned to rooms and passages between rooms; moreover, as each visitor will be provided with a mote acting as a tracking device, they may also be uniquely identified through that device's ID. In the following, such ID's will be indicated respectively as $RoomID$, $PassageID$, and $VisitorID$. As a group forms at the entrance, a list of $VisitorID$'s is created and is transmitted to the CCU in a SVC_SIG, CCU will then broadcast a SVC_REQ message to all robots through the WiFi backbone. The message will include the room where service is required (i.e. the starting room for the tour). Each robot will reply with a SVC_REPLY message containing an estimate for its service time, as explained above. CCU will then assign the task to one of the robots whose reply has been received and that provided the best bid, and the corresponding TASK_ASS message contains the list of $VisitorID$ and the list of $RoomID$ (i.e. the description of the "visit"). The selected robot will finally signal its acceptance by sending a TASK_ACC message to CCU. The complete set of messages is shown in Table 4, together with a brief description.

6   An Application Scenario

In the course of the years, the Robotics Lab of University of Palermo developed a robotic architecture that takes into account several suggestions from cognitive science. The architecture has been successfully tested in the CiceRobot project on tasks related to guided tours in the Archaeological Museum of Agrigento [5]. For the purpose of the current research, it is important to point out that the

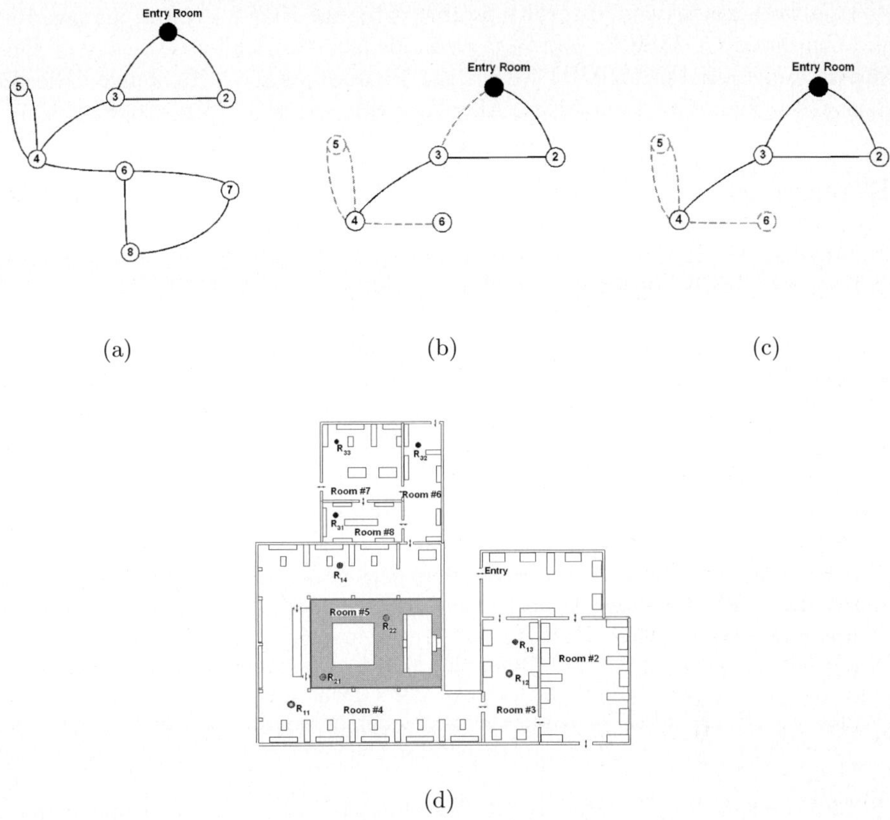

Fig. 2. (a) and (d) are respectively the graph representation and the map of the whole environment. (b) and (c) are the connectivity graph for R_{13} and R_{12} respectively.

robot planning system is based on a 3D Robot/Environment Simulator. The planning by simulation paradigm allows to easily and carefully perform those forms of planning that are more directly related to perceptual information. The proposed architecture has been deployed in the Archaeological Museum of Agrigento and is currently under test. Let us consider the multi-robot coordination in our experimental setup. Supposing that a group of visitors is waiting at the entrance; the CCU multi-casts a SVC_REQ message to those robots that are able to reach the entry (red and yellow/red robots in Figure 2). Each robot replies with its estimated performance relative to the current task, i.e. the time it takes to reach the entry: the simulated interaction between the robot and the environment allows to compute an accurate estimate of the robot performance. In the example reported in Figure 2 both robots R_{11} and R_{14} are busy guiding visitors, while robots R_{12} and R_{13} are idle. Even if R_{13} is the nearest robot to the entry, the CCU allocates the task to the robot R_{12} as its performance estimate is better. Actually R_{13} is not able to directly go from *Room #3* to *Entry Room* due to a slope that is too steep for it but not so for R_{12}.

This work makes use of results produced by the PI2S2 Project managed by the Consorzio COMETA, a project co-funded by the Italian Ministry of University and Research (MIUR) within the Piano Operativo Nazionale "Ricerca Scientifica, Sviluppo Tecnologico, Alta Formazione" (PON 2000-2006).

References

1. Akyildiz, I.F., Su, W., Sankarasubramaniam, Y., Cayirci, E.: A survey on sensor networks. IEEE Communication Magazine 40(8), 102–114 (2002)
2. Alami, R., Fleury, S., Herrb, M., Ingrand, F., Robert, F.: Multi-robot cooperation in the MARTHA project. Robotics & Automation Magazine, IEEE 5(1), 36–47 (1998)
3. Balakrishnan, H., Baliga, R., Curtis, D., Goraczko, M., Miu, A., Priyantha, N.B., Smith, A., Steele, K., Teller, S., Wang, K.: Lessons from developing and deploying the cricket indoor location system. Technical report, MIT Computer Science and AI Lab (2003)
4. Balch, T., Parker, L.E.: Robot Teams: From Diversity to Polymorphism. AK Peters (2002)
5. Chella, A., Macaluso, I.: Sensations and Perceptions in "Cicerobot" a Museum Guide Robot. In: Proc. of BICS 2006 Symposium on Brain Inspired Cognitive systems, Greece (2006)
6. Dudek, G., Jenkin, M.R.M., Milios, E., Wilkes, D.: A taxonomy for multi-agent robotics. Autonomous Robots 3(4), 375–397 (1996)
7. Matarić, M.J.: Behaviour-based control: examples from navigation, learning, and group behaviour. Journal of Experimental & Theoretical Artificial Intelligence 9(2), 323–336 (1997)
8. McMickell, M B., Goodwine, B., Montestruque, L.A.: Micabot: A robotic platform for large-scale distributed robotics. In: Proc. of the IEEE Int. Conf. on Robotics and Automation, Taipei, Taiwan, IEEE Computer Society Press, Los Alamitos (September 2003)
9. Moore, K.L., Chen, Y.Q., Song, Z.: Diffusion based path planning in mobile actuator-sensor networks (mas-net) - some preliminary results. In: Proc. of SPIE Conf. on Intelligent Computing: Theory and Applications II, Orlando, FL, USA (April 2004)
10. Priyantha, N.B., Chakraborty, A., Balakrishnan, H.: The cricket location-support system. In: MOBICOM. Proc. of the Sixth Annual ACM International Conference on Mobile Computing and Networking, Boston, MA, USA, ACM Press, New York (2000)
11. Smith, A., Balakrishnan, H., Goraczko, M., Priyantha, N.B.: Tracking moving devices with the cricket location system. In: Proc. of the 2nd ACM MobiSys, Boston, MA, USA, pp. 190–202. ACM Press, New York (June 2004)
12. Smith, R.G.: The contract net protocol: High-level communication and control in a distributed problem solver. IEEE Trans. Computers 29(12), 1104–1113 (1980)
13. Thrun, S., Burgard, W., Fox, D.: Probabilistic robotics. MIT Press, Cambridge (2005)

Design of a Multiagent Solution for Demand-Responsive Transportation

Claudio Cubillos[1], Sandra Gaete[1], Franco Guidi-Polanco[1],
and Claudio Demartini[2]

[1] Pontificia Universidad Católica de Valparaíso, Escuela de Ingeniería Informática,
Av. Brasil 2241, Valparaíso, Chile
`claudio.cubillos@ucv.cl, sandra.gaete@gmail.com, franco.guidi@ucv.cl`
[2] Politecnico di Torino, Dip. Automatica e Informatica,
Cso. Duca Degli Abruzzi 24, 10129, Torino, Italia
`claudio.demartini@polito.it`

Abstract. Mobility patterns in large cities has changed in the last decades making traditional fix-line public transportation no longer efficient to tackle the increasing complexity. Demand-responsive transportation leverages as an alternative where routes, departure times, vehicles and even operators, can be matched to the identified demand, allowing a more user-oriented and cost effective approach to service provision. In this context, the design of a multiagent system is presented following the agent-oriented software engineering methodology (AOSE) PASSI.

1 Introduction

In the last two decades, the mobility needs of European citizens have radically changed. Several factors are responsible for these changes, mostly linked to modifications in the organization of work and lifestyle pattern in urban environments, moving to an increase of activity at the neighborhood level. These modifications have greatly diminished the ability of regular public transport to satisfy the travel needs of the citizens. Conventional public transport, based on buses and trams operating on fixed lines is particularly efficient for well defined corridors of movement with clustered travel demand.

The need to cover more diffuse travel patterns, varying periods of low demand, city-peripheral journeys, as well as commuting trips often make conventional public transport systems unable to guarantee the level of service required to address the user needs. The use of Demand-Responsive Transport services (DRTS), where routes, departure times, vehicles and even operators, can be matched to the identified demand allows a more user-oriented and cost effective approach to service provision. The adaptation of the transport services to match actual demand enables cost savings to the operators, society and passengers.

On the other hand, software agents are defined as autonomous entities capable of flexible behavior denoted by reactiveness, pro-activeness and social ability [1]. Multiagent systems (MAS) consist of diverse agents that communicate and coordinate generating synergy to pursue a common goal. This higher level

R. Basili and M.T. Pazienza (Eds.): AI*IA 2007, LNAI 4733, pp. 797–804, 2007.

of abstraction has allowed agents to tackle the increasing complexity of nowadays open software systems where integration, transparency and interoperation among heterogeneous components are a must. Under such an scenario, the agent paradigm has leveraged as an important modeling abstraction, in areas such as web and grid service, peer to peer and ambient intelligence architectures just to mention some cases.

The present work describes the design of a multiagent system using a particular AOSE methodology called PASSI [2] for the passenger transportation under a flexible approach. It gives continuity to our past research [3] [4] on heuristics for solving scheduling of passenger trips.

2   Related Work

The research on Multi-Agent Systems (MAS) has deserved an increasing interest in the Intelligent Transportation Systems (ITS) domain. One ITS area of MAS development has been Urban Traffic Control (UTC) systems. In 2000, Ou [5] presented a UTC, which adopted MAS technology based on recursive modeling method (RMM) and Bayesian learning. Ferreira et al. [6] presented a multi-agent decentralized strategy where each agent was in charge of managing the signals of an intersection and optimized an index based on its local state and "opinions" coming from adjacent agents. Roozemond and Danko [7] proposed a UTC model primarily based on several coupled intersection control Intelligent Traffic Signaling Agents (ITSA), some authority agents and some Road Segment Agents (RSA). In 2002, Cai and Song [8] introduced a traffic control model with MAS, in which a more flexible agent self-control framework was described and a multi-agent negotiating strategy was conceived.

Advanced Transportation Information System (ATIS) is necessary in ITS. Adopting the agent technique can help to realize simple operations to obtain driver information. In this sense, Kase and Hattori [9] proposed the InfoMirror application that provides agent-based information assistance to drivers through car navigation systems or on-board PCs. Adorni [10] presented a distributing route guidance system, which allowed dynamic route searching using the coordination capabilities of MAS.

Bus-holding control tackles the coordination of multiple lines of fixed-route buses and the different stops, seeking the global optimality. In 2001, Jiamin et al. [11] proposed a distributed bus-holding control approach in which a MAS negotiation between a Bus Agent and a Stop Agent was conducted based on marginal cost calculations.

In the solutions above, no AOSE methodology is used for specifying the system, mainly due to a lack of maturity of AOSE methodologies at that time. The aim of this work is to provide an experience in the design of multiagent systems using the PASSI methodology and to present the design of an agent system devoted to demand-responsive passenger transportation.

3   Flexible Public Transport Services

Demand Responsive Transport (DRT) services aim to meet the needs of different users for additional transport supply. The use of flexible transport services, where routes, departure times, vehicles and even operators, can be matched to the identified demand allows a more user-oriented and cost effective approach to service provision. The adaptation of the transport services to match actual demand enables cost savings to the operators, society and passengers.

DRT can be seen as an element of a larger intermodal service chain, providing local mobility and complementary to other conventional forms of transportation (e.g. regular buses and trams, regional trains). In this context, DRT provides a range of Intermediate Transport solutions, filling the gap between traditional public bus services and individual taxis.

With respect to process implementation and management, the flexibility of the system is expressed along two main directions: on one hand, users of DRT systems must be provided with user-friendly instruments for accessing the services (such as information, reservation, query update) in several different flexible ways (the so called "anywhere and anytime" access). On the other hand, the organization providing flexible services must be itself flexible, with the capability of managing dynamic relationships in a pool of transport resources (vehicles), which may sometimes have to change to better adapt the transport supply to the dynamic demand.

To give answer to the above requirements, the architecture of a DRT system involves a number of advanced telecommunications and IT tools. It often considers a booking and reservation system to manage the customer requests and a Travel Dispatch Center (TDC) for allocating trips and optimizing resources, together with On-Board Units (OBU) in each of the vehicles to support the driver. Communication systems and equipment are also needed to link the TDC with both drivers (e.g. GPS/GSM-based vehicle location) and customers (e.g. Internet, IVRS and palm-top top devices to assist customer booking). Finally, smart-card based fare collection systems can be used additionally.

The final DRT service can be offered through a range of vehicles including regular service bus, mini-bus, maxi-vans, buses and vans adapted for special needs and regular cars. The use of each vehicle type depends on the transport service to offer, the covered area and the target users.

4   PASSI Methodology

The Process for Agent Societies Specification and Implementation (PASSI) is a step-by-step methodology for designing and developing multi-agent societies. PASSI integrates design models and concepts from both OO software engineering and artificial intelligence approaches using the UML notation. The design process with PASSI is supported by PTK (PASSI ToolKit [17]) to be used as an add-in for Rational Rose. Figure 1 shows the PASSI methodology, which is made up of five models containing twelve steps in the process of building multi-agent. The models are: System Requirements Model, Agent Society Model, gent Implementation Model, Code Model and Deployment Model. Because of space restrictions, the present work will focus in the first model. Please refer to [2] for a more detailed description on the whole PASSI methodology.

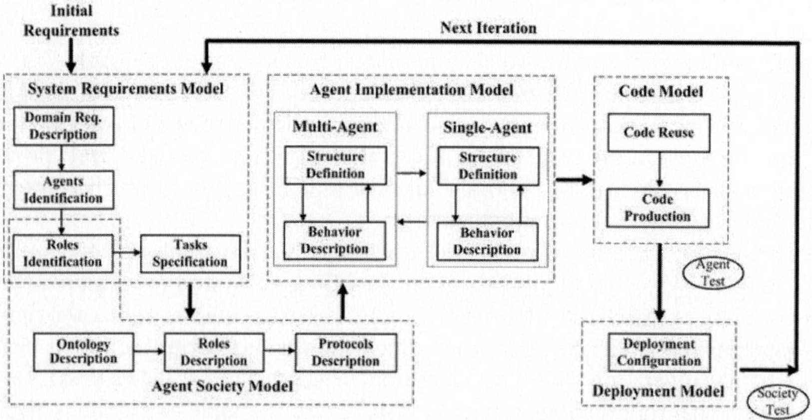

Fig. 1. The PASSI methodology

The System Requirements Model corresponds to an anthropomorphic model of the system requirements in terms of agency and purpose. It involves 4 steps: 1) a Domain Description (D.D.), which provides a functional description of the system using conventional use-case diagrams, 2) an Agent Identification (A.Id.), leveraging the separation of responsibility concerns into agents, represented as UML packages, 3) a Role Identification (R.Id.), consisting in use of sequence diagrams to explore each agent's responsibilities through role-specific scenarios and 4) a Task Specification (T.Sp.), detailing through activity diagrams the capabilities of each agent.

5   The Agent Architecture

The multiagent transportation system stands over the Jade Agent Platform[12], which provides a full environment for agents to work. In the following subsections, the agent architecture is described in terms of the PASSI methodology phases. In the following the agent system is described in terms of its System Requirements PASSI model.

5.1   Agent Identification (A.Id.)

In this step the use cases capturing the system requirements are grouped together to conform an agent. The diagram in Fig. 2 shows the identified use cases for the transport systems and the leveraged agents.

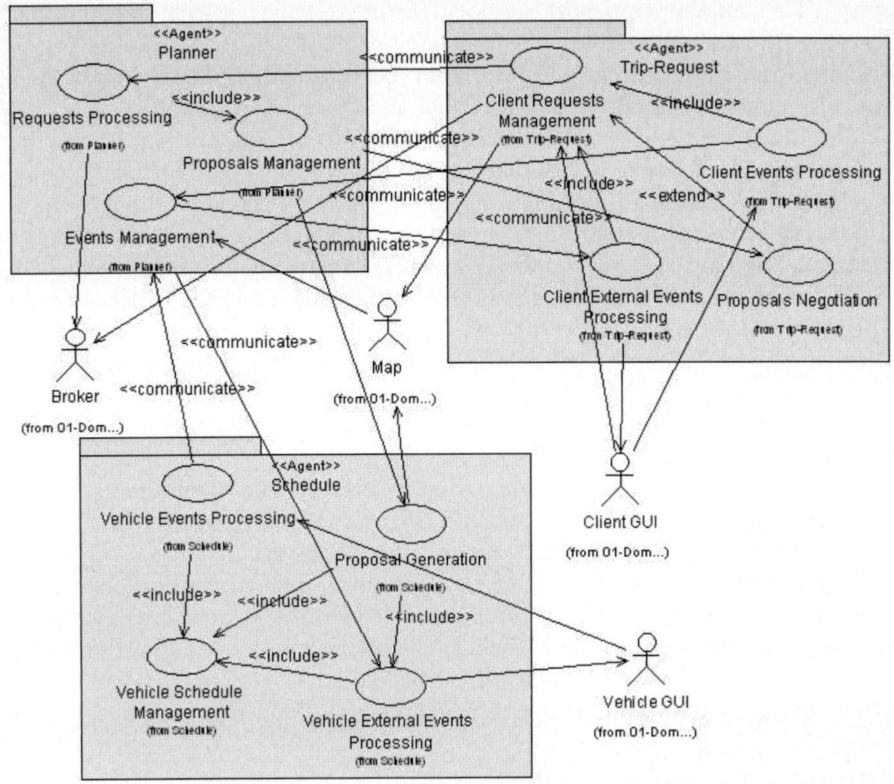

Fig. 2. Portion of the Agents' Identification Diagram

The Client GUI plays an interface role, providing the means for the end user (requester) to generate a trip request. They are also in charge of capturing the description of the desired transportation service through a *Trip Request Profile*. It also provides a channel for client-to-system events' communication (e.g. a delay or change on the agreed service) and for system-to-client events' communication (e.g. a traffic jam, or vehicle break down).

Vehicle GUIs are interface agents in charge of capturing the properties and status of the real vehicle. The most important role of the Vehicle GUI is to monitor the real vehicle while in service and inform their Drivers and Schedule agents about any differences with respect to the planned trip plan or any eventualities (e.g client no show, delay, detour, etc).

Trip-Request agent's main role is to represent the client and his decisions concerning the transportation request, residing on a device with more processing power. This agent is responsible of having the client's request fulfilled and of communicating him about the result. It is also responsible for events pre-processing and managing the negotiation with the Planner.

The Broker's main role is provides a publish/subscribe infrastructure that allows vehicles to enter or leave the system freely and allows clients to query the system for available transport services. Hence, it knows which transportation services are available and their characteristics. The Map is wrapping the underlying Geographical Information System (GIS) providing the routes, distances and times between points within the zone under service coverage.

The Planner processes all the clients' requests coming through their Trip-request agents. It starts a contract-net (CNP) [18] with the Schedule agents. Therefore it manages all the proposals for a given trip-request coming from the diverse Schedule agents representing each available vehicle. It is also in charge of managing inbound and outbound events once an agreement has been reached.

The main role of a Schedule agent is to manage the trip plan (work-schedule) of the vehicle. In practical terms, the agent will have to make proposals upon Planner request and in case of winning will have to include the trip into its actual plan. Upon changes (vehicle or client events) informed either by the Vehicle GUI or Planner agents, the Schedule agent will update the plan and reschedule the remaining requests.

Upon differences in the planning (due to breakdowns, traffic jam, etc) the Schedule agent re-plans. In the case of having an infeasible trip request (mainly due to the time-window restrictions), it informs the Planner agent about the situation. The Planner makes a call for trip-proposals to try reallocating the request in other available vehicle. In any case, the result is communicated to the corresponding Trip-request agent, which will inform the client about the change. This change may imply a different vehicle processing the trip only or also a delay or an anticipation of the pickup and delivery times defined previously.

5.2   Roles Identification (R.Id.)

Roles Identification consists in exploring all the possible paths of the preceding Agents' Identification Diagram in Fig. 2. In fact, each "communicate" relationship among two agents can be in one or more scenarios showing interacting agents working together to achieve a certain desired system behavior.

As example, the following Fig. 3 shows the scenario in which the Driver actor communicates the system that the passenger did not show at the pickup point. Each object in the diagram is described following the $\langle role \rangle : \langle agent \rangle$ convention. Therefore, this scenario involves the Driver and Accountability System actors plus the vehicle, Schedule and Planner agents.

The scenario starts with the Driver communicating the absence of the passenger at the pickup point through the Vehicle (agent) interface. This last one requests its Schedule agent to process the absence, providing the trip details. This request is processed by the Events' Processing role of the Schedule. This role performs two tasks: the first is the corresponding trip deletion from the actual schedule while the second is the communication of such event to the Planner. The first part is carried out by the schedule but through another role, the Schedule Management. Finally the Planner informs the rest of the system (the Accountability System in this case) about the event(*Passenger Absence Confirmation* as defined in the ontology) in order to update its corresponding trip-service registry.

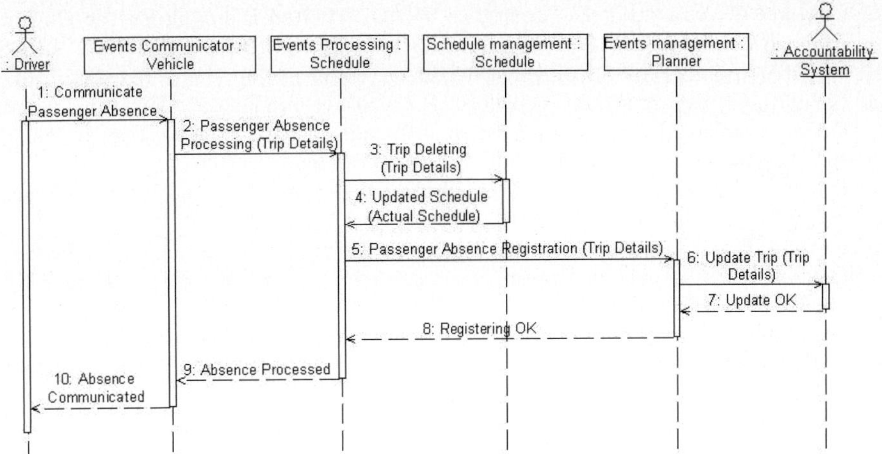

Fig. 3. Roles Identification for the "Driver Communicates Passenger Absence at Pickup Point" scenario

6 Conclusions

An agent system devoted to passenger transportation under a demand-responsive approach was described. The PASSI methodology used allowed an appropriate level of specification along its diverse phases. The present work focused in the Agent Requirements model, providing a functional description of the system in terms of use-cases, the identification of agents and the identification of agents' roles through sequence diagrams.

Future work considers the inclusion of other actors and subsystems such as the paying system, the accountability and traffic informants. Other issue is the implementation of a high-level communication mechanism in order to provide a dynamic participation in such a system.

Acknowledgement

This work is part of Project No. 209.746/2007 entitled "Coordinación en una sociedad multiagente dedicada a la programación y control bajo ambiente dinámico", funded by the Pontifical Catholic University of Valparaíso (www.pucv.cl).

References

1. Weiss, G.: Multiagent Systems: A Modern Approach to Distributed Artificial Intelligence. MIT Press, Massachusetts, USA (1999)
2. Burrafato, P., Cossentino, M.: Designing a multiagent solution for a bookstore with the passi methodology. In: AOIS-2002. Fourth International Bi-Conference Workshop on AgentOriented Information Systems (2002)

3. Cubillos, C., Crawford, B., Rodríguez, N.: Distributed Planning for the On-Line Dial-a-Ride Problem. In: Preparata, F.P., Fang, Q. (eds.) FAW 2007. LNCS, vol. 4613, pp. 124–135. Springer, Heidelberg (2007)
4. Cubillos, C., Rodríguez, N., Crawford, B.: A Study on Genetic Algorithms for the DARP Problem. In: Mira, J., Alvarez, J.R. (eds.) IWINAC 2007, Part I., 2007th edn. LNCS, vol. 4527, pp. 498–507. Springer, Heidelberg (2007)
5. Ou, H.T.: Urban Traffic Multi-Agent System based on RMM and Bayesian Learning. In: Proc. American Control Conference, pp. 2782–2783 (2000)
6. Ferreira, E.D., Subrahmanian, E.: Intelligent Agents in Decentralized Traffic Control. In: IEEE Intelligent Transportation Systems Conference Proceedings, USA, pp. 705–709. IEEE Computer Society Press, Los Alamitos (August 2001)
7. Roozemond, D.A.: Using Intelligmt Agents for Pro-active Real-time Urban Intersection Control. European Joumal of Operational Research 131(2), 293–301 (2001)
8. Cai, Z H., Song, J.Y.: Model of Road Traffic Flow Control based on Multi-agent. Journal of Highway and Transportation Research and Development 19(2), 105–109 (2002)
9. Kase, N., Hattori, M.: InfoMirror - Agent-based Information Assistance to Drivers. In: IEEE/IEEJ/JSAI Intelligent Transportation Systems Conference Proceedings, pp. 734–739 (1999)
10. Adorni, G.: Route Guidance as a Just-In-Time Multiagent Task. Journal of Applied Artificial Intelligence 10(2), 95–120 (1996)
11. Zhao, J., Dessouky, M., Bukkapatnam, S.: Distributed Holding Control of Bus Transit Operations. In: IEEE Intelligent Transportation Systems Conference Proceedings, Oakland - USA, pp. 976–981. IEEE Computer Society Press, Los Alamitos (August 2001)
12. Bellifemine, F., et al.: JADE - A FIPA Compliant Agent Framework. C SELT Internal Technical Report (1999)
13. Bürckert, H., Fischer, K., et al.: TeleTruck: A Holonic Fleet Management System. In: 14th European Meeting on Cybernetics and Systems Research, pp. 695–700 (1998)
14. Fischer, K., Müller, J.P., Pischel, M.: Cooperative Transportation Scheduling: An application Domain for DAI. Journal of Applied Artificial Intelligence 10 (1996)
15. Kohout, R., Erol, K., Robert, C.: In-Time Agent-Based Vehicle Routing with a Stochastic Improvement Heuristic. In: Proc. Of the AAAI/IAAI Int. Conf., Orlando, Florida, pp. 864–869 (1999)
16. Perugini, D., Lambert, D., et al.: A distributed agent approach to global transportation scheduling. In: IEEE/ WIC Int. Conf. on Intelligent Agent Technology, pp. 18–24 (2003)
17. PASSI Toolkit (PTK), Available at http://sourceforge.net/projects/ptk
18. Smith, R.G., Davis, R.: Distributed Problem Solving: The Contract Net Approach. In: Proceedings of the 2nd National Conference of the Canadian Society for Computational Studies of Intelligence (1978)

Planning the Behaviour of a Social Robot Acting as a Majordomo in Public Environments

Berardina De Carolis and Giovanni Cozzolongo

Department of Computer Science
University of Bari - Italy
www.di.uniba.it

Abstract. In this paper we propose the use of a social robot as a majordomo interface between users and Smart Environments. We focus, in particular, on the need for the robot to plan its behaviour by taking into account factors that are relevant in public environments in which the robot has a "social" role. In this context, once the situation has been recognized, the robot uses a probabilistic model to trigger social attitudes towards the user that influence, as a consequence, the activation of its high-level goals. According to the most probable goals, the behaviour plan is computed by applying a utility-based approach that allows selecting the most convenient actions in that situation.

Keywords: Social Robots, behaviour planning, ambient intelligence.

1 Introduction

In this paper we propose the use of a robot that acts as a kind of majordomo in public environments in which it embodies a "social" role. In this application context, taking into account social aspects become even more relevant when media are not boxed in a desktop computer but are integrated pervasively in everyday life environments [1]. Therefore, in evaluating possible approaches to the planning of the robot behaviour it is important to consider the interaction not only from the task oriented point of view, but also it is also important to take into account how social and affective attitudes influence its behaviour that may consist in a change in the environment configuration, in the presentation of information, in a direct dialog with the user or in a combination of these actions. In a previous phase of this project, we worked mainly on the recognition of the user requests by developing a model for recognizing the user attitude and communicative intent [2]. Now we are developing the behaviour planner in which we adopt a two-levels approach: first we use a probabilistic model for triggering the robot's high level goals according to the recognized situation and then we select the plan that allow achieving these goals by maximizing the expected utility both from the social and the task points of view. In particular, we show our preliminary results in the context of planning the answer of a social robot acting as a responsible of a public space in which it substitutes a human responsible and reacts appropriately to social situations according to the social rules of the place as the human would do. To test our approach we decided to use our research laboratory as

R. Basili and M.T. Pazienza (Eds.): AI*IA 2007, LNAI 4733, pp. 805–812, 2007.

smart environment and Sony Aibo as social robot responsible for the environment. In this case Aibo had to perform the main task of dealing with people that show up in the laboratory by adopting a behaviour appropriate to the type of user request not only from the service point of view but also to the type of social relation that typically exists between the responsible of the laboratory and that type of user.

For instance, let's suppose that *an unknown student enters in the laboratory without asking any permission and browses around, the human responsible for the laboratory is not present and the other people in the lab are busy in a meeting.*

A suitable behaviour that we would expect from the robot would consists in a combination of polite behaviour acts that make the student understand that there are not available resources and that he/she should come back in another moment, for instance when the human responsible is present, and then should dismiss the student. Considering the social and affective attitude, the robot should express to be sorry for not being able to help the student. In the remainder of this paper we will consider this as an example scenario for showing how our approach to planning works in this context.

The paper is then structured as follows. In Section 2 we illustrate briefly the architecture of the agent acting as the environment majordomo; Section 3 focuses on behaviour planning and Section 4 shows how the adapted approach is instantiated in the scenario explained previously; Section 5 concludes the paper by outlining the preliminary results of the work and the elements that need further investigation.

2   The Environment Majordomo Architecture

The long term goal of our research is to develop an interface agent able to facilitate the interaction with public social environments. In particular, this agent should be able to answer appropriately to the user's request, engage the user in social relations typical of that type of environment, provide context-aware information and explanation about the environment situation [3, 4]. To this aim, after having designed the agent basic architecture following the principle of the BDI approach [5], we started to develop its behavioural models (Figure 1).

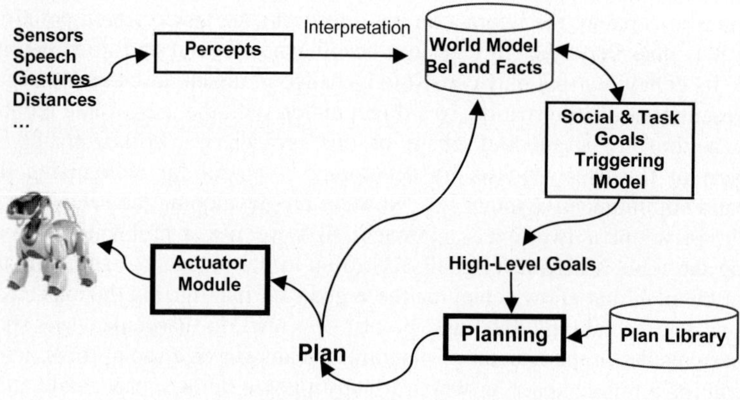

Fig. 1. Reasoning Schema

Such an agent has to be capable to translate a set of percepts, deriving from environment sensors and user's inputs (requests, commands or actions in the environment), into as a set of beliefs, to build in its mind a view of the world in which it operates (*World Model*). According to the current state of the world the robot has to be capable to reason in order to trigger a set of high-level goals concerning its behaviour both from the social and the task/service levels. These high level goals are used to plan the agent actions in the environment that are most appropriate to the recognized situation. These actions may correspond to changes in the environment configuration and/or to communicative actions toward the user. Obviously, the reasoning process has to be dynamic and the agent has to monitor continuously the effects of its actions in achieving the triggered goals and eventually revise them accordingly.

3 Behaviour Planning

Deciding the behaviour of the environment majordomo agent requires a real-time approach to planning that takes into account: i) the domain dynamicity, ii) the uncertainty related to situation recognition and to action outcomes, iii) the possibility that the agent has incomplete knowledge of the world, iv) the activation of multiple goals with different priorities and v) the monitoring and eventually the revision of these goals as a consequence of failures or changes in its perception of the world.

In order to meet these requirements, first we tried to formalize a general reasoning model; then, we tried to instantiate and apply it in the scenario described in the Introduction of this paper.

3.1 Triggering High-Level Goals

For reasoning about high-level goals and, afterward, about actions to perform, the robot needs to use a model that is able to handle uncertainty and incomplete world representation typical of this kind of domain [6]. In fact, interaction with smart environments contains various uncertainties that are mostly caused by the imperfectness and incompleteness of data or by the difficulty of a certain correct interpretation of human behaviour. Modelling approaches that employ the concept of probability, especially in combination with Bayesian methods, are promising candidates to solve these problems [7]. For this reason we use a combination Bayesian Networks (BN) and planning. In particular, high-level goal triggering is represented the BN model illustrated in Figure 2.

In this model, root nodes represent contextual data deriving from the perceptions layer that handle data from sensors, user input and actions and also more stable user features such as age, role, sex, etc. These data can be used by the robot agent to recognize the current contextual situation according to which is the most probable state of the environment and of the user. Then, it is possible to infer which are the probable beliefs of the agent about the user and the environment situation. These beliefs are used to trigger the most probable goals, related to the task that the robot has to perform in the environment, and to the social and affective attitudes that the robot has to show in order to answer appropriately to the recognized situation.

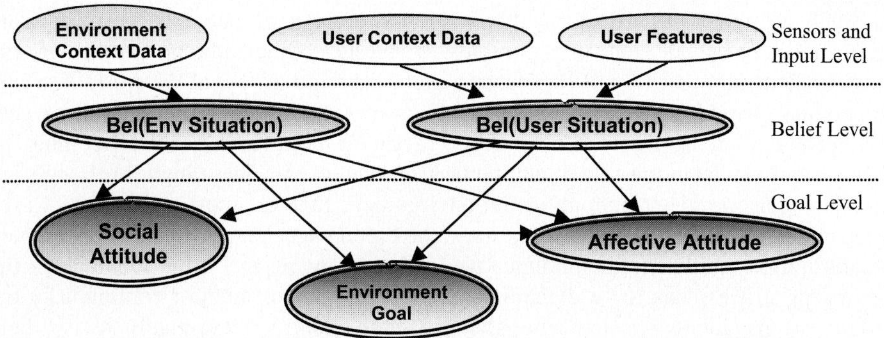

Fig. 2. Abstract BN Model for triggering high level environment goals

In our model, in order to keep some generality at this reasoning level, we adopted a nested approach to BN structuring. The root nodes of the network can be simple variables or can represent the result, in terms of probability distribution, of another BN that allows to reason on that particular context factor.

3.2   Deciding the Most Appropriate Plan to Execute

Triggered goals have to be actuated through plans of actions. When more than one action is possible in the current context, the robot has to decide which one to execute by considering its utility. Then, according to the set of possible actions that allow satisfying that goal, the robot selects the ones having a higher utility in the current context. Therefore, at a lower level, the decisional behaviour is modelled as a simplified probabilistic planning process. In the proposed approach, we use principles of decision theoretic planning for computing the expected utilities of plans and choose the plan candidate with maximal expected utility giving the evidences or probabilities outcomes of the variables as computed by the goal triggering BN.

In particular given a ***plan P*** in the plan library associated to an intended ***goal G*** it is represented as a sequence of actions. Each ***action A_i*** in P consists in a set of preconditions and effects. Effects can be non-deterministic. The likelihood of preconditions and effects is represented by probability values. Those related to preconditions come from the probability values related to nodes in the high-level BN, while those related to effects have been computed empirically by gathering experimental data in the selected domain, as well as the values of the utility of each action in the plan. Since our agent uses plan recipes, we use a hierarchical conditional approach to their representation. In particular, actions A_i in a plan ***P*** can be primitive, and they can be directly executed by the agent through its effectors, or complex. Complex action can be further decomposed in a sequence of primitive or complex sub-actions. Obviously, if a node in the plan can be decomposed in multiple ways it is important to consider the outcome of each path of actions in order to select the most appropriate one. Then, the expected utility of a plan can be computed by considering the utility of all the actions that maximize the global outcome. Each action operator of the domain is represented as follows:

```
Name: A;

Precond_list: ∀ pc precondition of A we denote with Precond(A,
pc, prob)  the  probability  of  that  precondition  pc  in  the
current context;

Effect_list: ∀ e effect of A we indicate with
      Effect_Prob(A, e, prob) the probability that an action A
      have that effect in the current contex,
      Effect_SocUtil(A, e, su) its expected social utility
      Effect_TaskUtil(A, e, tu) its expected utility in achieving
      the environment goal form the task point of view.
```

The following is the procedure that the robot agent applies to calculate which is the best action sequence for maximizing the expected outcome.

Given a goal G_i and a conditional plan P_i that formalizes a recipe for achieving that that goal, according to [8], we denote with E the evidence deriving by the observation of the world, or by the value of a variable in the BN after the propagation of the evidences characterizing the world, that influence a precondition of an action A.

In this case, (1) computes the probability of the action A in the plan P_i to contribute at achieving successfully the goal G_i through its effects.

$$P(A|E)= \prod_{x \in \Pr econd(A)} P(x \mid E) \times Effect\_\Pr ob(A) \tag{1}$$

Given the probability of each action A_j in the plan P_i, we can compute the expected utility of the plan P_i according to (2), where ***Utility(A_j)*** represents the utility value of the effect of an action in the plan. In our case we can compute the social utility or the task utility values or we can consider the sum of both values as expected utility.

$$EU(Pi|E)= \sum_{j=1...k} (P(Aj \mid E) \times Utility(Aj)) \tag{2}$$

4   Testing the Approach

In order to test our approach we collect data useful for building the BN model and the plan recipes we conducted a study based on the interview technique. The experiment setting corresponded to the scenario described in the Introduction.

We interviewed six people responsible for as many research laboratories asking them questions aiming at detecting which factors were influencing the behaviour of the responsible of the laboratory in terms of: a) environment context; b) user features and category; c) types of user's requests; d) types of user's behaviours. On the other hand, we asked to the interviewed subjects to describe their behaviours in relation to possible combinations of the factors mentioned above.

The data collected as answers to these questionnaire were used as a training dataset for learning the model described in Figure 3, which represents the goal-triggering model in the described domain. In particular, context nodes are used to compute the probability distributions relative to the agent's beliefs on the user situation (Bel(User_Sit)),   on his/her   intentions   in   entering   in   the   laboratory (Bel(User_Intention)), on the current situation of the laboratory (Bel(Lab_Sit)) and on the availability of the requested resource. This is a nested node whose probability distribution is derived by another BN that infers which is the most probable situation

810   B. De Carolis and G. Cozzolongo

of the laboratory taking into account the devices and people situation in the
laboratory. Moreover, from the results of the data collection study, we discovered that
the user attitude (Bel(User_Attitude)) had an influence on the social behaviour of the
responsible of the laboratory. This node is also a nested node, whose probability
values change according to the result of another model, described in [2].

According to the current beliefs, high level environment goals are inferred,
together with the social and affective attitude that are most appropriate to the
situation. For instance, let's suppose that the smart environment detects, through its
and the robot's sensors, the presence of an unknown student that with a quite
unfriendly attitude browse into the laboratory without asking anything or without
talking to anybody else present in the laboratory.

As evident from the probability values of the BN in Figure 3, the robot will infer
that, since the user is unknown to people in the laboratory that in that moment is quite
busy, probably his/her intention is to use the laboratory devices without permission or
to look for someone that is usually present in the laboratory or to talk to the
responsible in order, for instance, to ask for a permission.

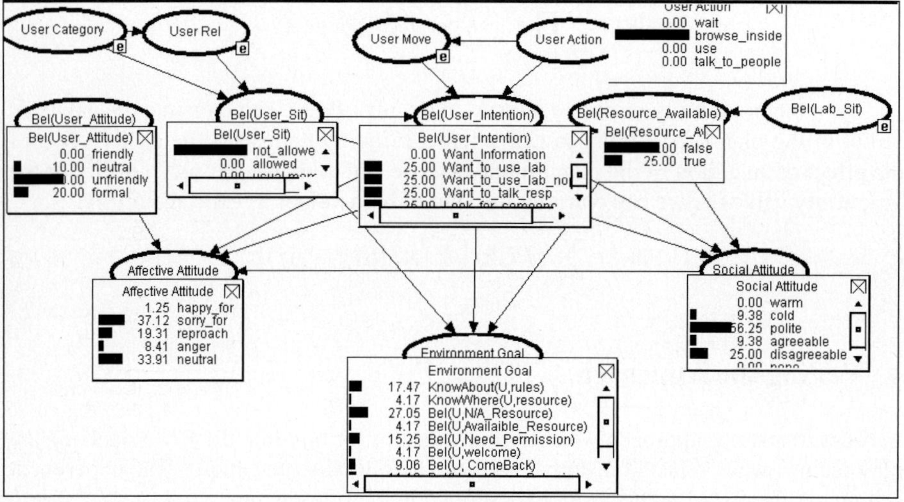

Fig. 3. BN formalizing goal triggering for AIBO acting as responsible of a research laboratory

In this case, the most probable goals that the robot has to achieve in order to
imitate the behaviour of the human responsible will be: to show information about the
laboratory rules (16%), to make the user understand the fact that the resources in the
laboratory are not available (24%) and to dismiss the student (10%).

On the basis of the triggered goals and in relation to their probability, the robot
agent mind has to evaluate the utility of achieving the goal through a certain sequence
of actions instead of another. In fact, a table look-up containing the relation among
intended goals and conditional plan recipes aiming at achieving those goals will be
consulted. Then, the agent will calculate the expected utility of all paths of actions
present in the plans that allows achieving the selected high-level goal and will execute
the one with the higher utility in the current context.

Now, taking into account the scenario introduced previously in this Section and the probabilities values coming from the BN illustrated in Figure 3 we can compute the Expected Social Utility (ESU) and the Expected Task Utility (ETU) of each sequence of actions in the conditional plan in Figure 4 leading at the expected outcome (Bel(U,N/A_Resource)). In particular by applying (1) we have:

P(A1|E)=0.1875 , P(A2|E)=0.3, P(A3|E)=0.33, P(A4|E)=0.37 and so on…

and by applying (2) we have:

ESU(P1.1[A1,A2,A3])=4,85 and ETU(P1.1[A1,A2,A3])= 4,45
ESU(P1.2[A4])=0 and ETU(P1.2[A4])= 3,7

and so on.

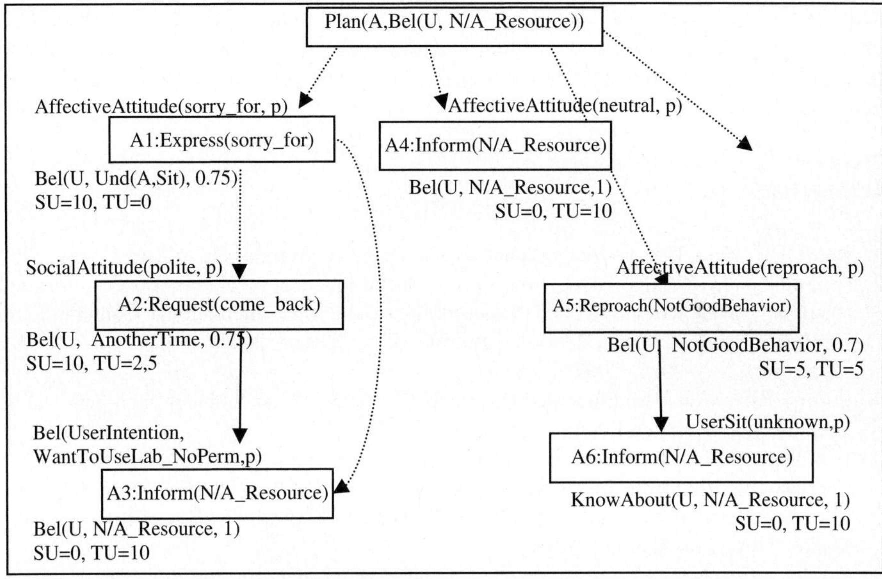

Fig. 4. A conditional plan recipe with effects probabilities and utilities

Therefore according to the weight we want to give to the social part of the interaction or to the task accomplishment we can select the more appropriate path. Since several studies proven that robots acceptance in interacting with humans is higher when they show and establish a social relation with people [9][10] we decided to take into account the social utility of a plan of actions by giving the same weight to both components (ESU and ETU). In this case, the plan of actions that seems to be the most appropriate according to the situation consists in executing A1 (the robot shows to be sorry for the situation), A2 (it asks to the student to come back later) and A3 (it informs the student that the laboratory is quite busy and the resources are not available). The plan will be then executed by Aibo by performing a sequence of informative and expressive actions.

5 Conclusions and Future Work Directions

This paper has explored the potential of utilising a social robot as a smart environment majordomo. In this phase of the project we are focussing on developing the behaviour planner of this agent. In particular, it has been designed and implemented as a two-levels process. First, a Bayesian Network is used to model the triggering of the agent high-level goals. Then, based on the assumption that a rational agent should adopt a plan that maximizes the expected utility of its actions, we adopt a simple approach to planning that explicitly takes into account the utility of each action in the plan according to decision-theoretic approaches. In particular, the robot is able to plan and adapt its interactive behaviour not only from the service point of view but also to the type of social relation that typically exists between the human responsible of the laboratory and that type of user. From the first results, the approach seems sufficient for our practical application. In the future we need to deal with several open problems that concern mainly the dynamicity typical of this domain and the possibility to consider conflicts in computing a plan for satisfying social and task needs.

References

1. Reeves, B., Nass, C.: The Media Equation. Cambridge University Press, New York (1996)
2. Cozzolongo, G., De Carolis, B., Pizzutilo, S.: Social robots as mediators between users and smart environments. In: IUI '07. Proceedings of the 12th international Conference on intelligent User interfaces, Honolulu, Hawaii, USA, January 28 - 31, 2007, pp. 353–356. ACM Press, New York (2007)
3. Bartnek, C.: eMuu – An Embodied Emotional Character for the Ambient Intelligent Home, Technische Universiteit Eindhoven (2002)
4. von Wichert, G., Lawitzky, G.: Man-Machine Interaction for Robot Applications in Everyday Environments. In: ROMAN 2001. Proc of the IEEE Int. Workshop on Robot and Human Interaction 2001, Paris, Bordeaux, Frankreich, September 18-21, IEEE Computer Society Press, Los Alamitos (2001)
5. Rao, A., Georgeff, M.: BDI agents: from theory to practice. In: Proceedings of the International Conference on Multi-Agent Systems (1995)
6. Horvitz, E., Breese, J., Heckerman, D., Hovel, D., Rommelse, K.: The Lumi're Project: Bayesian User Modelling for Inferring the Goals and Needs of Software Users. In: AUAI. Proceedings of the Fourteenth Conference on Uncertainty in Arti.cial Intelligence, pp. 256–265. Morgan Kaufman, San Francisco (1998)
7. Pearl, J.: Belief networks revisited. Artificial Intelligence 59, 49–56 (1993)
8. Mao, W., Gratch, J.: A Utility-Based Approach to Intention Recognition. In: Proceedings of the AAMAS 2004 Workshop on Agent Tracking: Modeling Other Agents from Observations (July 2004)
9. Bickmore, T.W., Picard, R.: Establishing and maintaining long-term human-computer relationships. Transactions on Computer-Human Interaction (2004)
10. Dautenhahn, K.: Robots as social actors: Aurora and the case of autism. In: Proc. CT99, The Third International Cognitive Technology Conference, San Francisco, August, pp. 359–374 (1999)

Enhancing Comprehension of Ontologies and Conceptual Models Through Abstractions

C. Maria Keet

Faculty of Computer Science, Free University of Bozen-Bolzano, Italy
`keet@inf.unibz.it`

Abstract. In addition to the Database Comprehension Problem, where diagrammatic conceptual data models are too large for a modeller or domain expert to comprehend or manage, an Ontology Comprehension Problem is emerging. Formal ontologies are, however, more amenable to automated abstractions to improve understandability. Three ways of abstraction are defined with 11 abstraction functions that use foundational ontology categories. Usability of the abstraction functions is enhanced by associating the functions with a basic framework of levels and abstraction hierarchy, thereby facilitating querying and visualizing ontologies.

1   Introduction

Information systems are rapidly increasing in size and complexity. This is caused by, among others, database integration through global schemas (integrated conceptual models) or large ontologies, such as [23,24,25], resulting from company mergers or the desire to link scientific databases on the Internet. Moreover, within the scope of the Semantic Web, large formal ontologies are being developed mainly by domain experts who often have not had any training in logics and therefore rely on more convenient GUIs as interface to the logical theories, such as the diagrammatic renderings with OntoViz and GrOWL. While this makes ontology development more accessible to domain experts, it has the major drawbacks that large diagrammatic logical theories do not fit onto one computer screen or printable figure and the GUIs are poor in ontology browsing and querying options, thereby making the full contents of the ontology difficult to comprehend; hence, in addition to the Database Comprehension Problem [2,8,9,19], there is an analogous Ontology Comprehension Problem. Compared to most conceptual data models, ontologies have at runtime a formal underpinning integrated with it, which therefore makes it easier to develop solutions for managing user interaction with those ontologies. An obvious solution is to avail of abstractions as mechanism to go from finer to coarser-grained information to avoid detailed representations that are not of interest for the user who *chooses to ignore* undesired aspects whilst maintaining both levels of detail in the background in the system (see also [20] and references therein). Extant proposals for abstractions differ along three dimensions: language to which it is applied, methodology, and semantics of what one does when abstracting. Concerning the latter, we identify

R. Basili and M.T. Pazienza (Eds.): AI*IA 2007, LNAI 4733, pp. 813–821, 2007.

three distinct ways of performing abstraction, which propagates to the types of abstraction functions needed to manage ontologies and conceptual data models. In addition, we use foundational ontological categories to type the functions, thereby facilitating consistent implementation and reusability. Third, we introduce more precisely the notion of abstraction level and abstraction hierarchy as an additional framework, which eases computation in particular regarding querying that can be executed as pre-processing step for visualisation of sections of ontologies. Section 2 contains a summary of extant approaches of abstraction and section 3 contains the main solutions we propose. We conclude in §4.

2   Related Works

A range of approaches to abstractions are described by [2,5,9,19]. The earlier works on theories of abstraction differ along three dimensions—language, axioms, and rules—and, as summarised by [5], concern topics such as abstraction for planning, reduction of search, and logical theories; we are interested in the latter. [2,9,19] provide overviews that focus on abstractions for conceptual models and ontologies, which are logical theories that have essential graphical 'syntactic sugar' for improved usability from the perspective of the domain expert. We illustrate main issues with extant approaches.

Manual abstraction is used for UML modularisation, EER clustering and 'abstraction hierarchies', *e.g.*, [8,13,19,21,27], that have the drawbacks that it is a laborious, intuitive, not scalable, and *ad hoc* method. Concerning methodology for abstractions, [2] introduced heuristics to simplify large ORM conceptual models, but they are tailored to ORM only and thus not directly applicable to other knowledge representation languages [9]. Limited syntax-focused formalisation of abstraction using Local Model Semantics of context reasoning is proposed by [4], which address taxonomic generalisation (subsumption), which concurs with [3,22,16]. This, however, ignores a crucial aspect of collapsing sub-processes into a grander process and overloads their *abs* function, thereby in itself abstracting away the finer details of the process of abstraction. Syntax abstraction augmented with semantics was investigated by [14,16], extending [6,7]. [14] addresses the important notion of "folding" formally: *e.g.*, for a biology domain, the catalytic reactions and proteins involved in the **Second messenger system** collapse into that one entity type, and **Cell** contains (modular) subsystems (*e.g.*, [18]). The approaches can be structured according to topic and implementation foci and the nature of the abstraction operations (see [9]). These solutions exhibit three main problems: abstraction focuses only on the contents of a level, thereby lacking a surrounding *framework*; a general abstraction function *abs* does neither reveal *what* it is abstracting nor *how*; extant proposed solutions are mainly theoretical and not developed for or assessed on its potential for reusability and scalability. In the next section, we introduce a basic framework, three types of abstraction, and abstraction functions for both basic and complex folding operations, respectively, so that abstractions become scalable, are unambiguous to implement, and amenable to automation.

3   Abstractions

The various abstractions have different purposes at the conceptual level, regardless implementation issues. What is abstracted away depends on multiple factors; we focus on the type of abstraction, the procedure of (consecutive steps of) abstraction, and on what type of representation/model the abstraction is performed. The types are depicted in Fig.1, and they are defined as follows.

Definition 1 (R-abs). *An abstraction is an* R-ABS *iff the more-detailed type ϕ abstracts into its related parent type ψ.*

Definition 2 (F-abs). *An abstraction is a* F-ABS *iff a more-detailed theory T_0 (with $\phi_1...\phi_n$ entity types, relations, and constraints among them) abstracts into a single related parent type ψ in T_1 that is distinct from any ϕ_i.*

Definition 3 (D-abs). *An abstraction is a* D-ABS *iff a more-detailed theory T_0 with $\phi_1...\phi_n$ entity types, relations, and constraints abstracts into theory T_1 with $\phi'_1...\phi'_m$ entity types, relations, and constraints, and $m < n$ through deletion of elements either from T_0 to obtain T_1 or from T_0's user interface.*

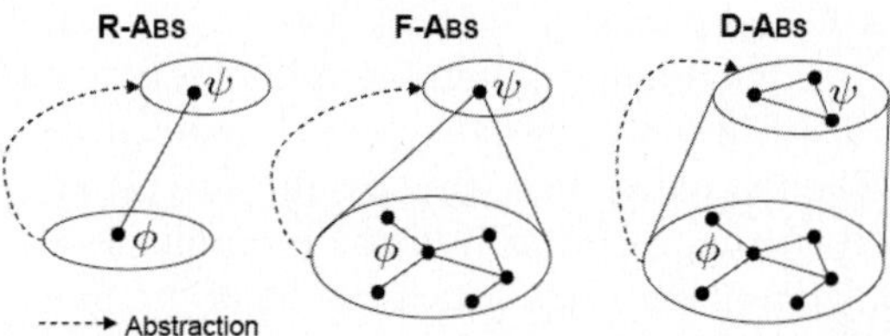

Fig. 1. Three conceptually distinct kinds of abstraction operations. R-ABS: the relation is remodelled as a function; F-ABS: folding multiple entities and relations into a different type of entity; D-ABS: hiding or deleting semantically less relevant entities and relations.

[4,5,7,9,16] mention 'levels' of abstraction, depicted in Fig.1 with the ovals, but to the best of our knowledge, the notion of level has not been specified and used specifically for abstractions. To be able to manage better both the abstraction functions and complex base- & simple theory resulting from an abstraction, we define an abstraction level as follows.

Definition 4 (Abstraction level). *Given a base theory T_0 and a simpler theory T_1 into which T_0 is abstracted, an abstraction level, denoted with λ_i, is the surrounding frame that contains T_i, which form a tuple $\langle \Lambda, \mathcal{T} \rangle$, where $\lambda_i \in \Lambda$ and $T_i \in \mathcal{T}$, and $\lambda_0 \preceq \lambda_1$.*

Observe that for any logical theory T_i (*i.e.*, ontology or conceptual data model), obviously the individual entity types, relations, and constraints are in T_i's level of abstraction λ_i and considered to be accessible for abstraction individually as well. To put levels to use, we need a function to retrieve the level where a theory or its entity types reside, *labs* : $\mathcal{T} \rightarrow \Lambda$, which is analogous to such functions for granularity [11]; *e.g.*, $labs(T_1) = \lambda_1$ (with $\lambda_1 \in \Lambda$), which thus also holds for any type in T_1 (if $\phi_1 \in T_1$ then $labs(\phi_1) = \lambda_1$). Last, to improve abstraction functions as introduced in [4,14] and make a significant step toward their usability for ontologies, we will avail of several ontological categories from DOLCE foundational ontology [15]. DOLCE has an OWL version—the ontology language for the Semantic Web—, is comprehensive and used across subject domains (see for an overview: http://www.loa-cnr.it/DOLCE.html). In particular, we will use DOLCE's endurant ED for entity types (OWL classes), perdurant PD, and PT for particular as top-type that subsumes any other type (`owl:Thing` in OWL). With these preliminaries, we can proceed to the abstraction functions.

3.1 Basic and Compound Abstraction Functions

The basic abstractions for R-ABS, (1-5), are listed in Table 1. They are straightforward relation-turned-into-function along a hierarchy in the formal ontology or conceptual data model, with the two distinctions that functions (1-5) are typed with ontological categories and have additional constraints to relate the entity types to their abstraction level. The functions conform to the main relations in the OBO Relation Ontology for bio-ontologies and the latest results on types of part-whole relations [10,17]. Note that abstraction for spatial containment (4) refers to both the type and region it occupies [10], and an addiitonal abstraction function for *proper* parthood may be useful for bio-ontologies; that is, an abs_{ppo}: $PT \rightarrow PT$ where $abs_{ppo}(\phi) = \psi$, $ppart\_of(\phi, \psi)$, $labs(\phi) = \lambda_i$, $labs(\psi) = \lambda_j$, and $\lambda_i \prec \lambda_j$ hold. The basic functions are trivially extensible for other ontological categories and recurring relations in domain ontologies even if one were to use a different foundational ontology, which can be of use in an implementation. Considering DOLCE foundational ontology [15], several examples are given to illustrate some of the possibilities to refine the *abs* functions further.

Example. i) Refinement of *abs* with EDs: Abstract non-agentive physical objects ($NAPO$) or amounts of matter (M) into amounts of matter (M), using (sub-)quantities; *e.g.*, **Air** and its M-part **Oxygen** or its $NAPO$-parts the types of molecule such as O_2 and CO_2. Abstracting social agents (SAGs) like citizens into society (SC), locusts into swarm, and so forth for entities denoted with collective nouns and their members. ii) Refinement with PDs: Mapping processes (PRO) into one event (EV), *e.g.*, **Running** into **Marathon.**   ◇

The last basic operation, abs_{d1}, covers one of the two functions for D-ABS, where some type is deleted, which is primarily applicable to conceptual data models; thus, $\phi \in T_0$, $\phi \notin T_1$, with $labs(T_0) = \lambda_0$, $labs(T_1) = \lambda_1$, $\lambda_0 \prec \lambda_1$, and $T_1 \subset T_0$. Note that when an attribute that is the sufficient condition of ϕ is removed, then the deletion implies $\phi \subset \varphi$, hence a taxonomic abstraction (abs_{isa}).

With these basic abstraction functions, we have covered the most widely used relations to construct hierarchies in 'simple' formal ontologies. Compound abstractions are required to manage comprehension and visualisation of complex formal ontologies and to enable abstractions for formal conceptual data models. The compound abstractions address F-ABS and D-ABS, folding two entities or types in λ_i into a simpler entity or type in λ_j where $\lambda_i \prec \lambda_j$. They are

Table 1. List of basic and compound abstraction functions

	Abstraction	Constraints; comment
(1)	$\mathrm{abs}_{isa} : PT \to PT$	$\mathrm{abs}_{isa}(\phi) = \psi$, $\phi \subseteq \psi$, $labs(\phi) = \lambda_i$, $labs(\psi) = \lambda_j$, $\lambda_i \prec \lambda_j$; sub-supertype (class) abstraction
(2)	$\mathrm{abs}_{po} : PT \to PT$	as (1), but $part\_of(\phi, \psi)$; part into its whole
(3)	$\mathrm{abs}_{in} : PD \to PD$	as in (1), but $involved\_in(\phi, \psi)$; Abstract a part-process into the whole-process
(4)	$\mathrm{abs}_{ci} : ED \to ED$	as in (1), but $contained\_in(\phi, \psi)$; Abstract a smaller contained type into larger type
(5)	$\mathrm{abs}_{pi} : ED \to PD$	as in (1), but $participates\_in(\phi, \psi)$; Abstract an endurant into a perdurant
(6)	$\mathrm{abs}_{d1} : PT \to \emptyset$	$labs(\phi) = \lambda_i$, $\lambda_i \prec \lambda_j$; Abstract a type into 'nothing', deleting it from the theory
(7)	$\mathrm{abs}_{p1} : ED \times ED \to ED$	$\mathrm{abs}_{p1}(\phi, \psi) = \varphi$, where $labs(\phi) = \lambda_i$, $labs(\psi) = \lambda_i$, $labs(\varphi) = \lambda_j$, and $\lambda_i \prec \lambda_j$. Abstract two endurants into another endurant
(8)	$\mathrm{abs}_{p2} : PD \times PD \to PD$	as in (7); Abstract two perdurants into a perdurant
(9)	$\mathrm{abs}_{p3} : ED \times PD \to ED$	as in (7); Abstract an endurant and a perdurant into an endurant
(10)	$\mathrm{abs}_{p4} : ED \times PD \to PD$	as in (7); Abstract an endurant and a perdurant into a perdurant
(11)	$\mathrm{abs}_{d2} : ED \times Q \to ED$	as in (7), but $\lambda_i \preceq \lambda_j$, $\phi = \varphi$; Remove an attribute

summarised in Table 1, (7-11). $abs_{p1}(\phi, \psi) = \varphi$, has, *e.g.*, **Blood cell** (a $NAPO$) and **Plasma** (an M) as direct parts of **Blood** (an M). One could add more specific functions that satisfy (8), such as an abs'_{p2}: $PRO \times ST \to EV$ for abstracting **Running** and **Being thirsty** into **Marathon**. For F-ABS, we have (9) that combines perdurants and endurants into 'systems' that are endurants, such as **Second messenger system** that is composed of enzymes and catalysis processes, and (10) has its analogue with EER clustering and abstractions [8,19]; for example **Orders** in the fact type "Customer Orders Book", where the ordering process involves, a.o., **Billing**, **Paying**, **Supplier**, and **Shipment**. Both functions require a constraint, being that the input types have to be related to each other, ensuring that no two arbitrary types are folded, but ones that are related so that a connected subset of T_i is folded into a type in T_j, *i.e.*, upon firing abs_{p3} or $abs_{p4} \geq 1$ times for elements in T'_i, where $T'_i \subseteq T_i$, then T'_i is abstracted into φ where $\varphi \in T_j$.

Constraint 1 (folding). *For each ϕ, ψ where $abs_{p3}(\phi, \psi) = \varphi$ or $abs_{p4}(\phi, \psi) = \varphi$, $labs(\varphi) = \lambda_j$, there must be either i) a predicate p such that $p(\phi, \psi) \in T_i$ that is contained in λ_i or ii) $\phi = ED$, $\psi = p'$ and $\forall x(ED(x) \to \exists y(p'(x, y)))$ in T_i.*

Here, as with deletion (abs_{d1}), compositionality of the theory is i mportant, which is a desirable feature from a computational viewpoint [5,16]; from the perspective of a domain expert it is debatable, because some details in the logical theory really may be undesirable to develop tractable systems biology simulations and making ontologies usable for ontology-guided applications [18,24,25]. For F-ABS this can be effectively managed with the current abstraction functions in conjunction with the levels. φ in T_j (in λ_j) is not a 'new' entity, but can be represented as element in the encompassing theory T_Δ for the whole system that is the union of $T_0, ..., T_n$; hence, soundness and completeness can be preserved.

With the last main abstraction function, abs_{d2}, we address the remainder of D-ABS. Suppressing details from the interface to a logical theory can already be done through toggle features, which lets the user select displaying more or less relations, attributes, and so forth, like with the OntoViz plugin [26] for the Protégé ontology development tool. This can be formally defined with $abs_{d2}(\phi, \psi)$, where attribute ψ (a quality Q in DOLCE) folds away. But for (11), because nothing changes to the underlying theory, we have $labs(\varphi) = \lambda_j$, $\varphi = \phi$ and $T_i = T_j$ and $\lambda_i \preceq \lambda_j$. More functions can be defined for the other to-be-hidden elements analogous to abs_{d2}. A software developer may want to label the abstraction not φ but ϕ' as approximation for ϕ, thereby communicating to the user that incomplete information is shown in the GUI and that further exploration (up to the base theory T_i) is possible. This simple hiding breaks down with theories of over about 100 entity types, and may need to be augmented with a generalisation [9] of Campbell *et al.*'s [2] rules and their weights; a.o., hiding based on prioritization where, *e.g.*, existential quantification takes precedence over all other constraints, and identification is more important than a non-key attribute. Thus, for a large diagram—with logical theory in the background—one can find out what the *important* elements are. Reformulation of the rules, which are written by [2] as "if ϕ then keep it" instead of "if ϕ then abstract it away", is feasible; *e.g.*, "*Rule 3: [keep] non-leaf object types*" can be rewritten for parthood relations, where $\neg(part\_of = R)$, as "*Rule 3'*: if $part\_of(\phi, \psi) \wedge \neg R(\phi, \varphi)$, then $abs_{po}(\phi) = \psi$."; hence, the functions proposed here are compatible with [2,9] and are applicable also to other conceptual modelling languages and ontologies.

3.2 Abstraction Hierarchy

By using abstraction functions (1-11) and Definition 1 for abstraction level, one can create abstraction hierarchies. We define an abstraction hierarchy as follows.

Definition 5 (Abstraction hierarchy). *Let T be set of theories, $\mathcal{F}$ denote a set of abstraction functions, and Λ the set of levels obtained from using $abs_i \in \mathcal{F}$ on a theory $T_0 \in T$, then an* abstraction hierarchy $H \in \mathcal{H}$ *is the ordered sequence of levels $\lambda_0, ..., \lambda_n \in \Lambda$, with $n > 1$, obtained from firing $abs_i \geq 1$ times successively on $T_0, T_1, ..., T_{n-1}$ such that $\lambda_0 \preceq \lambda_1 .... \lambda_{n-1} \preceq \lambda_n$ and $labs(T_0) = \lambda_0 ... labs(T_n) = \lambda_n$ hold.*

For purposes of understandability on what the system does as well as ease of implementation, we have restricted the abstraction hierarchy to one that is obtained by firing only *one type of abstraction function* to create each hierarchy. This definition differs with the k-level abstraction hierarchy from Knoblock *et al.* [12], because they differ in both the scope and usage of abstraction: planning vs. improving comprehensibility of large formal ontologies and conceptual models.

3.3   Toward Implementation

Foundational aspects of abstraction generally suffer from the trade-off to make a workable implementation: theory is there to guide implementation but for various reasons, such as computational complexity, usability, and relative importance, is not always strictly adhered to. The basic abstraction functions for R-ABS, however, have straightforward mappings to recursive queries with an additional clause for the ontological category or type of relation. This is supported in, *e.g.*, ontology query languages such as XQuery and nRQL and database query languages SQL and StruQL for ontologies that are stored in a database like the FMA and GO [24,25]. The compound abstraction functions require engineering work in CASE tools in addition to the recent results by [19,27]. Regarding F-ABS abstractions and any combination thereof for stepwise more elaborate folding, they are useful for, *e.g.*, coordinated UML-like modularisation and the 'black box' software modules in biology and ecology [27,18]. Provided one uses a formal version of UML (*e.g.*, [1]), one can marry the functions with the UML-as-logical-theory, yet have user-friendly interfaces like provided with CASE tools such as Rational Rose. Such CASE tools also have UML packages, which can be reused as diagrammatic support for abstraction levels and the hierarchies constructed with them. With the indexing of abstraction levels, one can keep track of what is abstracted into what more easily, and let a user select (query), say, 3 levels more abstract in one go instead of step-wise clicking in the GUI. For instance, from **Hepatic Macrophage** (a type of cell) in λ_7 at once to the organ it is part of in λ_3 (which is the **Liver**), although behind the scene this involves recursively going up the abstraction hierarchy with firing abs_{po} 3 times.

4   Conclusions

Three conceptually distinct ways of abstraction were identified, consisting of remodelling a relation between finer- and coarser-grained entities as a function (R-ABS), folding multiple entities and relations into a different type of entity (F-ABS), and hiding or deleting less relevant entities and relations (D-ABS). Six basic and five complex abstraction functions were introduced, which use foundational ontological types for unambiguous specification and are easily extensible. Abstraction level and abstraction hierarchy were defined, thereby providing a means for consist use of the functions and quick cross-level navigation in applications. By having the abstraction functions at the conceptual level and their corresponding formalisation, it simplifies understanding, provides space for extensions with more abstraction functions, and makes them usable and reusable across implementations of formal ontologies and conceptual data models. Thereby abstraction is scalable and straightforward to implement as queries over the ontology or conceptual data model or methods in software applications. We are currently investigation in more detail the interplay between abstraction and granularity.

References

1. Berardi, D., Calvanese, D., De Giacomo, G.: Reasoning on UML class diagrams. AI 168(1-2), 70–118 (2005)
2. Campbell, L.J., Halpin, T.A., Proper, H.A.: Conceptual Schemas with Abstractions: Making flat conceptual schemas more comprehensible. DKE 20(1), 39–85 (1996)
3. Degtyarenko, K., Contrino, S.: COMe: the ontology of bioinorganic proteins. BMC Structural Biology 4(3) (2004)
4. Ghidini, C., Giunchiglia, F.: A semantics for abstraction. TR DIT-03-082, University of Trento, Italy (2003)
5. Giunchiglia, F., Villafiorita, A., Walsh, T.: Theories of abstraction. AI Communications 10(3-4), 167–176 (1997)
6. Giunchiglia, F., Walsh, T.: A theory of abstraction. AI 57(2-3), 323–389 (1992)
7. Hobbs, J.R.: Granularity. In: Proc. of IJCAI85, pp. 432–435 (1985)
8. Jaeschke, P., Oberweis, A., Stucky, W.: Extending ER Model Clustering by relationship clustering. In: Elmasri, R.A., Kouramajian, V., Thalheim, B. (eds.) ER 1993. LNCS, vol. 823, Springer, Heidelberg (1994)
9. Keet, C.M.: Using abstractions to facilitate management of large ORM models and ontologies. In: Meersman, R., Tari, Z., Herrero, P. (eds.) OTM 2005 Workshops. LNCS, vol. 3762, pp. 603–612. Springer, Heidelberg (2005)
10. Keet, C.M.: Part-whole relations in Object-Role Models. In: Meersman, R., Tari, Z., Herrero, P. (eds.) On the Move to Meaningful Internet Systems 2006: OTM 2006 Workshops. LNCS, vol. 4278, Springer, Heidelberg (2006)
11. Keet, C.M.: A taxonomy of types of granularity. In: IEEE Conference on Granular Computing (GrC2006), Atlanta, USA, vol. 1, pp. 106–111. IEEE Xplore (2006)
12. Knoblock, C.A., Tenenberg, J., Yang, Q.: Characterizing abstraction hierarchies for planning. In: Proc. of AAAI '91, pp. 692–697. AAAI Press, California, USA (1991)
13. Lind, M.: Making sense of the abstraction hierarchy. In: Cognitive Science Approaches to Process Control (CSAPC99), Villeneuve d'Ascq, France, September 21-24 (1999)
14. Mani, I.: A theory of granularity and its application to problems of polysemy and underspecification of meaning. In: Proc. of KR'98, pp. 245–255 (1998)
15. Masolo, C., Borgo, S., Gangemi, A., Guarino, N., Oltramari, A.: Ontology Library. WonderWeb Deliverable D18 1 (December 31, 2003)
16. Pandurang Nayak, P., Levy, A.Y.: A semantic theory of abstractions. In: Proc. of IJCAI'95, pp. 196–203. Morgan Kaufmann, San Mateo (1995)
17. Smith, B., Ceusters, W., Klagges, B., Köhler, J., Kumar, A., Lomax, J., et al.: Relations in biomedical ontologies. Genome Biology 6, R46 (2005)
18. Sontag, E.D.: Some new directions in control theory inspired by systems biology. Systems biology 1(1), 9–18 (2004)
19. Tavana, M., Joglekar, P., Redmond, M.A.: An automated entity-relationship clustering algorithm for conceptual database design. Information Systems (2007) (EPub ahead of print: 4-8-2006)
20. Tzitzikas, Y., Hainaut, J-L.: On the visualization of large-sized ontologies. In: Proc. of AVI2006, pp. 99–102 (2006)
21. Yu, X., Lau, E., Vicente, K.J., Carter, M.W.: Toward theory-driven, quantitative performance measurement in ergonomics science: the abstraction hierarchy as a framework for data analysis. Th. Issues in Ergonomics Sci. 3(2), 124–142 (2002)

22. Zhang, J., Silvescu, A., Honavar, V.: Ontology-Driven Induction of Decision Trees at Multiple Levels of Abstraction. TR ISU-CS-TR 02-13, Iowa State University (2002)
23. Cell Cycle Ontology, http://www.cellcycleontology.org
24. Foundational Model of Anatomy.
    http://fme.biostr.washington.edu:8089/FME/index.html
    FMA-lite. http://obo.sourceforge.net/cgi-bin/detail.cgi?fma_lite
25. Gene Ontology & GO-slim, http://www.geneontology.org/GO.slims.shtml
26. OntoViz, http://protege.cim3.net/cgi-bin/wiki.pl?OntoViz
27. SemTalk, Semtation. http://www.semtalk.com

Recognizing Chinese Proper Nouns with Transformation-Based Learning and Ontology

Peifeng Li, Qiaoming Zhu, and Lei Wang

School of Computer Science & Technology, Soochow University, Suzhou, 215006, China
{pfli,qmzhu,lwang}@suda.edu.cn

Abstract. This paper proposes an approach based on the Ontology and transformation-based error-driven learning (TBL) to recognize Chinese proper nouns. Firstly, our approach redefines the label set and tags Chinese words according to the usage of proper nouns and their context, and then it extracts Characteristic Information (CI) of the proper noun from the text and merges them based on the Ontology. Secondly, it tags the training corpus following the new definition of Multi-dimension Attribute Points (MAP), and then extracts rules using the TBL approach. Finally, it recognizes proper nouns by utilizing the rule set and Ontology. The experimental results in our open test show that the precision is 92.5% and the recall is 86.3%.

Keywords: Chinese proper nouns recognition; TBL; MAP; rule.

1 Introduction and Methodology

Chinese Proper Nouns (PN) includes Chinese person name, translated person name, location name, organization name, etc. The approaches used to recognize Chinese PN include the rule-based, the statistic-based approach and the hybrid approach which combining above two ones. Currently popular statistic-based models include HMM [1], cascaded HMM [2], SVM [3], ME [4], etc. Otherwise, as for the rule-based and hybrid approach, Tan [5] computed the certainty degree to recognize place name. Li [6] used boundary templates to recognize person name. Lv [7] used dynamic programming searching the best path to recognize the person name, location name and organization name, etc.

Our research focuses on how to extract rules from the training set automatically and how to improve the quality of rules to achieve higher precision and recall. From our research, we found out that the context of PN and Characteristic Words (CW, defined in section 2.1) in PN were the most important information for Chinese PN recognition. We called them as Characteristic Information (CI, defined in section 2.1).

Current approaches still have many limitations to use that CI set. Firstly, they usually extract PN following "Single Point Activation" principle, which means they just select the string as the candidate PN while there are characteristic words in that string. Therefore, sometimes the proper noun without the distinct characteristic words in it would be ignored. Secondly, some approaches just recognize PN from fragments after word segmentation. So they can't recognize those PN when a part of them also is

R. Basili and M.T. Pazienza (Eds.): AI*IA 2007, LNAI 4733, pp. 822–830, 2007.

a word, or the boundary character of PN and its previous or following character/word can form a word. Those limitations will cause the recall decreased by about 10% [8]. Furthermore, rule and statistic models are almost all come from experiences and experiments, so building those models are expensive and time-consuming.

Therefore, we consider that a rule-based approach with a machine learning method to extract rules based on CI automatically is an appropriate way to solve above problems. This paper proposes an approach based on TBL and Ontology to recognize Chinese PN. Our approach extracts the CI set and then tags the training corpus following the definition of MAP (defined in section 3). Then it learns rules automatically from the Basic PN String (BPNS, defined in section 2.1) using TBL. Finally, it recognizes PN from the text using the rule set and reasons in the Ontology. In a word, our approach is illustrated as Figure 1.

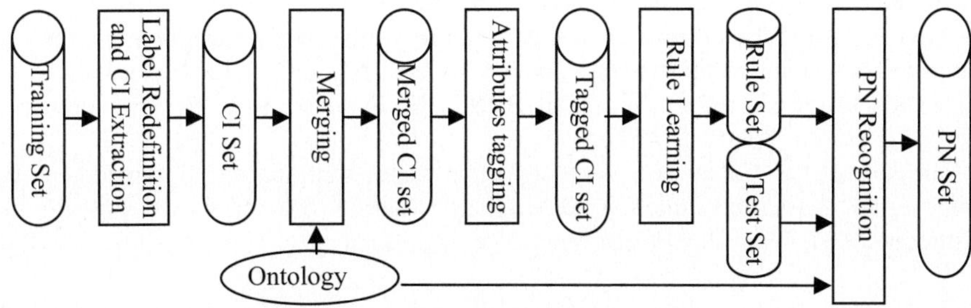

Fig. 1. The process of Chinese PN recognition

2 Extracting Characteristic Information

Our training set is a Chinese news corpus with 6,060,060 words from the People's Daily (Jan. 1 – May 31, 1998). The number of PN is 369,980, about 6% in that corpus and the basic approach we used to extract CI is the instance-based learning.

Table 1. A part of redefined labels

Labels	Significance	Examples
CW	Characteristic words have two types: PCW (CW at the beginning of PN) and SCW (CW at the end of PN).	苏州市（**Suzhou City**）　北京电视台 **(Beijing TV) 王蕾 (Wang Lei)**
FW	Filling Word in PN	苏州市　北京电视台　王蕾
NB	Neighboring words in front of PN	对苏州市来说(As For **Suzhou City**)
NF	Neighboring words following PN	王蕾说 （**Wang Lei** said）
CO	Conjunction in PN	学生和学者联谊会 (The Association of Student and Scholar)
WI	Word formed by its neighbor and head or tail of PN	我对于平说 （I told **Yu Ping**） "told Yu" in Chinese forms the word "toward"

The original label set in the tagged news corpus can't be used to extract CI, so we redefined a new label set and a part of them is showed as Table 1. The bold strings are PN and the underline strings are samples of label.

The PN consists of PrePN and SufPN, and is defined as follows:

Definition 1. <PN>={<PrePN> | <SufPN>}
     <PrePN>=<PCW> <FW>
     <SufPN>=<FW> <SCW>

Definition 2. BPNS (Basic PN String): BPNS is a string including PN and its context, and defined as follow:
     <BPNS>= {<NB><PN><NF> | <NB><PN> | <PN><NF>| <PN><CO><PN>}

Definition 3. Characteristic Information (CI): CI is the characteristic to recognize PN and it consists of CW, NB, NF, CO, WI, FW, etc.

After we re-tag the original corpus with the new label set, we can obtain a PNS set with new labels and them we can extract CW, NB, NF, CO and FW easily from the BPNS set following the definition of BPNS. As for extracting WI, the comparing method is used to build the WI set.

The size of the CI set is a very important factor that should be considered. We propose an evaluation function to evaluate whether one of CI is valuable for extracting rules. The value of that function C_i is defined as:

$$C_i = fr_i / fa_i \tag{1}$$

where fa_i is the total number that a string s_i appears in the corpus and fr_i is the total number that s_i is tagged as CI.

Giving a threshold C_f, we delete those CI whose C_i is less than C_f. So most useless CI with low frequency are filtered. We set 0.01 to C_f from our experiments so that the CI set could cover 99.2% BPNS in the training set.

Another way to reduce the size of CI set is to merge the similar CI based on merging rules and Ontology. After the merging work based on rules, we could get some combining BPNS, such as <NB><PN$_1$|PN$_2$|PN$_3$……>, <NB> <FW$_1$|FW$_2$| FW$_3$……><SCW>, etc. We also have built a language Ontology [9] to represent the hierarchical relation of words and Figure 1 shows a sample of that Ontology.

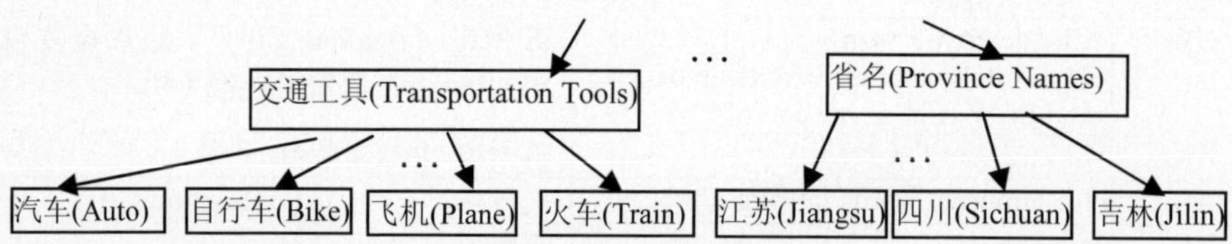

Fig. 2. A sample of the Ontology

Based on that Ontology, we can categorize some words to a class and use its super class to replace them. For example, there are three BPNS as follows:

在(At)/NB江苏*(Jiangsu)*/FW立达*(Lida)*/FW自行车*(Bike)*/FW厂*(Factory)*/SCW
在(At)/NB吉林*(Jilin)*/FW|第一*(No. 1)*/FW飞机*(Plane)*/FW厂*(Factory)*/SCW
在(At)/NB四川*(Sichuan)*/FW文三*(Wensan)*/FW汽车*(Auto)*/FW厂*(Factory)*/SCW

Those BPNS can be merged to "在/NB <省名>/FW <立达|第一|文三>/FW <交通工具>/FW 厂/SCW" while those words with underline are merged. Obviously that combined BPNS can be more general than above three ones. If there are 50 province names and 500 transportation tools, we can deduce 50*500=25,000 new BPNS instances from that BPNS.

3 Tagging Attributes

The original attribute tagging method provided by Eric Brill [10] is based on each single word, so each word is a one-dimension attribute point. We propose a novel conception - MAP which is based on multiple points and tags all attributes simultaneously. Our method doesn't compose all adjacent points to a legal attribute point, but composes them just when those points could form a PN.

Definition 4. Multi-dimension Attribute Points (MAP): MAP is a vector that points out the place of NB, PN, NF, etc in the BPNS. It is defined as:

$$MAP= (P_1, P_2, P_3) \mid (P_1, P_2)$$

where P_i ($1{\leq}i{\leq}3$) is the word position in the BPNS, and the relation between BPNS and MAP is showed in Table 2.

Table 2. The relation between the BPNS and MAP

BPNS Type	P_1	P_2	P_3
<NB><PN><NF>	The position of NB	The position of PN	The position of NF
<NB><PN>	The position of NB	The position of PN	NULL
<PN><NF>	The position of PN	The position of NF	NULL
<PN$_1$><CO><PN$_2$>	The position of PN$_1$	The position of CO	The position of PN$_2$

Definition 5. MAP relation

For any two $MAP=(P_1, P_2, P_3) \mid (P_1, P_2)$ and $MAP'=(P_1{'}, P_2{'}, P_3{'}) \mid (P_1{'}, P_2{'})$,

If $(P_1{>}P_1{'})$ or $(P_1{=}P_1{'}$ and $P_2{>}P_2{'})$ or $(P_1{=}P_1{'}$ and $P_2{=}P_2{'}$ and $P_3{>}P_3{'})$ Then $MAP{>}MAP'$, which means the size of MAP is bigger than that of MAP';

If $(P_1{=}P_1{'})$ and $(P_2{=}P_2{'})$ and $(P_3{=}P_3{'})$ then $MAP{=}MAP'$;

If $(P_1{<}P_1{'})$ or $(P_1{=}P_1{'}$ and $P_2{<}P_2{'})$ or $(P_1{=}P_1{'}$ and $P_2{=}P_2{'}$ and $P_3{<}P_3{'})$ then $MAP{<}MAP'$.

We tag attribute on words using the enumerative tagging method which extracts all MAP from the text and then tags them with the ascending order of the size of MAP.

We assume a sentence s is denoted as $W_1W_2...W_n$, and for each word $W_i(1\leq i\leq n)$ in s,

(1) If $W_i \in CI$, then it seeks the legal MAP beginning at W_i; if not, it picks up the next word and re-executes this step;

(2) If $W_i \in NB$ or $W_i \in PCW$, it seeks the MAP from left to right in the sentence; If $W_i \in NF$ or $W_i \in SCW$, it seeks the MAP from right to left;

(3) If the legal MAP is not found, it picks up the next word and go to step (1);

(4) The found MAP is tagged. If it has not only one attribute, the attribute with the highest frequency is selected;

(5) If there is FW in BPNS, it uses the following method to tag FW:
    If that BPNS is <NB><PN><NF> or <NB><FW><CW> or <CW><FW><NF>, then the word in the middle of the MAP is FW;
    If that BPNS is <NB><CW><FW>, then the fragment following the CW is FW;
    If that BPNS is <FW><CW><NF>, then the fragment in front of the CW is FW.

(6) If there is WI in BPNS, which means a segmentation error is occurred during the word segmentation. Firstly that WI should be divided into two parts: the boundary word of PN and other part of the NB or NF. If there is a legal MAP, it segments that WI and tags the found MAP.

4 Rule Learning

TBL [10] is one of the most successful rule-based machine learning algorithms and we introduce the following rule system into our approach [11].

Definition 6. <Rule Set>=<Rule Chunk> [<Rule Chunk>]
              <Rule Chunk>=<Transform Rule> [<Transform Rule>]
              <Transform Rule>=<Trigger Condition> <Transform Action>
              <Trigger Condition>=<Test Item> [<Test Item>]
              <Transform Action>=<To modify the current tags>

In the definition 6, a rule set contains many rule chunks, and each rule chunk is a set of transform rules for one special BPNS in which CI are used to identify such rule chunk. Each transform rule has two factors: the trigger condition and the transform action. The trigger condition is a set of CI for a special BPNS while the transform action is the action to modify BPNS's labels.

Definition 7. Transform Actions

  A-0: It modifies current label to invalid one according to the trigger condition;
  A-1: It affirms current label valid according to the trigger condition.

Following that definition, the transform action of Positive Rule (rules indicate the existence of PN) is A-1 while that of the Negative Rule (rules indicate inexistence of PN) is A-0 and they come from trigger environment defined as Table 3.

  The purpose of building such trigger environment is to mine more general rules based on CW. The trigger conditions are extracted from trigger environment and the number of them is 92, so there are 184 transform rules that can be used in the rule set.

Table 3. The definition of trigger environment

BPNS Type	PS1	PS2	PS3	PS4
<NB><PN><NF>	word in front of NB	word following NB	word in front of NF	word following NB
<NB><PN>	word in front of NB	NB	word in front of CW	—————
<PN><NF>	word in front of CW	NF	word following NB	—————
<PrePN$_1$><CO><PrePN$_2$>	word in front of CW in PrePN$_1$	word following CW in PrePN$_1$	word in front of CO	word CW in PrePN$_2$
<SufPN$_1$><CO><SufPN$_2$>	word CW in SufPN$_1$	word following CO	word in front of CW in SufPN$_2$	word following CW in SufPN$_2$

Our method to learn rules from each BPNS is based on TBL and Ontology.

The first stage is to tag MAP in the training set and then creates a tagged corpus. The tagging method is described in section 2.

The second stage mainly compares the original tagged corpus with our new tagged corpus and finds error labels in our corpus. Then it creates the candidate rule set following the definition of transform rule while the rule condition is the context of the word and the action is to correct the wrong label.

The last stage defines another evaluation function $F(r)$ to select the rule in the process of transformation-based learning firstly and the function $F(r)$ is as follow:

$$F(r) = C(r) - E(r) \tag{2}$$

where r is the rule, $C(r)$ is the number of labels which are corrected by using rule r while $E(r)$ is the number of labels which are modified to incorrect by using rule r.

The algorithm to learn rules is as follows: For one type BPNS, it extracts all possible trigger conditions according to the trigger environment;

(1) It calculates C_i in each BPNS and then selects the action from the type of CI;
(2) According to the trigger condition and transformation action, it applies them to tag MAP and then calculates $F(r)$;
(3) It selects the rule with highest $F(r)$ as the legal rule to apply to that MAP;
(4) It goes to step (3) until $F(r)$ is equal to 0 or less than 0;
(5) It stores the extracted rule. If there are any other type BPNS which hasn't processed, it selects one and goes to step (1); otherwise, the process is end.

Otherwise, we also create 213 reasons to extend rules based on Ontology and the detail categories please refer to document [9]. Here is a sample:

If word w_1 in the trigger condition tc_i and word $w_2=SubClassOf(w_1)$ then w_2 can replace w_1 in tc_i and form a new trigger condition in the rule.

$w_2=SubClassOf(w_1)$ means w_2 is a subclass of w_1. So using the reasoning mechanism, we can expand the rule set to increase the percent of recognized PN.

5   Chinese PN Recognition

Firstly, we segment words sentence by sentence using our segmentation tool [12] which doesn't recognize unknown registered words. The precision of it is about 96%.

Secondly, we modify the result of word segmentation using the WI set. It compares the words in the text with the WI set. If there is a word W_i in the text is also existing in the WI set and the context of W_i is equal or similar to the context of such WI, the word W_i should be segmented to W_{i1}/W_{i2} where $W_i = W_{i1}/W_{i2}$.

Thirdly, we recognize all possible BPNS from the segmented text (section 3);

Fourthly, we filter the illegal BPNS as follows: for each BPNS $bpns_i$:

(1) If there is WI in $bpns_i$, it seeks a rule chunk which includes that WI;
(2) It applies each rule in that rule chunk to $bpns_i$. If that WI of $bpns_i$ meets the trigger condition of a rule or a new rule deduced from a reason based on such rule, it sets $bpns_i$ to legal or illegal one following the rule's action;
(3) If all rules have been applied to $bpns_i$, then go to (4); otherwise, go to (1);
(4) If $bpns_i$ is a legal one, it keeps it; otherwise, it deletes it.

Finally, we sort all BPNS by their $F(r)$ from high to low and keep the highest one. Then PN set will be extracted easily following the structure of BPNS.

6 Experiments and Discussion

As usually, we conducted experiments on the Precision (P), Recall (R) and F-1 measure (F-1). In our experiments, we used the above news corpus from January 1 to May 31 as the training set while the other one month (June 1 to June 30) data is used as the open test data and the data in January is used as close set.

We firstly tag the corpus with our label set and there are 2,927,470 words with incorrect tag. By comparing incorrect tags with standard tags and using TBL approach, we extract 41,823 rule chunks and 142,185 transformation rules. Then rules are merged on Ontology, and we get 32,569 rule chunks and 67,483 transformation rules. So the size of rules is reduced by 52.5%. But with reasons based on Ontology, those rules can be deduced to a large rule set and cover more PN instance.

The experimental results are showed in Table 4. When only using un-merged rules without Ontology, the open test show that the precision is 93.2%, the recall is 80.7% and the F-1 is 86.5%. When using merged rules with Ontology, the open test show that the precision is 92.5%, the recall is 86.3% and the F-1 is 89.8%. Using merged rules with Ontology, it achieves an improvement of the precision by -0.7%, recall by 5.6% and F-1 by 3.3%. That result indicates that the merging method based on Ontology is an efficient method to improve the recall, because it makes the rules more general and high coverage. Furthermore, the reasoning mechanism of Ontology could be used to mine more PN. However, the precision decreases a little, but it's acceptable and intelligible. The reason is the reasoning mechanism would expand the number of rules and merged rules are abstract and not accurate as the instance.

By compared with other statistic-based approaches [2, 7] on the same corpus, our approach achieves a higher precision and F-measure while our recall is a little lower than them. Furthermore, our approach is good at extracting PN with complex structure, so our precision and recall of organization name is higher than that of other approaches. In our open test, the recall of complex structure PN including location name, organization name is 80.5% and the precision of that is 87.6%.

Table 4. The Precision, Recall and F-1

Test Type	Rules Without Ontology			Rules based on Ontology		
	P	R	F-1	P	R	F-1
Close Test	98.7%	95.6%	97.1%	97.5%	98.6%	98.0%
Open Test	93.2%	80.7%	86.5%	92.5%	86.3%	89.8%

One reason causes low recall is that we introduced CW into PN structure and some PN without CW in it would be missed. But if we ignore CW, the precision would be very low. So how to improve the representative of CW is our future work.

The Ontology acts an important role in our approach, but currently our Ontology is in building and its size is quite small. It only contains about 62,000 words and their relations now. As is well known, there are many PN libraries available, including last name libraries, foreign person name and location name libraries, etc. So we should introduce them into our Ontology.

7   Conclusion

In this paper we introduce the TBL and Ontology to extract rules automatically from the tagged corpus and then applied those rules to recognize Chinese PN. The experimental results showed it can achieve higher precision and F-measure than that of other approaches. We also propose a novel MAP conception and the tagging method, and it would make extracted rules more efficient and representative.

Acknowledgments. The authors would like to thank those anonymous reviewers for their comments on this paper. This research was supported by the National Natural Science Foundation of China under Grant No. 60673041 and Nation 863 Project of China under Grant No. 2006AA01Z147.

References

1. Yu, H., Zhang, H., Liu, Q.: Recognition of Chinese Organization Name Based on Role Tagging. In: Proc. of 20th Int. Conf. on Computer Processing of Oriental Languages, pp. 79–87 (2003)
2. Yu, H., Zhang, H., Liu, Q., Lv, X., Shi, S.: Chinese NE Identification Using Cascaded Hidden Markov Model. Journal of Communications 27(2), 87–94 (2006)
3. Li, L., Huang, D., Mao, T., Xu, X.: Auto Recognition of Person Names from Chinese Texts Based on SVM. Computer Engineering 32(19), 188–210 (2006)
4. Qian, J., Zhang, Y., Zhang, T.: Research on Chinese Person Name and Location Name Recognition Based on ME Model. Mini-Micro Systems 27(9), 1761–1765 (2006)
5. Tan, H., Zheng, J., Liu, K.: Design and Realization of Chinese Place Name Automatic Recognition System. Computer Engineering 28(8), 128–129 (2002)
6. Li, Z., Liu, Y.: Chinese Name Recognition Based on Boundary Templates and Local Frequency. Journal of Chinese Information Processing 20(5), 44–50 (2006)

7. Lv, Y., Zhao, T., Yang, M., Yu, H., Li, S.: Unknown Chinese Words Resolution by Dynamic Programming. Journal of Chinese Information Processing 15(1), 123–128 (2001)
8. Manning, C., Schutze, H.: Foundations of Statistical Natural Language Processing. MIT Press, Cambridge (1999)
9. Li, P., Zhu, Q., Qian, P.: The Construction of a Multilingual Language Ontology Framework. Journal of Computer Application 27(3), 646–649 (2007)
10. Brill, E.: Transformation-based Error-drive Learning and Natural Language Processing: a Case Study in Part of Speech Tagging. Computational Linguistic 21(4), 543–565 (1995)
11. Zhou, M., Wu, J., Wang, C.: A Fast Learning Algorithm for Part of Speech Tagging: An Improvement on Brill's Transformation-based Algorithm. Chinese Journal of Computer 21(4), 357–366 (1998)
12. Zhu, Q., Wen, T., Li, P., Qian, P.: Self-Adaptive Chinese Ambiguous Word Segmentation Method Based on Multi-Gram Library. Mini-micro Systems 27(8), 1597–1600 (2006)

Toward Image-Based Localization for AIBO Using Wavelet Transform

Alberto Pretto[1], Emanuele Menegatti[1], Enrico Pagello[1,2],
Yoshiaki Jitsukawa[3], Ryuichi Ueda[3], and Tamio Arai[3]

[1] Dept. of Information Engineering, The University of Padua, Italy
[2] *also with* ISIB-CNR corso Stati Uniti, Padua, Italy
[3] The University of Tokyo, Tokyo, Japan

Abstract. This paper describes a similarity measure for images to be used in image-based localization for autonomous robots with low computational resources. We propose a novel signature to be extracted from the image and to be stored in memory. The proposed signature allows, at the same time, memory saving and fast similarity calculation. The signature is based on the calculation of the 2D Haar Wavelet Transform of the gray-level image. We present experiments showing the effectiveness of the proposed image similarity measure. The used images were collected using the AIBOs ERS-7 of the RoboCup Team Araibo of the University of Tokyo on a RoboCup field, however, the proposed image similarity measure does not use any information on the structure of the environment and do not exploit the peculiar features of the RoboCup environment.

1   Introduction

Three are the main problems to be solved by any techniques of image-based localization one can develop: (i) how to reduce the number of images necessary to fully describe the environment in which the robot is working; (ii) how to efficiently store a large data set of reference images without filling-up the robot's memory (it is common to have several hundred reference images for typical environments); (iii) how to calculate in a fast and efficient way the similarity of the input image against all the reference images in the data set.

Several works have been published that use the image-based localization approach (among the others [14][5]). Each work tried to solve these problem in a different way. One of the most effective approaches to reduce the number of images needed to describe the environment is to mount an omnidirectional camera on the robot. In fact, an omnidirectional camera can acquire a complete view of the surroundings in one shot avoiding the need to shot at different gazing directions. The most popular technique, to reduce the memory consumption of the reference data set, is to extract a set of eigenimages from the set of reference images and to project the images into eigenspaces. The drawback of such systems is that they need to further preprocess the panoramic cylinder images they created from the omnidirectional image in order to obtain the rotational

R. Basili and M.T. Pazienza (Eds.): AI*IA 2007, LNAI 4733, pp. 831–838, 2007.

invariance, as in [1], in [10] and in [7] or to constrain the heading of the sensor as in [11]. An approach that exploit the natural rotational invariance of the omnidirectional images is to create a signature for the image based on the colour histograms of vertical sub-windows of the panoramic image, as in [8] or in [6]. However, this approach based on colours might not be very effective in a general environment with poor color information. An alternative approach to preserve the rotational invariance of omnidirectional image is the one presented in [12], which exploit the properties of the Fourier signature of the omnidirectional images.

Despite the effectiveness of the approaches based on the omnidirectional cameras, it is not always possible to mount an omnidirectional camera on the robot. A solution can be to constrain the movements of the robot in order to keep the camera pointing at the same location [2], but this greatly limits the motion of the robot. An alternative solution can be to extract from the perspective images some features that reduce the amount of required memory while retaining a rich description of the image. A good example of this is reported in [17], where 936 images were stored in less than 4MB by extracting features invariant to translation and to some amount of scaling. However, to extract such a large amount of images is time consuming, even if an automatic procedure is available.

2   Image-Based Localization for ERS-7 AIBO

In order to minimize the reference images to be stored, our idea is to keep as reference images two 180 degree panoramic views of the environment at every reference location; whose two images fully captures the appearance of the environment at a reference location. How to store in a memory-saving way the reference images and how to efficiently compare them with the input images is particularly important when using a robot with limited storage memory and limited computational resources, as the AIBO ERS-7 used in our experiments. Nowadays, a very popular approach used also for image-based localization is the SIFT approach proposed in [15]. However this approach is computationally expensive and focuses on local features in the single images, rather than on the global appearance of the environment. We developed an algorithm that allows the ERS-7 robot to autonomously build two 180 degrees panorama images using its standard camera and to stitch them together.

At the running stage, the 208×160 pixels image grabbed by the AIBO is matched with subwindows of the 360 deg. panoramic image (the black sliding window in Fig. 1(c). This can be done in an extremely efficient way, by effectively exploiting properties of the wavelet signature we developed. The matching returns similarity values that can be used to localize the robot. The fundamental assumption in this matching strategy is the head and the neck of the ERS-7 are always in the same configuration: same height and parallel to the ground. Image grabbed in different situations simply are not used in the robot localization process.

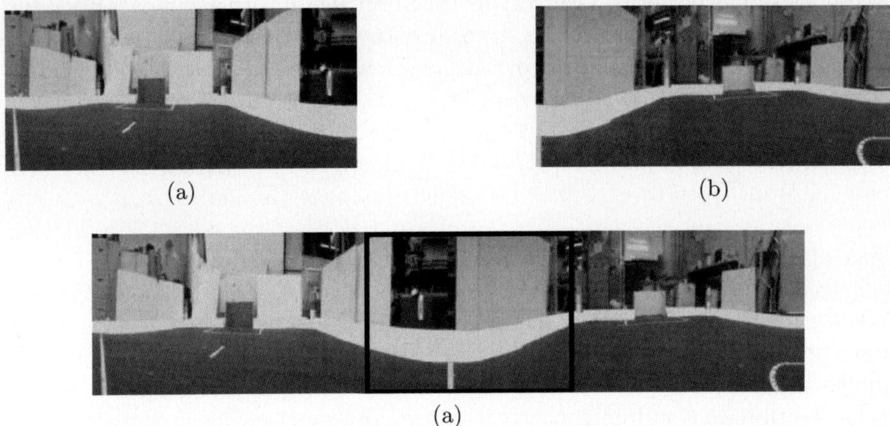

Fig. 1. In (a) and (b) two reference images, both taken by the ERS-7 at the same reference position, but with opposite heading. In (c) their composed 360 deg. panoramic image, with depicted the horizontal-sliding window used for input image matching. The position of the window is related to the returned bearing angle.

3   Discrete Wavelet Transform Image Signature

For an effective vision-based localization strategy, we need to store the visual memory of the environment (i.e., the reference images) in a compact and effective way. Images should be represented using specific *signatures* that characterize the content and some useful features of each image in the database. Signatures must have very small size compared with image sizes. The signature of a query image will be directly compared with the signatures of the reference images through a specific metric called *similarity measurement*. In the image-base localization context, a small similarity value between two images means that the two images have been grabbed one close to the other.

A tool for non-stationary signal analysis (whose frequency response varies in time, like in the images) is the Wavelet Transform [16]: it gives information about which frequency components exist and where these components appear. Wavelet features are successfully exploited in the image coding algorithms; for instance, the upcoming still image compression standard JPEG-2000 [3] is based on Wavelet Transform. As well, wavelet signatures are successfully used in image retrieval algorithms, e.g. [9,13], and texture retrieval algorithm, e.g. [4]. We exploited these properties of the Wavelet Transform using the Discrete Wavelet Transform (DWT) coefficients in order to represent images in a compact way, without losing information about location of the image discontinuity, shapes and texture [13].

Discrete Wavelet Transform are used to analyze signals at different scale, $scale = 1/frequency$. In single level discrete 1-D Wavelet Transform, the signal is decomposed into a coarse approximation and a detail information (Eq. 3,3).

Decomposition is performed convolving the input signal with a low-pass filter and an high-pass filter. After filtering, according to the Nyquist's rule, it is possible to eliminate half of the samples. $g()$ and $h()$ low and high-pass filter depend on chosen wavelet type.

$$y_{low}(k) = \sum_n x(n) * g(2k - n) \quad (1) \qquad y_{high}(k) = \sum_n x(n) * h(2k - n) \quad (2)$$

The single-level discrete Wavelet Transform can be recursively repeated for further decomposition of the previously y_{low}. In the 2-D case, the 1-D Wavelet Transform is applied first on each row of the image. The process results in two new matrices with half columns than the input image. A further 1-D DWT is applied to the columns of the resulting matrices. At the end of the one-level 2-D decomposition, $m \times m$ input matrix is decomposed in 4 $m/2 \times m/2$ matrices. In Fig. 2 is shown a multilevel 2-D Wavelet decomposition: I is the input image, C_i are the approximation coefficients, H_i, V_i and D_i are respectively the horizontal, vertical and diagonal detailed coefficients, $i = 1, 2, \ldots, n$ represent the recursion level of wavelet decomposition.

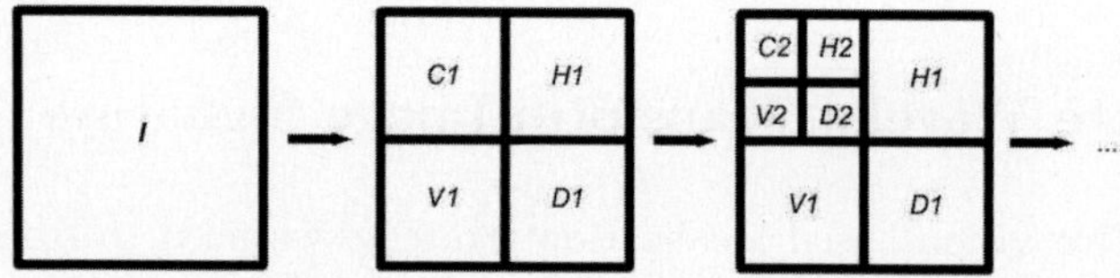

Fig. 2. Multilevel 2-D Wavelet decomposition

3.1   The Proposed Signature

We use as image signature a 2-D Haar Wavelet Transform of the grey-level values of the image. We decide to stop at 4-th level decomposition, and to characterize images only by the detailed coefficients (horizontal, vertical and diagonal) of this level. Thanks to the great properties of frequency localization given by the DWT, it is possible to store only a few of Discrete Wavelet Signatures for the references panoramic images: the subset of coefficients required for similarity measurement can be extracted using a simple sliding-window strategy.

Haar Wavelet is chosen as wavelet type because of it is very effective in detecting the exact instants when a signal changes: image discontinuity are one of the most important features chosen in image-based localization. Haar Wavelet can be easily implemented and they have very fast to compute. If one is interested in image reconstruction phase, the Haar Wavelets are not the good choice, because they tend to produce a lot of squared artifacts in the reconstructed image. However, we are not interested in the reconstruction phase, we exploit the DWT coefficients to calculate the similarity.

Other wavelet type was taken into account: Daubechies' Wavelets [16] family, commonly used in image coding, were tested. Surprisingly, growing the vanishing moments of the wavelets (i.e. the Daubechies' Wavelets order) performances decade. Those Wavelets are better suitable than Haar to detect a rupture in high-order derivative, but we are interested on detecting discontinuity and features directly in the signal.

Coupling the 180-degree references images, we obtain panoramic 720×160 pixels images. By applying recursively 2-D Haar Wavelet Transform, we can reduce a lot the signature size. On the other hand, high level failed on represent effectiveness feature of images, as edge and texture, useful for environment characterization. Choice of decomposition level 4 is a trade off between a compactness representation and a reliability similarity computation.

Coefficient of Haar Wavelet at level 4 pertains to 16×16 pixels square. In order to achieve horizontal 1-degree accuracy, we need to calculate only 8 global Discrete Wavelet Signature for every panoramic reference image, starting from pixels with $x = 0, 2, \ldots$ to 14. Given the bearing angle of an input image, the DWT coefficients can be effectively extracted from the right Wavelet table (from the eight precomputed, the index of the table depending on orientation) with a simple horizontal sliding-window strategy.

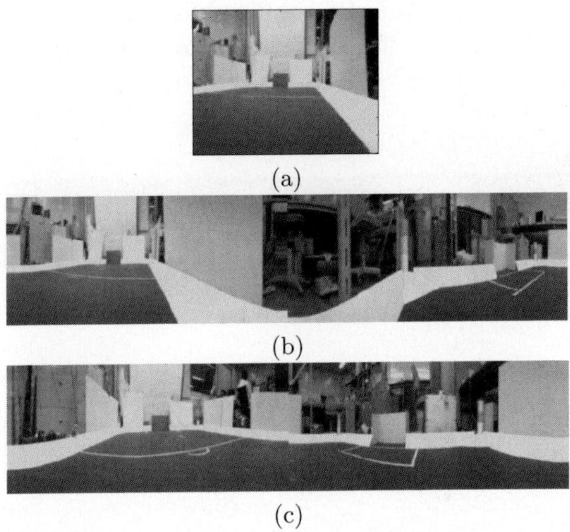

(a)

(b)

(c)

Fig. 3. (a) is an input image; (b) is the references image with the best match (100%); (c) is the second best match (61%)using the proposed DWT signature

In our experience, the approximation coefficients are not well suitable for image similarity computation: considering Haar Wavelet, those coefficients represent only the mean of the intensity of the pixels composing the macro-squares (16×16 pixels in our case). On the other hand, detailed coefficients can be used to well detected and highlight image discontinuities, shapes and patterns. Our image signature is based on those coefficients computed at level 4: approximation coefficients are simply discarded. As shown in [9], a coarse quantization of these coefficients doesn't affect the effectiveness of the Haar Wavelet coefficients in the image retrieval field. We tested a similar approach for our scope obtaining very good experimental results. We simply represent detailed coefficients d_i as -1 if $d_i < 0$ and as 1 if $d_i \geq 0$. In this way, it is possible to storage every detailed coefficient in only a single bit. Given the signature of an input images and the right subset of coefficients of a reference image, we compute our similarity measure as:

$$Sim = w_h * \sum_m \sum_n |H_i(m,n) - H_r(m,n)| + w_v * \sum_m \sum_n |V_i(m,n) - V_r(m,n)|$$

$$+ w_d * \sum_m \sum_n |D_i(m,n) - D_r(m,n)|$$

$$(3)$$

Where m, n represent rows and columns of the detailed coefficients matrices, H_i and H_r, V_i and V_r, D_i and D_r represent the horizontal, vertical and diagonal detailed coefficients respectively of the input and reference image. w_h, w_v, w_d are weights usefull to move importance through the three different set of coefficients in the localization process. Our default value are $w_h = 0.5, w_v = 0.25, w_d = 0.25$, because of the large amount of vertical characteristic in indoor environment. The memory saving of our approach is considerable: a gray-scale omnidirectional reference image $720 \times 160 = 115.2$ Kbyte of memory can be represented by our DWT signature with only 1.3 Kbyte. Experimental results will show the reliability of our approach.

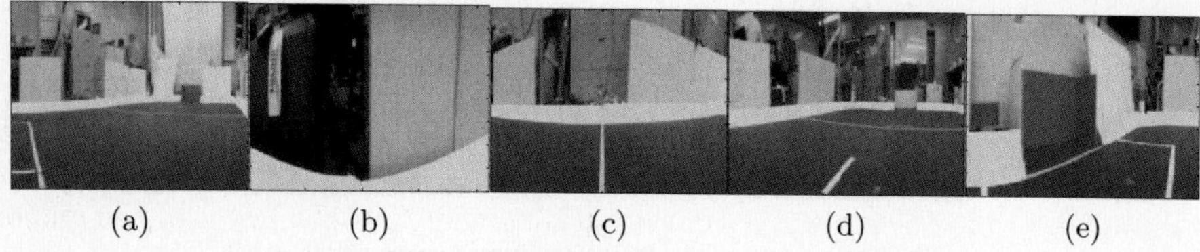

(a)   (b)   (c)   (d)   (e)

Fig. 4. Input images used for Fig. reffig:likelihoods

4   Experiments

We tested the system in a RoboCup Four-legged League 540×360 cm soccer field, using a grid of 13 by 9 reference images. The images have been grabbed in known poses regularly distributed all over the field. For every reference position two 180 deg. panoramic images were collected, using the technique explained in the previous sections. A set of input images, taken in distinct known positions and at different rotations, was used to test the proposed image similarity measure. The ground-truth position of the AIBO for every input image was measured by hand with an error less than 0.3 cm. In Fig. 4, five input images are depicted. In Fig. 5, the corresponding similarity values against the reference images are plotted. The similarity values have been interpolated to obtain a similarity value for every possible pose of the robot in the field. In the plot the darker areas correspond to a higher similarity. The white cross represents the actual pose of the robot.

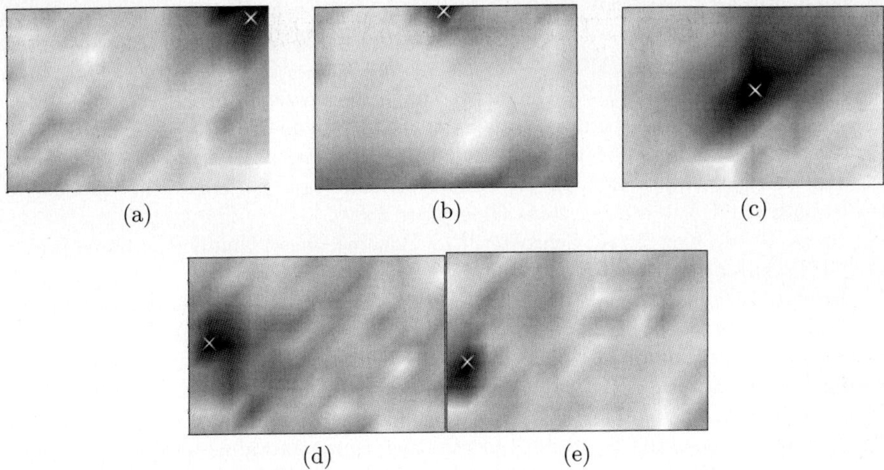

(a)   (b)   (c)

(d)   (e)

Fig. 5. Similarity values for all possible poses of the robot in the field, given the input images of Fig. 4. Darker areas correspond to a higher similarity. The cross represents the ground-truth robot position.

5 Conclusion and Future Works

We presented a new way to calculate the similarity between images to be used in the image-based localization approach on autonomous robot with low computational resources. The proposed technique exploit the properties of the Haar Wavelet Transform. We presented a technique that enables a quick set-up of the robot and of its localization system without requiring any previous knowledge on the environment. Successful experiments on the calculation of the image similarity of real images grabbed by a AIBO ERS-7 robot have been presented. These results encourage the creation of a Monte-Carlo localization system that uses this approach and make us feel more confident on exploring of the use of this similarity measure to develop a visual topological SLAM strategy.

References

1. Aihara, H., Iwasa, N., Yokoya, N., Takemura, H.: Memory-based self-localisation using omnidirectional images. In: Jain, A.K., Venkatesh, S., Lovell, B.C. (eds.) Proc. of the 14th International Conference on Pattern Recognition, vol. I, pp. 1799–1803 (1998)
2. Cassinis, R., Duina, D., Inelli, S., Rizzi, A.: Unsupervised matching of visual landmarks for robotic homing using Fourier-Mellin transform. Robotics and Autonomous Systems 40(2-3) (August 2002)
3. JPEG Committee. Jpeg home page, http://www.jpeg.org
4. Do, M.N., Vetterli, M.: Wavelet-based texture retrieval using generalized Gaussian density and Kullback-Leibler distance. IEEE Tr. Im. Proc. 11(2), 146–158 (2002)

5. Dudek, G., Jugessur, D.: Robust place recognition using local appearance based methods. In: ICRA'00. Proceedings IEEE International Conference on Robotics and Automation 2000, IEEE Computer Society Press, Los Alamitos (2000)
6. Frontoni, E., Zingaretti, P.: An efficient similarity metric for omnidirectional vision sensors. Robotics and Autonomous Systems 54(9), 750–757 (2006)
7. Gaspar, J., Winters, N., Santos-Victor, J.: Vision-based navigation and environmental representations with an omnidirectional camera. IEEE Transaction on Robotics and Automation 16(6) (December 2000)
8. Gross, H.-M., Koenig, A., Schroeter, Ch., Boehme, H.-J.: Omnivision-based probabilistic self-localization for a mobile shopping assistant continued. In: Gross, H.-M., Koenig, A. (eds.) IROS 2003. IEEE/RSJ Int. Conference on Intelligent Robots and Systems, Las Vegas USA, pp. 1505–1511 (October 2003)
9. Jacobs, C.E., Finkelstein, A., Salesin, D.H.: Fast multiresolution image querying. In: Proceedings of SIGGRAPH 95, Los Angeles, California,New York, August 6–11, 1995 (1995)
10. Jogan, M., Leonardis, A.: Robust localization using panoramic view-based recognition. In: ICPR00. Proc. of the 15th Int.Conference on Pattern Recognition, vol. 4, pp. 136–139. IEEE Computer Society, Los Alamitos (2000)
11. Krse, B.J.A., Vlassis, N., Bunschoten, R., Motomura, Y.: A probabilistic model for appareance-based robot localization. Image and Vision Computing 19(6), 381–391 (2001)
12. Menegatti, E., Maeda, T., Ishiguro, H.: Image-based memory for robot navigation using properties of the omnidirectional images. Robotics and Autonomous Systems, Elsevier 47(4), 251–267 (2004)
13. Natsev, A., Rastogi, R., Shim, K.: Walrus: a similarity retrieval algorithm for image databases. SIGMOD Rec. 28(2), 395–406 (1999)
14. Nayar, S.K., Murase, H., Nene, S.A.: Learning, positioning, and tracking visual appearance. In: Proceedings IEEE International Conference on Robotics and Automation, 1994, pp. 3237–3244. IEEE Computer Society Press, Los Alamitos (1994)
15. Se, S., Lowe, D., Little, J.: Mobile Robot Localization and Mapping with Uncertainty using Scale-Invariant Visual Landmarks. The International Journal of Robotics Research 21(8), 735 (2002)
16. Vetterli, M., Kovacevic, J.: Wavelets and Subband Coding. Signal Processing Series (1995)
17. Wolf, J., Burgard, W., Burkhardt, H.: Robust vision-based localization by combining an image retrieval system with monte carlo localization. IEEE Transactions on Robotics 21(2), 208–216 (2005)

Crosslingual Retrieval in an eLearning Environment

Cristina Vertan[1], Kiril Simov[2], Petya Osenova[2], Lothar Lemnitzer[3],
Alex Killing[4], Diane Evans[5], and Paola Monachesi[6]

[1] Natural Language Systems Division, Institute of Informatics, University Hamburg,
Germany
[2] LML, IPP, Bulgarian Academy of Sciences, Sofia, Bulgaria
[3] Seminar für Sprachwissenchaft, Universität Tübingen, Germany
[4] Center for Security Studies, ETH Zürich, Switzerland
[5] The Open University, Milton Keynes, UK
[6] Uil-OTS, Utrecht University, the Netherlands

Abstract. In this paper we are reporting about an ongoing project
LT4eL (Language Technolohy for eLearning) aiming at improving the
effectiveness of retrieval and accessibility of learning objects within a
learning management system. We elaborate the process of building the
domain ontology and present the multilingual support offered to the application.

1 Introduction

The aim of the Language Technology for eLearning project (LT4eL, www. lt4el.eu)
is to enhance eLearning with Language Technology tools and resources as well as
with semantic information [8], [9] in order to provide new functionalities which will
enhance the adaptability and the personalization of the learning process through
the software which mediates it.

An important objective of the project is to enhance LMSs with semantic
knowledge in order to improve the retrieval of the learning objects. We take two
groups of users into account: educators and authors of teaching material who
want to compile a course for a specific target group and who want to draw on
existing texts, media, as well as learners who are looking for content which suit
their current needs.

Ontologies, which are a key element in the architecture of the Semantic Web,
have been adopted to structure, query and navigate through the learning objects
which are part of the LMS. The ontology plays two roles. One the one hand,
it is employed in the classification of the learning objects. Each learning object
is connected to a set of concepts in the ontology. This classification allows for
ontological search, i.e. search based on concepts and their interrelations within
the ontology. On the other hand, it makes multilingual search for learning objects
possible. In this case the ontology plays the role of Interlingua between the
different languages. Thus the user might specify the query in one language and
get learning objects in other language(s).

R. Basili and M.T. Pazienza (Eds.): AI*IA 2007, LNAI 4733, pp. 839–847, 2007.

The ontology will be integrated in the ILIAS Learning Management System and we expect that the integration of ontologies within an LMS together with the appropriate tools for navigation, will facilitate the construction of user specific courses, by semantic querying for topics of interests; will allow direct access to ontological knowledge; will improve the creation of personalized content and will allow for decentralization and co-operation of content management.

The paper is structured as follows. In section 2, we present the developed methodology for building an ontology relevant for the domain under consideration, that is computer science for non experts. In section 3, we explain how multilingual material (lexicons and content) was linked to the ontology. In Section 4, we present the multilingual search scenarios which constitute the basis for the specification of the cross-lingual search engine. Section 5 concludes the paper and gives the directions for the future work.

2   Ontology Development

We intend to use the ontology to support cross-lingual semantic searches in a repository of learning objects. Two aspects are critical for the the ontology in that context and will therefore be evaluated carefully, i.e. consistency of the taxonomical structure and domain coverage. Consistency of the taxonomy is established by using the OntoClean methodology [4] and by linking our domain ontology to upper ontologies. Domain coverage is evaluated in the process of annotating our learning objects with concepts from the ontology, see below.

In this section we describe the methodology for the constructing a domain ontology, linking it to upper ontologies and formalizing the concepts.

2.1   LT4eL Methodology

Within the LT4eL project the domain chosen is Computer Science for non-specialists. Since no ontology covering the domain was available, we decided to create our own ontology. In the following we describe the major steps of the ontology creation process.

Processing of the Keywords. Once the learning objects for all languages involved were in place (cf. [7]), we started to build the ontology by annotating and extracting keywords from them using our keyword extractor(cf. [6], [8]).

The processing itself was performed in the following way:

– *Selection of appropriate keywords* We only considered those keywords which relevant for our domain. Admittedly, this domain is large or vaguely defined, and might contain concepts which are not, strictly speaking, related to computer science at large, but are nevertheless associated to it, such as the results of processes which involve computer, e.g. documents, and typical domains of computer use, e.g. distance learning, desktop publishing, and the web.

- *Collecting definitions*

  The Internet was searched for definitions of the selected keywords. The reason behind that was to provide non-formal accounts of the meaning(s) of the keywords. If possible, we selected several definitions for a concept in order to reflect various aspect of the meaning and to have a textual basis from which later on relations between concepts will be derived. From these sets of collected definition we selected or compiled one canonical definition for each concept.

- *Polysemy*

  For polysemous keywords, two or more senses and, consequently, concepts have to be established. For example the keyword *word* refers tothe linguistic unit as well as to the Microsoft product. MPEG can refer to the organization as well as the standard. Words senses which are irrelevant for our domain have been not taken into account though.

Formalization of the senses. The next step was to formalize definitions for the extracted concepts and relations in OWL-DL ([11]). For each meaning an appropriate class in the domain ontology was created. This resulted in an initial formal version of the ontology. This ontology was linked to upper ontologies.

Linking to upper ontologies. Linking our ontology to an upper ontology has two advantages. First, we can inherit relations from the upper ontologies, second, as a side product of this manual process the consistency and validity of our ontology is checked and improved.

We considered the following criteria for the selection of the upper ontology: (1) The ontology has to be constructed on a rigorous basis and to suit our domain; (2) it should be represented in an adequate formal language, preferably OWL; (3) domain ontologies exist which have been constructed using this upper ontology, and (4) support is provided by the authors of the upper ontology. After an initial evaluation of the alternatives and consultation of other evaluations of upper ontologies (cf. [12] and [10]) we selected DOLCE. This decision does not aim at ruling out mappings to other ontologies, though.

In order to get appropriate taxonomic relations between the concepts in the ontology and to facilitate the mapping to an upper ontology, we mapped each concept to synsets of OntoWordNet [2], which is a version of WordNet 1.6 mapped to DOLCE ontology. The mapping was performed via the two plug-in relations of *equality* and *hypernymy*. Thus, we created the taxonomical backbone of our ontology. Later on we will add more types of relations. The connection of OntoWordNet to DOLCE allows an evaluation of the defined concepts with respect to meta-ontological properties as they are defined in the OntoClean approach – cf. [3], [14] and [5].

Our ontology was also mapped onto WordNet 2.0. This mapping provides additional benefits. WordNet 2.0 is larger than OntoWordNet and has a richer set of relations. Therefore, the mapping will enable us to derive more relations between the concepts in our ontology. Furthermore, WordNet 2.0 is aligned to SUMO and thus we get an indirect mapping to another upper level ontology.

Since those two mappings have been performed independently of one another, the outcomes can be used to cross-check the validity of each concept and relation.

Results. Our ontology currently consists of 707 concepts / classes formalized in OWL and linked to WordNet and DOLCE ontology. In the following we present the concept 'WebPage' as an example.

```
<owl:Class rdf:about="http://www.lt4el.eu/CSnCS#WebPage">
    <rdfs:comment>A document (file) connected to the
    World Wide Web and viewable by anyone connected to
    the internet who has a web browser.</rdfs:comment>
    <rdfs:comment>Hyper CSnCS:
    http://www.lt4el.eu/CSnCS#TextFile</rdfs:comment>
    <rdfs:comment>Equal WN20: ENG20-05964213-n</rdfs:comment>
    <rdfs:comment>ID: id1757</rdfs:comment>
    <rdfs:subClassOf>
        <owl:Class rdf:about="http://www.lt4el.eu/CSnCS#TextFile">
        </owl:Class></rdfs:subClassOf>
</owl:Class>
```

3 Mapping Multilinguial Lexicons and Content on the Ontology

The main aim of the ontology in the learning management system is to enable a conceptual search through the learning objects. Moreover we intend to offer the user the possibility to perform this search multilingually. The connection between content, user's query and the ontology is realised through:

- mapping of lexicons in each involved language onto the ontology
- semantic annotation of the learning objects with ontology concepts.

In the following paragraphs we elaborate these two aspects.

3.1 Mapping of the Lexicons onto the Ontology

Terminological lexicons represent the main interface between the user's query and the ontological search engine. The terminological lexicons were constructed on the basis of the formal definitions of the concepts within the ontology. In this approach of construction of the terminological lexicon we escaped from the hard task of mapping different lexicons in several languages as it was done in EuroWordNet Project [13]. The main problems with this approach of construction of terminological lexicons are that (1) for some concepts there is no lexicalized term in a given language, and (2) some important term in a given language has no appropriate concept in the ontology which to represent its meaning. In order to solve these problems we, first, allow the lexicons to contains also non-lexicalized phrases which have the meaning of the concepts without lexicalization in a given language. Even more, we encourage the lexicon builders to add more terms and phrases to the lexicons for a given concept in order to represent as many ways of expressing the concept in the language as possible. These different phrases or terms for a given concept are used as a basis for construction of the regular grammar rules for annotation of the concept in the text. Having them, we could capture in the text different wordings of the same meaning. In order to solve the second problem we modify the ontology in such a way that it contains all the concepts that are important for the domain.

We could summarize the connection between the ontology and the lexicons in the following way: the ontology represents the semantic knowledge in form of concepts and relations with appropriate axioms; and the lexicons represent the ways in which these concepts can be realized in texts in the corresponding languages. Of course the ways in which a concept could be represented in text are potentially infinite in number, thus, we could hope to represent in our lexicons only the most frequent and important terms and phrases.

Here is an example of an entry from the Dutch lexicon:

```
<entry id="id60">
   <owl:Class rdf:about="http://www.lt4el.eu/CSnCS#BarWithButtons">
      <rdfs:subClassOf>
          <owl:Class rdf:about="http://www.lt4el.eu/CSnCS#Window"/>
      </rdfs:subClassOf>
   </owl:Class>
   <def>A horizontal or vertical bar as a part of a window,
        that contains buttons, icons.</def>
   <termg lang="nl">
      <term shead="1">werkbalk</term>
      <term>balk</term>
      <term type="nonlex">balk met knoppen</term>
      <term>menubalk</term>
   </termg>
</entry>
```

Each entry of the lexicons contains three type of information: (1) information about the concept from the ontology which represent the meaning for the terms in the entry; (2) explanation of the concept meaning in English; and (3) a set of terms in a given language that have the meaning expressed by the concept. The concept part of the entry provides minimum information for formal definition of the concept. The English explanation of the concept meaning facilitates the human understanding. The set of terms stands for different wordings of the concept in the corresponding language. One of the terms is the representative for the term set. This representative term will be used where just one of terms from the set is necessary to be used, for example as an item of a menu. In the example above we present the set of Dutch terms for the concept `http://www.lt4el.eu/CSnCS#BarWithButtons`. One of the term is non-lexicalized - attribute `type` with value `nonlex`. The first term is representative for the term set and it is marked-up with attribute `shead` with value 1.

3.2   Semantic Annotation of Learning Objects

After having mapped the lexicons to the ontology, we proceeded with the annotation of the Learning objects with the relevant parts of the ontology. The annotation was made within the textual content of the learning objects. This annotation allows us better search for learning content not only as whole learning objects, but also as parts of learning objects, for example paragraphs. The annotation was performed as regular grammars within CLaRK System[1], called annotation grammars. Ambiguous cases are resolved by using rules implemented as constraints within the system. For the purposes of the project the disambiguation was done manually and in this way we construct a gold standard corpus of LOs. As it was mentioned above in the lexicon we represent not only terms for the concepts in the ontology, but also non-lexicalized phrases. This allows us to construct better annotation grammars for corresponding concepts.

4   Crosslingual Search and Integration in the Learning Management System

As we mentioned in sections 2 and 3 the ontology and the lexicons constitute the backbone for the crosslingual search engine which we are integrating in the learning management system. The engine is currently under development. In this section we will present the user scenarios which constitute the basis of the specification for the multilingual search, as well as the architecture for the integration in the eLearning system. The user will specify within the learning management system the languages in which he intends to retrieve documents. The annotation described in section 3 has to be performed for all documents to be searched.

Under these assumtions a search scenario from the user's point of view implies following steps:

- Submit query. User submits a free text query.
- See document list. A list of documents is displayed with meta information like: title, length, original language, keywords and concepts that are common to both the query and the document, other keywords and concepts that are related to the document but not to the query.
- See concept browsing units. Each concept that is assumed to be related to the search query, is presented to the user together with its neighbourhood from the ontology (related concepts and relations between the concepts) calles "browsing unit". If no concept related to the search query is found, the root of the ontology with its neighbourhood is chosen as the browsing unit.
- View documents. User views the documents from the list.
- Browse ontology. User browses the ontology: starting from the presented concepts, he navigates to related concepts, and concepts that are related to those.

---

[1] CLaRK System is an XML-based system for corpora development:
  `http://www.bultreebank.org/clark/index.html`.

- Select concepts. User selects ontology fragments (sets of related concepts, possibly only indirectly related) from the presented browsing units.
- Select search option. this step will be detailed in the following paragraphs
- See new document list. A new list of documents is displayed, based on only ontologicalsearch
- See updated concept browsing units. As in step 3, but now, those concepts are presented, that are common to at least N of the found documents; this includes the concepts that were used as the search key but might include further concepts. The number of documents, specified by the parameter N, can be relative (a percentage of the number of found documents) or absolute.
- Repeat steps from step 6 (Select concepts). User selects another set of related concepts and submits it as the search key, etc.

With respect to the search option, we are implementing folowwing four startegies for combining ontology fragments

- fully disjunctive search: find documents, in which any of the concepts from any of the selected fragments occur
- disjunctive within fragments, conjunctive between different fragments: find documents, in which from each ontology fragment at least one concept occurs
- conjunctive within fragments, disjunctive between different fragments: find documents, in which at least one ontology fragment fully matches: every concept of the ontology fragment must occur in the document
- fully conjunctive search: find documents, in which all of the selected concepts from all of the ontology fragments occur

The steps 1 to 10 are currently formalized in functional modules composing the search engine.

The crosslingual search will be integrated together with the other component developed in the project (keyword extractor, definitory context finder) in the eLearning Management system ILIAS. The bases for the integration process are the use cases defined for the keyword extractor, the definitory context finder and the ontology enhanced searching and browsing capabilities. The use cases have been the major input for the specification of a web service interface between the language technology tools and the learning management system. It is a major goal of the project to make the language technology based functionalities re-usable for other learning management systems. To make the integration of the tools as easy as possible, the interface of the tools will be well-documented, standards-based and technology independent. The implementation of the interface as web services should ensure that these goals are met.

The major components of the integration setup are the language technology server and the learning management system. The language technology server provides the keyword extractor, definitory context finder and ontology management system functionalities. The tools are developed using the Java programming language and are hosted on a Java web server. The functionalities can be accessed directly on the webserver for test purposes or they can be used by the learning management system through the web service interface.

The fact that multiple developers are working on different parts of the overall structure has led to the decision to setup a Subversion server as a central code repository. The project partners have also decided to make the results immediately available to the general public and to give everyone the opportunity to join and collaborate with the project. The source code is available under an open source license and it is hosted on the SourceForget.net portal for open source projects at `https://sourceforge.net/projects/lt4el/`.

5   Conclusions and Further Work

In this paper we described a possible enhancement of search facilities in an learning management system through ontological support. Particulary we focused on the multilingual character of the problem.

We are currently working on the implementation of the multilingual engine and validation of the multilingual scenarios, as described in Section 5. The extension from monolingual search to multilingual search triggers additional problems like:

- Ranking throughout languages: The user is maybe less interested in receiving a list of documents classified per language. Another possibility is to display the complete list according to the same ranking criteria, and for each document indicate its language. In this way, the user can compare the relevance of two documents even if they are in a different language. A further refinement could be to include the language as a ranking criterion by giving a bonus which differs per language; the bonus could still be overruled by the annotation frequency criterion.
- Parameters: A number of decisions do not have to be taken when implementing the search functionality, but should be known at runtime and therefore treated as parameters:
  - Possible languages of search query (in which lexicons should we look?)
  - Retrieval languages
  - Show concepts that are shared in at least N of the found documents
  - If less than N documents are found for a certain concept: try with superconcept and subconcepts
- Documents annotation with relations: In the current approach, only concepts and no relations are annotated in the documents. Relations between concepts are only known to the ontology and serve as a connection between concepts. They are used to find related concepts, automatically as well as for manual ontology navigation. An extension could be to annotate in the documents those relations between the annotated concepts that are valid for the document. Then, for example, a user can search for documents that contain the concept 'computer memory' only if it is described as 'part-of' another concept. We are currently investigating the possibility of introducing relations corresponding to some pedagogical criteria, like the ACM-Ontology.

Within the learning management systme we already integrated a keword search engine (Lucene). The evaluation of the cross-lingual retrievel engine will be based on precision and recall measures comparing these 2 approaches. We are defining now also quality measures to prove that the ontologica search improves also the learning performance of users. We are intending also to compare the ontological search with statistical based methods like inverted index or LSA

References

1. Fellbaum, C. (ed.): WORDNET: an electronic lexical database. MIT Press, Cambridge (1998)
2. Gangemi, A., Navigli, R., Velardi, P.: The OntoWordNet Project: extension and axiomatisation of conceptual relations in WordNet. In: Meersman, R., Tari, Z., Schmidt, D.C. (eds.) CoopIS 2003, DOA 2003, and ODBASE 2003. LNCS, vol. 2888, Springer, Heidelberg (2003)
3. Gangemi, A., Guarino, N., Masolo, C., Oltramari, A.: Understanding top-level ontological distinctions. In: Proc. of IJCAI 2001 workshop on Ontologies and Information Sharing (2001)
4. Guarino, N.: Ontological Analysis and Ontology Design. In: An invited tutorial at the First Workshop on Ontologies and Lexical Knowledge Bases - OntoLex 2000, Sozopol, Bulgaria (2000)
5. Guarino, N., Welty, C.: Evaluating Ontological Decisions with OntoClean. Communications of the ACM 45(2), 61–65 (2002)
6. Lemnitzer, L., Degórski, L.: Language Technology for eLearning – Implementing a Keyword Extractor. Paper presented at the EDEN 2006 conferenc, Casteldelfels, Spain (2006)
7. Mossel, E., Lemnitzer, L., Vertan, C.: Language Technology for eLearning – A Multilingual Approach from the German Perspective. In: Proc. GLDV-2007 Spring Conference, Tübingen, pp. 125–134 (April 2007)
8. Lemnitzer, L., Vertan, C., Killing, A., Simov, K., Evans, D., Cristea, D., Monachesi, P.: Improving the search for learning objects with keywords and ontologies (2007) (Paper to be presented at ECTEL 2007, Crete, September 2007)
9. Monachesi, P., Cristea, D., Evans, D., Killing, A., Lemnitzer, L., Simov, K., Vertan, C.: Integrating Language Technology and Semantic Web techniques in eLearning. Villach, Austria (2006) (Presented at ICL 2006, September 27-29, 2006)
10. Oberle, D., et al.: DOLCE ergo SUMO: On Foundational and Domain Models in SWIntO (SmartWeb Integrated Ontology) 2006, (Submission to Journal of Web Semantics)
11. OWL: Web Ontology Language (Overview), http://www.w3.org/TR/owl-features/
12. Semy, S., Pulvermacher, M., Obrst, L.: Toward the Use of an Upper Ontology for U.S. government and Military Domains: An Evaluation. MITRE Technical Report 04B0000063 (September 2004)
13. Piek, V. (ed.): EuroWordNet General Document. Version 3, Final (July 19, 1999), http://www.hum.uva.nl/~ewn
14. Welty, C., Guarino, N.: Supporting Ontological Analysis of Taxonomic Relationships. Data and Knowledge Engineering (2001)

Constraint-Based School Timetabling Using Hybrid Genetic Algorithms

Tuncay Yigit

Suleyman Demirel University, Engineering and Architecture Faculty,
Computer Engineering, 32260, Cunur, Isparta, Turkey
tuncay@mmf.sdu.edu.tr

Abstract. In this paper, a hybrid genetic algorithm (HGA) has been developed to solve the constraint-based school timetabling problem (CB-STTP). HGA has a new operator called repair operator, in addition to standard crossover and mutation operators. A timetabling tool has been developed for HGA to solve CB-STTP. The timetabling tool has been tested extensively using real-word data obtained the Technical and Vocational High Schools in Turkey. Experimental results have presented that performance of HGA is better than performance of standard GA.

Keywords: school timetabling, genetic algorithms, planning and scheduling.

1   Introduction

The Timetabling problem is computationally NP-hard, therefore, it is very difficult to solve using conventional optimizations techniques. It has been frequently studied due to their wide range of applications, such as the traveling salesman problem, scheduling problem, employee timetabling, universities or high school timetabling. The School Timetabling Problem (STTP) is the planning of a number of meeting lessons or exams, involving a group of students or teachers for a given period and requiring given rooms or laboratories according with their availability and respecting some other constraints. The basic timetabling problem in a school consists of finding time-slots for a set of exams or lessons. A set of timetabling tasks is directly related to the satisfying a set of constraints. In most cases, although solutions are acceptable, there are many of hard and soft constraints remain violated [1].

There are many researcher have introduced models and algorithms for solving STTP problem. Recently, there has been a lot of attention paid to the problem of automating the construction of university and high school timetables. Many different methods have being tried, including simulated Annealing [2], tabu search [3], variations of genetic algorithms [4,5]. A standard GA does not yield desired timetables, because of violation of many constraints. This is a situation that has been noticed in several other implementations. Many researchers have used different hybrid operators to reduce of computing time and reduce the number of violations for some constraints. Wilke et. al. [6] are used Hybrid Genetic Algorithms for solving German High School. Their use direct representation of the problem and applies an

R. Basili and M.T. Pazienza (Eds.): AI*IA 2007, LNAI 4733, pp. 848–855, 2007.

adapted mutation operators as well as several specific repair operators. But, their using operators are applied randomly, according to a given hybrid repair probability parameter. Stefano et. al. [7], have used with two heuristics based on local search, implemented by the intelligence mutation and improvement operators for solving Italian school system. Burke et. al. [8], have proposed some heuristic operators to improve solutions. Deris et. al. [9], have proposed a hybrid algorithm with constraint-based reasoning. Michalewicz [10], has used special operators which are designed to generate feasible solutions.

This paper presents a new HGA approach to solve CB-STTP. HGA have been used to produce desired solutions and used an adaptive mutation and crossover operators. Repair operator is used to fix some chromosomes with duplications or absents of genes. The proposed algorithm is tested using the data of the Technical and Vocational High Schools in Turkey. The timetabling tool has been developed to using C++ Builder 5.0 language. The experimental results showed that the performance of the HGA is better than the standard GA.

2 School Timetabling

The school timetabling problem, which has an important role typically on planning of education, is a special kind of the optimization problems in real-word. School timetabling models must accommodate the characteristics and regulations of specific education systems. Therefore the problem under consideration varies from country to country.

2.1 Structure of the Problem

The data used this study, is the actual information of the Gazi Anatolian Technical and Vocational High Schools in Turkey. The students attend Technical High school up to 4 years and Vocational High Schools up to 3 years. Both of them, first year training is all nearly same. Timetable consists of 12 consecutive 40 minutes time-slots per day, having 5 minutes allocated as a break between courses, starting at 8:00 AM for 5 days. Vocational High School students go to industry to for vocational training in three days of a week. In these days, the students have no courses at school.

Structure of the data consists of the number of time-slot of lessons in a week. A timetabling is characterized by events, such as classes, teachers and rooms. Here, each one of event is automatically appointed ID. A graphical user interface has been developed to facilitate the input data, as can be seen in Figure 1. As can be seen from figure 1, the column dimension consists of weekdays, and the row dimension consists of several time-slots within each weekdays. These time-slots are directly related to the satisfying a set of constraints. These constraints are classified as hard constraints and soft constraints.

2.2 Constraints Definition

The constraints are the most important for the school timetabling to obtain good performance. These constraints are classified into two categorized. First, those constraints are called hard constraints. All of them, that must be satisfied completely

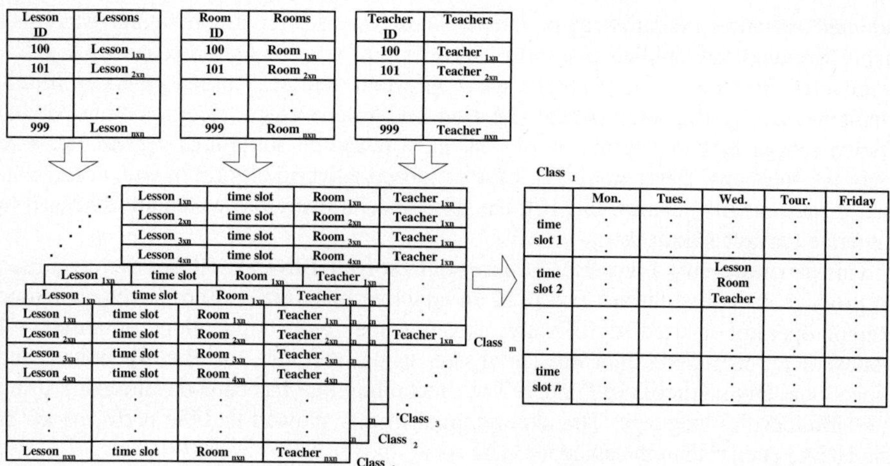

Fig. 1. Structure of data for STTP

in a timetabling. Second, those constraints are called soft constraints. Some or all of them may be violated provided that the penalty value. However, it is desired that all of the soft constraints should have minimum value. The school timetabling problem, based on a thorough analysis of the Turkish Technical and Vocational High School, the following a set of general constraints has been identified.

Typical hard constraints:

1. No teacher can teach two different classes at the same time
2. No two distinct classes can be held in the same room and time period.
3. Specific time-slot have to be closed or blocked, (no course hour is assigned)
4. Some of time-slots are closed for each of teacher. Consider a ten hour-long practical experiment.
5. Specific room requirements must be closed to take into considerations(i.e., lab)

Typical soft constraints:

6. Neither students nor teachers like timetables with a lot of empty slots (empty periods between lessons)
7. Teacher's preferences for time-slots for their classes
8. Time-slots of the same lesson should be distributed uniformly over the week.

3   Hybrid Genetic Algorithm for STTP

3.1   Background of Standard GA

GA's are a heuristic solution-search or optimization technique, originally motivated by the Darwinian principle of evolution through (genetic) selection. A GA is a parallel search method that manipulates a string of numbers (a chromosome) in a manner similar to the laws of evolution and biology. GA starts with an initial set of random solutions called populations and each individual in the population is called a chromosome. The operation of the GA changes slightly depending on the base of the numbers to apply the genetic operators such as, crossover, mutation, reproduction and elitism. The selection process evaluates each chromosome by some fitness mechanism and assigns it a fitness value. Although there are many techniques for the selection of parents, a commonly used method is the Roulette Wheel Selection, a proportionate selection scheme which bases the number of offspring on the average fitness of the population. Crossover is the procedure where two "parent" chromosomes exchange genetic information (i.e., a section of the string of numbers) to form two chromosome offspring's. Mutation is a form of global search where the genetic information of a chromosome is randomly altered. Elitism is used to transfer the fittest member of the population into the next generation without modification. However, in some situations, repair function is to be needed to fix problems in the any chromosome [11].

3.2 Chromosome Representation

GA work with a population of strings or chromosomes. The idea is to create a population of individuals, each individual representing a possible timetable. In our implementation an individual represents a school timetable that consists of a sequence of all classes timetable of the school, as shown in Figure 2. These chromosomes are constituted by genes which consisted of Lesson_ID, Room_ID and Teacher_ID. These genes are decimal strings and used for each activity in the timetable.

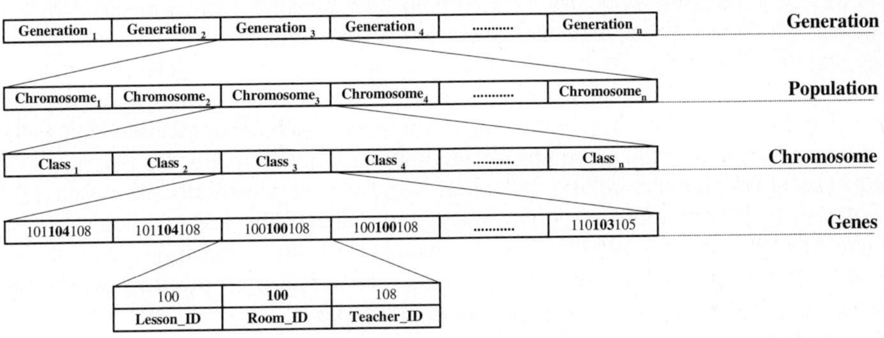

Fig. 2. Chromosome representation

3.3 Initialization

At the first stage of GA, it is necessary to form a beginning population in which the size of space and the chromosomes in this space will be determined. During initialization, a population of feasible solutions is created randomly without regard to their fitness value. The size of the beginning population is important in the sense of GA's activity. The small size of population causes the solution space to be small and not to reach the best solution merits. When solution space is too big, it causes both

GA's activity to minimize and solutions merits to turn towards very different and undesired points. In this study, during initialization, a population of candidate solution is created randomly for all lessons. Population size has been 20.

3.4   Fitness Function

The evaluation process is mainly deal with hard constraints and soft constraints and has a mechanism for assigning penalties whenever these types of constraints are violated. The fitness function for school timetabling is of the form [7], as follows;

$$f = \frac{1}{1 + \sum_i \alpha_i . h_i + \sum_j \beta_j . s_j} \tag{1}$$

where, $h_i \in \Re$ is the number violations of the ith hard constraint, whose penalty value is $\alpha_i \in \Re$, and $s_j \in \Re$ is the number violations of the jth soft constraint, whose penalty value is $\beta_j \in \Re$. The fitness of the chromosomes is inversely proportional to the number of violations of the hard and soft constraints. Those chromosomes with less penalty values are better solution. The penalty values for the violation of hard constraints are higher than those for soft constraints. The complete penalty value of the chromosomes is computed by adding the penalty values for all hard and soft constraints violations found. Thus the optimization process tries to generate a feasible solution with as few soft constraints violations as possible.

3.5   Genetic Operators

The selection operator evaluates each chromosome by some fitness mechanism and assigns it a fitness value. Although there are many techniques for the selection of parents, a commonly used method is the Roulette Wheel Selection [11], a proportionate selection scheme which bases the number of offspring on the average fitness of the population. But, in this mechanism it is possible that the individuals who were transferred from the preceding generation might not form a better individual. In that case, although better solution is expected in the next generation, the system may go worse. To prevent this, by applying a structure called elitism. The elitism is used to move into the next generation the fit member of the population without any modification into the next generation [11]. Crossover is the procedure where two parent (parents1 and parents2) chromosomes exchange a part of genetic information (i.e., a section of the string of numbers) to form two chromosome offspring. The simplest model is the single-point crossover, where the selection of a random position between 1 and $l - 1$, where l is the length of the chromosome, indicates which portions are interchanged between parents. Here, multi-point crossover has been used in this study, where each class timetable is selected randomly from one parent or the other. Mutation is a form of global search where the genetic information of a chromosome is randomly altered. In this presented algorithm, two gene swap for each classes in a random position. Repair operator is used to fix some with invalid solution for the problem. Because, the new gene structures formed after crossover and mutation operates turn into unsuitable gene structures. This operator use problem specific knowledge about the problem domain to repair missing, lost or extra lessons in timetable.

4 Experiments and Results

The developed timetabling tool has been tested using real-data obtained from Gazi Anatolian Technical and Vocational High School for 2004-2005 semesters. Table 1 summarizes information for this school. The parameter settings for the HGA reported in Table 2. Fitness function uses the penalty values for corresponding constraints as shown in Table 3. HGA attempts to solve the bigger penalty values ahead of others. By changing the penalties, constraints to be satisfied can be prioritized. In this study, those have been chosen using trial and error method. The implementation of the timetabling tool has been developed in C++ Builder. Experimental results are obtained by using PC which has Pentium Centrino 1.7 GHz processor and 512 MB RAM. Experimental results are obtained run standard GA and HGA.

Table 1. Summary of the School

Resources	Value
Teachers	111
Department	6
Classes	44
Size of the lessons	226
Rooms	70
Weekly time-slot of Timetable	60
Total time-slot of Timetable	2640

Table 2. Parameters of the HGA

Parameters	Value
Population size	20
Chromosome size	2640
Crossover rate(pc)	0,85
Mutation rate (pm)	0,08

Table 3. Penalty values of hard and soft constraints

Hard Constraints	Penalty Value
1	200
2	200
3, 4, 5	closed of time-slots

Soft Constraints	Penalty Value
6	50
7	50
8	50
9	50

As shown in Figure 3 and 4, those algorithms have been configurations computed are run 100.000 generations. Therefore, 2.000.000 configurations school timetables. Computing time for this problem was 6 hours on above PC. The total penalty value for the violation of all constraints is shown in figure 3. The best solutions with standard GA and HGA, respectively, about 17.000 and 4.000 penalty values were produced. In the run of GA and HGA completely are remained hard constraints violations as shown in figure 4. As shown in figure 4, HGA is better than the GA and it has less the computing time.

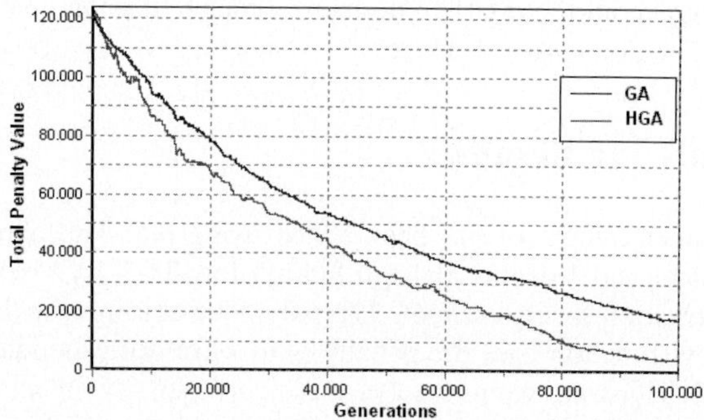

Fig. 3. The total penalty value for the violation of all constraints with GA and HGA

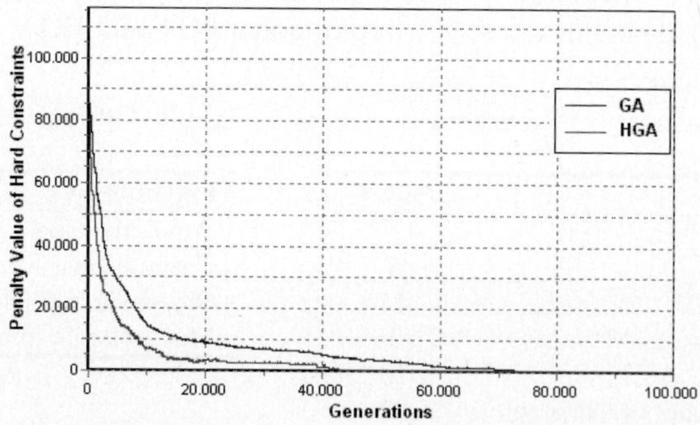

Fig. 4. Penalty value of hard constraints with GA and HGA

Especially, for reduce penalty value of hard constraint in the HGA are used repair algorithm. After the completely hard constraints are removed, HGA is run like GA. Thus, it has less computing time. In the timetable, blocked time-slot, in the initial and next generations are the same and not open. Table 4 is shown number of constraint violations in the initial and next generations. Hard constraints completely are removed at 42.857 in

Table 4. Number of constraints remained violated after GA and HGA

Hard Constraints	Initial Population	GA (72.682 generations)	HGA (42.857 generations)
1	201	0	0
2	204	0	0
3, 4, 5	blocked	blocked	blocked
Soft Constraints	**Initial Population**	**(100.000 generations)**	**(100.000 generations)**
6	26	6	2
7	210	82	13
8	252	104	23
9	342	142	41

HGA and 76.682 generations in GA, respectively. These experimental results are quite acceptable in the solution space. But, there were remain few soft constraints at 100.000 generation for two techniques. Accordingly, a solution will be acceptable if it satisfies all the hard constraints, and a feasible solution will be said to be more or less acceptable depending on the degree to which soft constraints are satisfied.

5 Conclusions

This paper deals with to solve the school timetabling problem using HGA with repair algorithm. HGA has so called a repair operator together with mutation and crossover operators. Significantly improvements have been achieved by using repair operator for the HGA. Paper discussed the application of a GA to the school timetabling problem, and show how the execution time can be reduced by using repair operator. The results obtained by HGA were compared with standard GA and experiments show.

References

1. de Werra, D.: An introduction to timetabling. Europan Journal Of Operations Research 19, 151–162 (1985)
2. Abramson, D.: Constructing school timetables using simulated annealing: sequential and parallel algorithms. Management Science 37, 98–113 (1991)
3. Hertz, A.: Tabu search for large scale timetabling problems. European Journal of Operations Research 54, 39–47 (1991)
4. Colorni, A., Dorigo, M., Maniezzo, V.: Genetic Algorithms and Highly Constrained Problems; The Timetable Case, Parallel Problem Solving from Nature I, pp. 55–59. Springer, Heidelberg (1990)
5. Calderia, J.P., Rosa, A.C.: School Timetabling using Genetic Search. In: Burke, E.K., Carter, M. (eds.) PATAT 1997. LNCS, vol. 1408, pp. 115–122. Springer, Heidelberg (1998)
6. Wilke, P., Grobner, M., Oster, N.: A Hybrid Genetic Algorithm for School Timetabling. In: McKay, B., Slaney, J. (eds.) AI 2002: Advances in Artificial Intelligence, pp. 455–464. Springer-Verlag, New York (2002)
7. Di Stefano, C., Tettamanzi, A.: An Evolutionary Algorithm for Solving the School Time-Tabling Problem. In: EvoWorkshops, pp. 452–462 (2001)
8. Burke, E.K., Petrovic, S., Qu, R.: Case Based Heuristic Selection for Timetabling Problems. Journal of Scheduling 9, 15–132 (2006)
9. Deris, S., Omatu, S., Ohta, H., Saad, P.: Incorporating Constraint Propagation in Genetic Algorithm for University Timetable Planning. Engineering Applications of Artificial Intelligence 12, 241–253 (1999)
10. Michalewicz, Z.: Genetic Algorithms+Data Structure=Evoluation Programs, 3rd edn. Springer, Heidelberg (1996)
11. Goldberg, D.E.: Genetic Algorithm in Search, Optimization, and Machine Learning. Addison- Wesley Publishing Company Inc, Canada (1989)

Author Index

Printing: Mercedes-Druck, Berlin
Binding: Stein+Lehmann, Berlin

Lecture Notes in Artificial Intelligence (LNAI)

Vol. 4481: J. Yao, P. Lingras, W.-Z. Wu, M. Szczuka, N.J. Cercone, D. Ślęzak (Eds.), Rough Sets and Knowledge Technology. XIV, 576 pages. 2007.

Vol. 4476: V. Gorodetsky, C. Zhang, V.A. Skormin, L. Cao (Eds.), Autonomous Intelligent Systems: Multi-Agents and Data Mining. XIII, 323 pages. 2007.

Vol. 4456: Y. Wang, Y.-m. Cheung, H. Liu (Eds.), Computational Intelligence and Security. XXIII, 1118 pages. 2007.

Vol. 4455: S. Muggleton, R. Otero, A. Tamaddoni-Nezhad (Eds.), Inductive Logic Programming. XII, 456 pages. 2007.

Vol. 4452: M. Fasli, O. Shehory (Eds.), Agent-Mediated Electronic Commerce. VIII, 249 pages. 2007.

Vol. 4451: T.S. Huang, A. Nijholt, M. Pantic, A. Pentland (Eds.), Artifical Intelligence for Human Computing. XVI, 359 pages. 2007.

Vol. 4441: C. Müller (Ed.), Speaker Classification. X, 309 pages. 2007.

Vol. 4438: L. Maicher, A. Sigel, L.M. Garshol (Eds.), Leveraging the Semantics of Topic Maps. X, 257 pages. 2007.

Vol. 4434: G. Lakemeyer, E. Sklar, D.G. Sorrenti, T. Takahashi (Eds.), RoboCup 2006: Robot Soccer World Cup X. XIII, 566 pages. 2007.

Vol. 4429: R. Lu, J.H. Siekmann, C. Ullrich (Eds.), Cognitive Systems. X, 161 pages. 2007.

Vol. 4428: S. Edelkamp, A. Lomuscio (Eds.), Model Checking and Artificial Intelligence. IX, 185 pages. 2007.

Vol. 4426: Z.-H. Zhou, H. Li, Q. Yang (Eds.), Advances in Knowledge Discovery and Data Mining. XXV, 1161 pages. 2007.

Vol. 4411: R.H. Bordini, M. Dastani, J. Dix, A.E.F. Seghrouchni (Eds.), Programming Multi-Agent Systems. XIV, 249 pages. 2007.

Vol. 4410: A. Branco (Ed.), Anaphora: Analysis, Algorithms and Applications. X, 191 pages. 2007.

Vol. 4399: T. Kovacs, X. Llorà, K. Takadama, P.L. Lanzi, W. Stolzmann, S.W. Wilson (Eds.), Learning Classifier Systems. XII, 345 pages. 2007.

Vol. 4390: S.O. Kuznetsov, S. Schmidt (Eds.), Formal Concept Analysis. X, 329 pages. 2007.

Vol. 4389: D. Weyns, H.V.D. Parunak, F. Michel (Eds.), Environments for Multi-Agent Systems III. X, 273 pages. 2007.

Vol. 4386: P. Noriega, J. Vázquez-Salceda, G. Boella, O. Boissier, V. Dignum, N. Fornara, E. Matson (Eds.), Coordination, Organizations, Institutions, and Norms in Agent Systems II. XI, 373 pages. 2007.

Vol. 4384: T. Washio, K. Satoh, H. Takeda, A. Inokuchi (Eds.), New Frontiers in Artificial Intelligence. IX, 401 pages. 2007.

Vol. 4371: K. Inoue, K. Satoh, F. Toni (Eds.), Computational Logic in Multi-Agent Systems. X, 315 pages. 2007.

Vol. 4369: M. Umeda, A. Wolf, O. Bartenstein, U. Geske, D. Seipel, O. Takata (Eds.), Declarative Programming for Knowledge Management. X, 229 pages. 2006.

Vol. 4343: C. Müller (Ed.), Speaker Classification I. X, 355 pages. 2007.

Vol. 4342: H. de Swart, E. Orłowska, G. Schmidt, M. Roubens (Eds.), Theory and Applications of Relational Structures as Knowledge Instruments II. X, 373 pages. 2006.

Vol. 4335: S.A. Brueckner, S. Hassas, M. Jelasity, D. Yamins (Eds.), Engineering Self-Organising Systems. XII, 212 pages. 2007.

Vol. 4334: B. Beckert, R. Hähnle, P.H. Schmitt (Eds.), Verification of Object-Oriented Software. XXIX, 658 pages. 2007.

Vol. 4333: U. Reimer, D. Karagiannis (Eds.), Practical Aspects of Knowledge Management. XII, 338 pages. 2006.

Vol. 4327: M. Baldoni, U. Endriss (Eds.), Declarative Agent Languages and Technologies IV. VIII, 257 pages. 2006.

Vol. 4314: C. Freksa, M. Kohlhase, K. Schill (Eds.), KI 2006: Advances in Artificial Intelligence. XII, 458 pages. 2007.

Vol. 4304: A. Sattar, B.-h. Kang (Eds.), AI 2006: Advances in Artificial Intelligence. XXVII, 1303 pages. 2006.

Vol. 4303: A. Hoffmann, B.-h. Kang, D. Richards, S. Tsumoto (Eds.), Advances in Knowledge Acquisition and Management. XI, 259 pages. 2006.

Vol. 4293: A. Gelbukh, C.A. Reyes-Garcia (Eds.), MICAI 2006: Advances in Artificial Intelligence. XXVIII, 1232 pages. 2006.

Vol. 4289: M. Ackermann, B. Berendt, M. Grobelnik, A. Hotho, D. Mladenič, G. Semeraro, M. Spiliopoulou, G. Stumme, V. Svátek, M. van Someren (Eds.), Semantics, Web and Mining. X, 197 pages. 2006.

Vol. 4285: Y. Matsumoto, R.W. Sproat, K.-F. Wong, M. Zhang (Eds.), Computer Processing of Oriental Languages. XVII, 544 pages. 2006.

Vol. 4274: Q. Huo, B. Ma, E.-S. Chng, H. Li (Eds.), Chinese Spoken Language Processing. XXIV, 805 pages. 2006.

Vol. 4265: L. Todorovski, N. Lavrač, K.P. Jantke (Eds.), Discovery Science. XIV, 384 pages. 2006.

Vol. 4264: J.L. Balcázar, P.M. Long, F. Stephan (Eds.), Algorithmic Learning Theory. XIII, 393 pages. 2006.

Vol. 4259: S. Greco, Y. Hata, S. Hirano, M. Inuiguchi, S. Miyamoto, H.S. Nguyen, R. Słowiński (Eds.), Rough Sets and Current Trends in Computing. XXII, 951 pages. 2006.

Vol. 4253: B. Gabrys, R.J. Howlett, L.C. Jain (Eds.), Knowledge-Based Intelligent Information and Engineering Systems, Part III. XXXII, 1301 pages. 2006.

Vol. 4252: B. Gabrys, R.J. Howlett, L.C. Jain (Eds.), Knowledge-Based Intelligent Information and Engineering Systems, Part II. XXXIII, 1335 pages. 2006.

Vol. 4251: B. Gabrys, R.J. Howlett, L.C. Jain (Eds.), Knowledge-Based Intelligent Information and Engineering Systems, Part I. LXVI, 1297 pages. 2006.

Vol. 4248: S. Staab, V. Svátek (Eds.), Managing Knowledge in a World of Networks. XIV, 400 pages. 2006.